KT-408-856

The Oxford Latin Minidictionary

Edited by
JAMES MORWOOD

...ated
over
...ondition
...haser

...wood.
...y Routledge in 1913.
...ood, James,

...kland

...ITY PRESS

Oxford University Press, Great Clarendon Street, Oxford OX2 6DP

Oxford New York
Athens Auckland Bangkok Bogota Bombay
Buenos Aires Calcutta Cape Town Dar es Salaam
Delhi Florence Hong Kong Istanbul Karachi
Kuala Lumpur Madras Madrid Melbourne
Mexico City Nairobi Paris Singapore
Taipei Tokyo Toronto

and associated companies in
Berlin Ibadan

Oxford is a trade mark of Oxford University Press

Published in the United States by
Oxford University Press Inc., New York

© Oxford University Press 1995
First edition published 1913 by
Routledge & Kegan Paul Ltd.
First published by Oxford University Press by
arrangement with Routledge 1994
Second edition published 1995
Reissued 1997

British Library Cataloguing in Publication Data

Data available

Library of Congress Cataloging in Publication Data

The Oxford Latin minidictionary | edited by James
p. cm.
Rev. ed. of Woodhouse's Latin dictionary, publishe
1. Latin language—Dictionaries—English. I. Mc
473'.21—dc20 PA2365.E5093 1955 94-46850

ISBN 0-19-860139-5

10 9 8 7 6 5

Typeset by Pure Tech India Ltd.
Printed in Great Britain by
Charles Letts (Scotland) Ltd., Dalkeith, S

Preface

The completion of the monumental *Oxford Latin Dictionary* in 1982 has created a need for a shorter, more accessible, and considerably less expensive dictionary to take account of the important philological advances which it made. This is the first dictionary to try to meet that need. Within its modest compass, it presents a Latin language cleansed of suspect accretions and a Victorian use of the English language.

It is in fact based on S. C. Woodhouse's Latin Dictionary, first published by Routledge & Kegan Paul in 1913 and subsequently reprinted many times. In the English into Latin section, the spirit of Woodhouse has been allowed some free play, even though the pruning knife, if not the axe, has had to be much at work on his inventive and lively luxuriance.

In a modern dictionary, the Latin into English section is of the greater importance. It is in this part of the present volume that the *Oxford Latin Dictionary* makes itself especially felt. I have centred this section on the Latin of the Golden Age (from 100 BC to the death of Livy) and it should prove a satisfactory guide to all of classical Latin. I have included macra (long markings) to indicate how the Latin words should be pronounced. The scholarly basis for the application of these is the important philological work of Professor W. Sidney Allen as expounded in his *Vox Latina* (2nd edn., Cambridge University Press, 1978). While the letter 'i' is both a vowel and a consonant and thus there is no 'j' in Latin, it unfortunately still appears necessary to make a distinction between 'u' as a vowel (as in English) and as a consonant, the latter being given as 'v'. This is unhistorical and philologically unsound and it is hoped that before too long the letter 'v' can be eradicated from this dictionary. Also included is a guide to pronunciation available for the first time in portable minidictionary format. We are offering an up-to-date guide to the Latin language which is none the less well suited to traditional demands. Two further sections cover the best-known historical and mythological figures of the ancient world as well as its geography.

JAMES MORWOOD

December 1994   Harrow School

Guide to Pronunciation

. . . .

Latin, unlike English, is spelt exactly as it is sounded. The Latin alphabet contains fifteen consonants (omitting the letters *x*, *y*, *z*, which are only found in words transliterated from Greek, and *k*, which occurs only in the word **Kalendae** and derivatives). It contains five vowels.

Consonants

Most of the consonants are pronounced, for practical purposes, as in English, except:

1 *i* consonantal, as in **iam**, is pronounced like English *y*.
2 *v* (= *u* consonantal), as in **vīdī**, is pronounced as English *w*.
3 *r* is rolled, as in Scottish, and is always sounded; e.g. **ars** – both **r** and **s** are sounded.
4 *c* is always hard as in *cat*.
5 *s* is always pronounced as in *sit*, never as in *rose*.
6 *g* is always hard as in *God*, except when followed by *n*; *gn* is pronounced *ngn* as in *hangnail*.
7 *h* is always sounded as in English *hope*.
8 *q* is never found except in the combination *qu*, sounded as in English.

Vowels

The five vowels each have a short and a long version:

1 *a* short, as in English *cup* (NB not as in *cap*).
2 *a* long, as in English *father*.
3 *e* short, as in English *pet*.
4 *e* long, as in French *gai*.

5 *i* short, as in English *dip*.
6 *i* long, as in English *deep*.
7 *o* short, as in English *pot*.
8 *o* long, as in French *beau*.
9 *u* short, as in English *put*.
10 *u* long, as in English *fool*.

Diphthongs

1 *ae* as in English *high*.
2 *au* as in English *how*.
3 *ei* as in English *day*.
4 *eu* e-u (occurs rarely, not properly a diphthong).
5 *oe* as in English *boy*.
6 *ui* u-i.

Throughout the Latin–English section, naturally long vowels are marked with a macron. All vowels not so marked are short.

List of Abbreviations

a.	adjective
abl.	ablative
acc.	accusative
ad.	adverb
c.	conjunction *or* (after Latin word) common (masculine or feminine in gender)
comp.	comparative
dat.	dative
def.	defective
dep.	deponent (passive in form, active in meaning)
e.g.	*exempli gratia* (for example)
etc.	*et cetera* (and so on)
f.	feminine
fig.	figurative meaning
gen.	genitive
gram.	grammatical
i.	interjection
impers.	impersonal
indecl.	indeclinable
inf.	infinitive
ir.	irregular
m.	masculine
med.	medical
mil.	military
mus.	musical
n.	noun
nt.	neuter
num.	numeral
p.	participle
pass.	passive
pl.	plural

pn.	pronoun
poet.	poetical usage
pr.	preposition
rel.	relative pronoun
sim.	similar
sing.	singular
subj.	subjunctive
sup.	superlative
v.	*vide*, i.e. see
v.	verb
v.i.	intransitive verb
v.t.	transitive verb

1. In the Latin–English section a word followed immediately by its genitive ending is a noun. From the genitive ending you can tell which of the five declensions it belongs to. The declensions of nouns are given on pp. 656–9 of the Summary of Grammar.

2. In the Latin–English section adjectives are given with their masculine, feminine (when different), and neuter endings in the nominative singular. From these you can tell which declension they belong to. The declensions of adjectives are given on pp. 660–1 of the Summary of Grammar.

3. For the formation of adverbs from adjectives, see p. 662 of the Summary of Grammar.

4. The numerals 1, 2, 3, 4 after verbs refer to their conjugation (see Summary of Grammar, pp. 671–84). Verbs marked '*ir.*' are given on pp. 685–93 of the Summary of Grammar.

5. In the English–Latin section, the first gender given in the case of nouns and the first conjugation given in the case of verbs apply to any unmarked words that precede them. For example, in the entry

aptness, *n.* convenientia, congruentia; (tendency, propensity) proclivitas, *f.*
all the nouns are feminine.

6. In the Latin–English section, all long vowels are marked with a macron (¯ over the vowel). These vowels are pronounced long. All other vowels are pronounced short. See Guide to Pronunciation (pp. v–vi).

A

ā, ab (abs), *pr. with abl.* from; by (of the agent); away from; since.

abacus, ī, *m.* counting-board; side-board; square stone on the top of columns.

abaliēnātiō, ōnis, *f.* legal transfer of property.

abaliēnō, [1] *v.* transfer by sale or contract; remove.

abavus, ī, *m.* great-great grandfather, ancestor.

abdicātiō, ōnis, *f.* renunciation; disowning (of a son).

abdicō, [1] *v.* resign; abolish; disinherit.

abdō, idī, itum, [3] *v.* hide, conceal; plunge; remove.

abdōmen, inis, *nt.* lower part of the belly, paunch; gluttony.

abdūcō, xī, ctum, [3] *v.* lead away, carry off.

abeō, īre, īvī (iī), itum, [4] *v.* go away, depart; vanish; escape; be changed.

aberrātiō, ōnis, *f.* diversion, relief.

aberrō, [1] *v.* go astray, deviate (from); disagree (with).

abhinc, *ad.* from this time, since, ago; from this place.

abhorreō, uī, [2] *v.* (usually with *ab* with *abl.*) be averse (to), shudder at; be inconsistent (with).

abiciō, iēcī, iectum, [3] *v.* throw away; slight; give up; humble, debase.

abiectē, *ad.* in a spiritless manner; in humble circumstances; negligently.

abiectus, a, um, *a.* downcast, mean, abject, base.

abiēgnus, a, um, *a.* made of fir.

abiēs, etis, *f.* white fir; ship; spear.

abigō, ēgī, āctum, [3] *v.* drive *or* send away.

abitus, ūs, *m.* going away; departure; way out, exit.

abiūdicō, [1] *v.* deprive by judicial verdict.

abiungō, nxī, nctum, *v.* unyoke, remove, separate.

abiūrō, [1] *v.* deny on oath, repudiate.

ablēgātiō, ōnis, *f.* sending away, dispatch.

ablēgō, [1] *v.* send away, remove.

abluō, uī, ūtum, [3] *v.* to wash away, blot out, to purify; quench, remove.

abnegō, [1] *v.* deny, refuse.

abnuō, uī, ūtum, [3] *v.* deny, refuse, reject.

aboleō, ēvī, itum, [2] *v.* abolish, destroy.

abolēscō, lēvī, [3] *v.* cease, be extinct, fall into disuse.

abolitiō, ōnis, *f.* abolition, cancellation, annulment.

abōminor, ārī, ātus, [1] *v. dep.* (seek to) avert (by prayer); detest.

aborior, orīrī, ortus, [4] *v. dep.* pass away, disappear; miscarry.

abortiō, ōnis, *f.* abortion, miscarriage.

abortīvus, a, um, *a.* abortive; addled.

abortus, ūs, *m.* miscarriage.

abrādō, sī, sum, [3] *v.* scratch off, shave; 'knock off', rob.

abripiō, ere, puī, eptum, [3] *v.* drag away by force; abduct, kidnap.

abrogātiō, ōnis, *f.* repeal of a law.

abrogō, [1] *v.* repeal wholly, abolish.

abrumpō, ūpī, uptum, [3] *v.* break off, tear asunder, cut through.

abruptiō, ōnis, *f.* breaking, breaking off.

abruptus, a, um, *a.* precipitous, steep; hasty, rash.

abs, *pr.,* v. **ab.**

abscēdō, cessī, cessum, [3] *v.* go away, depart; desist.

abscessus, ūs, *m.* going away, absence.

abscīdō, cīdī, cīsum, [3] *v.* cut off, remove.

abscindō, cīdī, cissum, [3] *v.* cut off, tear away; put an end to.

abscīsus, a, um, *a.* steep, abrupt.

abscondō, condī & condidī, conditum, [3] *v.* hide; keep secret.

absēns, entis, *a.* absent.

absentia, ae, *f.* absence.

absiliō, iī & uī, [4] *v.* leap away; fly apart.

absimilis, e, *a.* unlike.

absistō, stitī [3] *v.* stand off, go away; desist from, leave off.

absolūtē, *ad.* completely, perfectly.

absolūtiō, ōnis, *f.* finishing, acquittal, perfection.

absolūtus, a, um, *a.* free, complete, unconditional.

absolvō, vī, ūtum, [3] *v.* absolve (from), discharge, dismiss, release; finish.

absonus, a, um, *a.* out of tune, discordant, incongruous.

absorbeō, buī & psī, ptum, [2] *v.* absorb, suck in.

absque, *pr. with abl.* without, except.

abstēmius, a, um, *a.* sober, temperate; fasting.

abstergeō, rsī, rsum, [2] *v.* wipe off *or* dry *or* clean; remove.

absterreō, uī, itum, [2] *v.* frighten away.

abstinēns, entis, *a.* abstinent, temperate.

abstinenter, *ad.* abstinently.

abstinentia, ae, *f.* abstinence; fasting; moderation.

abstineō, uī, tentum, [2] *v.* restrain, keep away; abstain, forbear.

abstō, stitī, stitum, [1] *v.* stand at a distance.

abstrahō, xī, ctum, [3] *v.* drag away from; separate.

abstrūdō, ūsī, ūsum, [3] *v.* thrust away, conceal.

abstrūsus, a, um, *a.* secret, reserved.

absum, abesse, āfuī, *v.* be absent *or* away (from) *or* distant; be wanting.

absūmō, mpsī, mptum, [3] *v.* spend, waste, ruin.

absurdus, a, um, *a.* of a harsh sound; absurd, nonsensical.

abundanter, *ad.* abundantly, copiously.

abundantia, ae, *f.* abundance, plenty, riches.

abundē, *ad.* abundantly.

abundō, [1] *v.* abound (in), be rich.

abūsus, ūs, *m.* misuse, wasting.

abūtor, ūsus, [3] *v. dep.* use up, waste; misuse.

ac, *c.* and, and besides; than.

acadēmīa, ae, *f.* academy, university.

acadēmicus, a, um, *a.* academic.

acalanthis, idis, *f.* a small songbird.

acanthus, ī, *m.* bear's-foot; the gum arabic tree.

accēdō, cessī, cessum, *v.* go *or* come to, approach; attack; fall to one's share, be added, come over to; be like, enter upon.

accelerō, [1] *v.* accelerate, hasten; make haste.

accendō, ndī, nsum, [3] *v.* set on fire, light, illuminate; inflame.

accēnseō, uī, nsum, [2] *v.t.* attach as an attendant to.

accēnsus, ī, *m.* supernumerary soldier; attendant, orderly.

accentus, ūs, *m.* accent, intonation.

acceptiō, ōnis, *f.* taking, accepting; meaning, sense.

acceptus, a, um, *a.* welcome, well-liked; (of money) received.

accessiō, ōnis, *f.* approach; increase, addition; (*med.*) fit.

accessus, ūs, *m.* approach, admittance, attack.

accīdō, cīdī, cīsum, [3] *v.* cut short, weaken.

accidō, cidī, [3] *v.i.* fall at *or* near; happen.

accingō, nxī, nctum, [3] *v.* gird on *or* about; provide (with), prepare (for).

acciō, [4] *v.* send for, summon.

accipiō, cēpī, ceptum, [3] *v.* accept, receive; undertake; hear, learn, find; get; sustain; obey; treat.

accipiter, tris, *m.* hawk.

accītus, ūs, *m.* summons, call.

acclāmātiō, ōnis, *f.* acclamation, shout; crying against.

acclāmō, [1] *v.* shout (at), cry out against.

acclārō, [1] *v.* make clear, reveal.

acclīnis, e, *a.* leaning (on); sloping; inclined, disposed (to).

acclīnō, [1] *v.* lay down, rest (on), lean against, incline (to).

acclīvis, e, acclīvus, a, um, *a.* sloping upwards.

accola, ae, *m.* or *f.* neighbour.

accolō, coluī, cultum, [3] *v.* dwell near.

accommodātiō, ōnis, *f.* adjustment, willingness to oblige.

accommodātus, a, um, *a.* fit, suitable.

accommodō, [1] *v.* adjust, fit, suit; apply; synchronize.

accommodus, a, um, *a.* fit, convenient.

accrēdō, didī, ditum, [3] *v. with dat.* give credence to, believe.

accrēscō, ēvī, ētum, [3] *v.* grow on, increase, swell, be annexed to.

accrētiō, ōnis, *f.* increasing, increment.

accubitiō, ōnis, *f. a.* reclining (at meals).

accubō, āre, uī, itum, *v.* lie near *or* by; recline at table.

accumbō, cubuī, cubitum, [3] *v.* recline at table.

accumulātor, ōris, *m.* heaper up.

accumulō, [1] *v.* accumulate, heap up.

accūrātiō, ōnis, *f.* carefulness, painstakingness.

accūrātus, a, um, *a.* accurate, with care, meticulous.

accūrō, [1] *v.* take care of, attend to.

accurrō, currī, cursum, [3] *v.* run *or* hasten to.

accursus, ūs, *m.* rushing up; attack.

accūsābilis, e, *a.* blameable, reprehensible.

accūsātiō, ōnis, *f.* accusation.

accūsātor, ōris, *m.* accuser, plaintiff; informer.

accūsātōrius, a, um, *a.* accusatory.

accūsō, [1] *v.* accuse, blame, reprimand.

acer, eris, *nt.* maple-tree.

ācer, cris, cre, *a.* sharp, sour, pungent, piercing; violent; keen, furious, swift, active, ardent, courageous; drastic, critical.

acerbitās, ātis, *f.* acerbity, sourness; severity, bitterness; anguish, hardship.

acerbō, [1] *v.* embitter; aggravate.

acerbus, a, um, *a.* unripe, sour, bitter; crude; shrill, rough, violent; severe; grievous.

acernus, a, um, *a.* of maple.

acerra, ae, *f.* box *or* casket for incense.

acervātim, *ad.* in heaps, summarily, without any order.

acervō, [1] *v.* heap up.

acervus, ī, *m.* heap.

acēscō, acuī, [3] *v.* turn sour.

acētum, ī, *nt.* vinegar; sourness of disposition; sharpness of wit.

acidus, a, um, *a.* acid, sour.

aciēs, ēī, *f.* edge, point; battle-array, line of battle; the sight of the eyes; pupil of the eye; quickness of apprehension.

acinus, ī, *m.,* **acinum, ī,** *nt.* grape, ivy-berry; pip, seed.

acipēnser, eris, *m.* sturgeon.

aclys, ydis, *f.* javelin.

aconītum, ī, *nt.* wolf's-bane, aconite.

acquiēscō, ēvī, ētum, [3] *v.* lie down to rest; acquiesce (in), assent; subside.

acquīrō, sīvī, sītum, [3] *v.* acquire, get, obtain.

ācriculus, a, um, *a.* shrewd, acute.

ācrimōnia, ae, *f.* acrimony, sharpness, briskness.

ācriter, *ad.* sharply, vehemently; severely, steadfastly.

acroāma, atis, *nt.* item in an entertainment, act, 'turn'.

acroāsis, is, *f.* lecture.

ācta, ōrum, *nt. pl.* acts, exploits; chronicles, record.

acta, ae, *f.* sea-shore.

āctiō, ōnis, *f.* action; plot (of a play); legal process.

āctitō, [1] *v.* act *or* plead frequently.

āctīvus, a, um, *a.* active.

āctor, ōris, *m.* plaintiff, advocate; agent; player, actor; herdsman.

āctuārius, a, um, *a.* swift, speedy, light.

āctuārius, ī, *m.* short-hand writer, clerk, book-keeper, secretary.

āctuōsus, a, um, *a.* active, busy.

āctus, ūs, *m.* act, performance, action; delivery.

actūtum, *ad.* forthwith, instantly.

aculeātus, a, um, *a.* prickly; stinging, sharp, subtle.

aculeus, ī, *m.* sting, prickle, point; sarcasm.

acūmen, inis, *nt.* sharpened point, sting, sharpness, cunning, fraud.

acuō, uī, ūtum, [3] *v.* whet, sharpen; spur on, provoke.

acus, ūs, *f.* needle, pin.

acūtē, *ad.* acutely.

acūtulus, a, um, *a.* smart, subtle, clever.

acūtus, a, um, *a.* sharp, pointed; violent, severe; glaring; acute, sagacious; high-pitched.

ad, *pr. with acc.* to, towards, near by, at, before, up to, until, about; in comparison with, according to, in order to, for; in addition to, after, concerning.

adaequē, *ad.* equally, so much.

adaequō, [1] *v.* equalize, level, compare (to); be equal.

adamantēus, a, um, *a.* adamantine.

adamantinus, a, um, *a.* hard as steel, adamant.

adamās, antis, *m.* the hardest iron; diamond.

adamō, [1] *v.* love passionately.

adaperiō, uī, ertum, [4] *v.* throw open, uncover.

adapertilis, e, *a.* that may be opened.

adaptō, [1] *v.* adjust, fit.

adaquō, [1] *v.* water.

adauctus, ūs, *m.* increase, growth.

adaugeō, xī, ctum, [2] *v.* increase, intensify.

adbibō, bibī, [3] *v.* drink, drink in.

addecet, [2] *v. impers.* it is fitting.

addēnseō, [2] *v.* make more dense, close up (the ranks).

addīcō, xī, ctum, [3] *v.* be propitious; adjudge; confiscate; knock down to, award; consecrate; sacrifice.

addictiō, ōnis, *f.* adjudication, assignment.

addictus, ī, *m.* a person enslaved for debt *or* theft.

addiscō, didicī, [3] *v.* learn besides.

addītāmentum, ī, *nt.* addition.

addō, didī, ditum, *v.* add, give, bring to, say in addition.

addubitō, [1] *v.* doubt, hesitate.

addūcō, xī, ctum, [3] *v.* bring *or* lead to; induce, contract, tighten.

adedō, ēdī, ēsum, [3] *v.* eat up, eat into, squander.

adēmptiō, ōnis, *f.* taking away.

adeō, īvī & iī, itum, [4] *v.* go to *or* approach, address, accost, visit; attack; undergo, take a part in; enter on (an inheritance).

adeō, *ad.* so much, to such a degree, so, so far, just, even, much more, much less, 'you know'.

adeps, ipis, *m. or f.* fat, lard, grease; corpulence; bombast.

adeptiō, ōnis, *f.* obtaining, attainment.

adequitō, [1] *v.* ride up to.

adhaereō, haesī, haesum, [2] *or* **adhaerēscō,** [3] *v.* adhere, stick, cling to.

adhaesiō, ōnis, *f.* adhesion, linkage.

adhibeō, uī, itum, [2] *v.* apply, hold (to); use; invite, admit.

adhinniō, īvī, ītum, [4] *v.* whinny (to).

adhortātiō, ōnis, *f.* exhortation.

adhortātor, ōris, *m.* encourager.

adhortor, ātus, [1] *v. dep.* exhort, encourage.

adhūc, *ad.* to this point, hitherto; yet, still; besides.

adiaceō [2] *v. with dat.* lie beside *or* near to.

adiectiō, ōnis, *f.* addition.

adiciō, iēcī, iectum, [3] *v.* throw to, add to.

adigō, ēgī, āctum, [3] *v.* drive, bring, drive in, bind by oath.

adimō, ēmī, ēmptum, [3] *v.* take away, rescue, deprive.

adipīscor, eptus, [3] *v. dep.* reach, get, obtain, arrive (at), overtake.

aditus, ūs, *m.* access, way, means, opportunity.

adiūdicō, [1] *v.* adjudge, impute.

adiūmentum, ī, *nt.* help, assistance.

adiūnctiō, ōnis, *f.* union, addition.

adiūnctum, ī, *nt.* quality, characteristic.

adiungō, nxī, nctum, [3] *v.* join to, yoke, add to.

adiūrō, [1] *v.* swear solemnly.

adiūtō, [1] *v.* help.

adiūtor, ōris, *m.* assistant, helper, supporter.

adiūtōrium, ī, *nt.* help, assistance.

adiūtrix, īcis, *f.* female assistant, helper.

adiuvō, iūvī, iūtum, [1] *v.* assist, help, cherish, favour, mitigate.

admētior, mēnsus, [4] *v. dep.* measure out.

adminiculum, ī, *nt.* prop, support, stay, means, aid, assistance.

administer, trī, *m.* servant, assistant, supporter.

administrātiō, ōnis, *f.* administration; aid, assistance; execution, management, care of affairs.

administrātor, ōris, *m.* director, manager.

administrō, [1] *v.* administer, manage, serve.

admīrābilis, e, *a.* admirable, wonderful, strange.

admīrābilitās, ātis, *f.* wonderful character, remarkableness.

admīrābiliter, *ad.* admirably, astonishingly.

admīrātiō, ōnis, *f.* admiration, wondering.

admīrātor, ōris, *m.* admirer.

admīror, ātus, [1] *v. dep.* admire, wonder at.

admisceō, scuī, xtum, [2] *v.* mix, mingle with; mix up with, involve.

admissiō, ōnis, *f.* letting in, admission.

admissum, ī, *nt.* crime, offence.

admittō, mīsī, missum, [3] *v.* let in, admit, grant, permit, commit, let go, give rein to.

admixtiō, ōnis, *f.* (ad)mixture.

admodum, *ad.* quite, very, excessively; just so; certainly.

admoneō, uī, itum, [2] *v.* admonish, warn; remind; persuade.

admonitiō, ōnis, *f.* reminding, warning, advice; rebuke.

admonitor, ōris, *m.* one who reminds.

admonitus, ūs, *m.* admonition, warning.

admoveō, mōvī, mōtum, [2] *v.* move *or* bring to, apply, use, direct; lay on.

admurmurō, [1] *v.* murmur in protest *or* approval.

adnectō, exuī, exum, [3] *v.* tie on, annex.

adnītor, nīxus *or* **nīsus,** [3] *v. dep.* lean upon, strive.

adnō, [1] swim to, sail to *or* towards.

adnotō [1] note down, notice.

adnumerō, [1] *v.* count out, pay, count (in).

adnūntiō [1] *v.* announce

adnuō, uī, ūtum [3] *v.* nod at *or* to, assent, promise, grant, indicate by a nod.

adoleō, uī, ultum, [2] *v.* burn; honour by burnt offering.

adolēscō, ēvī, ultum, [3] *v.* grow up, increase.

adop(tā)tiō, ōnis, *f.* adoption of a child.

adoptīvus, a, um, *a.* adoptive.

adoptō, [1] *v.* select, adopt.

ador, ōris, *nt.* coarse grain.

adorior, ortus, [4] *v. dep.* attack, undertake, try.

adornō, [1] *v.* equip, set off, prepare, adorn.

adōrō, [1] *v.* adore, worship; beg.

adrādō, sī, sum, [3] *v.* scrape, shave, prune.

adsum, adesse, adfuī, *v.* be near, be present, arrive; (*with dat.*) aid.

adūlātiō, ōnis, *f.* fawning, flattery.

adūlātor, ōris, *m.* flatterer.

adūlātōrius, a, um, *a.* flattering, adulatory.

adulēscēns, entis, *m.* or *f.* young man *or* girl.

adulēscentia, ae, *f.* youth (time of life).

adulēscentulus, ī, *m.* young man, mere youth.

adūlor, ātus, [1] *v. dep.* fawn upon (as a dog); flatter.

adulter, erī, *m.,* **adultera, ae,** *f.* adulterer, adulteress.

adulter, a, um, *a.* adulterous; counterfeit.

adulterīnus, a, um, *a.* counterfeit, false.

adulterium, iī, *nt.* adultery.

adulterō, [1] *v.* commit adultery (with); falsify, corrupt.

adultus, a, um, *a.* full grown, adult.

adumbrātiō, ōnis, *f.* sketch.

adumbrō, [1] *v.t.* shadow out, sketch in outline; represent.

aduncitās, ātis, *f.* hookedness, curvature.

aduncus, a, um, *a.* crooked, hooked.

adurgeō, ursī, [2] *v.* press hard, pursue.

adūrō, ussī, ustum, [3] *v.* burn, scorch; consume.

adusque, *pr. with acc.* right up to, as far as; ~, *a.* wholly.

advectīcius, a, um, *a.* imported, foreign.

advehō, xī, ctum, [3] *v.* carry, bring, convey (to); **advehor,** arrive by travel, ride to.

advena, ae, *m.* or *f.* foreigner, stranger, interloper; ~, *a.* alien, foreign.

adveniō, vēnī, ventum, [4] *v.* come to, arrive at; develop.

adventīcius, a, um, *a.* coming from abroad, foreign, unusual.

adventō, [1] *v.* approach, arrive.

adventor, ōris, *m.* visitor, customer.

adventus, ūs, *m.* arrival, approach, attack.

adversārius, a, um, *a.* opposite; ~, *m.* opponent, enemy; ~ a, ōrum, *nt. pl.* memorandumbook.

adversātor, ōris, *m.* antagonist.

adversātrīx, īcis, *f.* female antagonist.

adversor, ātus, [1] *v. dep. with dat.* be against, oppose, withstand.

adversum, adversus, *ad.* opposite, against; ~, *pr. with acc.* towards, opposite to, against.

adversus, a, um, *a.* opposite, directly facing; adverse, evil, hostile; unfavourable; **adversō flūmine,** against the stream.

advertō, tī, sum, [3] *v.* turn or direct to, apply; **animum advertō,** notice, v. **animadvertō.**

advesperāscit, āvit, [3] *v. impers.* evening approaches.

advigilō, [1] *v.* watch by, take care.

advocātiō, ōnis, *f.* legal support; delay; pleading in the law courts.

advocātus, ī, *m.* counsellor, advocate, witness.

advocō, [1] *v.* call for, summon, call in as counsel.

advolō, [1] *v.* fly to, hasten towards.

advolvō, vī, volūtum, [3] *v.* roll to or towards; **genibus advolvor,** fall at the knees (of anyone).

adytum, ī, *nt.* innermost part of a temple, sanctuary.

aedēs (aedis), is, *f. sing.* temple; *pl.* house, room.

aedicula, ae, *f.* small house, chapel, niche, closet.

aedificātiō, ōnis, *f.* house-building; building.

aedificātor, ōris, *m.* builder, architect.

aedificium, iī, *nt.* building.

aedificō, [1] *v.* build, make, create.

aedīlicius, a, um, *a.* of an aedile.

aedīlis, is, *m.* aedile, Roman magistrate charged with the supervision of public buildings, games, markets, *etc.*

aedīlitās, ātis, *f.* aedileship.

aeditumus, ī, *m.* one who has charge of a temple, a sacristan.

aedituus, ī, *m.* sacristan.

aeger, gra, grum, *a.* sick, infirm, sad, sorrowful, painful, grievous.

aegis, idis, *f.* the aegis (Minerva's); shield, defence.

aegrē, *ad.* uncomfortably, reluctantly, with difficulty, scarcely.

aegrēscō, ere, [3] *v.* become sick, grow worse, grieve.

aegrimōnia, ae, *f.* sorrow, anxiety, melancholy.

aegritūdō, inis, *f.* sickness, disease, grief, sorrow.

aegrōtātiō, ōnis, *f.* sickness, disease, morbid desire.

aegrōtō, [1] *v.* be sick, be mentally ill.

aegrōtus, a, um, *a.* sick, diseased.

aemulātiō, ōnis, *f.* emulation, rivalry.

aemulātor, ōris, *m.* imitator, rival.

aemulātus, ūs, *m.* emulation, envy.

aemulor, ātus, [1] *v. dep.* emulate; be envious, jealous of.

aemulus, a, um, *a.* emulous; envious, grudging, (things) comparable (with); ~, *m.* rival.

aēneus, ahēneus, a, um, *a.* made of bronze.

aenigma, atis, *nt.* enigma, riddle, obscure saying.

aēnus, ahēnus, a, um, *a.* made of bronze.

aequābilis, e, *a.* equal, alike, uniform, steady, equable.

aequābilitās, ātis, *f.* equality, fairness, uniformity.

aequābiliter, *ad.* uniformly, equally.

aequaevus, a, um, *a.* of the same age.

aequālis, e, *a.* even, equal, of the same age, coeval; ~, *m.* or *f.* contemporary.

aequālitās, ātis, *f.* evenness; equality.

aequāliter, *ad.* equally, evenly.

aequanimitās, ātis, *f.* evenness of mind, patience, calmness.

aequātiō, ōnis, *f.* equal distribution.

aequē, *ad.* equally, in the same manner as, justly.

aequinoctiālis, e, *a.* equinoctial.

aequinoctium, iī, *nt.* equinox.

aequiperō, [1] *v.* compare, liken; (*with dat.*) become equal (with).

aequitās, ātis, *f.* evenness, conformity, symmetry, equanimity, fairness, impartiality.

aequō, [1] *v.* level; equal; compare; reach as high *or* deep as.

aequor, oris, *nt.* level surface, plain, surface of the sea, sea.

aequoreus, a, um, *a.* of the sea, bordering on the sea.

aequus, a, um, *a.* level, even, equal, like, just, kind, favourable, impartial, patient, contented.

āēr, āeris, *m.* air, atmosphere; cloud, mist.

aerārium, iī, *nt.* treasury.

aerārius, a, um, *a.* pertaining to copper, brass, *etc.*; ~, *m.* a citizen of the lowest class.

aerātus, a, um, *a.* covered with *or* made of copper *or* brass.

aereus, a, um, *a.* made of copper, bronze *or* brass.

aeripēs, edis, *a.* brazen-footed.

āerius, a, um, *a.* aerial, towering, airy.

aerūgō, inis, *f.* rust of copper, verdigris; canker of the mind, envy, ill-will, avarice.

aerumna, ae, *f.* toil, hardship, calamity.

aerumnōsus, a, um, *a.* full of trouble, wretched, calamitous.

aes, aeris, *nt.* copper ore, copper; bronze; money, pay, wages,

bronze statue, *etc.*; **aliēnum**, debt.

aesculus, ī, *f.* a variety of oak tree, perhaps either durmast or Hungarian oak.

aestās, ātis, *f.* summer; a year.

aestifer, a, um, *a.* producing heat, sultry.

aestimābilis, e, *a.* having worth *or* value.

aestimātiō, ōnis, *f.* valuation, value, price.

aestimātor, ōris, *m.* valuer, appraiser; judge.

aestimō, [1] *v.* value; estimate; consider.

aestīva, ōrum, *n. pl.* summer-quarters; the campaigning season.

aestīvō, [1] *v.* pass the summer.

aestīvus, a, um, *a.* summer-like, summer . . .

aestuārium, iī, *nt.* estuary, inlet, tidal opening.

aestuō, [1] *v.* boil, foam, billow; seethe; rage, waver, be undecided.

aestuōsus, a, um, *a.* hot, sultry, billowy.

aestus, ūs, *m.* heat, fire, tide, swell of the sea; passion; hesitation, anxiety.

aetās, ātis, *f.* life-time, age, period; generation.

aetātula, ae, *f.* the tender age of childhood.

aeternitās, ātis, *f.* eternity, immortality.

aeternō, [1] v. immortalize.

aeternus, a, um, a. eternal, everlasting, imperishable.

aethēr, eris, m. upper air, heaven, sky.

aetherius, a, um, a. ethereal, heavenly.

aethra, ae, f. brightness, splendour; clear sky.

aevum, ī, nt. time, life, time of life, age, old age, generation.

affābilis, e, easy of access, affable, friendly.

affatim, ad. sufficiently, amply.

affātus, ūs, m. address, speech, converse.

affectātiō, ōnis, f. seeking after; affectation.

affectiō, ōnis, f. mental condition, feeling, disposition, affection, love.

affectō, [1] v. aim at, desire, aspire, lay claim to, pretend.

affectus, ūs, m. disposition, state (of body and mind), affection, passion, love.

affectus, a, um, a. endowed with; disposed; impaired.

afferō, afferre, attulī, allātum, [3] v. bring to, bring word, allege, produce, contribute, cause.

afficiō, affēcī, affectum, [3] v. affect, move, influence.

affīgō, īxī, īxum, [3] v. with dat. fasten to, fix on; impress on.

affingō, īnxī, ictum, [3] v. add (to), embellish, counterfeit, attribute (wrongly).

affīnis, e, a. neighbouring, adjacent, related by marriage, connected (with).

affīnitās, ātis, f. neighbourhood; relationship (by marriage).

affirmātiō, ōnis, f. affirmation, assertion.

affirmō, [1] v. affirm, assert, confirm.

afflātus, ūs, m. breathing on, breeze, blast, breath; inspiration.

afflīctātiō, ōnis, f. grievous suffering, torment, affliction.

afflīctō, [1] v. strike repeatedly, damage, vex.

afflīgō, īxī, īctum, [3] v. afflict, throw down, crush, grieve, humble, weaken.

afflō, [1] v. blow or breathe on; inspire.

affluenter, ad. abundantly, copiously.

affluentia, ae, f. abundance, profusion, superfluity.

affluō, xī, xum, [3] v. flow on; flock together, abound.

affor, ārī, fātus sum, [1] v. dep. speak to, address.

affulgeō, ulsī, [2] v. with dat. shine on; smile upon.

affundō, ūdī, ūsum, [3] v. pour upon (into); **affundor,** prostrate oneself.

agāsō, ōnis, m. driver, groom, stable-boy; lackey.

age, agedum, *i* come! well! all right!

agellus, ī, *m.* little field, farm.

ager, grī, *m.* field, ground, territory, country, farm.

agger, eris, *m.* heap, mound, dam; mudwall; rampart; causeway.

aggerō, gessī, gestum, [3] *v.* carry to, bring, add, heap up, on *or* into.

aggerō, [1] *v.* heap up, fill up, increase.

aggestus, ūs, *m.* piling up.

agglomerō, [1] *v.* gather into a body.

agglūtinō, [1] *v.* glue to, fasten to.

aggravō, [1] *v.* aggravate, weigh down, oppress.

aggredior, gressus, [3] *v. dep.* approach, attack, undertake.

aggregō, [1] *v.* join together, attach; **sē aggregāre,** to ally oneself to.

agilis, e, *a.* agile, nimble, quick, busy.

agilitās, ātis, *f.* activity, quickness.

agitātiō, ōnis, *f.* agitation, exercise; violent motion.

agitātor, ōris, *m.* driver, charioteer.

agitō, [1] *v.* agitate, drive *or* shake *or* move about, revolve; consider, pursue, exercise, manage; keep, celebrate, disturb.

agmen, inis, *nt.* herd, flock, troop, swarm, army (on the march); **prīmum agmen,** the vanguard; **novissimum agmen,** the rear.

agna, ae, *f.* ewe lamb.

agnātus, ī, *m.* relation on the father's side; one born after a father has made his will.

agnīna, ae, *f.* flesh of a lamb.

agnōmen, inis, *nt.* an additional name denoting an achievement, a nickname.

agnōscō, nōvī, nitum, [3] *v.* recognize, acknowledge.

agnus, ī, *m.* lamb.

agō, ēgī, āctum, [3] *v.* drive, act, do, transact, carry off, steal, apply, rouse, cause to bring forth, urge, deal, think, manage, exercise, accuse, deliver (a speech), play (as an actor), behave (as), pass, spend, disturb; **grātiās agere,** to thank.

agrārius, a, um, *a.* agrarian.

agrestis, e, *a.* rustic, rude, wild, savage; **~,** *m.* countryman, peasant.

agricola, ae, *m.* farmer, cultivator.

ahēnus, ahēneus, v. aēnus.

ai, *i.* ah! alas!

aiō, *v.* say, say yes, assent, affirm.

āla, ae, *f.* wing; upper arm, armpit; an army's wing.

alacer, cris, cre, *a.* cheerful, brisk, active, courageous, eager, ready.

alacritās, ātis, *f.* cheerfulness, eagerness, liveliness.

ālāris, e, ālārius, a, um, *a.* pertaining to an army's wing, of the auxiliary cavalry.

ālātus, a, um, *a.* winged.

alauda, ae, *f.* lark.

albātus, a, um, *a.* clothed in white.

albeō, [2] *v.* be *or* grow white.

albēscō, [3] *v.* become white.

albicō, [1] *v.* be white.

albidus, a, um, *a.* whitish, pale.

album, ī, *nt.* white (the colour); white tablet, list of names, register.

albus, a, um, *a.* white, pale, hoary, bright, clear, favourable, fortunate.

alcēdō, inis, & alcyōn, onis, *f.* kingfisher.

alcēdonia, ōrum, *nt. pl.* halcyon days.

ālea, ae, *f.* die, dice-play, gambling, chance, venture, risk.

āleātor, ōris, *m.* dice-player, gambler.

āleātōrius, a, um, *a.* of dice; ~**ia damna**, losses at gambling.

āleō, ōnis, *m.* gambler.

āles, ālitis, *m.* or *f.* bird, fowl; augury; ~, *a.* winged, swift.

alga, ae, *f.* sea-weed; rubbish.

algeō, alsī, [2] *v.* be cold, feel chilly, endure cold.

algor, ōris, *m.* coldness.

aliā, *ad.* by another way.

aliās, *ad.* at another time, elsewhere, otherwise.

alibī, *ad.* elsewhere, in another place.

alicubi, *ad.* somewhere, anywhere.

alicunde, *ad.* from some place, from some source or other.

aliēnātiō, ōnis, *f.* transference, aversion, dislike.

aliēnigena, ae, *m.* stranger, foreigner.

aliēnō, [1] *v.* alienate, transfer by sale, estrange; **aliēnor, ārī**, *v. dep.* avoid (with antipathy); be insane.

aliēnus, a, um, *a.* another's, foreign; contrary, averse, hostile; unfavourable, insane; **aes aliēnum**, debt.

āliger, a, um, *a.* winged.

alimentum, ī, *nt.* nourishment, food.

aliō, *ad.* to another place; to another subject; to another purpose.

aliōquī(n), *ad.* in other respects, besides, else.

ālipēs, edis, *a.* wing-footed, swift.

aliquā, *ad.* somehow.

aliquamdiū, *ad.* for some time.

aliquandō, *ad.* sometimes, at length, formerly, hereafter.

aliquantō, *ad.* somewhat, to some (considerable) extent.

aliquantus, a, um, *a.* a certain quantity *or* amount *or* number of.

aliquī, aliquae, aliquod, *a.* some, any.

aliquis, aliquid, *pl.* **aliquī,** *pn.* someone, somewhat, something.

aliquō, *ad.* to some place *or* other.

aliquot, *a.* (indecl.) some, a number of.

aliquotiē(n)s, *ad.* several times.

aliter, *ad.* otherwise, else.

aliunde, *ad.* from another person *or* place.

alius ... alius, one ... another.

alius, a, ud, *a.* another, different, changed.

allābor, psus, *v. dep.* glide towards, move forwards.

allabōrō, [1] *v.* make a special effort.

allāpsus, ūs, *m.* gliding approach; flowing towards *or* near.

allātrō, [1] *v.* bark at; rail at.

allectō, [1] *v.* allure, entice.

allēgātiō, ōnis, *f.* intercession; allegation.

allēgō, [1] *v.* depute, commission.

allēgō, ēgī, ēctum, [3] *v.* choose, admit.

allevō, [1] *v.* lift up, raise; alleviate, diminish, weaken, console.

alliciō, lexī, lectum, [3] *v.* draw gently to, entice, attract.

allīdō, sī, sum, [3] *v.* dash against; shipwreck.

alligō, [1] *v.* bind to, bind, impede, entangle; bind by an obligation.

allinō, ēvī, itum, [3] *v.* smear over.

allocūtiō, ōnis, *f.* address, consolation, harangue.

alloquium, iī, *nt.* address, encouragement.

alloquor, cūtus, [3] *v. dep.* speak to, address, harangue.

allūdō, ūsī, ūsum, [3] *v.* frolic around, play with, jest.

alluō, uī, [3] *v.* wash against, bathe.

alluviēs, ēī, *f.* flood-land by a river.

almus, a, um, *a.* nourishing, kind, propitious.

alnus, ī, *f.* alder; plank, bridge, boat.

alō, aluī, altum & alitum, [3] *v.* nurse, nourish, maintain; promote; cherish.

Alpīnus, a, um, *a.* of the Alps.

alsius, a, um; alsus, a, um, *a.* liable to injury from cold, cool.

altāria, ium, *nt. pl.* altar.

altē, *ad.* on high, highly, deeply, far back.

alter, a, um, *a.* another, the other, any other, the former, the latter; **unus et alter,** one or two, a few.

altercātiō, ōnis, *f.* contention, dispute, debate.

altercor, ātus, [1] *v. dep.* bicker, dispute, quarrel; dispute in the law-courts.

alternō, [1] *v.* do by turns, vary; alternate, waver.

alternus, a, um, *a.* alternate, one after the other, by turns, mutual; **alternīs vicibus,** alternately, by turns.

alteruter, utra, utrum, either, one of two.

altisonus, a, um, *a.* high-sounding, lofty; sublime.

altitonāns, antis, *a.* thundering from on high.

altitūdō, dinis, *f.* height; depth; *fig.* loftiness, profundity, noble-mindedness, secrecy.

altivolāns, antis, *a.* high-flying.

altor, ōris, *m.* nourisher, foster-father.

altrīx, īcis, *f.* female nourisher, wet-nurse.

altus, a, um, *a.* high, deep, shrill, lofty, noble; deeply rooted; far-fetched; **altum, ī,** *nt.* the deep, the sea; a height.

ālūcinor, ātus, [1] *v. dep.* wander in mind, talk idly, dream.

alumnus, a, um, *a.* nourished, brought up; ~, *m.* nursling, foster-child, disciple.

alūta, ae, *f.* a piece of soft leather; a beauty patch.

alveus, ī, *m.* cavity; tub; tray; hold of a ship, boat; gaming-board; bee-hive; bathing-tub; river-bed.

alvus, ī, *f.* belly, paunch, womb, stomach; bee-hive.

amābilis, e, *a.* amiable, pleasant.

amābiliter, *ad.* lovingly, amicably, pleasantly.

āmandō, [1] *v.* send away, dismiss.

amāns, antis, *m.* or *f.* lover, sweetheart, mistress.

amanter, *ad.* lovingly, affectionately.

amāracus, ī, *m.* or *f.*, **amāracum, ī,** *nt.* marjoram.

amāritūdō, inis, *f.* bitterness; sharpness, disagreeableness.

amārus, a, um, *a.* bitter, harsh, shrill, sad, calamitous; ill-natured.

amātor, ōris, *m.* lover, devotee.

amātōrius, a, um, *a.* loving, amorous, procuring love.

amātrīx, īcis, *f.* sweetheart, mistress.

ambāgēs, is, *f., pl.* **ambāgēs, um,** round-about way, shifting, shuffling, prevarication; long-winded story; obscurity, ambiguity.

ambedō, ēdī, ēsum, [3] *v.* gnaw round the edge, consume.

ambigō, [3] *v.* hesitate, be in doubt, argue, wrangle.

ambiguitās, ātis, *f.* ambiguity.

ambiguus, a, um, *a.* changeable, varying, doubtful, dark, ambiguous, wavering, fickle.

ambiō, īvī & iī, ītum, [4] *v.* surround, solicit, ask, aspire to; canvass.

ambitiō, ōnis, *f.* ambition; currying favour, vain display; effort, canvassing.

ambitiōsus, a, um, *a.* ambitious, eager to please; importunate; showy.

ambitus, ūs, *m.* circuit; canvass, bribery; circumlocution; ostentation.

ambō, bae, bō, *a.* both (two together).

ambrosia, ae, *f.* food of the gods.

ambrosius, a, um, *a.* immortal, divine.

ambulātiō, ōnis, *f.* walking about; place for promenading.

ambulātiuncula, ae, *f.* little walk; small place for walking.

ambulō, [1] *v.* go about, take a walk, travel.

ambūrō, ussī, ustum, [3] *v.* burn around, scorch, burn wholly up; make frost-bitten.

āmēns, entis, *a.* mad, frantic.

āmentia, ae, *f.* madness, stupidity.

ames, itis, *m.* pole for supporting bird-nets.

amethystus, ī, *f.* amethyst.

amīca, ae, *f.* female friend, sweetheart, courtesan.

amiciō, icuī & ixī, ictum, [4] *v.* clothe, wrap about; veil.

amīcitia, ae, *f.* friendship, alliance, affinity.

amictus, ūs, *m.* upper garment, cloak, dress, clothing.

amīcula, ae, *f.* mistress, ladyfriend.

amiculum, ī, *nt.* mantle, cloak.

amīculus, ī, *m.* little friend, dear friend, humble friend.

amīcus, ī, *m.* friend, ally, lover, patron; counsellor, courtier, ~, **a, um,** *a.* friendly, fond of.

āmissiō, ōnis, *f.* loss.

amita, ae, *f.* father's sister, aunt.

āmittō, īsī, issum, [3] *v.* lose, dismiss, let fall, let slip.

amnis, is, *m.* stream, river.

amō, [1] *v.* love, like, be fond of; have a tendency to.

amoenitās, ātis, *f.* pleasantness, delight, charm.

amoenus, a, um, *a.* pleasant, agreeable, charming.

āmōlior, ītus, [4] *v. dep.* remove, obliterate; avert, refute.

amōmum, ī, *nt.* Eastern spice-plant; spice from this plant.

amor, ōris, *m.* love; the beloved; Cupid; eager desire.

āmoveō, mōvī, mōtum, [2] *v.* remove, steal; banish.

amphisbaena, ae, *f.* a species of serpent supposed to have a head at both ends of its body.

amphitheātrum, ī, *nt.* amphitheatre.

amphora, ae, *f.* large earthenware jar, usually two-handled.

amplector, exus, [3] *v. dep.* embrace, lay hold of; surround, contain; cherish; understand.

amplexor, ātus, [1] *v. dep.* v. **amplector;** love, esteem.

amplexus, ūs, *m.* embracing, embrace, surrounding.

amplificātiō, ōnis, *f.* enlargement, amplification.

amplificō, [1] *v.* amplify, enlarge, praise loudly.

ampliō, [1] *v.* make wider, enlarge, adjourn.

amplitūdō, inis, *f.* width, breadth, size, bulk; importance; fulness of expression.

amplius, *ad.* more, further.

amplus, a, um, *a.* ample, large, wide; distinguished.

ampulla, ae, *f.* bottle *or* flask for holding liquids; (*pl.*) inflated expressions, bombast.

amputātiō, ōnis, *f.* pruning, lopping off.

amputō, [1] *v.* lop off, prune, shorten.

amygdalum, ī, *nt.* almond tree.

an, *c.* whether? or, either.

anadēma, atis, *nt.* band for the hair.

anapaestus, ī, *m.* anapaest, metrical foot, two shorts followed by a long.

anas, anatis, *f.* duck.

anaticula, ae, *f.* duckling.

anatocismus, ī, *m.* compound interest.

anceps, cipitis, *a.* two-edged, two-headed; dangerous, doubtful; double, undecided.

ancīle, is, *nt.* small figure-of-eight shield.

ancilla, ae, *f.* maid-servant, female slave.

ancillula, ae, *f.* little serving-maid, young female slave.

ancora, ae, *f.* anchor.

ancorāle, is, *nt.* anchor cable.

andabata, ae, *m.* a gladiator who fought blindfolded.

androgynus, ī, *m.* hermaphrodite.

anēt(h)um, ī, *nt.* dill, anise.

anfrāctus, ūs, *m.* curving, bending, circuit, windings; circumlocution.

angiportus, ūs, *m.* **angiportum, ī,** *nt.* narrow street *or* alley.

angō, xī, ctum, [3] *v.* press tight, throttle; cause pain, vex, trouble.

angor, ōris, *m.* suffocation, choking, anguish, vexation.

anguicomus, a, um, *a.* with snaky hair.

anguifer, a, um, *a.* snake-bearing.

anguilla, ae, *f.* eel.

anguīnus, a, um, *a.* of a snake, snaky.

anguis, is, *m.* or *f.* snake, serpent; (constellation) the Dragon.

angulus, ī, *m.* angle, corner, nook, out-of-the-way spot.

angustiae, ārum, *f. pl.* strait, defile, narrowness; want, perplexity, trouble; narrow-mindedness.

angustō, [1] *v.* make narrow, constrict, crowd together.

angustus, a, um, *a.* narrow, confined; scanty, poor, needy, low, mean; narrow-minded.

anhēlitus, ūs, *m.* panting, puffing, breathing, breath, exhalation.

anhēlō, [1] *v.* pant, gasp, breathe out.

anhēlus, a, um, *a.* panting, puffing.

anicula, ae, *f.* little old woman.

anīlis, e, *a.* old-womanish.

anima, ae, *f.* air, breeze, breath, soul, life.

animadversiō, ōnis, *f.* observation, attention, reproach, punishment.

animadvertō, tī, sum, [3] *v.* observe, attend to, remark, notice, understand, perceive, avenge, punish, blame.

animal, ālis, *nt.* animal.

animālis, e, *a.* made of air, animal.

animāns, antis, *a.* living; ~, *m., f.,* & *nt.* being, animal.

animō, [1] *v.* animate, encourage, give life to, revive.

animōsus, a, um, *a.* courageous, bold, strong, ardent, energetic, stormy.

animula, ae, *f.* little life.

animus, ī, *m.* (rational) soul, mind, will, purpose, desire, character; courage; anger; pride; pleasure, inclination; memory, judgment, consciousness, opinion; vital power, life; **ex animō,** from the heart, with sincerity; **bonō animō esse,** to be of good heart; **aequō animō,** with equanimity.

annālēs, ium, *m. pl.* annals, year-books.

annālis, e, *a.* relating to the year, chronicle, history.

annatō, [1] *v.* swim towards.

anniversārius, a, um, *a.* annual, yearly.

annōna, ae, *f.* year's produce, provision, victuals, price of grain *or* other food.

annōsus, a, um, *a.* aged, old.

annōtinus, a, um, *a.* of last year.

annus, ī, *m.* year, season, year's produce; age.

annuus, a, um, *a.* yearly, lasting a year.

anquīrō, quīsīvī, ītum, [3] *v.* search diligently after, inquire into, examine judicially.

ānsa, ae, *f.* handle; opportunity.

ānser, eris, *m.* & *f.* goose.

ante, *pr. with acc.* before, in front of ~; *ad.* in front, before (of time), forwards.

anteā, *ad.* before this, formerly.

antecapiō, cēpī, ceptum, [3] *v.* take beforehand, anticipate.

antecēdēns, entis, *a.* previously existent.

antecēdō, essī, essum, [3] *v.* go before, precede, excel, surpass.

antecellō, [3] *v.* surpass, excel.

antecessiō, ōnis, *f.* going before; antecedent cause.

antecursor, ōris, *m.* (*pl.*) leading troops, vanguard.

anteeō, īvī & iī, [4] *v.* go before; surpass; anticipate; prevent.

anteferō, ferre, tulī, lātum, [3] *v.* carry before; prefer

antegredior, essus, [3] *v. dep.* go before, precede.

antehāc, *ad.* before this time; earlier.

antelūcānus, a, um, *a.* before daybreak.

antemerīdiānus, a, um, *a.* before noon.

antenna, ae, *f.* sail-yard; sail.

antepīlānī, ōrum, *m. pl.* men who fought in the first *or* second line.

antepōnō, suī, situm, [3] *v.* place before; prefer.

antequam, *c.* before.

antēs, ium, *m. pl.* rows (of plants).

antesignānus, ī, *m.* leader; (*pl.*) troops who fought in the front rank of a legion.

antestō *or* **antistō, stitī**, [1] *v. with dat.* surpass.

antestor, ātus, [1] *v. dep.* call as a witness.

anteveniō, vēnī, ventum, [4] *v.* come before; anticipate, forestall.

antevertō, tī, sum, [3] *v.* act first, precede; give priority to.

anticipātiō, ōnis, *f.* preconception.

anticipō, [1] *v.* occupy beforehand; anticipate.

antīquārius, iī, *m.* antiquarian, student of the past.

antīquē, *ad.* in the old way, in an old-fashioned manner.

antīquitās, ātis, *f.* antiquity: the ancients; virtue of olden time.

antīquitus, *ad.* in former times.

antīquō, [1] *v.* reject (a bill).

antīquus, a, um, *a.* old, ancient; aged; of the old stamp, simple, honest, venerable.

antistes, stitis, *m. & f.* high-priest; chief priestess; (*with gen.*) master (in).

antistita, ae, *f.*, *v.* antistes.

antrum, ī, *nt.* cave, cavern.

ānulārius, ī, *m.* ring-maker.

ānulus, ī, *m.* ring; signet-ring.

ānus, ī, *m.* ring, anus.

anus, ūs, *f.* old woman; sibyl; ~, *a.* old, aged.

ānxietās, ātis, *f.* anxiety; carefulness.

ānxius, a, um, *a.* anxious, uneasy; disturbed; concerned; careful.

apage, *i.* be off! get away with (you)!

aper, prī, *m.* wild boar.

aperiō, eruī, ertum, [4] *v.* open; discover; show, explain.

apertus, a, um, open; public; exposed; wide, extended; cloudless; clear; frank.

apex, icis, *m.* point, top, summit; cap, crown; conical cap of a priest; highest honour.

aphractus, ī, *f.* **aphractum, ī,** *nt.* undecked boat.

apis, is, *f.* bee.

apīscor, aptus, [3] *v. dep.* reach, obtain.

apium, iī, *nt.* wild celery *or* parsley.

aplustre, is, *nt.* ornamented stern-port of a ship.

apodýtērium, iī, *nt.* undressing-room in a bathing-house.

apologus, ī, *m.* narrative; fable.

apothēca, ae, *f.* store-house, store-room, wine-cellar.

apparātus, a, um, *a.* prepared, ready; splendid, sumptuous.

apparātus, ūs, *m.* preparation; provision; equipment; splendour, pomp.

appāreō, uī, itum, [2] *v.* appear; be evident; (*with dat.*) attend *or* serve; **appāret,** it is clear.

appāritiō, ōnis, *f.* service, attendance; servants.

appāritor, ōris, *m.* (public) servant; lictor, clerk.

apparō, [1] *v.* prepare, fit out, provide; attempt.

appellātiō, ōnis, *f.* appeal; calling by name; name, title; pronunciation.

appellātor, ōris, *m.* appellant.

appellitō, [1] *v.* call *or* name frequently.

appellō, [1] *v.* call upon; address; dun; appeal (to); bring into court; accuse; name, entitle; pronounce.

appellō, pulī, pulsum, [3] *v.* drive to; bring to land; come ashore.

appendix, icis, *f.* appendage; supplement.

appendō, endī, ēnsum, [3] *v.* weigh out.

appetēns, entis, *a.* with gen. eager for; avaricious.

appetentia, ae, *f.* longing after, appetite.

appetītiō, ōnis, *f.* desire; grasping (at).

appetītus, ūs, *m.* desire, appetite.

appetō, īvī & iī, ītum, [3] *v.* seek *or* grasp after; assail; strive eagerly after, long for; approach.

appingō, [3] *v.* paint upon; add in writing.

applaudō, sī, sum, [3] *v.* strike together; clap; applaud.

applicātiō, ōnis, *f.* application, inclination.

applicātus, a, um, *a.* situated close (to); devoted (to).

applicō, āvī & uī, ātum & itum, [1] *v.* join to, place near; apply (to); devote (to): connect.

appōnō, posuī, positum, [3] *v.* put *or* lay to; apply to; add to; serve up.

apportō, [1] *v.* carry, bring to; cause.

appositus, a, um, *a.* adjacent, near; fit, appropriate.

apprehendō, dī, sum, [3] *v.* seize, lay hold of.

approbātiō, ōnis, *f.* approbation; proof; decision.

approbō, [1] *v.* approve; prove; confirm; justify; allow; make good.

approperō, [1] *v.* hasten, hurry.

appropinquātiō, ōnis, *f.* approach, drawing near.

appropinquō, [1] *v.* approach, draw near.

appugnō, [1] *v.* attack, assault.

appulsus, ūs, *m.* driving to; landing; approach; influence.

aprīcātiō, ōnis, *f.* a basking in the sun.

aprīcor, [1] *v. dep.* sun oneself.

aprīcus, a, um, *a.* exposed to the sun; sunny.

Aprīlis, is, *m.* April.

aptē, *ad.* closely, snugly; fitly, suitably.

aptō, [1] *v.* fit, apply, put on; adjust; prepare, furnish.

aptus, a, um, *a.* attached to; connected, suitable, adapted;

(with ex with abl.) dependent (upon).

apud, *pr. with acc.* at the house of, at, by, near, with; among; in; before; in the time of; in the works of.

aqua, ae, *f.* water; rain; sea; lake; river.

aquaeductus, ūs, *m.* aqueduct.

aquārius, a, um, *a.* relating to water; ~, iī, *m.* water-carrier; overseer of the public water supply; Water-bearer (as a constellation).

aquāticus, a, um, *a.* aquatic; watery, rainy.

aquātiō, ōnis, *f.* fetching of water.

aquātor, ōris, *m.* water-carrier.

aquila, ae, *f.* eagle; standard of a Roman legion.

aquilifer, erī, *m.* standard-bearer.

aquilō, ōnis, *m.* north wind; north.

aquilōnius, a, um, *a.* northern.

aquor, ātus, [1] *v. dep.* fetch water.

aquōsus, a, um, *a.* abounding in water, humid, rainy.

āra, ae, *f.* altar; sanctuary; home; refuge, shelter.

arabarchēs, ae, *m.* Egyptian tax-gatherer.

arānea, ae, *f.* spider; cobweb.

arāneōsus, a, um, *a.* covered with spiders' webs.

arāneus, ī, *m.* spider.

arātiō, ōnis, *f.* ploughing; tilled ground.

arātor, ōris, *m.* ploughman, farmer.

arātrum, ī, *nt.* plough.

arbiter, trī, *m.* eye-witness; umpire, arbiter, lord, master.

arbitrātus, ūs, *m.* arbitration; choice.

arbitrium, iī, *nt.* judgment of an arbitrator; sentence; will, mastery, authority.

arbitror, ātus, [1] *v. dep.* observe, perceive, pass sentence; believe, think.

arbor, oris, *f.* tree; mast; oar; ship.

arboreus, a, um, *a.* of *or* belonging to trees.

arbustum, ī, *nt.* copse, plantation, grove of trees; shrub.

arbuteus, a, um, *a.* of the strawberry tree.

arbutum, ī, *nt.* wild strawberry; wild strawberry tree.

arbutus, ī, *f.* wild strawberry tree.

arca, ae, *f.* chest, strong-box, coffer; purse; coffin; prison-cell; ark.

arcānum, ī, secret, mystery.

arcānus, a, um, *a.* secret, hidden, mysterious.

arceō, cuī, [2] *v.* keep off, prevent; protect.

accessō, īvī, ītum, [3] *v.* send for, call; procure; summons, accuse.

architectūra, ae, *f.* architecture.

architectus, ī, *m.* architect; inventor, designer.

arcitenēns, entis, *a.* holding a bow (epithet of Apollo), (constellation) the Archer.

arctē, arctō, arctus, *v.* artē, artō, artus.

Arctos, ī, *f.* the Great Bear *or* the Little Bear; the north.

Arctōus, a, um, *a.* northern.

Arctūrus, ī, *m.* brightest star in the constellation Boötes.

arcula, ae, *f.* small box, casket.

arcus, ūs, *m.* arch; bow; rainbow; anything arched *or* curved.

ardea, ae, *f.* heron.

ardēns, entis, *a.* burning; glowing, fiery; eager, ardent, passionate.

ardeō, arsī, arsum, [2] *v.* burn, blaze; flash; glow, sparkle; be inflamed; be in a turmoil.

ardēscō, arsī, [3] *v.* take fire, kindle; be inflamed.

ardor, ōris, *m.* fire, flame, heat; brightness; ardour, love, intensity.

arduus, a, um, *a.* steep, high; difficult, arduous.

ārea, ae, *f.* open space; threshing-floor; granary; courtyard; field of action.

ārefaciō, fēcī, factum, [3] *v.* dry up.

arēna, ae, *f.* sand; sandy land *or* desert; seashore; place of contest, amphitheatre.

arēnāria, ae, *f.* sand-pit.

arēnōsus, a, um, *a.* sandy.

āreō, [2] *v.* be dry; be thirsty.

ārēscō, [3] *v.* become dry

argentāria, ae, *f.* banking-house, banking business; silver-mine.

argentārius, a, um, *a.* pertaining to silver *or* money; ~, **iī** , *m.* banker, financial agent.

argentātus, a, um *a.* silvered.

argenteus, a, um, *a.* of silver; silvery.

argentum, ī, *nt.* silver; silver plate; money.

argilla, ae, *f.* white clay, potter's earth.

argūmentātiō, ōnis, *f.* argumentation; proof.

argūmentor, ātus, [1] *v. dep.* support *or* prove by argument, reason.

argūmentum, ī, *nt.* argument, proof; subject, plot (of a play).

arguō, uī, ūtum, [3] *v.* prove, assert, accuse; convict; condemn.

argūtiae, ārum, *f. pl.* clever use of words; verbal trickery; wit.

argūtus, a, um, *a.* melodious; distinct, clear; sagacious, witty; cunning, sly; talkative, rustling, rattling.

āridum, ī, *nt.* dry land.

āridus, a, um, *a.* dry, parched; barren; thirsty; poor; shrivelled.

ariēs, ietis, *m.* ram; battering-ram; the Ram (in the zodiac).

arietō, [1] *v.* butt like a ram; strike violently.

arista, ae, *f.* beard of an ear of grain; ear of corn; grain crop.

arithmētica, ōrum, *nt. pl.* arithmetic.

arma, ōrum, *nt. pl.* arms, weapons; tools; tackling; shield; soldiers, army; war; battle; **vī et armīs**, by force of arms.

armāmenta, ōrum, *nt. pl.* tackle of a ship.

armāmentārium, iī, *nt.* arsenal, armoury.

armārium, iī, *nt.* cabinet, cupboard; book-case.

armātūra, ae, *f.* armour, harness; armed soldiers.

armentālis, e, *a.* of cattle.

armentum, ī, *nt.* herd (of large cattle); a head of cattle.

armifer, a, um, armiger, a um, *a.* armed, warlike; ~, *m.* armour-bearer, squire.

armilla, ae, *f.* bracelet.

armipotēns, entis, *a.* powerful in arms, valiant, warlike.

armisonus, a, um, *a.* sounding with the clash of arms.

armō, [1] *v.* equip; arm; kindle; incite to war; rig (a ship).

armus, ī, *m.* forequarter (of an animal), shoulder.

arō, [1] *v.* plough, till; furrow, wrinkle; produce by ploughing.

arrēpō, psī, ptum, [3] *v.* creep towards.

arrīdeō, rīsī, rīsum, [2] *v.* smile upon; please.

arrigō, rēxī, rēctum, [3] *v.* set upright, raise; animate, rouse.

arripiō, ripuī, reptum, [3] *v.* snatch away; take hold of; pick up (knowledge); appropriate; arrest; assail.

arrōdō, rōsī, rōsum, [3] *v.* gnaw *or* nibble at.

arrogāns, antis, *a.* arrogant.

arrogantia, ae, *f.* arrogance, conceit.

arrogō, [1] *v.* ask, question; arrogate to one's self, claim; confer (upon).

ars, artis, *f.* skill; art; work of art; profession; theory; manner of acting; cunning, artifice.

artē, *ad.* closely, tightly, briefly, in a confined space.

artēria, ae, *f.* windpipe; artery.

arthrīticus, a, um, *a.* affected with rheumatism.

articulus, ī, *m.* joint; part; moment of time, critical moment.

artifex, icis, *m.* artist, artificer; maker, author; ~, *a.* skilful; artful.

artificiōsus, a, um, *a.* skilful; ingenious; artificial, unnatural.

artificium, iī, *nt.* handicraft, art, trade; skill; theory, system; cunning.

artō, [1] *v.* compress, contract; abridge, limit.

artus, a, um, *a.* close, thick, narrow; short; strict; scanty, brief.

artūs, uum, *m. pl.* joints; limbs.

ārula, ae, *f.* small altar.

arundineus, a, um, *a.* of reeds; reedy.

arundō, inis, *f.* reed; fishing rod; arrow-shaft; arrow; pen; shepherd's pipe.

aruspex, *v.* haruspex.

arvīna, ae, *f.* fat, lard.

arvum, ī, *nt.* arable field; country; dry land; stretch of plain.

arvus, a, um, *a.* arable.

arx, arcis, *f.* stronghold, citadel; the Capitoline hill at Rome; defence, refuge.

as, assis, *m.* a copper coin of small value.

ascendō, ndī, nsum, [3] *v.* mount up, ascend.

ascēnsiō, ōnis, *f.* ascent; progress, advancement.

ascensus, ūs, *m.* ascending, ascent; approach; a stage in advancement.

asciō, [4] *v.* take to *or* associate, admit.

ascīscō, īvī, ītum, [3] *v.* receive, admit, approve of, associate; appropriate, adopt.

ascrībō, psī, ptum, [3] *v.* add in writing; ascribe, impute; appoint; enrol; reckon, number.

asella, ae, *f.* she-ass.

asellus, ī, *m.* ass, donkey.

asilus, ī, *m.* gadfly.

asinus, ī, *m.* ass; blockhead.

asōtus, ī, *m.* debauchee.

aspectō, [1] *v.* look *or* gaze at; observe; (geographically) look towards.

aspectus, ūs, *m.* looking at, glance, view; sight; horizon; appearance; aspect, mien.

asper, a, um, *a.* rough; uneven; harsh, sour; bitter; rude, violent, unkind, savage; wayward; austere; wild, fierce; critical, adverse.

aspergō, ersī, ersum, [3] *v.* besprinkle; defile, stain.

aspergō, inis, *f.* besprinkling; spray.

asperitās, ātis, *f.* roughness; severity; harshness; tartness; shrillness; fierceness.

aspernor, ātus, [1] *v. dep.* despise.

asperō, [1] *v.* make rough; sharpen; make fierce, violent.

aspersiō, ōnis, *f.* sprinkling.

aspiciō, exī, ectum, [3] *v.* look at, behold; (geographically) look towards; consider, contemplate.

aspīrātiō, ōnis, *f.* exhalation; aspiration; sounding an 'h'.

aspīrō, [1] *v.* breathe *or* blow upon; infuse; be favourable to; assist; aspire to.

aspis, idis, *f.* asp.

asportātiō, ōnis, *f.* carrying away.

asportō, *v.* carry away, remove.

asprētum, ī, *nt.* rough ground.

assa, ōrum, *nt. pl.* sweating bath.

assecla, assecula, ae, *m.* attendant, servant; hanger-on, sycophant.

assectātiō, ōnis, *f.* waiting on, attendance.

assectātor, ōris, *m.* follower, companion; disciple.

assector, ātus, [1] *v. dep.* accompany, attend; support.

assēnsiō, ōnis, *f.* assent, applause.

assēnsor, ōris, *m.* one who agrees or approves.

assēnsus, ūs, *m.* assent, approbation, applause.

assentātiō, ōnis, *f.* flattering agreement, toadyism.

assentātor, ōris, *m.* flatterer, 'yes-man.'

assentior, sēnsus, [4] *v. dep.* assent to, approve, comply with.

assentor, ātus, [1] *v. dep.* flatter.

assequor, secūtus, [3] *v. dep.* follow on, pursue; overtake; gain, attain to; equal, rival; understand.

asser, eris, *m.* pole, post, stake.

asserō, eruī, ertum, [3] *v.* assert; free; claim.

assertor, ōris, *m.* restorer of liberty; protector, advocate; champion.

asservō, [1] *v.* keep, preserve, watch, observe.

assessor, ōris, *m.* assessor, counsellor.

assevēranter, *ad.* earnestly, emphatically.

assevērātiō, ōnis, *f.* affirmation, asseveration; seriousness.

assevērō, [1] *v.* act with earnestness; assert strongly.

assideō, sēdī, sessum, [2] *v.* sit by; be an assessor; besiege; (*with dat.*) resemble.

assīdō, sēdī, [3] *v.* sit down.

assiduē, *ad.* continually, constantly.

assiduitās, ātis, *f.* attendance; assiduity; care; recurrence, repetition.

assiduus, a, um, *a.* assiduous; continual, unremitting.

assignātiō, ōnis, *f.* distribution *or* allotment of land; plot of land.

assignō, [1] *v.* assign; impute.

assiliō, siluī, sultum, [4] *v.* leap up, rush (at).

assimilis, e, *a.* similar, like.

assimulō, [1] *v.* make like; compare; counterfeit, pretend, feign.

assistō, astitī, [3] *v.* stand at *or* by, attend, be present at.

assoleō, [2] *v.* be accustomed *or* in the habit of.

assuēfaciō, fēcī, factum, [3] *v.* accustom (to).

assuēscō, ēvī, ētum, [3] *v.* accustom (to); become accustomed.

assuētūdō, inis, *f.* custom, habit; intimacy.

assuētus, a, um, *a.* accustomed, customary, usual.

assultō, [1] *v.* jump at; attack.

assultus, ūs, *m.* attack, assault.

assūmō, mpsī, mptum, [3] *v.* take up, adopt, receive; add to; usurp, arrogate.

assūmptiō, ōnis, *f.* adoption; minor premiss.

assuō, [3] *v.* sew *or* patch on.

assurgō, surrēxī, surrēctum, [3] *v.* claim, rise *or* stand up; rise, soar.

assus, a, um, *a.* roasted; dry.

ast, *c.* v. **at.**

asternō, [3] *v.* prostrate oneself, lie prone (on).

astō, stitī, [1] *v.* stand at *or* by; assist; stand upright.

astrepō, uī, [3] *v.* make a noise at, shout in support.

astrictus, a, um, *a.* bound by rules; terse, brief; parsimonious.

astringō, īnxī, ictum, [3] *v.* tighten, bind *or* fasten; oblige, contract.

astrologia, ae, *f.* astronomy, astrology.

astrologus, ī, *m.* astronomer, astrologer.

astrum, ī, *nt.* star, constellation; sky.

astruō, ūxī, ūctum, [3] v. build on; add to.

astupeō, [2] v. be stunned or astonished (at).

āstus, ūs, m. craft, cunning, trick.

āstūtia, ae, f. cunning, slyness, trick.

āstūtus, a, um, a. clever, expert; sly, cunning.

asȳlum, ī, nt. place of refuge, sanctuary.

at, ast, c. but, yet; but then; on the contrary; at least.

atat, i. ah!

atavus, ī, m. great-great-great grandfather; ancestor.

āter, tra, trum, a. black; gloomy, dismal, unlucky.

āthlēta, ae, m. wrestler, athlete.

atomus, ī, f. atom.

atque, c. and, and also, and even, and too; yet; nevertheless; (after words expressing comparison) as, than.

atquī, c. but, yet, notwithstanding, however, rather, but now; and yet; well now.

ātrāmentum, ī, nt. writing-ink; blacking.

ātrātus, a, um, a. darkened; wearing mourning.

ātriēnsis, is, m. steward.

ātriolum, ī, nt. small anteroom.

ātrium, iī, nt. hall in a Roman house; palace.

atrōcitās, ātis, f. fierceness; savageness, cruelty; severity.

atrōx, ōcis, a. savage, cruel, fierce, severe.

attāctus, ūs, m. touch.

attamen, ad. but yet, but however, nevertheless.

attendō, endī, entum, [3] v. turn towards; apply; attend to, listen carefully.

attentē, ad. diligently, carefully.

attentiō, ōnis, f. attention.

attentō, [1] v. try, attempt; assail, attack.

attentus, a, um, attentive; careful.

attenuō, [1] v. thin, weaken, lessen, diminish.

atterō, trīvī, trītum, [3] v. rub against; wear out, impair.

Atticē, ad. in the Attic manner; elegantly.

Atticus, a, um, a. Attic, Athenian; classic, elegant.

attineō, tinuī, tentum, [2] v. hold on or fast; delay; belong (to).

attingō, tigī, tāctum, [3] v. touch; arrive at; border upon; affect; mention in passing; achieve, win; relate to.

attollō, [3] v. lift up; erect, build; exalt; extol.

attondeō, tondī, tōnsum, [3] v. clip, prune.

attonitus, a, um, a. thunderstruck; stupefied, amazed; inspired, frenzied.

attonō, uī, itum, [1] *v.* strike with lightning; drive crazy.

attorqueō, [2] *v.* whirl at.

attrahō, xī, ctum, [3] *v.* attract; drag on.

attrectō, [1] *v.* touch, handle; deal with.

attribuō, uī, ūtum, [3] *v.* assign; attribute *or* impute to.

attribūtiō, ōnis, *f.* assignment of a debt; attribution of a quality.

au, *i.* oh! ow! oh dear!

auceps, cupis, *m.* bird-catcher; bird-seller.

auctificus, a, um, *a.* giving increase.

auctiō, ōnis, *f.* public sale, auction.

auctiōnārius, a, um, *a.* pertaining to an auction.

auctiōnor, ātus, [1] *v. dep.* put up to public sale.

auctō, [1] *v.* increase.

auctor, ōris, *m. or f.* creator, maker, inventor; father; teacher; leader; founder; author; promoter; adviser; protector; witness; vendor; bail; guardian, champion.

auctōrāmentum, ī, *nt.* wages, pay; reward.

auctōritās, ātis, *f.* authority, power; reputation, credit; opinion, judgment; command; influence, importance; credibility.

auctōror, ātus, [1] *v. dep.* bind oneself, hire oneself.

auctus, ūs, *m.* growth, increase, bulk.

aucupium, iī, *nt.* bird-catching; game birds.

aucupor, ātus, [1] *v. dep.* go bird-catching; lie in wait for.

audācia, ae, *f.* boldness; courage, valour; audacity.

audāciter, audacter, *ad.* boldly, courageously.

audāx, ācis, *a.* bold, courageous, audacious; desperate.

audēns, entis, *a.* daring, bold.

audentia, ae, *f.* boldness, courage.

audeō, ausus, [2] *v.* dare, venture.

audientia, ae, *f.* hearing; audience, attention.

audiō, īvī & iī, ītum, [4] *v.* hear; listen, hearken; regard; grant; obey.

audītiō, ōnis, *f.* hearing; report, hearsay.

audītor, ōris, *m.* hearer, auditor; disciple.

audītōrium, iī, *nt.* lecture-room, audience.

audītus, ūs, *m.* hearing; listening; sense of hearing; hearsay.

auferō, auferre, abstulī, ablātum, *v.* bear away; snatch away; carry off; obtain; destroy.

aufugiō, fūgī, [3] *v.* flee away *or* from.

augeō, auxī, auctum, [2] *v.* increase, augment; make a lot of.

augēscō, [3] *v.* grow, become greater.

augmen, inis, *nt.* growth, increase, bulk.

augur, uris, *m.* or *f.* augur; soothsayer.

augurālis, e, *a.* pertaining to augurs, relating to soothsaying.

augurātiō, ōnis, *f.* prediction by means of augury.

augurātō, *ad.* after taking the auguries.

augurātus, ūs, *m.* office of an augur; augury.

augurium, iī, *nt.* profession of an augur, soothsaying, prediction.

auguror, ātus, [1] *v. dep.* act as augur; foretell; conjecture.

augustus, a, um, *a.* sacred, venerable; majestic; august; ~, *m.* August (month).

aula, ae, *f.* inner court of a house; hall; palace; royal court; courtiers.

aulaeum, ī, *nt.* curtain of a theatre; canopy; tapestry.

aura, ae, *f.* air, gentle breeze; breath; wind; gleam, glittering; odour, exhalation; ~ populāris, the breath of popular favour.

aurātus, a, um, *a.* gilt, golden.

aureolus, a, um, *a.* golden, splendid.

aureus, a, um, *a.* golden; gilded; shining like gold; beautiful.

auricomus, a, um, *a.* golden-haired.

auricula, ae, *f.* ear.

aurifer, a, um, *a.* gold-bearing.

aurifex, icis, *m.* goldsmith.

aurīga, ae, *m.* charioteer; helmsman; (a constellation) the Waggoner; groom.

auris, is, *f.* ear; hearing.

aurītus, a, um, *a.* hearing well; long-eared.

aurōra, ae, *f.* dawn, daybreak.

aurum, ī, *nt.* gold.

auscultō, [1] *v.* listen to; overhear; obey.

auspex, icis, *m.* diviner by birds; soothsayer; patron, supporter.

auspicātō, *ad.* after taking the auspices; auspiciously.

auspicātus, a, um, *a.* consecrated by auguries; favourable, auspicious.

auspicium, iī, *nt.* auspices; the right of taking auspices; leadership, authority; sign, omen.

auspicor, ātus, [1] *v. dep.* take the auspices.

auster, trī, *m.* south wind; south.

austēritās, ātis, *f.* harshness; gloominess; severity.

austērus, a, um, *a.* austere; harsh; sour; sharp; rough, dark, stern; unornamented.

austrālis, e, *a.* southern.

austrīnus, a, um, *a.* southern.

ausum, ī, *nt.* daring attempt, enterprise; crime, outrage.

aut, *c.* or; or else, either.

autem, but; however; indeed; on the contrary.

autumnālis, e, *a.* autumnal.

autumnus, ī, *m.* autumn.

autumō, [1] *v.* say yes, affirm; say, mention.

auxiliāris, e, *a.* help-bringing, auxiliary.

auxiliārius, a, um, *a.* helping, auxiliary;

auxilior, ātus, [1] *v. dep.* give aid; (*with dat.*) assist.

auxilium, iī, *nt.* help, aid, assistance; auxiliary forces.

avāritia, ae, *f.* avarice, rapacity, miserliness.

avārus, a, um, *a.* avaricious, covetous, stingy.

āvehō, vēxī, vectum, [3] *v.* carry away; **avehī,** to ride away, go away.

āvellō, vellī & vulsī, vulsum, [3] *v.* pluck away, tear off; separate by force.

avēna, ae, *f.* oats; wild oats; stem, stalk, straw; oaten pipe, pan pipes.

avē, *i.* greetings!

aveō, [2] *v.* be eager *or* anxious; desire.

āverruncō, *v.* avert (something bad).

āversor, ātus, [1] *v. dep.* turn oneself away in disgust *or* horror; avoid, refuse; reject.

āversor, ōris, *m.* embezzler.

āversus, a, um, *a.* turned away; averse; hostile.

āvertō, tī, sum, [3] *v.* turn away from *or* aside; steal, misappropriate, divert, estrange.

avia, ae, *f.* grandmother.

aviārium, iī, *nt.* haunt of wild birds; aviary.

aviditās, ātis, *f.* covetousness, greed; ardent desire, lust.

avidus, a, um, *a.* eager, greedy; avaricious; lustful.

avis, is, *f.* bird; omen, portent.

avītus, a, um, *a.* ancestral; of a grandfather.

āvius, a, um, *a.* out of the way; pathless; straying.

āvocō, [1] *v.* call away; remove; divert the mind.

āvolō, [1] *v.* fly away; hasten away.

avunculus, ī, *m.* (maternal) uncle; great-uncle.

avus, ī, *m.* grandfather; ancestor.

axis, is, *m.* axle; chariot; axis (of the earth); north pole; heaven; sky; region, clime; board, plank.

....

B

....

bāca, bacca, ae, *f.* berry; olive-berry; pearl.

bācātus, a, um, *a.* set with pearls.

Baccha *or* **Bacchē, ae,** *f.* a votary of Bacchus.

Bacchānālia, um, *nt. pl.* Bac-chanalian orgies, feast of Bac-chus.

Bacchantēs, um, *f. pl.* votaries of Bacchus.

Bacchēus, a, um, *a.* Bacchic.

Bacchicus, a, um, *a.* Bacchic.

bacchor, ātus, [1] *v. dep.* cel-ebrate the rites of Bacchus; revel, rave; riot, run wild.

bācifer, a, um, *a.* berry-bear-ing.

bacillum, ī, *nt.* little staff; lictor's staff.

baculum, ī, *nt.* stick, walking-stick, lictor's staff.

bāiulus, ī, *m.* porter, carrier.

bālaena, ae, *f.* whale.

balanus, ī, *f.* acorn; balsam; shell-fish.

balatrō, ōnis, *m.* buffoon, joker.

bālātus, ūs, *m.* bleating of sheep.

balbus, a, um, *a.* stammering, stuttering.

balbūtiō, [4] *v.* stammer, stutter; speak obscurely, babble.

bal(l)ista, ae, *f.* large military en-gine for throwing stones and other missiles.

balneae, ārum, *f. pl.,* v. **balneum.**

balneārius, a, um, *a.* pertaining to baths.

balneātor, ōris, *m.* bath-attend-ant.

balneum, ī, *nt.* bath, place for bathing.

bālō, [1] *v.* bleat, baa.

balsamum, ī, *nt.* balsam-tree, balm.

balteus, ī, *m.* belt, sword-belt, baldric; woman's girdle.

barathrum, ī, *nt.* abyss, chasm; the infernal region.

barba, ae, *f.* beard.

barbaria, ae, *f.* foreign country; barbarousness; barbarism (in language); brutality.

barbaricus, a, um, *a.* outland-ish; barbarous.

barbariēs, v. **barbaria.**

barbarus, a, um, *a.* foreign, bar-barous; uncivilized; cruel, sav-age; ~, ī, *m.* foreigner, barbarian.

barbātulus, a, um, *a.* having a small beard.

barbātus, a, um, *a.* bearded; adult; ~, ī, *m.* ancient Roman, philosopher.

barbiton, *n.,* **barbitos, ī,** *m. & f.* lyre.

barbula, ae, *f.* little beard.

bārō, ōnis, *m.* block-head, lout.

barrus, ī, *m.* elephant.

bāsiātiō, ōnis, *f.* a kiss.

basilica, ae, *f.* oblong hall with double colonnade used for a law-court and as an exchange.

basiliscus, ī, *m.* basilisk.

bāsiō, [1] *v.* kiss.

basis, is, *f.* pedestal; base; foundation.

bāsium, iī, *nt.* a kiss.

beātitās, ātis, beātitūdō, inis, *f.* supreme happiness, blessedness.

beātus, a, um, *a.* happy, blessed; wealthy; abundant.

bellātor, ōris, *m.* warrior; ~, *a.* warlike.

bellātrīx, īcis, *f.* female warrior; ~, *a.* warlike.

bellicōsus, a, um, *a.* fond of war, warlike.

bellicus, a, um *a.* of *or* belonging to war, military; warlike.

belliger, a, um, *a.* waging war, martial.

belligerō, [1] *v.* wage *or* carry on war.

bellipotēns, entis, *a.* powerful in war.

bellō, [1] *v. (also* **bellor, [1])** wage war, fight.

bēllua, v. bēlua.

bellum, ī, *nt.* war; combat, fight; **bellī,** at the wars.

bellus, a, um, *a.* handsome, pretty, neat, agreeable, polite.

bēlua, ae, *f.* beast; monster; brute.

bēluōsus, a, um, *a.* abounding in beasts *or* monsters.

bene, *ad.* well, rightly, beautifully, pleasantly; opportunely.

benedīcō, xī, ctum, [3] *v. (with dat.)* speak well of; speak kindly to.

beneficentia, ae, *f.* beneficence, kindness.

beneficiāriī, ōrum, *m. pl.* soldiers exempted from certain military services.

beneficium, iī, *nt.* benefit, kindness; favour, help.

beneficus, a, um, *a.* beneficent, kind.

benevolēns, entis, *a.* benevolent, well-wishing, kind-hearted.

benevolentia, ae, *f.* benevolence, goodwill, kindness, favour.

benevolus, a, um, *a.* well-wishing, kind, friendly, devoted.

benignitās, ātis, *f.* good-heartedness, kindness, liberality, bounty.

benignus, a, um, *a.* kind-hearted, mild, affable; liberal, bounteous; fruitful.

beō, [1] *v.* make happy, bless.

bēs, bessis, *m.* two-thirds of any whole.

bēstia, ae, *f.* beast; wild beast.

bēstiārius, iī, *m.* fighter with wild beasts at public shows.

bēstiola, ae, *f.* little creature, insect.

bēta, ae, *f.* beet; beetroot.

bibliothēca, ae, *f.* library.

bibō, bibī, bibitum, [3] *v.* drink; imbibe; absorb, suck up; drink in.

bibulus, a, um, *a.* fond of drinking, ever thirsty; soaking, spongy.

biceps, cipitis, *a.* two-headed; with two summits.

bicolor, ōris, *a.* of two colours.

bicorniger, ī, the two-horned (god), epithet of Bacchus.

bicornis, e, *a.* two-horned; two-pronged.

bidēns, entis, *m.* two-pronged.

bidēns, entis, *m. f.* sheep; two-pronged hoe.

bīduum, ī, *nt.* period of two days.

biennium, iī, *nt.* period of two years.

bifāriam, *ad.* in two parts; in two ways.

bifer, a, um, *a.* bearing fruit *or* flowers twice a year.

bifidus, a, um, *a.* cloven, forked.

biforis, e, *a.* having two leaves *or* casements; from a double pipe.

biformis, e, *a.* two-shaped.

bifrōns, ontis, *a.* with two faces.

bifurcus, a, um, *a.* two-forked.

bīga, ae, *or* **bīgae, ārum,** *f. pl.* two-horsed chariot; pair of horses.

bīgātus, ī, *m.* a piece of money stamped with a representation of the bigae.

biiugis, e, biiugus, a, um, *a.* two-horsed.

bilībris, e, *a.* weighing two pounds.

bilinguis, e, *a.* two-tongued; speaking two languages; double-tongued, treacherous.

bīlis, is, *f.* gall, bile; wrath, anger; madness, folly.

bilūstris, e, *a.* lasting two lustres, lasting 10 years.

bimaris, e, *a.* situated between two seas.

bimembris, e, *a.* having limbs of two kinds, part man part beast.

bimestris, e, *a.* two months old; lasting two months.

bīmus, a, um, *a.* two years old; for two years.

bīnī, ae, a, two by two; two each.

bipatēns, entis, *a.* opening two ways; wide open.

bipedālis, e, *a.* two feet long, wide *or* thick.

bipennifer, a, um, *a.* bearing a two-edged axe.

bipennis, e, *a.* two-edged; ~, **is,** *f.* two-edged axe.

bipēs, edis, *a.* two-footed.

birēmis, is, *f.* ship with two banks of oars.

bis, *ad.* twice.

bisulcus, a, um, *a.* forked; cloven-footed.

bitūmen, inis, *nt.* bitumen, pitch, asphalt.

bivius, a, um, *a.* traversable both ways; **bivium, iī**, *nt.* a meeting-place of two roads.

blandīmentum, ī, *nt.* blandishment, flattery, charms.

blandior, ītus, [4] *v. dep.* flatter, coax; allure; please.

blanditia, ae, *f.* flattering, compliment; **ae**, *pl.* flatteries, courtship, blandishment.

blandus, a, um, *a.* flattering, pleasant, alluring, charming, gentle.

blatta, ae, *f.* cockroach; moth.

boārius, a, um, *a.* of oxen; **forum boārium**, the cattle market at Rome.

bōlētus, ī, *m.* mushroom.

bombus, ī, *m.* buzzing, booming.

bonitās, ātis, *f.* goodness; kindness, benevolence.

bonum, ī, *nt.* good; wealth, goods; benefit; advantage; profit; endowment, virtue; **summum bonum**, the supreme good (philosophical term).

bonus, a, um, *a.* good; kind; beautiful; pleasant; right; useful; considerable; rich; virtuous; promising, happy; favourable; high, honourable.

boō, [1] *v.* cry aloud, roar; call loudly upon.

boreas, ae, *m.* north wind.

boreus, a, um, *a.* northern.

bōs, bovis, *m.* or *f.* ox, bull; cow.

bovārius, *v.* boārius.

brācae, ārum, *f. pl.* trousers, breeches.

brācātus, a, um, *a.* breeched.

brāchium, iī, *nt.* arm; fore-arm; claw; branch, shoot; earthwork connecting fortified points; yard-arm.

brattea, ae, *f.* thin sheet of gold metal.

breviloquentia, ae, *f.* brevity of speech.

brevis, e, *a.* short, little, brief; small; concise; shallow; **brevi**, *ad.* briefly, in a few words; **(in) brevi**, soon.

brevitās, ātis, *f.* shortness; smallness; brevity.

breviter, *ad.* shortly, briefly.

brūma, ae, *f.* winter solstice; winter.

brūmālis, e, *a.* wintry.

brūtus, a, um, *a.* heavy, unwieldy; dull, stupid.

būbō, ōnis, *m.* horned *or* eagle owl.

bubulcus, ī, *m.* ploughman, farm-labourer.

bucca, ae, *f.* cheek.

buccula, ae, *f.* little cheek; cheek-piece of a helmet.

būcerus, a, um, *a.* ox-horned.

būcina, ae, *f.* trumpet; war-trumpet; watch-horn.

būcinātor, ōris, *m.* trumpeter; proclaimer.

būcolicus, a, um, *a.* pastoral, bucolic.

būcula, ae, *f.* heifer.

būfō, ōnis, *m.* toad.

bulbus, ī, *m.* bulb; onion.

bulla, ae, *f.* bubble; boss, knob, stud; locket hung round the necks of children.

bustum, ī, *nt.* pyre, tomb.

buxifer, a, um, *a.* bearing box-trees.

buxum, ī, *nt.* box-wood; top; flute.

buxus, ī, *f.* evergreen box-tree; box-wood; (*poet.*) flute.

....

C

....

caballus, ī, *m.* horse, riding horse, pack-horse.

cachinnātiō, ōnis, *f.* immoderate *or* boisterous laughter, guffawing.

cachinnō, [1] *v.* laugh loudly *or* boisterously.

cacūmen, inis, *nt.* tip, end; peak, summit.

cacūminō, [1] *v.* make pointed *or* tapered.

cadāver, eris, *nt.* dead body, corpse.

cadō, cecidī, cāsum, [3] *v.* fall (down, from); be slain; abate, decay; happen; end, close; fall through, fail.

cādūceum, ī, *nt.,* **cādūceus, ī,** *m.* herald's staff; wand of Mercury.

cādūcifer, a, um, *a.* staff-bearer, i.e. Mercury.

cādūcus, a, um, *a.* ready to fall; tottering, falling, fallen; frail, perishable, vain.

cadus, ī, *m.* large jar for wine, jar; funeral urn.

caecitās, ātis, *f.* blindness.

caecō, [1] *v.* blind; obscure; make morally blind.

caecus, a, um, *a.* blind; obscure; hidden, secret; confused; rash; vain, uncertain; dark, gloomy.

caedēs, is, *f.* felling; slaughter; murder; persons slain; blood, gore.

caedō, cecīdī, caesum, [3] *v.* fell, hew; cut; slaughter; murder.

caelātor, ōris, *m.* engraver, worker in bas-relief.

caelātūra, ae, *f.* engraving.

caelebs, libis, *a.* unmarried, single, widowed.

caeles, itis, *a.* heavenly; ~, *m.* a god.

caelestis, e, *a.* heavenly; divine; god-like; ~**ēs,** *m. pl.* the gods.

caelicola, ae, *m.* or *f.* inhabitant of heaven.

caelifer, a, um, *a.* supporting the sky.

caelō, [1] *v.* engrave, chase.

caelum, ī, *nt.* heaven; sky; climate, weather.

caelum, ī, *nt.* graving-tool, chisel.

caementum, ī, *nt.* small stones, rubble (used in concrete).

caenum, ī, *nt.* mud, filth; (of persons) scum.

caepa, ae, *f.,* **caepe, is,** *nt.* onion.

caerimōnia, ae, *f.* ritual; reverence; worship; sanctity.

caerul(e)us, a, um, *a.* blue, greenish-blue; dark-coloured.

caesariēs, ēi, *f.* long, flowing or luxuriant hair.

caesim, *ad.* by cutting; with the edge of the sword; in short clauses.

caespes, itis, *m.* turf, sod, grassy ground; altar.

caestus, ūs, *m.* boxing-glove.

calamister, trī, *m.* curling-tongs.

calamistrātus, a, um, *a.* curled with the curling-iron.

calamitās, ātis, *f.* disaster, ruin, misfortune; defeat.

calamitōsus, a, um, *a.* calamitous; miserable; ruinous; damaged.

calamus, ī, *m.* reed, cane; reed-pen; reed-pipe; arrow; angling-rod; stalk.

calathus, ī, *m.* wicker basket, flower basket; wine-cup; vessel for cheese or curdled milk.

calcar, āris, *nt.* spur.

calceō, [1] *v.* put shoes on.

calceus, ī, *m.* shoe.

calcitrō, [1] *v.* kick with the heels; be refractory.

calcō, [1] *v.* tread under foot; trample upon, spurn, despise.

calculus, ī, *m.* pebble, stone used for reckoning; reckoning, calculation.

caldārium, iī, *nt.* hot-bath.

calefaciō, fēcī, factum, [3] *v.* warm, heat; excite.

caleō, uī, [2] *v.* be warm or hot, be flushed; be in love; be excited.

calēscō, [3] *v.* grow warm or hot; become inflamed.

calidus, a, um, caldus, a, um, *a.* warm, hot; fiery, eager; fierce.

caliga, ae, *f.* soldier's boot.

cālīginōsus, a, um, *a.* foggy, misty.

cālīgō, inis, *f.* mist; darkness, gloom; moral or intellectual darkness.

cālīgō, [1] *v.* be dark.

calix, icis, *m.* cup, goblet.

calleō, [2] *v.* have experience or skill in, know; know how to.

calliditās, ātis, *f.* shrewdness, skilfulness; slyness.

callidus, a, um, *a.* expert, skilful; crafty, sly.

callis, is, *m.* rough track; path; pasturage.

callum, ī, *nt.* hardened skin, hide; callousness; lack of feeling.

cālō, ōnis, *m.* soldier's servant.

calor, ōris, *m.* warmth, heat; passion, zeal, ardour; love.

calt(h)a, ae, *f.* marigold.

calumnia, ae, *f.* sophistry; false accusation, false claim.

calumniātor, ōris, *m.* false accuser, pettifogger.

calumnior, ātus, [1] *v. dep.* contrive false accusations; depreciate, find fault with.

calvitium, iī, *nt.* baldness.

calvus, a, um, *a.* bald.

calx, cis, *f.* heel.

calx, cis, *f.* chalk, limestone, goal (because the goal-line was marked with chalk).

camēlus, ī, *m.* camel, dromedary.

Camēna, ae, *f.* Muse; poetry.

camīnus, ī, *m.* smelting furnace, forge; domestic stove.

campester, tris, tre, *a.* flat, level, open; of the Campus Martius.

campestre, is, *nt.* loin-cloth worn by athletes.

campus, ī, *m.* plain, field; field of battle; level surface; place for games, exercise, *etc.*; field of action; expanse of water, sea; **Campus Martius,** an open space by the side of the Tiber at Rome.

canālis, is, *m.* or *f.* channel, conduit, canal.

cancellī, ōrum, *m. pl.* railing, lattice; barrier; boundaries, limits.

cancer, crī, *m.* crab; Cancer, the sign of the zodiac; cancer.

candēla, ae, *f.* candle; waxed cord.

candēlābrum, ī, *nt.* stand for candles, candelabrum.

candeō, uī, [2] *v.* be of brilliant whiteness, shine; become *or* be hot.

candēscō, uī, [3] *v.* grow light; grow white; become hot.

candidātus, ī, *m.* candidate; aspirant.

candidus, a, um, *a.* dazzling white, clear, bright; clean, spotless; candid, frank; lucky; fairskinned.

candor, ōris, *m.* dazzling whiteness, brightness; beauty; candour; kindness, moral purity.

cāneō, uī, [2] *v.* be hoary, be white.

cānēscō, [3] *v.* grow hoary; grow old, be white.

canīcula, ae, *f.* bitch; dog-star, dog-days.

canīnus, a, um, *a.* canine; abusive, snarling.

canis, is, *m.* or *f.* dog; hound; subordinate, 'jackal'; dog-star; the lowest throw at dice.

canistrum, ī, *nt.* wicker basket.

cānitiēs, ēī, *f.* white or grey colouring; grey hair; old age.

canna, ae, *f.* reed, cane; reed-pipe.

canō, cecinī, cantum, [3] *v.* sing; crow; sound, play (an instrument); recite; celebrate in song *or* poetry; prophesy; blow (signals); sound (for a retreat).

canor, ōris, *m.* song, music, tune.

canōrus, a, um, *a.* melodious, harmonious.

cantharis, idis, *f.* blister-beetle; Spanish fly (used in medicine and as a poison).

cantharus, ī, *m.* large drinking vessel with handles.

cant(h)ērius, iī, *m.* poor-quality horse, gelding.

canticum, ī, *nt.* song; passage in a comedy chanted or sung.

cantiō, ōnis, *f.* incantation, spell.

cantitō, [1] *v.* sing over and over.

cantō, [1] *v.* sing; play; recite; praise; forewarn; enchant; bewitch.

cantor, ōris, *m.* singer; poet; eulogist.

cantus, ūs, *m.* song, poem; singing; melody; prophecy; incantation.

cānus, a, um, *a.* white, hoary, grey; foamy; old, aged.

capācitās, ātis, *f.* capacity, largeness.

capāx, ācis, *a.* spacious, roomy; capable.

capella, ae, *f.* she-goat; kid.

caper, prī, *m.* he-goat.

capessō, īvī, ītum, [3] *v.* seize eagerly; manage; undertake; pursue with zeal.

capillātus, a, um, *a.* having long hair.

capillus, ī, *m.* hair of the head; hair.

capiō, cēpī, captum, [3] *v.* take, seize; capture, occupy; get, obtain; captivate, win over; make choice of; find out; understand; choose, select; undertake.

capistrum, ī, *nt.* halter.

capitāl(e), *nt.* capital crime *or* the punishment due to it.

capitālis, e, *a.* belonging to the head *or* life; deadly, mortal; dangerous; excellent; first-rate.

Capitōlium, iī, *nt.* the Capitoline hill at Rome.

capra, ae, *f.* she-goat.

caprea, ae, *f.* roe-deer.

capreolus, ī, *m.* a young roebuck; rafter.

caprigenus, a, um, *a.* of goats.

capripēs, pedis, *a.* goat-footed.

capsa, ae, *f.* cylindrical case (for books).

capsula, ae, *f.* small box for books; chest.

captātor, ōris, *m.* legacy hunter; one who strives to obtain.

captiō, ōnis, *f.* deception; fraud; disadvantage; a piece of sophistry.

captiōsus, a, um, *a.* harmful, disadvantageous, captious.

captīvitās, ātis, *f.* captivity; capture.

captīvus, a, um, *a.* taken prisoner (in war, as booty); of captives; ~, ī, *m.* prisoner, captive.

captō, [1] *v.* snatch, endeavour to catch; strive after; hunt legacies; ensnare.

captus, ūs, *m.* capacity, ability, potentiality.

capulus, ī, *m.* handle; sword-hilt.

caput, itis, *nt.* head; top; end; source; beginning; principal point; mouth (of a river); article, chapter; life; person; civil rights; intelligence; author, leader, chief; capital city; capital as opposed to interest.

carbaseus, a, um, *a.* made of linen.

carbasus, ī, *f.* linen; sail; linen garment; awning.

carbō, ōnis, *m.* charcoal; glowing coal.

carcer, eris, *m.* prison, jail; barriers at the beginning of a racecourse; starting-point; beginning.

carchēsium, iī, *nt.* drinking-cup.

cardiacus, a, um, *a.* of the heart *or* stomach; suffering in the stomach.

cardō, inis, *m.* door-hinge; pole, axis; chief point *or* circumstance.

carduus, ī, *m.* thistle.

cārectum, ī, *nt.* bed of sedge.

careō, uī, itum, [2] *v. with abl.* be without, want; be absent from; miss, lose.

cārex, icis, *f.* reed-grass; sedge.

carīna, ae, *f.* bottom of a ship, keel; ship.

cariōsus, a, um, *a.* rotten.

cāritās, ātis, *f.* dearness; high price; love.

carmen, inis, *nt.* song, strain; poem; oracle; prophecy; magic formula; instrumental music.

carnifex, icis, *m.* executioner, murderer, butcher, torturer; scoundrel.

carnificīna, ae, *f.* work *or* trade of an executioner; torture.

carnificō, [1] *v.* execute, butcher.

carō, carnis, *f.* flesh; meat.

carpentum, ī, *nt.* two-wheeled carriage.

carpō, psī, ptum, [3] *v.* pick, pluck (off); gather; browse; tear off, rob, plunder; enjoy, use; slander; weaken; consume; harass; **carpere viam** *or* **iter,** to take one's way.

carptim, *ad.* in detached parts.

carrus, ī, *m.* Gallic wagon.

cārus, a, um, *a.* dear, costly; precious, loved.

casa, ae, *f.* hut, cottage; shop, booth.

cāseus, ī, *m.* cheese.

casia, ae, *f.* cinnamon.

cassida, ae, cassis, idis, *f.* helmet, usually of metal.

cassus, a, um, *a.* empty; lacking, deprived of; vain, fruitless; **in cassum,** in vain.

castanea, ae, *f.* chestnut-tree; chestnut.

castellānī, ōrum, *m. pl.* garrison of a fort.

castellum, ī, *nt.* fortified settlement, garrison; refuge, stronghold.

castīgātiō, ōnis, *f.* punishment, reprimanding.

castīgātor, ōris, *m.* corrector, reprover.

castīgō, [1] *v.* chastise, punish; correct, mend.

castimōnia, ae, *f.* chastity, abstinence; purity of morals.

castitās, ātis, *f.* chastity.

castoreum, eī, *nt.* aromatic secretion obtained from the beaver.

castrēnsis, e, *a.* of or connected with the camp or active military service.

castrō, [1] *v.* castrate; impair, weaken.

castrum, ī, *nt.* fortified post, settlement; **castra, ōrum,** *nt. pl.* military camp; war-service; day's march; field of activity;

pōnere castra, to pitch camp; **movēre castra,** to break camp.

castus, a, um, *a.* pure; spotless; chaste; pious; sacred.

cāsus, ūs, *m.* fall, overthrow; error; accident, chance, event; occasion; misfortune; danger, risk; death; (*gram.*) case; **cāsū,** by chance, by accident.

catafractēs *or* **ta, ae,** *m.* coat of mail.

catafractus, ī, *m.* soldier armed in mail.

catapulta, ae, *f.* machine for discharging bolts or other missiles, catapult.

catar(r)acta, ae, *f.* waterfall, rapid; portcullis.

catasta, ae, *f.* platform where slaves were exhibited for sale.

catella, ae, *f.* little chain.

catellus, ī, *m.* little dog, puppy.

catēna, ae, *f.* chain; fetter; bond, restraint.

catēnātus, a, um, *a.* chained, fettered.

caterva, ae, *f.* crowd; troop, company; flock.

catervātim, *ad.* in troops; in disordered masses.

cathedra, ae, *f.* arm-chair, easy chair; chair of a teacher.

catulus, ī, *m.* young dog, puppy, whelp.

catus, a, um, *a.* knowing, shrewd, wise, prudent.

cauda, ae, *f.* tail.

caudex, v. cōdex.

caulae, ārum, f. pl. railing, lattice barrier; holes, pores.

caulis, is, m. stalk; cabbage.

caupō, ōnis, m. shopkeeper; innkeeper.

caupōna, ae, f. inn, tavern, lodging-house.

caurus, v. cōrus.

causa, **caussa**, ae, f. cause, reason, motive; occasion; pretence; excuse; matter, subject; affair, business; process, suit; (political) party; blame, fault; connection, friendship; condition, state; ~, with gen. on account of, because of.

causidicus, ī, m. advocate, barrister.

causor, ātus, [1] v. dep. allege as an excuse; plead a cause, bring an action.

causula, ae, f. speech in a petty lawsuit.

cautēs, is, f. rough pointed rock; cliff, reef.

cautiō, ōnis, f. caution, heedfulness; stipulation; pledge.

cautus, a, um, a. cautious, heedful; made safe, secured.

cavea, ae, f. enclosure, cage, coop; audience's part of a theatre; theatre.

caveō, **cāvī**, **cautum**, [2] v. be on one's guard, take care; beware of; give security; get security; order or stipulate (by will, in writing).

caverna, ae, f. cavern, grotto, cave, hole; vault of the sky.

cavillātiō, ōnis, f. quibbling, banter, jeering.

cavillātor, ōris, m. jester, banterer, captious critic.

cavillor, ātus, [1] v. dep. cavil at; scoff, jeer, satirize.

cavō, [1] v. hollow out; pierce through; make by hollowing out.

cavum, ī, nt., **cavus**, ī, m. hole, cavity; cave, burrow.

cavus, a, um, a. hollow, concave; deep-channelled.

cēdō, **cessī**, **cessum**, [3] v. go, walk; turn out, come to pass; fall to, devolve; yield, give way; withdraw; go off; succeed; allow, grant; give up.

cedo, give here! pray! let us hear, tell! suppose, what if?

cedrus, ī, f. cedar; cedar-oil.

celeber, **bris**, **bre**, a. much frequented, populous; renowned, famous.

celebrātiō, ōnis, f. throng; celebrating of a festival.

celebrātus, a, um, a. crowded; festive; current, popular.

celebritās, ātis, f. crowded conditions; crowding; renown.

celebrō, [1] v. frequent, crowd; inhabit; practise, perform; celebrate; make known.

celer, **eris**, **ere**, a. swift, quick; lively; hurried; rash, hasty.

celerēs, um, *m. pl.* bodyguard of the Roman kings.

celeritās, ātis, *f.* swiftness, quickness.

celeriter, *ad.* quickly.

celerō, [1] *v.* quicken, accelerate; make haste.

cella, ae, *f.* cell; cellar; storehouse; larder; principal *or* subsidiary chamber in a temple; slave's room, 'garret'.

cēlō, [1] *v.* hide, conceal; keep in ignorance; keep dark.

celōx, ōcis, *f.* cutter, yacht.

celsus, a, um, *a.* high, lofty; great, sublime; haughty.

cēna, ae, *f.* dinner, supper, course for dinner.

cēnāculum, ī, *nt.* upper-room, attic.

cēnātiō, ōnis, *f.* dining-room.

cēnitō, [1] *v.* dine often.

cēnō, [1] *v.* dine, sup, dine on.

cēnseō, uī, cēnsum, [2] *v.* count, reckon; tax, assess; estimate, value; think, be of the opinion; decree; vote to.

cēnsor, ōris, *m.* censor; censurer, critic.

cēnsōrius, a, um, *a.* of *or* belonging to a censor; austere, moral.

cēnsūra, ae, *f.* censorship; judgment, control.

cēnsus, ūs, *m.* valuation of every Roman citizen's estate; registering of a man (his age, family, profession, *etc.*); sum assessed; property.

centaurēum, ī, *nt.* centaury (a herb).

centēnī, ae, a, *a.* a hundred each; a hundred.

centēsima, ae, *f.* hundredth part.

centēsimus, a, um, *a.* the hundredth.

centiceps, cipitis, *a.* hundred-headed.

centiē(n)s, *ad.* a hundred times.

centimanus, ūs, *a.* hundred-handed.

centō, ōnis, *m.* patched quilt, blanket *or* curtain.

centum, *a. indecl.* a hundred.

centumvirī, ōrum, *m. pl.* a panel of judges chosen annually to decide civil suits.

centuria, ae, *f.* century, company of 100 men; political unit for voting.

centuriātim, *ad.* by centuries.

centuriō, [1] *v.* arrange (recruits, *etc.*) in military centuries; **comitia centuriāta**, the assembly in which the Romans voted by centuries.

centuriō, ōnis, *m.* commander of a century, captain, centurion.

cēra, ae, *f.* wax; wax-covered writing-tablet; letter; seal of wax; waxen image.

cerasus, ī, *f.* cherry-tree; cherry.

Cereālis, e, *a.* of Ceres, of corn; **Cereālia, ium**, *nt. pl.* the festival of Ceres.

cerebrum, ī, *nt.* brain; understanding, anger.

cēreus, a, um, *a.* waxen; wax-coloured; pliant, soft; ~, ī, *m.* wax taper.

cernō, crēvī, crētum, [3] *v.* sift; discern, perceive; decide; determine; make formal acceptance of an inheritance.

cernuus, a, um, *a.* head foremost.

cerrītus, a, um, *a.* possessed by Ceres, frantic, mad.

certāmen, inis, *nt.* contest, struggle; battle, rivalry, combat; point of contention.

certātim, *ad.* with rivalry, in competition.

certātiō, ōnis, *f.* striving, contention.

certē, *ad.* certainly, surely; really; yet indeed, at least.

certō, *ad.* certainly, surely.

certō, [1] *v.* fight, contend; strive; contend at law.

certus, a, um, *a.* certain; sure, safe; distinct; fixed; agreed upon; steady, resolute; constant, faithful; unerring; **prō certō scīre**, to know for certain; **certiōrem facere**, to inform.

cērula, ae, *f.* red pencil.

cerva, ae, *f.* hind, doe; deer.

cervīcal, ālis, *nt.* pillow.

cervīnus, a, um, *a.* pertaining to a deer or stag.

cervīx, īcis, *f.* neck.

cervus, ī, *m.* hart, stag; **cervī**, chevaux- de-frise.

cessātiō, ōnis, *f.* relaxation, respite; idleness.

cessātor, ōris, *m.* idler, sluggard.

cessō, [1] *v.* hold back, leave off, delay, loiter; cease (from); idle; be wanting; go wrong.

cētārium, iī, *nt.* fish-pond.

cēterōquī, *ad.* in other respects, otherwise.

cēterum, *ad.* for the rest; but; besides.

cēterus, a, um, *a.* the other; **cēterī**, *pl.* the others, the rest.

cētus, ī, *m.* whale; porpoise; dolphin; sea-monster.

ceu, *ad.* as, just as; as if.

chalybs, ybis, *m.* steel, iron.

chalybēius, a, um, *a.* of steel.

Chaos (*acc.* Chaos, *abl.* Chaō), *nt.* formless state of primordial matter; pit of the Lower World.

charta, ae, *f.* (leaf of) paper; writing.

Chēlae, ārum, *f. pl.* the claws of Scorpio which extended into the sign Libra.

chelydrus, ī, *m.* venomous water-snake.

chelys (*acc.* ~yn), *f.* lyre.

chīrographum, ī, *nt.* handwriting; manuscript; bond.

chīrūrgia, ae, *f.* surgery.

chlamys, ydis, *f.* a Greek cloak or cape, frequently for military use.

chorda, ae, *f.* string of a musical instrument.

chorēa, ae, *f.* dance.

chorus, ī, *m.* dance with singing; chorus, choir; band, group.

chrȳsolithos, ī, *m.* or *f.* topaz.

cibus, ī, *m.* food; fare.

cicāda, ae, *f.* cricket, cicada.

cicātrīx, īcis, *f.* scar, cicatrice.

cicer, eris, *nt.* chick-pea.

cicōnia, ae, *f.* stork.

cicūta, ae, *f.* hemlock; shepherd's pipe.

cieō, cīvī, citum, [2] *v.* move; shake; rouse; disturb; provoke; call on, invoke; produce.

cīmex, icis, *m.* bed-bug.

cinaedus, ī, *m.* catamite.

cincinnātus, a, um, *a.* with curled hair.

cincinnus, ī, *m.* ringlet; *fig.* rhetorical flourish.

cīnctūtus, a, um, *a.* wearing a girdle *or* loin-cloth.

cingō, xī, nctum, [3] *v.* gird; surround; beleaguer; crown.

cingulum, ī, *nt.* band, belt; sword-belt.

cinis, eris, *m.* or *f.* ashes; ruins.

cip(p)us, ī, *m.* boundary stone *or* pillar; tombstone.

circā, ad. (all) around; ~, *pr. with acc.,* about, near to; concerning.

circēnsēs, m. pl. games and exercises of wrestling, running, fighting, *etc.,* in the circus.

circiter, ad. & pr. with acc., about, near; towards.

circu(m)itiō, ōnis, *f.* a going round; patrol; circumlocution.

circu(m)itus, ūs, *m.* going round, circuit; way round; circumference; circumlocution.

circulor, ātus, [1] *v. dep.* form groups round oneself.

circulus, ī, *m.* circle; orbit; ring, hoop; company.

circum, ad. (all) around, about; ~, *pr. with acc.,* around, about, among; at, near.

circumagō, ēgī, āctum, [3] *v.* drive in a circle, turn round; wheel.

circumcīdō, cīdī, cīsum, [3] *v.* cut around, clip; diminish; remove.

circumclūdō, sī, sum, [3] *v.* enclose on all sides.

circumcolō, [3] *v.* dwell round about.

circumdō, dedī, datum, [1] *v.* put round; surround; enclose.

circumdūcō, xī, ctum, [3] *v.* lead *or* draw around; lead out of the way; cheat; cancel.

circumeō *or* **circueō, īvī & iī, circuitum,** [4] *v.* go *or* march around; encompass; go about canvassing; circumvent.

circumferō, ferre, tulī, lātum, [3] *v.* carry about *or* round; spread round, divulge; purify; turn (eyes, face, hands, *etc.*) to a new direction.

circumfluō, xī, [3] *v.* flow round; be rich in.

circumfluus, a, um, *a.* circumfluent, surrounding; surrounded with water.

circumforāneus, a, um, *a.* connected with (the business of) the forum; itinerant.

circumfundō, fūdī, fūsum, [3] *v.* pour around; **circumfundor**, flow round; surround.

circumgredior, gressus, [3] *v.* go round behind by a flanking movement.

circumiaceō, [2] *v.* lie round about.

circumiectus, ūs, *m.* encompassing, embrace.

circumiciō, iēcī, iectum, [3] *v.* cast *or* place around; encompass with; **circumiectus, a, um**, surrounding.

circumligō, [1] *v.* bind round *or* to; encircle.

circumlinō, lēvī, litum, [3] *v.* (**circumliniō**, [4]) smear *or* anoint round, decorate.

circumluō, [3] *v.* wash *or* flow around.

circummittō, mīsī, missum, [3] *v.* send around.

circummūniō, īvī, ītum, [4] *v.* wall around, fortify.

circummūnītiō, ōnis, *f.* circumvallation.

circumplector, plexus, [3] *v. dep.* embrace, surround: circumvallate.

circumplicō, [1] *v.* coil round.

circumpōnō, suī, situm, [3] *v.* put *or* place around.

circumrētiō, tītum, [4] *v.* encircle with a net.

circumrōdō, sī, [3] *v.* gnaw all round; slander.

circumsaepiō, psī, ptum, [3] *v.* fence round, enclose.

circumscrībō, psī, ptum, [3] *v.* draw a line around; circumscribe; hem in; cheat; circumvent.

circumscrīptē, *ad.* concisely; in periodic style.

circumscrīptiō, ōnis, *f.* encircling; circle; boundary; outline; deceiving; periodic sentence.

circumscrīptor, ōris, *m.* cheat; defrauder.

circumsedeō, ēdī, essum, [2] *v.* sit around; besiege.

circumsīdō, [3] *v.* besiege.

circumsistō, stetī, [3] *v.* stand round.

circumsonō, [1] *v.* resound on every side, ring again with; echo round.

circumspectiō, ōnis, *f.* careful consideration.

circumspectō, [1] *v.* look about searchingly.

circumspectus, a, um, *a.* circumspect, cautious; wary; carefully considered.

circumspiciō, exī, ectum, [3] *v.* look about; take heed; survey; seek for.

circumstō, stetī, [1] *v.* stand round; surround.

circumstrepō, pitum, [3] *v.* make a noise around.

circumvādō, sī, [3] *v.* form a ring round, surround.

circumvagus, a, um, *a.* moving round, encircling.

circumvallō, [1] *v.* surround with siege works.

circumvectiō, ōnis, *f.* circular course; transport.

circumvector, ātus, [1] *v. dep.* sail round, travel round.

circumvehor, vectus, [3] *v. dep.* make the round of; travel round.

circumveniō, vēnī, ventum, [4] *v.* come round; surround; beat; oppress; circumvent.

circumvolitō, [1] *v.* fly around about.

circumvolō, [1] *v.* fly around.

circumvolvō, volūtum, [3] *v.* roll round, twine around.

circus, ī, *m.* circle; circus (at Rome).

cis, *pr. with acc.* on this side (of); within.

Cisalpīnus, a, um, *a.* lying on the south side of the Alps.

cisium, iī, *nt.* two-wheeled carriage.

cista, ae, *f.* chest, box.

cisterna, ae, *f.* cistern.

cistophorus, ī, *m.* an Asiatic coin.

citātus, a, um, *a.* quick, rapid; **equō citātō,** at full gallop.

citerior, us, *a.* on this side, hithermost; nearer.

cithara, ae, *f.* lyre.

citharista, ae, *m.* lyre-player.

citharoedus, ī, *m.* one who sings to the lyre.

citimus, a, um, *a.* nearest, next.

cito, ad. comp. citius; sup. citissimē, soon; quickly.

citō, [1] *v.* cite; summon; excite; encourage.

citrā, pr. with acc. on this side; within, short of; without, apart from.

citreus, a, um, *a.* of citron.

citrō, ad. to this side, hither; **ultrō citrōque,** to and fro; in and out; on both sides.

citus, a, um, *a.* quick, swift, rapid.

cīvicus, a, um, *a.* civic, civil; legal; **cīvica corōna,** a crown of oak leaves presented to one who had saved a fellow-countryman in war.

cīvīlis, e, *a.* civic, civil; political, public, polite, courteous.

cīvīliter, ad. in a civil sphere; in a manner suited to citizens.

cīvis, is, *m. or f.* citizen; countryman *or* woman.

cīvitās, ātis, *f.* citizenship; citizens; city; state.

clādes, is, *f.* defeat; destruction; ruin; plague; slaughter; calamity.

clam, ad. & pr. with abl. secretly; unknown to.

clāmātor, ōris, *m.* shouter.

clāmitō, [1] *v.* shout repeatedly; proclaim.

clāmō, [1] *v.* shout; shout the name of.

clāmor, ōris, *m.* shout, cry, clamour; applause; noise, din.

clanculum, *ad.* secretly.

clandestīnus, a, um, *a.* secret, hidden, clandestine.

clangor, ōris, *m.* clang, noise.

clārē, *ad.* brightly; clearly; aloud; lucidly.

clāreō, [2] *v.* shine; be famous.

clārēscō, uī, [3] *v.* begin to shine; become clear or evident; become famous.

clāritās, ātis, clāritūdō, inis, *f.* clearness, brightness; distinctness; celebrity, renown.

clārō, [1] *v.* make visible, brighten, make illustrious.

clārus, a, um, *a.* clear; bright; loud, distinct; evident; illustrious, famous.

classiārius, iī, *m.* mariner; sailor, seaman; *pl.* naval forces.

classicum, ī, *nt.* military trumpet-call.

classicus, a, um, *a.* belonging to the fleet; belonging to the highest class of citizen.

classis, is, *f.* class of the Roman people; army; fleet.

clāt(h)rī, ōrum, *m. pl.* lattices or bars; railings.

claudeō, [2] or **claudō, sum,** [3] *v.* limp, halt; be weak, be imperfect.

claudicō, [1] *v.* limp, be lame; waver, be defective.

claudō, sī, sum, [3] *v.* shut, close; conclude; finish; enclose; imprison; surround; besiege.

claudō, [3] *v.,* v. **claudeō**

claudus, a, um, *a.* limping; lame; defective, wavering, uncertain.

claustra, ōrum, *nt. pl.* bolts, bars; enclosure; barrier; door, gate; bulwark; dam.

clausula, ae, *f.* conclusion, end; close of a periodic sentence.

clāva, ae, *f.* cudgel, club.

clāviger, ī, *m.* club-bearer; key-bearer.

clāvis, is, *f.* door-key.

clāvus, ī, *m.* nail; tiller, helm, helm of the ship of state; rudder; **lātus clāvus,** a broad purple stripe worn on the robes of senators.

clēmēns, entis, *a.* merciful, gentle, mild; quiet, peaceable; courteous; moderate.

clēmentia, ae, *f.* clemency, mercy; mildness; calmness.

clepō, psī, ptum, [3] *v.* steal.

clepsydra, ae, *f.* water-clock.

cliēns, entis, *m.* client; vassal; dependent.

clientēla, ae, *f.* clientship; vassalage; patronage; clients; vassals.

clipeātus, a, um, *a.* furnished with a shield.

clipeus, ī, *m.* round, usually bronze shield; disc of the sun.

clītellae, ārum, *f. pl.* pack-saddle.

clīvōsus, a, um, *a.* hilly, steep.

clīvus, ī, *m.* sloping ground, slope.

cloāca, ae, *f.* sewer, drain.

clueō, [2] be called, be named, be reputed.

clūnis, is, *m.* or *f.* buttocks, haunches.

coacervātiō, ōnis, *f.* heaping together *or* up.

coacervō, [1] *v.* heap together *or* up; amass.

coacēscō, acuī, [3] *v.* become sour.

coāctor, ōris, *m.* collector (of money, taxes, *etc.*)

coaequō, [1] *v.* make level, regard as equal.

coagmentō, [1] *v.* join, connect; construct.

coagmentum, ī, *nt.* joint.

coalēscō, aluī, alitum, [3] *v.* grow together; close; become unified, strong.

coarguō, uī, [3] *v.* prove, make manifest; refute; convict.

coar(c)tō, [1] *v.* make narrower; pack together; abridge.

coccum, ī, *nt.* scarlet colour; scarlet cloth.

cochlea, ae, *f.* snail.

coctilis, e, *a.* baked (of bricks), built of baked bricks.

cōdex, icis, *m.* trunk of a tree; piece of wood; (bound) book; account-book.

cōdicillus, ī, *m.* rescript of the Emperor, petition to the Emperor; codicil; (*pl.*). set of writing tablets.

coemō, ēmī, ēmptum, [3] *v.* buy up.

coēmptiō, ōnis, *f.* (fictitious) sale of a woman to a man (legal term).

coeō, īvī & iī, itum, [4] *v.* go *or* come together, meet, clash; assemble; conspire; curdle; heal; unite.

coepiō, coepī, coeptum, [3] *v.* begin.

coeptō, [1] *v.* begin, attempt.

coeptum, ī, *nt.* beginning, undertaking.

coerceō, cuī, citum, [2] *v.* enclose; limit; correct, keep in order; punish; restrain.

coercitiō, ōnis, *f.* coercion, restraint; punishment.

coetus, ūs, *m.* meeting, assembly, company.

cōgitātiō, ōnis, *f.* thinking, meditation; thought; intention; plan; opinion; reasoning power.

cōgitō, [1] *v.* consider, ponder, think; meditate; intend; look forward to; imagine.

cognātiō, ōnis, *f.* relationship by birth; relatives, family; affinity.

cognātus, a, um, *a.* related by birth; related; similar; having affinity with.

cognitiō, ōnis, *f.* getting to know; idea, notion; examination, inquiry.

cognitor, ōris, *m.* attorney; guarantor of identity.

cognōmen, inis, *nt.* family name; sobriquet.

cognōmentum, ī, *nt.* surname; name.

cognōscō, gnōvī, gnitum, [3] *v.* learn, get to know; inform oneself of; understand; investigate; observe, perceive; identify.

cōgō, coēgī, coāctum, [3] *v.* drive together; collect; curdle; force, compel; prove conclusively.

cohaereō, sī, sum, [2] *v.* adhere (to); stick together; be consistent.

cohaerēscō, sī, [3] *v.* cohere; stick, adhere.

cohērēs, ēdis, *m.* or *f.* co-heir, joint-heir.

cohibeō, uī, itum, [2] *v.* hold together; restrain; curb; hinder; confine.

cohonestō, [1] *v.* honour, grace; make respectable.

cohorrēscō, uī, [3] *v.* shudder.

cohors, rtis, *f.* farmyard; cohort; bodyguard; attendants.

cohortātiō, ōnis, *f.* exhortation, encouragement.

cohortor, ātus, [1] *v. dep.* cheer up, encourage; exhort.

coitiō, ōnis, *f.* meeting; conspiracy, combination.

coitus, ūs, *m.* meeting; sexual intercourse.

collabefīō, fīerī, factus, *v.* collapse, break up; be overthrown politically.

collābor, lāpsus, [3] *v.* collapse, fall in ruins; fall in a swoon *or* in death.

collacrimō, [1] *v.* weep together, weep over.

collātiō, ōnis, *f.* placing together; payment of tribute; tax; comparison.

collaudātiō, ōnis, *f.* high praise.

collaudō, [1] *v.* praise very much.

collectiō, ōnis, *f.* collection; recapitulation.

collēga, ae, *m.* colleague.

collēgium, iī, *nt.* college, corporation; brotherhood; colleagueship.

collibuit *or* **bitum est.** [2] *v. impers. with dat.* it pleases.

collīdō, sī, sum, [3] *v.* strike, *or* dash together; crush; bring into conflict with each other.

colligō, ēgī, ēctum, [3] *v.* collect, assemble; acquire; pick up; infer; reckon; sum up; **sē colligere, animum colligere,** to recover oneself, to recover one's spirits.

colligō, [1] *v.* bind together, connect; fetter.

collinō, lēvī, litum, [3] *v.* besmear; pollute.

collis, is, *m.* hill.

collocātiō, ōnis, *f.* placing together; arrangement; marrying.

collocō, [1] *v.* put in a particular place together, arrange; bestow; employ; lay out; give in marriage.

collocūtiō, ōnis, *f.* conversation, conference; discussion.

colloquium, iī, *nt.* conversation, discourse, interview.

colloquor, locūtus, [3] *v. dep.* talk together, converse.

collūceō, [2] *v.* shine brightly.

collūdō, sī, sum, [3] *v.* play together; act in collusion.

collum, ī, *nt.* neck.

colluō, uī, ūtum, [3] *v.* wash, rinse out.

collūsiō, ōnis, *f.* secret understanding.

collūsor, ōris, *m.* playmate, fellow gambler.

collūstrō, [1] *v.* lighten up; survey on all sides.

colluviēs, ēī, colluviō, ōnis, *f.* filth, offscouring; 'cesspool'; turmoil.

collybus, ī, *m.* cost of exchange.

collȳrium, iī, *nt.* eye-salve.

colō, uī, cultum, [3] *v.* cultivate; take care of; dwell, inhabit; honour, pay court to, revere; worship; adorn; exercise; practise.

colocāsia, ae, *f.* the Egyptian bean.

colōnia, ae, *f.* colony.

colōnus, ī, *m.* farmer.

color, ōris, *m.* colour, complexion; outward show; excuse.

colōrātus, a, um, *a.* variegated; sunburnt.

colōrō, [1] *v.* colour, paint; dye; tan.

coluber, brī, *m.* serpent, snake.

colubra, ae, *f.* serpent, snake.

colubrifer, a, um, *a.* snaky; snake-haired.

columba, ae, *f.* dove, pigeon.

columbus, ī, *m.* male pigeon.

columella, ae, *f.* small column, pillar.

columen, inis, *nt.* height, peak; roof, gable; summit, head, chief.

columna, ae, *f.* column, pillar.

columnārium, iī, *nt.* a pillar-tax.

colurnus, a, um, *a.* made of hazel.

colus, ī, *m.*, **ūs,** *f.* distaff.

coma, ae, *f.* hair of the head; wool; foliage.

comāns, antis, *a.* hairy; long-haired; leafy.

comātus, a, um, *a.* long-haired; leafy; **Gallia Comāta,** Transalpine Gaul.

combibō, bibī, [3] *v.* drink up, absorb.

combūrō, bussī, bustum, [3] *v.* burn; burn up.

comedō, ēdī, ēsum, (ēstum), [3] v. eat up, consume; waste, squander.

comes, itis, m. or f. companion, comrade, partner; attendant.

comētēs, ae, m. comet.

cōmicus, a, um, a. comic; ~, ī, m. comic actor; writer of comedy.

cōminus, v. comminus.

cōmis, e, a. courteous, kind, friendly; elegant.

cōmis(s)ātiō, ōnis, f. merry-making, revelling.

cōmissātor, ōris, m. reveller.

cōmissor, ātus, [1] v. dep. carouse, revel.

cōmitās, ātis, f. courteousness, kindness, friendliness; good taste.

comitātus, ūs, m. escort, train, retinue; company.

cōmiter, ad. courteously, kindly, civilly, readily.

comitia, ōrum, v. comitium.

comitiālis, e, a. pertaining to the comitia.

comitium, iī, nt. a place in the forum, where the comitia were held; **comitia, ōrum,** nt. pl. elections.

comito, v. comitor.

comitor, ātus, [1] v. dep. accompany, attend.

commaculō, [1] v. stain deeply, pollute, defile; sully.

commeātus, ūs, m. passage; leave; merchandise; convoy; provisions.

commeminī, isse, v. recollect thoroughly, remember.

commemorātiō, ōnis, f. reminding, recalling, citation.

commemorō, [1] v. recall; mention.

commendābilis, e, a. praiseworthy.

commendātiō, ōnis, f. entrusting; recommendation; excellence; approval.

commendō, [1] v. commend to; recommend; entrust.

commentāriolum, ī, nt. notebook; treatise.

commentārius, iī, m. **commentārium, iī,** nt. note-book, memorandum; commentary; notes, jottings.

commentātiō, ōnis, f. thinking out, mental preparation.

commentīcius, a, um, a. invented, devised; imaginary; forged, false.

commentor, ātus, [1] v. dep. think about; study beforehand; imagine.

commentum, ī, nt. invention fiction, fabrication; scheme.

commeō, [1] v. go to and fro; pass; travel.

commercium, iī, nt. commercial intercourse, trade;

commereō, uī, itum, [2] v. dealings, relationship, merit fully; be guilty of.

commīlitium, iī, nt. companionship in military service; comradeship.

commīlitō, ōnis, *m.* fellow-soldier.

comminātiō, ōnis, *f.* threatening.

comminīscor, mentus, [3] *v. dep.* devise, invent; forge; fabricate; state falsely.

comminuō, uī, ūtum, [3] *v.* break into pieces; break up; crush.

comminus, *ad.* hand to hand; at hand, near.

commisceō, scuī, xtum, [2] *v.* mix together.

commiseror, ātus, [1] *v. dep.* pity; excite compassion.

commissum, ī, *nt.* enterprise, trust, secret; crime.

commissūra, ae, *f.* joint, seam.

committō, mīsī, missum, [3] *v.* join, unite; commit, entrust; match (one against another); compare; venture; begin; perpetrate; engage in; **committere proelium**, to join battle.

commoditās, ātis, *f.* fitness, convenience; advantage; obligingness.

commodō, [1] *v.* oblige, lend, provide, give.

commodum, ī, *nt.* convenience; profit; wages; advantage.

commodus, a, um, *a.* suitable, convenient, fit; advantageous; lucky; obliging, pleasant.

commonefaciō, fēcī, factum, [3] *v.* remind; impress upon.

commoneō, uī, itum, [2] *v.* remind.

commōnstrō, [1] *v.* point out.

commorātiō, ōnis, *f.* stay (at a place); delay; *fig.* dwelling on a point.

commorior, mortuus, [3] *v. dep.* die together.

commoror, ātus, [1] *v. dep.* sojourn, stay; stay long, be inactive; dwell upon.

commōtiō, ōnis, *f.* agitation; the arousing of emotion.

commoveō, mōvī, mōtum, [2] *v.* move vigorously; stir up; excite; disturb; astonish; affect.

commūnicātiō, ōnis, *f.* communication, an imparting.

commūnicō, [1] *v.* communicate; impart; share with; receive a share of.

commūniō, īvī (iī), ītum, [4] *v.* fortify; strengthen, reinforce, entrench.

commūniō, ōnis, *f.* mutual participation, association, sharing.

commūnis, e, *a.* shared by, joint, common, general, ordinary; affable; public.

commūnitās, ātis, *f.* joint possession, partnership; fellowship, kinship.

commūniter, *ad.* in common, commonly, generally.

commūtābilis, e, *a.* changeable, variable.

commūtātiō, ōnis, *f.* change; exchange.

commūtō, [1] *v.* change, alter; exchange, barter.

cōmō, mpsī mptum, [3] v. arrange, 'do' (hair); dress, adorn.

cōmoedia, ae, f. comedy.

cōmoedus, ī, m. comedian, comic actor.

compāgēs, is, compāgō, inis, f. the action of binding together; joint, structure, framework.

compar, aris, a. like, equal (to); equal, comrade; partner.

comparābilis, e, a. comparable.

comparātiō, ōnis, f. preparation; acquirement.

compāreō, uī, [2] v. appear, be visible; be present; be in existence.

comparō, [1] v. unite; compare; prepare; provide (for); acquire; raise (a force); appoint.

compellō, pulī, pulsum, [3] v. drive together or along; collect; impel; force.

compellō, [1] v. accost, address; chide, rebuke; abuse.

compendium, iī, nt. abridgement; a short cut; profit.

compēnsō, [1] v. balance, compensate.

comperendinō, [1] v. adjourn the trial of.

comperiō, perī, pertum, [4] v. find out, learn, know for certain.

compes, edis, f. shackle (for the feet); fetter.

compescō, uī, [3] v. confine, curb, restrain.

competītor, ōris, m. rival, competitor.

competō, īvī & iī, ītum, [3] v. meet; happen; coincide; suit, agree; correspond; be sound or capable.

compīlātiō, ōnis, f. burglary.

compīlō, [1] v. rob, pillage.

compingō, pēgī, pāctum, [3] v. join; fasten up; shut up.

Compitālia, ium, nt. pl. festival celebrated at cross-roads in honour of the rural gods.

compitum, ī, nt. cross-roads.

complector, xus, [3] v. dep. clasp around; encompass, embrace; lay hold of; contain; comprehend (mentally); comprise.

complēmentum, ī, nt. something that fills out or completes.

compleō, ēvī, ētum, [2] v. fill up; fill; complete; fulfil; perfect; supply; recruit; make good.

complexiō, ōnis, f. combination, connection; summary; dilemma.

complexus, ūs, m. embrace; sexual intercourse.

complicō, [1] v. fold up.

complōrātiō, ōnis, f., complōrātus, ūs, m. lamentation; (vocal) mourning.

complōrō, [1] v. bewail.

complūrēs, a, a. several, many.

compluvium, iī, nt. a quadrangular, inward-sloping, central portion of roof, designed to guide rain-water into the impluvium.

compōnō, posuī, positum, [3] *v.* put *or* lay together; arrange; compose; adjust; compare; match; construct; build; compose (books, *etc.*); soothe, appease, settle; bury.

comportō, [1] *v.* carry, transport, collect.

compos, ōtis, *a. usually with gen.* in possession of; participating, guilty of; ~ **mentis,** in full possession of one's faculties.

compositiō, ōnis, *f.* arrangement; matching.

compositor, ōris, *m.* writer, composer.

compositus, a, um, *a.* well-arranged; calm.

compōtor, ōris, *m.* drinking-companion.

comprānsor, ōris, *m.* table-companion.

comprecātiō, ōnis, *f. a.* public supplication *or* prayers.

comprecor, ātus, [1] *v. dep.* supplicate, implore, pray that.

comprehendō, dī, sum, [3] *v.* seize *or* grasp; comprise; include; attack; embrace; describe; express; arrest *or* lay hold of; understand.

comprehēnsiō, ōnis, *f.* arrest; comprehension, idea; dilemma.

comprimō, pressī, pressum, [3] *v.* press *or* squeeze together; keep *or* hold back *or* in; suppress.

comprobātiō, ōnis, *f.* approval.

comprobō, [1] *v.* approve; attest, confirm.

cōmptus, a, um, *a.* adorned; elegant, neat, polished.

compungō, nxī nctum, [3] *v.* prick, puncture.

computō, [1] *v.* calculate, count up, reckon.

cōnāmen, inis, *nt.* attempt; effort, exertion.

cōnātum, ī, *nt.* attempted action.

cōnātus, ūs, *m.* attempt, undertaking; effort; impulse.

concaedēs, ium, *f. pl.* barricade.

concalefaciō, fēcī, factum, [3] *v.* make warm, heat.

concalēscō, uī, [3] *v.* become warm, warm up.

concallēscō, uī, [3] *v.* become hard *or* callous; become insensible.

concavus, a, um, *a.* hollowed out, concave; hollow.

concēdō, cessī, cessum, [3] *v.* go away, depart, withdraw; yield to, submit; allow, grant; forgive.

concelebrō, [1] *v.* go to a place often *or* in large numbers, haunt; celebrate; publish.

concentus, ūs, *m.* singing together, harmony, melody; concord.

concerpō, psī, ptum, [3] *v.* tear in pieces.

concertātiō, ōnis, *f.* dispute, controversy.

concertō, [1] *v.* dispute, fight, argue over.

concessiō, ōnis, *f.* permission, grant, plea of excuse; the act of yielding.

concessus, ūs, *m.* concession; permission.

concha, ae, *f.* shell-fish, cockle; pearl; mussel-shell; oyster-shell; Triton's trumpet.

conchȳliātus, a, um, *a.* purple-dyed.

conchȳlium, iī, *nt.* shell-fish; purple, purple dye.

concidō, cidī, [3] *v.* fall down or into decay; fail; faint; be slain; die.

concīdō, cīdī, cīsum, [3] *v.* cut to pieces; break up; cudgel soundly; cut down, kill; weaken; destroy.

concieō, īvī, itum, [2] *v.* move, stir up; excite, incite.

conciliābulum, ī, *nt.* place of assembly.

conciliātiō, ōnis, *f.* union; winning over.

conciliātor, ōris, *m.* mediator, agent.

conciliō, [1] *v.* call together; unite; procure; win over; obtain; recommend; bring about, obtain.

concilium, iī, *nt.* assembly; council.

concinnitās, ātis, *f.* neatness, elegance.

concinnus, a, um, *a.* neat, pretty, elegant, pleasing.

concinō, cinuī, [3] *v.* sing together, celebrate in song; sound together.

concipiō, cēpī, ceptum, [3] *v.* take up; conceive; devise; understand; take in; produce, form.

concitātiō, ōnis, *f.* rapid motion; passion; excitement, disturbance.

concitātus, a, um, *a.* rapid; passionate, energetic.

concitō, [1] *v.* rouse, spur, excite; disturb; pursue; cause.

conclāmātiō, ōnis, *f.* shouting together; acclamation.

conclāmō, [1] *v.* cry (out) together, shout; bewail (the dead); proclaim.

conclāve, is, *nt.* room; public lavatory.

conclūdō, sī, sum, [3] *v.* enclose together; conclude, end; comprise; infer; stop; close.

conclūsiō, ōnis, *f.* conclusion, end; siege; peroration; logical conclusion from premisses.

concolor, ōris, *a.* of the same colour.

concoquō, coxī, coctum, [3] *v.* heat thoroughly; digest; mature; put up with; consider well; devise.

concordia, ae, *f.* harmony, concord.

concordō, [1] *v.* harmonize, be in agreement.

concors, cordis, *a.* agreeing, harmonious.

concrēdō, didī, ditum, [3] *v.* entrust for safe keeping, confide.

concremō, [1] v. burn up entirely.

concrepō, puī, pitum, [1] v. rattle, clash; snap (one's fingers).

concrēscō, ēvī, ētum, [3] v. grow together; curdle; congeal; clot.

concrētiō, ōnis, f. formation into solid matter.

concrētus, a, um, a. clotted, stiff, frozen; constructed, formed.

concubīna, ae, f. concubine.

concubitus, ūs, m. lying together; sexual intercourse.

concubius, a, um, a. ~ā nocte, in the early part of the night.

conculcō, [1] v. trample upon; oppress; despise.

concumbō, cubuī, cubitum, [3] v. lie with.

concupīscō, īvī & iī, ītum, [3] v. long much for, covet, desire ardently.

concurrō, currī, cursum, [3] v. run or assemble together; join battle; be in conflict; meet; happen simultaneously.

concursātiō, ōnis, f. running together; skirmish.

concursātor, ōris, m. skirmisher.

concursiō, ōnis, f. concourse, meeting; repetition.

concursō, [1] v. run hither and thither; run together; clash; run to visit.

concursus, ūs, m. concourse, crowd; encounter; combination.

concutiō, cussī, cussum, [3] v. shake violently, brandish; weaken; harass, rouse.

condemnō, [1] v. condemn, doom; convict.

condēnseō, [2] v. compress.

condēnsus, a, um, a. dense, thick; wedged together.

condiciō, ōnis, f. condition, situation, rank; stipulation; term, agreement; marriage; married person.

condīcō, xī, ctum, [3] v. agree (upon), declare; promise; undertake; give notice, engage oneself.

condīmentum, ī, nt. spice, seasoning.

condiō, īvī & iī, ītum, [4] v. preserve, pickle; embalm; spice; season, flavour; render pleasant.

condiscipulus, ī, m. schoolfellow, fellow-pupil.

condiscō, didicī, [3] v. learn thoroughly.

conditor, ōris, m. builder, founder, author.

condītus, a, um, a. seasoned, flavoured.

condō, didī, ditum, [3] v. build, found; compose, write; make; hide; sheathe; lay or treasure up; preserve, pickle; bury; thrust (into).

condolēscō, doluī, [3] v. be painful, ache; feel grief.

condōnō, [1] v. give as a present; forgive; remit; devote or sacrifice.

condūcō, xī, ctum, [3] v. lead together, assemble; hire; undertake; contract for; be of use; profit.

conductor, ōris, m. hirer; contractor; lessee.

conduplicō, [1] double, make twofold.

cōnfarreātiō, ōnis, a marriage ceremony, in which meal (fār) was given as an offering.

cōnfectiō, ōnis, f. making ready, preparation; compiling; mastication.

cōnfector, ōris, m. finisher; slayer.

cōnferciō, fertum, [4] v. stuff together, press close together.

cōnferō, cōnferre, contulī, collātum, [3] v. bring or carry together; collect; contribute, add; join; bestow; lay out; apply; discourse or talk together; match; compare; put off; refer; transfer; impute; compress; betake oneself, go.

cōnfertim, ad. in a compact body or bunch.

cōnfessiō, ōnis, f. confession, acknowledgement; admission; admission of guilt.

cōnfestim, ad. immediately, speedily.

cōnficiō, fēcī, fectum, [3] v. do, accomplish; finish; effect; arrange; produce, cause; conquer; kill; use up; consume, weaken, overwhelm; spend.

cōnfīdēns, entis, a. bold, daring; over-confident, presumptuous.

cōnfīdentia, ae, f. confidence; boldness; impudence, audacity.

cōnfīdō, fīsus sum, [3] v. with dat., trust to, have confidence in.

cōnfīgō, fīxī, fīxum, [3] v. fasten together; pierce through, strike down.

cōnfingō, fīnxī, fictum, [3] v. fashion, fabricate, invent, feign.

cōnfīnis, e, a. adjoining, contiguous, allied, akin.

cōnfīnium, iī, nt. common boundary; border.

cōnfirmātiō, ōnis, f. confirmation, encouragement.

cōnfirmō, [1] v. confirm; strengthen; encourage; prove; say boldly.

cōnfiteor, fessus, [2] v. dep. confess, admit; reveal.

cōnflagrō, [1] v. be burnt down; be utterly destroyed.

cōnflictō, [1] v. harass, torment; strike frequently, buffet.

cōnflīgō, xī, ctum, [3] v. strike together, collide, clash; strive; fight; dispute.

cōnflō, [1] v. blow on, ignite; melt; inflame; raise, bring about; arouse.

cōnfluō, xī, [3] v. flow together; flock together.

cōnfodiō, fōdī, fossum, [3] v. dig up; wound fatally; pierce.

cōnfōrmātiō, ōnis, f. shape, form; idea, notion; figure of speech.

cōnfōrmō, [1] v. shape, fashion; train, educate.

cōnfragōsus, a, um, confragus, a, um, a. rough, uneven; hard.

cōnfremō, uī, [3] v. murmur, echo.

cōnfricō, [1] v. rub.

cōnfringō, frēgī, frāctum, [3] v. break in pieces; ruin, subvert.

cōnfugiō, fūgī, [3] v. flee to, have recourse to.

cōnfundō, fūdī, fūsum, [3] v. pour or mix together; upset, confuse; bewilder.

cōnfūsiō, ōnis, f. mingling; confusion, disorder, trouble.

cōnfūtō, [1] v. check, repress; silence; disprove.

congelō, [1] v. congeal; curdle; freeze; grow hard.

congeminō, [1] v. redouble.

congemō, uī, [3] v. utter a cry of grief or pain; bewail.

congeriēs, ēī, f. heap, pile, mass; accumulation.

congerō, gessī, gestum, [3] v. heap up, get together; build; compile; confer.

congestus, ūs, m. bringing together, assembling; heap, pile, mass.

congiārium, iī, nt. largess for soldiers; gift in corn, oil, wine, etc.

conglobō, [1] v. make into a ball; crowd together.

conglūtinō, [1] v. glue together.

congrātulor, [1] v. dep. congratulate.

congredior, gressus, [3] v. dep. meet; join battle.

congregātiō, ōnis, f. society, association.

congregō, [1] v. collect (into a flock); unite.

congressiō, ōnis, f. meeting, visit, interview; conflict, attack; sexual intercourse.

congressus, ūs, m. conference, interview; encounter, fight; sexual intercourse.

congruēns, entis, a. consistent; harmonious, fitting.

congruō, uī, [3] v. come together; agree, accord; suit.

conicio, iēcī, iectum, [3] v. throw together; cast, fling; drive; direct; conjecture; interpret.

coniectō, [1] v. conjecture; interpret; think or imagine.

coniectūra, ae, f. conjecture; inference; interpretation; prophecy.

coniectus, ūs, m. throwing; directing; shot; glance.

cōnifer, a, um, a. coniferous.

cōnītor v. **con(n)ītor.**

coniugālis, e, a. conjugal, matrimonial.

coniugium, iī, nt. marriage, wedlock; wife; husband.

coniūnctim, ad. in combination, jointly.

coniūnctiō, ōnis, *f.* union, conjunction; agreement; mutual love; familiarity; match; fellowship.

coniūnx *or* **coniux, iugis**, *m. or f.* husband, wife, spouse, mate.

coniungō, nxī, nctum, [3] *v.* yoke together; connect; couple; ally; associate.

coniūrātiō, ōnis, *f.* conspiracy, plot; band of conspirators; taking an oath.

coniūrātus, a, um, *a.* leagued; **coniūrātī, ōrum**, *m. pl.* conspirators.

coniūrō, [1] *v.* swear together; conjure, conspire.

cōnīveō *v.* con(n)īveō

con(n)ectō, xuī, xum, [3] *v.* tie, fasten *or* join together, connect; implicate.

con(n)ītor, nīxus & nīsus, [3] *v. dep.* endeavour eagerly; struggle; strain, strive.

con(n)īveō, nīvī & nīxī, [2] *v.* close the eyes; wink at, overlook, turn a blind eye.

cōnōpēum, ī, *nt.* mosquito-net.

cōnor, ātus, [1] *v. dep.* try, venture, undertake.

conquassō, [1] *v.* shake violently; unsettle.

conqueror, questus, [3] *v. dep.* complain of, bewail.

conquiēscō, quiēvī, quiētum, [3] *v.* repose, rest; be inactive; go to sleep; find rest.

conquīrō, quīsīvī, quīsītum, [3] *v.* search for diligently; rake up; hunt down.

conquīsītiō, ōnis, *f.* levying.

cōnsaepiō, ptum, [4] *v.* enclose, fence.

cōnsalūtātiō, ōnis, *f.* greeting, exchange of greetings.

cōnsalūtō, [1] *v.* greet, hail; salute as.

cōnsanguineus, a, um, *a.* related by blood; brotherly, sisterly; ~ **eī**, *m. pl.* relatives.

cōnsanguinitās, ātis, *f.* blood-relationship, kinship.

cōnscelerātus, a, um, *a.* wicked, depraved; criminal.

cōnscelerō, [1] *v.* stain with crime, pollute.

cōnscendō, dī, sum, [3] *v.* mount, ascend; embark.

cōnscientia, ae, *f.* conscience, consciousness; knowledge; remorse.

cōnscindō, scidī, scissum, [3] *v.* rend to pieces; slaughter.

cōnscīscō, scīvī, scītum, [3] *v.* decree; ~ **mortem sibi cōnscīscere**, to commit suicide.

cōnscius, a, um, *a.* conscious; knowing; guilty.

cōnscrībō, psī, ptum, [3] *v.* enlist *or* enrol; compose, write; **patrēs cōnscrīptī**, the title by which senators were addressed.

cōnsecrātiō, ōnis, *f.* consecration; deification.

cōnsecrō, [1] v. consecrate; dedicate; hallow; deify.

cōnsector, ātus, [1] v. dep. go towards; seek after; imitate; pursue, hunt down; attack.

cōnsecūtiō, ōnis, f. consequence; order, sequence; logical consequence.

cōnsenēscō, nuī, [3] v. grow old; become weak; lose consideration or respect; fall into disuse.

cōnsēnsiō, ōnis, f. agreement, unanimity; conspiracy.

cōnsēnsus, ūs, m. unanimity, concord.

cōnsentāneus, a, um, a. agreeable; consistent, fitting.

cōnsentiō, sēnsī, sēnsum, [4] v. consent; agree; decree; conspire; be consistent with.

cōnsequēns, entis, a. following; following as a logical consequence; consistent.

cōnsequor, secūtus, [3] v. dep. follow after; overtake; get or obtain; procure, imitate; reach, come up to, befall; bring about, achieve.

cōnserō, sēvī, situm, [3] v. sow, plant.

cōnserō, seruī, sertum, [3] v. join; link; engage; **manum conserere**, to engage in hostilities.

cōnserva, ae, f. fellow-slave (female).

cōnservātiō, ōnis, f. keeping, preservation.

cōnservātor, ōris, m. keeper; defender; saviour.

cōnservō, [1] v. preserve, keep from danger; maintain.

cōnservus, ī, m. fellow-slave.

cōnsessor, ōris, m. assessor.

cōnsessus, ūs, m. assembly; audience; court.

cōnsīderātus, a, um, a. thought out, cautious, deliberate.

cōnsīderō, [1] v. inspect; consider, contemplate.

cōnsīdō, sēdī, sessum, [3] v. sit down; settle; sink down; encamp; take up one's residence; hold a session; abate; cease.

cōnsignō, [1] v. seal up; attest.

cōnsilior, ātus, [1] v. dep. take counsel; advise.

cōnsilium, iī, nt. counsel, advice; reason; purpose, plan; stratagem; resolution, will; judgment; prudence.

cōnsimilis, e, a. similar, like.

cōnsistō, stitī, stitum, [3] v. stand (together or fast); be frozen; make a stand; be steadfast; be in existence; consist (of); halt; cease.

cōnsitor, ōris, m. sower, planter.

cōnsociātiō, ōnis, f. association, uniting.

cōnsociō, [1] v. associate, unite; share.

cōnsōlātiō, ōnis, f. consolation, comfort; encouragement.

cōnsōlātor, ōris, m. comforter.

cōnsōlātōrius, a, um, *a.* consolatory, consoling.

cōnsōlor, ātus, [1] *v. dep.* console, solace; alleviate, allay.

cōnsonō, uī, [1] *v.* make a noise together, resound; agree; harmonize.

cōnsonus, a, um, *a.* sounding together; harmonious; accordant.

cōnsōpiō, ītum, [4] *v.* lull to sleep, make unconscious.

cōnsors, ortis, *a.* partaking of; brotherly, sisterly; ~, *m. and f.* colleague, partner; fellow.

cōnsortiō, ōnis, *f.* fellowship; partnership; association.

cōnsortium, iī, *nt.* fellowship, participation.

cōnspectus, a, um, *a.* visible; remarkable; ~, ūs, *m.* look, sight, view; presence; contemplation.

cōnspergō, sī, sum, [3] *v.* besprinkle, sprinkle.

cōnspiciō, spexī, spectum, [3] *v.* catch sight of, see; observe; descry.

cōnspicor, ātus, [1] *v. dep.* get a sight of, see.

cōnspicuus, a, um, *a.* in sight, visible; illustrious, remarkable.

cōnspīrātiō, ōnis, *f.* concord, harmony; unanimity; conspiracy.

cōnspīrō, [1] *v.* harmonize, agree; conspire.

cōnstāns, antis, *a.* steadfast, firm, immovable, constant; secure; consistent; sure, steady.

cōnstantia, ae, *f.* steadfastness, firmness, constancy, perseverance; resolution; agreement.

cōnsternātiō, ōnis, *f.* confusion, dismay; mutiny; sedition; disturbance, disorder.

cōnsternō, strāvī, strātum, [3] *v.* bestrew; throw down; pave.

cōnsternō, [1] *v.* terrify, confuse.

cōnstīpō, [1] *v.* crowd together.

cōnstituō, uī, ūtum, [3] *v.* put, set *or* place; constitute, appoint; decree, decide; fix *or* establish; range; build; establish; agree (upon); manage; determine; dispose; intend; settle.

cōnstitūtiō, ōnis, *f.* constitution, disposition; ordering; arrangement; ordinance.

cōnstitūtum, ī, *nt.* institution, law; agreement, compact.

cōnstō, stitī, stātum, [1] *v.* stand still; last; be settled *or* certain *or* known; cost; agree (with); exist *or* be; consist (of); stand firm; cōnstat, it is agreed.

cōnstringō, īnxī, ictum, [3] *v.* bind fast, tight; compress.

cōnstrūctiō, ōnis, *f.* building, construction.

cōnstruō, ūxī, ūctum, [3] *v.* heap up; make, build.

cōnstuprō, [1] *v.* ravish, rape.

cōnsuēfaciō, fēcī, factum, [3] *v.* accustom.

cōnsuēscō, suēvī, suētum, [3] *v.* accustom; become accustomed; be accustomed.

cōnsuētūdō, inis, *f.* custom, habit, use; manner; companionship, familiarity, conversation.

cōnsul, ulis, *m.* consul, one of the chief Roman magistrates.

cōnsulāris, e, *a.* consular; of *or* proper to a consul.

cōnsulātus, ūs, *m.* consulship.

cōnsulō, suluī, sultum, [3] *v.* take counsel; consider; consult (someone); take steps; ~ *with dat.* consult the interest of; take care of; provide for.

cōnsultātiō, ōnis, *f.* consultation, deliberation.

cōnsultē, cōnsultō, *ad.* deliberately, on purpose.

cōnsultō, [1] *v.* consult, to take counsel.

cōnsultor, ōris, *m.* adviser; consulter; lawyer.

cōnsultum, ī, *nt.* decision; decree.

cōnsultus, a, um, *a.* well-considered; knowing, experienced.

cōnsummō, [1] *v.* add up, finish.

cōnsūmō, sūmpsī, sūmptum, [3] *v.* use up; eat; consume; squander, destroy; employ.

cōnsurgō, surrēxī, surrēctum, [3] *v.* rise, stand; arise.

contabulō, [1] *v.* board over; cover.

contāctus, ūs, *m.* touch, contact; contagion.

contāgēs, is, *f.* contact; infection.

contāgiō, ōnis, *f.*, contāgium, iī, *nt.* contagion, contact, touch; influence; infection.

contāminō, [1] *v.* contaminate, pollute, debase, spoil.

contegō, xī, ctum, [3] *v.* cover (up); hide.

contemerō, [1] *v.* defile, pollute.

contemnō, tempsī, temptum, [3] *v.* scorn, contemn.

contemplātiō, ōnis, *f.* view, survey, contemplation; meditation.

contemplātus, ūs, *m.* contemplation.

contemplor, ātus, [1] *v. dep.* survey, observe; contemplate.

contemptim, *ad.* contemptuously; fearlessly.

contemptiō, ōnis, *f.* contempt, scorn, disdain.

contemptor, ōris, *m.* contemner; despiser.

contemptus, a, um, *a.* contemptible, vile; ~, ūs, *m.* contempt, scorn.

contendō, dī, tum, [3] *v.* stretch, strain; hurl; contend; fight; dispute; strive, exert; labour; demand; urge; state emphatically; go *or* march; hasten; compare.

contentē, *ad.* with great exertion.

contentiō, ōnis, *f.* exertion; contest, fight; dispute; comparison; contrast; antithesis.

contentus, a, um, *a.* tense, tight; energetic, vigorous.

contentus, a, um, *a.* contented, satisfied.

conterminus, a, um, *a.* bordering upon.

conterō, trīvī, trītum, [3] *v.* grind, bruise, crumble; waste; spend; exhaust.

conterreō, uī, itum, [2] *v.* frighten thoroughly.

contestor, ātus, [1] *v. dep.* call to witness.

contexō, xuī, xtum, [3] *v.* entwine, twist together; connect, compose.

contextus, ūs, *m.* connection, coherence; series.

conticēscō, ticuī, [3] *v.* cease to talk, fall silent.

contignātiō, ōnis, *f.* raftering; storey, floor.

contignō, [1] *v.* rafter, floor.

contiguus, a, um, *a.* adjoining, bordering upon.

continēns, entis, *a.* contiguous, adjacent; uninterrupted; temperate; ~, **entis**, *f.* mainland.

continenter, *ad.* without interruption; temperately.

continentia, ae, *f.* abstemiousness, continence, self-control.

contineō, uī, tentum, [2] *v.* hold together; bind; contain; retain; comprise; confine; keep secret; hinder, prevent; stop.

contingō, tigī, tactum, [3] *v.* touch; seize; border upon; reach; influence, affect; stain; befall; come to pass; be akin; be connected with.

continuātiō, ōnis, *f.* continuation, prolongation.

continuō, *ad.* immediately, forthwith.

continuō, [1] *v.* put in a line; join; deal with successively, prolong.

continuus, a, um, *a.* continuous; successive.

cōntiō, ōnis, *f.* assembly, meeting; oration.

cōntiōnābundus, a, um, *a.* delivering a public speech.

cōntiōnālis, e, *a.* belonging to a public assembly.

cōntiōnātor, ōris, *m.* haranguer of the people; demagogue.

cōntiōnor, ātus, [1] *v. dep.* deliver an oration to a public assembly.

cōntiuncula, ae, *f.* small *or* negligible meeting.

contorqueō, torsī, tortum, [2] *v.* brandish; fling; twist round.

contrā, *ad. & pr. with acc.* against; opposite to; contrary to; on the contrary; otherwise; mutually; face to face.

contractiō, ōnis, *f.* contraction; abridgement.

contractus, a, um, *a.* close; abridged; stinted.

contrādīcō, xī, ctum, [3] *v.* gainsay *or* contradict.

contrādictiō, ōnis, *f.* objection, contradiction.

contrahō, xī, ctum, [3] *v.* draw together; gather; tighten; abridge; check; agree; incur; get; cause.

contrārius, a, um, *a.* opposite, contrary; inimical; harmful; **ex contrāriō**, on the contrary.

contrectō, [1] *v.* touch repeatedly, handle.

contremīscō, muī, [3] *v.* tremble all over; tremble at.

contribuō, uī, ūtum, [3] *v.* incorporate; contribute.

contrīstō, [1] *v.* make sad, afflict; darken.

contrōversia, ae, *f.* controversy; dispute.

contrōversiōsus, a, um, *a.* much disputed, debatable.

contrucīdō, [1] *v.* cut down, slaughter.

contrūdō, sī, sum, [3] *v.* thrust, press in.

contubernālis, is, *m.* or *f.* tent-companion; comrade, mate.

contubernium, iī, *nt.* companionship in a tent; attendance on a superior; common war tent.

contueor, tuitus, [2] *v. dep.* look at, behold, see.

contumācia, ae, *f.* stubbornness.

contumāx, ācis, *a.* stubborn, defiant.

contumēlia, ae, *f.* insult, affront, ignominy; damage.

contumēliōsus, a, um, *a.* insolent, abusive.

contumulō, [1] *v.* bury.

contundō, tudī, tūsum, [3] *v.* bruise, crush; subdue utterly.

conturbātiō, ōnis, *f.* confusion, panic.

conturbātus, a, um, *a.* disturbed, perplexed.

conturbō, [1] *v.* upset; disquiet; go bankrupt.

contus, ī, *m.* long pole, pike.

cōnūbium, iī, *nt.* marriage.

cōnus, ī, *m.* cone; apex of a helmet.

convalēscō, luī, [3] *v.* recover, get better, grow strong.

convallis, is, *f.* a valley (much shut in).

convectō, [1] *v.* **convehō, vēxī, vectum**, [3] *v.* carry together, gather.

convellō, vellī, vulsum, [3] *v.* pull *or* pluck up; wrench; shatter; overthrow.

convenae, ārum, *m. pl.* refugees, immigrants.

conveniēns, entis, *a.* fitting; appropriate.

convenientia, ae, *f.* agreement, harmony; fitness.

conveniō, vēnī, ventum, [4] *v.* come together, assemble; meet; agree; fit, suit; be due; visit, prosecute.

conventiculum, ī, *nt.* small assemblage; place of assembly.

conventiō, ōnis, *f.*, **conventum, ī**, *nt.* agreement, compact.

conventus, ūs, *m.* meeting, assembly; provincial court; district.

conversō, [1] *v.* turn, turn over in the mind; **conversor**, be a constant visitor (to).

convertō, **tī**, **sum**, [3] *v.* turn round; convert; change *or* transform; translate.

convestiō, **īvī**, **ītum**, [4] clothe, dress, cover.

convexus, **a**, **um**, *a.* convex; arched, vaulted.

convīcium, **iī**, *nt.* cry, clamour; bawling; reproach, abuse.

convīctiō, **ōnis**, *f.* companionship, intimacy.

convīctor, **ōris**, *m.* messmate, friend.

convīctus, **ūs**, *m.* living together, intimacy; banquet, feast.

convincō, **vīcī**, **victum**, [3] *v.* convict, prove clearly.

convīva, **ae**, *m.* or *f.* table companion, guest.

convīvālis, **e**, *a.* convivial.

convīvātor, **ōris**, *m.* host.

convīvium, **iī**, *nt.* feast, entertainment, banquet.

convocō, [1] *v.* call together, convoke, assemble.

convolō, [1] *v.* fly together; *fig.* run together.

convolvō, **vī**, **volūtum**, [3] *v.* roll together *or* round, writhe.

cooperiō, **ruī**, **rtum**, [4] *v.* cover wholly, overwhelm.

cooptātiō, **ōnis**, *f.* co-option, adoption.

cooptō, [1] *v.* choose, elect, admit.

coorior, **ortus**, [4] *v. dep.* arise; break forth.

cōpia, **ae**, *f.* abundance, plenty; riches; store; provisions; ability; power; opportunity, means.

cōpiae, **ārum**, *f. pl.* (military) forces.

cōpiōsus, **a**, **um**, *a.* plentiful, rich, wealthy; eloquent.

cōpula, **ae**, *f.* bond, tie.

cōpulātiō, **ōnis**, *f.* connecting, uniting.

cōpulō, [1] *v.* couple, bind *or* tie together, connect, unite.

coquō, **xī**, **ctum**, [3] *v.* cook; boil, fry, bake; burn; parch; ripen; digest; mature, cherish, stir up.

coquus, **ī**, *m.* cook.

cor, **cordis**, *nt.* heart; mind, judgment; **cordī esse**, to be pleasing.

corallium, **iī**, *nt.* coral.

cōram, *ad.* & *pr. with abl.* in the presence of, face to face; personally.

corbis, **is**, *m.* or *f.* basket.

corium, **iī**, *nt.* skin, leather, hide.

corneus, **a**, **um**, *a.* of horn, resembling horn.

corneus, **a**, **um**, *a.* of the cornel-tree.

cornicen, **inis**, *m.* trumpeter, bugler.

corniger, **a**, **um**, *a.* horn-bearing, horned.

cornipēs, **edis**, *a.* horn-footed, hoofed.

cornīx, īcis, *f.* crow.

cornū, ūs, *nt.* horn; hoof; bill of a bird; horn of the moon; end, tip; peak, cone of a helmet; bow; trumpet; wing of an army; funnel.

cornum, ī, *nt.* cornel-berry.

cornus, ī, *f.* cornel-cherry-tree, cornel wood.

corōlla, ae, *f.* small garland.

corōna, ae, *f.* garland, wreath, crown; circle (of men); cordon of troops thrown round an enemy position.

corōnō, [1] *v.* crown, wreathe; surround.

corporeus, a, um, *a.* corporeal; fleshy.

corpus, oris, *nt.* body; flesh; corpse; trunk; frame; corporation.

corpusculum, ī, *nt.* little body, atom.

corrēctiō, ōnis, *f.* improvement, correction.

corrēctor, ōris, *m.* corrector, improver, reformer.

corrēpō, psī, [3] *v.* creep, move stealthily.

corrigō, rēxī, rēctum, [3] *v.* straighten, set right; correct.

corripiō, ripuī, reptum, [3] *v.* snatch up, lay hold of; rebuke; chastise; shorten; hasten; seize unlawfully; **corripere viam,** to hasten on one's way.

corrōborō, [1] *v.* strengthen, corroborate.

corrogō, [1] *v.* collect money by begging.

corrūgō, [1] *v.* make wrinkled.

corrumpō, rūpī, ruptum, [3] *v.* spoil, destroy, deface; falsify; bribe; corrupt, seduce.

corruō, uī, [3] *v.* break down, fall to the ground.

corruptēla, ae, *f.* corruption, enticement to sexual misconduct, bribery; corrupting influence.

corruptiō, ōnis, *f.* corruption; bribery.

corruptor, ōris, *m.* corrupter, seducer, briber.

cortex, icis, *m.* bark, rind; cork.

cortīna, ae, *f.* cauldron, cauldron on oracular tripod (at Delphi).

cōrus, ī, *m.* north-west wind.

coruscō, [1] *v.* brandish, shake; flash, coruscate.

coruscus, a, um, *a.* vibrating, tremulous; flashing.

corvus, ī, *m.* raven; military engine.

corylētum, ī, *nt.* copse of hazel-trees.

corylus, ī, *f.* hazel-tree.

corymbus, ī, *m.* cluster of ivy-berries *or* flowers *or* fruit.

cōs, cōtis, *f.* flint-stone; whet-stone; **cōtēs,** *pl.* rocks.

costa, ae, *f.* rib; side.

costum, ī, *nt.,* **costos, ī,** *f.* an aromatic plant *or* its powdered root.

cothurnātus, a, um, *a.* wearing the buskin; in lofty style.

cothurnus, ī, *m.* high boot worn by Greek tragic actors; elevated style, tragic poetry.

cot(t)īdiē, *ad.* every day, daily.

coturnīx, īcis, *f.* quail.

crābrō, ōnis, *m.* wasp, hornet; **irritāre ~nēs**, to disturb a hornets' nest.

crāpula, ae, *f.* drunkenness; next day's sickness.

crās, *ad.* tomorrow; in the future.

crassitūdō, inis, *f.* thickness, density.

crassus, a, um, *a.* thick, dense, fat, gross, stupid, crass.

crāstīnus, a, um, *a.* of tomorrow.

crātēr, ēris, *m.* **crātēra, ae**, *f.* mixing-bowl; crater of a volcano, basin of fountain; Cup (constellation).

crātis, is, *f.* wicker-work; harrow; frame-work.

creātor, ōris, *m.* creator, author, founder; father.

creātrīx, īcis, *f.* creatress, mother.

crēber, bra, brum, *a.* thick, close, pressed together, frequent, numerous; abundant.

crēbrēscō, bruī, [3] *v.* become frequent, increase.

crēbritās, ātis, *f.* frequency, closeness in succession.

crēdibilis, e, *a.* trustworthy, credible.

crēditor, ōris, *m.* lender, creditor.

crēditum, ī, *nt.* loan.

crēdō, didī, ditum, [3] *v. with dat.* believe, trust; entrust; think *or* to be of the opinion.

crēdulitās, ātis, *f.* credulity, trustfulness.

crēdulus, a, um, *a.* credulous.

cremō, [1] *v.* burn, consume by fire.

creō, [1] *v.* create, make, produce; choose; elect; cause; establish.

crepida, ae, *f.* slipper, sandal.

crepīdō, inis, *f.* pedestal; brink; pier, bank, sidewalk.

crepitāculum, ī, *nt.* rattle.

crepitō, [1] *v.* rattle, clatter, rustle.

crepitus, ūs, *m.* rattling, clashing, rustling; (of thunder) crash; (of the teeth) chattering; fart.

crepō, uī, itum, [1] *v.* rattle, rustle, clatter; snap the fingers; jingle; harp on, grumble at the way that.

crepundia, ōrum, *nt. pl.* child's rattle; cymbals.

crepusculum, ī, *nt.* twilight, dusk.

crēscō, crēvī, crētum, [3] *v.* grow; arise; spring; appear; get advantage; increase; attain honour, be advanced, be strengthened.

crēta, ae, *f.* chalk; clay; paint; clayey soil.

crētātus, a, um, *a.* marked with chalk; powdered.

crētiō, ōnis, *f.* declaration respecting the acceptance of an inheritance.

crētōsus, a, um, *a.* abounding in chalk *or* clay.

crīmen, inis, *nt.* crime, offence, fault; scandal; reproach; accusation.

crīminātiō, ōnis, *f.* accusation, indictment.

crīminor, ātus, [1] *v. dep.* accuse; charge (with).

crīminōsus, a, um, *a.* accusatory; reproachful, vituperative.

crīnālis, e, *a.* worn in the hair; covered with hair-like filaments.

crīnis, is, *m.* hair; tail of a comet.

crīnītus, a, um, *a.* hairy; having long locks; **stella ~a**, comet.

crispō, [1] *v.* curl, crisp; shake, brandish.

crispus, a, um, *a.* curled; curlyheaded; quivering.

crista, ae, *f.* crest; cock's comb; plume (of a helmet).

cristātus, a, um, *a.* tufted, crested; plumed.

criticus, ī, *m.* literary critic.

croceus, a, um, *a.* of saffron; saffron-coloured; yellow.

crocinus, a, um, *a.* of saffron, yellow.

crocinum, ī, *nt.* saffron oil used as a perfume.

crocodīlus, ī, *m.* crocodile.

crocus, ī, *m.* crocum, **ī**, *nt.* crocus; saffron; saffron-colour.

cruciāmentum, ī, *nt.* torture, torment.

cruciātus, ūs, *m.* torture; severe physical *or* mental pain.

cruciō, [1] *v.* torture; grieve.

crūdēlis, e, *a.* cruel, bloodthirsty;

crūdēlitās, ātis, *f.* cruelty, barbarity.

crūdēscō, duī, [3] *v.* become fierce *or* savage.

crūdus, a, um, *a.* raw; bloody; undigested; unripe, sour; fresh; immature; vigorous; harsh; cruel.

cruentō, [1] *v.* stain with blood.

cruentus, a, um, *a.* gory, bloody; blood-thirsty; blood-red.

cruor, ōris, *m.* gore, blood; murder.

crūs, ūris, *nt.* leg, shank, shin.

crusta, ae, *f.* rind, shell, crust, bark.

crustum, ī, *nt.* pastry, cake.

crux, ucis, *f.* cross; torture, trouble, misery, destruction.

cubiculārius, ī, *m.* *valet-de-chambre.*

cubiculum, ī, *nt.* bedroom.

cubīle, is, *nt.* couch, bed; marriage-bed; lair.

cubitō, [1] *v.* lie down.

cubitum, ī, *nt.* elbow; forearm; cubit.

cubō, uī, itum, [1] *v.* lie down; lie asleep; recline at table.

cucumis, eris, *m.* cucumber.

cucurbita, ae, *f.* gourd.

cūiās, ātis, *a.* of what country *or* town?

culex, icis, *m.* gnat, midge.

culīna, ae, *f.* kitchen; fare, victuals.

culmen, inis, *nt.* top, summit; gable; acme, eminence.

culmus, ī, *m.* stalk, stem; thatch.

culpa, ae, *f.* fault, crime, blame; negligence.

culpō, [1] *v.* blame, find fault with; accuse.

culter, trī, *m.* knife.

cultor, ōris, *m.* husbandman; cultivator, inhabitant; supporter; worshipper.

cultrīx, īcis, *f.* female inhabitant.

cultūra, ae, *f.* agriculture; care, culture, cultivation.

cultus, a, um, *a.* cultivated, polished, elegant, civilized; **culta, ōrum,** *nt. pl.* tilled land.

cultus, ūs, *m.* worship, reverence; culture; refinement; adorning; splendour, smartness.

culullus, ī, *m.* a drinking vessel *or* its contents.

cum, *pr. with abl.* with; along with; amid; with words expressing strife, contention, *etc.*, against.

cum, *c.* when; since; although; as soon as.

cumba, ae, *f.* small boat, skiff.

. . . -cumque, *ad.* . . . -ever, . . . -soever.

cumulātus, a, um, *a.* heaped, abundant, great.

cumulō, [1] *v.* heap up; accumulate; fill full.

cumulus, ī, *m.* heap, pile; surplus, increase; summit, crown.

cūnābula, ōrum, *nt. pl.* cradle; earliest dwelling-place; earliest childhood.

cūnae, ārum, *f. pl.* cradle; one's earliest years.

cūnctābundus, a, um, *a.* lingering, loitering.

cūnctāns, antis, *a.* hesitant, clinging; stubborn.

cūnctātiō, ōnis, *f.* delay, hesitation.

cūnctātor, ōris, *m.* delayer.

cūnctor, ātus, [1] *v. dep.* tarry, linger, hesitate.

cūnctus, a, um, *a.* all together, total, complete.

cuneātim, *ad.* in a closely packed formation.

cuneātus, a, um, *a.* wedge-shaped.

cuneus, ī, *m.* wedge; battalion, *etc.,* drawn up in the form of a wedge; rows of seats in a theatre.

cunīculus, ī, *m.* rabbit; underground passage; mine; channel.

cunnus, ī, *m.* the female puden-da.

-cunque, *v.* **-cumque.**

cupiditās, ātis, *f.* longing; desire; passion; avarice; ambition.

cupīdō, inis, *f.* desire, greedi-ness; appetite; love; desire of material gain; ~, *m.* the god of love.

cupidus, a, um, *a.* longing for, desiring, eager; loving; greedy, passionate.

cupiēns, entis, *a.* desirous, eager for, anxious.

cupiō, īvī & iī, ītum, [3] *v.* long for desire; covet.

cupresseus, a, um, *a.* of cypress.

cupressifer, era, erum, *a.* cy-press-bearing.

cupressus, ī, *f.* cypress-tree; spear of cypress-wood.

cūr, *ad.* why?

cūra, ae, *f.* attention, care; admin-istration; office; written work; task, responsibility; sorrow; anxiety, concern; trouble; love; object of love.

cūrātiō, ōnis, *f.* administra-tion, management; treatment, charge.

cūrātor, ōris, *m.* manager, superintendent; guardian.

curculiō, ōnis, *m.* corn-weevil.

cūria, ae, *f.* division of the Roman people, senate-house, senate.

cūriātus, a, um, *a.* pertaining to cūriae; **Comitia cūriāta,** *nt.*

pl. the assembly in which people voted according to cu-riae.

cūriō, ōnis, *m.* chief priest of a cūria.

cūriōsus, a, um, *a.* careful, dili-gent; curious, inquisitive.

cūrō, [1] *v.* take care of, mind; worry *or* care about; order; at-tend to; heal; cure.

curriculum, ī, *nt.* race; race-track; chariot; course of action.

currō, cucurrī, cursum, [3] *v.* run, hasten.

currus, ūs, *m.* chariot; triumphal chariot; triumph.

cursim, *ad.* swiftly, hastily.

cursitō, [1] **cursō,** [1] *v.* run to and fro.

cursor, ōris, *m.* runner; chariot-racer; courier.

cursus, ūs, *m.* running; course, voyage, journey; race; direc-tion; march; career.

curtus, a, um, *a.* mutilated; in-complete.

curūlis, e, *a.* of curule rank, i.e. of consuls, praetors, or curule aediles.

curvāmen, inis, *nt.* curvature; curved form, arc.

curvō, [1] *v.* make curved, bend; make (a person) stoop.

curvus, a, um, *a.* crooked, bent, curved, stooping.

cuspis, idis, *f.* point, spike; spear; trident (of Neptune); scorpion's sting.

custōdia, ae, _f._ watch, guard; care; watch-house; guard-post; confinement; prison.

custōdiō, īvī & iī, ītum, [4] _v._ watch, guard; preserve; take heed; retain.

custōs, ōdis, _m._ or _f._ keeper; guardian; protector; watchman; jailer; container.

cutis, is, _f._ skin.

cyathus, ī, _m._ wine-ladle, wine-measure.

cycnēus, a, um, _a._ of a swan; swan-like.

cycnus, cygnus, ī, _m._ swan.

cylindrus, drī, _m._ cylinder; roller (for levelling the ground).

cymbalum, ī, _nt._ cymbal.

cymbium, iī, _nt._ small cup, especially for wine.

Cynosūra, ae, _f._ the Lesser Bear (constellation).

cyparissus, ī, _v._ **cupressus.**

cytisus, ī, _m._ or _f._ a fodder plant, tree-medick.

....

D

....

D = 500.

daedalus, a, um, _a._ skilful; skilfully made.

damma, ae, _f._ fallow-deer, doe, small member of deer family.

damnātiō, ōnis, _f._ condemnation.

damnō, [1] _v._ condemn, sentence; discredit.

damnōsus, a, um, _a._ detrimental, injurious, destructive; prodigal.

damnum, ī, _nt._ damage, injury, loss; hurt, fine.

daps, dapis, _f._ sacrificial feast; banquet.

datiō, ōnis, _f._ giving, transfer, assigning.

dator, ōris, _m._ giver.

dē, _pr. with abl._ down from; from; away from, out of; about; (made) of; concerning; for; by reason of; after, according to.

dea, ae, _f._ goddess.

dēbellātor, ōris, _m._ conqueror.

dēbellō, [1] _v._ bring a battle _or_ war to an end; vanquish.

dēbeō, uī, itum, [2] _v._ owe, be in debt; be obliged _or_ bound _or_ destined.

dēbilis, e, _a._ weak, feeble; crippled.

dēbilitās, ātis, _f._ weakness, debility.

dēbilitō, [1] _v._ weaken; maim.

dēbitor, ōris, _m._ debtor.

dēbitum, ī, _nt._ debt; duty.

dēcantō, [1] _v._ reel off, chant; repeat.

dēcēdō, cessī, cessum, [3] *v.* go away; depart; retire; yield; cease; die; disappear; decrease.

decem, *a.* num. *indecl.* ten.

December, bris, *m.* December.

decempeda, ae, *f.* ten-foot measuring rod.

decemvirātus, ūs, *m.* office of decemvir.

decemvirī, ōrum, *m. pl.* commission of ten (magistrates at Rome).

decēns, entis, *a.* fitting; becoming, decent.

dēcernō, crēvī, crētum, [3] *v.* distinguish; judge; decide; settle; propose.

dēcerpō, psī, ptum, [3] *v.* pluck *or* pull off; destroy; catch, snatch, reap.

dēcertō, [1] *v.* fight out; dispute.

dēcessiō, ōnis, *f.* going away, departure; retirement; diminution; abatement.

dēcessor, ōris, *m.* magistrate retiring from his post.

dēcessus, ūs, *m.* departure; retirement; decrease; ebb; death.

decet, cuit, [2] *v. impers.* it is becoming *or* right *or* proper.

dēcidō, cīdī, [3] *v.* fall down; pass away; die.

dēcīdō, cīdī, cīsum, [3] *v.* cut off; determine, put an end to.

deciē(n)s, *ad.* ten times.

decima, ae, *f.* tenth part; tithe; **porta decimāna**, the rear gate of a Roman camp.

decimō, [1] *v.* choose by lot every tenth man (for punishment).

decimus, decumus, a, um, *a.* tenth.

dēcipiō, cēpī, ceptum, [3] *v.* deceive, cheat.

dēclāmātiō, ōnis, *f.* delivering of a set speech.

dēclāmō, [1] *v.* declaim, make speeches.

dēclārō, [1] *v.* declare; prove; mean.

dēclīnō, [1] *v.* turn aside; avoid; deviate.

dēclīvis, e, *a.* sloping downwards, declining; **dēclīve, is**, *nt.* slope, declivity.

dēclīvitās, ātis, *f.* falling gradient.

dēcoctor, ōris, *m.* insolvent person, defaulting debtor.

dēcolor, ōris, *a.* discoloured, faded; degenerate.

dēcoquō, xī, ctum, [3] *v.* boil down; waste away; become bankrupt.

decor, ōris, *m.* beauty, grace; charm.

decorō, [1] *v.* adorn, grace; glorify.

decōrus, a, um, *a.* decorous; proper; suitable; graceful; handsome; noble.

dēcrēscō, crēvī, crētum, [3] *v.* decrease; diminish; dwindle.

dēcrētum, ī, *nt.* decree, decision; principle, doctrine.

decuria, ae, *f.* group of ten, group.

decuriō, [1] *v.* divide into companies of ten.

decuriō, ōnis, *m.* the head of a decuria.

dēcurrō, (cu)currī, cursum, [3] *v.* run down; sail shorewards or downstream; have recourse to; drill.

dēcursus, ūs, *m.* downward course; declivity; charge downhill.

decus, oris, *nt.* grace, ornament; glory; beauty; virtue, decorum.

dēcutiō, cussī, cussum, [3] *v.* shake down or off.

dēdecet, cuit, *v. impers.* it is unsuitable for or unbecoming to.

dēdecorō, [1] *v.* disgrace.

dēdecōrus, a, um, *a.* dishonourable.

dēdecus, oris, *nt.* disgrace, infamy; shame; dishonour.

dēdicātiō, ōnis, *f.* dedication, consecration.

dēdicō, [1] *v.* dedicate, devote.

dēdignor, ātus, [1] *v. dep.* disdain; refuse, reject with scorn.

dēdīscō, didicī, [3] *v.* unlearn, forget.

dēditiō, ōnis, *f.* surrender.

dēditīcius, a, um, *a.* having surrendered.

dēditus, a, um, *a.* devoted to, fond of.

dēdō, didī, ditum, [3] *v.* surrender; abandon; yield.

dēdoleō, uī, [2] *v.* cease to grieve.

dēdūcō, xī, ctum, [3] *v.* lead or draw down; bring away or off; establish (a colony); launch; conduct; derive; compose; withdraw; subtract.

dēductiō, ōnis, *f.* transportation, deduction.

deerrō, [1] *v.* go astray.

dēfatīgātiō, ōnis, *f.* weariness, fatigue.

dēfatīgō, [1] *v.* tire, exhaust; lose heart.

dēfectiō, ōnis, *f.* failure, deficiency; defection, revolt.

dēfector, ōris, *m.* rebel, renegade.

dēfectus, ūs, *m.* failure; eclipse.

dēfendō, dī, sum, [3] *v.* defend, guard; preserve; keep off; affirm, maintain.

dēfēnsiō, ōnis, *f.* defence.

dēfēnsō, [1] *v.* protect.

dēfēnsor, ōris, *m.* defender, guardian, protector.

dēferō, ferre, tulī, lātum, *v.* bring or carry down or off; convey; bring word; bestow; present; tell; transfer; accuse, indict.

dēfetīscor, fessus, [3] *v. dep.* grow weary or faint.

dēficiō, fēcī, fectum, [3] *v.* fail; cease; faint; be discouraged; sink under; be wanting *or* defective; decay; die; desert, forsake.

dēfīgō, xī, xum, [3] *v.* fix down, fasten; thrust into; astound, bewitch.

dēfīniō, īvī, ītum, [4] *v.* limit; define; determine; end.

dēfīnītiō, ōnis, *f.* definition.

dēfīnītus, a, um, *a.* definite, precise, limited.

dēfīō, erī, [3] *v.* be lacking.

dēflagrō, [1] *v.* be burnt down; 'burn out'; burn down; destroy.

dēflectō, xī, xum, [3] *v.* bend *or* turn aside *or* off; divert, modify.

dēfleō, ēvī, ētum, [2] *v.* weep abundantly for, mourn the loss of.

dēflōrēscō, ruī, [3] *v.* fade, wither.

dēfluō, xī, xum, [3] *v.* flow down; glide down; fade; disappear; be ended.

dēfodiō, fōdī, fossum, [3] *v.* dig; bury.

dēformis, e, *a.* ill-formed, ugly; shapeless; odious; base.

dēformitās, ātis, *f.* deformity, ugliness, degradation; lack of good taste.

dēformō, [1] *v.* shape, fashion; delineate, describe.

dēformō, [1] *v.* disfigure; spoil, impair.

dēfraudō, [1] *v.* cheat, defraud.

dēfrēnātus, a, um, *a.* unbridled.

dēfricō, cuī, cātum & ctum, [1] *v.* rub hard.

dēfringō, frēgī, frāctum, [3] *v.* break off.

dēfugiō, fūgī, [3] *v.* avoid, run away (from), escape.

dēfundō, fūdī, fūsum, [3] *v.* pour down *or* out.

dēfungor, fūnctus, [3] *v. dep. with abl.* discharge, finish; have done with; have died.

dēgener, is, *a.* degenerate; lowborn; base.

dēgenerō, [1] *v.* degenerate; deteriorate, decline.

dēgō, dēgī, [3] *v.* spend *or* pass; live.

dēgravō, [1] *v.* weigh down; overpower.

dēgredior, gressus, [3] *v. dep.* march down, descend; dismount.

dēgustō, [1] *v.* taste, take a taste of; try; test.

dehinc, *ad.* after this; hence; henceforth; next; since then.

dehīscō, hīvī, [3] *v.* gape, split open.

dehonestāmentum, ī, *nt.* disfigurement, disgrace.

dehonestō, [1] *v.* disgrace.

dehortor, ātus, [1] *v. dep.* dissuade.

dēiciō, iēcī, iectum, [3] v. throw down; dislodge; fell; kill; rob of; to dispossess.

dēiectus, ūs, m. throwing down; fall; declivity, slope.

dein, v. deinde.

deinceps, ad. in succession; in a series.

deinde, ad. afterward; then; next.

dēlābor, lāpsus, [3] v. dep. slip or fall down; descend; sink.

dēlātiō, ōnis, f. accusation, denunciation.

dēlātor, ōris, m. accuser, informer.

dēlectābilis, e, a. delightful, agreeable.

dēlectātiō, ōnis, f. delight, pleasure, amusement.

dēlectō, [1] v. entice; delight; amuse; charm.

dēlectus, v. dīlectus.

dēlēgō, [1] v. assign; delegate, depute; transfer; attribute.

dēlēnīmentum, ī, nt. charm, allurement.

dēlēniō, īvī, ītum, [4] v. mitigate, smooth down; soften, bewitch; mollify.

dēleō, lēvī, lētum, [2] v. efface; suppress; destroy; kill; annul.

dēlīberābundus, a, um, a. deep in thought.

dēlīberātiō, ōnis, f. deliberation, consideration.

dēlīberō, [1] v. consult, deliberate; resolve.

dēlībō, [1] v. taste (of), touch on (a subject) lightly; diminish, detract (from).

dēlicātus, a, um, a. charming, elegant; delicate, tender; voluptuous; luxurious; effeminate.

dēliciae, ārum, f. pl. delight, pleasures; dalliance; airs and graces; darling, sweetheart.

dēlictum, ī, nt. fault, offence, crime.

dēligō, lēgī, lectum, [3] v. choose out, select, cull, pick off.

dēligō, [1] v. tie up, fasten.

dēlinquō, līquī, lictum, [3] v. fail (in duty); offend, do wrong.

dēliquēscō, licuī, [3] v. melt away; dissipate one's energy.

dēlīrō, [1] v. be crazy, speak deliriously.

dēlīrus, a, um, a. crazy, insane; senseless.

dēlitēscō, tuī, [3] v. go into hiding; withdraw.

delphīnus, ī, delphīn, īnis, m. dolphin.

dēlūbrum, ī, nt. shrine, temple.

dēlūdō, sī, sum, [3] v. deceive, dupe.

dēmēns, entis, a. senseless; mad, foolish.

dēmentia, ae, f. madness, folly.

dēmereō, uī, [2] v.t. oblige, win the favour of.

dēmergō, sī, sum, [3] v. plunge (into); sink; conceal.

dēmētior, mēnsus, [4] v. measure out.

dēmetō, messuī, messum, [3] v. mow, reap, cut off.

dēmigrō, [1] v. go away.

dēminuō, uī, ūtum, [3] v. lessen, diminish.

dēminūtiō, ōnis, f. diminution, decrease.

dēmīror, ātus, [1] v. dep. wonder, be amazed.

dēmissiō, ōnis, f. letting down; low spirits, dejection.

dēmissus, a, um, a. low-lying; hanging down; downcast; humble; unassuming; (of the voice) low.

dēmittō, mīsī, missum, [3] v. let sink, lower; send down; dismiss; thrust (into); plunge; sink; depose, demote.

dēmō, mpsī, mptum, [3] v. take away; subtract.

dēmōlior, ītus, [4] v. dep. pull down, demolish; destroy.

dēmōnstrātiō, ōnis, f. demonstration, clear proof.

dēmōnstrō, [1] v. point at; prove, demonstrate; describe; represent.

dēmorior, mortuus, [3] v. dep. die off.

dēmoror, ātus, [1] v. dep. keep back, delay; linger, stay.

dēmoveō, mōvī, mōtum, [2] v. move away, put away, remove.

dēmulceō, mulsī, mulctum, stroke, entrance.

dēmum, ad. at length, at last; **tum dēmum,** only then.

dēnārius, a, um, a. containing ten; ~, iī, m. Roman silver coin originally worth 10 **asses.**

dēnārrō, [1] v. relate fully.

dēnegō, [1] v. refuse, deny.

dēnī, ae, a, a. num. ten each, by tens.

dēnique, ad. at last, finally, in fact; in short.

dēnotō, [1] v. specify, point out; brand.

dēns, dentis, m. tooth; tusk; ivory.

dēnseō, ētum, [2] v. **dēnsō,** [1] v. thicken; press close together.

dēnsus, a, um, a. thick, dense; thickly planted with; frequent; concise.

dentāle, is, nt. the share-beam of a ploughshare.

dentātus, a, um, a. toothed; having prominent teeth.

dēnūbō, psī, ptum, [3] v. marry (away from her paternal home).

dēnūdō [1] v. make naked, uncover; reveal; rob, despoil.

dēnūntiātiō, ōnis, f. denunciation, declaration; threat; summons.

dēnūntiō, [1] v. announce, declare; foretell; threaten; summon (a witness).

dēnuō, ad. anew, afresh, again.

deonerō, [1] v. unload.

deorsum, deorsus, ad. downwards, beneath, below.

dēpacīscor, pactus, [3] v. dep. bargain for, agree upon.

dēpāscō, pāvī, pāstum, [3] v. pasture; eat up, waste, consume.

dēpellō, pulī, pulsum, [3] v. expel; dislodge; avert.

dēpendeō, [2] v. hang down, from or on; depend upon.

dēpendō, dī, sum, [3] v. pay, expend.

dēperdō, didī, ditum, [3] v. ruin; lose.

dēpereō, iī, [4] v. perish; be lost.

dēpingō, nxī, pictum, [3] v. paint, depict, portray; describe.

dēplangō, nxī, [3] v. mourn by beating the breast.

dēplōrō, [1] v. lament, mourn for; give up for lost.

dēpōnō, posuī, positum, [3] v. lay down or aside; deposit; commit; entrust; resign; fix or set or plant.

dēpopulō, [1] v. **dēpopulor, ātus,** [1] v. lay waste, plunder.

dēportō, [1] v. carry, convey.

dēposcō, poposcī, [3] v. ask for earnestly, require.

dēpositum, ī, nt. deposit, trust.

dēprāvō, [1] v. distort; deprave, corrupt.

dēprecātor, ōris, m. intercessor; one who pleads for the removal (of).

dēprecor, ātus, [1] v. dep. pray against; beg off; beg pardon; avert by prayer.

dēprehendō, dī, sum, [3] v. catch, find out; discern, perceive; reach or overtake; catch in the act; surprise.

dēprimō, pressī, pressum, [3] v. depress; keep down; sink; depress, humble.

dēprōmō, prōmpsī, prōmptum, [3] v. bring out.

dēpugnō, [1] v. fight it out or hard.

dērelinquō, līquī, lictum, [3] v. leave behind, abandon, neglect.

dērīdeō, rīsī, rīsum, [2] v. laugh at, deride.

dērīdiculum, ī, nt. laughingstock, ridiculousness.

dērigēscō, guī, [3] v. grow stiff or rigid.

dēripiō, ripuī, reptum, [3] v. tear off, remove.

dērīsor, ōris, m. mocker, scoffer.

dērīvātiō, ōnis, f. turning off (into another channel).

dērīvō, [1] v. divert, turn or draw off.

dērogō, [1] v. make or propose (modifications to a law); take away, diminish.

dēruptus, a, um, a. craggy, steep, precipitous.

dēsaeviō, iī, [4] v. work off or vent one's rage.

dēscendō, dī, sum, [3] v. descend; fall; alight; slope; penetrate; stoop, demean oneself.

dēscēnsus, ūs, *m.* climbing down.

dēscīscō, īvī & iī, ītum, [3] *v.* desert, defect.

dēscrībō, psī, ptum, [3] *v.* copy; describe; establish.

dēscrīptiō, ōnis, *f.* delineation; description.

dēsecō, cuī, ctum, [1] *v.* cut off.

dēserō, ruī, rtum, [3] *v.* forsake; desert; give up; fail.

dēserta, ōrum, *nt. pl.* wilderness.

dēsertor, ōris, *m.* abandoner; deserter; fugitive.

dēsertus, a, um, *a.* desert, lonely, waste.

dēserviō, [4] *v. with dat.* serve diligently, be devoted to.

dēsīderābilis, e, *a.* desirable; missed.

dēsīderium, iī, *nt.* desire, wishing, longing for; regret for what is absent; petition; request; favourite, darling.

dēsīderō, [1] *v.* wish for, desire; need, want; require; miss.

dēsidia, ae, *f.* idleness, sloth.

dēsidiōsus, a, um, *a.* indolent, lazy.

dēsīdō, sēdī, [3] *v.* sink, settle down.

dēsignātiō, ōnis, *f.* appointment, designation.

dēsignō, [1] *v.* mark out, designate; denote; appoint; choose.

dēsiliō, siluī, sultum, [4] *v.* leap down, alight.

dēsinō, īvī & iī, itum, [3] *v.* leave off, cease, desist.

dēsipiō, [3] *v.* be out of one's mind, lose one's reason.

dēsistō, stitī, stitum, [3] *v.* leave off, cease, desist from.

dēsōlō, [1] *v.* abandon, desert; empty.

dēspectō, [1] *v.* look down at; overlook; despise.

dēspectus, ūs, *m.* prospect, panorama; contempt.

dēspēranter, *ad.* despairingly.

dēspērātiō, ōnis, *f.* despair.

dēspērātus, a, um, *a.* desperate, despaired of.

dēspērō, [1] *v.* despair (of).

dēspicientia, ae, *f.* contempt (for).

dēspiciō, exī, ectum, [3] *v.* look down upon; despise.

dēspoliō, [1] *v.* rob, plunder.

dēspondeō, spondī, spōnsum, [2] *v.* promise (in marriage); **animum dēspondēre,** to despair.

dēspūmō, [1] *v.* skim off.

dēspuō, [3] *v.* spit (out), reject.

dēstillō, [1] *v.* trickle down.

dēstinātiō, ōnis, *f.* designation; resolution, determination.

dēstinō, [1] *v.* fix, determine, design; destine.

dēstituō, uī, ūtum, [3] *v.* leave, desert, abandon; give up; disappoint.

dēstringō, īnxī, ictum, [3] v. strip off; draw (a sword); graze (gently); censure.

dēstruō, xī, ctum, [3] v. pull down; destroy, ruin.

dēsubitō, ad. suddenly.

dēsuētūdō, inis, f. discontinuance, disuse.

dēsultor, ōris, m. a rider in the circus who jumped from one horse to another.

dēsum, fuī, esse, v. with dat. be wanting, fail.

dēsūmō, mpsī, [3] v. pick out, choose.

dēsuper, ad. from above.

dētegō, xī, ctum, [3] v. uncover, lay bare; reveal.

dētendō, dī, sum, [3] v. strike (tents), let down.

dētergeō, sī, sum, [2] v. wipe off, strip off, rub clean.

dēterior, ius, a. inferior; worse, meaner.

dēterminō, [1] v. set bounds to, limit, determine.

dēterō, trīvī, trītum, [3] v. wear away.

dēterreō, uī, itum, [2] v. deter, discourage.

dētestābilis, e, a. abominable, detestable.

dētestātiō, ōnis, f. solemn curse.

dētestor, ātus, [1] v. dep. call down a solemn curse on; detest; avert.

dētexō, xuī, xtum, [3] v. finish weaving, complete.

dētineō, tinuī, tentum, [2] v. hold down or off, detain; occupy; delay the end of.

dētondeō, totondī & tondī, tōnsum, [2] v. shear off, strip off.

dētonō, uī, [1] v. expend one's thunder.

dētorqueō, sī, tum, [2] v. turn or twist away; distort; divert.

dētractor, ōris, m. detractor, defamer.

dētrahō, xī, ctum, [3] v. draw off; remove; lessen; take away; detract from; impair.

dētrectātiō, ōnis, f. refusal.

dētrectō, [1] v. refuse; disparage, belittle.

dētrīmentum, ī, nt. detriment, loss, damage; defeat.

dētrūdō, sī, sum, [3] v. thrust down or from; expel; dispossess; reduce; postpone.

dētruncō, [1] v. lop off; behead; mutilate.

dēturbō, [1] v. dislodge; pull down; upset; topple.

deūrō, ussī, ustum, [3] v. burn down; (of cold) wither.

deus, ī, m. god.

dēvāstō, ātum, [1] v. lay waste.

dēvehō, xī, ctum, [3] v. carry away, convey; dēvehor, travel downstream.

dēveniō, vēnī, [4] v. arrive (at); land, turn (to).

dēversor, ātus, [1] v. dep. put up at an inn; lodge.

dēversōrium, iī, *nt.* inn, lodging-house.

dēverticulum, ī, *nt.* by-road; digression; port of call.

dēvertō, tī, sum, [3] *v.* turn aside; lodge; digress.

dēvexus, a, um, *a.* sloping, shelving.

dēvinciō, nxī, nctum, [4] *v.* bind fast, tie up; oblige.

dēvincō, vīcī, victum, [3] *v.* conquer entirely, subdue.

dēvītō, [1] *v.* avoid.

dēvius, a, um, *a.* out-of-the-way, devious; straying.

dēvocō, [1] *v.* call down *or* away, summon.

dēvolō, [1] *v.* fly down *or* away; hasten down, hasten away.

dēvolvō, volvī, volūtum, [3] *v.* roll down.

dēvorō, [1] *v.* devour; absorb; gulp down; check; drink in; use up.

dēvōtiō, ōnis, *f.* devoting; vow; curse.

dēvoveō, vōvī, vōtum, [2] *v.* vow, devote; curse; bewitch.

dexter, a, um, tra, trum, *a.* on the right side, right; dexterous, skilful; propitious.

dext(e)ra, ae, *f.* right hand; right side, pledge.

dexterē, *ad.* skilfully.

diadēma, ātis, *nt.* diadem, ornamental headband.

Diālis, e, *a.* of Jupiter.

dicācitās, ātis, *f.* mordant *or* caustic raillery.

dicāx, ācis, *a.* witty, smart, sarcastic.

dīciō, ōnis, *f.* sway; dominion; authority.

dīcō, [1] *v.* dedicate, consecrate; set apart; devote (oneself); assign.

dīcō, xī, ctum, [3] *v.* say, tell; order; call; declare; express; plead; designate.

dicrotum, ī, *nt.* a light galley, perhaps propelled by two banks of oars.

dictamnus, ī, *f.,* **dictamnum, ī,** *nt.* dittany.

dictāta, ōrum, *nt. pl.* dictated lessons *or* exercises.

dictātor, ōris, *m.* dictator; chief magistrate.

dictātōrius, a, um, *a.* of a dictator.

dictātūra, ae, *f.* dictatorship.

dictiō, ōnis, *f.* saying, delivery; speech; oracular utterance.

dictitō, [1] *v.* say often; plead often.

dictō, [1] *v.* say often; dictate (for writing); compose.

dictum, ī, *nt.* saying, word; maxim; *bon mot,* witticism; order.

dīdō, didī, ditum, [3] *v.* distribute, spread.

dīdūcō, xī, ctum, [3] *v.* draw *or* lead aside; separate; divide; scatter; open out.

diēs, ēī, *m.* day; daylight; festival; red letter day (*f.*); lifetime; **in diem,** each day.

diffāmō, [1] *v.* spread the news of; slander.

differō, differre, distulī, dīlātum, *v.* put off, delay; disperse; spread; publish; differ; disagree.

differtus, a, um, *a.* filled, crowded.

difficilis, e, *a.* difficult; obstinate, morose, intractable.

difficultās, ātis, *f.* difficulty; trouble; intractability.

diffīdentia, ae, *f.* mistrust, distrust.

diffīdō, fīsus sum, [3] *v. with dat.* lack confidence (in); despair.

diffindō, fidī, fissum, [3] *v.* split; put off.

diffingō, [3] *v.* remodel.

diffiteor, [2] *v. dep.* disavow, deny.

diffluō, [3] *v.* flow away in all directions; melt away; waste away.

diffugiō, [3] *v.* flee in different directions; scatter, disperse.

diffundō, fūdī, fūsum, [3] *v.* pour forth; diffuse, spread; cheer.

dīgerō, gessī, gestum, [3] *v.* distribute, spread over; arrange, dispose.

digitus, ī, *m.* finger; toe; a finger's-breadth.

dignātiō, ōnis, *f.* esteem; repute; rank.

dignitās, ātis, *f.* worthiness, merit; dignity; authority; office; grace; value, honour.

dignor, ātus, [1] *v. dep.* consider worthy.

di(g)nōscō, [3] *v.* distinguish, discern.

dignus, a, um, *a.* worthy, deserving; deserved.

dīgredior, gressus, [3] *v. dep.* depart, go away; leave (a subject of discussion).

dīgressiō, ōnis, *f.* going away; digression.

dīgressus, ūs, *m.* departure; digression.

dīiūdicō, [1] *v.* decide, determine; distinguish.

dīlābor, lāpsus, [3] *v. dep.* fall apart *or* to pieces; disperse; melt away; decay; disperse.

dīlacerō, [1] *v.* tear to pieces.

dīlaniō, [1] *v.* tear to pieces.

dīlargior, ītus, [4] *v. dep.* give away freely.

dīlātō, [1] *v.* make wider, enlarge, extend, dilate.

dīlectus, ūs, *m.* recruitment, levy; choice.

dīligēns, entis, *a.* careful, diligent, frugal, thrifty.

dīligentia, ae, *f.* carefulness, attentiveness; economy, frugality.

dīligō, lēxī, lēctum, [3] *v.* esteem highly; hold dear.

dīlūcēscō, lūxī, [3] *v.* dawn, become light.

dīlūcidus, a, um, *a.* plain, distinct, lucid.

dīluō, uī, ūtum, [3] *v.* wash (off); temper; dilute; dissolve; weaken; refute.

dīluviēs, ēī, *f.* inundation, flood.

dīluvium, iī, *nt.* inundation, flood.

dīmētior, mēnsus, [4] *v. dep.* measure out.

dīmicātiō, ōnis, *f.* fight, combat; struggle.

dīmicō, āvī & cuī, ātum, [1] *v.* fight; struggle, strive.

dīmidium, iī, *nt.* a half.

dīmidius, a, um, *a.* half.

dīminūtiō, *v.* **dēminūtiō**.

dīmittō, mīsī, missum, [3] *v.* send out *or* forth; dismiss; disband; release; divorce; break up; detach; let slip; give up; renounce.

dīmoveō, mōvī, mōtum, [2] *v.* separate; put aside; remove.

dīnōscō, *v.* **di(g)nōscō**.

dīnumerō, [1] *v.* count, enumerate.

diōta, ae, *f.* two-handled wine-jar.

diplōma, atis, *nt.* letter of recommendation.

dīrēctus, a, um, *a.* straight, vertical; steep; direct, simple.

dīreptiō, ōnis, *f.* plundering.

dīreptor, ōris, *m.* plunderer.

dīrigō, rēxī, rēctum, [3] *v.* direct, guide; steer; set in order.

dirimō, ēmī, ēmptum, [3] *v.* pull apart; separate; break up, dissolve.

dīripiō, uī, reptum, [3] *v.* snatch away; tear to pieces; rob, loot.

dīrumpō, rūpī, ruptum, [3] *v.* break apart, shatter, burst.

dīruō, ruī, rutum, [3] *v.* demolish, destroy.

dīrus, a, um, *a.* fearful, awful; horrible.

dīs, dītis, *a.* rich; *v.* **dīves**.

discēdō, cessī, cessum, [3] *v.* go off in different directions; march off; be divided; cease; die; depart from.

disceptātiō, ōnis, *f.* debate.

disceptātor, ōris, *m.* arbitrator.

disceptō, [1] *v.* dispute; debate; arbitrate.

discernō, crēvī, crētum, [3] *v.* separate; distinguish.

discerpō, psī, ptum, [3] *v.* pluck *or* tear in pieces; mangle.

discessiō, ōnis, *f.* withdrawal, dispersal.

discessus, ūs, *m.* going apart; separation; departure; marching off.

discidium, iī, *nt.* separation, divorce, discord.

discinctus, a, um, *a.* wearing loose clothes; easy-going.

discindō, scidī, scissum, [3] *v.* cut in two; divide.

disciplīna, ae, *f.* instruction; knowledge; discipline; system; method.

discipula, ae, *f.* female pupil.

discipulus, ī, *m.* pupil, disciple, trainee.

disclūdō, sī, sum, [3] *v.* separate; keep apart.

discō, didicī, [3] *v.* learn, acquire knowledge of.

discolor, ōris, *a.* of another colour; of various colours; variegated.

disconveniō, [4] *v.* be inconsistent, be different.

discordia, ae, *f.* disagreement, discord.

discordō, [1] *v.* be at variance, quarrel; be different.

discors, cordis, *a.* discordant, disagreeing; different.

discrepō, uī, [1] *v.* be out of tune; disagree, differ.

discrībō, psī, ptum, [3] *v.* divide, assign, distribute.

discrīmen, inis, *nt.* separating line; division; distinction, difference; crisis, risk.

discrīminō, [1] *v.* divide up, separate.

discrīptiō, ōnis, *f.* assignment, division.

discruciō, [1] *v.* torture.

discumbō, cubuī, cubitum, [3] *v.* lie down; recline at table; go to bed.

discurrō, cucurrī & currī, cursum, [3] *v.* run about.

discursus, ūs, *m.* running about; separation, dispersal.

discus, ī, *m.* discus.

discutiō, cussī, cussum, [3] *v.* shatter, shake violently; dissipate; bring to nothing.

disertus, a, um, *a.* eloquent; skilfully expressed.

disiciō, iēcī, iectum, [3] *v.* scatter; disperse; squander; frustrate.

disiungō, xī, ctum, [3] *v.* unyoke; separate; disjoin.

dispār, aris, *a.* unequal, unlike.

disparō, [1] *v.* separate, divide.

dispellō, pulī, pulsum, [3] *v.* drive apart *or* away; disperse.

dispendium, iī, *nt.* expense, cost; loss.

dispēnsātiō, ōnis, *f.* management; stewardship.

dispēnsātor, ōris, *m.* steward; treasurer.

dispēnsō, [1] *v.* manage; dispense; distribute; pay out; arrange.

disperdō, didī, ditum, [3] *v.* destroy *or* ruin utterly.

dispereō, iī, [4] *v.* perish, be destroyed.

dispergō, sī, sum, [3] *v.* scatter about, disperse.

dispertiō, īvī & iī, ītum, [4] *v.* distribute, divide; assign.

dispiciō, spexī, spectum, [3] *v.* look about (for); discover; espy; consider.

displiceō, uī, itum, [2] *v.* displease.

displōdō, ōsum, [3] *v.* burst apart.

dispōnō, posuī, positum, [3] *v.* distribute, set in order; post, station; arrange.

disputātiō, ōnis, *f.* discussion, argument, debate.

disputō, [1] *v.* argue, debate.

disquīsītiō, ōnis, *f.* inquiry.

dissēminō, [1] *v.* broadcast, disseminate.

dissēnsiō, ōnis, *f.* dissension, disagreement.

dissentiō, sī, sum, [4] *v.* dissent, disagree; differ.

disserō, ruī, rtum, [3] *v.* discuss, set out in words.

disserō, sēvī, situm, [3] *v.* sow.

dissertō, [1] *v.* discuss.

dissideō, sēdī, sessum, [2] *v.* be at variance; disagree; be separated.

dissiliō, uī, [4] *v.* leap *or* burst apart.

dissimilis, e, *a.* unlike, dissimilar.

dissimilitūdō, inis, *f.* unlikeness, difference.

dissimulanter, *ad.* dissemblingly.

dissimulātiō, ōnis, *f.* dissimulation, dissembling.

dissimulātor, ōris, *m.* dissembler.

dissimulō, [1] *v.* dissemble, disguise; hide; ignore.

dissipātiō, ōnis, *f.* squandering; scattering.

dissipō, [1] *v.* disperse; squander; destroy completely; circulate.

dissociābilis, e, *a.* incompatible; discordant.

dissociō, [1] *v.* separate, part; set at variance.

dissolūtiō, ōnis, *f.* disintegration, dissolution; destruction; disconnection; refutation.

dissolūtus, a, um, *a.* loose; lax; negligent; dissolute.

dissolvō, solvī, solūtum, [3] *v.* unloose; dissolve, destroy; melt; pay; refute; annul.

dissonus, a, um, *a.* dissonant, discordant; different.

dissuādeō, sī, sum, [2] *v.* dissuade, advise against.

dissuāsor, ōris, *m.* discourager, one who advises against.

dissultō, [1] *v.* fly *or* burst apart; bounce off.

distantia, ae, *f.* distance; difference.

distendō, dī, tum, [3] *v.* stretch in different directions, stretch out, extend; swell out; fill.

distillō, v. **dēstillō**.

distīnctiō, ōnis, *f.* distinction; difference.

distīnctus, a, um, *a.* separate, distinct; definite, lucid.

distineō, tinuī, tentum, [2] v. keep apart; separate; prevent, distract; hold up.

distinguō, nxī, nctum, [3] v. divide, part; distinguish; decorate.

distō, [1] v. stand apart, be distant; be different.

distorqueō, torsī, tortum, [2] v. twist this way and that.

distrahō, xī, ctum, [3] v. pull or draw apart, wrench; separate; sell; distract; set at variance; estrange.

distribuō, uī, ūtum, [3] v. divide, distribute.

distribūtiō, ōnis, f. division, distribution.

distringō, nxī, ctum, [3] v. stretch out; detain; distract; pull in different directions.

disturbō, [1] v. disturb; demolish; upset.

dītēscō, [3] v. grow rich.

dithyrambus, ī, m. a form of verse used especially for choral singing.

dītō, [1] v. enrich.

diū, ad. a long while; long since; **diūtius**, longer; **diūtissimē**, very long.

diurnus, a, um, a. daily.

dīus, a, um, daylit, divine.

diūtinus, a, um, a. lasting, long.

diūturnitās, ātis, f. long duration.

diūturnus, a, um, a. lasting long.

dīva, ae, f. goddess.

dīvellō, vellī, vulsum, [3] v. tear to pieces; tear away; estrange, break up.

dīvendō, ditum, [3] v. sell in small lots; sell up.

dīverberō, [1] v. split; strike violently.

dīversitās, ātis, f. difference.

dīversōrium, v. dēversōrium.

dīversus, a, um, a. opposite; separate, apart; unlike, different; hostile; contrary; distant; distinct.

dīves, itis, a. rich; talented.

dīvidō, vīsī, vīsum, [3] v. separate, divide; distribute; distinguish; break up.

dīviduus, a, um, a. divisible; divided; half; parted.

dīvīnātiō, ōnis, f. prophecy, prognostication.

dīvīnitus, ad. by divine agency or inspiration; divinely, excellently.

dīvīnō, [1] v. divine; prophesy; guess.

dīvīnus, a, um, a. divine; prophetic; blessed; excellent; ~, ī, m. prophet.

dīvīsiō, ōnis, f. division; distribution.

dīvīsor, ōris, m. distributor; a candidate's agent hired to distribute bribes.

dīvīsus, ūs, m. division.

dīvitiae, ārum, f. pl. riches, wealth.

dīvortium, iī, *nt.* separation; divorce; point of separation; watershed.

dīvulgō, [1] *v.* publish, disseminate news of.

dīvum, ī, *nt.* sky, open air; **sub dīvō**, in the open air.

dīvus, ī, *m.* god.

dō, dare, dedī, datum, [1] *v.* give; ascribe; grant, permit; furnish, offer; lend; tell of; enable, cause.

doceō, cuī, ctum, [2] *v.* teach; tell; show.

docilis, e, *a.* teachable, responsive.

doctor, ōris, *m.* teacher, instructor, trainer.

doctrīna, ae, *f.* teaching, instruction; science, learning; system of rules.

doctus, a, um, *a.* learned, wise, expert.

documentum, ī, *nt.* example; warning; instruction.

dōdrāns, antis, *m.* three-quarters.

dogma, atis, *nt.* doctrine, dogma, teaching.

doleō, uī, itum, [2] *v.* feel *or* suffer pain; grieve for.

dōlium, iī, *nt.* large earthenware vessel for storing liquids, grain, *etc.*.

dolor, ōris, *m.* pain; grief; anguish; sorrow; resentment.

dolōsus, a, um, *a.* crafty, deceitful.

dolus, ī, *m.* fraud, deceit; treachery, cunning.

domābilis, e, *a.* able to be tamed.

domesticus, a, um, *a.* domestic, familiar; native; private, personal.

domicilium, iī, *nt.* dwelling, abode, home.

domina, ae, *f.* mistress of a family; lady; wife; lady-love.

dominātiō, ōnis, *f.* dominion; despotism.

dominātus, ūs, *m.* absolute rule, dominion.

dominor, ātus, [1] *v. dep.* act as a despot, rule; be in control.

dominus, ī, *m.* master of the house; owner; lord, ruler; host; lover.

domitō, [1] *v.* tame, break in.

domitor, ōris, *m.* tamer; conqueror.

domō, uī, itum, [1] *v.* tame; conquer.

domus, ūs & ī, *f.* house; home; household; family; native country; **domī**, at home.

dōnārium, iī, *nt.* part of temple where votive offerings were received and stored; treasure chamber.

dōnātiō, ōnis, *f.* donation, gift.

dōnātīvum, ī, *nt.* gratuity.

dōnec, *c.* as long as, until.

dōnō, [1] *v.* present, bestow; forgive; give up.

dōnum, ī, *nt.* gift, present; offering.

dormiō, īvī & iī, ītum, [4] *v.* sleep; rest.

dormītō, [1] *v.* feel sleepy, drowsy; do nothing.

dorsum, ī, *nt.* back; slope of a hill, ridge.

dōs, dōtis, *f.* dowry; talent, quality.

dōtālis, e, *a.* forming part of a dowry, relating to a dowry.

drachma, ae, *f.* a Greek silver coin.

dracō, ōnis, *m.* snake.

dromas, ados, *m.* dromedary.

Druidae, ārum, Druides, um, *m. pl.* Druids.

dubitanter, *ad.* doubtingly; hesitatingly.

dubitātiō, ōnis, *f.* doubt; hesitation; irresolution.

dubitō, [1] *v.* doubt; be uncertain *or* irresolute; hesitate over.

dubius, a, um, *a.* doubtful; variable; uncertain; dangerous; critical.

ducēnī, ae, a, *a. pl.* two hundred each; two hundred.

ducentēsimus, a, um, *a.* two-hundredth.

ducentī, ae, a, *a. pl.* two hundred.

dūcō, xī, ctum, [3] *v.* lead, conduct, draw, bring; run (a wall, *etc.*); derive; guide; marry; persuade; deceive; prolong; think, esteem; reckon; pass; spend.

ductō, [1] *v.* lead.

ductor, ōris, *m.* leader, commander.

ductus, ūs, *m.* conducting; generalship.

dūdum, *ad.* a little while ago; formerly; **iam dūdum,** long ago.

dulcēdō, inis, *f.* sweetness; charm.

dulcis, e, *a.* sweet; pleasant, charming; dear, beloved.

dum, *c.* while, as long as; until; provided that.

dūmētum, ī, *nt.* thicket.

dummodo, *c.* provided that.

dūmōsus, a, um, *a.* overgrown with thorn, briar *or* the like.

dumtaxat, *ad.* only, at least; so far.

dūmus, ī, *m.* thorn *or* briar bush.

duo, ae, o, *a.* two.

duodecim, *a.* twelve.

duodecimus, a, um, *a.* twelfth.

duodēnī, ae, a, *a.* num. twelve each, by twelves.

duodēvīcēnī, ae, a, *a.* eighteen each.

duodēvīcēsimus, a, um, *a.* eighteenth.

duodēvīgintī, *a.* num. eighteen.

duovirī, ōrum, *m. pl.* board of two men.

duplex, icis, *a.* twofold, double; divided; 'two-faced'.

duplicō, [1] *v.* double; enlarge; bend double.

dūritia, ae, *f.* **dūritiēs, ēī,** *f.* hardness; austerity; rigour.

dūrō, [1] *v.* make hard; dry; harden, 'steel'; become hard *or* stern, *etc.*; endure; last out; survive.

dūrus, a, um, *a.* hard; harsh; hardy, vigorous; stern; unfeeling; inflexible; burdensome, difficult.

duumviri, v. **duovirī.**

dux, ducis, *m.* or *f.* leader, guide; commander, general.

ecce, *i.* look! see! behold! here!

echidna, ae, *f.* serpent, viper.

ēchō, ūs, *f.* echo.

ecloga, ae, *f.* a short poem.

ecquis, ecquae, ecqua, ecquod, *pn.* is there any?

ecquis, ecquid, *pn.* is there anyone who?

edāx, ācis, *a.* voracious, gluttonous; devouring.

edepol, *i.* by Pollux!

ēdīcō, xī, ctum, [3] *v.* publish, declare.

ēdictum, ī, *nt.* proclamation, edict.

ēdiscō, didicī, [3] *v.* learn by heart; study; get to know.

ēdisserō, ruī, rtum, [3] *v.* **ēdissertō,** [1] *v.* relate, expound.

ēditiō, ōnis, *f.* publishing; edition; statement.

ēditus, a, um, *a.* high, lofty.

edō, ēdī, ēsum, [3] *v.* eat; devour; spend (money) on food.

ēdō, didī, ditum, [3] *v.* put forth, emit; publish; relate; bring forth; beget; proclaim; bring about; cause.

ēdoceō, cuī, ctum, [2] *v.* teach *or* inform thoroughly.

ēdomō, uī, itum, [1] *v.* tame completely, conquer.

ēdormiō, īvī & iī, [4] *v.* sleep; sleep off.

ēducātiō, ōnis, *f.* bringing up; rearing.

E

ē, pr., v. **ex.**

eādem, *ad.* by the same route.

ēbibō, bī, bitum, [3] *v.* drink up, drain; absorb; squander.

ēblandior, ītus, [4] *v. dep.* obtain by flattery.

ēbrietās, ātis, *f.* drunkenness.

ēbriōsus, a, um, *a.* addicted to drink.

ēbrius, a, um, *a.* drunk; intoxicated.

ebulum, ī, *nt.* **ebulus, ī,** *m.* danewort.

ebur, oris, *nt.* ivory; ivory statue.

eburneus, eburnus, a, um, *a.* of ivory; white as ivory.

ēcastor, by Castor (interjection used by women).

ēducātor, ōris, *m.* bringer up, tutor; foster-father.

ēdūcō, xī, ctum, [3] *v.* lead or draw out; bring away; rear; educate; raise, produce.

ēducō, [1] *v.* bring up, rear.

edūlis, e, *a.* eatable.

ēdūrus, a, um, *a.* very hard.

effectus, ūs, *m.* execution, performance; effect.

effēminātus, a, um, *a.* womanish, effeminate.

effēminō, [1] *v.* emasculate; unman, enervate.

efferō, efferre, extulī, ēlātum, [3] *v.* bring or carry out; produce; utter; raise, advance; proclaim; carry out for burial.

efferō, [1] *v.* make savage.

efferus, a, um, *a.* savage, cruel, barbarous.

effervēscō, feruī, [3] *v.* boil up, seethe; become greatly excited.

effētus, a, um, *a.* exhausted, worn out.

efficāx, ācis, *a.* efficacious, effectual.

efficiō, fēcī, fectum, [3] *v.* effect, execute, accomplish, make; produce; prove; make up.

effigiēs, ēī, *f.* portrait, image, effigy, statue; ghost.

effingō, fīnxī, fictum, [3] *v.* form, mould; represent, portray; stroke.

efflāgitātiō, ōnis, *f.* urgent demand.

efflāgitō, [1] *v.* demand or ask urgently.

efflō, [1] *v.* blow or breathe out; breathe one's last.

effluō, xī, [3] *v.* flow out; escape; vanish; be forgotten.

effodiō, fōdī, fossum, [3] *v.* dig out; gouge out.

effor, ātus, [1] *v. dep.* utter; declare; speak.

effrēnō, ātum, [1] *v.* unbridle, let loose.

effrēnus, a, um, *a.* unbridled; unrestrained, unruly.

effringō, frēgī, frāctum, [3] *v.* break open.

effugiō, fūgī, [3]; *v.* escape; flee from, avoid; be unnoticed; escape the knowledge of.

effugium, iī, *nt.* flight; way of escape.

effulgeō, sī, [2] *v.* shine forth, glitter; be or become conspicuous.

effultus, a, um, *a.* propped up, supported (by).

effundō, fūdī, fūsum, [3] *v.* pour out, shed; send out; shoot in great numbers; discharge; let fall; give up; waste, squander; bring forth.

effūsē, *ad.* over a wide area; in a disorderly manner; immoderately.

effūsiō, ōnis, *f.* pouring forth; prodigality; excess.

effūsus, a, um, *a.* vast, wide; dishevelled; disorderly; extravagant.

effūtiō, ītum, [4] *v.* blurt out.

effutuō, uī, ūtum, [3] *v.* wear out with sexual intercourse.

ēgelidus, a, um, *a.* lukewarm, tepid.

egēns, entis, *a.* needy, very poor; destitute of.

egēnus, a, um, *a.* in want of, destitute of.

egeō, uī, [2] *v. with gen. or abl.* want; need; require, be without.

ēgerō, gessī, gestum, [3] *v.* carry *or* bear out; discharge; utter.

egestās, ātis, *f.* extreme poverty, want.

ego, *pn.* I; I myself.

egomet, *pn.* I myself; I for my part.

ēgredior, gressus, [3] *v. dep.* march *or* come out; set sail; land; go beyond; ascend; overstep.

ēgregius, a, um, *a.* excellent, eminent; illustrious.

ēgressus, ūs, *m.* departure; flight; landing; place of egress, mouth (of a river); digression.

ēheu, *i.* alas!

ei, v. hei.

eia, v. heia.

ēiaculor, ātus, [1] *v. dep.* shoot out; discharge.

ēiciō, iēcī, iectum, [3] *v.* throw *or* cast out; thrust out; expel; banish; vomit; dislocate; cast ashore; reject.

ēiectō, [1] *v.* cast out.

ēierō, v. ēiūrō.

ēiulātus, ūs, *m.* wailing, shrieking.

ēiūrō, [1] *v.* abjure; resign; reject on oath (of a judge); forswear, disown.

ēlābor, lāpsus, [3] *v. dep.* escape; slip away.

ēlabōrō, [1] *v.* take pains, exert oneself; bestow care on.

ēlanguēscō, guī, [3] *v.* begin to lose one's vigour; slacken, relax.

ēlēctiō, ōnis, *f.* choice, selection.

ēlectrum, ī, *nt.* amber; alloy of gold and silver.

ēlegāns, antis, *a.* elegant, fine, handsome; tasteful; fastidious, critical; discriminating, polite.

ēlegantia, ae, *f.* elegance; niceness; taste; politeness.

elegī, ōrum, *m. pl.* elegiac verses, elegy.

elegīa, ae, *or* **elegeia, ae**, *f.* elegy.

elementa, ōrum, *nt. pl.* elements; rudiments; beginnings.

elephā(n)s, antis, elephantus, ī, *m.* elephant; ivory.

ēlevō, [1] *v.* lift up, raise; alleviate; lessen; make light of.

ēlicēs, um, *m. pl.* trench, drain.

ēliciō, licuī, licitum, [3] *v.* entice, coax; call forth; draw forth.

ēlīdō, sī, sum, [3] *v.* strike *or* dash out; expel; shatter; crush out; strangle; destroy.

ēligō, lēgī, lēctum, [3] *v.* pick out, choose.

ēloquēns, entis, *a.* eloquent, articulate.

ēloquentia, ae, *f.* eloquium, iī, *nt.* eloquence, articulateness.

ēloquor, locūtus, [3] *v. dep.* speak out, utter.

ēlūceō, xī, [2] *v.* shine forth; show itself; be manifest.

ēluctor, ātus, [1] *v. dep.* force a way through; surmount a difficulty.

ēlūcubrō, [1] *v.* ēlūcubror, [1] *v. dep.* compose at night; burn the midnight oil over.

ēlūdō, sī, sum, [3] *v.* elude, escape from; parry; baffle; cheat; frustrate; mock, make fun of.

ēluō, uī, ūtum, [3] *v.* wash clean; wash away, clear oneself (of).

ēmancipō, [1] *v.* emancipate (a son from his father's authority); alienate; make subservient.

ēmānō, [1] *v.* flow out; arise, emanate from; become known.

emāx, ācis, *a.* fond of buying.

ēmendō, [1] *v.* correct; repair.

ēmentior, ītus, [4] *v. dep.* falsify, invent; feign.

ēmereō, uī, itum, [2] *v.* ēmereor, itus, [2] *v. dep.* earn; serve out one's time.

ēmeritus, ī, *m.* veteran.

ēmergō, sī, sum, [3] *v.* rise up out of the water, emerge; escape; appear; arrive.

ēmētior, mēnsus, [4] *v. dep.* measure out; pass through.

ēmicō, cuī, cātum, [1] *v.* spring forth, shine forth; appear suddenly.

ēminēns, entis, *a.* lofty; prominent; eminent.

ēmineō, uī, [2] *v.* project; stand out; be pre-eminent; excel.

**ēminus, ad.* at long range.

ēmittō, mīsī, missum, [3] *v.* send out or forth; set free; fling; let fall; publish; empty; drain off.

emō, ēmī, ēmptum, [3] *v.* buy; gain.

ēmolliō, iī, ītum, [4] *v.* soften; enervate, mellow.

ēmolumentum, ī, *nt.* advantage; benefit.

ēmorior, mortuus, [3] *v. dep.* die away; die; perish.

ēmoveō, mōvī, mōtum, [2] *v.* remove; dislodge.

emporium, iī, *nt.* centre of trade, mart.

ēmptor, ōris, *m.* buyer, purchaser.

ēmungō, nxī, nctum, [3] *v.* wipe the nose; trick, swindle.

ēmūniō, īvī & iī, ītum, [4] *v.* fortify; make roads through.

**ēn, i.* behold! see!

ēnārrābilis, e, *a.* that may be described or explained.

ēnārrō, [1] *v.* explain or relate in detail.

ēnatō, [1] v. escape by swimming.

ēnecō, cuī, ctum, or **necātum,** [1] v. kill, deprive of life.

ēnervō, [1] v. weaken, enervate.

enim, c. indeed, for, yes indeed; certainly; ~ **vērō,** positively! well, of course; certainly.

ēniteō, tuī, [2] v. shine forth; be outstanding.

ēnitēscō, tuī, [3] v. become bright; stand out.

ēnītor, nīsus & nīxus, [3] v. dep. force one's way up; strive; give birth to.

ēnō, [1] v. swim out.

ēnōdis, e, a. without knots; smooth.

ēnormis, e, a. irregular; immense, enormous.

ēnsis, is, m. sword.

ēnūbō, psī, [3] v. marry out of one's rank or outside one's community.

ēnumerō, [1] v. count up; pay out; specify, enumerate.

ēnūntiō, [1] v. speak out, say, express, declare; disclose.

eō, īre, īvī & iī, [4] v. go; walk, march; flow; come in; ride, sail; turn out.

eō, ad. to that place, thither; so far; therefore; so much (more or less).

eōdem, ad. to the same place or purpose.

Ēous, a, um, a. eastern; of the dawn.

ephippium, iī, nt. cloth on which the rider of a horse sits.

epistula, ae, epistola, ae, f. letter, dispatch.

epos, nt. (only in nom. and acc. sing.), epic poem.

ēpōtō, āvī, pōtum, [1] v. drink down; absorb; swallow up.

epulae, ārum, v. **epulum.**

epulor, ātus, [1] v. dep. dine sumptuously, feast.

epulum, ī, nt. banquet, feast.

equa, ae, f. mare.

eques, itis, m. horseman; rider; horse-soldier; **equitēs,** pl. cavalry; order of knights.

equester, tris, tre, a. equestrian; of, belonging to, or connected with cavalry; belonging to the order of knights.

equidem, ad. I for my part.

equīnus, a, um, a. concerning horses.

equitātus, ūs, m. cavalry.

equitō, [1] v. ride.

equus, ī, m. horse.

era, ae, f. mistress; lady of the house.

ergā, pr. with acc. opposite to; against, towards.

ergastulum, ī, nt. prison on large estate to which refractory slaves were sent for work in chain-gangs; in pl., convicts.

ergō, ad. therefore; then, now.

ēricius, iī, m. some kind of spiked barrier.

ērigō, rēxī, rēctum, [3] *v.* erect; raise; build; rouse, excite, stimulate.

erīlis, e, *a.* of a master or mistress.

ēripiō, ripuī, reptum, [3] *v.* snatch away, take by force; rescue.

ērogātiō, ōnis, *f.* paying out, distribution.

ērogō, [1] *v.* pay out, expend.

errābundus, a, um, *a.* wandering.

errāticus, a, um, *a.* roving, erratic; wild.

errātum, ī, *nt.* error, mistake; lapse.

errō, [1] *v.* wander *or* stray about; go astray; err, mistake; vacillate.

errō, ōnis, *m.* truant.

error, ōris, *m.* straying about; winding; maze; uncertainty; error; deception; derangement of the mind.

ērubēscō, buī, [3] *v.* redden; blush for shame.

ēructō, [1] *v.* bring up noisily; discharge violently.

ērudiō, īvī & iī, ītum, [4] *v.* educate, instruct, teach.

ērudītus, a, um, *a.* learned, skilled.

ērumpō, rūpī, ruptum, [3] *v.* break out; sally forth, break out of.

ēruō, uī, utum, [3] *v.* pluck *or* dig *or* root up; overthrow; destroy; elicit.

ēruptiō, ōnis, *f.* sally, sudden rush of troops from a position.

erus, ī, *m.* master; owner.

ervum, ī, *nt.* vetch.

ēsca, ae, *f.* food; bait.

ēscendō, dī, sum, [3] *v.* ascend, go up, mount.

essedārius, iī, *m.* fighter in a war-chariot.

essedum, ī, *nt.*, **esseda, ae**, *f.* war-chariot; light travelling carriage.

ēsuriō, ītum, [4] *v.* be hungry; desire eagerly.

et, *c.* and; also; even; moreover; et ... et ... both ... and. ...

etenim, and indeed, the fact is, for.

etēsiae, ārum, *m. pl.* etesian winds.

etiam, *c.* and also, too, besides; even now; yes indeed; yes; ~ atque ~, more and more.

etiamnum, etiamnunc, *c.* even now, still, yet.

etiamsī, *c.* even if, although.

etiamtum, *c.* even then; yet.

etsī, *c.* although, even if.

eu, *i.* well done! bravo!

euge! *i.* oh, good! fine!

euhāns, antis, *a.* uttering the name Euhan (Bacchus).

Euhius, iī, *a.* title given to Bacchus.

euhoe! *i.* cry of joy used by the votaries of Bacchus.

eunūchus, ī, *m.* eunuch.

eurōus, a, um, *a.* eastern.

eurus, ī, *m.* east (or south east) wind; the east.

ēvādō, sī, sum, [3] *v.* go *or* come out; escape, avoid; turn out.

ēvagor, ātus, [1] *v. dep.* wander off; spread; overflow.

ēvalēscō, luī, [3] *v.* increase in strength prevail, have sufficient strength (to).

ēvānēscō, nuī, [3] *v.* pass away, disappear, die out.

ēvānidus, a, um, *a.* vanishing, passing away.

ēvāstō, [1] *v.* devastate.

ēvehō, vēxī, vectum, [3] *v.* carry away, convey out; carry up; exalt; **evehī,** to ride out.

ēvellō, vellī, vulsum, [3] *v.* pluck *or* tear out; root out.

ēveniō, vēnī, ventum, [4] *v.* come out; come about.

ēventum, ī, *nt.* occurrence, event; issue, outcome.

ēventus, ūs, *m.* occurrence, event; result; success.

ēverberō, [1] *v.* beat violently.

ēversiō, ōnis, *f.* overthrowing; destruction.

ēversor, ōris, *m.* one who destroys *or* overthrows.

ēvertō, tī, sum, [3] *v.* turn upside down; churn up; ruin, overthrow.

ēvidēns, entis, *a.* apparent, evident.

ēvigilō, [1] *v.* be wakeful; watch throughout the night; devise *or* study with careful attention.

ēvinciō, nxī, nctum, [4] *v.* bind *or* wreathe round.

ēvincō, vīcī, victum, [3] *v.* defeat utterly; prevail; persuade.

ēviscerō, ātum, [1] *v.* disembowel; eviscerate.

ēvītābilis, e, *a.* avoidable.

ēvītō, [1] *v.* shun, avoid.

ēvocātī, ōrum, *m. pl.* veterans again called to service.

ēvocātor, ōris, *m.* one who orders out troops.

ēvocō, [1] *v.* call out; summon; lure *or* entice out.

ēvolō, [1] *v.* fly out; rush forth.

ēvolvō, volvī, volūtum, [3] *v.* unroll, unfold; extricate; peruse; explain; roll out *or* away; wrench out, eject.

ēvomō, uī, itum, [3] *v.* vomit out.

ēvulgō, [1] *v.* make public, divulge.

ex, ē (before consonants), *pr. with abl.* out of, from; down from, off; by; after; on account of; in accordance with.

exāctor, ōris, *m.* expeller; exactor; collector of taxes.

exāctus, a, um, *a.* exact, accurate.

exacuō, uī, ūtum, [3] *v.* make sharp *or* pointed; stimulate.

exaedificō, [1] *v.* complete the building of, construct.

exaequō, [1] v. equalize, make equal; regard as equal; be equal (to).

exaestuō, [1] v. boil up; seethe, rage.

exaggerō, [1] v. heap up, accumulate; magnify.

exagitō, [1] v. drive out; stir up; disturb continually; attack, scold; discuss.

exāmen, inis, nt. swarm (of bees); crowd; apparatus or process of weighing, balance.

exāminō, [1] v. weigh; consider, examine.

exanimis, e, a. lifeless, dead.

exanimō, [1] v. deprive of life; kill; alarm greatly; exhaust.

exanimus, a, um, v. **exanimis.**

exārdēscō, ārsī, ārsum, [3] v. catch fire; blaze, flare up.

exārēscō, ruī, [3] v. dry up.

exarō, [1] v. plough or dig up; plough; note down (by scratching the wax on the tablets).

exasperō, [1] v. roughen; irritate.

exauctōrō, [1] v. release or dismiss from military service.

exaudiō, īvī & iī, ītum, [4] v. hear; comply with, heed.

excēdō, cessī, cessum, [3] v. go out or away; withdraw; digress; go beyond; die; leave; surpass; exceed.

excellēns, entis, a. distinguished, excellent.

excellentia, ae, f. superiority, excellence.

excellō, celluī, celsum, [3] v. be pre-eminent, excel.

excelsus, a, um, a. lofty; high; sublime.

exceptiō, ōnis, f. exception, qualification.

exceptō, [1] v. take out, take up; inhale, take (to oneself).

excerpō, psī, ptum, [3] v. pick out; select.

excessus, ūs, m. departure; death; digression.

excidium, iī, nt. military destruction.

excidō, cidī, [3] v. fall out; escape; be deprived of; lose control of one's senses.

excīdō, cīdī, cīsum, [3] v. cut out or off, cut down; raze; destroy.

excieō, īvī, ītum, [2] **exciō, īvī & iī, ītum,** [4] v. rouse; call out, send for; summon; evoke.

excipiō, cēpī, ceptum, [3] v. exempt; except; catch; receive; listen to; follow after.

excitō, [1] v. rouse up, wake up; raise, erect; arouse.

exclāmātiō, ōnis, f. exclamation, saying.

exclāmō, [1] v. call or cry out; exclaim.

exclūdō, sī, sum, [3] v. shut out, exclude; hatch; prevent.

excōgitō, [1] v. think out, devise.

excolō, coluī, cultum, [3] *v.* improve; develop; honour.

excoquō, xī, ctum, [3] *v.* boil; temper (by heat); boil away; dry up, parch.

excors, cordis, *a.* silly, stupid.

excrēmentum, ī, *nt.* excrement; spittle, mucus.

excrēscō, ēvī, ētum, [3] *v.* grow out *or* up; grow up; grow.

excruciō, [1] *v.* torture; torment.

excubiae, ārum, *f. pl.* watching, watch, guard.

excubitor, ōris, *m.* watchman, sentinel.

excubō, buī, bitum, [1] *v.* sleep in the open; keep watch; be attentive.

excūdō, dī, sum, [3] *v.* strike out; forge; fashion.

excurrō, cucurrī (currī), cursum, [3] *v.* run out; make an excursion; sally; extend; project.

excursiō, ōnis, *f.* running forth; sally.

excursus, ūs, *m.* running out; excursion; sally, sudden raid.

excūsābilis, e, *a.* excusable.

excūsātiō, ōnis, *f.* excuse.

excūsō, [1] *v.* excuse; plead as an excuse; absolve.

excutiō, cussī, cussum, [3] *v.* shake out *or* off; cast out; search, examine.

exedō, ēdī, ēsum, [3] *v.* eat up, consume; hollow.

exemplar, āris, *nt.* model, pattern, example; copy.

exemplum, ī, *nt.* sample; example; precedent; warning; punishment; portrait; copy.

exenterō, [1] *v.* disembowel.

exeō, iī, itum, [4] *v.* go out *or* away; march out; escape; die; perish; rise; exceed.

exerceō, uī, itum, [2] *v.* drill, exercise; employ; practise; administer; cultivate; harass.

exercitātiō, ōnis, *f.* exercise, practice.

exercitātus, a, um, *a.* practised, skilled; troubled.

exercitium, iī, *nt.* exercise.

exercitō, [1] *v.* practise.

exercitus, ūs, *m.* army; swarm, flock.

exhālō, [1] *v.* breathe out; evaporate; die.

exhauriō, hausī, haustum, [4] *v.* drain; empty; drink up; exhaust; see through to the end.

exhibeō, uī, itum, [2] *v.* present; furnish; exhibit; produce.

exhorrēscō, ruī, [3] *v.* be terrified; tremble at.

exhortor, ātus, [1] *v. dep.* exhort, encourage, incite.

exigō, ēgī, āctum, [3] *v.* drive out; thrust; exact; finish; examine, weigh; make to conform with.

exiguitās, ātis, *f.* scarcity, smallness of size.

exiguus, a, um, *a*. scanty, small, petty, short, poor.

exīlis, e, *a*. small, thin; poor.

exilium, iī, v. **ex(s)ilium**.

exim, v. **exinde**.

eximius, a, um, *a*. select, extraordinary, excellent, fine.

eximō, ēmī, ēmptum, [3] *v*. take out, remove; free, release.

exin, *ad*., v. **exinde**.

exinde, *ad*. thence; after that; then.

existimātiō, ōnis, *f*. judgment; opinion; reputation; credit.

existimō, [1], **existumō**, [1] *v*. judge, value, think.

exitiābilis, e, **exitiālis, e**, *a*. destructive, deadly.

exitiōsus, a, um, *a*. destructive, pernicious, deadly.

exitium, iī, *nt*. ruin, mischief; death.

exitus, ūs, *m*. egress, departure; end; outlet; result; death.

exolēscō, ēvi, ētum, [3] *v*. grow up; grow out of use; die out.

exonerō, [1] *v*. unload, disburden, discharge.

exoptō, [1] *v*. long for.

exōrābilis, e, *a*. capable of being moved by entreaty.

exōrdior, ōrsus, [4] *v. dep*. begin, commence.

exōrdium, iī, *nt*. beginning; introduction, preface.

exorior, ortus, [4] *v. dep*. arise; begin; spring up; cheer up.

exōrnō, [1] *v*. furnish with, adorn, embellish.

exōrō, [1] *v*. obtain by entreaty; win over by entreaty.

exōsus, a, um, *a*. hating.

expallēscō, luī, [3] *v*. turn very pale.

expandō, pandī, passum & pānsum, [3] *v*. spread out, expand; expound.

expavēscō, pāvī [3] *v*. become frightened.

expediō, īvī & iī, ītum, [4] *v*. extricate; make ready; free; **expedit**, it is profitable *or* expedient.

expedītiō, ōnis, *f*. expedition, campaign.

expedītus, a, um, *a*. free, easy; ready; ready for action; without baggage; unencumbered.

expellō, pulī, pulsum, [3] *v*. expel; banish; reject.

expendō, dī, sum, [3] *v*. pay; pay out; weigh, judge; pay a penalty.

expergefaciō, fēcī, factum, [3] *v*. arouse, awake.

expergīscor, perrēctus, [3] *v. dep*. awake; bestir oneself.

experiēns, entis, *a*. active, enterprising.

experientia, ae, *f*. trial, experiment; experience.

experīmentum, ī, *nt*. trial, experiment, experience.

experior, pertus, [4] *v. dep*. make trial of, put to the test. experience, find; attempt.

expers, tis, *a. with gen.* destitute of, without; lacking experience; immune (from).

expertus, a, um, *a.* well-proved, tested.

expetō, īvī & iī, ītum, [3] *v.* ask for; desire; aspire to; demand; happen; fall on (a person).

expiātiō, ōnis, *f.* atonement, expiation, purification.

expilō, [1] *v.* plunder, rob, despoil.

expiō, [1] *v.* atone for, expiate; avert by expiatory rites.

explānō, [1] *v.* explain.

expleō, ēvī, ētum, [2] *v.* fill out or up, complete; finish; satisfy; satiate; fulfil, discharge.

explicō, āvī & uī, ātum & itum, [1] *v.* unfold; display; disentangle; exhibit; spread out.

explōdō, sī, sum, [3] *v.* drive (an actor) off the stage; reject.

explōrātor, ōris, *m.* spy, scout.

explōrō, [1] *v.* reconnoitre; test, try out; investigate.

expoliō, īvī, & iī, ītum, [4] *v.* polish; refine.

expōnō, posuī, positum, [3] *v.* set out; expose; disembark; publish; exhibit, explain.

exportō, [1] *v.* export, carry out.

exposcō, popōscī, [3] *v.* ask for, demand, request; demand the surrender of.

expostulātiō, ōnis, *f.* complaint, protest.

expostulō, [1] *v.* demand, call for; remonstrate, complain about.

exprimō, pressī, pressum, [3] *v.* squeeze, squeeze out; copy, portray; express; extort.

exprobrātiō, ōnis, *f.* reproaching, reproach.

exprobrō, [1] *v.* bring up as a reproach.

exprōmō, mpsī, mptum, [3] *v.* bring out; disclose, reveal.

expugnābilis, e, *a.* open to assault.

expugnātiō, ōnis, *f.* taking by storm.

expugnātor, ōris, *m.* conqueror.

expugnāx, ācis, *a.* effectual in overcoming resistance.

expugnō, [1] *v.* take by assault, storm; conquer; plunder; achieve; persuade.

expurgō, [1] *v.* cleanse, purify; exculpate.

exquīrō, sīvī, sītum, [3] inquire into; look for.

exsanguis, e, *a.* bloodless; pale, wan; feeble.

ex(s)atiō, [1] *v.* satisfy, satiate; glut.

exsaturābilis, e, *a.* capable of being satiated.

exsaturō, [1] *v.* satisfy, sate, glut.

ex(s)cindō, īdī, issum, [3] *v.* demolish, destroy.

exscrībō, psī, ptum, [3] *v.* copy, write out.

ex(s)ecō, cuī, ctum, [1] *v.* cut out or away; castrate.

ex(s)ecrābilis, e, *a.* accursed, detestable.

ex(s)ecrātiō, ōnis, *f.* imprecation, curse.

ex(s)ecror, ātus, [1] *v. dep.* curse; detest.

ex(s)equiae, ārum, *f. pl.* funeral procession.

ex(s)equor, cūtus, [3] *v. dep.* follow (to the grave); pursue; accomplish; relate; pursue with vengeance *or* punishment.

ex(s)erō, seruī, sertum, [3] *v.* stretch forth; thrust out, lay bare.

ex(s)iccō, [1] *v.* dry up; empty (a vessel).

ex(s)iliō, siluī, [4] *v.* spring forth, leap up.

ex(s)ilium, iī, *nt.* exile.

ex(s)istō, stitī, stitum, [3] *v.* step forth, appear; arise; become; prove to be.

ex(s)olvō, solvī, solūtum, [3] *v.* set free; pay; throw off; release; perform.

ex(s)ors, sortis, *a.* without share in, exempt from lottery.

ex(s)patior, ātus, [1] *v. dep.* wander from the course; spread out.

ex(s)pectātiō, ōnis, *f.* expectation, expectancy.

ex(s)pectō, [1] *v.* await, expect; anticipate; hope for.

ex(s)pēs, *a.* hopeless.

ex(s)pīrō, [1] *v.* breathe out; exhale; expire; die; cease.

ex(s)poliō, [1] *v.* plunder.

ex(s)puō, uī, ūtum, [3] *v.* spit out; eject; rid oneself of.

ex(s)ternō, [1] *v.* terrify, madden.

ex(s)timulō, [1] *v.* goad; stimulate.

ex(s)tinguō, nxī, nctum, [3] *v.* quench, extinguish; kill; destroy.

ex(s)tō, [1] *v.* stand out *or* forth; project; be visible; exist, be on record.

ex(s)truō, xī, ctum, [3] *v.* pile up; build up, raise.

ex(s)ūdō, [1] *v.* exude; sweat out.

ex(s)ul, ulis, *m.* or *f.* exile.

ex(s)ulō, [1] *v.* be an exile.

ex(s)ultātiō, ōnis, *f.* exultation, joy.

ex(s)ultō, [1] *v.* jump about; let oneself go; exult.

ex(s)uperābilis, e, *a.* able to be overcome.

ex(s)uperō, [1] *v.* excel; overtop; surpass; overpower.

ex(s)urgō, surrēxī, [3] *v.* rise, stand up; take action.

exsuscitō, [1] *v.* awaken; kindle; *fig.* stir up, excite.

exta, ōrum, *nt. pl.* bowels, entrails.

extemplō, *ad.* immediately, forthwith.

extendō, dī, tum & sum, [3] *v.* stretch out, extend; enlarge; prolong; continue.

extenuō, [1] *v.* make thin; diminish.

exter, tera, terum, *a.* outer, external, foreign; **exterior, exterius,** outer, exterior; **extrēmus & extimus,** uttermost, utmost, extreme, last.

exterior, ius, v. exter.

exterminō, [1] *v.* banish, expel; dismiss.

externus, a, um, *a.* external; foreign, strange.

exterreō, uī, itum, [2] *v.* strike with terror, scare.

exterus, a, um, v. exter.

extimēscō, muī, [3] *v.* take fright, be alarmed; dread.

extimus, a, um, v. exter.

extollō, [3] *v.* raise; lift up; extol, advance.

extorqueō, sī, tum, [2] *v.* twist or wrench out; extort.

extorris, e, *a.* exiled.

extrā, *ad. & pr. with acc.* outside, without; out of, beyond; except.

extrahō, xī, ctum, [3] *v.* draw out, extract; prolong.

extrāneus, a, um, *a.* external, extraneous, foreign; not belonging to one's family or household.

extraordinārius, a, um, *a.* supplementary; special; immoderate.

extrēmum, ī, *nt.* limit, outside; end.

extrēmus, a, um, v. exter.

extrīcō, [1] *v.* disentangle, extricate, free.

extrīnsecus, *ad.* from without; on the outside.

extrūdō, sī, sum, [3] *v.* thrust out; drive out.

extundō, tudī, tūsum, [3] *v.* beat or strike out; produce with effort.

exturbō, [1] *v.* thrust out; divorce; disturb.

exūberō, [1] *v.* surge or gush up; be abundant, be fruitful.

exul, v. ex(s)ul.

exulō, v. ex(s)ulō.

exululō, [1] *v.* invoke with howls.

exundō, [1] *v.* gush forth; overflow with.

exuō, uī, ūtum, [3] *v.* put off; doff; strip; deprive of; lay aside; cast off.

exūrō, ussī, ustum, [3] *v.* burn up; dry up; destroy; parch.

exuviae, ārum, *f. pl.* things stripped off; spoils, booty; something belonging to a person, serving as a memento.

F

faba, ae, *f.* bean.

fābella, ae, *f.* story, fable; play.

faber, brī, *m.* artisan, workman; smith; carpenter; ~, **bra, brum,** *a.* of the craftsman *or* his work.

fabrica, ae, *f.* art, craft.

fabricātor, ōris, *m.* maker, fashioner.

fabricō, [1] *v.,* **fabricor, ātus,** [1] *v. dep.* fashion, forge, shape; build, construct.

fabrīlis, e, *a.* of *or* belonging to a workman *of* a metal-worker, carpenter *or* builder.

fābula, ae, *f.* story; tale; fable; drama, play talk; **fābulae!** rubbish!

fābulōsus, a, um, *a.* storied, fabulous; celebrated in story.

facessō, cessī, ītum, [3] *v.* do; perpetrate; go away.

facētiae, ārum, *f. pl.* wit, joke.

facētus, a, um, *a.* witty, humorous; clever, adept.

faciēs, ēī, *f.* face, look, pretence; appearance, beauty.

facilis, e, *a.* easy; pliable; gentle; courteous; good-natured, affable.

facilitās, ātis, *f.* easiness, facility; readiness; good nature, courteousness, affability.

facinus, oris, *nt.* deed, crime, outrage.

faciō, fēcī, factum, [3] *v.* make; do; fashion; cause; compose; practise; commit; render; value.

factiō, ōnis, *f.* faction, party.

factiōsus, a, um, *a.* factious, seditious, turbulent.

factitō, [1] *v.* do frequently; practise.

factum, ī, *nt.* deed, exploit.

facultās, ātis, *f.* capability; possibility; means; opportunity; skill; quantity available; means.

fācundia, ae, *f.* eloquence.

fācundus, a, um, *a.* eloquent.

faecula, ae, *f.* lees of wine (used as a condiment or medicine).

faenebris, e, *a.* pertaining to usury; lent at interest.

faenerātiō, ōnis, *f.* usury, money-lending.

faenerātor, ōris, *m.* usurer, money-lender.

faenīlia, um, *nt. pl.* place for storing hay, barn.

faenum, ī, *nt.* hay.

faenus, eris, *nt.* interest; profit; gain.

faex, faecis, *f.* sediment, dregs; dregs of the people.

fāgin(e)us, a, um, *a.* of the beech tree; of beech-wood.

fāgus, ī, *f.* beech-tree.

falārica, ae, *f.* a heavy missile (thrown generally by a catapult).

falcārius, iī, *m.* scythe-maker.

falcātus, a, um, *a.* armed with scythes; sickle-shaped, curved.

falcifer, a, um, *a.* carrying a scythe; scythed.

Falernum, ī, *nt.* Falernian wine.

fallācia, ae, *f.* deceit, trick, stratagem.

fallāx, ācis, *a.* deceitful, fallacious; spurious.

fallō, fefellī, falsum, [3] *v.* cheat, deceive; disappoint; escape notice.

falsus, a, um, *a.* false; deceiving; deceived; spurious.

falx, falcis, *f.* sickle; scythe; curved blade.

fāma, ae, *f.* rumour; fame; renown; ill repute; news.

famēs, is, *f.* hunger; famine; craving.

familia, ae, *f.* household, all persons under the control of one man, whether relations, freedmen, or slaves; family; servants or slaves belonging to one master; estate.

familiāris, e, *a.* of the household; familiar; intimate; very friendly.

familiāritās, ātis, *f.* familiarity, intimacy, close friendship.

fāmōsus, a, um, *a.* famed, renowned; infamous, notorious; slanderous, libellous.

famula, ae, *f.* female slave; maidservant.

famulāris, e, *a.* of slaves, servile.

famulor, ātus, [1] *v. dep.* be a servant, attend.

famulus, ī, *m.* slave, servant; attendant; ~, **a, um,** *a.* servile, subject.

fānāticus, a, um, *a.* fanatic, frantic; belonging to a temple.

fandus, a, um, *a.* that may be spoken; proper, lawful.

fānum, ī, *nt.* sanctuary, temple.

fār, farris, *nt.* husked wheat, grain.

farciō, farsī, fartum, [4] *v.* stuff, cram.

farrāgō, inis, *f.* mixed fodder; a hotch-potch.

fās, *nt. indecl.* divine law; right; obligation.

fascia, ae, *f.* band.

fasciculus, ī, *m.* bundle, packet; bunch (of flowers).

fascinō, [1] *v.* cast a spell on, bewitch.

fascis, is, *m.* bundle, parcel; **fascēs,** *pl.* bundles of rods, carried before the highest magistrates of Rome, usually with an axe bound up in the middle of them; the power or office of a magistrate.

fāstī, ōrum, *m. pl.* list of festivals; calendar; list of consuls who gave their names to the year.

fastīdiō, īvī & iī, ītum, [4] *v.* disdain; be scornful; feel aversion to, be squeaming.

fastīdiōsus, a, um, *a.* squeamish; exacting; disdainful; nauseating.

fastīdium, iī, *nt.* squeamishness, loathing; scornful contempt; pride; fastidiousness.

fastīgium, iī, *nt.* slope, declivity; gable, roof; sharp point, tip; summit; height; depth; highest rank, dignity.

fāstus, a, um, *a.* **diēs ~,** day on which the courts could sit.

fastus, ūs, *m.* contempt; haughtiness.

fātālis, e, *a.* destined, fated; fatal.

fateor, fassus, [2] *v. dep.* confess; acknowledge.

fātidicus, a, um, *a.* prophetic.

fātifer, a, um, *a.* deadly; fatal.

fatīgō, [1] *v.* weary, tire, fatigue; harass; importune; overcome.

fatīscō, [3] *v.,* **fatīscor,** [3] *v. dep.* gape, crack; grow weak *or* exhausted.

fātum, ī, *nt.* fate, destiny; doom; ill-fate; death.

fatuus, a, um, *a.* foolish, silly; idiotic.

faucēs, ium, *f. pl.* throat; narrow entrance; defile; gulf, abyss.

Faunus, ī, *m.* a rustic god.

faustus, a, um, *a.* favourable; auspicious; lucky, prosperous.

fautor, ōris, *m.* patron; admirer; supporter.

faveō, fāvī, fautum, [2] *v. with dat.* favour, befriend; back up.

favīlla, ae, *f.* ashes, embers.

Favōnius, iī, *m.* west wind.

favor, ōris, *m.* favour, good-will; bias, applause.

favus, ī, *m.* honey-comb.

fax, facis, *f.* torch; firebrand; love-flame; fire, torment.

febris, is, *f.* fever, attack of fever.

februārius, iī, *m.* February.

fēcundītās, ātis, *f.* fertility, fecundity.

fēcundus, a, um, *a.* fruitful, fertile; abundant.

fel, fellis, *nt.* gall, bile; poison; bitterness, venom.

fēlīcitās, ātis, *f.* good fortune, felicity.

fēlīx, īcis, *a.* fruitful; lucky, happy, fortunate; successful.

fēmina, ae, *f.* female, woman.

fēmineus, a, um, *a.* womanly, feminine, womanish, effeminate.

femur, oris, *or* **inis,** *nt.* thigh.

fenestra, ae, *f.* window; loop-hole.

fera, ae, *f.* wild beast.

fērālis, e, *a.* funereal; deadly, fatal; **Fērālia, ium,** *nt. pl.* festival of the dead.

ferāx, ācis, *a.* fruitful, fertile.

ferculum, ī, *nt.* frame *or* stretcher for carrying things; dish; course (at dinner).

ferē, *ad.* nearly, almost; about; in general; (with negatives) hardly ever.

ferentārius, iī, *m.* light-armed soldier, skirmisher.

feretrum, ī, *nt.* bier.

fēriae, ārum, *f. pl.* holiday.

fēriātus, a, um, *a.* keeping holiday, at leisure.

ferīna, ae, *f.* game, flesh of wild animals.

ferīnus, a, um, *a.* of wild beasts.

feriō, [4] *v.* strike, knock; hit; slay, kill; strike (a bargain); strike (a treaty).

feritās, ātis, *f.* wildness, savageness.

fermē, *ad.* nearly, almost, about; (with negatives) hardly ever.

fero, ferre, tulī, lātum, *v.* carry; bring; bear away; plunder; bear with; lead; produce, bring forth; endure; receive; propose; exhibit; **ferunt,** they say; **fertur,** it is said.

ferōcia, ae, *f.* fierceness, ferocity; insolence.

ferōcitās, ātis, *f.* fierceness, savageness; excessive spirits; aggressiveness.

ferōx, ōcis, *a.* wild, bold; warlike; cruel; defiant, arrogant.

ferrāmentum, ī, *nt.* iron tool.

ferrāria, ae, *f.* iron mine.

ferrātus, a, um, *a.* bound *or* covered with iron; with iron points *or* studs.

ferreus, a, um, *a.* of iron; iron; hard, cruel; firm.

ferrūgineus, a, um, *a.* of the colour of iron-rust, sombre.

ferrūgō, inis, *f.* iron-rust; colour of iron-rust; dusky colour.

ferrum, ī, *nt.* iron; sword; any tool of iron; weapon.

fertilis, e, *a.* fruitful, fertile; abundant.

fertilitās, ātis, *f.* fruitfulness, fertility.

ferus, a, um, *a.* wild, savage; cruel; ~, ī, *m.;* wild beast.

fervefaciō, fēcī, factum, [3] *v.* make intensely hot, heat, boil.

fervēns, entis, *a.* boiling hot, burning; inflamed, impetuous.

ferveō, buī, [2] *v.* be intensely hot; boil; seethe, be roused.

fervēscō, [3] *v.* grow hot.

fervidus, a, um, *a.* boiling hot, fiery; torrid; roused; hot-blooded.

fervor, ōris, *m.* heat; ardour, passion.

fessus, a, um, *a.* wearied, tired; feeble.

festīnātiō, ōnis, *f.* haste, speed, hurry.

festīnō, [1] *v.* hasten; hurry.

fēstum, ī, *nt.* holiday, festival; feastday.

fēstus, a, um, *a.* festal; solemn, merry.

fētiālēs, ium, *m. pl.* Roman college of priests who represented the Roman people in their dealings with other nations.

fētidus, a, um, *a.* foul-smelling, stinking.

fētūra, ae, *f.* bearing, breeding; young offspring, brood.

fētus, a, um, *a.* pregnant with; fertile; full (of); having newly brought forth; ~, **ūs,** *m.* birth; offspring; produce.

fibra, ae, *f.* fibre, filament; entrails; leaf, blade (of grasses, *etc.*).

fībula, ae, *f.* clasp, buckle, brooch.

fictilis, e, *a.* made of earthenware; **fictile, is,** *nt.* earthenware vessel *or* statue.

fictor, ōris, *m.* one who devises *or* makes.

fictus, a, um, *a.* feigned, false; counterfeit.

fīcus, ī & ūs, *f.* fig-tree.

fidēlis, e, *a.* faithful; loyal; trustworthy; dependable.

fidēlitās, ātis, *f.* faithfulness, fidelity.

fīdēns, entis, *a.* confident; bold.

fidēs, ēī, *f.* faith, trust, confidence; belief, credence; loyalty; honesty; allegiance; promise; security; protection.

fidēs, is, *f.,* **fidēs, ium,** *pl.* lyre.

fidicen, inis, *m.* lyre-player.

fīdō, fīsus sum, [3] *v. with dat. or abl.* trust (in), have confidence (in).

fīdūcia, ae, *f.* trust, confidence; boldness, courage.

fīdūciārius, a, um, *a.* holding on trust; held on trust.

fīdus, a, um, *a.* trusty, faithful, loyal.

fīgō, xī, xum, [3] *v.* fix, fasten; transfix; establish.

figulus, ī, *m.* potter.

figūra, ae, *f.* shape, figure, form; image.

figūrō, [1] *v.* form, fashion, shape.

fīlia, ae, *f.* daughter.

fīliola, ae, *f.* little daughter.

fīliolus, ī, *m.* little son.

fīlius, iī, *m.* son.

filix, icis, *f.* fern, bracken.

fīlum, ī, *nt.* thread; cord; string; texture.

fimus, ī, *m.* **fimum, ī,** *nt.* dung, excrement.

findō, fidī, fissum, [3] *v.* cleave, split; divide.

fingō, fīnxī, fictum, [3] *v.* shape, form, fashion, make; contrive; invent; make a pretence of.

fīniō, īvī & iī, ītum, [4] *v.* limit; define; end, finish; mark out the boundaries of.

fīnis, is, *m. & f.* boundary, limit; end; purpose; death; **fīnēs, ium,** *pl.* country, territory.

fīnitimus, a, um, *a.* bordering on, adjoining, neighbouring.

fīō, fierī, factus sum, [4] *v.* be made *or* done; happen; become; take place.

firmāmen, inis (*poet.*), **firmāmentum, ī,** *nt.* support, prop, mainstay.

firmitās, ātis, *f.* firmness, strength.

firmiter, *ad.* firmly, strongly; steadfastly.

firmitūdō, inis, *f.* stability; strength.

firmō, [1] *v.* make firm *or* steady; strengthen; harden; confirm; establish; encourage.

firmus, a, um, *a.* firm; strong; steady; valid; bold.

fiscella, ae, *f.* small wicker-basket.

fiscina, ae, *f.* small basket of wicker-work.

fiscus, ī, *m.* money-bag, purse; imperial exchequer.

fissilis, e, *a.* easily split; split.

fistula, ae, *f.* pipe; tube; shepherd's pipe.

fīxus, a, um, *a.* fixed fast, immovable; fitted with.

flābra, ōrum, *nt. pl.* gusts *or* blasts of wind.

flaccidus, a, um, *a.* flaccid, flabby.

flagellum, ī, *nt.* whip, scourge; thong; vine-shoot.

flāgitātiō, ōnis, *f.* importunate request, demand.

flāgitātor, oris, *m.* importuner, dun.

flāgitiōsus, a, um, *a.* disgraceful, scandalous; infamous.

flāgitium, iī, *nt.* shameful *or* base action; crime; scandal, disgrace.

flāgitō, [1] *v.* demand importunely; ask repeatedly (for).

flagrāns, antis, *a.* blazing, glowing; ardent, passionate.

flagrō, [1] *v.* blaze, flame, burn; be inflamed; be excited.

flāmen, inis, *m.* priest of one particular deity; ~, **inis,** *nt.* blast; gale, wind.

flamma, ae, *f.* blaze, flame; ardour; fire of love; object of love.

flammeus, a, um, *a.* flaming, fiery; fiery red; ~**eum, eī,** *nt.* flame-coloured bridal veil.

flammō, [1] *v.* inflame, set on fire; excite.

flātus, ūs, *m.* blowing; snorting; breath; breeze.

flāveō, [2] *v.* be yellow *or* gold-coloured.

flāvēscō, [3] *v.* turn yellow *or* gold.

flāvus, a, um, *a.* yellow, flaxen, gold-coloured, blonde.

flēbilis, e, *a.* lamentable; doleful; tearful.

flectō, xī, xum, [3] *v.* bend, bow, curve, turn; prevail on, soften.

fleō, flēvī, flētum, [2] *v.* weep, cry; weep for.

flētus, ūs, *m.* weeping; tears.

flexibilis, e, *a.* flexible, pliant.

flexilis, e, *a.* pliant, pliable, supple.

flexus, ūs, *m.* turning, winding; swerve; bend; turning point.

flō, flāvī, flātum, [1] *v.* blow; sound; cast (by blowing).

floccus, ī, *m.* tuft of wool; **nōn floccī facere**, to consider of no importance.

flōreō, uī, [2] *v.* blossom; flourish; be in one's prime.

flōrēscō, [3] *v.* (begin to) blossom; increase in physical vigour *or* renown.

flōreus, a, um, *a.* flowery.

flōridus, a, um, *a.* blooming; flowery; florid.

flōrifer, a, um, *a.* flowery.

flōs, ōris, *m.* blossom, flower; youthful prime.

flōsculus, ī, *m.* little flower, floweret; the best of anything, the 'flower'.

fluctuō, [1] *v.*, **fluctuor, ātus**, [1] *v. dep.* rise in waves, surge; float; be in a state of agitation; waver.

fluctus, ūs, *m.* flood; wave, billow.

fluentum, ī, *nt.* stream; river.

fluidus, a, um, *a.* liquid; soft, feeble.

fluitō, [1] *v.* float; flow; waver.

flūmen, inis, *nt.* stream; river; **adversō flūmine**, against the current; **secundō flūmine**, with the current.

fluō, xī, xum, [3] *v.* flow; stream; emanate; proceed (from); fall gradually; hang loosely.

fluviālis, e, *a.* river...

fluvius, iī, *m.* river; running water.

fluxus, a, um, *a.* flowing; fluid; loose; transient; frail; dissolute.

focus, ī, *m.* fireplace, hearth; family, household.

fodiō, fōdī, fossum, [3] *v.* dig, dig up; stab.

foederātus, a, um, *a.* allied (to Rome).

foeditās, ātis, *f.* foulness; ugliness; shame.

foedō, [1] *v.* defile; pollute; disfigure, disgrace, sully.

foedus, a, um, *a.* foul, filthy; ugly; base, vile; abominable.

foedus, eris, *nt.* league, treaty; agreement.

foen . . ., v. **faen . . .**

folium, iī, *nt.* leaf.

folliculus, ī, *m.* bag *or* sack; pod; shell.

follis, is, *m.* pair of bellows; bag; scrotum.

fōmentum, ī, *nt.* poultice; alleviation, consolation.

fōmes, itis, *m.* chips of wood, *etc.* for kindling a fire.

fōns, fontis, *m.* spring, fountain; *fig.* source; principal cause.

fontānus, a, um, *a.* of a spring.

for, fātus, [1] *v. dep.* speak, talk; say.

forāmen, inis, *nt.* aperture, hole.

forās, *ad.* out of doors, abroad, forth, out.

forceps, cipis, *f.* pair of tongs, pincers.

forēnsis, e, *a.* public; pertaining to the courts.

foris, is, *f.* **forēs, um,** *f. pl.* door, gate; opening, entrance.

forīs, *ad.* out of doors; abroad.

fōrma, ae, *f.* form, figure, shape; mould; pattern; sort; beauty.

formīca, ae, *f.* ant.

formīdābilis, e, *a.* terrifying.

formīdō, [1] *v.* dread; be afraid of.

formīdō, inis, *f.* fear, terror, dread; a thing which frightens, bogy.

formīdolōsus, a, um, *a.* fearful; terrible.

fōrmō, [1] *v.* shape, fashion; form; model.

fōrmōsus, a, um, *a.* beautiful; handsome.

fōrmula, ae, *f.* set form of words, formula; principle, rule, legal process.

fornāx, ācis, *f.* furnace, oven.

fornicātus, a, um, *a.* arched, vaulted.

fornix, icis, *m.* arch, vault; brothel.

fors, fortis, *f.* fortune, chance; accident.

forsan, forsit, forsitan, fortasse, *ad.* perhaps.

forte, *ad.* by chance; as luck would have it.

fortis, e, *a.* strong, powerful; hardy; courageous; valiant; manful.

fortitūdō, inis, *f.* strength; firmness; courage, valour; manfulness.

fortuītus, a, um, *a.* casual; accidental.

fortūna, ae, *f.* fortune; chance; luck; prosperity; condition; wealth, property.

fortūnātus, a, um, *a.* lucky, happy, fortunate; rich.

forum, ī, *nt.* market; court of justice; forum (at Rome).

forus, ī, *m.* gangway in a ship; row of benches erected for spectators at games.

fossa, ae, *f.* ditch, trench.

fossor, ōris, *m.* one who digs the ground.

fovea, ae, *f.* pit; pitfall.

foveō, fōvī, fōtum, [2] *v.* keep warm; favour; cherish; maintain, foster.

frāga, ōrum, *nt. pl.* wild strawberries.

fragilis, e, *a.* brittle, frail; impermanent.

fragilitās, ātis, *f.* brittleness; frailty.

fragmen, inis, *nt.* fragment; **fragmina, um,** *pl.* fragments, ruins; chips.

fragmentum, ī, *nt.* fragment.

fragor, ōris, *m.* crash; noise.

fragōsus, a, um, *a.* brittle; ragged.

frāgrō, [1] v. smell strongly.

frangō, frēgī, frāctum, [3] v. break; crush; weaken; wear out; vanquish; break in.

frāter, tris, m. brother; cousin.

frāternus, a, um, a. brotherly, fraternal; friendly.

fraudō, [1] v. cheat; defraud; steal.

fraus, fraudis, f. deceit, fraud; crime; responsibility for an action.

fraxineus, a, um, fraxinus, a, um, a. of ash; ashen.

fraxinus, ī, f. ash-tree; spear or javelin of ash.

fremitus, ūs, m. roaring; shouting; clashing; muttering; loud murmur or buzz of applause, etc.

fremō, uī, itum, [3] v. roar; growl; rage; murmur; clamour for.

fremor. ōris, m. low, confused noise, murmur.

frendeō or frendō, uī, frēsum, [3] v. gnash the teeth, grind up small.

frēnō, [1] v. bridle; curb.

frēnum, ī, nt. bridle, bit; check.

frequēns, entis, a. frequent; usual, general; crowded; populous.

frequenter, ad. often, frequently; in crowds.

frequentia, ae, f. frequency; crowd; abundance of persons or things.

frequentō, [1] v. frequent; repeat often; haunt; throng; crowd; celebrate.

fretum, ī, nt. fretus, ūs, m. strait, narrow sea; sea.

frētus, a, um, a. with abl. relying upon, trusting to.

fricō, uī, ctum, [1] v. rub, chafe.

frīgeō, [2] v. be cold; lack vigour; have a cold reception.

frīgēscō, frīxī, [3] v. become cold.

frīgidus, a, um, a. cold, cool, chilly; dull; torpid.

frīgus, oris, nt. cold, coldness; frost, winter.

frīvolus, a, um, a. frivolous, trifling; silly; worthless; trashy.

frondātōr, ōris, m. pruner.

frondeō, [2] v. be in leaf, become leafy.

frondēscō, duī, [3] v. become leafy, shoot.

frondeus, a, um, a. leafy.

frondōsus, a, um, a. leafy, abounding in foliage.

frōns, dis, f. leafy branches; foliage, leaves.

frōns, frontis, f. forehead; brow; foremost part of anything.

frūctuōsus, a, um, a. fruitful; profitable.

frūctus, ūs, m. fruit, crops; profit.

frūgēs, um, frūgī, v. frūx.

frūgifer, a, um, a. fruit-bearing, fertile.

frūmentārius, a, um, *a.* of *or* concerned with corn.

frūmentātiō, ōnis, *f.* the collecting of corn; foraging.

frūmentātor, ōris, *m.* forager.

frūmentor, ātus, [1] *v. dep.* forage.

frūmentum, ī, *nt.* corn, grain.

fruor, frūctus & fruitus, [3] *v. dep. with abl.* enjoy, profit by.

frūstrā, *ad.* in vain, to no purpose.

frūstrātiō, ōnis, *f.* deceiving, disappointment.

frūstror, ātus, [1] *dep.* v. disappoint, frustrate; deceive.

frustum, ī, *nt.* morsel, scrap of food.

frutex, icis, *m.* shrub, bush.

fruticōsus, a, um, *a.* bushy.

frūx, frūgis, *f.*, **frūgēs, um**, *pl.* fruits, crops; **frūgī**, *ad.* honest; virtuous; thrifty.

fūcō, [1] *v.* colour; paint; dye.

fūcōsus, a, um, *a.* sham, bogus.

fūcus, ī, *m.* dye; bee-glue; drone; pretence, sham.

fuga, ae, *f.* flight; fleeing; avoidance; exile.

fugāx, ācis, *a.* flying swiftly; swift; avoiding; transitory.

fugiō, fūgī, [3] *v.* flee *or* fly, run away; go into exile; shun, avoid.

fugitīvus, a, um, *a.* fugitive; ~, **ī**, *m.* runaway.

fugō, [1] *v.* put to flight, chase away, rout; drive into exile.

fulciō, fulsī, fultum, [4] *v.* prop up, support.

fulcrum, ī, *nt.* head- *or* back-support of a couch.

fulgeō, fulsī, [2] *v.* gleam; glitter, shine forth, be bright.

fulgor, ōris, *m.* lightning; flash; glittering, brightness; glory.

fulgur, uris, *nt.* lightning.

fulica, ae, *f.* a water-fowl, probably the coot.

fūlīgō, inis, *f.* soot; lamp-black.

fulmen, inis, *nt.* lightning, thunderbolt; crushing blow.

fulmineus, a, um, *a.* of lightning; destructive.

fulminō, [1] *v.* lighten; cause lightning to strike; strike like lightning.

fulvus, a, um, *a.* reddish yellow, tawny.

fūmeus, a, um, *a.* smoky.

fūmidus, a, um, *a.* full of smoke, smoky.

fūmifer, a, um, *a.* smoky.

fūmō, [1] *v.* smoke, steam.

fūmōsus, a, um, *a.* full of smoke, smoky; smoked.

fūmus, ī, *m.* smoke, steam, vapour.

fūnāle, is, *nt.* torch of wax- or tallow-soaked rope; chandelier.

funda, ae, *f.* sling; casting-net.

fundāmen, inis, *nt.* foundation.

fundāmentum, ī, *nt.* foundation, groundwork, basis.

fundātor, ōris, *m.* founder.

funditor, ōris, *m.* slinger.

funditus, *ad.* from the very bottom; utterly, totally.

fundō, fūdī, fūsum, [3] *v.* pour out, shed; cast (metals); rout; scatter; produce; give birth to; utter freely.

fundō, [1] *v.* found; establish; give a firm base to.

fundus, ī, *m.* bottom; land; farm; estate.

fūnebris, e, *a.* funereal; deadly, fatal.

fūnereus, a, um, *a.* funereal; deadly; fatal.

fūnestō, [1] *v.* pollute by murder.

fūnestus, a, um, *a.* fatal, deadly; destructive.

fungor, fūnctus, [3] *v. dep. with acc. or abl.* perform; discharge (a duty).

fungus, ī, *m.* fungus, mushroom.

fūnis, is, *m.* rope, cable.

fūnus, eris, *nt.* burial; funeral; funeral rites; corpse; death.

fūr, fūris, *m. or f.* thief.

furca, ae, *f.* (two-pronged) fork; prop.

furcifer, ī, *m.* scoundrel, gallows bird.

furiae, ārum, *f. pl.* frenzy; mad craving for; Furies, avenging spirits.

furiālis, e, *a.* frenzied; mad; avenging.

furibundus, a, um, *a.* raging, mad, furious; inspired.

furiō, [1] *v.* madden, enrage.

furiōsus, a, um, *a.* furious, mad, frantic, wild.

furnus, ī, *m.* oven.

furō, uī, [3] *v.* rage, be mad *or* furious; be wild.

furor, ātus, [1] *v. dep.* steal, plunder.

furor, ōris, *m.* fury, rage, madness.

fūrtim, *ad.* by stealth, secretly; imperceptibly.

fūrtīvus, a, um, *a.* stolen; secret, furtive.

fūrtum, ī, *nt.* theft; stolen article; trick, deception.

fuscus, a, um, *a.* dark, swarthy, dusky; husky; hoarse.

fūsilis, e, *a.* molten.

fustis, is, *m.* staff; club; stick.

fustuārium, iī, *nt.* death by beating (a punishment meted out to soldiers).

fūsus, ī, *m.* spindle.

fūtilis, e, *v.* **futtilis**.

futtilis, e, *a.* vain; worthless.

futuō, uī, ūtum, [3] *v.* have sexual relations with (a woman).

futūrus, a, um, *a.* future.

G

gaesum, ī, *nt.* Gallic javelin.

galea, ae, *f.* helmet.

galērum, ī, *nt.* galērus, ī, *m.* cap *or* hat made of skin.

gallīna, ae, *f.* hen.

gallus, ī, *m.* cock.

gānea, ae, *f.* gāneum, ī, *nt.* common eating house (the resort of undesirable characters); gluttonous eating.

gāneō, ōnis, *m.* glutton, debauchee.

garriō, īvī & iī, ītum, [4] *v.* chatter, jabber; talk nonsense.

garrulus, a, um, *a.* chattering, garrulous; blabbing.

gaudeō, gāvīsus sum, [2] *v.* rejoice, be glad, be pleased with.

gaudium, iī, *nt.* joy, gladness; delight.

gausapa, ae, *f.*, gausape, is, *nt.* cloth of woollen frieze; cloak of this material.

gāza, ae, *f.* (royal) treasure.

gelidus, a, um, *a.* icy, cold; frozen.

gelū, ūs, *nt.* frost; ice, snow; cold, chilliness.

gemellus, a, um, *a.* twin-born; ~, ī, *m.* twin.

geminō, [1] *v.* double; repeat; double the force of; pair (with).

geminus, a, um, *a.* twin-born; double; both.

gemitus, ūs, *m.* sigh, groan; roaring.

gemma, ae, *f.* bud; jewel; cup; seal, signet.

gemmātus, a, um, *a.* jewelled.

gemmeus, a, um, *a.* set with precious stones.

gemō, uī, itum, [3] *v.* moan, groan; lament (over); grieve that.

gena, ae, *f.* cheek, eyes.

gener, erī, *m.* son-in-law.

generātim, *ad.* by kinds, by tribes; generally.

generātor, ōris, *m.* begetter, father, sire.

generō, [1] *v.* beget, father, produce.

generōsus, a, um, *a.* of noble birth; noble; of good stock.

genesta, ae, *v.* genista.

genetrīx, īcis, *f.* mother.

genetīvus, a, um, *a.* acquired at birth.

geniālis, e, *a.* connected with marriage; merry, genial; festive.

genista, ae, *f.* Spanish broom, greenweed and similar shrubs.

genitālis, e, *a.* generative; fruitful.

genitor, ōris, *m.* begetter, father; creator; originator.

genius, ī, *m.* tutelary deity *or* genius; talent.

genō, uī, itum, [3] v. gignō.

gēns, gentis, *f.* clan; tribe; family; race; nation.

gentīlicius, a, um, *a.* of *or* belonging to a particular Roman **gēns**.

gentīlis, e, *a.* of the same **gēns**.

genū, ūs, *nt.* knee.

genuīnus, ī, *m.* back-tooth, molar.

genus, eris, *nt.* birth, descent, origin; offspring; race; kind; family; nation; gender.

geōmetria, ae, *f.* geometry.

germānitās, ātis, *f.* brotherhood, sisterhood; affinity between things deriving from the same source.

germānus, a, um, *a.* (of brothers & sisters); full; genuine, true; ~, ī, *m.* brother; **germāna, ae**, *f.* sister.

germen, inis, *nt.* sprout; bud; shoot.

gerō, gessī, gestum, [3] v. wear, have; govern; carry on; administer; achieve; carry in the womb.

gestāmen, inis, *nt.* something worn *or* carried on the body.

gestiō, īvī & iī, ītum, [4] v. exult; desire eagerly.

gestō, [1] v. carry (about); wear.

gestus, ūs, *m.* movement of the limbs; bodily action, gesture; gesticulation.

gigā(n)s, antis, *m.* giant.

gignō, genuī, genitum, [3] v. beget, bear, bring forth, produce.

gingīva, ae, *f.* gum (in which the teeth are set).

glaber, ra, rum, *a.* hairless, smooth.

glaciālis, e, *a.* icy, frozen.

glaciēs, ēī, *f.* ice.

gladiātor, ōris, *m.* gladiator.

gladiātōrius, a, um, *a.* gladiatorial.

gladius, iī, *m.* sword.

glaeba, ae, *f.* clod; cultivated soil; lump, mass.

glāns, glandis, *f.* acorn, beach-nut; missile discharged from a sling.

glārea, ae, *f.* gravel.

glāreōsus, a, um, *a.* gravelly.

glaucus, a, um, *a.* bluish grey.

glēba, v. glaeba.

glīs, īris, *m.* dormouse.

glīscō, [3] v. swell; increase in power *or* violence.

globōsus, a, um, *a.* round, spherical.

globus, ī, *m.* sphere; dense mass; closely packed throng.

glomerō, [1] v. form into a ball; assemble, mass together.

glomus, eris, *nt.* ball-shaped mass.

glōria, ae, *f.* glory, fame, renown; vainglory, boasting.

glōrior, ātus, [1] *v. dep.* boast; glory in.

glōriōsus, a, um, *a.* glorious, famous; vainglorious, boasting.

glūten, inis, *nt.* glue.

gnārus, a, um, *a.* having knowledge *or* experience of; known.

gnātus, a, um, v. **nātus.**

gnāv. . . , v. **nāv. . .**

grabātus, ī, *m.* low couch or bed; camp-bed.

gracilis, e, *a.* thin, slender; meagre, lean; scanty, poor; simple, plain.

grāculus, ī, *m.* jackdaw.

gradātim, *ad.* step by step, by degrees.

gradior, gressus, [3] *v. dep.* step, walk.

gradus, ūs, *m.* step, pace; position; rank; degree; rung (ladder); stair.

Graeculus, a, um, *a.* Grecian, Greek (mostly in a contemptuous sense).

grāmen, inis, *nt.* grass; herb, plant.

grāmineus, a, um, *a.* of grass, grassy; made of grass *or* turf.

grammaticus, a, um, *a.* grammatical; ~, **ī,** *m.* grammarian, scholar, expert on linguistic and literary questions.

grandaevus, a, um, *a.* of great age, old.

grandēscō, [3] *v.* grow, increase in size *or* quantity.

grandis, e, *a.* old; grown up; great; grand; tall; lofty; powerful.

grandō, inis, *f.* hail, hail-storm.

grānum, ī, *nt.* grain, seed.

graphium, iī, *nt.* sharp-pointed writing implement; stylus.

grassor, ātus, [1] *v. dep.* march on, advance; roam in search of victims, prowl; proceed; run riot.

grātēs, *f. pl.* thanks; **grātēs agere,** to thank.

grātia, ae, *f.* grace; gracefulness; good-will; kindness; favour; obligation; **grātiās agere,** to thank; ~ *with gen.* for the sake of, for the purpose of.

grātificor, ātus, [1] *v. dep.* gratify; bestow.

grātiōsus, a, um, *a.* agreeable, enjoying favour; kind.

grātīs, *ad.,* without payment, for nothing.

grātor, [1] *v. dep. with dat.* congratulate; rejoice with.

grātuītus, a, um, *a.* free of charge; unremunerative.

grātulābundus, a, um, *a.* congratulating.

grātulātiō, ōnis, *f.* congratulation; rejoicing, joy.

grātulor, ātus, [1] *v. dep.* congratulate; rejoice.

grātus, a, um, *a.* agreeable; pleasing; thankful.

gravātē, *ad.* grudgingly; reluctantly.

gravēdō, inis, f. cold in the head, catarrh.

gravidus, a, um, a. pregnant; laden, weighed down with.

gravis, e, a. heavy; weighty, burdensome; burdened; important; solemn; serious; grievous; difficult; deep (of sound); strong (of smell).

gravitās, ātis, f. weight, heaviness; severity; authority.

graviter, ad. heavily, severely; grievously; with reluctance.

gravō, [1] v. load, burden; oppress, aggravate; **gravor,** show reluctance or annoyance.

gregārius, a, um, a. belonging to the rank and file; **mīles gregārius,** common soldier.

gregātim, ad. in flocks.

gremium, iī, nt. lap, bosom; female genital parts; interior.

gressus, ūs, m. going; step; (pl.) the feet.

grex, gregis, m. flock, herd; company; crew.

grūs, gruis, m. & f. crane.

grȳps, grȳphis, m. griffin.

gubernāculum, ī, nt. helm, rudder; helm of 'ship of state'.

gubernātiō, ōnis, f. steering; direction, control.

gubernātor, ōris, m. helmsman, pilot; one who directs or controls.

gubernō, [1] v. steer (a ship); govern.

gula, ae, f. gullet, throat; appetite.

gurges, itis, m. whirlpool, eddy; 'flood', 'stream'.

gustō, [1] v. taste; sip; have some experience of.

gutta, ae, f. drop; spot; speck.

guttur, uris, nt. gullet, throat; appetite.

gymnasium, iī, nt. sports centre.

gymnicus, a, um, a. gymnastic.

gȳrus, ī, m. circle; circuit; course.

H

habēna, ae, f. rein; thong; whip.

habeō, uī, itum, [2] v. have, hold, possess; contain; handle, use; manage; esteem; regard, treat (as).

habilis, e, a. handy, manageable; apt, fit.

habitābilis, e, a. habitable.

habitātiō, ōnis, f. lodging, residence.

habitātor, ōris, m. dweller, inhabitant.

habitō, [1] v. inhabit, dwell; live (in a place).

habitus, ūs, m. condition, state, dress, 'get-up'; expression, demeanour; character.

hāc, *ad.* by this way; on this side.

hāctenus, *ad.* hitherto; thus far; thus much.

haedus, ī, *m.* kid.

haereō, haesī, haesum, [2] *v.* stick, cling, adhere, be fixed; be in difficulties; doubt; linger.

haesitō, [1] *v.* stick hesitate, be undecided; be stuck.

hālitus, ūs, *m.* breath; steam, vapour.

hālō, [1] *v.* emit (vapour, *etc.*); be fragrant.

Hamadryas, ados, *f.* woodnymph, hamadryad.

hāmātus, a, um, *a.* hooked.

hāmus, ī, *m.* hook; fish-hook; barb of arrow.

hara, ae, *f.* coop, pigsty.

harēna v. **arēna**.

harmonia, ae, *f.* harmony; coupling.

harpagō, ōnis, *m.* grapplinghook.

harundō v. **arundō**.

haruspex, icis, *m.* soothsayer.

hasta, ae, *f.* spear, lance, pike; spear stuck in the ground at public auctions.

hastātus, a, um, *a.* armed with a spear; **hastātī, ōrum,** *m. pl.* first line of a Roman army.

hastīle, is, *nt.* shaft of a spear; spear; cane.

haud, *ad.* not, by no means; **~quāquam,** by no means, in no way.

hauriō, hausī, haustum, [4] *v.* draw (up *or* out); drink; drain; swallow; derive; have one's fill of; experience to the full.

haustus, ūs, *m.* drinking; drink, draught; the drawing (of water).

hebenus, ī, *m. & f.* ebony.

hebeō, [2] *v.* be blunt; be sluggish.

hebes, etis, *a.* blunt, dull; languid; stupid.

hebēscō, [3] *v.* grow blunt *or* feeble.

hebetō, [1] *v.* blunt, make dull; weaken.

hedera, ae, *f.* ivy.

hei, exclamation expressing anguish or similar.

heia, exclamation expressing deprecation, concession, astonishment, urgency.

hēlluō, ōnis, *m.* glutton, squanderer.

hēlluor, ātus, [1] *v. dep.* be a glutton; squander; spend immoderately.

hendecasyllabī, ōrum, *m.* verses consisting of eleven syllables.

hera v. **era**.

herba, ae, *f.* grass; herb.

herbidus, a, um, *a.* grassy.

herbifer, a, um, *a.* full of grass *or* herbs; bearing magical *or* medicinal plants.

hercle, hercule, *i.* by Hercules!

here v. **heri**.

hērēditās, ātis, *f.* heirship; inheritance.

hērēs, ēdis, *m. & f.* heir, heiress.

heri, *ad.* yesterday.

hērōicus, a, um, *a.* heroic, epic.

hērōs, ōos, *m.* hero.

hērōus, a, um, *a.* heroic.

Hesperia, ae, *f.* the western land, Italy.

hesperius, a, um, *a.* western.

Hesperus, ī, *m.* evening-star.

hesternus, a, um, *a.* of yesterday.

heu! *i.* oh! alas!

heus! *i.* ho! ho there! listen!

hiātus, ūs, *m.* opening, cleft; wide-opened jaw.

hīberna, ōrum, *nt. pl.* hībernāculum, ī, *nt.* winter-quarters.

hībernō, [1] *v.* spend the winter; be in winter-quarters.

hībernus, a, um, *a.* of winter, wintry.

(h)ibiscum, ī, *nt.* marsh mallow.

hic, haec, hoc, *pn.* this.

hīc, *ad.* here; in the present circumstances.

hicce, haecce, hocce, *pn.* this.

hiccine, haeccine, hoccine, *pn.* this?

hiemālis, e, *a.* of or belonging to winter, wintry.

hiemō, [1] *v.* pass the winter; be stormy.

hiems, emis, *or* hiemps, emis, *f.* winter; stormy weather.

hilaris, e, hilarus, a, um, *a.* cheerful, lively, light-hearted.

hilaritās, ātis, *f.* cheerfulness, light-heartedness.

hilarō, [1] *v.* gladden.

hinc, *ad.* from this place; henceforth; from this cause.

hinniō, [4] *v.* neigh.

hinnītus, ūs, *m.* neighing.

hiō, [1] *v.* be wide open, gape; be greedy for; be open-mouthed (with astonishment, *etc.*).

hircus, ī, *m.* he-goat.

hirsūtus, a, um, *a.* rough, shaggy, bristly, prickly; rude.

hirtus, a, um, *a.* rough, hairy, shaggy.

hirūdō, inis, *f.* leech.

hirundō, inis, *f.* swallow.

hīscō, [1] *v.* (begin to) open, gape; open the mouth to speak.

hispidus, a, um, *a.* rough, shaggy, hairy; bristly; dirty.

historia, ae, *f.* history; story.

historicus, a, um, *a.* historical.

histriō, ōnis, *m.* actor; performer in pantomime.

hiulcus, a, um, *a.* gaping, cracked.

hodiē, *ad.* today; at the present time.

hodiernus, a, um, *a.* of this day; present.

holus v. olus.

homicīda, ae, *m.* or *f.* murderer; killer of men.

homō, inis, *m.* human being, person; man, woman; fellow; **novus homō,** nouveau riche, upstart.

honestās, ātis, *f.* honourableness, honour; integrity.

honestō, [1] *v.* honour (with); adorn, grace.

honestus, a, um, *a.* worthy; decent; of high rank; honourable; handsome.

honor, honōs, ōris, *m.* honour; regard; office, dignity; grace.

honōrārius, a, um, *a.* complimentary, supplied voluntarily.

honōrificus, a, um, *a.* conferring honour.

honōrō, [1] *v.* honour.

honōrus, a, um, *a.* conferring honour.

honōs, oris, *v.* honor.

hōra, ae, *f.* hour; season (of the year); time; **Hōrae, ārum,** *f. pl.* the Seasons (personified).

hordeum, ī, *nt.* barley.

hornus, a, um, *a.* this year's.

horrendus, a, um, *a.* dreadful, terrible, horrible.

horreō, [2] *v.* stand on end, bristle; have a rough appearance; shiver, tremble; shudder at.

horrēscō, horruī, [3] *v.* bristle up, grow rough; begin to shake; tremble, shudder (at).

horreum, ī, *nt.* storehouse; barn.

horribilis, e, *a.* rough; terrible, horrible; monstrous.

horridus, a, um, *a.* rough, bristly; horrible; unkempt; grim.

horrifer, a, um, horrificus, a, um, *a.* dreadful, frightening; chilling.

horrisonus, a, um, *a.* sounding dreadfully.

horror, ōris, *m.* shivering; dread, awe; rigidity (from cold, *etc.*).

hortāmen, inis, *nt.* encouragement.

hortātiō, ōnis, *m.* encouragement; exhortation.

hortātor, ōris, *m.* encourager; exhorter.

hortātus, ūs, *m.* exhortation.

hortor, ātus, [1] *v. dep.* exhort; encourage.

hortulus, ī, *m.* small garden; (*pl.*) pleasure-grounds.

hortus, ī, *m.* garden; (*pl.*) pleasure-grounds.

hospes, itis, *m.* guest; visitor; host; stranger.

hospita, ae, *f.* female guest, hostess; landlady.

hospitālis, e, *a.* of *or* for a guest; hospitable.

hospitāliter, *ad.* in a hospitable manner.

hospitium, iī, *nt.* hospitality; entertainment; guest accommodation; lodgings.

hostia, ae, *f.* sacrificial animal.

hosticus, a, um, *a.* of *or* belonging to an enemy, hostile.

hostīlis, e, *a.* of an enemy, hostile.

hostis, is, *m.* or *f.* stranger, foreigner; enemy.

hūc, *ad.* hither; to this place; so far.

hūmānitās, ātis, *f.* human nature; civilization; culture; humane character.

hūmāniter, *ad.* moderately; in a friendly manner.

hūmānus, a, um, *a.* human; humane; civilized; considerate.

hūmidus, v. **ūmidus.**

humilis, e, *a.* low; low-lying; mean; humble, lowly.

humilitās, ātis, *f.* lowness; meanness; insignificance.

humō, [1] *v.* inter, bury.

hūmor, ōris, v. **ūmor.**

humus, ī, *f.* earth, soil, ground; **humī,** *ad.* on the ground.

hyacinthus, ī, *m.* hyacinth; sapphire.

Hyades, um, *f. pl.* group of five stars in the constellation of Taurus associated with rainy weather.

hyalus, ī, *m.* glass.

hydra, ae, *f.* water-serpent; snake.

hydrops, ōpis, *m.* dropsy.

hydrus, ī, *m.* water-snake.

Hymen, enis, Hymenaeus, ī, *m.* god of marriage; marriage; wedding-refrain.

hypocauston, ī, *nt.* system of hot-air channels for heating baths.

I

iaceō, cuī, [2] *v.* lie; be situated; be still; lie still; lie dead; lie in ruins.

iaciō, iēcī, iactum, [3] *v.* throw, cast, hurl; throw away; utter; pile up (structures).

iactanter, *ad.* arrogantly.

iactantia, ae, *f.* boasting, ostentation.

iactātiō, ōnis, *f.* shaking; boasting; showing off.

iactō, [1] *v.* throw, hurl; toss; utter with force; boast (of); torment; **sē iactāre,** to glory (in)

iactūra, ae, *f.* throwing (away, overboard); loss; cost.

iactus, ūs, *m.* throwing, throw, cast.

iaculātor, ōris, *m.* javelin-thrower.

iaculor, ātus, [1] *v. dep.* throw a javelin; hurl; shoot at.

iaculum, ī, *nt.* dart, javelin.

iam, *ad.* now, already.

iānitor, ōris, *m.* door-keeper, porter.

iānua, ae, *f.* door, house-door; entrance.

Iānuārius, ī, *m.* January.

Iānus, ī, *m.* a Roman god of gates and doorways.

iaspis, idis, *f.* jasper.

ibi, *ad.* there

ibidem, *ad.* in that very place; at that very instant.

ībis, idis *or* **is,** *f.* ibis (Egyptian bird).

īc(i)ō, īcī, ictum, [3] *v.* hit, strike; conclude a treaty.

ictus, ūs, *m.* blow, stroke; musical *or* metrical beat.

idcircō, *ad.* therefore, for that reason.

īdem, eadem, idem, *pn.* the same.

identidem, *ad.* continually; repeatedly; again and again.

ideō, *ad.* for the reason (that); for that reason, therefore.

idōneus, a, um, *a.* fit, suitable; able.

Īdūs, uum, *f. pl.* 15th day of March, May, July, October, 13th day of the other months.

iecur, iecoris, iecinoris, *nt.* liver.

iēiūnus, a, um, *a.* fasting; hungry; barren; insignificant; poor; uninteresting.

igitur, *ad.* therefore.

ignārus, a, um, *a.* ignorant (of), having no experience of; unknown.

ignāvia, ae, *f.* laziness; faintheartedness.

ignāvus, a, um, *a.* idle, sluggish; cowardly.

ignēscō, [3] *v.* take fire, kindle; become inflamed (with passion).

igneus, a, um, *a.* of fire; fiery; ardent.

ignifer, a, um, *a.* bearing *or* containing fire.

ignipotēns, entis, *a.* god of fire.

ignis, is, *m.* fire; brightness; glow of passion.

ignōbilis, e, *a.* unknown; ignoble; obscure; of low birth.

ignōbilitās, ātis, *f.* obscurity.

ignōminia, ae, *f.* ignominy, dishonour.

ignōminiōsus, a, um, *a.* disgraced; disgraceful.

ignōrantia, ae, *f.* ignorance.

ignōrātiō, ōnis, *f.* ignorance.

ignōrō, [1] *v.* be ignorant of; fail to recognize.

ignōscō, nōvī, nōtum, [3] *v. with dat.* forgive, pardon.

ignōtus, a, um, *a.* unknown; ignorant (of).

īlex, icis, *f.* holm-oak.

īlia, ium, *nt. pl.* side part of the body extending from the hips down to the groin; private parts; inwards.

īlignus, a, um, *a.* of the holm-oak.

illābor, psus, [3] *v. dep.* slide *or* flow (into); fall *or* sink (onto).

illacrimābilis, e, *a.* unlamented; inexorable.

illacrimō, [1] *v.* **illacrimor, ātus,** [1] *v. dep.* bewail, lament.

illaesus, a, um, *a.* uninjured; inviolate.

illaetābilis, e, *a.* joyless.

illaqueō, [1] *v.* ensnare, entangle.

ille, a, ud, illius, *pn.* he, she; it; that; the well-known; the former.

illecebra, ae, *f.* allurement, enticement.

illepidus, a, um, *a.* lacking grace *or* refinement.

illīc, *ad.* there, over there.

illiciō, lexī, lectum, [3] *v.* allure, entice.

illicitus, a, um, *a.* forbidden, unlawful, illicit.

illīdō, sī, sum, [3] *v.* strike *or* dash against.

illigō, [1] *v.* bind *or* tie up; bind.

illinc, *ad.* thence; on that side.

illinō, lēvī, litum, [3] *v.* smear over; anoint.

illō, *ad.* thither; to that point.

illūc, *ad.* thither.

illūcēscō, lūxī, [3] *v.* begin to dawn.

illūdō, sī, sum, [3] *v.* speak mockingly of; trick out; use for sexual pleasure.

illūminō, [1] *v.* light up; brighten.

illūstris, e, *a.* clear, bright; famous.

illūstrō, [1] *v.* illuminate; make famous *or* illustrious; make clear.

illuviēs, ēī, *f.* dirt, filth; filthy condition.

imāgō, inis, *f.* image, likeness; idea; appearance; echo; ghost, phantom.

imbēcillitās, ātis, *f.* weakness, feebleness; moral *or* intellectual weakness.

imbēcillus, a, um, *a.* weak, feeble.

imbellis, e, *a.* unwarlike; not suited *or* ready for war.

imber, bris, *m.* (shower of) rain; (any) liquid; shower of missiles.

imberbis, e, *a.* beardless.

imbibō, bī, [3] *v.* imbibe, absorb into one's mind.

imbrex, icis, *f. or m.* tile.

imbrifer, a, um, *a.* rain-bringing, rainy.

imbuō, uī, ūtum, [3] *v.* wet, soak; give initial instruction (in).

imitābilis, e, *a.* that may be imitated.

imitāmen, inis, *nt.* imitation; copy.

imitātiō, ōnis, *f.* imitation; mimicking; copy.

imitātor, ōris, *m.* one who imitates *or* copies.

imitātrīx, īcis, *f.* female imitator.

imitor, ātus, [1] *v. dep.* imitate; simulate; copy; resemble.

immadēscō, duī, [3] *v.* become wet *or* moist.

immānis, e, *a.* huge, vast, immense, monstrous; inhuman, savage.

immānitās, ātis, *f.* hugeness, vastness; brutality; barbarity.

immānsuētus, a, um, *a.* savage.

immātūrus, a, um, *a.* unripe, immature, untimely.

immedicābilis, e, *a.* incurable.

immemor, oris, *a.* forgetful; heedless.

immēnsus, a, um, *a.* endless, vast, immense; **immēnsum,** *ad.* to an enormous extent *or* degree.

immerēns, entis, *a.* undeserving (of ill-treatment); blameless.

immergō, sī, sum, [3] *v.* plunge into, immerse.

**immeritō, ** *ad.* unjustly; without cause.

immeritus, a, um, *a.* undeserving; undeserved.

immigrō, [1] *v.* move (into).

immineō, [2] *v.* overhang; threaten, be imminent; be a threat (to).

imminuō, uī, ūtum, [3] *v.* diminish; impair.

immīsceō, scuī, xtum & stum, [2] *v.* mix in, mingle; confuse.

immītis, e, *a.* harsh, sour; merciless.

immittō, mīsī, missum, [3] *v.* send (to); admit; throw (into); put in; give the rein to.

immō, *ad.* rather, more correctly.

immōbilis, e, *a.* immovable; unalterable.

immoderātus, a, um, *a.* unlimited; immoderate; disorderly.

immodicus, a, um, *a.* excessive, immoderate.

immolō, [1] *v.* offer (a victim) in sacrifice.

immorior, mortuus, [3] *dep. with dat.* die in (in a particular place, position, *etc.*).

immortālis, e, *a.* immortal; eternal.

immortālitās, ātis, *f.* immortality.

immōtus, a, um, *a.* unmoved, immovable; unchanged; inflexible.

immūgiō, īvī & iī, [4] *v.* bellow.

immundus, a, um, *a.* unclean, impure, filthy.

immūnis, e, *a.* exempt from tribute *or* taxation; free *or* exempt from.

immūnitās, ātis, *f.* freedom, community.

immūnītus, a, um, *a.* unfortified.

immurmurō, [1] *v.* murmur, mutter (at *or* to).

immūtābilis, e, *a.* unchangeable.

immūtō, [1] *v.* change, alter.

impācātus, a, um, *a.* not pacified.

impār, aris, *a.* uneven, unequal; inferior.

imparātus, a, um, *a.* not prepared; unready.

impatiēns, entis, *a.* impatient (of).

impatientia, ae, *f.* impatience.

impavidus, a, um, *a.* fearless, intrepid.

impedīmentum, ī, *nt.* hindrance, impediment; baggage of an army.

impediō, īvī & iī, ītum, [4] *v.* entangle; hamper; hinder.

impedītus, a, um, *a.* obstructed; not easily passable; difficult.

impellō, pulī, pulsum, [3] *v.* push *or* thrust against; impel; urge on.

impendeō, [2] *v.* hang over; impend; threaten.

impendium, iī, *nt.* expense, expenditure, payment.

impendō, dī, sum, [3] *v.* expend, spend; devote (to).

impēnsa, ae, *f.* outlay, cost, expense.

impēnsē, *ad.* without stint; lavishly.

impēnsus, a, um, *a.* immoderate, excessive.

imperātor, ōris, *m.* commander-in-chief; person in charge, ruler.

imperātōrius, a, um, *a.* of *or* belonging to a commanding officer; imperial.

imperātum, ī, *nt.* command, order.

imperfectus, a, um, *a.* unfinished, imperfect; not complete in every respect.

imperiōsus, a, um, *a.* masterful; domineering; dictatorial.

imperītia, ae, *f.* inexperience, ignorance.

imperītō, [1] *v.* command, govern.

imperītus, a, um, *a.* inexperienced (in), unskilled, ignorant (of).

imperium, iī, *nt.* command; rule; empire; supreme power.

imperō, [1] *v. with dat.* command, rule (over).

imperterritus, a, um, *a.* fearless.

impertiō, īvī & iī, ītum, [4] *v.* impart; give a share of.

impervius, a, um, *a.* impassable.

impetrābilis, e, *a.* easy to achieve *or* obtain.

impetrō, [1] *v.* get, obtain by request.

impetus, ūs, *m.* assault, attack; vigour; violent mental urge.

impexus, a, um, *a.* uncombed.

impietās, ātis, *f.* failure in duty *or* respect, *etc.*

impiger, gra, grum *a.* active, energetic.

impingō, pēgī, pāctum, [3] *v.* thrust, strike *or* dash against.

impius, a, um, *a.* irreverent; wicked; impious.

implācābilis, e, *a.* relentless, irreconcilable.

implācātus, a, um, *a.* not appeased, insatiable.

implacidus, a, um, *a.* restless, unquiet.

impleō, ēvī, ētum, [2] *v.* fill; fulfil.

implicō, āvī, ātum & uī, itum, [1] *v.* enfold; involve; encumber; entangle; **implicor,** *pass.*, be intimately connected with.

implōrō, [1] *v.t.* invoke, entreat, appeal to; ask for (help, protection, favours, *etc.*).

implūmis, e, *a.* unfledged.

impluvium, iī, *nt.* quadrangular basin in the floor of an atrium which receives the rain-water from the roof.

impōnō, suī, situm, [3] *v.* put upon *or* in; impose; assign; place in command *or* control (of).

importō, [1] *v.* bring *or* convey in, import; bring about, cause.

importūnitās, ātis, *f.* persistent lack of consideration for others; relentlessness.

importūnus, a, um, *a.* inconvenient; troublesome.

importuōsus, a, um, *a.* having no harbours.

impotēns, entis, *a.* powerless, impotent, wild, headstrong;

having no control (over), incapable (of).

impotentia, ae, *f.* weakness; immoderate behaviour, violence.

imprecor, ātus, [1] *v. dep.* call down upon, pray for; utter curses.

impressiō, ōnis, *f.* push, thrust, assault.

imprīmīs, *ad.* especially, above all; firstly.

imprimō, pressī, pressum, [3] *v.* impress, imprint; press upon; stamp.

improbitās, ātis, *f.* want of principle, shamelessness.

improbō, [1] *v.* express disapproval of, condemn.

improbus, a, um, *a.* morally unsound; disloyal; ill-disposed. shameless; excessive; presumptuous.

imprōvidus, a, um, *a.* improvident; thoughtless, unwary.

imprōvīsus, a, um, *a.* unforeseen, unexpected.

imprūdēns, entis, *a.* ignorant; foolish; unwarned.

imprūdentia, ae, *f.* imprudence; ignorance.

impūbēs, eris & is, *a.* below the age of puberty; beardless.

impudēns, entis, *a.* shameless, impudent.

impudentia, ae, *f.* shamelessness, effrontery.

impudīcitia, ae, *f.* sexual impurity (often of homosexuality).

impudīcus, a, um, *a.* unchaste, flouting the accepted sexual code.

impugnō, [1] *v.* fight against, attack, assail.

impulsor, ōris, *m.* instigator.

impulsus, ūs, *m.* shock, impact; incitement.

impūne, *ad.* safely, with impunity; scot-free.

impūnitās, ātis, *f.* impunity.

impūnītus, a, um, *a.* unpunished.

impūrus, a, um, *a.* unclean, filthy, foul; impure; morally foul.

imputō, [1] *v.* impute, charge; ascribe.

īmus, a, um, *a.* inmost, deepest, bottommost.

in, *pr.* (*with acc.*) to; into; against; for; towards; until; ~ **diēs,** day by day, every day; (*with abl.*) at; in; on; within; among.

inaccessus, a, um, *a.* inaccessible.

inaedificō, [1] *v.* build (in a place); wall up.

inaequālis, e, *a.* uneven; unequal.

inaestimābilis, e, *a.* beyond all price.

inamābilis, e, *a.* disagreeable, unattractive.

inambulō, [1] *v.* walk up and down.

inamoenus, a, um, *a.* unlovely, disagreeable.

inanimus, a, um, *a.* lifeless, inanimate.

inānis, e, empty, void; foolish; **ināne, is,** *nt.* the void; **ināniō, īvī** *or* **iī, ītum,** [4] *v.* empty.

inarātus, a, um, *a.* unploughed, untilled.

inardēscō, rsī, [3] *v.* kindle, take fire; become glowing.

inassuētus, a, um, *a.* unaccustomed.

inaudītus, a, um, *a.* unheard (of), novel, new.

inaugurō, [1] *v.* take omens by the flight of birds; consecrate by augury.

inaurō, [1] *v.* gild, make rich.

inausus, a, um, *a.* undared.

inb. . . v. imb. . .

incaeduus, a, um, *a.* not felled.

incalēscō, luī, [3] *v.* grow hot; become heated.

incallidus, a, um, *a.* not shrewd, simple.

incandēscō, duī, [3] *v.* become red-hot.

incānēscō, nuī, [3] *v.* turn grey *or* hoary.

incānus, a, um, *a.* quite grey, hoary.

incassum, *ad.* without effect, to no purpose.

incautus, a, um, *a.* incautious, off one's guard; unprotected.

incēdō, cessī, cessum, [3] *v.* step, walk, march along; advance; befall.

incelebrātus, a, um, *a.* unrecorded.

incendium, iī, *nt.* fire, conflagration; passion; fiery heat.

incendō, dī, sum, [3] *v.* set fire to, kindle; inflame; aggravate.

incēnsus, a, um, *a.* not registered at a census.

inceptum, ī, *nt.* beginning, undertaking.

incertus, a, um, *a.* uncertain; doubtful, inconstant; variable.

incessō, cessīvī & cessī, [3] *v.* assault, attack; reproach, abuse.

incessus, ūs, *m.* walking; advance; procession.

incestō, [1] *v.* pollute, defile.

incestus, a, um, *a.* unchaste; unholy.

incidō, cidī, cāsum, [3] *v.* fall (into); meet (with); arise, occur.

incīdō, cīdī, cīsum, [3] *v.* cut into; make an end to; engrave.

incingō, xī, ctum, [3] *v.* gird (with); wrap (tightly) round (with).

incipiō, cēpī, ceptum, [3] *v.* begin; undertake.

incitāmentum, ī, *nt.* incentive, stimulus.

incitātus, a, um, *a.* fast-moving, aroused, passionate; **equō incitātō**, at full gallop.

incitō, [1] *v.* incite; stir up, spur on; set in rapid motion.

incitus, a, um, *a.* rushing, headlong.

inclāmō, [1] *v.* cry out (to), call upon; abuse, revile.

inclēmēns, entis, *a.* harsh.

inclēmentia, ae, *f.* harshness.

inclīnātiō, ōnis, *f.* the act of leaning; tendency, inclination.

inclīnō, [1] *v.* bend; lower; incline; decay; grow worse; set (of the sun); deject.

inclitus, a, um, *a.* renowned, famous, celebrated.

inclūdō, sī, sum, [3] *v.* shut in or up; enclose.

inclutus, inclytus v. **inclitus**.

incognitus, a, um, *a.* not known, untried; untested.

incohō, [1] *v.* start; set going.

incola, ae, *m.* or *f.* inhabitant; resident alien.

incolō, luī, [3] *v.* dwell in, inhabit.

incolumis, e, *a.* uninjured, safe; unimpaired.

incolumitās, ātis, *f.* safety.

incomitātus, a, um, *a.* unaccompanied.

incommodum, ī, *nt.* inconvenience; misfortune; set-back.

incommodus, a, um, *a.* inconvenient, troublesome; disadvantageous, disagreeable.

incompertus, a, um, *a.* not known.

incompositus, a, um, *a.* clumsy, disorganized.

incōmptus, a, um, *a.* dishevelled; untidy; unpolished.

inconcessus, a, um, *a.* forbidden.

inconcinnus, a, um, *a.* awkward; clumsy.

inconditus, a, um, *a.* rough, crude; uncivilized; disordered, not disciplined.

incōnstāns, antis, *a.* changeable, fickle.

incōnstantia, ae, *f.* changeableness; fickleness.

incōnsultus, a, um, *a.* rash, ill-advised.

incontinēns, entis, *a.* intemperate.

incoquō, xī, ctum, [3] *v.* boil in *or* down; boil.

incorruptus, a, um, *a.* unspoilt, uncorrupted.

increbrēscō, bruī, [3] become stronger *or* more intense; spread.

incredibilis, e, *a.* incredible.

incredulus, a, um, *a.* disbelieving.

incrēmentum, ī, *nt.* growth, increase.

increpitō, [1] *v.* chide, utter (noisy) reproaches at.

increpō, uī, itum, [1] *v.* make a sharp, loud noise; protest at; remark indignantly.

incrēscō, ēvī, [3] *v.* grow (in *or* upon).

incruentus, a, um, *a.* bloodless, without shedding of blood.

incubō, (uī,) itum, [1] *v. with dat.* lie in *or* on; sit upon; brood over; keep a jealous watch (over).

incūdō, dī, sum, [3] *v.* hammer out.

inculcō, [1] *v.* force upon, impress, drive home.

incultus, a, um, *a.* uncultivated; unkempt; rough, uncouth.

incultus, ūs, *m.* want of cultivation *or* refinement; uncouthness, disregard.

incumbō, cubuī, cubitum, [3] *v.* lay oneself upon, lean *or* recline upon; apply oneself earnestly (to).

incūnābula, ōrum, *nt. pl.* the apparatus of the cradle; one's earliest years; birth-place.

incūria, ae, *f.* carelessness, neglect.

incūriōsus, a, um, *a.* careless, negligent; indifferent.

incurrō, currī (cucurrī), cursum, [3] *v.* run into *or* towards, attack, invade; meet (with); befall.

incursiō, ōnis, *f.* attack; raid.

incursō, [1] *v.* run against, dash against, attack; make raids upon.

incursus, ūs, *m.* attack, raid.

incurvō, [1] *v.* make crooked *or* bent; cause to bend down.

incurvus, a, um, *a.* crooked, curved.

incūs, ūdis, *f.* anvil.

incūsō, [1] *v.* blame; criticize; condemn.

incustōdītus, a, um, *a.* not watched over; unsuspected.

incutiō, cussī, cussum, [3] *v.* strike on *or* against; instil.

indāgō, inis, *f.* ring of huntsmen *or* nets.

inde, *ad.* thence, from that place; from that time; from that cause; thenceforwards; next.

indēbitus, a, um, *a.* that is not owed, not due.

indecoris, e, *a.* inglorious, shameful.

indecorō, [1] *v.* disgrace.

indecōrus, a, um, *a.* unbecoming, unseemly; ugly.

indēfēnsus, a, um, *a.* undefended; defenceless.

indēfessus, a, um, *a.* unwearied; indefatigable.

indemnātus, a, um, *a.* uncondemned.

index, icis, *m. or f.* informer, talebearer; sign, token.

indicium, iī, *nt.* information; token; disclosure; evidence (before a court).

indicō, [1] *v.* betray; reveal; give information.

indīcō, xī, ctum, [3] *v.* declare publicly; inflict (on) by one's pronouncement.

indictus, a, um, *a.* not said *or* mentioned; **indictā causā,**

without the case's being pleaded; unheard.

indidem, *ad.* from the same place, source *or* origin.

indigena, ae, *m.* native.

indigēns, entis, *a.* needy, indigent.

indigeō, uī, [2] *v.* need, require; lack.

indīgestus, a, um, *a.* chaotic; jumbled.

Indigitēs, um, *m. pl.* deified heroes, tutelary deities (local as opposed to foreign gods).

indignātiō, ōnis, *f.* indignation; anger; angry outburst.

indignitās, ātis, *f.* unworthiness, shamelessness; baseness; humiliation.

indignor, ātus, [1] *v. dep.* regard with indignation, resent; be indignant.

indignus, a, um, *a.* unworthy, undeserving; undeserved; shameful.

indigus, a, um, *a.* having need (of); lacking; needy.

indīligēns, entis, *a.* careless, negligent.

indīligentia, ae, *f.* negligence, want of care; want of concern (for).

indipīscor, deptus, [3] *v. dep.* overtake; acquire.

indiscrētus, a, um, *a.* indistinguishable.

indō, didī, ditum, [3] *v.* put in *or* on; introduce.

indocilis, e, *a.* unteachable, ignorant.

indoctus, a, um, *a.* untaught; unlearned; ignorant; untrained.

indolēs, is, *f.* innate character; inborn quality.

indolēscō, uī, [3] *v.* feel pain of mind; grieve.

indomitus, a, um, *a.* untamed; untamable; fierce.

indormiō, īvī, ītum, [4] *v.* sleep (in *or* over).

indōtātus, a, um, *a.* not provided with a dowry.

indubitō, [1] *v.* have misgivings (about).

indūcō, xī, ctum, [3] *v.* lead *or* conduct into; bring in; bring (performers) into the arena, on to the stage, *etc.*; introduce; put on; persuade; spread (with).

inductiō, ōnis, *f.* leading *or* bringing in; application.

indulgēns, entis, *a.* kind, mild.

indulgentia, ae, *f.* kindness; gentleness.

indulgeō, sī, tum, [2] *v. with dat.* be kind *or* lenient (to); grant; give way to; accede (to).

induō, uī, ūtum, [3] *v.* put on; dress oneself in; assume; fall *or* be impaled (upon).

indūrō, [1] *v.* make hard.

industria, ae, *f.* diligence, assiduity, industry; **dē** *or* **ex ~,** on purpose.

industrius, a, um, *a.* diligent, assiduous, industrious.

indūtiae, ārum, *f. pl.* truce, armistice.

inedia, ae, *f.* fasting, starvation.

inēlegāns, antis, *a.* lacking in taste; clumsy, infelicitous.

inēluctābilis, e, *a.* from which there is no escape.

inēmptus, a, um, *a.* not bought.

inēnarrābilis, e, *a.* indescribable.

ineō, īvī & iī, itum, [4] *v.* go into, enter (into *or* upon); commence; form a plan.

ineptus, a, um, *a.* silly, foolish; having no sense of what is fitting.

inermis, e, *a.* unarmed, defenceless; *fig.* unprepared.

iners, ertis, *a.* unskilful; sluggish; unadventurous; feeble.

inertia, ae, *f.* unskilfulness; idleness, sloth.

inēvītābilis, e, *a.* unavoidable.

inexcūsābilis, e, *a.* inexcusable.

inexōrābilis, e, *a.* inexorable, relentless.

inexpertus, a, um, *a.* inexperienced (in); untried.

inexpiābilis, e, *a.* inexpiable; implacable.

inexplēbilis, e, *a.* insatiable.

inexplōrātus, a, um, *a.* unexplored; not investigated.

inexpugnābilis, e, *a.* impregnable; invincible.

inexspectātus, a, um, *a.* unforeseen.

inexstīnctus, a, um, *a.* that is never extinguished.

inex(s)uperābilis, e, *a.* insurmountable; invincible; unsurpassable.

inextrīcābilis, e, *a.* impossible to disentangle *or* sort out.

īnfabrē, *ad.* without art, crudely.

īnfacētus, a, um, *a.* coarse, boorish.

īnfācundus, a, um, *a.* unable to express oneself fluently.

īnfāmia, ae, *f.* ill-fame, dishonour.

īnfāmis, e, *a.* disreputable, infamous.

īnfāmō, [1] *v.* bring into disrepute; defame.

īnfandus, a, um, *a.* unutterable, abominable.

īnfāns, antis, *a.* speechless; inarticulate; newly born, young; ~, *m.* or *f.* little child.

īnfantia, ae, *f.* infancy; inability to speak.

īnfaustus, a, um, *a.* unlucky, unfortunate; inauspicious.

īnfectus, a, um, *a.* not done, unmade; unfinished, impossible.

īnfēcunditās, ātis, *f.* barrenness.

īnfēcundus, a, um, *a.* unfruitful, infertile.

īnfēlīcitās, ātis, *f.* misfortune.

īnfēlīx, īcis, *a.* unfortunate, unhappy; unproductive.

īnfēnsus, a, um, *a.* hostile, bitterly hostile, enraged.

īnferiae, ārum, *f. pl.* offerings to the dead.

īnferior v. **īnferus.**

īnferius v. **īnfrā.**

īnfernus, a, um, *a.* lower; infernal.

īnferō, īnferre, intulī, illātum, [3] *v.* bring into *or* upon; bring forward (with hostile intention); produce, cause; inflict; bury.

īnferus, a, um, *a.* below, underneath, lower; **īnferī, ōrum**, *m. pl.* the dead; **inferior, ius,** lower; later; inferior; **īnfimus, īmus,** lowest.

īnfestus, a, um, *a.* hostile; dangerous; disturbed.

īnficiō, fēcī, fectum, [3] *v.* dye; stain; infect; imbue; corrupt.

īnfidēlis, e, *a.* treacherous, disloyal.

īnfidēlitās, ātis, *f.* faithlessness; inconstancy.

īnfīdus, a, um, *a.* faithless; treacherous.

īnfīgō, xī, xum, [3] *v.* fix, thrust in; fasten on.

īnfimus, a, um v. **īnferus.**

īnfindō, fidī, fissum, [3] *v.* cleave; plough a path into.

īnfīnītus, a, um, *a.* boundless, endless, infinite in quantity or amount.

īnfirmitās, ātis, *f.* weakness; sickness.

īnfirmō, [1] v. weaken; diminish; annul.

īnfirmus, a, um, a. weak, feeble; sickly; irresolute.

īnfit, v. def. he (or she) begins (to speak).

īnfitior, ātus, [1] v. dep. deny, disown.

īnflammō, [1] v. set on fire, kindle; excite; inflame.

īnflātus, a, um, a. puffed up; turgid, bombastic.

īnflectō, xī, xum, [3] v. bend; curve; change.

īnflīgō, xī, ctum, [3] v. knock or dash (against); inflict, impose.

īnflō, [1] v. blow into or upon; puff out.

īnfluō, xī, xum, [3] v. flow into.

īnfodiō, fōdī, fossum, [3] v. bury, inter.

īnfōrmis, e, a. shapeless; deformed, ugly.

īnfōrmō, [1] v. shape, form; fashion; form an idea of.

īnfortūnium, iī, nt. misfortune, punishment.

īnfrā, ad. & pr. with acc. below, underneath; under; later (than); less (than).

īnfrāctus, a, um, a. broken; humble in tone.

īnfremō, uī, [3] v. bellow, roar.

īnfrendō, [3] v. gnash the teeth (usually in anger).

īnfrēnis, e, īnfrēnus, a, um, a. not bridled; unrestrained.

īnfrēnō, [1] v. bridle.

īnfrequēns, entis, a. not crowded; below strength; present only in small numbers.

īnfrequentia, ae, f. insufficient numbers; depopulated condition (of a place).

īnfringō, frēgī, frāctum, [3] v. break, crush; weaken; diminish, dishearten; foil, invalidate.

īnfula, ae, f. woollen headband knotted with ribands.

īnfundō, fūdī, fūsum, [3] v. pour into or on; pour out.

īnfuscō, [1] v. darken; corrupt.

ingeminō, [1] v. redouble; increase in intensity.

ingemō, uī, [3] v. groan (over).

ingenerō, [1] v. implant.

ingeniōsus, a, um, a. clever, ingenious; naturally suited (to).

ingenium, (i)ī, nt. innate quality, nature; natural disposition; capacity; talent; gifted writer.

ingēns, entis, a. vast, huge; great; momentous.

ingenuus, a, um, a. indigenous, natural; free-born; generous; frank.

ingerō, gessī, gestum, [3] v. throw upon; heap on; obtrude; force or thrust on a person.

inglōrius, a, um, a. obscure, undistinguished.

ingluviēs, ēī, f. gullet, jaws; gluttony.

ingrātiīs, ingrātīs, *ad.* against the wishes (of); unwillingly.

ingrātus, a, um, *a.* unpleasant; unthankful.

ingravēscō, [3] *v.* grow heavy; increase in force *or* intensity.

ingravō, [1] *v.* aggravate, make worse.

ingredior, gressus sum, [3] *v. dep.* step *or* go into, enter; begin; walk.

ingruō, uī, [3] *v.* advance threateningly; make an onslaught (upon).

inguen, inis, *nt.* groin; the sexual organs.

inhabilis, e, *a.* difficult to handle; not fitted; awkward.

inhaereō, haesī, haesum, [2] *v.* stick in, cling (to); be firmly attached (to).

inhibeō, uī, itum, [2] *v.* restrain, curb; prevent.

inhiō, [1] *v.* gape; be open-mouthed with astonishment; covet.

inhonestō, [1] *v.* disgrace.

inhonestus, a, um, *a.* shameful; of ill repute.

inhonōrātus, a, um, *a.* not honoured.

inhorrēscō, horruī, [3] *v.* bristle up; quiver; tremble, shudder at.

inhūmānitās, ātis, *f.* churlishness.

inhūmānus, a, um, *a.* inhuman; uncivilized, churlish.

inhumātus, a, um, *a.* unburied.

iniciō, iēcī, iectum, [3] *v.* throw in *or* into; put on; instil (a feeling, *etc.*) in the mind.

inimīcitia, ae, *f.* hostility, enmity.

inimīcus, a, um, *a.* hostile, inimical, harmful; ~, ī, *m.* enemy, foe.

inīquitās, ātis, *f.* inequality; unfairness; unevenness of terrain.

inīquus, a, um, *a.* unequal, uneven; disadvantageous; unjust; unkind; hostile.

initiō, [1] *v.* initiate (into); admit (to) with introductory rites.

initium, iī, *nt.* beginning; **ab initiō**, from the beginning.

initus, ūs, *m.* entry, start.

iniūcundus, a, um, *a.* unpleasant.

iniungō, xī, ctum, [3] *v.* join *or* fasten (to); attach to; impose (upon).

iniūrātus, a, um, *a.* unsworn.

iniūria, ae, *f.* wrong, injury; abuse, insult; offence; sexual assault.

iniūriōsus, a, um, *a.* wrongful, insulting.

iniūrius, a, um, *a.* unjust, harsh.

iniussū, *ad. with gen.* without (the) orders (of).

iniussus, a, um, *a.* unbidden.

iniūstus, a, um, *a.* unjust, wrongful; severe; excessive, unsuitable.

innāscor, nātus sum, [3] *v. dep.* be born (in *or* on).

innatō, [1] *v.* swim (in *or* on); swim (into); float upon.

innātus, a, um, *a.* natural, inborn.

innāvigābilis, e, *a.* unnavigable.

innectō, xuī, xum, [3] *v.* tie, fasten (to); devise, weave (plots).

innītor, nīxus & nīsus, [3] *v. dep. with dat.* lean *or* rest (upon).

innō, [1] *v.* swim *or* float (in *or* on); sail (on).

innocēns, tis, *a.* harmless; innocent; virtuous.

innocentia, ae, *f.* harmlessness; innocence; integrity.

innocuus, a, um, *a.* harmless; innocent.

innōtēscō, nōtuī, [3] *v.* become known.

innoxius, a, um, *a.* harmless, innocuous; innocent; unhurt.

innūbō, nūpsī, [3] *v. with dat.* marry (into a family).

innumerābilis, e, *a.* countless.

innumerus, a, um, *a.* numberless.

innuō, uī, ūtum, [3] *v.* nod *or* beckon (to).

innūptus, a, um, *a.* unmarried.

inobservābilis, e, *a.* difficult to trace.

inobservātus, a, um, *a.* unobserved.

inoffēnsus, a, um, *a.* free from hindrance; uninterrupted.

inolēscō, ēvī, olitum, [3] *v. with dat.* grow in *or* on.

inopia, ae, *f.* want, scarcity; destitution; dearth.

inopīnāns, antis, *a.* not expecting, off one's guard.

inopīnātus, a, um, *a.* unexpected, unforeseen.

inopīnus, a, um, *a.* unexpected.

inops, opis, *a.* destitute (of), needy; helpless; poor, meagre.

inōrnātus, a, um, *a.* unadorned; uncelebrated.

inp . . . v. imp . . .

inquam v. inquiō.

inquiēs, ētis, *a.* restless, impatient; full of tumult.

inquiētus, a, um, *a.* restless; sleepless.

inquinō, [1] *v.* daub; stain, pollute; soil; 'smear'.

inquiō, [3] *v.* **inquam**, I say; **inquit**, he says.

inquīrō, quīsīvī, quīsītum, [3] *v.* search out; inquire into.

inquīsītiō, ōnis, *f.* search; inquiry.

īnsānābilis, e, *a.* incurable; irremediable.

īnsānia, ae, *f.* madness, folly; mad extravagance.

īnsāniō, īvī, & iī, ītum, [4] *v.* be mad, act crazily.

īnsānus, a, um, *a.* mad, insane; frenzied; wild.

īnsatiābilis, e, *a.* insatiable.

īnsciēns, entis, *a.* not knowing, unaware.

īnscientia, ae, *f.* **īnscītia, ae**, *f.* ignorance.

īnscītus, a, um, *a.* ignorant: uninformed.

īnscius, a, um, *a.* not knowing, ignorant; unskilled.

īnscrībō, psī, ptum, [3] *v.* write in or on, inscribe; brand; record as.

īnscrīptiō, ōnis, *f.* inscription.

īnsculpō, psī, ptum, [3] *v.* carve (in or on), engrave; engrave on the mind.

īnsecō, uī, ctum, [1] *v.* cut; incise.

īnsectātiō, ōnis, *f.* hostile pursuit; criticism.

īnsectō, [1] *v.*, **īnsector, ātus sum**, [1] *v. dep.* pursue with hostile intent; pursue with hostile speech, *etc.*

īnsenēscō, nuī, [3] *v.* grow old in; wane.

īnsepultus, a, um, *a.* unburied.

īnsequor, cūtus, [3] *v. dep.* follow closely, pursue; persecute; come after in time.

īnserō, sēvī, situm, [3] *v.* sow or plant in; graft on; implant.

īnserō, seruī, sertum, [3] *v.* put in; insert.

īnsertō, [1] *v.* thrust in, introduce.

īnserviō, īvī, ītum, [4] *v. with dat.* serve the interests of; take care of.

īnsideō, sēdī, sessum, [2] *v.* sit (at or on); lie in ambush (in); be troublesome (to).

īnsidiae, ārum, *f. pl.* ambush; plot, snare.

īnsidiātor, ōris, *m.* one who lies in wait (to attack, rob, *etc.*).

īnsidior, ātus sum, [1] *v. dep.* lie in ambush.

īnsidiōsus, a, um, *a.* deceitful; insidious; hazardous.

īnsīdō, sēdī, sessum, [3] *v.* sit down in or on, settle on; take possession of; be firmly implanted in.

īnsigne, is, *nt.* mark, emblem; badge of honour.

īnsigniō, īvī, ītum, [4] *v.* mark with a characteristic feature; distinguish.

īnsignis, e, *a.* notable; famous; remarkable; manifest.

īnsiliō, uī, [3] *v.* leap into or on.

īnsimulō, [1] *v.* accuse, charge; allege.

īnsincērus, a, um, *a.* corrupt; not genuine.

īnsinuō, [1] *v.* work in; insinuate; creep into.

īnsistō, stitī, [3] *v.* stand or tread on; stop; persevere (with); set about.

īnsociābilis, e, *a.* intractable, implacable.

īnsolēns, entis, *a.* unaccustomed (to); arrogant; insolent; excessive.

īnsolentia, ae, *f.* unfamiliarity; strangeness; haughtiness; extravagance.

īnsolēscō, [3] *v.* grow proud.

īnsolitus, a, um, *a.* unaccustomed (to).

īnsomnis, e, *a.* sleepless.

īnsomnium, iī, *nt.* wakefulness; vision, dream.

īnsonō, uī, itum, [1] *v.* make a loud noise; sound; resound.

īnsōns, ontis, *a.* guiltless; harmless.

īnsōpītus, a, um, *a.* unsleeping, wakeful.

īnspectō, [1] *v.* look at, observe; look on, watch.

īnspērāns, antis, *a.* not expecting.

īnspērātus, a, um, *a.* unhoped for, unexpected; unforeseen.

īnspiciō, exī, ectum, [3] *v.* look into *or* at, inspect; examine; observe.

īnspīrō, [1] *v.* blow into *or* on; inspire; excite.

īnstabilis, e, *a.* shaky; unstable; inconstant.

īnstāns, *a.* present; urgent.

īnstar, *nt. indecl.* counterpart, equal; moral worth; standard; to the extent, degree, *etc.* (of); image, likeness; manner.

īnstaurātiō, ōnis, *f.* renewal, repetition.

īnstaurō, [1] *v.* renew, repeat; restore.

īnsternō, strāvī, strātum, [3] *v.* spread *or* strew on; cover (with); lay over.

īnstīgō, [1] *v.* urge on; incite, rouse.

īnstillō, [1] *v.* pour in drop by drop, drop in.

īnstimulō, [1] *v.* goad on.

īnstīnctus, ūs, *m.* inspiration; instigation.

īnstīnctus, a, um, *a.* roused, fired; infuriated.

īnstita, ae, *f.* band on a dress.

īnstitor, ōris, *m.* shopkeeper; pedlar.

īnstituō, uī, ūtum, [3] *v.* set up; institute; found; build; make; establish; instruct, educate; start on.

īnstitūtiō, ōnis, *f.* arrangement; instruction, education.

īnstitūtum, ī, *nt.* plan; habit, custom; mode of life.

īnstō, stitī, [1] *v.* stand in *or* upon; threaten; press hard (on); press on (with).

īnstrepō, uī, itum, [3] *v.* make a loud noise.

īnstrūmentum, ī, *nt.* equipment, tools; an item of such equipment; means.

īnstruō, xī, ctum, [3] *v.* build, construct; draw up; set in order; instruct, teach; equip, furnish (with).

īnsuēscō, ēvī, ētum, [3] *v.* become accustomed (to); accustom.

īnsuētus, a, um, *a.* unaccustomed, unused, unusual.

īnsula, ae, *f.* island; tenement-house, block of flats.

īnsulsitās, ātis, *f.* dullness, stupidity.

īnsulsus, a, um, *a.* boring, stupid.

īnsultō, [1] *v.* leap, jump, dance *or* trample (upon *or* in); behave insultingly, mock (at).

īnsum, esse, fuī, *v.* be in *or* on; belong to; be involved in.

īnsuō, uī, ūtum, [3] *v.* sew up (in); sew (on *or* in).

īnsuper, *ad.* and *pr. with acc.* above, on top; in addition (to); over.

īnsuperābilis, e, *a.* insurmountable; unconquerable.

īnsurgō, rēxī, rēctum, [3] *v.* rise; rise up against.

intābēscō, buī, [3] *v.* pine away; melt away.

intāctus, a, um, *a.* untouched; intact; untried; virgin.

intectus, a, um, *a.* uncovered; naked; open.

integellus, a, um, *a.* unharmed.

integer, gra, grum, *a.* whole, entire; safe; healthful; fresh; undecided, open-minded; heart-whole; innocent; pure; upright; **ab (dē, ex) integrō**, afresh, anew.

integō, xī, ctum, [3] *v.* cover.

integritās, ātis, *f.* soundness; chastity; integrity.

integrō, [1] *v.* renew; refresh.

integumentum, ī, *nt.* covering, shield, guard.

intellegēns, entis, *a.* intelligent; discerning.

intellegentia, ae, *f.* intellect, understanding.

intellegō, lēxī, lēctum, [3] *v.* understand.

intemerātus, a, um, *a.* undefiled; chaste.

intemperāns, antis, *a.* unrestrained; licentious.

intemperiēs, ēī, *f.* lack of temperateness (of weather, *etc.*); outrageous behaviour.

intempestīvus, a, um, *a.* unseasonable, ill-timed; untimely.

intempestus, a, um, *a.* unseasonable; stormy, unhealthy; **nox intempesta**, the dead of night.

intendō, dī, tum & sum, [3] *v.* stretch; strain, exert; direct.

intentō, [1] *v.* point (at); point (weapons, *etc.*) in a threatening manner; threaten.

intentus, a, um, *a.* intent (upon); eager; strict.

intepēscō, uī, [3] *v.* become warm.

inter, *pr. with acc.* between, among; during.

intercalō, [1] *v.* insert (a day *or* month) into the calendar; postpone.

intercēdō, cessī, cessum, [3] *v.* come between, intervene; put a veto on; interrupt; go bail (for); forbid; oppose; interfere.

interceptor, ōris, *m.* usurper, embezzler.

intercessiō, ōnis, *f.* intervention; veto (of a magistrate).

intercessor, ōris, *m.* mediator; one who vetoes.

intercidō, cidī, [3] *v.* happen; perish; fall from memory; cease to exist.

intercīdō, cīdī, cīsum, [3] *v.* cut through; sever.

intercipiō, cēpī, ceptum, [3] *v.* intercept; steal; interrupt.

interclūdō, ūsī, ūsum, [3] *v.* cut off; hinder; blockade.

intercursō, [1] *v.* run in between.

intercursus, ūs, *m.* interposition.

interdīcō, xī, ctum, [3] *v.* forbid; interdict; prohibit, debar (from).

interdictum, ī, *nt.* prohibition; provisional decree of a praetor.

**interdiū, ** *ad.* by day.

**interdum, ** *ad.* sometimes, now and then.

**intereā, ** *ad.* meanwhile.

intereō, iī, itum, [4] *v.* perish, die; be ruined; cease.

interequitō, [1] *v.* ride among or between.

interfector, ōris, *m.* murderer, assassin.

interficiō, fēcī, fectum, [3] *v.* kill; destroy.

interfluō, flūxī, [3] *v.* flow between or through.

interfor, fātus sum, [1] *v. dep.* interrupt; break in upon a conversation.

interfūsus, a, um, *a.* poured or spread out between; suffused here and there.

interiaceō, [2] *v.* lie between.

interiaciō v. **intericiō.**

intericiō, iēcī, iectum, [3] *v.* throw between; introduce, insert.

interim, *ad.* meanwhile; at the same time.

interimō, ēmī, ēm(p)tum, [3] *v.* do away with; kill; destroy.

interior, ius, ōris, *a.* inner, more inward; more remote; more intimate.

interitus, ūs, *m.* violent or untimely death; extinction; dissolution.

interluō, [3] *v.* flow between.

intermisceō, scuī, xtum & stum, [2] *v.* intermingle, mix.

intermissiō, ōnis, *f.* intermission; pause.

intermittō, mīsī, missum, [3] *v.* leave off; leave off temporarily; leave a gap (between).

intermorior, tuus sum, [3] *v. dep.* perish; pass out.

internāscor, nātus sum, [3] *v. dep.* grow between or among.

internec\iō, ōnis, *f.* massacre; extermination.

internōdium, iī, *nt.* space between two joints in the body.

internōscō, nōvī, nōtum, [3] *v.* distinguish between; pick out.

internūntius, iī, *m.* intermediary, go-between.

internus, a, um, *a.* inward, internal; domestic.

interpellātiō, ōnis, *f.* interruption in speaking.

interpellō, [1] *v.* interrupt (in speaking); obstruct.

interpōnō, posuī, positum, [3] *v.* put, lay *or* set between; interpose; insert; introduce.

interpres, etis, *m.* or *f.* intermediary, go-between; interpreter; translator.

interpretātiō, ōnis, *f.* interpretation; meaning.

interpretor, ātus sum, [1] *v. dep.* interpret; explain; regard.

interrēgnum, ī, *nt.* space between two reigns, interregnum.

interrēx, rēgis, *m.* one who holds office between the death of a supreme magistrate and the appointment of a successor.

interritus, a, um, *a.* fearless.

interrogātiō, ōnis, *f.* question; inquiry; questioning.

interrogō, [1] *v.* ask, question; examine; indict.

interrumpō, rūpī, ruptum, [3] *v.* drive a gap in, break up; cut short, interrupt.

intersaepiō, psī, ptum, [4] *v.* separate; block.

interscindō, idī, issum, [3] *v.* cut through, sever.

intersum, esse, fuī, *v.* be *or* lie between, be in the midst; be present; take part in; be different; **interest,** it makes a difference, it matters; it is of advantage.

intervāllum, ī, *nt.* space between two things, interval; distance; respite.

interveniō, vēnī, ventum, [4] *v.* come between; intervene; occur, crop up; occur by way of a hindrance.

interventus, ūs, *m.* intervention; occurrence of an event.

intervertō, [3] *v.* embezzle; cheat.

intestābilis, e, *a.* detestable, infamous.

intestīnus, a, um, *a.* internal; domestic, civil.

intexō, xuī, xtum, [3] *v.* weave (into), embroider (on); cover by twining; insert (into a book, *etc.*).

intibum v. **intubum.**

intimus, a, um, *a.* inmost; most secret; most intimate.

intolerābilis, e, *a.* **intolerandus, a, um,** *a.* insupportable, insufferable.

intolerāns, antis, *a.* unable to endure, impatient (of); insufferable.

intolerantia, ae, *f.* impatience.

intonō, uī, [1] *v.* thunder; make a noise like thunder; thunder forth.

intōnsus, a, um, *a.* uncut; unshaven, unshorn; not stripped of foliage.

intorqueō, torsī, tortum, [2] *v.* twist *or* turn round, sprain; hurl *or* launch a missile at.

intrā, *ad. & pr. with acc.* within; within the space of; under, fewer than.

intractābilis, e, *a.* unmanageable, intractable.

intremō, uī, [3] *v.* tremble.

intrepidus, a, um, *a.* undaunted, fearless, untroubled.

intrīnsecus, *ad.* on the inside.

intrō, *ad.* within, inside, indoors.

intrō, [1] *v.* go into; enter; penetrate.

intrōdūcō, xī, ctum, [3] *v.* lead *or* bring in; introduce.

introeō, īvī & iī, itum, [4] *v.* go inside, enter; invade.

introitus, ūs, *m.* going in, entry; invasion.

intrōmittō, mīsī, missum, [3] *v.* send in; admit.

intrōrsum, intrōrsus, *ad.* to within, inwards; internally.

intrōspiciō, spexī, spectum, [3] *v.* examine, inspect; look upon.

intubum, ī, *nt.,* **intubus, ī,** *m.,* endive *or* chicory.

intueor, itus sum, [2] *v. dep.* look at *or* on; consider; observe; consider; bear in mind.

intumēscō, muī, [3] *v.* swell up, rise; become swollen.

intumulātus, a, um, *a.* unburied.

intus, *ad.* inside, within; at home.

intūtus, a, um, *a.* defenceless; unsafe.

inultus, a, um, *a.* unpunished; scot-free.

inumbrō, [1] *v.* cast a shadow.

inundō, [1] *v.* overflow, inundate, flood; swarm.

inurbānus, a, um, *a.* rustic, boorish, dull.

inūrō, ussī, ustum, [3] *v.* burn in (with a hot iron); brand (on *or* with).

inūsitātus, a, um, *a.* unusual.

inūtilis, e, *a.* useless; unprofitable; disadvantageous, inexpedient.

invādō, sī, sum, [3] *v.* go into; invade; rush into; take possession of, usurp; seize; attack; rush on (in order to embrace).

invalidus, a, um, *a.* infirm, weak, feeble; ineffectual.

invehō, vexī, vectum, [3] *v.* carry *or* bring in; import; **invehī,** to ride, drive, sail, *etc.* in; inveigh against.

inveniō, vēnī, ventum, [4] *v.* invent; contrive; find; discover; manage to get.

inventor, ōris, *m.* inventor; author, contriver; discoverer.

inventrīx, īcis, *f.* inventress.

inventum, ī, *nt.* invention, discovery.

invenustus, a, um, *a.* unlovely, unattractive.

invergō, [3] *v.* tip (liquids) upon.

invertō, vertī, versum, [3] *v.* turn upside down; pervert; change.

investīgō, [1] *v.* search out, track down.

inveterāscō, āvī, [3] *v.* grow old; become established *or* customary.

invicem, *ad.* by turns, in turn; reciprocally, mutually.

invictus, a, um, *a.* unconquered; invincible.

invideō, vīdī, vīsum, [2] *v. with dat.* envy, grudge; hate; refuse.

invidia, ae, *f.* envy, jealousy; spite; dislike.

invidiōsus, a, um, *a.* arousing hatred, odium *or* envy; envious.

invidus, a, um, *a.* ill-disposed; envious.

invigilō, [1] *v. with dat.* stay awake (over); watch (over) diligently.

inviolābilis, e, *a.* sacrosanct, imperishable.

inviolātus, a, um, *a.* unhurt; unviolated; inviolable.

invīsitātus, a, um, *a.* unvisited, unseen.

invīsō, sī, sum, [3] *v.* go to see, visit; watch over.

invīsus, a, um, *a.* hateful, hated.

invītāmentum, *ī, nt.* inducement.

invītātiō, ōnis, *f.* invitation.

invītō, [1] *v.* invite; entertain; allure, entice; incite.

invītus, a, um, *a.* against one's will, reluctant.

invius, a, um, *a.* impassable; inaccessible.

invocō, [1] *v.* call upon; invoke; pray for.

involō, [1] *v.* fly into *or* at, rush upon; seize on.

involvō, volvī, volūtum, [3] *v.* wrap (in), cover, envelop; roll along.

iō, *i.* ritual exclamation uttered under strong emotion.

iocor, ātus, [1] *v. dep.* jest, joke.

iocōsus, a, um, *a.* fond of jokes; full of fun; funny.

iocularis, e, *a.* laughable.

ioculor, [1] *v. dep.* jest; joke.

iocus, ī, *m.* jest, joke; sport.

ipse, a, um, ipsīus, ipsī, *pn.* he, she, it; self, very, identical.

īra, ae, *f.* anger, wrath, rage.

īrācundia, ae, *f.* irascibility; passion.

īrācundus, a, um, *a.* irascible, angry.

īrāscor, ātus sum, [3] *v. dep.* be angry, fly into a rage.

īrātus, a, um, *a.* angry; enraged.

irreligātus, a, um, *a.* unbound, unmoored.

irremeābilis, e, *a.* along *or* across which one cannot return.

irreparābilis, e, *a.* irreparable, irrecoverable.

irrepertus, a, um, *a.* not found, undiscovered.

irrēpō, psī, [3] *v.* creep in or into; steal into; insinuate oneself (into).

irreprehēnsus, a, um, *a.* blameless.

irrētiō, īvī or **iī, ītum,** [4] *v.* entangle; catch in a net.

irreverentia, ae, *f.* disrespect.

irrevocābilis, e, *a.* irrevocable, unalterable.

irrīdeō, rīsī, rīsum, [2] *v.* laugh at, mock, make fun of.

irridiculē, *ad.* without wit.

irrigō, [1] *v.* water, irrigate; inundate; wet, moisten; diffuse.

irriguus, a, um, *a.* watering; well-watered.

irrīsor, ōris, *m.* mocker, scoffer.

irrīsus, ūs, *m.* mockery; laughing-stock.

irrītābilis, e, *a.* easily provoked, sensitive.

irrītāmen, inis, irrītāmentum, ī, *nt.* incentive, stimulus.

irrītātiō, ōnis, *f.* incitement, provocation.

irrītō, [1] *v.* provoke, annoy; excite; stimulate; aggravate.

irritus, a, um, *a.* invalid, void; of no effect; vain, useless.

irrōrō, [1] *v.* wet with dew; besprinkle; water; rain on.

irrumpō, rūpī, ruptum, [3] *v.* break in or burst or rush into; interrupt; invade.

irruō, uī, [3] *v.* rush or dash in; charge (at).

irruptiō, ōnis, *f.* violent or forcible entry; assault.

is, ea, id, ēius, *pn.* he, she, it; this, that.

iste, a, ud, istīus, *pn.* this or that of yours; that which you refer to; the well-known.

isthmus, ī, *m.* isthmus; strait.

istic, aec, oc, (uc), *pn.* that of yours; that which you refer to.

istīc, *ad.* there by you; over there; here.

istinc, *ad.* from over there, from here; from or on your side.

istō, istūc, *ad.* to the place where you are; to the point you have reached.

ita, *ad.* so, thus; even so; yes.

itaque, *c.* and so; therefore, consequently.

item, *ad.* similarly, likewise.

iter, itineris, *nt.* journey; march; route; road, foot-way.

iterō, [1] *v.* do a second time, repeat; renew, revise.

iterum, *ad.* again, for the second time.

itidem, *ad.* in the same manner, likewise.

itus, ūs, *m.* going, gait; departure.

iuba, ae, *f.* mane of a horse; crest (of a helmet).

iubar, aris, *nt.* radiance of the heavenly bodies, brightness; first light of day; source of light.

iubeō, iussī, iussum, [2] *v.* order, command; decree; **salvēre iubeō,** greet, welcome.

iūcunditās, ātis, *f.* pleasantness, charm.

iūcundus, a, um, *a.* pleasant, agreeable; delightful.

iūdex, icis, *m.* or *f.* judge; arbitrator; umpire; juror; critic.

iūdicium, iī, *nt.* judicial investigation; judgment; verdict; opinion; discernment.

iūdicō, [1] *v.* judge, give judgement; sentence; decide; appraise.

iugālis, e, *a.* yoked together; nuptial.

iugerum, ī, *nt.* two-thirds of an acre of land.

iūgis, e, *a.* continual; ever-flowing.

iugō, [1] *v.* marry; join (to).

iugulō, [1] *v.* cut the throat, kill; butcher.

iugulum, ī, *nt.*, **iugulus, ī,** *m.* collar-bone; throat.

iugum, ī, *nt.* yoke (for oxen); team; pair (of horses, *etc.*); ridge (of a mountain).

iūmentum, ī, *nt.* beast of burden.

iūnctūra, ae, *f.* joint; association.

iuncus, ī, *m.* rush.

iungō, nxī, nctum, [3] *v.* yoke, harness; join; clasp (hands); unite.

iūnior, *a.* younger.

iūniperus, ī, *f.* juniper.

Iūnius, iī, *m.* June.

iūre, *ad.* justly, rightly; deservedly.

iūrgium, iī, *nt.* quarrel, dispute; abuse.

iūrgō, [1] *v.* quarrel, scold.

iūriscōnsultus, ī, *m.* lawyer, jurist.

iūrisdictiō, ōnis, *f.* jurisdiction, legal authority; administration of justice.

iūrō, [1] *v.* swear, take an oath; conspire.

iūs, iūris, *nt.* law; right; authority; court of justice; code; (war) convention(s).

iūs iūrandum, ī, *nt.* oath.

iussum, ī, *nt.* order, command.

iussū, *abl.* of **iussus,** by order of.

iūstitia, ae, *f.* justice; equity.

iūstitium, iī, *nt.* cessation of judicial and all public business, due to national calamity.

iūstus, a, um, *a.* just, equitable; lawful; legitimate; well grounded; proper; right; regular; impartial; **iūsta, ōrum,** *nt. pl.* due observances; funeral offerings.

iuvenālis, e, *a.* youthful, young.

iuvenca, ae, *f.* young cow, heifer.

iuvencus, ī, *m.* young bull; young man.

iuvenēscō, nuī, [3] *v.* grow up; grow young again.

iuvenīlis, e, *a.* youthful.

iuvenis, is, *a.* young, youthful; ~, **is,** *m.* or *f.* youth, young man *or* woman.

iuventa, ae, youth.

iuventās, ātis, *f.* youth.

iuventūs, ūtis, *f.* youth.

iuvō, iūvī, iūtum, [1] *v.* help, assist; delight; benefit; **iuvat, it** pleases.

iuxtā, *pr. with acc.* near by, near to; ~, *ad.* close; alike; equally; ~ **ac,** as much as.

....

K

....

Kalendae, ārum, *f. pl.* the first day of the month.

....

L

....

L = 50.

labāscō, [3] *v.* fall to pieces, break up; waver.

labefaciō, fēcī, factum, [3] *v.* loosen; shake; cause to totter; undermine.

labefactō, [1] *v.* shake; cause to waver; make unsteady, loosen; undermine.

labellum, ī, *nt.* lip.

labēs, is, *f.* land-slip; subsidence; disaster, débàcle; fault; stain, blemish, dishonour.

labō, [1] *v.* totter, be ready to fall; waver.

labor, ōris, *m.* labour, toil, exertion; hardship, distress.

lābor, psus, [3] *v. dep.* slide *or* glide down; fall down; drop; perish; go wrong.

labōriōsus, a, um, *a.* laborious, painstaking.

labōrō, [1] *v.* labour, take pains; strive; be sick; be oppressed *or* troubled; be in danger; work (at).

labōs v. **labor.**

lābrum, ī, *nt.* basin, vat; bathing-place.

labrum, ī, *nt.* lip; edge (of a vessel, ditch, river, *etc.*).

lābrusca, ae, *f.* wild vine.

labyrinthēus, a, um, *a.* of a labyrinth.

labyrinthus, ī, *m.* labyrinth, maze.

lac, lactis, *nt.* milk; milky juice.

lacer, a, um, *a.* mangled; torn; rent.

lacerātiō, ōnis, *f.* mangling; tearing.

lacerō, [1] *v.* tear, mangle; shatter, torment, harass; 'lash'.

lacerta, ae, *f.* lizard.

lacertōsus, a, um, *a.* muscular, brawny.

lacertus, ī, *m.* lizard; muscular part of the arm; strength.

lacessō, īvī & iī, ītum, [3] *v.* excite, provoke, challenge; harass; assail.

lacrima, ae, *f.* tear.

lacrimābilis, e, *a.* mournful; tearful.

lacrimō, [1] *v.* **lacrimor, ātus,** [1] *v. dep.* shed tears, weep.

lacrimōsus, a, um, *a.* tearful, weeping; causing tears.

lacruma, etc., v. **lacrima, etc.**

lactēns, entis, *a.* unweaned, sucking; juicy.

lacteus, a, um, *a.* milky; milkwhite; ~ **orbis** *or* **circulus,** Milky Way.

lacūna, ae, *f.* pool; hollow, pit, cavity.

lacūnar, āris, *nt.* panelled ceiling.

lacus, ūs, *m.* lake; pond; tank, reservoir, trough.

laedō, sī, sum, [3] *v.* hurt; injure; annoy.

laena ae, *f.* woollen double cloak.

laetābilis, e, *a.* joyful.

laetitia, ae, *f.* joy; gladness.

laetor, ātus, [1] *v. dep.* rejoice, be joyful.

laetus, a, um, *a.* joyful, cheerful, glad; fortunate; luxuriant, lush; pleasing, welcome, beautiful; rich.

laeva, ae, *f.* left hand.

laevus, a, um, *a.* left; unfavourable, harmful.

lagēna, ae, *f.* flask; bottle.

lambō, bī, [3] *v.* lick; wash.

lāmentābilis, e, *a.* doleful; lamentable.

lāmentātiō, ōnis, *f.* lamentation; wailing.

lāmentor, ātus, [1] *v. dep.* lament; bewail.

lamia, ae, *f.* witch.

lāmina, lāmna, ae, *f.* plate; veneer; thin sheet of metal.

lampas, adis, *f.* torch; lamp.

lāna, ae, *f.* wool; soft hair; down.

lānātus, a, um, *a.* woolly.

lancea, ae, *f.* light spear, lance.

lāneus, a, um, *a.* woollen.

langueō, [2] *v.* be sluggish; be unwell; wilt; lack vigour.

languēscō, guī, [3] *v.* become faint *or* languid *or* weak; wilt.

languidus, a, um, *a.* languid, faint, weak; ill; sluggish; inert.

languor, ōris, *m.* faintness, feebleness; languor; apathy.

lānificus, a, um, *a.* wool-working, spinning, weaving.

lāniger, a, um, a. wool-bearing, fleecy; woolly.

laniō, [1] v. tear, mutilate; pull to pieces.

lanista, ae, m. manager of a troop of gladiators, trainer.

lānūgō, inis, f. down, youth.

lānx, lancis, f. plate, dish; pan of a pair of scales.

lapathum, ī, nt.,

lapathus, ī, m. or f. sorrel.

lapideus, a, um, a. of stone; stony.

lapidō, [1] v. throw stones at; stone; **lapidat**, it rains stones.

lapidōsus, a, um, a. full of stones, stony; gritty.

lapillus, ī, m. little stone, pebble; precious stone, gem.

lapis, idis, m. stone; milestone; precious stone.

lappa, ae, f. bur; plant bearing burs.

lāpsō, [1] v. slip, lose one's footing.

lāpsus, ūs, m. gliding, sliding; slipping and falling.

laqueāre, āris, nt. panelled ceiling.

laqueātus, a, um, a. panelled.

laqueus, ī, m. noose, snare; trap.

lar, laris, m. tutelary household god; home.

largior, ītus, [4] v. dep. give bountifully; give presents corruptly; bestow, grant, permit; overlook, condone.

largitās, ātis, f. abundance; munificence.

largiter, ad. plentifully; liberally; greatly.

largītiō, ōnis, f. distribution of doles, land, etc., largess; bribery.

largītor, ōris, m. liberal giver; briber.

largus, a, um, a. lavish; plentiful; bountiful.

lāridum, ī, nt., **lārdum, ī**, nt. bacon.

lascīvia, ae, f. playfulness; wantonness, lasciviousness.

lascīviō, iī, ītum, [4] v. frisk; sport; run riot.

lascīvus, a, um, a. wanton; frolicsome; sportive; mischievous; free from restraint in sexual matters.

lassitūdō, inis, f. faintness, weariness.

lassō, [1] v. tire, weary; wear out.

lassus, a, um, a. languid, weary, tired.

lātē, ad. widely, far and wide.

latebra, ae, f. hiding-place, retreat; lair; subterfuge.

latebrōsus, a, um, a. full of lurking places; lurking in concealment.

lateō, uī, [2] *v.* lie hid, lurk; escape notice.

later, eris, *m.* brick; ingot.

latericius, a, um, *a.* made of bricks.

latex, icis, *m.* water; (any) liquid; spring water; juice; wine; oil.

latibulum, ī, *nt.* hiding-place, den.

Latīnē, *ad.* in Latin.

Latīnus, a, um, *a.* Latin.

latitō, [1] *v.* remain in hiding; be hidden.

lātitūdō, inis, *f.* breadth, width; extent.

lātomiae v. **lautumiae.**

lātor, ōris, *m.* mover *or* proposer (of a law).

lātrātor, ōris, *m.* barker, one who barks.

lātrātus, ūs, *m.* barking.

lātrō, [1] *v.* bark; bark at.

latrō, ōnis, *m.* brigand, bandit; plunderer.

latrōcinium, iī, *nt.* robbery with violence; bandit raid; pillage; band of robbers.

latrōcinor, ātus, [1] *v. dep.* engage in brigandage *or* piracy.

latrunculus, ī, *m.* robber, brigand.

lātus, a, um, *a.* broad, wide; spacious; extensive.

latus, eris, *nt.* side; flank.

laudābilis, e, *a.* praiseworthy.

laudātiō, ōnis, *f.* praising; eulogy.

laudātor, ōris, *m.* one who praises, eulogist.

laudō, [1] *v.* praise, extol; deliver a funerary eulogy of.

laurea, ae, *f.* laurel-tree; laurel wreath *or* branch; triumph, victory.

laureātus, a, um, *a.* adorned with a laurel; **laureātae litterae,** a despatch reporting a victory.

laureus, a, um, *a.* of the laurel tree, laurel.

lauriger, a, um, *a.* crowned with laurel.

laurus, ī, *f.* bay-tree, laurel; laurel crown; triumph.

laus, laudis, *f.* praise; glory; excellence; merit.

lautumiae, ārum, *f. pl.* stone-quarry, especially used as a prison.

lautus, a, um, *a.* clean; well-turned-out, fine; sumptuous.

lavō, lāvī, lautum, lavātum & **lōtum,** [1] & [3] *v.* wash; bathe; soak.

laxāmentum, ī, *nt.* respite; opportunity.

laxitās, ātis, *f.* roominess, largeness.

laxō, [1] *v.* expand, extend; open up; slacken; relax; weaken.

laxus, a, um, *a.* wide, loose; roomy; slack; open; lax.

lea, ae, leaena, ae, *f.* lioness.

lebēs, ētis, *m.* caldron.

lectīca, ae, *f.* litter.

lectīcārius, ī, *m.* litter-bearer.

lēctiō, ōnis, *f.* reading (aloud); perusal; choosing.

lectisternium, iī, *nt.* special feast of supplication at which a banquet was offered to the gods, couches being spread for them to recline upon.

lēctitō, [1] *v.* read repeatedly; be in the habit of reading.

lēctor, ōris, *m.* reader.

lectulus, ī, *m.* bed or couch.

lectus, ī, *m.* couch, (bridal-)bed.

lēgātiō, ōnis, *f.* embassy.

lēgātum, ī, *nt.* bequest, legacy.

lēgātus, ī, *m.* ambassador, legate; deputy; commander.

lēgifer, a, um, *a.* law-giving.

legiō, ōnis, *f.* Roman legion; army.

legiōnārius, a, um, *a.* of a legion, legionary.

lēgitimus, a, um, *a.* lawful, right; legitimate; real, genuine; just; proper.

lēgō, [1] *v.* send as an envoy; choose as deputy; bequeath.

legō, lēgī, lēctum, [3] *v.* gather; choose; furl; traverse; read.

legūmen, inis, *nt.* pulse, leguminous plant.

lembus, ī, *m.* small fast-sailing boat.

lemurēs, um, *m. pl.* malevolent ghosts of the dead, spectres, shades.

lēna, ae, *f.* procuress; brothel-keeper.

lēnīmen, inis, *nt.* alleviation, solace.

lēniō, īvī & iī, ītum, [4] *v.* mitigate; allay, ease; explain away.

lēnis, e, *a.* smooth, soft, mild, gentle, easy, calm.

lēnitās, ātis, *f.* slowness; gentleness, mildness.

lēnō, ōnis, *m.* brothel-keeper, bawd, procurer.

lēnōcinium, iī, *nt.* pandering; allurement, enticement; flattery.

lēns, tis, *f.* the lentil-plant.

lentēscō, [3] *v.* become sticky; relax.

lentitūdō, inis, *f.* slowness in action; apathy.

lentō, [1], *v.* bend under strain.

lentus, a, um, *a.* pliant; tough; clinging; slow; lazy; calm; procrastinating; phlegmatic.

lēnunculus, ī, *m.* skiff.

leō, ōnis, *m.* lion.

lepidus, a, um, *a.* agreeable, charming, delightful, amusing, witty.

lepōs, ōris, *m.* charm, grace; wit; humour.

lepus, oris, *m.* hare.

lētālis, e, *a.* deadly, fatal, mortal.

Lēthaeus, a, um, *a.* of Lethe; causing forgetfulness; of the underworld.

Lēthē, ēs, *f.* Lethe, the river of forgetfulness.

lētifer, a, um 149 librārius, a, um

lētifer, a, um, *a.* deadly; fatal.

lētum, ī, *nt.* death; death and destruction.

levāmen, inis, *nt.* alleviation, solace.

levāmentum, ī, *nt.* alleviation, mitigation, consolation.

levis, e, *a.* light; nimble; trivial, trifling; gentle; capricious; fickle, inconstant.

lēvis e, *a.* smooth; polished; free from coarse hair; smooth.

levitās, ātis, *f.* lightness; restlessness; mildness; fickleness; shallowness.

levō, [1] *v.* lift; support; relieve, lessen; free from.

lēvō, [1] *v.* smooth; polish.

lēx, lēgis, *f.* law; rule; principle; condition.

lībāmen, inis, lībāmentum, ī, *nt.* drink-offering; first-fruits.

lībella, ae, *f.* small silver coin; plumb-line, level.

libellus, ī, *m.* little book; memorial; petition; pamphlet, defamatory publication; programme.

libēns, entis, *a.* willing; cheerful.

liber, a, um, *a.* free; unimpeded; void of; frank, free-spoken; licentious; outspoken.

Līber, ī, *m.* Bacchus; wine.

liber, brī, *m.* inner bark of a tree; book; volume.

līberālis, e, *a.* gentlemanly; well-bred; liberal; open-handed; generous; lavish.

līberālitās, ātis, *f.* nobleness, kindness; frankness; liberality; gift.

līberātor, ōris, *m.* deliverer, liberator.

līberē, *ad.* freely; frankly; shamelessly.

līberī, ōrum, *m. pl.* children.

līberō, [1] *v.* release, free; acquit; absolve.

līberta, ae, lībertīna, ae, *f.* freedwoman.

lībertās, ātis, *f.* freedom; liberty; frankness of speech, outspokenness.

lībertīnus, a, um, *a.* of a freedman.

lībertīnus, libertus, ī, *m.* freedman.

libet, libuit, libitum est, [2] *v. impers.* it pleases, is agreeable; ~ mihi, I feel like, want.

libīdinōsus, a, um, *a.* lustful, wanton; capricious.

libīdō, inis, *f.* desire; lust; passion.

Libitīna, ae, *f.* goddess of funerals.

lībō, [1] *v.* nibble, sip; pour in offering; impair; graze, skim.

lībra, ae, *f.* Roman pound (about ¾ modern pound); level; balance; scales; one of the twelve signs of the zodiac.

lībrāmentum, ī, *nt.* weight, counterpoise.

librārius, a, um, *a.* of books; ~, iī, *m.* copyist, secretary; bookseller.

lībrō, [1] v. weigh; level; balance, poise.

lībum, ī, nt. cake; consecrated cake.

liburna, ae, f. light, fast-sailing warship.

licēns, entis, a. free, unrestrained.

licentia, ae, f. liberty, licence; freedom; disorderliness; outspokenness.

liceō, [2] v. fetch (a price).

liceor, licitus, [2] v. dep. bid at an auction.

licet, cuit, citum est, [2] v. impers. it is lawful or permitted; one may or can.

licitus, a, um, a. lawful; permitted.

līcium, iī, nt. thread; leash or heddle (in weaving).

līctor, ōris, m. lictor (attendant on a Roman magistrate).

ligāmen, inis, nt. bandage; string.

lignārius, iī, m. carpenter; timber-merchant.

lignātiō, ōnis, f. collecting firewood.

lignātor, ōris, m. one who collects firewood.

ligneus, a, um, a. of wood, wooden.

lignor, ātus, [1] v. dep. collect firewood.

lignum, ī, nt. wood; firewood; timber; 'stump'.

ligō, [1] v. bind, fasten; attach; tie up.

ligō, ōnis, m. mattock, hoe.

ligūr(r)iō, īvī & iī, ītum, [4] v. lick, lick up.

ligustrum, ī, nt. privet, white-flowered shrub.

līlium, iī, nt. lily.

līma, ae, f. file; polishing, revision.

limbus, ī, m. ornamental border to a robe.

līmen, inis, nt. lintel, threshold; entrance; house.

līmes, itis, m. strip of uncultivated ground to mark the division of land; stone to mark a boundary; boundary; track; channel; route.

līmō, [1] v. file; polish; file down; detract gradually from.

līmōsus, a, um, a. miry, muddy.

limpidus, a, um, a. clear.

līmus, a, um, a. oblique, side-long.

līmus, ī, m. mud; slime.

līnea, ae, f. string, cord; fishing-line; plumb-line; finishing-line.

līneāmentum, ī, nt. line; (pl.) outlines, features.

līneus, a, um, a. made of flax or linen.

lingua, ae, f. tongue; speech, language; dialect.

līniger, a, um, a. wearing linen.

linō, lēvī, litum, [3] v. smear, plaster (with); erase; befoul.

linquō, līquī, [3] *v.* leave, quit, forsake; abandon.

linter, tris, *f.* small light boat; trough, vat.

linteum, ī, *nt.* linen cloth; linen; sail; napkin; awning.

linteus, a, um, *a.* of linen.

līnum, ī, *nt.* flax; linen, thread; rope; fishing-line; net.

lippus, a, um, *a.* having watery *or* inflamed eyes.

liquefaciō, fēcī, factum, [3] *v.* melt, dissolve.

liqueō, licuī, & līquī, [2] *v.* be clear to a person; be evident.

liquēscō, licuī, [3] *v.* become liquid, melt; decompose.

liquidus, a, um, *a.* liquid, fluid; clear; manifest; smooth; melodious; evident.

liquō, [1] *v.* melt; strain.

līquor, [3] *v. dep.* dissolve; waste away; flow.

liquor, ōris, *m.* fluid, liquid.

līs, lītis, *f.* quarrel; lawsuit.

lītera, *etc.,* v. littera, *etc.*

lītigiōsus, a, um, *a.* quarrelsome, contentious.

lītigō, [1] *v.* quarrel; go to law.

litō, [1] *v.* obtain *or* give favourable omens from a sacrifice; make an (acceptable) offering (to).

lītoreus, a, um, *a.* of the seashore.

littera, ae, *f.* letter of the alphabet; **litterae, ārum,** *pl.* let-ter, literature; writings; the elements of education.

litterātus, a, um, *a.* learned; cultured.

litūra, ae, *f.* smearing; erasure; blot.

lītus, oris, *nt.* seashore, coast.

lituus, ī, *m.* curved staff carried by augurs; a kind of war-trumpet curved at one end.

līveō, [2] *v.* be livid *or* discoloured; be envious.

līvidus, a, um, *a.* livid, slate-coloured; discoloured by bruises; envious, spiteful.

līvor, ōris, *m.* bluish discoloration (produced by bruising, *etc.*), envy, spite.

lixa, ae, *m.* camp-follower.

locātiō, ōnis, *f.* hiring out *or* letting (of property).

locō, [1] *v.* place, station; contract (for); farm out (taxes) on contract.

locuplēs, ētis, *a.* rich, well-to-do; rich (in).

locus, ī, *m.* (*pl.* locī & loca, *nt. pl.*) place; position; rank; passage (in a book); topic.

lolium, iī, *nt.* a grass found as a weed in corn, darnel.

longaevus, a, um, *a.* of great age, ancient.

longē, *ad.* far off; far; a great while; very much; by a large margin; ~ lātēque, far and wide.

longinquitās, ātis, *f.* length; distance; duration.

longinquus, a, um, *a.* far off, distant; of long duration; **ē longinquō,** from a distance.

longitūdō, inis, *f.* length.

longus, a, um, *a.* long, tall; lasting a long time, tedious.

loquācitās, ātis, *f.* talkativeness.

loquāx, ācis, *a.* talkative, loquacious.

loquēla, ae, *f.* speech, utterance.

loquor, cūtus, [3] *v. dep.* speak, talk, say; mention.

lōrīca, ae, *f.* cuirass; parapet, breast-work.

lōrum, ī, *nt.* thong; rawhide whip.

lōtus, ī, *f.* lotus plant; nettle plant.

lubēns, *etc.,* v. **libēns,** *etc.*

lubet v. **libet.**

lubīdō v. **libīdō.**

lūbricus, a, um, *a.* slippery; sinuous; inconstant; hazardous, ticklish; deceitful.

lucellum, ī, *nt.* small *or* petty gain.

lūceō, lūxī, [2] *v.* shine; glitter; be conspicuous.

lucerna, ae, *f.* oil lamp.

lūcēscō, [3] *v.* begin to shine, grow light.

lūcidus, a, um, *a.* bright, shining; clear.

lūcifer, a, um, *a.* light-bringing; **~, ī,** *m.* morning star.

lūcifugus, a, um, *a.* avoiding the light of day.

Lūcīna, ae, *f.* goddess of childbirth; childbirth.

lucror, ātus, [1] *v. dep.* gain, win; make a profit (out of).

lucrōsus, a, um, *a.* gainful, lucrative.

lucrum, ī, *nt.* gain, profit; avarice.

luctāmen, inis, *nt.* struggling, exertion.

luctātor, ōris, *m.* wrestler.

luctificus, a, um, *a.* dire, calamitous.

luctor, ātus sum, [1] *v. dep.* wrestle; struggle; fight (against).

luctuōsus, a, um, *a.* mournful; grievous.

luctus, ūs, *m.* sorrow, lamentation; mourning; instance *or* cause of grief.

lūcubrō, [1] *v.* work by lamplight, 'burn the midnight oil'; make *or* produce at night.

lūculentus, a, um, *a.* excellent; fine; beautiful.

lūcus, ī, *m.* grove.

lūdibrium, ī, *nt.* mockery; laughing-stock.

lūdibundus, a, um, *a.* having fun; carefree.

lūdicer, cra, crum, lūdicrus, a, um, connected with sport *or* the stage.

lūdicrum, ī, *nt.* stage-play; show; source of fun, plaything.

lūdificātiō, ōnis, *f.* mockery.

lūdificor, ātus sum, [1] *v.* make sport of, trifle with.

lūdō, sī, sum, [3] *v.* play; sport; tease; trick.

lūdus, ī, *m.* play, game, pastime; sport, entertainment, fun; school, elementary school.

luēs, is, *f.* plague, pestilence; scourge, affliction.

lūgeō, xī, ctum, [3] *v.* mourn, lament; be in mourning.

lūgubris, e, *a.* mourning; mournful; grievous.

lumbus, ī, *m.* the loins; the loins as the seat of sexual excitement.

lūmen, inis, *nt.* light; daylight; day; lamp, torch; life; eye; (of a person) glory, cynosure.

lūna, ae, *f.* moon; month.

lūnāris, e, *a.* lunar.

lūnātus, a, um, *a.* crescent-shaped.

lūnō, [1] *v.* make crescent-shaped, curve.

luō, luī, [3] *v.* wash, lave.

luō, luī, ūtum & uitum, [3] *v.* pay; atone for; **poenam luere,** to suffer punishment.

lupa, ae, *f.* she-wolf; prostitute.

lupānar, āris, *nt.* brothel.

lupātus, a, um, *a.* furnished with jagged teeth; **lupātī, ōrum.** *m. pl.* jagged toothed bit.

Lupercālia, ium, *nt. pl.* festival promoting fertility held on 15 Feb.

Lupercus, ī, *m.* priest in this festival.

lupīnus, a, um, *a.* of *or* belonging to a wolf; made of wolf-skin.

lupus, ī, *m.* wolf; grappling iron.

lūridus, a, um, *a.* sallow, wan, ghastly.

luscinia, ae, *f.* nightingale.

lūsor, ōris, *m.* player; tease; one who treats (of a subject) lightly.

lūstrālis, e, *a.* relating to purification; serving to avert evil.

lūstrō, [1] *v.* purify; illuminate; move round, over *or* through; go about; review, survey.

lūstrum, ī, *nt.* purificatory ceremony; period of five years.

lustrum, ī, *nt.* haunts of wild beasts; (*pl.*) den of vice.

lūsus, ūs, *m.* play, game; sport, amusement; amorous sport.

lūteolus, a, um, *a.* yellow.

lūteus, a, um, *a.* yellow; saffron.

luteus, a, um, *a.* of mud *or* clay; good for nothing.

lutulentus, a, um, *a.* muddy; turbid; dirty; morally polluted.

lutum, ī, *nt.* mud, clay; dirt.

lūtum, ī, *nt.* yellow dye; any yellow colour.

lūx, lūcis, *f.* light (of the sun, stars, *etc.*); daylight, day; splendour; eyesight.

luxuria, ae, luxuriēs, ēī, *f.* luxury, extravagance, rankness, thriving condition.

luxuriō, [1] *v.* **luxurior, ātus,** [1] *v. dep.* grow rank *or* luxuriant; frisk; indulge oneself.

luxuriōsus, a, um, *a.* luxuriant, exuberant; immoderate; wanton; luxurious; self-indulgent.

luxus, ūs, *m.* luxury, soft living; sumptuousness.

lychnus, ī, *m.* lamp.

lympha, ae, *f.* water; water-nymph.

lymphāticus, a, um, *a.* frenzied.

lymphātus, a, um, *a.* frenzied, frantic.

lynx, lyncis, *m.* or *f.* lynx.

lyra, ae, *f.* lyre; lyric poetry; Lyre (constellation).

lyricus, a, um, *a.* lyric.

....

M

....

M = 1000.

macellum, ī, *nt.* provision-market.

macer, cra, crum, *a.* lean, meagre, poor.

māceria, ae, *f.* wall of brick *or* stone.

mācerō, [1] *v.* make soft, soak; worry, annoy.

māchina, ae, *f.* machine; siege-engine.

māchināmentum, ī, *nt.* siege-engine.

māchinātiō, ōnis, *f.* mechanism; engine of war.

māchinātor, ōris, *m.* engineer; *fig.* projector.

māchinor, ātus, [1] *v. dep.* devise; plot.

maciēs, ēī, *f.* leanness, meagreness; poverty.

macrēscō, cruī, [3] *v.* become thin, waste away.

mactō, [1] *v.* honour; sacrifice; slaughter.

macte, *i.* well done! bravo!

macula, ae, *f.* spot; stain, blemish; mesh in a net.

maculō, [1] *v.* spot; pollute; dishonour, taint.

maculōsus, a, um, *a.* spotted; disreputable.

madefaciō, fēcī, factum, [3] *v.* make wet; soak; **madefīō, fierī,** be moistened, be made wet.

madeō, uī, [2] *v.* be wet *or* sodden; be wet with tears, perspiration, *etc.*

madēscō, duī, [3] *v.* become moist *or* wet.

madidus, a, um, *a.* moist, wet; drenched; drunk.

maenas, adis, *f.* Bacchante, female votary of Bacchus; frenzied woman.

maereō, [2] *v.* be sad, grieve, lament; bewail.

maeror, ōris, *m.* sadness, grief, mourning.

maestitia, ae, *f.* sadness, grief.

maestus, a, um, *a.* sad, melancholy; gloomy; woeful; distressing.

māgālia, ium, *nt. pl.* huts.

magicus, a, um, *a.* magical.

magis, *ad.* more, rather.

magister, trī, *m.* master, chief; expert, tutor, teacher; pilot of a ship; ~ **equitum,** dictator's lieutenant; master of the horse.

magisterium, iī, *nt.* office of a president; instruction.

magistra, ae, *f.* instructress.

magistrātus, ūs, *m.* magistracy; office; magistrate.

magnanimus, a, um, *a.* noble in spirit, brave, generous.

magnēs, ētis, *m.* magnet.

magnificentia, ae, *f.* greatness, nobleness; grandeur; splendour.

magnificus, a, um, *a.* noble, eminent, stately; sumptuous, magnificent, boastful.

magniloquentia, ae, *f.* exalted diction; braggadocio.

magniloquus, a, um, *a.* boastful.

magnitūdō, inis, *f.* greatness, bulk; intensity; importance.

magnopere, *ad.* much, greatly, especially, strongly.

magnus, a, um, *a.* great, large, tall; loud; much; noble, grand; mighty.

magus, ī, *m.* magician, sorcerer; ~, **a, um,** *a.* magical.

māiestās, ātis, *f.* majesty; authority; grandeur; high treason.

maior, ōris, *a.* greater; older; **maiōrēs,** *m. pl.* ancestors.

Māius, ī, *m.* May.

māla, ae, *f.* cheeks, jaws.

malacia, ae, *f.* dead calm.

male, *ad.* badly, ill, wickedly, unfortunately; amiss; sometimes has the force of a negative, *e.g.* **male sānus** for **īnsānus.**

maledīcō, xī, ctum, [3] *v.* speak ill of, abuse.

maledictum, ī, *nt.* reproach, taunt.

malefaciō, fēcī, factum, [3] *v.* do evil or wrong, injure.

maleficium, iī, *nt.* misdeed, crime; injury.

maleficus, a, um, *a.* wicked, criminal, harmful.

malesuādus, a, um, *a.* ill-advising.

malevolus, a, um, *a.* spiteful, malevolent.

mālifer, a, um, *a.* apple-bearing.

malignitās, ātis, *f.* ill-will, spite, malice; niggardliness.

malignus, a, um, *a.* spiteful; niggardly; narrow.

malitia, ae, *f.* wickedness; vice, fault.

malleolus, ī, *m.* fire-dart.

malleus, ī, *m.* hammer, mallet.

mālō, mālle, māluī, *v.* wish or choose rather, prefer.

malum, ī, *nt.* evil, calamity, misfortune.

mālum, ī, *nt.* apple.

malus, a, um, *a.* bad, evil, wicked; unfortunate; weak.

mālus, ī, *m.* pole, mast of a ship; *f.* apple-tree.

malva, ae, *f.* mallow-plant.

mamma, ae, *f.* breast, udder.

manceps, ipis, *m.* contractor, agent.

mancipium, iī, *nt.* formal mode of purchase; property; right of ownership; slave.

mancipō, [1] *v.* transfer, sell; surrender.

mancus, a, um, *a.* maimed, crippled; powerless.

mandātum, ī, *nt.* order, commission.

mandō, [1] *v.* commit to one's charge, commission; command; entrust (to).

mandō, dī, sum, [3] *v.* chew, champ.

māne, *nt. indecl.* morning; ~, *ad.* in the morning; early next day.

maneō, nsī, nsum, [2] *v.* stay, remain; await; abide by; last; endure.

mānēs, ium, *m. pl.* gods of the Lower World; shades *or* ghosts of the dead; mortal remains; underworld; death.

manica, ae, *f.* long sleeve; handcuff.

manifestus, a, um, *a.* clear, evident; plainly guilty; flagrant.

manipulāris, e, *a.* belonging to the ranks, private; ~, **is,** *m.* common soldier; marine.

manipulātim, in handfuls; in companies.

manipulus, maniplus, ī, *m.* handful, bundle; company of soldiers.

mannus, ī, *m.* pony.

mānō, [1] *v.* flow, pour; be shed; be wet; spring.

mānsitō, [1] *v.* spend the night, stay.

mānsuēfaciō, fēcī, factum, [3] *v.* tame; civilize, make mild.

mansuēscō, suēvī, suētum, [3] *v.* tame; become *or* grow tame.

mānsuētūdō, inis, *f.* mildness, clemency.

mānsuētus, a, um, *a.* tame; mild, gentle.

mantēle, is, mantēlium, iī, *nt.* hand-towel; napkin.

mantica, ae, *f.* travelling-bag, knapsack.

manubiae, ārum, *f. pl.* general's share of the booty; prize-money; profits.

manūmittō, mīsī, missum, [3] *v.* set at liberty, emancipate, free.

manus, ūs, *f.* hand; fist; trunk (of an elephant); handwriting; band of soldiers; company; armed force of any size; workman; legal power of a husband; **conferre manum,** to join battle.

mapālia, ium, *nt. pl.* huts in which the Nomadic Africans lived.

mappa, ae, *f.* table-napkin; cloth dropped as a signal to start a race in the circus.

marceō, [2] *v.* be enfeebled, weak *or* faint.

marcēscō, [3] *v.* pine away; become weak, enfeebled *or* languid.

marcidus, a, um, *a.* withered, rotten; exhausted.

mare, is, *nt.* sea; sea-water.

margarītum, ī, *nt.* pearl.

marginō, [1] *v.* provide with borders.

margō, inis, *m. & f.* edge; rim; border.

marīnus, a, um, *a.* of *or* belonging to the sea, marine; sea-born; rōs~, rosemary.

marīta, ae, *f.* wife.

maritimus, a, um, *a.* sea . . . , maritime; (of people) used to the sea; **maritima, ōrum,** *nt. pl.* sea-coast.

marītō, [1] *v.* marry, give in marriage.

marītus, a, um, *a.* married, united, 'wedded'; ~, **ī,** *m.* husband; mate.

marmor, oris, *nt.* marble; marble statue; sea.

marmoreus, a, um, made of marble; marble-like.

Mars, tis, *m.* god of war; war, battle; warlike spirit; the advantage in war.

Martiālis, e, *a.* of *or* belonging to Mars.

Martius, a, um, *a.* of *or* belonging to Mars; March.

mās, maris, *a.* male; masculine; manly.

māsculus, a, um, *a.* male; manly; virile.

massa, ae, *f.* lump, mass; bulk, size.

Massicum, ī, *nt.* Massic wine.

mastīgia, ae, *m.* one who deserves a whipping, rascal.

māter, tris, *f.* mother; matron; origin, source; motherland, mother-city.

mātercula, ae, *f.* affectionate term for mother.

māterfamiliās, mātrisfamiliās, *f.* mistress of the house; respectable married woman.

māteria, ae, māteriēs, ēī, *f.* material; timber; subject-matter.

māternus, a, um, *a.* motherly, maternal.

mathēmaticus, ī, *m.* mathematician; astrologer.

mātrimōnium, iī, *nt.* marriage, matrimony.

mātrimus, a, um, *a.* having a mother living.

mātrōna, ae, *f.* wife, matron.

mātrōnālis, e, *a.* of *or* befitting a married woman.

mātūrēscō, ruī, [3] *v.* become ripe, ripen; mature.

mātūritās, ātis, *f.* ripeness.

mātūrō, [1] *v.* make ripe; hasten; make haste to.

mātūrus, a, um, *a.* ripe; mellow; mature; seasonable, timely; early; speedy.

mātūtīnus, a, um, *a.* of or belonging to the early morning.

Māvors, ortis v. **Mars.**

maximus, a, um, *a.* greatest, *etc.,* v. **magnus.**

mē, *acc. and abl.* of **ego.**

meātus, ūs, *m.* movement, course.

mēcum = cum mē.

medēns, entis, *m.* physician, doctor.

medeor, [2] *v. dep.* heal, cure; remedy.

mēdica, ae, *f.* a kind of clover, lucerne.

medicābilis, e, *a.* curable.

medicāmen, inis, *nt.* drug, remedy, medicine; dye.

medicāmentum, ī, *nt.* drug, remedy, medicine.

medicīna, ae, *f.* medical art; medicine; treatment, remedy.

medicō, [1] *v.* heal, cure; medicate; dye.

medicor, ātus, [1] *v. dep.* heal, cure.

medicus, a, um, *a.* healing, medical; ~, ī, *m.* physician, doctor.

medimnum, ī, *nt.* **medimnus, ī**, *m.* a dry measure, Greek 'bushel' (6 **modiī**).

mediocris, e, *a.* middling, moderate, tolerable, mediocre.

mediocritās, ātis, *f.* medium, moderateness; mediocrity.

meditāmentum, ī, *nt.* training exercise.

meditātiō, ōnis, *f.* contemplation, meditation; practising.

mediterrāneus, a, um, *a.* remote from the coast, inland.

meditor, ātus, [1] *v.* think about constantly, ponder; intend; devise; reflect; practise; work over in performance.

medium, iī, *nt.* middle; public, publicity.

medius, a, um, *a.* mid, middle; neutral; ambiguous; middling, ordinary; moderate.

medulla, ae, *f.* marrow, kernel; innermost part; quintessence.

mel, mellis, *nt.* honey; sweetness; darling.

melicus, a, um, *a.* musical, lyrical; ~, ī, *m.* a lyric poet.

melior, ius, ōris, *a. comp.* better, v. **bonus.**

mellifer, a, um, *a.* honey-producing.

mellītus, a, um, *a.* sweetened with honey; honey-sweet.

melos, ī, *nt.* song.

membrāna, ae, *f.* membrane; skin; parchment.

membrātim, *ad.* limb by limb.

membrum, ī, *nt.* limb; the genital member.

mēmet v. **mē**.

meminī, isse, v. remember; retain in the mind; attend to; recall in writing, speech, *etc.*

memor, oris, *a.* mindful (of), remembering, unforgetting; grateful; commemorative.

memorābilis, e, *a.* memorable, remarkable.

memoria, ae, *f.* memory; recollection; time within remembrance; history.

memorō, [1] *v.* remind of; mention; relate.

menda, ae, *f.,* v. **mendum**.

mendācium, iī, *nt.* lie; counterfeit.

mendāx, ācis, *a.* lying; false; deceitful; counterfeit.

mendīcō, [1] *v.* beg for; be a beggar.

mendōsus, a, um, *a.* faulty, erroneous; prone to error.

mendum, ī, *nt.* blemish, fault; error.

mēns, mentis, *f.* mind, intellect; reason, judgement; frame of mind; disposition, intention.

mēnsa, ae, *f.* table; meal; course (at a meal); banker's counter.

mēnsārius, iī, *m.* moneychanger, banker; treasury official.

mēnsis, is, *m.* month.

mēnsor, ōris, *m.* land-surveyor; surveyor of building-works.

mēnstruus, a, um, *a.* monthly.

mēnsūra, ae, *f.* measuring; length, area, capacity, *etc.*

mentiō, ōnis, *f.* mention.

mentior, ītus, [4] *v. dep.* lie, deceive; feign; speak falsely about; give a false impression; mimic.

mentula, ae, *f.* the male sexual organ.

mentum, ī, *nt.* chin.

meō, [1] *v.* go along, pass, travel.

merācus, a, um, *a.* undiluted, neat.

mercātor, ōris, *m.* trader, merchant.

mercātūra, ae, *f.* trade, commerce.

mercātus, ūs, *m.* gathering for the purposes of commerce; market; fair.

mercēnnārius, a, um, *a.* hired, mercenary; ~, **iī,** *m.* hired worker; mercenary.

mercēs, ēdis, *f.* hire, pay, wages, salary; reward; rent, price.

mercor, ātus, [1] *v. dep.* trade; buy.

merda, ae, *f.* dung, excrement.

mereō, uī, itum, mereor, itus, [2] *v.* earn, get; deserve; be rewarded; **merēre stipendia,** *v.* to serve as soldier; draw pay as a soldier.

meretrīcius, a, um, *a.* of, belonging to, *or* typical of a courtesan.

meretrīcula, ae, *f.* courtesan.

meretrīx, īcis, *f.* courtesan, kept woman.

merges, itis, *f.* sheaf of corn.

mergō, sī, sum, [3] *v.* immerse; plunge; bury; hide; drown; overwhelm; plunge in ruin.

mergus, ī, *m.* a sea-bird, probably a gull.

merīdiānus, a, um, *a.* pertaining to noon; southern.

merīdiēs, ēī, *m.* midday, noon; south.

meritum, ī, *nt.* desert; service, kindness; due reward.

meritus, a, um, *a.* deserved, due.

mersō, [1] *v.* dip (in); immerse; overwhelm, drown.

merula, ae, *f.* blackbird; a dark-coloured fish, the wrasse.

merum, ī, *nt.* wine unmixed with water.

merus, a, um, *a.* pure, unmixed; bare, only, mere; sheer.

merx, cis, *f.* a commodity; (*pl.*) goods, merchandise.

messis, is, *m.* or *f.* harvest, crop; harvest time.

messor, ōris, *m.* reaper, harvester.

. . .-met = self.

mēta, ae, *f.* cone-shaped turning post at either end of a race-track; limit; end; conical shape; cone.

metallum, ī, *nt.* metal; mine; quarry.

mētior, mēnsus, [4] *v. dep.* measure; traverse; walk or sail through; estimate, gauge.

metō, messuī, messum, [3] *v.* reap, mow, cut off.

mētor, ātus, [1] *v. dep.* measure off, mark out.

metuō, uī, ūtum, [3] *v.* be afraid of; be afraid to; fear.

metus, ūs, *m.* fear; anxiety; awe; object of dread.

meus, a, um, *a.* my, mine.

mī, *voc.* of **meus**.

mīca, ae, *f.* particle, grain, crumb.

micō, uī, [1] *v.* move quickly, quiver; dart; throb; flash, glitter.

migrātiō, ōnis, *f.* change of abode; move.

migrō, [1] *v.* change one's residence or position; pass into a new condition; move, shift.

mīles, itis, *m.* soldier; foot-soldier; soldiery.

mīlitāris, e, *a.* military; warlike.

mīlitia, ae, *f.* military service; campaign.

mīlitō, [1] *v.* serve as a soldier.

milium, iī, *nt.* millet.

mīlle, *pl.* **mīlia**, or **mīlia**, *a.* thousand; thousands; innumerable; ~ **passūs**, *m. pl.* a mile.

mīllēsimus, a, um, *a.* a thousandth.

mīlliārium (or mīl.), iī, *nt.* milestone.

mīlliēs (or mīl.), *ad.* a thousand times.

mīlvus, ī, *m.* kite.

mīma, ae, *f.* actress performing in mimes.

mīmus, ī, *m.* actor in mimes; mime; farce.

minae, ārum, *f. pl.* threats, menaces; warning signs.

mināx, ācis, *a.* threatening; boding ill.

Minerva, ae, *f.* a person's natural capacity, intelligence, tastes, *etc.*; weaving; spinning.

minimus, a, um, *a.* least, smallest, v. **parvus**.

minister, trī, *m.* attendant; servant; agent; accomplice.

ministerium, iī, *nt.* service; employment; commission.

ministrō, [1] *v. with dat.* attend (to), serve; furnish; supply.

minitor, ātus, [1] *v. dep. with dat.* threaten.

minor, ātus, [1] *v. dep. with dat.* threaten.

minor, us, ōris, *a.* smaller, lesser, younger, *etc.*, v. **parvus**; **minōrēs, um**, *m. pl.* descendants.

minuō, uī, ūtum, [3] *v.* lessen; impair; abate; make smaller; grow less.

minus, *ad.* less; not so well; not quite.

minūtātim, *ad.* bit by bit.

minūtus, a, um, *a.* small, insignificant, petty.

mīrābilis, e, *a.* wonderful, marvellous, extraordinary.

mīrābundus, a, um, *a.* wondering.

mīrāculum, ī, *nt.* wonder, marvel; amazing event.

mīrātor, ōris, *m.* admirer.

mīrificus, a, um, *a.* wonderful; amazing.

mīror, ātus, [1] *v. dep.* wonder at, be amazed (at); admire.

mīrus, a, um, *a.* wonderful, astonishing.

misceō, miscuī, mistum & mixtum, [2] *v.* mix, mingle; embroil; confound; stir up.

misellus, a, um, *a.* poor, wretched.

miser, a, um, *a.* wretched, unfortunate, miserable; distressing.

miserābilis, e, *a.* pitiable; wretched.

miserātiō, ōnis, *f.* pity, compassion.

miserē, *ad.* wretchedly; desperately.

misereor, itus sum, [2] *v. dep.* pity. **mē miseret, miserētur**, *v. impers. with gen.* it distresses me (for); I pity.

miserēscō, [3] *v. with gen.* have compassion (on).

miseria, ae, *f.* wretchedness, misery; distress; woe.

misericordia, ae, *f.* pity, compassion; pathos.

misericors, dis, *a.* merciful, tender-hearted.

miseror, ātus, [1] *v. dep.* feel sorry for.

missilis, e, *a.* that may be thrown, missile.

missiō, ōnis, *f.* sending (away); release; discharge (of soldiers); reprieve.

missitō, [1] *v.* send repeatedly.

missus, ūs, *m.* sending (away); despatch; shooting, discharge of missiles.

mītēscō, [3] *v.* become soft and mellow; ripen; grow mild; soften.

mītigō, [1] *v.* soften; lighten, alleviate; soothe; civilize.

mītis, e, *a.* mild; sweet and juicy, mellow; placid; soothing; clement.

mitra, ae, *f.* an oriental headdress.

mittō, mīsī, missum, [3] *v.* send; cast, hurl; throw away; dismiss; disregard, say nothing of; subject (to).

mōbilis, e, *a.* quick, active; movable; changeable; inconstant.

mōbilitās, ātis, *f.* agility, quickness of mind; mobility; inconstancy.

moderābilis, e, *a.* controllable.

moderāmen, inis, *nt.* rudder; management, government.

moderātiō, ōnis, *f.* moderation; guidance, government.

moderātor, ōris, *m.* governor, master; user; one who restrains.

moderātus, a, um, *a.* moderate; restrained; sober; temperate.

moderor, ātus, [1] *v. dep.* guide; control; regulate; govern.

modestia, ae, *f.* restraint, temperateness; discipline; modesty.

modestus, a, um, *a.* restrained, mild; modest; reserved; disciplined.

modicus, a, um, *a.* moderate; temperate, restrained.

modius, iī, *m.* Roman dry measure, peck.

modo, *ad.* only; just now; provided that; if only; **modo . . . , modo . . . ,** at one time . . . at another.

modulor, ātus, [1] *v. dep.* sing; play; set to music.

modus, ī, *m.* measure; size; rhythm; metre; mode; manner; bound, limit; end; moderation.

moecha, ae, *f.* adulteress.

moechor, ātus, [1] *v. dep.* commit adultery.

moechus, ī, *m.* adulterer.

moenia, ium, *nt. pl.* town walls, fortified town.

mola, ae, *f.* millstone; (*pl.*) mill; cake of ground barley and salt (for sacrifices); sacrificial meal.

molāris, is, *m.* rock as large as a millstone used as a missile; molar tooth.

mōlēs, is, *f.* huge, heavy mass, lump; monster; massive structure; danger; trouble; effort; vast undertaking.

molestus, a, um, *a.* troublesome, tiresome.

mōlīmen, inis, *nt.* effort, vehemence; bulk; weight.

mōlīmentum, ī, *nt.* exertion, labour.

mōlior, ītus, [4] *v.* labour to bring about; strive; *dep.* labour at, perform with effort; propel, set in motion; build.

mollēscō, [3] *v.* become soft; become gentle *or* effeminate.

molliō, īvī & iī, ītum, [4] *v.* soften; mitigate; make easier; tame, enfeeble.

mollis, e, *a.* soft, tender, mild; mellow; pleasant; weak; effeminate; impressionable; sensitive.

mollitia, ae, *f.,* **mollitiēs, ēī,** *f.* softness; tenderness; weakness; effeminacy.

mōmen, inis, *nt.* movement; impulse; a trend.

mōmentum, ī, *nt.* movement, impulse; effort; moment; importance; influence.

monēdula, ae, *f.* jackdaw.

moneō, uī, itum, [2] *v.* warn; advise; presage.

monīle, is, *nt.* necklace; collar; collar (for horses and other animals).

monitiō, ōnis, *f.* advice; warning.

monitor, ōris, *m.* counsellor; preceptor; prompter.

monitus, ūs, *m.* warning, command; advice, counsel.

mōns, tis, *m.* mountain; towering heap; huge rock.

mōnstrātor, ōris, *m.* guide, demonstrator.

mōnstrō, [1] *v.* show, point out; teach; reveal.

mōnstrum, ī, *nt.* unnatural thing *or* event regarded as on omen, portent, sign; monstrous thing; monster; atrocity.

mōnstruōsus, a, um, *a.* strange, monstrous, ill-omened.

montānus, a, um, *a.* mountain. . .; mountainous; ~, **ī,** *m.* mountain- *or* hill-dweller.

monticola, ae, *m. a.* mountain-dwelling.

montuōsus, a, um, *a.* mountainous.

monumentum, ī, *nt.* memorial, monument; tomb; record; a literary work, book; history.

mora, ae, *f.* delay; hindrance, obstacle.

morātor, ōris, *m.* delayer; loiterer.

mōrātus, a, um, *a.* endowed with character *or* manners of a specified kind; gentle, civilized.

morbidus, a, um, *a.* diseased; unhealthy.

morbus, ī, *m.* sickness, disease, illness, distress; weakness, vice.

mordāx, ācis, *a.* biting, snappish; tart; cutting, sharp; caustic.

mordeō, momordī, morsum, [2] *v.* bite; sting; hurt, distress; vex; criticize, carp at.

mordicus, *ad.* by biting, with the teeth; tenaciously.

moribundus, a, um, *a.* dying.

mŏrigerus, a, um, *a.* compliant, indulgent.

morior, morī, mortuus, [3] *v. dep.* die; fail; decay.

moror, ātus, [1] *v. dep.* delay, stay behind; devote attention to.

mōrōsus, a, um, *a.* hard to please, pernickety.

mors, tis, *f.* death; corpse; annihilation.

morsus, ūs, *m.* bite; sting; anguish, pain.

mortālis, e, *a.* mortal; transient; human; of human origin.

mortālitās, ātis, *f.* mortality; death.

mortifer, mortiferus, a, um, *a.* death-bringing, deadly.

mortuus, a, um, *a.* dead, deceased.

mōrum, ī, *nt.* fruit of the black mulberry.

mōrus, ī, *f.* black mulberry-tree.

mōs, mōris, *m.* custom, usage; manner; style; civilization; law; **mōrēs,** *pl.* character; behaviour; morals.

mōtō, [1] *v.* set in motion, shake, stir, *etc.*

mōtus, ūs, *m.* moving, motion; commotion; disturbance; emotion; prompting; manoeuvre.

moveō, mōvī, mōtum, [2] *v.* move, stir; brandish; agitate; af-fect; provoke; set in motion; shift; influence.

mox, *ad.* soon, next in position.

mucrō, ōnis, *m.* sharp point; sword.

mūcus, ī, *m.* mucus, snot.

mūgil, is, mūgilis, is, *m.* grey mullet.

mūgiō, īvī & ītum, [4] *v.* low, bellow; make a loud deep noise.

mūgītus, ūs, *m.* lowing, bellowing; roaring, rumble.

mūla, ae, *f.* she-mule; mule.

mulceō, sī, sum, [2] *v.* stroke, touch lightly; soothe, appease; charm, beguile.

Mulciber, eris & erī, *m.* Vulcan; fire.

mulcō, [1] *v.* beat up; worst.

mulctra, ae, *f. or* **mulctrum, ī,** *nt.* milking-pail.

mulgeō, sī, sum & ctum, [2] *v.* milk.

muliebris, e, *a.* womanly, female, feminine; womanish, effeminate; **muliebria patī,** to be used as a catamite.

mulier, is, *f.* woman; wife, mistress.

muliercula, ae, *f.* (little, weak, foolish, *etc.*) woman.

mūliō, ōnis, *m.* muleteer.

mullus, ī, *m.* red mullet.

mulsum, ī, *nt.* drink from honey and wine.

multa, ae, *f.* fine; penalty.

multicavus, a, um, *a.* porous.

multifāriam, *ad.* in many places.

multifidus, a, um, *a.* splintered.

multigenus, a, um, *a.* of many different sorts.

multiplex, icis, *a.* having many windings; having many layers *or* thicknesses; multifarious; changeable.

multiplicō, [1] *v.* multiply; increase.

multitūdō, inis, *f.* great number, multitude; crowd; mob.

multō, *ad.* much, by far; long (before *or* after).

multō, [1] *v.* punish; fine.

multum, *ad.* much, plenty.

multus, a, um, *a.* much, great; many a; large, intense; assiduous; tedious.

mūlus, ī, *m.* mule.

munditia, ae, munditiēs, ēī, *f.* cleanness, elegance of appearance, manners *or* taste.

mundus, a, um, *a.* clean, elegant; delicate, refined.

mundus, ī, *m.* toilet, ornaments; world; universe.

mūnia, ōrum. *nt. pl.* duties, functions.

mūniceps, ipis, *m.* citizen of a municipium; native of the same municipium.

mūnicipālis, e, *a.* of, belonging to *or* typical of a **municipium**; (in contempt) provincial.

mūnicipium, iī, *nt.* town subject to Rome, but governed by its own laws; free town.

mūnificentia, ae, *f.* bountifulness, munificence.

mūnificus, a, um, *a.* bountiful, liberal, munificent.

mūnīmen, inis, *nt.* fortification; defence.

mūnīmentum, ī, *nt.* fortification; bulwark; defence.

mūniō, īvī & iī, ītum, [4] *v.* fortify; build (a road); defend; safeguard.

mūnītiō, ōnis, *f.* fortifying; fortification.

mūnītor, ōris, *m.* one who builds fortifications.

mūnus, eris, *nt.* function, duty; gift; public show.

mūnusculum, ī, *nt.* small present *or* favour.

mūrālis, e, *a.* of walls; of *or* connected with a (city) wall; turreted.

mūrena ae, murena, *f.* kind of eel, the moray.

mūrex, icis, *m.* purple dye; purple cloth.

murmur, uris, *nt.* murmur(ing); humming; growling; whisper; rustling; roaring (of the sea, a lion *or* the thunder).

murmurō, [1] *v.* hum, murmur, mutter; roar.

murra, myrr(h)a, ae, *f.* myrrh, an aromatic gum.

murreus, a, um, *a.* having the colour of myrrh, i.e. reddish-brown.

mūrus, ī, *m.* wall; city wall.

mūs, mūris, *m.* mouse.

Mūsa, ae, *f.* Muse; poetic composition; ~ **ae,** *pl.* sciences, poetry.

muscōsus, a, um, *a.* mossy.

muscus, ī, *m.* moss.

mussitō, [1] *v.* mutter; keep quiet (about).

mussō, [1] *v.* say in an undertone, mutter; keep quiet (about).

mustēla, mustella, ae, *f.* weasel.

mustum, ī, *nt.* unfermented grape-juice, must.

mūtābilis, e, *a.* changeable; inconstant.

mūtātiō, ōnis, *f.* changing; exchange.

mutilō, [1] *v.* maim, mutilate; lop off.

mutilus, a, um, *a.* mutilated; hornless, having stunted horns.

mūtō, [1] *v.* alter, change; exchange; shift; substitute (for).

mūtuātiō, ōnis, *f.* borrowing.

mūtuor, ātus, [1] *v. dep.* borrow.

mūtus, a, um, *a.* silent, dumb, mute; speechless.

mūtuus, a, um, *a.* borrowed, lent; mutual, in return.

myoparōn, ōnis, *m.* light naval vessel.

myrīcē, ēs, *f.* tamarisk (bush).

myrtētum, ī, *nt.* myrtle-grove.

myrteus, a, um, *a.* of myrtle.

myrtum, ī, *nt.* myrtle-berry.

myrtus, ī, *f.* myrtle, myrtle-tree.

mystērium, iī, *nt.* sacred mystery; secret.

mysticus, a, um, *a.* belonging to the sacred mysteries; mysterious.

N

naevus, ī, *m.* mole (on the body); birth-mark.

Nāias, adis, Nāis, idis & idos, *f.* water-nymph; nymph.

nam, for.

namque, certainly; for; now, well then.

nancīscor, nactus or **nānctus sum,** [3] *v. dep.* get, obtain, receive; meet with.

nardum, ī, *nt.* **nardus, ī,** *f.* nard; nard-oil.

nāris, is, *f.* nose; **nārēs, ium,** *pl.* nostrils; nose.

nārrābilis, e, *a.* that can be narrated.

nārrātiō, ōnis, *f.* narrative, story.

nārrātus, ūs, *m.,* v. **nārrātiō.**

nārrō, [1] *v.* tell, narrate; describe, tell about.

nāscor, nātus, [3] *v. dep.* be born; proceed (from); rise; grow.

nāsus, ī, *m.* nose; sense of smelling.

nāsūtus, a, um, *a.* having a long nose.

nāta, ae, *f.* daughter.

nātālis, e, *a.* of *or* belonging to birth, natal; native; ~, **is,** *m.* birthday; **nātālēs, ium,** *m. pl.* parentage, origins.

natātor, ōris, *m.* swimmer.

natēs, ium, *f. pl.* buttocks.

nātiō, ōnis, *f.* race, nation, people; class, set.

nātīvus, a, um, *a.* innate; natural, native.

natō, [1] *v.* swim; float; be inundated; sway, lack firmness, waver.

nātūra, ae, *f.* nature; character; **rērum** ~, the way things happen.

nātūrālis, e, *a.* natural; innate.

nātus, ī, *m.* son; (*pl.*) children, offspring.

naufragium, iī, *nt.* shipwreck; ruin; wreckage.

naufragus, a, um, *a.* shipwrecked; causing shipwreck; ruined.

nausea, ae, *f.* sea-sickness; nausea.

nauseō, [1] *v.* be sea-sick; feel sick.

nauta, ae, *m.* sailor, seaman.

nauticus, a, um, *a.* nautical; **nauticī, ōrum,** *m. pl.* seamen, sailors.

nāvāle, is, *nt.* dock, slipway.

nāvālis, e, *a.* nautical, naval.

nāvicula, ae, *f.* little ship, boat.

nāvifragus, a, um, *a.* shipwrecking.

nāvigābilis, e, *a.* navigable, suitable for shipping.

nāvigātiō, ōnis, *f.* sailing, seavoyage.

nāviger, a, um, *a.* ship-bearing, navigable.

nāvigium, iī, *nt.* vessel, ship.

nāvis, is, *f.* ship; ~ **longa,** ship of war; ~ **onerāria,** merchant ship; **nāvem solvere,** to set sail.

nāvita v. **nauta.**

nāviter, *ad.* diligently; wholly.

nāvō, [1] *v.* devote oneself to; accomplish; **operam nāvāre,** to devote one's energies.

nāvus, a, um, *a.* active, industrious.

nē, verily; indeed.

nē, not; that not; in order that not; lest; **nē. . .quidem,** not even.

-ne, interrogative particle not implying anything about the answer expected; **vidēsne,** do you see?; (in indirect questions) whether.

nebula, ae, *f.* mist, fog; cloud.

nebulō, ōnis, *m.* rascal, scoundrel.

nec, *c.* neither; nor; and not; ~ **nōn,** and also; **nec. . .nec,** neither. . .nor.

necdum, *c.* and (but) not yet.

necessārius, a, um, *a.* necessary; indispensable; connected by close ties of friendship, relationship *or* obligation.; ~, **iī,** *m.* close relative; near friend.

necesse, *ad.* essential; inevitable.

necessitās, ātis, *f.* necessity; constraint; poverty.

necessitūdō, inis, *f.* obligation, affinity; compulsion.

necne, or not.

necnōn v. **nec.**

necō, [1] *v.* kill.

necopīnāns, antis, *a.* not expecting; unawares.

necopīnātus, a, um, *a.,* **necopīnus, a, um,** *a.* unexpected, unforeseen.

nectar, aris, *nt.* nectar, the drink of the gods; anything sweet, pleasant *or* delicious.

nectareus, a, um, *a.* sweet as nectar.

nectō, xuī & xī, xum, [3] *v.* bind, tie *or* join together, link; contrive.

nēcubi, *ad.* lest at any place; lest on any occasion.

nēcunde, *ad.* lest from anywhere.

nēdum, *c.* still less; not to speak of; much more;

nefandus, a, um, *a.* impious; wicked; abominable.

nefārius, a, um, *a.* offending against moral law, wicked.

nefās, *nt.* indecl. sin, crime (against divine law); wicked action; portent, horror; ~! *i.* oh horror!

nefāstus, a, um, *a.* contrary to divine law; **diēs nefāstī,** days unfit for public business.

negitō, [1] *v.* deny *or* refuse repeatedly.

neglegēns, entis, *a.* heedless, neglectful.

neglegentia, ae, *f.* heedlessness, neglect.

neglegō, lēxī, lēctum, [3] *v.* not to heed, neglect; overlook; do without.

negō, [1] *v.* say no, deny; refuse, decline.

negōtiātor, ōris, *m.* wholesale trader *or* dealer.

negōtior, ātus, [1] *v. dep.* do business, trade.

negōtiōsus, a, um, *a.* active, occupied.

negōtium, iī, *nt.* business; difficulty; trouble; situation.

nēmō, inis, *m.* or *f.* no one, nobody; ~ **nōn,** every.

nemorālis, e, *a.* belonging to a wood *or* forest, sylvan.

nemorivagus, a, um, *a.* forestroving.

nemorōsus, a, um, *a.* wellwooded.

nempe, *c.* without doubt; why, clearly; admittedly.

nemus, oris, *nt.* wood, forest.

nēnia, ae, *f.* funeral dirge sung; incantation, jingle.

neō, nēvī, nētum, [2] *v.* spin; weave; produce by spinning.

nepōs, ōtis, *m.* grandson; descendant; spendthrift, playboy; **nepōtēs**, *pl.* descendants.

neptis, is, *f.* granddaughter; female descendant.

Neptūnus, ī, *m.* Neptune; sea.

nēquam, *a. indecl.* worthless; bad.

nēquāquam, *ad.* by no means, not at all.

neque, *c.* not; and not; *cf.* **nec**.

nequedum v. **necdum**.

nequeō, īvī & iī, [4] *v.* to be unable (to).

nēquicquam *or* **nēquīquam**, *ad.* in vain.

nēquis, lest any one.

nēquiter, *ad.* badly; wickedly.

nēquitia, ae, nēquitiēs, ēī, *f.* (moral) badness, vice; villainy; naughtiness.

Nērēis, idos, *f.* sea-nymph.

Nēreus, ei *or* **eos**, *m.* Nereus; the sea.

nervōsus, a, um, *a.* sinewy; vigorous.

nervus, ī, *m.* sinew; nerve; bowstring; string (of a lute, *etc.*); fetter; strength, vigour.

nesciō, īvī & iī, ītum, [4] *v.* not to know; be unfamiliar with.

nescius, a, um, *a.* not knowing, ignorant.

neu v. **nēve**.

neuter, tra, trum, *a.* neither (of two).

neutrō, *ad.* to neither side.

nēve, *ad.* and not; nor, and that not; **nēve . . . nēve**, neither . . . nor.

nex, necis, *f.* violent death, murder.

nexilis, e, *a.* woven together, intertwined.

nexum, ī, *n.*, **nexus, ūs**, *m.* obligation between creditor and debtor.

nexus, ī *m.* one reduced to quasi-slavery for debt, bondman.

nī, *ad. & c.* if . . . not; unless; ~ **quid nī?** why not?

nictō, [1] *v.* blink.

nīdor, ōris, *m.* rich, strong smell, fumes.

nīdus, ī, *m.* nest; set of nestlings; eyrie.

niger, gra, grum, *a.* black, dark; discoloured, sombre. ill-omened.

nigrāns, antis, *a.* black, dark-coloured; shadowy; murky.

nigrēscō, gruī, [3] *v.* become black, grow dark.

nigrō, [1] *v.* be black.

nihil, *n. indecl.* nothing; ~, *ad.* not at all.

nihilōminus, *ad.* nevertheless, notwithstanding.

nihilum, *ad.* nothing as yet.

nihilum, **ī**, *nt.* nothing; **dē nihilō**, for nothing; for no reason.

nīl, contr. of **nihil**, nothing.

nimbōsus, **a**, **um**, *a.* full of, *or* surrounded by, rain clouds.

nimbus, **ī**, *m.* rain-cloud; cloud; cloud-burst; shower.

nimiō, *ad.* by a very great degree, far.

nīmīrum, *ad.* without doubt, evidently, forsooth.

nimis, *ad.* too much; exceedingly.

nimium, *ad.* too much, too, very much.

nimius, **a**, **um**, *a.* excessive, too great, too much; intemperate; over-confident.

ningit, **nxit**, [3] *v. impers.* it snows.

nisi, *c.* if not; unless.

nīsus, **ūs**, *m.* resting one's weight on the ground; endeavour; exertion; strong muscular effort; advance.

niteō, **uī**, [2] *v.* shine, glitter; be sleek and plump.

nitēscō, **tuī**, [3] *v.* begin to shine.

nitidus, **a**, **um**, *a.* shining, glittering, bright; polished; spruce; sleek.

nītor, **nīsus** & **nīxus**, [3] *v. dep.* lean *or* rest (on); endeavour; exert oneself; *fig.* rely (on).

nitor, **ōris**, *m.* brightness, splendour; beauty; elegance, smartness.

nivālis, **e**, *a.* snowy, snow-covered; snow-like.

niveus, **a**, **um**, *a.* snowy; snow-white.

nivōsus, **a**, **um**, *a.* full of snow, snowy.

nix, **nivis**, *f.* snow; white hair.

nixus, **ūs**, *m.* straining; (*pl.*) the efforts of childbirth, travail.

nō, [1] *v.* swim; float.

nōbilis, **e**, *a.* famous, celebrated; high-born; superior; ~, **is**, *m.* nobleman.

nōbilitās, **ātis**, *f.* renown, glory; high birth; excellence; nobleness.

nōbilitō, [1] *v.* make known; render famous; render notorious.

noceō, **cuī**, **citum**, [2] *v. with dat.* hurt, injure, impair.

noctivagus, **a**, **um**, *a.* night-wandering.

noctū, by night, at night.

noctua, **ae**, *f.* the little owl.

nocturnus, **a**, **um**, *a.* nocturnal; under conditions of night.

nōdō, [1] *v.* tie in a knot *or* knots.

nōdōsus, **a**, **um**, *a.* tied into many knots, full of knots; knotty.

nōdus, **ī**, *m.* knot; rope; difficulty; intricacy; bond.

nōlo, **nōlle**, **nōluī**, *v.* not to wish; be unwilling; refuse.

nōmen, inis, *nt.* name; family; celebrity.

nōminātim, *ad.* by name, expressly.

nōminātiō, ōnis, *f.* naming; nomination (to an office).

nōminitō, [1] *v.* name, term.

nōminō, [1] *v.* name; nominate; accuse, mention, speak of, make famous.

nōn, *ad.* not.

Nōnae, ārum, *f. pl.* the Nones; the fifth day of the month, except in March, May, July, and October, when the Nones fell on the seventh day.

nōnāgintā, *a. indecl.* ninety.

nōnānus, a, um, *a.* of the ninth legion.

nōndum, *ad.* not yet.

nōngentī, ae, a, *a.* nine hundred.

nōnne, *ad.* is it not the case that. . .?

nōnnēmō, inis, *m.* or *f.*, some persons, a few.

nōnnihil, *n. indecl.* a certain amount; ~ *ad.* in some measure.

nōnnūllus, a, um, *a.* not a little; some, several.

nōnnunquam, *ad.* sometimes.

nōnus, a, um, *a.* the ninth.

norma, ae, *f.* carpenter's square; standard, pattern.

nōs, *pn.* we.

nōscitō, [1] *v.* recognize; be acquainted with.

nōscō, nōvī, nōtum, [3] *v.* get a knowledge of, learn to know; know.

noster, stra, strum, *a.* our, our own, ours; one of us, our friend; favourable to us; dear, good.

nota, ae, *f.* mark; sign; letter; word; writing; spot; brand, tattoo-mark.

notābilis, e, *a.* remarkable, notable.

notātiō, ōnis, *f.* marking.

nōtēscō, tuī, [3] *v.* become known; become famous.

nothus, a, um, *a.* spurious; illegitimate; (animals) cross-bred.

nōtiō, ōnis, *f.* judicial examination *or* enquiry.

nōtitia, ae, nōtitiēs, ēī, *f.* celebrity; knowledge; conception; acquaintance; carnal knowledge.

notō, [1] *v.* mark; write down; observe; censure; brand, stain, scar.

nōtus, a, um, *a.* known; notorious; familiar.

Notus, Notos, ī, *m.* south wind.

novācula, ae, *f.* razor.

novālis, is, *f.* **novāle, is**, *nt.* fallow-land; enclosed land, field.

novellus, a, um, *a.* young, tender.

novem, *a.* nine.

November, Novembris, is, *m.* November.

novendiālis, e, *a.* lasting nine days; held on the ninth day after a person's death.

novēnus, a, um, *a. num.* nine each; nine at a time.

noverca, ae, *f.* stepmother.

noviē(n)s *ad.* nine times.

novissimus, a, um, *a.* last, rear; most recent; utmost.

novitās, ātis, *f.* newness, novelty; unfamiliarity, surprise.

novō, [1] *v.* make new, renew; alter.

novus, a, um, *a.* new; young, fresh, novel; **novus homō,** first in one's family to attain the consulate.

nox, noctis, *f.* night; darkness; blindness; **nocte, noctū,** by night.

noxa, ae, *f.* hurt, injury; crime; punishment; harm.

noxia, ae, *f.* wrongdoing, injury.

noxius, a, um, *a.* harmful, noxious; guilty, criminal.

nūbēs, is, *f.* cloud; smoke; swarm; gloominess; threat (of war, calamity, *etc.*).

nūbifer, a, um, cloud-capped; that brings clouds.

nūbigena, ae, *m.* cloud-born.

nūbilis, e, *a.* marriageable; nubile.

nūbilus, a, um, *a.* cloudy; lowering; **nūbilum, ī,** *nt.* cloudy sky or weather.

nūbō, psī, ptum, [3] *v. with dat.* marry (a husband).

nūdō, [1] *v.* bare; strip, uncover; plunder; reveal, disclose.

nūdus, a, um, *a.* naked, bare; destitute; unarmed.

nūgae, ārum, *f. pl.* trifles, nonsense; trash; frivolities; bagatelle(s).

nūgātor, ōris, *m.* one who plays the fool; teller of tall stories.

nūgātōrius, a, um, *a.* trifling, worthless, futile, paltry.

nūgor, ātus, [1] *v. dep.* play the fool, talk nonsense; trifle.

nūllus, a, um, nūllīus, *a.* not any, no.

num, (in direct questions when the answer 'no' is expected); whether (in indirect questions).

nūmen, inis, *nt.* nod; bias; divine will; divine presence; deity, god.

numerābilis, e, *a.* possible *or* easy to count.

numerō, [1] *v.* count, number.

numerōsus, a, um, *a.* numerous; harmonious.

numerus, ī, *m.* number; rhythm; poetry, metre; class.

nummātus, a, um, *a.* moneyed.

nummus, ī, *m.* coin, money.

numquam v. **nunquam**.

nūmus v. **nummus**.

nunc, *ad.* now, at present; **nunc . . . nunc,** one time . . . another time.

nunciam, *ad.* here and now; now at last.

nuncupō, [1] *v.* call, name; express.

nūndinae, ārum, *f. pl.* market-day; *fig.* traffic.

nūndinor, ātus, [1] *dep.* buy *or* sell in the market; practise trade of a discreditable kind.

nūndinum, ī, *nt.* the period from one market-day to the next.

nunquam, *ad.* at no time, never; not in any circumstances.

nūntiō, [1] *v.* announce; relate, inform.

nūntius, a, um, *a.* bringing tidings, reporting; ~, **iī**, *m.* messenger; message.

nūper, *ad.* recently, not long ago; in modern times.

nūpta, ae, *f.* wife, married woman.

nūptiae, ārum, *f. pl.* marriage.

nūptiālis, e, *a.* nuptial.

nurus, ūs, *f.* daughter-in-law; young woman.

nusquam, *ad.* nowhere, in no place; to no place; on no occasion; ~ **esse**, not to exist.

nūtō, [1] *v.* nod; sway to and fro; waver; waver in allegiance.

nūtrīcius, iī, *m.* tutor; foster-father.

nūtrīcula, ae, *f.* nurse.

nūtrīmen, inis, *nt.* **nūtrīmentum, ī**, *nt.* nourishment, sustenance.

nūtriō, īvī & iī, ītum, [4] *v.* suckle, nourish, foster, bring up; tend; deal gently with.

nūtrīx, īcis, *f.* wet-nurse, nurse.

nūtus, ūs, *m.* nod; will, command.

nux, nucis, *f.* nut; thing of no value.

nympha, ae, nymphē, ēs, *f.* nymph, young wife, maiden.

••••••••••••••••••••••••••

O

••••••••••••••••••••••••••

ō, i. oh! ~ (**sī**), if only.

ob, *pr. with acc.* for; by reason of.

obaerātus, a, um, *a.* involved in debt; ~, **ī**, *m.* debtor.

obambulō, [1] *v.* walk up to, so as to meet; traverse.

obarmō, [1] *v.* arm.

obarō, [1] *v.* plough up.

obc . . . v. occ . . .

obdō, didī, ditum, [3] *v.* put before *or* against; shut; expose to danger.

obdūcō, xī, ctum, [3] *v.* lead *or* draw before; cover *or* lay over; overspread; wrinkle; screen.

obdūrēscō, ruī, [3] *v.* be persistent, endure.

obdūrō, [1] *v.* persist, endure.

obeō, īvī & iī, itum, [4] *v.* meet with; visit; review; enclose; accept; die; set.

obequitō, [1] *v.* ride up to.

obēsus, a, um, *a.* fat, stout, plump.

obex, obicis, *m.* or *f.* bolt, bar; barrier; obstacle.

obf . . . v. off . . .

obiciō, iēcī, iectum, [3] *v.* throw before *or* towards; expose (to); interpose; lay to one's charge.

obiaceō, uī, [2] *v.* lie at hand.

obiectō, [1] *v.* expose (to); lay to one's charge.

obiectus, ūs, *m.* placing something in the way of; barrier.

obitus, ūs, *m.* approaching; approach, visit; setting (of the sun, *etc.*); death.

obiurgō, [1] *v.* chide; rebuke.

oblectāmen, inis, *nt.,* **oblectāmentum, ī,** *nt.* delight, pleasure, source of pleasure.

oblectātiō, ōnis, *f.* delighting.

oblectō, [1] *v.* delight, please, amuse.

obligō, [1] *v.* bind *or* tie around; swathe, render liable; place under a moral obligation; bind (by oath, *etc.*).

oblīmō, [1] *v.* cover with mud; silt up.

oblinō, lēvī (līvī), litum, [3] *v.* smear, daub; sully, defame.

oblīquus, a, um, *a.* slanting, oblique; indirect; zigzag.

oblitterō, [1] *v.* cause to be forgotten.

oblīviō, ōnis, *f.* oblivion; forgetfulness.

oblīvīscor, lītus, [3] *v.* dep. forget.

oblīvium, iī, *nt.* forgetfulness, oblivion.

obloquor, cūtus, [3] *v.* dep. with dat. interpose remarks, interrupt.

obluctor, ātus sum, [1] dep. with dat. struggle against.

obmōlior, lītus sum, [4] *v.* dep. put in the way as an obstruction; block up.

obmurmurō, [1] *v.* murmur in protest (at).

obmūtēscō, mūtuī, [3] *v.* lose one's speech; become silent.

obnītor, sus, xus, [3] *v.* dep. thrust *or* press against; struggle against.

obnoxius, a, um, *a.* indebted, accountable, subservient (to); exposed to; submissive; vulnerable.

obnūbō, psī, ptum, [3] *v.* veil, cover (the head).

obnūntiō, [1] *v.* announce adverse omens.

oboediēns, entis, *a.* obedient, submissive.

oboediō, īvī *or* **iī, ītum,** [4] *v.* with dat. obey; comply with.

oborior, ortus, [4] *v.* dep. arise, appear *or* spring up before; well up (of tears).

obp . . . v. opp . . .

obrēpō, psī, ptum, [3] *v.* creep up to; approach unawares; sneak in.

obruō, uī, utum, [3] *v.* overwhelm; bury; sink; drown; suppress; smother (in).

obsaepiō, psī, ptum, [4] *v.* enclose, seal up; block, obstruct.

obscēnus, a, um, *a.* inauspicious; repulsive; ill-boding; detestable; foul; obscene; (applied to the sexual and excretory parts).

obscūritās, ātis, *f.* darkness; obscurity; unintelligibility.

obscūrō, [1] *v.* darken, obscure; conceal; make indistinct; cause to be forgotten.

obscūrus, a, um, *a.* dark, shady, obscure; gloomy; uncertain; incomprehensible.

obsecrātiō, ōnis, *f.* supplication, entreaty; public act of prayer.

obsecrō, [1] *v.* implore; beg.

obsequenter, *ad.* compliantly; obediently; with deference.

obsequium, (i)ī, *nt.* compliance (with), deference; servility; discipline.

obsequor, cūtus, [3] *v. dep. with dat.* comply (with), gratify, submit (to).

obserō, [1] *v.* bolt, fasten; obstruct.

obserō, sēvī, situm, [3] *v.* sow, plant; sow (with).

observō, [1] *v.* watch, observe; attend to; respect; pay court to.

obses, idis, *m.* or *f.* hostage; security, bail.

obsessiō, ōnis, *f.* besieging, blockade.

obsessor, ōris, *m.* besieger; frequenter.

obsideō, sēdī, sessum, [2] *v.* besiege, blockade; frequent; surround; occupy; throng.

obsidiō, ōnis, *f.* siege, blockade.

obsidium, iī, *nt.* siege, occupy.

obsīdō, [3] *v.* besiege; occupy.

obsignō, [1] *v.* seal up; stamp; impress.

obsistō, stitī, stitum, [3] *v. with dat.* stand in the way; resist, oppose; hinder.

obsitus, a, um, *a.* overgrown, covered (with).

obsolēscō, lēvī, lētum, [3] *v.* fall into disuse; be forgotten about.

obsolētus, a, um, *a.* worn-out, dilapidated; hackneyed.

obstetrīx, īcis, *f.* midwife.

obstinātiō, ōnis, *f.* firmness; stubbornness.

obstinātus, a, um, *a.* steady; stubborn.

obstinō, [1] *v.* be determined to.

obstipēscō v. **obstupēscō.**

obstīpus, a, um, *a.* awry, crooked, bent sideways *or* at an angle.

obstō, stitī, itum, [1] *v. with dat.* stand in the way of; block the path of; withstand; hinder.

obstrepō, uī, itum, [3] *v.* roar against; make a loud noise.

obstringō, nxī, ctum, [3] *v.* bind, tie *or* fasten up; place under an obligation; involve or implicate in.

obstruō, xī, ctum, [3] v. pile before or against; block up; stop, stifle.

obstupefaciō, fēcī, factum, [3] v. strike dumb with any powerful emotion, daze; paralyse; be **stupefīō, fierī, factus**, be astonished.

obstupēscō, puī, [3] v. be stupefied; be struck dumb; be astounded.

obsum, obesse, obfuī & offuī, v. with dat. hurt; be a nuisance to; tell against.

obsuō, uī, ūtum, [3] v. sew up.

obtegō, xī, ctum, [3] v. cover over; conceal; protect.

obtemperō, [1] v. with dat. comply with, obey.

obtendō, dī, tum, [3] v. stretch or spread before; conceal; plead in excuse.

obtentus, ūs, m. spreading before; cloaking, disguising, pretext.

obterō, trīvī, trītum, [3] v. crush; destroy; trample on, speak of or treat with the utmost contempt.

obtestātiō, ōnis, f. earnest entreaty, supplication.

obtestor, ātus, [1] v. call upon as a witness; invoke, entreat; aver.

obtexō, uī, [3] v. veil, cover.

obticēscō, ticuī, [3] v. meet a situation with silence.

obtineō, tinuī, tentum, [2] v. hold; support; obtain; gain; prevail.

obtingō, tigī, [3] v. with dat. fall to one's lot; occur to the benefit or disadvantage of.

obtorpēscō, puī, [3] v. become numb; lose feeling.

obtorqueō, sī, tum, [2] v. bend back; twist or turn.

obtrectātiō, ōnis, f. detraction, disparagement.

obtrectātor, ōris, m. detractor, malicious critic.

obtrectō, [1] v. detract from; disparage, belittle.

obtruncō, [1] v. cut to pieces, mutilate, kill.

obtundō, tudī, tūsum, [3] v. strike, beat, batter; make blunt; deafen.

obtūsus, a, um, a. blunt; dull; obtuse.

obtūtus, ūs, m. gaze; contemplation.

obumbrō, [1] v. overshadow; darken; conceal; defend.

obuncus, a, um, a. bent, hooked.

obustus, a, um, a. having the extremity burnt to form a point; scorched by burning.

obveniō, vēnī, ventum, [4] v. with dat. come to one by chance; happen; fall to the lot of; come up.

obversor, ātus, [1] v. dep. appear before one; go to and fro publicly.

obvertō, tī, sum, [3] *v.* turn or direct towards; direct against.

obviam, *ad. with dat.* in the way of; towards, against; to meet; at hand.

obvius, a, um, *a.* in the way, easy; hostile; exposed (to).

obvolvō, vī, ūtum, [3] *v.* wrap round, muffle up, cover; cloak.

occaecō, [1] *v.* blind; darken; conceal.

occallēscō, luī, [3] *v.* become callous; acquire a thick skin.

occāsiō, ōnis, *f.* opportunity, right *or* appropriate time.

occāsus, ūs, *m.* sun-setting, west; ruin, end, death.

occidēns, entis, *m.* quarter of the setting sun, the west.

occīdiō, ōnis, *f.* massacre; wholesale slaughter.

occidō, cidī, cāsum, [3] *v.* fall down; set (of the sun, *etc.*); die, perish; be ruined.

occīdō, cīdī, cīsum, [3] *v.* kill, slay.

occiduus, a, um, *a.* going down, setting; western; declining.

occinō, uī, [3] *v.* break in with a song *or* call; interpose a call.

occipiō, cēpī, ceptum, [3] *v.* begin.

occō, [1] *v.* harrow (ground).

occubō, [1] *v.* lie dead.

occulcō, [1] *v.* trample down.

occulō, culuī, cultum, [3] *v.* cover up; conceal.

occultātiō, ōnis, *f.* concealment.

occultō, [1] *v.* keep hidden, conceal; cover up.

occultus, a, um, *a.* hidden, concealed.

occumbō, cubuī, cubitum, [3] *v.* meet with (death); meet one's death.

occupātiō, ōnis, *f.* taking possession of; preoccupation with business, *etc.*, employment.

occupō, [1] *v.* occupy; seize; reach (a destination); engross.

occurrō, currī, cursum, [3] *v.* with dat. run towards or to meet; appear before; counteract; occur.

occursō, [1] *v.* run repeatedly or in large numbers; mob; obstruct.

occursus, ūs, *m.* meeting.

Ōceanus, ī, *m.* ocean.

ocellus, ī, *m.* (little) eye; darling.

ōcior, ōcius, *a.* swifter, more speedy; sooner.

ocrea, ae, *f.* greave, leg-covering.

octāvus, a, um, *a.* eighth.

octiē(n)s, *ad.* eight times.

octingentē(n)simus, a, um, *a.* num. eight hundredth.

octingentī, ae, a, *a.* eight hundred.

octō, *a.* eight.

Octōber, bris, *m.* October.

octōgēnī, ae, a, *a.* eighty each.

octōgē(n)simus, a, um, *a.* eightieth.

octōgintā, *ad.* eighty.

octōnī, ae, a, *a. num.* eight each.

octuplus, a, um, *a.* eightfold.

octussis, is, *m.* eight 'asses'.

oculus, ī, *m.* eye; eyesight; bud.

ōdī, ōdisse, *v.* hate; dislike.

odium, iī, *nt.* hatred, spite; unpopularity.

odor, ōris, *m.* smell, scent, odour; perfume.

odōrātus, a, um, *a.* sweet-smelling, fragrant.

odōrifer, a, um, *a.* fragrant.

odōrō, [1] *v.* perfume, make fragrant.

odōror, ātus, [1] *v. dep.* smell out, scent; get a smattering (of).

odōrus, a, um, *a.* odorous, fragrant; keen-scented.

odōs v. odor.

oestrus, ī, *m.* gad-fly.

offa, ae, *f.* lump of food, cake.

offendō, dī, sum, [3] *v.* strike or dash against; light upon; stumble; offend, displease; upset; harm.

offēnsa, ae, *f.* offence, displeasure; offence to a person's feelings; resentment.

offēnsiō, ōnis, *f.* striking against, stumbling-block; offence.

offēnsō, [1] *v.* knock or strike against, bump into.

offēnsus, ūs, *m.* collision, knock.

offerō, offerre, obtulī, oblātum, [3] *v.* bring before; offer;

exhibit; bring forwards; inflict; offer one's services.

officīna, ae, *f.* workshop.

officiō, fēcī, fectum, [3] *v. with dat.* block the path (of); check; impede.

officiōsus, a, um, *a.* dutiful, attentive; officious.

officium, iī, *nt.* service; duty; courtesy.

offirmō, [1] *v.* secure; make inflexible.

offulgeō, lsī, [2] *v. with dat.* shine forth in the path of.

offundō, fūdī, fūsum, [3] *v.* pour or spread over.

ōh, *i.* oh! ah!

ohē, *i.* hey! hey there!

olea, ae, *f.* olive; olive-tree.

oleaster, trī, *m.* wild olive-tree.

oleō, oluī, [2] *v.* smell; smell of; be fragrant; stink.

oleum, ī, *nt.* olive-oil; oil.

olfaciō, fēcī, factum, [3] *v.* smell.

olidus, a, um, *a.* stinking.

ōlim, *ad.* formerly, in times past; at a future time, some day; sometimes.

olitor, ōris, *m.* vegetable-grower.

olitōrius, a, um, *a.* pertaining to vegetables.

olīva, ae, *f.* olive; olive-tree; olive-branch; staff of olive-wood.

olīvētum, ī, *nt.* olive-yard.

olīvifer, a, um, *a.* olive-bearing.

olīvum, ī, *nt.* olive-oil; wrestling.

ōlla, ae, *f.* pot, jar.

ollus v. **ille.**

olor, ōris, *m.* swan.

olōrīnus, a, um, *a.* belonging to a swan or swans.

olus, eris, *nt.* vegetables.

ōmen, inis, *nt.* augury, sign, token (of good or bad luck).

ōminor, ātus, [1] *v. dep.* forebode, presage.

omittō, mīsī, missum, [3] *v.* let go; lay aside; give up; neglect; disregard; cease.

omnigenus, a, um, *a.* of every kind.

omnimodīs, *ad.* in every way.

omnīnō, *ad.* altogether, utterly; in all; in general.

omniparēns, entis, *a.* parent or creator of all things.

omnipotēns, entis, *a.* almighty.

omnis, e, *a.* all, every.

onager, onagrus, ī, *m.* wild ass.

onerārius, a, um, *a.* that carries loads, cargo, *etc.*; **nāvis onerāria,** merchant-ship.

onerō, [1] *v.* load, burden, freight; overload; overwhelm; oppress; aggravate.

onerōsus, a, um, *a.* burdensome, heavy; tiresome.

onus, eris, *nt.* load, burden; affliction, trouble, responsibility.

onustus, a, um, *a.* laden, burdened, freighted; weighed down.

onyx, ychis, *m.* yellow marble; onyx box.

opācō, [1] *v.* shade, overshadow.

opācus, a, um, *a.* shady; darkened, overshadowed; retired.

opella, ae, *f.* little effort; trifling duties.

opera, ae, *f.* pains, work, labour; task; care, attention, endeavour; **operae,** *pl.* labourers; hired rowdies; **operam dare,** *with dat.* to apply oneself to.

operīmentum, ī, *nt.* cover, lid, covering.

operiō, uī, ertum, [4] *v.* cover over; shut; conceal.

operōsus, a, um, *a.* painstaking; laborious; elaborate.

opertus, a, um, *a.* hidden; obscure, secret.

opēs v. **ops.**

opifer, a, um, *a.* bringing help.

opifex, icis, *m.* or *f.* craftsman, artificer; artisan.

ōpiliō v. **ūpiliō.**

opīmus, a, um, *a.* fruitful; rich; sumptuous; plentiful; **spolia opīma,** spoils taken by a victorious Roman general from the enemy leader he had killed in single combat.

opīniō, ōnis, *f.* opinion, belief; report, imagination; reputation.

opīnor, ātus, [1] *v. dep.* hold as an opinion, think, believe.

opitulor, ātus, [1] *v. dep. with dat.* bring aid to; help; bring relief to.

oportet, uit, [2] v. impers. it is necessary or proper (that); it is inevitable that.

opperior, perītus & pertus, [4] v. dep. wait (for); await.

oppetō, īvī & iī, ītum, [3] v. meet, encounter; perish.

oppidānus, a, um, a. of or in a town (other than Rome); provincial, local; **oppidānī, ōrum,** m. pl. townsmen, townsfolk.

oppidō, ad. exceedingly, utterly, altogether.

oppidulum, ī, nt. small town.

oppidum, ī, nt. town.

oppīlō, [1] v. stop up, block.

oppleō, ēvī, ētum, [2] v. fill (completely); overspread.

oppōnō, suī, situm, [3] v. put against or before; oppose; pledge; wager; object, say in answer.

opportūnitās, ātis, f. convenience, advantageousness; right time; opportuneness; opportunity.

opportūnus, a, um, a. convenient; opportune; advantageous; ready to hand; liable to.

opprimō, pressī, pressum, [3] v. press on or against; crush; overpower; beat down; surprise; suppress; conceal, cover.

opprobrium, iī, nt. scandal, disgrace; reproach, taunt.

oppugnātiō, ōnis, f. assault.

oppugnātor, ōris, m. attacker.

oppugnō, [1] v. attack, assault; batter.

ops, opis, f. power, might, strength, ability, help; **opes, um,** f. pl. wealth; resources, assistance.

optābilis, e, a. desirable.

optimās, ātis, m. aristocrat; (pl.) the best class of citizens.

optimus, a, um, a. best.

optiō, ōnis, f. choice; ~ m. junior officer.

optō, [1] v. choose; wish for, desire.

optumus v. optimus.

opulentia, ae, f. riches, wealth; sumptuousness.

opulentus a, um, a. wealthy; abounding with resources; well supplied (with); sumptuous.

opus, eris, nt. work, effort; structure; (pl.) siege-works.

opus, nt. indecl. need, necessity; ~ est, it is needful; ~ est mihi, with abl. of thing needed, I have need of.

opusculum, ī, nt. little work, trifle.

ōra, ae, f. border, edge; sea-coast; bank; region; climatic region.

ōrāculum, ī, nt. oracle.

ōrātiō, ōnis, f. speech; conversation.

ōrātor, ōris, m. speaker, orator; ambassador; advocate.

orbis, is, m. disc, circle; orb; ring; wheel; circuit; the world; ~ terrārum, or terrae, the world.

orbita, ae, f. wheel-track, rut; orbit.

orbitās, ātis, *f.* bereavement; loss of a child; orphanhood; childlessness.

orbō, [1] *v.* bereave (of parents, children, *etc.*), deprive (of).

orbus, a, um, *a.* bereaved; parentless; childless; deprived *or* destitute (of anything); ~, ī, *m.* & **orba, ae,** *f.* orphan.

Orcus, ī, *m.* the god of the underworld, Dis; death; the underworld.

ōrdinārius, a, um, *a.* regular; usual.

ōrdinātim, *ad.* in good order.

ōrdinō, [1] *v.* set in order, arrange, regulate.

ōrdior, ōrsus, [4] *v. dep.* begin; undertake; embark on.

ōrdō, inis, *m.* row, regular series; order; class of citizens; arrangement; method; degree; rank.

Orēas, adis, *f.* mountain-nymph, Oread.

orgia, ōrum, *nt. pl.* secret rites (of Bacchus).

orichalcum, ī, *nt.* yellow copper ore, brass.

oriēns, entis, *m.* east, orient; daybreak, dawn.

orīgō, inis, *f.* beginning, source; birth, origin.

orior, ortus, [4] *v. dep.* rise; appear on the scene; arise; begin; be born.

oriundus, a, um, *a.* descended; originating from.

ōrnāmentum, ī, *nt.* equipment; ornament, decoration; (mark of) distinction.

ōrnātus, ūs, *m.* military equipment; armour; costume, garb, get-up; adornment.

ōrnō, [1] *v.* adorn; honour; praise.

ornus, ī, *f.* ash-tree.

ōrō, [1] *v.* plead; pray (to); beseech, supplicate.

ōrsa, ōrum, *nt. pl.* words, utterance.

ortus, ūs, *m.* rising, sunrise; birth; beginnings, origin.

ōs, ōris, *nt.* mouth; speech; face; assurance.

os, ossis, *nt.* bone.

oscen, inis, *m.* bird which gives omens by its cry; song-bird.

ōscillum, ī, *nt.* a small mask hung on trees.

ōscitō, [1] *v.* gape; yawn.

ōsculātiō, ōnis, *f.* kissing.

ōsculor, ātus, [1] *v. dep.* kiss.

ōsculum, ī, *nt.* mouth; kiss.

ostendō, dī, sum & tum, [3] *v.* hold out for inspection; show; exhibit; demonstrate; offer.

ostentātiō, ōnis, *f.* exhibition, display; 'showing off'.

ostentō, [1] *v.* show off, display; offer.

ostentum, ī, *nt.* prodigy; marvel.

ostentus, ūs, *nt.* display; demonstration, advertisement.

ōstium, iī, *nt.* mouth (of a river); entrance; exit; door.

ostrea, ae, *f.* oyster; sea-snail.

ostrifer, a, um, *a.* bearing oysters.

ostrum, ī, *nt.* purple; anything dyed purple.

ōtior, ātus, [1] *v. dep.* be at leisure, enjoy a holiday.

ōtiōsus, a, um, *a.* at leisure, unoccupied; free from public affairs; quiet; free, unemployed; undisturbed (by); superfluous; useless.

ōtium, iī, *nt.* leisure; rest; peace; ease; lull.

ovīle, is, *nt.* sheepfold.

ovis, is, *f.* sheep.

ovō, [1] *v.* celebrate a minor triumph; exult, rejoice.

ovum, ī, *nt.* egg; wooden balls set up in the Circus, and removed one by one at the completion of each lap; **ab ovō usque ad māla,** from the hors d'œuvre to the dessert, i.e. from beginning to end.

. . . .

P

. . . .

pābulātiō, ōnis, *f.* foraging.

pābulātor, ōris, *m.* forager.

pābulor, ātus, [1] *v. dep.* forage.

pābulum, ī, *nt.* food, nourishment; fodder; food, sustenance.

pācālis, e, *a.* associated with peace.

pācātus, a, um, *a.* peaceful, calm.

pācifer, a, um, *a.* bringing peace, peaceful.

pācificātiō, ōnis, *f.* peace-making.

pācificō, [1] *v.* negotiate about peace, appease.

pācificus, a, um, *a.* making *or* tending to make peace.

pacīscō, pactum, [3] *v.,* **pacīscor, pactus sum,** [3] *v. dep.* make a bargain *or* agreement; agree, enter into a marriage contract; negotiate.

pācō, [1] *v.* impose a settlement on; bring under control.

pactiō, ōnis, *f.* agreement, compact.

pactum, ī, *nt.,* v. **pactiō;** manner, way; **quō pactō?** how?

paeān, ānis, *m.* hymn, hymn usually of victory.

paedīcō, [1] *v.* commit sodomy with.

paedor, ōris, *m.* filth, dirt.

paelex v. **pellex.**

paene, *ad.* nearly, almost, practically.

paenīnsula, ae, *f.* peninsula.

paenitentia, ae, *f.* regret; change of mind.

paenitet, uit, [2] *v. impers.* it gives reason for regret; **mē paenitet,** I repent.

paenula, ae, *f.* hooded weather-proof cloak.

paenulātus, a, um, *a.* wearing a paenula.

paetus, a, um, *a.* having a cast in the eye, squinting slightly.

pāgānus, a, um, *a.* rustic; civilian.

pāgina, ae, *f.* column *or* page of writing; piece of writing.

pāgus, ī, *m.* country district *or* community.

pāla, ae, *f.* spade.

palaestra, ae, *f.* wrestling-place; gymnastics.

palam, *ad.* openly, publicly; *prep. with abl.* openly in the presence of.

Palātīnus, a, um, *a.* the name of one of the hills of Rome, the Palatine.

Palātium, iī, *nt.* the Palatine Hill.

palātum, ī, *nt.* palate; sense of taste.

palea, ae, *f.* chaff, husk.

palear, āris, *nt.* dewlap.

Palīlia, ium, *nt. pl.* Feast of Pales (a tutelary deity of sheep and herds) on 21 April.

paliūrus, ī, *m.* the shrub, Christ's thorn.

palla, ae, *f.* rectangular outdoor garment worn by women, mantle of a tragic actor.

palleō, uī, [2] *v.* be *or* look pale; fade; become pale at.

pallēscō, palluī, [3] *v.* grow pale; blanch; fade.

pallidus, a, um, *a.* pale.

pallolum, ī, *nt.* small cloak.

pallium, ī, *nt.* rectangular outdoor garment worn by men; bed-cover.

pallor, ōris, *m.* paleness, wanness.

palma, ae, *f.* palm of the hand; hand; palm-tree; date; oar; victory, first place.

palmātus, a, um, *a.* having a palm-leaf pattern.

palmes, itis, *m.* vine-branch or -shoot.

palmētum, ī, *nt.* palm-grove.

palmifer, a, um, *a.* palm-bearing.

palmula, ae, *f.* oar.

pālor, ātus, [1] *v. dep.* wander abroad, stray; scatter; wander aimlessly.

palpitō, [1] *v.* throb, beat, pulsate.

palūdāmentum, ī, *nt.* military cloak; general's cloak.

palūdātus, a, um, *a.* wearing a military cloak.

palūdōsus, a, um, *a.* fenny, boggy, marshy.

palumbēs, is, *m.* or *f.* wood-pigeon, ring-dove.

pālus, ī, *m.* stake, prop.

palūs, ūdis, *f.* flood-water, fen, swamp.

paluster, tris, tre, *a.* marshy; of marshes.

pampineus, a, um, *a.* of *or* covered with vine-shoots *or* foliage.

pampinus, ī, *m. or f.* vine-shoot, vine foliage.

pandō, pandī, pānsum & passum, [3] *v.* spread out, extend; unfold; reveal.

pandus, a, um, *a.* spreading round in a wide curve; arched.

pangō, pēgī & pepigī, pāctum, [3] *v.* fix; drive in; *fig.* settle, stipulate for; conclude; compose.

pānicum, ī, *nt.* Italian millet.

pānis, is, *m.* bread, loaf; food.

pannōsus, a, um, *a.* dressed in rags, tattered.

pannus, ī, *m.* cloth, garment; charioteer's coloured shirt; rags.

panthēra, ae, *f.* leopard.

panticēs, um, *m. pl.* belly, paunch, guts.

pantomīmus, ī, *m.* mime performer in a pantomime.

papāver, eris, *nt.* poppy; poppy-seed.

papāvereus, a, um, *a.* of poppy, poppy-.

pāpiliō, ōnis, *m.* butterfly, moth.

papilla, ae, *f.* nipple, teat, dug (of mammals).

papula, ae, *f.* pimple, pustule.

papȳrifer, a, um, *a.* papyrus-bearing.

papȳrus, ī, *f.* **papȳrum, ī**, *nt.* paper-reed; papyrus.

pār, paris, *a.* equal; fair; fit; ~, *m. or f.* equal; mate, partner.

pār, paris, *nt.* pair; couple.

parābilis, e, *a.* procurable, easily obtainable.

parasītus, ī, *m.* guest; parasite.

parātus, a, um, *a.* prepared, ready; equipped.

parātus, ūs, *m.* preparation; equipment, paraphernalia; attire.

parcō, pepercī (parsī), [3] *v.* *with dat.* act sparingly, be thrifty with; spare; pardon; forbear; refrain from.

parcus, a, um, *a.* sparing, economical; niggardly, parsimonious; moderate.

parēns, entis, *m. or f.* father, mother, parent; ancestor; originator; producer, source.

parentālis, e, *a.* of *or* belonging to parents.

parentō, [1] *v.* perform the rites at the tombs of the dead; make an offering of appeasement (to the dead).

pāreō, uī, [2] *v.* be visible; (*with dat.*) obey; comply with; be subject to; submit to.

pariēs, etis, *m.* wall (of a house).

parilis, e, *a.* like, equal.

pariō, peperī, paritum & partum, [3] *v.* bring forth, bear; produce, create; procure, get.

pariter, *ad.* equally, as well; together; in the same manner; simultaneously.

parma, ae, *f.* small round shield.

parō, [1] *v.* get ready, prepare, furnish, provide; intend; plan; obtain; buy.

parochus, ī, *m.* commissary.

parricīda, ae, *m.* or *f.* parricide (murderer); murderer of a near relative; traitor.

parricīdium, iī, *nt.* parricide (murder); murder of a near relation, treason, rebellion.

pars, partis, *f.* part, piece, portion, share; function, office; role; party, side; **pars . . . pars,** some . . . others; **partēs, ium,** *f. pl.* party; faction.

parsimōnia, ae, *f.* frugality, thrift, parsimony; temperance.

particeps, cipis, *a.* sharing in; ~ *m.* or *f.* participant, sharer.

participium, iī, *nt.* participle.

participō, [1] *v.* inform of; share with others in; partake of; make a party to.

particula, ae, *f.* small part, little bit, particle, atom.

partim, *ad.* partly, in part.

partiō, iī & īvī, ītum, [4] *v.* **partior, ītus sum,** [4] *v. dep.* share, divide up.

parturiō, īvī & iī, [4] *v.* be in travail *or* labour; bring forth; produce; be pregnant with.

partus, ūs, *m.* bringing forth, birth; foetus, embryo; offspring, progeny.

parum, *n. indecl. & ad.* too little, not enough; encore!

parumper, *ad.* for a short while.

parvulus, a, um, *a.* tiny, small, little, petty, slight.

parvus, a, um, *a.* little, small, petty, mean; young; cheap.

pāscō, pāvī, pāstum, [3] *v.* feed, pasture; provide food for; nurture; feast.

pāscuum, ī, *nt.* pasture.

passer, eris, *m.* sparrow; blue thrush.

passim, *ad.* here and there, hither and thither; at random.

passum, ī, *nt.* raisin-wine.

passus, ūs, *m.* step, pace (5 Roman feet); track, trace; **mīlle passūs,** *pl.* a mile.

passus, a, um, *a.* spread out; dried (of grapes, *etc.*).

pāstor, ōris, *m.* herdsman, shepherd.

pāstōrālis, e, *a.* pastoral.

pāstus, ūs, *m.* pasture, feeding ground; pasturage.

patefaciō, fēcī, factum, [3] *v.* open, throw open; disclose, bring to light.

patella, ae, *f.* small dish *or* plate.

pateō, uī, [2] *v.* be open; be accessible; be visible; be exposed to; stretch out, extend; be evident; be available.

pater, tris, *m.* father; ~ **familiās,** head of a family; **patrēs, patrēs cōnscrīptī,** *pl.* senators; **patrēs,** forefathers.

patera, ae, *f.* broad, shallow offering dish.

paternus, a, um, *a.* fatherly; paternal.

patēscō, uī, [3] *v.* open; extend; become clear *or* known.

patibulum, ī, *nt.* fork-shaped yoke; gibbet.

patiēns, entis, *a.* patient; capable of enduring.

patientia, ae, *f.* patience; forbearance; submissiveness.

patior, passus sum, *v. dep.* bear, undergo; suffer; allow; leave, let be.

patria, ae, *f.* fatherland, native country; home, source.

patricīda v. **parricīda**.

patricius, a, um, *a.* patrician, noble.

patrimōnium, iī, *nt.* private possessions, estate, fortune.

patrīmus, a, um, *a.* having a father still living.

patrius, a, um, *a.* belonging to a father, paternal; hereditary; of one's native land.

patrō, [1] *v.* accomplish, bring to completion.

patrōcinium, iī, *nt.* protection, defence, patronage, legal defence.

patrōna, ae, *f.* protectress, patroness.

patrōnus, ī, *m.* protector, patron; pleader, advocate.

patruēlis, is, *m. or f.* of *or* belonging to a paternal uncle.

patruus, ī, *m.* paternal uncle; type of harshness and censoriousness.

patulus, a, um, *a.* wide open, gaping; wide-spreading.

paucitās, ātis, *f.* small number, fewness.

paucus, a, um, *a.* few, little; **pauca**, *nt. pl.* a few words.

paul(l)ātim, *ad.* by degrees, gradually.

paul(l)īsper, *ad.* for a little while, for a short time.

paul(l)ō, *a.* by a little; somewhat.

paul(l)um, *ad.* a little, somewhat.

paul(l)us, a, um, *a.* little, small; **paul(l)um, ī**, *nt.* a little, a little bit.

pauper, eris, *a.* poor; meagre, unproductive.

pauperiēs, ēī *f.* **paupertās, ātis**, *f.* poverty.

pavefaciō, fēcī, factum, [3] *v.* terrify.

paveō, pāvī, [2] *v.* be frightened or terrified at.

pavēscō, [3] *v.* become alarmed.

pavidus, a, um, *a.* fearful, terrified, panic-struck.

pavīmentum, ī, *nt.* paved surface *or* floor, pavement.

pavitō, [1] *v.* be in a state of fear *or* trepidation (at).

pāvō, ōnis, *m.* peacock.

pavor, ōris, *m.* fear, dread, alarm, terror, anxiety.

pāx, pācis, *f.* peace; tranquillity of mind; favour, grace; leave; **pāce tuā**, by your leave.

peccātum, ī, *nt.* error, sin.

peccō, [1] v. make a mistake; err; commit a fault; sin.

pecten, inis, m. comb; quill with which the lyre is struck.

pectō, pexī, pexum & pectitum, [3] v. comb: card (wool, etc.).

pectus, oris, nt. breast; soul; feeling; courage; understanding.

pecuārius, iī, m. cattle-breeder, grazier.

pecūlātor, ōris, m. embezzler of public money.

pecūlātus, ūs, m. embezzlement of public money or property.

pecūlium, iī, nt. private property of a son, daughter, or slave, held with the father's or master's consent.

pecūnia, ae, f. property, wealth; money.

pecus, pecoris, nt. cattle; herd, flock.

pecus, udis, f. farm animal; animal; sheep.

pedālis, e, a. measuring a foot.

pedes, itis, m. pedestrian, footsoldier; **peditēs,** pl. infantry

pedester, tris, tre, a. on foot, pedestrian.

pedetem(p)tim, ad. step by step, slowly; cautiously.

pedica, ae, f. shackle, fetter; snare.

pedisequus, ī, m. **pedisequa, ae,** f. male attendant, manservant; waiting-woman.

peditātus, ūs, m. infantry.

pedum, ī, nt. shepherd's crook.

pēierō, [1] v. swear falsely.

pēior, us, a. worse.

pelagus, ī, nt. open sea.

pellāx, ācis, a. seductive, glib.

pellex, icis, f. mistress.

pelliciō, lexī, lectum, [3] v. attract; seduce; charm; inveigle.

pellicula, ae, f. skin, hide.

pellis, is, f. skin, hide; leather.

pellītus, a, um, a. covered with skins.

pellō, pepulī, pulsum, [3] v. push, strike; drive out, banish; impel.

pelōris, idis, f. mussel.

pelta, ae, f. crescent-shaped shield.

peltātus, a, um, a. armed with the pelta.

pēlvis, is, f. shallow bowl or basin.

Penātēs, ium, m. pl. the household gods; the gods of the state; one's home; dwelling.

pendeō, pependī, [2] v. hang (down); be suspended; hang loose; be unstable, movable; be uncertain; depend (on).

pendō, pependī, pēnsum, [3] v. weigh; pay, pay out; consider.

pendulus, a, um, a. hanging down; suspended.

penes, pr. with acc. in the possession or power of.

penetrābilis, e, a. that can be pierced; penetrable; piercing.

penetrāle, is, *nt.* inner part of a place; inner shrine.

penetrālis, e, *a.* innermost; penetrating.

penetrō, [1] *v.* pierce, penetrate (into); gain entrance.

pēnis, is, *m.* male sexual organ, penis.

penitus, *ad.* inwardly; deep(ly); far within; utterly, completely.

penna, ae, *f.* feather; wing.

pennātus, a, um, *a.* winged.

pēnsō, [1] *v.* weigh, weigh out; pay *or* punish for; counterbalance, compensate; ponder, examine.

pēnsum, ī, *nt.* quantity of wool given to be spun *or* woven; task, stint.

pēnūria, ae, *f.* want, need, scarcity.

penus, ūs *or* **ī**, *m.* or *f.* provisions, food.

per, *pr. with acc.* through, throughout, all over; during; by (means of); for·the·sake of; (in compounds) thoroughly, very; by (in oaths, *etc.*).

perabsurdus, a, um, *a.* highly ridiculous.

perācer, cris, cre, *a.* very sharp.

peracūtus, a, um, *a.* very penetrating; very sharp.

peraequē, *ad.* equally.

peragitō, [1] *v.* harass with repeated attacks.

peragō, ēgī, āctum, [3] *v.* execute, finish, accomplish;

pierce through; pass through; relate.

peragrō, [1] *v.* travel over every part of, scour.

perambulō, [1] *v.* walk about in, tour; make the round of.

perangustus, a, um, *a.* very narrow.

perantīquus, a, um, *a.* very ancient.

perarō, [1] *v.* furrow; inscribe (scratch on a waxen tablet).

perbeātus, a, um, *a.* very fortunate.

perbibō, bibī, [3] *v.* drink deeply, drink in.

percallēscō, uī, [3] *v.* become callous.

percelebrō, [1] *v.* make thoroughly known.

percellō, culī, culsum, [3] *v.* strike down; strike; overpower; dismay, demoralize, upset.

percieō, [2] **perciō, ciī, citum**, [4] *v.* excite; set in motion.

percipiō, cēpī, ceptum, [3] *v.* take possession of; perceive, take in.

percommodus, a, um, *a.* very convenient.

percontātiō, ōnis, *f.* question, interrogation.

percontor, ātus sum, [1] *v. dep.* question; investigate.

percoquō, xī, ctum, *v.* cook thoroughly; bake, heat.

percrēbēscō, uī, percrēbrēscō, bruī, [3] *v.* become very frequent, become very widespread.

percurrō, percucurrī & percurrī, cursum, [3] *v.* run *or* hasten through *or* over; traverse; pass quickly over.

percussor, ōris, *m.* assassin.

percussus, ūs, *m.* buffeting; beating.

percutiō, cussī, cussum, [3] *v.* strike forcibly; kill; shock, make a deep impression on.

perdiscō, didicī, [3] *v.* learn thoroughly.

perditor, ōris, *m.* destroyer.

perditus, a, um, *a.* ruined, lost, desperate, abandoned, morally depraved.

perdiū, *ad.* for a long while.

perdīx, īcis, *m. or f.* partridge.

perdō, didī, ditum, [3] *v.* lose; destroy; ruin; waste; spoil, impair.

perdoceō, uī, ctum, [3] *v.* teach (thoroughly).

perdomō, uī, itum, [1] *v.* tame thoroughly, subjugate completely.

perdūcō, xī, ctum, [3] *v.* lead *or* bring through, conduct; prolong; cover over, coat.

perduelliō, ōnis, *f.* treason.

perduellis, is, *m.* national enemy.

peredō, ēdī, ēsum, [3] *v.* eat up, consume, waste.

peregrē, *ad.* abroad; to, in, *or* from foreign parts.

peregrīnātiō, ōnis, *f.* foreign travel.

peregrīnor, ātus, [1] *v. dep.* travel about *or* abroad; reside abroad.

peregrīnus, a, um, *a.* outlandish, strange, foreign, ~, ī, *m.* foreigner, alien.

perendinus, a, um, *a.* after tomorrow.

perennis, e, *a.* continuing throughout the year; constant, uninterrupted; enduring.

pereō, iī (īvī), itum, [4] *v.* pass from view, vanish, disappear; be destroyed, perish; be desperately in love (with); **periī,** I am ruined.

perequitō, [1] *v.* ride (through *or* over), traverse; ride hither and thither, ride *or* drive about.

pererrō, [1] *v.* wander through, roam *or* ramble over.

perexiguus, a, um, *a.* very little *or* small.

perfacilis, e, *a.* very easy.

perfectus, a, um, *a.* finished, complete, perfect.

perferō, ferre, tulī, lātum, *v.* bear *or* carry through; convey; report; tell; endure; undergo.

perficiō, fēcī, fectum, [3] *v.* finish, perform; complete; accomplish.

perfidia, ae, *f.* faithlessness, treachery.

perfidiōsus, a, um, *a.* treacherous.

perfidus, a, um, *a.* faithless, treacherous, false, deceitful.

perflō, [1] *v.* blow through *or* over.

perfluō, xī, [3] *v.* flow (through).

perfodiō, fōdī, fossum, [3] *v.* dig *or* pierce through.

perforō, [1] *v.* bore through; pierce.

perfringō, frēgī, frāctum, [3] *v.* break through; break *or* dash in pieces; smash.

perfruor, ctus, [3] *v. dep. with abl.* have full enjoyment of, enjoy.

perfuga, ae, *m.* deserter.

perfugiō, fūgī, [3] *v.* take refuge, escape; go for refuge (to the enemy).

perfugium, iī, *nt.* refuge; asylum; excuse.

perfundō, fūdī, fūsum, [3] *v.* pour over, wet; overspread, imbue.

perfungor, nctus, [3] *v. dep. with abl.* perform, discharge; have done with.

perfurō, [3] *v.* rage, storm (throughout).

pergō, perrēxī, perrēctum, [3] *v.* advance; continue; proceed, go on.

pergrandis, e, *a.* very large, of very advanced age.

pergrātus, a, um, *a.* very agreeable *or* pleasant.

perhibeō, uī, itum, [2] *v.* present, give, bestow; regard, hold; name.

perhorrēscō, ruī, [3] *v.* tremble *or* shudder greatly; recoil in terror from.

perīclitor, ātus, [1] *v. dep.* risk; try, test; be in danger; risk.

perīculōsus, a, um, *a.* dangerous, hazardous, perilous.

perīculum, ī, *nt.* trial, proof; danger, peril; risk; liability.

peridōneus, a, um, *a.* very suitable, very well-fitted.

perimō, ēmī, ēmptum [3] *v.* destroy; kill; prevent.

perinde, *ad.* just (as), equally; ~ ac, just, as if.

perītia, ae, *f.* practical knowledge, skill, expertise.

perītus, a, um, *a.* experienced, practised, skilful, expert.

periūcundus, a, um, *a.* very welcome, agreeable.

periūrium, iī, *nt.* false oath, perjury.

periūrō *v.* pēierō.

periūrus, a, um, *a.* perjured; false, lying.

perlābor, lāpsus sum, [3] *v. dep.* glide along, over *or* through, skim.

perlegō, lēgī, lēctum, [3] *v.* scan, survey; read through.

perlitō, [1] *v.* make auspicious sacrifice.

perlūceō, [2] *v.* be transparent; shine through; shine out.

perlūcidus, a, um, *a.* transparent, pellucid.

perluō, uī, ūtum, [3] *v.* wash off *or* thoroughly; bathe.

perlūstrō, [1] *v.* go *or* wander all through; view all over, scan, scrutinize.

permagnus, a, um, *a.* very great.

permaneō, mānsī, mānsum, [2] *v.* continue *or* persist in staying; persist.

permānō, [1] *v.* flow through; leak through; permeate.

permeō, [1] *v.* go *or* pass through, cross, traverse; pervade.

permētior, mēnsus, [4] *v.* measure exactly; travel over.

permisceō, scuī, stum & xtum, [2] *v.* mix *or* mingle together; confound; embroil; disturb thoroughly.

permissus, ūs, *m.* permission, authorization.

permittō, mīsī, missum, [3] *v.* let go through; allow full scope to, give rein to; allow, permit; leave (to another) to do *or* decide; grant.

permoveō, mōvī, mōtum, [2] *v.* move *or* stir up thoroughly; move deeply; excite.

permulceō, sī, sum & ctum, [2] *v.* rub gently, stroke, touch gently; charm, please, beguile; soothe, alleviate.

permultus, a, um, *a.* very much, very many.

permūniō, īvī, *or* **iī, ītum**, [4] *v.* fortify thoroughly.

permūtātiō, ōnis, *f.* change; exchange, barter.

permūtō, [1] *v.* exchange (for); swap.

perniciēs, ēī, *f.* destruction, ruin; fatal injury.

perniciōsus, a, um, *a.* destructive, ruinous, fatal.

pernīcitās, ātis, *f.* nimbleness.

pernīx, īcis, *a.* nimble, agile, travelling quickly.

pernoctō, [1] *v.* spend the night.

pernōscō, nōvī, nōtum, [3] *v.* get a thorough knowledge of.

pernox, octis, *a.* lasting all night.

pērō, ōnis, *m.* thick boot of raw hide.

perobscūrus, a, um, *a.* very obscure, very vague.

perōdī, ōsus sum, *v.* hate greatly, detest.

peropportūnus, a, um, *a.* very favourably situated, very convenient.

perōrō, [1] *v.* deliver the final part of a speech, conclude.

perpācō, [1] *v.* subdue completely.

perparvus, a, um, *a.* very little, very trifling.

perpaucus, a, um, *a.* very few.

perpellō, pulī, pulsum, [3] *v.* compel, constrain, prevail upon; enforce.

perpendiculum, ī, *nt.* plummet; **ad perpendiculum**, perpendicularly.

perpendō, pendī, pēnsum, [3] *v.* weigh carefully; assess carefully.

perperam, *ad.* wrongly, incorrectly.

perpetior, pessus, [3] *v. dep.* endure to the full.

perpetrō, [1] *v.* carry through, accomplish.

perpetuitās, ātis, *f.* continuity, permanence.

perpetuus, a, um, *a.* uninterrupted; continuous; lasting; invariable.

perplexus, a, um, *a.* entangled, muddled; intricate, cryptic.

perpoliō, īvī *or* **iī, ītum**, [4] *v.* polish thoroughly; put the finishing touches to.

perpopulor, ātus, [1] *v. dep.* ravage, devastate completely.

perpōtō, [1] *v.* drink heavily; drink up.

perquam, *ad.* extremely.

perquīrō, sīvī, sītum, [3] *v.* search everywhere for.

perrārus, a, um, *a.* very rare, exceptional.

perrumpō, rūpī, ruptum, [3] *v.* break *or* rush through, force one's way through; cleave, sever; violate.

persaepe, *ad.* very often.

perscrībō, psī, ptum, [3] *v.* write in full *or* at length; give a full account *or* report of in writing.

perscrūtor, [1] *v.* search high and low; study carefully.

persequor, cūtus, [3] *v. dep.* follow perseveringly, pursue; pursue with hostile intent; strive

after; go through with; catch up with.

perseverantia, ae, *f.* steadfastness, persistence.

persevērō, [1] *v.* persist, persevere in.

persolvō, solvī, solūtum, [3] *v.* pay in full; pay off.

persōna, ae, *f.* mask; personage, character, part.

persōnātus, a, um, *a.* masked.

personō, uī, itum, [1] *v.* resound, ring with; cause to resound; make loud music; shout out.

perspiciō, exī, ectum, [3] *v.* look *or* see through, look into, look at, examine, inspect; study, investigate.

perspicuus, a, um, *a.* transparent, clear; evident.

perstō, stitī, stātum, [1] *v.* stand firm; last, endure; persevere, persist in.

perstringō, nxī, ctum, [3] *v.* graze, graze against; make tight all over; offend, make unfavourable mention of.

persuādeō, sī, sum, [2] *v. with dat.* persuade, convince; prevail upon, persuade to do.

persultō, [1] *v.* leap *or* skip *or* prance about; range (over), scour.

pertaedet, taesum est, [2] *v. impers.* be very wearied with.

pertemptō *v.* pertentō.

pertendō, dī, sum, [3] *v.* persevere, persist; press on.

pertentō, [1] v. test, try out; explore thoroughly; agitate thoroughly.

perterreō, **uī**, **itum**, [2] v. frighten or terrify thoroughly.

pertica, **ae**, f. pole, long staff, measuring-rod, perch.

pertimēscō, **muī**, [3] v. become very scared (of).

pertinācia, **ae**, f. obstinacy, defiance.

pertināx, **ācis**, a. firm, constant, steadfast, obstinate.

pertineō, **uī**, [2] v. continue or extend through or to; reach; belong or pertain to, be relevant to.

pertrahō, **xī**, **ctum**, [3] v. draw or drag through or to, bring or conduct forcibly to; draw on, lure.

pertundō, **tudī**, **tūsum**, [3] v. bore through, perforate.

perturbātiō, **ōnis**, f. confusion, disturbance; mental disturbance, perturbation; passion.

perturbō, [1] v. disorder, confuse; disturb; frighten.

perūrō, **ussī**, **ustum**, [3] v. burn up; fire; scorch; make sore.

pervādō, **sī**, **sum**, [3] v. go or come through; spread through; penetrate; pervade.

pervagor, **ātus**, [1] v. dep. wander or range through, rove about; pervade, spread widely; extend.

pervastō, [1] v. devastate completely.

pervehō, **xī**, **ctum**, [3] v. bear, carry or convey through; **pervehī**, pass. to sail to, ride to.

perveniō, **vēnī**, **ventum**, [4] v. come through to, arrive at, reach.

perversus, **a**, **um**, a. askew, awry; perverse, evil, bad.

pervertō, **tī**, **sum**, [3] v. overthrow; subvert; destroy, ruin, corrupt.

pervestīgō, [1] v. make a thorough search of; explore fully.

pervetus, **eris**, a. very old.

pervicācia, **ae**, f. stubbornness, obstinacy; firmness, steadiness.

pervicāx, **ācis**, a. stubborn, obstinate; firm, steadfast.

pervideō, **vīdī**, **vīsum**, [2] v. take in with the eyes or mind.

pervigil, **is**, a. keeping watch or sleepless all night long.

pervigilō, [1] v. remain awake all night; keep watch all night.

pervincō, **vīcī**, **victum**, [3] v. conquer completely; carry (a proposal), gain an objective; persuade.

pervius, **a**, **um**, a. passable, traversable; penetrable.

pervolō, [1] v. fly or flit through; wing one's way; move rapidly through the air.

pervulgō, [1] v. make publicly known, spread abroad.

pēs, pedis, m. foot; metrical foot; foot (as a linear measure); sheet (of a sail).

pessimus, a, um, *a.* worst.

pessum, *ad.* to the lowest part, to the bottom; ~ **dare,** to destroy, ruin.

pestifer, a, um, *a.* pestilential; destructive.

pestilēns, entis, *a.* pestilential, unhealthy, unwholesome; destructive.

pestilentia, ae, *f.* pestilence, unhealthy atmosphere *or* region; plague.

pestis, is, *f.* plague, pestilence; destruction, ruin, death.

petītiō, ōnis, *f.* attack, thrust; request, petition; candidature; lawsuit.

petītor, ōris, *m.* seeker, striver after; applicant, candidate; claimant, plaintiff.

petō, īvī, ītum, [3] *v.* make for; seek; fetch; seek after; attack; ask for; desire; be a candidate for.

petulāns, antis, *a.* pert, saucy, impudent, petulant; wanton, lascivious.

petulantia, ae, *f.* impudent *or* boisterous aggressiveness; wantonness, immodesty.

petulcus, a, um, *a.* butting.

phalānx, angis, *f.* body of soldiers drawn up in close order.

phalerae, ārum, *f. pl.* ornaments worn by men of arms and horses.

pharetra, ae, *f.* quiver.

pharetrātus, a, um, *a.* wearing a quiver.

pharmacopōla, ae, *m.* drugseller; quack.

phasēlus, ī, *m.* or *f.* kidney-bean; light ship.

philomēla, ae, *f.* nightingale.

philosophia, ae, *f.* philosophy.

philosophor, ātus, [1] *v. dep.* philosophize.

philtrum, ī, *nt.* love-potion.

philyra, ae, *f.* linden-tree, lime-tree.

phōca, ae, phōcē, ēs, *f.* seal.

piāculāris, e, *a.* atoning, expiatory.

piāculum, ī, *nt.* expiatory offering *or* rite; sin.

piāmen, inis, *nt.* atonement.

pīca, ae, *f.* magpie; jay.

picea, ae, *f.* spruce.

piceus, a, um, *a.* made of pitch; pitchblack.

pictor, ōris, *m.* painter.

pictūra, ae, *f.* art of painting; picture; mental image.

pictūrātus, a, um, *a.* decorated with colour.

pietās, ātis, *f.* piety; dutifulness; affection, love; loyalty; gratitude.

piget, *v. impers.* it affects with revulsion *or* displeasure, it irks.

piger, gra, grum, *a.* slow, sluggish, inactive; inert.

pignerō, [1] *v.* pledge, pawn; appropriate.

pignus, oris & eris, *nt.* pledge, pawn, surety; token, proof; stake.

pigritia, ae, pigritiēs, ēī, *f.* sloth, sluggishness, laziness, indolence.

pīla, ae, *f.* squared pillar; pier, pile.

pila, ae, *f.* ball.

pīlānus, ī, *m.* a soldier of the third rank.

pīlentum, ī, *nt.* luxurious carriage used by women.

pīleum, ī, *nt.,* **pīleus, ī,** *m.* felt cap; freedom, liberty.

pilleus v. **pīleus.**

pīlum, ī, *nt.* javelin.

pilus, ī, *m.* hair; trifle.

pīlus, ī, *m.* the first century of the first cohort of a legion; **prīmum pīlum dūcere,** to command the first century of the first cohort of a legion.

pīnētum, ī, *nt.* pine-wood.

pīneus, a, um, *a.* of the pine, covered in pines.

pingō, nxī, pictum, [3] *v.* paint; embroider; embellish; tattoo.

pinguēscō, [3] *v.* grow fat; become strong *or* fertile.

pinguis, e, *a.* fat; plump; rich; dull, slow-witted; slothful.

pīnifer, a, um, pīniger, a, um, *a.* pine-bearing.

pinna, ae, *f.* feather; wing; raised part of an embattled parapet.

pinniger, a, um, *a.* winged; finny.

pīnus, ūs & ī, *f.* pine-tree; ship; pine-wood torch.

piō, [1] *v.* appease, propitiate; cleanse, expiate.

pīrāta, ae, *m.* corsair, pirate.

pīrāticus, a, um, *a.* piratical.

pirum, ī, *nt.* pear.

pirus, ī, *f.* pear-tree.

piscātor, ōris, *m.* fisherman.

piscātōrius, a, um, *a.* of *or* for fishing.

piscīna, ae, *f.* fish-pond; swimming-pool.

piscis, is, *m.* fish.

piscor, ātus, [1] *v. dep.* fish.

piscōsus, a, um, *a.* teeming with fish.

pistrīnum, ī, *nt.* mill, bakery (as a place of punishment *or* drudgery).

pistris, is, *f.* sea monster; whale.

pius, a, um, *a.* pious, religious, faithful, devout; dutiful.

pix, picis, *f.* pitch.

plācābilis, e, *a.* easily appeased, placable; appeasing, pacifying.

plācātus, a, um, *a.* kindly disposed; peaceful, calm.

placenta, ae, *f.* a kind of flat cake.

placeō, cuī, citum, [2] *v.* with *dat.* be pleasing (to), satisfy; **placet,** it seems good (to); it is resolved *or* agreed on (by).

placidus, a, um, *a.* gentle, calm, mild, peaceful, placid.

plācō, [1] *v.* calm, assuage, placate, appease, reconcile (with).

plāga, ae, *f.* blow, stroke; wound.

plaga, ae, *f.* open expanse (of land, sea or sky), tract; hunting-net.

plāgōsus, a, um, *a.* lavish with blows.

plānē, *ad.* plainly, clearly; utterly, quite.

planēta, ae, *m.* wandering star, planet.

plangō, nxī, nctum, [3] *v.* strike, beat; beat the breast in mourning, mourn for.

plangor, ōris, *m.* beating, striking; lamentation.

plānitiēs, ēī, *f.* flat or even surface, level ground, plain.

planta, ae, *f.* sprout, shoot; sole of the foot.

plantāria, ium, *nt. pl.* slips, cuttings.

plānus, a, um, *a.* level, flat, plane, even; obvious.

platanus, ī, *f.* plane-tree.

platēa (platea), ae, *f.* street.

plaudō, sī, sum, [3] *v.* clap, strike, beat; (*with dat.*) applaud.

plausor, ōris, *m.* applauder.

plaustrum, ī, *nt.* waggon, cart; Charles's Wain.

plausus, ūs, *m.* clapping; applause.

plēbēcula, ae, *f.* mob, common people.

plēbēius, a, um, *a.* pertaining to the common people, plebeian; common, everyday.

plēbēs, is & ēī v. **plēbs.**

plēbicola, ae, *m.* one who courts the favour of the people.

plēbiscītum, ī, *nt.* resolution of the people.

plēbs, plēbēs, is & ēī & ī, *f.* common people, plebeians; mob, common herd, masses.

plectō, xī, ctum, [3] *v.* plait, twine.

plectō, [3] *v.* buffet, beat; punish.

plectrum, ī, *nt.* quill to strike the strings of a musical instrument.

plēnus, a, um, *a.* full, filled with; plump, stout; plenteous; entire, whole.

plērīque, raeque, raque v. **plērusque.**

plērumque, *ad.* generally, mostly, commonly, often.

plērusque, raque, rumque, *a.* the greater part or number of, most of; (*pl.*) most (people), very many.

plicō, [1] *v.* fold, bend; twine, coil.

plōdō v. **plaudō.**

plōrātus, ūs, *m.* wailing, crying.

plōrō, [1] *v.* wail, weep aloud, weep over.

pluit, *v. impers.* it rains; v. **pluō.**

plūma, ae, *f.* feather, plumage; down.

plumbeus, a, um, *a.* leaden; blunt, dull; heavy; stupid.

plumbum, ī, *nt.* lead.

plūmeus, a, um, *a.* feathery; composed of *or* filled with feathers.

pluō, pluī & plūvī, [3] *v.* rain; fall like rain.

plūmōsus, a, um, *a.* feathered.

plūrēs, plūra, *a. pl.* more, a number of; very many.

plūrimus, a, um, *a.* very much *or* many, (the) most, very long *or* large *or* big.

plūs, *ad.* more; plūris, of more value.

pluteus, ī, *m.* movable screen of wood or wickerwork used for protection in siege warfare; upright board forming the back of a couch.

pluvia, ae, *f.* rain.

pluviālis, e, *a.* rainy; consisting of rain; rain-swollen.

pluvius, a, um, *a.* rainy, causing *or* bringing rain.

pōculum, ī, *nt.* drinking-vessel, cup; drink.

podagra, ae, *f.* gout.

poēma, atis, *nt.* poem.

poena, ae, *f.* punishment, penalty; dare poenās, to pay the penalty.

poēsis, is, *f.* poetry; poem.

poēta, ae, *m.* poet.

poēticus, a, um, *a.* poetic.

pol, *i.* by Pollux!

polenta, ae, *f.* barley-meal.

poliō, īvī, ītum, [4] *v.* smooth, polish; refine, give finish to.

polītus, a, um, *a.* refined, polished.

pollēns, entis, *a.* strong, potent, exerting power.

polleō, [2] *v.* exert power *or* influence; be strong.

pollex, icis, *m.* thumb.

polliceor, itus, [2] *v. dep.* promise.

pollicitātiō, ōnis, *f.* promise.

pollicitor, [1] *v. dep.* promise (assiduously).

polluō, uī, ūtum, [3] *v.* soil, defile, pollute; contaminate; violate; defile with illicit sexual conduct.

polus, ī, *m.* pole; heaven, sky.

polypus, ī, *m.* octopus, nasal tumour.

pōmārium, iī, *nt.* orchard.

pōmerium v. pōmoerium.

pōmifer, a, um, *a.* fruit-bearing.

pōmoerium, iī, *nt.* space left free from buildings round the walls of a Roman *or* Etruscan town.

pōmōsus, a, um, *a.* rich in fruit.

pompa, ae, *f.* ceremonial procession.

pōmum, ī, *nt.* fruit; fruit-tree.

pōmus, ī, *f.* fruit; fruit-tree.

ponderō, [1] *v.* weigh; weigh up.

pondō, *ad.* in *or* by weight.

pondus, eris, *nt.* weight; burden; value; importance, gravity; pound's weight.

pōne, *ad. & pr. with acc.* behind.

pōnō, posuī, positum, [3] *v.* put, place; lay; station; plant; lay aside; appoint.

pōns, ntis, *m.* bridge; deck (of a ship); floor of a tower.

ponticulus, ī, *m.* little bridge.

pontifex, icis, *m.* Roman high priest.

pontificalis, e, pontificius, a, um, *a.* pontifical, of *or* pertaining to a **pontifex**.

pontificātus, ūs, *m.* pontificate, the office of **pontifex**.

pontus, ī, *m.* sea.

popīna, ae, *f.* cook-shop, bistro, low-class eating house.

poples, itis, *m.* knee.

populābilis, e, *a.* that may be ravaged *or* laid waste.

populāris, e, *a.* popular; of the common people; of the same country; ~ **aura**, the breeze of popular favour; ~, **is**, *m.* fellow-citizen, compatriot; member of the 'popular' party.

populāritās, ātis, *f.* courting of popular favour.

populāriter, *ad.* in everyday language; in a manner designed to win popular support.

populātiō, ōnis, *f.* plundering, devastation.

populātor, ōris, *m.* devastator, ravager, plunderer.

pōpuleus, a, um, *a.* of a poplar.

populō, [1] *v.* **populor, ātus**, [1] *v. dep.* ravage, devastate; plunder; despoil.

populus, ī, *m.* people, nation.

pōpulus, ī, *f.* poplar-tree.

porca, ae, *f.* female pig, sow.

porcus, ī, *m.* hog, pig.

porrigō, rēxī, rēctum, [3] *v.* put forward, extend; stretch *or* spread (oneself) out; offer.

porrō, *ad.* onward, further off; further; besides; again, more-over.

porrum, ī, *nt.*, **porrus, ī**, *m.* leek.

porta, ae, *f.* gate; entrance.

portendō, dī, tum, [3] *v.* portend, presage; reveal by portents.

portentum, ī, *nt.* omen, portent; something unnatural *or* extra-ordinary, monster, monstros-ity; fantastic story.

porticus, ūs, *f.* colonnade, porti-co.

portiō, ōnis, *f.* part, portion, share; proportion; **prōpor-tiōne**, proportionally.

portitor, ōris, *m.* ferryman; Cha-ron; toll-collector, customs-officer.

portō, [1] *v.* carry, bear, convey.

portōrium, iī, *nt.* duty, toll.

portuōsus, a, um, *a.* well pro-vided with harbours.

portus, ūs, *m.* harbour, haven, port; mouth of a river.

poscō, poposcī, [3] *v.* ask for in-sistently, demand; demand for punishment, trial, *etc.*

positor, ōris, *m.* builder, founder.

positus, ūs, *m.* situation, position; arrangement.

possessiō, ōnis, *f.* possession; estate.

possessor, ōris, *m.* owner, occupier.

possibilis, e, *a.* possible.

possideō, sēdī, sessum, [2] *v.* possess, have.

possum, posse, potuī, *v.* be able; have power; can.

post, *ad. & pr. with acc.* behind, back; backwards; after; inferior to.

posteā, *ad.* hereafter, thereafter, afterwards.

posteāquam, *ad.* after, ever since.

posterior, us, *a.* later in order; later, latter; inferior.

posteritās, ātis, *f.* future time; posterity.

posterus, a, um, *a.* following, next, ensuing, future; **posterī, ōrum,** *m. pl.* posterity, descendants.

posthabeō, uī, itum, [2] *v.* esteem less, subordinate (to); postpone.

posthāc, *ad.* hereafter, henceforth, in future.

postīcus, a, um, *a.* back, rear; **postīcum, ī,** *nt.* back door.

postis, is, *m.* post, door-post; door.

postmodo, postmodum, *ad.* afterwards, presently, later.

postpōnō, posuī, positum, [3] *v.* esteem less than; postpone.

postquam, *c.* after, since.

postrēmō, *ad.* at last.

postrēmus, a, um, *a.* last; worst.

postrīdiē, *ad.* on the day after, on the following *or* next day.

postulātiō, ōnis, *f.* petition, request.

postulātum, ī, *nt.* demand, request.

postulō, [1] *v.* ask for, demand, require, request, desire; accuse, prosecute.

postumus, a, um, *a.* last; lastborn; born after the death of the father.

potēns, entis, *a.* able, mighty, powerful, potent, efficacious.

potentātus, ūs, *m.* dominion, command.

potentia, ae, *f.* power; efficacy, virtue; ability.

potestās, ātis, *f.* power, faculty, opportunity; authority; dominion; command.

pōtiō, ōnis, *f.* drink, draught; potion, philtre.

potior, ītus, [4] *v. dep.* take possession of, get, obtain, acquire, receive; possess.

potior, ius, *a.* more powerful; preferable.

potis, pote, *a.* able (to), capable (of); possible.

potissimus, a, um, *a.* principal; most powerful, chief.

potius, *ad.* rather, preferably; more (than).

pōtō, ātum & pōtum, [1] *v.* drink; tipple; drink to excess.

prae, *pr. with abl.* before, in front of; in comparison with; in the face of, under the pressure of.

praeacūtus, a, um, *a.* sharpened at the end, very sharp.

praealtus, a, um, *a.* very high; very deep.

praebeō, uī, itum, [2] *v.* offer; present; show; give; expose.

praecaveō, cāvī, cautum, [2] *v.* guard (against), beware.

praecēdō, cessī, cessum, [3] *v.* go before, precede; surpass.

praecellō, [3] *v.* excel; surpass.

praecelsus, a, um, *a.* exceptionally high *or* tall.

praeceps, cipitis, *a.* headlong; impetuous, sheer; involving risk of sudden disaster; **in ~**, headlong.

praeceptor, ōris, *m.* teacher, instructor.

praeceptum, ī, *nt.* rule, precept; order, instruction; teaching.

praecerpō, psī, ptum, [3] *v.* pluck before time; pluck *or* cut off.

praecīdō, cīdī, cīsum, [3] *v.* cut off in front; cut back, cut short.

praecingō, nxī, nctum, [3] *v.* gird, surround, encircle.

praecinō, uī, centum, [3] *v.* sing before; predict.

praecipiō, cēpī, ceptum, [3] *v.* take *or* obtain in advance, anticipate; teach, recommend, order.

praecipitō, [1] *v.* throw down headlong, precipitate; destroy; suffer ruin; drive headlong; fall headlong.

praecipuus, a, um, *a.* particular, peculiar, especial; special.

praecīsus, a, um, *a.* abrupt, precipitous; clipped, staccato.

praeclārus, a, um, *a.* very bright; beautiful; splendid, noble, excellent, brilliant; glorious.

praeclūdō, sī, sum, [3] *v.* block up, bar; prevent; forbid access to.

praecō, ōnis, *m.* crier; auctioneer.

praecōnsūmō, mpsī, mptum, [3] *v.* use up prematurely.

praecordia, ōrum, *nt. pl.* vitals, diaphragm; breast; chest as the seat of feelings.

praecox, cocis, praecoquis, e, *a.* ripened too soon; premature; unseasonable; precocious.

praecurrō, cucurrī (currī), cursum, [3] *v.* run before, hasten on before; precede; anticipate.

praecursor, ōris, *m.* forerunner; member of advance-guard.

praeda, ae, *f.* booty, spoil, loot; prey, game.

praedābundus, a, um, *a.* pillaging.

praedātor, ōris, *m.* plunderer, pillager; hunter.

praedātōrius, a, um, *a.* plundering, rapacious; piratical.

praedicātiō, ōnis, *f.* proclamation, publication; commendation.

praedicō, [1] *v.* publish; proclaim; cite; describe (as), call; praise.

praedīcō, xī, ctum, [3] *v.* say *or* mention beforehand; foretell; warn; recommend.

praedictum, ī, *nt.* prediction; forewarning; command.

praediscō, [3] *v.* learn in advance.

praeditus, a, um, *a.* endowed (with).

praedium, iī, *nt.* land, estate.

praedīves, itis, *a.* very rich; richly supplied.

praedō, ōnis, *m.* brigand; pirate.

praedor, ātus, [1] *v. dep.* plunder, loot, pillage, spoil; take as plunder.

praedūcō, xī, ctum, [3] *v.* run (a ditch *or* a wall) in front.

praedulcis, e, *a.* very sweet.

praedūrus, a, um, *a.* very hard; very strong.

praeeō, īvī & iī, itum, [4] *v.* go before, precede; dictate.

praefectūra, ae, *f.* command; office of praefectus.

praefectus, ī, *m.* director, president, chief; governor.

praeferō, ferre, tulī, lātum, *v.* bear before; prefer; display, reveal; give precedence to.

praeferōx, ōcis, *a.* very high-spirited.

praeficiō, fēcī, fectum, [3] *v.* put in charge (of); appoint to the command (of).

praefīgō, xī, xum, [3] *v.* fasten before; fix on the end *or* surface (of); obstruct.

praefīniō, īvī *or* **iī, ītum,** [4] *v.* fix the range of; determine.

praefodiō, fōdī, [3] *v.* dig a trench in front of; bury beforehand.

praefor, fātus, [1] *v. dep.* say *or* utter beforehand, mention first; recite (a preliminary formula); address with a preliminary prayer.

praefrīgidus, a, um, *a.* very cold.

praefringō, frēgī, frāctum, [3] *v.* break off at the end, break off short.

praefulgeō, sī, tum, [2] *v.* shine with outstanding brightness; be outstanding.

praegelidus, a, um, *a.* outstandingly cold.

praegnā(n)s, a(n)tis, *a.* with child, pregnant.

praegravis, e, *a.* very heavy; burdensome.

praegravō, [1] *v.* weigh down; burden.

praegredior, gressus, [3] *v. dep.* go ahead; go before, precede; surpass.

praegustō, [1] *v.* taste in advance.

praeiūdicium, iī, *nt.* precedent, example; prejudgement.

praeiūdicō, [1] v. prejudge.

praelābor, lāpsus sum, [3] v. dep. flow, glide ahead or past.

praelegō, lēgī, lēctum, [3] v. sail along.

praelongus, a, um, a. exceptionally long.

praelūceō, xī, [2] v. shine forth; outshine; light the way (for).

praemeditor, ātus sum, [1] v. dep. consider in advance.

praemetuō, [3] v. fear beforehand.

praemittō, mīsī, missum, [3] v. send in advance (of).

praemium, iī, nt. booty, plunder, prize; reward; punishment; payment.

praemoneō, uī, itum, [2] v. forewarn.

praemonitus, ūs, m. forewarning.

praemorior, mortuus sum, [3] v. dep. die beforehand.

praemūniō, īvī, ītum, [4] v. fortify, defend in advance; safeguard.

praenatō, [1] v. swim by; flow by.

praenōmen, inis, nt. first name.

praenōscō, [3] v. foreknow.

praenūntiō, [1] v. announce in advance.

praenūntius, a, um, a. acting as harbinger; heralding.

praeoccupō, [1] v. seize upon beforehand; anticipate.

praeoptō, [1] v. choose in preference; prefer.

praeparātiō, ōnis, f. preparation.

praeparō, [1] v. furnish beforehand; provide in readiness; plan in advance; prepare.

praepediō, (i)ī, ītum, [4] v. shackle, fetter; hinder.

praependeō, [2] v. hang down in front.

praepes, etis, a. flying straight ahead; nimble, fleet; winged.

praepinguis, e, a. outstandingly rich.

praepōnō, posuī, positum, [3] v. put before; prefer (to); put in charge (of).

praeposterus, a, um, a. in the wrong order; wrong-headed; topsy-turvy.

praepotēns, entis, a. very powerful.

praeproperus, a, um, a. very hurried, precipitate; too hasty.

praeripiō, ripuī, reptum, [3] v. snatch away (before the proper time); seize first; forestall.

praerogātīva, ae, f. tribe which voted first.

praerumpō, rūpī, ruptum, [3] v. break off.

praeruptus, a, um, a. broken off; precipitous; hasty, rash.

praes, praedis, m. surety, bondsman.

praesaepe, is, nt. **praesaepēs, is**, f., **praesaepium, iī**, nt. stall; brothel.

praesaepiō, psī, ptum, [4] v. fence in front.

praesāgiō, īvī, [4] v. have a presentiment (of); portend.

praesāgium, iī, nt. sense of foreboding; prognostication.

praesāgus, a, um, a. having a foreboding; ominous.

praescius, a, um, a. foreknowing, prescient.

praescrībō, psī, ptum, [3] v. write before; prescribe, appoint.

praescrīptum, ī, nt. precept, rule; route.

praesecō, uī, ctum or **cātum**, [1] v. cut in front, cut.

praesēns, entis, a. present, in person, at hand, ready; prompt; favourable; effectual; immediate; present, aiding; **in ~**, for the present.

praesentia, ae, f. presence; helpful presence.

praesentiō, sēnsī, sēnsum, [4] v. feel or perceive beforehand; have a presentiment of.

praesēpe, is, v. praesaepe.

praesēpiō v. praesaepiō.

praesertim, ad. especially, particularly.

praeses, idis, m. guardian, warden, custodian.

praesideō, sēdī, [2] v. with dat. preside (over); guard, protect, defend; superintend.

praesidium, iī, nt. help, assistance; defence, protection; convoy, escort; garrison; stronghold.

praesignis, e, a. pre-eminent, outstanding.

praestābilis, e, a. pre-eminent, distinguished, excellent.

praestāns, antis, a. excellent; distinguished (for).

praestituō, uī, ūtum, [3] v. determine in advance.

praestō, ad. ready, at one's service.

praestō, stitī, stitum, & **stātum**, [1] v. stand out; be superior (to); surpass; answer for; fulfil; maintain; show; furnish.

praestōlor, ātus sum, [1] v. dep. expect; await.

praestringō, īnxī, ictum, [3] v. bind or tie up; graze, weaken, blunt.

praestruō, xī, ctum, [3] v. block up, contrive beforehand.

praesultō, [1] v. dance before.

praesum, esse, fuī, v. with dat. be in charge (of), be in control (of); take the lead (in).

praesūmō, m(p)sī, mptum [3] v. consume beforehand; perform beforehand; spend or employ beforehand; presuppose.

praetendō, dī, tum, [3] v. stretch out; spread before; extend in front; allege in excuse.

praeter, ad. & pr. with acc. past; except; excepting; along; beyond; besides; unless, save.

praetereā, ad. besides; moreover.

praetereō, īvī & iī, itum, [4] *v.* go by *or* past; pass by; escape the notice of; neglect; surpass.

praeterfluō, [3] *v.* flow past.

praetergredior, gressus, [3] *v.* march *or* go past.

praeteritus, a, um, *a.* past.

praeterlābor, psus, [3] *v. dep.* glide *or* slip past.

praetermittō, mīsī, missum, [3] *v.* let pass; omit, neglect; pass over, make no mention of.

praeterquam, *ad.* beyond, besides; except, save.

praetervehor, ctus sum, [3] *v. dep.* drive, ride *or* sail by; pass by.

praetervolō, [1] *v.* fly past; slip by.

praetexō, xuī, xtum, [3] *v.* weave in front, fringe; cloak (with); pretend.

praetexta, ae, *f.* toga with a purple border worn by curule magistrates and children.

praetextātus, a, um, *a.* wearing the **toga praetexta.**

praetextus, ūs, *m.* show; pretext.

praetor, ōris, *m.* Roman magistrate concerned chiefly with judicial functions.

praetōrium, iī, *nt.* general's headquarters building *or* tent; imperial bodyguard.

praetōrius, a, um, *a.* of *or* belonging to a commander (of a Roman military force), praetorian; ~, **iī,** *m.* an ex-**praetor.**

praetūra, ae, *f.* praetorship.

praeūrō, ussī, ustum, [3] *v.* scorch at the extremity *or* on the surface.

praevaleō, uī, [2] *v.* have greater power, influence *or* worth; prevail.

praevalidus, a, um, *a.* very strong; strong in growth.

praevehor, ctus, [3] *v.* travel past *or* along.

praeveniō, vēnī, ventum, [4] *v.* arrive first *or* beforehand; anticipate, forestall.

praevertō, tī, [3] *v.* anticipate; preoccupy; attend to first; outstrip, outrun.

praevideō, vīdī, vīsum, [2] *v.* foresee, see in advance.

praevius, a, um, *a.* going before, leading the way.

prandeō, dī, nsum, [2] *v.* eat one's morning *or* midday meal.

prandium, iī, *nt.* meal eaten about midday, luncheon.

prātum, ī, *nt.* meadow.

prāvitās, ātis, *f.* bad condition; viciousness, perverseness, depravity.

prāvus, a, um, *a.* crooked; misshapen, deformed; perverse, vicious, corrupt; faulty; bad.

precārius, a, um, *a.* obtained by prayer; doubtful, precarious.

precātiō, ōnis, *f.* prayer, supplication.

precor, ātus, [1] *v. dep.* pray to, beseech, entreat; ask for; invoke.

prehendō, prendō, dī, sum, [3] *v.* take hold of, seize hold of; catch in the act.

prēlum, ī, *nt.* wine- or oil-press.

premō, pressī, pressum, [3] *v.* press; squeeze; oppress; curb; thrust; overpower; keep in subjection; afflict; pursue; have intercourse with.

prēnsō, [1] *v.* grasp at; accost; canvass.

pressō, [1] *v.* press, squeeze.

pressus, a, um, *a.* firmly planted, deliberate.

pretiōsus, a, um, *a.* valuable, precious; costly.

pretium, iī, *nt.* price, worth, value; wages, reward; bribe; ~ est, *or* operae ~ est, it is worth while.

prex, ecis, *f.* prayer, entreaty; curse; good wishes.

prīdem, *ad.* some time ago, previously.

prīdiē, *ad.* on the day before.

prīmaevus, a, um, *a.* youthful.

prīmipīlus, prīmōpilus, ī, *m.* senior centurion of a legion.

prīmitiae, ārum, *f. pl.* firstfruits; beginnings.

prīmordium, iī, *nt.* beginnings, origin.

prīmōris, is, *a.* first; foremost; extreme; **prīmōrēs,** *m. pl.* nobles, men of the first rank.

prīmum, *ad.* first, in the first place, at the beginning; for the first time.

prīmus, a, um, *a.* first, foremost; most distinguished; **prīma lux,** early dawn.

prīnceps, ipis, *a.* first; ~, *m.* or *f.* chief; general; prime mover; ~ **senātūs,** senator whose name stood first on the censors' list.

prīncipālis, e, *a.* first, original, principal.

prīncipātus, ūs, *m.* preeminence; supremacy, post of commander-in-chief; rule; beginning.

prīncipium, iī, *nt.* beginning, origin, principle.

prior, prius, ōris, *a.* former, previous; in front; better; **priōrēs,** *m. pl.* ancestors.

prīscus, a, um, *a.* old, ancient; archaic.

prīstinus, a, um, *a.* former, antique, ancient.

prius, *ad.* before, sooner.

priusquam, *c.* before.

prīvātim, *ad.* in private, privately.

prīvātus, a, um, *a.* private.

prīvigna, ae, *f.* stepdaughter.

prīvignus, ī, *m.* stepson.

prīvō, [1] *v.* deprive (of); free or release (from).

prīvus, a, um, *a.* one's own, private; separate, single.

prō, *pr. with abl.* before, in front of; from the front of; for, in favour of; instead of; in proportion to.

prō i. with voc., acc. and nom. Good God! good heavens!

proavia, ae, f. great-grand-mother.

proavītus, a, um, a. ancestral.

proavus, ī, m. great-grandfather; remote ancestor.

probābilis, e, a. probable; commendable.

probātor, ōris, m. one who approves.

probitās, ātis, f. honesty, probity; virtue.

probō, [1] v. test; recommend; approve of; prove.

probrōsus, a, um, a. shameful; disreputable.

probrum, ī, nt. disgrace; abuse, insult; disgrace, shame.

probus, a, um, a. good; clever; honest, virtuous.

procāx, ācis, a. pushing, impudent; undisciplined; frivolous.

prōcēdō, cessī cessum, [3] v. go forward or before, proceed; advance; get on; be successful; make progress.

procella, ae, f. storm, gale; tumult, commotion.

procellōsus, a, um, a. stormy, boisterous.

procer, eris, m. great man, nobleman.

procerēs, um v. procer.

prōcērus, a, um, a. high, tall; long.

prōcessus, ūs, m. advance, progress.

prōcidō, cidī, [3] v. fall prostrate, collapse.

prōcīnctus, ūs, m. readiness for battle.

prōclāmō, [1] v. call or cry out; appeal noisily.

prōclīnō, [1] v. tilt forward; cause to totter.

prōclīvis, e, a. sloping down; downward; prone (to); easy.

prōcōnsul, is, m. ex-consul; governor of a province.

prōcōnsulāris, e, a. proconsular.

prōcrāstinō, [1] v. put off till the next day, postpone; delay.

prōcreō, [1] v. bring into existence, beget, procreate; produce, create.

prōcrēscō, [3] v. grow on to maturity, grow larger.

prōcubō, [1] v. lie outstretched.

prōcūdō, dī, sum, [3] v. forge, hammer out, beat out.

procul, ad. far, some way off, far away.

prōculcō, [1] v. trample on.

prōcumbō, cubuī, cubitum, [3] v. lean or bend forward; sink down, prostrate oneself.

prōcūrātiō, ōnis, f. charge, management; superintendence.

prōcūrātor, ōris, m. manager, overseer; agent; deputy.

prōcūrō, [1] v. attend to; administer; expiate (by sacrifice).

prōcurrō, cucurrī & currī, cursum, [3] v. run or rush forwards; extend, project.

prōcursātiō, ōnis, f. sudden charge, sally.

prōcursō, [1] v. run frequently forward, dash out.

prōcursus, ūs, m. forward movement; outbreak.

prōcurvus, a, um, a. curved outwards or forwards.

procus, ī, m. wooer, suitor.

prōdeō, iī, itum, [4] v. go or come forward or forth; project; appear in public, appear on the stage; advance, proceed.

prōdicō, xī ctum, [3] v. give notice of or fix a day.

prōdigiōsus, a, um, a. prodigious, strange, wonderful, unnatural.

prōdigium, iī, nt. omen, portent, monster; marvel; monstrous creature.

prōdigus, a, um, a. wasteful, lavish, prodigal.

prōditiō, ōnis, f. betrayal, treachery.

prōditor, ōris, m. traitor; betrayer.

prōdō, didī, ditum, [3] v. give birth to; nominate; publish; betray; hand down.

prōdūcō, xī, ctum, [3] v. lead or bring forward; draw out; accompany to the tomb; lengthen; prolong; bring forth.

proelior, ātus, [1] v. dep. join battle, fight; contend.

proelium, iī, nt. battle, combat; conflict, dispute.

profānō, [1] v. desecrate, profane.

profānus, a, um, a. secular, profane; not initiated; impious.

profectiō, ōnis, f. setting out; departure.

profectō, ad. without question, undoubtedly, assuredly.

prōfectus, ūs, m. progress, success.

prōferō, ferre, tulī, lātum, v. carry or bring out, bring forth; extend; prolong; defer; reveal; utter; produce; publish.

profēstus, a, um, a. not kept as a holiday; common, ordinary.

prōficiō, fēcī, fectum, [3] v. make headway; advance; help; develop, be successful.

proficīscor, fectus, [3] v. dep. set out, depart; proceed, arise or spring from.

profiteor, fessus, [2] v. dep. declare publicly; promise, volunteer; profess (oneself) to be.

prōflīgātus, a, um, a. profligate, depraved.

prōflīgō, [1] v. defeat decisively, crush, overwhelm; ruin or destroy utterly.

prōflō, [1] v. blow out, exhale.

prōfluō, xī, xum, v. flow forth or along; emanate (from).

profor, fātus sum, [1] v. dep. speak out.

profugiō, fūgī, [3] v. flee, run away (from).

profugus, a, um, *a.* fugitive; run-away; refugee.

profundō, fūdī, fūsum, [3] *v.* pour out; lavish, squander; break out.

profundus, a, um, *a.* deep, profound; boundless; insatiable; **profundum, ī**, *nt.* depths, abyss, chasm; boundless expanse.

profūsus, a, um, *a.* excessive; lavish; extravagant.

prōgeniēs, ēī, *f.* race, family, progeny.

prōgenitor, ōris, *m.* ancestor.

prōgignō, genuī, genitum, [3] *v.* beget; produce.

prōgnātus, a, um, *a.* born (of), descended (from).

prōgredior, gressus, [3] *v. dep.* march forwards, go on, proceed.

prōgressus, ūs, *m.* advance, progress.

prohibeō, uī, itum, [2] *v.* keep off, hold at bay; prevent, restrain; stop, forbid; avert; defend.

prōiciō, iēcī, iectum, [3] *v.* throw forth or before, fling down or away; expose; expel; renounce.

prōiectus, a, um, *a.* jutting out, projecting; precipitate; abject, grovelling.

proinde, *ad.* accordingly, so then; ~ ac, just as if.

prōlābor, lāpsus, [3] *v. dep.* glide or slip forwards, fall into decay, go to ruin; collapse.

prōlātiō, ōnis, *f.* postponement; enlargement.

prōlātō, [1] *v.* lengthen, enlarge; prolong; put off, defer.

prōlectō, [1] *v.* lure, entice.

prōlēs, is, *f.* offspring, progeny, descendants, race.

prōliciō, [3] *v.* lure forward, lead on.

prōloquor, cūtus sum, [3] *v. dep.* speak out, declare.

prōlūdō, sī, sum, [3] *v.* carry out preliminary exercises before a fight; rehearse for.

prōluō, luī, lūtum, [3] *v.* wash out; wash away; wash up; purify.

prōluviēs, ēī, *f.* overflow, flood; bodily discharge.

prōmereō, uī, itum, [2] *v.* **prōmereor, itus sum**, [2] *v. dep.* deserve, merit; deserve well of; earn; gain.

prōmineō, uī, [2] *v.* jut out, stick up.

prōmiscuus, a, um, *a.* common, shared; general, indiscriminate.

prōmissum, ī, *nt.* promise.

prōmissus, a, um, *a.* hanging down, long.

prōmittō, mīsī, missum, [3] *v.* send or put forth, let hang down; promise, guarantee.

prōmō, mpsī (msī), mptum, [3] *v.* take or bring out or forth; bring into view; bring out or display on the stage; make known.

prōmonturium, iī, *nt.* promontory, headland; mountain spur.

prōmoveō, mōvī, mōtum, [2] *v.* move forwards; advance, push forward.

prōmptus, a, um, *a.* plainly visible, evident; at hand, ready, prompt, quick.

prōmptus, ūs, *m.,* **in prōmptū sum,** be in full view; be obvious; be within easy reach for use.

prōmulgō, [1] *v.* make known by public proclamation; publish.

prōmus, ī, *m.* butler; steward.

pronepōs, ōtis, *m.* great-grandson.

prōnuba, ae, *f.* a married woman who conducted the bride to the bridal chamber.

prōnūntiātiō, ōnis, *f.* proclamation; delivery; verdict.

prōnūntiō, [1] *v.* proclaim, announce; recite, declaim; tell, report; promise publicly.

prōnus, a, um, *a.* stooping, bending down; inclined downwards; setting, sinking; disposed, prone to; easy.

propāgātiō, ōnis, *f.* propagation; prolongation; the action of extending.

propāgō, [1] *v.* propagate; extend, enlarge, increase.

propāgō, inis, *f.* a layer *or* set by which a plant is propagated; offspring, children, race, breed.

prōpalam, *ad.* openly.

prope, *ad.* & *pr. with acc.* near, almost.

propediem, *ad.* before long, shortly.

prōpellō, pulī, pulsum, [3] *v.* drive *or* push forwards; propel; drive away; impel.

propemodo, propemodum, *ad.* just about, pretty well.

prōpēnsus, a, um, *a.* ready, eager, willing; favourably disposed.

properanter, *ad.* hurriedly, hastily.

properō, [1] *v.* hasten; do with haste.

properus, a, um, *a.* quick, speedy.

prōpexus, a, um, *a.* combed so as to hang down.

propinquitās, ātis, *f.* nearness, proximity; relationship, affinity; intimacy.

propinquō, [1] *v.* bring near; draw near.

propinquus, a, um, *a.* near, neighbouring; ~, **ī,** *m.* kinsman.

propior, ius, ōris, *a.* nearer; more like; closer.

propitius, a, um, *a.* favourably inclined, well-disposed, propitious.

prōpōnō, posuī, positum, [3] *v.* put out; set *or* post up; display; expose (to); report; purpose.

prōpositum, ī, *nt.* intention, purpose; theme, point.

prōpraetor, ōris, *m*. an ex-praetor; one sent to govern a province as **praetor**.

proprietās, ātis, *f*. quality; special character; ownership.

proprius, a, um, *a*. one's own; personal; special; peculiar, proper.

propter, *ad*. & *pr. with acc.* near, hard by, at hand; because of; on account of.

proptereā, *ad*. therefore, on account of that.

prōpugnāculum, ī, *nt*. bulwark, rampart; defence.

prōpugnātor, ōris, *m*. defender; champion.

prōpugnō, [1] *v*. fight; fight in defence of.

prōpulsō, [1] *v*. drive off; ward off, repel.

prōquaestor, ōris, *m*. deputy or treasurer; ex-quaestor.

prōra, ae, *f*. prow; ship.

prōrēpō, psī, ptum, [3] *v*. crawl *or* creep forth.

prōripiō, puī, reptum, [3] *v*. drag *or* snatch away; rush *or* burst forth.

prōrogātiō, ōnis, *f*. extension of a term of office; postponement.

prōrogō, [1] *v*. prolong, keep going; put off, defer.

prōrsus, *ad*. forward; straight ahead; absolutely.

prōrumpō, rūpī, ruptum, [3] *v*. rush forth, break out.

prōruō, ruī, rutum, [3] *v*. rush forward; tumble down; overthrow; hurl forward.

prōsāpia, ae, *f*. family, lineage.

proscaenium, iī, *nt*. scaffold before the scene for the actors to play on; stage.

proscindō, scidī, scissum, [3] *v*. cut, plough; castigate, lash.

prōscrībō, psī, ptum, [3] *v*. announce publicly; post up, advertise (for sale); outlaw, proscribe.

prōscrīptiō, ōnis, *f*. advertisement; proscription.

prōscrīptus, ī, *m*. proscribed person, outlaw.

prōsequor, cūtus, [3] *v. dep*. follow up, pursue; accompany.

prōsiliō, uī, [4] *v*. leap *or* spring forth; start out; gush.

prōspectō, [1] *v*. gaze out (at); look out on.

prōspectus, ūs, *m*. view, prospect.

prōspeculor, *v*. look out for.

prosperō, [1] *v*. cause to succeed, further.

prosperus, a, um, *a*. favourable, prosperous; propitious.

prōspiciō, exī, ectum, [3] *v*. see in front; foresee; take care (that); see to.

prōsternō, strāvī, strātum, [3] *v*. throw to the ground, overthrow, prostrate; cause the downfall of.

prōstituō, uī, ūtum, [3] *v*. prostitute; dishonour.

prōstō, stitī, stātum, [1] v. prostitute oneself.

prōsubigō, ēgī, āctum, [3] v. dig up in front of one.

prōsum, prōdesse, fuī, v. with dat. do good, benefit, profit.

prōtegō, xī, ctum, [3] v. cover; furnish with a projecting roof; protect; defend.

prōtendō, dī, sum & tum, [3] v. stretch out, extend; prolong.

prōterō, trīvī, trītum, [3] v. crush, tread under foot; oppress.

prōterreō, uī, itum, [2] v. frighten off or away.

protervus, a, um, a. violent, reckless; impudent, shameless.

prōtinus, ad. forward, straight on; forthwith; immediately.

prōtrahō, xī, ctum, [3] v. drag forward; bring to light, reveal; prolong.

prōtrūdō, sī, sum, [3] v. thrust forwards or out; put off.

prōturbō, [1] v. drive or push out of the way.

prout, ad. according as, in proportion as; inasmuch as.

prōvectus, a, um, a. advanced, late; elderly.

prōvehō, xī, ctum, [3] v. carry forward; convey out to sea.

prōveniō, vēnī, ventum, [4] v. come forth; come into being; prosper.

prōventus, ūs, m. growth; crop, produce; success; successful course.

prōverbium, iī, nt. proverb, saying.

prōvidentia, ae, f. foresight, foreknowledge; providence.

prōvideō, vīdī, vīsum, [2] v. provide (for); foresee.

prōvidus, a, um, a. prophetic; provident; characterized by forethought.

prōvincia, ae, f. command, government, administration, province.

prōvinciālis, e, a. provincial.

prōvīsor, ōris, m. one who foresees; one who takes care (of).

prōvocātiō, ōnis, f. challenge; appeal; right of appeal.

prōvocō, [1] v. call forth, call out; challenge, excite.

prōvolō, [1] v. fly forth; rush out.

prōvolvō, volvī, volūtum, [3] v. roll forward or along, bowl over; **prōvolvor,** prostrate oneself.

proximitās, ātis, f. near relationship; resemblance; similarity.

proximus, a, um, a. nearest; next; immediately preceding, immediately following; next of kin.

prūdēns, entis, a. foreseeing, aware (of); intelligent, prudent; skilled (in).

prūdentia, ae, f. practical understanding; intelligence, prudence; practical grasp; foreknowledge.

pruīna, ae, f. hoar-frost, rime.

pruīnōsus, a, um, *a.* frosty.

prūna, ae, *f.* glowing charcoal, a live coal.

prūnum, ī, *nt.* plum.

prūriō, [4] *v.* itch; be sexually excited.

psallō, llī, [3] *v.* play on the cithara.

psaltria, ae, *f.* female player on the lute.

psittacus, ī, *m.* parrot.

. . . . -pte, emphatic suffix of pronouns, = self.

pūbēns, entis, *a.* full of sap, vigorous.

pūbertās, ātis, *f.* puberty; virility.

pūbēs, eris, *a.* adult, grown-up; full of sap.

pūbēs, is, *f.* manpower, adult population; private parts.

pūbēscō, buī, [3] *v.* reach physical maturity; ripen.

pūblicānus, ī, *m.* contractor for public works, farmer of the Roman taxes.

pūblicō, [1] *v.* confiscate; make public property.

pūblicus, a, um, *a.* public, common; ~, ī, *m.* public slave; **pūblicum, ī,** *nt.* public purse; public property.

pudendus, a, um, *a.* disgraceful, scandalous.

pudēns, entis, *a.* modest; bashful.

pudeō, uī, puditum, [2] *v.* be ashamed; make ashamed; **mē pudet,** I am ashamed.

pudibundus, a, um, *a.* shame-faced, blushing.

pudīcitia, ae, *f.* chastity, purity.

pudīcus, a, um, *a.* chaste, virtuous.

pudor, ōris, *m.* shame, shyness, modesty; decency; dishonour.

puella, ae, *f.* girl, maiden; sweetheart.

puellāris, e, *a.* girlish, maidenly.

puer, erī, *m.* boy, son, young male slave; **ā puerō,** from boyhood.

puerīlis, e, *a.* childish, boyish, youthful; immature.

pueritia, ae, *f.* boyhood; callowness.

puerperium, (i)ī, *nt.* childbirth.

puerpera, ae, *f.* a woman in labour.

pugil, ilis, *m.* boxer, pugilist.

pugillārēs, ium, *m. pl.* writing-tablets.

pugiō, ōnis, *m.* dagger; poniard.

pugna, ae, *f.* fight; battle, combat; conflict, dispute.

pugnātor, ōris, *m.* fighter, combatant.

pugnāx, ācis, *a.* combative, pugnacious; quarrelsome.

pugnō, [1] *v.* fight; contend, clash.

pugnus, ī, *m.* fist.

pulcer, cra, crum, pulcher, chra, chrum, *a.* beautiful, handsome; glorious; illustrious; noble.

pulcritūdō, inis, *f.* beauty; attractiveness.

pullārius, iī, *m.* keeper of the sacred chickens.

pullulō, [1] *v.* sprout, send forth new growth; spring forth.

pullus, ī, *m.* young animal; young chicken; darling, pet.

pullus, a, um, *a.* dingy, sombre.

pulmō, ōnis, *m.* lungs.

pulpitum, ī, *nt.* stage.

pulsō, [1] *v.* push, strike, beat, batter; assail.

pulsus, ūs, *m.* stroke; beat; pulse; impulse.

pulvereus, a, um, *a.* dusty.

pulverulentus, a, um, *a.* dusty.

pulvīnar, āris, *nt.* pulvīnus, ī, *m.* cushioned couch on which images of the gods were placed.

pulvis, eris, *m.* dust, powder, arena, battlefield.

pūmex, icis, *m.* pumice.

pūnctim, *ad.* with the point.

pūnctum, ī, *nt.* prick, small hole, puncture; spot; vote; ~ **temporis**, a moment.

pungō, pupugī, pūnctum, [3] *v.* prick, puncture; vex, trouble.

pūniceus, a, um, *a.* scarlet, crimson.

pūniō, īvī & iī, ītum, [4] *v.* punish; avenge.

pūpillus, ī, *m.* ward.

puppis, is, *f.* stern, poop; ship.

pūpula, ae, *f.* pupil of the eye.

pūrgāmen, inis, *nt.* impurity; means of purification.

pūrgō, [1] *v.* make clean, clean, cleanse, purify; justify, excuse, clear, exonerate.

purpura, ae, *f.* purple colour, purple; purple dye; purple-dyed cloth.

purpurātus, a, um, *a.* dressed in purple.

purpureus, a, um, *a.* purple-coloured, purple; radiant, glowing.

pūrus, a, um, *a.* clean, pure, undefiled; clear, chaste, naked, unadorned; without an iron point.

pusillus, a, um, *a.* very little, petty, insignificant.

putātor, ōris, *m.* pruner.

puteal, ālis, *nt.* structure surrounding the mouth of a well (in the Comitium at Rome).

puteālis, e, derived from a well.

pūteō, [2] *v.* stink.

puter, tris, tre, *a.* rotten, decaying; stinking, putrid, crumbling.

pūtēscō, [3] *v.* begin to rot, go off.

puteus, ī, *m.* well.

pūtidus, a, um, *a.* rotten; stinking; unpleasant; offensive; tiresomely affected; pedantic.

putō, [1] *v.* trim, prune; assess, estimate, regard(as); think, suppose, believe.

putrefaciō, fēcī, factum, [3] *v.* cause to rot, putrefy.

putrēscō, [3] *v.* rot, putrefy; crumble, moulder.

putris, e v. **puter.**

pyra, ae, *f.* funeral pile, pyre.

pȳramis, idis, *f.* pyramid.

pyrōpus, ī, *m.* an alloy of gold and bronze; a red precious stone.

• • • • • • • • • • • • • • • • •

Q

• • • • • • • • • • • • • • • • •

quā, *ad.* in which direction; where; by what means, how; in so far as.

quācumque, *ad.* wherever.

quadra, ae, *f.* segment, slice.

quadrāgēnī, ae, a, *a.* forty each.

quadrāgēsimus, a, um, *a.* fortieth.

quadrāgiē(n)s, *ad.* forty times.

quadrāgintā, *a.* forty.

quadrāns, antis, *m.* fourth part, quarter; coin worth a quarter of an *as.*

quadrātus, a, um, *a.* squared, square-set.

quadrīduum, ī, *nt.* period of four days.

quadrifāriam, *ad.* in four ways, into four parts.

quadrifidus, a, um, *a.* split into four.

quadrīgae, ārum, *f. pl.* chariot with four horses.

quadriiugus, a, um, *a.* yoked four abreast.

quadrīmus, a, um, *a.* four years old.

quadringēnārius, a, um, *a.* of four hundred each.

quadringēnī, ae, a, *a.* four hundred each.

quadringentē(n)simus, a, um, *a.* the four hundredth.

quadringentī, ae, a, *a.* four hundred.

quadrirēmis, is, *f.* galley with four rowers to every 'room'.

quadrō, [1] *v.* quadruple; form a rectangular pattern.

quadrupedāns, antis, *a.* galloping.

quadrupēs, edis, *a.* four-footed; ~, *m.* or *f.* quadruped.

quadruplex, icis, *a.* fourfold; quadruple.

quaeritō, [1] *v.* seek; search for.

quaerō, sīvī & siī, sītum, [3] *v.* look *or* search for; get, procure; inquire into.

quaesītiō, ōnis, *f.* inquisition.

quaesītus, a, um, *a.* elaborate, recherché.

quaesō, īvī & iī, [3] *v.* ask (for); pray; please.

quaestiō, ōnis, *f.* inquiry, investigation, question; examination by torture.

quaestor, ōris, *m.* quaestor (Roman magistrate), financial officer.

quaestōrius, a, um, *a.* of a quaestor . . . ; ~, **iī,** *m.* ex-quaestor.

quaestuōsus, a, um, *a.* profitable.

quaestūra, ae, *f.* quaestorship; public money.

quaestus, ūs, *m.* gaining, acquiring; gain, profit, income.

quālibet, *ad.* wherever one likes; no matter how.

quālis, e, *pn.* & *a.* of what sort, kind *or* nature, of what kind.

quāliscumque, quālecumque, *a.* of whatever sort *or* quality; any kind of.

quālum, ī, *n.,* **quālus, ī,** *m.* wicker basket.

quam, *ad.* in what way; how; how much; than; **tam . . . ~,** as . . . as.

quamdiū, *ad.* as long as; how long.

quamlibet, *ad.* however, however much.

quamobrem, *ad.* why? for what reason? for which reason.

quam prīmum, *ad.* as soon as possible.

quamquam, *c.* although; yet.

quamvīs, *ad.* & *c.* to any degree you like; although; however.

quandō, at what time? when? when; at any time.

quandōcumque, *ad.* whenever, as often as, as soon as.

quandōque, *ad.* whenever; at some time *or* other.

quandoquidem, *c.* since, seeing that.

quantō, *ad.* (by) how much.

quantopere, *ad.* how greatly; in what degree.

quantulus, a, um, *a.* how little, how small, how trifling.

quantuluscumque, acumque, umcumque, *a.* however small *or* insignificant.

quantus, a, um, *a.* how great, as great as.

quantuscumque, tacumque, tumcumque, *a.* however great (or small); whatever.

quantuslibet, talibet, tumlibet, *a.* no matter how great; however great.

quantusvīs, tavīs, tumvīs, *a.* however great.

quāpropter, *ad.* wherefore; why.

quārē, *ad.* in what way? how? whereby; wherefore, why.

quārtus, a, um, *a.* fourth.

quasi, *ad.* as if, just as; as good as, practically.

quassātiō, ōnis, *f.* violent shaking.

quassō, [1] *v.* shake repeatedly; wave, flourish; batter; weaken.

quassus, a, um, *a.* shaking, battered, bruised.

quātenus, *ad.* how far; to what extent; how long, seeing that, since.

quater, *ad.* four times.

quaternī, ae, a, *a. pl.* four each, by fours; four together.

quatiō, quassum, [3] *v.* strike, shatter; shake; agitate, discompose; urge on.

quattuor, *a.* four.

quattuordecim, fourteen.

quattuorvirī, ōrum, *m. pl.* body of four men; board of chief magistrates.

-que, *c.* and (attached to the word it connects); **-que . . . et,** both . . . and.

quemadmodum, *ad.* how, in what way.

queō, īvī & iī, [4] *v. dep.* be able (to).

quercus, ūs, *f.* oak, oak-tree; garland of oak leaves.

querēla, ae, *f.* complaint; plaintive sound.

querimōnia, ae, *f.* complaint; 'difference of opinion'.

quernus, a, um, *a.* of oak, made of oak-wood.

queror, questus, [3] *v. dep.* complain; protest that *or* at.

querulus, a, um, *a.* complaining, querulous; giving forth a mournful sound.

questus, ūs, *m.* complaint.

quī, quae, quod, who, which, that; which? any.

quī, *ad.* why? by what means? how?

quia, *c.* because.

quianam, *ad.* why ever?

quīcumque, quaecumque, quodcumque, whoever, whatever.

quīdam, quaedam, quoddam, a certain.

quidem, *ad.* indeed, certainly, in fact; **nē . . . ~,** not . . . even.

quidnam, *ad.* what? how?

quidnī, *ad.* why not?

quiēs, ētis, *f.* rest, quiet, repose; peace; sleep; death.

quiēscō, ēvī, ētum, [3] *v.* rest, keep quiet; repose in sleep.

quiētus, a, um, *a.* calm, quiet; peaceful, sleeping; undisturbed.

quīlibet, quaelibet, quodlibet & quidlibet, whoever *or* whatever you please.

quīn, *c.* that not; (but) that; indeed; why not? nay more.

quīncūnx, uncis, *m.* five-twelfths (of an *as*); a pattern in which trees were planted; interest at 5 per cent.

quīndecim, *a.* fifteen.

quīndecimvirī, ōrum, *m. pl.* college *or* board of fifteen; college of priests who had charge of the Sibylline books.

quīngēnī, ae, a, *a.* five hundred each.

quīngentēsimus, a, um, *a.* five-hundredth.

quīngentī, ae, a, *a.* five hundred.

quīnī, ae, a, *a.* five each; five apiece; five at a time.

quīnquāgēnī, ae, a, *a.* fifty each; fifty at a time.

quīnquāgē(n)simus, a, um, *a.* fiftieth.

quīnquāgintā, *a.* fifty.

quīnquātria, ōrum, *nt. pl.* **quīnquātrūs, uum,** *f. pl.* feast in honour of Minerva on 19–23 March.

quīnque, *a.* five.

quīnquennālis, e, *a.* quinquennial, occurring every five years.

quīnquennis, e, *a.* five years old; lasting for five years.

quīnquennium, iī, *nt.* (period of) five years.

quinquerēmis, e, *a.* (of a galley) with five rowers to each 'room'.

quīnquevirī, ōrum, *m. pl.* board of five.

quīnquiēs *or* **quīnquiēns,** *ad.* five times.

quīntadecumānī, ōrum, *m. pl.* soldiers of the fifteenth legion.

quīntāna, ae, *f.* street *or* market in a Roman camp.

quīntānī, ōrum, *m. pl.* soldiers of the fifth legion.

Quīn(c)tīlis, is, *m.* July.

quīntō, quīntum, *ad.* for the fifth time.

quīntus, a, um, *a.* num. fifth.

quippe, the reason is that; for; of course, naturally; seeing that; inasmuch as; as being; indeed, namely.

Quirīnālia, ium, *nt. pl.* a festival in honour of Romulus, cel-

ebrated on the 17th of February.

Quirītēs, *m. pl.* citizens of Rome collectively in their peacetime functions.

quis, quid, *pn.* who? which? what? anyone; anything; someone; something.

quisnam, quaenam, quidnam, *pn.* who tell me? what, tell me?

quispiam, quaepiam, quodpiam & quidpiam *or* **quippiam,** *pn.* anyone, anybody, anything, any; someone, something, some.

quisquam, quaequam, quicquam, *pn.* any, any one, anybody, anything.

quisque, quaeque, quodque & quicque (quidque), *pn.* each, every, everybody, everything; **optimus ~,** all the best people.

quisquis, quodquod & quicquid (quidquid), *pn.* whoever, whatever, everyone who.

quīvīs, quaevīs, quodvīs & quidvīs, *pn.* who *or* what you please, anyone, anything.

quō, whither; whither? for what purpose? what for? so that thereby.

quoad, *ad.* how soon? how far? till, until; as far as; for as long as.

quōcircā, *c.* on account of which; wherefore.

quōcunque, *ad.* whithersoever.

quod, *c.* that, in that, because; as to the fact that; although; since.

quōlibet, *ad.* whithersoever you please.

quōminus, *c.* so as to prevent (something happening); so that ... not.

quōmodo, *ad.* in what manner, in what way, how.

quōnam, *ad.* to whatever place.

quondam, *ad.* formerly; some day; at times.

quoniam, *ad.* seeing that, since, because.

quōpiam, *ad.* somewhere.

quōquam, *ad.* to any place, anywhere.

quoque, *c.* also, too.

quōquō, *ad.* whithersoever.

quōrsum, quōrsus, *ad.* to what end? to what place?

quot, *a.* how many? as many as; every.

quotannīs, *ad.* every year.

quotiē(n)s, *ad.* how often? how many times? whenever; ~cumque, as often as.

quotquot, *a.* however many.

quotus, a, um, *a.* having what position in a numerical series? bearing what proportion to the total?

quōusque, *ad.* until what time? till when? how long?

R

rabidus, a, um, *a.* mad, raging, frenzied, wild.

rabiēs, em, ē, *f.* savageness, ferocity; passion, frenzy.

rabiōsus, a, um, *a.* raving, rabid, mad.

racēmifer, a, um, *a.* bearing clusters.

racēmus, ī, *m.* bunch or cluster (of grapes or other fruit).

rādīcitus, *ad.* by the roots; utterly.

radiō, [1] *v.* beam, shine.

radius, iī, *m.* pointed rod used by teachers, *etc.,* for drawing diagrams, *etc.;* spoke (of a wheel); beam, ray.

rādīx, īcis, *f.* root; radish; foot of a hill; origin; base.

rādō, rāsī, rāsum, [3] *v.* scrape, scratch, shave (off); erase; skirt, graze; strip off; hurt, offend.

raeda, ae, *f.* four-wheeled carriage.

raedārius, iī, *m.* coachman.

rāmālia, ium, *nt. pl.* brushwood, twigs.

rāmeus, a, um, *a.* of a bough.

rāmōsus, a, um, *a.* having many branches, branching.

rāmulus, ī, *m.* twig, little bough.

rāmus, ī, *m.* branch, twig.

rāna, ae, *f.* frog.

rancidus, a, um, *a.* rotten, putrid, nauseating.

rapāx, ācis, *a.* rapacious; inordinately greedy.

rapiditās, ātis, *f.* swiftness, rapidity.

rapidus, a, um, *a.* swift, rapid.

rapīna, ae, *f.* plunder, booty; the carrying off of a person.

rapiō, rapuī, raptum, [3] *v.* snatch, tear *or* drag away; carry off; plunder; ravish.

raptim, *ad.* hastily, hurriedly.

raptō, [1] *v.* drag violently off; ravage.

raptor, ōris, *m.* robber, ravisher.

raptum, ī, *nt.* plunder; prey.

raptus, ūs, *m.* violent snatching *or* dragging away; robbery, carrying off, abduction.

rāpulum, ī, *nt.* little turnip.

rāpum, ī, *nt.* turnip.

rārēfaciō, fēcī, factum, [3] *v.* rarefy.

rārēscō, [3] *v.* thin out, open out; become sparse.

rārō, *ad.* seldom, rarely.

rārus, a, um, *a.* thin, loose in texture; scattered; rare; few; sporadic.

rāsilis, e, *a.* worn smooth, polished.

rāstrum, ī, *nt.* drag-hoe.

ratiō, ōnis, *f.* account; calculation, computation; sum, number; transaction, business; matter, affair; consideration of; judgement, reason; method, order; system, theory.

ratis, is, *f.* raft; boat.

ratus, a, um, *a.* established, authoritative; fixed, certain.

raucisonus, a, um, *a.* hoarsesounding, raucous.

raucus, a, um, *a.* hoarse; husky; raucous.

rāvus, a, um, *a.* greyish, tawny.

re- (before vowels **red-**), *inseparable particle,* back again, anew.

rebellātrīx, īcis, *f.* a. rebellious.

rebelliō, ōnis, *f.* revolt, rebellion.

rebellis, e, *a.* insurgent, rebellious.

rebellō, [1] *v.* revolt, rebel.

reboō, [1] *v.* resound.

recaleō, luī, [2], **recalēscō,** [3] *v.* grow warm again.

recalfaciō, [3] *v.* make warm again.

recandēscō, duī, [3] *v.* glow again with heat; become white.

recantō, ātum, [1] *v.* charm away; withdraw.

recēdō, cessī, cessum, [3] *v.* retire, withdraw; depart; recede; vanish.

recēns, entis, *a.* fresh, recent; ~ ā vulnere, fresh from a wound.

recēnseō, suī, sum [2] *v.* review, count; review the roll of.

receptāculum, ī, *nt.* receptacle; place of refuge, shelter.

receptō, [1] *v.* recover; receive, admit (frequently).

receptus, ūs, *m.* withdrawal, retreat; refuge.

recessus, ūs, *m.* retiring, retreat; recess; haunt, refuge.

recidīvus, a, um, *a.* recurring.

recidō, cidī, cāsum, [3] *v.* fall back, lapse; rebound (onto its author).

recīdō, dī, sum, [3] *v.* cut away; curtail.

recingō, [3] *v.* ungird, unfasten.

recinō, [3] *v.* chant back, echo; call out.

reciper . . . , v. **recuper . . .**

recipiō, cēpī, ceptum, [3] *v.* get back; retake, regain, recover; withdraw; admit; accept; entertain; undertake; **sē recipere,** to retreat.

recitātor, ōris, *m.* reciter.

recitō, [1] *v.* read out, recite.

reclāmō, [1] *v.* cry out in protest at.

reclīnis, e, *a.* leaning back, reclining.

reclīnō, [1] *v.* bend *or* lean back.

reclūdō, sī, sum, [3] *v.* open; open up, lay open; disclose, reveal.

recognōscō, gnōvī, gnitum, [3] *v.* recognize; recollect; examine; inspect.

recolligō, lēgī, lēctum, [3] *v.* recover.

recolō, coluī, cultum, [3] *v.* cultivate afresh; go over in one's mind.

reconciliātiō, ōnis, *f.* reconciliation; the restoration (of good relations, *etc.*).

reconciliātor, ōris, *m.* restorer.

reconciliō, [1] *v.* restore; reconcile.

reconditus, a, um, *a.* hidden, concealed; abstruse, recherché.

recondō, didī, ditum, [3] *v.* shut up; hide, bury, store away; replace; close again.

recoquō, coxī, coctum, [3] *v.* renew by cooking, rehash; reheat, melt down.

recordātiō, ōnis, *f.* recollection.

recordor, ātus, [1] *v. dep.* think over; call to mind, remember.

recreō, [1] *v.* make anew, restore; refresh, revive.

recrepō, uī, [1] *v.* sound in answer, resound.

recrēscō, ēvī, ētum, [3] *v.* grow again.

recrūdēscō, duī, [3] *v.* become raw again; break out again.

rēctā, *ad.* directly, straight.

rēctē, *ad.* vertically; rightly, correctly, properly, well.

rēctor, ōris, *m.* guide, director, helmsman; horseman; driver; leader, ruler, governor; preceptor.

rēctus, a, um, *a.* straight, upright; direct; honest; proper; morally right.

recubō, [1] v. recline, lie at ease.

recumbō, cubuī, [3] v. lie down; recline at table; sink down.

recuperō, [1] v. get again; regain, recover.

recūrō, [1] v. cure.

recurrō, currī, [3] v. run or hasten back; return; have recourse (to).

recursō, [1] v. keep rebounding or recoiling; keep recurring to the mind.

recursus, ūs, m. running back, retreat, return.

recurvō, [1] v. bend back.

recurvus, a, um, a. bent back on itself, bent round.

recūsātiō, ōnis, f. refusal; objection; counterplea.

recūsō, [1] v. decline, reject, refuse.

recutiō, cussī, cussum, [3] v. strike so as to cause to vibrate.

redārdēscō, [3] v. blaze up again.

redarguō, uī, [3] v. refute; prove untrue.

reddō, didī, ditum, [3] v. give back, return, restore; give up, resign; assign; render; utter in reply.

redēmptiō, ōnis, f. ransoming; purchasing.

redēmptor, ōris, m. contractor.

redeō, iī, itum, [4] v. go or come back; return.

redigō, ēgī, āctum, [3] v. drive back, return; restore; bring down (to); reduce.

redimīculum, ī, nt. female headband.

redimiō, iī, ītum, [4] v. encircle with a garland; surround.

redimō, ēmī, ēmptum, [3] v. buy back; ransom, redeem; buy off; rescue; buy; contract for.

redintegrō, [1] v. restore, renew, refresh.

reditiō, ōnis, f. return(ing).

reditus, ūs, m. returning, return; revenue.

redivīvus, a, um, a. re-used, second-hand.

redoleō, uī, [2] v. emit a scent, be odorous.

redōnō, [1] v. give back again; forgive.

redūcō, xī, ctum, [3] v. lead or bring back; escort home; withdraw; draw back; bring or reduce (to).

reductor, ōris, m. restorer.

reductus, a, um, a. receding deeply, set back.

redundō, [1] v. flow back; overflow; abound (in).

redux, ucis, a. coming back, returning.

refellō, fellī, [3] v. refute, rebut.

referciō, sī, tum, [4] v. stuff or cram full.

referō, referre, rettulī, relātum, [3] v. carry, bring or put back; tell; propose; record; ascribe; restore; repay; render an account; answer; **pedem referre,** to return, go back.

rĕfert, tulit, *v. impers.* it concerns, is of importance to; **meā ~**, it matters to me.

refertus, a, um, *a.* crammed full to bursting with; crowded.

reficiō, fēcī, fectum, [3] *v.* make again, restore, rebuild, repair; reappoint.

reffīgō, xī, xum, [3] *v.* unfix, unfasten, detach.

reflectō, xī, xum, [3] *v.* bend back; turn back; turn round.

reflō, [1] *v.* blow back again.

refluō, [1] *v.* flow back.

refluus, a, um, *a.* flowing back.

reformīdō, ātum, [1] *v.* dread, shun, shrink from.

reformō, [1] *v.* transform, remould; form (a new shape); restore.

refoveō, fōvī, fōtum, [2] *v.* refresh; revive; warm again.

refrēnō, [1] *v.* curb, check; restrain.

refricō, [1] *v.* gall; excite again.

refrīgerō, [1] *v.* make cool.

refrīgēscō, frīxī, [3] *v.* grow cold, cool down.

refringō, frēgī, frāctum, [3] *v.* break open.

refugiō, fūgī, [3] *v.* run away; flee to; shrink back; recoil from.

refugium, iī, *nt.* refuge.

refugus, a, um, *a.* fleeing back; receding, drawing back.

refulgeō, sī, [2] *v.* radiate light; gleam.

refundō, fūdī, fūsum, [3] *v.* pour back.

refūtō, [1] *v.* check; refute.

rēgālis, e, *a.* kingly, royal, regal.

regerō, gessī, gestum, [3] *v.* carry back; throw back; throw back by way of retort.

rēgia, ae, *f.* palace.

rēgificus, a, um, *a.* fit for a king.

regimen, inis, *nt.* control, steering; direction.

rēgīna, ae, *f.* queen.

regiō, ōnis, *f.* line; district, locality, region; boundary-line.

rēgius, a, um, *a.* kingly, royal; splendid, princely.

rēgnātor, ōris, *m.* king, lord.

rēgnō, [1] *v.* have royal power; reign; hold sway, lord it.

rēgnum, ī, *nt.* kingship, monarchy, tyranny; kingdom.

regō, xī, ctum, [3] *v.* guide, conduct, direct; govern, rule.

regredior, gressus, [3] *v. dep.* go *or* come back, return; retire, retreat.

regressus, ūs, *m.* going back, return.

rēgula, ae, *f.* ruler, rod, bar; basic principle, rule.

rēgulus, ī, *m.* petty king.

rēicio, iēcī, iectum, [3] *v.* reject; refuse; repulse; refer (a matter) for consideration, *etc.*; put off.

relābor, lāpsus, [3] *v. dep.* slide *or* glide back; recede, ebb.

relanguēscō, guī, [3] *v.* become faint; abate; lose one's passion *or* ardour.

relaxō, [1] *v.* loosen; open up.

relēgātiō, ōnis, *f.* banishment.

relēgō, [1] *v.* banish; remove; remove from the scene.

relegō, lēgī, lēctum, [3] *v.* pick up again; pick out; read over *or* out; recount.

relevō, [1] *v.* lift, raise; lighten; relieve; alleviate; refresh.

rēligiō, ōnis, *f.* supernatural feeling of constraint; scruple; sanction; religious awe; superstition; sanctity; ritual; conscientiousness.

religiōsus, a, um, *a.* pious, devout, religious; scrupulous.

religō, [1] *v.* tie out of the way; bind fast; moor.

relinquō, līquī, lictum, [3] *v.* leave behind; leave; disregard.

reliquiae, ārum, *f. pl.* remains, relics, remnants.

reliquum, ī, *nt.* remainder, residue; the future.

reliquus, a, um, *a.* remaining; future; remaining alive.

relūceō, xī, [2] *v.* shine out.

relūcēscō, lūxī, [3] *v.* grow bright again.

reluctor, ātus, [1] *v. dep.* struggle (against), resist.

remaneō, mānsī, [2] *v.* stay behind; remain, continue to be; persist.

remedium, iī, *nt.* cure; remedy.

remeō, [1] *v.* go *or* come back, return.

remētior, mēnsus, [4] *v. dep.* go back over.

rēmex, igis, *m.* rower, oarsman.

rēmigium, iī, *nt.* rowing; oarage; crew of rowers.

rēmigō, [1] *v.* row.

remigrō, [1] *v.* return.

reminīscor, [3] *v. dep.* recall to mind, recollect.

remissiō, ōnis, *f.* sending back; relaxation.

remissus, a, um, *a.* mild, gentle; subdued.

remittō, mīsī, missum, [3] *v.* send back; relax, slacken; grant, concede; remit.

remōlior, ītus sum, [4] *v. dep.* heave back.

remollēscō, [3] *v.* become soft again; grow soft.

remordeō, sum, [2] *v.* bite back; gnaw, nag.

remoror, ātus, [1] *v. dep.* wait, linger; delay, hold up, check.

remōtus, a, um, *a.* distant, remote.

removeō, mōvī, mōtum, [2] *v.* move back; remove; withdraw.

remūgiō, [4] *v.* bellow back, moo in reply; resound.

remulceō, sī, sum, [2] *v.* stroke back.

remulcum, ī, *nt.* tow-rope.

remūnerō, [1] *v.,* **remūneror, ātus,** [1] *v. dep.* reward, recompense, remunerate.

rēmus, ī, *m.* oar.

renārrō, [1] *v.* tell over again.

renāscor, nātus, [3] *v. dep.* be born again; be renewed, be revived.

renīdeō, [2] *v.* shine (back), gleam; smile back (at).

rēnō, ōnis, *m.* reindeer-skin.

renovō, [1] *v.* make new again; restore; refresh; resume.

renūntiō, [1] *v.* report, declare, announce; renounce, call off.

renuō, uī, [3] *v.* give a refusal, disapprove; refuse.

reor, ratus, [2] *v. dep.* think, suppose, imagine, deem.

repāgula, ōrum, *nt. pl.* doorbars.

repandus, a, um, *a.* spread out, flattened back.

reparābilis, e, *a.* capable of being recovered or restored.

reparō, [1] *v.* recover, restore, repair, renew; revive.

repellō, reppulī, pulsum, [3] *v.* drive or push back; reject; repulse.

rependō, dī, sum, [3] *v.* weigh or balance (against); weigh out in return; pay in return; purchase, compensate.

repēns, entis, *a.* sudden, unexpected; completely new.

repente, repentīnō, *ad.* suddenly, unexpectedly; all at once.

repentīnus, a, um, *a.* sudden, done to meet a sudden contingency.

repercutiō, cussī, cussum, [3] *v.* cause to rebound; reflect; strike against.

reperiō, repperī, repertum, [4] *v.* find, find out; discover; invent.

repertor, ōris, *m.* discoverer, inventor, author.

repertum, ī, *nt.* discovery.

repetō, īvī & iī, ītum, [3] *v.* return to; get back; demand back; repeat; recall; attack again.

repetundae, ārum, *f. pl.* the recovery of extorted money.

repleō, ēvī, ētum, [2] *v.* fill again; fill up, replenish; restore to its full number.

replētus, a, um, *a.* full (of).

rēpō, psī, ptum, [3] *v.* creep, crawl.

repōnō, posuī, positum, [3] *v.* put or lay back; replace; stage (a play) again; store away.

reportō, [1] *v.* carry or bring back; report; bring home from war.

reposcō, [3] *v.* demand back; claim as one's due.

repraesentō, [1] *v.* exhibit, pay in ready money; revive.

reprehendō, dī, sum, [3] *v.* catch hold of; censure, reprehend, rebuke.

reprimō, pressī, pressum, [3] *v.* hold in check; check, restrain; repress.

repudiō, [1] v. divorce, repudiate; refuse.

repugnō, [1] v. fight back, offer resistance (to); object (to); be inimical (to).

repulsa, ae, f. electoral defeat; rebuff.

repulsō, [1] v. drive back; reject.

reputō, [1] v. think over, reflect on.

requiēs, ētis, f. rest, relaxation, recreation.

requiēscō, ēvī, ētum, [3] v. rest, repose; take a holiday; quieten down; rest (upon).

requiētus, a, um, a. rested; improved by lying fallow.

requīrō, quīsīvī & sii, quīsītum, [3] v. seek; search for; need; ask about.

rēs, reī, f. thing; matter; affair; fact; condition; property; profit, advantage; world, universe, case (in law), suit; power; valour; exploit; ~ **novae,** political changes, revolution; ~ **pūblica,** republic, state; ~ **secundae,** prosperity; **rē vērā,** actually, really.

resānēscō, nuī, [3] v. be healed.

rescindō, scidī, scissum, [3] v. cut away; tear open; annul, rescind.

rescrībō, psī, ptum, [3] v. write in return or in answer; enrol in place of another.

resecō, cuī, ctum, [1] v. cut back, prune; cut at the base.

resēminō, [1] v. reproduce.

resequor, cūtus sum, [3] v. dep. reply to.

reserō, [1] v. unbar; open; disclose, uncover.

reservō, [1] v. keep back, hold in reserve; preserve; reserve (for).

reses, idis, a. motionless, inactive, idle, sluggish.

resideō, sēdī, [2] v. sit, remain in a place; be left.

resīdō, sēdī, [3] v. sit down; settle; abate; subside, quieten down.

resignō, [1] v. unseal; open; resign.

resiliō, uī, [4] v. leap or spring back; recoil; rebound; shrink (back again).

resīmus, a, um, a. turned up, snub.

resipīscō, īvī & iī, & uī, [3] v. become reasonable again.

resistō, stitī, [3] v. come to a standstill, stop; (with dat.) resist, stand up (to).

resolvō, solvī, solūtum, [3] v. loosen, release, disperse, melt; relax; pay; enervate; pay back; break up; finish.

resonō, [1] v. resound, re-echo.

resonus, a, um, a. echoing.

resorbeō, [2] v. swallow down.

respectō, [1] v. keep on looking round or back; await; have regard for.

respectus, ūs, m. looking back (at); refuge; regard, consideration (for).

respergō, sī, sum, [3] *v.* sprinkle, spatter.

respiciō, exī, ectum, [3] *v.* look round (for), look back (at); take notice of.

respīrāmen, inis, *nt.* means or channel of breathing.

respīrātiō, ōnis, *f.* taking of breath.

respīrō, [1] *v.* breathe out; take breath; enjoy a respite.

resplendeō, [2] *v.* shine brightly (with reflected light).

respondeō, dī, sum, [2] *v.* reply; say (write) in answer; say in refutation; answer a summons to appear.

respōnsō, [1] *v.* answer, reply (to); re-echo.

respōnsum, ī, *nt.* answer, reply; answer given by an oracle; opinion of one learned in the law.

rēs pūblica, reī pūblicae, *f.* republic; state; the public good.

respuō, uī, [3] *v.* spit out; refuse or reject (with abhorrence).

restāgnō, [1] *v.* overflow; be covered with flood-water.

restinguō, nxī, nctum, [3] *v.* quench, extinguish; slake; neutralize.

restis, is, *f.* rope, cord.

restituō, uī, ūtum, [3] *v.* replace, restore; rebuild; revive; give back, reverse; reinstate.

restitūtiō, ōnis, *f.* rebuilding; reinstatement.

restō, stitī, [1] *v.* stay put; stand firm; resist; remain, be left.

restringō, īnxī, ictum, [3] *v.* draw tight; fasten behind one; tie up.

resultō, [1] *v.* leap back, rebound; echo.

resūmō, mpsī, mptum, [3] *v.* pick up again; resume; recover.

resupīnus, a, um, *a.* lying flat on; leaning back.

resurgō, surrēxī, surrēctum, [3] *v.* rise (again); flare up again, revive.

resuscitō, [1] *v.* rouse again, reawaken.

retardō, [1] *v.* delay, hold up.

rēte, is, *nt.* net.

retegō, xī, ctum, [3] *v.* uncover, lay bare, reveal; disclose.

retentō, [1] *v.* hold fast; hold back.

retexō, xuī, xtum, [3] *v.* unweave, unravel; destroy gradually.

rētiārius, iī, *m.* net-fighter in the arena.

reticeō, cuī, [2] *v.* keep silent; leave unsaid.

rēticulum, ī, *nt.,* **rēticulus, ī,** *m.* (little) net; mesh-work bag.

retināculum, ī, *nt.* rope; hawser; rein; towing-rope.

retineō, uī, tentum, [2] *v.* hold fast; hold back; detain; retain; maintain; restrain; cling to.

retorqueō, sī, tum, [2] *v.* twist back; cast back; fling back; turn aside.

retractō, [1] *v.* undertake anew; draw back, be reluctant; reconsider; withdraw.

retrahō, xī, ctum, [3] *v.* drag *or* pull backwards; summon back; win back; withdraw.

retrō, *ad.* backwards, behind; back again, conversely.

retrōrsum, retrōrsus, retrōversus, *ad.* back, backwards; in reverse order.

retundō, (t)tudī, tū(n)sum, [3] *v.* blunt; weaken; repress, quell.

reus, ī, *m.*, **rea, ae,** *f.* defendant; guilty party; debtor.

revalēscō, luī, [3] *v.* grow well again.

revehō, xī, ctum, [3] *v.* carry *or* bring back; **revehor,** *pass.* ride *or* sail back.

revellō, vellī, vulsum, [3] *v.* wrench off, tear down; tear out; remove.

reveniō, vēnī, ventum, [4] *v.* come back, return.

rē vērā, *ad.* in reality, in fact.

reverentia, ae, *f.* respect, deference; awe, reverence.

revereor, itus, [2] *v. dep.* stand in awe of; venerate.

revertō, vertī, [3] *v.* turn back; **revertor,** *pass.* come back, return.

revinciō, vīnxī, vīnctum, [4] *v.* hold down *or* restrain with bonds; hold firmly in place.

revincō, vīcī, victum, [3] *v.* conquer in one's turn; refute; convict.

revirēscō, ruī, [3] *v.* grow green again; grow strong *or* young again.

revīsō, [3] *v.* revisit, go back and see.

revīvīscō, vīxī, [3] *v.* come to life again, revive (in spirit).

revocābilis, e, *a.* capable of being revoked *or* retracted.

revocāmen, inis, *nt.* summons to return.

revocō, [1] *v.* call back, recall, summon back; restrain; reduce; refer (to); revoke.

revolō, [1] *v.* fly back.

revolūbilis, e, *a.* that may be rolled back to the beginning; rolling backward.

revolvō, volvī, volūtum, [3] *v.* roll back; unroll; revolve; go back over in thought *or* speech.

revomō, uī, [3] *v.* vomit up again, spew out.

rēx, rēgis, *m.* king, tyrant, despot; master; leader, head; patron; great man.

rhētor, oris, *m.* a teacher of public speaking, rhetorician.

rhētoricus, a, um, *a.* rhetorical.

rhombus, ī, *m.* instrument whirled on a string to produce a whirring noise; turbot.

rictus, ūs, *m.* the open mouth *or* jaws.

rīdeō, rīsī, rīsum, [2] *v.* laugh; smile; mock; laugh at *or* over.

rīdiculum, ī, *nt.* joke, piece of humour.

rīdiculus, a, um, *a.* laughable, funny; silly; ~, ī, *m.* buffoon, jester.

rigeō, [2] *v.* be stiff *or* numb; stand on end; be solidified.

rigēscō, guī, [3] *v.* grow stiff *or* numb; stiffen, harden.

rigidus, a, um, *a.* stiff, hard, rigid; inflexible; stern.

rigō, [1] *v.* moisten, wet, water, irrigate.

rigor, ōris, *m.* stiffness, rigidity, coldness, numbness, hardness, inflexibility; severity.

riguus, a, um, *a.* irrigating; well-watered.

rīma, ae, *f.* narrow cleft, crack, chink, fissure; flash of lightning.

rīmor, ātus, [1] *v. dep.* probe, search; rummage about for, examine, explore.

rīmōsus, a, um, *a.* full of cracks *or* fissures.

rīpa, ae, *f.* bank; shore of the sea.

rīsor, ōris, *m.* one who laughs.

rīsus, ūs, *m.* laughter.

rīte, *ad.* with the proper rites; duly, correctly.

rītus, ūs, *m.* religious observance *or* ceremony; rite; **rītū** (*with the gen.*), in the manner of.

rīvālis, is, *m.* rival.

rīvus, ī, *m.* brook, stream; channel.

rixa, ae, *f.* violent *or* noisy quarrel, brawl, dispute.

rixor, ātus, [1] *v. dep.* quarrel violently, brawl, dispute.

rōbīgō, inis, *f.* rust; mildew, blight; a foul deposit in the mouth.

rōboreus, a, um, *a.* made of oak.

rōborō, [1] *v.* give physical strength to; reinforce.

rōbur, oris, *nt.* any hard wood; oak; oak-wood; trunk (of such wood); strength, power, might; man-power; courage; resolve.

rōbustus, a, um, *a.* made of oak; hard, firm, strong, hardy, robust; physically mature.

rōdō, sī, sum, [3] *v.* gnaw; eat away, erode; backbite, carp at.

rogālis, e, *a.* of a funeral pyre.

rogātiō, ōnis, *f.* proposed measure.

rogitō, [1] *v.* ask frequently *or* insistently.

rogō, [1] *v.* ask, question; propose (a law, a magistrate); request, solicit for favours.

rogus, ī, *m.* funeral-pyre; remains.

rōrifer, a, um, *a.* bringing dew.

rōrō, [1] *v.* drop *or* distil dew; drip *or* run with moisture.

rōs, rōris, *m.* dew; ~ **marīnus,** rosemary.

rosa, ae, *f.* rose.

rosārium, iī, *nt.* rose-garden.

rōscidus, a, um, *a.* dewy; wet.

rosētum, ī, *nt.* garden of roses.

roseus, a, um, *a.* of roses; rose-coloured.

rōstrātus, a, um, *a.* having a beaked prow.

rōstrum, ī, *nt.* snout *or* muzzle (of an animal), beak, bill; ship's beak; **rōstra, ōrum,** *nt. pl.* platform for speakers in the Roman forum.

rota, ae, *f.* wheel; chariot.

rotō, [1] *v.* whirl round; revolve, rotate.

rotundō, [1] *v.* make round, round off.

rotundus, a, um, *a.* round, circular; smooth and finished.

rubefaciō, fēcī, factum, [3] *v.* redden.

rubēns, entis, *a.* coloured *or* tinged with red.

rubeō, [2] *v.* be red, become red.

ruber, bra, brum, *a.* red (including shades of orange).

rubēscō, buī, [3] *v.* turn red, redden, become red.

rubētum, ī, *nt.* bramble-thicket.

rubeus, a, um, *a.* of *or* produced from a bramble.

rubia, ae, *f.* madder.

rubicundus, a, um, *a.* suffused with red, ruddy.

rūbīgō, v. **rōbīgō.**

rubor, ōris, *m.* redness; blush; modesty, feeling of shame; cause for shame.

rubus, ī, *m.* bramble, blackberry.

rudēns, entis, *m.* rope.

rudīmentum, ī, *nt.* first lesson(s); early training.

rudis, e, *a.* rough, unwrought; raw; untrained; unbroken; ill-made, rudely finished, coarse; ignorant (of).

rudis, is, *f.* wooden sword used in practice fights *or* presented to a gladiator on his discharge.

rudō, īvī, ītum, [3] *v.* bellow, roar, bray, creak loudly.

rūga, ae, *f.* wrinkle; crease, small fold.

rūgōsus, a, um, *a.* full of wrinkles, folds *or* creases.

ruīna, ae, *f.* tumbling down, downfall, ruin; ruins; debris, disaster; landslide.

ruīnōsus, a, um, *a.* ruinous; ruined.

rūminō, [1] *v.* **rūminor,** *v. dep.* chew over again; chew the cud.

rūmor, ōris, *m.* hearsay, rumour; reputation; ill repute.

rumpō, rūpī, ruptum, [3] *v.* burst, break down; force open; violate; rupture; break off.

ruō, uī, utum, [3] *v.* collapse, fall, go to ruin; rush (headlong) (towards), hurry (on); sweep headlong; disturb violently; overthrow.

rūpēs, is, *f.* steep rocky cliff, crag.

ruptor, ōris, *m.* one who breaks *or* violates.

rūricola, ae, *m. or f.* one who tills the land; country-dweller.

rūrigena, ae, *m.* born in the country.

rūrsum, rūrsus, *ad.* backwards; on the other hand; again; in one's turn.

rūs, rūris, *nt.* country; country estate.

ruscum, ī, *nt.* butcher's broom.

russus, a, um, *a.* red.

rūsticānus, a, um, *a.* living in the country.

rūsticitās, ātis, *f.* lack of sophistication.

rūsticus, a, um, *a.* rural, rustic; agricultural; coarse, boorish; crude, clumsy; simple; ~, ī, *m.* countryman; **rūstica, ae,** *f.* countrywoman.

rūta, ae, *f.* rue.

rutilō, [1] *v.* glow with a bright *or* golden red colour; colour bright *or* golden red.

rutilus, a, um, *a.* red, reddish; ruddy.

rūtrum, ī, *nt.* shovel.

••••••••••••••••••••••

S

••••••••••••••••••••••

saburra, ae, *f.* gravel (for ballast).

sacculus, ī, *m.* little bag.

saccus, ī, *m.* large bag; sack.

sacellum, ī, *nt.* shrine.

sacer, sacra, sacrum, *a.* holy, sacred; divine.

sacerdōs, ōtis, *m.* or *f.* priest; priestess.

sacerdōtium, iī, *nt.* priesthood.

sacrāmentum, ī, *nt.* oath taken by newly enlisted soldiers; oath, solemn obligation.

sacrārium, iī, *nt.* sanctuary, shrine.

sacrātus, a, um, *a.* hallowed, holy, sacred.

sacrifer, a, um, *a.* carrying sacred objects.

sacrificium, iī, *nt.* sacrifice, offering to a deity.

sacrificō, [1] *v.* sacrifice, offer up as a sacrifice.

sacrificulus, ī, *m.* sacrificing priest.

sacrificus, a, um, *a.* sacrificial.

sacrilegium, iī, *nt.* sacrilege; robbery of sacred property.

sacrilegus, a, um, *a.* sacrilegious; profane, impious; ~, ī, *m.* temple-robber.

sacrō, [1] *v.* consecrate; devote to destruction; doom; make subject to religious sanction; hallow, sanctify.

sacrōsānctus, a, um, *a.* sacrosanct, inviolable.

sacrum, ī, *nt.* sacred object; consecrated place; temple.

saeculāris, e, *a.* of a generation; lūdī saeculārēs, games celebrated at fixed intervals; **car-men saeculāre**, hymn sung at the **lūdī saeculārēs**.

saeculum, saeclum, ī, *nt.* generation, life-time; race; century; indefinitely long period; the times.

saepe, *ad.* often, oftentimes, frequently; **saepenumerō,** oftentimes, very often.

saepēs, is, *f.* hedge; fence.

saepīmentum, ī, *nt.* fence; enclosure.

saepiō, saepsī, saeptum, [4] *v.* fence in; enclose; surround.

saeptum, ī, *nt.* fold, paddock; enclosure; voting enclosure in the Campus Martius.

saeta, ae, *f.* hair; bristle; fishing-line.

saetiger, a, um, *a.* bristly.

saetōsus, a, um, *a.* bristly, shaggy.

saeviō, iī, ītum, [4] *v.* be fierce *or* furious, rage; be violent.

saevitia, ae, *f.* rage, fierceness, ferocity; cruelty, barbarity, violence.

saevus, a, um, *a.* raging, furious, ferocious, barbarous, cruel; violent.

sāga, ae, *f.* witch, sorceress, wise woman.

sagāx, ācis, *a.* keen-scented; acute, sharp, perceptive.

sagitta, ae, *f.* arrow.

sagittārius, iī, *m.* archer, bowman; Archer (constellation).

sagittifer, a, um, *a.* carrying arrows.

sagulum, ī, *nt.* small military cloak.

sagum, ī, *nt.* coarse woollen cloak; military cloak.

sal, salis, *m.* salt; sea-water; sea; shrewdness; a quality which gives 'life' to a person or thing; **salēs,** *pl.* jokes, witticisms.

salārium, iī, *nt.* regular official payment to the holder of a civil *or* military post.

salārius, a, um, *a.* of salt, salt . . .

salāx, ācis, *a.* highly sexed; aphrodisiac.

salebra, ae, *f.* rut, irregularity; roughness (of style or speech).

salictum, ī, *nt.* collection of willows, osier-bed.

saliēns, ntis, *f.* fountain, jet d'eau.

salillum, ī, *nt.* little salt-cellar.

salīnae, ārum, *f. pl.* salt-pans.

salīnum, ī, *nt.* salt-cellar.

saliō, iī & uī, saltum, [4] *v.* leap, jump; move suddenly; gush, spurt; (of male animals) mount, cover.

salīva, ae, *f.* spittle; distinctive flavour.

salix, icis, *f.* willow-tree, willow.

salsus, a, um, *a.* salted; salty, briny; salted with humour, witty, funny.

saltātor, ōris, *m.* dancer.

saltātus, ūs, *m.* dancing, a dance.

saltem, *ad*. at least, at all events; **nōn** *or* **neque ~**, not *or* nor even, not so much as.

saltō, [1] *v*. dance, jump; portray *or* represent in a dance.

saltuōsus, a, um, *a*. characterized by wooded valleys.

saltus, ūs, *m*. leap, spring, jump; **saltus, ūs**, *m*. narrow passage through forest, mountainous country, defile, pass; woodland interspersed with glades, passes, *etc*.

salūber, salūbris, e, *a*. healthy, salutary, beneficial.

salūbritās, ātis, *f*. good health; wholesomeness.

salum, ī, *nt*. sea in motion, swell, billow.

salūs, ūtis, *f*. health, well-being, safety; greeting, salutation.

salūtāris, e, *a*. healthful, salutary.

salūtātiō, ōnis, *f*. greeting, salutation; formal morning call paid by a client on his patron.

salūtifer, a, um, *a*. health-giving.

salūtō, [1] *v*. greet, salute; call to pay one's respects to.

salvē! *ad*. hail! welcome! farewell! good-bye! **salvēre iubēre**, to greet; to bid good day.

salvus, a, um, *a*. safe, well, sound, undamaged, intact.

sambūcistria, ae, *f*. female player on a small harp.

sānābilis, e, *a*. curable.

sanciō, xī, ctum, [4] *v*. ratify solemnly, confirm; enact.

sānctitās, ātis, *f*. sacrosanctity; moral purity, virtue.

sānctus, a, um, *a*. sacred, inviolable; venerable; holy; upright, virtuous.

sandyx, ycis & ȳcis, *f*. red dye; scarlet cloth.

sānē, *ad*. certainly; truly, 'and that's a fact'; admittedly.

sanguineus, a, um, *a*. bloody, blood-stained; blood-red.

sanguinolentus, a, um, *a*. bloody; blood-red; blood-stained.

sanguis, inis, *m*. blood; race, family, consanguinity; life; vigour.

saniēs, em, ē, *f*. matter discharged from a wound, ulcer.

sānitās, ātis, *f*. health; soundness of mind, good sense.

sānō, [1] *v*. heal, cure, restore to health.

sānus, a, um, *a*. healthy; sound in mind, rational.

sapa, ae, *f*. new wine.

sapiēns, entis, *a*. wise, sensible, understanding; **~**, *m*. wise man.

sapientia, ae, *f*. wisdom.

sapiō, īvī & iī, [3] *v*. taste (of); be intelligent, show good sense.

sapor, ōris, *m*. taste, flavour; sense of taste.

sarcina, ae, *f*. bundle, burden, load, pack.

sarcinārius, a, um, *a.* employed in carrying packs.

sarcinula, ae, *f.* (little) pack, bundle.

sarciō, sarsī, sartum, [4] *v.* make good; redeem; restore.

sarculum, ī, *nt.* hoe.

sarmentum, ī, *nt.* shoot; (*pl.*) twigs, cut twigs, brushwood.

sat, *v.* **satis.**

sata, ōrum, *nt. pl.* crops, cultivated plants.

satelles, itis, *m.* attendant, bodyguard, (*pl.*) retinue; accomplice, violent supporter.

satiās, ātis, *f.* sufficiency, abundance; distaste caused by excess.

satietās, ātis, *f.* satiety; the state of being sated.

satiō, [1] *v.* satisfy; satiate; fill to repletion.

satiō, ōnis, *f.* planting, sowing.

satis, *ad.* sufficient, enough; adequately, sufficiently; **satius,** better, preferable.

satisfaciō, fēcī, factum, [3] *v. with dat.* give satisfaction (to), satisfy; make amends; give sufficient attention (to).

satisfactiō, ōnis, *f.* satisfaction for an offence, apology, indemnification.

sator, ōris, *m.* sower, planter; founder, originator.

satur, a, um, *a.* well-fed, replete; rich; saturated.

satura, ae, *f.* stage medley, satire.

Sāturnālia, ium, *nt. pl.* festival in honour of Saturn, beginning on the 17 December.

saturō, [1] *v.* fill to repletion, sate, satisfy; drench, saturate.

satus, a, um, *a.* sprung (from); native.

satyrus, ī, *m.* satyr; satyric play.

sauciō, [1] *v.* wound; gash.

saucius, a, um, *a.* wounded; physically distressed, afflicted; pierced; stricken.

saxeus, a, um, *a.* rocky, stony, made of stones.

saxificus, a, um, *a.* petrifying.

saxōsus, a, um, *a.* rocky, stony.

saxum, ī, *nt.* rock, boulder; stone.

scaber, bra, brum, *a.* scurfy, scabbed, having a rough surface.

scabiēs, ēī *f.* scurf; scab, mange, itching.

scabō, scābī, [3] *v.* scratch.

scaena, ae, *f.* stage of a theatre; background; the drama; sphere in which actions, *etc.*, are on public display.

scaenicus, a, um, *a.* theatrical; ~, **ī,** *m.* actor.

scālae, ārum, *f. pl.* ladder; flight of steps.

scalprum, ī, *nt.* tool for scraping, paring *or* cutting away.

scamnum, ī, *nt.* bench, stool.

scandō, dī, sum, [3] *v.* climb, mount, ascend.

scapha, ae, *f.* light boat, skiff.

scapulae, ārum, *f. pl.* shoulderblades; shoulders.

scatebra, ae, *f.* gush of water from the ground, bubbling spring.

scateō, [2] *v.* gush out; swarm (with); be alive (with).

scatūrīgō, inis, *f.* bubbling spring.

scelerātus, a, um, *a.* accursed; heinously criminal; sinful.

scelerō, [1] *v.* defile.

scelerōsus, a, um, *a.* steeped in wickedness.

scelestus, a, um, *a.* wicked, villainous.

scelus, eris, *nt.* crime.

scēptrifer, a, um, *a.* bearing a sceptre.

scēptrum, ī, *nt.* sceptre; phallus; kingship.

schola, ae, *f.* lecture; school.

scholasticus, ī, *m.* student, teacher.

sciēns, entis, *a.* expert, knowledgeable.

scientia, ae, *f.* knowledge; understanding, expert knowledge.

scīlicet, *ad.* one may be sure (that), it is clear (that); naturally; yes, but at the same time; evidently; to be sure, doubtless; I ask you!

scindō, scidī, scissum, [3] *v.* split, cleave, tear apart; separate.

scintilla, ae, *f.* spark.

scintillō, [1] *v.* send out sparks.

sciō, īvī & iī, ītum, [4] *v.* know; know of.

scīpiō, ōnis, *m.* ceremonial rod, baton.

scirpea, ae, *f.* large basket made of bulrushes.

scīscitor, ātus, [1] *v. dep.* inquire (of).

scissūra, ae, *f.* cleft, fissure.

scītor, [1] *v. dep.* seek to know; inquire (about); question.

scītum, ī, *nt.* ordinance, statute.

scītus, a, um, *a.* having practical knowledge of, neat, ingenious; nice, excellent.

scomber, brī, *m.* mackerel.

scopulus, ī, *m.* rock, boulder.

scorteus, a, um, *a.* of hide, leathern.

scortillum, ī, *nt.* young prostitute.

scortum, ī, *nt.* harlot, prostitute; male prostitute.

scrība, ae, *m.* public clerk; secretary.

scrībō, psī, ptum, [3] *v.* write; compose; draft.

scrīnium, iī, *nt.* receptacle for holding letters *or* papers, writing-case.

scrīptor, ōris, *m.* writer, scribe, copyist.

scrīptum, ī, *nt.* something written; written communication; literary work.

scrīptūra, ae, *f.* writing; literary work, composition.

scrobis, is, *m.* or *f.* pit.

scrūpeus, a, um, *a.* composed of sharp rocks.

scrūta, ōrum, *nt. pl.* trash, a job lot.

scrūtor, ātus, [1] *v. dep.* search, examine; inquire into.

sculpō, psī, ptum, [3] *v.* carve, engrave, chisel.

sculptilis, e, *a.* engraved.

scurror, [1] *v. dep.* play the 'man about town', i.e. dine off one's jokes.

scūtātus, a, um, *a.* armed with a long wooden shield.

scutica, ae, *f.* strap.

scūtum, ī, *nt.* (oblong wooden) shield, buckler.

scyphus, ī, *m.* two-handled drinking-vessel.

sē, sēsē (*acc.*), **suī** (*gen.*), **sibi** (*dat.*), **sē** (*abl.*), *pn.* himself, herself, itself, themselves.

sēbum, ī, *nt.* suet, tallow, hard animal fat.

sēcēdō, cessī, cessum, [3] *v.* draw aside, withdraw; retire; secede.

sēcernō, crēvī, crētum, [3] *v.* separate off; cut off; set aside; treat as distinct.

sēcessiō, ōnis, *f.* withdrawal; secession; estrangement.

sēcessus, ūs, *m.* withdrawal; secluded place.

sēclūdō, sī, sum, [3] *v.* shut off, shut up.

secō, cuī, ctum, [1] *v.* cut, cut off; cut up; make an incision in; cleave a path through; form by cutting.

sēcrētus, a, um, *a.* separate, apart (from); private, secret; remote; hidden; **sēcrētum, ī,** *nt.* secret, mystic rite; retired haunt.

sectilis, e, *a.* capable of being cut into thin layers.

sector, ātus, [1] *v. dep.* follow continually; pursue; pursue with punishment; hunt out; run after; attend.

sectūrae, ārum, *f. pl.* quarry.

sēcubitus, ūs, *m.* sleeping apart from one's spouse or lover.

sēcubō, uī, [1] *v.* sleep apart from one's spouse or lover.

sēcum = **cum sē**.

secundānī, ōrum, *m. pl.* soldiers of the second legion.

secundō, [1] *v.* (of winds) make (conditions) favourable for travel.

secundum, *ad. & pr. with acc.* after; along; next to; in favour of; in conformity with.

secundus, a, um, *a.* second; following; next; inferior, secondary; favourable; **rēs secundae,** prosperity.

secūrifer, secūriger, a, um, *a.* armed with an axe.

secūris, is, f. axe, hatchet; authority.

sēcūritās, ātis, f. freedom from care; carelessness; safety, security.

sēcūrus, a, um, a. unconcerned; careless; safe, secure; untroubled; nonchalant.

secus, ad. otherwise; wrongly; nōn ~, just so.

sed, c. but; however; yet; but also; ~ enim, but in fact; ~ etiam, but also.

sēdātus, a, um, a. calm, untroubled.

sēdecim, a. sixteen.

sedeō, sēdī, sessum, [2] v. be seated, sit; remain; rest; be decided on.

sēdēs, is, f. seat; home, residence.

sedīle, is, nt. seat, bench, chair.

sēditiō, ōnis, f. violent political discord, mutiny, sedition.

sēditiōsus, a, um, a. factious, seditious; turbulent.

sēdō, [1] v. settle, allay; restrain; calm down.

sēdūcō, xī, ctum, [3] v. lead aside; separate off.

sēductus, a, um, a. distant; retired, secluded.

sēdulitās, ātis, f. assiduity, painstaking attention (to).

sēdulus, a, um, a. attentive, painstaking, sedulous.

seges, etis, f. corn-field; crop.

sēgnis, e, a. slow, sluggish, inactive, unenergetic.

sēgnitia, ae, f., sēgnitiēs, ēī, f. sloth, sluggishness.

sēgregō, [1] v. separate (into parts); break off.

sēiungō, nxī, nctum, [3] v. separate; exclude.

sēlibra, ae, f. half-pound.

sēligō, lēgī, lēctum, [3] v. select, choose.

sella, ae, f. seat, chair, stool; sella curūlis, magistrate's chair.

semel, ad. once, a single time; once and for all; the first time; at any time, once, ever; ~ atque iterum, once and again.

sēmen, inis, nt. seed; shoot; slip, cutting; parentage, descent; germ, spark.

sēmē(n)stris, e, a. half-yearly; of six months' duration.

sēmentis, is, f. sowing; crop.

sēmēsus, a, um, a. half-eaten.

sēmet, pn. himself; herself; themselves.

sēmi, inseparable particle = half, demi...

sēmiadapertus, a, um, a. half-open.

sēmianimis, e, sēmianimus, a, um, a. half-alive.

sēmiapertus, a, um, a. half-open.

sēmibōs, bovis, m. half-bull (i.e. the Minotaur).

sēmicaper, prī, *m.* half-goat (Pan).

sēmicremātus, a, um, *a.,* **sēmicremus, a, um,** *a.* half-burned.

sēmiermis, e, sēmiermus, a, um, *a.* half-armed.

sēmifer, a, um, *a.* half-wild; half-monster.

sēmihiāns, antis, *a.* half-open.

sēmihomō, inis, *m.* half-man, half-human.

sēmilacer, a, um, *a.* half-mangled.

sēmimarīnus, a, um, *a.* half belonging to the sea.

sēmimās, aris, *m.* half-male.

sēmin(ex), ecis, *a.* half-dead.

sēminō, [1] *v.* plant, sow.

sēminūdus, a, um, *a.* half-naked.

sēmiplēnus, a, um, *a.* half-full; half-manned.

sēmiputātus, a, um, *a.* half-pruned.

sēmireductus, a, um, *a.* half bent back.

sēmirefectus, a, um, *a.* half-repaired.

sēmirutus, a, um, *a.* half-ruined *or* demolished.

sēmis, issis, *m.* half an *as*; half; 6% per annum.

sēmisepultus, a, um, *a.* half-buried.

sēmisomnus, a, um, *a.* half-asleep, drowsy.

sēmisupīnus, a, um, *a.* half-lying on one's back.

sēmita, ae, *f.* side-path, track, lane.

sēmiustus, a, um, *a.,* v. **sēmustus.**

sēmivir, ī, *m.* half man; ~, *a.* effeminate.

sēmivīvus, a, um, *a.* half-alive, almost dead.

sēmōtus, a, um, *a.* distant, remote.

semper, *ad.* always.

sēmuncia, ae, *f.* twenty-fourth part (of a pound, *etc.*); a minimal amount.

sēmustus, a, um, *a.* half-burnt, singed.

senātor, ōris, *m.* member of the senate, senator.

senātōrius, a, um, *a.* senatorial.

senātus, ūs, *m.* senate.

senātūs cōnsultum, ī, *nt.* recommendation of the senate.

senecta, ae, senectūs, ūtis, *f.* old age; old men collectively.

seneō, [2] *v.* be old.

senēscō, nuī, [3] *v.* grow old; grow weak, be in a decline; become exhausted.

senex, senis, *m.* old man; ~, *a.* old, aged.

sēnī, ae, a, *a.* six apiece; six.

senīlis, e, *a.* aged, senile.

senior, ōris, *a.* older.

senium, iī, *nt.* condition of old age; melancholy, gloom.

sēnsim, *ad.* slowly, gradually, cautiously.

sēnsus, ūs, *m.* faculty of feeling, perception, sensation, sense; emotion; idea; epigrammatic notion; meaning.

sententia, ae, *f.* opinion, sentiment; judgment; advice; vote; meaning; period; sentence.

sentīna, ae, *f.* bilgewater; scum *or* dregs of society.

sentiō, sī, sum, [4] *v.* discern by the senses; feel, hear, see; undergo; perceive, notice; think, deem; vote, declare; intend.

sentis, is, *m.* any thorny bush *or* shrub, briar, bramble.

sentus, a, um, *a.* rough, rugged, uneven.

s(e)orsum, s(e)orsus, *ad.* separately, apart from the rest.

sēpar, aris, *a.* separate.

sēparātim, *ad.* separately, individually.

sēparō, [1] *v.* separate, divide; cut off, isolate.

sepeliō, īvī & iī, pultum, [4] *v.* bury, submerge, overcome; suppress.

sēpia, ae, *f.* cuttle-fish; ink.

sēpōnō, posuī, positum, [3] *v.* put away from one; disregard; isolate; reserve.

septem, *a.* seven.

September, bris, *a.* of September; seventh (later the ninth) month of the Roman year.

septemdecim, v. **septendecim.**

septemfluus, a, um, *a.* that flows in seven streams.

septemgeminus, a, um, *a.* sevenfold.

septemplex, icis, *a.* sevenfold; of seven layers.

septemtriō, v. **septentriōnēs.**

septendecim, *a.* seventeen.

septēnī, ae, a, *a.* seven each; seven at a go; seven.

septentriōnēs, um, *m. pl.* Great Bear; Little Bear; north, northern regions, north wind.

septiē(n)s, *ad.* seven times.

septimus, a, um, *a.* seventh.

septingentēsimus, a, um, *a.* seven hundredth.

septingentī, ae, a, *a.* seven hundred.

septuāgēnī, ae, a, *a.* seventy each.

septuāgē(n)simus, a, um, *a.* seventieth.

septuāgintā, *a.* seventy.

sepulcrālis, e, *a.* sepulchral, of the tomb.

sepulcrētum, ī, *nt.* graveyard.

sepulcrum, ī, *nt.* grave, sepulchre, tomb; (*pl.*) the dead.

sepultūra, ae, *f.* burial.

sequāx, ācis, *a.* that follows closely *or* eagerly; pliant, tractable.

sequester, tra, trum, *a.* intermediary.

sequestra, ae, f. female go-be-tween, mediatress.

sequor, secūtus, [3] v. dep. follow, come or go after, attend; pursue; aim at; comply (with), conform (to); succeed.

sera, ae, f. bar (for fastening doors).

serēnitās, ātis, f. fine weather; favourable conditions.

serēnō, [1] v. clear up, brighten; lighten.

serēnum, ī, nt. fair weather.

serēnus, a, um, a. clear, fine, bright, cloudless; cheerful, glad, joyous, tranquil.

serēscō, [3] v. grow dry.

sēria, ae, f. large earthenware jar.

sēricus, a, um, a. silken.

seriēs, em, ē, f. row, succession, series; line of ancestors or descendants.

sērius, a, um, a. serious, weighty, important; sober, grave.

sērius, ad. later, too late; ~ **aut citius,** sooner or later.

sermō, ōnis, m. speech, talk; conversation; gossip; subject of talk; language, dialect.

sērō, ad. late, at a late hour; too late.

serō, (seruī,) sertum, [3] v. string together; join, engage (in).

serō, sēvī, satum, [3] v. sow, plant; beget; broadcast; foment.

serpēns, entis, f. snake, serpent; the constellation Draco.

serpō, psī, ptum, [3] v. crawl; move slowly on, glide; creep on.

serpyllum, ī, nt. wild thyme.

serra, ae, f. saw.

serta, ae, f. garland.

serta, ōrum, nt. pl. chains of flowers, garlands, festoons.

serum, ī, nt. whey.

sērus, a, um, a. late; too late; slow, tardy.

serva, ae, f. female slave.

servābilis, e, a. capable of being saved.

servātor, ōris, m. watcher, observer; preserver, saviour.

servātrīx, īcis, f. female preserver, protectress.

servīlis, e, a. slavish, servile; of or belonging to slaves.

serviō, īvī & iī, ītum, [4] v. with dat. be a slave, serve, wait on; be of use (to); be subject (to); labour for.

servitium, iī, nt. slavery, servitude; slaves; the slave class.

servitūs, ūtis, f. slavery, servitude, bondage.

servō, [1] v. save, preserve; protect; keep, observe; look after; pay attention to.

servolus, ī, m. young (worthless) slave.

servus, ī, *m.* slave; ~, **a, um,** *a.* having the status of a slave, servile.

sescentī, ae, a, *a.* six hundred; an indefinitely large number.

sēsē, *pn.* himself, herself; themselves.

sesquipedālis, e, *a.* of a foot and a half; (of words) a foot and a half long.

sessilis, e, *a.* fit for sitting upon.

sēstertium, *nt.* (originally *gen. pl.* after **centēna mīlia**), a hundred thousand sesterces.

sēstertius, a, um, *a.* two and a half; ~, **iī,** *m.* $2\frac{1}{2}$ asses, sesterce.

seu, *v.* **sīve.**

sevēritās, ātis, *f.* gravity, sternness, strictness, severity.

sevērus, a, um, *a.* grave, strict, austere, stern, severe; forbidding.

sēvocō, [1] *v.* call apart, draw aside; separate, appropriate.

sex, *a.* six.

sexāgēnī, ae, a, *a.* sixty each; sixty at a time.

sexāgintā, *a.* sixty.

sexangulus, a, um, *a.* six-cornered, hexagonal.

sexc . . . , *v.* **sesc . . .**

sexiē(n)s, *ad.* six times.

sextādecimānī, ōrum, *m. pl.* soldiers of the sixteenth legion.

sextāns, antis, *m.* one-sixth of any unit.

Sextīlis, e, *a.* of the sixth, later the eighth month of the Roman year; ~, *m.* (month) August.

sextus, a, um, *a.* sixth.

sexus, ūs, *m.* sex.

sī, *c.* if.

sībilō, [1] *v.* hiss; hiss at.

sībilus, ī, *m.* **sībilum, ī,** *nt.* hissing, whistling; hiss of contempt *or* disfavour; ~, **a, um,** *a.* hissing.

Sibylla, ae, *f.* prophetess, a sibyl.

Sibyllīnus, a, um, *a.* of *or* connected with a sibyl, sibylline.

sīc, *ad.* in this *or* in such a manner, so, thus; to such an extent.

sīca, ae, *f.* dagger.

sīcārius, iī, *m.* assassin, murderer.

siccitās, ātis, *f.* dryness; drought; dried up condition.

siccō, [1] *v.* dry, staunch; dry up by evaporation; empty; suck dry.

siccum, ī, *nt.* dry ground.

siccus, a, um, *a.* dry; rainless, not carrying moisture; thirsty; abstemious.

sīcine, *ad.* so? thus?

sīcubi, *ad.* if anywhere, if at any place.

sīcunde, *ad.* if from any place *or* source.

sīcut, sīcutī, *ad.* just as, in the same way as; as it were; just as for instance; just as if; as indeed (is the case).

sīdereus, a, um, *a.* relating to stars; starry; heavenly; star-like.

sīdō, sīdī, [3] *v.* settle; sink down; sit down; run aground.

sīdus, eris, *nt.* star, constellation; climate, weather; glory; (*pl.*) star, the stars.

sigillum, ī, *nt.* statuette; embossed figure, relief; figure woven in tapestry.

signātor, ōris, *m.* witness (to a will, *etc.*).

signifer, a, um, *a.* holding the constellations; ~, **ī,** *m.* standard-bearer.

significātiō, ōnis, *f.* giving signs *or* signals; expression, indication, sign; suggestion, hint.

significō, [1] *v.* show, point out, indicate; intimate, signify; express.

signō, [1] *v.* mark; affix a seal to, seal up; coin, stamp; inscribe; indicate.

signum, ī, *nt.* mark, token, sign; standard, ensign; cohort; signal, password; image, picture, statue; seal, signet; constellation.

silēns, entis, *a.* silent; **silentēs, um,** *m. pl.* the dead.

silentium, (i)ī, *nt.* stillness, silence; repose, tranquillity; omission to speak *or* write of; neglect.

sileō, uī, [2] *v.* be silent, not to speak (about); be quiet; not to function.

silēscō, uī, [3] *v.* grow quiet.

silex, icis, *m. or f.* pebble-stone, flint; boulder, stone.

siliqua, ae, *f.* pod.

silva, ae, *f.* wood, forest; brushwood; thicket-like growth; branches and foliage of trees, bushes, *etc.*; trees.

silvānī, ōrum, *m. pl.* gods associated with forest and uncultivated land.

silvestris, e, *a.* covered with woods, wooded; found in woodland; living in woodlands; wild, untamed, savage.

silvicola, ae, *a.* inhabiting woodlands.

similis, e, *a.* like, resembling, similar.

similitūdō, inis, *f.* likeness, resemblance, similarity; comparison, simile.

simplex, icis, *a.* simple, unmixed; artless, ingenuous, naïve.

simplicitās, ātis, *f.* simplicity; plainness, frankness, candour.

simpliciter, *ad.* simply, just; candidly, frankly.

simul, *ad.* together, at the same time, as well.

simulac, simulatque, *ad.* as soon as, the moment that.

simulācrum, ī, *nt.* likeness, image, statue; pictorial representation; ghost, phantom; shade; sham.

simulāmen, inis, *nt.* imitation, simulation.

simulātiō, ōnis, *f.* pretence, simulation; excuse, pretext.

simulātor, ōris, *m.* one who copies *or* imitates; feigner.

simulatque, v. **simulac**.

simulō, [1] *v.* imitate, copy, represent; simulate, counterfeit, pretend; act the part of; cause to resemble.

simultās, ātis, *f.* state of animosity, quarrel, feud.

sīmulus, a, um, sīmus, a, um, *a.* flat-nosed, snub-nosed.

sīn, *c.* if however, but if; but if (despite what has been said).

sincērus, a, um, *a.* sound, whole; genuine, pure; faithful, straightforward.

sine, *pr. with abl.* without.

singillātim, *ad.* singly, one by one.

singulāris, e, *a.* single, singular; unusual, remarkable.

singulī, ae, a, *a.* one to each recipient; every single; individual; isolated.

singultim, *ad.* sobbingly, with sobs.

singultō, ātum, [1] *v.* catch the breath, gasp; utter with sobs; gasp out (one's life).

singultus, ūs, *m.* sobbing; convulsive catching of breath.

sinister, tra, trum, *a.* left, on the left; unlucky, bad; auspicious, lucky, favourable; perverted.

sinistra, ae, *f.* left hand *or* side.

sinistrā, *ad.* on the left.

sinistrō(r)sum, sinistrō(r)sus, *ad.* to the left.

sinō, sīvī *or* **sīī, situm**, [3] *v.* let, leave; allow, permit, leave alone, let be; grant.

sīnum, ī, nt. sīnus, ī, m. bowl for serving wine, *etc.*

sinuō, [1] *v.* bend into a curve; bend; billow out.

sinuōsus, a, um, *a.* characterized by the action of bending; winding, sinuous; full of folds *or* recesses.

sinus, ūs, *m.* curve; fold; hollow; bosom, lap; bay, gulf; pocket for money; asylum; inmost part; hiding-place; embrace.

sī quandō, *ad.* if ever, if at any time.

sī quidem, *c.* at any rate if, always assuming that; if it is really the case that; seeing that, inasmuch as.

sī quis, qua, quid, *pn.* if any one, if any person.

Sīrius, iī, *m.* greater dog-star, Sirius; ~, **a, um**, *a.* of the dog-star.

sistō, stetī & stitī, statum, [3] *v.* set up, erect, place firmly, plant, station; stand still; stand firm.

sistrum, ī, nt. metal rattle used in the worship of Isis.

sitiēns, entis, *a.* thirsting, producing thirst, arid, dry, parched; thirsty (for).

sitiō, īvī & iī, [4] *v.* be thirsty; long greatly for; be in need of water.

sitis, is, *f.* thirst; aridity, dryness; violent craving (for).

situs, a, um, *a.* laid up, stored; positioned, situated; centred (on).

situs, ūs, *m.* situation, position, site; structure; neglect, disuse, stagnation; rottenness, mould.

sīve, *c.* or if; ~ ... ~, whether ... or.

smaragdus, ī, *m.* emerald; beryl, jasper.

smyrna, ae, *f.* myrrh.

sōbrius, a, um, *a.* sober; staid, sensible, temperate.

soccus, ī, *m.* low-heeled, loose-fitting shoe *or* slipper, worn by Greeks; shoe worn by comic actors; comedy.

socer, erī, *m.* father-in-law; **socerī,** parents-in-law.

socia, *f.,* v. **socius.**

sociālis, e, *a.* social; of *or* relating to allies; conjugal.

societās, ātis, *f.* association; partnership; trading company; society; fellowship; connection, affinity.

sociō, [1] *v.* unite in partnership *or* an alliance; associate (one's resources, *etc.*) with those of a partner; share; combine.

socius, ī, *m.* **socia, ae,** *f.* sharer, partner, companion, associate; spouse; ally, confederate.

socius, a, um, *a.* sharing, associated; allied, confederate.

sōcordia, ae, *f.* sluggishness, torpor, inaction.

sōcorditer, *ad.* negligently.

sōcors, ordis, *a.* sluggish, inactive.

sodālicium, iī, *nt.* close association, partnership.

sodālis, is, *m.* companion, comrade, crony.

sōdēs(= sī audēs) if you do not mind, please.

sōl, sōlis, *m.* sun; east; sunlight; heat of the sun; day.

sōlācium, iī, *nt.* solace, comfort, consolation.

sōlāmen, inis, *nt.* source of comfort, solace.

sōlātium, v. **sōlācium.**

solea, ae, *f.* sole, sandal; sandal worn by a beast of burden.

soleō, itus sum, [2] *v.* be accustomed (to), be apt (to), be the common practise.

solidō, [1] *v.* make solid; strengthen, consolidate.

solidus, a, um, *a.* solid, firm, complete, entire; unwavering, strong; solid, lasting, real.

sōlitūdō, inis, *f.* loneliness, solitariness; desert, waste; emptiness, solitude.

solitus, a, um, *a.* accustomed, usual, customary, normal.

solium, iī, *nt.* throne; bath-tub.

sollemnis, e, *a.* solemn, ceremonial; traditional, customary.

sollers, tis, *a.* clever, skilled, resourceful.

sollertia, ae, *f.* skill, cleverness; resourcefulness.

sollicitātiō, ōnis, *f.* incitement to disloyalty *or* crime.

sollicitō, [1] *v.* harass, molest; tug at, shake up; disturb, pester; torment; rouse, stimulate; strive to influence; incite to revolt; attempt to seduce.

sollicitūdō, inis, *f.* anxiety, uneasiness.

sollicitus, a, um, *a.* restless; in a state of turmoil; uneasy, apprehensive; accompanied by anxiety *or* uneasiness.

sōlor, ātus, [1] *v. dep.* comfort, console; relieve, mitigate.

solstitiālis, e, *a.* of *or* belonging to the summer solstice.

solstitium, iī, *nt.* solstice; summer-time, heat of the summer-solstice.

solum, ī, *nt.* base, foundation; earth, ground, soil; sole of the foot *or* shoe.

sōlum, *ad.* only, merely; **nōn ~ . . . sed,** not only . . . but.

sōlus, a, um, *a.* alone, sole; solitary; lonely; deserted.

solūtiō, ōnis, *f.* payment.

solūtus, a, um, *a.* unbound; free; unrestrained, profligate; free to act as one pleases; lax, careless.

solvō, solvī, solūtum, [3] *v.* loosen, unbind; separate, disengage; dissolve; melt; open; fulfil,

perform; pay, deliver, release; acquit; **nāvem solvere,** to set sail.

somnifer, a, um, somnificus, a, um, *a.* inducing sleep.

somniō, [1] *v.* dream; dream of *or* see in a dream.

somnium, iī, *nt.* dream, vision; fantasy, day-dream.

somnus, ī, *m.* sleep; sloth.

sonābilis, e, *a.* noisy, resonant.

sonipes, edis, *m.* horse, steed.

sonitus, ūs, *m.* noise, loud sound.

sonō, uī, itum, [1] *v.* make a noise; sound, resound (with); utter; be heard.

sonor, ōris, *m.* sound, noise, din.

sonōrus, a, um, *a.* noisy, loud, resounding, sonorous.

sōns, sontis, *a.* guilty, criminal; ~, *m.* or *f.* criminal.

sonus, ī, *m.* noise, sound.

sōpiō, īvī & iī, ītum, [4] *v.* cause to sleep; render insensible by a blow *or* sudden shock.

sopor, ōris, *m.* sleep.

sopōrifer, a, um, *a.* bringing sleep *or* unconsciousness.

sopōrō, atum, [1] *v.* rend to sleep, render unconscious, stupefy.

sopōrus, a, um, *a.* that induces sleep.

sorbeō, uī, [2] *v.* suck up, drink up, absorb, soak up; engulf.

sorbum, ī, *nt.* sorb, service-berry.

sordeō, [2] *v.* be dirty; seem mean, unworthy, not good enough, *etc.*

sordēs, is, *f.* dirt, filth, nastiness, squalor; baseness, lowness; niggardliness.

sordidātus, a, um, *a.* shabbily dressed; wearing mourning clothes.

sordidus, a, um, *a.* dirty, foul, filthy; vulgar, low; poor; paltry, niggardly, sordid.

soror, ōris, *f.* sister; **sorōrēs,** *pl.* the Muses; the Fates.

sorōrius, a, um, *a.* of or concerning a sister.

sors, tis, *f.* lot, drawing of lots; decision by lot; response of an oracle; fate, destiny; part; share.

sortior, ītus sum, [4] *v. dep.* cast or draw lots; obtain by lot; appoint by lot; choose.

sortītus, ūs, *m.* process of lottery.

sospes, itis, *a.* safe and sound, unscathed.

sospita, ae, *f.* female preserver (cult title of Juno at Lanuvium).

sospitō, [1] *v.* preserve, defend.

spadō, ōnis, *m.* eunuch.

spargō, sparsī, sparsum, [3] *v.* strew, scatter; sprinkle; discharge in large numbers, shower; let stream out in all directions; place in scattered positions; spread about.

sparus, ī, *m.* hunting-spear, javelin.

spatior, ātus, [1] *v. dep.* walk about, range, stalk; spread out.

spatiōsus, a, um, *a.* roomy, ample, spacious, long; protracted.

spatium, iī, *nt.* room, space; place for walking, interval; period; length; time available for a purpose.

speciēs, ēī, *f.* visual appearance; look; sight; outward appearance; semblance; pretence; display, splendour, beauty; vision; image, likeness; species; artistic representation.

specimen, inis, *nt.* sign, evidence; token, symbol.

speciōsus, a, um, *a.* showy, handsome, beautiful, splendid, brilliant; specious, plausible.

spectābilis, e, *a.* able to be seen or looked at; worth looking at.

spectāculum (āclum), ī, *nt.* show, sight, spectacle; place occupied by spectators in a theatre.

spectātor, ōris, *m.* witness, spectator; sightseer; critical observer.

spectātrīx, īcis, *f.* female observer or watcher.

spectō, [1] *v.* look at; watch, observe; (geographically) lie, face; examine; test, prove; consider, pay regard to, regard (as).

specula, ae, *f.* raised look-out post.

speculātor, ōris, *m.* spy, scout; look-out man.

speculor, ātus, [1] *v. dep.* keep a close watch on, observe, spy out; look out, watch for.

speculum, ī, *nt.* looking-glass, mirror.

specus, ūs, *m., f.,* or *nt.* cave, abyss, chasm; hole, pit; hollow (of any kind).

spēlunca, ae, *f.* cave, grotto, cavern.

spernō, sprēvī, sprētum, [3] *v.* reject with scorn, disdain; scorn; disregard.

spērō, [1] *v.* look forward to, hope for; hope; anticipate.

spēs, speī, *f.* hope; expectation; object of hope; joy.

spīca, ae, *f.* ear of corn.

spīceus, a, um, *a.* consisting of ears of corn.

spīculum, ī, *nt.* sting; javelin; arrow; sharp point of a weapon.

spīna, ae, *f.* thorn; spine; backbone; thorn-bush.

spīnētum, ī, *nt.* thicket (of thorn-bushes).

spīneus, a, um, *a.* thorny, covered with thorns.

spīnōsus, a, um, *a.* thorny, prickly; crabbed, difficult.

spīnus, ī, *f.* thorn-bush.

spīra, ae, *f.* coil.

spīrāculum, ī, *nt.* air-hole, vent.

spīrāmentum, ī, *nt.* breathing-passage.

spīritus, ūs, *m.* breath of air, breeze; breath, breathing; soul, mind; life.

spīrō, [1] *v.* breathe; blow; live; breathe out; exhale; breathe the spirit of.

spissēscō, [3] *v.* become more compact, thicken.

spissō, [1] *v.* thicken, condense.

spissus, a, um, *a.* thick, dense; closely packed, crowded.

splendeō, [2] *v.* shine, be bright; be brilliant *or* distinguished.

splendēscō, duī, [3] *v.* become bright, begin to shine.

splendidus, a, um, *a.* bright, shining, glittering, brilliant; splendid, sumptuous; illustrious; showy, striking.

splendor, ōris, *m.* brightness; brilliance, splendour; magnificence; personal distinction.

spoliātiō, ōnis, *f.* robbing, plundering, spoliation.

spoliātor, ōris, *m.* one who plunders *or* despoils.

spoliō, [1] *v.* strip *or* rob of clothing; plunder, rob, despoil.

spolium, iī, *nt.* skin, hide (of an animal, stripped off); booty, spoil; **spolia opīma,** spoils taken by a general after a single combat with the opposing general.

sponda, ae, *f.* bed, couch.

spondeō, spopondī, spōnsum, [2] *v.* give a pledge *or* undertaking; guarantee; act as surety for.

spondēus, ī, *m.* spondee (metrical foot of 2 long syllables).

spōnsa, ae, *f.* betrothed, fiancée.

spōnsālia, ōrum, *nt. pl.* betrothal.

spōnsiō, ōnis, *f.* solemn promise; wager at law.

spōnsor, ōris, *m.* one who guarantees the good faith of another; surety.

spōnsus, ī, *m.* affianced husband.

sponte, *ad.* of one's own accord, freely, voluntarily, spontaneously; by oneself, alone.

sporta, ae, *f.* basket, hamper.

sportella, ae, *f.* little basket.

sportula, ae, *f.,* v. **sportella**; food *or* money given by patrons to clients.

sprētor, ōris, *m.* one who despises *or* scorns.

spūma, ae, *f.* foam, froth.

spūmēscō, [3] *v.* become foamy.

spūmeus, a, um, *a.* foamy, frothy.

spūmō, [1] *v.* foam; be covered with foam.

spūmōsus, a, um, *a.* foaming, frothy.

spuō, uī, ūtum, [3] *v.* spit, spit out.

spurcō, [1] *v.* soil, infect; deprave.

spurcus, a, um, *a.* dirty, foul; morally polluted.

spūtō, [1] *v.* spit out.

spūtum, ī, *nt.* spittle.

squāleō, uī, [2] *v.* be covered with a rough *or* scaly layer; be dirty.

squālidus, a, um, *a.* having a rough surface; coated with dirt, filthy.

squālor, ōris, *m.* dirtiness, filthiness, dirty *or* neglectful state as a sign of mourning.

squāma, ae, *f.* scale; metal-plate used in the making of scale-armour.

squāmeus, squāmiger, squāmōsus, a, um, *a.* scaly.

st, *i.* hush! sh!

stabiliō, īvī, ītum, [4] *v.* make firm *or* steady; hold still; fix *or* establish firmly.

stabilis, e, *a.* firm, steady, stable; lasting, immovable, constant.

stabulō, [1] *v.* house (domestic animals, poultry, *etc.*); be housed.

stabulum, ī, *nt.* stall, shed, fold, stable; bee-hive; stabling.

stadium, iī, *nt.* running-track.

stāgnō, [1] *v.* form *or* lie in pools; be under water.

stāgnum, ī, *nt.* pool, lagoon; water.

stāmen, inis, *nt.* warp (in the loom); thread (on the distaff, to spin); thread of life spun by the Fates.

stāmineus, a, um, *a.* of *or* consisting of threads.

statārius, a, um, *a.* stationary.

statim, *ad.* at once, immediately, instantly.

statiō, ōnis, *f.* standing (still); halting-place; armed post;

guard-duty; guard; station, place; anchorage.

statīvus, a, um, *a.* stationary, permanent.

stator, ōris, *m.* one who establishes *or* upholds (cult-title of Jupiter).

statua, ae, *f.* statue.

statūmen, inis, *nt.* support.

statuō, uī, ūtum, [3] *v.* place, put up; set up, appoint; determine, resolve (to); decide; judge.

statūra, ae, *f.* the height of the body in an upright position, stature.

status, a, um, *a.* fixed, appointed; regular.

status, ūs, *m.* standing, position; posture; condition, circumstance, state; rank.

stēlla, ae, *f.* star.

stēllāns, antis, *a.* starry; having the appearance of stars.

stellātus, a, um, *a.* furnished with star-like points of light.

stel(l)iō, ōnis, *m.* lizard, gecko.

stercus, oris, *nt.* dung, excrement, muck.

sterilis, e, *a.* barren, sterile; fruitless; unprofitable, futile.

sternāx, ācis, *a.* liable to throw its rider (of a horse).

sternō, strāvī, strātum, [3] *v.* spread, strew; extend; level, knock down; cause to subside; lay low, defeat utterly.

sternuō, uī, [3] *v.* sneeze.

stertō, uī, [3] *v.* snore.

stillicidium, iī, *nt.* fall (of a liquid) in successive drops.

stillō, [1] *v.* fall in drops; drip; cause to drip, pour in drops.

stilus, ī, *m.* spike, stem; stylus, pen.

stimulō, [1] *v.* urge forward with a goad, torment, 'sting'; incite, rouse to frenzy.

stimulus, ī, *m.* goad; spur; pointed stake; incitement.

stinguō, [3] *v.* extinguish, put out; annihilate.

stīpātor, ōris, *m.* one of the train surrounding a king; bodyguard, close attendant.

stīpendiārius, a, um, *a.* mercenary; paying tribute in the form of cash.

stīpendium, (i)ī, *nt.* tax, contribution; pay; (a year of) military service; campaign; **stīpendia merērī**, to complete (so many years of) military service.

stīpes, itis, *m.* trunk (of a tree); stake.

stīpō, [1] *v.* crowd, press together, compress, surround closely.

stips, stipis, *f.* small offering.

stipula, ae, *f.* stalk; stubble; straw; reed played on as a pipe.

stīria, ae, *f.* icicle.

stirps, pis, *f.* stock, stem, stalk; root; plant, shrub; family, ancestral race; offspring, posterity.

stīva, ae, *f.* shaft of a plough-handle.

stō, stetī, statum, [1] *v.* stand; stand still; be fixed; be erect; be *or* become upright, endure, persist; remain; adhere (to); be one's fault; **per tē stetit quōminus vincerem,** it was due to you that I did not conquer.

Stōicus, a, um, *a.* Stoic.

stola, ae, *f.* long upper garment.

stolidus, a, um, *a.* dull, stupid, brutish.

stomachor, ātus, [1] *v. dep.* be angry, boil with rage.

stomachōsus, a, um, *a.* irritable, short-tempered.

stomachus, ī, *m.* gullet; stomach; annoyance; ill-temper.

storea, storia, ae, *f.* matting of rushes.

strāgēs, is, *f.* overthrow; massacre, slaughter, cutting down; havoc; confused heap; destruction, devastation.

strāmen, inis, *nt.* straw for bedding, *etc.*, litter.

strāmentum, ī, *nt.* straw, litter; coverings.

strāmineus, a, um, *a.* made of straw.

strangulō, [1] *v.* choke; suffocate, smother.

strātum, ī, *nt.* coverlet; bed, couch; horse-blanket.

strēnuitās, ātis, *f.* strenuous behaviour, activity.

strēnuus, a, um, *a.* active, vigorous, energetic.

strepitō, [1] *v.* make a loud *or* harsh noise.

strepitus, ūs, *m.* noise, din; crashing, rustling, clattering sound (of a musical instrument); noisy talk, uproar.

strepō, uī, itum, [3] *v.* make a loud noise; shout confusedly; resound.

strictūra, ae, *f.* hardened mass of iron.

strīdeō, dī, [2] **strīdō, dī,** [3] *v.* creak, hiss, whistle, buzz, rattle; produce a high-pitched utterance; be filled with a shrill sound.

strīdor, ōris, *m.* hissing, buzzing, rattling, whistling; high-pitched sound.

strīdulus, a, um, *a.* making a high-pitched *or* shrill sound.

strigilis, is, *f.* instrument with a curved and channelled blade for scraping oil, *etc.* from the skin.

strigōsus, a, um, *a.* lean, scraggy.

stringō, īnxī, ictum, [3] *v.* draw *or* tie tight; skin, brush; graze; pluck, strip off; prune; unsheathe.

strix, strigis, *f.* owl.

strophium, iī, *nt.* twisted breast-band; head-band.

strūctūra, ae, *f.* building, construction; structure; masonry, concrete.

struēs, is, *f.* heap, pile; row of sacrificial cakes.

struō, xī, ctum, [3] *v.* build, construct; arrange; devise, contrive.

studeō, uī, [2] *v. with dat.* devote oneself to, concern oneself (with); strive after; concentrate on; support; study.

studiōsus, a, um, *a.* eager, zealous, studious, scholarly; affectionate, fond; devoted.

studium, (i)ī, *nt.* zeal, eagerness (for), study, application; devotion, goodwill, support.

stultitia, ae, *f.* stupidity, folly, fatuity.

stultus, a, um, *a.* foolish, silly; inept.

stupefaciō, fēcī, factum, [3] *v.* stun with amazement, stupefy; **stupefīō,** [4] be astonished.

stupeō, uī, [2] *v.* be stunned *or* benumbed; be astonished *or* stupefied (at).

stupor, ōris, *m.* numbness, torpor; stupefaction; stupidity.

stuppa, ae, *f.* tow, coarse flax.

stuppeus, a, um, *a.* of tow.

stuprō, [1] *v.* have illicit sexual intercourse with.

stuprum, ī, *nt.* dishonour, shame; illicit sexual intercourse.

stylus, ī, v. **stilus.**

suādeō, sī, sum, [2] *v.* advise, recommend, urge; advocate.

suāsor, ōris, *m.* adviser, counsellor.

suāvidicus, a, um, *a.* speaking pleasantly.

suāviloquēns, entis, *a.* speaking agreeably.

s(u)āviolum, ī, *nt.* tender kiss.

suāvior, ātus sum, [1] *v. dep.* kiss.

suāvis, e, *a.* sweet, pleasant, agreeable, delightful.

s(u)āvium, iī, *nt.* kiss; sweetheart.

sub, *pr. (with abl.)* under, below, beneath; under the power of; *(with acc.)* near to; about; a little before; to a position under; up to; directly after.

subc . . . , v. **succ . . .**

subdō, didī, ditum, [3] *v.* place *or* insert below; place under; subject, expose (to); substitute fraudulently; supply.

subdolus, a, um, *a.* sly, deceitful, treacherous.

subdūcō, xī, ctum, [3] *v.* draw from under *or* from below; withdraw (from); extricate; steal (away); reckon up, calculate.

subductiō, ōnis, *f.* hauling up of a ship onto the beach.

subedō ēdī, [3] *v.* eat away below.

subeō, iī & īvī, itum, [4] *v.* go, move *or* pass underneath; come up to, approach; undergo, endure; come next; succeed to; steal in on, come over; suggest itself.

subf . . . , v. **suff . . .**

subg . . . , v. **sugg . . .**

sūbiciō, iēcī, iectum, [3] v. throw up; place below; place under; lay before; put under the control of; expose; place next; interpose; suborn; introduce.

subiectō, [1] v. throw up from below; apply below.

subiectus, a, um, a. with dat. situated under; open or exposed (to); subject (to).

subigō, ēgī, āctum, [3] v. conquer, subjugate; plough; force; drive under.

subinde, ad. immediately after, thereupon; constantly, repeatedly.

subitārius, a, um, a. got together to meet an emergency, hastily enrolled.

subitō, ad. suddenly, unexpectedly; at short notice; in no time at all.

subitus, a, um, a. sudden, unexpected; **subitum, ī**, nt. emergency, crisis.

subiungō, xī, ctum, [3] v. yoke; subjoin; add; bring under the control of.

sublābor, lāpsus sum, [3] v. dep. collapse; sink or ebb away; creep up.

sublegō, lēgī, lectum, [3] v. pick up from the ground, steal away.

sublevō, [1] v. lift, raise, support; lighten, alleviate; assist, encourage.

sublica, ae, f. wooden stake or pile.

sublīgō, [1] v. fasten (to).

sublīmis, e, a. high, lofty, exalted; imposingly tall; sublime; eminent.

sublūceō, [2] v. shine faintly, glimmer.

subluō, lūtum, [3] v. wash; flow at the foot of.

sublūstris, e, a. faintly lit, dim.

submergō, sī, sum, [3] v. cause to sink, submerge.

subministrō, [1] v. supply, furnish, afford.

submissus, a, um, a. stooping; quiet.

submittō, īsī, issum, [3] v. raise, rear; send up; send (reinforcements); drop; make subject (to).

submoveō, ōvī, ōtum, [3] v. remove; drive off, dislodge; expel; ward off; keep at a distance.

subnectō, nexuī, xum, [3] v. bind under, add, subjoin, fasten up.

subnīxus, a, um, a. with abl. relying on; elated by.

subnūbilus, a, um, a. somewhat cloudy, overcast.

subolēs, is, f. shoot, sucker; race; offspring; progeny.

subolēscō, [3] v. grow up.

suborior, ortus sum, [4] v. dep. come into being, be provided.

subortus, ūs, m. the springing up (of a fresh supply).

subp . . . , v. **supp . . .**

subrēmigō, [1] v. make rowing movements underneath.

subrēpō, psī, ptum, [3] *v.* creep, creep (up to); steal on, insinuate itself.

subrīdeō, sī, [2] *v.* smile.

subripiō, ripuī, reptum, [3] *v.* steal, kidnap, remove by stealth.

subrubeō, [2] *v.* be tinged with red *or* purple.

subruō, uī, utum, [3] *v.* weaken at the base, undermine.

subscrībō, psī, ptum, [3] *v.* write underneath; append; inscribe at the foot; give support (to).

subsecō, cuī, ctum, [1] *v.* cut away below; pare (the nails).

subsellium, iī, *nt.* bench, low seat; court, courts.

subsequor, cūtus, [3] *v. dep.* follow close behind, follow, succeed; follow the lead of.

subsidiārius, a, um, *a.* acting as a support to the front line; **subsidiāriī, ōrum,** *m. pl.* the reserves.

subsidium, iī, *nt.* body of troops in reserve; aid; support; safeguard; means of assistance.

subsīdō, sēdī, sessum, [3] *v.* squat down; settle down; subside; lie in wait (for); fall to the ground.

subsistō, stitī, [3] *v.* stop short; stand firm; stop short, cease from; remain, tarry, settle down.

substernō, strāvī, strātum, [3] *v.* spread out (as an underlay).

substringō, nxī, ctum, [3] *v.* draw in close, gather up; draw tight; **aurem substringere,** to strain your ears.

substrūctiō, ōnis, *f.* (building of) a foundation, substructure.

substruō, xī, ctum, [3] *v.* build up from the base; support by means of substructures.

subsum, *v. ir.* be underneath; be a basis for discussion; be close at hand as a reserve *or* refuge.

subsūtus, a, um, *a.* stitched at the bottom.

subtē(g)men, inis, *nt.* the weft, the transverse threads woven in between the warp threads; threads of the Fates.

subter, *ad. & pr. with acc.* below, beneath, under, underneath; to underneath.

subterfugiō, fūgī, [3] *v.* evade, avoid by a stratagem.

subterlābor, [3] *v. dep.* glide *or* flow beneath, slip away.

subtexō, xuī, xtum, [3] *v.* weave beneath; veil; subjoin, attach as a sequel (to).

subtīlis, e, *a.* fine-spun; fine; slender, delicate, exact; minutely thorough.

subtrahō, xī, ctum, [3] *v.* draw from under, undermine; withdraw (from); detach from the main body; rescue from the threat (of); remove.

subūcula, ae, *f.* under-tunic worn by both sexes.

subulcus, ī, *m.* swineherd.

Subūra, ae, *f.* valley between the Esquiline *and* Viminal hills of Rome (a centre of night life).

suburbānī, ōrum, *m. pl.* people dwelling near the city.

suburbānus, a, um, *a.* situated close to the city; growing or cultivated near the city.

suburgeō, [2] *v.* drive up close.

subvectiō, ōnis, *f.* transporting (of supplies) to a centre.

subvectō, [1] *v.* convey (often *or* laboriously) upwards.

subvehō, vēxī, vectum, [3] *v.* convey upwards; convey up; (*pass.*) sail upstream.

subveniō, vēnī, ventum, [4] *v. with dat.* come to the help (of); relieve.

subvertō, tī, sum, [3] *v.* overturn, cause to topple; overthrow, destroy, subvert.

subvexus, a, um, *a.* sloping up.

subvolō, [1] *v.* fly upwards.

subvolvō, [3] *v.* roll uphill.

succēdō, cessī, cessum, [3] *v.* go below *or* under; come to the foot (of), come up (to); move on upwards; move up into the position (of); take the place (of); succeed (to).

succendō, dī, sum, [3] *v.* set alight, kindle from below; inflame.

succēnseō, suī, sum, [2] *v.* be angry.

successor, ōris, *m.* successor.

successus, ūs, *m.* the action of coming up close; success, good result.

succidō, cidī, [3] *v.* collapse through the lower parts giving way.

succīdō, cīdī, cīsum, [3] *v.* cut from below, cut down.

succiduus, a, um, *a.* giving way under one.

succingō, nxī, nctum, [3] *v.* gather up with a belt *or* girdle; prepare for action; surround.

succlāmātiō, ōnis, *f.* answering shout.

succlāmō, [1] *v.* shout in response (to).

succrēscō, [3] *v.* grow up from below; grow up as a replacement *or* successor.

succumbō, cubuī, cubitum, [3] *v.* sink to the ground; collapse; lie down (under); lower itself; give in (to).

succurrō, currī, cursum, [3] *v. with dat.* run *or* move quickly to the rescue (of); come into one's mind.

succutiō, cussī, cussum, [3] *v.* shake from below.

sūcus, ī, *m.* juice, sap; vital fluid in trees and plants.

sūdārium, iī, *nt.* handkerchief, napkin.

sudis, is, *f.* stake, pointed stick; spike.

sūdō, [1] *v.* sweat, perspire; become damp with surface moisture.

sūdor, ōris, *m.* sweat, perspiration.

sūdus, a, um, *a.* clear and bright.

suēscō, suēvī, suētum, [3] *v.* become accustomed (to).

suētus, a, um, *a.* wont, accustomed; usual, familiar.

sufferō, sufferre, sustulī, sublātum, *v.* submit to, endure, to suffer.

sufficiō, fēcī, fectum, [3] *v.* supply, provide; suffuse, imbue, steep; appoint in place of another; have sufficient strength (to), stand up (to); have sufficient wealth *or* resources for; be sufficient for; be available for.

suffigō, xī, xum, [3] *v.* fasten beneath as a support; crucify.

suffīmen, inis, suffīmentum, ī, *nt.* a substance used to fumigate.

suffiō, īvī & iī, ītum, [4] *v.* fumigate.

sufflō, [1] *v.* puff up.

suffodiō, fōdī, fossum, [3] *v.* undermine, dig under; pierce *or* prod below.

suffrāgātiō, ōnis, *f.* public expression of support (for).

suffrāgium, iī, *nt.* voting; vote; right of voting; recommendation.

suffrāgor, ātus, [1] *v. dep.* express public support (for), canvass *or* vote for; lend support (to).

suffugium, iī, *nt.* shelter.

suffulciō, sī, tum, [4] *v.* underprop, keep from falling.

suffundō, fūdī, fūsum, [3] *v.* pour in *or* on; cause to well up to the surface; cover *or* fill with a liquid that wells up from below.

suggerō, gessī, gestum, [3] *v.* heap up; supply, feed; subjoin.

sūg(g)illō, [1] *v.* insult, humiliate.

suggestus, ūs, *m.* raised surface; platform, dais.

sūgō, xī, ctum, [3] *v.* suck; *fig.* take in.

suī, sibi, sē (sēsē), v. **sē**.

suillus, a, um, *a.* of pigs.

sulcō, [1] *v.* furrow, plough; cleave.

sulcus, ī, *m.* furrow; rut; trail of a meteor; track, wake.

sulfur, uris, *nt.* brimstone, sulphur.

sulp(h)ur, v. **sulfur**.

sulp(h)ureus, a, um, *a.* sulphurous.

sum, esse, fuī, *v.* be, exist; live; happen; remain; be possible *or* allowable.

summa, ae, *f.* total number *or* amount; sum; sum-total; a whole; the whole of a thing; the overall matter in question; an activity's general purpose.

summātim, *ad.* summarily, briefly.

summē, *ad.* in the highest degree, intensely.

summus, a, um, *a.* highest, greatest, very great; chief, principal; the farthest, utmost, last, extreme; very deep; ~ **mōns**, the top of the mountain.

sūmō, sūmpsī, sūmptum, [3] *v.* take, take up; take hold of; receive; spend; have recourse to; adopt as suitable; adopt; embrace; assume; take on.

sūmptuārius, a, um, *a.* concerned with the spending of money.

sūmptuōsus, a, um, *a.* expensive, costly, sumptuous.

sūmptus, ūs, *m.* expense, lavish expenditure; expenses; charge.

suō, suī, sūtum, [3] *v.* sew, stitch together.

suovetaurīlia, ium, *nt. pl.* purificatory sacrifice consisting of a boar, a ram, and a bull.

supellex, lectilis, *f.* furniture, furnishings; outfit, paraphernalia.

super, *ad. & pr. with acc.* above, on, over; beyond; on top of; besides; (*with abl.*) about; concerning; in addition to.

supera, ōrum, *nt. pl.* heaven.

superābilis, e, *a.* that may be got over *or* surmounted; that may be conquered.

superaddō, idī, itum, [3] *v.* add *or* affix on the surface.

superātor, ōris, *m.* conqueror.

superbia, ae, *f.* pride, lofty self-esteem, disdain.

superbiō, [4] *v. with abl.* show pride *or* disdain on account (of), plume oneself (on).

superbus, a, um, *a.* haughty, proud, arrogant; disdainful; glorying (in); that is a source of pride; grand, proud, sumptuous.

supercilium, iī, *nt.* eyebrow; gravity, haughtiness, stern looks, pride; overhanging edge, brow.

superēmineō, [2] *v.* overtop, stand out above the level of.

superfluō, [3] *v.* overflow; superabound; be superabundantly supplied with.

superfundō, fūdī, fūsum, [3] *v.* pour over.

supergredior, gressus, [3] *v. dep.* pass over *or* beyond; exceed, surpass.

superī, ōrum, *m. pl.* gods above.

superimmineō, [2] *v.* stand above in a threatening position.

superimpōnō, positum, [3] *v.* place on top *or* over.

superincidēns, entis, *a.* falling on top.

superincubāns, antis, *a.* lying on top.

superincumbō, cubuī, [3] *v.* lean over.

superiniciō, iēcī, iectum, [3] *v.* throw *or* scatter on over the surface.

superīnsternō, strāvī, [3] *v.* lay on over the surface.

superior, ius, *a.* higher, upper, superior, better; past, previous; elder, stronger; victorious.

superiaciō, iēcī, iectum, [3] *v.* throw *or* scatter on top *or* over the surface; shoot over the top of.

supernē, *ad.* at *or* to a higher level, above; in the upper part; on top.

supernus, a, um, *a.* situated above.

superō, [1] *v.* climb over; overtop; rise to a higher level; get beyond; surpass; be superior; defeat, surmount; survive; be present in excess of one's needs; abound; remain; remain alive; be situated beyond; vanquish.

superoccupō, [1] *v.* take by surprise from above.

superpendēns, entis, *a.* overhanging.

superpōnō, posuī, positum, [3] *v.* place over *or* on top; put in charge.

superscandō, [3] *v.* climb over.

supersedeō, sēdī, sessum, [2] *v.* with *abl.* refrain (from), desist (from).

supersternō, strāvī, strātum, [3] *v.* spread *or* lay on top.

superstes, itis, *a.* outliving, surviving; standing over.

superstitiō, ōnis, *f.* superstition; irrational religious awe.

superstitiōsus, a, um, *a.* superstitious, full of unreasoning religious awe.

superstō, [1] *v.* stand over *or* on top (of).

supersum, esse, fuī, *v.* have the strength (for); be superfluous (to); be left over; remain alive, survive; remain to be performed.

superus, a, um, *a.* upper; earthly; heavenly, celestial.; **super-um mare,** the Adriatic Sea; see also **superior, suprēmus.**

supervacāneus, a, um, *a.* redundant; unnecessary.

supervacuus, a, um, *a.* superfluous, redundant; unnecessary.

supervādō, [3] *v.* surmount.

supervehor, vectus sum, [3] *v.* ride, sail, *etc.*, over *or* past.

superveniō, vēnī, ventum, [4] *v.* arrive on the scene; (*with dat.*) come up (with a person, catching him in a given activity *or* situation).

supervolitō, [1] *v.* fly to and fro over.

supervolō, [1] *v.* fly over.

supīnō, [1] *v.* lay on the back; turn up; tilt back.

supīnus, a, um, *a.* lying face upwards, flat on one's back; turned palm upwards; directed *or* flowing backwards; flat, lowlying; languid, passive.

suppeditō, [1] *v.* be available when required, supply the needs (of); make available as required; supply (with).

suppetō, īvī & iī, ītum, [3] *v.* turn up as a support, give backing (to); be available for one's needs; suggest itself.

supplēmentum, ī, *nt.* supplement; reinforcement.

suppleō, ēvī, ētum, [2] *v.* complete, fill up; make (a whole).

supplex, icis, *a.* suppliant, making humble entreaty; expressing *or* involving supplication.

supplicātiō, ōnis, *f.* offering of propitiation to a deity.

suppliciter, *ad.* suppliantly, in an attitude of humble entreaty.

supplicium, iī, *nt.* act performed to propitiate a deity; punishment; torment; penalty, punishment.

supplicō, [1] *v. with dat.* make humble petition to; make propitiary offerings to, do worship.

suppōnō, posuī, positum, [3] *v.* place under; substitute; introduce fraudulently into a situation.

supportō, [1] *v.* transport (supplies, *etc.*) to a centre.

supprimō, pressī, pressum, [3] *v.* press down *or* under; suppress; keep back, contain; stop, check.

suprā, *pr. with acc.* above, over, on the upper side of; beyond; earlier than; more than.

suprāscandō, [3] *v.* climb on top of.

suprēma, ōrum, *nt. pl.* funeral rites *or* offerings.

suprēmus, a, um, *a.* highest; topmost; last, latest, dying; greatest.

sūra, ae, *f.* calf of the leg.

surculus, ī, *m.* twig; cutting, graft.

surditās, ātis, *f.* deafness.

surdus, a, um, *a.* deaf; unresponsive to what is said; falling on deaf ears; muffled, muted.

surgō, surrēxī, surrēctum, [3] *v.* rise, get up; rouse oneself to action; stand high; grow tall.

surr . . . , v. subr . . .

surrigō, v. surgō.

sūrsum, *ad.* upwards; on high, above.

sūs, suis, *m. or f.* pig, sow.

suscipiō, cēpī, ceptum, [3] *v.* take (up), catch from below; support; receive; take under one's protection; adopt; undertake, perform; venture upon; accept; acknowledge (a newborn child); get *or* have a child.

suscitō, [1] *v.* dislodge, cause to rise; restore to health; venture upon; enter on the performance of; face, accept; rouse.

suspectus, ūs, *m.* looking up; high regard.

suspendium, iī, *nt.* the act of hanging oneself.

suspendō, dī, sum, [3] *v.* hang (up); keep poised; keep in suspense.

suspēnsus, a, um, *a.* in a state of anxious uncertainty *or* suspense; light.

suspicāx, ācis, *a.* mistrustful.

suspiciō, spexī, ctum, [3] *v.* look upwards (to); look up at; esteem, admire; be suspicious of.

suspiciō, ōnis, *f.* suspicion, mistrustful feeling; trace.

suspicor, ātus, [1] *v. dep.* suspect; have an inkling of; infer.

suspīrātus, ūs, *m.* sigh; deep breath.

suspīritus, ūs, *m.* sigh.

suspīrium, iī, *nt.* sigh; heart-throb.

suspīrō, [1] *v.* sigh; utter with a sigh.

sustentō, [1] *v.* support, hold up; uphold, bear up against; delay.

sustineō, tinuī, tentum, [2] *v.* hold up, support, sustain; stand up to, withstand; shoulder; have the necessary endurance (to); submit (to); endure; hold back.

sustollō, [3] *v.* raise on high.

susurrō, [1] *v.* whisper; rustle.

susurrus, ī, *m.* whisper, whispered report; soft rustling sound.

susurrus, a, um, *a.* whispering.

sūtilis, e, *a.* made by sewing, consisting of things stitched together.

sūtor, ōris, *m.* shoemaker; cobbler.

sūtūra, ae, *f.* seam, stitch, piece of sewing.

suus, a, um, *pn.* his own, her own, its own, their own; especially dear to him; belonging to him at birth; normal to him; due *or* allotted to him; convenient for him.

syllaba, ae, *f.* syllable.

symphōnia, ae, *f.* harmony, group of singers *or* musicians.

T

tabella, ae, *f.* tablet; voting-tablet; board for games; placard; board; (*pl.*) wax-coated wooden tablets, threaded together to form a notebook.

tabellārius, iī, *m.* letter-carrier, courier.

tābeō, [2] *v.* rot away, decay.

taberna, ae, *f.* hut, booth, inn; tavern; shop *or* stall.

tabernāculum, ī, *nt.* tent.

tābēs, is, *f.* wasting away; decay; putrefaction; fluid resulting from corruption *or* decay.

tābēscō, buī, [3] *v.* waste *or* dwindle away; melt away; decompose.

tābidus, a, um, *a.* wasting away, emaciated, putrefying, rotten; accompanied by wasting.

tābificus, a, um, *a.* causing decay *or* wasting.

tābitūdō, inis, *f.* wasting away.

tabula, ae, *f.* board, plank; votive-tablet; writing-tablet; letter, will; panel; picture; game board; tablet of stone *or* metal set up as a permanent record; (*pl.*) account-books; document; will.

tabulārium, iī, *nt.* collection of (inscribed) tablets; record-office, registry.

tabulātiō, ōnis, *f.* structure of boards, boarding.

tabulātum, ī, *nt.* floor, storey, tier formed by the horizontal branches of a tree.

tābum, ī, *nt.* viscous fluid consisting of putrid matter.

taceō, cuī, citum, [2] *v.* be silent; say nothing about.

taciturnitās, ātis, *f.* maintaining silence.

taciturnus, a, um, *a.* saying nothing, making no noise.

tacitus, a, um, *a.* silent; quiet; secret, hidden; unmentioned; tacit.

tāctilis, e, *a.* able to be touched.

tāctus, ūs, *m.* touch, sense of touch.

taeda, ae, *f.* pine-wood, pine-torch; wedding; pine-tree.

taedet, duit, taesum est, [2] *v. impers. with gen. or inf. and acc. of person affected* be tired *or* sick (of).

taedifer, a, um, *a.* torch-bearing.

taedium, iī, *nt.* weariness, ennui; an object of weariness.

taenia, ae, *f.* ribbon.

taeter, tra, trum, foul, monstrous, vile, horrible.

tālāria, ium, *nt. pl.* skirts; winged sandals.

tālāris, e, *a.* reaching down to the ankles.

tālea, ae, *f.* long, thin piece of wood, metal, etc.

talentum, ī, *nt.* talent of silver (currency).

tālis, e, *a.* such, of such a kind; such (a).

talpa, ae, *f.* or *m.* (animal) mole.

tālus, ī, *m.* ankle, ankle-bone; knuckle-bone of a sheep, (*pl.*) the game played with such bones.

tam, *ad.* so; so much (as).

tamen, *c.* nevertheless, all the same; yet.

tamen etsī, *c.* even though.

tametsī, *c.* even though.

tamquam, *ad.* just as; just as if.

tandem, *ad.* at length, at last, after some time; really, I ask you, after all.

tangō, tetigī, tāctum, [3] *v.* touch; put one's hand on; reach; be next to, border on; arrive (at); affect, move; touch on, make a mention of.

tanquam, v. **tamquam.**

tantillus, a, um, *a.* so small; so small a quantity.

tantīsper, *ad.* for so long (as); for the present.

tantopere, *ad.* so very, to such a great degree.

tantulus, a, um, *a.* so small, such a little.

tantum, *ad.* so much, to such a degree, so; only, just, merely; ~ **nōn**, all but, almost.

tantummodo, *ad.* only, merely.

tantundem, tantīdem, *nt.* the same quantity, just as much.

tantus, a, um, *a.* so great.

tantusdem, tantadem, tantundem, *a.* just as great; *nt.* just as much.

tapēs, ētis, *m.*, **tapēte, is, tapētum, ī**, *nt.* woollen cloth *or* rug used as a covering, hanging, *etc.*

tardēscō, [3] *v.* become slow.

tardipēs, edis, *a.* slow-footed, lame.

tarditās, ātis, *f.* slowness of movement, action, *etc.*

tardō, [1] *v.* delay, check.

tardus, a, um, *a.* slow; tardy, late; dull, stupid.

Tartareus, a, um, *a.* of *or* belonging to the underworld; Tartarean.

Tartarus, ī, *m.*, **Tartara, ōrum**, *nt. pl.* the infernal regions, the underworld.

taurea, ae, *f.* leather whip.

taureus, a, um, *a.* derived from a bull.

tauriformis, e, *a.* having the form of a bull.

taurīnus, a, um, *a.* of *or* derived from a bull; made of ox-hide.

taurus, ī, *m.* bull; the constellation Taurus.

taxus, ī, *f.* yew-tree.

tēctum, ī, *nt.* roof; house, dwelling; (rough *or* improvised) shelter.

tegimen, inis, *nt.* covering, cover.

tegō, xī, ctum, [3] *v.* cover; hide, conceal; roof over; shield, protect.

tēgula, ae, *f.* roof-tile.

tēla, ae, *f.* cloth in the process of being woven on a loom; the upright threads in a loom; a loom.

tellūs, ūris, *f.* earth; ground.

tēlum, ī, *nt.* missile, javelin; sword; (any offensive) weapon; sunbeam, thunderbolt.

temerārius, a, um, *a.* accidental; rash, foolhardy, thoughtless, reckless, hasty.

temere, *ad.* blindly, heedlessly; without due thought *or* care; without reason; at random, casually; readily, easily.

temeritās, ātis, *f.* recklessness, thoughtlessness, impetuosity.

temerō, [1] *v.* violate; defile, pollute; violate sexually.

tēmētum, ī, *nt.* strong wine; intoxicating liquor.

temnō, [3] *v.* scorn, despise.

tēmō, ōnis, *m.* beam *or* pole of a cart, chariot, *etc.*; Charles's Wain.

temperāns, antis, *a.* restrained, self-controlled.

temperantia, ae, *f.* moderation, restraint, self-control.

temperātus, a, um, *a.* temperate, moderate.

temperī, *ad.* at the right time, seasonably.

temperiēs, ēī, *f.* mixture of substances, qualities, *etc.* in due proportion; climate, temperateness; (moderate) temperature.

temperō, [1] *v.* exercise restraint, exercise moderation (in respect of); be moderate in one's conduct (towards); restrain oneself, refrain (from); temper; cause to moderate violence, *etc.*; modify; control physically; control, regulate.

tempestās, ātis, *f.* portion of time, season; weather; storm; violent disturbance.

tempestīvus, a, um, *a.* seasonable; opportune, physically in one's prime, ripe (for marriage); timely.

templum, ī, *nt.* temple, shrine; zone, space, region; plank.

temporī, *ad.* at the right time.

temp . . . , tempt . . . , v. tent . . .

tempus, oris, *nt.* time, season; a sufficiency of time (for a particular purpose); opportunity; season (of the year); condition; (*pl.*) times; temples of the head.

tēmulentus, a, um, *a.* drunken.

tenācitās, ātis, *f.* the quality of holding on to a thing.

tenāx, ācis, *a.* holding fast, tenacious; persistent, steadfast; stubborn, obstinate.

tendō, tetendī, tentum & tēnsum, [3] *v.* stretch out, extend; pitch tents; encamp; string *or* draw (a bow, *etc.*); distend; direct one's course, proceed; reach; exert oneself; aim (at); aim (to do).

tenebrae, ārum, *f. pl.* darkness, obscurity; night; dark corner; ignorance; concealment; gloomy state of affairs.

tenebricōsus, a, um, *a.* dark.

tenellulus, a, um, *a.* tender, delicate.

tenellus, a, um, *a.* tender.

teneō, tenuī, tentum, [2] *v.* hold, keep, possess; occupy; retain; hold a position; include; reach in journeying; maintain; detain, hold up; keep in check; bind.

tener, era, erum, *a.* soft, delicate, tender; immature, young; soft, effeminate.

tenor, ōris, *m.* a sustained and even course of movement; course, tenor.

tēnsa, ae, *f.* wagon on which the images of the gods were carried to public spectacles.

tentābundus, a, um, *a.* testing every stop *or* move.

tentāmen, inis, *nt.* attempt, effort.

tentāmentum, ī, *nt.* trial, attempt, experiment.

tentō, [1] *v.* handle; feel; attempt, try; prove; test; try out; attack; brave; make an attempt on.

tentōrium, iī, *nt.* tent.

tenuis, e, *a.* thin, slender; slight, faint; fine; weak; trivial.

tenuō, [1] *v.* make thin; reduce, lessen; wear down.

tenus, *pr. with abl.* reaching to, as far as, up to.

tepefaciō, fēcī, factum, [3] *v.* make warm.

tepeō, [2] *v.* be (luke)warm; feel the warmth of love, glow; be lukewarm in one's feelings.

tepēscō, puī, [3] *v.* become warm.

tepidārium, iī, *nt.* 'warm' room in Roman baths.

tepidus, a, um, *a.* lukewarm, tepid; mild, warm.

tepor, ōris, *m.* warmth, mild heat.

ter, *ad.* three times.

terebinthus, ī, *f.* terebinth tree *or* its wood.

terebrō, [1] *v.* bore through, drill a hole in.

teres, etis, *a.* smooth and rounded.

tergeminus, a, um, *a.* threefold, triple.

tergeō, tergō, sī, sum, [2] *or* [3] *v.* rub clean, polish; press.

tergiversor, ātus sum, [1] *v. dep.* turn one's back on a task *or* challenge; hang back.

tergum, ī, tergus, oris, *nt.* back; hide, skin; surface; **terga dare**

or **terga vertere**, to turn tail, flee.

Termīnālia, ium, *nt. pl.* festival of the god of boundaries (Terminus) on 23 Feb.

terminātiō, ōnis, *f.* marking the boundaries of a territory.

terminō, [1] *v.* mark the boundaries of, form the boundaries of; restrict; conclude.

terminus, ī, *m.* boundary, limit; end; post, stone, *etc.* marking the boundary of a property.

ternī, ae, a, *a.* three each; three.

terō, trīvī, trītum, [3] *v.* rub, bruise, grind; polish, rub smooth; wear out *or* away; handle constantly; use up (time).

terra, ae, *f.* earth; land, ground, soil; country; region.

terrēnus, a, um, *a.* belonging to the ground, earthy, earthly; mortal.

terreō, uī, itum, [2] *v.* terrorize, overawe, terrify; deter.

terrestris, e, *a.* by *or* on land, terrestrial.

terreus, a, um, *m.* one born of the earth.

terribilis, e, *a.* frightening, terrible.

terrificō, [1] *v.* terrify.

terrificus, a, um, *a.* terrifying, awe-inspiring.

terrigena, ae, *m.* one born of the earth.

terriloquus, a, um, *a.* uttering frightening words.

territō, [1] *v.* frighten, terrify; try to scare.

terror, ōris, *m.* dread, terror.

tersus, a, um, *a.* neat, spruce.

tertium, *ad.* for a third time.

tertius, a, um, *a.* third.

tessera, ae, *f.* square tile; die; tablet on which the password was written; fragment of earthenware, shard.

testa, ae, *f.* object made from burnt clay; earthenware jar; fragment of earthenware, shard.

testāmentum, ī, *nt.* will, testament.

testātiō, ōnis, *f.* action of testifying to a fact.

testātus, a, um, *a.* known on good evidence.

testificor, ātus sum, [1] *v. dep.* assert solemnly, testify (to a fact); demonstrate; invoke as a witness.

testimōnium, iī, *nt.* testimony; proof.

testis, is, *m.* or *f.* witness; spectator.

testis, is, *m.* testicle.

testor, ātus sum, [1] *v. dep.* be a witness, testify (to); declare solemnly; invoke as a witness.

testū, *indecl.,* **testum, ī,** *nt.* earthenware pot.

testūdineus, a, um, *a.* made of tortoise shell.

testūdō, inis, *f.* tortoise; tortoise shell; lyre; roof; a covering formed of the shields of soldiers held over their heads; movable wooden screen for siege-engines *or* men engaged in siege operations.

tetrarchēs, ae, *m.* tetrarch (a minor king under Roman protection).

texō, xuī, xtum, [3] *v.* weave; plait (together); construct with elaborate care.

textilis, e, *a.* woven.

textor, ōris, *m.* weaver.

textum, ī, *nt.* woven fabric, cloth; framework; web.

textūra, ae, *f.* weaving, texture.

thalamus, ī, *m.* an inner chamber; bedroom; marriage.

theātrālis, e, *a.* theatrical, of the stage.

theātrum, ī, *nt.* theatre.

thermae, ārum, *f. pl.* hot baths.

thēsaurus, ī, *m.* treasure-chamber, vault; treasure.

thiasus, ī, *nt.* orgiastic Bacchic dance.

tholus, ī, *m.* circular building with a domed roof, rotunda.

thōrāx, ācis, *m.* breastplate, cuirass.

T(h)rāx, ācis, *m.* Thracian; gladiator with sabre and short shield, gladiator.

thronus, ī, *m.* throne.

thūs, thūris, v. **tūs.**

thymbra, ae, *f.* an aromatic plant, perhaps Cretan thyme.

thymum, ī, *nt.* thyme.

thynnus, ī, *m.* tunny-fish.

thyrsus, ī, *m.* Bacchic wand tipped with a fir-cone, tuft of ivy *or* vine leaves.

tiāra, ae, *f.,* **tiārās, ae,** *m.* ornamented felt head-dress.

tībia, ae, *f.* reed-pipe.

tībīcen, inis, *m.* piper, prop.

tībīcina, ae, *f.* female performer on the tibia.

tigillum, ī, *nt.* small plank *or* beam.

tignum, ī, *nt.* timber, beam, board.

tigris, is, & idis, *m.* or *f.* tiger; tigress.

tilia, ae, *f.* lime-tree.

timeō, uī, [2] *v.* fear, be afraid (of); be afraid (to).

timidus, a, um, *a.* fearful, timid.

timor, ōris, *m.* fear; object *or* source of fear.

tīnctilis, e, *a.* obtained by dipping.

tīnctus, ūs, *m.* dyeing; dipping.

tinea, ae, *f.* grub, maggot.

tingō (tinguō), nxī, nctum, [3] *v.* wet, dye, tint, stain, tinge.

tinnītus, ūs, *m.* ringing, clanging, jangling.

tinnulus, a, um, *a.* emitting a ringing *or* jangling sound.

tintinnō *or* **tintinō,** [1] *v.* make a ringing *or* jangling sound.

tīnus, ī, *m.* laurustinus (kind of bay-tree).

tīrō, ōnis, *m.* recruit; beginner, novice.

tīrōcinium, iī, *nt.* inexperience in military service; first campaign; apprenticeship, youthful inexperience.

tītillō, [1] *v.* tickle, titillate; provoke; stimulate sensually.

titubō, [1] *v.* stagger, totter; falter.

titulus, ī, *m.* placard, tablet, label; inscription; title; pretext; distinction, honour.

tōfus, ī, *m.* tufa.

toga, ae, *f.* the formal outer garment of a Roman citizen, toga; peace; ~ **candida,** toga worn by candidates for office; ~ **praetexta,** toga worn by magistrates and children with a purple border; ~ **virīlis,** toga worn by adults (without the purple border).

togātus, a, um, *a.* dressed in *or* wearing a toga; having a civilian occupation.

tolerābilis, e, *a.* bearable, tolerable, patient; able to be withstood.

tolerō, [1] *v.* bear, endure, tolerate; support; provide food for.

tollō, sustulī, sublātum, [3] *v.* lift, raise; acknowledge (a newborn child); remove; eliminate; steal.

tondeō, totondī, tōnsum, [2] *v.* shear, clip; prune back; browse on.

tonitrus, ūs, *m.* thunder.

tonō, uī, itum, [1] *v.* thunder; speak in thunderous tones, utter thunderously; make *or* resound with a noise like thunder.

tōnsa, ae, *f.* oar.

tōnsūra, ae, *f.* shearing, clipping.

tōphus, v. **tōfus.**

tormentum, ī, *nt.* twisted rope; machine for discharging missiles in war, catapult, ballista, *etc.*; torture; torment.

tornus, ī, *m.* turner's lathe.

torōsus, a, um, *a.* muscular, brawny.

torpeō, [2] *v.* be numb *or* lethargic; be struck motionless from fear.

torpēscō, puī, [3] *v.* grow numb, become slothful.

torpidus, a, um, *a.* numbed, paralysed.

torpor, ōris, *m.* numbness, torpor, paralysis.

torquātus, a, um, *a.* wearing a collar *or* necklace.

torqueō, torsī, tortum, [2] *v.* turn, twist; hurl; torture; torment; bend, distort; spin, whirl; wind (round).

torquēs, torquis, is, *m.* or *f.* collar of twisted metal; wreath.

torrēns, entis, *a.* burning hot; rushing; torrential.

torrēns, entis, *m.* torrent, rushing stream.

torreō, torruī, tostum, [2] *v.* parch, roast, scorch, burn; dry up.

torrēscō, [3] *v.* be scorched.

torridus, a, um, *a.* parched, dried up; shrivelled, desiccated.

torris, is, *m.* firebrand.

tortilis, e, *a.* twisted, coiled.

tortor, ōris, *m.* torturer.

tortuōsus, a, um, *a.* winding; tortuous.

tortus, a, um, *a.* crooked, twisted.

torus, ī, *m.* muscle; marriage-bed, marriage; bolster, palliasse.

torvus, a, um, *a.* pitiless, grim; savage.

tot, *a. indecl.* so many.

totidem, *a. indecl.* the same number as, as many.

totiēns, totiēs, *ad.* so often, so many times, as often.

tōtus, a, um, tōtīus, *a.* all, the whole of, entire.

toxicum, ī, *nt.* poison.

trabālis, e, *a.* of *or* used for wooden beams.

trabea, ae, *f.* short purple *or* partly purple garment.

trabēs, is, trabs, trabis, *f.* tree-trunk, beam, timber; ship.

tractābilis, e, *a.* manageable; tractable; easy to deal with.

tractātiō, ōnis, *f.* management; treatment; discussion.

tractim, *ad.* in a long-drawn-out manner.

tractō, [1] *v.* handle, manage; practise; manipulate; perform;

examine, discuss, treat (a subject).

tractus, ūs, *m.* dragging *or* pulling along; drawing out; extent; tract, region; lengthening.

trādō, didī, ditum, [3] *v.* hand *or* pass over; deliver; surrender; hand down, bequeath; entrust; introduce; relate, tell of.

trādūcō, xī, ctum, [3] *v.* lead *or* bring across *or* over; lead along *or* parade; transfer; convert.

tragicus, a, um, *a.* tragic; suitable to tragedy; ~, ī, *m.* tragic poet, tragic actor.

tragoedia, ae, *f.* tragedy.

tragoedus, ī, *m.* tragic actor.

trāgula, ae, *f.* spear fitted with a throwing strap.

trahea, ae, *f.* a drag used as a threshing implement.

trahō, xī, ctum, [3] *v.* draw, drag, haul; drag along; trail; draw *or* stretch out; extend; contract; drink; breathe in; carry off as plunder; attract; protract, delay; spend *or* get through (time).

trāiectus, ūs, *m.* crossing over; way *or* route across.

trāiciō, iēcī, iectum, [3] *v.* throw, cast *or* shoot over *or* across; convey across, transport; transfix, thrust through; transfer; cross over.

trāmes, itis, *m.* footpath; track; bed (of a stream).

trānō, [1] *v.* swim across *or* through; fly across.

tranquillitās, ātis. *f.* tranquillity; calmness, fair weather.

tranquillum, ī, *nt.* calm weather; calm state of affairs.

tranquillus, a, um, *a.* quiet, calm, still, peaceful.

trāns, *pr. with acc.* across, over, beyond, through.

trānsabeō, iī, [4] *v.* go away beyond.

trānsadigō, adēgī, adāctum, [3] *v.* pierce through; thrust through.

trānscendō, dī, sum, [3] *v.* climb *or* step over, transgress, overstep.

trānscrībō, psī, ptum, [3] *v.* copy; transfer.

trānscurrō, currī & cucurrī, cursum, [3] *v.* run across; run *or* hasten through.

trānscursus, ūs, *m.* rapid movement across a space.

trānsdūcō, *etc.,* v. **trādūcō,** *etc.*

trānseō, iī & īvī, itum, [4] *v.* go over *or* across, pass over; pass by; go through; go over (to a side, *etc.*); omit, say nothing of; pass away.

trānsferō, tulī, lātum, *v.* carry *or* bring over; transport; transfer; bring over (to a new course of action).

trānsfīgō, xī, xum, [3] *v.* pierce through; thrust (through).

trānsfodiō, fōdī, fossum, [3] *v.* dig through to the other side of; run through.

trānsformis, e, *a.* that undergoes transformation.

trānsformō, [1] *v.* change in shape, transform.

trānsfuga, ae, *m.* deserter.

trānsfugiō, fūgī, [3] *v.* go over to the enemy, desert.

trānsfugium, iī, *nt.* desertion.

trānsgredior, gressus, [3] *v. dep.* step over; change one's policy; surpass; omit.

trānsgressus, ūs, *m.* crossing to the other side.

trānsigō, ēgī, āctum, [3] *v.* thrust *or* run through, pierce through; come to terms about, settle; conclude, finish, settle.

trānsiliō, īvī & uī, [4] *v.* leap across *or* over; skip; overstep, exceed.

trānsitiō, ōnis, *f.* passing over, passage; desertion; infection, contagion.

trānsitus, ūs, *m.* passage; passage over; transition.

trānslūceō, [2] *v.* shine through *or* across; be transparent.

trānslūcidus, a, um, *a.* transparent.

trānsmigrō, [1] *v.* change one's residence from one place to another.

trānsmissus, ūs, *m.* crossing.

trānsmittō, mīsī, missum, [3] *v.* send *or* pass over; go to the other side of; travel to the other side (of).

trānsmūtō, [1] *v.* change about.

trānsnō, [1] *v.* swim across, sail across; swim to the other side.

trānsportō, [1] *v.* carry across; convey across.

trānstrum, ī, *nt.* cross-beam; rower's seat.

trānsultō, [1] *v.* spring across.

trānsuō, uī, ūtum, [3] *v.* pierce through.

trānsvehō, trāvehō, xī, ctum, [3] *v.* carry across; carry past; trānsvehī, to sail, ride *or* travel to the other side.

trānsverberō, [1] *v.* transfix.

trānsversus, a, um, *a.* lying across, moving across.

trānsvolitō, [1] *v.* fly over *or* through.

trānsvolō, [1] *v.* fly across.

trecēnī, ae, a, *a.* three hundred each; three hundred; lots of three hundred (men).

trecentī, ae, a, *a.* three hundred; (used to denote a large number).

tredecim, *a.* thirteen.

tremebundus, a, um, *a.* trembling, quivering, vibrating.

tremefaciō, fēcī, factum, [3] *v.* cause to tremble.

tremendus, a, um, *a.* terrible, awe-inspiring.

tremēscō, [3] *v.* tremble, quiver, vibrate; tremble at.

tremō, uī, [3] *v.* tremble, quake; tremble (at).

tremor, ōris, *m.* trembling, shuddering; quivering, quaking.

tremulus, a, um, *a.* shaking; moving tremulously; quivering.

trepidanter, *ad.* tremblingly, anxiously.

trepidātiō, ōnis, *f.* trepidation, perturbation.

trepidō, [1] *v.* be in a state of alarm *or* trepidation; scurry, bustle; tremble, quiver, shake; be nervous.

trepidus, a, um, *a.* alarmed, anxious; marked by apprehensiveness *or* alarm; behaving in an excited manner; quivering, trembling.

trēs, tria, *a.* three.

trēsvirī, ōrum, *m. pl.* board of three.

triāriī, ōrum, *m. pl.* the third line of the early Roman army; the reserves.

tribūlis, is, *m.* fellow tribesman.

tribūnal, ālis, *nt.* dais, platform.

tribūnātus, ūs, *m.* the office of tribune.

tribūnicius, tribūnitius, a, um, *a.* belonging to a tribune; ~, **iī,** *m.* ex-tribune.

tribūnus, ī, *m.* tribune; military tribune.

tribuō, uī, ūtum, [3] *v.* grant, bestow, award (to); allocate.

tribus, ūs, *f.* (division of the people) tribe.

tribūtim, *ad.* by tribes.

tribūtum, ī, *nt.* tribute, tax.

tribūtus, a, um, *a.* organized by tribes.

trīciē(n)s, *ad.* thirty times.

trīclīnium, iī, *nt.* dining-room.

tricorpor, oris, *a.* having three bodies.

tricuspis, idis, *a.* having three prongs.

tridēns, entis, *a.* three-pronged; ~, *m.* trident.

tridentifer, tridentiger, ī, *m.* carrying a trident.

trīduum, iī, *nt.* space of three days.

triennia, ium, *nt. pl.* triennial festival.

triennium, iī, *nt.* period of three years.

triēns, entis, *m.* third part; third; third part of an **as.**

trietēricus, a, um, *a.* triennial; ~ **a, ōrum,** *nt. pl.* triennial rites.

trifāriam, *ad.* in three ways, into three parts.

trifaucis, e, *a.* having three throats.

trifidus, a, um, *a.* divided to form three prongs.

triformis, e, *a.* of three forms, triple, threefold.

trīgeminus, a, um, *a.* born as one of triplets; v. **tergeminus.**

trīgintā, *a.* thirty.

trilībris, e, *a.* of three pounds weight.

trilinguis, e, *a.* that has three tongues.

trilīx, īcis, *a.* having a triple thread.

trīmus, a, um, *a.* three years old.

trīnī, ae, a, *a.* three in each case, three at a time; three, triple.

trinōdis, e, *a.* having three knots or bosses.

Triōnēs, um, *m. pl.* the constellations Great and Little Bear.

tripēs, edis, *a.* three-legged.

triplex, icis, *a.* threefold, triple, tripartite.

tripodes, um, *m. pl.*, v. **tripūs**.

tripudiō, [1] *v.* leap, jump, dance, caper.

tripudium, iī, *nt.* solemn religious dance; favourable omen (when the sacred chickens ate so greedily that the food dropped to the ground).

tripūs, odis, *m.* three-legged stand, tripod; the oracle at Delphi.

triquetrus, a, um, *a.* three-cornered, triangular.

trirēmis, e, *a.* having three oars to each bench; ~, **is**, *f.* trireme.

trīste, *ad.* sadly, sorrowfully; harshly, severely.

trīstis, e, *a.* depressed, gloomy, unhappy; bitter; ill-humoured; stern, austere; unhappy; grim, unpleasant; sour.

trīstitia, ae, *f.* unhappiness, despondency, gloom; sourness.

trisulcus, a, um, *a.* divided into three forks or prongs.

trīticeus, a, um, *a.* of wheat.

trīticum, ī, *nt.* wheat.

trītūra, ae, *f.* rubbing, friction; threshing.

trītus, a, um, *a.* well-trodden, well-worn; worn; common; familiar.

triumphālia, ium, *nt. pl.* the insignia of a triumph.

triumphālis, e, *a.* of or associated with the celebration of a triumph; having triumphal status; triumphant.

triumphō, [1] *v.* triumph; celebrate a triumph; exult, triumph over.

triumphus, ī, *m.* triumphal procession, triumph.

triumvir, v. **triumvirī**.

triumvirātus, ūs, *m.* triumvirate.

triumvirī, ōrum & um, *m. pl.* board of three, triumvirate; ~ **capitālēs**, superintendents of public prisons and executions.

trivium, iī, *nt.* place where three roads meet; 'the gutter'.

trivius, a, um, *a.* having a temple at a spot where three roads meet.

trochus, ī, *m.* metal hoop (used for games or exercise).

Trōiugena, ae, *a.* born of Trojan stock.

tropaeum, ī, *nt.* trophy; monument, victory.

trucīdātiō, ōnis, *f.* slaughtering, massacre.

trucīdō, [1] *v.* slaughter, butcher, massacre.

truculentus, a, um, *a.* ferocious, aggressive.

trudis, is, *f.* metal-tipped pole; barge-pole.

trūdō, sī, sum, [3] *v.* thrust, push, shove; drive, force; drive on.

truncō, [1] *v.* maim, mutilate; strip of branches, foliage; cut off.

truncus, ī, *m.* trunk (of a tree); body of a man, trunk, torso.

truncus, a, um, *a.* maimed, mutilated, dismembered; trimmed of its branches; stunted in growth.

trux, ucis, *a.* harsh, savage, pitiless, cruel.

tū, tē, tuī, tibi, tē, *pn.* you (sing.).

tuba, ae, *f.* (straight) trumpet; war-trumpet.

tūber, eris, *nt.* tumour, protuberance, excrescence.

tubicen, inis, *m.* trumpeter.

Tubilūstrium, iī, *nt.* feast of trumpets (on the 23rd of March and 23rd of May).

tueor, tuitus sum, [2] *v. dep.* look at, scan, view; keep safe, protect, watch over; preserve from danger; defend; look after; uphold; **torva tuerī,** to look grim.

tugurium, iī, *nt.* primitive dwelling, hut, shack.

tum, *ad.* then; at that time; besides; afterwards; in that case; at that moment; **quid ~?** what then? what further?; **tum . . . tum,** both . . . and; as well . . . as; first . . . then; at this moment . . . at that moment; **cum . . . tum,** both . . . and especially; not only . . . but also; **tum dēmum, tum dēnique,** then and not till then; **tum prīmum,** then for the first time.

tumefaciō, fēcī, factum, [3] *v.* cause to swell; puff up.

tumeō, [2] *v.* swell, become inflated; be puffed up; be bombastic; be swollen with conceit, presumption, *etc.*

tumēscō, muī, [3] *v.* (begin to) swell; become inflamed with pride, passion, *etc.*

tumidus, a, um, *a.* swollen, swelling, distended; puffed up with pride *or* self-confidence; bombastic.

tumor, ōris, *m.* swollen *or* distended condition; swell (of the sea, waves); excitement, passion, conceit.

tumulō, [1] *v.* cover with a burial mound.

tumulōsus, a, um, *a.* full of hillocks.

tumultuārius, a, um, *a.* raised to deal with a sudden emergency; improvised; unplanned; harphazard.

tumultuātiō, ōnis, *f.* confused uproar.

tumultuō, [1] v. **tumultuor, ātus sum**, [1] v. dep. make a confused uproar; make an armed rising.

tumultuōsus, a, um, a. turbulent, full of commotion or uproar.

tumultus, ūs, m. tumult, uproar, disturbance; turbulence; alarm; agitation (of the mind or feelings); sudden outbreak of violence or disorder; muddle.

tumulus, ī, m. rounded hill, knoll; burial-mound, grave.

tunc, ad. then, at the very time, at that; v. **tum**.

tundō, tutudī, tūnsum & tūsum, [3] v. beat; bruise, pulp, crush.

tunica, ae, f. tunic.

tunicātus, a, um, a. wearing a tunic.

turba, ae, f. disorder; dense or disorderly mass of people, multitude, crowd; confusion, disturbance.

turbāmentum, ī, nt. means of disturbing.

turbātiō, ōnis, f. disturbance.

turbātor, ōris, m. one who disturbs.

turbidus, a, um, a. wild, confused, disordered; muddy, turbid; foggy; troubled, turbulent; gloomy; unruly, mutinous.

turbineus, a, um, a. gyrating like a spinning-top.

turbō, [1] v. disturb, confuse, trouble, disorder; make muddy or turbid.

turbō, inis, m. whirlwind, tornado; whirlpool, eddy; spinning-top; whirling motion; whorl or fly-wheel of a spindle.

turbulentus, a, um, a. violently disturbed, stormy, turbulent; turbid; marked by turmoil or violent unrest; unruly, riotous.

turdus, ī, m. thrush.

tūreus, a, um, a. of or connected with incense.

turgeō, tursī, [2] v. swell out, become swollen or tumid.

turgēscō, [3] v. begin to swell.

turgidulus, a, um, a. (poor little) swollen.

turgidus, a, um, a. swollen, inflated.

tūribulum, ī, nt. censer.

tūricremus, a, um, a. burning incense.

tūrifer, a, um, a. yielding or producing incense.

tūrilegus, a, um, a. incense-gathering.

turma, ae, f. small troop, squadron (of cavalry); company.

turmālis, e, a. belonging to a squadron of cavalry.

turmātim, ad. in troops or squadrons of cavalry.

turpiculus, a, um, a. somewhat ugly.

turpis, e, a. ugly; foul; disgraceful, dishonourable, degrading; loathsome; guilty of disgraceful behaviour; indecent, obscene.

turpō, [1] *v.* make ugly; pollute, disfigure.

turriger, a, um, *a.* bearing a tower; wearing a turreted crown.

turris, is, *f.* tower; howdah.

turrītus, a, um, *a.* crowned with towers; tower-shaped.

turtur, uris, *m.* turtle-dove.

t(h)ūs, t(h)ūris, *nt.* frankincense.

tussis, is, *f.* cough.

tūtāmen, inis, *nt.* means of protection.

tūtāmentum, ī, *nt.* means of protection.

tūte, *pn.* emphatic form of **tū.**

tūtēla, ae, *f.* protection, guardianship, tutelage, defence; charge.

tūtō, [1] *v.,* v. **tūtor,** [1].

tūtor, ōris, *m.* protector; guardian.

tūtor, ātus sum, [1] *v. dep.* guard, protect, defend; guard against, avert.

tūtus, a, um, *a.* safe, secure; watchful; free from risk; that may safely be trusted.

tuus, a, um, *pn. a.* your (sing.).

ty(m)panum, ī, *nt.* small drum; revolving cylinder.

tyrannis, idis, *f.* tyranny, position *or* rule of a tyrant.

tyrannus, ī, *m.* despot, tyrant; monarch.

U

ūber, eris, *nt.* teat, pap, udder; soil rich in nourishing quality.

ūber, eris, *a.* plentiful, abundant, copious; rich, luxuriant.

ūbertās, ātis, *f.* fruitfulness, fertility; abundance, plenty.

ūbertim, *ad.* plentifully, copiously.

ubi, *ad.* where; where? when.

ubicumque, ubīcumque, *ad.* wherever; in any place whatever.

ubinam, *ad.* where in the world?

ubiquāque, *ad.* everywhere.

ubīque, *ad.* everywhere, anywhere, wherever.

ubivīs, *ad.* anywhere you like, no matter where.

ūdus, a, um, *a.* wet.

ulcerō, [1] *v.* cause to fester.

ulcerōsus, a, um, *a.* full of sores.

ulcīscor, ultus, [3] *v. dep.* take vengeance (on) *or* revenge (for); avenge.

ulcus, eris, *nt.* ulcer, sore.

ūlīgō, inis, *f.* waterlogged ground, marsh.

ūllus, a, um, ūllīus, *a.* any, any one.

ulmeus, a, um, *a.* of elm.

ulmus, ī, *f.* elm-tree; elm-wood.

ulna, ae, *f.* forearm; the span of the outstretched arms.

ulterior, us, *a.* farther away, more distant; additional, further.

ulterius, *ad.* farther away; to a further degree; any more.

ultimus, a, um, *a.* last; utmost; farthest; greatest; lowest, meanest, least; latest; earliest; **ultima ratiō,** the last resort.

ultiō, ōnis, *f.* revenge, vengeance, retribution.

ultor, ōris, *m.* avenger, revenger.

ultrā, *ad.* beyond, farther off, more, besides; ~, *pr. with acc.* beyond, past; more than.

ultrīx, īcis, *f. a.* avenging, vengeful.

ultrō, *ad.* into the bargain; conversely; of one's own accord, on one's own initiative; ~ **citrōque,** to and fro.

ulula, ae, *f.* the tawny owl.

ululātus, ūs, *m.* howling, yelling.

ululō, [1] *v.* howl, yell, shriek; celebrate *or* proclaim with howling.

ulva, ae, *f.* sedge.

umbilīcus, ī, *m.* navel; centre of a country, region; ornamental end of the cylinder on which a book was rolled, middle, centre.

umbō, ōnis, *m.* boss (of a shield).

umbra, ae, *f.* shade, shadow; ghost (of a dead person); sheltered conditions, privacy; darkness; empty form, phantom.

umbrāculum, ī, *nt.* shelter, shade; parasol.

umbrifer, a, um, *a.* providing shade, shady.

umbrō, [1] *v.* cast a shadow on, shade.

umbrōsus, a, um, *a.* shady, shadowy.

ūmectō, [1] *v.* moisten, make wet.

ūmeō, [2] *v.* be wet; be moist.

umerus, ī, *m.* shoulder.

ūmēscō, [3] *v.* become moist *or* wet.

ūmidulus, a, um, *a.* somewhat moist.

ūmidus, a, um, *a.* moist, wet; full of sap.

ūmor, ōris, *m.* moisture; liquid; bodily fluid *or* discharge.

umquam, v. **unquam.**

ūnā, *ad.* at the same time; in one company, together.

ūnanimitās, ātis, *f.* unity of purpose, concord.

ūnanimus, a, um, *a.* acting in accord.

uncia, ae, *f.* twelfth part, twelfth; ounce; inch.

unciārius, a, um, *a.* concerned with a twelfth part.

ūnctus, a, um, *a.* oily, greasy; anointed, oiled.

uncus, ī, *m.* hook; hook used to drag executed criminals, clamp.

uncus, a, um, *a.* hooked, curved round at the extremity.

unda, ae, *f.* wave, sea; sea-water; river, spring; water; advancing mass.

unde, *ad.* from what place? where ... from? whence? from whom; out of which; from what source, cause, *etc.*? from what stock, family, rank, *etc.*?

undecim, *a.* eleven.

undecimus, a, um, *a.* eleventh.

undēvīcē(n)simus, a, um, *a.* nineteenth.

undēvīgintī, *a.* nineteen.

undique, *ad.* from all sides *or* directions, from every side *or* place; in all respects.

undō, [1] *v.* rise in waves; surge, seethe; well up; billow; undulate.

undōsus, a, um, *a.* abounding in waves, flowing water, *etc.*

ungō *or* **unguō, ūnxī, ūnctum,** [3] *v.* smear with oil, grease, *etc.*; anoint with oil, unguents, *etc.*

unguen, inis, *nt.* fat, grease.

unguentārius, iī, *m.* dealer in ointments, maker of ointments.

unguentātus, a, um, *a.* anointed *or* greased with ointments.

unguentum, ī, *nt.* ointment, unguent.

unguis, is, *m.* nail (of a human finger *or* toe), claw, talon, hoof;

ad (in) unguem, to an exact measurement *or* standard.

ungula, ae, *f.* hoof.

unguō, *v.* ungō.

ūnicē, *ad.* to a singular degree; especially.

ūnicus, a, um, *a.* one and only, sole; unique, singular.

ūnigena, ae, *a.* one sharing a single parentage, i.e. brother or sister.

ūnimanus, a, um, *a.* one-handed.

ūniter, *ad.* so as to form a singular entity.

ūniversus, a, um, *a.* occurring all at once; the whole of, entire; whole; (*pl.*) all without exception; taken all together.

unquam, *ad.* at any time, ever; at some time.

ūnus, a, um, *a.* one; a, an; only; a single, alone, sole; one and the same; the one and only; a certain; **in ūnum,** so as to form a single mass; **ad ūnum,** to a man; without exception.

ūnusquisque, ūnaquaeque, ūnumquodque *or* **ūnumquidque,** *pn.* everyone.

ūpiliō, ōnis, *m.* shepherd, herdsman.

urbānitās, ātis, *f.* sophistication, polish, suavity.

urbānus, a, um, *a.* of *or* belonging to the city; elegant, sophisticated, witty; polished, refined.

urbs, urbis, *f.* city; (city of) Rome.

urgeō, ursī, [2] *v.* press, squeeze; push, thrust, shove; spur on; weigh down; be oppressive to; press hard in attack; follow hard on the heels of; crowd in; 'keep on at'; pursue with vigour.

ūrīnātor, ōris, *m.* diver.

urna, ae, *f.* water-jar; urn; cinerary urn; urn used in drawing lots; voting urn; *fig.* urn of fate; a liquid measure (about 13 litres).

ūrō, ussī, ustum, [3] *v.* burn; burn up; destroy by fire; scorch; make sore, cause to smart; corrode; inflame with desire; keep alight.

ursa, ae, *f.* she-bear; Great Bear.

ursus, ī, *m.* bear.

urtīca, ae, *f.* stinging-nettle.

ūrus, ī, *m.* aurochs, the long-horned wild ox of primeval Europe.

ūsitātus, a, um, *a.* familiar, everyday.

uspiam, *ad.* anywhere, somewhere.

usquam, *ad.* at *or* in any place, anywhere; to any place; at any juncture.

usque, *ad.* continuously, constantly; all along, all the way; all the while, as long *or* as far as, until; ~ **ad** *with acc.* right up to.

usquequāque, *ad.* in every conceivable situation; wholly, altogether.

ustulō, [1] *v.* scorch, char, burn partially.

ūsūcapiō, cēpī, captum, [3] *v.* acquire ownership of (a thing) by virtue of uninterrupted possession.

ūsūrpō, [1] *v.* make use of; employ; practise, perform; carry out; take possession of; take to oneself; assert one's possession of (a right *or* privilege) by exercising it; make frequent use of (a word, expression); call habitually (by a name); speak habitually of (as).

ūsus, ūs, *m.* use, employment; practical experience; practice; habitual dealings; value, utility; requirement, need.

ut, utī, *ad. & c.* in what manner, how; in the manner that, as; however; such as; for, as being, inasmuch as; how much *or* greatly; when, as soon as; ~ . . . **ita,** as well as . . . no less; while . . . while; ~, *c.* so that; in order that; as if; as if it were: to wit, namely; although; as is usual.

utcumque, utcunque, *ad.* in whatever manner *or* degree; no matter how; whenever; in any event; as best one can.

ūter, tris, *m.* leather bag for wine, oil, *etc.*; inflated bag to keep one afloat.

uter, utra, utrum, *a.* whichever *or* which of the two, either one of the two.

uterque, utraque, utrumque, *pn.* each of the two.

uterus, ī, *m.* womb; belly, abdomen.

ūtilis, e, *a.* useful, serviceable, advantageous, profitable, helpful.

ūtilitās, ātis, *f.* the quality of being useful, usefulness, utility, advantage, expediency.

utinam, *ad.* how I wish that! if only!

utīque, *ad.* in any case; certainly; at all costs.

ūtor, ūsus, [3] *v. dep. with abl.* use, make use of, employ, apply, enjoy; practise, exercise; experience.

utpote, *ad.* as one might expect, as is natural.

ūtrārius, iī, *m.* water-carrier.

utrimque, *ad.* from *or* on both sides; at both ends.

utrō, *ad.* to which side (of two).

utrōbīque, *ad.*, v. **utrubīque**.

utrōque, *ad.* to both sides, in both directions.

utrubīque, *ad.* in both places; in both cases.

utrum, *ad.* whether; whether?

ūva, ae, *f.* grapes; bunch of grapes; cluster.

ūvēscō, [3] *v.* become wet.

ūvidulus, a, um, *a.* wet, damp.

ūvidus, a, um, *a.* wet, soaked, dripping; moistened with drinking.

uxor, ōris, *f.* wife.

uxōrius, a, um, *a.* of *or* belonging to a wife; excessively fond of one's wife.

V

vacātiō, ōnis, *f.* exemption, immunity; vacation; exemption from military service.

vacca, ae, *f.* cow.

vaccīnium, iī, *nt.* whortleberry.

vacēfīō, fierī, *v. pass.* become empty.

vacillō, [1] *v.* stagger, totter; be in a weak condition.

vacō, [1] *v.* be empty *or* unfilled; be without occupants; be devoid (of), be free (from); be available (for); have leisure; be unemployed; have time for; **vacat**, there is room, space *or* opportunity (to).

vacuō, [1] *v.* empty.

vacuus, a, um, *a.* empty, void; insubstantial; destitute *or* devoid (of); empty-handed; plain, bare; unobstructed, clear; unoccupied, deserted; ownerless; idle, having leisure; fancy-free.

vadimōnium, iī, *nt.* bail, security, surety.

vādō, [3] *v.* go, advance, proceed.

vador, ātus sum, [1] *v. dep.* accept sureties from (the other party) for his appearance or reappearance in court at an appointed date.

vadōsus, a, um, *a.* full of shallows.

vadum, ī, *nt.* shallow, ford; bottom of the sea; shoal; (*pl.*) waters.

vae, *i.* ah! alas! woe! ~ **victīs**, alas! for the conquered.

vafer, fra, frum, *a.* sly, cunning, crafty.

vagē, *ad.* so as to move in different directions over a wide area.

vāgīna, ae, *f.* scabbard, sheath.

vāgiō, īvī & iī, [4] *v.* utter cries of distress, wail, squall.

vāgītus, ūs, *m.* cry of distress, wail, howl, squalling.

vagor, ātus sum, [1] *v. dep.* wander, roam, rove; move freely to and fro; vary, fluctuate.

vagus, a, um, *a.* roving, wandering; moving at random, shifting, inconstant; scattered.

valdē, *ad.* in a high degree, intensely, strongly; exceedingly.

valē, v. **valeō**.

valēns, entis, *a.* strong, stout, vigorous; healthy; powerful; potent, effective.

valeō, uī, itum, [2] *v.* be healthy, be well; be strong or vigorous; have the ability or power to; take effect; be powerful; have influence; be worth; **valēre iubēre** or **dīcere**, to bid farewell or good-bye; **valē,** goodbye!

valēscō, [3] *v.* become sound in health; become powerful.

valētūdō, inis, *f.* health, soundness; good health; bad health, indisposition, illness.

validus, a, um, *a.* strong, stout, sturdy, powerful; healthy, sound, well; fit, active; brisk; influential, telling.

vāllāris, e, *a.* **corōna** ~, crown or garland awarded to the first soldier to cross the **vallum** surrounding an enemy camp.

vallis, or **vallēs, is,** *f.* valley.

vāllō, [1] *v.* surround or fortify (a camp, *etc.*) with a palisaded rampart; furnish with a palisade.

vāllum, ī, *nt.* a palisade of stakes on top of an **agger**, a palisaded earthwork.

vāllus, ī, *m.* stake; palisade, palisaded earthwork.

valvae, ārum, *f. pl.* double or folding-door.

vānēscō, [3] *v.* melt into nothingness, vanish; become useless.

vāniloquentia, ae, *f.* idle talk, chatter; boastful speech.

vānitās, ātis, *f.* emptiness; untruthfulness; futility, foolishness, empty pride.

vannus, ī, *f.* winnowing basket.

vānus, a, um, *a.* empty, hollow, illusory; vain, useless; foolish, fatuous, trifling; silly; unreliable, ineffectual; devoid (of).

vapor, ōris, *m.* steam, exhalation, vapour; heat.

vapōrō, [1] *v.* cover or fill with vapour; heat, warm; be hot.

vappa, ae, *f.* flat wine; ~, *m.* a worthless person.

vāpulō, [1] *v.* be beaten *or* thrashed; be battered.

variantia, ae, *f.* diversity, variety.

variātiō, ōnis, *f.* divergence of behaviour.

vāricus, a, um, *a.* straddling.

varietās, ātis, *f.* diversity, variety; change, vicissitude.

variō, [1] *v.* mark with contrasting colours, variegate; vary; cause (opinions) to be divided; waver; fluctuate, undergo changes.

varius, a, um, *a.* variegated; various; changeable, inconstant; wavering; multifarious; many-sided.

vārus, a, um, *a.* bent-outwards; bandy; bow-legged; contrasting.

vas, vadis, *m.* surety.

vās, vāsis, *nt.*, **vāsa, ōrum,** *nt. pl.* vessel, utensil; equipment, kit.

vastātiō, ōnis, *f.* laying waste, ravaging.

vastātor, ōris, *m.* destroyer, ravager.

vastitās, ātis, *f.* desolation; devastation.

vastō, [1] *v.* leave desolate; plunder, destroy, lay waste; ravage.

vastus, a, um, *a.* desolate; vast, huge, enormous; awe-inspiring; clumsy, ungainly.

vātēs, is, *m.* or *f.* prophet; poet, bard.

vāticinātiō, ōnis, *f.* prophesying, predicting.

vāticinātor, ōris, *m.* prophet.

vāticinor, ātus, [1] *v. dep.* prophesy; rave, talk wildly.

vāticinus, a, um, *a.* prophetic.

-ve, *c.* or.

vēcordia, ae, *f.* frenzy.

vēcors, dis, *a.* mad; frenzied.

vectīgal, ālis, *nt.* revenue derived from public property.

vectīgālis, e, *a.* yielding taxes, subject to taxation.

vectis, is, *m.* crowbar, lever.

vectō, [1] *v.* carry, convey; (*pass.*) ride, travel.

vector, ōris, *m.* passenger; one that carries *or* transports.

vectōrius, a, um, *a.* used for transporting *or* conveying.

vectūra, ae, *f.* transportation, carriage.

vēgrandis, e, *a.* far from large, puny.

vehemēns, entis, *a.* violent, vehement; vigorous, powerful, strong.

vehiculum, ī, *nt.* cart, waggon.

vehō, xī, ctum, [3] *v.* carry, convey; vehī, to ride; sail; travel.

vel, *c.* or; even; for instance; or rather; even; (with superlatives) quite, altogether; ~ . . . ~, either . . . or.

vēlāmen, inis, *nt.* covering, clothing.

vēlāmentum, ī, *nt.* cover; olive-branch wrapped in wool carried by a suppliant.

vēles, itis, *m.* light-armed foot-soldier.

vēlifer, a, um, *a.* carrying a sail.

vēlitāris, e, *a.* of *or* belonging to the **vēlitēs.**

vēlitēs, um, v. **vēles.**

vēlivolus, a, um, *a.* speeding along under sail; characterized by speeding sails.

vellicō, [1] *v.* pinch, nip; criticize carpingly.

vellō, vellī, vulsum, [3] *v.* pluck *or* pull out, tear *or* pull up; tug at, pluck.

vellus, eris, *nt.* fleece; hide, fur; piece *or* lump of wool.

vēlō, [1] *v.* cover, clothe; conceal, cover up.

vēlōcitās, ātis, *f.* swiftness, rapidity, speed.

vēlōx, ōcis, *a.* swift, rapid, speedy.

vēlum, ī, *nt.* sail; curtain, awning: a woven cloth; **vēla dare,** to expose one's sails to the wind.

velut, velutī, *ad.* just as, just like; as for example; as it were; as if, as though; as being.

vēmēns, v. **vehemēns.**

vēna, ae, *f.* blood-vessel, vein; artery; pulse; fissure, pore, cavity, (underground) stream; vein of ore, *etc.*; supply *or* store (of talent).

vēnābulum, ī, *nt.* hunting-spear.

vēnālis, e, *a.* for sale; (that is) on hire; open to the influence of bribes.

vēnāticus, a, um, *a.* for hunting.

vēnātiō, ōnis, *f.* hunting, chase; beasts hunted, game; animal hunt in the arena.

vēnātor, ōris, *m.* hunter.

vēnātrīx, īcis, *f.* huntress.

vēnātus, ūs, *m.* hunting, hunt.

vēndibilis, e, *a.* that can (easily) be sold, marketable.

vēnditō, [1] *v.* offer for sale; cry up; pay court (to).

vēndō, didī, ditum, [3] *v.* sell, betray for money; promote the sale of.

venēfica, ae, *f.* female poisoner; sorceress.

venēficium, iī, *nt.* poisoning; magic, sorcery.

venēficus, a, um, *a.* of *or* connected with sorcery; ~, **ī,** *m.* poisoner.

venēnātus, a, um, *a.* poisonous, venomous; poisoned.

venēnifer, a, um, *a.* venomous.

venēnō, [1] *v.* imbue *or* infect with poison.

venēnum, ī, *nt.* poison; potent herb used for medical *or* magical purposes.

vēneō, īvī & iī, itum, [4] *v.* be sold (as a slave); be disposed of for financial gain.

venerābilis, e, *a.* venerable, august.

venerābundus, a, um, *a.* expressing religious awe (towards).

venerātiō, ōnis, *f.* reverence, veneration.

venerātor, ōris, *m.* one who reveres.

veneror, ātus sum, [1] *v. dep.* **venerō**, [1] *v.* worship, revere, venerate; honour; supplicate.

venia, ae, *f.* pardon, forgiveness; leave, permission; favour, indulgence; relief, remission.

veniō, vēnī, ventum, [4] *v.* come; go; arrive; arise, come to pass; proceed.

vēnor, ātus sum, [1] *v. dep.* hunt.

venter, tris, *m.* belly; paunch, abdomen; stomach; swelling; embryo.

ventilō, [1] *v.* expose to a draught; fan; brandish.

ventitō, [1] *v.* come frequently, resort.

ventōsus, a, um, *a.* windy; swift (as the wind); fickle, changeable; vain, puffed up.

ventus, ī, *m.* wind; puff, breeze.

vēnum dō, dedī, datum, [1] *v.* put up for sale.

Venus, eris, *f.* goddess of love; beloved person; object of love; loveliness; beauty; charm; (planet) Venus; best throw at dice; sexual intercourse.

venustās, ātis, *f.* attractiveness, charm, grace.

venustus, a, um, *a.* attractive, charming, graceful, pretty, neat.

vēpallidus, a, um, *a.* deathly pale.

vepris, is, *m.* thorn-bush.

vēr, vēris, *nt.* spring; spring-time of life.

vērāx, ācis, *a.* speaking the truth, truthful.

verbēna, ae, *f.* a leafy branch *or* twig from various aromatic trees *or* shrubs used in religious ceremonies *or* for medicinal purposes.

verber, eris, *nt.* lash, thong of a sling; blow, stroke; (*pl.*) an instrument for flogging.

verberō, [1] *v.* lash, scourge, flog; batter, hammer; assail.

verbōsus, a, um, *a.* prolix, lengthy; long-winded.

verbum, ī, *nt.* word; language; discourse, wording; talk; **verba dare** (*with dat.*), to deceive.

vērē, *ad.* truly, really, indeed; correctly.

verēcundia, ae, *f.* modesty; respect; uncertainty, diffidence; sense of shame.

verēcundus, a, um, *a.* modest.

verendus, a, um, *a.* that is to be regarded with awe *or* reverence.

vereor, itus, [2] *v.* show reverence *or* respect for; be afraid of, fear; be afraid (to do something); be afraid (that).

vergō, [3] *v.* slope down (towards); look towards; sink (towards something); tilt down.

vērīsimilis, e, *or* **vērī similis,** *a.* having the appearance of truth.

vēritās, ātis, *f.* truth, truthfulness, frankness.

vermiculus, ī, *m.* grub, larva.

vermis, is, *m.* worm, maggot.

verna, ae, *m. & f.* slave born in the master's household.

vernāculus, a, um, *a.* domestic, home-grown; indigenous, native, belonging to the country; low-bred, proletarian.

vernīlis, e, *a.* servile, obsequious.

vernīliter, *ad.* obsequiously, fawningly.

vernō, [1] *v.* carry on *or* undergo the process proper to spring.

vernus, a, um, *a.* of the spring, vernal.

vērō, *ad.* in fact, certainly, to be sure; however; moreover; on the other hand; yet.

verrō, verrī, versum, [3] *v.* sweep clean; sweep together; sweep (to the ground); skim; sweep; sweep along.

verrūca, ae, *f.* wart.

verruncō, [1] *v.* turn out.

versābundus, a, um, *a.* revolving.

versātilis, e, *a.* revolving; versatile.

versicolor, ōris, *a.* having colours that change.

versiculus, ī, *m.* brief line of verse.

versō, [1] *v.* keep turning round, spin, whirl; keep going round, keep turning over; turn over and over; stir; drive this way and that; turn this way and that; manoeuvre; sway, 'manipulate'; adapt; ponder; maintain; (*pass.*) come and go frequently; be in operation; be involved (in), concern oneself (in); dwell (upon); pass one's time (in).

versum, *ad. & pr.,* v. **versus.**

versus, ūs, *m.* line; row; furrow; bench of rowers; line of writing; line of verse.

versus, *ad. & pr. with acc.* towards, facing.

versūtia, ae, *f.* cunning, craft.

versūtus, a, um, *a.* full of stratagems *or* shifts, wily, cunning, adroit.

vertex, icis, *m.* whirlpool, eddy; crown of the head; peak, top, summit (of anything); pole.

verticōsus, a, um, *a.* full of whirlpools *or* eddies.

vertīgō, inis, *f.* whirling *or* spinning movement, gyration, giddiness, dizziness.

vertō, tī, sum, [3] *v.* turn, turn around *or* about; turn upside down; overthrow; alter, change; transform; turn out; cause to develop (into); pass into a new frame of mind; translate; **tergum vertere,** to turn tail, flee.

verū, ūs, *nt.* spit, point of javelin.

verum, ī, *nt.* spit; v. verū.

vērum, ī, *nt.* truth.

vērum, *c.* but; but at the same time.

vērumtamen, *c.* nevertheless, but even so.

vērus, a, um, *a.* true, real, genuine; just; right; proper.

verūtum, ī, *nt.* short throwing spear.

vervēx, ēcis, *m.* wether.

vēsānia, ae, *f.* madness, frenzy.

vēsāniēns, entis, *a.* raging, frenzied.

vēsānus, a, um, *a.* mad, frenzied; wild.

vēscor, [3] *v. dep.* take food, eat; enjoy, put to use; feed on, devour.

vēscus, a, um, *a.* thin, attenuated.

vēsīca, ae, *f.* bladder; balloon.

vēsīcula, ae, *f.* small bladder-like formation.

vespa, ae, *f.* wasp.

vesper, eris & erī, *m.* evening; evening-star; west; **sub vesperum,** towards evening; **~ e** *or* **~ ī,** in the evening.

vespera, ae, *f.* evening.

vesperāscō, āvī, [3] *v.* grow towards evening.

vespertīnus, a, um, *a.* evening . . . , of the evening; situated in the west.

vester, tra, trum, your (*pl.*).

vestibulum, ī, *nt.* fore-court, entrance.

vestīgium, ī, *nt.* footprint; track; sole of the foot; trace, mark, imprint, vestige; instant; **ē vestīgiō,** at once, immediately.

vestīgō, [1] *v.* track down, search for; search out; try to find out by searching; investigate.

vestīmentum, ī, *nt.* clothing; (*pl.*) clothes.

vestiō, īvī & iī, ītum, [4] *v.* dress, clothe; cover.

vestis, is, *f.* garments, clothing, clothes; cloth; **mūtāre vestem,** to change into mourning garments.

vestītus, ūs, *m.* clothes, dress; **redīre ad vestītum,** to resume (one's normal) dress (after mourning).

veterānus, a, um, *a.* veteran, having experience of action.

veternus, ī, *m.* morbid state of torpor.

vetō, uī, itum, [1] *v.* forbid; prohibit, be an obstacle to.

vetulus, a, um, *a.* elderly, ageing.

vetus, eris, *a.* aged, old; as he was in previous days; **veterēs, um,** *m. pl.* 'old-timers'; old authors or writers.

vetustās, ātis, *f.* old age; antiquity; long duration.

vetustus, a, um, *a.* ancient, old-established; long-established.

vexāmen, inis, *nt.* **vexātiō, ōnis**, *f.* shaking; disturbance, upheaval.

vexillārius, iī, *m.* standard-bearer; **vexillariī**, *pl.* troops serving for the time being in a special detachment.

vexillum, ī, *nt.* standard, banner; detachment of troops.

vexō, [1] *v.* agitate, buffet; harry, ravage; afflict, upset; persecute; disturb.

via, ae, *f.* way; road, passage; channel; march, journey; manner, method, means.

viāticum, ī, *nt.* provision for a journey, travelling allowance; money saved by soldiers from day to day.

viātor, ōris, *m.* traveller.

vibrō, [1] *v.* brandish, wave; crimp, corrugate; rock; propel suddenly; flash; dart; glitter.

vīburnum, ī, *nt.* guelder rose.

vicārius, iī, *m.* substitute, deputy; successor.

vīcātim, *ad.* by (urban) districts, street by street; in *or* by villages.

vīcēnī, ae, a, twenty each.

vīcē(n)simus, a, um, *a.* twentieth.

vicia, ae, *f.* vetch.

vīciē(n)s, *ad.* twenty times.

vīcīnālis, e, *a.* of *or* for the use of local inhabitants.

vīcīnia, ae, *f.* neighbourhood; nearness; neighbours.

vīcīnitās, ātis, *f.* neighbourhood; nearness; neighbours.

vīcīnum, ī *nt.* neighbourhood, neighbouring place, vicinity (of).

vīcīnus, a, um, *a.* neighbouring, in the neighbourhood, near; similar; ~, ī, *m.* neighbour.

vicis, *gen.* no *nom.*, *f.* change; succession; place, turn; part; exchange, retaliation, return, interchange; **in vicem** *or* **invicem**, by turns; reciprocally; instead of; **vicem**, after the manner of; **vice**, after the manner of.

vicissim, *ad.* in turn; conversely.

vicissitūdō, inis, *f.* change, alternation vicissitude.

victima, ae, *f.* an animal offered in sacrifice; a full-grown victim.

victor, ōris, *m.* conqueror, victor.

victōria, ae, *f.* victory.

victrīx, īcis, *f.* female conqueror; ~, *a.* (*f.*) victorious.

victus, ūs, *m.* livelihood, food; way of life.

vīculus, ī, *m.* small village, hamlet.

vīcus, ī, *m.* street; village; district of Rome.

vidēlicet, *ad.* it is clear (that), evidently, plainly; namely; (expressing irony) of course, no doubt.

videō, vīdī, vīsum, [2] *v.* see; look at, behold, observe, per-

ceive; understand; regard; take
care; pay regard to.

videor, [2] *v. pass.* appear, seem;
be seen; be deemed; **vidētur,** it
seems good.

viduitās, ātis, *f.* widowhood.

viduō, [1] *v.* widow; bereave of a
husband.

viduus, a, um, *a.* bereft, deprived
(of); widowed; divorced; not
supporting a climbing plant,
unsupported.

viētus, a, um, *a.* shrivelled,
wrinkled.

vigeō, [2] *v.* be strong *or* vigorous;
thrive, flourish, be active; be effective.

vigēscō, guī, [3] *v.* acquire
strength.

vigil, ilis, *a.* awake, on the watch,
alert; wakeful; ~, *m.* or *f.*
sentry, guard; member of fire
brigade.

vigilāns, antis, *a.* watchful, vigilant.

vigilantia, ae, *f.* vigilance, alertness.

vigilia, ae, *f.* wakefulness, lying
awake; watch, guard; patrol;
watchfulness, vigilance.

vigilō, [1] *v.* watch; be awake; stay
awake; spend time (on a task)
by remaining awake; spend (a
night, *etc.*) awake; be watchful
or alert.

vīgintī, *a.* twenty.

vigor, ōris, *m.* vigour; physical
or mental energy.

vīlica, ae, *f.* wife of a farm overseer.

vīlicus, ī, *m.* farm overseer, manager.

vīlipendō, [3] *v.* despise, slight.

vīlis, e, *a.* cheap; worthless; contemptible; humble, mean, com-
mon.

vīlitās, ātis, *f.* cheapness; worthlessness.

vīlla, ae, *f.* rural dwelling with
associated farm buildings.

villōsus, a, um, *a.* shaggy, hairy.

vīllula, ae, *f.* small farmstead *or*
country-house.

villus, ī, *m.* shaggy hair, tuft of
hair.

vīmen, inis, *nt.* flexible branch;
withy; basket.

vīmineus, a, um, *a.* of wicker-
work.

Vīnālia, ium, *n. pl.* wine-festi-
vals (on 22 April and 19–20 of
August).

vīnārius, iī, *m.* wine-merchant.

vinciō, vīnxī, vīnctum, [4] *v.* tie
up; bind, encircle; bond; link;
fetter.

vinclum, v. **vinculum.**

vincō, vīcī, victum, [3] *v.* conquer, overcome; defeat; subdue;
win; surmount; exceed, excel;
prevail.

vinculum, ī, *nt.* band, bond, cord,
rope, chain, fetter; band;
prison; imprisonment; tether;
mooring-rope; restraint, tie.

vīndēmia, ae, *f.* grape-gathering; produce of a vineyard in any given year.

vindex, icis, *m.* or *f.* champion, defender; protector; avenger, revenger; one who punishes (an offence).

vindiciae, ārum, *f. pl.* interim possession (of disputed property).

vindicō, [1] *v.* vindicate, lay legal claim to; save, preserve; free; avenge, punish; defend, protect.

vindicta, ae, *f.* the ceremonial act of claiming as free one who contends he is wrongly held in slavery; vengeance; punishment.

vīnea, ae, *f.* vines; movable penthouse used to shelter siege-workers.

vīnētum, ī, *nt.* vineyard.

vīnitor, ōris, *m.* vineyard worker.

vīnōsus, a, um, *a.* immoderately fond of wine; intoxicated with wine.

vīnum, ī, *nt.* wine.

viola, ae, *f.* violet stock, gillyvor; violet colour.

violābilis, e, *a.* that may be violated or suffer outrage.

violāceus, a, um, *a.* violet-coloured.

violārium, iī, *nt.* bed of violets.

violātiō, ōnis, *f.* profanation, violation.

violātor, ōris, *m.* profaner, violator.

violēns, entis, *a.* vehement, violent.

violentia, ae, *f.* violence, aggressiveness.

violentus, a, um, *a.* violent, aggressive.

violō, [1] *v.* profane; defile, pollute; dishonour, outrage; transgress against; pierce, wound; violate.

vīpera, ae, *f.* viper.

vīpereus, vīperīnus, a, um, *a.* of vipers.

vir, virī, *m.* man; male; husband, lover; a true man; solider.

virāgō, inis, *f.* a warlike or heroic woman.

virectum, ī, *nt.* area of greenery.

vireō, uī, [2] *v.* be green or verdant; be lively or vigorous; be full of youthful vigour.

vīrēs, ium, *f. pl.* strength; control; resources, assets; value; meaning.

virēscō, [3] *v.* turn green.

virga, ae, *f.* twig, shoot, spray, rod, stick; magic wand.

virgātus, a, um, *a.* made of twigs; striped.

virgeus, a, um, *a.* consisting of twigs or shoots.

virgineus, a, um, *a.* of, belonging to or characteristic of a girl of marriageable age; virgin.

virginitās, ātis, *f.* maidenhood, virginity.

virgō, inis, *f.* a girl of marriageable age; virgin; Virgo (constellation); aqueduct at

Rome noted for the coolness of its water.

virgultum, ī, *nt.* shrub; (*pl.*) low shrubby vegetation, brush-wood.

viridis, e, *a.* green; fresh, blooming, sappy; marked by youthful vigour.

viridō, [1] *v.* make green; be green.

virīlis, e, *a.* male, masculine; of a man; manly; bold; firm; vigorous; **prō virīlī parte,** with the utmost effort; as far as a man may; **toga ~,** the plain white toga worn by a Roman on reaching puberty.

virītim, *ad.* man by man, per man, individually.

virōsus, a, um, *a.* having an unpleasantly strong taste *or* smell, rank.

virtūs, ūtis, *f.* manliness, manhood; goodness, virtue; excellence, worth; resolution, valour.

virus, ī, *nt.* venom; poisonous fluid; malignant quality; secretion with medicinal *or* magical potency.

vīs, vim (*acc.*), **vī** (*dat. & abl.*), *f.,* **vīrēs, ium,** *pl.* strength, force; vigour, power, energy; violence; meaning, signification; nature; efficacy, virtue (of drugs, *etc.*); **vīrēs** (*pl.*) strength; power; military strength.

vīscātus, a, um, *a.* smeared with bird-lime.

vīscera, um, *nt. pl.,* v. **vīscus,** *nt.*

vīscerātiō, ōnis, *f.* a communal sacrificial feast at which the flesh of the victim was shared among the guests.

viscum, ī, *nt.* mistletoe; bird-lime.

vīscus, eris, *nt.,* **vīscera, um,** *nt. pl.* the soft fleshy parts of the body, internal organs; entrails, flesh; offspring; innermost part, heart (of).

vīsum, ī, *m.* v. **viscum.**

vīsō, sī, sum, [3] *v.* go and look (at), look, view; visit.

vīsum, ī, *nt.* vision.

vīsus, ūs, *m.* the faculty of seeing; sight, vision; supernatural manifestation.

vīta, ae, *f.* life; living, manner of life; the course of a life.

vītābilis, e, *a.* to be avoided.

vītābundus, a, um, *a.* taking evasive action.

vītālis, e, *a.* of life; vital; life-giving, alive.

vītāliter, *ad.* so as to endow with life.

vitellus, ī, *m.* little calf; yolk of an egg.

vīteus, a, um, *a.* belonging to a vine.

vītigenus, a, um, *a.* produced from the vine.

vitiō, [1] *v.* spoil, harm, impair; deflower; invalidate.

vitiōsus, a, um, *a.* faulty, defective; corrupt; wicked, vicious.

vītis, is, *f.* vine; vine-branch; centurion's staff.

vītisator, ōris, *m.* vine-planter.

vitium, iī, *nt.* fault, defect, blemish; error; shortcoming.

vītō, [1] *v.* avoid, shun, keep clear of.

vitreus, a, um, *a.* of glass; resembling glass in its colour (greenish), translucency, *or* glitter.

vītricus, ī, *m.* stepfather.

vitrum, ī, *nt.* glass; woad.

vitta, ae, *f.* linen headband; woollen band.

vittātus, a, um, *a.* wearing *or* carrying a ritual **vitta.**

vitula, ae, *f.* calf, young cow.

vitulus, ī, *m.* (bull-)calf.

vituperō, [1] *v.* find fault with, criticize adversely.

vīvārium, iī, *nt.* game enclosure *or* preserve.

vīvāx, ācis, *a.* long-lived, tenacious of life; vivifying; lively, vigorous.

vīvēscō, vīxī, [3] *v.* come to life.

vīvidus, a, um, *a.* lively, vigorous, spirited; lifelike.

vīvō, vīxī, vīctum, [3] *v.* live, be alive; really live; live (on); live (by); pass one's life (in); survive.

vīvus, a, um, *a.* alive, living; lively.

vix, ad. hardly, scarcely, not easily.

vixdum, ad. scarcely yet, only just.

vocābulum, ī, *nt.* word used to designate something, term, name.

vōcālis, e, *a.* able to speak; having a notable voice; tuneful.

vōcāmen, inis, *nt.* designation, name.

vocātiō, ōnis, *f.* invitation.

vocātus, ūs, *m.* peremptory *or* urgent call.

vōciferātiō, ōnis, *f.* loud outcry, shout, roar.

vōciferor, ātus sum, [1] *v. dep.* utter a loud cry, shout, yell, cry out, announce loudly.

vocitō, [1] *v.* call.

vocō, [1] *v.* call; call upon, summon; name; invite; challenge; demand.

volaemum, ī, *nt.* a large kind of pear.

volantēs, ium, *m. pl.* birds.

volātilis, e, *a.* equipped to fly, flying, fleeing; fleeting, transient.

volātus, ūs, *m.* flying, flight.

Volcānus, v. **Vulcānus.**

volēns, entis, *a.* willing, welcome.

volitō, [1] *v.* fly about; flutter, move swiftly through the air; go to and fro.

volō, velle, voluī, *v.* be willing; wish, desire; want; mean, signify; maintain, claim.

volō, [1] *v.* fly; speed.

volō, ōnis, *m.* volunteer.

voltur, uris, v. **vultur.**

volturius, iī, v. vulturius.

voltus, ūs, v. vultus.

volūbilis, e, *a.* spinning, rotating; rolling; coiled; flowing, fluent.

volūbilitās, ātis, *f.* rotundity.

volucer, cris, cre, *a.* flying, winged; swift; fleeting, transitory.

volucris, is, *f.* bird.

volūmen, inis, *nt.* roll of papyrus, book; coil, twist.

voluntārius, a, um, *a.* of one's own free will, voluntarily undergone.

voluntās, ātis, *f.* will, wish, choice, desire, inclination; good-will, sympathy; approval.

voluptās, ātis, *f.* delight; pleasure; source of pleasure; sexual intercourse.

volūtābrum, ī, *nt.* place where pigs wallow.

volūtō, [1] *v.* roll, wallow; turn over in one's mind; think *or* talk over.

volvō, volvī, volūtum, [3] *v.* roll, roll over; cause to roll, wrap up; cause (the eyes) to travel restlessly; unroll; turn over in the mind; grovel; turn round.

vōmer, eris, *m.* ploughshare.

vomō, uī, itum, [3] *v.* be sick, vomit; discharge, spew out; belch out.

vorāgō, inis, *f.* deep hole, chasm, watery hollow.

vorāx, ācis, *a.* ravenous; insatiable; devouring.

vorō, [1] *v.* devour; engulf, eat away.

vortex, *etc.*, v. vertex.

voster, tra, trum, v. **vester.**

vōtīvus, a, um, *a.* offered in fulfilment of a vow.

vōtum, ī, *nt.* vow; votive offering; prayer; desire, hope.

voveō, vōvī, vōtum, [2] *v.* vow; pray *or* long for.

vōx, vōcis, *f.* voice, sound, word, words; speech; language.

Vulcānus, ī, *m.* Vulcan, the god of fire; fire.

vulgāris, e, *a.* usual, common, commonplace, everyday; of the common people; shared by all.

vulgātor, ōris, *m.* divulger.

vulgātus, a, um, *a.* common, ordinary; conventional; wellknown.

vulgivagus, a, um, *a.* widely ranging; promiscuous.

vulgō, [1] *v.* make common to all; make public, publish; spread abroad; prostitute; publish the news (that).

vulgō, *ad.* commonly, publicly; en masse; far and wide.

vulgus, ī, *nt.* the common people, general public, crowd.

vulnerō, [1] *v.* wound, hurt, distress.

vulnificus, a, um, *a.* causing wounds.

vulnus, eris, *nt.* wound; emotional hurt; injury.

vulpēcula, ae, *f.* (little) fox.

vulpēs, is, *f.* fox.

vultur, uris, *m.* vulture.

vulturius, iī, *m.* vulture.

vultus, ūs, *m.* countenance, facial expression; face; looks, features.

X

X = 10.

xiphiās, ae, *m.* swordfish.

Z

Zephyrus, ī, *m.* a west wind.

zōna, ae, *f.* belt, girdle; celestial zone.

English– Latin Dictionary

A

a, indefinite article, generally unexpressed in Latin; unus (a, um); quidam; is (ea, id).

aback, taken ~, *fig.* stupefactus, attonitus, consternatus.

abandon, *v.t.* (de)relinquo, desero, destituo, abicio, omitto, neglego, [3].

abandoned, *a.* derelictus; desertus; *fig.* flagitiosus, perditus.

abandoning, abandonment, *n.* derelictio, destitutio, *f.*

abashed, *a.* pudibundus.

abbreviate, *v.t.* imminuo, contraho, [3].

abbreviation, *n.* contractio, *f.*

abdicate, *v.t. & i.* me abdico, [1] (*with abl.*); depono, [3].

abdomen, *n.* abdomen, *nt.*

abduct, *v.t.* rapio, [3].

abduction, *n.* raptus, us, *m.*

aberration, *n.* error, *m.*

abet, *v.t.* adiuvo, instigo, [1]; faveo, [2] (*with dat.*).

abetter, *n.* instigator, impulsor, *m.*

abhor, *v.t.* abhorreo, [2]; detestor, aversor, [1].

abhorrence, *n.* odium, *nt.*

abhorrent, *a.* perosus; odiosus; alienus.

abide, *v.t.* (endure) patior, [3]; tolero, [1]; subeo, [4]; expecto, [1]; ~, *v.i.* (dwell) habito, [1]; maneo, [2]; ~ **by**, sto, [1] (*with abl.*).

ability, *n.* facultas; peritia, *f.*; ingenium, *nt.*; **to the best of one's ~**, summa ope.

abject, *a.* abiectus, vilis; humilis.

ablaze, *a.* ardens, fervens.

able, *a.* potens; capax, peritus; ingeniosus; **be ~ (to)**, posse, valere, [2]; quire, [4]; sufficere, [3].

able-bodied, *a.* validus, robustus, firmus.

aboard, *ad.* in nave; **go ~ a ship**, navem conscendere, [3].

abode, *n.* domicilium, *nt.*; sedes, *f.*; (sojourn) commoratio; mansio, *f.*

abolish, *v.t.* aboleo, [2]; exstinguo, tollo, rescindo, [3].

abolition, *n.* abolitio, dissolutio, *f.*

abominable, *a.* detestabilis, exsecrabilis, infandus; odiosus.

abomination, *n.* detestatio, *f.*; odium, *nt.*; **abominations**, (vile acts) nefaria, *nt. pl.*

abortive, *a.* abortivus; *fig.* irritus.

abound, *v.i.* abundo, redundo, [1]; supersum; supero, [1]; ~ **in**, abundo, [1] (*with abl.*).

abounding, *a.* abundans; copiosus, largus; creber.

about, *pr.* circa, circum ad, apud; circiter; sub (*all with acc.*); de (*with abl.*); ~, *ad.* circiter; ferme; (*more or less*) quasi; **be ~ to** . . . (*e.g.* write, *etc.*), scripturus, *etc.*; **go ~**, aggredior, incipio, [3]; **bring ~**, efficio, [3].

above, *pr.* (higher) super, supra; (beyond, more than) ante; praeter, ultra (*all with acc.*); ~, *ad.* supra; insuper; plus, magis; (upwards) sursum; **from ~**, desuper, superne; **be ~**, emineo, [2]; *fig.* dedignor, [1]; fastidio, [4]; **over and ~**, insuper; ~ **all**, super omnia.

above-board, *ad. fig.* aperte, candide.

above-mentioned, *a.* quod supra dictum est.

abrasion, *n.* attritus, us, *m.*

abreast, *ad.* ex adverso.

abridge, *v.t.* contraho, [3].

abridgement, *n.* contractio, *f.*

abroad, *ad.* (out of doors) foris; (to the outside of a house) foras; (in foreign parts) peregre; (here and there) passim, undique; **from ~**, extrinsecus; peregre; **be** (*or* **live**) **~**, peregrinor, [1]; patria careo, [2].

abrupt, *a.* praeruptus; praeceps; *fig.* subitus, repentinus; improvisus.

abruptly, *ad.* raptim.

abscess, *n.* ulcus, *nt.*

abscond, *v.i.* me clam subduco, me abdo, lateo, [2]; latito, [1].

absence, *n.* absentia; peregrinatio, *f.*; *fig.* (of mind) oblivio, *f.*

absent, *a.* absens; **be ~**, abesse, peregrinari.

absentee, *n.* peregrinator, *m.*

absent-minded, *a.* obliviosus.

absolute, *a.* absolutus; summus.

absolutely, *ad.* absolute; prorsus; (entirely) penitus.

absolution, *a.* absolutio; indulgentia, *f.*

absolve, *v.t.* veniam do, [1]; absolvo, [3]; libero, [1]; dimitto, [3].

absorb, *v.t.* absorbeo, [2]; haurio, [4]; combibo, [3]; *fig.* teneo, [2].

absorbent, *a.* bibulus.

abstain, *v.i.* abstineo, [2].

abstemious, *a.* abstemius; sobrius.

abstinence, *n.* abstinentia, *fig.* (fasting) ieiunium, *nt.*

abstinent, *a.* abstinens; ~**ly**, *ad.* abstinenter, continenter.

abstracted, *a.* (in mind) parum attentus; ~**ly**, *ad.* parum attente.

abstraction, *n.* (concept) imago, *f.*

abstruse, *a.* abstrusus; reconditus; obscurus, occultus; ~**ly**, *ad.* abdite, occulte.

absurd, *a.* absurdus, insulsus; ineptus, ridiculus; ~**ly**, *ad.* inepte, absurde.

absurdity, *n.* ineptia; insulsitas; res inepta, *f.*

abundance, *n.* abundantia, copia, ubertas, *f.*

abundant, *a.* abundans; amplus; copiosus, plenus; uber; **be ~**, abundo, [1].

abundantly, *ad.* abunde, abundanter, copiose; effuse; (fruitfully) feliciter.

abuse, *v.t.* (misuse) abutor, [3]; *fig.* (insult, *etc.*) maledico, [3] (*with dat.*); convicior, lacero, [1].

abuse, *n.* (wrong use) abusus; perversus mos, *m.*; (insult) iniuria, *f.*, convicium, *nt.*; violatio, *f.*

abusive, *a.* contumeliosus; maledicus; ~**ly**, *ad.* contumeliose; maledice.

abyss, *n.* profundum, *nt.*; (whirlpool) gurges, *m.*; *fig.* vorago, *f.*

academic, *a.* academicus; ~**ally**, *ad.* ut solent academici.

academy, *n.* Academia, *f.*; collegium, *nt.*

accede, *v.i.* accedo, annuo, [3]; assentior, [4].

accelerate, *v.t.* accelero, festino, appropero, [1].

acceleration, *n.* festinatio, *f.*

accent, *n.* accentus; tenor; *fig.* sonus, *m.*; lingua, *f.*

accent, *v.t.* (in speaking) acuo, [3]; (in writing) fastigo, [1].

accept, *v.t.* accipio; recipio, [3]; (approve of) probo, [1]; (agree to) assentior, [4] (*with dat.*).

acceptable, *a.* acceptus, gratus; iucundus.

acceptance, *n.* acceptio; approbatio, *f.*

access, *n.* aditus; accessus, *m.*; **gain ~**, admitti, [3].

accessible, *a.* patens; *fig.* affabilis, facilis.

accession, *n.* (to the throne) regni principium, *nt.*

accessory, *a.* adiunctus; (of crimes) conscius; ~, *n.* particeps, *c.*, conscius, *m.*

accident, *n.* casus, *m.*; **by ~**, casu, fortuito, temere.

accidental, *a.* fortuitus; ~**ally**, *ad.* casu; fortuito.

acclamation, *n.* acclamatio, *f.*, clamor, consensus, plausus, *m.*

acclimatize, *v.t.* assuefacio, [3].

accommodate, *v.t.* accommodo, apto, [1]; *fig.* (have room for) capio, [3].

accommodation, *n.* (lodging) deversorium, *nt.*

accompany, *v.t.* comitor, [1]; (escort) deduco, [3]; (*mus.*) concino, [3].

accomplice, *n.* particeps, conscius (rei); (of crimes or vices) satelles, *m.*

accomplish, *v.t.* exsequor, perficio; perago, [3]; impleo, [2].

accomplished, *a.* *fig.* eruditus; doctus.

accomplishment, *n.* exsecutio, effectio; (skill) ars, *f.*

accord, *n.* consensus, *m.*; concordia, *f.*; **of one's own ~**, sponte; ultro; **with one ~**, uno ore.

accord, *v.t.* (grant) concedo, [3]; (agree) *v.i.* congruo, [3]; concordo, [1]; convenio, [4].

accordance, *n.*, v. accord, *n.*; **in ~ with**, secundum (*with acc.*).

according, *pr.* ~ **to**, de, ex, pro (*all with abl.*); secundum (*with acc.*).

accordingly, *ad.* itaque; ita; (therefore) igitur, ergo.

account, *n.* (reckoning, of money) ratio, *f.*; (narrative) memoria; narratio, *f.*; (esteem) reputatio, *f.*; (advantage) commodum, *nt.*; *fig.* **on ~ of . . .**, ob, propter (*with acc.*); **on that ~**, propterea; ideo; **call to ~**, rationem poscere, [3]; **of little** *or* **no ~**, nullius pretii, vilis; **take into ~**, rationem habere (*with gen.*).

account, *v.t.* (esteem) aestimo, [1]; habeo, [2]; pendo, pono, [3]; ~, *v.i.* ~ **for**, rationem reddo, [3].

accountable, *a.* reus, rationem reddere debens.

accountant, *n.* tabularius, *m.*

accrue, *v.i.* orior; accresco, [3]; provenio, [4].

accumulate, *v.t.* accumulo, coacervo, [1]; congero, [3]; ~, *v.i.* cresco; congeror, [3].

accumulation, *n.* (heap, *etc.*) cumulus; acervus; *fig.* congestus, *m.*

accuracy, *n.* cura; subtilitas, *f.*

accurate, *a.* accuratus; subtilis; **~ly**, *ad.* accurate, subtiliter.

accusation, *n.* accusatio, *f.*; crimen, *nt.*

accuse, *v.t.* accuso; criminor, [1]; (blame) reprehendo, [3].

accuser, *n.* accusator; (informer) delator, *m.*

accustom, *v.t.* assuefacio, [3]; ~ **oneself**, assuefieri, consuescere, [3]; **be ~ed**, solitus esse.

accustomed, *a.* assuetus, consuetus, solitus.

ache, *v.i.* doleo, [2]; **my head ~s**, caput mihi dolet.

ache, *n.* dolor, *m.*

achieve, *v.t.* patro, [1]; consequor, conficio, perficio, [3].

achievement, *n.* res gesta, *f.*; facinus, *nt.*

aching, *n.* dolor, *m.*

acid, *a.* acidus; acidulus.

acidity, *n.* aciditas, *f.*

acknowledge, *v.t.* agnosco, recognosco, [3]; fateor, confiteor, [2].

acknowledgement, *n.* agnitio; confessio, *f.*

acme, *n.* fastigium, *nt.*; (the acme of folly) summa dementia.

aconite, *n.* aconitum, *nt.*

acorn, *n.* glans, *f.*; **~-bearing**, *a.* glandifer.

acquaint, *v.t.* certiorem facio, [3]; ~ **oneself (with),** noscere, cognoscere, [3].

acquaintance, *n.* scientia; (friendship with) familiaritas; notitia, *f.*; (person) familiaris, *c.*

acquainted, *a.* gnarus (rei); (with) prudens (locorum, *etc.*); peritus (rei *or* re); **become ~,** noscere, cognoscere.

acquiesce, *v.i.* (in) acquiesco, [3]; assentior, [4]; probo, [1].

acquiescence, *n.* assensus, *m.*; approbatio, *f.*

acquire, *v.t.* comparo, [1]; nanciscor, consequor, pario, adipiscor, [3]; *fig.* disco, [3].

acquisition, *n.* (acquiring) conciliatio, comparatio, *f.*; (thing acquired) quaesitum, *nt.*

acquit, *v.t.* absolvo, [3]; libero, purgo, [1]; ~ **oneself,** se gerere, [3].

acquittal, *n.* absolutio, *f.*

acre, *n.* iugerum, *nt.*

acrid, *a.* acerbus, acer.

acrimonious, *a.* acerbus; *fig.* asper, truculentus.

acrimony, *n.* acrimonia; amaritudo, *f.*

acrobat, *n.* funambulus, *m.*

across, *pr.* trans (*with acc.*); *ad.* ex transverso, in transversum.

act, *v.i.* ago, facio; gero, [3]; (behave) me gero, [3]; (exert force) vim habeo, [2]; (on the stage) in scaenam prodeo, [4]; ~, *v.t.* (as actor) (comoediam, primam partem) ago, [3].

act, *n.* (deed, action) factum; gestum, *nt.*; (exploit) facinus, *nt.*; (decree) decretum, *nt.*; (in a play) actus, *m.*; **be caught in the ~,** deprehendi; ~**s,** *pl.* acta, *nt. pl.*

action, *n.* actio, *f.*; actus, *m.*; (battle) pugna, *f.*; (gesture) gestus, *m.*; (law) actio, *f.*; **bring an ~ against someone,** actionem alicui intendere, [3].

active, *a.* agilis; impiger, industrius, operosus; strenuus; vividus; ~**ly,** *ad.* impigre; strenue.

activity, *n.* agilitas, mobilitas; industria, navitas, *f.*

actor, *n.* (in a play) comoedus, histrio; mimus; artifex scaenicus; (doer) auctor; qui agit, *m.*

actress, *n.* mima, *f.*

actual, *a.* verus, ipse; ~**ly,** *ad.* re vera, re ipsa.

acumen, *n.* sagacitas, *f.*; ingenium, *nt.*

acute, *a.* acutus; acer; (of the understanding) sagax, subtilis; ~**ly,** *ad.* acute; acriter; (shrewdly) sagaciter.

adamant, *f.* adamas, *m.*

adapt, *v.t.* accommodo, apto, [1].

adaptable, *a.* habilis.

adaptation, *n.* accommodatio, *f.*

add, *v.t.* addo; appono, adiungo, adicio, [3]; (in speaking) adicio, [3]; (in writing) subiungo, [3]; ~ **up,** computo, [1]; **be ~ed,** accedo, [3].

adder, *n.* coluber, *m.*, vipera, *f.*

addicted, *a.* deditus, studiosus; **be ~ (to),** deditus esse.

addition, *n.* additamentum, *nt.*; adiectio; accessio; **in ~,** *ad.* insuper.

addle-headed, *a. fig.* inanis, vanus, fatuus, stultus.

address, *v.t.* (direct to) inscribo, [3]; (speak to) alloquor, aggredior, [3].

address, *n.* (speaking to) alloquium, *nt.* allocutio; (direction) inscriptio, *f.*; (petition) libellus supplex, *m.*; *fig.* dexteritas, ars; (speech) oratio, contio, *f.*

adduce, *v.t.* (witnesses) profero, [3]; (quote) cito, [1]; adduco, [3].

adept, *a.* peritus.

adequate, *a.* sufficiens, par.

adhere, *v.i.* adhaereo; cohaereo, [2]; *fig.* sto (in), [1] (*with abl.*).

adherent, *n.* assectator; fautor; particeps, *c.*; socius, *m.*; (dependent) cliens, *m.*

adhesive, *a.* tenax, lentus.

adieu, *i.* ave, salve, vale; **bid ~,** valedico, [3]; valere iubeo, [2].

adjacent, *a.* confinis, conterminus; vicinus.

adjoining, *a.* adiacens, confinis, vicinus.

adjourn, *v.t.* comperendino, [1]; differo, profero, [3]; **~,** *v.i.* differri.

adjournment, *n.* dilatio, prolatio, *f.*

adjudge, *v.t.* adiudico, [1].

adjudicate, *v.t.* addico, decerno, [3].

adjudication, *n.* addictio; (verdict) sententia, *f.*, arbitrium, *nt.*

adjust, *v.t.* apto, [1]; dispono, [3]; (settle) compono, [3]; ordino [1].

adjustment, *n.* accommodatio, compositio, *f.*

adjutant, *n.* optio, *m.*

administer, *v.t.* (manage, *etc.*) administro, curo, procuro, [1]; (medicine, *etc.*) adhibeo, [2]; (an oath) adigo, [3]; (justice) exerceo, [2]; reddo, [3].

administration, *n.* administratio; cura; procuratio, *f.*; magistratus, *m.*; (of public affairs) summa rerum.

administrator, *n.* administrator; procurator, *m.*

admirable, *a.* admirabilis; mirabilis, admirandus; insignis.

admirably, *ad.* admirabiliter; praeclare, insigniter.

admiral, *n.* praefectus classis, *m.*

admiration, *n.* admiratio, *f.*

admire, *v.t.* admiror; amo, [1].

admirer, *n.* admirator; mirator; laudator; amans, *m.*

admission, *n.* admissio, *f.*; aditus, accessus, *m.*; (confession) confessio, *f.*

admit, *v.t.* admitto; recipio; introduco; (adopt) ascisco, [3]; (confess) fateor, confiteor, [2]; **it is ~ted,** constat.

admittance, *n*. admissio, aditus, accessus, *m*.

admonish, *v.t.* moneo, commoneo, [2].

admonition, *n*. monitio, admonitio; adhortatio, *f*.; monitum, *nt*.

admonitory, *a*. monitorius.

ado, *n*. tumultus, *m*.; **with much ~**, aegre, vix; **without more ~**, statim.

adolescence, *n*. adolescentia, *f*.

adolescent, *a*. adolescens.

adopt, *v.t.* (a child) adopto, (an adult) arrogo, [1]; *fig.* ascisco; assumo, [3]; (a policy, *etc.*) capio, [3]; ineo, [4].

adoption, *n*. adoptio, adoptatio; (of an adult) arrogatio; *fig.* assumptio, *f*.

adoptive, *a*. adoptivus.

adorable, *a*. adorandus, venerandus; (lovable) amandus.

adoration, *n*. adoratio, *f*.; (love) amor, *m*.

adore, *v.t.* adoro, veneror, *fig.* admiror, amo, [1].

adorer, *n*. cultor, *m*.; (lover) amator, *m*.

adorn, *v.t.* orno, decoro, illustro, [1]; excolo, como, [3].

adornment, *n*. exornatio, *f*.; ornatus, *m*.; ornamentum, *nt*.

adrift, *ad*. in salo fluctuans; **be ~**, *v*. fluctuor, [1].

adroit, *a*. callidus, dexter, sollers, peritus, ingeniosus; **~ly**, *ad*.

callide, sollerter, perite, ingeniose.

adroitness, *n*. dexteritas, *f*.

adulation, *n*. adulatio, assentatio, *f*.

adult, *a*. adultus; pubes; **~**, *n*. adultus homo, *m*.

adulterate, *v.t.* adultero, vitio, [1]; corrumpo, [3].

adulterer, *n*. adulter; moechus, *m*.

adulteress, *n*. adultera; moecha, *f*.

adulterous, *a*. adulterinus; **~ly**, *ad*. adulterio, per adulterium.

adultery, *n*. adulterium; stuprum, *nt*.; **commit ~**, moechor, [1].

advance, *v.t.* promoveo, [2]; (lift up) tollo, attollo, [3]; exalto, [1]; (an opinion) exhibeo, [2]; profero, [3]; (lend) commodo, [1]; (accelerate) maturo, [1]; **~ someone's interests**, alicui consulo, [3]; rebus alicuius studeo, [2]; **~**, *v.i.* procedo, progredior, incedo, [3]; (*mil.*) gradum (pedem) infero, [3]; *fig.* proficio, [3].

advance, *n*. progressus; (attack) incursio, *f*.; (in rank) accessio dignitatis, *f*.; (increase, rise) incrementum, *nt*.

advanced, *a*. provectus; (of age) grandis.

advance-guard, *n*. antecursores, *m. pl.*, primum agmen, *nt*.

advantage, *n*. lucrum, commodum, emolumentum, *nt*.;

utilitas, *f.*; fructus; usus, *m.*;
(blessings) bona, *nt. pl.*; **have
the ~ over**, praesto, [1] (*with
dat.*); superior sum; **make ~**
or take ~ of, utor, [3] (*with abl.*);
be of ~ to, prosum (*with dat.*).

advantageous, *a.* fructuosus;
utilis; commodus; **~ly**, *ad.*
utiliter; bene; commode.

advent, *n.* adventus, us, *m.*

adventure, *n.* casus, *m.*; (as action) facinus, *nt.*

adventurous, *a.* audax; **~ly**, *ad.*
audacter.

adversary, *n.* adversarius, *m.*; inimicus, *m.*; inimica, *f.*

adverse, *a.* adversus, infestus;
fig. asper; **~ly**, *ad.* secus, infeliciter.

adversity, *n.* res adversae, *f. pl.*;
calamitas, *f.*; res asperae, *f. pl.*

advertise, *v.t.* (publish) divulgo,
[1]; (try to sell) vendito, [1].

advertisement, *n.* venditatio, *f.*

adviser, *n.* venditator, *m.*

advice, *n.* consilium, *nt.*; **ask ~**,
consulo, [3]; **give ~**, moneo, [2];
(information, intelligence) indicium, *nt.*

advisable, *a.* commodus, utilis; **it
is ~**, expedit, [4].

advise, *v.t.* moneo; (recommend)
suadeo, [2] (*with dat.*); (with)
consulo, [3]; (against) dissuadeo, [2]; (exhort) hortor, [1]; (inform) certiorem facio, [3].

adviser, *n.* consultor, monitor,
suasor, auctor, *m.*

advocacy, *n.* patrocinium, *nt.*

advocate, *n.* advocatus, causidicus; patronus; (one who recom-
mends) suasor, *m.*; (defender)
defensor, *m.*

advocate, *v.t.* suadeo, [2].

aedile, *n.* aedilis, *m.*

aegis, *n.* aegis, *f.*

afar, *ad.* procul, longe; **from ~**, e
longinquo.

affability, *n.* comitas, affabilitas,
facilitas, *f.*

affable, *a.* affabilis, comis, facilis.

affably, *ad.* comiter.

affair, *n.* res, *f.*; negotium, *nt.*

affect, *v.t.* afficio, [3]; commoveo,
[2]; percutio, [3]; (pretend) simulo, [1].

affection, *n.* (of mind *or* body) affectus, *m.*; affectio, *f.*; (love)
amor, *m.*; gratia; benevolentia,
f.; (feeling) affectus, impetus,
motus; sensus, *m.*

affectionate, *a.* amans, benevolus, pius; blandus; **~ly**, *ad.*
amanter; pie, blande.

affinity, *n.* affinitas; cognatio,
proximitas, *f.*

affirm, *v.t.* affirmo, assevero, testificor, [1].

affirmation, *n.* affirmatio, *f.*; asseveratio, *nt.*

affix, *v.t.* affigo, [3].

afflict, *v.t.* torqueo, [2]; vexo, crucio, [1].

affliction, *n.* miseria, *f.*; res adversae, *f. pl.*

affluence, *n.* abundantia, copia, *f.*; (wealth) divitiae, *f. pl.*

affluent, *a.* abundans, affluens; (rich) dives.

afford, *v.t.* praebeo, [2]; (yield) reddo, fero, fundo, [3]; (supply) sufficio, [3]; (buy) emo, [3].

affront, *v.t.* irrito, [1]; contumelia afficio, [3]; ~, *n.* contumelia, iniuria, *f.*

afloat, be, *v.i.* navigo, [1], navi vehor, [3].

afoot, *ad.* be ~, parari.

afraid, *a.* timidus, pavidus; **be ~ (of)** timeo, [2]; (much) pertimesco, [2]; expavesco, [3]; **make ~,** terreo, [2]; territo, [1]; **not ~,** impavidus, intrepidus.

afresh, *ad.* de integro, ab integro, iterum, denuo.

after, *pr.* post (*with acc.*); a, de, e, ex (*with abl.*); (one after another) alius ex alio; (following immediately upon) sub; (of degree *or* succession) iuxta; secundum; (in imitation of) ad (*all with acc.*); ~, *ad.* (afterwards) exinde, postea, posterius; post; ~ **all,** tamen; saltem; **a little ~,** paulo post; **the day ~,** postridie; ~, *c.* (when) postquam, posteaquam.

after-ages, *n.* posteritas, *f.*

afternoon, *n.* post meridiem, *nt.*; ~, *a.* postmeridianus, pomeridianus.

afterthought, *n.* posterior cogitatio, *f.*

afterwards, *ad.* post; postea; deinde, deinceps, dehinc.

again, *ad.* iterum, denuo, rursum, rursus; (likewise, in turn) invicem, mutuo, vicissim; contra; (besides) praeterea; **over ~,** ab integro; ~ **and ~,** iterum atque iterum.

against, *pr.* (opposite to), contra; adversus; (denoting attack) in; (by, at) ad, ante (*all with acc.*); **be ~,** adversor, oppugno, [1]; **fight ~,** pugno cum.

age, *n.* aetas, *f.*; (century) saeculum; (time in general) tempus, *nt.*; (old ~) senectus, *f.*; **under ~,** impubis; **of the same ~,** aequaevus.

aged, *a.* aetate provectus; senilis; (of a certain age) natus (*with acc. of* annus), ~ **five,** natus annos quinque.

agent, *n.* actor, *m.*; auctor; (assistant) satelles, *c.*; administer, *m.*

aggrandize, *v.t.* amplifico, [1]; attollo, [3]; augeo, [2].

aggrandizement, *n.* amplificatio, *f.*; incrementum, *nt.*

aggravate, *v.t.* augeo, [2]; exaggero, [1].

aggravation, *n.* exaggeratio, *f.*

aggression, *n.* incursio, *f.*

aggressive, *a.* arma (ultro) inferens; (pugnacious) pugnax.

aggrieved, *a.* **feel ~,** aegre fero, [3].

aghast, *a.* attonitus, consternatus.

agile, *a.* agilis; pernix.

agility, *n.* agilitas; pernicitas, *f.*

agitate, *v.t.* agito, [1]; commoveo, [2]; perturbo, [1]; **~d,** *a.* tumultuosus; turbulentus; (anxious) sollicitus.

agitation, *n.* agitatio; commotio; iactatio, *f.*; *fig.* tumultus, *m.*; trepidatio, *f.*

agitator, *n.* concitator; turbator (populi *or* vulgi), *m.*

ago, *ad.* abhinc; **long ~,** iamdudum; **how long ~?** quamdudum; **some time ~,** pridem.

agog, *ad.* (astonished) attonitus.

agonizing, *a.* crucians.

agony, *n.* dolor, *m.*; cruciatus, *m.*

agree, *v.i.* (be in agreement) congruo, [3]; concordo, [1]; concino, [3]; consentio, [4]; (make a bargain) paciscor, [3]; (be agreeable) placeo, [2]; (assent) annuo, [3]; assentior, [4]; **it is ~d,** constat.

agreeable, *a.* gratus, acceptus; amabilis; **very ~,** pergratus.

agreeably, *ad.* grate, iucunde; suaviter.

agreement, *n.* consensus, *m.*; (covenant) pactum, *nt.*; stipulatio, *f.*; conventum, *nt.*; (bargain) condicio, *f.*; (harmonious arrangement) concinnitas, *f.*; (*fig.* harmony) consensio, *f.*

agricultural, *a.* rusticus.

agriculture, *n.* agri cultura, *f.*; res rustica, *f.*

aground, *ad.*; **run ~,** in terram appello, [3]; (be stranded) eicior,

[3]; **be ~,** (touch bottom) sido, [3].

ah, *i.* ah! eia! vah! vae!

ahead, *ad.* ante, (get ~ of) praetereo, [4].

aid, *n.* auxilium; subsidium, *nt.*; **with the ~ of,** opera.

aid, *v.t.* adiuto, iuvo, [1] (*with acc.*); succurro, [3] (*with dat.*); subvenio, [4]. (*with dat.*).

aide-de-camp, *n.* optio, *m.*

ailment, *n.* malum, *nt.*; morbus, *m.*; aegritudo, aegrotatio, *f.*

aim, *n.* propositum, *nt.*

aim, *v.t.* intendo; dirigo, tendo, [3]; *fig.* (~ at) affecto; specto, [1]; expeto, [3]; molior, [4].

air, *n.* aer, *m.*, aura, *f.*; (sky) caelum, *nt.*; *fig.* habitus; gestus, *m.*; (appearance) species, *f.*; (tune) numeri, *m. pl.*; modus, *m.*; **in the open ~,** sub divo.

air, *v.t.* sicco, [1]; **~ opinions,** profero, [3].

airy, *a.* aerius; apertus, patens, ventosus; *fig.* levis.

aisle, *n.* ala, *f.*

ajar, *a.* (of doors) semiapertus; semiadapertus.

akin, *a.* cognatus; propinquus; *fig.* finitimus, cognatus.

alacrity, *n.* alacritas, *f.*; studium, *nt.*

alarm, *n.* (signal in war, *etc.*) classicum, *nt.*; (sudden fear) trepidatio, *f.*; tumultus, *m.*

alarm　303　**alloy**

alarm, *v.t.* terreo, [2]; consterno, territo, [1]; **be ~ed**, perturbor, [1].

alarming, *a.* terribilis.

alas, *i.* eheu! heu, hei mihi misero! (alas for the conquered!) vae victis!

alcove, *n.* (corner) angulus, *m.*

alder, *n.* alnus, *f.*

alert, *a.* alacer, promptus, vigil.

alertness, *n.* alacritas, *f.*

alien, *a. & n.* peregrinus; alienigena, *m.*

alienate, *v.t.* alieno; abalieno, [1]; *fig.* averto, [3].

alienation, *n.* abalienatio; alienatio; (estrangement) disiunctio, alienatio, *f.*

alight, *v.i.* descendo, [3]; (from a horse) desilio, [4]; (of birds, *etc.*) insido, [3].

alight, *a.* ardens.

alike, *a.* aequus, par, similis; ~, *ad.* pariter, similiter.

alive, *a.* vivus; *fig.* vividus, alacer; **be ~**, vivo, [3]; supersum.

all, *a.* omnis, cunctus; universus; (whole) totus; (every one in particular) unusquisque; **by ~ means**, quoquomodo; **on ~ sides**, ubique, passim, undique; **~ this while**, usque adhuc; **~ the better**, tanto melius; **~ the more**, eo plus; **it is ~ over with**, actum est de; **it is ~ one to me**, nihil mea interest.

all, *n.* omnia, *nt. pl.*; **at ~**, omnino; **not at ~**, nihil *or* nullus, *etc.*, admodum; **in ~**, in summa.

allay, *v.t.* lenio, [4]; mitigo, [1]; (quench) restinguo, [3]; sedo, [1].

allegation, *n.* affirmatio, *f.*

allege, *v.t.* arguo, [3]; affirmo, [1]; (bring forward) affero, [3].

allegiance, *n.* fides, *f.*

alleviate, *v.t.* levo, allevo, sublevo, [1].

alleviation, *n.* levamen, *nt.*

alley, *n.* (narrow street) angiportus, *m.*; ambulatio, *f.*

alliance, *n.* (by blood) consanguinitas, *f.*; (by marriage) affinitas, *f.*; (of states) foedus, *nt.*; (mutual connection) societas, *f.*

allied, *a.* cognatus; propinquus; (of states) foederatus, socius.

all-mighty, **all-powerful**, *a.* omnipotens

allot, *v.t.* distribuo, [3]; assigno, [1]; tribuo, [3]; do, [1].

allotment, *n.* assignatio, portio, *f.*; pars, *f.*

allow, *v.t.* concedo, permitto, [3]; (permit) patior, sino, [3]; ~ **of**, admitto, [3]; (confess) fateor, confiteor, [2]; ~ **for**, indulgeo, [2] (*with dat.*); **it is ~ed**, licet.

allowable, *a.* licitus, concessus.

allowance, *n.* (daily ration of food) cibarium, *nt.*; **make ~s for**, indulgeo, [2] (*with dat.*).

alloy, *n.* mixtura, *f.*

alloy, *v.t.* misceo, [2]; vitio, [3]; adultero, [1].

allude, *v.i.* (to) attingo, [3]; designo, denoto; specto, [1].

allure, *v.t.* allicio, [3]; allecto, [1].

allurement, *n.* illecebra, *f.*; *fig.* blandimentum, *nt.*; blanditiae, *f. pl.*

alluring, *a.* blandus; ~ly, *ad.* blande.

allusion, *n.* significatio, *f.*

allusive, *a.* obliquus; ~ly, *ad.* oblique.

ally, *n.* socius, *m.*

ally, *v.t.* socio, [1].

almighty, *a.* omnipotens.

almond, *n.* amygdala, *f.*; amygdalum, *nt.*

almost, *ad.* fere, paene, prope; tantum non.

alms, *n.* stips, *f.*

aloft, *ad.* sublime.

alone, *a.* solus; unus; solitarius; ~, *ad.* solum; tantum; **leave ~**, desero, [3]; **let ~**, omitto, mitto, [3].

along, *pr.* secundum, praeter (*with acc.*); ~ **with**, cum (*with abl.*).

aloof, *ad.* procul, longe; **stand ~**, discedo, [3]; removeo (me ab), [2]; non attingo, [3].

aloud, *ad.* clara voce, clare.

alpine, *a.* Alpinus.

already, *ad.* iam.

also, *ad.* etiam; item, quoque, necnon; (moreover) praeterea, porro, insuper.

altar, *n.* ara, *f.* altaria, *nt. pl.*

alter, *v.t.* muto, commuto, vario, novo, [1]; verto, [3]; ~, *v.i.* mutor, commutor, [1] *etc.*

alterable, *a.* mutabilis, commutabilis.

alteration, *n.* mutatio; commutatio, *f.*

altercation, *n.* altercatio, *f.*, iurgium, *nt.*

alternate, *a.* alternus.

alternate, *v.t. & i.* alterno, vario, [1].

alternately, *ad.* in vicem, per vices; alternis.

alternation, *n.* vicissitudo, *f.*; vices, *f. pl.*

alternative, *n.* (condition) condicio, *f.*; (refuge) refugium, *nt.*; **I have no ~**, nihil mihi reliqui est; ~, *a.* alternus.

although, *c.* etsi, tametsi, quamquam, quamvis, licet.

altitude, *n.* altitudo, sublimitas, *f.*

altogether, *ad.* omnino; prorsus; plane, penitus.

always, *ad.* semper; in aeternum.

am, sum, v. **be.**

amain, *ad.* vi, strenue.

amalgamate, *v.t.* misceo, [2]; ~, *v.i.* coeo, [4].

amalgamation, *n.* mixtura, *f.*; (combination) coitus, *m.*

amaranth, *n.* amarantus, *m.*

amass, *v.t.* coacervo, cumulo, [1].

amateur, *a.* (unskilful) rudis, imperitus.

amaze, *v.t.* obstupefacio, [3].

amazed, *a.* attonitus, stupefactus; **be ~**, stupeo, [2]; obstupesco, [3].

amazement *n.* stupor, *m.*

amazing, *a.* mirus, mirabilis, mirandus; **~ly**, *ad.* (ad)mirabiliter.

ambassador, *n.* legatus, *m.*

amber, *n.* sucinum, electrum, *nt.*; **~**, *a.* sucineus.

ambiguity, *n.* ambiguitas, *f.*, ambages, *f. pl.*

ambiguous, *a.* ambiguus, dubius, anceps; **~ly**, *ad.* ambigue.

ambition, *n.* ambitio, *f.*

ambitious, *a.* laudis *or* gloriae cupidus; ambitiosus; **~ly**, *ad.* ambitiose.

amble, *v.i.* tolutim incedo, [3].

amblingly, *ad.* tolutim.

ambrosia, *n.* ambrosia, *f.*

ambrosial, *a.* ambrosius.

ambush, *n.* insidiae, *f. pl.*; **lie in ~**, insidior, [1].

ameliorate, *v.t. & i.* meliorem *or* melius facere; melior *or* melius fio.

amenable, *a.* oboediens, docilis.

amend, *v.t.* emendo, [1]; corrigo, [3]; **~**, *v.i.* proficio, [3].

amendment, *n.* correctio, emendatio, *f.*

amends, *n.* make **~**, expio, [1]; satisfacio, luo, [3]; compenso, [1].

amenity, *n.* amoenitas, *f.*

amiability, *n.* lenitas, humanitas, suavitas, *f.*

amiable, *a.* amabilis, suavis, lenis, humanus.

amiably, *ad.* amabiliter, suaviter, leniter, humaniter.

amicable, *a.* pacatus; benevolus; benignus.

amicably, *ad.* pacate; amice, benevole.

amid(st), *pr.* inter (*with acc.*).

amiss, *ad.* perperam, prave, male; secus.

ammunition, *n.* arma, *nt. pl.*; apparatus bellicus, *m.*

amnesty, *n.* impunitas, venia, oblivio, *f.*

amok, *ad.* run **~**, furo, [3].

among(st), *pr.* inter; apud; ad with *acc.*; **from ~**, e, ex (*with abl.*)

amorous, *a.* amatorius; amore captus.

amount, *n.* summa, *f.*

amount, *v.i.* it **~s to the same thing**, idem est, par est.

amphitheatre, *n.* amphitheatrum, *nt.*

ample, *a.* amplus; copiosus; largus; (enough) satis.

amplification, *n.* amplificatio, *f.*

amplify, *v.t.* dilato; amplifico, [1].

amply, *ad.* ample, abunde, satis.

amputate, *v.t.* amputo; seco, [1].

amputation, *n.* amputatio; sectio, *f.*

amuse, *v.t.* oblecto, delecto, [1]; ~ **oneself**, ludo, [3]; mihi placeo, [2].

amusement, *n.* delectatio, oblectatio, *f.*; delectamentum, oblectamentum, *nt.*; (game) ludus, *m.*

amusing, *a.* festivus; (funny) iocosus.

analyse, *v.t.* enodo, explico, [1].

anarchical, *a. fig.* turbulentus.

anarchist, *n.* civis seditiosus et turbulentus, *m.*

anarchy, *n.* licentia, *f.*

ancestor, *n.* avus, proavus, atavus; auctor, *m.*; ~**s**, *pl.* maiores; priores, *m. pl.*

ancestral, *a.* avitus, proavitus.

ancestry, *n.* prosapia; stirps, *f.*; genus, *nt.*; v. **ancestors**.

anchor, *n.* ancora, *f.*; **weigh ~**, ancoram tollere *or* solvere, [3]; **cast ~**, ancoram iacere; **ride at ~**, in ancoris consistere.

anchor, *v.t. & i.* ancoras iacio, [3]; (of ships) sto, [1].

anchorage, *n.* statio, *f.*

ancient, *a.* antiquus, vetus, vetustus; priscus; (former) pristinus; **from ~ times**, antiquitus; **the ~s**, (fore-fathers, ancestors) veteres, priores, *m. pl.*; (authors) antiqui, *m. pl.*; (abstractly) antiquitas, *f.*

and, *c.* et, ac, atque; -que; necnon.

anecdote, *n.* fabella; narratiuncula, *f.*

anew, *ad.* denuo; ab integro.

anger, *n.* ira, iracundia, bilis, *f.*; furor, *m.*

anger, *v.t.* irrito, exacerbo, [1]; commoveo, [2].

angle, *n.* angulus, *m.*

angler, *n.* piscator, *m.*

angrily, *ad.* iracunde, irate.

angry, *a.* iratus, iracundus; **be ~**, irascor, [3]; suscenseo, [2]; stomachor, [1]; **make ~**, irrito, exacerbo, [1].

anguish, *n.* angor, dolor, *m.*

anguished, *a.* animo fractus.

angular, *a.* angularis; (full of angles) angulosus.

animal, *n.* animal, *nt.*; (wild beast) fera, *f.*; (beast) pecus, *f.*

animate, *v.t.* (give life to) animo; *fig.* hortor; excito, [1]; erigo, [3].

animate, *a.* (living) animans; (of nature) vividus.

animated, *a.* (lively) vividus, alacer.

animation, *n.* alacritas *f.*; ardor; spiritus, *m.*

animosity, *n.* (grudge) simultas, acerbitas, malevolentia, *f.*; odium, *nt.*

ankle(-bone), *n.* talus, *m.*

annals, *n.* annales, fasti, *m. pl.*

annex, *v.t.* annecto, adiungo, suppono, [3]; (seize) rapio, [3].

annihilate, *v.t.* deleo, [2]; exstinguo, everto, [3].

annihilation, *n.* exstinctio; internecio, *f.*; (ruin) excidium, *nt.*

anniversary, *a.* anniversarius; annuus; ~, *n.* festus dies anniversarius, *m.*

annotate, *v.t.* annoto, commentor, [1].

annotation, *n.* annotatio; nota, *f.*

announce, *v.t.* nuntio; (report) renuntio, [1]; (of laws, *etc.*) promulgo, [1].

announcement, *n.* nuntiatio; renuntiatio, *f.*; (news) nuntius, *m.*

annoy, *v.t.* incommodo, [1]; male habeo, [2]; (vex) irrito, [1]; **be ~ed,** stomachor, [1]; offensus sum.

annoyance, *n.* molestia, *f.*; (anger) ira, *f.*

annoying, *a.* molestus, incommodus.

annual, *a.* anniversarius, annuus; **~ly,** *ad.* quotannis.

annul, *v.t.* abrogo, [1]; rescindo, tollo, [3].

annulment, *n.* abolitio, abrogatio, *f.*

anoint, *v.t.* ungo, inungo, perungo, [3].

anointer, *n.* unctor, *m.*

anointing, *n.* unctio, *f.*

anon, *ad.* statim, illico; mox.

anonymous, *a.* **~ly,** *ad.* sine nomine.

another, *a.* alius; **~'s,** alienus; **one ~,** alius alium, inter se.

answer, *v.t.* respondeo, [2]; (in writing) rescribo, [3]; (correspond to) respondeo, [2]; **~ for,** rationem reddo, [3]; praesto, [1].

answer, *n.* responsio, *f.*, responsum, *nt.*; (of an oracle) sors, *f.*; (solution of a problem) explicatio, *f.*

answerable, *a.* (responsible) reus; obnoxius; **be ~,** praesto, [1]; **make ~,** obligo, [1].

answering, *a.* congruens; (echoing) resonus.

ant, *n.* formica, *f.*

antagonism, *n.* adversitas, *f.*; (dislike) inimicitia, *f.*

antagonist, *n.* adversarius, *m.*; adversatrix, *f.*; aemulus, hostis, inimicus, *m.*

antechamber, *n.* vestibulum, *nt.*

antelope, *n.* dorcas, *f.*

anthem, *n.* canticum, *nt.*

anticipate, *v.t.* anticipo, [1]; praesumo, [3]; (forestall) praevenio, [4].

anticipation, *n.* anticipatio; praesumptio, *f.*

antidote, *n.* antidotum, *nt.*; antidotus, *f.*; remedium, *nt.*

antipathy, *n.* odium, fastidium, *nt.*

antiquarian, antiquary, *n.* antiquarius, rerum antiquarum studiosus; rerum antiquarum peritus, *m.*

antiquated, *a.* obsoletus.

antique, *a.* antiquus.

antique, *n.* opus antiqui artificis; monumentum antiquitatis, *nt.*

antiquity, *n.* antiquitas; vetustas, *f.*

antler, *n.* ramus, *m.*

anvil, *n.* incus, *f.*

anxiety, *n.* anxietas; sollicitudo, trepidatio, *f.*

anxious, *a.* anxius; sollicitus; trepidus; **be ~ (to)**, laboro (ut *or* ne), [1]; anxium esse de aliqua re.

anxiously, *ad.* anxie; sollicite; trepide.

any, anybody, *pn.* quisquam, quivis, quilibet; quis (after si, nisi, num, ne); (interrogatively) ecquis; (all) omnis; **any longer**, diutius; **any more**, amplius; **at any time**, unquam.

anyhow, *ad.* quoquomodo.

anything, *pn.* quicquam, quidpiam, quodvis.

anywhere, *ad.* ubilibet, alicubi, ubivis.

apace, *ad.* celeriter; cito, propere.

apart, *ad.* seorsum, separatim; ~ **from**, praeter, extra (*with acc.*); **stand ~**, disto, [1]; **set ~**, sepono, [3].

apartment, *n.* conclave, *nt.*

apathetic, *a.* lentus; socors.

apathy, *n.* stupor, *m.*; ignavia, socordia, lentitudo, *f.*

ape, *n.* simius, *m.*; simia, *f.*; ~, *v.t.* imitor, [1].

aperture, *n.* apertura, *f.*; foramen, *nt.*

apex, *n.* cacumen, *nt.*; apex, *m.*

aphorism, *n.* sententia, *f.*

apiece, *ad.* singuli, ae, a; quisque.

apologize, *v.t.* excuso, [1]; defendo, veniam peto, [3].

apology, *n.* excusatio; defensio; (written treatise) apologia, *f.*; **make an ~ for**, excuso, [1].

appal, *v.t.* exterreo, [2]; percello, [3].

appalling, *a.* horrendus.

apparatus, *n.* apparatus, *m.*

apparel, *n.* vestis, *f.*, vestitus, *m.*

apparent, *a.* manifestus; (feigned) simulatus, fictus; **be ~**, appareo, [2].

apparently, *ad.* (plainly) aperte, manifeste; (pretendedly) per speciem; **he is ~ dead**, mortuus esse videtur.

apparition, *n.* spectrum, simulacrum, *nt.*

appeal, *v.i.* appello; provoco; obsecro, [1].

appeal, *n.* (law) appellatio; provocatio; (entreaty) obsecratio, *f.*

appealing, *a.* (pleading) supplex; (charming) lepidus.

appear, *v.i.* appareo, compareo, [2]; se ostendere, [3]; (seem) videor, [2]; (arise) exorior, [4]; surgo, [3]; (before a court) me sisto, [3]; **it ~s**, patet, liquet.

appearance, *n.* (becoming visible) aspectus, *m.*; (outward show) species, f.; (vision) spectrum, nt.; (arrival) adventus, m.; **first ~**, exortus, m.; **to all ~s he has been killed,** occisus esse videtur.

appease, v.t. placo, mitigo, expio, (hunger, etc.) sedo, [1].

append, v.t. addo, [3].

appendage, n. appendix; accessio; appendicula, f.

appertain to, v.t. pertineo, ad; attineo, ad [2].

appetite, n. appetitus, m. cupiditas, f.; **have an ~,** esurio, [4].

applaud, v.t. applaudo, [3]; laudo, [1]; plaudo, [3].

applause, n. plausus, applausus, m.; laus, f.

apple, n. malum, pomum, nt.; (of the eye) pupula, pupilla, f.

apple-tree, n. malus, f.

appliance, n. (instrument) instrumentum, nt.

applicable, a. commodus, conveniens; **not be ~,** alienum esse.

applicant, n. petitor, m.

application, n. (use) usus, m.; usurpatio, f.; (zeal) studium, nt., sedulitas, diligentia, cura, f.

apply, v.t. adhibeo; admoveo, [2]; appono, [3]; apto, accommodo, [1]; **~,** v.i. pertineo, [2]; (~ to someone for something) aggredior, [3].

appoint, v.t. creo, [1]; facio, [3]; designo, destino, [1]; constituo, [3].

appointment, n. (office) munus, nt.; (order) mandatum, nt.; (rendezvous) constitutum, nt.

apportion, v.t. divido, distribuo, [3].

apposite, a. aptus, idoneus; appositus; **~ly,** ad. apte; apposite.

appraise, v.t. aestimo, [1].

appraisal, n. aestimatio, f.

appreciable, a. quod aestimari potest.

appreciate, v.t. aestimo, [1]; (value highly) magni facio, [3].

appreciation, n. aestimatio; (praise) laus, f.

apprehend, v.t. comprehendo, apprehendo; percipio, [3]; (fear) timeo, [2]; (suspect) suspicor, [1]; (seize) capio, [3]; (take unawares) intercipio, [3]; (arrest) comprehendo, [3].

apprehension, n. (fear) timor, m.; (suspicion) suspicio; (seizing) comprehensio f.; (understanding) ingenium, nt., intelligentia, n.

apprehensive, a. timidus.

apprentice, n. discipulus; tiro, m.

apprenticeship, n. tirocinium, nt.

approach, v.t. & i. appropinquo, [1]; accedo, [3]; adeo, [4]; (be imminent) immineo, [2]; insto, [1].

approachable, a. patens; fig. affabilis, facilis.

approbation, n. approbatio, laus, f.

appropriate, *v.t.* mihi arrogo, [1]; mihi assero, [3]; vindico, [1]; assumo, [3].

appropriate, *a.* proprius; congruens.

appropriately, *ad.* apte, congruenter.

appropriateness, *n.* convenientia, *f.*

approval, *n.* approbatio, *f.*

approve, *v.t.* approbo, probo, laudo, [1].

approximate, *a.* propinquus.

approximately, *ad.* fere, prope.

appurtenance, *n.* appendix, *f.*

April, *n.* Aprilis, *m.*

apron, *n.* subligaculum, *nt.*

apt, *a.* aptus, idoneus; (inclined, prone) pronus, propensus, proclivis.

aptitude, *n.* habilitas, *f.*; ingenium, *nt.*

aptly, *ad.* apte, apposite.

aptness, *n.* convenientia, congruentia; (tendency, propensity) proclivitas, *f.*

aquatic, *a.* aquatilis; aquaticus.

aqueduct, *n.* aquae ductus, aquarum ductus, *m.*

Arab, *n.* Arabs, *m.*

arable, *a.* arabilis; ~ **land**, *n.* arvum, novale, *nt.*; novalis, *f.*

arbiter, *n.* arbiter; dominus, *m.*

arbitrarily, *ad.* ad arbitrium; ad libidinem.

arbitrary, *a.* imperiosus; superbus.

arbitrate, *v.t. & i.* discepto, [1].

arbitration, *n.* arbitrium, *nt.*

arbitrator, *n.* arbiter; (private) disceptator, *m.*

arbour, *n.* umbraculum, *nt.*

arbute, *n.* (tree) arbutus, *f.*; (fruit) arbutum, *nt.*; ~-**berry**, *n.* arbutum, *nt.*

arc, *n.* arcus, *m.*

arcade, *n.* porticus, *f.*

arch, *n.* arcus, fornix, *m.*

arch, *v.t.* arcuo, [1].

archaeology, *n.* scientia antiquitatis, *f.*

archaic, *a.* obsoletus.

arched, *a.* curvus.

archer, *n.* sagittarius, *m.*

archery, *n.* ars sagittandi, *f.*

archetype, *n.* archetypum, exemplum, *nt.*

architect, *n.* architectus, *m.*; artifex, *m.*

architectural, *a.* architectonicus.

architecture, *n.* architectura, *f.*

archives, *n.* tabulae, *f. pl.*; tabularium, *nt.*

archway, *n.* porticus, *f.*

arctic, *a.* arcticus; Arctous.

ardent, *a.* ardens, fervidus; ~**ly**, *ad.* ardenter.

ardour, *n.* ardor, fervor, *m.*

arduous, *a.* (difficult) arduus; difficilis; ~**ly,** *ad.* difficulter.

area, *n.* area; superficies, *f.*

arena, *n.* arena, *f.*

argonaut, *n.* argonauta, *m.*

argue, *v.t. & i.* disputo, discepto, [1]; dissero, [3]; (prove) arguo, evinco, [3]; probo, [1].

argument, *n.* disceptatio, disputatio, *f.*; (subject) argumentum, *nt.*

argumentative, *a.* (fond of dispute) litigiosus.

arid, *a.* aridus, siccus.

aridity, *n.* ariditas, siccitas, *f.*

aright, *ad.* recte, bene.

arise, *v.i.* surgo, [3]; orior, [4]; (proceed from) nascor, [3].

aristocracy, *n.* optimates, nobiles, *m. pl.*

aristocrat, *n.* optimas, patricius, *m.*

aristocratic, *a.* patricius; ~**ally,** *ad.* more patricio.

arithmetic, *n.* arithmetica, *nt. pl.*

arithmetical, *a.* arithmeticus.

arm, *n.* bracchium, *nt.*; lacertus, *m.*; (weapon) telum, *nt.*; v. **arms.**

arm, *v.t.* armo, [1]; ~, *v.i.* armor, [1]; arma capio, [3]; bellum paro, [1].

armament, *n.* armatura, *f.*; apparatus bellicus, *m.*

armed, *a.* armatus.

armistice, *n.* indutiae, *f. pl.*

armour, *n.* armatura, *f.*; armatus, *m.*; arma, *nt. pl.*; ~-**bearer,** *n.* armiger, *m.*

armoury, *n.* armamentarium, *nt.*

arms, *n.* arma; *fig.* bellum, *nt.*; **lay down** ~, ab armis discedere; arma dedere; **take (up)** ~, sumere arma; **be under** ~, in armis esse.

army, *n.* exercitus, *m.*; (in battle array) acies, *f.*; (on the march) agmen, *nt.*; (forces) copiae, *f. pl.*

aroma, *n.* odor, *m.*

aromatic, *a.* fragrans.

around, *pr. & ad.* circum, circa (*with acc.*); **all** ~, undique.

arouse, *v.t.* suscito, excito, concito, [1]; (produce) cieo, moveo, [2]; conflo, [1]; (encourage) erigo, [3]; ~ **oneself,** expergisci, [3].

arraign, *v.t.* accuso, [1].

arraignment, *n.* accusatio, *f.*

arrange, *v.t.* instruo, struo, (battle) instituo, [3]; ordino, [1]; dispono, [3]; colloco, [1]; (make a plan) constituo, [3].

arrangement, *n.* collocatio, compositio; dispositio; (of battle) ordinatio, *f.*; (plan) consilium, *nt.*

array, *n.* (of battle) acies, *f.*; (clothing) vestitus, *m.*; (arrangement, order) ordo, *m.*; dispositio, compositio, *f.*

array, *v.t.* vestio, [4]; adorno, [1]; compono, instruo, [3].

arrears, *n.* reliqua, *nt. pl.* residuae (of taxes, vectigalium), *f. pl.*; **be in ~,** reliquor, [1].

arrest, *n.* comprehensio, *f.*

arrest, *v.t.* comprehendo, [3]; (detain) detineo, [2]; (stop) sisto, [3].

arrival, *n.* adventus, *m.*

arrive, *v.i.* advenio, pervenio, [4]; (as a ship) advehor, appellor, [3].

arrogance, *n.* arrogantia; superbia, insolentia, *f.*

arrogant, *a.* arrogans; superbus; insolens; **~ly,** *ad.* arroganter, insolenter.

arrow, *n.* sagitta, arundo, *f.*; telum, *nt.*

arsenal, *n.* armamentarium, *nt.*; navalia, *nt. pl.*

arson, *n.* incendium, *nt.*

art, *n.* ars, *f.*; (cunning) artificium, *nt.*; (skill) sollertia, *f.*; **fine ~s,** artes elegantes *or* ingenuae, *pl.*; **black ~,** magice, *f.*

artery, *n.* arteria; vena, *f.*

artful, *a.* callidus, subtilis; subdolus; **~ly,** *ad.* callide, subtiliter, subdole.

artfulness, *n.* artificium *nt.*; calliditas, *f.*

arthritic, *a.* arthriticus.

article, *n.* (item) res; (condition) condicio; pactio; (for sale) merx, *f.*

articulate, *a.* distinctus; dilucidus.

articulate, *v.t.* articulo, enuntio, [1].

artifice, *n.* artificium, *nt.*; ars, *f.*; dolus, *m.*; fraus, *f.*

artificer, *n.* artifex, *m.*; opifex, *c.*

artificial, *a.* artificiosus; facticius; **~ly,** *ad.* arte.

artillery, *n.* tormenta, *nt. pl.*

artisan, *n.* faber, *m.*; artifex, *m.*; opifex, *c.*

artist, *n.* artifex, *m.*

artistic, *a.* artificiosus; **~ally,** *ad.* artificiose; affabre.

artless, *a.* incomptus; incompositus; ingenuus, simplex; **~ly,** *ad.* incompte; ingenue.

artlessness, *n.* simplicitas, *f.*

as, *c. & ad.* (of time) dum, cum; (of manner) ut; quam; ita ut; sicut; velut; **~ far ~,** quoad, usque ad, quantum; **~ for,** de (*with abl.*); **~ if,** quasi, perinde ac si; ita ut si; **~ it were,** ceu, tanquam; **~ long ~,** quamdiu; **~ many ~,** quotquot, quotcunque; **~ much,** tantum; **~ often ~,** quoties; **~ soon ~,** cum primum, simul atque; **~ yet,** adhuc; **not ~ yet,** nondum.

ascend, *v.t. & i.* ascendo, conscendo, scando, [3].

ascension, *n.* ascensio, *f.*; ascensus, *m.*

ascent, *n.* ascensio, *f.*; ascensus, *m.*; acclivitas, *f.*

ascertain, *v.t.* comperio, pro certo scio, [4]; cognosco, [3].

ascribe, *v.t.* imputo, [1]; ascribo, tribuo, [3].

ash, *n.* (tree) fraxinus, *f.*; (cinders) cinis, *m.*; v. **ashes.**

ashamed, *a.* pudibundus; **be ~,** erubesco, [3]; **I am ~ of,** use me pudet, [2] (*with genitive or infinitive*).

ashen, *a.* (of the tree) fraxineus; (pale) pallidus.

ashes, *n.* cinis, *m.*; (hot ~) favilla, *f.*

ashore, *ad.* in terram, ad litus; **be cast ~,** eicior; **go ~,** egredior; **put ~,** expono, [3].

Asian, *a.* Asiaticus, Asius.

aside, *ad.* seorsum, oblique; **call ~,** sevoco, [1]; **lay** or **set ~,** sepono, [3].

asinine, *a.* asininus.

ask for, *v.t.* rogo, [1], posco, peto, quaero, [3]; (a question) interrogo, [1].

askance, *ad.* **look ~,** torva tueor, [2].

askew, *ad.* in obliquum.

aslant, *ad.* oblique, in obliquum.

asleep, *a.* dormiens; **be ~,** dormio, [4]; **fall ~,** obdormio; **lull ~,** sopio, consopio, [4].

aspect, *n.* (what is seen) aspectus; prospectus; (face) vultus, us, *m.*, facies, *f.*

asperity, *n.* acerbitas, *f.*

asphalt, *n.* bitumen, *nt.*

aspiration, *n.* (desire) affectatio, *f.*; (longing) votum, *nt.*

aspire to, *v.t.* affecto, aspiro, [1]; peto, annitor, [3].

aspiring, *a.* appetens (*with genitive*).

ass, *n.* asinus, *m.,* asina, *f.*; (wild ~) onager; **~-driver,** *n.* asinarius, *m.*

assail, *v.t.* aggredior, [3]; oppugno, [1]; invehor, [3].

assassin, *n.* sicarius, *m.*

assassinate, *v.t.* insidiis interficio, [3].

assassination, *n.* caedes, *f.*

assault, *n.* impetus, *m.*; oppugnatio; (violence) vis, *f.*; v. **attack.**

assault, *v.t.* adorior, [4]; oppugno, [1]; manus infero, [3].

assemblage, *n.* congregatio; (multitude) multitudo, *f.*

assemble, *v.t.* congrego, convoco, [1]; contraho, [3]; **~,** *v.i.* convenio, [4].

assembly, *n.* coetus, conventus, *m.*; concilium; (in politics) comitia, *nt. pl.*; contio, *f.*; (small) conventiculum, *nt.*; (of people standing round) corona, *f.*

assembly-room, *n.* curia, *f.*

assent, *v.i.* assentior, [4]; annuo, [3].

assent, *n.* assensus, us, *m.*

assert, *v.t.* affirmo, assevero, [1]; (vindicate) defendo, [3]; tueor, [2].

assertion, *n.* affirmatio, asseveratio; sententia, *f.*

assess, *v.t.* (tax) censeo, [2]; (value) aestimo, [1].

assessment, *n.* census, *m.*; aestimatio, *f.*; (tax) vectigal; tributum, *nt.*

assessor, *n.* (judge) assessor; (of taxes) censor, *m.*

assets, *n.* bona, *nt. pl.*

assiduity, *n.* assiduitas, diligentia, *f.*

assiduous, *a.* assiduus, sedulus; ~ly, *ad.* assidue, sedulo.

assign, *v.t.* attribuo, [3]; delego, assigno, [1]; (determine) statuo, constituo, [3].

assignation, *n.* constitutum, *nt.*

assignment, *n.* assignatio; attributio, *f.*

assimilate, *v.t.* assimulo; (make equal) aequo, [1]; (digest) concoquo, [3].

assimilation, *n.* assimulatio, *f.*

assist, *v.t.* iuvo, adiuvo, auxilior, [1]; succurro, [3], subvenio, [4]. (*both with dat.*)

assistance, *n.* auxilium, *nt.*, opis, *f.*, *gen. sing.*

assistant, *n.* adiutor, *m.*, adiutrix, *f.*, administer, auxiliator, advocatus, *m.*

associate, *v.t.* consocio, [1]; adscisco, [3]; (impute) ascribo; ~, *v.i.* (with) versor cum, [1].

associate, *a.* socius.

associate, *n.* socius, *m.*; consors, *c.*; particeps, *c.*

association, *n.* societas; communitas; consociatio; congrega-tio, *f.*; (corporation) collegium, *nt.*

assuage, *v.t.* allevo, levo, [1]; lenio, [4].

assume, *v.t.* induo; assumo, [3]; (claim) arrogo, [1]; (pretend) simulo, [1]; (take for granted) pono, [3].

assumption, *n.* (the taking for granted) sumptio, *f.*

assurance, *n.* fiducia; (confidence) audacia, (presumptuousness) impudentia, *f.*; (pledge) pignus, *nt.*

assure, *v.t.* confirmo, affirmo, [1]; promitto, [3]; (encourage) adhortor, [1]; **be ~d**, confido, [3].

assuredly, *ad.* profecto, certe.

astern, *ad.* in puppi; a puppi.

asthma, *n.* dyspnoea, *f.*, asthma, *nt.*

asthmatic, *a.* asthmaticus.

astonish, *v.t.* obstupefacio, [3]; **be ~ed**, miror, [1]; obstupesco, [3].

astonishing, *a.* mirabilis, mirandus.

astonishingly, *ad.* admirabiliter.

astonishment, *n.* admiratio, *f.*; stupor, *m.*

astound, *v.t.* (ob)stupefacio, [3].

astray, *a.* **go ~**, erro, [1]; **lead ~**, via recta abducere, transversum agere, [3].

astringent, *a.* astrictorius.

astrologer, *n.* astrologus; mathematicus, *m.*

astrological, *a.* Chaldaicus.

astrology, *n.* astrologia; mathematica, *f.*

astronomer, *n.* astrologus; astronomus, *m.*

astronomical, *a.* astronomicus.

astronomy, *n.* astrologia; astronomia, *f.*

astute, *a.* callidus, astutus, sagax.

astutely, *ad.* callide, astute, sagaciter.

astuteness, *n.* calliditas, sagacitas, *f.*

asunder, *ad.* seorsum, separatim; (in two) dis . . . ; **cut ~,** disseco, [1]; **pull ~,** distraho, [3].

asylum, *n.* asylum, *nt.*

at, *pr.* ad, apud; (during) inter (*all with acc.*); in (*with abl.*); (of time) use *abl.*; (of cost) use *gen.* or *abl.*

athirst, *ad.* sitiens.

athlete, *n.* athleta, *m.*

athletic, *a.* athleticus.

atmosphere, *n.* aër, *m.*; caelum; inane, *nt.*

atom, *n.* atomus, *f.*; corpus individuum, corpus insecabile, *nt.*; *fig.* mica, particula, *f.*; **not an ~ of,** nihil omnino (*with gen.*).

atone, *v.t.* pio; expio, [1]; solvo, luo, [3].

atonement, *n.* piaculum, *nt.* expiatio; compensatio, satisfactio, *f.*

atrocious, *a.* nefarius, nefandus; (monstrous) immanis; (of crimes) dirus; atrox.

atrocity, *n.* atrocitas, *f.*; nefas, facinus, *nt.*

attach, *v.t.* annecto, adiungo, [3]; applico, [1]; (belong to) attineo (*ad.*); **be ~ ed (to),** haereo, adhaereo, [2]; (be fond of) amo, [1].

attachment, *n.* (affection) amor, *m.*, caritas, *f.*

attack, *n.* (onset) impetus, *m.*; oppugnatio, *f.*; incursus, *m.*; *fig.* (of a disease, *etc.*) tentatio, *f.*

attack, *v.t.* (the enemy) aggredior, irruo, [3]; (a town) oppugno; *fig.* provoco, [1]; lacesso, [3]; (verbally) invehor, [3]; (of diseases) corripio, invado, [3]; tento, [1].

attacker, *n.* oppugnator; provocator, *m.*

attain, *v.t.* adipiscor, consequor, [3]; pervenio ad, [4].

attainable, *a.* impetrabilis.

attainment, *n.* comparatio, impetratio, *f.*

attempt, *n.* conatum; inceptum, ausum, periculum, *nt.*; **a first ~,** tirocinium, *nt.*

attempt, *v.t.* conor, [1]; nitor, [3]; molior, [4]; audeo, [2]; tento, [1].

attend, *v.t.* (accompany) comitor, [1]; (escort) deduco, [3]; (be present) intersum, (be present at) adesse (*with dat.*); **~ to,** curo, procuro, [1]; servio, [4]; (comply with) obtempero, invigilo, [1]; (pay attention) animum adverto, [3].

attendance, *n.* (service) obsequium; officium, ministerium, *nt.*; (care) cura, diligentia, *f.*; (retinue) comitatus, *m.*; (presence) praesentia, *f.*

attendant, *n.* comes; assectator, assecla, apparitor; famulus, *m.*; famula, *f.*; **~s,** *pl.* comitatus, *m.*

attention, *n.* animus attentus, *m.*; intentio; sedulitas, *f.*; cultus, *m.*; observantia, *f.*; **pay ~ to,** observo, [1]; operam do, [1]; colo, [3]; studeo, [2].

attentive, *a.* attentus; sedulus; officiosus; **~ ly,** *ad.* attente, intento animo; sedulo; officiose.

attest, *v.t.* testor, testificor, [1].

attire, *n.* ornatus; vestitus, *m.*

attire, *v.t.* adorno, [1]; vestio, [4].

attitude, *n.* (appearance) habitus; status, *m.*; (opinion) sententia, *f.*

attorney, *n.* cognitor, causidicus, advocatus, *m.*

attract, *v.t.* traho, attraho; allicio, [3].

attraction, *n.* illecebra, *f.*; *v.* **charm.**

attractive, *a.* lepidus, blandus.

attractiveness, *n.* lepos, *m.*

attribute, *v.t.* tribuo, attribuo, ascribo, [3]; (falsely) affingo, [3]; imputo, [1].

attribute, *n.* (characteristic) proprium, *nt.*

attrition, *n.* attritus, *m.*

attune, *v.t.* modulor, [1].

auburn, *a.* flavus; aureus.

auction, *n.* auctio, *f.*; **sell by ~,** auctionor, [1]; sub hasta vendo, [3].

auctioneer, *n.* praeco, *m.*

audacious, *a.* audax; confidens; **~ ly,** *ad.* audacter; confidenter.

audacity, *n.* confidentia, audacia, *f.*

audible, *a.* quod audiri potest.

audibly, *ad.* clara voce, ut omnes exaudire possint.

audience, *n.* (admittance) aditus, *m.*; (conversation) colloquium, *nt.*; (hearers) auditores, *m. pl.*; (bystanders) corona, *f.*

audit, *v.t.* rationes inspicio, [3].

auditor, *n.* (hearer) auditor, *m.*

auditorium, *n.* auditorium, *nt.*

auger, *n.* terebra, *f.*

augment, *v.t.* augeo, [2]; amplio, [1]; **~,** *v.i.* (be augmented) augeor, [2]; cresco, accresco, [3].

augmentation, *n.* incrementum, *nt.*

augur, *n.* augur, *c.*; hariolus, haruspex, *m.*

augur, *v.i. & t.* auguror; vaticinor, hariolor, [1].

augury, *n.* augurium, auspicium, *nt.*; auguratio, *f.*

august, *a.* augustus; magnificus.

August, *n.* Sextilis, Augustus, *m.*

aunt, *n.* (on the father's side) amita; (on the mother's side) matertera, *f.*

auspices, *n.* auspicium, *nt.*; **under your ~**, te auspice.

auspicious, *a.* faustus; secundus, prosperus; auspicatus; **~ly**, *ad.* auspicato; feliciter; prospere.

austere, *a.* austerus, severus.

austerity, *n.* austeritas, severitas, *f.*

authentic, *a.* certus; verus; fide dignus.

authentically, *ad.* certo auctore; cum auctoritate.

authenticate, *v.t.* recognosco, [3]; firmo, confirmo, [1].

authentication, *n.* auctoritas; confirmatio, *f.*

authenticity, *n.* auctoritas; fides, *f.*

author, *n.* auctor; scriptor; (inventor) conditor, inventor; (beginner) princeps, *m.*; (of a crime) caput (sceleris), *nt.*

authoritative, *a.* auctoritate firmatus; (imperious) imperiosus.

authority, *n.* auctoritas; potestas; (leave) licentia, *f.*; (power) ius; imperium, *nt.*; (office or official) magistratus, *m.*

authorization, *n.* confirmatio, licentia, *f.*

authorize, *v.t.* potestatem or copiam do, [1]; (excuse) excuso; (approve) probo, [1].

autobiography, *n.* res gestae, *f. pl.*

autocrat, *n.* dominus, *m.*

autograph, *n.* chirographum, *nt.*

autumn, *n.* autumnus, *m.*

autumnal, *n.* autumnalis.

auxiliary, *a.* auxiliaris, auxiliarius; **~**, *n.* adiutor, *m.*; **~ auxiliaries**, *n. pl.* (mil.) auxilia, *nt. pl.*

avail, *v.* **~ oneself of**, utor, [3] (with abl.).

avail, *n.* **be of no ~**, usui non esse.

available, *a.* utilis; efficax; (at hand) praesto (indecl.).

avalanche, *n.* nivis casus, *m.*

avarice, *n.* avaritia, parsimonia, sordes, *f.*

avaricious, *a.* avarus, sordidus; **~ly**, *ad.* avare, sordide.

avenge, *v.t.* vindico, [1]; ulciscor, [3].

avenger, *n.* ultor, *m.*, ultrix, *f.*; vindex, *c.*

avenging, *a.* ultrix, vindex.

avenue, *n.* aditus, introitus; (of trees) xystus, *m.*

average, *n.* medium inter maximum et minimum, *nt.*; aequa distributio, *f.*; **on ~**, peraeque (about) circiter.

average, *a.* medius inter maximum minimumque.

averse, *a.* alienus; aversus, abhorrens; **be ~ to**, abhorreo, [2] (with dat.).

aversion, *n.* odium, fastidium, *nt.*; **~ to**, taedium (with gen.), *nt.*

avert, *v.t.* amoveo, [2]; averto, depello, [3]; (beg off) deprecor, [1].

aviary, *n.* aviarium, *nt.*

avid, *a.* avidus.

avidity, *n.* aviditas, *f.*

avoid, *v.t.* fugio, [3]; (de)vito, [1]; (turn aside, decline) declino, detrecto, [1].

avoidable, *a.* evitabilis, quod effugi potest.

avoidance, *n.* vitatio; declinatio; (flight from) fuga (*with gen.*), *f.*

avow, *v.t.* profiteor, confiteor, [2].

avowal, *n.* professio, confessio, *f.*

avowedly, *ad.* ex professo, aperte.

await, *v.t.* exspecto, [1].

awake, *a.* vigil, vigilans; (sleepless) exsomnis; **be ~**, vigilo, [1].

awake, awaken, *v.t.* excito, suscito, [1]; expergefacio, [3]; **~**, *v.i.* expergiscor, [3].

award, *n.* sententia, *f.*; iudicium, arbitrium, *nt.*

award, *v.t.* adiudico, [1]; addico, tribuo, [3]; assigno, [1].

aware, *a.* gnarus, sciens; **not ~**, ignarus, nescius; **be ~ (of)**, sentio, scio, [4].

awareness, *n.* scientia, *f.*

away, *ad.* procul; **~!**, abi! apage! **be ~**, abesse; **go ~**, abeo, [4]; **take ~**, aufero, tollo, [3].

awe, *n.* reverentia, *f.*; (fear) metus, terror, *m.*; formido, *f.*; **stand in ~**, metuo, [3]; timeo, [2].

awestruck, *a.* pavefactus.

awful, *a.* (awe-inspiring) verendus; (dreadful) formidolosus, terribilis, dirus; **~ly**, *ad.* formidolose.

awhile, *ad.* paulisper.

awkward, *a.* ineptus; rusticus, rudis, inscitus; (things) incommodus; **~ly**, *ad.* inepte; rustice; inscite.

awkwardness, *n.* imperitia, rusticitas, *f.*; (inconvenience) incommoditas, *f.*

awning, *n.* velarium, velum, *nt.*

awry, *a.* obliquus; **~**, *ad.* oblique; perverse; prave, perperam.

axe, *n.* securis, ascia; (battleaxe) bipennis; (pick-axe) dolabra, *f.*

axis, *n.* axis, *m.*

axle, *n.* axis, *m.*

azure, *a.* caeruleus.

B

ba, *v.i.* (like a sheep) balo, [1].

babble, *n.* garrulitas, *f.*

babble, *v.i.* blatero, [1]; garrio, [4].

babbling, *a.* garrulus, loquax.

baby, *n.* infans, parvulus, *m.*

babyhood, *n.* infantia, *f.*

babyish, *a.* puerilis.

Bacchanalia, n. Bacchanalia, nt. pl.

bacchanalian, a. bacchanalis.

Bacchante, n. Baccha, f.

Bacchic, a. Bacchicus.

bachelor, n. caelebs, m.

back, n. tergum, dorsum, nt.; **wound in the ~,** aversum vulnero, [1]; **turn one's ~,** tergum verto, [3].

back, ad. retro; retrorsum; re . . .

back, v.t. (help) adiuvo, [1]; (support) faveo, [2] (with dat.); **~ water,** navem remis inhibere; **~** v.i. me recipio; (back out of) evado, [3].

backbite, v.t. maledico (with dat.), dente carpo, [3].

backbiter, n. maledicus, obtrectator, m.

backbiting, n. obtrectatio, f.

backbone, n. spina, f.

back door, n. posticum ostium, m.

backer, n. adiutor, m.

background, n. scaena, f.; fig. recessus, us, m.; (keep in the background) abscondo, [3].

backing, a. (help) auxilium, (political) suffragium, nt.

backward(s), ad. retro; retrorsum.

backward, a. (lying on the back) supinus; (slow) piger, tardus, segnis; (averse to) alienus; **be ~,** cunctor, [1].

backwardness, n. tarditas; pigritia, f.

bacon, n. lardum, nt.

bad, a. malus, pravus, nequam; improbus; (ill) aeger; (unfortunate) malus, tristis; **~ weather,** tempestas adversa, f.

badge, n. insigne, signum, indicium, nt.

badger, n. meles, melis, f.

badly, ad. male, prave; improbe.

badness, n. nequitia; improbitas, f.

baffle, v.t. decipio, fallo, eludo, [3].

bag, n. saccus; crumena, f.; (of leather) uter, m.; (of netting) reticulum, nt.

baggage, n. sarcinae, f. pl.; impedimenta, nt. pl.

bail, n. vadimonium, f. nt.; (surety) vas (vadis); (for debt) praes, dis, m.

bail, v.t. (give ~ for) spondeo, [2]; fidepromitto, [3]; (accept ~ for) vador, [1].

bailiff, n. (of a farm) vilicus; (of a court of justice) apparitor, m.

bailiwick, n. iurisdictio, f.

bait, n. esca, f.; fig. incitamentum, nt.

bait, v.t. inesco, [1]; (tease) lacesso, [3].

bake, v.t. torreo, [2]; coquo, [3]; igne obduro, [1].

bakery, n. pistrina, f.

baker, n. pistor, m.; **~'s shop,** n. pistrina, f.; pistrinum, nt.

balance, n. (scales) libra, statera, trutina, f.; (equipoise) aequipondium, *nt.*; (in book-keeping) reliquum, *nt.*; **lose one's ~**, labi.

balance, *v.t.* libro, [1], pendo, [3]; (weigh one thing against another) penso, compenso, [1]; (accounts) dispungo, [3].

balcony, *n.* maeniana, *nt. pl.*

bald, *a.* calvus, glaber; *fig.* ieiunus, aridus.

balderdash, *n.* farrago, *f.*

baldness, *n.* calvitium, *nt.*

baldric, *n.* cingulum, *nt.*, balteus, *m.*

bale, *n.* sarcina, *f.*, fascis, *m.*

baleful, *a.* funestus; perniciosus, exitialis, noxius.

balk, *v.t.* (frustrate) frustror, [1]; eludo, decipio, fallo, [3].

ball, *n.* globus, globulus, *m.*; (to play with) pila, *f.*

ballad, *n.* nenia, *f.*; carmen triviale, *nt.*

ballast, *n.* saburra, *f.*

ballet, *n.* pantomimus, *m.*; embolium, *nt.*

ballet-dancer, *n.* pantomimus, *m.*; pantomima, *f.*

ballot, *n.* (token used in voting) tabella, *f.*; (voting) suffragor, *f.*

ballot, *v.i.* tabella or tabellis suffragor, [1].

ballot-box, *n.* cista, *f.*

balm, *n.* balsamum, *f.*; *fig.* solatium, *nt.*

balustrade, *n.* (rails enclosing a place) cancelli, *m. pl.*

ban, *n.* interdictio, *f.*

ban, *v.t.* interdico, [3].

banal, *a.* ieiunus.

band, *n.* (chain) vinculum; (headband) redimiculum, *nt.*; (troop) caterva, *f.*; (chorus) grex, *m.*; *fig.* catena, copula, *f.*; vinculum, *nt.*

band, *v.t.* socio, consocio; **~**, *v.i.* (league together) coniuro, [1].

bandage, *n.* fascia, *f.*

bandage, *v.t.* deligo, [1].

bandit, *n.* latro, *m.*

bandy-legged, *a.* loripes, valgus.

bane, *n.* venenum, *nt.*; pestis; pernicies, *f.*

baneful, *a.* pestifer; perniciosus; funestus; exitialis.

bang, *v.t. & i.* crepo, [1].; (hit) ferio [4].

bang, *n.* crepitus, sonitus, *m.*; (blow) plaga, *f.*; (shock) percussus, *m.*

banish, *v.t.* in exilium mitto, pello, [3]; relego, [1]; *fig.* pono, [3].

banishment, *n.* (act) eiectio; relegatio, *f.*; (state) exilium, *nt.*; fuga, *f.*

bank, *n.* (hillock) tumulus, *m.*; (of a river) ripa, *f.*; (for money) argentaria taberna, *f.*

banker, *n.* argentarius, mensarius, tarpezita, *m.*

bankrupt, *n.* decoctor, *m.*; **be ~ or go ~**, rationes conturbare, [1]; decoquo, [3].

bankruptcy, n. novae tabulae, f. pl.

banner, n. vexillum, nt.

banquet, n. convivium, nt.; epulae, dapes, f. pl.

banquet, v.i. convivor; epulor, [1]: ~, v.t. convivio excipio, [3].

banqueter, n. epulo, conviva, m.

banqueting, n. epulatio, f.

banter, n. iocus, m.; cavillatio, f.

banter, v.t. cavillor, [1]; derideo, [2].

banteringly, a. per ludibrium.

bar, n. vectis; (of a door) obex, m.; repagulum, nt.; pessulus, m.; fig. impedimentum, nt.; (ingot) later, m.; (in a court of justice) cancelli, m. pl.; claustra, nt. pl.; (barristers) advocati, m. pl.; iudiciale, nt.

bar, v.t. (a door, etc.) obsero, [1]; (shut out) excludo, [3]; (prevent) prohibeo, [2]; veto, [1].

barb, n. (hook) uncus; hamus, m.

barbacan, n. turris; specula, f.

barbarian, a. & n. barbarus, m.

barbaric, a. barbaricus.

barbarity, n. barbaries; feritas, truculentia, f.

barbarous, a. barbarus; ferus; immanis; saevus, truculentus; (uncultivated) rudis, barbarus; ~ly, ad. barbare; saeve.

barbed, a. hamatus.

barber, n. tonsor, m., tonstrix, f.; ~'s shop, tonstrina, f.

bard, n. vates, c.

bare, a. (unclothed) nudus; (mere) merus; (of style) pressus; (plain) manifestus; (empty) nudus, vacuus.

bare, v.t. nudo, denudo, [1]; aperio, [4].

barefaced, a. impudens; audax.

barefoot, barefooted, a. nudo pede, nudis pedibus; discalceatus.

bareheaded a. nudo capite.

barely, ad. vix, aegre.

bargain, n. pactio, f., pactum, nt.

bargain, v.i. stipulor, [1]; paciscor, [3].

barge, n. navicula, linter, f.

bargeman, n. portitor, m.

bark, n. (of trees) cortex, c.; (inner bark) liber; (of dogs) latratus, us, m.

bark, (sound) v.i. latro, [1]; ~ at, allatro, [1] (also fig.).

barking, n. latratus, m.

barley, n. hordeum, nt.

barmaid, n. ministra cauponae, f.

barn, n. granarium, horreum, nt.

barque, n. navicula, ratis, linter, f.

barracks, n. castra (stativa), nt. pl.

barrel, n. (cask) cadus, m.; dolium, nt.; orca, f.; (cylinder) cylindrus, m.

barren, a. sterilis; infecundus.

barrenness, *n.* sterilitas, infecunditas, *f.*

barricade, *n.* agger, *m.*; vallum, *nt.*

barricade, *v.t.* obstruo, [3].

barrier, *n.* cancelli, *m. pl.*; saepta, *nt. pl.*; (in the circus) carcer, *m.*; claustra, *nt. pl.*; *fig.* impedimentum, *nt.*

barrister, *n.* advocatus, causidicus, *m.*

barrow, *n.* (vehicle) ferculum, *nt.*; (mound) tumulus, *m.*

barter, *n.* permutatio, *f.*; commercium, *nt.*

barter, *v.t.* & *i.* (per)muto, (com)muto, [1]; paciscor, [3].

base, *a.* humilis, ignobilis, obscurus; inferior; infamis, vilis, turpis; foedus; ~**ly,** *ad.* abiecte; turpiter.

base, *n.* basis, *f.*; fundus, *m.*; fundamentum, *nt.*

baseless, *a.* vanus, inanis; falsus.

baseness, *n.* humilitas; turpitudo; nequitia, *f.*

bashful, *a.* pudens; pudicus, pudibundus, modestus; verecundus; ~**ly,** *ad.* timide; modeste, verecunde; pudenter.

bashfulness, *n.* pudor; rubor, *m.*; verecundia, modestia, *f.*

basin, *n.* (for washing the hands) pelvis, *f.*, trulleus, *m.*; (tub) labrum, *nt.*; (lake) lacus, *m.*; (dock) navalia, *nt. pl.*

basis, *n.* fundamentum, *nt.*; (cause) causa *f.*

bask, *v.i.* apricor, [1].

basket, *n.* corbis, *f.*; canistrum; qualum, *nt.*; calathus, *m.*; (large basket) cophinus, *m.*

bass, *n.* (sound) sonus gravis, *m.*

bastard, *n.* nothus, spurius, *m.*; *fig.* fictus, falsus; ~, *a.* spurius.

baste, *v.t.* perfundo, conspergo, [3].

bastion, *n.* propugnaculum, castellum, *nt.*

bat, *n.* (animal) vespertilio, *m.*; (club) clava, *f.*

batch, *n.* (troop) turma, *f.*; (of things) numerus, *m.*; **in** ~**es,** *ad.* turmatim.

bath, *n.* balneum, *nt.*; lavatio, *f.*; (tub) alveus, *m.*, labrum, *nt.*

bathe, *v.t.* lavo; (steep) macero, [1]; (sprinkle) perfundo, [3]; ~, *v.i.* lavor, [1].

bathing, *n.* lavatio, *f.*

bath-keeper, *n.* balneator, *m.*

battalion, *n.* cohors, *f.*; (army in battle-array) acies, *f.*

batter, *v.t.* verbero, pulso, [1]; percutio, obtundo, diruo, [3]; ferio, [4].

battering-ram, *n.* aries, *m.*

battery, *n.* (mound for artillery) agger, *m.*; (artillery) tormenta, *nt. pl.*; (assault) vis, *f.*

battle, *n.* proelium, *nt.*, pugna, *f.*

battle, *v.i.* proelior, pugno, [1]; (with someone) contendo, [3].

battle-array, *n.* acies, *f.*

battle-axe, *n.* bipennis, *f.*

battlefield, *n.* acies, *f.*; campus, *m.*

battlement, *n.* pinna, *f.*

bauble, *n.* tricae, nugae, *f. pl.*

bawd, *n.* lena, *f.*; leno, *m.*

bawdy, *a.* impudicus, immodestus.

bawl, *v.i.* clamito, vociferor, [1].

bawling, *n.* vociferatio, *f.*; clamor, *m.*

bay, *n.* (of the sea) sinus, *m.*; (tree) laurus, laurea, *f.*; **at ~**, ad pugnam paratus.

bazaar, *n.* forum, *nt.*

be, *v.i.* sum, esse, fui; (exist) existo, [3]; **how are you?** quid agis? **~ against**, adversor, [1]; abhorreo, [2]; **~ amongst or between**, intersum; **~ away**, absum; **~ for** (one), faveo [2]; cum aliquo sto, [1]; **~ in**, inesse; **so ~ it**, ita fiat, esto! **let ~**, mitto, [3]; **~ present**, adsum; **~ without**, careo, [2].

beach, *n.* litus, *nt.*; (coast) ora, *f.*

beacon, *n.* specula, *f.*; (lighthouse) pharus, *m.*; (fire) ignis, *m.*

bead, *n.* globus, globulus, *m.*

beak, *n.* rostrum, *nt.*; (of ships) rostra, *nt. pl.*

beaked, *a.* rostratus.

beaker, *n.* poculum, carchesium, *nt.*

beam, *n.* (wooden) tignum, *nt.*, trabs, *f.*; (of ships) transtrum, *nt.*; (of a balance) scapus; (light) radius, *m.*

beam, *v.i.* radio, [1]; refulgeo, niteo, [2].

beaming, *a.* nitens, lucidus; **~**, *nt.* nitor, *m.*

bear, *v.t.* fero; *fig.* patior; gero, [3]; subeo, [4]; sustineo, [2]; tolero, [1]; (of children) pario, (bring forth) fero, effero, fundo, profundo, [3]; **away or off**, aufero, [3]; **~ out**, effero, [3], *fig.*; praesto, [1]; **~ witness**, testor, [1]; **~ with**, indulgeo, [2] (*with dat.*).

bear, *n.* ursus, *m.*, ursa, *f.*; (constellation) septentriones, *m. pl.*

bearable, *a.* tolerandus, tolerabilis.

beard, *n.* barba; (of corn) arista, *f.*

bearded, *a.* barbatus; intonsus.

beardless, *a.* imberbis.

bearer, *n.* (porter) baiulus; (of litters, *etc.*) lecticarius; (of corpses) vispillo, *m.*

bearing, *n.* (physical) gestus, *m.*; **have a ~ on**, pertinere ad.

beast, *n.* belua; bestia, *f.*; (cattle) pecus, *nt.*; **wild ~**, fera, *f.*; **~ of burden**, iumentum, *nt.*

beat, *v.t.* verbero; (knock) pulso, [1]; caedo, [3]; (conquer) vinco; (bruise) tero, [3]; (excel) supero, [1]; **~ back or off**, repello, [3]; **~**, *v.i.* (of the heart) palpito, [1].

beaten, *a.* victus; (of a path, *etc.*) tritus.

beating, *n.* verberatio, *f.*; (blow) ictus, *m.*; verbera, *nt. pl.*; (of time in music) percussio, *f.*; (of the heart) palpitatio, *f.*

beautiful, *a.* pulcher, chra, chrum; (of form) formosus.

beautifully, *ad.* pulchre.

beautify, *v.t.* decoro, orno, [1]; excolo, [3].

beauty, *n.* pulcritudo; forma; (grace, *etc.*) Venus, *f.*

beaver, *n.* castor, fiber, *m.*; (cheek-piece of a helmet) buccula, *f.*

becalm, *v.t.* paco, sedo, [1]; ~ed, vento destituitus.

because, *c.* quia, quod; ~ of, ob, propter (*with acc.*).

beckon, *v.i.* nuto, [1]; annuo, innuo, [3].

become, *v.i.* fio, *ir.*

becoming, *a.* decorus; decens; conveniens; ~ly, *ad.* decenter; honeste.

bed, *n.* lectus, torus, *m.*; cubile, *nt.*; (in a garden) areola, *f.*; (of a river) alveus, *m.*

bedaub, *v.t.* lino, perunguo, [3]; inquino, conspurco, [1].

bedclothes, bedding, *n.* stragulum, *nt.*; vestis, *f.*

bedeck, *v.t.* decoro, orno, exorno, [1]; excolo, [3].

bedew, *v.t.* irroro, umecto, [1]; perfundo, [3].

bed-fellow, *n.* socius (*m.*) *or* socia (*f.*) tori.

bedpost, *n.* fulcrum, *nt.*

bedridden, *a.* lecto affixus.

bedroom, *n.,* cubiculum, *nt.*

bedstead, *n.* sponda, *f.*

bedtime, *n.* hora somni, *f.*

bee, *n.* apis, *f.*; ~ hive, *n.* alveus, *m.*; apiarium, alvearium, *nt.*; ~, keeper, *n.* apiarius, *m.*

beechen, *a.* faginus, fagineus, fageus.

beech, *n.* fagus, *f.*

beef, *n.* bubula (caro), *f.*

beer, *n.* cervisia, *f.*

beet, *n.* beta, *f.*

beetle, *n.* scarabaeus, *m.*

befall, *v.i.* contingo, accido, [3]; evenio, [4].

befit, *v.t.* convenio, [4]; it ~s, par est, convenit, [4]; decet, [2] (*all with dat.*).

befitting, *a.* decens; conveniens, idoneus.

before, *pr.* ante (*with acc.*); prae, pro; (in the presence of) coram (*with abl.*); apud (*with acc.*); ~, *ad.* ante; antea prius; ~ now, antehac; ~, *c.* antequam, priusquam; long ~, iamdudum; a little ~, paulo ante.

before, *a.* prior.

beforehand, *ad.* ante; prius; prae . . . .

befriend, *v.t.* sublevo, adiuvo, [1], faveo, [2] (*with dat.*).

beg, *v.t. & i.* peto, posco, [3]; oro, precor, obsecro, flagito, rogo, [1]; (be a beggar) mendico, [1].

beget, *v.t.* gigno, [3]; procreo, creo, genero, [1].

beggar, *n.* mendicus, *m.*, mendica, *f.*

beggar, *v.t.* ad inopiam redigo, [3].

beggarly, *a.* mendicus; vilis, abiectus; (wretched) exilis.

beggary, *n.* mendicitas, egestas, paupertas, *f.*

begin, *v.t. & i.* initium facio, [3]; incoho, [1]; ordior, [4]; coepi, incipio, [3]; (arise) exorior, [4].

beginner, *n.* auctor; *fig.* tiro, *m.*

beginning, *n.* inceptio, *f.*; initium; principium, exordium, *nt.*; origo, *f.*

begrudge, *v.t.* invideo (*with acc.* (rem) *and dat.* (alicui)).

beguile, *v.t.* fraudo, frustror, [1]; fallo, [3]; circumvenio, [4].

behalf, *n.* on ~ of, pro (*with abl.*), propter (*with acc.*), causa (*with gen.*).

behave, (conduct) ~ **oneself,** *v.i. & t.* me gero; (towards) utor, [3] (*with abl.*).

behaviour, *n.* mores, *m. pl.*; (actions) facta, *nt. pl.*; **good ~,** urbanitas, *f.*; **bad ~,** rusticitas, *f.*

behead, *v.t.* decollo, [1]; securi percutio, [3].

behind, *ad.* pone, a tergo, post; (remaining) reliquus; **be left ~,** relinquor, [3]; *pr.* post (*with acc.*).

behold, *v.t.* conspicio, [3]; obtueor, [2]; specto, [1]; cerno, [3]; aspicio, [3].

behold, *i.* ecce! en! aspice!

beholden, *a.* obnoxius; **be ~,** obligor, [1]; gratiam debeo, [2].

being, *n.* natura; (essence) essentia, *f.*; (man) homo, *m.*; **supreme ~,** numen, *nt.*

belabour, *v.t.* verbero, pulso, [1].

belated, *a.* serus.

belch, *v.i.* ructo; eructo, [1].

belch, *n.* ructus, *m.*

beleaguer, *v.t.* obsideo, [2].

belief, *n.* fides, opinio, persuasio, religio, *f.*; (teaching) doctrina, *f.*

believe, *v.t.* credo, [3]; (trust to) confido, [3]; (think) existimo, opinor, arbitror, puto, [1]; ~ **in the gods,** deos esse credo, [3].

belittle, *v.t.* rodo, [3].

bell, *n.* tintinnabulum, *nt.*

bellow, *v.i.* rugio, mugio, [4].

bellowing, *n.* mugitus, *m.*

bellows, *n.* (a pair of ~) follis, *m.*

belly, *n.* venter, *m.*; abdomen, *nt.*; alvus, *f.*; stomachus, uterus, *m.*

belong, *v.i.* (to) pertineo ad, [2].

belongings, *n.* bona, *nt. pl.*

beloved, *a.* delectus, carus; amatus.

below, *pr.* infra; subter (*with acc.*); ~, *ad.* infra; deorsum, subter; **from ~,** ab inferiore parte.

belt, *n.* cingulum, *nt.*; zona, *f.*; (sword-belt) balteus, *m.*

bemoan, *v.t.* ingemo, [3]; deploro, [1]; defleo, [2].

bench, *n.* scamnum, sedile, (of the senate) subsellium, *nt.*; (court of justice) subsellia, *nt. pl.*

bend, *v.t.* flecto, [3]; curvo, inclino, [1]; *fig.* domo, [1]; **~ down,** deflecto, [3]; **~,** *v.i.* use pass. of verbs given.

bend, *n.* sinus, flexus, *m.;* curvamen, *nt.; fig.* inclinatio, *f.*

beneath, v. **below; it is ~ me to . . . ,** me indignum est.

benefaction, *n.* largitio, *f.;* beneficium, *nt.*

benefactor, *n.* patronus, *m.*

benefactress, *n.* patrona, *f.*

beneficent, *a.* beneficus, benignus, liberalis.

beneficial, *a.* utilis, commodus, salutaris; **~ly,** *ad.* utiliter.

benefit, *n.* beneficium, *nt.,* gratia, *f.*

benefit, *v.t.* iuvo, [1]; prosum, *u ir. (with dat.);* **~,** *v.i.* lucror, [1].

benevolence, *n.* benevolentia; largitio, *f.*

benevolent, *a.* benevolus; benignus; **~ly,** *ad.* benevole, benigne.

benign, *a.* benignus.

bent, *a.* curvus, flexus; (backwards) recurvus; (forwards) pronus; (inwards) camur; (winding) sinuosus.

bent, *n. fig.* (inclination) ingenium, *nt.;* animus, *m.;* voluntas, *f.*

bequeath, *v.t.* lego, [1]; relinquo, [3].

bequest, *n.* legatum, *nt.*

bereave, *v.t.* (of) orbo, spolio, privo, [1].

bereavement, *n.* orbitas; spoliatio; (loneliness) solitudo, *f.*

bereft (of), *a.* orbus *(with abl.).*

berry, *n.* baca, *f.;* acinus, i, *m.*

berth, *n.* (of ship) statio, *f.;* (sleeping-place) cubiculum, *nt.;* (place, office) munus, *nt.*

beseech, *v.t.* obsecro, imploro, supplico, obtestor, [1].

beset, *v.t.* circumdo, [1]; obsideo; circumsideo; urgeo, [2]; vexo, [1].

beside, besides, *pr.* (in addition to) ad, (outside) extra, (near) iuxta, (except) praeter; (along) secundum *(all with acc.);* **~,** *ad.* porro, praeterea, praeterquam; insuper; **be ~ oneself,** deliro, [1].

besiege, *v.t.* circumsedeo, obsideo, [2].

besieger, *n.* obsessor, *m.*

best, *a.* optimus, praestantissimus; **~ of all,** *ad.* optime, potissimum; **to the ~ of one's ability,** pro viribus.

best, *ad.* optime.

bestir, **~ oneself,** *v.i.* expergiscor, (make an effort) incumbo, [3].

bestow, *v.t.* tribuo, confero, [3]; dono, [1]; largior, [4].

bet, *n.* pignus, *nt.;* sponsio, *f.;* v. **wager.**

bet, *v.t.* pignore contendo, [3].

betoken, *v.t.* indico, [1]; portendo, [3].

betray, *v.t.* trado, prodo, [3], (leave in the lurch) desum *(with* *dat.*); *fig.* (reveal one's presence) oleo, [2] (*with acc.*); (show) profero; (give proof of) arguo, [3].

betrayal, *n.* proditio, *f.*

betrayer, *n.* proditor, *m.*

betroth, *v.t.* spondeo, despondeo, [2].

betrothal, *n.* sponsalia, *nt. pl.*

betrothed, *a. & n.* sponsus, *m.*; sponsa, *f.*

better, *a.* melior, potior, praestantior; superior; **get the ~ (of)**, supero, [1]; vinco, [3]; praevaleo, [2]; **it is ~**, praestat, [1].

better, *ad.* melius, potius; rectius; satius; **get ~**, (in health) convalesco, [3].

better, *v.t.* emendo, [1]; corrigo, [3].

between, *pr.* inter (*with acc.*), in medio (*with gen.*).

beverage, *n.* potio, *f.*, potus, *m.*

bewail, *v.t.* deploro, [1]; ingemo, queror, [3]; lamentor, [1]; defleo, [2].

beware, *v.i. & t.* caveo, praecaveo, [2].; ~! cave, cavete.

bewilder, *v.t.* perturbo, [1]; confundo, [3].

bewilderment, *n.* perturbatio, *f.*

bewitch, *v.t.* fascino, [1]; (charm) demulceo, [2]; capio, [3].

beyond, *pr.* ultra, supra; praeter; (across) trans (*all with acc.*); ~, *ad.* supra, ultra; ulterius.

bias, *n.* inclinatio, *f.*; momentum, *nt.*; impetus, *m.*

bias, *v.t.* inclino, [1].

bicker, *v.i.* altercor, rixor, [1].

bibulous, *a.* bibulus, vinosus.

bickering, *n.* altercatio, rixa, *f.*; iurgium, *nt.*

bid, *v.t.* iubeo, [2]; impero (*with dat.*), mando; (invite) invito, rogo, (money for wares) licitor, [1]; liceor, [2]; ~ **goodbye**, valedico, [3].

bid, *n.* licitatio, *f.*

bidding, *n.* iussum, mandatum, *nt.*; (at the bidding of) iussu (*with gen.*), *f.*; (auction) licitatio, *f.*

bide one's time, *v.i.* exspecto, [1].

bier, *n.* feretrum, *nt.*, sandapila, *f.*

big, *a.* ingens, immanis, vastus, grandis; (in bulk) crassus; *fig.* potens; (with pride) tumidus; **talk ~**, ampullor, [1].

bigamist, *n.* bimaritus, *m.*; bigamus, *m.*

bigoted, *a.* superstitiosus; (obstinate) pervicax.

bigotry, *n.* superstitio, *f.*; (obstinacy) pervicacia, *f.*

bile, *n.* bilis, *f.*

bilge-water, *n.* sentina, *f.*

bilious, *a.* biliosus.

bill, *n.* (of a bird) rostrum, *nt.*; (in writing) libellus, *m.*; (law proposed) rogatio; lex, *f.*; plebiscitum, *nt.*; (account) syngrapha, *f.*

billet, *v.t.* milites per hospitia dispono, [3].

bill-hook, *n.* falx, falcula, *f.*

billow, *n.* fluctus, *m.*

billowy, *a.* fluctuosus, undabundus.

bin, *n.* (in a wine-cellar) loculus, *m.*

bind, *v.t.* ligo, [1]; necto, stringo, [3]; vincio, [4]; *fig.* astringo, [3]; (legibus) obligo, [1]; devincio, [4]; ~ **down**, deligo, [1]; ~ **over**, obligo; vador, [1]; ~ **together**, colligo, [1]; ~ **up**, ligo; alligo, colligo, [1]; substringo, [3]; (be bound up in) *fig.* contineri, [2].

binding, *a.* obligatorius.

binding, *n.* religatio, *f.*; (wrapper) involucrum, *nt.*

biographer, *n.* vitae rerumque gestarum alicuius scriptor, *m.*

biography, *n.* vitae descriptio, *f.*

birch, *n.* betula, *f.*

bird, *n.* avis, volucris, ales, *f.*; (bird of omen) praepes, *f.*; oscen, *m.*

birdcage, *n.* cavea, *f.*

birdcatcher, *n.* auceps, cupis, *m.*

birdcatching, *n.* aucupium, *nt.*

birdlime, *n.* viscum, *nt.*

bird's nest, *n.* nidus, *m.*

birth, *n.* partus; ortus, *m.*; (race) stirps, *f.*, genus, *nt.*, natales, *m. pl.*; give ~, pario, [3].

birthday, *n.* dies natalis, *m.*

birthplace, *n.* solum natale *or* genitale, *nt.*

birthright, *n.* ius ex genere ortum, *nt.*

bit, *n.* (for a horse) frenum; (little piece) frustum, *nt.*, offa, offula, *f.*

bitch, *n.* canis, *f.*

bite, *n.* morsus, *m.*

bite, *v.t.* mordeo, [2]; (as pepper, *etc.*) uro, [3].

biting, *a.* mordax; *fig.* asper.

bitter, *a.* amarus; acerbus; asper; gravis; infensus; ~**ly**, *ad.* amare; acerbe, aspere; graviter; infense.

bitterness, *n.* amaritudo; acerbitas; asperitas, gravitas, *f.*

bitumen, *n.* bitumen, *nt.*

bivouac, *n.* excubiae, *f. pl.*

bivouac, *v.i.* excubo, [1].

black, *a.* niger; ater; *fig.* (gloomy) tristis; scelestus, improbus; ~ **and blue**, lividus; ~ **eye**, sugillatio, *f.*

black, *n.* nigrum, *nt.*; **dressed in** ~, pullatus.

blackberry, *n.* morum, *nt.*; ~ **bush**, rubus, *m.*

blackbird, *n.* merula, *f.*

blacken, *v.t.* nigro; denigro (also *fig.*), [1].

blacking, *n.* atramentum, *nt.*

blackish, *a.* subniger.

blackness, *n.* nigritia, nigrities, nigritudo, *f.*

Black Sea, *n.* Pontus, *m.*

blacksmith, *n.* ferrarius faber, *m.*

bladder, *n.* vesica, *f.*

blade, *n.* lamina, *f.;* (of grass, *etc.*) caulis, *m.;* herba, *f.;* culmus, *m.;* (of an oar) palma, palmula, *f.*

blame, *v.t.* reprehendo, [3]; culpo, vitupero, [1].

blame, *n.* reprehensio; culpa, *f.*

blameless, *a.* integer, innoxius; innocens, innocuus; irreprehensus; ~ly, *ad.* integre, innocenter.

blamelessness, *n.* integritas; innocentia, *f.*

blanch, *v.i.* expallesco, [3]; palleo, [2]; pallesco, [3].

bland, *a.* blandus.

blandishment, *n.* blanditiae, *f. pl.,* blandimentum; (charm) lenocinium, *nt.*

blank, *a.* (empty) vacuus; (unwritten on) purus; **look** ~, confundor, [3].

blank, *n.* inane, *nt.;* res vana, *f.*

blanket, *n.* stragulum, *nt.;* lodix, *m.*

blare, *v.i.* clango [3].

blare, *n.* sonus, strepitus, *m.*

blast, *n.* (of wind) flatus, *m.;* flamen, *nt.;* flabra, *nt. pl.;* (blight) sideratio, rubigo, *f.;* (sound) clangor, *m.*

blaze, *n.* flamma, *f.;* fulgor, *m.;* incendium, *nt.*

blaze, *v.i.* flagro, [1]; ardeo, [2]; ardesco, [3].

bleach, *v.t.* candefacio, [3]; *v.i.* albesco, [3].

bleak, *a.* algidus, frigidus; immitis.

bleakness, *n.* algor, *m.;* frigus, *nt.*

blear-eyed, *a.* lippus; **be** ~, lippio, [4].

bleat, *v.i.* (as a sheep) balo, [1].

bleating, *n.* balatus, *m.*

bleed, *v.i.* (of blood) fluo, [3]; (emit blood) sanguinem effundo.

bleeding, *a.* (of wounds) crudus.

bleeding, *n.* (flowing of blood) sanguinis profluvium, *nt.*

blemish, *n.* (flaw) vitium, *nt.,* labes, macula, *f.*

blend, *v.t.* misceo, immisceo, commisceo, [2].

bless, *v.t.* benedico, [3]; (consecrate) consecro, [1]; (with good success) bene verto, [3]; prospero, aspiro, secundo, [1].

blessed, *a.* beatus; pius; (fortunate) felix, fortunatus.

blessing, *n.* benedictio; (good wish) fausta precatio, *f.;* (benefit) beneficium, bonum, munus, *nt.*

blight, *n.* lues; (of corn, *etc.*) robigo, uredo; sideratio, *f.*

blight, *v.t.* uro, [3]; (ruin) deleo, [2]; (frustrate) frustror, [1]; fallo, [3].

blind, *a.* caecus.

blind, *n.* (screen of cloth) velum, *nt.; fig.* praetextum, *nt.*

blind, *v.t.* caeco, occaeco, [1]; (deceive) fallo, [3].

blindness, *n.* caecitas, *f.*; tenebrae, *f. pl.*

blink, *v.i.* coniveo, [2]; nicto, [1].

bliss, *n.* beatitudo, *f.*

blissful, *a.* beatus; **~ly,** *ad.* beate.

blister, *n.* pustula, *f.*

blister, *v.t. & i.* pustulo, [1].

bloated, *a.* sufflatus; inflatus, tumefactus, tumidus; (immense) immanis.

block, *n.* (lump) massa, *f.*

block, *v.t.* **~ up,** obstruo, intercludo, [3].

blockade, *n.* obsidium, *nt.*; obsidio, *f.*; **~,** *v.t.* obsideo, [2].

blockage, *n.* impedimentum, *nt.*

blockhead, *n.* caudex, *m.*

blood, *n.* sanguis, *m.*; (gore) cruor, *m.*; *fig.* (slaughter) caedes; (lineage) natura, *f.*, genus, *nt.*

bloodless, *a.* exsanguis; (without bloodshed) incruentus.

blood-red, *a.* cruentus; sanguineus, sanguinolentus.

bloodshed, *n.* caedes, *f.*

bloodshot, *a.* cruore suffusus.

bloodstained, *a.* cruentus, cruentatus, sanguinolentus.

bloodthirsty, *a.* sanguinarius; sanguinolentus; sanguineus; cruentus.

blood-vessel, *n.* arteria, vena, *f.*

bloody, *a.* sanguineus; sanguinolentus; sanguinarius; cruentus.

bloom, *n.* flos, *m.* (also *fig.*); robur, *nt.*

bloom, *v.i.* floreo, vigeo, [2]; (also *fig.*).

blooming, *a.* florens; floridus; nitidus.

blossom, *n. & v.i.,* v. **bloom.**

blot, *n.* macula, litura; *fig.* labes, *f.*, dedecus, *nt.*

blot, *v.t.* maculo, [1]; **~ out,** deleo, [2]; exstinguo, [3]; (erase) oblittero, [1].

blow, *n.* (stroke) plaga, *f.*, ictus, *m.*; (with the fist) colaphus, *m.*; plaga, *f.*; vulnus, *nt.*; **it came to ~s,** res ad pugnam venit.

blow, *v.i.* flo; (breathe) spiro, [1]; (musical instruments) cano, [3]; (pant) anhelo, [1]; **~,** *v.t.* flo, afflo; (a wind instrument) inflo, [1]; (blow the nose) emungo, [3]; **~ out,** exstinguo, [3].

blue, *a.* caeruleus, caerulus; (dark blue) cyaneus; **~,** *n.* caeruleum, *nt.*

bluff, *a.* (unsophisticated) rusticus; (steep) declivis; (windy) ventosus; (hearty) vehemens.

bluish, *a.* lividus, livens.

blunder, *n.* mendum, erratum, *nt.*; error, *m.*

blunder, *v.i.* offendo, [3]; erro, [1].

blunt, *a.* hebes; obtusus; retusus; *fig.* inurbanus, rusticus; (plain) planus; **~ly,** *ad.* plane, libere.

blunt, *v.t.* hebeto, [1]; obtundo, retundo, [3].

blur, *v.t.* maculo, [1]; (darken) obscuro, [1].

blurt, *v.t.* ~ out, divulgo, vulgo, [1].

blush, *v.i.* erubesco, rubesco, [3]; rubeo, [2].

blush, blushing, *n.* rubor, *m.*

blushing, *a.*, ~ly, *ad.* rubens, erubescens.

boar, *n.* aper; verres, *m.*

board, *n.* (plank) tabula; (table) mensa, *f.*; (food, *etc.*) victus; (playing-table) abacus, alveus lusorius, *m.*; (council, *etc.*) collegium; consilium; *nt.*; on ~, in nave.

board, *v.t.* (cover with boards) contabulo, [1]; (a ship) navem conscendo, [3].

boarder, *n.* convictor; hospes, *m.*

boast, *v.i.* iacto, glorior, [1].

boast, *n.* iactantia, iactatio, gloriatio, vanitas, *f.*

boaster, *n.* iactator, *m.*

boastful, boasting, *a.* gloriosus, vaniloquus.

boat, *n.* linter, scapha, navicula, cumba, *f.*

boat-hook, *n.* contus, *m.*

boatman, *n.* nauta, *m.*; (ferryman) portitor, *m.*

bode, *v.t.* portendo, [3]; praesagio, [4]; praemonstro, [1].

bodiless, *a.* incorporalis; sine corpore.

bodily, *a.* corporeus; corporalis; ~, *ad.* corporaliter.

body, *n.* corpus; (corpse) cadaver, *nt.*; (trunk) truncus, (*mil.*) numerus, *m.*, vis, *f.*; (collection of people) societas; multitudo, *f.*; collegium, *nt.*

bodyguard, *n.* stipatores, satellites, *m. pl.*; cohors praetoria, *f.*

bog, *n.* palus, *f.*

boggy, *a.* paludosus, palustris.

boil, *v.i.* ferveo, [2]; effervesco, [3]; aestuo, exaestuo, [1]; ~, *v.t.* fervefacio; coquo, [3].

boil, *n.* furunculus, *m.*; ulcus, *nt.*

boisterous, *a.* procellosus; violentus; turbidus.

bold, *a.* audax; fortis; impavidus; intrepidus; (free) liber; (rash) temerarius; (impudent) insolens; procax.

boldly, *ad.* audacter; libere; insolenter; fortiter.

boldness, *n.* audacia; fidentia; (of speech) libertas; impudentia; (rashness) temeritas, *f.*

bolster, *n.* pulvinus, *m.*; (of a bed) cervical, *nt.*

bolster up, *v.t.* fulcio, [4].

bolt, *n.* (of a door) pessulus, *m.*; claustrum, *nt.*; obex, *m.*; (dart) iaculum, pilum, *nt.*; (of thunder) fulmen, *nt.*; (rivet) clavus, *m.*

bolt, *v.t.* obsero, [1]; occludo, [3].

bombard, *v.t.* tormentis verbero, [1].

bombastic, *a.* inflatus, tumidus.

bond, *n.* vinculum, *nt.*; nodus, *m.*; copula; catena; (imprisonment) custodia, *f.*; (obligation) necessitas, necessitudo, *f.;* (legal document) syngrapha, *f.*

bondage, *n.* servitus, *f.,* servitium, *nt.;* captivitas, *f.*

bondsman, *n.* servus; addictus, *m.;* verna, *c.*

bone, *n.* os (ossis), *nt.;* (of fish) spina, *f.*

bone, *v.t.* exosso, [1].

boneless, *a.* exos, exossis.

bonfire, *n.* ignes festi, *m. pl.*

bonnet, *n.* mitra, *f.*

bony, *a.* osseus, (thin) macer.

booby, *n.* stultus, *m.*

book, *n.* liber, libellus, *m.;* volumen, *nt.;* codex, *m.*

bookcase, *n.* foruli, *m. pl.*

bookish, *a.* libris deditus.

bookseller, *n.* bibliopola, librarius, *m.;* ~'s shop, taberna (libraria), *f.*

bookshelf, *n.* pluteus, *m.*

bookworm, *n. fig.* be a ~, libris helluor, [1].

boom, *n.* (of a ship) longurius, *m.;* (noise) stridor, *m.*

boom, *v.i.* resono, [1].

boon, *n.* bonum, donum, *nt.;* gratia, *f.*

boor, *n.* rusticus, *m.*

boorish, *a.* agrestis, rusticus; ~ly, *ad.* rustice.

boorishness, *n.* rusticitas, *f.*

boot, *n.* calceus, *m.;* caliga, *f.*

booth, *n.* taberna, *f.,* tabernaculum, *nt.*

booty, *n.* praeda, *f.;* spolia, *nt. pl.;* (stripped from a foe) exuviae, *f. pl.*

border, *n.* (edge) margo, *c.;* (of dress) limbus, *m.;* (boundary) finis, terminus, *m.;* confinium, *nt.*

border, *v.i.* tango, attingo, [3]; circumiaceo, [2]; ~, *v.t.* praetexo, [3].

bordering, *a.* affinis, finitimus.

bore, *v.t.* terebro, perforo; cavo, [1]; *fig.* fatigo, [1].

bore, *n.* (hole) foramen, *nt.;* (tool) terebra, *f.; fig.* importunus, molestus, odiosus, *m.*

boredom, *n.* taedium, *nt.*

boring, *a.* molestus.

born, *a.* natus; genitus; be ~, nascor, gignor, [3]; *fig.* orior, [4]; a ~ soldier, aptus militiae.

borough, *n.* municipium, *nt.*

borrow, *v.t.* mutuor, [1]; mutuum sumo, [3]; *fig.* imitor, [1].

borrowed, *a.* mutuatus, mutuus; alienus.

bosom, *n.* (breast) pectus, *nt.,* sinus, *m.;* gremium, *nt.;* ~ friend, amicus coniunctissimus.

Bosphorus, *n.* Bosphorus, *m.*

boss, *n.* (of a shield) umbo, *m.*

botanist, *n.* herbarius, *m.*

botany, *n.* herbarum scientia, *f.*

botch, *v.t. fig.* male gero, [3].

both, *a.* ambo; (pair) geminus; duo; uterque; ~ ways, bifariam.

both, c. ~ . . . **and**, et . . . et, cum . . . tum; que . . . que.

bother, v.t. vexo, [1].

bother, n. vexatio, sollicitudo, cura, f.

bottle, n. ampulla; (with handles) lagena, f.

bottle, v.t. in ampullas infundo, [3].

bottom, n. fundus, m.; (of a ship) carina, f.; (dregs) faex, f.; (of a mountain) radix, f.; (depth of a thing) profundum, nt.; **at** ~, ad imum (imam) . . . ; **go to the** ~, subsido, resido, [3]; (sink) mergor, [3]; **from top to** ~, funditus, penitus; **get to the** ~ **of**, scrutor, [1].

bottom, a. imus, infimus.

bottomless, a. fundo carens, immensus; profundus.

bough, n. ramus, m., bracchium, nt.

bounce, v.i. resilio, [4]; resulto, [1].

bound, n. finis, terminus, limes, m.; meta, f.; (leap) saltus, m.

bound, v.t. finio, definio, [4]; termino, [1]; (set ~s to) circumscribo, [3]; ~, v.i. salio, exsilio, [4].

boundary, n. finis, terminus, limes, m.; confinium, nt.

boundless, a. infinitus; immensus.

boundlessness, n. infinitas; immensitas, f.

bounteous, bountiful, a. benignus, largus, munificus; ~**ly**, ad. benigne, large, munifice.

bounty, n. largitas; benignitas, munificentia, f.; praemium, munus, nt.

bouquet, n. fasciculus (florum), m.; (of wine) flos, m.

bovine, a. bubulus.

bow, v.t. flecto, [3]; inclino, [1]; (one's head) demitto, [3]; fig. submitto, [3]; ~, v.i. flector, [3]; (yield) cedo, [3].

bow, n. arcus, m.; (of a ship) prora, f.

bowels, n. intestina, viscera, nt. pl.; fig. misericordia, f.

bowl, n. cratera; patera, phiala, f.; (shallow bowl) pelvis, f.

bow-legged, a. valgus.

bowman, n. sagittarius, m.

bowstring, n. nervus, m.

box, n. arca; cista, f.; loculus, m.; capsa, f.; (for letters, etc.) scrinium, nt.; (for ointments, etc.) pyxis, f.; ~ **on the ear**, alapa, f.

box, n. (tree) buxus, f.

box, v.i. pugnis certo, [1].

boxer, n. pugil, m.

boxing-match, n. pugilatio, f.

boy, n. puer; (little ~) puerulus, m.

boyhood, n. pueritia; aetas puerilis, f.

boyish, a. puerilis; ~**ly**, ad. pueriliter.

brace, n. (strap) fascia, f.; copula, f.; (couple) par, nt.

brace oneself, v.i. contendo, [3].

bracelet, *n.* armilla, *f.*, bracchiale, *nt.*

brag, *v.i.* iacto, [1].

braggart, *n.* iactator, *m.*

braggart, *a.* gloriosus.

braid, *n.* limbus, *m.*; (of hair) cincinnus, *m.*

braid, *v.t.* plecto, texo, praetexo, [3].

brain, *n.* cerebrum; (sense) cor, *nt.*; (understanding) mens, *f.*

bramble, *n.* (blackberry-bush) rubus, *m.*; (thicket) rubetum, *nt.*; (thorny bush) sentis, vepris, *m.*

bran, *n.* furfur, *nt.*

branch, *n.* (of a tree) ramus, *m.*; bracchium; (of a river) cornu, *nt.*; (of a pedigree) stemma, *nt.*; *fig.* pars, *f.*

branching, *a.* ramosus; (widespreading) patulus.

brand, *n.* (mark) nota, *f.*; (torch) torris, *m.*; fax, taeda, *f.*

branding-iron, *n.* cauter, *m.*; cauterium, *nt.*

brandish, *v.t.* vibro, libro, corusco, [1].

brand-new, *a.* recentissimus.

brass, *n.* orichalcum, aes, *nt.*

brass, *a.* aēnus, aereus, aēneus, aeratus.

brat, *n.* infans, *c.*

brave, *a.* fortis; strenuus; animosus.

brave, *v.t.* provoco, [1]; lacesso, [3].

bravely, *ad.* fortiter; animose.

bravery, *n.* fortitudo; virtus; magnanimitas, *f.*; (finery) splendor, *m.*

bravo, *i.* eu! euge!

brawl, *v.i.* rixor, iurgo, [1].

brawl, *n.* rixa, *f.*; iurgium, *nt.*

brawler, *n.* rixator; rabula, *m.*

brawny, *a.* lacertosus, torosus.

bray, *v.i.* (of asses) rudo, [3]; (cry out) vociferor, [1].

bray, **braying**, *n.* (noise) strepitus, *m.*

brazen, *a.* (of brass) aēnus, aēneus, aereus, aeratus; *fig.* ~-**faced**, impudens.

brazier, *n.* aerarius, *m.*; (coalpan) foculus, *m.*

breach, *n.* ruptura; ruina; (of a treaty) violatio, *f.*; (falling out) discidium, *nt.*; discordia, *f.*; ~ **of law**, lex violata, *f.*; **commit ~ of duty**, officium neglego, [3].

bread, *n.* panis; *fig.* victus, *m.*

bread-basket, *n.* panarium, *nt.*

bread-making, *n.* panificium, *nt.*

breadth, *n.* latitudo, *f.*

break, *v.t.* frango; rumpo, [3]; *fig.* violo, [1]; ~, *v.i.* frangor, [3]; (cease) desino; ~ **apart**, diffringo, dirumpo, [3]; ~ **down**, demolior, [4]; destruo, [3]; ~ **forth**, erumpo, [3]; ~ **in**, (tame) domo, [1]; subigo, [3]; ~ **into**, irrumpo; invado, [3]; ~ **loose**, eluctor, [1]; ~ **off**, abrumpo; (friendship) dirumpo; (a conference) dirimo; (a conversation) interrumpo, [3]; *v.i.* praefringor; ~ **open**, effringo, [3]; ~ **out**, erumpo; (a calamity, *etc.*) prorumpo, [3]; (a war) exorior, [4]; ~ **through**, perrrumpo, [3]; ~ **up**, frango, effringo, dissolvo; (an army, assembly) dimitto; (ground) fodio, [3]; ~ **with**, dissideo, [2].

break, *n.* intermissio, *f.*; intervallum; (of day) diluculum, *nt.*

breakable, *a.* fragilis.

breakage, *n.* fractura, *f.*

breaker, *n.* (wave) fluctus, *m.*

breakfast, *n.* prandium, ientaculum, *nt.*

breakfast, *v.t.* prandeo, [2]; iento, [1].

break-up, *n.* dissolutio, *f.*

breakwater, *n.* moles, pila, *f.*

breast, *n.* pectus, *nt.*; (of a woman) mamma, papilla, *f.*; (full of milk) uber, *nt.*; *fig.* praecordia, *nt. pl.*, pectus, cor, *nt.*

breastplate, *n.* lorica, *f.*; thorax, *m.*

breath, *n.* halitus, spiritus, flatus, *m.*; anima; (of air) aura, *f.*; take ~, respiro, [1].

breathe, *v.t.* duco, [3]; (pant) anhelo; (whisper) susurro, [1]; ~ **out**, exspiro; (the life) exhalo, [1]; ~, *v.i.* spiro, respiro, [1].

breathing, *n.* respiratio, *f.*

breathing-hole, *n.* spiraculum, spiramen, spiramentum, *nt.*

breathless, *a.* exanimis, exanimus; exanimatus; (panting) anhelus.

bred, *a.* **well** ~, humanus, urbanus.

breeches, *n.* bracae, *f. pl.*

breed, *v.t.* pario, gigno, [3]; genero, creo, [1]; (cause) produco, [3]; (engender) procreo, [1]; (horses, *etc.*) pasco; alo, [3]; nutrio, [4]; (bring up) educo, [1]; alo, [3].

breed, *n.* genus, *nt.*

breeding, *n.* fetura; (education) educatio, *f.*; **good** ~, humanitas, urbanitas, *f.*

breeze, *n.* aura, *f.*

breezy, *a.* ventosus.

brevity, *n.* brevitas, *f.*

brew, *v.t.* coquo, [3]; *fig.* concito, conflo, [1]; ~, *v.i.* excitor, concitor, [1]; **be ~ing**, immineo, [2].

briar, *n.*, *v.* **bramble.**

bribe, *n.* pretium, *nt.*, merces, pecunia, *f.*

bribe, *v.t.* corrumpo, [3].

bribery, *n.* corruptio, corruptela, largitio, *f.*; ambitus, *m.*

brick, *n.* later, *m.*

bricklayer, *n.* caementarius, *m.*

brickmaker, *n.* laterarius, *m.*

brickwork, *n.* latericium, *nt.*

bridal, *a.* nuptialis; ~ **song**, *n.* epithalamium, *nt.*

bridal-chamber, *n.* thalamus, *m.*

bride, *n.* sponsa; nupta, nympha, *f.*

bridegroom, *n.* sponsus; novus maritus, *m.*

bridesmaid, *n.* pronuba, *f.*

bridge, *n.* pons, *m.*; (of instrument *or* nose) iugum, *nt.*

bridge, *v.t.* ~ **over,** flumen ponte iungo, [3].

bridle, *n.* frenum, *nt.* (also *fig.*); habena, *f.*

bridle, *v.t.* freno; *fig.* infreno, refreno, [1]; coerceo, [2].

brief, *a.* brevis, concisus.

briefly, *ad.* breviter; paucis (verbis).

briefness, *n.* brevitas, *f.*

brier, *n.*, v. **bramble.**

brigade, *n.* (of infantry) legio; (of cavalry) turma, *f.*

brigadier, *n.* tribunus militum, *m.*

brigand, *n.* latro, latrunculus, *m.*

bright, *a.* clarus; lucidus, splendidus; nitidus; candidus; (flashing) fulgidus; (smart, clever) argutus, sollers; (cloudless) serenus.

brighten, *v.t.* polio, [4]; ~, *v.i.* lucesco; splendesco; claresco, [3]; (gladden) hilaro, exhilaro, [1].

brightly, *ad.* lucide, clare, splendide, nitide.

brightness, *n.* splendor; nitor; fulgor, *m.*; (of the sun) lumen, *nt.*; *fig.* hilaritas, *f.*; (of intellect) sollertia, *f.*

brilliance, brilliancy, *n.* splendor, *m.*; *fig.* (of style) lumen, *nt.*

brilliant, *a.* splendidus; nitens; nitidus; *fig.* luculentus; praeclarus; (clever) ingeniosus; **be ~,** splendeo, niteo, [2].

brim, *n.* ora, *f.*, margo, *c.*, labrum, *nt.*

brimstone, *n.* sulfur, sulpur, *nt.*

brine, *n.* muria, *f.*, salsamentum; (sea) salum, *nt.*

bring, *v.t.* fero, affero, infero; gero, duco, [3]; porto, [1]; (by carriage, *etc.*) adveho, [3]; ~ **about,** effero, [3]; ~ **back,** refero, reduco, [3]; reporto; *fig.* revoco, [1]; (by force) redigo, [3]; ~ **before,** defero; produco, [3]; ~ **down,** defero; deduco; (by force) deicio, [3]; ~ **forth,** prodo; depromo, [3]; pario; (yield) fero, effero, [3]; ~ **forward,** profero, effero; ago, [3]; ~ **in(to),** infero; inveho; induco; (as income) reddo, [3]; ~ **off,** praesto, [1]; (carry through) perficio, [3]; ~ **on,** affero; adduco; *fig.* obicio, [3]; ~ **out,** effero; produco, [3]; excio, [4]; ~ **over,** perduco, traduco; *fig.* perduco, traho, [3]; concilio, [1]; ~ **to,** adduco; appello, [3]; *fig.* persuadeo, [2]; ~ **together,** confero; (assemble, *etc.*) contraho, [3]; *fig.* concilio, [1]; ~ **up,** subduco, [3]; (children) educo, [1]; (vomit) evomo, [3].

brink, *n.* margo, *c.*

briny, *a.* salsus; subsalsus.

brisk, *a.* alacer, agilis, vividus; laetus; impiger, acer; **~ly,** *ad.* alacriter, acriter, impigre.

briskness, *n.* alacritas, *f.*, vigor, *m.*

bristle, *n.* saeta, *f.*

bristle, *v.i.* horreo, [2]; horresco, [3].

bristly, *a.* saetiger, saetosus; hirsutus.

Britain, *n.* Britannia, *f.*

British, *a.* Britannicus.

brittle, *a.* fragilis, caducus.

brittleness, *n.* fragilitas, *f.*

broach, *v.t.* (a cask) (dolium) relino, [3]; (publish) in medium profero, [3].

broad, *a.* latus, largus, amplus; *fig.* manifestus, apertus.

broadly, *ad.* late.

broadness, *n.* amplitudo, latitudo, *f.*

broken, *a.* fractus; intermissus; dirutus; (off) abruptus; (open) effractus; (in pieces) contusus; (up) dismissus; violatus; (of the heart) vulneratus.

broken-hearted, *a.* abiectus, spe deiectus, afflictus.

broker, *n.* (money-changer) nummularius, *m.*

bronze, *n.* aes, *nt.*

bronze, *a.* aēnus, aēneus, aereus, aeratus.

brooch, *n.* fibula, *f.*

brood, *n.* proles; progenies; suboles; (of chickens) pullities, *f.*

brood, *v.i.* (as a hen) incubo, [1]; *fig. v.t.* (upon) foveo, [2]; agito, [1].

brook, *n.* amniculus, rivulus, *m.*

brook, *v.t.* fero, patior, [3]; tolero, [1].

broom, *n.* scopae, *f. pl.*

broomstick, *n.* scoparum manubrium, *nt.*

broth, *n.* ius, *nt.*

brothel, *n.* lupanar, lustrum, *nt.*

brother, *n.* frater, germanus, *m.*; ~ **-in-law,** *n.* levir, sororis maritus, *m.*

brotherhood, *n.* germanitas; fraternitas, *f.*; *fig.* sodalicium, collegium, *nt.*

brotherly, *a.* fraternus.

brow, *n.* supercilium, *nt.*; frons, *f.*

browbeat, *v.t.* terreo, [2]; deprimo, [3].

brown, *a.* fulvus, fuscus, pullus, spadix; ~, *n.* fulvus color, *m.*

brownish, *a.* subniger, suffuscus.

browse, *v.t.* (graze on) carpo, depasco, [3]; tondeo, [2].

bruise, *v.t.* contundo, [3]; sugillo, [1]; infringo, [3].

bruise, *n.* contusio; sugillatio, *f.*

brush, *n.* scopula, *f.*; (painter's ~) penicillus, *m.*; (bushy tail) muscarium, *nt.*; (fray, skirmish) concursatio, *f.*

brush, *v.t.* verro, [3]; tergeo; detergeo; ~ **away,** amoveo, [2]; ~ **up,** orno, [1]; reficio, [3].

brushwood, *n.* sarmenta, virgulta, ramalia, *nt. pl.*

brusque, *a.* praeceps.

brutal, *a.* ferus; immanis; inhumanus; saevus; furiosus; **~ly**, *ad.* inhumane; saeve.

brutality, *n.* feritas, ferocitas, saevitia; immanitas, *f.*

brute, *n.* bestia, pecus, *f.*

brutish, *a.* ferus; fatuus, stupidus.

bubble, *n.* bulla, *f.*

bubble, *v.i.* bullio, [4]; (gush up) scateo, [2].

buccaneer, *n.* pirata, praedo, *m.*

bucket, *n.* hama, situla, *f.*

buckle, *n.* fibula, *f.*

buckle, *v.t.* fibula necto, [3]; **~ on**, accomodo, [1].

buckler, *n.* parma, *f.*, v. **shield.**

bucolic, *a.* bucolicus, pastoralis, pastorius, rusticus, agrestis.

bud, *n.* gemma, *f.*, germen, *nt.*; (of a flower) calyx; (in grafting) oculus, *m.*

bud, *v.i.* gemmo, germino, [1].

budge, *v.i.* me moveo, [2]; cedo, loco cedo, [3].

buff, *a.* luteus.

buffet, *n.* (blow) alapa, *f.*, colaphus, *m.*

buffet, *v.t.* (strike) ferio, [4].

buffoon, *n.* scurra; sannio, balatro, *m.*; **play the ~**, scurror, [1].

buffoonery, *n.* scurrilitas, *f.*; lascivia, *f.*; iocus, *m.*

bug, *n.* cimex, *m.*

bugle, *n.* bucina, *f.*; cornu, *nt.*

build, *v.t.* aedifico, [1]; struo, construo, exstruo, condo, [3]; fabrico, [1]; (upon) inaedifico, [1]; *fig.* (rely on) nitor, [3] (*with abl.*).

builder, *n.* aedificator; conditor, structor; *fig.* auctor, fabricator, *m.*

building, *n.* (act) aedificatio, exstructio, *f.*; (structure) aedificium, *nt.*

bulb, *n.* bulbus, *m.*

bulge, *v.i.* tumeo, turgeo, [2]; procurro, [3]; **~ out**, tumesco, [3].

bulk, *n.* amplitudo; moles, *f.*

bulky, *a.* crassus; ingens; gravis; onerosus.

bull, *n.* taurus, bos, *m.*; (edict) edictum, *nt.*

bull-dog, *n.* canis molossus, *m.*

bullet, *n.* glans, *f.*

bullock, *n.* taurus castratus; iuvencus, *m.*

bully, *n.* salaco, rixator, *m.*

bully, *v.t.* insulto, [1]; lacesso, [3].

bulrush, *n.* scirpus; iuncus, *m.*

bulwark, *n.* agger, *m.*; propugnaculum, *nt.*; moenia, munimenta, *nt. pl.*; *fig.* praesidium, propugnaculum, *nt.*

bump, *n.* (swelling) tuber, *nt.*; (thump) plaga, *f.*

bump (into), *v.t.* offendo, [3]; pulso, [1].

bumpkin, *n.* rusticus, *m.*

bun, *n.* libum, crustulum, *nt.* placenta, *f.*

bunch, n. (bundle) fasciculus; ~ **of grapes,** racemus, m.

bundle, n. fascis, fasciculus, m.; (pack) sarcina, f.; (of rods) fasces, m. pl.

bundle, v.t. colligo, [1].

bungle, v.t. rem inscite gero, inscite ago, [3]; v.i. erro, [1].

bungler, n. homo rudis; imperitus, m.

buoy, v.t. (up) attollo, [3]; sustineo, [2]; sustento, [1]; fulcio, [4].

buoyancy, n. levitas; fig. hilaritas, f.

buoyant, a. levis; fig. hilaris.

bur, n. lappa, f.

burden, n. onus, nt.; fascis, m.; sarcina, f.

burden, v.t. onero, gravo, [1]; opprimo, [3]; **beast of ~,** iumentum, nt.

burdensone, a. onerosus, gravis, molestus, iniquus.

burglar, n. fur, m.

burglary, n. effractura, f.

burial, n. (act of burying) sepultura, f.; funus, nt.; exsequiae, f. pl.

burial-place, n. locus sepulturae, m.; sepulcrum, nt.

burly, a. corpulentus, robustus, lacertosus.

burn, v.t. uro, [3]; cremo, [1]; (set on fire) incendo, [3]; ~, v.i. flagro, [1]; ardeo, [2]; (with love, etc.) ardeo, [2]; flagro, [1]; caleo, [2]; calesco, [3]; ~ **down,** deuro,

[3]; **be ~t down,** deflagro, [1]; ~ **out,** exuro; (v.i.) exstinguor, [3]; ~ **up,** concremo, [1].

burning, n. ustio, adustio; deflagratio, f. incendium, nt.

burning, a. ardens; fig. fervens.

burnish, v.t. polio, expolio, [4]; levigo, [1].

burrow, n. cuniculus, i, m.; cubile, nt.

burrow, v.i. (dig down) defodio, [3].

burst, v.t. rumpo, dirumpo; (with a noise) displodo, [3]; ~ **forth,** v.i. erumpo, prorumpo, [3]; ~ **into tears,** in lacrimas effundor; ~ **open,** effringo, [3]; dirumpor, [3]; dissilio, [4].

burst, n. (noise) fragor, m.

bury, v.t. sepelio, [4]; humo, [1]; (hide, etc.) abdo, condo; (put into the ground) infodio, defodio, [3].

bush, n. frutex, dumus, sentis, vepres, m.

bushy, a. dumosus; fruticosus; (of hair) hirsutus, horridus.

busily, ad. industrie, sedulo.

business, n. negotium, nt.; (calling, trade) ars; (matter) res; (employment) occupatio, f.; studium; (duty) officium; (work) opus, nt.

bust, n. statua, effigies, f.

bustle, n. festinatio, f.; tumulus, m.

bustle, v.i. (hurry) festino, [1]; (run to and fro) discurro, [3].

bustling, *a.* operosus.

busy, *a.* occupatus; negotiosus; (industrious) strenuus, industrius, navus; (meddling) curiosus, molestus; (active, laborious) operosus.

busybody, *n.* ardelio, *m.*

but, *c. & pr.* sed, ast, at; autem; ceterum; vero, verum; ~ **for,** absque; (except) praeter, nisi; (only) modo, solum, tantum; ~ **if,** sin, sin autem; ~ **if not,** sin aliter, sin minus; ~ **yet,** nihilominus, veruntamen; **I cannot** ~, non possum facere quin (*with subj.*).

butcher, *n.* lanius; *fig.* carnifex, *m.*; ~'**s shop,** *n.* macellum, *nt.*

butcher, *v.t.* caedo, [3]; trucido, [1].

butchery, *n.* caedes, trucidatio, *f.*

butler, *n.* promus, *m.*

butt, *n.* (mark) meta, *f.*; (cask) dolium, *nt.*; *fig.* (laughing-stock) ludibrium, *nt.*

butt, *v.i.* arieto, [1]; **butting,** *a.* petulcus.

butter, *n.* butyrum, *nt.*

butterfly, *n.* papilio, *m.*

buttock, *n.* clunis, *c.*; natis, *f.*

buttress, *v.t.* ulcio, suffulcio, [4].

buxom, *a.* alacer, hilaris, laetus, lascivus, procax; (fat) pinguis.

buy, *v.t.* emo, [3]; mercor, [1]; ~ **back** *or* **off,** redimo, [3]; ~ **up,** emercor, [1]; coemo, [3].

buyer, *n.* emptor, *m.*

buying, *n.* emptio, mercatura, *f.*

buzz, *v.i.* murmuro, susurro, [1]; (in the ear) insusurro, [1].

buzz, buzzing, *n.* bombus, *m.*, murmur, *nt.*; susurrus, *m.*

buzzard, *n.* buteo, *m.*

by, *pr.* (of place) ad, apud; sub; (along) secundum, praeter; (near) propter, iuxta; (of time) sub; (denoting the instrument *or* cause) per; (in oaths) per (*all with acc.*); (of the agent, *e.g.* by a soldier) a, ab (*with abl.*); ~ **oneself,** solus, solum; ~ **and** ~, mox, brevi, postmodo; **go** ~, praetereo, [4].

bygone, *a.* praeteritus; priscus.

by-law, *n.* praescriptum, *nt.*

bystander, *n.* arbiter, *m.*; ~**s,** *pl.* circumstantes, *m. pl.*

byword, *n.* proverbium, *nt.*; *fig.* fabula, *f.*; **be a** ~, ludibrio sum.

....

C

....

cabbage, *n.* brassica, *f.*, caulis, *m.*; crambe, *f.*

cabin, *n.* (hut) tugurium, *nt.*; (small room) cellula, *f.*

cabinet, *n.* conclave; (piece of furniture) scrinium, armarium, *nt.*, cistula, *f.*; (government) summum principis consilium, *nt.*

cable, *n.* ancorale, *nt.*, rudens, *m.*

cackle, *v.i.* strepo, [3]; clango, [3]; (of hens) gracillo, [1]; *fig.* garrio, [4].

cackle, *n.* strepitus, clangor, *m.*; *fig.* gerrae, *f. pl.*

cadaverous, *a.* cadaverosus; (thin) macer.

cadet, *n.* tiro, *m.*

cage, *n.* cavea, *f.*, avarium, *nt.*; (prison) carcer, *m.*; (for large animals) saeptum, *nt.*

cage, *v.t.* includo, [3].

cajole, *v.t.* adulor, [1]; illicio, [3]; blandior, [4].

cajolery, *n.* blanditiae, *f. pl.*; adulatio, *f.*

cake, *n.* placenta, *f.*, libum, *nt.*; (doughy mass) massa, *f.*

cake, *v.i.* concresco, [3].

calamitous, *a.* calamitosus; lacrimosus; funestus; gravis; infelix; ~**ly**, *ad.* calamitose, infeliciter.

calamity, *n.* calamitas; clades, *f.*; malum, *nt.*; res adversa, *f.*

calculate, *v.t. & i.* computo, supputo; aestimo, existimo, [1].

calculated, *a.* aptus, ad rem accommodatus; (intentional) meditatus.

calculation, *n.* computatio, ratio, *f.*, calculus, *m.*; *fig.* ratiocinatio, *f.*

calculator, *n.* abacus, *m.*

calendar, *n.* kalendarium, *nt.*, fasti, *m. pl.*; (diary) ephemeris, *f.*

calf, *n.* vitulus, *m.*; (of the leg) sura, *f.*

calibre, *n. fig.* ingenium, *nt.*, indoles, *f.*

call, *v.t.* voco, [1]; (name) appello, nomino, [1]; ~ **aside**, sevoco, [1]; ~ **away**, avoco, [1]; *fig.* devoco, [1]; ~ **back**, revoco, [1]; ~ **down**, devoco, [1]; ~ **for**, postulo, [1]; flagito; ~ **forth**, evoco, provoco, [1]; *fig.* excieo, [2]; elicio, [3]; ~ **in**, introvoco, [1]; (money) cogo, [3]; ~ **off**, avoco, revoco, [1]; ~ **on**, inclamo, [1]; cieo, [2]; appello, [1]; (visit) viso, [3]; saluto, [1]; ~ **out**, evoco, [1]; (*v.i.*) exclamo, [1]; ~ **to**, advoco, [1]; ~ **to mind**, recordor, [1]; ~ **to witness**, testor, [1]; ~ **together**, convoco, [1]; ~ **up**, excito; suscito, [1]; elicio, [3].

call, *n.* (summons) vocatio; (sound of the voice) vox, *f.*; (shout) clamor, *m.*; (short visit) salutatio, *f.*

caller, *n.* salutator, *m.*

calling, *n.* (summoning) vocatio, *f.*; (profession) studium, *nt.*; ars, *f.*; (bent) impetus, *m.* (rank, position) condicio, *f.*; ~ **in** (of money), coactio, *f.*; ~ **together**, convocatio, *f.*; ~ **upon**, invocatio, *f.*

callous, *a.* callosus; *fig.* (insensible) durus; **become** ~, occallesco; obduresco, [3].

callousness, *n.* duritia, *f.*

calm, *a.* tranquillus, placidus, sedatus, placatus, quietus, serenus.

calm, *n.* tranquillitas, quies, *f.*; (a calm sea) tranquillum, *nt.*

calm, *v.t.* paco, placo, sedo, [1]; mulceo, [2]; tranquillo, [1].

calmly, *ad.* placide, sedate, tranquille.

calmness, *n.* tranquillitas; serenitas, quies, *f.*; **bear with ~,** aequo animo fero, [3].

calumny, *n.* maledictum, *nt.*, criminatio, *f.*

camel, *n.* camelus, *m.*

camp, *n.* castra, *nt. pl.*; **winter ~,** hiberna, *nt. pl.*; **summer ~,** aestiva, *nt. pl.*

camp, *v.i.* castra pono, [3].

camp-follower, *n.* lixa, *m.*

campaign, *n.* expeditio, *f.*; (service) militia, *f.*; stipendium; (war) bellum, *nt.*; *fig.* **one's first ~,** tirocinium, *nt.*

campaign, *v.i.* expeditioni interesse.

can, *n.* hirnea, hirnula, *f.*

can, *v.i.* possum, *ir.*; queo, [4]; **I ~not,** nequeo; nescio, [4].

canal, *n.* fossa, *f.*; canalis, *m.*

cancel, *v.t.* deleo, [2]; rescindo, [3]; abrogo, [1]; tollo, [3].

cancer, *n.* (disease, and sign of the zodiac) cancer, *m.*

candelabrum, *n.* candelabrum, *nt.*

candid, *a.* candidus; apertus; sincerus; **~ly,** *ad.* candide; sincere; sine fraude.

candidate, *n.* candidatus, *m.*

candidateship, *n.* petitio, *f.*

candle, *n.* candela, *f.*

candlelight, *n.* lucerna, *f.*; **study by ~,** lucubro, [1].

candlestick, *n.* candelabrum, *nt.*

candour, *n.* candor, *m.*, sinceritas, *f.*

cane, *n.* canna, arundo, *f.*; baculus, calamus, *m.*; (rod for striking) ferula, *f.*

cane, *v.t.* ferula ferio, [4].

canine, *a.* caninus.

canister, *n.* pyxis, *f.*

canker, *n.* (of plants) robigo, *f.*; *fig.* lues, *f.*; pestis, *f.*

cannibal, *n.* anthropophagus, *m.*

canoe, *n.* linter, *f.*

canopy, *n.* vela; (curtain) aulaea, *nt. pl.*

cantankerous, *a.* difficilis, morosus.

canteen, *n.* caupona, *f.*

canter, *v.i.* curro, [3]; volo, [1]; **~ing,** *a.* quadrupedans.

canter, *n.* cursus incitatus, *m.*

canvas, *n.* linteum, *nt.*; carbasus, *f.* (for sails); (for painters) textile, *nt.*

canvassing, *n.* ambitio, petitio, *f.*; (unlawful) ambitus, *m.*

canvass, *v.t.* ambio; circumeo, [4]; prenso, [1]; (be a candidate) peto, [3].

cap, *n.* pilleus, galerus, *m.*; mitra, *f.*

capability, *n.* facultas, *f.*

capable, *a.* capax; idoneus, potens.

capacious, *a.* capax; amplus.

capaciousness, *n.* capacitas; amplitudo, *f.*; spatium, *n.*

capacity, *n.* (measure) mensura, *f.*; modus, *m.*; (intelligence) ingenium, *nt.*; facultas, *f.*

cape, *n.* (headland) promunturium; (garment) umerale, *nt.*; lacerna, *f.*

caper, *n.* saltus, *m.*, exsultatio, *f.*

caper, *v.i.* tripudio, exsulto, [1].

capital, *a.* (of crimes) capitalis; *fig.* (outstanding) insignis, eximius.

capital, *n.* (chief city) caput; (money) caput, *nt.*, sors, *f.*

Capitol, *n.* Capitolium, *nt.*

capitulate, *v.i.* arma trado, me dedo, [3].

capitulation, *n.* deditio, *f.*

caprice, *n.* libido; inconstantia, *f.*

capricious, *a.* levis, inconstans; mobilis; ventosus; ~ly, ex libidine; inconstanter.

capsize, *v.i.* evertor, [3].

captain, *n.* (of infantry) centurio; (of cavalry) praefectus; (of a merchantship) navicularius, magister, *m.*; (general) dux, imperator, *m.*

captivate, *v.t.* mulceo, [2]; capto, [1]; capio, allicio, [3].

captive, *n.* captivus, *m.*; ~, *a.* captivus.

captivity, *n.* captivitas, *f.*; (confinement) custodia, *f.*; (chains) vincula, *nt. pl.*

captor, *n.* expugnator, *m.*

capture, *n.* captura; expugnatio, *f.*

capture, *v.t.* capio, excipio, [3]; expugno, [1].

carbuncle, *n.* (tumour) carbunculus, furunculus; (precious stone) carbunculus, *m.*

carcass, *n.* cadaver, *nt.*

card, *v.t.* (wool) pecto, carpo, [3]; carmino, [1].

carder, *n.* carminator, *m.*

cardinal, *a.* (chief) praecipuus.

care, *n.* cura, sollicitudo; (heed) cautio; (diligence) diligentia; (anxiety) anxietas; (protection, guardianship) tutela; (management) procuratio; curatio; custodia, *f.*; **take ~**, caveo, [2]; **take ~ of**, curo, [1].

care, *v.i.* curo, [1]; ~ **for**, *v.t.* provideo, [2], invigilo, [1] (*with dat.*); **I don't ~**, non mihi curae est.

career, *n.* curriculum, *nt.*; cursus, decursus, *m.*; (life) vita, *f.*

carefree, *a.* hilarus, hilaris.

careful, *a.* (diligent) diligens; attentus; (cautious) cautus, providus; (of things) accuratus; ~ly, *ad.* caute; diligenter; accurate, exquisite; **be ~!** cave, cavete.

carefulness, *n.* cura; (diligence) diligentia; (caution) cautio, *f.*

careless, *a.* securus; neglegens; imprudens; **~ly,** *ad.* neglegenter; secure; incuriose.

carelessness, *n.* incuria; neglegentia; imprudentia; securitas, *f.*

caress, *n.* blanditiae, *f. pl.*; complexus, *m.*

caress, *v.t.* blandior, [4]; foveo, permulceo, [2]; osculor, [1].

cargo, *n.* onus, *nt.*

carnage, *n.* caedes, strages, trucidatio, *f.*

carnival, *n.* saturnalia, *nt. pl.*; festum, *nt.*

carnivorous, *a.* carnivorus.

carouse, *v.t. & i.* comissor, poto, perbacchor, [1].

carp at, *v.t.* carpo, rodo, [3]; vellico, [1]; mordeo, [2].

carpenter, *n.* faber tignarius, *m.*

carpentry, *n.* ars fabrilis, opera fabrilis, *f.*

carpet, *n.* tapete, *nt.*; stragulum, *nt.*

carping, *n.* cavillatio, *f.*

carriage, *n.* (act of carrying) vectura, *f.*; (vehicle) vehiculum, *nt.*; raeda, *f.*; currus, *m.*; carpentum, *nt.*; *fig.* habitus, gestus, incessus, *m.*

carrion, *n.* cadaver, *nt.*, caro morticina, *f.*

carrot, *n.* pastinaca, *f.*

carry, *v.t.* porto, [1]; fero; gero, [3]; gesto, [1]; (by carriage) veho; (lead) duco, conduco, [3]; ~ away, aufero; aveho; *fig.* rapio, [3]; ~ along, perduco; ago, [3]; ~ back, refero; reveho, [3]; ~ in, importo, [1]; inveho, [3]; ~ off, aufero; rapio; abstraho, [3]; ~ on, (continue) permaneo, [2] (*with* in + *abl.*), perduco, [3]; *fig.* exerceo, [2]; gero, [3]; ~ out, effero, [3]; exporto, [1]; eveho; *fig.* exsequor, [3]; ~ round, circumfero, [3]; ~ together, comporto, [1]; confero, [3]; ~ through, perfero; *fig.* exsequor, [3].

cart, *n.* carrus, *m.*, plaustrum, vehiculum, *nt.*; **put the ~ before the horse,** *fig.* praeposteris consiliis uti, [3].

cart-horse, *n.* caballus, *m.*; iumentum, *nt.*

cartilage, *n.* cartilago, *f.*

cartwright, *n.* faber carpentarius, *m.*

carve, *v.t.* sculpo, exsculpo, [3]; caelo, [1]; incido, [3]; (meat) seco, [1].

carver, *n.* (artist) caelator; (of meat) carptor, scissor, *m.*

carving, *n.* caelatura, *f.*; **~-knife,** *n.* cultellus, *m.*

cascade, *n.* aquae lapsus *or* deiectus, *m.*

case, *n.* (sheath) involucrum, *nt.*, theca; vagina; (matter) res; (in law) causa; (condition, state, *etc.*) condicio, *f.*, status, *m.*, quaestio, *f.*; (event) eventus, *m.*; **it is often the ~,** saepe accidit; **nothing to do with the ~,** nihil ad rem.

cash, *n.* pecunia numerata; (~ down) praesens pecunia, *f.*

cash-book, *n.* codex, *m.*

cask, *n.* cadus, *m.*; dolium, *nt.*

casket, *n.* arca, arcula; pyxis, cista, cistula, *f.*

cast, *v.t.* (throw) iacio; conicio; mitto, [3]; iaculor, iacto, [1]; (metal) fundo, [3]; ~ **away** or **aside**, abicio, reicio, [3]; ~ **down**, deicio; *fig.* affligo; ~ **off**, (the skin) exuo, [3]; *fig.* amoveo [2]; pono, [3]; repudio, [1]; ~ **out**, eicio, expello, [3].

cast, *n.* (throw and distance) iactus; missus, *m.*; (pattern) imago, *f.*

castanet, *n.* crotalum, *nt.*

castaway, *n.* (shipwrecked) naufragus, *m.*

castigate, *v.t.* castigo, [1].

castigation, *n.* castigatio, *f.*

casting, *n.* (of metals) fusura, *f.*; (throwing) iactatura, iactus, *m.*

casting-net, *n.* iaculum, rete iaculum, *nt.*

castle, *n.* castellum, *nt.*; turris, arx, *f.*

castrate, *v.t.* castro, exseco, [1]; excido, [3].

castration, *n.* castratio, castratura, *f.*

casual, *a.* fortuitus; ~**ly**, *ad.* fortuito; temere; (by the way) obiter.

casualty, *n.* casus, *m.*

cat, *n.* feles, *f.*

catacombs, *n.* puticuli, *m. pl.*

catalogue, *n.* index, *m.*; tabula, *f.*

catapult, *n.* catapulta, *f.*

cataract, *n.* cata(r)racta, *f.*, catarractes, *m.*; (disease of the eye) glaucoma, *nt.*

catarrh, *n.* gravedo, *f.*

catastrophe, *n.* exitus, eventus, *m.*; (ruin) pernicies, *f.*; exitium, *nt.*

catastrophic, *a.* damnosus, exitialis.

catch, *v.t.* capio, [3]; capto, [1]; (by surprise) deprehendo; (understand) intellego [3]; comprehendo, [3]; (in a net) illaqueo; (with bait) inesco, [1]; (fire) concipio; (a disease) contraho, [3]; ~ **up**, excipio, [3].

catch, *n.* (prize) captura, *f.*; (of locks, *etc.*) ansa, *f.*

catching, *a.* contagiosus.

category, *n.* categoria, *f.*; (class) genus, *nt.*

cater, *v.i.* obsonor; cibos suppedito, [1].

caterer, *n.* obsonator, *m.*

caterpillar, *n.* eruca, *f.*

cattle, *n.* boves, *m. pl.*

cattle-market, *n.* forum boarium, *nt.*

cauldron, *n.* aēnum, *n.*, lebes, *m.*; cortina, *f.*

cauliflower, *n.* brassica, *f.*

cause, *n.* causa, *f.*; (source) fons, *m.*; origo, *f.*; (matter) res; (reason) ratio; (action at law) actio, lis, *f.*

cause, *v.t.* facio, efficio, [3]; creo, [1]; excito, [1]; moveo, [2]; (induce) suadeo, [2]; adduco, [3].

causeway, *n.* agger viae, *m.*

caustic, *a.* causticus; *fig.* mordax, acerbus.

caution, *n.* cautio; cura; prudentia; (warning) monitio, *f.*

caution, *v.t.* (ad)moneo, [2].

cautious, *a.* cautus, consideratus; circumspectus; providus, prudens; **~ly**, *ad.* caute; pedetem(p)tim.

cavalcade, *n.* pompa equestris, *f.*

cavalier, *n.* eques, *m.*

cavalry, *n.* equitatus, *m.*, equites, *m. pl.*, copiae equestres, *f. pl.*

cave, *n.* specus, *m.*, *f.*, or *nt.*, antrum, *nt.*; caverna, spelunca, *f.*

cavern, *n.* spelunca, caverna, *f.*, antrum, *nt.*; specus, *m.*, *f.*, or *nt.*

cavernous, *a.* cavus.

caw, *v.i.* crocio, [4]; crocito, [1].

cease, *v.t.* desino; omitto; intermitto; **~**, *v.i.* (*with infin.*) mitto, desino; desisto; omitto, [3]; cesso, [1]; (come to an end) desino, desisto, [3]; cesso, [1].

ceaseless, *a.* perpetuus; assiduus; **~ly**, *ad.* perpetuo; assidue; usque; continenter.

cedar, *n.* cedrus, *f.*

cedar, *a.* cedrus.

cede, *v.t.* cedo, dedo, [3]; **~**, *v.i.* cedo, decedo, [3].

ceiling, *n.* lacunar, laquear, *nt.*

celebrate, *v.t.* celebro, laudo, [1]; (solemnize) ago, [3]; agito, celebro, [1].

celebrated, *a.* celeber; nobilis; clarus, praeclarus, illustris.

celebration, *n.* celebratio, *f.*

celebrity, *n.* fama, celebritas, *f.*

celery, *n.* apium, *nt.*

celestial, *a.* caelestis; divinus; **~**, *n.* caeles, *m.*; caelicola, *c.*

cell, *n.* cella, *f.*

cellar, *n.* cella, *f.*, cellarium, *nt.*

cement, *n.* ferrumen, caementum, *nt.*

cement, *v.t.* conglutino; ferrumino, [1]; *fig.* (confirm) firmo, confirmo, [1].

cemetery, *n.* sepulcretum, *nt.*

cenotaph, *n.* tumulus inanis, *m.*; cenotaphium, *nt.*

censer, *n.* turibulum, *nt.*

censor, *n.* censor; (one who blames) reprehensor, castigator, *m.*

censorious, *a.* austerus, severus.

censorship, *n.* censura, *f.*

censure, *n.* vituperatio, censura, reprehensio, *f.*

censure, *v.t.* animadverto, reprehendo, [3]; vitupero, improbo, [1].

census, *n.* census, *m.*

centaur, *n.* centaurus, *m.*

centenary, *a.* centenarius; **~**, *n.* centenarius numerus; centesimus annus, *m.*

centipede, *n.* centipeda, *f.*

central, *a.* medius; **~ly**, *ad.* in medio.

centralize, *v.t.* in unum contra-ho, [3].

centre, *n.* centrum, *nt.*; medius locus, *m.*; (the centre of the line) media acies, *f.*

centurion, *n.* centurio, *m.*

century, *n.* (political division, subdivision of a legion) centuria, *f.*; (number of years) saeculum, *nt.*

ceremonial, *a.* sollemnis; **~ly**, *ad.* rite; sollemniter.

ceremonious, *a.* sollemnis; **~**, *ad.* sollemniter.

ceremony, *n.* caerimonia, *f.*; sollemne, officium, *nt.*; ritus; (pomp) apparatus, *m.*

certain, *a.* certus; compertus; **a ~**, quidam; **for ~**, certe, pro certo; **it is ~**, constat.

certainly, *ad.* certe, certo; profecto.

certainty, *n.* certum, *nt.*, veritas, fides, *f.*

certify, *v.t.* confirmo, affirmo, [1].

cessation, *n.* cessatio; intermissio, *f.*; (end) finis, *c.*

cesspool, *n.* cloaca, *f.*

chafe, *v.* (with the hand) frico, [1]; (make sore) attero, [3]; (vex) vexo, [1].

chaff, *n.* palea, *f.*; acus, *nt.*

chaffinch, *n.* fringilla, *f.*

chagrin, *n.* vexatio, *f.*

chain, *n.* catena, *f.*; vinculum, *nt.*; (ornament) torques, *c.*; *fig.* series, *f.*; (of mountains) iugum, *nt.*

chain, *v.t.* catenis constringo; catenas alicui inicio, [3].

chair, *n.* sella; cathedra, sedes, *f.*; sedile, *nt.*; (sedan) lectica, *f.*

chairman, *n.* (of a club, *etc.*) praeses, *m.*

chalice, *n.* calix, *m.*

chalk, *n.* creta, *f.*

chalk, *v.t.* creta noto, [1]; creta illino, [3]; **~ out**, designo, [1].

chalky, *a.* (chalk-like) cretaceus; (full of chalk) cretosus.

challenge, *n.* provocatio; (law) reiectio, *f.*

challenge, *v.t.* provoco, [1]; lacesso; (law) reicio, [3].

chamber, *n.* cubiculum, conclave, *nt.*; (bedroom) thalamus, *m.*

chambermaid, *n.* ancilla, *f.*

champ, *v.t. & i.* mando, [3]; mordeo, [2].

champion, *n.* propugnator; defensor, *m.*; vindex, *c.*

chance, *n.* (accident) casus, *m.*; fors, fortuna, *fig.* alea; (probability) spes, *f.*; (opportunity) occasio, *f.*; **by ~**, casu, fortuito, forte.

chance, *a.* fortuitus; inexpectatus.

change, *v.t.* muto, commuto; novo, vario; (one's place) demigro, [1]; (money) permuto; **~**, *v.i.* mutor, vario, [1].

change, *n.* mutatio; commutatio; vicissitudo, *f.*; vices, *f. pl.*;

(variety) varietas, *f.*; (small money) nummuli, *m. pl.*

changeable, *a.* mutabilis; inconstans; levis; (of colour) versicolor.

changeableness, *n.* mutabilitas; mobilitas, inconstantia, levitas, volubilitas, *f.*

changeless, *a.* immutabilis, immutatus.

channel, *n.* canalis; (of rivers) alveus, *m.*; (arm of the sea) fretum, *nt.*; *fig.* cursus, *m.*; via, *f.*

chant, *n.* cantus, *m.*

chant, *v.t. & i.* canto, [1].

chaos, *n.* chaos, *nt.*; *fig.* confusio, *f.*

chaotic, *a.* confusus; indigestus.

chapel, *n.* sacellum, sacrarium, *nt.*

chaplet, *n.* sertum, *nt.*; corona, *f.*

chapter, *n.* caput, *nt.*

char, *v.t.* amburo, [3].

charwoman, *n.* operaria, *f.*

character, *n.* mores, *m. pl.*; indoles, *f.*; ingenium, *nt.*; habitus, *m.*; natura; proprietas, *f.*

characteristic, *a.* proprius (*with gen.*); ~ally, *ad.* ex more (tuo, suo, *etc.*).

characteristic, *n.* proprium, *nt.*

characterize, *v.t.* describo, [3].

charcoal, *n.* carbo, *m.*

charge, *v.t.* accuso, [1]; arguo, [1]; criminor, [1]; (attack) adorior, [4]; aggredior, [3]; (burden) onero; (command) impero, [1];

(entrust) committo, credo, [3]; mando, [1]; (exact) exigo, [3]; ~, *v.i.* irruo, invado, [3].

charge, *n.* accusatio, *f.*; crimen, *nt.*; (attack) impetus, incursus, *m.*; (command) mandatum, *nt.*; (trust) cura, custodia, *f.*; (office) munus, *nt.*; (cost) impensa, *f.*; sumptus, *m.*

charger, *n.* (war-horse) equus bellator, sonipes, quadrupedans, *m.*

chariot, *n.* currus, *m.*, curriculum, *nt.*; (for war) essedum, *nt.*

charioteer, *n.* auriga, *m.*

charitable, *a.* benignus, beneficus; *fig.* mitis.

charitably, *ad.* benigne; indulgenter, in meliorem partem.

charity, *n.* (love) caritas; (alms) stips, *f.*; (goodwill) benevolentia, *f.*; (indulgence) indulgentia, venia, *f.*

charlatan, *n.* pharmacopola circumforaneus; *fig.* ostentator, iactator, *m.*

charm, *n.* (incantation) cantus, *m.*; carmen, *nt.*; cantio, *f.*; incantamentum, *nt.*; *fig.* illecebra; gratia, *f.*; (physical charms) venustas, *f.*; veneres, *f. pl.*; (amulet) amuletum, *nt.*

charm, *v.t.* incanto, fascino, canto, [1]; (delight) capio, [3]; delecto, [1].

charming, *a.* venustus, amoenus, lepidus, blandus.

charnel-house, *n.* ossuarium, *nt.*

chart, *n.* tabula, *f.*

charter, *n.* (privilege) licentia, *f.*

charter, *v.t.* conduco, [3].

chase, *v.t.* persequor, [3]; venor, sector, [1]; (drive) pello, ago, [3]; agito, [1].

chase, *n.* (hunting) venatio, *f.*; venatus, *m.*

chasm, *n.* hiatus, *m.*; specus, *m., f.,* or *nt.*

chaste, *a.* castus, pudicus; purus.

chasten, *v.t.* castigo, [1].

chastise, *v.t.* castigo, [1].

chastisement, *n.* castigatio; animadversio, *f.*

chastity, *n.* pudicitia, castitas, *f.*; (modesty) pudor, *m.*

chat, *v.i.* fabulor, [1]; garrio, [4].

chat, *n.* sermo, *m.*; **have a ~,** fabulor, [1]; garrio, [4].

chattel, *n.* bona, *nt. pl.*; res, *f.*

chatter, *v.i.* nugor, [1]; garrio, effutio, [4]; (of the teeth) crepito, [1].

chatter, chattering, *n.* strepitus, *m.*; (idle talk) garrulitas, *f.*; nugae, *f pl.*; (of the teeth) crepitus, *m.*

chatterbox, *n.* lingulaca, *f.*

chattering, *a.* garrulus.

chatty, *a.* garrulus.

cheap, *a.* vilis.

cheaply, *ad.* bene, vili.

cheapness, *n.* vilitas, *f.*

cheat, *v.t.* decipio, fallo, eludo, [3]; fraudo, [1].

cheat, *n.* (act) fraus, ars, *f.*, dolus, *m.*; (person) fraudator, *m.*

check, *v.t.* (restrain) cohibeo, inhibeo, [2]; reprimo, [3]; (stop) retardo, tardo, [1]; (bridle) refreno, [1]; (accounts) dispungo, [3]; (verify) confirmo, probo, [1].

check, *n.* (hindrance) impedimentum, *nt.*; (disadvantage) detrimentum, *nt.*; (delay) mora, *f.*; (verification) probatio, *f.*

cheek, *n.* gena, bucca, *f.*; **~-bone,** *n.* mala, maxilla, *f.*

cheeky, *a.* impudens.

cheer, *v.t.* (gladden) hilaro, exhilaro, [1]; (encourage) hortor, adhortor, [1]; (comfort) solor, [1]; (applaud) plaudo, [3].

cheer, *n.* (shout) clamor, plausus, *m.*; (cheerfulness) hilaritas, *f.*; **be of good ~,** bono animo esse.

cheerful, *a.* hilaris, alacer, laetus, *f.*; **~ly,** *ad.* hilare, laete; (willingly) libenter.

cheerfulness, *n.* alacritas, hilaritas, *f.*

cheering, *n.* acclamatio, *f.*, plausus, *m.*

cheery, *a.*, v. cheerful.

cheese, *n.* caseus, *m.*

chemist, *n.* pharmacopola, *m.*

chequered, *a.* tessellatus, distinctus; varius.

cherish, *v.t.* (nourish) alo, [3]; (treat tenderly) foveo, [2]; *fig.* colo, [3].

cherry, *n.* cerasus, *f.*; cerasum, *nt.*; ~**-tree**, *n.* cerasus, *f.*

chess, *n.* ludus latruncularius; ~**board**, *n.* tabula latruncularia; ~**man**, *n.* latrunculus, calculus, *m.*

chest, *n.* (breast) pectus, *nt.*; (box) cista, arca, capsa, *f.*; (for clothes) vestiarium, *nt.*; (cabinet) scrinium, *nt.*

chestnut, *n.* castanea, *f.*; ~**-tree**, *n.* castanea, *f.*

chew, *v.t.* mando, [3]; manduco, [1]; (the cud) rumino, [1]; *fig.* meditor, [1].

chick, chicken, *n.* pullus (gallinaceus), *m.*

chick-pea, *n.* cicer, *nt.*

chicory, *n.* cichorium, *nt.*; intubus, *m.*

chide, *v.t. & i.* obiurgo, vitupero, [1]; reprehendo, [3]; (sharply) corripio, [3].

chiding, *n.* obiurgatio, reprehensio, *f.*

chief, *a.* primus; praecipuus, summus, supremus.

chief, *n.* princeps, procer, dux, auctor, *m.*; caput, *nt.*

chiefly, *ad.* praecipue, imprimis.

chieftain, *n.* dux, ductor, *m.*

chilblain, *n.* pernio, *m.*

child, *n.* infans, *c.*; puer, filius, *m.*; puella, filia, *f.*; (children) liberi, *m. pl.*; **bear a** ~, parturio, [4]; **with** ~, gravida.

child-bed, *n.* puerperium, *nt.*; **woman in** ~, puerpera, *f.*

childbirth, *n.* partus, *m.*; Lucinae labores, *m. pl.*

childhood, *n.* infantia; pueritia, *f.*; **from** ~, a puero *or* pueris; a parvo.

childish, *a.* puerilis, infans; ~**ly**, *ad.* pueriliter.

childishness, *n.* puerilitas, *f.*

childless, *a.* orbus.

childlike, *a.* puerilis.

chill, *n.* frigus, *nt.*; algor, *m.*; horror, *m.*; (fever) febris, *f.*

chill, *v.t.* refrigero, [1].

chilly, *a.* alsiosus; frigidulus.

chime, *n.* (harmony) concentus, *m.*

chime, *v.i.* (of bells) cano, [3]; ~ **in**, succino, [3].

chimera, *n.* chimaera, *f.*

chimney, *n.* caminus, *m.*

chin, *n.* mentum, *nt.*

china, *n.* murrha, *f.*, murrhina, *nt. pl.*

chine, *n.* tergum, *nt.*, spina, *f.*

chink, *n.* rima, fissura, *f.*; (sound) tinnitus, *m.*

chip, *n.* segmen, *nt.*, assula, *f.*; (for lighting fire) fomes, *m.*; (fragment) fragmentum, fragmen, *nt.*

chip, *v.t.* dolo, dedolo, [1].

chirp, chirrup, *v.i.* (of birds) pipio, [1]; pipilo, [1]; (of crickets) strideo, [2].

chirp, chirping, chirrup, *n.* pipatus, *m.*

chisel, *n.* scalprum, caelum, *nt.*

chisel, *v.t.* scalpo, [3].

chit-chat, *n.* garrulitas, *f.*; nugae, *f. pl.*

chivalrous, *a.* magnanimus, nobilis.

chivalry, *n.* virtus, *f.*, magnanimitas, *f.*

choice, *n.* delectus, *m.*; electio; (power of choosing) optio; (diversity) varietas, *f.*

choice, *a.* electus, exquisitus, praestans, eximius.

choir, *n.* chorus, *m.*

choke, *v.t.* suffoco; strangulo, [1]; fauces elido, [3]; *fig.* praecludo, [3]; ~, *v.i.* suffocor; strangulor, [1].

choler, *n.* ira, bilis, *f.*

cholera, *n.* cholera, *f.*

choose, *v.t.* eligo, deligo, lego, [3]; opto, [1]; ~, *v.i.* (prefer) malo; (be willing) volo, *v. ir.*

chop, *v.t.* abscido, [3]; trunco; ~ off, detrunco, [1]; abscido; ~ up, concido, [3].

chop, *n.* (of meat) ofella, *f.*

chord, *n.* (string) chorda, *f.*, nervus, *m.*

chore, *n.* officium, munus, eris, *nt.*

chorus, *n.* chorus, *m.*; concentus, *m.*

Christ, *n.* Christus, *m.*

Christian, *a.* Christianus.

chronicle, *n.* annales, fasti, *m. pl.*

chronicle, *v.t.* in annales refero, [3].

chronicler, *n.* annalium scriptor, *m.*

chronology, *n.* aetatum ordo, *m.*; ratio temporum, *f.*

chrysalis, *n.* chrysallis, *f.*

chubby, *a.* bucculentus.

chuckle, *v.i.* cachinno, [1].

chum, *n.* contubernalis, *m.*

chunk, *n.* (of food) frustum, *nt.*

churchyard, *n.* caemeterium, sepulcretum, *nt.*

churl, *n.* homo rusticus, homo illiberalis, *m.*

churlish, *a.* inhumanus; agrestis; ~ly, *ad.* inhumaniter.

churlishness, *n.* inhumanitas, rusticitas, *f.*

cinder, *n.* cinis, *m.*; favilla, *f.*

cinnamon, *n.* cinnamum, *nt.*

circle, *n.* circulus, orbis; (whirling motion) gyrus, *m.*; (of people) corona, *f.*; (social meeting) circulus, *m.*

circle, *v.t.* circumdo, [1]; cingo, [3]; ~, *v.i.* (move round) circumvolvor, [3].

circuit, *n.* circuitus; ambitus, *m.*; circumscriptio, *f.*; (of judges) conventus, *m.*; **make a ~,** circumire, [4].

circuitous, *a.* devius.

circular, *a.* orbiculatus, rotundus.

circulate, *v.t.* spargo, differo, [3]; ~, *v.i.* circulor, [1].

circulation, *n.* circumactus, *m.*; **come into ~,** in usum venire.

circumcise, *v.t.* circumcido, [3].

circumcision, *n.* circumcisio, *f.*

circumference, *n.* peripheria, *f.*, circulus, orbis, *m.*

circumlocution, *n.* circumlocutio, *f.*; ambages, *f. pl.*

circumnavigate, *v.t.* circumvehor, [3].

circumstance, *n.* res, *f.*; tempus, *nt.*; condicio, *f.*; status, *m.*; **under these ~s,** cum res ita se habeant.

circus, *n.* circus, *m.*

cistern, *n.* cisterna, *f.*; puteus, *m.*

citadel, *n.* arx, *f.*

citation, *n.* vocatio, prolatio, *f.*

cite, *v.t.* (law) cito, evoco, [1]; (quote) profero, [3].

citizen, *n.* civis, *c.*; (townsman) oppidanus, *m.*

citizenship, *n.* civitas, *f.*

city, *n.* urbs, *f.*

city, *a.* urbanus; urbicus.

civic, *a.* civilis, civicus.

civil, *a.* civilis; (polite) comis, urbanus; **~ly,** *ad.* comiter, urbane.

civilian, *n.* (non-military person) togatus, *m.*

civility, *n.* urbanitas, *f.*

civilization, *n.* cultus, *m.*

civilize, *v.t.* excolo, [3]; expolio, emollio, [4].

clad, *a.* vestitus, indutus, amictus.

claim, *v.t.* postulo; flagito, [1]; exposco, exigo, [3]; (demand for oneself) vindico, [1].

claim, *n.* vindicatio; postulatio, *f.*; postulatum, *nt.*; **legal ~,** vindiciae, *f. pl.*

claimant, *n.* petitor, *m.*

clamber, *v.i.* scando, conscendo, [3].

clammy, *a.* lentus, viscidus.

clamour, *n.* clamor, tumultus, *m.*

clamp, *n.* confibula, *f.*

clan, *n.* gens, *f.*

clandestine, *a.* clandestinus, furtivus.

clang, *n.* clangor, *m.*

clang, *v.i.* clango; strepo, [3].

clap, *v.i.* (hands) plaudo, [3].

clap, *n.* (blow) ictus; (noise) crepitus; (of thunder) fragor; (with the hands) plausus, *m.*

clarify, *v.t.* deliquo, defaeco, [1].

clarity, *n.* claritas, *f.*

clash, *n.* crepitus, *m.*; concursus, *m.*; (opposition) repugnantia, *f.*

clash, *v.i.* crepito, [1]; concurro, [3]; *fig.* confligo, [3]; repugno, [1].

clasp, *n.* fibula, *f.*; (embrace) amplexus, *m.*

clasp, *v.t.* fibulo, [1]; (embrace) amplector; (grasp) comprehendo, [3].

class, *n.* classis, *f.*; ordo, *m.*; genus, *nt.*; (of pupils) classis, *f.*

class, *v.t.* in classes distribuo, [3]; (value) aestimo, [1].

classification, *n.* distributio, *f.*

classify, *v.t.* in classes distribuo, [3].

clatter, *v.i.* crepo, crepito, [1].

clatter, **clattering**, *n.* strepitus, crepitus, *m.*

claw, *n.* unguis, *m.*; ungula, *f.*; (of a crab) bracchium, *nt.*

claw, *v.t.* (scratch) scalpo, [3]; lacero, [1]; ~ away *or* off, diripio, [3].

clay, *n.* argilla; creta, *f.*; lutum, *nt.*

clean, *a.* mundus, purus; nitidus.

clean, *v.t.* mundo, purgo, [1]; (sweep) verro, [3]; (by wiping, brushing *or* rubbing) tergeo, detergeo, [2]; (by washing) abluo, [3].

cleanness, *n.* munditia, *f.*; nitor, *m.*; *fig.* innocentia, *f.*

cleanse, *v.t.* purgo, depurgo, expurgo, purifico, [1].

cleansing, *n.* purgatio, *f.*

clear, *a.* (bright) lucidus, clarus; (of fluids) limpidus; (transparent) liquidus; (clean) purus; (fair) serenus; (of voice) candidus; (manifest) conspicuus, manifestus; (of space) apertus, patens; (of style) lucidus; *fig.* (in the head) sagax; ~ of, (free from) solutus, liber; **keep** ~ **of**, caveo, [2].

clear, *v.t.* purgo, [1]; (acquit) absolvo, [3]; (a doubt) explano; (from) libero; (land, forests) ex-

trico; (exculpate) purgo (de aliqua re), [1]; ~ away, detergeo; amoveo, [2]; (a debt) solvo, [3]; ~ out, emundo, [1]; ~ up, (*v.t.*) enodo; explano, illustro; (*v.i.*) (of the weather) sereno, [1].

clearly, *ad.* clare; (of sounds) liquide; *fig.* dilucide; plane; aperte, haud dubie, manifesto.

clearness, *n.* claritas; (of sky) serenitas, *f.*; *fig.* candor, *m.*

cleft, *n.* rima, fissura, *f.*

clemency, *n.* clementia, mansuetudo, indulgentia, *f.*

clement, *a.* clemens, mitis.

clench, *v.t.* contraho, astringo, [3].

clerk, *n.* (scholar) doctus; (accountant) actuarius; scriba, *m.*

clever, *a.* sollers; dexter; ingeniosus; (knowing) scitus; (quick) versutus; (sly, cunning) callidus, astutus.

cleverly, *ad.* sollerter, perite; ingeniose; scite; astute; callide.

cleverness, *n.* dexteritas, sollertia, astutia, calliditas, *f.*

click, *v.i.* crepito, [1].

client, *n.* cliens, *m.*; (one who consults another) consultor, *m.*

clientele, *n.* clientela, *f.*

cliff, *n.* (sharp rock) cautes, rupes, *f.*, scopulus; (hill) collis, *m.*

climate, *n.* regio, *f.*; aer, *m.*; caelum, *nt.*; **a mild** ~, temperies, *f.*

climb, *v.t. & i.* ascendo, conscendo, scando, enitor, evado, [3].

clinch, *v.t.* (an argument) astringo, [3].

cling, *v.i.* adhaereo, haereo, [2]; amplector, [3]; (remain) maneo, [2].

clinging, *a.* lentus, tenax, sequax.

clink, *v.i.* tinnio, [4].

clink, *n.* tinnitus, *m.*

clip, *v.t.* tondeo, [2]; circumcido, praecido, [3]; amputo, [1].

clipper, *n.* (ship) celox, *f.*

clipping, *n.* tonsura, *f.*

clique, *n.* factio, *f.*

cloak, *n.* pallium, sagum, *nt.*; lacerna, laena, chlamys, *f.*; amictus, *m.*

cloak, *v.t.* pallio vestio, [4]; *fig.* dissimulo, [1]; praetendo, tego, [3].

clock, *n.* horologium, *nt.*

clod, *n.* glaeba, *f.*

clog, *n.* (heavy shoes) sculponeae, *f. pl.*; *fig.* impedimentum, *nt.*; mora, *f.*

clog, *v.t.* impedio, praepedio, [4]; onero, [1].

close, *v.t.* claudo, [3]; operio, [4]; (end) finio, [4]; termino, [1]; ~ **in,** includo, [3]; ~, *v.i.* (come together) coeo, [4]; (end) terminor, [1]; ~ **up,** praecludo, occludo, [3].

close, *a.* (thick) densus; (narrow) angustus; artus; (near to) contiguus; *fig.* taciturnus, tectus; ~

by, vicinus, propinquus; ~ **together,** confertus, continuus.

close, *ad.* dense; (near) prope, proxime.

close, *n.* (end) finis, *c.*; (~ of a speech) peroratio, *f.*; **bring to a** ~, finio, [4]; termino, [1]; **draw to a** ~, terminor, [1].

closeness, *n.* (nearness) proximitas, *f.*

closet, *n.* cella, *f.*, conclave; (for clothes) vestiarium, *nt.*

clot, *v.i.* concresco, [3].

cloth, *n.* pannus, *m.*; (linen) linteum; (for horses) stragulum, *nt.*

clothe, *v.t.* vestio, amicio, [4]; induo, [3]; velo, [1].

clothes, *n.* vestis, *f.*; vestitus, *m.*; vestimenta, *nt. pl.*

clothing, *n.* vestitus, *m.*, vestimenta, *nt. pl.*

cloud, *n.* nubes, nebula, *f.*; nubila, *nt. pl.*

cloudless, *a.* serenus, sudus.

cloudy, *a.* nubilus; (of liquids) turbidus; **grow** ~, nubilo, [1].

cloven, *a.* bisulcus, bifidus.

clover, *n.* trifolium, *nt.*

clown, *n.* (buffoon) scurra, *m.*

club, *n.* (cudgel) clava, *f.* fustis, *m.*; (of people) sodalicium, *nt.*; sodalitas, *f.*; circulus, *m.*

cluck, *v.i.* singultio, [4].

clue, *n.* glomus, *nt.*; (trace, mark) indicium, *nt.*

clump, *n.* massa, *f.*; globus, *m.*; ~ **of bushes,** dumentum, *nt.*

clumsily, *ad.* crasse; rustice; inscite, ineleganter, male.

clumsiness, *n.* rusticitas, *f.*

clumsy, *a.* inhabilis; inelegans; inscitus; rusticus, agrestis.

cluster, *n.* (of grapes, *etc.*) racemus; (of flowers) corymbus, *m.*

cluster, *v.i.* congregor, conglobor, [1].

clutch, *v.t.* arripio, [3].

clutch, *n. fig.* **in one's ~es,** in sua potestate.

coach, *n.* currus, *n.*, raeda, *f.*; pilentum, petoritum, *nt.*

coachman, *n.* raedarius, *m.*, auriga, *c.*

coagulate, *v.i.* concresco, [3].

coal, *n.* carbo, *m.*; (burning) pruna, *f.*

coalesce, *v.i.* coalesco, [3]; *fig.* coeo, [4].

coalition, *n.* societas, *f.*

coalmine, *n.* fodina, *f.*

coarse, *a.* crassus; *fig.* incultus; rudis, rusticus, infacetus, illiberalis; ~**ly,** *ad.* crasse; infacete.

coarseness, *n.* crassitudo; rusticitas, *f.*

coast, *n.* ora, *f.*, litus, *nt.*

coastal, *a.* maritimus.

coat, *n.* vestis; tunica, *f.*; ~ **of arms,** insignia, *nt. pl.*; ~ **of mail,** lorica, *f.*; (skin) pellis, *f.*; corium, *nt.*; tegumentum, *nt.*

coat, *v.t.* illino, induco, [3].

coax, *v.t.* mulceo, [2]; blandior, [4]; (persuade) adduco, [3].

coaxing, *n.* blandimenta, *nt. pl.*; blanditiae, *f. pl.*

coaxing, *a.* blandus.

cobble, *v.t.* resarcio, [4].

cobbler, *n.* sutor, veteramentarius, *m.*

cobweb, *n.* aranea tela, aranea, *f.*; aranea texta, *nt. pl.*

cock, *n.* gallus, *m.*

cockle, *n.* (shell-fish) chema, *f.*

cockroach, *n.* blatta, *f.*

cocoon, *n.* globulus, *m.*

code, *n.* leges *f. pl.*

coerce, *v.t.* coerceo, [2]; refreno, [1]; cogo, [3].

coercion, *n.* coercitio, *f.*; (force) vis, *f.*; (necessity) necessitas, *f.*

coffin, *n.* arca, *f.*; loculus, *m.*

cog, *n.* (of a wheel) dens, *m.*

cogent, *a.* gravis, efficax; ~**ly,** *ad.* efficaciter, graviter.

cogitate, *v.i.* meditor, reputo, [1].

cogitation, *n.* reputatio, *f.*

cohabitation, *n.* concubitus, *m.*

cohere, *v.i.* cohaereo, [2]; *fig.* consentio, [4]; concordo, [1].

coherence, *n.* contextus, *m.*; (order) ordo, *m.*

coherent, *a.* contextus, continens; (clear) clarus.

cohesive, *a.* tenax, lentus.

cohort, *n.* cohors, *f.*

coil, n. spira, f.; volumen, glomus, nt.

coil, v.t. & i. glomero; glomeror, [1]; (wind) volvo, volvor, [3].

coin, n. nummus, m.; (collectively) pecunia, f.; (small ~) nummulus, m.

coin, v.t. (money) cudo, [3]; ferio, [4]; fig. (invent) fingo, [3].

coinage, n. res nummaria; (coined money) pecunia publice signata, moneta; (invention) fictio, f.

coincide, v.i. congruo, [3]; convenio, [4].

coincidence, n. concursus fortuitorum, f.; (agreement) consensus, m.

colander, n. colum, nt.

cold, a. frigidus, gelidus; **be ~,** frigeo, algeo, [2]; **become ~,** frigesco, [3].

cold, n. frigus, nt., algor, m.; (illness) gravedo, f.; **catch ~,** perfrigesco, algesco, [3].

coldly, ad. fig. frigide, gelide, lente.

coldness, n. frigus, nt. algor, m.; fig. lentitudo, f.

collapse, v.i. collabor; concido, corruo, [3].

collapse, n. lapsus, casus, m.; labes, ruina, f.

collar, n. (of a garment) collare, nt.; (ornament) torques, c.; monile, nt.; (for horses) helcium, nt.; (for dogs) mellum, nt.

colleague, n. collega, m.; consors, c.

collect, v.t. lego, colligo, confero, [3]; (an army) comparo, convoco, [1]; (gather) cogo, [3]; comporto, [1]; (money) exigo, [3]; (heap up) coacervo, [1]; ~ oneself, se or animum colligere; ~, v.i. convenio, [3], coeo, [4]; congregor, [1].

collection, n. collectio; conquisitio; (of money) collatio, f.

college, n. collegium, nt.; academia, f.

collide, v.i. confligo, concurro, [3].

colliery, n. fodina, f.

collision, n. conflictio, f.; concursus, m.

colloquial, a. communis (sermo), m.

collusion, n. collusio; praevaricatio, f.

colonist, n. colonus, m.

colonize, v.t. coloniam deduco (in with acc.).

colonnade, n. porticus, f., xystus, m.

colony, n. colonia, f.

colossal, a. (of statues) colossicus, colosseus; (huge) ingens, immanis.

colossus, n. colossus, m.

colour, n. color, m., pigmentum, nt.; (ensign) vexillum, signum, nt.

colour, v.t. coloro, [1]; (dye) tingo, inficio, imbuo, [3]; ~, v.i. erubesco, [3].

coloured, a. coloratus.

colouring, *n.* color; *fig.* ornatus, *m.*

colt, *n.* equulus, pullus equinus, *m.*

column, *n.* columna, *f.*

comb, *n.* pecten, *m.*

comb, *v.t.* pecto, [3].

combat, *n.* pugna, *f.*, proelium, certamen, *nt.*

combat, *v.t. & i.* pugno, proelior, [1]; certo, dimico, [1]; contendo, [3]; (oppose) repugno, adversor, [1] (*both with dat.*).

combatant, *n.* miles, pugnator, proeliator, *m.*

combination, *n.* coniunctio, iunctura, *f.*; concursus, *m.*

combine, *v.t.* coniungo, [3]; misceo, [2]; ~, *v.i.* coeo, [4].

combustion, *n.* crematio, deflagratio, *f.*

come, *v.i.* venio, [4]; (arrive) pervenio ad (+ *acc.*), [4]; (happen) fieri, *v.* ~ **about,** evenio, [4]; ~ **after,** sequor, [3]; ~ **again,** revenio, [4]; ~ **along,** procedo, [3]; ~ **away,** abscedo, [3]; abeo, [4]; ~ **back,** revenio; redeo, [4]; ~ **before,** praevenio, [4]; ~ **by,** praetereo, [4]; (get) acquiro, [3]; ~ **down,** descendo, [3]; (fall down) decido, [3]; ~ **forth,** exeo, [4]; egredior, [3]; *fig.* exorior, [4]; ~ **forward,** procedo, [3]; ~ **in(to),** introeo, [4]; ~ **in!** intra, intrate; ~ **near,** appropinquo, [1]; accedo, [3]; ~ **of,** originem traho (de, e, *both with abl.*); ~ **off,** recedo; *fig.* disce-

do, [3]; (of hair, *etc.*) cado, [3]; ~ **on,** procedo, pergo, [3]; ~ **on!** agite! ~ **out,** *v.* ~ **forth &** ~ **off;** (be published) edi, emitti, [3]; (become known) evulgor, [1]; ~ **round,** circumagi; *fig.* adduci, [3]; ~ **to,** advenio ad, [4] pervenio ad; *fig.* ~ **to pass,** evenio, [4]; fio, *v. ir.*; ~ **together,** convenio, coeo, [4]; ~ **up,** subvenio, [4]; (spring up) provenio, [4]; (surprise) deprehendo, [3].

come! *i.* age! eia!

comedian, *n.* comoedus; comicus, *m.*

comedy, *n.* comoedia, *f.*; soccus, *m.*

comely, *a.* decens, pulcher, venustus.

comet, *n.* cometes, *m.*, stella crinita, *f.*

comfort, *v.t.* consolor, solor, [1].

comfort, *n.* solacium, solamen, *nt.*, consolatio, *f.*

comfortable, *a.* (commodious) commodus.

comfortably, *ad.* commode.

comforter, *n.* consolator, *m.*

comic(al), *a.* comicus; ridiculus.

comically, *ad.* comice; ridicule.

coming, *n.* adventus, *m.*

coming, *a.* venturus, futurus.

command, *v.t.* impero, [1], praecipio, [3] (*both with dat.*); iubeo, [2].

command, *n.* mandatum, praeceptum, imperium, *nt.*; (order) iussus, *m.*; iussum, *nt.*; (office, place) praefectura, *f.*, imperium, *nt.*

commander, *n.* dux, praefectus, imperator, *m.*

commandment, *n.* imperium, *nt.*

commemorate, *v.t.* celebro, [1].

commemoration, *n.* celebratio, *f.*

commence, *v.t. & i.* incipio, [3]; incoho, [1]; ordior, [4]; coepi, [3].

commencement, *n.* initium, principium, *nt.*

commend, *v.t.* (commit) commendo, [1]; committo, [3]; (approve) approbo, laudo, probo, [1].

commendable, *a.* commendabilis, probabilis, laudabilis.

commendably, *ad.* laudabiliter.

commendation, *n.* commendatio, laus, *f.*

comment, commentary, *v.t. & i.* commentor, interpretor, [1]; (remark) animadverto, [3].

comment, commentary, *n.* commentarius, *m.*, commentarium, *nt.*; (criticism) animadversio, *f.*

commentator, *n.* interpres, *c.*

commerce, *n.* commercium, *nt.*; mercatus, *m.*; mercatura, *f.*

commiserate, *v.i.* ~ **with,** *v.t.* miseror, commiseror, [1]; miseresco, [3] (*with gen.*).

commiseration, *n.* miseratio, *f.*

commission, *n.* mandatum, *nt.*; (in the army) tribunatus, *m.*; **a** ~ **of two,** duumviri, *m. pl.*

commission, *v.t.* delego, [1].

commit, *v.t.* (give) do, [1]; (trust) committo, [3]; (be guilty of) patro, perpetro, [1]; admitto, [3]; (imprison) in custodiam do, [1]; ~ **oneself,** se dedere, [3].

committee, *n.* delecti; ~ **of ten,** decemviri, *m. pl.*

commodity, *n.* res venalis, merx, *f.*

common, *a.* communis; publicus; (ordinary, *etc.*) vulgaris; (well known) pervulgatus; *fig.* tritus; mediocris; (social status) plebeius.

common, in ~, *ad.* in medium, in commune; communiter; promiscue.

commoner, *n.* plebeius, *m.*

commonly, *ad.* vulgo, fere, plerumque.

commonplace, *n.* locus communis, *m.*; ~, *a.* (hackneyed) vulgaris, pervulgatus, tritus; ~ **book,** *n.* commentarius, *m.*

commonwealth, *n.* respublica, civitas, *f.*

commotion, *n.* agitatio, *f.* tumultus, motus, concursus, *m.*

communicate, *v.t.* impertio, [4]; communico, [1].

communication, *n.* communicatio, *f.*; commercium; colloquium, *nt.*; (message) nuntius, *m.*; (*mil.*), **cut off** ~**s,** omnes aditus intercludere.

communicative, *a.* affabilis, apertus.

community, *n.* communitas; (partnership) societas; (state) civitas, respublica, *f.*

compact, *a.* densus, spissus; solidus; (of style) pressus; **~ly,** *ad.* dense, spisse; presse.

compact, *n.* pactum, *nt.;* conventio, *f.;* foedus, *nt.*

companion, *n.* socius, sodalis; comes; (as soldier) contubernalis; (in games and gambling) collusor, *m.;* **boon ~,** compotor, *m.*

companionship, *n.* sodalitas, *f.;* contubernium, *nt.*

company, *n.* societas, sodalitas; (of soldiers) cohors, *f.,* manipulus, *m.;* (at table) convivium, *nt.;* (troop) caterva; turba, manus, *f.;* (corporation) collegium, *nt.*

comparable, *a.* comparabilis.

comparative, *a.* comparativus.

comparatively, *ad.* use the comparative, *e.g.* **~ slow,** tardior.

compare, *v.t.* comparo, aequo, [1]; confero, [3].

comparison, *n.* comparatio, collatio, *f.;* **in ~ with,** *pr.* prae (*with ablative*).

compartment, *n.* loculus, *m.,* cella, *f.*

compass, *n.* (circuit) ambitus, circuitus, *m.;* (limits) fines, *m. pl.;* (pair of compasses) circinus, *m.*

compassion, *n.* misericordia, miseratio, *f.*

compassionate, *a.* misericors; **~ly,** *ad.* misericorditer.

compatibility, *n.* congruentia; (conformity) convenientia, *f.*

compatible, *a.* congruus, conveniens.

compatriot, *n.* civis, *c.;* popularis, *m.*

compel, *v.t.* cogo, compello, [3].

compensate for, *v.t.* penso, compenso, [1].

compensation, *n.* compensatio, *f.*

compete, *v.i.* contendo, [3]; certo, [1].

competence, competency, *n.* facultas, *f.*

competent, *a.* capax; (suitable) congruens, idoneus; (of authorities) locuples; **~ly,** *ad.* idonee, satis.

competition, *n.* contentio, aemulatio, *f.,* certamen, *nt.*

competitive, *a.* aemulus.

competitor, *n.* aemulus, rivalis, *m.*

compilation, *n.* collectio, *f.;* excerpta, *nt. pl.*

compile, *v.t.* colligo, conscribo, compono, [3].

complacency, *n.* delectatio, *f.*

complacent, *a.* (contented) contentus; (smug) qui sibi placet.

complacently, *ad.* aequo animo.

complain of, *v.t.* queror, conqueror, [3]; ploro, [1]; **~,** *v.i.* gemo, [3]; lamentor, [1].

complaining, *a.* querulus.

complaint, *n.* querela, querimonia, *f.*; (charge) crimen, *nt.*; lamentatio, *f.*; (disease) morbus, *m.*

complaisant, *a.* officiosus, comis, facilis, humanus.

complement, *n.* complementum, supplementum, *nt.*

complete, *a.* plenus; integer; perfectus; ~ly, *ad.* plane, prorsus.

complete, *v.t.* compleo; suppleo; expleo, [2]; (accomplish) perficio, [3].

completeness, *n.* integritas; perfectio, *f.*

completion, *n.* (accomplishment) perfectio, *f.*

complex, *a.* multiplex.

complexion, *n.* (of the skin) color, *m.*

complexity, *n.* ambages, *f. pl.*; difficultas, *f.*

compliance, *n.* obtemperatio, *f.*, obsequium, *nt.*

compliant, *a.* officiosus; facilis.

complicate, *v.t.* impedio, [4]; confundo, [3]; turbo, [1].

complicated, *a.* nodosus, difficilis, perplexus.

complication, *n.* nodus, *m.*; ambages, *f. pl.*; difficultas, *f.*

complicity, *n.* conscientia, *f.*

compliment, *n.* verba honorifica, *nt. pl.*; blanditiae, *f. pl.*; **pay one's ~s (to),** saluto, [1].

compliment, *v.t.* laudo, [1].

complimentary, *a.* honorificus; blandus.

comply, *v.i.* (with) concedo (*with dat.*); cedo, [3]; pareo, [2]; (humour) morigeror; (me) accommodo, [1]; (accept) accipio, [3].

component, *n.* pars, *f.*, elementa, *nt. pl.*

compose, *v.t.* compono; (arrange) digero, dispono, [3]; (calm) sedo; ~ **oneself,** tranquillor, [1].

composed, *a.* quietus, tranquillus; ~ly, *ad.* quiete, aequo animo.

composer, *n.* scriptor, *m.*

composition, *n.* compositio; confectio, *f.*; (book) liber, *m.*

compost, *n.* stercus, *nt.*

composure, *n.* tranquillitas, *f.*, animus aequus, *m.*

compound, *v.t.* compono, [3]; misceo, [2].

compound, *a.* compositus; concretus.

comprehend, *v.t.* (embrace) contineo, [2], complector; (understand) capio, percipio, comprehendo, intellego, [3].

comprehensible, *a.* comprehensibilis.

comprehension, *n.* intellectus, *m.*, intelligentia, comprehensio, *f.*

comprehensive, *a.* amplus.

compress, *v.t.* comprimo, astringo, [3] coarto, [1].

compression, *n.* compressio, *f.*

comprise, *v.t.* contineo, cohibeo, [2]; comprehendo, complector, [3].

compromise, *n.* compromissum, *nt.*; (agreement) pactum, *nt.*

compromise, *v.t.* compromitto, [3]; (bring into disrepute) in invidiam adduco; ~, *v.i.* paciscor, [3].

compulsion, *n.* vis, necessitas, *f.*

compulsorily, *ad.* vi, per vim.

compulsory, *a.* necessarius.

computer, *n.* calculator, *m.*

comrade, *n.* sodalis, socius; (military) contubernalis, *m.*

concave, *a.* cavus; concavus.

conceal, *v.t.* celo, occulto, [1]; abdo, condo, occulo, [3]; (dissemble) dissimulo, [1].

concealment, *n.* occultatio; dissimulatio, *f.*

concede, *v.t.* concedo, permitto, [3]; do, [1].

conceit, *n.* (fancy) opinio; (pride) arrogantia, superbia, *f.*; **witty ~,** lepos, *m.*

conceited, *a.* arrogans, superbus, tumidus.

conceivable, *a.* comprehensibilis.

conceive, *v.t.* concipio; (comprehend) percipio, intellego, [3]; (imagine) fingo, [3].

concentrate, *v.t.* in unum locum contraho; ~, *v.i. fig.* animum intendo (in aliquid), [3].

concentration, *n.* in unum locum contractio, *fig.* animi intentio, *f.*

concept, *n.* imago, notio, opinio, *f.*

conception, *n.* (in the womb) conceptus, *m.*; (idea) imago, species, notio, *f.*

concern, *n.* (affair) res, *f.*, negotium, *nt.*; cura, *f.*; (importance) momentum, *nt.*; (anxiety, trouble) sollicitudo, *f.*

concern, *v.t.* pertineo, [2]; **it ~s,** (mea, tua, *etc.*) interest, refert; **be ~ed,** occupor, [1]; particeps sum; (be anxious) sollicitus sum; **it does not ~ me,** non mihi curae est.

concerning, *pr.* (about) de (*with abl.*); (as to) quod ad (*with acc.*).

concession, *n.* concessio, *f.*; (thing) concessum, *nt.*; (allowance) venia, *f.*

conch, *n.* concha, *f.*

conciliate, *v.t.* concilio, [1].

conciliation, *n.* conciliatio, *f.*

conciliatory, *a.* pacificus; pacificatorius.

concise, *a.* brevis, concisus; (style) pressus; **~ly,** *ad.* breviter, concise.

conciseness, *n.* brevitas, *f.*

conclude, *v.t. & i.* concludo, [3]; finio, [4]; (end) perficio; (settle) statuo, [3]; (infer) concludo, [3].

conclusion, *n.* (end) conclusio, *f.*; finis, *c.*; (of a speech) peroratio, *f.*; epilogus, *m.*; (inference) conclusio, *f.*

conclusive, *a.* (of arguments) certus.

concoct, *v.t.* concoquo, [3]; (contrive) excogito, machinor, [1].

concord, n. concordia; conspiratio, f.; consensus, m.; (mus.) concentus, m.

concourse, n. concursus; conventus, m.; frequentia, f.

concrete, a. concretus.

concubinage, n. concubinatus, m.

concubine, n. concubina, f.

concur, v.i. convenio; (agree) consentio, [4].

concurrence, n. concursus, consensus, m.

concurrently, ad. una, simul.

concussion, n. concussio, f.

condemn, v.t. damno, condemno; (blame) vitupero, [1].

condemnation, n. damnatio, condemnatio, f.

condemnatory, a. damnatorius.

condensation, n. densatio, spissatio, f.

condense, v.t. (con)denso, spisso, [1]; fig. coarto, [1].

condescend, v.i. dignor, [1]; descendo, me summitto, [3].

condescending, a. comis, facilis, officiosus.

condescendingly, ad. comiter, officiose.

condescension, n. obsequium, nt.; comitas, f.

condiment, n. condimentum, nt.

condition, n. condicio, f., status, m.; (of agreement) pactum, nt., lex, f.; (rank) ordo, m.

condolence, n. consolatio, f.

condone, v.t. condono, veniam do, [1]; ignosco, [3] (all with dat.).

conduct, n. vita, ratio, f.; mores, m. pl.; (management) administratio, cura, f.; (deeds) facta, nt. pl.

conduct, v.t. adduco; deduco; perduco, [3]; administro, [1]; (direct) dirigo, [3]; (preside over) praesum (with dat.).

conduit, n. canalis, m., aquaeductus, m.

cone, n. conus, m.

confectioner, n. crustularius, pistor dulciarius, m.

confectionery, n. cuppedia, nt. pl.

confederacy, n. (alliance) foedus, nt.; societas, f.

confederation, n. foedus, nt.; societas, f.

confer, v.t. (bestow) confero, [3]; (compare) comparo, [1]; ~ with, colloquor, [3]; convenio, [4].

conference, n. colloquium, nt.; congressus, m.

confess, v.t. fateor, confiteor, [2].

confession, n. confessio, f.

confidant, n. familiaris, c.; ~, a. conscius.

confide, v.t. confido, committo; credo, [3]; ~ in, (trust) confido, fido, [3] (both with dat.).

confidence, n. fides; fiducia; confidentia; (boldness) audacia, f.;

(self-confidence) sui fiducia, *f.*; **in ~,** (secretly) clam.

confident, *a.* confidens; securus; (bold) audax; **~ly,** *ad.* confidenter.

confidential, *a.* (secret) arcanus.

confine, *v.t.* claudo, includo, [3]; coerceo, cohibeo, [2]; circumscribo, [3]; termino, [1].

confinement, *n.* inclusio; (imprisonment) custodia, *f.*; carcer, *m.*; (childbirth) puerperium, *nt.*

confirm, *v.t.* confirmo; firmo; (prove) comprobo, [1]; (ratify) sancio, [4].

confirmation, *n.* confirmatio, *f.*

confirmed, *a.* inveteratus.

confiscate, *v.t.* proscribo, [3]; publico, confisco, [1].

confiscation, *n.* publicatio, confiscatio, proscriptio, *f.*

conflagration, *n.* incendium, *nt.*

conflict, *n.* contentio; controversia, *f.*; certamen, *nt.*; pugna, *f.*

conflict, *v.i.* contendo, [3]; (struggle) luctor, [1]; (be at variance) discrepo, [1].

conflicting, *a.* contrarius, adversus.

conform to, *v.i.* (comply with) obtempero, [1] (*with dat.*).

conformity, *n.* convenientia, congruentia, *f.*; **in ~ with,** secundum (*with acc.*).

confound, *v.t.* confundo, [3]; permisceo, [2]; perturbo, [1]; (destroy) deleo, [2]; perimo, [3].

confront, *v.t.* (match) committo, [3]; **~,** *v.i.* (meet) congredior cum (*with abl.*).

confuse, *v.t.* confundo, [3]; perturbo, [1].

confused, *a.* confusus, perplexus; indistinctus; pudibundus.

confusion, *n.* confusio; perturbatio, *f.*; tumultus; pudor, *m.*

confute, *v.t.* confuto, refuto, [1]; refello, redarguo, [3].

congeal, *v.t.* congelo, glacio, [1]; **~,** *v.i.* consisto, concresco, [3].

congenial, *a.* (pleasant) gratus, consentaneus; (amicably shared) concors.

congestion, *n.* congestus, *m.*

congratulate, *v.t.* gratulor, grator, [1] (*both with dat.*).

congratulation, *n.* gratulatio, *f.*

congratulatory, *a.* gratulatorius.

congregate, *v.i.* congregor, conglobor, [1]; convenio, [4].

congregation, *n.* contio, *f.*; coetus, *m.*; auditores, *m. pl.*

conifer, *n.* arbor conifera, *f.*

conjectural, *a.* opinabilis, coniecturalis; **~ly,** *ad.* ex coniectura.

conjecture, *n.* coniectura, *f.*

conjecture, *v.t.* coniecto, [1]; conicio, [3].

conjugal, *a.* coniugalis; coniugialis.

conjunction, *n.* coniunctio, *f.*; concursus, *m.*

conjure, *v.t.* (entreat) obtestor; [1]; ~, *v.i.* praestigiis utor, [3].

conjurer, *n.* magus; (juggler) praetigiator, *m.*

conjuring, *n.* (juggling) praestigiae, *f. pl.*

connect, *v.t.* connecto, [3]; copulo [1]; (in a series) sero, [3].

connected, *a.* coniunctus; continuus; **be ~,** cohaereo, [2].

connection, *n.* coniunctio, *f.*; contextus, *m.*; (relation) affinitas; cognatio, *f.*; **have a ~ with,** pertineo ad (*with acc.*), [2].

connive, *v.i.* coniveo, indulgeo, [2].

connoisseur, *a.* homo doctus, peritus, intellegens, elegans.

connubial, *a.* coniugalis.

conquer, *v.t.* vinco, [3]; supero; domo, [1]; (gain) capio, [3]; potior, [4].

conqueror, *n.* victor; domitor, *m.*, victrix, *f.*

conquest, *n.* victoria, *f.*; (what is gained) partum, *nt.*

conscience, *n.* conscientia, *f.*

conscientious, *a.* religiosus; sanctus; (hard-working) diligens.

conscientiousness, *n.* aequi reverentia, religio, fides, *f.*; (application) diligentia, *f.*

conscious, *a.* conscius; ~**ly,** *ad.* use *a.* sciens, prudens.

consciousness, *n.* conscientia, *f.*; (feeling) sensus, *m.*; **lose ~,** concido, [3]; exanimor, [1].

conscript, *n.* tiro, *m.*

conscription, *n.* (of soldiers) delectus, *m.*

consecrate, *v.t.* sacro, consecro; dedico, [1].

consecration, *n.* consecratio; dedicatio, *f.*

consecutive, *a.* continuus; ~**ly,** *ad.* per ordinem; continenter; deinceps.

consent, *v.i.* assentior, consentio, [4].

consent, *n.* consensus, *m.*, consensio, *f.*; **without my ~,** me invito.

consequence, *n.* consequentia, consecutio; (logical) conclusio, *f.*; (issue) exitus, *m.*; (importance) momentum, *nt.*

consequent, *a.* consequens, consectarius; ~**ly,** *ad.* ergo, igitur, proinde.

conservation, *n.* conservatio, *f.*

conservative, *a.* (moderate) mediocris; **a ~ in politics,** optimatium fautor.

conserve, *v.t.* conservo, servo, [1].

consider, *v.t.* considero, contemplor, [1]; intueor, contueor, [2]; (turn over in the mind) volvo, [3]; verso, voluto, reputo, [1]; (regard) aestimo; (reckon) numero, [1].

considerable, *a.* aliquantus; (of size) amplus.

considerably, *ad.* aliquantum; multum, maxime.

considerate, *a.* consideratus, prudens; (kind) humanus; ~**ly,**

ad. considerate; (kindly) humaniter.

consideration, *n.* consideratio; contemplatio; prudentia, *f.*; (regard) respectus, *m.*; (kindness) humanitas, *f.*; **take into ~,** rationem habeo, [2] *(with gen.)*; **without ~,** inconsulte.

considering, *pr.* (having regard to) pro *(with abl.)*; **~ that,** utpote, (since) quoniam, quando.

consign, *v.t.* confido, [3]; assigno, [1]; trado, [3].

consist, *v.i.* **~ of,** consto, [1]; consisto, [3]; (be) sum.

consistency, *n.* convenientia; constantia, *f.*; (hardness) firmitas, *f.*; (thickness) densitas, *f.*

consistent, *a.* constans; congruens; consentaneus; **~ly,** *ad.* constanter; congruenter.

consolable, *a.* consolabilis.

consolation, *n.* consolatio, *f.*; solamen, solacium, *nt.*

console, *v.t.* solor, consolor, [1].

consolidate, *v.t.* consolido, firmo, [1]; stabilio, [4].

consort, *v.i.* **~ with,** vivo cum *(with abl.)*; familiariter utor, [3] *(with abl.)*.

conspicuous, *a.* conspicuus; insignis; manifestus; **~ly,** *ad.* manifesto.

conspiracy, *n.* coniuratio, conspiratio, *f.*

conspirator, *n.* coniuratus, conspiratus, *m.*

conspire, *v.i.* coniuro, conspiro, [1].

constancy, *n.* constantia, firmitas; perseverantia, *f.*

constant, *a.* constans, firmus; perpetuus; assiduus; fidelis; fidus; **~ly,** *ad.* constanter, fideliter; perpetuo, assidue.

constellation, *n.* sidus, astrum, *nt.*

consternation, *n.* consternatio, trepidatio, *f.*, pavor, *m.*

constitute, *v.t.* constituo, facio, [3], creo, [1]; (be) sum.

constitution, *n.* (of the body, *etc.*) habitus, *m.*, constitutio, *f.*; (political) civitas, *f.*; *fig.* condicio, natura, *f.*

constitutional, *a.* legitimus, e republica; natura insitus.

constrain, *v.t.* cogo, compello, [3].

constraint, *n.* vis, coercitio, necessitas, *f.*

constrict, *v.t.* constringo, [3].

construct, *v.t.* construo, struo, exstruo, [3]; aedifico, [1].

construction, *n.* constructio, aedificatio; figura, forma, *f.*; (meaning, sense) sensus, *m.*; **put a bad ~ on,** in malam partem accipio, [3].

consul, *n.* consul, *m.*

consular, *a.* consularis.

consulate, consulship, *n.* consulatus, *m.*

consult, *v.t. & i.* consulo, [3]; consulto; delibero, [1]; **~ a person's**

interests, consulo, [3] (*with dat.*).

consultation, n. consultatio; deliberatio, f.

consume, v.t. (destroy, use up) consumo, absumo, conficio; (squander) effundo, [3]; dissipo, [1]; (eat) edo, [3].

consumer, n. consumptor, m.

consumption, n. consumptio; (disease) tabes; phthisis, f.

contact, n. contactus, m.

contagion, n. contagium, nt.

contagious, a. pestilens, pestifer, contagiosus.

contain, v.t. contineo, habeo, [2]; comprehendo, [3]; ~ **oneself,** se tenere, [2].

container, n. arca, f.

contaminate, v.t. inquino, [1]; polluo, inficio, [3]; foedo, violo, [1].

contamination, n. contagium, nt.

contemn, v.t. temno, contemno, sperno, despicio, [3]; fastidio, [4].

contemplate, v.t. & i. contemplor, [1]; intueor, contueor, [2].

contemplation, n. contemplatio, meditatio, f.

contemplative, a. contemplativus.

contemporary, a. aequalis, contemporaneus.

contemporary, n. aequalis, aequaevus, m.

contempt, n. contemptio, f., contemptus, m.; fastidium, nt.

contemptible, a. contemnendus; abiectus; sordidus.

contemptuous, a. fastidiosus, superbus; ~ly, ad. fastidiose, contemptim.

contend, v.i. contendo, [3]; pugno, certo, [1]; (struggle) luctor, [1]; (dispute) verbis certo, [1]; (maintain) confirmo, affirmo, [1]; ~ **against,** repugno, adversor, [1] (*both with dat.*).

contending, a. adversus; rivalis.

content, a. contentus.

content, v.t. satisfacio, [3]; placeo, [2] (*both with dat.*).

content, n. aequus animus, m.

contented, a., v. content, a.

contentedly, ad. aequo animo, placide.

contention, n. contentio, lis, f.; certamen, nt.

contentious, a. litigiosus; pugnax.

contentment, n., v. content, n.

contents, n. quod inest; (of a book) argumentum, nt.

contest, v.t. & i. (oppose) repugno, [1] (*with dat.*).

contest, n. certatio, contentio; controversia; lis, f.; certamen, nt.

context, n. contextus, m.

continent, a. abstinens, continens; castus, pudicus; ~ly, ad. temperanter.

continent, *n.* continens, *f.*

continental, *a.* continentem incolens; in continenti positus, ad continentem pertinens.

contingency, *n.* casus, eventus, *m.*

contingent, *a.* (accidental) fortuitus; **be ~ on,** pendere ex (*abl.*).

contingent, *n.* numerus, *m.*

continual, *a.* continuus; perpetuus; assiduus; perennis; **~ly,** *ad.* continenter; perpetuo; semper; assidue.

continuation, *n.* continuatio; series, *f.*

continue, *v.t.* persevero in (*with abl.*), [1]; (prolong) produco, [3]; **~,** *v.i.* (re)maneo, [2]; duro, [1]; persisto, [3]; (go on) pergo, [3].

continuity, *n.* continuitas; perpetuitas, *f.*

continuous, *a.* continens; continuus; perpetuus; **~ly,** *ad.* continenter, perpetuo.

contort, *v.t.* distorqueo, [2].

contortion, *n.* distortio, *f.*

contour, *n.* lineamenta, *nt. pl.*

contraband, *a.* illicitus, vetitus.

contraband, *n.* merces vetitae, *f. pl.*

contract, *v.t.* (compress) contraho, astringo, [3]; (a disease, *etc.*) contraho, [3]; **~ for,** loco, [1]; (undertake by contract) redimo, [3]; **~,** *v.i.* (make an arrangement by bargaining) paciscor, [3]; (shrink) contrahor, [3].

contract, *n.* (bargain) locatio, *f.*; pactum, *nt.*

contraction, *n.* contractio, *f.*; compendium, *nt.*

contractor, *n.* (of work) susceptor, redemptor, conductor, *m.*

contradict, *v.t.* contradico, obloquor, [3]; adversor, [1] (*all with dat.*).

contradiction, *n.* contradictio; (of things) repugnantia, *f.*

contradictory, *a.* contrarius, repugnans.

contrary, *a.* (opposite) contrarius; diversus; adversus; repugnans.

contrary, *ad. & pr.* **~ to,** contra; praeter (*both with acc.*).

contrary, *n.* contrarium, *nt.*, contraria pars, *f.*; **on the ~,** contra, e contrario; immo.

contrast, *n.* diversitas; varietas; dissimilitudo, *f.*

contrast, *v.t.* comparo, [1]; confero, [3]; **~,** *v.i.* discrepo, [1].

contravene, *v.t.* violo, [1]; frango, [3].

contribute, *v.t.* confero, [3]; (give) do, [1].

contribution, *n.* collatio; (of money) collecta, *f.*; (gift) donum, *nt.*

contrivance, *n.* inventio, machinatio, *f.*; (thing contrived) inventum, *nt.*; machina, *f.*

contrive, *v.t.* (invent) fingo, [3]; excogito, [1]; invenio, [4]; machinor, [1]; **~ to,** efficio ut (*with subj.*).

control, n. (power) potestas, dicio, f; (check) coercitio, f; (command) imperium, regimen, nt.; (management) administratio, f; self~, moderatio, f.

control, v.t. (check) reprimo, [3]; (restrain) coerceo, [2]; (be at the head of) praesum (with dat.); (manage) administro, moderor, [1]; (rule) rego, [3].

controversial, a. controversus.

controversy, n. controversia, f; concertatio; (debate) disceptatio; (disagreement) dissensio, f.

contumely, n. contumelia, f, probrum, opprobrium, nt.

contusion, n. contusio, f, contusum, nt.

convalesce, v.i. convalesco, [3].

convalescent, a. convalescens.

convene, v.t. convoco, [1].

convenience, n. commoditas, f; commodum, nt.; utilitas, f.

convenient, a. commodus, idoneus, opportunus; ~ly, ad. commode; opportune.

convention, n. conventus, m.; (agreement) pactum, conventum, nt.; (custom) mos, m.

conventional, a. usitatus, translaticius.

converge, v.i. vergo, [3].

conversant, a. peritus, exercitatus.

conversation, n. colloquium, nt., sermo, m.

converse, v.i. colloquor, [3].

conversion, n. conversio, f.

convert, v.t. converto, [3]; commuto, [1]; reduco, transfero, [3].

convex, a. convexus.

convexity, n. convexitas, f.

convey, v.t. veho, [3], asporto, deporto, [1]; adveho, [3]; porto, vecto; (transfer) abalieno; fig. significo, [1].

conveyance, n. (act) advectio, vectura, f; (vehicle) vehiculum, nt.; (law) abalienatio, f.

convict, v.t. convinco, [3]; (detect) comperio, [4]; (by sentence) condemno, [1].

convict, n. convictus, ad poenam damnatus, m.

conviction, n. (condemnation) damnatio; (belief) persuasio, f.

convince, v.t. suadeo, persuadeo, [2] (with dat.).

convincing, a. gravis; ~ly, ad. graviter.

convivial, a. hilaris, laetus.

convoke, v.t. convoco, [1].

convoy, n. (escort) praesidium, nt.

convulse, v.t. concutio, convello, [3].

convulsed, a. convulsus.

convulsion, n. convulsio, f, spasmus, m.

cook, n. coquus, m., coqua, f.

cook, v.t. & i. coquo, [3].

cookery, n. ars coquinaria, f.

cooking, n. coctura, f; ~, a. coquinarius.

cool, *a.* frigidus; frigidulus; (shady) opacus; *fig.* sedatus; (shady) opacus; *fig.* sedatus; immotus; impavidus; (indifferent) lentus; (impudent) impudens.

cool, *n.,* v. coolness.

cool, *v.t. & i.* refrigero; refrigeror, [1]; *fig.* frigesco, defervesco, languesco, [3].

coolly, *ad.* frigide; *fig.* sedate; aequo animo; lente; impudenter.

coolness, *n.* frigus, *nt.*; (pleasant ~) refrigeratio, *f.*; (shadiness) opacum, *nt.*; *fig.* lentitudo; cautela, *f.*; aequus animus, *m.*

coop, *n.* (for hens) cavea, *f.*

coop, *v.t.* ~ **up,** includo, [3].

co-operate, *v.i.* una ago, [3]; adiuvo, cooperor, [1].

co-operation, *n.* auxilium, adiumentum, *nt.,* cooperatio, *f.*

coot, *n.* fulica, *f.*

cope, *v.i.* ~ **with,** certo, [1], contendo, [3], cum (*with abl.*) ~, *v.t.* (manage) gero, [3]; tracto, administro, [1].

copious, *a.* copiosus, abundans, uber; ~**ly,** *ad.* abundanter, copiose.

copper, *n.* aes; cyprium, *nt.*

copper, *a.* aëneus, aënus, cypreus.

copper-smith, *n.* faber aerarius, *m.*

coppice, copse, *n.* dumetum, fruticetum, *nt.*

copulate, *v.* coeo (*ir.*).

copulation, *n.* concubitus, *m.*

copy, *n.* exemplar, exemplum, *nt.*; imitatio; imago, *f.*

copy, *v.t. & i.* transcribo, [3]; imitor, [1]; (follow) sequor, [3].

coral, *n.* corallium, *nt.*

cord, *n.* funis, *m.*

cordial, *a.* benignus; sincerus; ~**ly,** *ad.* ex animo; benigne; sincere.

cordiality, *n.* animus benignus, *m.*; comitas, *f.*

cordon, *n.* corona, *f.*

core, *n.* (of fruit) vulva, *f.*

cork, *n.* (tree) suber, *nt.*; (bark) cortex, *c.*

cork, *a.* subereus.

cork, *v.t.* (seal up a container) obturo, [1].

corn, *n.* frumentum, *nt.*; (cereals) fruges, *f. pl.*; annona, *f.*; (on the toes) callus, *m.*

corner, *n.* angulus, *m.*; (lurking-place) latebra, *f.*, recessus, *m.*; (of a street) compitum, *nt.*

cornfield, *n.* seges, *f.*, arvum, *nt.*; ~**s,** *pl.* sata, *nt. pl.*

corn-merchant, *n.* frumentarius, *m.*

cornucopia, *n.* cornu copiae, *nt.*

coronet, *n.* diadema, *nt.*

corporal, *n.* decurio, *m.*

corporal, corporeal, *a.* corporeus, corporalis.

corporation, *n.* societas, *f.*, sodalicium, *n.*

corps, *n.* legio, *f.*

corpse, *n.* cadaver, *nt.*

corpulent, *a.* corpulentus, pinguis, obesus.

correct, *a.* emendatus; rectus; accuratus; elegans; ~ly, *ad.* emendate; recte; accurate; eleganter.

correct, *v.t.* corrigo, [3]; emendo, [1]; *fig.* animadverto, [3]; castigo, [1].

correction, *n.* correctio, emendatio; *fig.* animadversio; castigatio, *f.*

correspond, *v.i.* congruo, [3]; respondeo, [2].

correspondence, *n.* congruentia; (letters) epistulae, *f. pl.*

correspondent, *n.* scriptor, *m.*

corresponding, *a.* par (*with dat.*).

corridor, *n.* andron, *m.*

corroborate, *v.t.* confirmo, [1].

corrode, *v.t.* erodo; peredo, [3].

corroding, *a. fig.* mordax.

corrosion, *n.* rosio, *f.*

corrosive, *a.* mordax.

corrupt, *v.t.* corrumpo, [3]; depravo, [1]; ~, *v.i.* putresco, [3].

corrupt, *a.* corruptus, putridus; *fig.* pravus; impurus; venalis.

corruptible, *a.* corruptibilis; venalis.

corruption, *n.* corruptio; putredo, *f.; fig.* depravatio, pravitas; (by money) corruptela, *f.*

corselet, *n.* lorica, *f.;* thorax, *m.*

cortège, *n.* pompa, *f.*

cosmetic, *n.* medicamen, *nt.*

cosmopolitan, *a.* cosmicus.

cost, *n.* (price) pretium, *nt.;* (expense) impensa, *f.*

cost, *v.t. & i.* consto, sto, [1].

costliness, *n.* caritas, *f.*

costly, *a.* pretiosus, carus, sumptuosus.

costume, *n.* vestitus, *m.*

cosy, *a.* commodus.

cot, *n.* (bed) lectulus, *m.*

cottage, *n.* casa, *f.,* tugurium, *nt.*

couch, *n.* cubile; pulvinar, *nt.;* lectus, torus, *m.*

cough, *n.* tussis, *f.;* **have a bad ~,** male tussio, [4].

cough, *v.i.* tussio, [4].

council, *n.* concilium, consilium, *nt.,* senatus, *m.*

councillor, *n.* consiliarius, *m.*

counsel, *n.* (advice) consilium, *nt.;* (person) advocatus, *m.*

counsel, *v.t.* consulo, [3]; moneo, [2].

counsellor, *n.* consiliarius, consiliator; advocatus, *m.*

count, *v.t. & i.* numero, [1]; censeo; (consider, deem) habeo, [2]; existimo, [1]; duco, [3]; ~ **on,** confido, [3] (*with dat.*).

count, *n.* (calculation) computatio, *f.*

countenance, *n.* (face, look) facies, *f.,* vultus, aspectus; (encouragement) favor, *m.*; **put out of ~**, confundo, [3]; perturbo, [1].

counter, *n.* (of a shop) mensa, *f.*; (for games) calculus, *m.*

counter, *ad.* contra; **run ~ to,** adversor, repugno, [1] (*with dat.*).

counteract, *v.t.* obsisto, [3] (*with dat.*).

counterbalance, *v.t.* exaequo, penso, compenso, [1].

counterfeit, *v.t.* imitor; adultero; simulo, [1].

counterfeit, *a.* ficticius; simulatus; fictus; adulterinus.

counterfeiter, *n.* imitator; falsarius, *m.*

countermand, *v.t.* renuntio, [1].

countless, *a.* innumerabilis, innumerus, infinitus.

country, *n.* (as opposed to the town) rus, *nt.*; regio; terra, *f.*; loca, *nt. pl.*; **native ~**, solum natale, *nt.*

country-house, *n.* villa, *f.*

countryman, *n.* rusticus, *m.*

countryside, *n.* rus, *nt.*

couple, *n.* par, *nt.*

couple, *v.t.* copulo, [1]; connecto, coniungo, [3].

courage, *n.* animus, *m.*, virtus, audacia, fortitudo, *f.*

courageous, *a.* animosus, ferox; audax; fortis; **~ly,** *ad.* ferociter; audacter; fortiter.

courier, *n.* cursor; nuntius; (letter-carrier) tabellarius, *m.*

course, *n.* (running) cursus; (of water) ductus, *m.*; (means) ratio, *f.*; **of ~**, *ad.* profecto, sane.

court, *n.* (palace) regia domus, aula, *f.*; (retinue) comitatus, *m.*; (in law) forum, tribunal, *nt.*; iudices, *m. pl.*

court, *v.t.* (cultivate friendship of) colo, [3]; ambio, blandior, [4]; observo, [1]; (of a suitor) peto, [3].

courteous, *a.* comis, humanus, benignus; affabilis; **~ly,** *ad.* comiter, humaniter, benigne, affabiliter.

courtesan, *n.* meretrix, *f.*

courtesy, *n.* comitas, affabilitas, urbanitas, *f.*

courtier, *n.* aulicus, purpuratus, *m.*

court martial, *n.* iudicium castrense, *nt.*

courtship, *n.* amor, *m.*

courtyard, *n.* area, *f.*, atrium, *nt.*

cousin, *n.* consobrinus, *m.*; consobrina, *f.*; patruelis, *c.*

cove, *n.* (small bay) sinus, *m.*

covenant, *n.* pactum, *nt.*; conventio, *f.*

cover, *v.t.* tego, [3]; operio, [4]; celo, [1]; instruo, [3]; *fig.* (protect) protego, [3].

cover, *n.* tegmen; (lid) operculum; (wrapper) involucrum; (shelter) praesidium, *nt.*; (for game) operimentum, *nt.*; lustra, *nt. pl.*; *fig.* praetextus, *m.*

covering, *n.* (act) obductio, *f.*; (cover) tegmen, velamen;

(wrapper) involucrum; (lid) operculum; (of a bed) stragulum, *nt.*

coverlet, *n.* stragulum, *nt.*

covert, *n.* perfugium, latibulum, lustrum, *nt.*

covert, *a.* tectus; occultus; (indirect) obliquus; **~ly**, *ad.* tecte, occulte; oblique.

covet, *v.t.* concupisco, cupio, appeto, [3].

covetous, *a.* avidus, avarus, appetens, cupidus; **~ly**, *ad.* avide, avare; appetenter.

covetousness, *n.* avaritia, aviditas, cupiditas, *f.*

cow, *n.* vacca, bos, *f.*

coward, *n.* ignavus, timidus, *m.*

cowardice, *n.* ignavia; timiditas, *f.*

cowardly, *a.* ignavus, timidus.

cower, *v.i.* subsido, [3].

cowherd, *n.* bubulcus, armentarius, *m.*

cowshed, *n.* bubile, *nt.*

coy, *a.* modestus; timidus; verecundus; **~ly**, *ad.* verecunde, timide.

coyness, *n.* modestia; timiditas, *f.*

cozen, *v.t.* fallo, [3]; ludificor, [1].

crab, *n.* cancer, *m.*

crabbed, *a.* morosus; (sour) acerbus.

crack, *v.t.* findo; frango, [3]; (a whip) flagello insono, [1]; **~**, *v.i.* dehisco, displodor, [3]; dissilio, [4].

crack, *n.* fissura, rima, *f.*; (noise) crepitus, *m.*

cracked, *a.* (of walls, *etc.*) rimosus.

crackle, *v.i.* crepito, [1].

cradle, *n.* cunae, *f. pl.*; *fig.* cunabula, incunabula, *nt. pl.*

craft, *n.* (cunning) astutia, *f.*; astus, *m.*; (calling, trade) ars, *f.*; (ship) navicula, linter, *f.*

craftily, *ad.* astute, callide.

craftiness, *n.* astutia, calliditas; (skill) sollertia, *f.*

crafty, *a.* astutus, callidus; (deceitful) subdolus, fallax, dolosus.

craftsman, *n.* artifex, *m.*

crag, *n.* scopulus, *m.*

craggy, *a.* scopulosus; (rough) asper.

cram, *v.t.* farcio, [4]; **~ together**, constipo, [1].

cramp, *n.* (disease) spasmus, *m.*; (tool) uncus, *m.*

crane, *n.* (bird) grus, *c.*; (machine) tolleno, *f.*

cranny, *n.* rima, fissura, *f.*

crash, *n.* fragor, strepitus, *m.*

crash, *v.i.* strepo, [3]; sono, fragorem do, [1].

crass, *a.* crassus.

crate, *n.* corbis, *f.*

crater, *n.* (of a volcano) crater, *m.*

crave, *v.t.* (beg) rogo, imploro, efflagito, [1], posco, expeto, [3]; (desire) cupio, [4].

craven, *a.* ignavus, timidus.

craving, *n.* desiderium, *nt.*; appetitus, *m.*; sitis, fames, *f.*

crawl, *v.i.* repo, serpo, [3]; repto, [1].

craziness, *n.* imbecillitas, vesania, insania, *f.*, furor, *m.*

crazy, *a.* imbecillus, insanus, vesanus.

creak, *v.i.* strideo, [2]; crepito, [1].

creak, creaking, *n.* stridor, crepitus, *m.*

creaking, *a.* stridulus.

cream, *n.* flos lactis, *m.*; *fig.* (the pick of) flos, *m.*; robur, *nt.*

crease, *n.* ruga, *f.*

crease, *v.t.* corrugo, rugo, replico, [1].

create, *v.t.* creo, [1]; pario, gigno, [3]; *fig.* formo, [1]; fingo, [3]; invenio, [4]; (appoint) creo, [1].

creation, *n.* (act) creatio, *f.*; (origin) origo, *f.*; (whole world) mundus, *m.*; *fig.* (work of art) opus, *nt.*, ars, *f.*

creative, *a.* creatrix; effectrix.

creator, *n.* creator, procreator; *fig.* fabricator; auctor, *m.*

creature, *n.* res creata, *f.*; animal, *nt.*; (person) caput, *nt.*; (dependant, tool) minister, *m.*

credence, *n.* (belief) fides, *f.*; **give ~ to,** credo, [3] (*with dat.*).

credentials, *n.* auctoritates, litterae, *f. pl.*

credibility, *n.* fides, probabilitas, *f.*

credible, *a.* credibilis.

credibly, *ad.* credibiliter.

credit, *n.* (authority) auctoritas; (belief, faith) fides; (reputation) fama, existimatio; (praise) laus, *f.*; (financial) fides, *f.*

credit, *v.t.* credo; (financial) acceptum refero (alicui), [3].

creditable, *a.* honorificus, honestus.

creditor, *n.* creditor, *m.*

credulity, *n.* credulitas, *f.*

credulous, *a.* credulus.

creed, *n.* fides, doctrina, opinio, *f.*

creek, *n.* aestuarium, *nt.*

creep, *v.i.* repo, serpo, [3]; repto, [1].

crescent-shaped, *a.* lunatus; (of the moon) crescens.

crest, *n.* (of animals) crista; (of a horse) iuba; (of a helmet) crista, *f.*; (heraldic) insigne, *nt.*; (of a hill) apex, *m.*

crested, *a.* cristatus.

crestfallen, *a.* *fig.* demissus, deiectus.

crevice, *n.* rima, rimula, *f.*

crew, *n.* grex, *m.*, turba, multitudo, *f.*; (of a ship) remiges, nautae, *m. pl.*

cricket, *n.* (insect) gryllus, *m.*, cicada, *f.*

crime, *n.* crimen, delictum, maleficium; facinus; (shameful deed) flagitium, *nt.*

criminal, *n.* nocens, *m.*

criminal, *a.* scelestus, sceleratus, nefarius; (of a charge) capitalis.

crimson, *n.* coccum, *nt.*; ~, *a.* coccineus, coccinus.

cringe to, *v.t.* adulor, [1].

cripple, *n.* claudus, *m.*

cripple, *v.t.* aliquem claudum facio, [3]; *fig.* debilito, [1]; accido, [3].

crippled, *a.* claudus, mancus.

crisis, *n.* discrimen, momentum, *nt.*

crisp, *a.* crispus; (brittle) fragilis.

criterion, *n.* signum, insigne, indicium, *nt.*

critic, *n.* existimator; iudex; criticus, censor, *m.*

critical, *a.* criticus; (censorious) mordax.

criticism, *n.* ars critica, *f.*; iudicium, *nt.*; censura, reprehensio, *f.*

criticize, *v.t.* iudico, examino, [1]; carpo, reprehendo, [3].

croak, *v.i.* (as frogs) coaxo, [1]; (as ravens) crocio, [4].

croak, croaking, *n.* crocitus, *m.*

crockery, *n.* (vasa) fictilia, *nt. pl.*

crocodile, *n.* crocodilus, *m.*

crocus, *n.* crocus, *m.*, crocum, *nt.*

crone, *n.* anicula, vetula, *f.*

crook, *n.* (of shepherds) pedum, *nt.*; **by hook or by ~**, quocumque modo.

crooked, *a.* curvatus, curvus, incurvus, flexus; *fig.* (dishonest) pravus; dolosus; ~**ly**, *ad.* torte; prave.

crookedness, *n.* curvatura, *f.*, curvamen, *nt.*; *fig.* (dishonesty) pravitas, *f.*

crop, *n.* (of corn) messis, *f.*; (yield) reditus, *m.*

crop, *v.t.* abscido, [3], decurto, [1]; tondeo, [2]; (browse) carpo, depasco, [3]; tondeo, [2].

cross, *n.* crux; *fig.* molestia, *f.*; cruciatus, *m.*; infortunium, *nt.*

cross, *a. fig.* (ill-tempered) morosus; ~**ly**, *ad.* morose.

cross, *v.t.* (pass over) transeo, *ir.*; (send across) transmitto, traicio, [3]; *fig.* (thwart) frustror, [1]; ~ **one's mind**, subeo, *ir.*; succurro, [3]; ~, *v.i.* ~ **over**, transcendo, traicio, transgredior, [3].

crossbar, *n.* repagulum, *nt.*

crossbow, *n.* arcuballista, *f.*

crossbowman, *n.* arcuballistarius, *m.*

cross-examination, *n.* interrogatio, percontatio, *f.*

cross-examine, *v.t.* percontor, [1].

crossing, *n.* transitus; traiectus, *m.*; (of roads) bivium; (of three *or* four roads) trivium, quadrivium, *nt.*

crossness, *n.* morositas, *f.*

cross-question, *v.t.* percontor, [1].

crossroads, *n.* trames, *m.*

crouch, *v.i.* me demitto, subsido, [3]; (hide) delitesco, [3].

crow, *n.* (bird) cornix, *f.*; (voice of the cock) cantus, *m.*; gallicinium, *nt.*

crow, *v.i.* (of cocks) cano, [3]; canto; *fig.* (boast) iacto, [1].

crowbar, *n.* (lever) vectis, *m.*

crowd, *n.* turba; frequentia, caterva, multitudo, *f.*; concursus, *m.*

crowd, *v.t.* arto, stipo, [1]; premo, [3]; ~, *v.i.* (around) circumfundor, [3]; (together) convolo, congregor, [1]; concurro, confluo, [3].

crowded, *a.* condensus, confertus; frequens; celeber.

crowing, *n.* (of the cock) gallicinium, *nt.*, cantus, *m.*

crown, *n.* corona, *f.*, diadema, *nt.*; (top) vertex, *m.*; (completion) cumulus, *m.*; *fig.* (royal power) regnum, *nt.*

crown, *v.t.* corono, [1]; (with a garland, *etc.*) cingo, [3]; (add finishing touch to) cumulo, [1]; **be ~ed with success,** felicem exitum habeo, [2].

crucial, *a.* maximi momenti (= of the greatest importance).

crucifixion, *n.* summum supplicium, *nt.*

crucify, *v.t.* cruci suffigo, [3].

crude, *a.* crudus; *fig.* rudis; incultus; ~ly, *ad.* imperfecte, inculte.

cruel, *a.* crudelis, atrox, saevus; immanis; barbarus, durus, ferus; ~ly, *ad.* crudeliter, saeve; dure; atrociter.

cruelty, *n.* crudelitas; atrocitas, saevitia, *f.*

cruise, *v.i.* pervagor, circumvector, [1].

cruise, cruising, *n.* navigatio, *f.*

crumb, *n.* (of bread) mica, *f.*; frustum, *nt.*

crumble, *v.t.* frio, [1]; comminuo, contero, [3]; ~, *v.i.* frior, [1]; collabor, corruo, [3].

crumple, *v.t.* rugo, corrugo, [1].

crunch, *v.i.* dentibus frango, morsu divello, [3].

crush, *v.t.* contundo, contero; (press) premo, comprimo, [3]; elido; *fig.* opprimo; affligo, [3]; (weaken) debilito, [1].

crust, *n.* crusta, *f.*

crusty, *a.* crustosus; *fig.* morosus.

crutch, *n.* baculum, *nt.*; (support) fulcrum, *nt.*

cry, *v.t. & i.* clamo, exclamo, conclamo; (weep) lacrimo, [1]; fleo, [2]; ~ **against,** obiurgo, [1]; ~ **out,** exclamo, vociferor, [1].

cry, *n.* clamor, *m.*, vox, exclamatio, *f.*; (of infants) vagitus; (weeping) ploratus, *m.*

crying, *n.* fletus, ploratus, *m.*

crypt, *n.* crypta, *f.*

cryptic, *a.* ambiguus.

crystal, *n.* crystallum, *nt.*

crystal, *a.* crystallinus, vitreus; pellucidus.

cub, *n.* catulus, *m.*

cube, *n.* cubus, *m.*

cubic, *a.* cubicus.

cubit, *n.* cubitum, *nt.*, ulna, *f.*

cuckoo, *n.* coccyx, cuculus, *m.*

cucumber, *n.* cucumis, *m.*

cud, chew the ~, rumino, [1].

cuddle, *v.t.* amplector, [3].

cudgel, *n.* fustis, *m.*, baculum, *nt.*

cudgel, *v.t.* fustibus verbero, [1].

cue, *n.* (hint) nutus, *m.*; (watchword) signum, *nt.*; tessera, *f.*

cuff, *n.* (blow) colaphus, *m.*; alapa, *f.*

cuirass, *n.* lorica, *f.*; thorax; cataphracta, *m.*

culinary, *a.* culinarius; coquinarius.

cull, *v.t.* carpo, lego, decerpo, [3].

culminate, *v.i.* ad summum fastigium pervenio, [4].

culmination, *n.* fastigium, *nt.*

culpable, *a.* culpandus; nocens.

culprit, *n.* (person accused) reus, *m.*, rea, *f.*; (guilty person) nocens, noxius, *m.*

cult, *n.* cultus, *m.*

cultivate, *v.t.* colo, [3]; (develop) formo, [1]; fingo, excolo, [3]; (train) exerceo; (show attentions to) foveo, [2]; observo, [1].

cultivation, *n.* cultura, *f.*, cultus, *m.*

culture, *n.* cultura, *f.*, cultus, *m.*; (of the mind) humanitas, *f.*

cumbersome, *a.* iniquus, gravis, incommodus, onerosus.

cunning, *a.* doctus, peritus; sollers; (in a pejorative sense) astutus, vafer.

cunningly, *ad.* docte, perite, sollerter; astute, vafre, dolose.

cunning, *n.* peritia; astutia, calliditas, ars, *f.*

cup, *n.* poculum, *nt.*, calix, *m.*; (beaker) patera, *f.*

cup-bearer, *n.* pocillator, *m.*

cupboard, *n.* armarium, *nt.*

Cupid, *n.* Cupido, Amor, *m.*

cupidity, *n.* cupiditas, *f.*

cur, *n.* canis, *c.*

curable, *a.* medicabilis, sanabilis.

curative, *a.* medicabilis.

curator, *n.* curator; custos, *m.*

curb, *n.* frenum, *nt.*; *fig.* coercitio, *f.*

curb, *v.t.* freno, refreno, [1]; compesco, comprimo, [3]; coerceo, [2].

curdle, *v.t.* cogo, [3]; coagulo, [1]; ~, *v.i.* coeo, [4]; concresco, [3].

cure, *n.* (of wounds) sanatio, *f.*; (remedy) remedium, *n.*, medicina, *f.*

cure, *v.t.* (heal) sano, [1], medeor, [2]; (preserve) salio, [4].

curiosity, *n.* curiositas; audiendi *or* spectandi studium, *nt.*; (object) res rara, raritas, *f.*

curious, *a.* (inquisitive) curiosus; (wondrously made) elaboratus; rarus; mirus; **~ly,** *ad.*

curiose; mirabiliter; arte (*abl.* of *ars*).

curl, *v.t.* (hair) crispo, [1]; torqueo, [2]; ~, *v.i.* crispor, [1].

curl, *n.* (natural) cirrus; (artificial) cincinnus, *m.*; (curve) flexus, *m.*

curling-iron, *n.* calamister, *m.*; ferrum, *nt.*

curly, *a.* crispus.

currency, *n.* (money) moneta, *f.*; nummi, *m. pl.*; (use) usus, *m.*

current, *a.* vulgaris, usitatus; (be ~) valeo, [2]; ~ly, *ad.* vulgo.

current, *n.* (of a river) flumen, *nt.*; (of the sea) aestus; (of air) afflatus, *m.*; aura, *f.*

curry, *v.t.* ~ **favour with**, morem gero (*with dat.*) [3].

curse, *n.* exsecratio, *f.*, maledictum, *nt.*

curse, *v.t.* exsecror, detestor, [1]; devoveo, [2].

cursed, *a.* exsecrabilis.

cursory, *a.* brevis, properatus.

curt, *a.* brevis, abruptus; ~ly, *ad.* breviter.

curtail, *v.t.* decurto, mutilo, [1]; praecido, [3]; *fig.* coarto, [1]; minuo, [3].

curtain, *n.* velum; (in a theatre) aulaeum, *nt.*; (for beds, *etc.*) plagula, *f.*; (mosquito net) conopium, *nt.*

curtness, *n.* brevitas, *f.*

curve, *n.* curvamen, *nt.*, flexus; sinus, *m.*; (thing curved) curvatura, *f.*

curve, *v.t.* (in)curvo, sinuo, [1]; flecto, [3].

curved, *a.* curvus, incurvus, recurvus; curvatus; sinuosus; (as sickle) falcatus.

cushion, *n.* pulvinar, *nt.*, pulvinus, *m.*, culcita, *f.*

custody, *n.* custodia, tutela, *f.*; (imprisonment) carcer, *m.*

custom, *n.* (use) usus, mos, *m.*, consuetudo, *f.*; (fashion) institutum, praescriptum, *nt.*; (rite) ritus, *m.*; ~s **duty**, portorium, vectigal, *nt.*

custom-house, *n.* telonium, *nt.*; ~s-**officer**, *n.* portitor, *m.*

customary, *a.* usitatus, consuetus, translaticius.

customer, *n.* emptor, *m.*

cut, *v.t.* seco, [1]; (fell) caedo; (mow) succido, meto, [3]; ~ **apart**, intercido, [3]; disseco, [1]; ~ **away**, recido, abscindo, [3]; amputo, [1]; ~ **down**, caedo; (kill) occido, [3]; ~ **to pieces**, concido, [3]; ~ **off**, praecido; abscindo, [3]; (amputate) amputo, [1]; (the head) detrunco, [1]; (intercept) intercludo, [3]; prohibeo, [2]; *fig.* (destroy, *etc.*) exstinguo, perimo, adimo, [3]; ~ **open**, incido, [3]; ~ **out**, exseco, [1]; (out of a rock, *etc.*) excido, [3]; ~ **short**, intercido; (abridge) praecido, [3]; *fig.* (interrupt) intermitto, [3]; ~ **through**, disseco, [1]; (e.g. the enemy) perrumpo, [3]; ~ **up**, minutatim concido, [3].

cut, *n.* incisura, *f.*; (slice) segmentum; (wound) vulnus, *nt.*, plaga,

f; (a short cut) via compendia-
ria, *f.*

cutlery, *n.* ferramenta, *nt. pl.*

cutpurse, *n.* saccularius, sector
zonarius, *m.*

cut-throat, *n.* sector collorum,
sicarius, *m.*

cutting, *a.* (sharp) acutus; *fig.*
mordax.

cutting, *n.* (act) sectio; (of a
plant) propago, talea, *f.*

cuttle-fish, *n.* loligo, sepia, *f.*

cycle, *n.* orbis, *m.*

cylinder, *n.* cylindrus, *m.*

cylindrical, *a.* cylindratus.

cymbal, *n.* cymbalum, *nt.*

cynic, *a. &* *n.* cynicus, *m.*

cynical, *a.* mordax, difficilis,
severus; ~ly, *ad.* cynice, mordaciter, severe.

cypress, *n.* cupressus, cyparissus, *f.*

....

D

....

dab, *v.t.* illino, [3].

dabble in, *v.t.* strictim attingo, [3].

daffodil, *n.* narcissus, *m.*

dagger, *n.* pugio, *m.*, sica, *f.*

daily, *a.* diurnus; quotidianus; ~,
ad. cotidie, in dies.

daintiness, *n.* fastidium, *nt.*

dainty, *a.* (of people) fastidiosus;
elegans; (of things) delicatus;
exquisitus, mollis.

daisy, *n.* bellis, *f.*

dale, *n.* vallis, convallis, *f.*

dalliance, *n.* blanditiae, *f. pl.*

dam, *n.* (mole) moles, pila, *f.*,
agger, *m.*; (barrier) obex, *m.*

dam, *v.t.* coerceo, [2]; obstruo, [3];
oppilo, [1].

damage, *n.* damnum, incommodum; (loss) detrimentum, *nt.*;
(injury) iniuria, noxa, *f.*

damage, *v.t.* (hurt) laedo, [3]; (impair) obsum.

damn, *v.t.* (condemn) damno, condemno, [1].

damnation, *n.* damnatio, *f.*

damp, *a.* umidus, udus.

damp, *n.* umor, *m.*

damp, dampen, *v.t.* umecto, [1];
fig. infringo; restinguo, [3].

dampness, *n.* uligo, *f.*; umor, *m.*

damsel, *n.* puella, virgo, *f.*

dance, *n.* saltatus, *m.*, saltatio, *f.*;
chorus, *m.*; chorea, *f.*

dance, *v.i.* salto, [1].

dancer, *n.* saltator, *m.*

dancing, *n.* saltatio, *f.*, saltatus,
m.

dancing-girl, *n.* saltatrix, *f.*

dandruff, *n.* furfur, *m.*; porrigo, *f.*

danger, *n.* periculum, discrimen,
nt.

dangerous, *a.* periculosus, gravis; ~ly, *ad.* periculose; graviter.

dangle, *v.i.* pendeo, dependeo, [2]; fluctuo, [1].

dangling, *a.* pendulus.

dank, *a.* umidus, uvidus, udus.

dappled, *a.* variatus, varius.

dare, *v.i.* audeo, [2]; ~, *v.t.* provoco, [1].

daring, *a.* audens; ferox; audax; animosus; ~ly, *ad.* audenter, audacter, animose.

dark, *a.* obscurus; opacus; niger; caecus; tenebrosus; caliginosus; (of mourning-dress) pullus; *fig.* obscurus, ambiguus, dubius, anceps; (gloomy) atrox.

dark, *n.* tenebrae, *f. pl.*; obscurum, *nt.*; nox, *f.*

darken, *v.t.* obscuro; (of colours) infusco; *fig.* occaeco, [1].

darkly, *ad.* obscure; *fig.* per ambages.

darkness, *n.* obscuritas, caligo, *f.*; (shadiness) opacitas, *f.*; tenebrae, *f. pl.*; color fuscus, *m.*

darling, *n.* deliciae, *f. pl.*; amores, *m. pl.*; corculum, *nt.*; ~, *a.* suavis, mellitus; amatus.

darn, *v.t.* resarcio, [4].

darnel, *n.* lolium, *nt.*

dart, *n.* iaculum, spiculum, missile, *nt.*; hasta, lancea, *f.*

dart, *v.i.* provolo, [1]; se inicere, [3].

dash, *v.t.* (against) allido, illido; offendo, [3]; (frustrate) frustror,

[1]; (confound) confundo, [3]; ~ to pieces, discutio, [3]; ~ out, (*v.t.*) elido, [3]; (*v.i.*) ruo, feror, [3]; ~, *v.i.* (rush) ruo, feror [3].

dash, *n.* (onset) impetus, *m.*

dashing, *a.* acer, alacer; splendidus.

date, *n.* (of time) dies, *m. & f.*; tempus, *nt.*; (fruit) balanus, *c.*; palma, *f.*; out of ~, obsoletus, desuetus.

date, *v.t.* diem ascribo, [3]; ~, *v.i.* (from) incipio, originem traho, [3].

daub, *v.t.* oblino, illino, [3].

daub, *n.* litura, *f.*

daughter, *n.* filia, *f.*

daughter-in-law, *n.* nurus, *f.*

daunt, *v.t.* pavefacio, [3]; terreo, perterreo, [2].

dauntless, *a.* impavidus, intrepidus.

dawdle, *v.i.* (loiter) moror, cesso, [1].

dawn, *v.i.* illucesco, dilucesco, [3]; *fig.* eluceo, [2]; ~ upon, *fig.* subeo, [4]; succurro, [3] (*both with dat.*).

dawn, *n.* aurora, prima lux, *f.*, diluculum, *nt.*

day, *n.* dies, *c.*; lux, *f.*, sol, *m.*; tempus, *nt.*; the ~ before, pridie; the ~ after, postridie.

day, *a.* diurnus.

daybreak, *n.* lux prima, *f.*

daylight, *n.* lux, *f.*, dies, *m.*

daytime, *n.* tempus diurnum, *nt.*

daze, v.t. obstupefacio, [3].

dazzle, v.t. praestringo, [3]; *fig.* capio, [3].

dazzling, a. fulgidus, splendidus.

dead, a. mortuus; vita defunctus; (lifeless, senseless) exanimis; *fig.* torpidus; (dull) segnis.

dead, n. manes, m. pl.; (of night) intempesta (nox), f.

deaden, v.t. hebeto, [1]; obtundo, [3]; (weaken) debilito, enervo, [1]; (lessen) imminuo, [3].

deadly, a. mortifer, letalis; *fig.* capitalis, implacabilis.

deadness, n. torpor; stupor, m., inertia; (dullness) insulsitas, f.

deaf, a. surdus.

deafen, v.t. exsurdo, [1]; obtundo, [3].

deafness, n. surditas, f.

deal, n. (quantity) numerus, m.; vis, copia, f.; (business) negotium, nt.; **a great ~,** multum.

deal, v.t. distribuo, [3]; (handle) tracto, [1]; **~ in,** (sell) vendo; **~ with,** utor, [3] (with abl.); **~,** v.i. mercor, negotior, [1].

dealer, n. mercator, negotiator, m.

dealing, n. (trade) negotiatio, mercatura, f., commercium, nt.; usus, m.; (doing) factum, n.; (treatment) tractatio, f.

dear, a. (costly) carus, pretiosus; (beloved) dilectus, carus; **~ly,** ad. care; valde.

dearness, n. caritas, f.

dearth, n. inopia, penuria; fames, f.

death, n. mors, f.; letum, nt.; interitus, obitus, m.; **violent ~,** nex, f.; funus, nt.

deathbed, n. **on one's ~,** moriens.

debar, v.t. excludo, [3]; prohibeo, arceo, [2].

debase, v.t. depravo; adultero; vitio, [1]; corrumpo, [3]; *fig.* dedecoro, [1].

debatable, a. disputabilis, controversiosus, dubius.

debate, v.t. disputo, discepto, [1]; dissero, [3]; **~,** v.i. cogito, medi-tor, [1].

debate, n. controversia, disceptatio f.; (friendly) colloquium, n.

debauch, v.t. stupro; vitio, [1]; corrumpo, [3].

debauchery, n. libido, luxuria, f., stuprum, nt.

debit, n. expensum, nt.

debit, v.t. expensam pecuniam alicui ferre.

debris, n. ruina, f.

debt, n. (of money) debitum, aes alienum; *fig.* debitum, nt.

debtor, n. debitor (also fig.), m.

decade, n. decennium, nt.

decay, v.i. (of buildings) dilabor, labor; (of flowers) defloresco; (rot) putresco; (waste away) tabesco, [3]; *fig.* deficio, [3]; declino, [1].

decay, n. tabes, caries; *fig.* defectio; deminutio, f.

deceased, *a.* mortuus, defunctus.

deceit, *n.* fraus, fallacia, *f.*, dolus, *m.*

deceitful, *a.* fallax; dolosus; fraudulentus; falsus; ~**ly,** *ad.* fallaciter; fraudulenter; dolose; per fallacias.

deceive, *v.t.* decipio, fallo, [3]; (cheat) fraudo, [1]; circumduco, [3]; circumvenio, [4] ~, *v.i. fig.* mentior, [4].

deceiver, *n.* fraudator, *m.*

December, *n.* December, *m.*

decency, *n.* decorum, *nt.*; pudor, *m.*

decent, *a.* decens; decorus; pudicus; honestus; ~**ly,** *ad.* decore, decenter, honeste.

deception, *n.* fraudatio, fraus, fallacia, *f.*

deceptive, *a.* fallax, vanus.

decide, *v.t. & i.* discepto, dijudico, [1]; decerno; constituo, [3].

decided, *a.* firmus, constans; (of things) certus; ~**ly,** *ad.* certe.

decimate, *v.t.* decimo; *fig.* depopulor, [1].

decipher, *v.t.* explico, [1].

decision, *n.* sententia, *f.*, arbitrium, iudicium, *nt.*

decisive, *a.* decretorius, haud dubius, certus; ~**ly,** *ad.* haud dubie.

deck, *n.* pons, *m.*; transtra, *nt. pl.*

declaim, *v.t. & i.* declamo, declamito, [1]; invehor (in . . .), [3] (*with acc.*).

declamation, *n.* declamatio, *f.*

declaration, *n.* professio; (of war) denuntiatio, *f.*; (speech) oratio, *f.*; (opinion) sententia, *f.*

declare, *v.t.* declaro, [1]; aperio, [4]; profiteor, [2]; (war) denuntio; (as a judge) iudico, [1]; ~, *v.i.* affirmo, [1].

decline, *v.t.* (recoil from) detrecto; (refuse) recuso, [1]; ~, *v.i.* (slope) vergo, [3]; inclino, [1]; (decay) deficio, minuor, [3]; (abate) laxo, [1].

decline, *n.* defectio; (wasting away) tabes, *f.*

decompose, *v.t.* dissolvo; ~, *v.i.* dissolvor, putresco, [3].

decomposition, *n.* dissolutio; (decay) tabes, *f.*

decorate, *v.t.* orno, exorno, decoro, [1].

decoration, *n.* (act) ornatio, exornatio, *f.*; ornatus, *m.*; (ornament) ornamentum, *nt.*

decorator, *n.* exornator, *m.*

decorous, *a.* decorus; ~**ly,** *ad.* decore.

decorum, *n.* decorum, quod decet, *nt.*

decoy, *v.t.* inesco, [1]; *fig.* allicio, illicio, pellicio, [3].

decoy, *n.* illecebra, *f.*, illicium, *nt.*; (bird) allector, *m.*

decrease, *v.t.* minuo, imminuo, deminuo, [3]; ~, *v.i.* decresco, minuor, [3]; minor fio, *ir.*

decrease, *n.* deminutio, imminutio, *f.*

decree, *n.* decretum, edictum, *nt.*; (judgment) sententia, *f.*

decree, *v.t.* statuo; decerno, edico, [3].

decrepit, *a.* decrepitus, debilis, enervatus.

decry, *v.t.* detrecto, obtrecto, [1].

dedicate, *v.t.* dedico; consecro, [1]; voveo, [2].

dedication, *n.* dedicatio; consecratio; (of a book) nuncupatio, *f.*

deduce, *v.t.* (infer) concludo, [3].

deduct, *v.t.* detraho, subtraho, deduco, [3].

deduction, *n.* deductio, *f.*; (in logic) conclusio, *f.*

deed, *n.* factum; facinus, *nt.*; (law) syngrapha, *f.*, instrumentum, *nt.*

deem, *v.t.* iudico, puto, existimo, [1]; duco, [3].

deep, *a.* altus, profundus; (of sounds) gravis; (of colours) satur.

deep, *n.* profundum; (sea) mare, *nt.*

deepen, *v.t.* excavo, [1]; defodio, deprimo, [3]; ~, *v.i.* altior fio, *ir.*; (night, *etc.*) densor, [1].

deeply, *ad.* alte, profunde; (inwardly) penitus; *fig.* graviter, valde.

deepness, *v.* depth.

deer, *n.* cervus, *m.*; cerva, *f.*

deface, *v.t.* deformo, turpo, [1].

defamation, *n.* obtrectatio, *f.*

defamatory, *a.* probrosus.

defame, *v.t.* diffamo, calumnior, obtrecto, [1].

default, *v.i.* (fail) deficio, [3]; **let a legal case go by ~**, ad vadimonium non venio, [4].

defeat, *n.* clades, calamitas; (frustration) frustratio, *f.*

defeat, *v.t.* (baffle) frustror, [1]; (conquer) vinco, [3]; supero, [1].

defect, *n.* vitium, mendum, *nt.*; menda, *f.*; (want) defectus, *m.*

defect, *v.i.* deficio, [3].

defection, *n.* defectio, *f.*

defective, *a.* mancus, vitiosus; imperfectus.

defence, *n.* (act) defensio; (excuse) excusatio; (means of) tutela, *f.*; tutamen, *f.*; ~s, munimentum, *nt.*

defenceless, *a.* inermis; defensoribus nudatus.

defend, *v.t.* defendo, [3]; (at law) patrocinor, [1] (*with dat.*).

defendant, *n.* reus, *m.*, rea, *f.*; **the ~**, iste.

defender, *n.* defensor; patronus, *m.*

defensible, *a.* quod defendi potest; excusabilis.

defer, *v.t.* differo, profero, produco, [3]; ~ **to**, obsequor, [3] (*with dat.*).

deference, *n.* observantia; reverentia, *f.*

defiance, *n.* provocatio, *f.*; **in ~ of**, contra (*with acc.*).

defiant, *a.* ferox.

deficiency, *n.* defectio, *f,* defectus, *m.* pars relicta; (want) lacuna, *f.*

deficient, *a.* mancus; (deficient in) inops (gen.); **be ~ in,** deficio, [3].

deficit, *n.* lacuna, *f.*

defile, *v.t.* contamino, inquino, maculo, commaculo; *fig.* foedo; incesto, violo, [1].

defile, *n.* fauces, angustiae, *f. pl.;* saltus, *m.*

define, *v.t.* circumscribo, [3]; termino, [1]; definio, [4].

definite, *a.* certus, status, definitus; **~ly,** *ad.* definite, certe.

definition, *n.* definitio, *f.*

definitive, *a.* definitivus, decretorius.

deflect, *v.t. & i.* deflecto, [3]; declino, [1].

deform, *v.t.* deformo, [1].

deformed, *a.* deformis; deformatus; distortus.

deformity, *n.* deformitas; pravitas, *f.*

defraud, *v.t.* fraudo, defraudo, [1].

deft, *a.* habilis.

defunct, *a.* vita defunctus, defunctus, mortuus.

defy, *v.t.* (challenge) provoco, [1]; (spurn) contemno, [3].

degenerate, *v.i.* degenero, [1].

degenerate, *a.* degener.

degradation, *n.* ignominia; deiectio, *f.*

degrade, *v.t.* deicio, [3]; loco moveo, [2]; *fig.* ignominia afficio, [3].

degree, *n.* gradus, ordo, *m.;* **in the highest ~,** summe; **by ~s,** paulatim, sensim, pedetentim, gradatim.

deification, *n.* apotheosis, consecratio, *f.*

deify, *v.t.* divum habeo, [2]; in numero deorum colloco, [1].

deign, *v.i.* dignor; non aspernor, non gravor, [1]; sustineo, [2].

deity, *n.* numen, *nt.;* deus, *m.;* dea, *f.*

dejected, *a.* demissus; tristis.

dejection, *n.* animi demissio, *f;* animus afflictus, *m.*

delay, *n.* mora, cunctatio; dilatio, retardatio, *f.*

delay, *v.t.* detineo, [2]; tardo; retardo; (keep back) remoror, [1]; **~,** *v.i.* cunctor; moror, cesso, [1].

delectable, *a.* amoenus.

delegate, *n.* legatus, *m.*

delegate, *v.t.* (depute) delego; (commit) commendo, [1].

delegation, *n.* delegatio, *f.*

deliberate, *a.* deliberatus, consideratus, cautus, prudens; lentus; **~ly,** *ad.* deliberate, cogitate; lente; consulto.

deliberate, *v.i.* consulto, delibero, considero, reputo, verso, voluto, [1]; volvo [3].

deliberation, *n.* deliberatio, *f.*

delicacy, *n.* subilitas, tenuitas; elegantia, *f*; cuppediae, *f pl.*; (weakness) infirmitas, *f*.

delicate, *a.* delicatus; mollis, tener; exquisitus; elegans; fastidiosus; (of texture) subtilis; (in taste) suavis; (weak) infirmus; ~ly, *ad.* delicate; exquisite; subtiliter; molliter.

delicious, *a.* delicatus, suavis; exquisitus.

delight, *n.* delectatio, *f*; deliciae, *f pl.*; gaudium, *nt.*; voluptas, *f*.

delight, *v.t.* delecto, [1]; ~, *v.i.* gaudeo, [2]; laetor, [1].

delightful, *a.* suavis, iucundus, amoenus; ~ly, *ad.* iucunde, suaviter.

delinquency, *n.* delictum, *nt.*

delinquent, *n.* nocens, *m.*

delirious, *a.* non sui compos, mente alienatus.

delirium, *n.* mentis alienatio, *f*; delirium, *nt.*

deliver, *v.t.* do, [1]; (hand over) trado, [3]; (free) libero, [1]; (surrender) prodo, [3]; (a speech) habeo, [2]; (sentence) dico (ius), [3]; (an opinion) promo, [3]; (a message) perfero, [3]; (of childbirth) parienti adsum; (~ up) cedo, [3].

deliverance, *n.* liberatio, *f*.

deliverer, *n.* liberator, conservator, *m.*; vindex, *c.*

delivery, *n.* liberatio; (of goods) traditio; (utterance) pronuntiatio, *f*; (child-birth) partus, *m.*

delude, *v.t.* decipio, deludo, [3]; derideo, [2].

deluge, *n.* diluvies, inundatio, *f*, diluvium, *nt.*

deluge, *v.t.* inundo, [1].

delusion, *n.* error, *m.*; fraus, *f*.

delve, *v.t., v.* **dig.**

demand, *v.t.* postulo, flagito, [1]; posco, deposco, peto, [3].

demand, *n.* postulatio, petitio, *f*; **be in ~,** a multis expetor, [3].

demarcation, *n.* designatio, *f*; (boundary) confinium, *nt.*

demean, *v.i.* ~ oneself, (condescend to) descendo ad (*with acc.*), [3].

demeanour, *n.* mores, *m. pl.*; (deportment) gestus, *m.*

democracy, *n.* civitas popularis, *f*; liber populus, *m.*

democrat, *n.* plebicola, homo popularis, *m.*

democratic, *a.* popularis; ~ally, *ad.* populi voluntate, per populum.

demolish, *v.t.* demolior, [4]; everto, disicio, [3].

demolition, *n.* demolitio, eversio, *f*.

demon, *n.* daemon, *m.*

demonstrable, *a.* demonstrabilis, manifestus.

demonstrate, *v.t.* demonstro, firmo, [1]; convinco, [3].

demonstration, *n.* demonstratio, *f*.

demur, *v.i.* haesito, dubito, [1]; ~ to, nego, repudio, [1].

demur, demurral, *n.* mora; (objection) exceptio, *f.*

demure, *a.* modestus, gravis, severus; ~ly, *ad.* modeste.

den, *n.* (cave) specus, *m., f., & nt.*; (of beasts) latibulum, *nt.*; spelunca, latebra, *f.*; lustra, *nt. pl.*

denial, *n.* negatio; infitiatio; (refusal) repudiatio; repulsa, *f.*

denote, *v.t.* significo, [1].

denounce, *v.t.* (accuse) accuso; (blame) culpo, [1].

dense, *a.* densus, spissus, confertus; ~ly, *ad.* dense; crebro.

density, *n.* densitas, *f.*

dent, *n.* (mark) nota, *f.*

dent, *v.t.* (mark) noto, [1].

dentist, *n.* dentium medicus, *m.*

denude, *v.t.* denudo, nudo, [1]; detego, [3]; (rob) spolio, [1].

denunciation, *n.* denuntiatio; accusatio, *f.*

deny, *v.t.* nego, infitior; (refuse) nego, recuso, denego, [1]; renuo, abnuo, [3].

depart, *v.i.* abeo; exeo, [4]; (leave) discedo, [3]; (move) demigro, [1]; (set out) proficiscor, [3].

department, *n.* (area of responsibility) provincia, *f.*; cura, *f.*; munus, *nt.*; (branch) genus, *nt.*

departure, *n.* abitus, discessus, *m.*; profectio; (deviation) digressio, *f.*

depend on, *v.i.* pendeo, [2], (*with ab or ex with abl.*); (trust) confido, fido (*with dat.*).

dependable, *a.* fidus.

dependant, *n.* cliens, *c.*; assecla, *c.*

dependence, dependency, *n.* servitus; (reliance) fiducia, fides, *f.*; (poverty) inopia, *f.*

dependent, *a.* subiectus; (poor) inops.

depict, *v.t.* (de)pingo; effingo; describo; exprimo, [3].

deplorable, *a.* miserabilis, flebilis, lugendus, plorabilis, calamitosus.

deploy, *v.t.* explico, [1].

depopulate, *v.t.* desolo, vasto, [1].

deportment, *n.* gestus, habitus, *m.*

depose, *v.t.* abrogo, [1]; amoveo, [2].

deposit, *v.t.* depono, [3]; (commit) commendo, [1].

deposit, *n.* depositum; (pledge) pignus, *nt.*; (first instalment) arrabo, *m.*

deposition, *n.* (evidence) testimonium, *nt.*

depraved, *a.* corruptus.

depravity, *n.* pravitas, *f.*

deprecate, *v.t.* deprecor, [1].

deprecation, *n.* deprecatio, *f.*

depredation, *n.* praedatio, spoliatio, *f.*; latrocinium, *nt.*

depress, *v.t.* deprimo; *fig.* infringo; affligo, [3].

depressed, *a.* (downcast) afflictus; (flat) planus; (hollow) cavus.

depressing, *a.* tristis.

depression, *n.* *fig.* animi demissio,*f.*; animus afflictus, *m.*

deprivation, *n.* (act) privatio; spoliatio; (state) orbitas, inopia, *f.*

deprive, *v.t.* privo; spolio, orbo, [1]; (take away) adimo, eripio, [3].

deprived, *a.* expers, exsors.

depth, *n.* altitudo, *f.*; profundum, *nt.*; (sea) pontus; (bottom) fundus, *m.*

deputation, *n.* legati; (spokesmen) oratores, *m. pl.*

depute, *v.t.* lego, mando, [1].

deputy, *n.* legatus; vicarius, *m.*

deranged, *a.* (mentally) mente captus, delirus.

derangement, *n.* (of mind) mens alienata, mentis alienatio,*f.*

derelict, *a.* derelictus.

deride, *v.t.* rideo, derideo, irrideo, [2].

derision, *n.* risus, derisus, *m.*; irrisio,*f.*

derisive, *a.* acerbus.

derivation, *n.* derivatio; etymologia,*f.*

derive, *v.t.* duco, deduco, [3]; ~, *v.i.* proficiscor, [3]; orior, [4].

derogatory, *a.* inhonestus, turpis.

descend, *v.t. & i.* descendo; (fall suddenly) delabor, [3]; **be ~ed**

from, orior ab (*with abl.*), [4]; originem traho ab (*with abl.*), [3].

descendant, *n.* progenies, proles, stirps,*f.*

descent, *n.* descensus, *m.*; descensio; (slope) declivitas,*f.*; *fig.* lapsus, *m.*; (origin) origo,*f.*; genus, *nt.*

describe, *v.t.* describo; depingo, [3]; narro, [1].

description, *n.* descriptio; narratio,*f.*

desecrate, *v.t.* profano, violo, [1]; polluo, [3].

desecration, *n.* violatio,*f.*

desert, *n.* (wilderness) desertum, *nt.*, vastitas, solitudo,*f.*

desert, *n.* meritum, *nt.*

desert, *v.t.* desero, relinquo, destituo, [3]; ~, *v.i.* transfugio, signa relinquo, [3].

deserter, *n.* desertor; transfuga, *m.*

desertion, *n.* derelictio; (betrayal) proditio,*f.*

deserve, *v.t. & i.* mereo, mereor, [2]; dignus sum.

deservedly, *ad.* merito, iure.

deserving, *a.* dignus; bonus, optimus, probus.

design, *v.t.* describo, [3]; *fig.* machinor, excogito, [1]; molior, [4]; (destine) destino, [1].

design, *n.* (drawing) descriptio,*f.*; *fig.* (purpose) consilium, propositum, *nt.*

designate, *v.t.* designo; nomino, [1].

designation, *n.* designatio, *f.*; (name) nomen, *nt.*

designer, *n.* inventor; fabricator; machinator, *m.*

designing, *a.* callidus, subdolus.

desirable, *a.* optabilis, expetendus.

desire, *v.t.* desidero, opto, [1]; expeto, cupio, [3].

desire, *n.* desiderium, *nt.*; cupido, *f.*; appetitus, *m.*; appetitio, *f.*

desirous, *a.* cupidus, appetens.

desist, *v.i.* desisto; absisto; (cease) desino, [3].

desk, *n.* scrinium; pulpitum, *nt.*

desolate, *a.* solus, desertus, vastus, desolatus; *fig.* (of persons) afflictus.

desolation, *n.* vastitas; solitudo, *f.*; (bereavement) orbitas, *f.*

despair, *n.* desperatio, *f.*

despair, *v.i.* despero (de aliqua re), [1].

despairingly, *ad.* desperanter.

despatch, *v.t.* mitto; dimitto, [3]; (finish) absolvo; exsequor; (settle) transigo; conficio; (kill) interficio, [3].

desperate, *a.* (without hope) exspes, desperatus; (dangerous) periculosus; **~ly**, *ad.* ita ut spes amittatur; **be ~ly in love**, perdite amo, [1].

desperation, *n.* desperatio, *f.*

despicable, *a.* aspernandus, vilis.

despicably, *ad.* turpiter.

despise, *v.t.* despicio, sperno, temno, contemno, [3]; aspernor, [1].

despite, *c.* etiamsi (= even if).

despoil, *v.* **spoil**, *v.t.*

despondency, *n.* animi demissio, *f.*

despondent, *a.* demissus.

despot, *n.* dominus; tyrannus, *m.*

despotic, *a.* imperiosus, superbus, tyrannicus; **~ally**, *ad.* tyrannice.

despotism, *n.* dominatio, regia potestas, *f.*

dessert, *n.* secunda mensa, *f.*; bellaria, *nt. pl.*

destination, *n.* (purpose) destinatio, *f.*; propositum, *nt.*; (goal) meta, *f.*

destine, *v.t.* destino; (mark out) designo, [1].

destiny, *n.* fatum, *nt.*; sors, *f.*

destitute, *a.* egens, egenus, inops; destitutus, expers; viduus.

destitution, *n.* inopia; egestas, *f.*; mendicitas, *f.*

destroy, *v.t.* destruo, perdo, everto, tollo, consumo, [3]; aboleo, deleo, [2]; vasto, [1]; **be ~ed**, intereo, [4].

destruction, *n.* eversio, *f.*; exitium, *nt.* clades, *f.*

destructive, *a.* exitialis, perniciosus; calamitosus.

detach, *v.t.* seiungo; solvo, secerno, [3].

detached, *a.* seiunctus.

detachment, *n.* separatio; (of troops) manus, *f.*; (fairness) aequitas, *f.*

detail, *v.t.* enumero, [1]; singillatim dico, [3].

detail, *n.* singulae res, *f. pl.*; singula, *nt. pl.*

detain, *v.t.* retineo, [2]; retardo, [1].

detect, *v.t.* comperio, [4]; deprendo, [3].

detection, *n.* deprehensio, *f.*; indicium, *nt.*

detective, *n.* inquisitor, *m.*

detention, *n.* mora, *f.*

deter, *v.t.* deterreo, absterreo, [2]; averto, [3].

deteriorate, *v.i.* deterior fio, *ir.*, in peius mutor, [1].

deterioration, *n.* depravatio, corruptio, *f.*

determination, *n.* definitio, *f.*; arbitrium, iudicium, *nt.*; mens, voluntas, *f.*; (purpose) consilium, *nt.*; (resoluteness) constantia, *f.*

determine, *v.t.* determino, [1]; definio, [4]; statuo, constituo, decerno, [3]; diiudico, [1]; **I am ~d,** certum est mihi.

detest, *v.t.* abominor, detestor, [1]; odi, perodi, [3].

detestable, *a.* detestabilis, foedus, odiosus.

detestation, *n.* odium, *nt.*; detestatio, *f.*

dethrone, *v.t.* regno expello, [3].

detract, *v.t.* detraho, imminuo, [3]; (slander) detrecto, obtrecto, [1].

detraction, *n.* obtrectatio, *f.*

detriment, *n.* detrimentum, damnum, *nt.*

detrimental, *a.* damnosus, iniuriosus, iniquus.

devastate, *v.t.* vasto, populor, depopulor, [1]; *fig.* percello, [3].

devastation, *n.* (act) vastatio, populatio; (state) vastitas, *f.*

develop, *v.t.* evolvo, [3]; explico, [1]; *fig.* excolo, [3]; ~, *v.i.* cresco, [3].

development, *n.* explicatio, *f.*; (issue) exitus, *m.*

deviate, *v.i.* aberro, [1]; digredior, [3].

deviation, *n.* aberratio; declinatio; digressio, *f.*; *fig.* error, *m.*

device, *n.* (emblem) insigne, is, *nt.*; (motto) inscriptio, *f.*; (contrivance) artificium, *nt.*; machina, *f.*

devious, *a.* devius; vagus; erraticus; ~ **course,** ambages, *f. pl.*

devise, *v.t.* fingo, [3]; excogito, [1]; concoquo, [3]; molior, [4]; machinor, [1].

devoid, *a.* inanis, vacuus; liber; expers.

devote, *v.t.* devoveo, [2]; consecro, dico, [1]; (set apart) sepono, [3]; ~ **oneself to,** studeo, [2]; incumbo, [3] (*both with dat.*).

devoted, *a.* studiosus; (loving) pius.

devotedly, *ad.* studiose, summo studio.

devotion, *n.* devotio, *f.*; (affection) pietas, *f.*; (zeal) studium, *nt.*; diligentia, *f.*

devour, *v.t.* voro, devoro, [1]; haurio, [4]; consumo, [3].

devout, *a.* pius, devotus; ~**ly**, *ad.* pie, religiose, sancte.

dew, *n.* ros, *m.*

dewy, *a.* roscidus, roridus, rorulentus.

dexterity, *n.* calliditas, sollertia, *f.*

dexterous, dextrous, *a.* callidus, sollers, sciens, habilis; ~**ly**, *ad.* callide, scienter, sollerter.

diabolical, *a.* diabolicus.

diagnosis, *n.* (examination) exploratio, *f.*; (judgment) sententia, *f.*

diagonal, *a.* diagonalis; ~, *n.* diagonalis linea, *f.*; ~**ly**, *ad.* in quincuncem, in transversum.

diagram, *n.* forma; forma geometrica, *f.*

dial, *n.* solarium, *nt.*

dialect, *n.* dialectos, *f.*; sermo, *m.*

dialogue, *n.* sermo, *m.*; colloquium, *nt.*; (written discussion) dialogus, *m.*

diameter, *n.* diametros, dimetiens, *f.*

diamond, *n.* adamas, *m.*

diaphragm, *n.* praecordia, *nt. pl.*

diarrhoea, *n.* profluvium, *nt.*

diary, *n.* diarium, *nt.*; ephemeris, *f.*

dice, *n. pl.* tali, *m. pl.*; tesserae, *f. pl.*; (the game) alea, *f.*

dictate, *v.t.* dicto, [1]; praescribo, [3]; (command) impero, [1] (*with dat.*).

dictation, *n.* dictatum, *nt.*; (command) imperium, praescriptum, *nt.*

dictator, *n.* dictator, *m.*

dictatorial, *a.* dictatorius; arrogans; imperiosus.

dictatorship, *n.* dictatura, *f.*

diction, *n.* dictio, *f.*

dictionary, *n.* lexicon, *nt.*; thesaurus, *m.*

die, *n.* (for gaming) talus, *m.*; **the ~ is cast**, alea iacta est.

die, *v.i.* morior; *fig.* extinguor; (decay) labor, [3]; pereo, intereo, [4]; (fade) cado, [3].

diet, *n.* (food) victus, *m.*; (*med.*) diaeta, *f.*

differ, *v.i.* differo, [3]; discrepo, disto, [1]; (in opinion, *etc.*) dissentio, [4]; dissideo, [2].

difference, *n.* differentia; diversitas; varietas, *f.*; discrimen, *nt.*; (of opinion) discrepantia; dissensio, *f.*

different, *a.* diversus; alius; dispar; (unlike) dissimilis, (various) diversus, varius; ~**ly**, *ad.* aliter; diverse.

difficult, *a.* difficilis; arduus.

difficulty, *n.* difficultas, *f.*; (dilemma, need) angustiae, *f. pl.*; **with ~**, aegre.

diffident, *a.* diffidens; verecundus, timidus; modestus.

dig, *v.t. & i.* fodio; ~ **up**, eruo, effodio, [3].

digest, *v.t.* (food) concoquo, [3]; (*also fig.*).

digestion, *n.* (of food) concoctio, *f.*; (stomach) stomachus, *m.*

digit, *n.* digitus, numerus, *m.*

dignified, *a.* gravis.

dignify, *v.t.* honesto, honoro, orno, [1].

dignity, *n.* dignitas, gravitas, *f.*, honor, *m.*

digress, *v.i.* digredior, [3]; aberro, [1].

digression, *n.* digressio, *f.*

dike, *v.* **dyke**.

dilapidated, *a.* ruinosus, prolapsus.

dilapidation, *n.* ruina, *f.*

dilate, *v.t. & i.* dilato; dilator, [1]; ~ **on**, uberius dico de (*with abl.*).

dilatory, *a.* cunctabundus, lentus, tardus.

dilemma, *n.* dilemma, *nt.*; *fig.* (difficulty) angustiae, *f. pl.*

diligence, *n.* diligentia, sedulitas, *f.*

diligent, *a.* diligens, sedulus, ~**ly**, *ad.* diligenter, sedulo.

dilute, *v.t.* diluo, [3]; misceo, [2]; tempero, [1].

dilution, *n.* temperatio, mixtura, *f.*

dim, *a.* hebes; obscurus; **be** ~, hebeo, [2]; **become** ~, hebesco, [3].

dimension, *n.* dimensio, mensura, *f.*

diminish, *v.t.* minuo, imminuo, deminuo, [3]; (reduce) extenuo, [1]; ~, *v.i.* minuor, [3]; extenuor, [1].

diminution, *n.* imminutio, deminutio, *f.*

dimly, *ad.* obscure.

dimness, *n.* hebetatio; obscuritas; caligo, *f.*

din, *n.* strepitus, sonitus, fragor, *m.*; **make a** ~, strepo, [3].

dine, *v.i.* ceno, [1]; prandeo, [2].

dingy, *a.* fuscus, squalidus, sordidus, subniger.

dining-room, *n.* cenatio, *f.*

dinner, *n.* cena, *f.*

dinner-party, *n.* convivium, *nt.*

dint, *n.*, **by** ~ **of**, per (*with acc.*).

dip, *v.t.* immergo; tingo, [3]; ~, *v.i.* mergor; tingor; (sink) premor, vergo, [3]; declino, [1].

dip, *n.* declivitas, *f.*

diploma, *n.* diploma, *nt.*

diplomacy, *n. fig.* ars, astutia, *f.*

diplomatist, diplomatist, *n.* (ambassador) legatus, *m.*

dire, *a.* dirus, terribilis.

direct, *a.* rectus, directus; ~**ly**, *ad.* directe, recta (via); (immediately) statim, confestim.

direct, *v.t.* dirigo; (turn) flecto, verto; (address) inscribo, [3];

(order) iubeo, [2]; (rule) guberno; (manage) curo, procuro, [1].

direction, *n.* (act) directio, *f.*; (way) iter, *nt.*; via; (quarter) regio; (ruling) gubernatio; (management) administratio, *f.*; (order) praeceptum, *nt.*; **in both ~s,** utroque.

director, *n.* rector; magister; praeses, praefectus; gubernator; (manager) curator, *m.*

dirge, *n.* nenia, *f.*, carmen funebre, *nt.*

dirt, *n.* sordes, *f.*; caenum, lutum, *nt.*; limus, *m.*

dirtiness, *n.* spurcitia, *f.*; *fig.* obscenitas, *f.*

dirty, *a.* spurcus, sordidus, immundus, lutulentus, caenosus; (unwashed) illotus; *fig.* obscenus.

dirty, *v.t.* foedo, spurco, maculo, commaculo, [1].

disability, *n.* impotentia, *f.*

disable, *v.t.* debilito; enervo, [1].

disabled, *a.* debilis; mancus.

disadvantage, *n.* incommodum, detrimentum, damnum, *nt.*; (inequality) iniquitas, *f.*

disadvantageous, *a.* incommodus; iniquus.

disaffected, *a.* alienatus; aversus; seditiosus.

disaffection, *n.* alienatus animus, *m.*; seditio, *f.*

disagree, *v.i.* discrepo, [1]; dissideo, [2]; dissentio, [4].

disagreeable, *a.* iniucundus; ingratus; molestus; insuavis; gravis; (of people) difficilis, morosus.

disagreement, *n.* dissensio, discordia, *f.*

disappear, *v.i.* vanesco; evanesco; dilabor, [3].

disappearance, *n.* exitus, *m.*

disappoint, *v.t.* fallo, [3]; frustror, fraudo, [1].

disappointment, *n.* frustratio, *f.*; (inconvenience) incommodum, *nt.*

disapprobation, disapproval, *n.* improbatio, reprehensio, *f.*

disapprove, *v.t.* reprehendo, [3]; improbo, [1].

disarm, *v.t.* exarmo, [1]; armis exuo, [3]; *fig.* mitigo, [1].

disaster, *n.* calamitas, clades, *f.*; incommodum, *nt.*

disastrous, *a.* calamitosus, funestus; pestifer; **~ly,** *ad.* calamitose; pestifere.

disband, *v.t.* dimitto, [3]; missum facio, [3].

disbelief, *n.* diffidentia; incredulitas, *f.*

disbelieve, *v.t.* fidem non habeo, [2]; non credo, [3].

disc, *n.* discus, *m.*; orbis (solis, lunae), *m.*

discard, *v.t.* repudio, [1]; reicio, excutio, [3].

discern, *v.t.* discerno, distinguo, [3].

discerning, *a.* perspicax, acutus.

discernment, *n.* perspicientia, *f.*; (faculty) prudentia, *f.*; acumen, *nt.*

discharge, *u.t. & i.* (unload) exonero, [1]; (dismiss) dimitto, [3]; (of rivers) effundo, [3]; (perform) fungor, perfungor, [3]; (pay) solvo, [3]; (shoot, let fly) mitto, immitto; (acquit) absolvo, [3].

discharge, *n.* (unloading) exoneratio; (dismissal) missio; (acquittal) absolutio; (payment) solutio, *f.*; (efflux) profluvium, effluvium, *nt.*

disciple, *n.* discipulus, *m.*; discipula, *f.*; *fig.* sectator, *m.*

discipline, *n.* disciplina, *f.*

discipline, *u.t.* instituo; assuefacio, [3].

disclaim, *u.t.* infitior, [1]; diffiteor, [2]; nego, [1]; (let go) remitto, dimitto, [3].

disclaimer, *n.* negatio, infitiatio, *f.*

disclose, *u.t.* patefacio, pando, detego, [3]; aperio, [4]; enuntio, vulgo, [1].

disclosure, *n.* indicium, *nt.*

discolour, *u.t.* decoloro, [1].

discomfort, *n.* incommoda, *nt. pl.*; molestiae, *f. pl.*; vexatio, *f.*

disconcert, *u.t.* conturbo, [1]; (frustrate) frustror, [1].

disconnect, *u.t.* disiungo, seiungo, [3].

disconsolate, *a.* afflictus, tristis; ~**ly**, *ad.* insolabiliter; triste.

discontent, *n.* animus parum contentus, *m.*; (anger) ira, *f.*; (hatred) odium, *nt.*

discontented, *a.* parum contentus; (disagreeable) morosus.

discontinue, *u.t. & i.* intermitto; desino, desisto, [3].

discord, *n.* discordia, *f.*

discordant, *a.* discors; discrepans; dissonus; absonus.

discount, *u.t.* deduco; (disregard) neglego, [3].

discourage, *u.t.* deterreo, [2]; examino, [1]; (dissuade) dissuadeo, [2]; **be ~d**, animum demitto, [3].

discouragement, *n.* animi demissio, *f.*; (dissuasion) dissuasio, *f.*

discouraging, *a.* adversus, incommodus.

discourse, *n.* sermo, *m.*; colloquium, *nt.*; (written) libellus, *m.*

discourteous, *a.* inurbanus; inhumanus; ~**ly**, *ad.* inurbane; inhumaniter.

discourtesy, *n.* inhumanitas, *f.*

discover, *u.t.* comperio, [4]; (search out) exploro, investigo, [1].

discoverer, *n.* inventor; repertor, *m.*; inventrix, repertrix, *f.*; (searcher) investigator, *m.*

discovery, *n.* inventio; (searching out) investigatio, *f.*; (thing found out) inventum, *nt.*; (making known) patefactio, *f.*

discreet, *a.* cautus, prudens; ~**ly**, *ad.* caute, prudenter.

discrepancy, *n.* discrepantia, *f.*

discretion, *n.* prudentia, circumspectio, *f.*; **at the ~ of,** arbitrio (*with gen.*), ad arbitrium (*with gen.*).

discriminate, *v.t.* diiudico, [1]; distinguo, [3].

discriminating, *a.* proprius; (intelligent) acutus, perspicax, sagax.

discrimination, *n.* (distinguishing) distinctio, *f.*; (discernment) iudicium; (distinction) discrimen, *nt.*

discuss, *v.t.* disputo, [1]; dissero, ago, [3].

discussion, *n.* disputatio, disceptatio, controversia, *f.*

disdain, *v.t.* dedignor, aspernor, [1]; despicio, sperno, contemno, [3]; fastidio, [4].

disdain, *n.* contemptus, *m.*; fastidium, *nt.*; superbia, *f.*

disdainful, *a.* fastidiosus, superbus; **~ly,** *ad.* fastidiose, contemptim, superbe.

disease, *n.* morbus, *m.*, malum, *nt.*; (plague) pestilentia, pestis, lues, *f.*

diseased, *a.* aegrotus, aeger.

disembark, *v.t. & i.* e navi (navibus) expono; e navi egredior (in terram), [3].

disembowel, *v.t.* eviscero, [1].

disengage, *v.t.* solvo, exsolvo, [3]; avoco, [1].

disentangle, *v.t.* extrico, explico, [1]; expedio, [4].

disfavour, *n.* invidia, *f.*

disfigure, *v.t.* deformo, turpo, mutilo, [1].

disfigurement, *n.* deformatio; deformitas, foeditas, *f.*; (blemish) vitium, *nt.*; labes, *f.*

disgorge, *v.t.* revomo, evomo, [3].

disgrace, *n.* (shame) infamia; ignominia, *f.*; dedecus, *nt.*; (disfavour) offensa, invidia, *f.*

disgrace, *v.t.* dedecoro, dehonesto, [1].

disgraceful, *a.* turpis, inhonestus, ignominiosus; **~ly,** *ad.* turpiter, inhoneste, ignominiose.

disguise, *n.* (mask) persona, *f.*; *fig.* dissimulatio, *f.*; (false appearance) species, *f.*; (pretence) praetextum, *nt.*

disguise, *v.t.* vestem muto; *fig.* celo; dissimulo, [1].

disgust, *n.* (loathing) fastidium, taedium, odium, *nt.*

disgust, *v.t.* fastidium moveo, [2]; **be ~ed,** piget (me rei), [2]; aegre fero, [3].

disgusting, *a.* foedus; *fig.* odiosus.

dish, *n.* catinus, *m.*; (flat ~) patina; (a large dish) lanx, *f.*; (course) mensa, *f.*, ferculum, *nt.*

dish, *v.t.* ~ **up,** appono, [3].

dishearten, *v.t.* animum frango, [3]; exanimo, [1]; **be ~ed,** animum demitto, [3].

dishevelled, *a.* passus, effusus, irreligatus.

dishonest, *a.* improbus, malus, perfidus, fradulentus; **~ly,** *ad.*

improbe, dolo malo, fraude ac dolo.

dishonesty, *n.* improbitas, fraus, *f.*; dolus malus, *m.*

dishonour, *n.* infamia, *f.*; dedecus, *nt.*; ignominia, *f.*

dishonour, *v.t.* dehonesto; dedecoro, [1].

dishonourable, *a.* inhonestus, turpis.

disinherit, *v.t.* exheredo, [1].

disinterested, *a.* aequus, integer.

disjointed, *a.* intermissus.

dislike, *v.t.* aversor, non amo, [1].

dislike, *n.* aversatio, *f.*; odium, fastidium, *nt.*

dislocate, *v.t.* luxo, [1].

dislocation, *n.* luxatura, *f.*

dislodge, *v.t.* deturbo, [1]; depello, [3].

disloyal, *a.* infidelis, perfidus, perfidiosus.

disloyalty, *n.* infidelitas, perfidia, *f.*

dismal, *a.* tristis, miser; maestus; (dreadful) dirus; **~ly,** *ad.* misere, maeste.

dismantle, *v.t.* diruo, [3].

dismay, *n.* consternatio, perturbatio, *f.*; pavor, *m.*

dismay, *v.t.* perterrefacio, [3]; territo, consterno, perturbo, [1].

dismiss, *v.t.* dimitto, [3]; demoveo, [2].

dismissal, *n.* missio, demissio, *f.*

dismount, *v.i.* ex equo desilio, [4].

disobedience, *n.* contumacia, *f.*

disobedient, *a.* non oboediens; contumax; **~ly,** *ad.* contra (alicuius) iussum.

disobey, *v.i.* non pareo [2] *or* non oboedio, [4] (*with dat.*); neglego, [3]; detrecto, [1].

disorder, *n.* confusio, *f.*; (disturbance of the peace) tumultus, *m.*; (illness) aegrotatio; (of mind) perturbatio (animi), *f.*

disorderly, *a.* inordinatus, turbatus; turbidus; incompositus; tumultuosus.

disorganization, *n.* dissolutio, *f.*

disorganized, *a.* dissolutus.

disown, *v.t.* diffiteor, [2]; infitior, [1].

disparage, *v.t.* obtrecto, detrecto, [1].

disparagement, *n.* obtrectatio, *f.*

disparity, *n.* inaequalitas, diversitas, *f.*

dispatch, v. **despatch.**

dispel, *v.t.* dispello, depello, solvo, [3].

dispense, *v.t.* distribuo, [3]; **~ with,** careo (*with abl.*), [2].

dispenser, *n.* dispensator, *m.*

disperse, *v.t.* spargo, dispergo, [3]; dissipo, [1]; (put to flight) fundo, [3]; fugo, [1]; **~,** *v.i.* dilabor; diffugio, [3].

dispersion, *n.* dissipatio, *f.*

dispirited, *a.* abiectus, animo fractus.

displace, *v.t.* summoveo, [2]; (a person) loco moveo, [2].

display, *n.* (show) ostentus, *m.*; *fig.* iactatio, ostentatio, *f.*

display, *v.t.* (expose) expono; (spread) expando, [3]; *fig.* iacto, ostento, [1]; (exercise) praesto, [1]; exhibeo, [2].

displease, *v.t.* displiceo, [2] (*with dat.*).

displeasure, *n.* offensa; offensio; (grudge) ira, *f.*

disposable, *a.* in promptu.

disposal, *n.* arbitrium, *nt.*; **at the ~ of,** *pr.* penes (*with acc.*).

dispose, *v.t.* dispono, [3]; ordino, [1]; (induce) adduco, [3]; **~ of,** (sell) vendo, [3]; (get rid of) tollo, [3].

disposed, *a.* inclinatus (ad *with acc.*); propensus (ad); pronus (ad); **well-~,** aequus; **ill-~,** malevolus, iniquus.

disposition, *n.* (arrangement) dispositio; (nature) natura, indoles, *f.*; ingenium, *nt.*; mens, *f.*; animus, *m.*

disproof, *n.* refutatio, *f.*

disproportionate, *a.* inaequalis, impar; **~ly,** *ad.* inaequaliter, impariter.

disprove, *v.t.* confuto, refuto, [1]; refello, redarguo, [3].

disputable, *a.* disputabilis; (doubtful) dubius, ambiguus.

dispute, *n.* disputatio, disceptatio, contentio; controversia, *f.*; (quarrel) rixa, *f.*; iurgium, *nt.*

dispute, *v.t. & i.* disputo, [1]; contendo, [3]; **it is ~d,** ambigitur.

disqualification, *n.* impedimentum, *nt.*

disqualify, *v.t.* impedimento esse (*with dat.*).

disquiet, *n.* sollicitudo, inquies, *f.*

disregard, *n.* incuria, neglegentia, *f.*; contemptus, *m.*

disregard, *v.t.* neglego; parvi facio, [3].

disreputable, *a.* infamis.

disrepute, *n.* infamia, *f.*

disrespect, *n.* neglegentia, irreverentia, *f.*

disrespectful, *a.* irreverens; **~ly,** *ad.* irreverenter.

disrupt, *v.* disturbo, [1].

disruption, *n.* diruptio, *f.*; *fig.* discidium, *nt.*

dissatisfaction, *n.* taedium, fastidium, *nt.*; indignatio, *f.*

dissatisfied, *a.* male (parum) contentus.

dissect, *v.t.* disseco, [1]; incido, [3].

dissection, *n.* sectio, incisio, anatomia, *f.*

dissemble, *v.t. & i.* dissimulo, [1].

dissembler, *n.* dissimulator, *m.*

dissension, *n.* dissensio, *f.*; dissidium, *nt.*

dissent, *v.i.* dissentio, [4]; dissideo, [2].

dissent, *n.* dissensio, *f.*

dissident, *n. & a.* rebellis.

dissimilar, *a.* dissimilis, dispar.

dissimilarity, *n.* dissimilitudo, *f.*

dissimulation, *n.* dissimulatio, *f.*

dissipate, *v.t. & i.* dissipo; dissipor, [1].

dissipation, *n.* dissipatio, *f.*; (licentiousness) libido, luxuria, *f.*

dissipated, *a.* perditus, dissolutus.

dissolute, *a.* dissolutus, corruptus, immoderatus.

dissoluteness, *n.* mores dissoluti, *m. pl.*

dissolution, *n.* dissolutio; mors, *f.*

dissolve, *v.t.* dissolvo; (melt) liquefacio, [3]; liquo, [1]; (break up) dirimo, [3]; ~, *v.i.* liquesco, [3]; (break up) dissolvor, [3].

dissonant, *a.* dissonus, absonus.

dissuade, *v.t.* dissuadeo, [2] (*with dat.*); abduco, [3].

distaff, *n.* colus, *f.*

distance, *n.* distantia, *f.*; intervallum, (space) spatium, *nt.*; (remoteness) longinquitas, *f.*; **at a** ~, procul, longe.

distant, *a.* distans, disiunctus, longinquus, remotus, amotus.

distaste, *n.* fastidium, *nt.*

distasteful, *a. fig.* odiosus, molestus, gravis.

distend, *v.t.* distendo, [3].

distended, *a.* tumidus, tumefactus.

distil, *v.t. & i.* stillo, destillo; exsudo, [1].

distinct, *a.* (different) diversus, alius; (clear) clarus; distinctus; ~**ly,** *ad.* clare, distincte.

distinction, *n.* distinctio, *f.*; (difference) differentia, *f.*; discrimen, *nt.*

distinctive, *a.* proprius.

distinguish, *v.t. & i.* distinguo, discerno, [3]; ~ **oneself,** eniteo, [2]; praecello, [3].

distinguishable, *a.* qui (quae, quod) secerni, internosci potest.

distinguished, *a.* insignis; clarus, praeclarus, celeber, notus, eximius.

distort, *v.t.* distorqueo; detorqueo, [2]; depravo, [1].

distortion, *n.* distortio, depravatio, *f.*

distract, *v.t.* distraho, [3]; (divert) avoco, [1].

distracted, *a.* amens, demens, mente alienatus, vesanus, vecors.

distress, *n.* dolor, *m.*; miseria, tristitia, *f.*; angustiae, *f. pl.*; (poverty) inopia, *f.*

distress, *v.t.* affligo, ango, [3].

distressing, *a.* molestus, gravis.

distribute, *v.t.* distribuo, divido, [3]; dispertio, [4].

distribution, *n.* distributio, *f.*

district, *n.* regio, *f.*

distrust, *n.* diffidentia, *f.*

distrust, *v.t.* diffido, [3] (*with dat.*).

distrustful, *a.* diffidens, suspicax, suspiciosus; **~ly**, *ad.* diffidenter.

disturb, *v.t.* perturbo; sollicito, inquieto, [1]; (break up) dirimo, [3].

disturbance, *n.* perturbatio; confusio, *f.*; tumultus, *m.*; seditio, *f.*

disuse, *n.* desuetudo, *f.*

ditch, *n.* fossa, *f.*

dive, *v.i.* mergor, [3].

dive, *n.* (den of vice) lustrum, *nt.*

diverge, *v.i.* deflecto, [3]; declino, [1].

divergence, *n.* declinatio; *fig.* discrepantia, *f.*

divergent, *a.* diversus; (contrary) contrarius.

diverse, *a.* alius, varius, diversus.

diversification, *n.* variatio, *f.*; vices, *f. pl.*

diversify, *v.t.* vario, [1]; distinguo, [3].

diversion, *n.* (turning aside) derivatio; *fig.* oblectatio, *f.*; oblectamentum, *nt.*

diversity, *n.* diversitas, varietas, *f.*

divert, *v.t.* diverto, [3]; *fig.* oblecto, [1]; (distract) avoco, [1].

divide, *v.t.* divido, [3]; partior, [4]; distribuo, [3]; ~, *v.i.* discedo; (gape open) dehisco, [3].

divination, *n.* divinatio, vaticinatio, *f.*

divine, *a.* divinus; caelestis.

divinity, *n.* divinitas, *f.*; numen, *nt.*; (god) deus, *m.*

divisible, *a.* dividuus, divisibilis.

division, *n.* divisio, distributio, partitio; (part) pars; *fig.* (dissent) seditio, discordia, *f.*; dissidium, *nt.*

divorce, *n.* divortium, discidium, *nt.*

divorce, *v.t.* repudio, [1]; dimitto, [3].

divulge, *v.t.* vulgo, divulgo, [1]; palam facio, in medium profero, [3].

dizziness, *n.* vertigo, *f.*

dizzy, *a.* vertiginosus; (precipitous) praeceps.

do, *v.t.* ago, facio, efficio, [3]; **~ away with**, tollo, perdo, [3]; **~ for**, conficio, [3]; **~ up**, (bind) constringo, [3]; **~ without**, egeo, careo (*both with abl.*); **~**, *v.i.* (be suitable) convenio, [4].

docile, *a.* docilis; tractabilis.

dock, *n.* navale, *nt.*

dock, *v.t.* (ships) subduco, [3]; (curtail) curto, [1].

dockyard, *n.* navalia, *nt. pl.*

doctor, *n.* (physician) medicus, *m.*

doctrine, *n.* doctrina, *f.*

document, *n.* litterae, *f. pl.*

dodge, *v.t.* eludo, [3].

doe, *n.* cerva, *f.*

dog, *n.* canis, *c.*

dog, *v.t.* indago, [1].

dogged, *a.* pervicax; **~ly,** *ad.* pervicaciter.

doggedness, *n.* pervicacia, *f.*

doggerel, *n.* versus inculti, *m. pl.*

dogma, *n.* dogma, placitum, praeceptum, *nt.*

dogmatic, *a.* imperiosus.

doing, *n.* factum, facinus, *nt.*

dole, *v.t.* ~ out, metior, [4].

dole, *n.* donatio, *f.*; congiarium, *nt.*; diurnus victus, *m.*

doll, *n.* pupa, *f.*

dolphin, *n.* delphinus, delphin, *m.*

dolt, *n.* caudex, stipes, *m.*

domestic, *a.* domesticus, familiaris; intestinus; (private) privatus.

domesticate, *v.t.* (tame) mansuefacio, [3].

domicile, *n.* domicilium, *nt.*; domus, *f.*

dominant, *a.* praevalens.

dominate, *v.i.* dominor, [1] (*with* in *and* acc.).

domination, *n.* dominatio, *f.*

domineer, *v.i.* dominor, [1]; imperito, [1].

domineering, *a.* arrogans, imperiosus.

dominion, *n.* imperium, *nt.*; potestas, *f.*; dicio, *f.*; regnum, *nt.*

donate, *v.t.* dono, [1].

donation, *n.* donum, munus, *nt.*; stips, *f.*

donkey, *n.* asinus, asellus, *m.*

donor, *n.* donator, dator, *m.*; donatrix, *f.*

doom, *n.* fatum, exitium, *nt.*

doom, *v.t.* damno, condemno, [1]; ~ to, destino, [1] (*with dat.*).

door, *n.* ianua, foris, *f.*; ostium *nt.*; folding ~, valvae, *f. pl.*

doorkeeper, *n.* ianitor, *m.*; ianitrix, *f.*; custos, *c.*

door-post, *n.* postis, *m.*

doorway, *n.* ianua, *f.*; ostium, *nt.*

dormant, *a.* (lying idle) reses; (hidden) latens.

dormitory, *n.* cubiculum, dormitorium, *nt.*

dormouse, *n.* glis, *m.*

dot, *n.* punctum, *nt.*

dotage, *n.* deliratio, *f.*; (old age) senium, *nt.*; senectus, *f.*

dotard, *n.* senex delirus, *m.*

dote on, *v.t.* depereo, *ir.*; deamo, [1].

double, *a.* duplex; (of pairs) geminus; (as much again) duplus.

double, *n.* duplum, *nt.*

double, *v.t.* duplico, [1].

double-dealer, *n.* homo duplex, *m.*

double-dealing, *n.* fraus, fallacia, *f.*; dolus, *m.*

doubly, *ad.* dupliciter; bis.

doubt, *n.* dubitatio, *f.*; scrupulus, *m.*; **there is no ~,** non est dubium.

doubt, *v.t.* dubito, suspicor, [1]; (distrust) diffido, [3] (*with dat.*); ~, *v.i.* haesito, dubito.

doubtful, *a.* (of people) dubius; (of things) incertus; ambiguus; anceps; ~ly, *ad.* (of people) dubie; (of things) ambigue.

doubtless, *ad.* sine dubio, haud dubie.

dove, *n.* columbus, *m.*; columba, *f.*

dove-coloured, *a.* columbinus.

dove-cot, *n.* columbarium, *nt.*

down, *ad.* deorsum; (on the ground) humi.

down, *pr.* ~ **from,** de (*with abl.*); ~ **to,** usque ad (*with acc.*); **up and** ~, sursum deorsum.

down, *a.* declivis; (sad) tristis.

downcast, *a.* (of the eyes *or* head) deiectus, demissus; *fig.* afflictus.

downfall, *n.* occasus, *m.*; ruina, *f.*; exitium, *nt.*

downhill, *a.* declivis.

downstream, *ad.* secundo flumine.

downward, *a.* declivis; pronus.

downwards, *ad.* deorsum.

dowry, *n.* dos, *f.*

doze, *v.i.* dormito, [1].

dozen, *n.* duodecim; *a.* duodeni.

drab, *a.* cinereus; pullus.

draft, *v.* (levy) conscribo, scribo, [3].

draft, *n.* (first copy) exemplar, *nt.*

drag, *v.t.* traho; ~, *v.i.* (on the ground) trahor, [3].

dragon, *n.* draco; anguis, serpens, *m.*

drain, *n.* cloaca; fossa, *f.*

drain, *v.t.* sicco, [1]; (drink) exhaurio, [4]; ebibo, [3]; epoto, exsicco, [1].

drake, *n.* anas, *m.*

drama, *n.* drama, *nt.*; fabula, *f.*

dramatic, *a.* dramaticus, scaenicus; ~ally, *ad.* scaenice.

dramatist, *n.* poeta scaenicus, *m.*

dramatize, *v.t.* fabulam ad scaenam compono, [3].

drape, *v.t.* induo, [3]; amicio, [4]; velo, [1].

drapery, *n.* (cloth) vestis, *f.*

draught, *n.* (of drink) haustus, *m.*; (of air) aura, *f.*

draughty, *a.* ventosus.

draw, *v.t.* (pull) veho; duco, [3]; (a picture, *etc.*) delineo, [1]; describo, [3]; (the sword) stringo, destringo; (teeth) extraho, [3]; (water) haurio, [4]; (attract) illicio, [3]; ~ **aside,** abduco, seduco, [3]; ~ **away,** averto, distraho, [3]; ~ **back,** (*v.t.*) retraho; (*v.i.*) pedem refero, cedo; *fig.* recedo, [3]; ~ **near,** *v.i.* appropinquo; insto, [1]; ~ **off,** *v.t.* detraho; abduco; (wine) promo; (*v.i.*) cedo, [3]; ~ **out,** *v.t.* (sword, *etc.*) educo; (prolong) extendo, [3]; *fig.* elicio, [3]; ~ **together,** contraho, [3]; ~ **up,** subduco; scribo; (troops) instruo, constituo, [3].

drawback, *n.* impedimentum; detrimentum; incommodum, *nt.*; mora, *f.*; retardatio, *f.*

drawing, *n.* (art) pictura linearis; (picture) tabula, imago, *f.*

drawing-room, *n.* exedra, *f.*

dread, *n.* terror, pavor, *m.*; formido, *f.*

dread, *v.t.* timeo, [2]; metuo, expavesco, [3]; formido, [1].

dreadful, *a.* terribilis, horribilis; dirus; (violent) atrox; ~**ly,** *ad.* foede, atrociter.

dream, *n.* somnium, *nt.*; quies, *f.*

dream, *v.t. & i.* somnio; *fig.* dormito, [1].

dreamer, *n.* somniator, *m.*

dreamy, *a.* somniculosus.

dreary, *a.* vastus, solus, incultus; horridus; tristis.

dregs, *n.* faex; sentina, *f.*

drench, *v.t.* madefacio, [3]; irrigo, [1].

dress, *n.* (clothing) habitus, vestitus, *m.*; vestis, *f.*; ornatus, *m.*

dress, *v.t.* vestio, [4]; induo, [3]; (ex)orno; (wounds) curo, [1]; ~, *v.i.* (I get dressed) me vestio, [4].

dressing, *n.* ornatus, *m.*; (of food) coctura; (wounds, *etc.*) curatio, *f.*; (poultice) fomentum, *nt.*

dribble, *v.i.* stillo, [1].

drift, *n.* (meaning) propositum, *nt.*; (purpose) consilium; (of sand) cumulus, *m.*; (of snow) vis, *f.*

drift, *v.i.* feror, [3]; fluito, [1].

drill, *v.t.* terebro, perforo, [1]; (troops) exerceo, [2]; (discipline) instituo, [3].

drill, *n.* terebra; (of troops) exercitatio, *f.*

drink, *v.t. & i.* bibo, [3]; poto, [1]; ~ **in,** absorbeo, [2]; bibo, [3]; ~ **up,** ebibo, [3]; haurio, [4]; epoto, [1]; ~ **to,** propino, [1] (*with dat.*)

drink, *n.* potus, *m.*; potio, *f.*

drinkable, *a.* potabilis.

drinker, *n.* potor, potator, *m.*

drinking, *n.* (act) potatio; (drunkenness) ebrietas, *f.*; ~**-bout,** *n.* compotatio, *f.*

drip, *v.i.* stillo; roro, mano, [1].

drip, *n.* stillicidium, *nt.*

drive, *v.t.* ago; pello; impello; (force) compello, cogo, [3]; (horses, carriages) ago, [3]; ~, *v.i.* (in a carriage) vehor; (be carried along) deferor, [3]; ~ **along,** v. ~ **on;** ~ **away,** abigo; depello, [3]; fugo, [1]; ~ **back,** repello, [3]; ~ **in(to),** (a nail, *etc.*) infigo; (sheep, *etc.*) cogo; *fig.* compello, [3]; ~ **off,** abigo; (*v.i.*) avehor, [3]; ~ **on,** impello; ~ **out,** expello, [3]; ~ **past,** praetervehor, [3].

drivel, *n. fig.* ineptiae, *f. pl.*

driver, *n.* agitator; agaso, *m.*; (of carriages) auriga, *c.*

drizzle, *v.i.* roro, irroro, [1].

drizzle, *n.* pluvia, *f.*

droll, *a.* facetus, iocosus; ridiculus.

drone, *n.* fucus; (person) deses; (noise) bombus, *m.*

drone, *v.i.* murmuro, susurro, [1].

droop, *v.i.* langueo, [2]; marcesco; tabesco, [3]; ~, *v.t.* demitto, [3].

drop, *n.* gutta, stilla, *f.*; (a little bit) paululum, *nt.*; ~ **by** ~, guttatim, stillatim.

drop, *v.t.* (pour) stillo, [1]; (let slip) omitto, [3]; (pour out) effundo; (dismiss) dimitto, [3]; ~, *v.i.* stillo, [1]; (fall *or* glide down) delabor, [3]; (decrease) deminuor, [3].

dross, *n.* scoria; spurcitia, *f.*; (dropsy) aqua intercus, *f.*; *fig.* quisquiliae, *f pl.*; faex, *f.*

drought, *n.* siccitas, ariditas, *f.*

drover, *n.* pecuarius, armentarius, *m.*

drown, *v.t.* immergo, demergo; *fig.* opprimo, [3]; **his voice was ~ed by shouts**, vox prae clamoribus audiri non potuit.

drowsily, *ad.* somniculose.

drowsiness, *n.* somni cupiditas, *f.*

drowsy, *a.* somniculosus.

drudge, *v.i.* me exerceo, [2]; laboro, [1].

drudge, *n.* (a slave) mediastinus; *fig.* homo clitellarius, *m.*

drudgery, *n.* opera servilis, *f.*

drug, *n.* medicamentum, medicamen, *nt.*; medicina, *f.*

drug, *v.t.* medico, [1].

Druids, *n. pl.* Druidae, *m. pl.*

drum, *n.* tympanum, *nt.*

drummer, *n.* tympanista, *m.*

drunk, *a.* ebrius, potus.

drunkard, *n.* (use *a.*) temulentus, ebriosus, vinolentus, *m.*

drunken, *v.* **drunk**.

drunkenness, *n.* ebrietas, temulentia, *f.*

dry, *a.* aridus, siccus; (thirsty) siticulosus; *fig.* ieiunus; insulsus.

dry, *v.t.* sicco, desicco, [1]; arefacio, [3]; (in the sun) insolo, [1]; ~, *v.i.* aresco, [3].

dryness, *n.* ariditas, siccitas, *f.*

dual, *a.* duplex.

dub, *v.t.* (name) nomino, [1].

dubious, *a.* dubius; ~ly, *ad.* dubie.

duck, *n.* anas, *f.*

duck, *v.t.* mergo, submergo, demergo, [3]; ~, *v.i.* (head) caput demitto, [3].

duckling, *n.* anaticula, *f.*

dudgeon, *n.* ira, indignatio, *f.*

due, *a.* debitus; iustus; meritus; idoneus, aptus.

due, *n.* debitum; ius; (tax) vectigal, *nt.*

duel, *n.* singulare certamen, *nt.*

duet, *n.* bicinium, *nt.*

dull, *a.* hebes; obtunsus; surdus; (cloudy) caliginosus; nebulosus; *fig.* tardus; languidus; tristis; segnis; insulsus; stupidus.

dull, *v.t.* hebeto, [1]; obtundo; stupefacio, [3].

duly, *ad.* rite; recte.

dumb, *a.* mutus; **be ~**, obmutesco, [3].

dumbfound, *v.t.* obstupefacio, [3].

dunce, *n.* homo stupidus, stipes, *m.*

dung, *n.* stercus, *nt.*; fimus, *m.*

dungeon, *n.* carcer, *m.*; ergastulum, *nt.*

dung-hill, *n.* sterculinium, fimetum, *nt.*

dupe, *n.* homo credulus, *m.*; victima, *f.*

dupe, *v.t.* decipio, [3]; ludifico, [1]; fallo, [3].

duplicate, *a.* duplex.

duplicate, *n.* exemplum, exemplar, apographum, *nt.*

duplicity, *n.* fraus; fallacia, *f.*

durable, *a.* stabilis; durabilis; solidus; constans.

duration, *n.* spatium (temporis), *nt.*; diuturnitas, *f.*

during, *pr.* per; inter (*both with acc.*).

dusk, *n.* crepusculum, *nt.*

dusky, *a.* obscurus, tenebrosus; fuscus.

dust, *n.* pulvis, *m.*; (of filing *or* sawing) scobis, *f.*

dust, *v.t.* detergeo, [2].

duster, *n.* peniculus, *m.*

dustman, *n.* scoparius, *m.*

dusty, *a.* pulverulentus, pulvereus.

dutiful, *a.* pius; officiosus; oboediens, obsequens; ~**ly**, *ad.* pie; officiose; oboedienter.

duty, *n.* officium; munus; (tax) vectigal, *nt.*; (*mil.*) statio, *f.*

dwarf, *n.* nanus, pumilio, *m.*

dwarf, *v.t.* (diminish) imminuo, [3]; (overtop) supereminео, [2].

dwell, *v.i.* habito, [1]; incolo, [3]; *fig.* (upon) commoror, [1].

dwelling-place, *n.* domicilium, *nt.*; sedes, domus, habitatio, *f.*

dwindle, *v.i.* decresco, imminuor, [3].

dye, *v.t.* tingo, inficio, imbuo, [3]; coloro, [1].

dye, *n.* tinctura, *f.*; color, *m.*

dying, *a.* moriens, moribundus; (last) extremus, ultimus.

dyke, *n.* (ditch) fossa, *f.*; (dam, mound) agger, *m.*

dynasty, *n.* imperium, *nt.*; domus regnatrix, *f.*

dysentery, *n.* dysenteria, *f.*

....

E

....

each, *a.* (every) quisque; (every one) unusquisque; ~ **other**, alter alterum; ~ **of two**, uterque; **one** ~, singuli.

eager, *a.* acer, studiosus, cupidus, avidus; (fierce) ferox; (earnest) vehemens; ~**ly**, *ad.* acriter; avide, cupide.

eagerness, *n.* aviditas, cupiditas; *fig.* alacritas, *f.*; impetus, *m.*; studium, *nt.*

eagle, *n.* aquila, *f.* (also as standard).

ear, *n.* auris; (of corn) spica, *f.*; (hearing) aures, *f. pl.*

ear-ache, *n.* aurium dolor, *m.*

earliness, *n.* maturitas, *f.*

early, *a.* (in the morning) matutinus; (of early date) antiquus; (beginning) novus; (forward) maturus, praematurus, praecox.

early, *ad.* (in the morning) mane; (untimely) mature; (too ~) praemature; (quickly, soon) cito.

earn, *v.t.* lucror, [1]; mereo, [2]; consequor, quaero, [3].

earnest, *ad.* intentus; impensus; vehemens; ardens; (important) gravis; (serious) serius; **~ly,** *ad.* acriter; impense, intente.

earnest, *ad.* **in ~,** serio; bona fide.

earnings, *n.* stipendium, *nt.*

earring, *n.* inaures, *f. pl.*

earshot, *n.* unde quis exaudiri potest.

earth, *n.* (land) terra, tellus, *f.*; (world) orbis, *m.*; (of a fox) specus, *m., f.,* or *nt.*; (ground) solum, *nt.*; humus, *f.*

earthenware, *n.* fictilia, *nt. pl.*

earthly, *a.* terrenus; terrestris; humanus.

earthquake, *n.* terrae motus, *m.*

earth-work, *n.* agger, *m.*

earthy, *a.* terrosus; *fig.* terrenus.

ease, *n.* otium, *nt.*; quies, requies, *f.*; *fig.* (grace) lepor, *m.*; facilitas; (pleasure) voluptas, *f.*; **with ~,** facile.

ease, *v.t.* levo, exonero, laxo, [1].

easily, *ad.* facile.

east, *a.* orientalis.

east, *n.* oriens; ortus, *m.*

easterly, eastern, *a.* orientalis; ad orientem vergens.

eastwards, *ad.* ad orientem versus.

east wind, *n.* Eurus, *m.*

easy, *a.* facilis; solutus; expeditus; (at leisure) otiosus; quietus; (graceful) lepidus; (of temper) facilis.

eat, *v.t. & i.* edo, comedo, vescor; *fig.* rodo, [3]; **~ away,** peredo, *fig.* corrodo, [3]; **~ up,** comedo, [3]; voro, devoro, [1].

eatable, *a.* esculentus; edulis.

eating, *n.* esus, *m.*; **~-house,** *n.* popina, *f.*

eaves, *n.* suggrunda, *nt. pl.*

eavesdrop, *v.i.* subausculto, [1].

eavesdropper, *n.* auceps, *m.*

ebb, *n.* recessus, *m.*

ebb, *v.i.* recedo; *fig.* decresco, [3].

echo, *n.* imago, echo; resonantia, *f.*

echo, *v.t.* repercutio, [3]; resono, [1]; **~,** *v.i.* resulto, [1]; (resound, be loud) sono, resono, persono, [1].

eclipse, *n.* defectus, *m.*; defectio, *f.*

eclipse, *v.t.* obscuro, obumbro, [1]; **be ~d,** deficio, [3].

economic(al), *a.* oeconomicus; (sparing) parcus; **~ly,** *ad.* parce.

economize (with), *v.t. & i.* parco, [3] (*with dat.*).

economy, *n.* oeconomia; (stinginess) parsimonia, *f.*

ecstasy, *n.* ecstasis, insania, *f;* furor, *m.*

ecstatic, *a.* furibundus, lymphatus.

eddy, *n.* vortex, *m.*

eddy, *v.i.* circumferor, *ir.*

edge, *n.* (brink) margo, *c.;* (of a knife, *etc.*) acies; (of a forest, *etc.*) ora, *f;* (lip) labrum, *nt.*

edible, *a.* esculentus, edulis.

edict, *n.* edictum, decretum, *nt.*

edit, *v.t.* edo, [3].

edition, *n.* editio, *f.*

educate, *v.t.* educo, [1]; erudio, [4].

education, *n.* educatio; eruditio; disciplina, *f*

educational, *a.* scholasticus.

eel, *n.* anguilla, *f.*

eerie, *n.* nidus, *m.*

eerie, *a.* lugubris.

effect, *n.* vis, *f;* effectus, *m.;* **in ~,** re vera; etenim; **take ~,** bene succedere, [3]; efficax esse.

effective, *a.* efficax; potens; **~ly,** *ad.* efficaciter.

effects, *n. pl.* bona, *nt. pl.*

effectual, *a.* efficax, valens, potens.

effeminacy, *n.* mollitia, *f.*

effeminate, *a.* effeminatus, mollis, muliebris.

efficacious, *a.* efficax; **~ly,** *ad.* efficaciter.

efficacy, efficiency, *n.* efficacitas, vis, *f.*

efficient, *a.* efficiens; efficax; **~ly,** *ad.* efficaciter.

effigy, *n.* imago, effigies, *f.*

effort, *n.* conatus, nisus, impetus, labor, *m.;* **make an ~,** nitor, [3], molior, [4].

effrontery, *n.* audacia, impudentia, *f.*

egg, *n.* ovum, *nt.;* **lay ~s,** ova pario, [3].

egg on, *v.t.* impello, incendo, [3]; excito, [1].

eggshell, *n.* ovi putamen, *nt.;* ovi testa, *f.*

egotism, *n.* sui iactantia, *f*

eight, *a.* octo; **~ times,** octies.

eighteen, *a.* duodeviginti.

eighteenth, *a.* duodevicesimus.

eighth, *a.* octavus; **~,** *n.* octava pars, *f.*

eight hundred, *a.* octingenti.

eightieth, *a.* octogesimus.

eighty, *a.* octoginta.

either, *pn.* alteruter; uter; alter; **~ of two,** utervis, uterlibet; **not either,** neuter.

either, *c.* **either . . . or,** aut . . . aut; vel . . . vel.

eject, *v.t.* eicio; expello, [3].

ejection, *n.* eiectio, *f*

eke, *v.t.* **~ out,** suppleo, [2]; (livelihood) colligo, [3].

elaborate, v.t. elaboro, evigilo, [1].

elaborate, a. elaboratus; accuratus; ~ly, ad. accurate.

elapse, v.i. praetereo, [4]; labor, [3].

elastic, a. (pliant) lentus.

elasticity, n. lentitia, f.

elate, v.t. inflo, [1]; effero, [3]; **be ~d**, intumesco, [3].

elation, n. superbia, f.; animus elatus, m.

elbow, n. cubitum, nt.; ulna, f.

elbow-room, n. fig. spatium, nt.

elder, a. maior natu; (in date) prior.

elderly, a. aetate provectior.

eldest, a. maximus natu; antiquissimus.

elect, v.t. eligo, [3]; creo, [1].

election, n. electio, f., delectus, m.; (political) comitia, nt. pl.

electioneering, n. petitio, ambitio, prensatio, f.; ~, a. candidatorius.

elegance, n. elegantia, f.; nitor, m.

elegant, a. elegans; nitidus; lautus; concinnus; ~ly, ad. eleganter, nitide, laute.

elegy, n. elegia, f.; elegi, m. pl.

element, n. elementum, nt.; ~s, pl. principia rerum; fig. rudimenta, nt. pl.

elementary, a. simplex, puerilis, primus.

elephant, n. elephantus, elephas, m.

elevate, v.t. levo, [1]; effero, attollo, [3]; fig. inflo, [1].

elevation, n. elatio; (loftiness) altitudo, f.; (rising ground) locus superior, m.

eleven, a. undecim; ~ **times**, undecies.

eleventh, a. undecimus.

elicit, v.t. elicio, [3]; evoco, [1].

eligible, a. dignus.

eliminate, v.t. amoveo, [2].

elm, n. ulmus, f.

elocution, n. elocutio, f.

elongate, v.t. produco, [3].

elope, v.i. (domo) clam fugio, aufugio, [3].

elopement, n. fuga clandestina, f.

eloquence, n. eloquentia, facundia, f.; eloquium, nt.

eloquent, a. eloquens, disertus, facundus; ~ly, ad. diserte, eloquenter.

else, a. alius; **no one ~**, nemo alius; nemo alter.

else, ad. praeterea; (otherwise) aliter; (if not) si non.

elsewhere, ad. alibi.

elucidate, v.t. illustro, explico, [1].

elucidation, n. explicatio, f.

elude, v.t. eludo, effugio, [3]; frustror, [1]; evito, [1].

elusive, a. fallax, fugax.

emaciated, a. macer, macilentus.

emaciation, n. macies; tabes, f.

emanate, v.i. emano, [1]; orior, [4].

emancipate, v.t. emancipo, [1]; manumitto, [3]; *fig.* libero, [1].

emancipation, n. (of a slave) manumissio; (of a son) emancipatio; *fig.* liberatio, *f.*

embalm, v.t. condio, [4], pollingo, [3].

embankment, n. agger, *m.*; moles, *f.*

embark, v.t. in navem impono, [3]; ~, v.i. in navem conscendo, [3].

embarkation, n. (in navem) consensio, *f.*

embarrass, v.t. (hinder) impedio, [4]; (entangle) implico; *fig.* perturbo, [1].

embarrassment, n. implicatio, *f.*; angustiae, *f. pl.*; scrupulus, *m.*; perturbatio, *f.*; (hindrance) impedimentum, *nt.*; mora, *f.*

embassy, n. legatio, *f.*; legati, *m. pl.*

embellish, v.t. orno, exorno, [1].

embellishment, n. ornamentum, decus, insigne, *nt.*

embers, n. cinis, *c.*; (live coals) favilla, *f.*

embezzle, v.t. averto, [3].

embezzlement, n. peculatus, *m.*

embezzler, n. interceptor, peculator, *m.*

embitter, v.t. exacerbo, [1].

emblem, n. signum, *nt.*; imago, *f.*; (example) exemplum, *nt.*

embolden, v.t. animo, confirmo, [1].

emboss, v.t. caelo, [1].

embrace, v.t. complector, [3]; (contain) contineo, [2]; amplector, [3].

embrace, n. amplexus, complexus, *m.*

embroider, v.t. acu pingo, [3].

embroidery, n. (art) ars plumaria, *f.*

embroil, v.t. confundo, [3]; permisceo, [2]; *fig.* implico, [1]; impedio, [4]; (match, set to fight) committo, [3].

embryo, n. semen, *nt.*

emerald, n. smaragdus, *m.*

emerge, v.i. emergo; (arise) exsisto, [3].

emergency, n. (accident) casus, *m.*; (crisis) discrimen, *nt.*; necessitas, *f.*

emigrant, n. colonus, *m.*

emigrate, v.i. migro, [1].

emigration, n. migratio (in alias terras), *f.*

eminence, n. praestantia, *f.*

eminent, a. eminens; egregius, eximius, insignis, praestans; ~ly, ad. eximie, insigniter.

emit, v.t. emitto, [3]; (breathe out) exhalo, [1].

emolument, n. lucrum, emolumentum, *nt.*; quaestus, *m.*

emotion, n. animi motus, affectus, *m.*; commotio; perturbatio, *f.*

emperor, *n.* imperator, princeps, *m.*

emphasis, *n.* vis, *f.*; pondus, *nt.*

emphasize, *v.* vehementer dico, [3].

emphatic, *a.* gravis; **~ally**, *ad.* graviter.

empire, *n.* imperium, regnum, *nt.*

employ, *v.t.* adhibeo; exerceo, [2]; occupo, [1]; (use) utor, [3] (*with abl.*); usurpo, [1].

employer, *n.* conductor; dominus, *m.*

employment, *n.* occupatio, *f.*; (business) negotium, studium, *nt.*

empower, *v.t.* potestatem (alicui) facio, [3]; copiam (alicui) do, [1].

empress, *n.* imperatrix, *f.*

emptiness, *n.* inanitas; *fig.* vanitas, *f.*

empty, *a.* vacuus, inanis; *fig.* vanus.

empty, *v.t.* vacuo, [1]; vacuefacio, [3]; exinanio, [4]; (drink up) haurio, exhaurio, [4].

emulate, *v.t.* aemulor; imitor, [1].

emulation, *n.* aemulatio, *f.*

enable, *v.t.* facultatem (alicui) facio, [3].

enact, *v.t.* decerno, [3]; sancio, [4].

enactment, *n.* sanctio; (law) lex, *f.*; decretum, *nt.*

enamoured, *a.* be **~**, amo, deamo, [1].

encampment, *n.* castra, *nt. pl.*

enchant, *v.t.* fascino, [1]; *fig.* capio, [3]; delecto, [1].

enchanted, *a.* cantatus, incantatus.

enchanting, *a. fig.* venustus, suavissimus, pulcherrimus.

enchantment, *n.* incantamentum, *nt.*; *fig.* illecebrae, *f. pl.*; (magic) carmen, *nt.*

enchantress, *n.* maga; cantatrix, *f.*; (beloved one) amata, *f.*

encircle, *v.t.* circumplector; cingo, [3]; circumdo, [1].

enclose, *v.t.* saepio, [4]; includo; (encircle) cingo, [3]; circumdo, [1].

enclosure, *n.* saeptum, *nt.*

encounter, *n.* (meeting) congressus, *m.*; (fight) certamen, *nt.*; pugna, *f.*

encounter, *v.t. & i.* congredior, [3] (*with cum with abl.*); obviam eo, [4], incurro, [3] (*both with dat.*).

encourage, *v.t.* hortor, cohortor, animo, confirmo, [1].

encouragement, *n.* hortatus, *m.*; cohortatio, confirmatio, *f.*

encroach, *v.i.* usurpo, [1]; praesumo, [3].

encroachment, *n.* usurpatio, *f.*

encumber, *v.t.* onero, [1]; impedio, [4]; (weigh down) praegravo, [1].

encumbrance, *n.* impedimentum; onus, *nt.*; (trouble) molestia, *f.*

end, *n.* finis, *c.*; terminus; exitus, *m.*; (aim, design) propositum, *nt.*; (death) mors, *f.*; obitus, *m.*

end, *v.t.* finio, [4]; termino, [1]; concludo, [3]; ~, *v.i.* (cease) desino, [3]; finior, [4].

endanger, *v.t.* periclitor, [1]; in periculum deduco, [3].

endearing, *a.* carus.

endearment, *n.* blanditiae, *f. pl.*; blandimenta, *nt. pl.*

endeavour, *v.i.* tempto, conor, [1]; nitor, enitor, [3]; contendo, [3].

endeavour, *n.* conatus, nisus, *m.*; conamen, *nt.*

ending, *n.* exitus, *m.*

endless, *a.* infinitus; perpetuus; aeternus; sempiternus; ~ly, *ad.* sine fine, perpetuo; in aeternum.

endorse, *v.* confirmo, [1].

endorsement, *n.* confirmatio, *f.*

endow, *v.t.* doto, [1]; instruo, [3]; orno, [1]; ~ed with, praeditus (*with abl.*).

endowment, *n.* dos, *f.*

endurable, *a.* tolerabilis.

endurance, *n.* patientia; (stability) stabilitas, *f.*

endure, *v.t.* tolero, [1]; patior, perpetior, fero, [3]; sustineo, [2]; ~, *v.i.* duro, [1]; permaneo, [2].

enemy, *n.* hostis, inimicus, *m.*

energetic, *a.* strenuus; alacer, acer; ~ally, *ad.* strenue; acriter.

energy, *n.* vis; alacritas; vehementia, *f.*; impetus, *m.*

enervate, *v.t.* enervo; debilito, [1].

enfeeble, *v.t.* debilito, infirmo, labefacto, [1].

enforce, *v.t.* (compel) cogo, [3]; (put in execution) exerceo, [2].

enfranchise, *v.t.* libero, [1]; manumitto, [3]; civitatem do, [1].

engage, *v.t.* (hire) conduco, [3]; (involve, entangle) implico, [1]; (occupy) occupo, [1]; ~, *v.i.* (in battle) confligo, [3]; (promise) spondeo, [2]; (undertake) suscipio, [3].

engaged, *a.* (to marry) sponsus.

engagement, *n.* (agreement) stipulatio, *f.*; pactum, *nt.*; (occupation) occupatio, *f.*; (battle) proelium, *nt.*; (betrothal) pactio nuptialis, *f.*; (promise) fides, *f.*

engine, *n.* machina; machinatio, *f.*

engineer, *n.* machinator; architectus, *m.*

England, *n.* Anglia, *f.*

English, *a.* Anglicus, Britannicus.

Englishman, *n.* Anglus, *m.*

engrave, *v.t.* scalpo, sculpo; incido, [3]; caelo, [1].

engraver, *n.* sculptor, sculptor, *m.*

engraving, *n.* (art) scalptura, sculptura, *f.*

engulf, *v.t.* devoro, ingurgito, [1].

engrossed in, deditus (*with dat.*).

enhance, *v.t.* augeo, [2]; amplifico, orno, [1]; (raise) accendo, [3].

enigma, *n.* aenigma, *nt.*; ambages, *f. pl.*

enigmatic, *a.* aenigmaticus, ambiguus; ~**ally**, *ad.* ambigue.

enjoin, *v.t.* iubeo, [2]; iniungo, praecipio, [3] (*both with dat.*).

enjoy, *v.t.* fruor, [3] (*with abl.*); percipio, [3]; (rejoice in) gaudeo (*with in with abl.*); (possess) possideo, [2]; ~ **oneself**, me oblecto, [1].

enjoyable, *a.* gratus.

enjoyment, *n.* fructus, *m.*; gaudium, *nt.*; possessio, *f.*; oblectatio; voluptates, *f. pl.*

enlarge, *v.t.* amplifico; dilato, [1]; ~, *v.i.* amplificor, [1], *etc.*; ~ **upon** (a subject), uberius dico de (*with abl.*), [3].

enlargement, *n.* amplificatio, *f.*; (increase) auctus, *m.*

enlighten, *v.t. fig.* erudio, [4]; doceo, [2].

enlightened, *a.* (cultivated) cultus.

enlightenment, *n. fig.* eruditio, *f.*; (culture) humanitas, *f.*

enlist, *v.t.* conscribo, [3]; (win over) concilio, [1]; ~, *v.i.* sacramentum dico, [3].

enliven, *v.t.* animo; incito; exhilaro, [1].

enmity, *n.* inimicitia, *f.*; odium, *nt.*

enormity, *n.* immanitas; *fig.* atrocitas, *f.*

enormous, *a.* ingens, enormis, immensus; vastus, immanis;

~**ly**, *ad.* admodum, multum, mire.

enough, *ad.* satis, sat, affatim; ~ **of this**, sed haec hactenus.

enquire, v. **inquire**.

enrage, *v.t.* irrito; exaspero, [1].

enraged, *a.* iratus, furens.

enrich, *v.t.* locupleto, dito, [1].

enrol, *v.t.* inscribo, [3]; ~, *v.i.* (enlist) sacramentum dico, [3].

ensign, *n.* (flag) vexillum; (mark) insigne, *nt.*; (officer) signifer, *m.*

enslave, *v.t.* subigo, in servitutem redigo, [3].

enslavement, *n.* servitus, *f.*; servitium, *nt.*

ensnare, *v.t.* illaqueo, [1]; irretio, [4]; (*fig.*) illicio, capio, [3].

ensue, *v.i.* sequor, insequor, [3].

ensuing, *a.* sequens, insequens, posterus, proximus.

ensure, *v.t.* (guarantee) praesto, [1]; (see to it that) curo ut (*with subj.*), [1].

entail, *v.t. fig.* affero, [3].

entangle, *v.t.* implico, illaqueo, [1]; irretio; impedio, [4].

enter, *v.t. & i.* intro, [1]; ineo, [4]; ingredior, [3]; ~ **in a book**, refero, [3]; ~ **on** *or* **upon**, (undertake) incipio, suscipio, [3].

enterprise, *n.* (undertaking) inceptum; ausum, *nt.*; (boldness) audacia, *f.*

enterprising, *a.* audax, strenuus, acer.

entertain, *v.t.* (a guest) accipio, excipio, [3]; (an opinion) habeo, [2]; (amuse) oblecto, [1].

entertainment, *n.* (by a host) hospitium; (feast) convivium, *nt.*; (amusement) oblectatio, delectatio, *f.*

enthral, *v.t.* mancipo, [1]; servum facio, [3]; *fig.* capio, [3].

enthusiasm, *n.* fervor, *m.*; alacritas, *f.*

enthusiast, *n.* fanaticus, *m.*

enthusiastic, *a.* fervidus, fanaticus; **~ally,** *ad.* fanatice.

entice, *v.t.* allicio, [3]; allecto, [1].

enticement, *n.* allectatio; illecebra, *f.*

enticing, *a.* blandus.

entire, *a.* integer, totus; **~ly,** *ad.* omnino; penitus, prorsus.

entitle, *v.t.* (name) appello, nomino, [1]; inscribo (titulum), [3]; (give a right) potestatem do (*with dat.*), [1].

entrails, *n.* viscera, *nt. pl.*

entrance, *n.* aditus; introitus, *m.*; (beginning) principium, *nt.*

entrance, *v.t.* rapio, capio, [3].

entrance-hall, *n.* vestibulum, *nt.*

entreat, *v.t.* obsecro; oro; deprecor, obtestor, [1]; (beg) peto, [3].

entreaty, *n.* obsecratio, *f.*; preces, *f. pl.*

entrust, *v.t.* committo, credo, [3]; mando, commendo, [1].

entry, *n.* (act of entering) introitus, *m.*; (in a book) nomen, *nt.*

entwine, *v.t.* implico; circumplico, [1]; necto, [3].

enumerate, *v.t.* enumero, [1]; recenseo, [2].

envelop, *v.t.* involvo, [3]; amicio, [4].

envelope, *n.* involucrum, *nt.*

enviable, *a.* dignus cui invideatur, fortunatus.

envious, *a.* invidus, invidiosus.

envoy, *n.* nuntius, legatus, *m.*

envy, *n.* invidia; malignitas, *f.*; livor, *m.*

envy, *v.t.* invideo (*with dat.*), [2].

ephemeral, *a. fig.* brevis; caducus.

epic, *a.* epicus; ~ **poem,** epos, *nt.*

epidemic, *n.* lues, pestilentia, *f.*

epidemic, *a.* epidemus.

epigram, *n.* epigramma, *nt.*

epilepsy, *n.* morbus comitialis, morbus caducus, *m.*; epilepsia, *f.*

epileptic, *a.* epilepticus.

epilogue, *n.* epilogus, *m.*

episode, *n.* embolium, *nt.*; (affair) res, *f.*

epistle, *n.* epistula, *f.*; litterae, *f. pl.*

epitaph, *n.* epitaphium; carmen, *nt.*

epitome, *n.* epitome, *f.*; breviarium, *nt.*

epoch, *n.* saeculum, *nt.*; aetas, *f.*; tempus, *nt.*

equal, *a.* aequalis, aequus, par.

equal, *n.* par, *c.*

equal, *v.t.* aequo, adaequo, aequiparo, [1]; assequor, [3].

equality, *n.* aequalitas, *f.*; aequum, *nt.*

equalize, *v.t.* aequo, adaequo, exaequo, [1].

equally, *ad.* aeque; aequaliter; pariter.

equanimity, *n.* aequus animus, *m.*

equestrian, *a.* equestris; ~, *n.* eques, *m.*

equilibrium, *n.* aequilibrium, *nt.*

equinoctial, *a.* aequinoctialis.

equinox, *n.* aequinoctium, *nt.*

equip, *v.t.* armo; exorno, [1]; instruo, [3].

equipment, *n.* armamenta, *nt. pl.*; armatura, *f.*

equitable, *a.* aequus, iustus.

equivalent, *a.* tantusdem; par.

era, *n.* tempus, *nt.*; aetas, *f.*; saeculum, *nt.*

eradicate, *v.t.* eradico, exstirpo, [1]; tollo, [3].

eradication, *n.* exstirpatio, *f.*; excidium, *nt.*

erase, *v.t.* erado, [3]; deleo, [2].

erect, *a.* erectus, arrectus.

erect, *v.t.* (raise) erigo, educo; (build up) exstruo *fig.* statuo, (found) condo, [3].

erection, *n.* exstructio; aedificatio, *f.*

erode, *v.* erodo, [3].

erotic, *a.* amatorius.

err, *v.i.* (ab)erro; *fig.* pecco, [1]; delinquo, [3].

errand, *n.* mandatum, *nt.*

erratic, *a.* erraticus; *fig.* inconstans.

erroneous, *a.* falsus, vanus; ~ly, *ad.* falso.

error, *n.* (fault) delictum, peccatum, erratum, *nt.*; (mistake) fraus, *f.*, error, *m.*

erudite, *a.* eruditus, doctus.

erudition, *n.* eruditio, *f.*

eruption, *n.* (of a volcano) eruptio; (of the skin) scabies, *f.*

escapade, *n.* ausum, *nt.*

escape, *v.t. & i.* evado, effugio, elabor, [3]; (secretly) subterfugio, [3]; (with difficulty) eluctor, [1].

escape, *n.* fuga, *f.*; effugium, *nt.*

escort, *n.* comitatus, *m.*; (protection) praesidium, *nt.*; custodia, *f.*

escort, *v.t.* comitor, [1]; deduco, [3]; prosequor, [3].

especial, *v.* special.

especially, *ad.*, *v.* **specially.**

espy, *v.t.* conspicor, [1]; aspicio, [3]; video, [2]; ~, *v.i.* speculor, [1].

essay, *n.* (treatise) libellus, tractatus, *m.*

essence, *n.* essentia; natura, vis, *f.*

essential, *a.* proprius, necessarius; ~ly, *ad.* natura, necessario.

establish, *v.t.* statuo; constituo, [3]; firmo, confirmo, [1]; stabilio, [4].

estate, *n.* fundus, ager, *m.*; (means, wealth) bona, *nt. pl.*; divitiae, *f. pl.*; (class, in politics) ordo, *m.*; dignitas, *f.*

esteem, *v.t.* aestimo, puto, [1]; habeo, [2]; (judge) existimo, [1]; (respect) magni facio, [3].

esteem, *n.* aestimatio, *f.*; honor, *m.*; reverentia, *f.*

estimate, *v.t.* aestimo, [1]; (assess) censeo, [2].

estimate, *n.* (valuation) aestimatio, *f.*; pretium; iudicium, *nt.*

estimation, *n.* aestimatio; opinio, *f.*

estrangement, *n.* alienatio, *f.*; discidium, *nt.*

estuary, *n.* aestuarium, *nt.*

eternal, *a.* aeternus, sempiternus, immortalis; ~ly, *ad.* in aeternum, semper.

eternity, *n.* aeternitas; immortalitas, *f.*

ethereal, *a.* aethereus.

eulogistic, *a.* panegyricus, laudativus

eulogize, *v.t.* collaudo, [1].

eulogy, *n.* laus, laudatio, *f.*; panegyricus, *m.*

eunuch, *n.* eunuchus, *m.*

evacuate, *v.t.* vacuo, [1]; vacuefacio, [3]; (leave) relinquo, [3].

evacuation, *n.* (departure) excessus, *m.*

evade, *v.t.* subterfugio, eludo, [3].

evaporate, *v.i.* evaporor, [1]; evanesco, [3]; ~, *v.t.* evaporo, exhalo, [1].

evaporation, *n.* evaporatio, exhalatio, *f.*

evasion, *n.* effugium, *nt.*; fuga; tergiversatio, *f.*

evasive, *a.* vafer; subdolus; ambiguus; ~ly, *ad.* vafre; subdole; ambigue.

eve, *n.* vesper, *m.*; (of a feast) vigiliae, *f. pl.*

even, *a.* aequalis, aequus; (level) planus; (of numbers) par.

even, *ad.* etiam, quoque; (with superlatives) vel; **not** ~, ne . . . quidem; ~ **as**, perinde ac si, quemadmodum; ~ **if**, etiamsi.

evening, *n.* vesper, *m.*

evening, *a.* vespertinus.

Evening-star, *n.* Vesper, Hesperus, *m.*

evenly, *ad.* aequaliter, aequabiliter.

event, *n.* eventus, exitus, casus, *m.*

eventful, *a.* (remarkable) memorabilis.

eventually, *ad.* denique, aliquando, tandem.

ever, *ad.* unquam; aliquando; semper; **for** ~, in aeternum; **who**~, quicumque.

evergreen, *a.* semper viridis.

everlasting, *a.* sempiternus.

every, *a.* quisque, quaeque, quodque; omnis; ~ **day**, cotidie, in dies.

everybody, *pn.* quisque; unusquisque; nemo non; omnes; quivis; quilibet.

everyday, *a.* quotidianus; usitatus.

everything, *n.* omnia (*nt. pl.*); quidvis; quidlibet.

everywhere, *ad.* ubique, ubivis, undique.

evict, *v.t.* expello, [3]; deturbo, [1].

eviction, *n.* (law) expulsio, [4].

evidence, *n.* (proof) argumentum; (in law) testimonium, *nt.*; (witness) testis, *c.*; (information) indicium, *nt.*

evident, *a.* apertus, manifestus, clarus, liquidus; **it is ~,** apparet, liquet; **~ly,** *ad.* aperte, manifesto, liquide.

evil, *a.* malus, pravus, improbus; **~,** *n.* malum, incommodum, *nt.*

evince, *v.t.* praesto, [1].

evoke, *v.t.* evoco, [1]; elicio, [3].

evolve, *v.t.* evolvo, [3].

ewe, *n.* ovis femina, *f.*

exact, *a.* (attentive to detail) diligens, subtilis; (of things) exactus; **~ly,** *ad.* exacte, ad unguem.

exact, *v.t.* exigo, [3].

exaggerate, *v.t.* exaggero, aggravo, [1]; augeo, [2].

exaggeration, *n.* amplificatio, *f.*; immoderatio, *f.*

exalted, *a.* celsus, altus, sublimis.

examination, *n.* investigatio, inspectio; (of witnesses) interrogatio, *f.*

examine, *v.t.* investigo; exploro, [1]; inspicio, [3]; (witnesses) interrogo, [1].

example, *n.* exemplum, exemplar, documentum, *nt.*; **for ~,** verbi gratia.

exasperate, *v.t.* exaspero, exacerbo, irrito, [1].

exasperation, *n.* ira, *f.*; animus iratus, *m.*

excavate, *v.t.* excavo, [1]; effodio, [3].

excavation, *n.* excavatio, *f.*

exceed, *v.t.* excedo, [3]; supero, [1].

exceedingly, *ad.* valde, egregie, magnopere; vehementer.

excel, *v.t.* praesto (*with dat.*), [1]; supero, [1]; **~,** *v.i.* excello, [3].

excellence, *n.* excellentia, praestantia, *f.*

excellent, *a.* excellens, praestans, egregius, eximius.

except, *v.t.* excipio, eximo, [3].

except, excepting, *pr.* extra, praeter (*with acc.*); (unless) nisi; **~ that,** nisi quod, nisi.

exception, *n.* exceptio, *f.*; **take ~ to,** reprehendo, [3]; culpo, [1]; **with the ~ of,** excepto (*excepta*) (*ablat. absol.*).

exceptional, *a.* rarus; **~ly,** *ad.* raro; (outstandingly) eximie; (contrary to custom) praeter solitum.

excess, *n.* exsuperantia, immoderatio; (licence) intemperantia, licentia, *f.*; **to ~,** nimis.

excessive, *a.* nimius; immodicus; immoderatus; **~ly,** *ad.* nimis; immodice; immoderate.

exchange, *n.* (barter) mutatio, permutatio, *f.*; (of money) collybus, *m.*

exchange, *v.t.* muto, permuto, [1].

excitable, *a.* irritabilis; fervidus.

excite, *v.t.* excito, incito, stimulo, [1]; (inflame) incendo, [3]; (thrill) agito, [1]; commoveo, [2]; (produce) cieo, moveo, [2]; conflo, [3].

excited, *a.* agitatus.

excitement, *n.* commotio; perturbatio, *f.*

exclaim, *v.t.* exclamo; (several voices) conclamo, [1].

exclamation, *n.* vox; exclamatio; (of several people) conclamatio, *f.*

exclude, *v.t.* excludo, [3]; arceo; prohibeo; removeo, [2].

exclusion, *n.* exclusio, *f.*

exclusive, *a.* (one's own) proprius; (especial) praecipuus.

exclusively, *ad.* (only) solum.

excrement, *n.* excrementum; stercus, *nt.*; proluvies, *f.*

excruciating, *a.* acerbissimus.

excursion, *n.* excursio, incursio; *fig.* digressio, *f.*

excusable, *a.* excusabilis.

excuse, *v.t.* excuso; (exculpate) purgo, [1]; (pardon) ignosco, [3]; condono, [1].

excuse, *n.* excusatio, *f.*; causa, *f.*; (pretence) praetextum, *nt.*

execute, *v.t.* (fulfil, perform) exsequor, persequor, perficio, perago, [3]; (as punishment) securi ferio, [4].

execution, *n.* (performance) exsecutio, *f.*; (punishment) supplicium, *nt.*; (death) mors, *f.*; **place of ~,** furca, *f.*

executioner, *n.* carnifex, *m.*

exemplary, *a.* egregius, eximius, excellens.

exemplify, *v.t.* (give example of) exemplum do (*with gen.*).

exempt, *v.t.* eximo, [3]; immunitatem do; [1].

exempt, *a.* immunis.

exemption, *n.* vacatio, immunitas, *f.*

exercise, *n.* exercitatio, *f.*; (of soldiers) exercitium, *nt.*; (task) pensum, *nt.*

exercise, *v.t.* exerceo, [2]; (an office) fungor, [3] (*with abl.*); **~,** *v.i.* exerceor, [2].

exert, *v.t.* exhibeo, exerceo, [2]; **~ oneself,** contendo, nitor, [3].

exertion, *n.* contentio, *f.*; nisus, *m.*

exhalation, *n.* exhalatio, *f.*; vapor, *m.*

exhale, *v.t.* exhalo, exspiro, [1]; spargo, emitto, [3].

exhaust, *v.t.* exhaurio, [4]; conficio, [3]; debilito, infirmo, [1].

exhausted, *a.* fessus, defessus, confectus, languidus.

exhaustion, *n.* *fig.* languor, *m.*; lassitudo, defectio (virium), *f.*

exhibit 415 **expiration**

exhibit, *v.t.* exhibeo, [2]; expono, propono, profero, ostendo, [3]; (qualities) praesto, [1].

exhibition, *n.* prolatio, *f.*; (show) spectaculum, *nt.*

exhilarate, *v.t.* exhilaro, [1].

exhilaration, *n.* hilaritas, *f.*

exhort, *v.t.* hortor, [1].

exhortation, *n.* hortatio, *f.*

exile, *n.* (banishment) ex(s)ilium, *nt.*; fuga, *f.*; (person banished) ex(s)ul, extorris, *c.*

exile, *v.t.* relego, [1]; in exilium pello, [3].

exist, *v.i.* sum, exsisto; vivo, [3].

existence, *n.* vita, *f.*

existing, *a.* qui (quae, quod) nunc est.

exit, *n.* exitus, *m.*; effugium, *nt.*

exonerate, *v.t.* culpa libero, excuso, [1].

exorbitant, *a.* nimius, immodicus.

exotic, *a.* externus, peregrinus.

expand, *v.t.* expando; extendo, [3]; dilato, [1]; augeo, [2]; ~, *v.i.* expandor, extendor, cresco, [3]; dilator, [1].

expanse, *n.* spatium, *nt.*

expect, *v.t. & i.* exspecto; spero, [1].

expectant, *a.* suspensus.

expectation, *n.* exspectatio; spes, *f.*

expediency, *n.* utilitas, *f.*

expedient, *a.* utilis, commodus, salutaris; **it is ~,** expedit.

expedient, *n.* modus, *m.*; ratio, *f.*

expedite, *v.t.* maturo, [1].

expedition, *n.* (mil.) expeditio, *f.*

expel, *v.t.* expello, eicio, [3].

expend, *v.t.* expendo, impendo; consumo, [3].

expenditure, *n.* sumptus, *m.*; impensa, *f.*

expense, *n.* impensa, *f.*; sumptus, *m.*

expensive, *a.* sumptuosus, pretiosus, carus; **~ly,** *ad.* sumptuose, pretiose, care.

expensiveness, *n.* caritas, *f.*; magnum pretium, *nt.*

experience, *n.* experientia; peritia, *f.*; usus, *m.*

experience, *v.t.* experior, [4]; utor (*with abl.*), cognosco, [3].

experienced, *a.* peritus, experiens; callidus.

experiment, *n.* experimentum, periculum, *nt.*

experiment, *v.t.* experimentum facio, [3].

experimental, *a.* usu comparatus; **~ly,** *ad.* usu, experimentis.

expert, *n.* artifex, *m.*

expert, *a.* callidus, sciens; **~ly,** *ad.* callide, scienter.

expertise, *n.* ars, calliditas, sollertia, *f.*

expiate, *v.t.* expio, [1]; luo, [3].

expiration, *n.* exspiratio, *f.*; finis, *c.*; exitus, *m.*

expire, *v.i.* (die) exspiro, [1]; (terminate) exeo, [4].

explain, *v.t.* explano, explico, [1]; expono, [3].

explanation, *n.* explanatio, explicatio, *f.*

explicit, *a.* explicatus; apertus; ~ly, *ad.* aperte, plane, nominatim.

explode, *v.t.* (blow up) displodo; *fig.* explodo, reicio; ~, *v.i.* displodor, [3].

exploit, *v.* utor, [3] (*with abl.*).

exploit, *n.* res gesta, *f.*; facinus, *nt.*

exploration, *n.* indagatio, investigatio, *f.*

explore, *v.t.* exploro; perscrutor; vestigo, indago, [1].

explorer, *n.* explorator, *m.*

explosion, *n.* crepitus, fragor, *m.*

export, *v.t.* eveho, [3]; exporto, [1].

export, exportation, *n.* exportatio, *f.*

expose, *v.t.* expono, retego, [3]; nudo, [1]; ~ **to,** obicio, [3]; obiecto, [1].

exposition, *n.* explicatio, expositio; interpretatio, *f.*

exposure, *n.* expositio, *f.*; (disclosure) indicium, *nt.*; (cold) frigus, *nt.*

expound, *v.t.* expono, [3]; interpretor, [1].

express, *v.t.* exprimo, loquor, dico, [3]; significo, [1].

express, *a.* clarus; certus; expressus; ~ly, *ad.* expresse, nominatim.

expression, *n.* (word) vox; (maxim, epigram) sententia, *f.*; *fig.* (of the face) vultus, *m.*

expressive, *a.* significans; *fig.* (of) index; (speaking) loquax; (clear) argutus; ~ly, *ad.* significanter.

expulsion, *n.* exactio, *f.*

expurgate, *v.t.* expurgo, [1].

exquisite, *a.* conquisitus; exquisitus; elegans, subtilis, eximius; ~ly, *ad.* exquisite, eximie, eleganter.

exquisiteness, *n.* elegantia; subtilitas, *f.*

extant, *a.* superstes; **be ~,** *v.i.* exsto, [1].

extemporary, *a.* extemporalis.

extempore, *ad.* subito; ex tempore.

extemporize, *v.t.* ex tempore dico, [3].

extend, *v.t.* extendo; produco, [3]; propago, [1]; ~, *v.i.* extendo; porrigor, [3].

extension, *n.* extensio; propagatio; (of boundaries, *etc.*) prolatio, *f.*; (space) spatium, *nt.*

extensive, *a.* late patens, amplus, diffusus; ~ly, *ad.* late.

extent, *n.* spatium, *nt.*; (of a country) tractus, *m.*; fines, *m. pl.*; (range) circuitus, *m.*; (amount) vis, *f.*

exterior, *a.* externus, exterior.

exterior, *n.* species, facies, forma, *f.*

exterminate, *v.t.* exstirpo, extermino, [1]; deleo, [2]; tollo, exstinguo, [3].

extermination, *n.* exstirpatio, *f.*

external, *a.* externus; extraneus; ~**ly,** *ad.* extrinsecus.

extinct, *a.* exstinctus; obsoletus; **become** ~, exstinguor, obsolesco, [3].

extinction, *n.* exstinctio, *f.*; interitus, *m.*

extinguish, *v.t.* exstinguo, [3].

extol, *v.t.* laudibus effero, [3]; laudo, [1].

extort, *v.t.* extorqueo, [2]; exprimo, [3].

extortion, *n.* (pecuniae) repetundae, *f. pl.*

extra, *a.* praecipuus.

extra, *ad.* insuper, praeterea; ~, *n.* supplementum, *nt.*

extract, *v.t.* extraho, [3].

extract, *n.* (juice) sucus, *m.*; (literary) excerptum; (epitome) compendium, *nt.*

extraction, *n.* (birth) stirps; origo, *f.*; genus, *nt.*

extraordinarily, *a.* extra modum; praeter solitum.

extraordinary, *a.* extraordinarius, insolitus, mirabilis.

extravagance, *n.* intemperantia, effusio; luxuria, *f.*

extravagant, *a.* immodicus, nimius; profusus; effusus; luxuriosus; (dissolute) perditus; ~**ly,** *ad.* immodice; effuse; prodige; nimis.

extreme, *a.* extremus; ultimus; summus; *fig.* ingens; ~**ly,** *ad.* summe.

extreme, *n.* extremum, summum, *nt.*

extremity, *n.* extremitas, *f.*; extremum, *nt.*; (distress) miseria, *f.*; (danger) discrimen, periculum, *nt.*; (difficulty) angustiae, *f. pl.*

extricate, *v.t.* expedio, [4]; extraho, [3]; libero, [1].

exuberance, *n.* luxuria, redundantia; ubertas, *f.*

exuberant, *a.* luxuriosus; redundans; *fig.*

exude, *v.t. & i.* exsudo, [1].

exult, *v.i.* exsulto, ovo, [1]; gestio, [4].

exultant, *a.* laetus, ovans.

exultation, *n.* laetitia, *f.*; gaudium, *nt.*

eye, *n.* oculus, ocellus, *m.*; lumen, *nt.*; (of a needle) foramen, *nt.*; (sight) acies, *f.*

eye, *v.t.* aspicio, [3]; intueor, [2]; contemplor, [1].

eyeball, *n.* pupula, *f.*

eyebrow, *n.* supercilium, *nt.*

eyelid, *n.* palpebra, *f.*

eyesight, *n.* acies oculi, *f.*

eyesore, *n.* res odiosa, *f.*

eyewitness, *n.* arbiter, *m.*; testis, *c.*; spectator, *m.*

F

fable, *n.* fabula, *f.*

fabric, *n.* (woven material), textile, textum, *nt.*

fabricate, *v.t.* fabrico, [1]; struo, [3].

fabrication, *n.* (construction) fabricatio, *f.*; *fig.* mendacium, *nt.*

face, *n.* facies, *f.*; os, *nt.*; vultus; *fig.* conspectus, *m.*; (boldness) audacia, impudentia, *f.*; (appearance) species, *f.*; ~ **to** ~, coram.

face, *v.t.* aspicio, [3]; intueor, [2]; (of position) specto ad (*with acc.*), [1]; (meet) obeo, [4] (*with dat.*); (cover in part) praetexo, [3].

facetious, *a.* facetus, lepidus; ~**ly,** *ad.* facete, lepide.

facetiousness, *n.* facetiae, *f. pl.*; lepos, *m.*

facilitate, *v.t.* facilius reddo, [3].

facility, *n.* facilitas, *f.*; (opportunity) copia, facultas, *f.*

facing, *pr.* adversus, ante, (*both with acc.*).

facing, *a.* contrarius, adversus.

facsimile, fax, *n.* imago scripturae, *f.*

fact, *n.* factum, *nt.*; res, *f.*; **in** ~, re ipsa; re vera, enim.

faction, *n.* (party) factio, *f.*

factor, *n.* (agent) procurator, *m.*; (element) pars, *f.*

factory, *n.* officina, *f.*

faculty, *n.* facultas; vis, *f.*; ingenium, *nt.*

fade, *v.t.* marcesco, defloresco, [3]; langueo, [2]; (decay) deficio, [3]; (become pale) albesco, [3].

faggot, *n.* fascis, *m.*; sarmenta, *nt. pl.*

fail, *v.t.* (disappoint) deficio, desero, [3]; ~, *v.i.* (break down) succumbo, [3]; (of duty) delinquo, [3]; (become bankrupt) decoquo, [3]; (be unsuccessful) cado, [3]; male cedo, [3].

fail, *n.* **without** ~, certo.

failing, *n.* (deficiency) defectus, *m.*; (fault) culpa, *f.*; delictum *nt.*

failure, *n.* defectio, *f.*; defectus, *m.*; (fault) culpa, *f.*; delictum, *nt.*

faint, *n.* exanimatio, *f.*

faint, *a.* (weary) defessus; (dropping) languidus; (of sight, smell, *etc.*) hebes; (of sound) surdus; (unenthusiastic) frigidus; (timid) demissus; ~**ly,** *ad.* languide; timide.

faint, *v.i.* (swoon) collabor, [3].

faintness, *n.* defectio, *f.*; languor, *m.*

fair, *a.* (of complexion) candidus; (beautiful) formosus, pulcher; (of weather) serenus, sudus; (of winds) secundus, idoneus; (of hair) flavus; *fig.* aequus; mediocris; modicus; ~ **play**, *n.* aequitas, *f.*

fairly, *ad.* iuste; (moderately) mediocriter.

fairness, *n.* (beauty) forma, pulchritudo, *f.*; (justice) aequitas, *f.*; candor animi, *m.*

faith, *n.* (trust) fides, (confidence) fiducia, (religion) religio, *f.*

faithful, *a.* fidelis; fidus; ~**ly**, *ad.* fideliter, fide.

faithfulness, *a.* fides, fidelitas, integritas, *f.*

faithless, *a.* infidus, infidelis, perfidus; perfidiosus.

fake, *a.* falsus.

falcon, *n.* falco, *m.*

fall, *v.i.* cado; concido; (die) occido; (decrease) decresco; (violently and completely) corruo, [3]; ~ **apart**, dilabor, [3]; ~ **away**, deficio, [3]; ~ **back**, recido; relabor; (retreat) pedem refero; *fig.* recurro, [3]; ~ **down**, decido; (completely) concido, [3]; ~ **forwards**, procido; procumbo; prolabor, [3]; ~ **in(to)**, incido; ~ **in with**, (meet) incido, [3]; (find) invenio, [4]; (agree) assentior, [4]; ~ **in love with**, adamo, [1]; ~ **off**, decido; ~ **on**, v. ~ **upon**; ~ **out**, excido; (happen) contingo, accido, [3]; evenio, [4]; (with someone) dissideo, [2]; ~ **short of**, non contingo, [3]; ~ **sick**, in morbum incido, [3]; ~ **under**, succumbo, [3]; (be classed) pertineo (ad *with acc.*), [2]; (be sub

jected to) patior, [3]; ~ **upon**, accido; incido; (assail) invado, ingruo, incurro, [3]; occupo, [1]; **let** ~, demitto; (out of the hand) emitto, [3].

fall, *n.* casus; lapsus, *m.*; (ruin) ruina, *f.*; labes, *f.*; (of ground, *etc.*) libramentum, *nt.*; (waterfall) cataracta; (diminution) deminutio, *f.*; (autumn) autumnus, *m.*; (death) mors, *f.*

fallacious, *a.* fallax, fictus, falsus; ~**ly**, *ad.* fallaciter, ficte, falso.

fallible, *a.* errori obnoxius.

fallow, *a.* (of land) inaratus; (never having been ploughed) novalis; (~ land) novalis, *m.*; novale, *nt.*

false, *a.* falsus; fictus; (counterfeit) adulterinus; ~**ly**, *ad.* falso, perperam, ficte.

falsehood, *n.* (untrue story) commentum; (lie) mendacium, *nt.*

falseness, *n.* perfidia, *f.*; dolus, *m.*

falsification, *n.* adulteratio, corruptio, *f.*

falsify, *v.t.* suppono, corrumpo, [3]; depravo, (documents) vitio, [1]; interlino, [3].

falter, *v.i.* haereo, [2]; haesito, labo; (reel, totter) titubo, [1].

fame, *n.* fama; laus, gloria, *f.*; nomen, decus, *nt.*; (famousness) claritas; celebritas, *f.*

familiar, *a.* familiaris; solitus; notus; intimus; ~**ly**, *ad.* familiariter.

familiarity, *n.* familiaritas; necessitudo, notitia; (in bad sense) licentia, *f.*

familiarize, *v.t.* assuefacio, [3].

family, *n.* familia; domus, *f.*; genus, *nt.*; cognatio, *f.*; (clan) gens, *f.*

famine, *n.* fames, *f.*; *fig.* inopia, *f.*

famished, *a.* famelicus; fame enectus.

famous, *a.* clarus, praeclarus, notus, celeber, inclutus; ~ly, *ad.* praeclare; insigniter.

fan, *n.* flabellum, *nt.*; (for winnowing) vannus, *f.*

fan, *v.t.* ventilo, [1]; (fire) accendo, [3]; *fig.* excito, conflo, [1].

fanatic(al), *a.* fanaticus; ~ally, *ad.* fanatice.

fanciful, *a.* vanis imaginibus deditus; (capricious) inconstans, levis; libidinosus.

fancy, *n.* opinio, imaginatio, *f.* (mind) animus, *m.*; (caprice) libido, *f.*; (dream) somnium, *nt.*; (liking, inclination) voluntas, *f.*

fancy, *v.t.* & *i.* imaginor; somnio; (like) amo, [1].

fang, *n.* dens; (claw) unguis, *m.*

fantasy, *n.* phantasia, *f.*

fantastic, *a.* (unreal) vanus; (absurd) absurdus.

far, *a.* longinquus, remotus.

far, *ad.* procul, longe; ~ off, procul; by ~, multo; from ~, procul (*with abl.*); how ~, quousque? as ~ as, quantum; quatenus; so ~, hactenus; ~ be

it from me, longe absit; ~ and near, longe lateque.

farce, *n.* mimus, *m.*

farcical, *a.* mimicus; ~ly, *ad.* mimice.

fare, *n.* (food) cibus, victus, *m.*; (money) vectura, *f.*; naulum, *nt.*

fare, *v.i.* ago, [3]; habeo (me) [2]; cedo, [3].

farewell, *ad.* & *i.* vale! salve! bid ~, valere *or* salvere iubeo, [2]; valedico (*with dat.*), [3].

far-fetched, *a.* quaesitus; longe petitus.

farm, *n.* fundus, agellus, *m.*; praedium, *nt.*

farm, *v.t.* (till) aro, [1]; colo, [3].

farmer, *n.* agricola; colonus, *m.*

farm-house, *n.* villa, *f.*

farming, *n.* agricultura, *f.*; res rusticae, *f. pl.*

farther, *a.* ulterior; ~, *ad.* longius, ulterius.

farthest, *a.* ultimus, extremus.

fascinate, *v.t.* fascino, [1]; *fig.* capio, [3].

fascination, *n.* fascinatio, *f.*; illecebrae, *f. pl.*; gratia, *f.*

fashion, *n.* (form) figura, forma, *f.*; (manner) mos, modus; ritus, *m.*; (custom) consuetudo, *f.*; usus, *m.*; (sophistication) urbanitas, *f.*

fashion, *v.t.* (shape) formo, informo, fabrico, [1]; effingo, [3].

fashionable, *a.* elegans; concinnus; be ~, in usu esse, valere, [2].

fashionably, *ad.* ad morem; eleganter.

fast, *a.* (firm) firmus, stabilis; (tight) astrictus; (swift) celer; (shut) occlusus.

fast, *ad.* firmiter; (quickly) celeriter.

fast, *v.i.* cibo abstineo, [2]; ieiuno, [1].

fast, *n.* ieiunium, *nt.*

fasten, *v.t.* astringo, affigo, [3]; *fig.* infero, *ir.*, [3]; (down) defigo; (to) annecto; impingo *ir.*, [3]; (together) colligo, [1]; configo, [3].

fastening, *n.* vinculum, *nt.*

fastidious, *a.* fastidiosus; delicatus; elegans; morosus.

fat, *a.* pinguis, obesus; opimus.

fat, *n.* adeps, *c.*; pingue, *nt.*; arvina, *f.*; (suet) sebum, *nt.*; (of a pig) lardum, *nt.*; (in general) pinguitudo, *f.*

fatal, *a.* mortifer, letifer; exitialis; funebris; funestus; **~ly**, *ad.* fataliter; fato.

fate, *n.* Fatum, *nt.*; sors, *f.*; **the Fates**, *pl.* Parcae, *f. pl.*; (fortune) fortuna, *f.*; (chance) casus, *m.*

fated, *a.* fatalis; **ill-~**, infaustus.

father, *n.* pater, genitor, parens, *m.*; **~ of a family**, paterfamilias, *m.*

fatherhood, *n.* paternitas, *f.*

father-in-law, *n.* socer, *m.*

fatherless, *a.* orbus.

fatherly, *a.* paternus, patrius.

fathom, *n.* ulna, *f.*

fatigue, *n.* (de)fatigatio, lassitudo, *f.*

fatness, *n.* pinguitudo, sagina, *f.*

fatten, *v.t.* sagino, [1]; farcio, [4].

fattening, *n.* saginatio; (cramming of fowls), fartura, *f.*

fatty, *a.* pinguis.

fatuous, *a.* stultus, fatuus.

fault, *n.* delictum, mendum, vitium, *nt.*; (responsibility) culpa, *f.*; (mistake) error, *m.*; (blemish) menda, labes, macula, *f.*; **at ~**, in culpa; **find ~ with**, vitupero, [1]; carpo, [3].

faultless, *a.* perfectus; integer.

faulty, *a.* vitiosus; mendosus.

favour, *n.* favor, *m.*; gratia; (goodwill) benevolentia, *f.*; beneficium, *nt.*; (present) munus, *nt.* **do a ~**, gratificor, [1] (*with dat.*).

favour, *v.t.* faveo, [2] (*with dat.*); secundo, [1].

favourable, *a.* prosperus, felix, faustus; commodus, idoneus; benignus; (of the gods) propitius, aequus, secundus.

favourably, *ad.* prospere, feliciter, fauste; benigne, opportune.

favourite, *a.* dilectus, gratus; (popular) gratiosus; **~**, *n.* (darling, *etc.*) deliciae, *f. pl.*

favouritism, *n.* gratia, *f.* studium, *nt.*

fawn, *n.* hinnuleus, *m.*

fawn, *v.i.* (on, upon) adulor, [1].

fawning, *a.* adulatorius, blandus.

fear, *n.* timor, metus, *m.*; formido, *f.*

fear, *v.t. & i.* timeo, paveo, [2]; metuo, [3]; formido, [1]; (reverentially) vereor, [2].

fearful, *a.* timidus, pavidus; (terrible) dirus, formidolosus; ~**ly**, *ad.* timide, formidolose.

fearfulness, *n.* timiditas, *f.*

fearless, *a.* impavidus, intrepidus; ~**ly**, *ad.* impavide.

fearlessness, *n.* audacia, audentia, *f.*

feasible, quod fieri potest.

feast, *n.* (holiday) dies festus, *m.*; sollemne, *nt.*; (banquet) convivium, *nt.*; epulae, dapes, *f.pl.*

feast, *v.i.* epulor, convivor, [1]; *fig.* (~ one's eyes on) oculos pasco, [3].

feat, *n.* facinus; factum, *nt.*; res gesta, *f.*

feather, *n.* (big *or* wing ~) penna; (small, downy) pluma, *f.*

feathered, *a.* pennatus; plumosus, penniger.

feature, *n.* lineamentum, *nt.*; vultus, *m.*; os, *nt.*; *fig.* (part) pars, *f.*

February, *n.* Februarius, *m.*

federal, *a.* foederatus.

federation, *n.* societas, *f.*

fee, *n.* (pay) merces, *f.*; praemium, pretium, *nt.*

feeble, *a.* infirmus, debilis, languidus; **grow** ~, languesco, [3].

feebleness, *n.* infirmitas, debilitas, *f.*; languor, *m.*

feebly, *ad.* infirme; languide.

feed, *v.t.* (animals) pasco; (nourish) alo, [3]; (support) sustento, [1]; ~, *v.i.* pascor; vescor, [3].

feel, *v.t. & i.* (touch) tango, [3]; (handle) tracto, [1]; (perceive) sentio, [4]; concipio, percipio, [3]; (be moved, affected) moveor, commoveor, [3]; **how do you** ~? quid agis? ~ **for**, doleo (cum *with abl.*), misereor (*with gen.*), [2].

feel, *n.* tactus, *m.*

feeler, *n.* (of an insect) crinis, *m.*; *fig.* tentamen, *n.*

feeling, *n.* (touch) tactus; (sensibility in general) sensus; (emotion) affectus, *m.*; (judgement) iudicium, *nt.*

feign, *v.t. & i.* fingo, comminiscor, [3]; (pretend) dissimulo, simulo, [1]; (lie) mentior, [4].

feint, *n.* simulatio; (in fencing) captatio, *f.*

fell, *v.t.* (trees) caedo; (knock down) sterno, prosterno, everto, [3].

fellow, *n.* (companion) socius; (in office) collega; (any individual) homo; (equal) par, *m.*

fellow-citizen, fellow-countryman, *n.* civis, *c.*

fellow-creature, *n.* homo, *m.*

fellow-feeling, *n.* (pity) misericordia, *f.*

fellow-servant, *n.* conservus, *m.*; conserva, *f.*

fellowship, *n.* societas, communitas, *f*; sodalicium, *nt.*

fellow-traveller, *n.* convector; socius itineris, *m.*

felt, *n.* coactilia, *nt. pl.*

female, *n.* femina, mulier, *f*

female, *a.* femineus, muliebris.

feminine, *a.* femineus, muliebris; femininus.

fence, *n.* saepes, *f*; saeptum, *nt.*

fence, *v.t.* saepio, [4]; defendo, [3]; ~, *v.i.* battuo, [3].

fencer, *n.* gladii peritus, gladiator, lanista, *m.*

fencing, *n.* ars gladii, *f*

fend, *v.i.* ~ **for oneself,** suis opibus nitor, [3].

fennel, *n.* faeniculum, *nt.*

ferment, *n.* fermentum, *nt.*; *fig.* aestus, *m.*

ferment, *v.t. & i.* fermento; fermentor, [1].

fern, *n.* filix, *f*

ferocious, *a.* ferus, truculentus, saevus, atrox; ~**ly,** *ad.* truculente, saeve, atrociter.

ferociousness, ferocity, *n.* saevitia, feritas, atrocitas, *f*

ferret, *n.* viverra, *f*

ferret, *v.t.* ~ **out,** rimor, expiscor, [1].

ferry, *v.t.* traicio, transveho, [3].

ferry-boat, *n.* scapha, cumba, *f*

ferry-man, *n.* portitor, *m.*

fertile, *a.* fertilis, fecundus, ferax, uber.

fertility, *n.* fertilitas, ubertas, *f*

fertilize, *v.t.* fecundo, [1].

fervent, *a.* ardens, fervidus; vehemens; ~**ly,** *ad.* ardenter; vehementer.

fervour, *n.* ardor, fervor, impetus, *m.*

fester, *v.i.* suppuro, ulceror, [1].

festival, *n.* dies festus, *m.*; sollemne, *nt.*

festive, *a.* festus, festivus.

festivity, *a.* sollemnia, *nt. pl.*; (gaiety) festivitas, *f*

festoon, *n.* sertum, *nt.*; ~, *v.t.* corono, adorno, [1].

fetch, *v.t.* adduco, [3], affero, *ir.*; arcesso, peto, [3]; ~ **back,** reduco, [3]; ~ **down,** deveho, [3]; ~ **in,** importo, [1]; ~ **out,** depromo; (cause to appear) elicio, [3].

fetter, *v.t.* compedes impingo (alicui), [3]; colligo, [1]; vincio, [4]; *fig.* impedio, [4]; illaqueo, [1].

fetter, *n.* compes, pedica, *f*

feud, *n.* lis, simultas; inimicitia, *f*; odium, *nt.*

fever, *n.* febris, *f*

feverish, *a.* febriculosus; *fig.* ardens.

few, *a.* pauci, perpauci; aliquot, (*indecl.*); **in a ~ words,** paucis, breviter.

fib, *n.* mendaciolum, mendaciunculum, *nt.*

fibre, *n.* fibra, *f*; filum, *nt.*

fickle, *a.* inconstans, mobilis; instabilis; levis.

fickleness, *n.* inconstantia; mutabilitas; mobilitas, levitas, *f.*

fiction, *n.* fictio, *f.*; commentum, *nt.*; fabula, *f.*

fictitious, *a.* fictus, commenticius; (simulated), simulatus; ~ly, *ad.* ficte.

fiddle, *n.* fides, *f.*

fidelity, *n.* fidelitas; constantia, fides, *f.*

fidget, *v.i.* cursito, [1].

fidgety, *a.* inquietus.

field, *n.* campus, ager, *m.*; arvum, rus, *nt.*; ~ **of grass,** pratum; (battle) proelium, *nt.*; *fig.* (scope) area, *f.*

field-mouse, *n.* mus agrestis, *m.*

fiend, *n.* Erinys, *f.*

fierce, *a.* atrox; saevus; vehemens; ~ly, *ad.* atrociter; saeve; ferociter; vehementer.

fierceness, *n.* atrocitas; saevitia; ferocitas; ferocia; vehementia, *f.*

fiery, *a.* igneus; *fig.* ardens, fervidus, iracundus.

fifteen, *a.* quindecim.

fifteenth, *a.* quintus decimus.

fifth, *a.* quintus.

fifth, *n.* quinta pars, *f.*

fifthly, *ad.* quintum, quinto.

fiftieth, *a.* quinquagesimus.

fifty, *a.* quinquaginta.

fig, *n.* (fruit and tree) ficus, *f.*

fight, *n.* pugna, *f.*; proelium, *nt.*; (struggle) contentio, *f.*

fight, *v.t. & i.* pugno; dimico, [1]; contendo, [3]; (in battle) proelior; (with sword) digladior; (hand to hand) comminus pugno, [1]; ~ **against,** repugno, [1].

fighter, *n.* pugnator, proeliator, *m.*

figurative, *a.* translatus; ~ly, *ad.* per translationem, tropice.

figure, *n.* figura; forma; (shape) imago, *f.*; (appearance) species, *f.*; (of speech) tropus, *m.*; (number) numerus, *m.*

figured, *a.* sigillatus; (chased) caelatus.

filament, *n.* fibrae, *f. pl.*; filum, *nt.*

filch, *v.t.* surripio, [3]; suffuror, [1].

file, *n.* (tool) lima, *f.*; (for *or* of papers) scapus; (line, string, row) ordo, *m.*; series, *f.*; **the rank and ~,** milites gregarii, *m. pl.*

file, *v.t.* (rub smooth) limo, [1].

filial, *a.* pius; ~ly, *ad.* pie.

filings, *n.* scobis, *f.*

fill, *v.t.* compleo; impleo, expleo; (supply) suppleo, [2]; ~ **out,** impleo, [2]; ~ **up,** expleo; (completely) compleo, [2]; (heap) cumulo, [1].

fill, *n.* satietas, *f.*; **have one's ~ of,** satior, [1] (*with abl.*).

filter, *n.* colum, *nt.*

filter, *v.t. & i.* percolo; percolor, [1].

filth, *n.* sordes, colluvies, illuvies, *f.*; v. **dirt.**

filthiness, _n._ foeditas, _f.;_ squalor, _m.; fig._ obscenitas, _f._

filthy, _a._ sordidus, foedus, spurcus; _fig._ obscenus.

fin, _n._ pinna, _f._

final, _a._ ultimus, extremus, postremus; **~ly**, _ad._ postremo; denique.

finance, _n._ res familiaris, _f.,_ fiscus, aerarii reditus, _m._

financial, _a._ aerarius.

finch, _n._ fringilla, _f._

find, _v.t._ invenio, reperio, [4]; (hit upon) offendo, [3]; (catch in the act) deprehendo, [3]; **~ out**, comperio, [4]; (discover) rescisco, [3]; (guess) conicio, [1].

fine, _a._ (of texture) subtilis; (thin) tenuis; (of gold) purus; (handsome) bellus; elegans; (excellent) optimus, (ironically) bonus, egregius, praeclarus.

fine, _n._ mul(c)ta, _f._

fine, _v.t._ mul(c)to, [1].

finely, _ad._ subtiliter; tenuiter; _fig._ pulchre; egregie.

fineness, _n._ subtilitas; tenuitas; _fig._ pulchritudo; elegantia, praestantia, _f._

finery, _n._ ornatus, cultus, _m.;_ lautitia, _f._

finger, _n._ digitus, _m._

finger, _v.t._ tango, [3]; tracto, [1].

finish, _v.t._ conficio, perficio, [3]; (put an end to) termino, [1]; finio, [4]; **~ off**, consummo, [1]; ultimam manum operi impono, [3]; **~**, _v.i._ finio, [4].

finish, _n._ (end) finis, _c._

finishing-touch, _n._ ultima manus, _f._

finite, _a._ caducus, moriturus.

fir(-tree), _n._ abies, pinus, _f.;_ (of fir) _a._ abiegnus, pineus.

fire, _n._ ignis, _m.;_ (conflagration) incendium, _nt.; fig._ fervor, ardor, impetus, _m.;_ **catch ~**, ignem concipio, [3]; **set ~ to**, incendo, [3]; **on ~**, incensus, inflammatus.

fire, _v.t._ (weapons) mitto, dirigo, [3].

firebrand, _n._ torris, _m._

fire-engine, _n._ sipho, _m._

firemen, _n._ excubiae vigilesque adversus incendia, _m. pl._

fireplace, _n._ caminus; focus, _m._

fireproof, _a._ ignibus impervius.

fireside, _n._ focus, _m._

firewood, _n._ lignum, _nt._

firm, _a._ firmus; solidus; (of purpose) tenax; **be ~**, (endure) persevero, persto, [1].

firm, _n._ (company) societas, _f._

firmly, _ad._ firme, firmiter; solide; (of purpose) tenaciter.

firmness, _n._ firmitas; constantia, _f._

first, _a._ primus; princeps.

first, _ad._ primum; **at ~**, primo; **~ of all**, imprimis.

fiscal, _a._ fiscalis.

fish, _n._ piscis, _m._

fish, _v.t. & i._ piscor; _fig._ expiscor, [1].

fish-bone, n. spina piscis, f.

fisher, fisherman, n. piscator, m.

fish-hook, n. hamus, m.

fishing, n. piscatus, m.; piscatio, f.

fishing-boat, n. piscatoria navis, f.

fishing-line, n. linum, nt.

fishing-net, n. funda, f.; iaculum, everriculum, nt.

fishing-rod, n. arundo, f.; calamus, m.

fishmonger, n. cetarius, piscarius, m.

fish-pond, n. piscina, f.; vivarium, nt.

fishy, a. piscosus, pisculentus; fig. suspectus.

fissure, n. rima, fissura, f.

fist, n. pugnus, m.

fit, n. (of a disease) accessio, f.; **epileptic ~**, morbus caducus, m.; (whim) libido, f.; **by ~s and starts**, ad. carptim.

fit, a. aptus, idoneus; conveniens, opportunus; habilis; (becoming) decens; (ready) paratus; (healthy) sanus.

fit, v.t. accommodo, apto; (apply) applico, [1]; (furnish) instruo, [3]; orno, [1]; **~ out**, instruo, [3]; orno, adorno, [1]; suppedito, [1]; **~**, v.i. (of dress) sedeo, [2]; fig. convenio, [4].

fitful, a. mobilis, mutabilis, inconstans.

fitness, n. convenientia; (healthiness) valetudo, f.

fitting, n. decens, v. fit, a.

five, a. quinque; **~ times**, quinquies.

fix, v.t. figo, [3]; (the eyes, etc.) intendo, [3]; (establish) stabilio, [4]; (on, upon) eligo, [3]; (appoint) statuo, constituo, [3]; (repair) reficio, [3]; **~**, v.i. (be fixed, stick) inhaereo, [2].

fixed, a. fixus, firmus; certus; (intent upon) intentus; **~ly**, ad. firmiter, constanter.

flabby, a. flaccidus, flaccus; fluidus; (drooping) marcidus.

flaccid, a. flaccidus.

flag, n. (banner) vexillum; insigne, nt.

flag, v.i. languesco; refrigesco, remittor, [3]; laxor, [1].

flagon, n. lagena, f.

flagrant, a. immanis, insignis; atrox, nefarius; (open) apertus.

flag-ship, n. navis praetoria, f.

flake, n. floccus, m.; frustum, nt.; squama, f.; **snow ~s**, nives, f. pl.

flaky, a. squameus.

flame, n. flamma, f.; ardor, m.

flame, v.i. flammo, flagro, [1]; **~ up**, fig. exardesco, [3].

flamingo, n. (bird) phoenicopterus, m.

flank, n. (of an animal) ilia, nt. pl.; (of an army) latus, nt.

flap, n. lacinia, f.

flap, *v.t. & i.* (wings) alis plaudo, [3]; (hang loosely) fluito, [1]; dependeo, [2].

flare, *v.i.* flagro, [1]; fulgeo, [2].

flash, *n.* fulgor, *m.*; (of lightning) fulmen, *nt.*

flash, *v.i.* fulgeo, splendeo, [2]; corusco, [1].

flask, *n.* ampulla, laguncula, *f.*

flat, *a.* (even, level) planus; (not mountainous) campester; (lying on the face) pronus; (sheer) merus; (insipid, of drinks) vapidus; *fig.* frigidus; insulsus; ieiunus.

flatness, *n.* planities; (evenness) aequalitas; (of a discourse, *etc.*) ieiunitas; (of drinks) vappa, *f.*

flatten, *v.t.* complano, aequo, [1].

flatter, *v.t.* adulor, assentor, [1]; blandior, [4].

flatterer, *n.* adulator, assentator, *m.*

flattering, *a.* adulans, blandus, adulatorius.

flattery, *n.* adulatio, assentatio, *f.*; blanditiae, *f. pl.*

flaunt, *v.t.* obicio, [3].

flautist, *n.* tibicen, *m.*

flavour, *n.* sapor, *m.*

flavour, *v.t.* condio, [4].

flavouring, *n.* condimentum, *nt.*

flaw, *n.* (defect) vitium, *nt.*; menda, macula, labes, *f.*; (chink) rima, *f.*

flawless, *a.* sine mendo, perfectus, integer.

flax, *n.* linum, *nt.*

flaxen, *a.* lineus; (of colour) flavus.

flay, *v.t.* pellem detraho, [3].

flea, *n.* pulex, *m.*

fleck, *n.* macula, *f.*

fleck, *v.t.* maculo, [1].

flee, *v.t. & i.* fugio, [3]; ~ **away**, aufugio, [3]; ~ **to**, confugio, [3]; ~**from**, effugio, [3].

fleece, *n.* vellus, *nt.*

fleece, *v.t.* (shear) tondeo, [2]; *fig.* spolio; privo; expilo, [1].

fleecy, *a.* laniger.

fleet, *n.* classis, *f.*

fleeting, *a.* fugax; fluxus; lubricus; caducus.

flesh, *n.* caro, *f.*; viscera, *nt. pl.*; *fig.* (body) corpus, *nt.*; (sensuality) libido, *f.*

fleshy, *a.* (abounding in flesh) carnosus.

flexibility, *n.* mollitia, facilitas, *f.*

flexible, *a.* flexibilis, flexilis, mollis, lentus; *fig.* exorabilis.

flicker, *v.i.* (flutter) volito; (flash) corusco, [1].

flight, *n.* fuga, *f.*; (escape) effugium *nt.*; (of birds) volatus, *m.*; (of stairs) scala, *f.*; **put to ~**, in fugam impello, [3]; fugo, [1]; fundo, [3]; **take (to) ~**, aufugio, [3].

flimsiness, *n.* tenuitas, exilitas, *f.*

flimsy, *a.* tenuis, praetenuis; *fig.* frivolus.

flinch, *v.i.* abhorreo, [2].

fling, *v.t.* iacio, mitto, [3]; ~ away, abicio, [3]; ~ down, deicio, [3]; ~ off, reicio, [3].

flint, *n.* silex, *c.*

flippancy, *n.* levitas, protervitas, *f.*

flippant, *a.* levis, protervus, petulans; ~ly, *ad.* proterve, petulanter.

flirt, *v.i.* ludo, [3].

flirtation, *n.* lusus, *m.*

flit, *v.i.* volito, circumvolito, [1].

float, *v.i.* fluito, (in)nato; fluctuor, [1]; pendeo, [2]; (hang loosely) volito, [1]; *v.t.* (launch) deduco, [3].

flock, *n.* (of sheep, birds, *etc.*) grex, *m.*

flock, *v.i.* (together) coeo, convenio, [4], congregor; convolo, [1].

flog, *v.t.* verbero, [1]; caedo, [3].

flogging, *n.* verberatio, *f.*; verbera, *nt. pl.*

flood, *n.* (inundation) diluvies, *f.*; (stream) flumen, *nt.*; (tide) aestus, *m.*; *fig.* flumen, *nt.*

floor, *n.* solum, *nt.*; (paved ~) pavimentum, *nt.*; (of a barn) area; (storey) contignatio, *f.*; tabulatum, *nt.*

floor, *v.t.* pavimentum struo, [3]; (with planks) contabulo, [1]; (throw down) sterno, [3]; (silence) confuto, [1].

flooring, *n.* contabulatio, *f.*, v. floor, *n.*

floral, *a.* florens.

florid, *a.* (of complexion) rubicundus; *fig.* (of style) floridus.

flounder, *v.i.* voluto, titubo, [1].

flour, *n.* farina, *f.*

flourish, *v.i.* floreo; vireo, [2].

flourish, *n.* ornamentum, *nt.*; (of style) calamistri, flosculi, *m. pl.*; (of a trumpet) cantus, *m.*

flourishing, *a.* florens.

floury, *a.* farinulentus.

flout, *v.t.* derideo, [2]; repudio, [1].

flow, *v.i.* fluo, feror, [3]; mano, [1]; (of the tide) affluo, accedo, [3].

flow, *n.* fluxus, *m.*; (gliding motion) lapsus; (of the tide) accessus, *m.*; (stream) flumen, *nt.*; (course) cursus, *m.*

flower, *n.* flos, flosculus, *m.*; *fig.* (the best) flos, *m.*

flower, *v.i.* floreo, [2]; floresco, [3].

flower-bed, *n.* area, *f.*

flowery, *a.* floreus; floridus; florifer.

fluctuate, *v.t.* fluctuo; fluito, iactor, [1].

fluctuation, *n.* fluctuatio; *fig.* mutatio, *f.*

flue, *n.* cuniculus fornacis, *m.*

fluency, *n.* volubilitas linguae; copia verborum, *f.*

fluent, *a.* volubilis; profluens; (eloquent) disertus; ~ly, *ad.* volubiliter.

fluid, *a.* fluidus, liquidus.

fluid, *n.* liquor, umor, latex, *m.*

flurry, *n.* perturbatio, *f.*; tumultus, *m.*

flush, *n.* (sudden attack) impetus, *m.*; (abundance) copia, *f.*; (blush) rubor, *m.*

flush, *v.i.* erubesco, [3].

fluster, *v.t.* perturbo; inquieto, [1]; sollicito, [1].

flute, *n.* tibia, *f.*

flutter, *v.t.* agito, perturbo, sollicito, [1]; ~, *v.i.* (of birds) volito; (with alarm) trepido, [1].

fly, *n.* musca, *f.*

fly, *v.i.* volo, volito, [1]; (flee) fugio, [3]; ~ **off,** avolo, [1]; ~ **open,** dissilio, [4]; ~ **out,** provolo, [1]; ~ **up,** subvolo, [1].

flying, *a.* volatilis; volucer; ales.

foal, *n.* (of the horse) equulus, *m.*

foam, *n.* spuma, *f.*

foam, *v.i.* spumo, [1].

foamy, *a.* spumans; spumeus, spumosus, spumifer.

fodder, *n.* pabulum, *nt.*

foe, *n.* hostis, inimicus, *m.*

fog, *n.* caligo, nebula, *f.*

foggy, *a.* caliginosus, nebulosus.

foible, *n.* vitium, *nt.*; error, *m.*

foil, *n.* (for fencing) rudis, *f.*; (leaf of metal) lamina, *f.*; (very thin) brattea, *f.*; (contrast) exemplum contrarii, *nt.*

foil, *v.t.* frustror, [1]; repello, [3]; **be ~ed,** spe deici.

fold, *n.* sinus, *m.*; (wrinkling) ruga, *f.*; (for cattle) stabulum; (for sheep) ovile, *nt.*

fold, *v.t.* plico, complico, [1].

folding-doors, *n.* valvae, *f. pl.*

foliage, *n.* frons, coma, *f.*; folia, *nt. pl.*

folk, *n.* homines, *m. pl.*

follow, *v.i.* sequor, insequor, consequor, [3]; (close) insto, sector, assector, [1]; (on) persequor; (out) exsequor, prosequor; (up) subsequor, [3].

follower, *n.* sectator, assectator; *fig.* discipulus, i, *m.*

following, *a.* (in)sequens; posterus, proximus; (uninterruptedly) continuus; **on the ~ day,** postridie.

folly, *n.* stultitia; insipientia; (madness) dementia, *f.*

foment, *v.t.* foveo, [2]; (disorder, *etc.*) stimulo, [1]; cieo, [2].

fond, *a.* amans; deditus; cupidus; (indulgent) indulgens; (foolishly infatuated) demens; **be ~ of,** amo, [1].

fondle, *v.t.* permulceo, foveo, [2].

fondly, *ad.* amanter, peramanter.

fondness, *n.* amor, *m.*; indulgentia; caritas, *f.*

food, *n.* (for cattle, *etc.*) pabulum; (any nourishing substance) alimentum, *nt.*; (of people) cibus, *m.*; esca, *f.*

fool, *n.* stultus, insipiens; (idiot) fatuus; (in a play) sannio, *m.*; **make a ~ of,** ludificor (aliquem), [1]; **play the ~,** ineptio, [4]; nugor, [1].

fool, *v.t.* ludificor, [1]; ludo, illudo, [3]; ~ **around**, ineptio, [4]; nugor, [1].

foolery, *n.* ineptiae, nugae, *f. pl.*

foolhardiness, *n.* temeritas, *f.*

foolhardy, *a.* temerarius.

foolish, *a.* stultus, fatuus, ineptus, stolidus; ~**ly**, *ad.* stulte, inepte.

foot, *n.* pes, *m.*; (of a mountain) radix, *f.*; (of a pillar, *etc.*) basis, *f.*; on ~, pedester (tris, tre).

football, *n.* pila, *f.*

footing, *a.* (condition) status, *m.*; condicio, *f.*

footpath, *n.* semita, *f.*; callis, trames, *m.*

footprint, *n.* vestigium, *nt.*

foot-soldier, *n.* pedes, *m.*

footstep, *n.* vestigium, *nt.*

footstool, *n.* scabellum, *nt.*

for, *pr.* (on behalf of) pro (*with abl.*); (for the sake of) causa (*with gen.*); (because of) ob, propter (*with acc.*); (after negatives) prae (*with abl.*); ~, *c.* nam, enim; ~ **some time**, aliquandiu; food ~ **a day**, cibus unius diei.

forage, *v.t. & i.* pabulor; frumentor, [1]; *fig.* rimor, [1].

forager, *n.* pabulator; frumentator, *m.*

foraging, *n.* pabulatio; frumentatio, *f.*

foray, *n.* incursio, populatio, *f.*

forbear, *v.i.* abstineo, [2]; (leave off) desisto, [3].

forbearance, *n.* patientia; indulgentia, *f.*

forbid, *v.t.* veto, [1]; prohibeo, [2]; interdico, [3].

forbidding, *a.* insuavis, odiosus; (ugly) deformis; (frightful) immanis.

force, *n.* vis; (law) manus, *f.*; (mil.) copiae, *f. pl.*; (weight) momentum, pondus, *nt.*; (strength) vires, *f. pl.*; robur, *nt.*; in ~, valens, validus.

force, *v.t.* cogo; (a door, a wall, *etc.*) perrumpo; (drive away) expello, [3]; ~ **down**, detrudo, [3]; ~ **in**, (a nail, *etc.*) infigo, [3]; ~ **out**, extorqueo, [2]; depello, [3]; ~ **open**, rumpo, [3].

forced, *a.* (unnatural) accersitus, quaesitus; ~ **march**, magnum *or* maximum iter, *nt.*

forceful, *a.* validus.

forcible, *a.* per vim factus; (violent) vehemens; (compulsory) coactus.

forcibly, *ad.* per vim, vi; violenter.

ford, *n.* vadum, *nt.*

ford, *v.t.* vado transeo, [4].

forearm, *n.* bracchium, *nt.*

forearm, *v.t.* praemunio, [4].

forebode, *v.t.* portendo, [3]; praesagio, [4]; (forewarn) moneo, [2].

foreboding, *n.* portentum, praesagium, *nt.*; (prophetic feeling) praesensio, *f.*

forecast, *v.t.* praevideo, [2]; prospicio, [3]; auguror, [1].

forecast, *n.* providentia, *f.*; augurium, *nt.*

forefather, *n.* atavus, *m.*; ~s, *pl.* maiores, *m. pl.*

forefinger, *n.* digitus index, *m.*

foregoing, *a.* prior, proximus.

forehead, *n.* frons, *f.*

foreign, *a.* externus, alienus, peregrinus.

foreigner, *n.* peregrinus, externus; (stranger) advena, *m.*

foreknowledge, *n.* providentia, *f.*

foreland, *n.* promontorium, *nt.*; lingua, *f.*

forelock, *n.* cirrus, *m.*

foremost, *a.* primus; princeps, praecipuus.

forensic, *a.* forensis.

forerunner, *n.* praenuntius, antecursor, *m.*

foresee, *v.t.* praevideo, [2]; prospicio, [3].

foresight, *n.* providentia, prospicientia, prudentia; (precaution) provisio, *f.*

forest, *n.* silva, *f.*; nemus, *nt.*; saltus, *m.*; ~, *a.* silvestris, nemorensis.

forestall, *v.t.* anticipo, [1]; praecipio, [3].

foretaste, *n.* gustus, *m.*

foretell, *v.t.* praedico, [3]; vaticinor, [1].

forethought, *n.* providentia, prospicientia, *f.*

forever, *ad.* in aeternum.

forewarn, *v.t.* praemoneo; moneo, [2].

forfeit, *n.* mul(c)ta, poena, *f.*

forfeit, *v.t.* mul(c)tor, [1]; (lose) amitto, [3].

forfeiture, *n.* (loss) amissio; (of goods) publicatio, *f.*

forge, *v.t.* (metal, *etc.*) cudo, procudo, [3]; fabricor, [1]; (devise) fingo; (counterfeit) corrumpo, [3]; (a document) interlino, [3]; *v.i.* ~ ahead, progredior, [3].

forge, *n.* fornax, *f.*

forger, *n.* fabricator; (of writings) falsarius, *m.*

forgery, *n.* (of documents) subiectio; (forged document) litterae falsae, *f. pl.*

forget, *v.t.* obliviscor; (unlearn) dedisco, [3].

forgetful, *a.* obliviosus, immemor.

forgetfulness, *n.* oblivio, *f.*; oblivium, *nt.*

forgive, *v.t.* condono, [1]; ignosco, [3] (*with dat.*).

forgiveness, *n.* venia, *f.*

forgiving, *a.* ignoscens; clemens.

forgo, *v.t.* renuntio, [1]; dimitto, [3]; (abstain from) abstineo ab (*with abl.*), [2]; (lose) amitto, [3].

fork, *n.* furca, *f.*; (of roads) bivium, trivium, quadrivium, *nt.*

fork, *v.i.* scindor, [3].

forked, *a.* bifurcus, bicornis.

forlorn, *a.* solus, desertus, miser.

form, *n.* forma, figura, *f.;* (bench) scamnum, *nt.;* (rite) ritus, *m.;* (class in a school) classis, *f.*

form, *v.t.* formo, [1]; fingo; (produce) efficio, [3]; (constitute) sum.

formal, *a.* formalis; *fig.* frigidus; (stiff) rigidus, durus.

formality, *n.* ritus, *m.*

formation, *n.* conformatio; forma, figura, *f.*

former, *a.* prior, priscus, pristinus; (immediately preceding) superior; **~ly,** *ad.* antea, prius, antehac; olim; quondam.

formidable, *a.* formidabilis, formidolosus, metuendus.

formless, *a.* informis; *fig.* rudis.

formula, *n.* formula, *f.;* exemplar, *nt.*

forsake, *v.t.* desero, derelinquo, relinquo, destituo, [3].

fort, *n.* castellum, *nt.;* arx, *f.*

forth, *ad.* foras; (of time) inde; **and so ~,** et cetera.

forthcoming, *a.* promptus; in promptu.

forthwith, *ad.* extemplo, protinus, statim, continuo.

fortieth, *a.* quadragesimus.

fortification, *n.* munitio, *f.;* munimen, munimentum, *nt.*

fortify, *v.t.* munio, circummunio, [4].

fortitude, *n.* fortitudo, virtus, *f.*

fortnight, *n.* semestrium, *nt.;* dies quatuordecim, *m. pl.*

fortress, *n.* arx, *f.;* castellum, *nt.*

fortuitous, *a.* fortuitus; **~ly,** *ad.* fortuito.

fortunate, *a.* fortunatus, felix, prosperus; **~ly,** *ad.* fortunate, prospere, feliciter.

fortune, *n.* fortuna, fors, sors, *f.;* casus, *m.;* **good ~,** fortuna, *f.;* (wealth) divitiae, opes, *f. pl.;* **tell ~s,** hariolor, [1].

fortune-teller, *n.* hariolus, *m.;* hariola, *f.*

forty, *a.* quadraginta.

forum, *n.* forum, *nt.*

forward(s), *ad.* porro, prorsus, prorsum.

forward, *a.* (early, soon ripe) praecox; (bold) audax; (saucy) protervus.

forward, *v.t.* (despatch) mitto, [3]; (promote) promoveo, [2]; consulo (*with dat.*), [3].

foster, *v.t.* foveo, [2]; nutrio, [4]; alo, [3].

foster-child, *n.* alumnus, *m.;* alumna, *f.*

foster-father, *n.* nutricius, nutritor, *m.*

foster-mother, *n.* nutrix, altrix, educatrix, *f.*

foul, *a.* (dirty) foedus, lutulentus, squalidus; (of language) obscenus; (of weather, stormy) turbidus; *fig.* turpis.

foul, *v.t.* foedo, inquino, [1].

foul-mouthed, *a.* maledicus.

foulness, n. foeditas, f.; (dirt) squalor, m.; (of a crime) atrocitas; fig. turpitudo; obscenitas, f.

found, v.t. fundo, [1]; condo, constituo, construo, [3].

foundation, n. fundamentum, fundamen, nt.; substructio, sedes, f.

founder, n. fundator, conditor; auctor, m.

founder, v.i. (of ships) submergor, deprimor, [3].

foundling, n. expositicius, m.

fountain, n. fons, m.

four, a. quattuor; ~ **times,** quater; **on all** ~**s,** repens.

fourfold, a. quadruplex, quadruplus.

four-footed, a. quadrupes.

fourteen, a. quattuordecim.

fourteenth, a. quartus decimus.

fourth, a. quartus; ~**ly,** ad. quarto.

fowl, n. avis, volucris, f.; **domestic** ~, gallina, f.

fox, n. vulpes, vulpecula, f.; fig. homo astutus.

fraction, n. pars exigua, f.; fragmentum, fragmen, nt.

fractious, a. difficilis, morosus.

fractiousness, n.; morositas, f.

fracture, n. fractura, f.; ~, v.t. frango, [3].

fragile, a. fragilis; fig. caducus.

fragility, n. fragilitas, f.

fragment, n. fragmentum, fragmen, nt.

fragrance, n. odor, m.

fragrant, a. suaveolens, odorus; odorifer.

frail, a. fragilis; caducus; infirmus.

frailty, n. fragilitas; infirmitas, f.

frame, n. compages; (of body) figura, f.; (of a window, etc.) forma; (of a bed) sponda, f.; (edge) margo, c.; fig. habitus animi, m.

frame, v.t. (shape) formo; (build) fabrico, [1]; (join together) compingo, [3]; (contrive) molior, [4].

framework, n. compages, f.

franchise, n. ius suffragii, nt.

frank, a. candidus, liber, ingenuus, sincerus, simplex.

frankly, ad. candide, libere, ingenue, sincere, simpliciter.

frankness, n. libertas f.; candor, m.; ingenuitas; simplicitas; sinceritas, f.

frantic, a. fanaticus, furens, insanus, amens; ~**ly,** ad. insane.

fraternal, a. fraternus; ~**ly,** ad. fraterne.

fraternity, n. (association) sodalitas, f.

fraternize, v.i. amice convenio, [4].

fratricide, n. (murderer) fratricida, m.; (murder) fraternum parricidium, nt.

fraud, n. fraus, fallacia, f.; dolus, m.

fraudulent, *a.* fraudulentus, dolosus; **~ly**, *ad.* fraudulenter, dolo malo.

fray, *n.* rixa, pugna, *f.*; certamen, *nt.*

fray, *v.t.* (wear away) attero, [3].

freak, *n.* (monster) monstrum, portentum, *nt.*

freckles, *n.* lentigo, *f.*

freckled, *a.* lentiginosus.

free, *a.* liber; (from business) otiosus; (not bound by . . .) solutus; (of space) vacuus; (immune) immunis; (gratuitous) gratuitus; (impudent) procax; *fig.* candidus, sincerus; **~ from**, expers (*with gen.*), vacuus (*with abl.*).

free, *v.t.* libero, [1]; (a slave) manumitto, [3].

freebooter, *n.* praedo, latro; (at sea) pirata, *m.*

freeborn, *a.* ingenuus.

freedman, *n.* libertus, libertinus, *m.*

freedom, *n.* libertas; immunitas; (from) vacuitas, *f.*; (franchise) civitas, *f.*

freedwoman, *n.* liberta, libertina, *f.*

freely, *ad.* libere; (of one's own accord) sponte; (liberally) large; copiose; liberaliter; munifice; (far and wide) late; (for nothing) gratis.

freeman, *n.* liber, *m.*

free-will, *n.* voluntas, *f.*; liberum arbitrium, *nt.*

freeze, *v.t.* congelo, gelo, glacio, [1]; **~**, *v.i.* consisto, rigesco, [3]; **it is freezing**, gelat.

freight, *n.* onus, *nt.*

frenzied, *a.* furens, lymphatus.

frenzy, *n.* furor, *m.*; insania, *f.*

frequency, *n.* crebritas; frequentia, *f.*

frequent, *a.* creber; frequens; **~ly**, *ad.* crebro; frequenter, saepe.

frequent, *v.t.* frequento, celebro, [1].

fresco, *n.* tectorium, *nt.*; **al ~**, sub divo.

fresh, *a.* (new) recens, novus; (cool) frigidulus; (lusty) vigens; (not tired) integer; (green) viridis; (not salt) dulcis.

freshen, *v.t.* recreo, [1]; **~**, *v.i.* increbresco, [3].

freshly, *ad.* recenter.

freshness, *n.* (newness) novitas, *f.*; (vigour) vigor, *m.*

fret, *v.i.* (grieve) doleo, [2]; crucior, [1]; aegre fero, [3].

fretful, *a.* morosus; difficilis.

fretfulness, *n.* morositas, *f.*

fretwork, *n.* caelatum opus, *nt.*

friction, *n.* frictio, *f.*; tritus, attritus, *m.*

friend, *n.* amicus, *m.*; amica, *f.*; familiaris, *c.*; necessarius, *m.*; sodalis, *m.*

friendless, *a.* amicorum inops, desertus.

friendliness, *n.* benevolentia; comitas, affabilitas, *f.*

friendly, *a.* benevolus; comis; amicus.

friendship, *n.* amicitia, sodalitas, necessitudo, familiaritas, *f.*

frieze, *n.* (in architecture) zoophorus, *m.*

frigate, *n.* navis longa, *f.*

fright, *n.* pavor, terror, metus, *m.*; formido, *f.*

frighten, *v.t.* (per)terreo, [2]; ~ **away,** absterreo, [2].

frightful, *a.* terribilis, terrificus; dirus; **~ly,** *ad.* terribilem in modum.

frigid, *a.* frigidus; **~ly,** *ad.* frigide.

frigidity, *n.* frigiditas, *f.*

frill, *n.* segmentum, *nt.*

frilly, *a.* segmentatus.

fringe, *n.* fimbriae, *f. pl.*; limbus, *m.*

frisk, *v.i.* lascivio; salio, exsilio, [4]; luxurio, [1].

frisky, *a.* lascivus, procax, protervus.

fritter, *v.t.* ~ **away,** contero; comminuo, [3]; *fig.* dissipo, [1].

frivolity, *n.* levitas, inconstantia, *f.*

frivolous, *a.* levis; frivolus, futilis; **~ly,** *ad.* nugatorie, tenuiter.

fro, *ad.* **to and ~,** huc illuc; ultro citroque.

frock, *n.* palla, stola, *f.*

frog, *n.* rana, *f.*

frolic, *n.* lascivia, *f.*; (play, prank) ludus, *m.*

frolic, *v.i.* exsulto, [1]; lascivio, [4].

from, *pr.* a, ab, de, ex (all with *abl.*); (owing to) propter (with *acc.*); ~ **above,** desuper; ~ **day to day,** de die in diem; ~ **time to time,** continuo.

front, *n.* frons, prior pars, *f.*; (*mil.*) primum agmen, *nt.*

front, *a.* prior, primus; (*mil.*) primoris; **in ~,** ex adverso.

frontage, *n.* frons, *f.*

frontier, *n.* finis, terminus, *m.*

frost, *n.* gelu, *nt.*; (hoar-frost) pruina, *f.*

frostbitten, *a.* frigore adustus.

frosty, *a.* gelidus, glacialis; *fig.* (of manner) frigidus.

froth, *n.* spuma, *f.*; *fig.* (empty words) vaniloquentia, *f.*

froth, *v.i.* spumo, [1].

frothy, *a.* spumeus, spumosus; *fig.* tumidus.

frown, *n.* contractio frontis, *f.*; vultus severus, *m.*

frown, *v.i.* frontem contraho, [3]; *fig.* (~ upon) aversor, [1].

frozen, *a.* conglaciatus, gelatus, gelu rigens, concretus.

frugal, *a.* abstinens, parcus, frugalis; **~ly,** *ad.* frugaliter, parce.

frugality, *n.* parsimonia; frugalitas, *f.*

fruit, n. fructus, m.; frux, f.; fig.
(gain) lucrum, nt.; (result) fructus, m.

fruitful, a. fecundus, fertilis;
ferax, uber; ~ly, ad. fecunde,
feraciter.

fruitfulness, n. fecunditas, fertilitas, ubertas, f.

fruition, n. fructus, m.

fruitless, a. fig. irritus; ~ly, ad.
frustra; re infecta.

fruit-tree, n. pomum, nt.

frustrate, v.t. frustror, [1];
(baffle) decipio, fallo, [3]; (break
up) dirimo, [3].

frustration, n. frustratio, f.

fry, v.t. frigo, [3].

frying-pan, n. sartago, f.

fuck, v. futuo, [3].

fuel, n. fomes, m.; ligna, nt. pl.;
nutrimen, nt.

fugitive, a. fugitivus; fugax.

fugitive, n. profugus, m.; profuga,
f.

fulfil, v.t. expleo, [2]; exsequor, [3].

fulfilment, n. exsecutio, perfectio, f.; (result) exitus, m.

full, a. plenus; (filled up) expletus; (entire) integer; solidus;
(satiated) satur; (of dress)
fusus; ~, ad. v. **fully.**

full-grown, a. adultus.

full moon, n. plenilunium, nt.

fully, ad. plene; copiose; omnino;
prorsus.

fume, n. vapor, halitus, m.

fume, v.t. & i. exhalo, [1]; (fig.)
irascor, [3].

fumigate, v.t. fumigo, [1]; suffio, [4].

fumigation, n. suffitus, m.; suffitio, f.

fun, n. iocus, ludus, m.; ludibrium, nt.

function, n. munus, officium, nt.

functional, a. utilis.

fund, n. pecunia, f.; opes, f. pl.; fig.
copia, f.

fundamental, a. primus, simplex, necessarius, stabilis; ~ly,
ad. (by nature) natura; (essentially) necessario; (altogether)
penitus, omnino.

funeral, n. funus, nt.; exsequiae,
f. pl.

funeral, a. funebris, funereus; ~
rites, iusta funebria, nt. pl.; ~
pile, n. rogus, m.; pyra, f.

fungus, n. fungus, m.

funnel, n. infundibulum, nt.

funny, a. ridiculus, festivus.

fur, n. villi, m. pl.; pellis, f.

furious, a. (frenzied) furialis, furiosus, furens; (angry) iratus.

furl, v.t. contraho, lego, [3].

furnace, n. fornax, f.

furnish, v.t. ministro, suppedito;
orno, exorno, [1]; instruo, [3].

furniture, n. supellex, f.; apparatus, m.

furrow, n. sulcus, m.; (groove)
stria, f.

furrow, v.t. sulco; aro, [1].

furry, *a.* pellicius.

further, *ad.* ultra, longius, ulterius; ~, *a.* ulterior.

further, *v.t.* promoveo, [2]; proveho, consulo (*with dat.*) [3]; (aid) adiuvo, [1].

furthermore, *ad.* porro, insuper.

furthest, *a.* extremus, ultimus.

furtive, *a.* furtivus; ~ly, *ad.* clam, furtim, furtive.

fury, *n.* furor, *m.*; ira, rabies, *f.*

fuse, *v.t.* fundo, liquefacio, [3]; conflo, [1].

fusion, *n.* fusura, *f.*

fuss, *n.* tumultus, *m.*; turba, *f.*

fussy, *a.* curiosus.

futile, *a.* futilis, frivolus, vanus.

futility, *n.* futilitas, *f.*

future, *a.* futurus.

future, *n.* futura, *nt. pl.*; posterum tempus, *nt.*; **in, for the ~,** in posterum.

·····················

G

·····················

gabble, *v.i.* blatero, [1]; garrio, [4].

gable, *n.* fastigium, *nt.*

gad-fly, *n.* tabanus, oestrus, asilus, *m.*

gag, *n.* oris obturamentum, *nt.*

gag, *v.t.* os obturo, praeligo, [1]; obstruo, [3].

gaiety, *n.* festivitas, hilaritas, *f.*; nitor, splendor, *m.*

gain, *v.t.* lucror, [1]; consequor, acquiro, [3]; (get possession of) potior, [4].

gain, *n.* lucrum, emolumentum, *nt.*; quaestus, *m.*

gainful, *a.* lucrosus.

gait, *n.* incessus, ingressus, *m.*

galaxy, *n.* via lactea, *f.*

gale, *n.* ventus, *m.*; aura, tempestas, procella, *f.*

gall, *n.* bilis, *f.*; fel, *nt.*

gallant, *a.* nitidus, elegans; urbanus; (brave) fortis.

gallantry, *n.* virtus, *f.*; (politeness) urbanitas, elegantia, *f.*

galleon, *n.* navis oneraria, *f.*

gallery, *n.* porticus, *f.*; (open) peristylium, *nt.*; (top seats) summa cavea, *f.*

galley, *n.* navis longa, biremis, triremis, *f.*

gallop, *n.* cursus citatus, *m.*

gallop, *v.i.* citato equo contendo, [3]; (of the horse) quadrupedo, [1].

gallows, *n.* patibulum, *nt.*

gamble, *v.i.* alea ludo, [3]; ~ **away,** ludo amitto, [3].

gambler, *n.* aleator; lusor, *m.*

gambling, *n.* alea, *f.*

gambling-house, *n.* aleatorium, *nt.*

gambling-table, *n.* alveus, *m.*

gambol, *v.i.* lascivio, [4]; ludo, [3]; exsulto, [1].

game, *n.* ludus; (act of playing) lusus, *m.*; (in hunting) ferae, *f. pl.*; ~ **of chance,** alea, *f.*; **make ~ of,** ludificor, [1].

gamekeeper, *n.* saltuarius, *m.*

gaming, *v.* **gambling.**

gander, *n.* anser, *m.*

gang, *n.* grex, *m.*; (troop) caterva, *f.*; sodalicium, *nt.*

gangrene, *n.* gangraena, *f.*

gangway, *n.* (in a ship) forus, *m.*

gaol, *etc.,* *v.* **jail,** *etc.*

gap, *n.* rima, fissura; lacuna, *f.*; hiatus, *m.*

gape, *v.i.* hio, [1]; dehisco, [3]; (with mouth open) oscito, [1]; *fig.* stupeo, [2]; ~ **at,** inhio, [1].

gaping, *a.* hians, hiulcus; *fig.* stupidus.

garb, *n.* vestitus, *m.*

garbage, *n.* quisquiliae, *f. pl.*

garden, *n.* hortus, *m.*

gardener, *n.* hortulanus; **market-~,** holitor, *m.*

gardening, *n.* hortorum cultus, *m.*

gargle, *v.i.* gargarizo, [1].

garland, *n.* sertum, *nt.*; corona, *f.*

garlic, *n.* allium, *nt.*

garment, *n.* vestimentum, *nt.*; vestitus, *m.*

garnish, *v.t.* decoro, orno, [1]; (season) condio, [4]; ~, *n.* ornamentum, *nt.*

garotte, *v.t.* laqueo strangulo, [1].

garret, *n.* cenaculum, *nt.*

garrison, *n.* praesidium, *nt.*; ~, *v.t.* praesidium colloco, [1].

garrulous, *a.* garrulus, loquax.

gash, *n.* vulnus, *nt.*; plaga, *f.*; ~, *v.t.* seco, vulnero, [1].

gasp, *n.* anhelitus, *m.*

gasp, *v.i.* anhelo, [1].

gate, *n.* ianua, *f.*; ostium, *nt.*; fores, *f. pl.*; (of a town) porta, *f.*

gateway, *n.* porta, *f.*

gather, *v.t.* (assemble) congrego, [1]; (bring together) colligo; (of fruits) decerpo, lego; (pluck) carpo; (in logic) concludo, [3]; (suspect) suspicor, [1]; ~, *v.i.* (assemble) convenio, [4]; ~ **round,** *v.i.* convolo, [1]; confluo, [3]; ~ **up,** colligo; (pick up) sublego, [3].

gathering, *n.* collectio, *f.*; (assembling) congregatio, *f.*; (assembly) coetus, *m.*

gaudiness, *n.* ornatus, nitor, *m.*; lautitia, *f.*

gaudy, *a.* lautus, splendidus, speciosus.

gauge, *v.t.* metior, [4].

gauge, *n.* modulus, *m.*

gaunt, *a.* macer.

gay, *a.* laetus, hilaris; floridus; splendidus.

gaze, *n.* conspectus; (fixed look) obtutus, *m.*

gaze, *v.i.* intueor, [2]; specto, contemplor, [1].

gear, *n.* instrumenta, *nt. pl.*; arma, *nt. pl.*; supellex, *f.*

gem, *n.* gemma; baca, *f.*

gender, *n.* genus, *nt.*

general, *a.* generalis; vulgaris, publicus, universus; **in ~**, in universum; (for the most part) plerumque.

general, *n.* dux, imperator, *m.*

generally, *ad.* generatim; universe; (commonly) plerumque, vulgo.

generalship, *n.* ductus, *m.*; (skill of a commander) ars imperatoria, *f.*

generate, *v.t.* genero, procreo, [1]; gigno, [3].

generation, *n.* generatio, *f.*; (lineage) genus, *nt.*; (age) saeculum, *nt.*

generosity, *n.* liberalitas, generositas, *f.*; munificentia, *f.*

generous, *a.* generosus, liberalis; munificus; magnanimus.

generously, *ad.* liberaliter, munifice.

genial, *a.* genialis, hilaris.

geniality, *n.* geniale ingenium, *nt.*

genitals, *n.* genitalia, *nt. pl.*

genius, *n.* ingenium, *nt.*; (nature) indoles, *f.*; (person) vir ingeniosus, *m.*

genteel, *a.* elegans, urbanus.

gentle, *a.* (mild) lenis, mitis, clemens; (gradual) mollis.

gentleman, *n.* homo nobilis; *fig.* vir honestus; (well-bred man) homo liberalis, *m.*

gentleness, *n.* lenitas, clementia, *f.*

gently, *ad.* leniter; clementer; placide; (gradually) sensim; paulatim; pedetemptim.

genuine, *a.* sincerus; purus; verus; germanus; **~ly**, *ad.* sincere, vere.

genus, *n.* genus, *nt.*

geography, *n.* geographia, *f.*

geometrical, *a.* geometricus.

geometry, *n.* geometria, *f.*

germ, *n.* germen, *nt.*

germinate, *v.i.* germino, pullulo, [1].

germination, *n.* germinatio, *f.*; germinatus, *m.*

gesticulate, *v.i.* gestum ago, [3].

gesticulation, *n.* gestus, *m.*

gesture, *n.* gestus, motus, *m.*

get, *v.t.* adipiscor, consequor, acquiro, [3]; (by entreaty) impetro, [1]; **~ something done**, curo aliquid faciendum; **~** *v.i.* (become) fio, *ir.*; **~ away**, aufugio, [3]; **~ back**, (*v.t.*) recupero [1]; (*v.i.*) reverto [3]; **~ the better of**, *fig.* supero, [1]; praevaleo, [2]; **~ down**, (*v.i.*) descendo [3]; **~ hold of**, prehendo, [3]; occupo, [1]; **~ off**, (*v.i.*) aufugio [3]; **~ on**, (succeed) bene cedo, succedo, [3]; **~ out**, (*v.i.*) exeo [4]; (e curru) descendo [3]; **~ over**, (*v.t.*) traicio, transgredior, [3]; supero, [1]; **~ rid of**, amoveo [2]; tollo, [3]; **~ through**, pervenio, [4]; *fig.* perago, perficio [3];

~ **together**, (*v.t.*) colligo, cogo, [3]; (*v.i.*) congrego, [1]; ~ **up**, surgo, [3].

ghastly, *a.* (sallow) luridus; (pale) pallidus, pallens; (horrid, shocking) foedus.

ghost, *n.* (phantom) larva, *f.*; (of a dead person) umbra, *f.*; manes, *m. pl.*

ghostly, *a.* (unsubstantial) inanis.

giant, *n.* gigas, *m.*; ~, *a.* praegrandis.

gibberish, *n.* inanis strepitus, *m.*

gibbet, *n.* furca, *f.*; patibulum, *nt.*

gibe, *n.* (sneer) sanna, *f.*; (mockery) ludibrium, *nt.*; ~, *v.t.* illudo, [3].

giddiness, *n.* vertigo, *f.*; *fig.* levitas, inconstantia, *f.*

giddy, *a.* vertiginosus; *fig.* levis, inconstans.

gift, *n.* donum; beneficium, munus, *nt.*; (talent) dos, *f.*

gifted, *a.* (endowed) praeditus; *fig.* ingeniosus.

gigantic, *a.* praegrandis, ingens.

giggle, *v.i.* cachinno, [1].

gild, *v.t.* inauro, [1].

ginger, *n.* zingiberi, *nt.*

giraffe, *n.* camelopardalis, *f.*

girdle, *n.* cingulum, *nt.*; balteus, *m.*; (of women) zona, *f.*

girl, *n.* puella, virgo, *f.*

girlhood, *n.* puellaris aetas, *f.*

girlish, *a.* puellaris; virginalis; virgineus.

girth, *n.* fascia; (of a horse) cingula, *f.*; (circuit) ambitus, *m.*

gist, *n.* (main point) summa, *f.*

give, *v.t.* do, dono, [1]; confero, [3]; praebeo, [2]; (deliver) trado, [3]; ~ **away**, dono, [1]; ~ **back**, reddo, [3]; ~ **in**, (*v.i.*) (yield) cedo, [3]; ~ **out**, edo; emitto, [3]; nuntio, [1]; distribuo, [3]; (*v.i.*) (fail) deficio; ~ **up**, (*v.t.*) trado; (betray) prodo; (abandon) dimitto, [3]; ~ **way**, pedem refero; (yield) cedo; (comply with) obsequor, [3] (*with dat.*).

glad, *a.* laetus, contentus; hilaris, libens; **be** ~, gaudeo, [2]; laetor, [1].

gladden, *v.t.* laetifico, hilaro, exhilaro, [1].

glade, *n.* nemus, *nt.*; saltus, *m.*

gladiator, *n.* gladiator, *m.*

gladly, *ad.* laete; libenter.

gladness, *n.* gaudium, *nt.*; laetitia, *f.*

glamour, *n.* pulchritudo, *f.*

glance, *n.* aspectus, obtutus, *m.*

glance, *v.i.* aspicio; *fig.* ~ **at**, stringo, perstringo, [3].

gland, *n.* glandula, *f.*

glare, *n.* fulgor, ardor, *m.*; (fierce look) oculi torvi, *m. pl.*

glare, *v.i.* (of light) fulgeo, ardeo, [2]; (of expression) torvis oculis aspicio, [3].

glaring, *a.* fulgens; *fig.* manifestus.

glass, *n.* vitrum; (mirror) speculum, *nt.*; (for drinking) calix, *m.*; (glassware) vitrea, *nt. pl.*

glass, *a.* vitreus.

gleam, *n.* fulgor, splendor, *m.* iubar, *nt.*; *fig.* aura, *f.*

gleam, *u.i.* corusco, mico, [1]; fulgeo, [2].

gleaming, *a.* coruscus, renidens.

glee, *n.* laetitia, *f.*; gaudium, *nt.*

gleeful, *a.* laetus.

glib, *a.* volubilis; ~**ly**, *ad.* volubiliter.

glide, *u.i.* labor, prolabor, [3].

glimmer, *n.* lux dubia, *f.*; crepusculum, *nt.*, v. **gleam**.

glimmer, *u.i.* subluceo, [2].

glimpse, *n.* aspectus, *m.*; **have a ~ of**, dispicio, [3].

glisten, *u.i.* luceo, fulgeo, [2]; radio, [1].

glitter, *n.* fulgor, *m.*

glitter, *u.i.* fulgeo, [2]; radio, mico, corusco, [1].

gloat, *u.i.* (over) oculos pasco, [3].

globe, *n.* globus; *fig.* orbis terrae *or* terrarum, *m.*

globule, *n.* globulus, *m.* pilula, *f.*

gloom, *n.* tenebrae, *f. pl.*; caligo; *fig.* tristitia, *f.*

gloominess, *n.*, v. **gloom**.

gloomy, *a.* tenebrosus, nubilus; *fig.* maestus, tristis.

glorify, *u.t.* celebro, glorifico, [1].

glorious, *a.* gloriosus, illustris, splendidus; eximius.

glory, *n.* gloria; laus, fama, *f.*

glory, *u.i.* glorior, [1]; superbio, [4].

gloss, *n.* (lustre) nitor, *m.*

glossy, *a.* nitidus; expolitus; levis.

glove, *n.* digitabulum, *nt.*

glow, *n.* ardor, fervor, calor, *m.*

glow, *u.i.* candeo, caleo, [2]; excandesco, [3].

glowing, *a.* candens, fervens; *fig.* fervidus.

glow-worm, *n.* cicindela, lampyris, *f.*

glue, *n.* gluten, glutinum, *nt.*

glue, *u.t.* glutino, conglutino, [1].

glum, *a.* tristis, deiectus.

glut, *n.* satietas, *f.*

glut, *u.t.* satio, saturo, [1]; (feast) pasco, [3].

glutton, *n.* helluo, homo gulosus, *m.*

gluttonous, *a.* gulosus, edax.

gluttony, *n.* gula, *f.*

gnarled, *a.* nodosus.

gnash, *u.t.* frendeo, infrendeo, [2]; dentibus strido, [3].

gnat, *n.* culex, *m.*

gnaw, *u.t. & i.* rodo, [3].

go, *u.i.* eo, ir.; proficiscor, incedo, [3]; cedo, [3]; ~ **around**, circumeo, *ir.*; *fig.* aggredior, [3]; ~ **abroad**, peregre abeo, *ir.*; ~ **after**, sequor, [3]; ~ **astray**, aberro, vagor, [1]; ~ **away**, abeo, *ir.*; ~ **back**, revertor, [3]; ~ **before**, praeeo, *ir.*; antecedo, [3]; ~ **beyond**, egredior; *fig.* excedo, [3]; ~ **by**, praetereo, *ir.*; *fig.* (adhere to) sto, [1] (with *abl.*); ~ **down**, descendo; (of the sun) occido, [3]; ~ **for**, peto, [3]; ~ **forth**, exeo, *ir.*; ~ **in**(to), ineo, *ir.*; ~ **off**, abeo, *ir.*; ~ **on**, pergo, [3]; (happen) fio, *ir.*; (succeed, thrive) succedo, [3]; ~ **out**, exeo, *ir.*; *fig.* (of fire) extinguor, [3]; ~ **over**, transgredior; *fig.* (a subject) percurro, [3]; ~ **round**, circumeo (locum), *ir.*; ~ **through**, transeo; obeo, *ir.*, pertendo, [3]; (endure) patior, [3]; ~ **to**, adeo, *ir.*; accedo, [3]; ~ **towards**, peto, [3]; ~ **under**, subeo, *ir.*; ~ **up**, ascendo, [3]; let ~, dimitto; (let fall) omitto, [3]; ~ **without**, careo, egeo, [2] (*both with abl.*).

goad, *n.* pertica, *f.*; stimulus, *m.*

goad, *v.t.* instigo; *fig.* stimulo, [1].

goal, *n.* (in the Roman circus) meta, calx, *f.*; *fig.* finis, *c.*

goat, *n.* caper, *m.*; (she-~) capra, *f.*

gobble, *v.i.* voro, devoro, [1]; exsorbeo, [2].

go-between, *n.* internuntius, *m.*; internuntia, *f.*; conciliator, *m.*; conciliatrix, *f.*

goblet, *n.* poculum, *nt.*; scyphus, *m.*, v. **cup**.

god, *n.* deus, *m.*; divus, *m.*; numen, *nt.*

goddess, *n.* dea, diva, *f.*

godly, *a.* pius, sanctus.

gold, *n.* aurum, *nt.*; ~, *a.* aureus.

golden, *a.* aureus; (yellow) flavus.

goldfinch, *n.* carduelis, *f.*

goldfish, *n.* hippurus, *m.*

gold-mine, *n.* aurifodina, *f.*

goldsmith, *n.* aurifex, *m.*

good, *a.* bonus; (effective) efficax; salutaris; utilis; (kind-hearted) benevolus; ~ **for nothing**, nequam; **do ~ to**, prodesse (*with dat.*); **make ~**, compenso, [1]; restituo, [3]; sano, [1].

good, *n.* (profit) commodum, lucrum, *nt.*; salus; utilitas, *f.*; (in abstract sense) bonum, *nt.*

good, *i.* bene! euge!

goodbye, *i.* vale, valete.

good-humoured, *a.* facilis.

good-natured, *a.* comis, benignus, facilis.

goodness, *n.* bonitas; probitas; benignitas, *f.*

goods, *n.* bona, *nt. pl.*; res, *f.*

goodwill, *n.* benevolentia; gratia, *f.*

goose, *n.* anser, *m.*

gore, *n.* cruor, *m.*; sanies, *f.*

gore, *v.t.* cornu ferio, [4].

gorge, *n.* fauces; angustiae, *f. pl.*

gorge, *v.i.* devoro, ingurgito, [1].

gorgeous, *a.* nitidus, lautus, splendidus; magnificus.

gorse, *n.* ulex, *m.*

gory, *a.* cruentus, cruentatus, sanguineus, sanguinolentus.

gossip, *n.* (idle talk) nugae, gerrae, *f. pl.*; (person) homo garrulus, *m.*; mulier loquax, *f.*

gossip, *v.i.* garrio, [4].

gouge, v.t. evello, eruo, [3].

gout, n. morbus articularis, m.; (in the feet) podagra, f.

govern, v.t. impero, imperito, [1] (*both with dat.*); rego, [3]; (check) coerceo, [2]; moderor, [1].

governess, n. magistra, f.

government, n. gubernatio (civitatis); administratio, f.; imperium, regnum, nt.; provincia, f.

governor, n. gubernator; praefectus; dominus, m.

gown, n. (woman's garment) stola; (of a Roman citizen) toga, f.

grab, v. corripio, [3].

grace, n. gratia; (elegance, *etc.*) venustas, f.; veneres, f. pl.; decor, lepos, m.; (pardon) venia, f.; **Graces**, pl. Gratiae, f.pl.

graceful, a. elegans; lepidus, venustus; ~**ly**, ad. venuste; eleganter, lepide.

gracious, a. benignus; clemens; humanus; (propitious) aequus, propitius; ~**ly**, ad. benigne; humane.

graciousness, n. benignitas, humanitas, clementia, f.

grade, n. gradus, ordo, m.

gradient, n. clivus, m.

gradual, a. per gradus; ~**ly**, ad. gradatim, pedetemptim, paulatim.

graft, n. (of plants) insitum, nt.; surculus, m.

graft, v.t. insero, [3].

grain, n. granum, nt.; fig. particula, [1].

grammar, n. grammatica, f.

grammatical, a. grammaticus.

granary, n. horreum, granarium, nt.

grand, a. grandis, magnificus; praeclarus, splendidus.

grandchild, n. nepos, m.; neptis, f.

granddaughter, n. neptis, f.

grandeur, n. magnificentia; granditas; sublimitas; maiestas, f.; splendor, m.

grandfather, n. avus, m.

grandmother, n. avia, f.

grandson, n. nepos, m.

grant, v.t. concedo, permitto, [3]; (acknowledge) fateor, [2]; do, [1]; praebeo, [2].

grant, n. concessio, f.

grape, n. acinus, m.; uva, f.; **bunch of** ~**s**, racemus, m.

graphic, a. expressus; ~**ally**, ad. expresse.

grapple, v.i. luctor, [1].

grasp, v.t. prehendo, corripio, [3]; affecto, [1]; (understand) teneo, [2]; ~ **at**, capto, [1]; fig. appeto, [3].

grasp, n. complexus, m.; (power) potestas; (hand) manus, f.

grasping, a. avidus, cupidus; avarus.

grass, n. gramen, nt.; herba, f.

grasshopper, n. grillus, m.

grassy, *a.* graminosus, gramineus, herbosus, herbidus.

grate, *n.* clathri, cancelli, *m. pl.*

grate, *v.t.* (grind) tero, contero, [3]; ~, *v.i.* strideo, [2].

grateful, *a.* gratus, iucundus; ~ly, *ad.* grate; (thankfully) grato animo.

gratification, *n.* expletio; gratificatio; (pleasure, delight) voluptas; oblectatio, *f.*

gratify, *v.t.* (indulge) indulgeo, [2]; gratificor, [1] (*both with dat.*).

gratifying, *a.* gratus.

grating, *n.* clathri, cancelli, *m. pl.*; (sound) stridor, *m.*

gratitude, *n.* gratia, *f.*; gratus animus, *m.*

gratuitous, *a.* gratuitus.

gratuity, *n.* stips, *f.*; munus, praemium, *nt.*

grave, *a.* gravis, serius; (stern) severus; ~ly, *ad.* graviter; severe.

grave, *n.* sepulcrum, bustum, *nt.*; tumulus, *m.*

gravel, *n.* glarea, *f.*; sabulo, *m.*

gravely, *ad.* graviter, serio, severe.

gravestone, *n.* monumentum, *nt.*

gravity, *n.* gravitas, *f.*; pondus, *nt.*; (personal) severitas; dignitas; tristitia, *f.*

graze, *v.t.* (pasture) pascor; (touch lightly) stringo, perstringo, [3]; (scrape) rado, [3].

graze, *n.* vulnus, *nt.*

grease, *v.t.* ungo, perungo, illino, [3].

grease, *n.* unguen, pingue, *nt.*; arvina, *f.*; (for wheels) axungia, *f.*

greasy, *a.* pinguis; unctus; (dirty) squalidus.

great, *a.* magnus; ingens; amplus, grandis; (powerful) potens; **so** ~, tantus; **as** ~ **as**, tantus, quantus.

great-grandfather, *n.* proavus, *m.*

great-hearted, *a.* magnanimus.

greatly, *ad.* magnopere, valde.

greatness, *n.* magnitudo, *f.*

greaves, *n.* ocreae, *f. pl.*

Greece, *n.* Graecia, *f.*

greed, **greediness**, *n.* aviditas; voracitas, *f.*

greedily, *ad.* avide, cupide.

greedy, *a.* avidus, avarus, cupidus; vorax.

Greek, *a.* & *n.* Graecus, *m.*

green, *a.* viridis; virens; prasinus; *fig.* recens; (unripe) crudus, immaturus; **become** ~, viresco, [3]; ~, *n.* color viridis; (lawn) locus *or* campus herbidus, *m.*; ~s, holera, *nt. pl.*

greengrocer, *n.* holerum venditor, *m.*

greenish, *a.* subviridis.

greenness, *n.* color viridis, *m.*; (in abstract sense) viriditas, *f.*; *fig.* immaturitas, *f.*

greet, *v.t.* saluto, [1]; salutem dico, [3] (*with dat.*).

greeting, *n.* salutatio, salus, *f.*

gregarious, *a.* gregalis.

grey, *a.* cinereus; (blue-grey) glaucus; (with age) canus; **become ~,** canesco, [3].

grey-headed, *a.* canus.

greyish, *a.* canescens.

greyness, *n.* canities, *f.*

grief, *n.* dolor, maeror; luctus, *m.*; aegritudo; molestia, tristitia, *f.*

grievance, *n.* querimonia, querela, iniuria, *f.*; malum, *nt.*

grieve, *v.t.* dolore afficio (aliquem), [3]; excrucio, sollicito, [1]; ~, *v.i.* doleo, lugeo, [2].

grievous, *a.* gravis, durus, atrox, acerbus.

griffin, *n.* gryps, *m.*

grill, *v.t.* torreo, [2].

grim, *a.* torvus; trux, truculentus, horridus; ~**ly,** *ad.* horride.

grimace, *n.* vultus distortus, *m.*; oris depravatio, *f.*

grime, *n.* squalor, *m.*, v. **dirt**.

grimy, *a.* squalidus.

grin, *v.i.* ringor, [3]; (laugh) rideo, [2].

grin, *n.* rictus, *m.*

grind, *v.t.* (corn) molo, [3]; (in a mortar) contundo, [3]; (on a whetstone) exacuo, [3]; (the teeth) dentibus frendeo, [3].

grindstone, *n.* cos, *f.*

grip, *n.* manus, *f.*

grip, *v.* comprehendo, [3].

grisly, *a.* horrendus, horridus.

gristle, *n.* cartilago, *f.*

gristly, *a.* cartilagineus, cartilaginosus.

grit, *n.* glarea, *f.*; arena, *f.*, sabulo, *m.*

gritty, *a.* arenosus, sabulosus.

groan, *v.i.* gemo, ingemo, [3].

groan, groaning, *n.* gemitus, *m.*

grocer, *n.* condimentarius, *m.*

groin, *n.* inguen, *nt.*

groom, *n.* agaso, equiso, *m.*

groom, *v.t.* (equum) curo, [1]; ~, *n.* (bridegroom) sponsus, *m.*

groove, *n.* canalis, *m.*; stria, *f.*

grope, *v.i.* praetento, [1].

gross, *a.* (fat) crassus, densus; pinguis; (coarse) rusticus, incultus; (dreadful) atrox; (whole) totus; ~**ly,** *ad.* graviter; crasse; turpiter.

grotesque, *a.* absurdus, ridiculus.

ground, *n.* solum, *nt.* terra; humus, *f.*; (place) locus, *m.*; fig. causa, *f.*; **on the ~,** humi; **gain ~,** proficio, [3]; **lose ~,** recedo, [3]; ~**s,** (sediment) faex, *f.*

groundless, *a.* vanus, falsus; fictus.

groundwork, *n.* subtructio, *f.*; *fig.* fundamentum, *nt.*

group, *n.* corona, turba, *f.*; globus, circulus, *m.*

group, *v.t.* dispono, [3]; ~, *v.i.* circulor, [1].

grouse, *n.* lagopus, tetrao, *m.*

grove, *n.* lucus, saltus, *m.*; nemus, *nt.*

grovel, *v.i.* provolvor, [3]; *fig.* servio, [4].

grovelling, *a.* humilis, supplex, servilis.

grow, *v.i.* cresco, [3]; (increase) augeor, [2]; adolesco, [3]; (become) fio, *ir.*; ~, *v.t.* (cultivate) sero, [3]; (a beard, *etc.*) promitto, [3]; ~ **out of,** *fig.* orior, [4]; nascor, [3]; (grow up) adolesco, [3].

grower, *n.* cultor, *m.*

growl, *n.* fremitus, *m.*

growl, *v.i.* fremo, [3]; mussito, murmuro, [1].

grown-up, *a.* adultus; puber.

growth, *n.* incrementum, *nt.*; auctus; **full ~,** maturitas, *f.*

grub, *n.* vermiculus, *m.*

grudge, *n.* odium, *nt.*; simultas, *f.*; **hold a ~ against,** succenseo (*with dat.*), [2].

grudge, *v.t.* invideo, [2].

grudgingly, *ad.* invite, gravate.

gruff, *a.* asper, taetricus, torvus; **~ly,** *ad.* aspere.

grumble, *v.i.* murmuro, mussito, [1]; queror, [3].

grunt, *v.i.* grunnio, [4].

grunt, *n.* grunnitus, *m.*

guarantee, *n.* fides, satisdatio, *f.*

guarantee, *v.t.* satisdo, praesto, [1]; (promise) spondeo, [2].

guard, *n.* custodia; tutela, *f.*; (military) praesidium, *nt.*; (person) custos, *c.*; **be on one's ~,** caveo, [2].

guard, *v.t.* custodio, [4]; defendo, protego, [3]; munio, [4]; (against) caveo, [2].

guarded, *a.* cautus, circumspectus.

guardian, *n.* custos; praeses, *c.*; defensor; (of orphans) tutor; curator, *m.*

guess, *v.t. & i.* conicio, [3]; divino, suspicor, [1]; (solve) solvo, [3].

guess, *n.* coniectura, *f.*

guest, *n.* hospes; (stranger) advena; (at a feast) conviva, *c.*

guidance, *n.* ductus, *m.*; cura, curatio, administratio, *f.*

guide, *n.* dux, *c.*; ductor, *m.*

guide, *v.t.* duco, [3]; (rule) guberno, [1]; rego, [3].

guidebook, *n.* itinerarium, *nt.*

guild, *n.* collegium, *nt.*

guile, *n.* dolus, astus, *m.*; astutia, *f.*

guilt, *n.* culpa, noxa, *f.*; crimen, peccatum, *nt.*

guiltless, *a.* innocens, insons, innocuus.

guilty, *a.* sons, nocens, noxius (*with abl. or gen.*); sceleratus.

guise, *n.* (manner) modus; mos, *m.*; (appearance) species, *f.*

guitar, *n.* cithara, *f.*

gulf, *n.* sinus, *m.*; (abyss) vorago, *f.*

gullet, *n.* gula, *f.*; fauces, *f. pl.*

gullibility, *n.* credulitas, *f.*

gullible, *a.* credulus.

gum, *n.* (of the mouth) gingiva, *f.*; (adhesive) cummi, *nt.*, cummis, *f.*

gum, *v.t.* glutino, [1].

gush, *v.i.* (out) effluo, profluo, [3]; prosilio, [4]; scateo, [2].

gust, *n.* flatus, *m.*; flamen, *nt.*

gusty, *a.* procellosus.

gut, *n.* intestinum, *nt.*; ~s, viscera, *nt. pl.*

gut, *v.t.* exentero, [1]; *fig.* exinanio, [4].

gutter, *n.* canalis, *m.*; (of streets) colliciae, *f. pl.*

gymnasium, *n.* gymnasium, *nt.*; palaestra, *f.*

gymnastic, *a.* gymnicus, gymnasticus.

gymnastics, *n.* palaestrica, *f.*

gyrate, *v.i.* volvor, [3].

gyration, *n.* gyrus, *m.*

....

H

....

habit, *n.* (custom) consuetudo, *f.*; mos, *m.*; (dress) vestitus, *m.*; (state) habitus, *m.*

habitable, *a.* habitabilis; not ~, inhabitabilis.

habitation, *n.* habitatio, domus, *f.*

habitual, *a.* inveteratus, assuetus, consuetus, solitus; ~ly, *ad.* de (ex) more.

hack, *v.t.* concido, [3]; mutilo, [1].

hackneyed, *a.* tritus; pervulgatus.

hag, *n.* anus, *f.*

haemorrhage, *n.* haemorrhagia, *f.*

haggard, *a.* macer, exsanguis.

haggle, *v.t.* cavillor; (bargain) licitor, [1].

hail, *n.* grando, *f.*

hail, *v.t.* (salute) saluto, [1]; ~, *v.i.* grandino, [1].

hail, *i.* salve!

hailstone, *n.* grando, *f.*

hair, *n.* capillus, crinis, *m.*, caesaries, coma, *f.*; (single) pilus; (of animals) villus, *m.*; grey ~, canities, *f.*

hairdresser, *n.* capitis et capilli concinnator, *m.*; ornatrix, *f.*

hairy, *a.* pilosus; crinitus; comatus; (shaggy) hirsutus.

halcyon, *n.* alcedo, alcyon, *f.*

half, *a.* dimidius; ~, *n.* dimidia pars, *f.*; dimidium, *nt.*

half-..., semi-...

half-dead, *a.* semianimis.

half-eaten, *a.* semiesus.

half-hearted, *a.* piger.

half-yearly, *a.* semestris.

hall, *n.* atrium; (entrance-~) vestibulum; (for business) conciliabulum, *nt.*; (of the senate) curia, *f.*

hallucination, *n.* alucinatio, *f.*; error, *m.*; somnium, *nt.*

halt, *v.i.* consisto, [3]; *fig.* haesito, [1].

halt, *n.* pausa, mora, *f.*

halve, *v.t.* ex aequo divido, [3].

hammer, *n.* malleus, *m.*

hammer, *v.t.* cudo, [3].

hamper, *n.* qualus, *m.*; fiscina, *f.*

hamper, *v.t.* impedio, [4]; implico, retardo, [1].

hand, *n.* manus, palma, *f.*; (handwriting) chirographum, *nt.*; (of a dial) gnomon, *m.*; **at ~**, ad manum; prae manibus; praesto; **by ~**, manu; **~ in ~**, iunctis manibus; **~ to ~**, comminus; **in ~**, (of money) prae manu; **on the other ~**, altera parte; **on the right ~**, ad dextram.

hand, *v.t.* trado, [3]; **~ out**, distribuo, [3]; **~ over**, trado, [3]; **~ round**, circumfero, [3].

handcuffs, *n. pl.* manicae, *f. pl.*

handful, *n.* manipulus, pugillus, *m.*

handicap, *n.* impedimentum, *nt.*

handicraft, *n.* ars, *f.*; artificium, *nt.*

handiwork, *n.* opus, *nt.*; opera, *f.*

handkerchief, *n.* sudarium, *nt.*

handle, *v.t.* tracto, [1].

handle, *n.* manubrium, *nt.*; ansa, *f.*; (of a sword) capulus, *m.*

handsome, *a.* pulcher, formosus; honestus; elegans, bellus.

handwriting, *n.* manus, *f.*; (manuscript) chirographum, *nt.*

handy, *a.* (useful) utilis.

hang, *v.t.* suspendo; (let ~) demitto, [3]; ~, *v.i.* pendeo, dependeo, [2]; **~ back**, haesito, [1]; **~ over**, immineo, [2] (*with dat.*).

hanger-on, *n.* assecla, *fig.* parasitus, *m.*

hangman, *n.* carnifex, *m.*

hanker, *v.i.* desidero, [1]; expeto, [3].

haphazard, *a.* fortuitus.

happen, *v.i.* accido, [3]; evenio, [4]; contingo, [3]; fio, *ir.*

happiness, *n.* vita beata; (good fortune) felicitas, *f.*

happy, *a.* felix, fortunatus, faustus; beatus.

harangue, *n.* contio, *f.*; ~, *v.t. & i.* contionor, [1].

harass, *v.t.* fatigo; vexo; inquieto, [1]; lacesso, [3].

harbinger, *n.* praenuntius, antecursor, *m.*

harbour, *n.* portus, *m.*; *fig.* refugium, perfugium, *nt.*

harbour, *v.t.* excipio, [3]; (feelings, *etc.*) habeo, [2]; afficior, [3] (*with abl.*).

hard, *a.* durus; *fig.* (difficult) arduus; (severe) acer, rigidus; (hard-hearted) crudelis.

harden, *v.t.* duro; induro, [1]; ~, *v.i.* duresco; obduresco, [3].

hard-hearted, *a.* durus, ferreus, inhumanus, crudelis.

hard-heartedness, *n.* crudelitas, *f.*; ingenium durum, *nt.*

hardihood, *n.* audacia, *f.*

hardiness, *n.* robur, *nt.*

hardly, *ad.* (with difficulty, scarcely) vix; aegre.

hardness, *n.* duritia, *f.*

hardship, *n.* aerumna; difficultas, *f.*; labor, *m.*; dura, *nt. pl.*

hardware, *n.* ferramenta, *nt. pl.*

hardy, *a.* durus; robustus.

hare, *n.* lepus, *m.*

harem, *n.* gynaeceum, *nt.*

harm, *n.* damnum, *nt.*; iniuria; fraus, noxa; calamitas, *f.*

harm, *v.t.* laedo, [3]; noceo, [2] (*with dat.*).

harmful, *a.* noxius, perniciosus.

harmless, *a.* (things) innocuus; innoxius; (person) innocens.

harmonious, *a.* concors, consonus; canorus; *fig.* concors, consentiens.

harmonize, *v.t.* compono, [3]; ~, *v.i.* concino, [3]; *fig.* consentio, [4].

harmony, *n.* harmonia, *f.*; concentus, *m.*; *fig.* concordia, *f.*

harness, *n.* ornatus, *m.*

harness, *v.t.* adiungo, iungo, subiungo, [3]; (saddle) insterno, [3].

harp, *n.* lyra, *f.*

harpist, *n.* psaltes, *m.*; psaltria, *f.*

harpoon, *n.* iaculum, *nt.*; ~, *v.t.* iaculor, [1], transfigo, [3].

harridan, *n.* anus, vetula, *f.*

harrow, *n.* rastrum, *nt.*; ~, *v.t.* occo, [1]; *fig.* crucio, excrucio, [1].

harsh, *a.* asper; (in sound) discors, stridulus; (hoarse) raucus; (in taste) acer; *fig.* gravis; severus, durus; ~**ly,** *ad.* aspere; graviter, acerbe, duriter.

harshness, *n.* asperitas; acerbitas; saevitia; severitas, *f.*

harvest, *n.* messis, *f.*; ~, *v.t.* meto, [3].

harvester, *n.* messor, *m.*

hash, *n. fig.* **make a ~ of,** male gero (*with acc.*).

haste, *n.* celeritas; festinatio, properatio, *f.*; **in ~,** propere; properanter; **make ~,** propero, festino, [1].

hasten, *v.t.* accelero, propero; (hurry on) praecipito, [1]; ~, *v.i.* propero, festino, [1].

hastily, *ad.* propere; raptim.

hastiness, *n.* celeritas, *f.*

hasty, *a.* properus; praeceps; *fig.* iracundus.

hat, *n.* pilleus, galerus, petasus, *m.*

hatchet, *n.* ascia, securis, bipennis, *f.*

hate, *v.t.* odi, perodi, [3]; destestor, [1].

hate, *n.*, v. **hatred**.

hateful, *a.* odiosus, invisus; inamabilis.

hatred, *n.* odium, *nt.*; invidia, simultas, inimicitia, *f.*

haughtiness, *n.* superbia; arrogantia, *f.*; fastidium, *nt.*

haughty, *a.* superbus; arrogans; fastidiosus.

haul, *v.t.* traho, subduco, [3].

haunt, *v.t.* frequento, [1]; *fig.* (of spirits) adsum, *ir.*

haunt, *n.* latebra, *f.*; lustra, *nt. pl.*

have, *v.t.* habeo; possideo, teneo, [2]; ~ on, gero, [3]; I would ~ you know, velim scias.

haven, *n.* portus, *m.*; (*fig.*) salus, *f.*

havoc, *n.* strages, caedes, *f.*

hawk, *n.* accipiter, *m.*

hay, *n.* faenum, *nt.*

hazard, *n.* periculum, discrimen, *nt.*; (chance) alea, *f.*

hazardous, *a.* periculosus; anceps.

haze, *n.* nebula, *f.*; vapor, *m.*

hazel, *n.* (tree) corylus, *f.*

hazel, *a.* colurnus; (of colour) spadix, flavus.

hazy, *a.* nebulosus, caliginosus; *fig.* (doubtful) dubius, ambiguus.

he, *pn.* hic, is, ille.

head, *n.* caput, *nt.*; vertex, *m.*; (also *fig.*) (mental faculty) ingenium, *nt.*; (chief) princeps, *c.*; (top) culmen, cacumen, *nt.*

head, *a.* princeps, summus.

head, *v.t.* dux sum (*with gen.*); ~ for, peto, [3].

headache, *n.* capitis dolor, *m.*

head-band, *n.* vitta, *f.*

heading, *n.* titulus, *m.*

headland, *n.* promontorium, *nt.*

headlong, *a.* praeceps; temerarius.

headquarters, *n.* praetorium, *nt.*

headstrong, *a.* pervicax, contumax, v. **stubborn**.

heal, *v.t.* sano, [1]; medeor, [2]; ~, *v.i.* sanesco; (wounds) coalesco, [3]; coeo, [4].

healing, *a.* salutaris, saluber; ~, *n.* sanatio, *f.*

health, *n.* sanitas, valetudo, salus, *f.*

healthful, *a.* salutaris, saluber.

healthiness, *n.* firma valetudo; (of place *or* things) salubritas, *f.*

healthy, *n.* sanus; integer; (places *or* things) saluber.

heap, *n.* acervus, cumulus, *m.*; congeries, *f.*

heap, *v.t.* acervo, coacervo, accumulo, [1].

hear, *v.t. & i.* audio; exaudio, [4]; ausculto, [1]; (find out) certior fio, *ir.*

hearing, *n.* (act) auditio, *f.*; (sense) auditus, *m.*

hearsay, *n.* fama, *f.*; rumor, *m.*

hearse, *n.* feretrum, *nt.*

heart, *n.* cor, *nt.*; *fig.* (feeling) pectus, *nt.*; (courage) animus, *m.*; **have the ~ to,** sustineo, audeo, [2].

heartbreaking, *a.* miserabilis.

heartbroken, *a.* angoribus confectus, afflictus.

hearten, *v.* confirmo, [1].

hearth, *n.* focus, *m.*

heartily, *ad.* sincere; effuse; valde; vere; ex animo.

heartless, *a.* ferreus, crudelis, inhumanus; **~ly,** *ad.* inhumane, crudeliter.

heartlessness, *n.* inhumanitas, saevitia, *f.*

heat, *n.* calor, ardor; fervor, aestus, *m.*

heat, *v.t.* calefacio, incendo, [3]; **~,** *v.i.* calesco, [3].

heating, *n.* calefactio, *f.*

heave, *v.t.* attollo, [3]; levo, [1]; (sighs, *etc.*) traho, duco, [3]; **~,** *v.i.* tumeo, [2]; fluctuo, [1].

heaven, *n.* caelum, *nt.*; *fig.* di, superi, *m. pl.*

heavenly, *a.* caelestis, divinus.

heaviness, *n.* gravitas; (slowness) tarditas; (dullness) stultitia, *f.*; (drowsiness) sopor, *m.*

heavy, *a.* gravis; onerosus, ponderosus.

hedge, *n.* saepes, *f.*; saeptum, *nt.*

hedgehog, *n.* erinaceus, ericius, *m.*

heed, pay ~ to, *v.t.* curo, [1]; *v.i.* **take ~,** (prae)caveo, [2].

heedless, *a.* incautus; temerarius.

heel, *n.* calx, *f.*

heifer, *n.* iuvenca, *f.*

height, *n.* altitudo; (tallness) proceritas, *f.*; (top) culmen, *nt.*; (hill) clivus, collis, tumulus, *m.*

heighten, *v.t.* altius effero, [3]; *fig.* amplifico; exaggero, [1].

heinous, *a.* atrox; nefarius; foedus.

heir, heiress, *n.* heres, *c.*

heirloom, *n.* res hereditaria, *f.*

hell, *n.* Tartarus, *m.*

hellish, *a.* infernus, nefarius.

hello, *i.* ave, avete.

helm, *n.* gubernaculum, *nt.*; calvus, *m.*

helmet, *n.* cassis, galea, *f.*

helmsman, *n.* gubernator, rector navis, *m.*

help, *n.* auxilium, *nt.*; opem, *f.* (*acc. sing.*).

help, *v.t.* (ad)iuvo, [1]; succurro, [3]; subvenio, [4] (*both with dat.*); auxilior, sublevo, [1].

helper, *n.* adiutor, auxiliator, *m.*

helpful, *a.* utilis.

helpless, *a.* inops.

helplessness, *n.* inopia, *f.*

hem, *n.* ora, *f.*; limbus, *m.*

hem, *v.t.* praetexo; *fig.* cingo, [3]; ~ **in,** circumsideo, [2].

hemisphere, *n.* hemisphaerium, *nt.*

hemlock, *n.* cicuta, *f.*

hen, *n.* gallina, *f.*

hence, *ad.* hinc.

henceforth, *ad.* posthac; dehinc, in posterum.

henhouse, *n.* gallinarium, *nt.*

henpecked, *a.* uxorius.

her, *a.* suus.

herald, *n.* caduceator; (crier) praeco, *m.*

herald, *v.t.* nuntio, [1].

herb, *n.* herba, *f.*

herd, *n.* grex, *m.*; *fig.* (in contempt) vulgus, *m.*

herd, *v.i.* congregor, [1].

herdsman, *n.* pastor; armentarius; bubulcus, *m.*

here, *ad.* hic; (hither) huc; ~ **and there,** raro.

hereditary, *a.* hereditarius.

heritage, *n.* hereditas, *f.*

hero, *n.* heros, vir fortis; (in a play) qui primas partes agit, *m.*

heroic, *a.* heroicus; ~**ally,** *ad.* fortiter.

heroine, *n.* heroina; virago; (of a play) quae primas partes agit, *f.*

heroism, *n.* virtus, fortitudo, *f.*

heron, *n.* ardea, *f.*

herring, *n.* harenga, *f.*

hers, *pn.* eius, illius (*gen.* of ea, illa).

herself, *n.* ipsa; (reflexive) se.

hesitant, *a.* haesitans; ~**ly,** *ad.* cunctanter.

hesitate, *v.i.* dubito, haesito, cunctor, cesso, [1].

hesitation, *n.* dubitatio; haesitatio, *f.*

hew, *v.t.* dolo, [1]; caedo, [3]; seco, [1].

hey, *i.* ohe!

hiccough, hiccup, *n.* singultus, *m.*

hiccough, hiccup, *v.i.* singulto, [1].

hide, *n.* pellis, *f.*; corium, *nt.*

hide, *v.t.* abdo, condo, occulo, abscondo, [3]; celo, [1]; (dissemble) dissimulo, [1]; ~, *v.i.* lateo, [2].

hideous, *a.* foedus, turpis, deformis.

hiding, *n.* (beating) verberatio, *f.*

hiding-place, *n.* latebra, *f.*; latibulum, *nt.*

hierarchy, *n.* sacerdotium, collegium, *nt.*; (ranking) ordo, *m.*

high, *a.* altus, excelsus; sublimis; (tall) procerus; (of price) pretiosus; carus; *fig.* magnus; amplus; ~, *ad.* alte; sublime; valde; vehementer; **aim** ~, magnas res appeto, [3].

highland, *n.* regio aspera *or* montuosa, *f.*

highly, *ad.* (much) valde, multum; (value) magni, permagni.

high priest, *n.* summus sacerdos, pontifex maximus, *m.*

high-spirited, *a.* generosus, animosus.

highway, *n.* via, *f.*

highwayman, *n.* latro, grassator, *m.*

hike, *v.* ambulo, [1].

hilarious, *a.* hilaris, festivus.

hill, *n.* collis; tumulus; (slope) clivus, *m.*

hilly, *a.* montuosus, clivosus.

hilt, *n.* (of a sword) capulus, *m.*

him, *pn.* eum, hunc, illum; **of ~,** eius, huius; illius; de illo.

himself, *pn.* ipse; (reflexive) se.

hind, *a.* posterior, aversus.

hinder, *v.t.* impedio, [4]; obsto, [1] (*with dat.*); retardo, [1]; (prevent) prohibeo, [2].

hindrance, *n.* impedimentum, *nt.*

hinge, *n.* cardo, *m.*

hint, *n.* indicium, *nt.*; nutus, *m.*; significatio, *f.*

hint, *v.t. & i.* innuo, suggero, [3]; summoneo, [2]; **~ at,** perstringo, [3].

hip, *n.* coxa, coxendix, *f.*

hippopotamus, *n.* hippopotamus, *m.*

hire, *n.* merces, *f.*; stipendium, *nt.*

hire, *v.t.* conduco, [3]; loco, [1].

hired, *a.* conductus, conducticius; mercenarius.

his, *pn.* eius, huius; illius, ipsius; **~ own,** suus, proprius.

hiss, *v.t. & i.* sibilo, [1]; strideo, [2].

hiss, hissing, *n.* sibilus; stridor, *m.*

historian, *n.* historicus, *m.*

historic(al), *a.* historicus; **~(al)ly,** *ad.* historice.

history, *n.* historia, memoria rerum gestarum, *f.*; res, *f.*; (narrative) narratio, *f.*

hit, *v.t.* ferio, [4]; percutio, [3]; **~ upon,** (discover) invenio, reperio, [4].

hitch, *n.* impedimentum, *nt.*; mora, *f.*

hither, *ad.* huc.

hitherto, *ad.* adhuc.

hive, *n.* alvus, *f.* alvearium, *nt.*

hoard, *n.* acervus, *m.*; **~,** *v.t.* coacervo, [1].

hoarder, *n.* accumulator, *m.*

hoar-frost, *n.* pruina, *f.*

hoarse, *a.* raucus; **get ~,** irraucesco, [3].

hoarsely, *ad.* rauca voce.

hoarseness, *n.* raucitas, *f.*

hoax, *n.* ludificatio, *f.*; fraus, *f.*; dolus, *m.*; **~,** *v.t.* ludificor, [1].

hobble, *v.i.* claudico, [1].

hobby, *n.* studium, *nt.*; cura, *f.*

hoe, *n.* sarculum, pastinum, *nt.*; **~,** *v.t.* sarculo, [1]; pastino, [1]; (weeds) pecto, [3].

hog, *n.* sus, porcus, *m.*

hoist, *v.t.* sublevo, [1]; tollo, [3].

hold, *v.t.* teneo; possideo, habeo, [2]; (contain) capio, [3]; ~, *v.i.* permaneo, [2]; (think) existimo, [1]; censeo, [2]; ~ **back**, retineo, [2]; (*v.i.*) cunctor, [1]; ~ **forth**, (*v.i.*) contionem habeo, [2]; ~ **in**, inhibeo, cohibeo, [2]; ~ **off**, abstineo, [2]; ~ **out**, porrigo, extendo, [3]; (offer) praebeo, [2]; *fig.* ostendo, [3]; (endure) duro, [1]; (persevere) obduro, persevero, [1]; ~ **together**, contineo, [2]; ~ **up**, (lift up) attollo, [3]; sustineo, [2]; (delay) moror, [1]; ~ **with**, consentio, [4].

hold, *n.* manus; custodia, *f.*; (influence) momentum, *nt.*; potestas, *f.*; (of a ship) alveus, *m.*

holder, *n.* possessor, *m.*; colonus, *m.*; (handle) manubrium, *nt.*

hole, *n.* foramen, *nt.*; rima, *f.*; *fig.* latebra, *f.*; (of mice, *etc.*) cavum, *nt.*

holiday, *n.* dies festus, *m.*; ~**s**, *pl.* feriae, *f. pl.*

holiness, *n.* sanctitas, religio, pietas, *f.*

hollow, *a.* cavus; concavus; *fig.* vanus.

hollow, *n.* caverna, *f.*; cavum, *nt.*; (depression) lacuna, *f.*

hollow, *v.t.* cavo, excavo, [1].

hollowness, *n. fig.* vanitas, *f.*

holm-oak, *n.* ilex, *f.*

holy, *a.* sanctus; sacer, religiosus; (dutiful) pius.

homage, *n.* obsequium, *nt.*; cultus, *m.*; observantia, *f.*; **pay ~ to**, colo, [3]; observo, [1].

home, *n.* domicilium, *nt.*; domus, *f.*; **at ~**, domi.

home, *a.* domesticus; ~, *ad.* (homewards) domum.

home-bred, *a.* domesticus, vernaculus.

homeless, *a.* tecto carens, profugus.

homely, *a.* (unsophisticated) simplex; rudis; incompositus; rusticus.

home-made, *a.* domesticus, vernaculus.

homesick, *n.* suorum desiderium, *nt.*

homeward, *ad.* domum.

homicide, *n.* (person) homicida, *m.*; (deed) homicidium, *nt.*

honest, *a.* probus; sincerus; integer, verus; ~**ly**, *ad.* probe, sincere, integre, vere.

honesty, *n.* probitas, sinceritas, integritas, *f.*

honey, *n.* mel, *nt.*

honeycomb, *n.* favus, *m.*

honorary, *a.* honorarius.

honour, *n.* honos, *m.*; fama, laus, gloria; honestas, fides, *f.*; (high position) dignitas, *f.*

honour, *v.t.* honoro; celebro, [1]; (hold in ~) in honore habeo, [2]; (pay homage to) colo, [3]; observo, [1].

honourable, *a.* honestus; honorificus; bonus.

hood, n. cucullus, m.; palliolum, nt.

hoodwink, v.t. ludificor, [1].

hoof, n. ungula, f.

hook, n. hamus; uncus, m.

hook, v.t. inunco, [1]; fig. capio, [3].

hooked, a. hamatus; (crooked) curvatus, aduncus, curvus, recurvus.

hoop, n. circulus, m.

hoot, v.t. & i. gemo, queror, [3]; acclamo, [1]; explodo, [3].

hop, v.i. salio, [4]; subsulto, [1].

hope, n. spes, f.

hope, v.t. spero, [1]; ~ **for,** expecto, [1].

hopeful, a. bonae spei; ~**ly,** ad. cum magna spe.

hopeless, a. exspes; desperatus; ~**ly,** ad. sine spe, desperanter.

horde, n. turba, f.; v. **crowd.**

horizon, n. orbis finiens, m.

horizontal, a. libratus; ~**ly,** ad. ad libram.

horn, n. cornu, nt.; (to blow on) bucina, f.; cornu, nt.

hornet, n. crabro, m.

horoscope, n. horoscopus, m.; genesis, f.

horrible, a. horribilis, foedus, nefarius.

horrid, a. horridus, horrens, immanis.

horrific, a. horrificus, terribilis.

horrify, v.t. horrifico, [1]; terreo, exterreo, [2].

horror, n. horror, pavor, m.; (hatred) odium, nt.

horse, n. equus, m.; equitatus, m.

horseback, n. **on ~, (in)** equo, **ex equo; ride on ~,** equito, [1].

horseman, n. eques, m.

horse-race, n. curriculum equorum, nt.; certatio equestris, f.

horseshoe, n. solea, f.

horticulture, n. hortorum cultus, m.

hose, n. (pipe) tubulus, m.

hospitable, a. hospitalis, liberalis, munificus.

hospital, n. valetudinarium, nt.

hospitality, n. hospitium, nt.; hospitalitas; liberalitas, f.

host, n. (of guests) hospes, m.; (at an inn) caupo, m.; (crowd) multitudo, f.; (army) exercitus, m.

hostage, n. obses, c.

hostess, n. hospita, f.; (at an inn) caupona, f.

hostile, a. hostilis, hosticus, inimicus, infestus.

hostility, n. inimicitia, f.; **hostilities,** (war) bellum, nt.

hot, a. calidus; fervens, candens; fervidus; (of spices) acer; (furious) furens, iratus; (keen) vehemens, acer; **grow ~,** excandesco, [3].

hotchpotch, *n.* farrago, *f.*; miscellanea, *nt. pl.*

hotel, *n.* hospitium, *nt.*; caupona, *f.*; deversorium, *nt.*

hotly, *ad.* acriter, ardenter, vehementer.

hound, *n.* catulus, *m.*; canis, *c.*

hour, *n.* hora, *f.*; **half an ~**, semihora, *f.*; **three-quarters of an ~**, dodrans horae, *m.*

hourglass, *n.* horarium, *nt.*

hourly, *a.* & *ad.* in singulas horas; in horas, singulis horis.

house, *n.* domus, sedes, *f.*; tectum; domicilium, *nt.*; *fig.* familia; domus, gens, *f.*; (in politics) (senatorum, *etc.*) ordo, *m.*

house, *v.t.* domo excipio; (store) condo, [3].

household, *n.* domus, familia, *f.*; **~**, *a.* domesticus, familiaris.

householder, *n.* paterfamilias, *m.*

household-god, *n.* Lar, *m.*; **~s**, Penates, *m. pl.*

housekeeper, *n.* promus; dispensator, *m.*; (female) dispensatrix, *f.*

housekeeping, *n.* cura rei familiaris, *f.*

housewife, *n.* materfamilias, *f.*

hovel, *n.* tugurium, *nt.*; casa, *f.*

hover, *v.i.* pendeo, [2]; volito, [1]; libror, [1]; (over) immineo, [2].

how, *ad.* quomodo; ut; (to what degree) quam; **~ many**, quot, quam multi; **~ often**, quoties; **~ much**, quantum.

how, ut! quam!

however, *ad.* ~cumque, quamvis, utcumque; quantumvis; **~**, *c.* nihilominus, tamen.

howl, *v.i.* ululo, [1]; **~**, *n.* ululatus, *m.*

hubbub, *n.* tumultus, *m.*; turba, *f.*

hue, *n.* color, *m.*; **~ and cry**, conclamatio, *f.*

huff, *n.* ira, *f.*

hug, *n.* complexus, amplexus, *m.*

hug, *v.t.* complector, amplector, [3].

huge, *a.* ingens; vastus; immanis; **~ly**, *ad.* immaniter, egregie.

hull, *n.* (of a ship) alveus, *m.*

hum, *v.i.* susurro; murmuro, [1].

hum, *n.* bombus, *m.*; fremitus, *m.*; murmur, *nt.*; susurrus, *m.*

human, *a.* humanus; mortalis.

human (being), *n.* homo, *m.*

humane, *a.* humanus, misericors; **~ly**, *ad.* humaniter; misericorditer.

humanity, *n.* (humaneness) humanitas; misericordia, *f.*; (mankind) homines, mortales, *m. pl.*

humble, *a.* humilis; summissus, supplex; (mean) obscurus.

humble, *v.t.* infringo, deprimo, [3]; **~ myself**, me demitto, [3].

humbly, *ad.* humiliter, summisse.

humid, *a.* umidus.

humidity, *n.* umor, *m.*

humiliate, *v.t.* humilio, [1]; deprimo, [3].

humiliation, *n.* humiliatio, *f*; dedecus, *nt.*; ignominia, turpitudo, *f*

humility, *n.* animus summissus, *m.*; modestia, *f*

humorous, *a.* facetus; lepidus; ridiculus.

humour, *n.* (frame of mind) ingenium, *nt.*; (whim) libido, *f*; (liveliness) festivitas, *f*; lepos, *m.*; facetiae, *f pl.*

humour, *v.t.* obsequor, morem gero, [3]; indulgeo, [2] (*all with dat.*).

hump, *n.* gibber, gibbus, *m.*

humpbacked, *a.* gibber.

hundred, *a.* centum; ~, *n.* centuria, *f*; ~ **times,** centiens.

hundredth, *a.* centesimus.

hunger, *n.* fames, *f*; ieiunium, *nt.*; ~, *v.i.* esurio, [4]; *fig.* cupio, [3].

hungrily, *ad.* voraciter.

hungry, *a.* esuriens; ieiunus; *fig.* avidus, vorax.

hunt, *v.i.* venor, [1]; ~ **for,** *v.t.* peto, quaero, [3].

hunt, hunting, *n.* venatio, *f*; venatus, *m.*

hunter, *n.* venator; (hunting horse) equus venaticus, *m.*

hunting-spear, *n.* venabulum, *nt.*

huntress, *n.* venatrix, *f*

huntsman, *n.* venator, *m.*

hurdle, *n.* crates, *f*

hurl, *v.t.* iacio, proicio, [3]; iacto, [1]; iaculor, [1].

hurly-burly, *n.* tumultus, *m.*

hurrah, hurray, *i.* euge!

hurricane, *n.* procella, tempestas, *f*; turbo, *m.*

hurriedly, *ad.* raptim; festinanter.

hurry, *v.i.* festino, propero, praecipito, [1]; curro, [3]; ~, *v.t.* urgeo, [2]; festino, propero, praecipito, [1]; ~ **along,** *v.i.* curro, [3]; ~ **away,** *v.i.* propero, [1]; aufugio, [3].

hurry, *n.* festinatio, properatio, *f*; **in a ~,** festinanter.

hurt, *v.t.* noceo, [2] (*with dat.*); laedo, [3]; *fig.* offendo, [3]; ~, *v.i.* doleo, [2].

hurt, *n.* vulnus; damnum, *nt.*; iniuria, *f*

hurtful, *a.* noxius, perniciosus; (cruel) crudelis.

husband, *n.* maritus, vir, uxor, coniunx, *m.*, [1].

hush, *i.* st! tace, tacete.

hush, *v.t.* paco, [1]; comprimo, [3]; ~ **up,** *fig.* celo, [1]; ~, *v.i.* taceo, [2].

husk, *n.* folliculus, *m.*; siliqua, *f*; (of corn) gluma, *f*

husky, *a.* (of voice) surraucus.

hustle, *v.t.* proturbo, [1].

hut, *n.* tugurium, *nt.*; casa, *f*

hutch, *n.* cavea, *f*; mapalia, *nt. pl.*

hyacinth, *n.* hyacinthus, *m.*

hydraulic, *a.* hydraulicus.

hyena, *n.* hyaena, *f.*

hygiene, *n.* munditia, *f.*

hygienic, *a.* mundus.

hymn, *n.* hymnus, *m.*

hypochondria, *n.* atra bilis, *f.*

hypocrisy, *n.* simulatio, dissimulatio; pietas ficta, *f.*

hypocrite, *n.* simulator, dissimulator; hypocrita, *m.*

hypocritical, *a.* simulatus, fictus.

hypothesis, *n.* (guess) coniectura; (opinion) sententia, *f.*

hysteria, *n.* animi concitatio, *f.*

....

I

....

I, ego; ~ **myself,** egomet, ipse ego.

ice, *n.* glacies, *f.*; gelu, *nt.*

icicle, *n.* stiria, *f.*

icy, *a.* glacialis; gelidus.

idea, *n.* species, forma; imago; notitia; notio; (opinion) opinio, sententia; (suspicion) suspicio; (guess) coniectura, *f.*

ideal, *a.* perfectus; mente conceptus.

ideal, *n.* exemplar (perfectum), *nt.*

identical, *a.* idem; unus atque idem.

identify, *v.t.* agnosco, [3]; ~ **with,** sto cum (*with abl.*).

idiocy, *n.* fatuitas, stultitia, *f.*

idiomatic, *a.* proprius linguae; vernaculus.

idiosyncrasy, *n.* proprium, *nt.*

idiot, *n.* fatuus; stupidus, stultus; excors, *m.*

idiotic, *a.* fatuus.

idle, *a.* (at leisure) otiosus, vacuus; (of people) ignavus, piger, segnis, desidiosus, iners.

idleness, *n.* otium, *nt.*; ignavia, segnitia, desidia, *f.*

idly, *ad.* otiose; segniter; *fig.* frustra, incassum.

idol, *n.* idolum, simulacrum, *nt.*; *fig.* deliciae, *f. pl.*

idolize, *v.t.* (be desperately in love with) depereo, [4] (*with acc.*).

if, *c.* si; **as** ~, quasi, tamquam; **even** ~, etiamsi; ~ **only,** dummodo; ~ **not,** ni, nisi, si non.

ignite, *v.t.* accendo; ~, *v.i.* exardesco, excandesco, [3].

ignominious, *a.* contumeliosus, ignominiosus, turpis.

ignorance, *n.* ignoratio, ignorantia, inscitia, *f.*

ignorant, *a.* (unaware) inscius, ignarus, nescius; (unlearned) indoctus, inscitus; **be** ~ **of,** ignoro, [1]; nescio, [4].

ignore, *v.t. fig.* praetereo, [4].

ill, *a.* malus; (in health) aegrotus; **be** ~, aegroto, [1]; **fall** ~, in morbum incido, [3].

ill, *n.* malum, *nt.*; **take it** ~, aegre fero, [3].

ill-advised, *a.* inconsideratus, inconsultus, temerarius.

ill-bred, *a.* agrestis, inurbanus.

ill-disposed, *a.* malevolus, malignus.

illegal, *a.* quod contra leges fit; illicitus; **~ly,** *ad.* contra leges; illicite.

illegible, *a.* quod legi non potest.

illegitimacy, *n.* (of birth) ortus infamia, *f.*

illegitimate, *a.* (of birth) haud legitimus; spurius; nothus; (wrong) vitiosus.

ill health, *n.* (infirma) valetudo, *f.*

illicit, *a.* illicitus; **~ly,** *ad.* illicite.

illiterate, *a.* illitteratus.

ill-natured, *a.* malevolus, malignus.

illness, *n.* morbus, *m.*; aegrotatio, *f.*

illogical, *a.* vitiosus.

ill-omened, *a.* dirus, infaustus.

ill-temper, *n.* iracundia, morositas, *f.*

ill-tempered, *a.* iracundus, acerbus, stomachosus; difficilis.

ill-treat, *v.* lacesso, [3].

illuminate, *v.t.* illustro; illumino, [1].

illumination, *n.* lux, *f.*; lumen, *nt.*; festi ignes, *m. pl.*

illusion, *n.* error, *m.*

illusory, *a.* fallax.

illustrate, *v.t.* illustro; *fig.* explano, [1]; patefacio, [3].

illustration, *n.* illustratio, *f.*; *fig.* exemplum, *nt.*

illustrious, *a.* clarus, illustris, praeclarus, inclutus, insignis.

ill will, *n.* malevolentia, malitia, malignitas, *f.*

image, *n.* simulacrum, *nt.*; (likeness, portrait) effigies, imago, *f.*; (form) species, forma, *f.*

imaginary, *a.* (unreal) imaginarius, fictus, falsus.

imagination, *n.* cogitatio; imaginatio, *f.*; (dream) somnium, *nt.*

imaginative, *a.* ingeniosus.

imagine, *v.t.* imaginor, [1]; fingo, [3]; (think) existimo, arbitror, [1]; (guess) conicio, [3]; (dream) somnio, [1].

imbecile, *n.* fatuus, *m.*

imbecility, *n.* imbecillitas animi, *f.*

immigrant, *n.* advena, *c.*

imitate, *v.t.* imitor, assimulo, [1].

imitation, *n.* imitatio, *f.*; imitamentum, *nt.*

immaculate, *a.* castus, integer, inviolatus.

immaterial, *a.* simplex, incorporalis; (unimportant) levis.

immature, *a.* immaturus.

immaturity, *n.* immaturitas, *f.*

immeasurable, *a.* immensus, infinitus.

immediate, *a.* praesens; **~ly,** *ad.* confestim, extemplo, protinus; continuo.

immemorial, *a.* from time ~, ex omni memoria aetatum.

immense, *a.* ingens, immensus, enormis; **~ly,** *ad.* immensum, multum.

immensity, *n.* immensitas; vastitas, *f.*

immerse, *v.t.* mergo, demergo, immergo, [3].

immersion, *n.* immersio, *f.*

imminent, *a.* instans, praesens.

immobile, *a.* immobilis.

immobility, *n.* immobilitas, *f.*

immoderate, *a.* immodicus, nimius, immoderatus.

immoral, *a.* corruptus, pravus, improbus.

immorality, *n.* improbitas morum, *f.*

immortal, *a.* immortalis; aeternus.

immortality, *n.* immortalitas, *f.*

immortalize, *v.t.* aeterno, [1]; immortalem reddo, [3].

immovable, *a.* immobilis; immotus.

immune, *a.* immunis.

immunity, *n.* immunitas, *f.*

impact, *n.* impetus, *m.*

impair, *v.t.* laedo; imminuo; attero, [3]; debilito, [1].

impart, *v.t.* impertio, [4]; communico, [1].

impartial, *a.* aequus; **~ly,** *ad.* sine ira et studio.

impartiality, *n.* aequitas, aequabilitas, *f.*

impassable, *a.* insuperabilis, invius, impervius.

impassioned, *a.* vehemens, ardens.

impatience, *n.* impatientia, *f.*

impatient, *a.* impatiens; iracundus; **~ly,** *ad.* impatienter.

impeach, *v.t.* accuso, [1].

impede, *v.t.* impedio, [4]; retardo, [1].

impediment, *n.* impedimentum, *nt.*; mora, *f.*; (in speech) haesitatio, *f.*

impel, *v.t.* impello, [3]; excito, stimulo, [1]; cieo, [2].

impending, *a.* praesens.

impenetrable, *a.* impenetrabilis, impervius; *fig.* occultus.

imperceptible, *a.* quod sensu percipi non potest.

imperceptibly, *ad.* (little by little) sensim; (step by step) pedetentim; obscure.

imperfect, *a.* imperfectus, mancus; (faulty) mendosus; vitiosus.

imperfection, *n.* defectus, *m.*; vitium, *nt.*

imperial, *a.* imperatorius; imperialis.

imperious, *a.* imperiosus; superbus; arrogans.

imperishable, *a.* perennis; *fig.* immortalis.

impersonate, *v.t.* partes (alicuius) sustineo, [2].

impersonation, *n.* partes (actoris), *f. pl.*

impertinence, *n.* insolentia, *f.*

impertinent, *a.* insolens; (things) ineptus, absurdus; ~ly, *ad.* insolenter.

impervious, *a.* impervius; (inexorable) inexorabilis.

impetuous, *a.* vehemens, fervidus; ~ly, *ad.* vehementer.

impetus, *n.* vis, *f.*; impetus, impulsus, *m.*

impious, *a.* impius; scelestus, sceleratus; nefandus, nefarius; ~ly, *ad.* impie; sceleste, scelerate; nefarie.

implacable, *a.* implacabilis, inexorabilis.

implant, *v.t.* ingigno; insero, [3].

implement, *n.* instrumentum, *nt.*; arma, *nt. pl.*

implicate, *v.t.* implico, [1]; be ~d, particeps sum.

implicit, *a.* tacitus; ~ly, *ad.* tacite.

implore, *v.t.* imploro, obsecro, supplico, obtestor, [1].

imply, *v.t.* significo, [1]; be implied, subesse.

impolite, *a.* inurbanus; ~ly, *ad.* inurbane.

impoliteness, *n.* rusticitas, importunitas, *f.*

import, *v.t.* importo, [1]; inveho, [3]; (mean) significo, [1].

import, *n.* (meaning) significatio; (of goods) invectio, *f.*

importance, *n. fig.* momentum, pondus, *nt.*; gravitas, *f.*

important, *a.* magni momenti, gravis.

importer, *n.* qui merces peregrinas invehit.

impose, *v.t.* (a task) iniungo, impono, [3]; ~ upon, (deceive) fraudo, [1].

impossibility, *n.* impossibilitas, *f.*

impossible, *a.* impossibilis.

impostor, *m.* fraudator, praestigiator, *m.*; planus, *m.*

impotent, *a.* infirmus, impotens.

impound, *v.t.* confisco, [1]; (animals) includo, [3].

impoverish, *v.t.* pauperem reddo, [3]; *fig.* vitio, [1].

impracticable, *a.* quod fieri non potest.

impregnable, *a.* inexpugnabilis.

impress, *v.t.* (stamp, imprint) imprimo, [1]; (mark) signo, [1]; *fig.* inculco, [1]; (move) moveo, [2].

impression, *n.* (stamping) impressio, *f.*; (track, footstep) vestigium, *nt.*; (of a book) editio, *f.*; *fig.* animi motus, *m.*; (effect) momentum, *nt.*

impressive, *a.* gravis.

imprint, *n.* (mark) vestigium, *nt.*

imprint, *v.t.* imprimo, [3].

imprison, *v.t.* includo, in vincula conicio, [3].

imprisonment, *n.* captivitas, custodia, *f.*

improbable, *a.* haud verisimilis.

impromptu, *a.* ex tempore dictus.

improper, *a.* indecorus; indignus.

impropriety, *n.* improprietas, *f.*; indecorum, *nt.*

improve, *u.t.* emendo, [1]; excolo, corrigo, [3]; ~, *u.i.* melior fio, *ir.*, proficio, [3].

improvement, *n.* cultura, *f.*; (progress) profectus, *m.*

improvise, *u.t.* ex tempore dico *or* compono, [3].

impudence, *n.* impudentia, procacitas, protervitas, *f.*

impudent, *a.* impudens; procax, protervus; **~ly**, *ad.* impudenter; procaciter, proterve.

impulse, *n.* impulsus, impetus, *m.*

impulsive, *a.* vehemens, ardens, temerarius.

impunity, *n.* with ~, impune.

impure, *a.* (of morals) impurus; incestus; impudicus.

impurity, *n.* impuritas, *f.*

impute, *u.t.* (ascribe) attribuo, [3]; do, [1]; verto, [3]; (as a fault) imputo, [1].

in, *pr.* in (*with abl.*); (in the works of) apud (*with acc.*).

inability, *n.* infirmitas; (lack of means) inopia, *f.*

inaccessible, *a.* inaccessus, difficilis aditu.

inaccuracy, *n.* neglegentia, *f.*; error, *m.*

inaccurate, *a.* parum accuratus, minime exactus; falsus.

inactive, *a.* iners, ignavus, otiosus.

inactivity, *n.* inertia, socordia; cessatio, *f.*

inadequate, *a.* impar; mancus; **~ly**, *ad.* haud satis.

inadvertent, *a.* imprudens.

inadvertently, *ad.* imprudenter.

inane, *a.* ineptus.

inanimate, *a.* inanimus.

inanity, *n.* ineptiae, *f. pl.*

inapplicable, *a.* be ~, non pertineo ad (*with acc.*).

inappropriate, *a.* haud idoneus, parum aptus.

inarticulate, *a.* indistinctus, confusus.

inattention, *n.* animus parum attentus, *m.*; neglegentia, incuria, *f.*

inattentive, *a.* haud *or* parum attentus; neglegens; **~ly**, *ad.* animo parum attento; neglegenter.

inaudible, *a.* quod audiri nequit.

inaugurate, *u.t.* inauguro, [1].

inauguration, *n.* inauguratio, consecratio, *f.*

inauspicious, *a.* infaustus; infelix, funestus.

inborn, **inbred**, *a.* ingenitus, innatus, insitus.

incalculable, *a.* quod aestimari nequit; *fig.* immensus; incredibilis.

incapable, *a.* inhabilis, imperitus.

incapacitate, *u.t.* noceo, [2] (*with dat.*); laedo, [3].

incense, *n.* tus, *nt.*

incense, *u.t. fig.* exaspero, [1]; incendo, [3].

incentive, *n.* incitamentum, *nt.*; stimulus, *m.*

incessant, *a.* continuus, assiduus, perpetuus; **~ly**, *ad.* assidue; perpetuo.

incest, *n.* incestum, *nt.*; incestus, *m.*

incestuous, *a.* incestus.

inch, *n.* uncia, *f.*; **~ by ~**, unciatim; *fig.* paulatim, sensim.

incident, *n.* (event) eventus, *m.*; res, *f.*; casus, *m.*

incidental, *a.* fortuitus; **~ly**, *ad.* fortuito.

incision, *n.* incisura, *f.*; incisus, *m.*

incisive, *a. fig.* acer, acerbus.

incite, *v.t.* incito, stimulo, [1]; impello, [3].

incitement, *n.* incitamentum, *nt.*; incitatio, *f.*; stimulus *m.*

inclination, *n.* (tilt) inclinatio; (slope) acclivitas; *fig.* voluntas, inclinatio, *f.*

incline, *v.t.* inclino, [1] (also *fig.*); *fig.* adduco, [3]; **~**, *v.i.* propendeo, [2]; inclino, [1].

incline, *n.* acclivitas, *f.*

inclined, *a.* proclivis; propensus.

include, *v.t.* includo, comprehendo, [3].

incognito, *ad.* dissimulato nomine.

incoherent, *a.* confusus.

income, *n.* reditus; fructus, *m.*

incomparable, *a.* incomparabilis, unicus.

incompatibility, *n.* repugnantia, *f.*

incompatible, *a.* discors, repugnans, contrarius.

incompetence, *n.* inscitia, imperitia, *f.*

incompetent, *a.* inhabilis; inscitus, imperitus.

incomplete, *a.* imperfectus, incohatus; mancus.

incomprehensible, *a.* quod comprehendi non potest.

inconceivable, *a.* quod cogitari *or* mente percipi non potest.

inconclusive, *a.* levis; infirmus.

incongruous, *a.* inconveniens, male congruens; **~ly**, *ad.* parum apte.

inconsiderate, *a.* inconsideratus.

inconsistency, *n.* inconstantia, mutabilitas; repugnantia, *f.*

inconsistent, *a.* inconstans; contrarius, absonus; **~ly**, *ad.* inconstanter.

inconsolable, *a.* inconsolabilis.

inconspicuous, *a.* obscurus.

inconstant, *a.* inconstans, levis, mutabilis, mobilis.

incontrovertible, *a.* certus.

inconvenience, *n.* incommodum, *nt.*; **~**, *v.t.* incommodo, [1].

inconvenient, *a.* incommodus; molestus; **~ly**, *ad.* incommode.

incorporate, *v.t.* adiungo, [3]; admisceo, [2].

incorrect, *a.* mendosus, falsus.

incorrigible, *a.* insanabilis.

increase, *v.t.* augeo, [2]; amplifico, [1]; ~, *v.i.* augeor, [2]; cresco; ingravesco, [3].

increase, *n.* incrementum, *nt.*; auctus, *m.*

incredible, *a.* incredibilis.

incredibly, *ad.* incredibiliter; incredibile quantum; ultra fidem.

incredulity, *n.* incredulitas, *f.*

incredulous, *a.* incredulus.

incriminate, *v.t.* accuso, [1].

incubate, *v.i.* incubo, [1].

incubation, *n.* incubatio, *f.*; incubitus, *m.*

inculcate, *v.t.* inculco, [1].

incur, *v.t.* incurro (in *with acc.*), [3]; mereor, [2].

incurable, *a.* insanabilis, immedicabilis.

indebted, *a.* obaeratus; **I am ~ to you for this,** hoc tibi debeo.

indecency, *n.* indecorum, *nt.*; indignitas, *f.*

indecent, *a.* indecens, indecorus; **~ly,** *ad.* indecenter, indecore.

indecision, *n.* haesitatio, dubitatio, *f.*

indecisive, *a.* dubius, incertus, anceps, ambiguus.

indeed, *ad.* (it is true) re vera, profecto; **~?** itane? **very good ~,** vel optimum.

indefinite, *a.* incertus; anceps, obscurus.

indelible, *a.* indelebilis.

indemnity, *n.* indemnitas, *f.*; **act of ~,** impunitas, *f.*

indentation, *n.* incisura, *f.*

independence, *n.* libertas, *f.*

independent, *a.* sui potens; liber; *fig.* sui iuris; **~ly,** *ad.* libere; suis legibus; (each by itself) singillatim.

indescribable, *a.* inenarrabilis, infandus.

index, *n.* (of a book) index, *m.*; *fig.* indicium, *nt.*

indicate, *v.t.* indico; significo, [1].

indication, *n.* signum, indicium, *nt.*

indict, *v.t.* accuso, [1]; defero, [3].

indictment, *n.* (accusation) accusatio, *f.*

indifference, *n.* (neutrality) aequus animus, *m.*; (carelessness) neglegentia, *f.*; (contempt) contemptus, *m.*

indifferent, *a.* aequus, medius; remissus, neglegens, frigidus.

indigent, *a.* egens, inops.

indigestion, *n.* cruditas, *f.*

indignant, *a.* indignans, indignabundus, iratus; **~ly,** *ad.* indignanter.

indignation, *n.* indignatio; ira, *f.*

indirect, *a.* obliquus; **~ly,** *ad.* oblique; **touch on ~,** perstringo, [3].

indiscreet, *a.* inconsultus.

indiscretion, *n.* imprudentia, *f.*

indiscriminate, *a.* promiscuus; **~ly,** *ad.* promiscue.

indispensable, *a.* necessarius.

indisposed, *a.* (in health) minus valens.

indisposition, *a.* (illness) aegrotatio, commotiuncula, *f.*

indisputable, *a.* certus; haud dubius.

indisputably, *ad.* haud dubie.

indistinct, *a.* indistinctus, obscurus.

individual, *a.* individuus, proprius; ~**ly,** *ad.* singillatim.

individual, *n.* homo, *m.*

indolence, *n.* inertia, desidia, ignavia, socordia, *f.*

indolent, *a.* iners, ignavus, deses, socors, segnis.

indomitable, *a.* indomitus, invictus.

indoor, *a.* domesticus, umbratilis.

indoors, *ad.* domi.

indubitable, *a.* indubitabilis, haud dubius, certus.

indubitably, *ad.* haud dubie.

induce, *v.t.* adduco, impello, [3]; persuadeo, [2] (*with dat.*); incito, [1].

inducement, *n.* incitamentum, *nt.*; causa, *f.*; stimulus, *m.*

indulge, indulge in, *v.t.* indulgeo, [2] (*with dat.*).

indulgence, *n.* indulgentia; (pardon) venia; (kindness) clementia, *f.*

indulgent, *a.* indulgens, facilis, clemens; ~**ly,** *ad.* indulgenter, clementer.

industrious, *a.* industrius; diligens; sedulus; strenuus; ~**ly,** *ad.* industrie, diligenter, sedulo, strenue.

industry, *n.* industria; sedulitas; diligentia, *f.*; studium, *nt.*; (manufacturing) officina, *f.*

inebriated, *a.* ebrius.

ineffective, ineffectual, *a.* inefficax, inutilis.

inefficiency, *n.* inutilitas, *f.*

inefficient, *a.* inefficax; inhabilis; inutilis.

inelegant, *a.* inelegans; inconcinnus.

inept, *a.* ineptus.

inequality, *n.* inaequalitas, *f.*

inert, *a.* iners, segnis.

inertia, *n.* inertia, *f.*

inevitable, *v.* **unavoidable.**

inexcusable, *a.* inexcusabilis.

inexhaustible, *a.* inexhaustus.

inexorable, *a.* inexorabilis, durus, implacabilis.

inexpensive, *a.* vilis.

inexperience, *n.* imperitia, inscitia, *f.*

inexperienced, *a.* imperitus; inexpertus inscitus; rudis.

inexplicable, *a.* inexplicabilis, inenodabilis.

inexpressible, *a.* inenarrabilis, infandus.

infallible, *a.* qui errare non potest; certus, haud dubius.

infallibly, *ad.* haud dubie.

infamous, *a.* infamis; turpis, inhonestus, foedus, ignominiosus.

infamy, *n.* infamia, ignominia, *f.;* opprobrium, probrum, *nt.*

infancy, *n.* infantia, aetas iniens, *f.*

infant, *n.* infans, *c.*

infantile, *a.* infantilis, puerilis.

infantry, *n.* peditatus, *m.;* pedestres copiae, *f. pl.*

infatuated, be ~ with, *u.t.* depereo, [4].

infect, *u.t.* inficio, [3]; contamino, [1].

infection, *n.* contagium, *nt.;* contagio, *f.;* contactus, *m.*

infectious, *a.* contagiosus.

infer, *u.t.* conicio, infero, colligo, [3].

inference, *n.* coniectura, conclusio, *f.*

inferior, *a.* inferior, deterior, minor; ~, *n.* impar, *c.*

infernal, *a.* infernus.

infertile, *a.* sterilis.

infertility, *n.* sterilitas, *f.*

infidelity, *n.* infidelitas, *f.*

infinite, *a.* infinitus; immensus; ~ly, *ad.* infinite; infinito.

infinity, *n.* infinitas, infinitio, *f.*

infirm, *a.* infirmus, debilis, imbecillus.

infirmity, *n.* infirmitas, imbecillitas, debilitas, *f.*

inflame, *u.t.* inflammo, [1]; incendo, [3].

inflammation, *n.* inflammatio, *f.*

inflammatory, *a.* *fig.* turbulentus, seditiosus.

inflate, *u.t.* inflo, [1]; (also *fig.*); be ~d, tumeo, [2].

inflexibility, *n.* rigor, *m.*

inflexible, *a.* rigidus; *fig.* obstinatus.

inflict, *u.t.* infligo; impono, [3]; irrogo, [1].

influence, *n.* momentum, pondus, *nt.;* auctoritas, gratia, *f.;* (prompting) impulsus, *m.*

influence, *u.t.* moveo, [2]; impello, [3]; valeo, [2].

influential, *a.* (auctoritate) gravis, potens.

inform, *u.t.* (teach) doceo, [2]; instruo; (give information) certiorem facio; (against) defero, [3].

informal, *a.* privatus.

informant, *n.* (messenger) nuntius, *m.*

information, *n.* (news) nuntius, *m.;* (knowledge) scientia, *f.*

informer, *n.* delator, *m.*

infringe, *u.t.* violo, [1].

infringement, *n.* violatio, *f.*

infuriate, *u.t.* effero, exaspero, [1].

ingenious, *a.* sollers; subtilis; ingeniosus.

ingenuity, *n.* ingenium, *nt.*

ingot, *n.* later, *m.*

ingrained, *a.* insitus, inveteratus.

ingratiate, ~ oneself, *v.i.* gratiam ineo apud (aliquem), [4]; gratiam (mihi) concilio, [1].

ingratitude, *n.* animus ingratus, *m.*; beneficii oblivio, *f.*

ingredient, *n.* pars, *f.*

inhabit, *v.t.* colo, incolo, [3]; habito, [1].

inhabitant, *n.* incola, *c.*; habitator, colonus, *m.*

inhale, *v.t.* duco, [3]; haurio, [4].

inherent, *a.* inhaerens, proprius.

inherit, *v.t.* hereditate accipio, [3].

inheritance, *n.* hereditas, *f.*; patrimonium, *nt.*

inhibit, *v.t.* coerceo, [2].

inhospitable, *a.* inhospitalis, inhospitus.

inhuman, *a.* inhumanus; crudelis; ~ly, *ad.* inhumane; crudeliter.

inhumanity, *n.* inhumanitas; crudelitas, *f.*

inimitable, *a.* inimitabilis.

initial, *a.* primus; ~, *n.* prima verbi littera, *f.*

initiate, *v.t.* initio, [1].

initiation, *n.* initiatio, *f.*; initiamenta, *nt. pl.*

initiative, *n.* take the ~, initium capio, [3].

inject, *v.t.* infundo, immitto, [3].

injection, *n.* (act) infusio, *f.*; infusus, *m.*

injure, *v.t.* noceo, [2] (*with dat.*); laedo; offendo, [3].

injury, *n.* iniuria, *f.*; damnum, detrimentum, *nt.*

injustice, *n.* iniustitia; iniquitas; iniuria, *f.*

ink, *n.* atramentum, *nt.*

inkling, *n.* (hint) rumusculus, *m.*; (suspicion) suspicio, *f.*

inlet, *n.* (of the sea) aestuarium, *nt.*

inmate, *n.* incola, inquilinus, *m.*

inmost, *a.* intimus, imus; ~ recesses, penetralia, *nt. pl.*

inn, *n.* caupona, taberna, *f.*; deversorium, hospitium, *nt.*

innate, *a.* innatus; insitus; ingenitus.

inner, *a.* interior.

innermost, *a.* intimus; imus.

innkeeper, *n.* caupo, *m.*

innocence, *n.* innocentia; integritas; castitas, *f.*

innocent, *a.* innocuus; innocens; insons; (chaste) castus; ~ly, *ad.* innocue; innocenter; caste.

innocuous, *a.* innocuus.

innovation, *n.* res novae, *f. pl.*

innumerable, *a.* innumerabilis, innumerus.

inoffensive, *a.* innocens, innoxius.

inopportune, *a.* intempestivus.

inordinate, *a.* immoderatus; ~ly, *ad.* immoderate.

inquest, *n.* inquisitio, *f.*

inquire, *v.t. & i.* quaero, inquiro, [3]; investigo, [1].

inquiry, *n.* inquisitio, *f.*

inquisitive, *a.* curiosus; **~ly**, *ad.* curiose.

inroad, *n.* incursio, irruptio, *f.*; **make ~s into**, incurro in (*with acc.*), [3].

insane, *a.* insanus; vecors; amens; demens.

insanity, *n.* insania, dementia, amentia, vecordia, *f.*

insatiable, *a.* insatiabilis, inexplebilis, inexpletus.

inscribe, *v.t.* inscribo; insculpo; incido, [3].

inscription, *n.* inscriptio, *f.*; titulus, *m.*; carmen, *nt. pl.*

insect, *n.* insectum, *nt.*

insecure, *a.* intutus, periculosus; infestus, lubricus.

insecurity, *n.* periculum, *nt.*

inseparable, *a.* inseparabilis.

insert, *v.t.* insero; ascribo, interpono, [3].

inside, *n.* interior pars, *f.*; interiora, *nt. pl.*

inside, *a.* interior; **~**, *ad.* intrinsecus; intra, intro, intus; **~** *pr.* intra (*with acc.*).

insidious, *a.* insidiosus; subdolus; **~ly**, *ad.* insidiose; subdole.

insight, *n.* prudentia, cognitio, *f.*

insignificant, *a.* exiguus; nullius momenti; levis.

insincere, *a.* insincerus, simulatus; fallax; dolosus.

insincerity, *n.* fallacia; simulatio, *f.*

insinuate, *v.t.* **~ oneself into**, irrepo, [3]; (hint) significo, [1].

insinuation, *n.* insinuatio, *f.*; (suspicion) suspicio, *f.*; **make ~s against**, oblique perstringo, [3].

insipid, *a.* insulsus; *fig.* hebes; frigidus.

insist, *v.i.* insto, [1]; urgeo, [2]; exigo, [3]; **~ on**, flagito, [1].

insolence, *n.* insolentia, arrogantia, superbia, *f.*

insolent, *a.* insolens, arrogans, superbus; **~ly**, *ad.* insolenter; impudenter; superbe.

inspect, *v.t.* inspicio, introspicio, [3].

inspection, *n.* inspectio; cura, *f.*

inspector, *n.* curator; praefectus, *m.*

inspiration, *n.* (divine) afflatus, *m.*; numen, *nt.*; instinctus, *m.*

inspire, *v.t.* inspiro, [1]; inicio, [3]; (kindle) incendo, [3]; excito, [1].

instability, *n.* instabilitas, inconstantia, *f.*

install, *v.t.* inauguro, [1]; constituo, [3].

instalment, *n.* (payment in part) pensio, portio, *f.*

instance, *n.* exemplum, *nt.*; **for ~**, exempli gratia.

instant, *a.* (immediate) praesens; **~ly**, *ad.* (at once) statim.

instant, *n.* momentum, punctum temporis, *nt.*; **this ~**, statim, actutum.

instantaneous, a. quod momento temporis fit; ~ly, ad. continuo; statim.

instead, ad. ~ of, loco, vice (*both with gen.*); pro (*with abl.*).

instigate, v.t. instigo, stimulo, incito, [1]; cieo, [2].

instigation, n. incitatio, f.; stimulus, m.

instil, v.t. instillo, [1].

instinct, n. natura, f.

instinctive, a. naturalis; ~ly, ad. naturaliter.

institution, n. (thing instituted) institutum, nt.

instruct, v.t. (teach) doceo, [2]; instruo, instituo, [3]; erudio, [4]; (order, command) mando, [1].

instruction, n. institutio, disciplina, f.; (order, commission) mandatum, nt.

instructor, n. praeceptor, magister, m.; magistra, f.

instrument, n. instrumentum, nt.

instrumental, a. aptus, utilis.

insubordinate, a. seditiosus.

insubordination, n. seditio, f.; tumultus, m.

insufferable, a. intolerandus, intolerabilis.

insufficiency, n. inopia, egestas, f.

insufficient, a. non or parum sufficiens, impar; ~ly, ad. haud satis.

insulate, v.t. insulo, [1].

insult, n. opprobrium, probrum, convicium, nt.; contumelia, f.

insult, v.t. maledico, [3] (*with dat.*).

insulting, a. contumeliosus.

insurmountable, a. inexsuperabilis, insuperabilis.

insurrection, n. rebellio, seditio, f.; tumultus, m.

intact, a. integer; incolumis.

integral, a. necessarius.

integrity, n. integritas, probitas; sinceritas, innocentia, f.

intellect, n. intellectus, m.; intellegentia, mens, f.

intelligence, n. ingenium, nt.; (cleverness) sollertia, f.; (news) nuntius, m.

intelligent, a. intellegens; sollers; ~ly, ad. intellegenter.

intelligible, a. intellegibilis.

intend, v.t. destino, [1]; (resolve) constituo, decerno, [3].

intense, a. acer, vehemens; (excessive) nimius; ~ly, ad. acriter; vehementer; (extremely) valde, magnopere.

intensity, n. vehementia, vis, f.; (of winter, etc.) asperitas, f.

intent, a. intentus, attentus; ~ly, ad. intente.

intent, intention, n. consilium, propositum, nt.; (meaning) significatio, f.

intentionally, ad. de industria, consilio, consulto.

intercede, v.i. intercedo, [3]; deprecor, [1].

intercept, *v.t.* intercipio, intercludo; deprehendo, [3].

interchange, *v.t.* permuto, commuto, [1].

interchange, *n.* permutatio; vicissitudo, *f.*

intercourse, *n.* (sexual) coitus, concubitus, *m.*

interest, *v.t.* teneo, [2]; capio, [3]; delecto, [1].

interest, *n.* (advantage) emolumentum, *nt.*; utilitas, *f.*; (for money) faenus, *nt.*, usura, *f.*; (concern) studium, *nt.*

interesting, *a.* (appealing) iucundus.

interfere, *v.i.* intercedo, [3]; intervenio, [4]; (hinder) obsto, [1] (*with dat.*).

interference, *n.* intercessio, *f.*; interventus, *m.*

interim, *n.* intervallum, *nt.*; **in the ~**, interim.

interior, *a.* interior, internus; ~, *n.* pars interior, *f.*

interjection, *n.* interiectio, *f.*

interlude, *n.* (entr'acte) embolium, *nt.*

intermarriage, *n.* conubium, *nt.*

intermediate, *a.* medius.

interminable, *a.* infinitus.

intermingle, *v.t.* intermisceo, immisceo, [2].

intermission, *n.* intermissio; cessatio, remissio, *f.*

intermittent, *a.* rarus.

internal, *a.* intestinus, domesticus; ~**ly**, *ad.* intus.

international, *a.* ~ law, *n.* ius gentium, *nt.*

interpret, *v.t.* interpretor, [1]; (figure out) conicio, [3].

interpretation, *n.* interpretatio, coniectio, *f.*

interpreter, *n.* interpres, *c.*

interrogate, *v.t.* interrogo, percontor, [1].

interrogation, *n.* interrogatio, percontatio, *f.*

interrupt, *v.t.* interrumpo, intermitto, [3]; interpello, [1].

interruption, *n.* interruptio; interpellatio, *f.*

intersect, *v.t.* interseco, [1].

intersection, *n.* decussatio, *f.*

intersperse, *v.t.* intermisceo, immisceo, [2].

interval, *n.* intervallum, spatium, *nt.*

intervene, *v.i.* (be between) interiaceo, [2]; (come between) intercedo, [3]; (hinder) intervenio, [4] (*with dat.*).

intervening, *a.* medius.

intervention, *n.* interventus, interiectus, *m.*

interview, *n.* colloquium, *nt.*; congressus, *m.*

interview, *v.t.* convenio, [4].

interweave, *v.t.* intertexo; intexo, [3].

intestines, *n. pl.* intestina; viscera, *nt. pl.*

intimacy, *n.* familiaritas, consuetudo, *f.*

intimate, *a.* familiaris, intimus;
~**ly,** *ad.* familiariter, intime.

intimidate, *v.t.* metum inicio, [3];
minor, [1] (*with dat.*); terreo, [2].

intimidation, *n.* minae, *f. pl.*

into, *pr.* in (*with acc.*).

intolerable, *a.* intolerabilis, intolerandus.

intolerance, *n.* intolerantia, impatientia, *f.*

intolerant, *a.* intolerans, impa-
tiens.

intoxicate, *v.t.* ebrium reddo, [3].

intoxication, *n.* ebrietas, *f.*

intrepid, *a.* intrepidus, impavidus.

intricacy, *n.* ambages, *f. pl.*

intricate, *a.* contortus, perplexus; ~**ly,** *ad.* contorte; perplexe.

intrigue, *n.* consilium clandesti-
num, *nt.*; fraus, ars, *f.*; (amour)
amores, *m. pl.*

intrinsic, *a.* internus; innatus;
~**ally,** *ad.* intrinsecus.

introduce, *v.t.* introduco; (institute) instituo, [3].

introduction, *n.* inductio; (to a
person) introductio; (preface)
praefatio, *f.*; exordium, prooemium, *nt.*

introductory, *a.* introductorius.

intrude, *v.t. & i.* immitto, me immitto, [3]; molestus sum.

intrusion, *n.* importunitas; usurpatio, *f.*

intrusive, *a.* molestus.

inundate, *v.t.* inundo, [1].

inundation, *n.* inundatio, *f.*; diluvium, *nt.*

inure, *v.t.* assuefacio, [3].

invade, *v.t.* invado, irrumpo, bellum infero, [3].

invader, *n.* invasor, *m.*

invalid, *a.* infirmus, vitiosus,
nugatorius, irritus.

invalid, *n.* aeger, aegrotus, vale-
tudinarius, *m.*

invalidate, *v.t.* irritum reddo;
rescindo, [3].

invaluable, *a.* inaestimabilis.

invariable, *a.* constans, immutabilis, immobilis.

invariably, *ad.* immutabiliter;
semper.

invasion, *n.* incursio, irruptio, *f.*

invective, *n.* convicium, *nt.*

inveigle, *v.t.* illicio, pellicio, [3].

invent, *v.t.* invenio, reperio, [4];
(contrive) excogito, [1]; fingo,
[3].

invention, *n.* (act) inventio, *f.*;
(thing invented) inventum, *nt.*;
(lie, *etc.*) commentum, *nt.*

inventive, *a.* habilis, ingeniosus.

inventor, *n.* inventor, repertor,
m.

inventress, *n.* inventrix, *f.*

inverse, *a.* inversus, conversus.

inversion, *n.* inversio, conversio,
f.

invert, *v.t.* inverto, [3].

invest, *v.t.* do, mando; (money) colloco, [1]; pono, [3]; (besiege) obsideo, [2].

investigate, *v.t.* investigo, indago, scrutor, [1]; inquiro, cognosco, [3].

investigation, *n.* investigatio, inquisitio, *f.*

investment, *n.* (of money) pecunia in faenore posita.

inveterate, *a.* inveteratus.

invidious, *a.* invidus, malignus, invidiosus; ~ly, *ad.* invidiose; maligne.

invigorate, *v.t.* corroboro, confirmo, [1].

invincible, *a.* invictus; insuperabilis.

invisible, *a.* invisibilis.

invitation, *n.* invitatio, *f.*

invite, *v.t.* invito, voco, [1].

inviting, *a.* gratus, blandus, suavis.

invocation, *n.* obtestatio, *f.*

invoke, *v.t.* invoco, imploro, obtestor, [1].

involuntary, *a.* invitus, coactus.

involve, *v.t.* (contain) contineo, [2]; (entangle) implico, [1]; (imply) habeo, [2].

involved, *a.* (intricate) perplexus.

invulnerable, *a.* invulnerabilis.

inward, *a.* interior.

inwardly, inwards, *ad.* intus, intrinsecus, introrsus.

irascible, *a.* iracundus.

irate, *a.* iratus.

iris, *n.* (plant) iris, *f.*

irksome, *a.* molestus, odiosus.

iron, *n.* ferrum, *nt.*; ~s, *pl.* vincula, *nt. pl.*

iron, *a.* ferreus; *fig.* durus.

ironic(al), *a.* deridens; ~(al)ly, *ad.* ironice.

ironmonger, *n.* negotiator ferrarius, *m.*

irony, *n.* ironia, dissimulatio, *f.*

irrational, *a.* rationis expers, irrationalis.

irreconcilable, *a.* implacabilis; (incompatible) repugnans.

irrefutable, *a.* quod confutari non potest.

irregular, *a.* (disorderly) tumultuarius; (spasmodic) rarus, infrequens; (uneven) iniquus.

irrelevant, *a.* non pertinens, alienus.

irreligious, *a.* impius, irreligiosus, religionis neglegens.

irreparable, *a.* irreparabilis; irrevocabilis.

irresistible, *a.* invictus; cui nullo modo resisti potest.

irresolute, *a.* incertus animi; dubius; parum firmus; ~ly, *ad.* dubitanter.

irresolution, *n.* dubitatio, *f.*; animus parum firmus, *m.*

irresponsible, *a.* levis.

irreverent, *a.* irreverens, parum reverens.

irrevocable, *a.* irrevocabilis.

irrigate, *v.t.* rigo, irrigo, [1].

irrigation, *n.* irrigatio, inductio aquae, *f.*

irritability, *n.* iracundia, *f.*

irritable, *a.* irritabilis, stomachosus, iracundus.

irritate, *v.t.* irrito; inflammo, [1].

irritation, *n.* irritatio, *f.*; stomachus, *m.*; ira, *f.*

island, *n.* insula, *f.*

isolate, *v.t.* seiungo, secerno, [3].

isolation, *n.* solitudo, *f.*

issue, *n.* (outlet) egressus, *m.*; (result) eventus, exitus, *m.*; (end) finis, *c.*; (matter) res, *f.*; (offspring) liberi, *m. pl.*; (of money) erogatio, *f.*; (profit) reditus, *m.*

issue, *v.t.* (publish) edo; (post up) propono, [3]; (money) erogo, [1]; ~, *v.i.* emano, [1]; egredior, [3]; (end) evenio, [4].

isthmus, *n.* isthmus, *m.*

it, *pn.* id, hoc.

Italy, *n.* Italia, *f.*

itch, *n.* scabies, prurigo, *f.*

itch, *v.i.* prurio, [4].

itchy, *a.* scabrosus.

item, *n.* res, *f.*

itinerary, *n.* itinerarium, *nt.*

itself, *pn.* ipsum.

ivory, *n.* ebur, *nt.*

ivory, *a.* eburneus; eburnus.

ivy, *n.* hedera, *f.*

J

jackal, *n.* canis aureus, *m.*

jackdaw, *n.* monedula, *f.*

jade, *n.* (horse) caballus, *m.*; *fig.* (woman) importuna mulier, *f.*

jaded, *a.* defessus.

jagged, *a.* dentatus, serratus.

jail, *n.* carcer, *m.*

jail, *v.t.* in carcerem conicio, [3].

jailer, *n.* custos, *m.*

jam, *n.* conditae baccae, *f. pl.*

jam, *v.t.* comprimo, [3].

jangle, *v.i.* (make a jangling sound) tinnio, [4]; tintinno, [1].

January, *n.* Ianuarius, *m.*

jar, *n.* (pitcher, bottle, cask) olla; amphora, *f.*; urceus, *m.*

jar, *v.i.* discrepo, discordo, [1].

jargon, *n.* confusae voces, *f. pl.*; barbarus sermo, *m.*

jarring, *a.* dissonus, discors.

jasper, *n.* iaspis, *f.*

jaundice, *n.* morbus regius, icterus, *m.*

jaundiced, *a.* ictericus; *fig.* morosus; invidiosus.

jaunt, *n.* excursio, *f.*

javelin, *n.* pilum, iaculum; telum, veru, *nt.*

jaw, *n.* mala; maxilla, *f.; fig.* fauces, *f. pl.*

jawbone, *n.* maxilla, *f.*

jay, *n.* corvus glandarius, *m.*

jealous, *a.* invidus; aemulus; invidiosus.

jealousy, *n.* invidia; aemulatio, *f.*; livor, *m.*

jeer, *v.i.* derideo, irrideo, [2].

jeer, jeering, *n.* risus; irrisus, *m.*

jelly, *n.* cylon, quilon, *nt.*

jellyfish, *n.* pulmo, halipleumon, *m.*

jeopardize, *v.t.* in periculum adduco, [3].

jeopardy, *n.* periculum, discrimen, *nt.*

jerk, *n.* impetus, subitus motus, *m.*

jerk, *v.t.* subito moveo, [2].

jest, *n.* iocus, lusus, *m.*; facetiae, *f. pl.*; **in ~,** ioco, iocose.

jest, *v.i.* iocor, [1]; ludo, [3].

jester, *n.* ioculator; (buffoon) scurra, *m.*

jet, *n.* (spout of water) scatebra, *f.*; (mineral) gagates, *m.*

jet-black, *a.* nigerrimus.

jetty, *n.* moles, pila, *f.*

Jew, *n.* Iudaeus, *m.*

jewel, *n.* gemma, *f.*

jewelled, *a.* gemmeus, gemmifer.

jeweller, *n.* gemmarius, *m.*

jewellery, *n.* gemmae, *f. pl.*

jig, *n.* saltatio, *f.*

jilt, *v.t.* fallo, [3].

jingle, *v.i.* tinnio, [4].

jingling, *n.* tinnitus, *m.*

job, *n.* negotiolum, *nt.*; res lucrosa, *f.*

jockey, *n.* agaso, *m.*

jocular, *a.* iocularis, iocosus, facetus; **~ly,** *ad.* ioculariter, facete, iocose.

jocularity, *n.* facetiae, *f. pl.*, animus iocosus, *m.*

jog, *v.t.* concutio, quatio, [3].

join, *v.t.* iungo, coniungo, [3]; (border on) contingo; **~ battle,** *v.i.* confligo, manum consero, [3]; congredior cum (*with abl.*); **~,** *v.i.* adiungor, [3]; cohaereo, [2]; **~ in** (take part in) particeps or socius sum (alicuius rei).

joiner, *n.* lignarius, *m.*

joint, *n.* commissura, *f.*; articulus, *m.*; vertebra; iunctura, *f.*

jointly, *ad.* coniuncte, coniunctim, una, communiter.

joist, *n.* tignum transversarium, *nt.*

joke, *n.* iocus, *m.*; sales, *m. pl.*; facetiae, *f. pl.*

joke (at), *v.t. & i.* iocor, [1]; ludo, [3]; irrideo, [2].

joker, *n.* ioculator, *m.*

jollity, *n.* festivitas, hilaritas, *f.*

jolly, *a.* festivus, hilaris.

jolt, *v.t.* concutio, [3]; iacto, quasso, [1]; **~,** *v.i.* concutior, [3]; iactor, quassor, [1].

jolt, *n.* iactatio, *f.*

jostle, *v.t.* pulso, deturbo, [1].

journal, *n.* ephemeris, *f*; diarium, *nt.*; (newspaper) acta diurna, *nt. pl.*

journey, *n.* iter, *nt.*; profectio, *f*; via, *f*.

Jove, *n.* Iupiter, *m.*

jovial, *a.* hilaris, festivus.

joviality, *n.* hilaritas, festivitas, *f*.

joy, *n.* gaudium, *nt.*; laetitia, *f*.

joyful, joyous, *a.* laetus, hilaris; ~ly, *ad.* laete, hilare; libenter.

jubilant, *a.* laetitia exsultans; ovans.

jubilation, *n.* triumphus, *m.*; gaudium, *nt*.

Judaism, *n.* Iudaismus, *m.*

judge, *n.* iudex; quaesitor, arbiter; (critic) existimator, censor, *m.*; (umpire) arbiter, *m.*

judge, *v.t. & i.* iudico; existimo, [1]; censeo, [2]; (value) aestimo, [1].

judgment, *n.* sententia, *f*; arbitrium; *fig.* (opinion, faculty of judging) iudicium, *nt*.

judicial, *a.* iudicialis.

judicious, *a.* sapiens, prudens; ~ly, *ad.* sapienter, prudenter.

jug, *n.* urceus, *m.*

juggle, *v.i.* praestigias ago, [3].

juggler, *n.* praestigiator; pilarius, *m.*

juggling, *n.* praestigiae, *f. pl.*

juice, *n.* sucus, *m.*

juicy, *a.* sucosus.

July, *n.* Quintilis, *m.*

jumble, *v.t.* confundo, [3]; permisceo, [2].

jumble, *n.* confusio, congeries, strages, *f*.

jump, *v.i.* salio, exsilio, [4]; exsulto, [1].

jump, *n.* saltus, *m.*

junction, *n.* coniunctio, iunctura, *f*.

June, *n.* Iunius, *m.*

jungle, *n.* locus virgultis obsitus, *m.*

junior, *a. & n.* iunior, minor.

jurisdiction, *n.* iurisdictio, *f*.

juror, *n.* iudex, *m.*

jury, *n.* iudices, *m. pl.*

just, *a.* iustus; meritus; aequus.

just, *ad.* (a moment ago) modo; (only) modo; (only just) vix; ~ so, haud secus.

justice, *n.* iustitia, aequitas, *f*.

justifiable, *a.* excusandus.

justifiably, *ad.* iure; cum causa, excusate.

justification, *n.* excusatio, purgatio, *f*.

justify, *v.t.* purgo; excuso, [1].

justly, *ad.* iuste; iure; merito.

jut out, *v.i.* promineo, [2]; procurro, [3].

juvenile, *a.* iuvenilis, puerilis.

K

Kalends, n. Kalendae, f. pl.

keel, n. carina, f.

keen, a. acer; alacer; sagax; (sharp) acutus; **~ly,** ad. acute, acriter; sagaciter.

keenness, n. sagacitas, subtilitas, f.

keen-sighted, a. perspicax.

keep, v.t. teneo; habeo, [2]; (preserve) servo, conservo, [1]; (guard) custodio, [4]; (store) recondo; (support) alo, [3]; sustineo, [2]; (animals) pasco, [3]; (a holiday) celebro, [1]; ago, [3]; (reserve) reservo, [1]; (one's word, law, *etc.*) servo, [1]; **~,** v.i. maneo, [2]; duro, [1]; **~ away,** arceo, prohibeo; (v.i.) abstineo, [2]; **~ back,** retineo, cohibeo, [2]; (conceal) celo, [1]; **~ company,** comitor, [1]; **~ down,** comprimo, [3]; **~ from,** (v.t.) prohibeo, [2]; (v.i.) abstineo, [2]; **~ in,** includo, [3]; **~ off,** v. **~ away,** (v.i.) persevero, [1]; **~ out,** (v.t.) excludo, [3]; **~ up,** (maintain) tueor, [2]; sustineo, [2]; (v.i.) subsequor, [3].

keep, n. (citadel) arx, f.; (food) cibus, m.

keeper, n. custos, c.

keeping, n. tutela; custodia; cura, f.

keepsake, n. pignus, nt.

keg, n. cadus, m.; testa, f.

kennel, n. cubile, nt.; stabulum, nt.

kernel, n. (of a fruit) nucleus, m.

kettle, n. lebes, m.; aënum, nt.

key, n. clavis, f.; (key position controlling access) claustra, nt. pl.; fig. cardo, m.

kick, v.i. calcitro, [1]; calce ferio, [4].

kick, n. calcitratus, m.

kid, n. (young goat) haedus, m.

kidnap, v.t. surripio, [3].

kidnapper, n. plagiarius, m.

kidneys, n. renes, m. pl.

kill, v.t. interficio, caedo, occido, interimo, perimo, [3]; neco, [1].

killer, n. interfector, m.

kiln, n. fornax, f.

kin, n. consanguinitas, f.; genus, nt.; v. **relation.**

kind, n. genus, nt.; modus, m.; species, f.; **of what ~,** qualis, cuiusmodi.

kind, a. amicus; benignus; benevolus; comis; humanus; suavis.

kind-hearted, a. benignus.

kindle, v.t. accendo, [3]; fig. inflammo, [1]; **~,** v.i. exardesco, [3].

kindly, a., v. **kind; ~,** ad. amice; benigne; humane; comiter.

kindness, n. benignitas; humanitas, f.; (kind act) beneficium, nt.

king, *n.* rex, *m.*

kingdom, *n.* regnum, *nt.*

kingfisher, *n.* alcedo, *f.*

kinsman, *n.* necessarius, cognatus, consanguineus, *m.*

kiss, *n.* suavium, osculum, basium, *nt.*

kiss, *v.t.* suavior, osculor, basio, [1].

kitchen, *n.* culina, *f.*

kit, *n.* impedimenta, *nt. pl.*

kite, *n.* (bird) milvus, *m.*

kitten, *n.* catulus felinus, *m.*

knack, *n.* ars, sollertia, *f.*

knapsack, *n.* sarcina, *f.*

knavish, *a.* scelestus, nefarius, *m.*

knead, *v.t.* depso, subigo, [3].

knee, *n.* genu, *nt.*

kneecap, *n.* patella, *f.*

kneel, *v.i.* in genua procumbo, genibus nitor, [3].

knife, *n.* culter, cultellus, *m.*

knight, *n.* eques, *m.*

knighthood, *n.* equestris dignitas, *f.*

knit, *v.t.* ~ **the brow,** supercilium (frontem) contraho, [3].

knob, *n.* tuber, *nt.* nodus, *m.*; (of a door) bulla, *f.*

knock, *v.t. & i.* pulso, [1]; ferio, [4]; tundo, [3]; ~ **against,** (one's head, *etc.*) offendo, [3]; ~ **at** (a door), pulso, [1]; ferio, [4]; ~ **down,** deicio, sterno, [3]; *fig.* (at an auction) addico (bona ali-

cui), [3]; ~ **over,** deturbo, [1]; ~ **up,** (awake) suscito, [1].

knock, knocking, *n.* pulsatio, *f.*

knock-kneed, *a.* varus.

knoll, *n.* tumulus, *m.*

knot, *n.* nodus, *m.*; geniculum, *nt.*; *fig.* (of people) circulus, *m.*; *fig.* difficultas, *f.*

knot, *v.t.* nodo, [1].

knotty, *a.* nodosus; *fig.* spinosus, difficilis.

know, *v.t.* scio, [4]; (learn, become acquainted with) cognosco, [3]; (be acquainted with) nosco, [3]; ~ **how to,** scio, [4] (*with inf.*) **not** ~, ignoro, [1]; ~ **again,** recognosco, [3].

knowing, *a.* sciens, prudens; (cunning) astutus; **~ly,** *ad.* scienter; prudenter; (cunningly) astute.

knowledge, *n.* scientia, cognitio; (skill) peritia; (learning) eruditio, *f.*; (understanding) intellectus, *m.*

knowledgeable, *a.* sciens.

known, *a.* notus; **be ~,** enotesco, [3]; **it is ~,** constat; **become ~,** emano, [1]; **make ~,** palam facio, [3]; divulgo, [1]; **well ~,** (famous) celeber.

knuckle, *n.* condylus, articulus, *m.*; ~ **-bones,** *pl.* (game) tali, *m. pl.*

....

L

....

label, *n.* titulus, *m.*

label, *v.t.* titulum affigo, [3].

laborious, *a.* laboriosus; (difficult) operosus, *f.*; *ad.* laboriose; operose; multo labore.

labour, *n.* labor, *m.*; (manual) opera, *f.*; (work) opus, *nt.*; (of childbirth) partus, *m.*

labour, *v.t. & i.* laboro, operor, [1]; (struggle, *etc.*) contendo, [3].

labourer, *n.* operarius, *m.*; opifex, *c.*

labyrinth, *n.* labyrinthus, *m.*

lace, *v.t.* (edge) praetexo, [3]; (tie) necto, astringo, [3].

lacerate, *v.t.* lacero, lanio, [1].

laceration, *n.* laceratio, *f.*

lack, *v.t.* egeo, careo, [2] (*with abl.*).

lack, *n.* inopia, egestas, *f.*

laconic, *a.* Laconicus, brevis.

lad, *n.* puer, adulescens, *m.*

ladder, *n.* scala, *f.*

laden, *a.* onustus, oneratus.

ladle, *n.* ligula, spatha, trulla, *f.*; coclear, *nt.*

lady, *n.* domina; matrona, era, *f.*

lag, *v.i.* cesso, cunctor, moror, [1].

lagoon, *n.* lacuna, *f.*

lair, *n.* cubile; latibulum, lustrum, *nt.*

lake, *n.* lacus, *m.*; stagnum, *nt.*

lamb, *n.* agnus, *m.*; agna, *f.*

lame, *a.* claudus, debilis; *fig.* inconcinnus, ineptus.

lame, *v.t.* mutilo; debilito, [1].

lament, *v.t. & i.* lamentor; deploro, [1]; fleo, [2].

lament, *n.*, v. **lamentation.**

lamentable, *a.* miserandus; lamentabilis; luctuosus, flebilis, miser.

lamentation, *n.* lamentatio, *f.*; lamenta, *nt. pl.*; (act) ploratus, fletus, *m.*

lamp, *n.* lucerna, lampas, *f.*; lychnus, *m.*

lance, *n.* lancea, hasta, *f.*

land, *n.* (soil) terra, tellus, *f.*; (country) regio, *f.*; (estate) fundus, *m.*; praedium, *nt.*; (field) ager, *m.*

land, *v.t.* in terram expono, [3]; ~, *v.i.* egredior, [3].

land-forces, *n. pl.* copiae terrestres, *f. pl.*

landing, *n.* egressus, *m.*

landlord, *n.* (innkeeper) caupo; (owner of land) dominus, *m.*

landmark, *n.* limes, *m.*

landscape, *n.* forma et situs agri; (picture) topia, *f.*

landslide, *n.* lapsus terrae, *m.*

lane, *n.* angiportus, *m.*

language, *n.* lingua, oratio, *f.*; sermo, *m.*; verba, *nt. pl.*

languid, *a.* languidus.

languish, *v.i.* langueo, [2]; languesco, [3].

lank, lanky, *a.* macer.

lantern, *n.* lanterna, *f.*

lap, *n.* sinus, *m.*; gremium, *nt.*; (of a racecourse) spatium, *nt.*

lap, *v.t.* (lick) lambo, [3].

lap-dog, *n.* catellus, *m.*

lapse, *n.* lapsus, *m.*; *fig.* (error) erratum, peccatum, *nt.*

lapse, *v.i.* labor, [3]; (come to an end) exeo, [4]; (err) pecco, [1].

lard, *n.* laridum, lardum, *nt.*

larder, *n.* carnarium, *nt.*; cella, *f.*

large, *a.* magnus, amplus, grandis, largus.

largess, *n.* largitio, *f.*; donativum, *nt.*

lark, *n.* alauda, *f.*

lascivious, *a.* salax; lascivus, petulans; **~ly,** *ad.* lascive; petulanter.

lasciviousness, *n.* salacitas, lascivia; petulantia, *f.*

lash, *n.* (stroke) verber, *nt.*; (whip) scutica, *f.*; flagellum, *nt.*

lash, *v.t.* (whip) verbero, flagello; (fasten) alligo; *fig.* castigo, [1].

last, *a.* postremus, ultimus; summus, extremus, (most recent) novissimus; **~ but one,** paenultimus; **at ~,** demum, tandem; denique, postremo.

last, *ad.* postremum; novissime.

last, *v.i.* duro, perduro, [1]; maneo, [2].

lasting, *a.* mansurus; perennis; stabilis.

lastly, *ad.* postremo, denique.

latch, *n.* obex, c.; pessulus, *m.*

late, *a.* serus; tardus; (new) recens; (dead) mortuus; **~,** *ad.* sero; **it grows ~,** vesperascit.

lately, *ad.* nuper, modo.

latent, *a.* latens, latitans, occultus.

later, *a.* posterus.

lateral, *a.* lateralis.

lathe, *n.* tornus, *m.*

lather, *n.* spuma, *f.*

Latin, *a. & n.* Latinus; (language) lingua Latina, *f.*

latitude, *n.* latitudo; (liberty) licenta, *f.*

latter, *a.* posterior; **the ~,** hic; **~ly,** *ad.* nuperrime.

lattice, *n.* cancelli, clathri, *m. pl.*

laudable, *a.* laudabilis, laude dignus.

laudatory, *a.* laudativus.

laugh, *v.i.* rideo, [2]; **~ at,** derideo, irrideo, [2].

laugh, *n.* risus, *m.*

laughable, *a.* ridiculus.

laughing-stock, *n.* ludibrium, *nt.*

laughter, *n.* risus, *m.*

launch, *v.t.* deduco, [3]; (hurl) iaculor, [1]; contorqueo, [2].

laurel, *n.* (tree) laurus, *f.*; laurea, *f.*

laurel, *a.* laureus.

laurelled, *a.* laureatus, laurifer, lauriger.

lava, *n.* torrens igneus, *m.*, liquefacta massa, *f.*

lavatory, *n.* latrina, *f.*

lavish, *a.* prodigus; profusus; ~ly, *ad.* profuse, prodige.

lavish, *v.t.* prodigo, profundo, effundo, [3].

law, *n.* lex, *f.*; (right) ius, *nt.*; (rule) norma, *f.*; (court of justice) iurisdictio, *f.*; ~suit, lis, *f.*; international ~, ius gentium, *nt.*

lawful, *a.* legitimus; iustus; licitus; ~ly, *ad.* legitime; lege.

lawless, *a.* exlex; illicitus; inconcessus; ~ly, *ad.* contra leges.

lawlessness, *n.* licentia, *f.*

lawn, *n.* (of grass) pratum, *nt.*; (fine linen) carbasus, sindon, *f.*

lawsuit, *n.* lis, causa, *f.*

lawyer, *n.* iurisconsultus; causidicus, advocatus, *m.*

lax, *a.* remissus; *fig.* neglegens.

laxity, laxness, *n.* remissio, neglegentia, *f.*

lay, *v.t.* pono; (eggs) pario; (spread) spargo, expando, [3]; ~ **aside,** amoveo, [2]; repono; ~ **by,** repono, recondo, sepono, [3]; ~ **claim to,** vindico, [1]; ~ **down,** depono; (state) statuo, ~ **on,** impono, [3]; *fig.* imputo, [1]; ~ **out,** expono; (money) expendo, [3]; ~ **waste,** vasto, [1].

laziness, *n.* segnities, pigritia; desidia, *f.*

lazy, *a.* iners, ignavus, piger, segnis, desidiosus.

lead, *n.* plumbum, *nt.*

lead, *v.t.* duco, [3]; praeeo, [4]; (pass. spend) ago, dego, [3]; (manage) moderor, [1]; ~ **away,** abduco, [3]; ~ **off,** diverto; adduco, [3]; ~ **on,** (induce) conduco, [3].

leaden, *a.* plumbeus.

leader, *n.* dux, *c.*; ductor; *fig.* auctor, *m.*

leadership, *n.* ductus, *m.*

leading, *a.* princeps; primarius.

leaf, *n.* folium, *nt.*; (of paper) pagina; (of metal) brattea, *f.*

leafless, *a.* fronde nudatus.

leafy, *a.* frondosus, frondeus, frondifer.

league, *n.* (confederacy) foedus, *nt.*; societas, *f.*; **be in ~ with,** consocio cum (*with abl.*), [1].

leak, *n.* rima, *f.*; hiatus, *m.*

leak, *v.i.* perfluo; humorem transmitto, [3].

leaky, *a.* rimosus.

lean, *a.* macer; exilis, gracilis.

lean, *v.t.* inclino, acclino, [1]; ~ **on,** (*v.i.*) innitor (*with dat.*); ~ **(over),** (*v.i.*) incumbo ad (*with acc.*), [3]; ~, *v.i.* inclino, [1].

leap, *v.i.* salio, [4]; *fig.* exsulto, [1]; ~ **across,** transilio, [4].

leap year, *n.* bisextilis annus, *m.*

learn, *v.t. & i.* disco; cognosco, [3]; (hear) audio, [4]; **~ by heart**, edisco, perdisco, [3].

learned, *a.* eruditus, doctus.

learner, *n.* discipulus, *m.*

learning, *n.* doctrina, humanitas, *f.*; litterae, *f. pl.*; (knowledge) eruditio, *f.*

lease, *n.* conductio, locatio, *f.*

lease, *v.t.* conduco, [3]; loco; (out) eloco, [1].

leash, *n.* (thong) lorum, *nt.*; (rein) habena, (leash) copula, *f.*

least, *a.* minimus; **~**, *ad.* minime; **at ~**, saltem; **not in the ~**, ne minimum quidem.

leather, *n.* corium, *nt.*; (tanned) aluta, *f.*

leather, *a.* scorteus.

leave, *v.t.* linquo, relinquo, desero, [3]; (entrust) mando, [1]; trado, [3]; (bequeath) relinquo, [3]; lego, [1]; **~ behind**, relinquo, [3]; **~ off**, (*v.i.*) desino; (*v.t.*) fig. depono; (through interruption) intermitto, [3]; **~ out**, omitto, [3]; praetereo, [4].

leave, *n.* permissio, licentia, copia, potestas, *f.*; (of absence) commeatus, *m.*

lecherous, *a.* libidinosus, salax.

lecture, *n.* schola, acroasis, *f.*; praelectio, *f.*

lecture, *v.t.* praelego, [3]; (reprove) obiurgo, [1]; corripio, [3].

lecturer, *n.* praelector, *m.*

ledge, *n.* dorsum, *nt.*; ora, *f.*

ledger, *n.* codex, *m.*

leech, *n.* sanguisuga, hirudo, *f.*

leek, *n.* porrum, allium, *nt.*

leer, *v.i.* limis oculis intueor, [3].

left, *a.* sinister, laevus; **~**, *n.* manus sinistra, *f.*; **on the ~**, a sinistra; **to the ~**, ad sinistram, sinistrorsum.

leg, *n.* tibia, *f.*; crus, *nt.*; (of a table, *etc.*) pes, *m.*

legacy, *n.* legatum, *nt.*

legal, *a.* legalis, legitimus; iudicialis; **~ly**, *ad.* legitime; legibus.

legalize, *v.t.* legibus confirmo, [1].

legate, *n.* legatus, *m.*

legation, *n.* legatio, *f.*

legend, *n.* fabula, *f.*

legendary, *a.* fabulosus.

legible, *a.* quod legi potest.

legion, *n.* legio, *f.*

legionary soldier, *n.* legionarius, *m.*

legislate, *v.t.* legem fero, [3].

legislation, *n.* legum datio, *f.*

legislator, *n.* legum lator, *m.*

legitimate, *a.* legitimus; licitus; fig. sincerus, verus.

leisure, *n.* otium, *nt.*; **at ~**, otiosus; vacuus.

lemon, *n.* citrum, *nt.*

lend, *v.t.* pecuniam mutuam do; commodo; (at interest) faeneror, [1]; fig. praebeo, [2].

lender, *n.* qui pecuniam mutuam dat, *m.*

length, *n.* longitudo; (of time) longinquitas; (tallness) proceritas, *f.*; **at ~,** tandem, demum.

lengthen, *v.t.* extendo, protraho; *fig.* produco, [3].

lengthy, *a.* longus; prolixus.

leniency, *n.* lenitas, clementia, mansuetudo, indulgentia, *f.*; (pardon) venia, *f.*

lenient, *a.* mitis, lenis, clemens; mansuetus.

lentil, *n.* lens, *f.*

leopard, *n.* leopardus, *m.*

leprosy, *n.* leprae, *f. pl.*

less, *a.* minor; **~,** *ad.* minus.

lessen, *v.t.* minuo, imminuo; **~,** *v.i.* decresco, minuor, [3].

lesson, *n.* schola, *f.*

lest, *c.* ne . . .

let, *v.t.* permitto, [3] (*with dat.*); sino; patior, [3]; (lease) loco, [1]; **~ alone,** omitto, [3]; **~ down,** demitto, [3]; **~ in,** admitto, [3]; **~ out,** emitto, [3]; (hire) eloco, [1]; **~ pass,** omitto, [3]; praetereo, [4].

lethal, *a.* letalis.

lethargic, *a.* languidus.

lethargy, *n.* languor; veternus, *m.*

letter, *n.* (of alphabet) littera, *f.*; (communication) epistula, *f.*; litterae, *f. pl.*; **~s,** *pl.* (learning) litterae, *f. pl.*

lettering, *n.* titulus, *m.*

lettuce, *n.* lactuca, *f.*

levee, *n.* salutantium comitatus, *m.*

level, *a.* planus, aequus.

level, *n.* planities, *f.*

level, *v.t.* aequo, coaequo, complano, [1].

lever, *n.* vectis, *m.*

levity, *n.* levitas; iocatio, *f.*

levy, *n.* delectus, *m.*

levy, *v.t.* (troops) conscribo, [3]; (money) exigo, [3].

lewd, *a.* incestus, impudicus; libidinosus.

liability, *n.* (obstacle) impedimentum, *nt.*

liable, *a.* obnoxius; **~ to,** obnoxius (*with dat.*).

liaison, *n.* amicitia, *f.*

liar, *n.* mendax, *c.*

libel, *n.* libellus famosus, *m.*

libel, *v.t.* diffamo, [1].

libellous, *a.* probrosus; famosus.

liberal, *a.* liberalis, munificus; *fig.* ingenuus; **~ly,** *ad.* liberaliter, munifice; ingenue.

liberality, *n.* liberalitas, munificentia, *f.*

liberate, *v.t.* libero, [1]; (in law) manumitto, [3].

liberation, *n.* liberatio, *f.*

liberator, *n.* liberator, *m.*

liberty, *n.* libertas; licentia, *f.*; **at ~,** liber.

librarian, *n.* bibliothecae praefectus, *m.*

library, *n.* bibliotheca, *f.*

licence, *n.* licentia; (lack of restraint) licentia, intemperantia, *f.*; venia, *f.*

licentious, *a.* dissolutus, impudicus, lascivus; incestus; **~ly,** *ad.* inceste, lascive.

licentiousness, *n.* mores dissoluti, *m. pl.*; licentia, lascivia, intemperantia, *f.*

lick, *v.t.* lambo, [3]; (daintily) ligurrio, [4].

lictor, *n.* lictor, *m.*

lid, *n.* operculum; operimentum, *nt.*

lie, *n.* mendacium, *nt.*; **tell a ~,** mentior, [4].

lie, *v.i.* (tell falsehoods) mentior, [4].

lie, *v.i.* iaceo, [2]; (in bed, *etc.*) cubo, [1]; (be situated) situs esse; **~ down,** decumbo, [3]; **~ in wait,** insidior, [1]; **~ on,** incubo, [1]; incumbo, [3] (*both with dat.*).

lieu, *n.* **in ~ of,** loco (*with gen.*).

life, *n.* vita; anima, *f.*; spiritus, *m.*; *fig.* vigor, *m.*; alacritas, *f.*

lifeless, *a.* inanimus; exanimis; *fig.* exsanguis, frigidus.

lifetime, *n.* aetas, *f.*; aevum, *nt.*

lift, *v.t.* tollo, attollo, erigo, [3]; levo, sublevo, [1].

ligament, *n.* ligamentum, ligamen, *f.*

light, *n.* lux, *f.*; lumen, *nt.*; (lamp) lucerna, *f.*; **bring to ~,** in lucem profero, [3].

light, *a.* (bright, *etc.*) lucidus, fulgens; (in weight) levis; (of colours) candidus, dilutus; (easy) facilis; (nimble) agilis; pernix; (inconstant) instabilis.

light, *v.t.* accendo, [3]; **~ up,** illumino, [1]; **~,** *v.i.* exardesco, [3].

lighten, *v.t.* (illumine) illumino, illustro, [1]; (a weight) allevo; exonero, [1].

light-hearted, *a.* hilaris, laetus, alacer.

lighthouse, *n.* pharus, *f.*

lightly, *ad.* leviter; perniciter; *fig.* neglegenter; temere.

lightness, *n.* levitas; (quickness) agilitas, pernicitas, *f.*

lightning, *n.* fulmen, *nt.*

like, *a.* similis; assimilis, consimilis; (equal) par, aequus (*all with dat.*); **~,** *ad.* tamquam, velut; (in ~ manner) pariter, similiter.

like, *v.t. & i.* (approve) comprobo, [1]; (be fond of) amo, [1]; **would you ~?** velis?

likelihood, *n.* verisimilitudo, *f.*

likely, *a.* probabilis, verisimilis; **~,** *ad.* probabiliter.

liken, *v.t.* assimulo, comparo, [1]; confero, [3].

likeness, *n.* similitudo; (portrait) imago, effigies, *f.*

likewise, *ad.* pariter, similiter.

liking, *n.* approbatio, *f.*; favor, *m.*; (fancy) libido, *f.*

lily, *n.* lilium, *nt.*

limb, *n.* membrum, *nt.*; artus, *m.*

lime, *n.* calx, *f.*; **bird-~**, viscum, *n.* (tree) tilla, *f.*

lime, *v.t.* visco illino, [3].

limestone, *n.* calx, *f.*; lapis calcarius, *m.*

limit, *n.* limes, terminus, *m.*; finis, *c.*; modus, *m.*

limit, *v.t.* termino, [1]; finio, [4]; circumscribo, [3].

limitation, *n. fig.* exceptio, *f.*

limited, *a.* circumscriptus.

limitless, *a.* infinitus.

limp, *v.i.* claudico, [1]; ~, *n.* claudicatio, *f.*

limp, *a.* flaccidus, lentus.

line, *n.* (drawn) linea, *f.*; (row) series, *f.*; ordo, *m.*; (lineage) stirps, progenies, *f.*; genus, *nt.*; (cord) funiculus, *m.*; (in poetry) versus, *m.*; (entrenchment) vallum, *nt.*; (fishing-~) linea, *f.*

line up, *v.t.* in ordinem instruo, [3].

lineage, *n.* stirps, *f.*; genus, *nt.*

linear, *a.* linearis.

linen, *n.* linteum, *nt.*; carbasus, *f.*; (fine) sindon, *f.*

linen, *a.* linteus, lineus, carbaseus.

linger, *v.i.* cunctor, cesso, moror, [1].

lingering, *a.* cunctabundus; tardus.

linguist, *n.* linguarum peritus, *m.*

link, *n.* (of a chain) anulus, *m.*; (bond) vinculum, *nt.*

link, *v.t.* connecto, [3].

lintel, *n.* limen superum, *nt.*

lion, *n.* leo, *m.*

lioness, *n.* leaena, lea, *f.*

lip, *n.* labrum, labellum, *nt.*; *fig.* os, *nt.*; (edge) ora, *f.*

liquefy, *v.t.* liquefacio, [3]; ~, *v.i.* liquefio, [3].

liquid, *a.* liquidus; (transparent) pellucidus.

liquid, *n.* liquidum, *nt.*; liquor, *m.*

liquor, *n.* umor, liquor, *m.*

lisp, *n.* os blaesum, *nt.*

lisp, *v.i.* balbutio, [4].

list, *n.* index, *m.*

listen, *v.i.* ausculto, [1]; audio, [4].

listener, *n.* auscultator, auditor, *m.*

listless, *a.* remissus, neglegens, languidus.

listlessness, *n.* inertia, socordia, *f.*; languor, *m.*

literal, *a.* accuratus; **~ly**, *ad.* ad litteram, ad verbum.

literary, *a.* ad litteras pertinens.

literature, *n.* litterae, *f. pl.*

litigant, *n.* litigator, *m.*

litigation, *n.* lis, *f.*

litter, *n.* (of straw, *etc.*) substramen, substramentum, stramentum, *nt.*; (vehicle) lectica, *f.*; (brood) partus, *m.*

little, *a.* parvus, exiguus; **~**, *ad.* parum; **a ~**, paulum.

little, *n.* paulum, exiguum; (somewhat) aliquantulum; non-nihil, *n.*; ~ **by** ~, paulatim.

live, *v.i.* vivo, dego, [3]; spiro, [1]; vitam ago, [3]; (reside) habito, [1]; (on) vescor, [3].

live, *a.* vivus; vivens.

livelihood, *n.* (trade) ars, *f.*; (means of maintenance) victus, *m.*

liveliness, *n.* vigor, *nt.*

lively, *a.* vivus, vividus, alacer; vegetus.

liver, *n.* iecur, *nt.*

livid, *a.* (of colour) lividus, livens.

living, *a.* vivus, vivens, spirans.

living, *n.* (way of life, food) victus, *m.*

lizard, *n.* lacertus, *m.*; lacerta, *f.*

load, *n.* onus, *nt.*; sarcina, *f.*; (quantity) vehis, *f.*

load, *v.t.* onero, [1].

loaf, *n.* panis, *m.*

loan, *n.* mutua pecunia, *f.*

loathe, *v.t.* fastidio, [4]; aspernor, [1]; odi, perodi, [3].

loathing, *n.* fastidium, taedium, *nt.*; satietas, *f.*

loathsome, *a.* foedus; odiosus.

lobby, *n.* vestibulum, *nt.*

lobster, *n.* locusta, *f.*; cammarus, *m.*

local, *a.* loci, locorum (*both gen.*); (neighbouring) vicinus.

locality, *n.* locus, *m.*

locate, *v.t.* (place) loco, [1]; (find) invenio, [4].

location, *n.* locus, *m.*

lock, *n.* sera, *f.*; claustrum, *nt.*; (of hair, wool, *etc.*) cirrus; floccus, *m.*

lock, *v.t. & i.* (a door) obsero, [1]; ~ **in,** includo, [3]; ~ **out,** excludo, [3]; ~ **up,** occludo, [3].

locker, *n.* loculamentum, *nt.*; capsa, *f.*

locksmith, *n.* claustrarius artifex, *m.*

locust, *n.* locusta, *f.*

lodge, *v.i.* habito, [1]; (stick fast in) haereo, [2] (*with* in *with abl.*).

lodge, *n.* casa, cella, *f.*

lodger, *n.* inquilinus, *m.*

lodging, *n.* (stay) commoratio, *f.*; (room) cubiculum; (inn) deversorium, *nt.*

loft, *n.* cella, *f.*; tabulatum, cenaculum, *nt.*

lofty, *a.* altus; (ex)celsus; sublimis; *fig.* superbus, elatus, arrogans.

log, *n.* lignum, *nt.*; stipes; (trunk) truncus, *m.*

loggerhead, *n.* **be at** ~**s,** rixor, [1] (*with* cum *with abl.*)

logic, *n.* logica, dialectica, *f.*

logical, *a.* logicus, dialecticus; ~**ly,** *ad.* dialectice.

loiter, *v.i.* cesso, cunctor; moror, [1].

loll, *v.i.* dependo, [3]; langueo, [2]; ~**on,** innitor, [3] (*with dat.*).

lone, lonely, *a.* solus; solitarius; (of places) desolatus; avius.

loneliness, *n.* solitudo, *f.*

long, *a.* longus; (of time) diuturnus; diutinus; (lengthened) productus.

long, *ad.* diu; ~ **after**, multo post; ~ **ago**, iamdudum; ~ **before**, multo ante.

long, *v.i.* aveo, [2]; (for) desidero, [1]; cupio, [3].

longevity, *n.* longaevitas, *f.*

longing, *n.* desiderium, *nt.*; appetitus, *m.*; cupido, *f.*

longitude, *n.* longitudo, *f.*

long-suffering, *a.* patiens.

look, *v.i.* video, [2]; aspicio, conspicio, [3]; specto, [1]; ~ **fierce**, torva tueor, [2]; v. **seem**; ~ **around**, circumspicio, [3]; ~ **after**, *fig.* curo, [1]; ~ **at**, intueor, [2]; ~ **back**, respicio; ~ **down on**, despicio, [3]; ~ **for**, (seek) quaero, [3]; ~ **forward**, prospicio, [3]; ~ **in**, in(tro)spicio, [3]; (examine) perscrutor, [1]; ~ **on**, intueor, [2]; ~ **out**, prospicio, [3]; (for) quaero, [3]; ~ **out!** cave! cavete!; ~ **round**, circumspicio; respicio, [3]; ~ **through**, per . . . aspicio; *fig.* perspicio, [3]; ~ **to**, *fig.* curo, [1]; ~ **up**, suspicio, [3]; ~ **upon**, *fig.* (value) habeo, [2]; aestimo, [1]; ~ **up to**, *fig.* veneror, [1].

look, *n.* aspectus, vultus, *m.*; os, *nt.*; facies, *f.*; (glance) obtutus, *m.*

look, *i.* ecce! en! aspice!

looking-glass, *n.* speculum, *nt.*

look-out post, *n.* specula, *f.*

loom, *n.* tela, *f.*

loom, *v.i.* appareo, obscure videor, [2].

loop, *n.* laqueus, *m.*

loophole, *n. fig.* effugium, *nt.*

loose, *a.* laxus; solutus; neglegens; dissolutus.

loose, loosen, *v.t.* solvo, resolvo, [3]; laxo, relaxo, [1]; ~, *v.i.* solvor, [3].

loot, *n.* praeda, *f.*

looter, *n.* raptor, *m.*

loquacious, *a.* loquax, garrulus.

lord, *n.* dominus, *m.*

lordly, *a.* superbus, imperiosus.

lordship, *n.* imperium, *nt.*

lore, *n.* doctrina; eruditio, *f.*; (rites) ritus, *m. pl.*

lose, *v.t.* amitto, perdo, [3]; (be deprived of) privor, [1] (*with abl.*); (be defeated) vincor, [3]; ~ **one's way**, aberro, [1]; **be lost**, pereo, [4].

loss, *n.* (act) amissio, iactura, *f.*; damnum, detrimentum, *nt.*; (*mil.*) clades, *f.*

lot, *n.* pars, portio; (chance) sors, *f.*; casus, *m.*; **by** ~, sorte; ~ **of**, multus.

lotion, *n.* medicamen, *nt.*

lottery, *n.* sortitio, *f.*

loud, *a.* clarus, sonorus; ~**ly**, *ad.* clare, magna voce.

loudness, *n.* claritas, *f.*

lounge, *v.i.* cesso, otior, [1].

lounge, *n.* lectulus, *m.*

louse, *n.* pedis, pediculus, *m.*

lout, *n.* homo agrestis, rusticus, *m.*

loutish, *a.* agrestis, rusticus.

love, *n.* amor, ardor, *m.*; flamma, *f.*; (desire) desiderium, *nt.*; (dearness) caritas, *f.*; in ~, *a.* amans.

love, *v.t.* amo, [1]; diligo, [3].

love-letter, *n.* nota blanda, *f.*

loveliness, *n.* venustas; forma, pulchritudo, *f.*

lovely, *a.* formosus pulcher; venustus.

love-potion, *n.* philtrum, *nt.*

lover, *n.* amator, amans; (devotee) studiosus, *m.*

lovingly, *ad.* amanter, blande.

low, *a.* humilis; (of price) vilis; (of birth) obscurus; (of the voice) summissus; *fig.* turpis; (downcast) abiectus.

low, *ad.* humiliter; summissa voce.

low, *v.i.* mugio, [4].

lower, *v.t.* (let down) demitto; (humiliate) abicio; (the price) imminuo, [3]; (the voice) submitto, [3].

lower, *a.* inferior.

lowermost, *a.* infimus, imus.

lowing, *n.* mugitus, *m.*

lowliness, *n.* humilitas, *f.*; *fig.* animus demissus, *m.*

lowly, *a.* humilis, obscurus.

loyal, *a.* fidelis; ~ly, *ad.* fideliter.

loyalty, *n.* fides, fidelitas, *f.*

lucid, *a.* lucidus; (transparent) pellucidus.

luck, *n.* fortuna, *f.*; successus, *m.*; bad ~, res adversae, *f. pl.*; good ~, res secundae, *f.pl.*

luckily, *a.* feliciter; fauste, prospere, fortunate.

lucky, *a.* felix, faustus, prosperus, fortunatus.

lucrative, *a.* quaestuosus, lucrosus.

ludicrous, *a.* ridiculus, iocularis.

lug, *v.t.* traho, [3].

luggage, *n.* sarcinae, *f. pl.*; impedimenta, *nt. pl.*; onus, *nt.*

lukewarm, *a.* egelidus, tepidus; *fig.* frigidus.

lull, *v.t.* sopio, [4]; *fig.* demulceo, [2].

lull, *n.* quies, *f.*

luminous, *a.* illustris, lucidus.

lump, *n.* glaeba; massa; (heap) congeries, *f.*

lumpy, *a.* glaebosus.

lunacy, *n.* alienatio mentis, *f.*; amentia, dementia, *f.*

lunar, *a.* lunaris.

lunatic, *a.* insanus, demens; ~, *n.* homo insanus, *m.*

lunch, luncheon, *n.* merenda, *f.*; prandium, *nt.*

lunch, *v.i.* prandeo, [2].

lung, *n.* pulmo, *m.*

lunge, *n.* ictus, *m.*; plaga, *f.*

lurch, *n.*; leave in the ~, desero, destituo, [3].

lurch, *v.i.* titubo, [1].

lure, *n.* illecebra, (bait) esca, *f.*

lure, *v.t.* allicio, pellicio, [3].

lurk, *v.i.* lateo, [2]; latito, [1].

luscious, *a.* suavis, praedulcis

lust, *n.* libido, cupido, cupiditas, *f.*; appetitus, *m.*

lust for, *v.t.* concupisco, [3].

lustful, *a.* libidinosus, salax, lascivus.

lustre, *n.* splendor, *m.* (*also fig.*)

lusty, *a.* robustus, vegetus.

luxuriant, luxurious, *a.* luxuriosus; sumptuosus; *fig.* luxurians.

luxury, *n.* luxus, *m.* luxuria, *f.*

lying, *a.* mendax; fallax; vanus.

lynx, *n.* lynx, *c.*; ~-eyed, *a.* lynceus.

lyre, *n.* cithara; lyra, *f.*

lyric(al), *a.* lyricus.

....

M

....

mace, *n.* sceptrum, *nt.*

machination, *n.* dolus, *m.*; (trick) machina; ars, *f.*

machine, *n.* machina, *f.*; machinamentum, *nt.*

machinery, *n.* machinamentum, *nt.*; machinatio, *f.*

mackerel, *n.* scomber, *m.*

mad, *a.* insanus, vesanus, demens, amens.

madam, *n.* domina, era, *f.*

madden, *v.t.* mentem alieno; *fig.* furio, [1]; ad insaniam adigo, [3].

maddening, *a. fig.* furiosus; (troublesome) molestus.

madly, *ad.* insane, dementer; furiose.

madman, *n.* homo furiosus; *fig.* demens, *m.*

madness, *n.* insania; rabies; amentia, dementia, *f.*; furor, *m.*

maggot, *n.* vermiculus, termes, *m.*

magic, *a.* magicus; ~, *n.* magica ars, *f.*; veneficium, *nt.*

magician, *n.* magus, veneficus, *m.*

magistracy, *n.* magistratus, *m.*

magistrate, *n.* magistratus, *m.*

magnanimity, *n.* magnanimitas, magnitudo animi, *f.*

magnanimous, *a.* magnanimus; ~ly, *ad.* pro magnitudine animi.

magnet, *n.* magnes, *m.*

magnetic, *a.* magnes.

magnificence, *n.* magnificentia, *f.*; splendor, *m.*

magnificent, *a.* magnificus, splendidus; ~ly, *ad.* magnifice; splendide.

magnify, *v.t.* amplifico, [1].

magnitude, *n.* magnitudo, *f.*

magpie, *n.* corvus pica, *f.*

maid, *n.* (female servant) ancilla, famula, *f.*

maiden, *a.* ~ **speech,** *n.* prima oratio, *f.*

maidenhood, *n.* virginitas, *f.*

mail, *n.* (letter-carrier) tabellarius, *m.*; (coat) lorica, *f.*; thorax, *m.*

maim, *v.t.* mutilo; trunco, [1].

main, *a.* praecipuus, primus, maximus; ~**ly,** *ad.* praecipue, maxime; praesertim.

mainland, *n.* terra continens, *f.*

maintain, *v.t. & i.* affirmo, [1]; (defend) tueor, sustineo, [2]; (keep) nutrio, [4]; sustento, [1]; alo, [3]; (keep in good condition) conservo, [1].

maintenance, *n.* (support) defensio, *f.*; (means of living) alimentum, *nt.*; victus, *m.*

maize, *n.* zea, *f.*

majestic, *a.* augustus; sublimis; imperatorius.

majesty, *n.* maiestas; dignitas, sublimitas, *f.*

majority, *n.* pars maior, *f.*; plures, *m. & f. pl.*

make, *v.t.* facio, [3]; (elect) creo, [1]; (form, fabricate) conficio; fingo, [3]; (render) reddo, [3]; ~ **for,** peto, [3]; ~ **good,** resarcio, [4]; ~ **much of,** magni facio, [3]; ~ **up,** (compensate) resarcio, [4]; (resolve) decerno, [3]; (nu-

merically) expleo, [2]; (invent) fingo, [3].

maker, *n.* fabricator, *m.*; auctor, *c.*

makeshift, *a.* subitarius.

maladministration, *n.* administratio mala, *f.*

male, *a.* mas; masculinus, masculus, virilis.

male, *n.* mas, masculus, *m.*

malefactor, *n.* maleficus, *m.*

malevolence, *n.* malevolentia, malignitas, invidia, *f.*

malevolent, *a.* malevolus, malignus.

malice, *n.* malevolentia, malitia, *f.*

malicious, *a.* malevolus, malitiosus; ~**ly,** *ad.* malevolo animo, malitiose.

malign, malignant, *a.* malevolus.

malign, *v.t.* obtrecto, [1].

malleable, *a.* ductilis, mollis.

mallet, *n.* malleus, *m.*

malpractice, *n.* male facta, delicta, *nt. pl.*; maleficium, *nt.*

maltreat, *v.t.* vexo, [1]; laedo, [3].

maltreatment, *n.* iniuria, *f.*

mammal, *n.* animal, *nt.*

man, *n.* homo; vir; mas, *m.*; **a** ~, (some one) aliquis; ~ **of war,** navis longa, *f.*

man, *v.t.* (a ship) compleo, [2].

manacle, *n.* manicae, *f. pl.*; compes, *f.*

manacle, *v.t.* manicas (alicui) inicio, [3].

manage, *v.t.* administro; curo, tracto, [1]; gero, [3].; ~, *v.i.* (cope) rem prospere gero, [3].

manageable, *a.* tractabilis.

management, *n.* administratio; cura, procuratio, *f.*

manager, *n.* curator; (steward) procurator, vilicus, *m.*

mandate, *n.* mandatum, *nt.*

mandatory, *a.* necessarius.

mane, *n.* iuba, *f.*

mange, *n.* scabies, *f.*

mangle, *v.t.* lacero, lanio, dilanio, [1].

mangle, *n.* prelum, *nt.*

mangy, *a.* scaber.

manhood, *n.* pubertas; virilitas; fortitudo, *f.*

mania, *n. fig.* insania, amentia, *f.*

maniac, *n.* homo furiosus, *m.*

manifest, *a.* manifestus, clarus, apertus, evidens; ~ly, *ad.* manifeste, aperte; evidenter.

manifest, *v.t.* declaro, [1]; ostendo, [3]; praebeo, [2].

manifestation, *n.* patefactio, *f.*

manifesto, *n.* edictum, *nt.*

manifold, *a.* multiplex; varius.

maniple, *n.* manipulus, *m.*

manipulate, *v.t.* (manibus) tracto, [1].

manipulation, *n.* tractatio, *f.*

mankind, *n.* genus humanum, *nt.*; homines, *m. pl.*

manliness, *n.* virtus, fortitudo, *f.*

manly, *a.* virilis; strenuus; fortis.

manner, *n.* modus, *m.*; ratio, consuetudo, *f.*; ~s, mores, *m. pl.*; **good** ~s, urbanitas, *f.*; **bad** ~s, rusticitas, *f.*

mannerism, *n.* mala affectatio, *f.*

manoeuvre, *n. (mil.)* decursus, *m.*; *fig.* artificium, *nt.*

manoeuvre, *v.i. (mil.)* decurro, [3]; (plot) machinor, [1].

mansion, *n.* domus, sedes, *f.*

manslaughter, *n.* homicidium, *nt.*

manual, *a.* manualis; ~ **labour,** *n.* opera, *f.*

manufacture, *n.* fabrica, *f.*; opificium, *nt.*

manufacture, *v.t.* fabricor, [1]; fabrefacio, [3].

manufacturer, *n.* fabricator, *m.*, opifex, *c.*

manumission, *n.* manumissio, *f.*

manumit, *v.t.* manumitto, [3].

manure, *n.* stercus, *nt.*; fimus, *m.*

manure, *v.i.* stercoro, [1].

manuscript, *n.* codex, *m.*

many, *a.* multi; plerique; complures; **as ~ as,** quot . . . tot; **how ~,** quot; **so ~,** tot; ~ **ways,** multifarie.

map, *n.* tabula geographica, *f.*

map, *v.t.* (out) designo, [1].

maple, *n.* acer, *nt.*

maple, *a.* acernus.

mar, *v.t.* foedo, vitio, [1]; corrumpo, [3].

marauder, *n.* praedator, *m.*

marauding, *n.* praedatio, *f.*

marble, *n.* marmor, *nt.*; ~, *a.* marmoreus.

March, *n.* (month) Martius, *m.*

march, *n.* iter, *nt.*; (step) gradus, *m.*

march, *v.i.* iter facio, incedo, gradior, proficiscor, [3]; ~ **in**, ingredior, [3]; ~ **off**, recedo, [3]; ~, *v.t.* exercitum duco, [3].

mare, *n.* equa, *f.*

margin, *n.* margo, *c.*

marginal, *a.* in margine positus, margini ascriptus.

marine, *a.* marinus, maritimus.

mariner, *n.* nauta, *m.*

marital, *a.* conubialis.

maritime, *a.* maritimus.

marjoram, *n.* amaracum, origanum, *nt.*

mark, *n.* nota, *f.*; signum; (brand) stigma; (impression) vestigium, *nt.*; (to shoot at) scopus, *m.*; (of a stripe) vibex; (of a wound) cicatrix, *f.*; *fig.* indicium, *nt.*

mark, *v.t.* noto, signo, [1]; (observe) animadverto, [3]; (with a pencil, *etc.*) designo, [1]; ~ **out**, metor, [1]; metior, [4].

market, *n.* (place) forum, *nt.*; mercatus, *m.*

market-day, *n.* nundinae, *f. pl.*

marketing, *n.* emptio, mercatura, *f.*

market-place, *n.* forum, *nt.*

marksman, *n.* iaculator, *m.*

marriage, *n.* conubium, coniugium, matrimonium, *nt.*; nuptiae, *f. pl.*

marriage, *a.* nuptialis, coniugalis, conubialis.

marriageable, *a.* nubilis, adultus.

married, *a.* (of a woman) nupta; (of a man) maritus.

marrow, *n.* (of bones) medulla, *f.*

marry, *v.t.* (of a priest) conubio iungo; (as the man) uxorem duco; (as the woman) viro nubo, [3].

marsh, *n.* palus, *f.*

marshal, *v.t.* dispono, [3].

marshy, *a.* paluster, paludosus.

martial, *a.* bellicosus, ferox; militaris, bellicus; **court** ~, *n.* castrense iudicium, *nt.*

martyr, *n.* martyr, *c.*

marvel, *n.* res mira, *f.*; mirum, *nt.*; miraculum, *nt.*

marvellous, *a.* mirus, mirabilis; ~**ly**, *ad.* mire; mirabiliter.

masculine, *a.* masculus; mas; virilis.

mask, *n.* persona, larva, *f.*; *fig.* praetextum, *nt.*

mask, *v.t.* personam induo, [3]; *fig.* dissimulo, [1].

mason, *n.* lapicida, structor, *m.*

masonry, *n.* saxa, *nt. pl.*

mass, *n.* moles, massa; immensa copia, *f.*; ingens pondus, *nt.*; (of people) multitudo, turba, *f.*

massacre, *n.* caedes, trucidatio *f.*; ~, *v.t.* trucido, [1].

massive, *a.* solidus.

mast, *n.* (of a ship) malus, *m.*

master, *n.* dominus, erus; (teacher) magister, praeceptor, *m.*; *fig.* potens, compos (*with gen.*) *c.*; (expert) peritus, *m.*

master, *v.t.* supero, [1]; vinco, [3]; dominor, [1]; (learn) perdisco, [3].

masterly, *a.* (of an artist) artificiosus.

masterpiece, *n.* opus palmare, *nt.*

master-stroke, *n.* artificium singulare, *nt.*

mastery, *n.* dominatus, *m.*; imperium, *nt.*; (skill) peritia, *f.*

mat, *n.* matta, teges, *f.*; stragulum, *nt.*

match, *n.* (marriage) nuptiae, *f. pl.*; (contest) certamen, *nt.*; (an equal) par, compar, *c.*

match, *v.t.* compono, [3]; adaequo, exaequo; ~, *v.i.* (be suitable) quadro, [1].

matchless, *a.* incomparabilis, eximius, singularis.

matchmaker, *n.* conciliator (conciliatrix) nuptiarum, *m.* (& *f.*).

mate, *n.* socius, collega, *m.*; coniunx, *c.*

mate, *v.i.* (of animals) coniungor, [3].

material, *a.* corporeus; *fig.* (important) magni momenti.

material, *n.* materia, *f.*; (cloth) textile, *nt.*; ~**s,** *pl.* res necessariae, *f. pl.*

maternal, *a.* maternus.

maternity, *n.* condicio matris, *f.*

mathematical, *a.* mathematicus.

mathematician, *n.* mathematicus, *m.*

mathematics, *n.* mathematica, *f.*

matricide, *n.* (murder) matricidium, *nt.*; (murderer) matricida, *c.*

matrimonial, *a.* coniugalis, conubialis, nuptialis.

matted, *a.* concretus.

matter, *n.* (substance) materia; (affair, business, *etc.*) res, *f.*; negotium; (purulent) pus, *nt.*; sanies, *f.*; **no** ~, nihil interest.

matter, *v.i. impers.* **it does not** ~, nihil interest, nihil refert.

matting, *n.* tegetes, *f. pl.*

mattress, *n.* culcita, *f.*

mature, *a.* maturus; tempestivus; ~, *v.t. & i.* maturo, [1].

maturity, *n.* maturitas; aetas matura, *f.*

maul, *v.t.* mulco, [1].

mausoleum, *n.* mausoleum, *nt.*

mawkish, *a.* (of taste) putidus; fastidiosus; ~**ly,** *ad.* putide, fastidiose.

maxim, *n.* praeceptum, *nt.*; sententia, *f.*

May, *n.* (month) Maius, *m.*

may, *v.i.* possum; licet.

maybe, *ad.* forsitan, forsan.

mayor, *n.* praefectus urbanus, *m.*

maze, *n.* labyrinthus, *m.*; ambages, *f. pl.*

me, *pr.* me; **to ~**, mihi.

meadow, *n.* pratum, *nt.*

meagre, *a.* macer; *fig.* aridus; ieiunus; exilis.

meal, *n.* (flour) farina, *f.*; (food) cibus, *m.*; (dinner, *etc.*) epulae, *f. pl.*

mealtime, *n.* cibi hora, *f.*

mean, *a.* (middle) medius; (moderate) mediocris; (low) humilis; (miserly) avarus; (unkind) malignus; *fig.* sordidus; vilis; **in the ~time**, interea.

mean, *n.* medium, *nt.*; (manner) modus, *m.*; ratio, *f.*; **by all ~s**, quam maxime; **by no ~s**, nullo modo.

mean, *ut. & i.* volo; mihi volo, *ir.*; cogito; significo, [1].

meander, *n.* cursus; flexus, *m.*

meander, *ui.* labor, [3]; sinuor, [1].

meaning, *n.* significatio, *f.*; animus, sensus, *m.*

meanness, *n.* humilitas; *fig.* avaritia; ignobilitas, *f.*

means, *n.* (method) modus, *m.*, ratio, *f.*

meanwhile, *ad.* interea, interim.

measurable, *a.* quod metiri potes, mensurabilis.

measure, *n.* mensura, *f.*; (of land, liquids) modus, *m.*; **~s**, *pl.* consilium, *nt.*; **in some ~**, aliquatenus.

measure, *ut.* metior, [4]; metor, [1]; **~out**, admetior, [4].

measurement, *n.* mensura, *f.*

meat, *n.* caro, *f.*

mechanical, *a.* mechanicus; **~ly**, *ad.* mechanica quadam arte.

mechanic, *n.* opifex, *c.*, faber, *m.*

mechanics, mechanica ars; machinalis scientia, *f.*

mechanism, *n.* machinatio; mechanica ratio, *f.*

medal, medallion, *n.* nomisma, *nt.*

meddle, *ui.* (with) me immisceo, [2]; intervenio, [4].

mediate, *ui.* intercedo [3].

mediation, *n.* intercessio, *f.*

mediator, *n.* intercessor, conciliator, *m.*

medical, *a.* medicus, medicinalis.

medicinal, *a.* medicus; salutaris.

medicine, *n.* (science) medicina, *f.*; (remedy) medicamentum, medicamen, *nt.*

mediocre, *a.* mediocris, modicus.

mediocrity, *n.* mediocritas, *f.*

meditate, *ui.* meditor, cogito, [1].

meditation, *n.* meditatio, cogitatio, *f.*

meditative, *a.* cogitabundus.

Mediterranean, *n.* mare mediterraneum *or* internum *or* medium, *nt.*

medium, *n.* (middle) medium, *nt.*; (mode, method) modus, *m.*, ratio, *f.*; (agent) conciliator, *m.*

medium, *a.* mediocris.

medley, *n.* farrago, *f.*

meek, *a.* mitis; *fig.* summissus, humilis; **~ly**, *ad.* summisse.

meekness, *n.* animus summissus, *m.*

meet, *v.t.* obvenio, [4]; occurro, [3]; obviam eo, [4] (*all with dat.*); congredior, [3] (*with cum with abl.*); **~ with**, offendo, [3]; (bad) subeo, [4]; patior, [3]; (good) nanciscor, [3].

meeting, *n.* congressio, *f.*; congressus, *m.*; (assembly) conventus, *m.*

melancholy, *n.* tristitia, maestitia, *f.*

melancholy, *a.* melancholicus, maestus, tristis.

mellow, *a.* maturus, mitis.

mellow, *v.i.* maturesco, [3].

melodious, *a.* canorus, numerosus.

melody, *n.* melos, *nt.*; modulatio, *f.*; numerus, *m.*

melt, *v.t.* liquefacio, solvo, dissolvo, [3]; **~**, *v.i.* liquefio, *ir.*, liquesco, [3].

membrane, *n.* membrana, *f.*

memento, *n.* monumentum, *nt.*

memoir, *n.* commentarius, *m.*

memorable, *a.* memorabilis, notabilis, memoria dignus.

memorial, *n.* monumentum, *nt.*

memory, *n.* memoria, *f.*

menace, *n. & v.t.*, *v.* **threat, threaten**.

menagerie, *n.* vivarium, *nt.*

mend, *v.t.* emendo, [1]; corrigo, [3]; reparo, [1]; (clothes) sarcio, [4]; **~**, *v.i.* melior fio, *ir.*

menial, *a.* servilis; sordidus.

mental, *a.* mentis, animi (*gen. sing.*); mente conceptus, internus; **~ly**, *ad.* mente, animo.

mention, *n.* commemoratio, mentio, *f.*

mention, *v.t.* commemoro, [1]; mentionem facio (*with gen.*), [3]; **not to ~**, silentio praetereo, [4].

mercenary, *a.* mercenarius, venalis; **~**, *n.* miles conductus, *m.*

merchandise, *n.* merx; (trade) mercatura, *f.*

merchant, *n.* mercator, negotiator, *m.*

merciful, *a.* misericors, clemens.

merciless, *a.* immisericors, inclemens; immitis, durus.

mercury, *n.* (metal) argentum vivum, *nt.*

mercy, *n.* misericordia, clementia, indulgentia, *f.*; **at the ~ of**, in manu (*with gen.*)

mere, *a.* merus; **~ly**, *ad.* tantummodo, solummodo, nihil nisi.

merge, *v.t.* confundo, [3]; misceo, [2]; **~**, *v.i.* commisceor (*cum with abl.*).

merit, *n.* meritum, *nt.*; virtus, *f.*

merit, *v.t.* mereo, demereor, promereo, [2].

merry, *a.* hilaris, festivus.

merrymaking, *n.* festivitas, *f.*

mesh, *n.* (of a net) macula, *f.*

mesmerize, *v.t.* consopio, [4].

mess, *n.* (*mil.*) contubernium, *nt.*; (dirt) squalor, *m.*; *fig.* (confusion) turba, *f.*

mess about, *v.i.* ludo, [3].

message, *n.* nuntius, *m.*

messenger, *n.* nuntius; (letter-carrier) tabellarius, *m.*

metal, *n.* metallum, *nt.*

metallic, *a.* metallicus.

metamorphose, *v.t.* transformo, transfiguro, [1].

metamorphosis, *n.* transfiguratio, *f.*

metaphor, *n.* translatio, *f.*

metaphorical, *a.* translaticius; ~ly, *ad.* per translationem.

meteor, *n.* fax caelestis, *f.*

method, *n.* ratio, via, *f.*

methodical, *a.* dispositus, ratione et via factus; ~ly, *ad.* ratione et via; disposite.

meticulous, *a.* curiosus, diligens.

metre, *n.* metrum, *nt.*; numerus, *m.*; versus, *m.*

metrical, *a.* metricus.

mettle, *n.* vigor, animus, *m.*; (courage) virtus, fortitudo; magnanimitas, *f.*

mid, *a.* medius.

midday, *n.* meridies, *m.*; meridianum tempus, *nt.*; ~, *a.* meridianus.

middle, *a.* medius.

middle, *n.* medium, *nt.*; (waist) medium corpus, *nt.*

middling, *a.* mediocris; modicus.

midnight, *n.* media nox, *f.*

midst, *n.* medium, *nt.*; **in the ~ of,** inter (*with acc.*).

midsummer, *n.* media aestas, summa aestas, *f.*

midway, *n.* media via, *f.*

midwife, *n.* obstetrix, *f.*

midwinter, *n.* media hiems, *f.*

mien, *n.* vultus, *m.*; os, *nt.*; species, *f.*

might, *n.* vis, potestas, potentia, *f.*; **with all one's ~,** summa ope.

might, I ~, *v.i.* possem.

mighty, *a.* potens, pollens, validus; magnus.

migrate, *v.i.* migro, transmigro, [1]; abeo, *ir.*

migration, *n.* migratio, peregrinatio, *f.*

mild, *a.* mitis, lenis; placidus; clemens; mansuetus; ~ly, *ad.* leniter, clementer, placide, mansuete.

mildew, *a.* (mould) mucor, situs, *m.*

mildness, *n.* clementia, lenitas, mansuetudo, *f.*

mile, *n.* mille passus, *m. pl.*

milestone, *n.* miliarium, *nt.*

militant, *a.* pugnax.

military, *a.* militaris; ~, *n.* milites, *m. pl.*

milk, *n.* lac, *nt.*

milk, *v.t.* mulgeo, [2].

milky, *a.* lacteus, lactans; ~ **way**, *n.* orbis lacteus, *m.*; via lactea, *f.*

mill, *n.* mola, *f.*; pistrinum, *nt.*

miller, *n.* molitor, *m.*

millet, *n.* milium, *nt.*

million, *n.* decies centena milia, *f.*

millionaire, *n.* homo praedives, *m.*

millstone, *n.* mola, *f.*; molaris, *m.*

mime, *n.* (play and player) mimus, *m.*

mimic, *n.* mimus, *m.*

mimic, *v.t.* imitor, [1].

mimicry, *n.* imitatio, *f.*

mince, *v.t.* concido, [3].

mind, *n.* animus, *m.*; mens, *f.*; ingenium, *nt.*; sensus, *m.*; (desire) desiderium, *nt.*; (recollection) voluntas, cupido, *f.*; (recollection) memoria, *f.*

mind, *v.t.* (look after) curo, [1]; (regard) respicio, [3]; (consider) animadverto, [3]; considero, [1]; **I don't ~**, nihil moror, [1].

mindful, *a.* attentus, diligens; memor.

mine, *n.* fodina, *f.*; metallum, *nt.*; (mil.) cuniculus, *m.*

mine, *v.t. & i.* effodio, [3]; (mil.) cuniculos ago, [3].

mine, *a.* meus.

miner, *n.* (of metals) metallicus, *m.*

mineral, *n.* metallum, *nt.*; ~, *a.* metallicus.

mingle, *v.t.* misceo, commisceo, [2]; confundo, [3]; ~, *v.i.* commisceor, [2].

minimum, *n.* minimum, *nt.*

minion, *n.* satelles, *m.*

minister, *n.* minister; (of state) rerum publicarum administer, *m.*

minor, *n.* pupillus, *m.*; pupilla, *f.*

minority, *n.* minor pars, *f.*; (under age) pupillaris aetas, *f.*

minstrel, *n.* fidicen, *m.*

mint, *n.* moneta, *f.*; (plant) menta, *f.*

mint, *v.t.* cudo, [3]; signo, [1].

minute, *n.* punctum temporis, *nt.*

minute, *a.* minutus, exiguus.

miracle, *n.* miraculum, *nt.*

miraculous, *a.* prodigiosus, mirabilis; ~**ly**, *ad.* divinitus.

mirror, *n.* speculum, *nt.*

mirth, *n.* hilaritas; laetitia; festivitas, *f.*

misadventure, *n.* infortunium, *nt.*

misapprehension, *n.* falsa conceptio, *f.*; error, *m.*

misbehave, *v.i.* indecore se gerere, [3].

misbehaviour, *n.* morum pravitas, *f.*

miscalculate, *v.t.* erro, [1]; fallor, [3].

miscalculation, *n.* error, *m.*

miscarriage, *n.* (in childbirth) abortus; *fig.* malus successus, *m.*

miscarry, *v.i. fig.* parum succedo, [3].

miscellaneous, *a.* promiscuus, miscellaneus.

miscellany, *n.* coniectanea, miscellanea, *nt. pl.*

mischief, *n.* (harm, loss) incommodum, damnum; (injury, wrong) maleficium, malum, *nt.*; (nuisance) pestis, *f.*

mischievous, *a.* maleficus; noxius, funestus.

misconception, *n.* falsa opinio, *f.*

misconduct, *n.* delictum, peccatum, *nt.*

misconstrue, *v.t.* male *or* perverse interpretor, [1].

misdeed, *n.* delictum, peccatum, *nt.*; scelus, *nt.*

misdemeanour, *n.* vitium, *nt.*

miser, *n.* avarus, *m.*

miserable, *a.* miser, miserabilis, miserandus, aerumnosus.

miserly, *a.* avarus.

misery, *n.* miseria, *f.*; aerumnae, *f. pl.*; angor, *m.*

misfortune, *n.* adversa fortuna, calamitas, *f.*; infortunium, incommodum, *nt.*

misgivings, have ~, **parum confido, diffido,** [3].

misguided, *a. fig.* demens.

mishap, *n.* incommodum, *nt.*

misinterpret, *v.t.* male interpretor, [1].

misinterpretation, *n.* falsa interpretatio, *f.*

misjudge, *v.t.* male iudico, [1].

mislay, *v.t.* amitto, [3].

mislead, *v.t.* decipio, fallo, [3].

mismanage, *v.t.* male gero, [3].

misnomer, *n.* falsum nomen, *nt.*

misplace, *v.t.* alieno loco pono, [3].

misrepresent, *v.t.* perverse interpretor; calumnior, [1]; detorqueo, [2].

miss, *n.* error, *m.*; (loss) damnum, *nt.*; (failure) malus successus, *m.*

miss, *v.t. & i.* (pass over) omitto, [3]; (one's aim) non attingo, [3]; (be disappointed) de spe decido, [3]; (not find) reperire non possum, *ir.*; (feel the loss of) desidero, [1]; careo, [2] *(with abl.)*.

misshapen, *a.* deformis, pravus.

missile, *n.* telum, missile, *nt.*

mission, *n.* legatio; missio, *f.*; (instructions) mandatum, *nt.*

mist, *n.* nebula; caligo, *f.*

mistake, *n.* erratum, mendum, vitium, *nt.*; error, *m.*

mistake, *v.t.* male interpretor, [1].

mistaken, *a.* falsus; be ~, erro, [1].

mistletoe, *n.* viscum, *nt.*

mistress, *n.* domina, era; (sweetheart) amica; (teacher) magistra, *f.*

mistrust, *n.* diffidentia, suspicio, *f.*

mistrust, *v.i.* diffido, [3]; suspicor, [1].

mistrustful, *a.* diffidens.

misty, *a.* nebulosus, caliginosus; *fig.* obscurus.

misunderstand, *v.t.* perperam intellego, [3].

misunderstanding, *n.* error, *m.*; (disagreement) offensa, offensio, *f.*

misuse, *v.t.* abutor, [3] (*with abl.*).

misuse, *n.* abusus, *m.*; (ill-treatment) iniuria, *f.*

mitigate, *v.t.* mitigo, levo, [1]; lenio, [4]; remitto, [3]; extenuo, [1].

mitre, *n.* mitra, *f.*

mix, *v.t.* misceo, commisceo, permisceo, [2]; ~ **up,** admisceo, [2]; ~ **with,** (socially) me immisceo, [2].

mixed, *a.* mixtus, promiscuus, confusus.

mixture, *n.* (act and result) mixtura, *f.*; (hotchpotch) farrago, *f.*

moan, *v.i.* gemo, ingemisco, [3].

moan, *n.* gemitus, *m.*

moat, *n.* fossa, *f.*

mob, *n.* turba, *f.*; vulgus, *nt.*

mobile, *a.* mobilis, expeditus.

mobility, *n.* mobilitas, *f.*

mock, *v.t. & i.* ludo, [3]; ludificor, [1]; irrideo, [2].

mock, *a.* fictus, fucatus, simulatus.

mockery, *n.* irrisio, *f.*; irrisus, *m.*

mode, *n.* modus, *m.*; ratio, *f.*; (fashion) usus, *m.*

model, *n.* exemplar, exemplum, *nt.*

model, *v.t.* formo; delineo, [1].

moderate, *a.* moderatus; mediocris; modicus; ~**ly,** *ad.* moderate; modice; mediocriter.

moderate, *v.t.* moderor, tempero, [1]; (restrain) coerceo, [2].

moderation, *n.* moderatio; temperantia, modestia, *f.*

modern, *a.* recens; hodiernus.

modest, *a.* (moderate) mediocris, modicus; (not proud) verecundus; modestus; ~**ly,** *ad.* modeste, verecunde, mediocriter.

modesty, *n.* pudor, *m.*; modestia, pudicitia, verecundia, *f.*

modification, *n.* immutatio, *f.*

modify, *v.t.* immuto, [1].

moist, *a.* umidus, uvidus, udus, madidus.

moisten, *v.t.* umecto, irroro, rigo, [1].

moisture, *n.* umor, *m.*; uligo, *f.*

molar, *n.* molaris, *m.*

mole, *n.* (massive structure, pile) moles, pila, *f.*; (earthwork) agger, *m.*; (on the body) naevus, *m.*; (animal) talpa, *c.*

molest, *v.t.* vexo, sollicito, [1].

molten, *a.* fusus, fusilis; liquidus.

moment, *n.* (of time) punctum temporis; (importance) momentum, pondus, *nt.*; (opportunity) occasio, *f.*; **in a** ~, statim; **of great** ~, magni ponderis; **this** ~, ad tempus.

momentarily, *ad.* subito.

momentary, *a.* brevis, brevissimus, subitus.

momentum, *n.* impetus, *m.*

momentous, *a.* magni momenti.

monarch, *n.* rex, *m.;* princeps, *c.*

monarchy, *n.* regnum, *nt.*

Monday, *n.* dies lunae, *m.*

money, *n.* pecunia, *f.;* argentum, *nt.;* nummus, *m.*

moneylender, *n.* faenerator, *m.*

monitor, *n.* admonitor *m.*

monkey, *n.* simius, *m.;* simia, *f.*

monologue, *n.* soliloquium, *nt.*

monopolize, *v.i.* monopolium exerceo, [2]; *fig.* solus habeo, [2].

monopoly, *n.* monopolium, *nt.*

monotonous, *a.* *fig.* continuus; nulla varietate delectans.

monster, *n.* monstrum; portentum, prodigium, *nt.* ~

monstrous, *a.* monstruosus, portentosus, prodigiosus.

month, *n.* mensis, *m.*

monthly, *a.* menstruus.

monument, *n.* monumentum; (tomb) mausoleum, *nt.*

monumental, *a.* monumentalis.

mood, *n.* animi affectus, habitus, *m.,* voluntas, *f.*

moody, *a.* morosus; tristis.

moon, *n.* luna, *f.*

moonlight, *n.* lunae lumen, *nt.;* **by** ~, per lunam.

moor, *n.* loca patentia et ericis obsita, *nt. pl.*

moor, *v.t.* (a ship) navem religo, [1].

mop, *n.* peniculus, *m.;* ~, *v.t.* detergeo, [2].

mope, *v.i.* tristis sum.

moral, *a.* moralis; qui ad mores pertinet; (virtuous) integer, honestus.

morality, *n.* mores, *m. pl.;* (virtue) virtus, *f.;* (duty) officium, *nt.*

morals, *n.* mores, *m. pl.;* instituta, *nt. pl.*

morbid, *a.* morbidus, morbosus.

more, *a.* plus, maior; ~, *ad.* plus, magis; amplius; ultra; ~ **and** ~, magis et magis; ~ **than enough,** plus satis; **nothing** ~, nihil amplius.

moreover, *ad.* praeterea, ultra.

morning, *n.* mane, *nt. indecl.;* matutinum tempus, *nt.;* **early** ~, prima lux, *f.;* **good** ~, *i.* salve! (when parting) ave!

morning, *a.* matutinus.

morose, *a.* morosus, difficilis, serverus.

morsel, *n.* offa, *f.;* frustum, *nt.*

mortal, *a.* mortalis; (deadly) mortifer, letifer, letalis; *fig.* (of an enemy) infensissimus.

mortal, *n.* homo, *c.;* ~**s,** *pl.* mortales, *m. pl.*

mortality, *n.* mortalitas; mors; pestis, *f.*

mortar, *n.* mortarium, *nt.*

mortgage, *n.* hypotheca, *f*; pignus, *nt.*; ~, *v.t.* pignori oppono, [3].

mosaic, *n.* tessellatum (opus), *nt.*; ~, *a.* tessellatus.

mosquito, *n.* culex, *m.*

moss, *n.* muscus, *m.*

mossy, *a.* muscosus.

most, *a.* plurimus, maximus, plerique.

most, *ad.* maxime, plurimum; ~**ly,** *ad.* (usually) plerumque; vulgo.

moth, *n.* blatta, tinea, *f.*

mother, *n.* mater; genetrix, *f.*

mother-in-law, *n.* socrus, *f.*

mother-of-pearl, *n.* concha Persica, *f.*

motherhood, *n.* condicio matris, *f.*

motherless, *a.* matre orbus.

motherly, *a.* maternus.

motion, *n.* motio, *f.*; motus, *m.*; (proposal) rogatio, *f.*

motionless, *a.* immotus, immobilis, fixus.

motivate, *v.t.* incito, [1].

motive, *n.* causa, ratio, *f.*; incitamentum, *n.*

motto, *n.* sententia, *f.*; praeceptum, *nt.*

mould, *n.* (for casting) forma, *f.*; (mustiness) mucor, situs, *m.*

mould, *v.t.* formo; fingo; (knead) subigo, [3].

moulder, *v.i.* putresco, dilabor, [3].

mouldy, *a.* mucidus; situ corruptus; **go** ~, putresco, [3].

moult, *v.i.* plumas exuo, [3].

mound, *n.* tumulus, agger, *m.*; moles, *f.*

mount, *v.t. & i.* scando, ascendo, [3]; supero, [1]; (rise) sublime feror, [3]; subvolo, [1]; (get on a horse) equum conscendo, [3].

mountain, *n.* mons, *m.*

mountaineer, *n.* homo montanus, *m.*

mountainous, *a.* montuosus, montanus.

mounted, *a.* (on horseback) eques.

mourn, *v.t. & i.* lugeo; maereo, doleo, [2]; lamentor, [1].

mourner, *n.* plorator; pullatus, *m.*

mournful, *a.* luctuosus, lugubris; maestus; tristis, lamentabilis, flebilis; ~**ly,** *ad.* maeste; flebiliter.

mourning, *n.* luctus, maeror, *m.*; (clothes) vestis lugubris, *f.*; **be in** ~, lugeo, [2]; **go into** ~, vestitum muto, [1].

mouse, *n.* mus, *m.*

mouse-hole, *n.* cavum (muris), *nt.*

mousetrap, *n.* muscipulum, *nt.*

mouth, *n.* os, *nt.*; rictus, *m.*; (of a bird) rostrum, *nt.*; (of a bottle) lura, *f.*; (of a river) ostium, *nt.*

mouthful, *n.* buccella, *f.*

mouthpiece, *n. fig.* (speaker) interpres, *c.*; orator *m.*

movable, *a.* mobilis.

move, *v.t.* moveo, [2]; (also *fig.*); ~, *v.i.* moveor, [2]; feror, [3]; (change dwelling, *etc.*) migro, [1]; ~ **on,** progredior, [3].

move, *n.* motus, *m.*; *fig.* artificium, *nt.*

movement, *n.* motus, *m.*

moving, *a. fig.* flebilis, miserabilis; ~**ly,** *ad.* flebiliter.

mow, *v.t.* meto, [3].

mower, *n.* faenisex, *m.*; messor, *m.*

much, *a.* multus; ~, *ad.* multum; (with comparative) multo; **as** ~ **as,** tantus ... quantus; tantum ... quantum; **how** ~, quantus; quantum; **so** ~, tantus; tantum; **too** ~, nimius; (*ad.*) nimis; **very** ~, plurimus; plurimum.

muck, *n.* stercus, *nt.*

mud, *n.* caenum, lutum, *nt.*; limus, *m.*

muddle, *v.t.* turbo; perturbo, [1].

muddle, *n.* confusio, turba, *f.*

muddy, *a.* lutosus, lutulentus; limosus, caenosus; (troubled) turbidus.

muffle, *v.t.* obvolvo, [3].

mug, *n.* poculum, *nt.*, v. **cup.**

muggy, *a.* umidus.

mulberry, *n.* morum, *nt.*; ~ **tree,** *n.* morus, *f.*

mule, *n.* mulus, *m.*; mula, *f.*

muleteer, *n.* mulio, *m.*

multiple, *a.* multiplex.

multiplication, *n.* multiplicatio, *f.*

multiply, *v.t.* multiplico, [1]; ~, *v.i.* cresco, [3]; augeor, [2].

multitude, *n.* multitudo; turba, plebs, *f.*; vulgus, *nt.*

mumble, *v.i.* murmuro, musso, [1].

munch, *v.t.* manduco, [1]; mando, [3].

mundane, *a.* mundanus.

municipal, *a.* municipalis.

municipality, *a.* municipium, *nt.*

munificence, *n.* munificentia, largitas, *f.*

murder, *n.* caedes, *f.*; homicidium, *nt.*

murder, *v.t.* neco, trucido, obtrunco, [1].

murderer, *n.* homicida, *c.*; sicarius, *m.*

murderous, *a. fig.* sanguinarius, cruentus.

murky, *a.* caliginosus, tenebrosus, obscurus.

murmur, *n.* murmur, *nt.*; susurrus, *m.*; fremitus, *m.*; (complaint) questus, *m.*; querela, *f.*

murmur, *v.t. & i.* murmuro, musso, mussito, susurro, *m.*; fremo, [3]; (complain) queror, [3].

muscle, *n.* musculus; lacertus; torus; *m.*

muscular, a. musculosus; lacertosus; robustus, torosus.

Muse, n. Musa, f.

muse, v.i. cogito, meditor, [1].

museum, n. museum, nt.

mushroom, n. fungus; boletus, m.; agaricum, nt.

music, n. (art) musica, f.; (of instruments and voices) cantus; concentus, m.

musical, a. musicus; (tuneful) canorus.

musician, n. musicus, m.

muslin, n. sindon, f.

mussel, n. (shell-fish) mytilus, m.; conchylium, nt.

must, v.i. necesse est; I ~, debeo, [2]; oportet me (with inf.), [2].

mustard, n. sinapi, nt.; sinapis, f.

muster, v.t. colligo, [1]; fig. (up) colligo, [3]; ~, v.i. convenio, [4].

muster, n. **pass ~,** approbor, [1].

musty, a. mucidus.

mute, a. mutus, tacitus; ~ly, ad. tacite, silenter.

mutilate, v.t. mutilo, trunco, [1].

mutilation, n. mutilatio, detruncatio, f.

mutineer, n. seditiosus; homo turbulentus, m.

mutinous, a. seditiosus, turbulentus.

mutiny, n. seditio; tumultus, m.; ~, v.i. tumultuor, [1].

mutter, v.t. & i. murmuro, musso, mussito, [1]; ~, n. murmur, nt.; murmuratio, f.

mutton, n. ovilla (caro), f.

mutual, a. mutuus; ~ly, ad. mutuo, invicem.

muzzle, n. capistrum, nt.; ~, v.t. capistro, [1], constringo, [3].

my, pn. meus; ~ **own,** proprius.

myriad, n. decem milia, nt. pl.

myrtle, n. myrtus, f.

myrtle, a. myrteus.

myself, pn. ipse, ego; I ~, egomet.

mysterious, a. arcanus; occultus; mysticus; ~ly, ad. occulte.

mystery, n. mysterium, arcanum, nt.; fig. res occultissima, f.

mystical, a. mysticus

mystify, v.t. ludificor, [1]; fallo, [3].

myth, n. fabula, f.

mythical, a. fabulosus.

mythological, a. mythologicus.

mythology, n. mythologia, f.

N

nab, v.t. prehendo, [3].

nag, v.t. sollicito, [1].

Naiad, n. Naias, f.

nail, n. unguis; (of metal) clavus, m.

nail, *v.t.* clavum pango *or* defigo, [3].

naïve, *a.* ingenuus, simplex.

naïvety, *n.* ingenuitas, simplicitas, *f.*

naked, *a.* nudus, apertus; (of a sword) strictus.

nakedness, *n.* nuditas, *f.*

name, *n.* nomen, vocabulum, *nt.* appellatio; *fig.* (reputation) fama; celebritas, *f.*; **by ~**, nominatim.

name, *v.t.* nomino, appello, nuncupo, [1]; (mention) mentionem facio, [3].

nameless, *a.* sine nomine, nominis expers.

namely, *ad.* scilicet, videlicet.

namesake, *n.* cognominis, eodem nomine dictus, *m.*

nap, *n.* somnus brevis, *m.*; (of cloth) villus, *m.*; **take a ~**, obdormisco, [3]; (at noon) meridior, [1].

nape, *n.* **~ of the neck**, cervix, *f.*

napkin, *n.* (serviette) mappa, *f.*; (little towel) mantele, *nt.*

narcotic, *a.* somnificus, somnifer; **~**, *n.* medicamentum somnificum, *nt.*

narrate, *v.t.* narro, enarro, [1].

narration, narrative, *n.* narratio; expositio, *f.*

narrator, *n.* narrator, *m.*

narrow, *a.* angustus; artus; **~ly**, *ad.* (with difficulty) aegre.

narrow, *v.t.* coarto, [1]; contraho, [3].

narrow-minded, *a.* animi angusti *or* parvi.

narrowness, *n.* angustiae, *f. pl.*

nastiness, *n.* foeditas; obscenitas, *f.*

nasty, *a.* (foul) foedus; obscenus; (ill-natured) malignus.

nation, *n.* gens, natio, *f.*; (as political body) populus, *m.*

national, *a.* popularis.

nationality, *n.* totum populi corpus, *nt.*

native, *a.* nativus, vernaculus.

native, *n.* indigena, *m.*

native land, *n.* patria, *f.*

natural, *a.* naturalis; nativus, innatus; proprius; *fig.* sincerus; simplex; **~ly**, *ad.* naturaliter; (unaffectedly) simpliciter; (of its own accord) sponte; (of course) plane.

naturalist, *n.* rerum naturalium investigator, *m.*

naturalization, *n.* civitatis donatio, *f.*

naturalize, *v.t.* aliquem civitate dono, [1].

nature, *n.* natura, *f.*; (natural disposition) indoles, *f.*, ingenium, *nt.*; (peculiarity) proprietas, *f.*; (universe) mundus, *m.*

naughtiness, *n.* malitia, petulantia, *f.*

naughty, *a.* improbus, malus.

nausea, *n.* (seasickness, feeling sick) nausea, *f.*; (squeamishness) fastidium, *nt.*

nauseate, *v.t.* fastidium pario, [3]; satio, [1].

nautical, *a.* nauticus.

naval, *a.* navalis, maritimus.

navel, *n.* umbilicus, *m.*

navigable, *a.* navigabilis.

navigate, *v.t.* guberno, [1]; ~, *v.i.* navigo, [1].

navigation, *n.* navigatio, *f.*

navigator, *n.* nauta, navigator, *m.*

navy, *n.* classis, *f.*; copiae navales, *f. pl.*

near, *a.* propinquus, vicinus; (of relationship) proximus.

near, *ad.* prope; iuxta; proxime; ~, *pr.* ad, apud, prope, iuxta (*all with acc.*); ~ **at hand**, propinquus, in promptu; **far and** ~, longe lateque.

near, *v.t.* appropinquo, [1] (*with dat.*).

nearby, *a.* propinquus, vicinus.

nearly, *ad.* prope; fere; ferme; (almost) paene.

nearness, *n.* propinquitas; vicinia; (of relationship) propinquitas, *f.*

neat, *a.* mundus; lautus; lepidus; nitidus; concinnus, elegans.

neatness, *n.* munditia; concinnitas, *f.*

necessaries, *n. pl.* (of life) necessitates, *f. pl.*; necessaria, *nt. pl.*

necessarily, *ad.* necessario.

necessary, *a.* necessarius; **it is** ~, necesse est.

necessitate, *v.t.* cogo, [3].

necessity, *n.* necessitas; (want) egestas, necessitudo; (indispensable thing) res omnino necessaria, *f.*

neck, *n.* collum, *nt.*; cervix, *f.*; (of a bottle) collum, *nt.*

necklace, *n.* monile, *nt.*; (as ornament) torques, *c.*

nectar, *n.* nectar, *nt.*

need, *n.* (necessity) opus, *nt.*, necessitas; (want) egestas, penuria, *f.*

need, *v.t.* (require) requiro, [3]; egeo, [2] (*with abl.*); ~, *v.i.* (must) debeo, [2].

needle, *n.* acus, *f.*

needlework, *n.* opus acu factum, *nt.*

needless, *a.* minime necessarius, supervacaneus; ~**ly**, *ad.* sine causa.

needy, *a.* egens, indigens, egenus, inops.

negative, *a.* negativus.

negative, *n.* negatio; repulsa, *f.*; **answer in the** ~, nego, [1].

neglect, *v.t.* neglego; desero, praetermitto, [3].

neglect, *n.* neglegentia, incuria, *f.*; neglectus, *m.*

neglectful, *a.* neglegens.

negligence, *n.* neglegentia; incuria, *f.*

negligent, *a.* neglegens, indiligens, remissus; incuriosus; ~ly, *ad.* neglegenter, incuriose.

negligible, *a.* minimi momenti.

negotiable, *a.* mercabilis.

negotiate, *v.t.* agere, gero, [3]; ~, *v.i.* negotior, [1].

negotiation, *n.* actio, *f.*

negotiator, *n.* conciliator; (spokesman) orator, *m.*

neigh, *v.i.* hinnio, [4].

neigh, neighing, *n.* hinnitus, *m.*

neighbour, *n.* vicinus, finitimus, propinquus, *m.*

neighbourhood, *n.* vicinitas; vicinia; proximitas; propinquitas, *f.*

neighbouring, *a.* vicinus; finitimus; propinquus.

neither, *a. & pn.* neuter; ~, *c.* nec, neque; ~ . . . **nor,** nec . . . nec.

nephew, *n.* fratris *or* sororis filius, *m.*; nepos, *m.*

nerve, *n.* nervus, *m.*; *fig.* fortitudo, *f.*

nervous, *a.* nervosus; (fearful) timidus, trepidus, anxius; ~ly, *ad.* nervose; (fearfully) trepide, timide, anxie.

nervousness, *n.* anxietas, *f.*; timor, *m.*

nest, *n.* nidus, *m.*

nestle, *v.i.* recubo, [1].

net, *n.* (for hunting) rete, *nt.*; iaculum, *nt.*; plaga, *f.*; (for fishing) funda, *f.*

netting, *n.* opus reticulatum, *nt.*

nettle, *n.* urtica, *f.*

network, *n.* reticulum, *nt.*

neuter, *a.* neuter.

neutral, *a.* medius; neuter, aequus.

neutrality, *n.* aequitas, *f.*

neutralize, *v.t.* aequo; compenso, [1].

never, *ad.* nunquam; ~**more,** nunquam posthac.

nevertheless, *ad.* nihilominus, tamen, attamen.

new, *a.* novus, novellus, recens; integer.

newcomer, *n.* advena, *c.*; hospes, *m.*

newfangled, *a.* novicius.

newly, *ad.* nuper, modo; recenter.

newness, *n.* novitas, *f.*

news, *n.* res novae, *f. pl.*; (report) fama, *f.*; rumor, nuntius, *m.*

newspaper, *n.* acta diurna, *nt. pl.*

next, *a.* proximus; (of time) insequens.

next, *ad.* proxime; iuxta; (of time) deinde.

nib, *n.* (of a pen) acumen, *nt.*

nibble, *v.t.* rodo, arrodo, [3].

nice, *a.* (dainty) delicatus; (choice) exquisitus; (exact) accuratus; subtilis; (fine) bellus; (pleasant) iucundus; (amiable) suavis; ~ly, *ad.* delicate; exquisite; subtiliter; accurate; belle.

niche, *n.* loculamentum, *nt.*

nick, *n.* (cut, notch) incisura, *f.*; **in the very ~ of time**, in ipso articulo temporis.

nickname, *n.* nomen probrosum, *nt.*

niece, *n.* fratris *or* sororis filia, *f.*

niggardly, *a.* parcus, tenax; avarus.

night, *n.* nox, *f.*; **by ~**, nocte, noctu.

nightfall, *n.* **at ~**, sub noctem, primis tenebris.

nightingale, *n.* luscinia, Philomela, *f.*

nightly, *a.* nocturnus; **~**, *ad.* noctu, de nocte.

nightmare, *n.* incubo, *m.*; suppressio, *f.*

night-watch, *n.* vigilia, *f.*; (person) vigil, *m.*

nimble, *a.* pernix; agilis, mobilis.

nimbleness, *n.* pernicitas, agilitas, mobilitas, *f.*

nimbly, *ad.* perniciter.

nine, *a.* novem (*indecl.*); **~ times**, novies.

nineteen, *a.* undeviginti (*indecl.*).

nineteenth, *a.* undevicesimus.

ninetieth, *a.* nonagesimus.

ninety, *a.* nonaginta (*indecl.*).

ninth, *a.* nonus.

nip, *v.t.* vellico, [1]; (of cold) uro, [3]; **~ off**, deseco, [1].

nipple, *n.* papilla, *f.*

no, *a.* nullus; nemo; nihil (*indecl.*); **~ one**, nemo, *c.*

no, *ad.* haud, non; minime.

nobility, *n.* nobilitas, *f.*; nobiles, *m. pl.*; *fig.* magnanimitas, *f.*

noble, *a.* nobilis, *fig.* generosus; magnanimus.

noble, nobleman, *n.* vir nobilis, *m.*

nobly, *ad.* praeclare; generose.

nobody, *n.* nemo, *c.*

nocturnal, *a.* nocturnus.

nod, *n.* nutus, *m.*; **~**, *v.i.* nuto, [1]; annuo, innuo, [3]; (be drowsy) dormito, [1].

noise, *n.* strepitus, stridor; fragor; sonus, sonitus; (of voices) clamor, *m.*; **make a ~**, strepito, sono, [1]; fremo, strepo, [3].

noiseless, *a.* tacitus; silens; **~ly**, *ad.* tacite.

noisily, *ad.* cum strepitu.

noisy, *a.* tumultuosus.

nomad, *n.* vagus, *m.*

nominal, *a.* nominalis; **~ly**, *ad.* nomine, verbo.

nominate, *v.i.* nomino, designo, [1].

nomination, *n.* nominatio, designatio; (of an heir) nuncupatio, *f.*

nonchalantly, *ad.* aequo animo.

nondescript, *a.* nulli certo generi ascriptus.

none, *a. & pn.* nemo, nullus.

nones, *n.* Nonae, *f. pl.*

nonplus, *v.t.* (checkmate) ad incitas redigo, [3].

nonsense, *n.* ineptiae, nugae, *f. pl.*; ~! *i.* gerrae! fabulae! somnia! **talk** ~, absurde loquor, [3]; garrio, [4].

nonsensical, *a.* ineptus, absurdus.

nook, *n.* angulus, *m.*; latebra, *f.*

noon, *n.* meridies, *m.*

noose, *n.* laqueus, *m.*

nor, *c.* nec, neque; neve, neu.

normal, *a.* secundum normam.

normally, *ad.* ut solet.

north, *n.* septentrio, *m.*

north, northern, *a.* septentrionalis, aquilonius, boreus.

northerly, *a.* septentrionem spectans.

north pole, *n.* Arctos, *f.*

northward, *ad.* septentrionem versus.

north wind, *n.* aquilo, *m.*; boreas, *m.*

nose, *n.* nasus, *m.*; nares, *f. pl.*

nostril, *n.* naris, *f.*

not, *ad.* non; haud; minime; (in prohibitions) ne; ~ **at all**, nullo modo; ~ **yet**, nondum.

notable, *a.* notabilis, insignis.

notably, *ad.* insignite, insigniter, notabiliter; (especially) praecipue, praesertim.

notch, *n.* incisura, *f.*; ~, *v.t.* incido, [3].

note, *n.* (mark) nota, *f.*; signum, indicium, *nt.*; (writing) chirographum, *nt.*

note, *v.t.* (mark) noto, [1]; (in a book) annoto, [1]; *v.* **notice**.

notebook, *n.* commentarius, *m.* tabulae, *f. pl.*

noted, *a.* nobilis; insignis, notus; clarus, praeclarus, celeber.

noteworthy, *a.* notandus, notabilis.

nothing, *n.* nihil, *nt.* **for** ~, gratis.

notice, *n.* (noticing) animadversio, observatio, *f.*; (proclamation) edictum, *nt.*; **public** ~, proscriptio, *f.*; (placard) titulus, *m.*; **escape** ~, lateo, [2]; **give** ~, edico, [3].

notice, *v.t.* observo, [1]; animadverto, [3]; **take no** ~ **of**, ignoro, [1].

notification, *n.* denuntiatio, proscriptio, *f.*

notify, *v.t.* significo, denuntio, [1].

notion, *n.* notio, notitia; opinio, *f.*

notoriety, *n.* notitia, *f.*

notorious, *a.* (in a bad sense) famosus.

noun, *n.* nomen, *nt.*

nourish, *v.t.* nutrio, [4]; alo, [3].

nourishment, *n.* alimentum, *nt.*; cibus, *m.*

novel, *a.* novus.

novel, *n.* fabula, *f.*

novelist, *n.* fabulator, *m.*

novelty, *n.* novitas, *f.*

November, *n.* Novembris, *m.*

novice, *n.* tiro, *m.*; novicius, *m.*; novicia, *f.*

now, *ad.* nunc; ~ **and then**, non-nunquam.

nowadays, *ad.* hodie, his temporibus.

nowhere, *ad.* nusquam, nullo in loco.

noxious, *a.* nocens, noxius, perniciosus.

nude, *a.* nudus.

nudge, *n.* cubiti ictus, *m.*; ~, *v.t.* fodico, [1].

nudity, *n.* nudatio, *f.*

nugget, *n.* massa, *f.*

nuisance, *n.* incommodum, *nt.*; molestia, *f.*

null, and void, *a.* irritus; nullus.

numb, *a.* torpens, torpidus, hebes.

numb, *v.t.* hebeto, [1]; obstupefacio, [3].

number, *n.* numerus, *m.*; (of things) copia; vis; (of people) frequentia, multitudo, *f.*

number, *v.t.* numero, computo, [1].

numberless, *a.* innumerus, innumerabilis.

numbness, *n.* torpor; *fig.* stupor, *m.*

numerous, *a.* frequens, creber, multus.

nuptial, *a.* nuptialis, coniugalis, conubialis, coniugialis.

nurse, *n.* nutrix, altrix, *f.*

nurse, *v.t.* nutrio, [4]; *fig.* foveo, [2]; (to the sick) ancillor, [1] (*with dat.*).

nursery, *n.* (for children) cubiculum infantium, *n.*; (of plants) seminarium, *nt.*

nurture, *v.t.* educo, [1]; nutrio, [4].

nut, *n.* nux, *f.*

nutcracker, *n.* nucifrangibulum, *nt.*

nutrition, *n.* nutrimentum, *nt.*

nutritious, nutritive, *a.* alibilis.

nutshell, *n.* putamen, *nt.*; *fig.* **in a** ~, paucis verbis.

nymph, *n.* nympha; (girl) puella, *f.*

O

oaf, *n.* stultus, hebes, *m.*

oak, *n.* quercus, aesculus, ilex, *f.*; robur, *nt.*

oar, *n.* remus, *m.*

oarsman, *n.* remex, *m.*

oat, oats, *n.* avena, *f.*

oath, *n.* iusiurandum, (*genit.*) iurisiurandi, *nt.*; (of soldiers) sacramentum, *nt.*; **take an** ~, iuro, [1] (in verba).

obedience, *n.* oboedientia, *f.*; obsequium, *nt.*

obedient, *a.* oboediens, obsequens; ~**ly**, *ad.* oboedienter.

obese, *a.* obesus; v. **fat.**

obesity, *n.* obesitas, *f.*

obey, *v.t.* pareo, [2], oboedio, [4], obtempero, [1] (*all with dat.*).

object, *n.* obiectum, *nt.*; res, *f.*; (aim, design) consilium, *nt.*

object, *v.t.* (to) repugno (*with dat.*), improbo, [1].

objection, *n.* impedimentum, *nt.*; mora, *f.*; **if you have no ~**, si per te licet.

objectionable, *a.* improbabilis.

objective, *a.* medius.

obligation, *n.* officium; beneficium, *nt.*

oblige, *v.t.* cogo, [3]; obligo, [1]; devincio, [4]; (by kindness) bene de aliquo mereor, [2]; **be ~d to**, debeo, [2] (*with inf.*)

obliging, *a.* officiosus, comis, blandus; benignus, beneficus; **~ly**, *ad.* comiter; benigne; officiose.

oblique, *a.* obliquus; **~ly**, *ad.* oblique.

obliterate, *v.t.* deleo, [2]; oblittero, [1].

oblivion, *n.* oblivio, *f.*; oblivium, *nt.*

oblivious, *a.* obliviosus, immemor.

oblong, *a.* oblongus.

obnoxious, *a.* (hateful) invisus; (hurtful) noxius.

obscene, *a.* obscenus, spurcus, turpis.

obscenity, *n.* obscenitas; turpitudo, *f.*

obscure, *a.* obscurus; *fig.* perplexus; (intricate, puzzling) difficilis; (of style) intortus; (of people) ignobilis, ignotus.

obscure, *v.t.* obscuro, obumbro, [1].

obscurity, *n.* obscuritas, *f.*; tenebrae, *f. pl.*; *fig.* ignobilitas, humilitas, *f.*

obsequious, *a.* officiosus, morigerus; **~ly**, *ad.* cum nimia obsequentia; assentatorie.

observance, *n.* observantia, observatio, *f.*

observant, *a.* attentus; oboediens.

observation, *n.* observatio; animadversio, *f.*; (remark) dictum, *nt.*

observe, *v.t.* observo, [1]; animadverto, [3]; (utter) dico, [3]; (spy out) speculor, [1]; (obey) pareo, [2], obtempero, [1] (*both with dat.*).

observer, *n.* spectator, *m.*

obsolete, *a.* obsoletus.

obstacle, *n.* impedimentum, *nt.*; mora, *f.*

obstinacy, *n.* obstinatio, pertinacia, pervicacia, contumacia, *f.*

obstinate, *a.* obstinatus, pertinax; pervicax, contumax; **~ly**, *ad.* obstinate; pervicaciter, contumaciter, pertinaciter.

obstruct, *v.t.* obstruo, [3]; (hinder) impedio, [4].

obstruction, *n.* obstructio, *f.*; impedimentum, *nt.*

obtain, *v.t.* paro, [1]; consequor, quaero, nanciscor; adipiscor, [3]; (by entreaty) impetro, [1].

obtainable, *a.* impetrabilis.

obtrusive, *a.* molestus; importunus.

obtuse, *a.* obtusus; hebes.

obvious, *a.* apertus, perspicuus, manifestus; ~ly, *ad.* aperte, manifesto.

occasion, *n.* occasio, causa, *f.*

occasional, *a.* rarus, infrequens; ~ly, *ad.* per occasionem, occasione oblata.

occult, *a.* occultus, arcanus.

occupant, *n.* possessor, *m.*

occupation, *n.* (including military) possessio, *f.*; (employment) quaestus, *m.*; (business) studium, negotium, *nt.*

occupier, *n.* possessor, *m.*

occupy, *v.t.* occupo, [1]; (possess) teneo, [2]; (inhabit) habito, [1]; (detain) detineo, [2].

occur, *v.i.* occido, contingo, [3]; evenio; obvenio; *fig.* in mentem venio, [4].

occurrence, *n.* casus, eventus, *m.*; res, *f.*

ocean, *n.* oceanus, *m.*

octagon, *n.* octagonon, *nt.*

octagonal, *a.* octagonos.

October, *n.* October, *m.*

odd, *a.* (of number) impar; (strange) insolitus, inusitatus; ~ly, *ad.* inusitate.

oddity, *n.* res inusitata, *f.*; monstrum, *nt.*

odds, *n.* discordia, dissensio, contentio, *f.*; (difference) discrimen, *nt.*; **be at ~ with someone,** ab aliquo dissideo, [2].

odious, *a.* odiosus, invisus; (disgusting) foedus; ~ly, *ad.* odiose.

odorous, *a.* odoratus.

odour, *n.* odor, *m.*

of, the meaning of the genitive.

off, *pr.* (out of) extra (*with acc.*); (from, of) de, ex (*with abl.*).

off, *ad.* procul, longe; **be well ~,** bene me habeo, [2].

offal, *n.* quisquiliae, *f. pl.*

offence, *n.* (fault) offensa, culpa, *f.*; (insult) iniuria, contumelia, *f.*; (displeasure) offensio, *f.*

offend, *v.t.* (insult, *etc.*) offendo; laedo, [3]; (transgress) pecco, [1] (*v.i.*); (against) violo, [1].

offender, *n.* reus, *m.*

offensive, *a.* iniuriosus; (things) odiosus; foedus.

offer, *v.t.* offero, [3]; do, [1]; praebeo, [2]; (at an auction) licitor, [1].

offer, *n.* oblatio; (proposal) condicio, *f.*

offering, *n.* oblatio, *f.*; donum, *nt.*; (of a sacrifice) immolatio, *f.*

office, *n.* (duty) officium, munus; (room) tabularium, *nt.*

officer, *n.* magistratus, *m.*; (in the army) praefectus, tribunus militaris, *m.*

official, *a.* publicus; (holding an official position) magistratui praepositus.

official, *n.* minister; accensus, lictor, *m.*

officiate, *v.i.* officium praesto, [1]; (in religious ceremonies) rem divinam facio, [3]; (for another) alterius vice fungor, [3].

officious, *a.* molestus.

offspring, *n.* proles, progenies, stirps, suboles, *f.*

often, *ad.* saepe; **very ~,** persaepe.

ogle, *v.t.* limis oculis intueor, [2].

ogre, *n.* larva, *f.*

oh, *i.* oh! ah! ohe!

oil, *n.* oleum, *nt.*; olivum, *nt.*

oily, *a.* (like oil) oleaceus; oleosus.

ointment, *n.* unguentum, unguen; (as medicament) collyrium, *nt.*

old, *a.* (in age) aetate provectus, senex; (ancient) vetus, vetustus; (out of use) obsoletus; (worn) exesus, tritus; (of former days) antiquus, priscus, pristinus; **~ man,** *n.* senex, *m.*; **~ woman,** *n.* anus, *f.*; **~ age,** *n.* senectus, *f.*; **of ~,** olim, quondam; **~er,** senior; vetustior; **~est,** natu maximus; **grow ~,** senesco, [3].

old-fashioned, *a.* priscus, antiquus.

oldness, *n.* antiquitas, vetustas, *f.*

oligarchy, *n.* paucorum potestas, *f.*

olive, *n.* olea, oliva, *f.*

Olympic, *a.* Olympicus; **the ~ games,** Olympia, *nt. pl.*

omen, *n.* omen, auspicium, augurium, ostentum, *nt.*

ominous, *a.* infaustus, infelix; **~ly,** *ad.* malis ominibus.

omission, *n.* praetermissio, *f.*

omit, *v.t.* praetermitto, omitto; (temporarily) intermitto, [3].

on, *pr.* in, super (*both with abl.*); (near) ad (*with acc.*); (depending, hanging on) de; (immediately, after) e, ex (*all with abl.*); **~ his side,** cum illo.

on, *ad.* porro; (continually) usque; **and so ~,** et cetera; **go ~,** procedo, pergo, [3].

once, *ad.* (one time) semel; (formerly) olim, quondam; aliquando; **at ~,** illico, statim; (at the same time) simul, uno tempore; **~ (and) for all,** semel.

one, *a.* unus; (a certain person *or* thing) quidam; **~ another,** alius alium; **~ after another,** alternus; (*ad.*) invicem; **~ by ~,** singillatim; **it is all ~,** perinde est; **~ or the other,** alteruter.

onerous, *a.* gravis, praegravis, onerosus.

oneself, *pn.* ipse; (with reflexive verbs) se.

one-sided, *a.* inaequalis, iniquus.

onion, *n.* caepa, *f.*

only, *a.* unicus; unus, solus.

only, *ad.* solum, tantum, dumtaxat; (except) non nisi.

onset, onslaught, n. impetus, incursus, m.; incursio, f.

onwards, ad. porro; protinus.

ooze, v.i. mano, emano; (de)stillo, [1].

opal, n. opalus, m.

opaque, a. densus, opacus.

open, v.t. aperio, [4]; patefacio, pando, [3]; (uncover) retego, [3]; (a letter) resigno, [1]; (begin) ordior, [4]; ~, v.i. patesco, [3]; (gape open) dehisco, [3].

open, a. (not shut) apertus, patens; (visible) in conspectu positus; (evident) manifestus; (sincere) candidus, ingenuus; (public) communis, publicus; **in the ~ air**, sub divo.

opening, n. (act of making accessible) apertio, f.; (aperture) foramen, nt.; (air-hole) spiramentum, nt.

openly, ad. aperte; manifesto; (publicly) palam; fig. libere, simpliciter.

operate, v.t. & i. operor, [1]; ago, [3]; (cut open) seco, [1]; (have force) vim habeo, [2].

operation, n. effectus, m.; (surgical) sectio, f.; (business) negotium, nt.

operative, a. efficax; potens.

opinion, n. opinio, sententia; censura; mens, f.; iudicium, nt.; animus, m.; (esteem) existimatio, f.; **in my ~**, mea sententia.

opponent, n. adversarius, m.

opportune, a. opportunus, idoneus, commodus.

opportunity, n. occasio; opportunitas, facultas, copia, f.

oppose, v.t. oppono, obicio, [3]; ~, v.i. (resist) repugno, adversor, obsto, [1]; resisto, [3] (all with dat.).

opposed, a. adversus; adversarius; contrarius.

opposite, a. adversus, contrarius, diversus; ~, n. contrarium, nt.

opposite, ad. & pr. ~ **to**, contra (with acc.), ex adverso.

opposition, n. oppositio; repugnantia; discrepantia, f.; (obstacle) impedimentum, nt.

oppress, v.t. affligo, [3]; vexo; gravo, onero, [1].

oppression, n. gravatio; iniuria; vexatio, f.

oppressive, a. gravis; acerbus, molestus, iniquus.

oppressor, n. tyrannus, m.

opt for, v.t. opto, [1].

optical, a. oculorum, gen. pl.

option, n. optio, f.

optional, a. cuius rei optio est.

opulence, n. opulentia, f.

opulent, a. opulens, opulentus, dives; ~**ly**, ad. opulenter.

or, c. vel; aut; (interrogatively) an; **either . . . ~**, vel . . . vel, aut . . . aut; **whether . . . ~**, sive . . . sive, seu . . . seu.

oracle, n. oraculum, responsum, nt.; sors, f.

oral, *a.* verbo traditus; praesens; ~**ly,** *ad.*

orange, *a.* luteus.

oration, *n.* oratio; (before the people or to the army) contio. *f.*

orator, *n.* orator, *m.*

oratory, *n.* oratoria ars, rhetorica; (eloquence) eloquentia. *f.*

orbit, *n.* orbis, *m.* orbita, *f.*; (in astronomy) ambitus, *m.*

orchard, *n.* pomarium, *nt.*

orchestra, *n.* (body of musical performers) symphoniaci, *m. pl.*

orchid, *n.* orchis, *f.*

ordain, *ut.* ordino, [1]; iubeo, [2]; instituo, [3].

ordeal, *n. fig.* discrimen, *nt.*

order, *n.* ordo, *m.*; (rank) ordo, *m.*; (row) series, *f.*; (command) praeceptum, mandatum, decretum, *nt.*; (custom) mos, *m.*; consuetudo, *f.*; (instruction) rescriptum; (decree) edictum, *nt.* (association) societas, *f.*; **in** ~, ordine, ex ordine; **out of** ~, (out of turn) extra ordinem.

order, *ut.* (put in order) dispono, [3]; ordino, [1]; (give orders to) impero, [1] (*with dat.*); iubeo, [2].

orderly, *a.* compositus, ordinatus; (of people) oboediens; (quiet, sober) modestus, temperatus.

orderly, *n.* (*mil.*) tesserarius, *m.*

ordinarily, *ad.* usitate, fere, plerumque, vulgo.

ordinary, *a.* usitatus, solitus, vulgaris.

ordination, *n.* ordinatio, *f.*

ore, *n.* metallum, *nt.*

organ, *n.* (musical instrument) organum, *nt.*; (of the body) membrum, *nt.*

organism, *n.* compages, natura, *f.*

organist, *n.* organicus, *m.*

organization, *n.* ordinatio; temperatio, *f.*

organize, *ut.* ordino, [1]; constituo, dispono, [3]; formo, [1].

orgies, *n.* orgia, *nt. pl.*

orgy, *n.* (revelry) comissatio, *f.*

oriental, *a.* orientalis.

origin, *n.* origo, *f.*; principium, *nt.*; ortus, *m.*

original, *a.* primitivus; pristinus; principalis; ~**ly,** *ad.* ab origine; primum.

original, *n.* archetypum, exemplar; (writing) autographum, *nt.*

originality, *n.* proprietas quaedam ingenii, *f.*

originate, *ui.* orior, [4]; proficiscor, [3].

ornament, *n.* ornamentum, *nt.*; ornatus, *m.*; decus, *nt.*

ornament, *ut.* orno, decoro, [1].

ornamental, *a.* quod ornamento, decori est.

ornate, *a.* ornatus; pictus.

orphan, *a. & n.* orbus.

orthodox, *a.* orthodoxus.

oscillate, *v.i.* fluctuo, [1].

oscillation, *n.* fluctuatio, *f.*

osier, *n.* vimen, *nt.*; salix, *f.*

ostensible, *a.* simulatus, fictus.

ostensibly, *ad.* specie, per speciem.

ostentation, *n.* ostentatio; iactatio, *f.*

ostentatious, *a.* ambitiosus; gloriosus; vanus; ~**ly**, *ad.* ambitiose, gloriose, iactanter.

ostracism, *n.* testarum suffragia, *nt. pl.*

ostrich, *n.* struthiocamelus, *m.*

other, *a.* (another) alius; alter; the ~**s**, ceteri, reliqui.

otherwise, *ad.* alio modo, aliter; (if not) si non; (besides) insuper.

otter, *n.* lutra, *f.*

ought, *v.i.* debeo, oportet, [2].

our, ours, *pr.* noster; (of ~ country) nostras.

ourselves, *pr.* nosmet, nosmet ipsi.

oust, *v.t.* eicio, [3].

out, *ad.* (out of doors) foris; (to outside) foras; **get ~!** apage!

out, *pr.* ~ **of**, e, ex (*with abl.*); (on account of) propter; (~side, beyond) extra (*both with acc.*); ~ **of the way**, devius.

outbreak, *n.* eruptio; *fig.* (revolt) seditio, *f.*

outcast, *n.* exsul, extorris, profugus, *m.*

outcome, *n.* eventus, *m.*

outcry, *n.* clamor, *m.*; acclamatio, *f.*

outdo, *v.t.* supero, [1].

outer, *a.* exterior.

outfit, *n.* apparatus, *m.*

outflank, *v.t.* circumeo, [4].

outgrow, *v.t. fig.* dedisco, [3].

outlandish, *a.* externus; barbarus.

outlast, *v.t.* durando supero, [1].

outlaw, *n.* proscriptus, *m.*

outlaw, *v.t.* aqua et igni interdico (*with dat.*), proscribo, [3].

outlay, *n.* sumptus, *m.*; impensa, *f.*

outlet, *n.* exitus, egressus, *m.*

outline, *n.* forma rudis, *f.*

outlive, *v.t.* supervivo, [3]; supersum; supero, [1]; superstes sum.

outlook, *n.* prospectus, *m.*

outlying, *a.* (distant) remotus.

outnumber, *v.t.* numero supero, [1].

outpost, *n.* statio, *f.*

outrage, *n.* iniuria, *f.*; (outrageous deed) flagitium, *nt.*

outrage, *v.t.* iniuria afficio, [3]; laedo, [3].

outrageous, *a.* iniuriosus; atrox; (exaggerated) immodicus; immanis; immoderatus.

outright, *ad.* (completely) prorsus.

outrun, *v.t.* praecurro, [3]; cursu supero, [1].

outset, *n.* principium, initium, *nt.*

outside, *n.* pars exterior; superficies; (appearance) species, *f.*; ~, *a.* exterus.

outside, *ad.* foris, extrinsecus.

outside, *pr.* extra. (*with acc.*)

outskirts, *n.* (of towns) suburbium, *nt.*

outspoken, *a.* candidus.

outstanding, *a.* prominens; (excellent) egregius; (of debts) solvendus.

outstretch, *v.t.* expando, extendo, [3].

outstrip, *v.t.* cursu supero, [1]; praeverto, [3].

outvote, *v.t.* suffragiis supero, [1].

outward, *a.* externus, exterus; ~, *ad.* foras.

outwardly, *ad.* extrinsecus, extra.

outwards, *ad.* in exteriorem partem; extra.

outweigh, *v.t.* praepondero, [1].

outwit, *v.t.* deludo, [3]; circumvenio, [4].

oval, *a.* ovatus.

ovation, *n.* ovatio, *f.*

oven, *n.* furnus, *m.*

over, *pr.* super; supra, trans; ~, *ad.* super; supra (*all with acc.*); ~ **and** ~ **again,** iterum ac saepius; **all** ~, per totum; ~ **and above,** insuper.

overawe, *v.t.* metu coerceo, [2].

overbalance, *v.t.* praepondero, [1].

overbearing, *a.* insolens, superbus.

overcast, *a.* nubilus, tristis.

overcharge, *v.i.* (in price) plus aequo exigo, [3].

overcoat, *n.* lacerna, paenula, *f.*; pallium, *nt.*

overcome, *v.t.* supero, [1]; vinco, [3].

overdo, *v.t.* nimis studeo, [2] (*with dat.*); nimis incumbo, [3] (*with in with acc.*).

overdue, *a.* iamdudum solvendus.

overflow, *v.i.* exundo, redundo, restagno, [1]; superfluo, [3]; ~, *v.t.* inundo, [1].

overgrown, *a.* obductus, obsitus.

overhang, *v.i.* impendeo, immineo, [2] (*both with dat.*).

overhead, *ad.* desuper; supra, superne.

overhear, *v.t.* subausculto, [1].

overjoyed, *a.* ovans, exsultans.

overlap, *v.t.* excedo, [3].

overload, *v.t.* nimio pondere onero, [1].

overlook, *v.t.* (not notice) praetermitto; (have view of) prospecto, [1].

overpower, *v.t.* opprimo, [3]; supero, exsupero, [1].

overrate, *v.t.* nimis aestimo, [1].

override, *v.t.* (cancel) rescindo, [3].

overripe, *a.* praematurus.

overrule, *v.t.* (check) coerceo, [2]; (cancel) rescindo, [3].

overrun, *v.t.* (devastate) vasto, [1]; ~ **with**, *a.* obsitus.

oversee, *v.t.* curo, [1]; inspicio, [3].

overshadow, *v.t.* obumbro, opaco; *fig.* obscuro, [1].

oversight, *n.* (carelessness) incuria; neglegentia, *f.*; error, *m.*; (guardianship) cura, custodia, *f.*

overt, *a.* manifestus, apertus; ~**ly**, *ad.* manifesto, aperte.

overtake, *v.t.* assequor, excipio, [3]; supervenio, [4].

overthrow, *v.t.* subverto, everto, proruo; (the enemy) devinco, prosterno; *fig.* opprimo, [3].

overture, *n.* (proposal) condicio, *f.*; (beginning) exordium, *nt.*

overturn, *v.t.* everto, subverto, [3].

overvalue, *v.t.* nimis aestimo, [1].

overwhelm, *v.t.* obruo; opprimo, [3].

owe, *v.t.* debeo, [2]; **be ~ing (to)**, per (aliquem) stat ut (*with subj.*).

owing, *pr.* (to) propter, ob (*with acc.*).

owl, *n.* bubo, *m.*; strix, noctua, ulula, *f.*

own, *a.* proprius, peculiaris; **one's ~**, suus, proprius.

own, *v.t.* possideo, teneo, habeo; (acknowledge) confiteor, [2]; (claim) vindico, [1].

owner, *n.* dominus, possessor, erus, *m.*

ownership, *n.* dominium, *nt.*

ox, *n.* bos, iuvencus, *m.*

oyster, *n.* ostrea, *f.*

···

P

···

pace, *n.* gressus; incessus; passus, *m.*

pace, *v.i.* incedo, [3]; spatior, [1]; ~, *v.t.* passibus emetior, [4].

pacific, *a.* pacificus; tranquillus; placidus, pacifer.

pacify, *v.t.* placo, sedo, paco, pacifico, [1]; lenio, [4].

pack, *n.* (bundle) sarcina, *f.*; fasciculus, *m.*; (crowd) grex, *m.*; turba, *f.*

pack, *v.t.* (cram) stipo, suffarcino, [1]; (bring together) colligo, [3].

package, *n.* sarcina, *f.*; fasciculus, *m.*

packet, *n.* fasciculus, *m.*

pact, *n.* foedus, *nt.*

pad, *n.* (cushion) pulvinus, *m.*

paddle, *n.* remus, *m.*

paddock, *n.* saeptum, *nt.*

padlock, *n.* sera, *f.*

page, *n.* (of a book) pagina, *f.*; (~ boy) puer, *m.*

pageant, *n.* spectaculum, *nt.*; pompa; *fig.* species, *f.*

pageantry, *n.* species atque pompa, *f.*

pail, *n.* hama, situla, *f.*

pain, *n.* dolor; angor, cruciatus, *m.*

painful, *a.* gravis, aeger; (laborious) operosus.

painless, *a.* sine dolore, doloris expers.

pains, *n.* cura, *f.*; studium, *nt.*; take ~, operam do, [1].

painstaking, *a.* operosus.

paint, *v.t.* (colour) (colore) induco; pingo, depingo, [3]; (the face) fuco, [1]; ~, *v.i.* (as artist) pingo, [3].

paint, *n.* pigmentum, *nt.*

paintbrush, *n.* penicilus, *m.*

painter, *n.* (artist) pictor, *m.*

painting, *n.* (art) pictura; (picture) tabula, pictura, *f.*

pair, *n.* (couple) par, *nt.*

pair, *v.t.* iungo, coniungo, [3]; copulo, [1].

palace, *n.* regia (domus), *f.*; palatium, *nt.*

palatable, *a.* sapidus; iucundus.

palate, *n.* palatum, *nt.*

pale, *a.* pallidus; exsanguis; be ~, palleo, [2]; grow ~, pallesco, [3].

paleness, *n.* pallor, *m.*

pall, *n.* pallium, *nt.*

pall, *v.i.* nil sapio, [3].

palm, *n.* (of the hand) palma, *f.*; (tree) palma, *f.*

palm, *v.t.* ~ off, vendito, [1].

palpitate, *v.i.* palpito, [1].

palpitation, *n.* palpitatio, *f.*

paltry, *a.* vilis; (trifling) minutus, exiguus.

pamper, *v.t.* indulgeo, [2] (*with dat.*).

pamphlet, *n.* libellus, *m.*

pan, *n.* (vessel) patina, *f.*

panacea, *n.* panacea, *f.*; panchrestum medicamentum, *nt.*

pander, *n.* leno, *m.*; ~ to, *v.i.* lenocinor, [1]; indulgeo, [2] (*with dat.*).

panegyric, *n.* laudatio, *f.*; panegyricus, *m.*

panel, *n.* (of a door) tympanum, *nt.*; (list of names) index, *m.*; album, *nt.*

pang, *n.* dolor, angor, *m.*

panic, *n.* terror, pavor, metus, *m.*; formido, *f.*

panic-stricken, panic-struck, *a.* pavidus, exterritus.

panorama, *n.* prospectus, *m.*

pant, *v.i.* palpito; trepido; anhelo, [1].

panther, *n.* panthera, *f.*

panting, *a.* anhelus; ~, *n.* anhelitus, *m.*

pantry, *n.* cella penaria, *f.*; promptuarium, *nt.*

paper, *n.* (for writing on) charta, *f.*; (newspaper) acta diurna, *nt. pl.*; ~s, *pl.* scripta, *nt. pl.*; litterae, *f. pl.*

parable, *n.* parabola, *f.*

parade, *n.* (mil.) decursus; locus exercendi; (display) apparatus, *m.*; pompa, ostentatio, *f.*

parade, *v.t.* (mil.) instruo, [3]; *fig.* ostento, [1]; ~, *v.i.* (march ceremonially) decurro, [3].

paradise, *n.* Elysii campi, *m. pl.*

paradox, *n.* quod contra opinionem omnium est.

paradoxical, *a.* praeter opinionem accidens.

paragon, *n.* specimen, exemplum, *nt.*

paragraph, *n.* caput, *nt.*

parallel, *a.* parallelos; *fig.* consimilis.

parallel, *n.* parallelos, *m.*; (comparison) collatio, comparatio, *f.*

parallel, *v.t.* exaequo; (compare) comparo, [1]; (be equal) par esse.

paralyse, *v.t.* debilito, enervo, [1].

paralysis, *n.* paralysis; *fig.* torpedo, *f.*; torpor, *m.*

paralytic, *n.* paralyticus, *m.*

paramount, *a.* supremus; summus.

parapet, *n.* pluteus, *m.*

paraphernalia, *n.* apparatus, *m.*

paraphrase, *n.* paraphrasis, *f.*

paraphrase, *v.t.* liberius interpretor, [1].

parasite, *n.* parasitus, assecla, *m.*

parasitic, *a.* parasiticus.

parasol, *n.* umbella, *f.*; umbraculum, *nt.*

parcel, *n.* pars, *f.*; (bundle) fasciculus, *m.*

parch, *v.t.* arefacio, [3]; torreo, [2]; **parched,** torridus.

parchment, *n.* membrana, *f.*

pardon, *n.* venia, *f.*

pardon, *v.t.* ignosco, [3]; condono, [1] (*both with dat.*).

pardonable, *a.* condonandus.

parent, *n.* parens, *c.*

parentage, *n.* genus, *nt.*; prosapia, origo, *f.*

parental, *a.* paternus; maternus.

parenthesis, *n.* interpositio, interclusio, *f.*

park, *n.* (for game) vivarium; (for pleasure) viridarium, *nt.*; horti, *m. pl.*

parley, *n.* colloquium, *nt.*; ~, *v.i.* colloquor, [3].

parrot, *n.* psittacus, *m.*

parry, *v.t.* averto, defendo, [3]; propulso, [1].

parsimonious, *a.* parcus, sordidus.

parsimony, *n.* parsimonia, *f.*

part, *n.* pars, portio; (in a play) persona, *f.*, partes, *f. pl.*; (duty) officium, *nt.*; (of a town) regio, *f.*; **in ~,** partim.

part, *v.t.* separo, [1]; divido, [3]; ~, *v.i.* (go away) discedo, [3]; digredior, [3], abeo, *ir.*; (gape open) dehisco, fatisco, [3]; ~ **with**, dimitto, [3].

partial, *a.* per partes; (biased) iniquus; ~**ly**, *ad.* partim; ~ **to**, cupidus (*with gen.*).

partiality, *n.* gratia; iniquitas, *f.*

participant, *n.* particeps, *c.*

participate, *v.i.* particeps sum *or* fio, [4].

participation, *n.* participium, *nt.*; societas, *f.*

particle, *n.* particula, *f.*

particoloured, *a.* versicolor; varius.

particular, *a.* proprius; peculiaris; singularis; (fastidious) fastidiosus; (special) praecipuus; ~**ly**, *ad.* particulatim; singillatim; (especially) praesertim, praecipue.

particular, *n.* singula, *nt. pl.*; **in** ~, *v.* **particularly**.

parting, *n.* divisio, *f.*; (from) discessus, *m.*

partisan, *n.* fautor, homo factiosus, *m.*

partition, *n.* partitio, *f.*; (enclosure) saeptum, *nt.*; (of rooms) paries, *m.*

partly, *ad.* partim; nonnulla ex parte, in parte.

partner, *n.* socius, *m.*; socia, *f.*; particeps, consors, *c.*

partnership, *n.* societas, consociatio, consortio, *f.*

partridge, *n.* perdix, *c.*

party, *n.* factio; secta, *f.* partes, *f. pl.*; (detachment) manus, *f.*

pass, *v.t.* (go) eo, *ir.*; vado, cedo, [3]; (go by) praetereo, *ir.*; (cross) transeo, *ir.*; (a law, *etc.*) fero, [3]; (approve) approbo, [1]; ~, *v.i.* praetereo, *ir.*; praetervehor, [3]; (of time) praetereo, *ir.*; (from one to another) migro, [1]; (for) habeor, [2]; (hand over) trado, [3]; ~ **away**, transeo, *ir.*; (die) pereo, *ir.*; labor, effluo, [3]; (cease) cesso, [1]; ~ **by**, praetereo, *ir.* (*also fig.*); ~ **over**, traicio, transgredior, [3]; *fig.* praetereo, *ir.*; ~ **round**, circumfero, trado, [3]; **let** ~, praetermitto, dimitto, [3].

pass, *n.* fauces, angustiae, *f. pl.*; saltus, *m.*; (ticket) tessera, *f.*

passable, *a.* (of a way) pervius; *fig.* mediocris, tolerabilis.

passage, *n.* (action) transitus, *m.*; transitio, *f.*; transmissio, traiectio; (thoroughfare) transitio pervia, *f.*; (of a book) locus, *m.*

passenger, *n.* viator; (by water) vector, *m.*

passing, *a.* transiens; praeteriens; *fig.* brevis, caducus.

passion, *n.* cupiditas, *f.*; fervor, *m.*; impetus, animi motus, *m.*; (anger) ira, *f.*; (for) studium, *nt.*; (love) amor, *m.*

passionate, *a.* fervidus, ardens, vehemens; iracundus; ~**ly**, *ad.* ardenter; iracunde, vehementer.

passive, *a.* patibilis; passivus; ~**ly**, *ad.* passive.

passport, *n.* syngraphus, *m.*

password, *n.* tessera, *f.*

past, *a.* praeteritus; (immediately preceding) proximus, superior; ~, *n.* praeteritum tempus, *nt.;* actum tempus, *nt.*

past, *pr.* praeter; (beyond) ultra (*both with acc.*).

paste, *n.* gluten, *nt.*

paste, *u.t.* glutino, [1].

pastime, *n.* oblectamentum, *nt.;* ludus, *m.*

pastoral, *a.* pastoralis; pastorius.

pastry, *n.* crustum, *nt.,* bellaria, *nt. pl.;* crustula, *nt. pl.*

pasture, *n.* pabulum, *nt.*

pat, *n.* plaga levis, *f.*

patch, *n.* pannus, *m.*

patch, *u.t.* sarcio, resarcio, [4]; assuo, [3].

patent, *a.* apertus, manifestus; ~ly, plane.

patent, *n.* diploma, *nt.*

paternal, *a.* paternus, patrius.

paternity, *n.* paternitas, *f.*

path, *n.* semita, *f.;* trames, callis, *m.; fig.* (course) via, *f.*

pathetic, *a.* patheticus; ~ally, *ad.* pathetice.

pathway, *n.* semita, *f.;* callis, *m.*

patience, *n.* patientia, *f.;* tolerantia.

patient, *a.* patiens; tolerans; ~ly, *ad.* patienter; aequo animo.

patient, *n.* aegrotus, *m.;* aegrota, *f.*

patrician, *a. & n.* patricius.

patrimony, *n.* patrimonium, *nt.;* hereditas, *f.*

patriot, *n.* amans patriae, *m.;* bonus civis, *m.*

patriotic, *a.* amans patriae; bonus, pius.

patriotism, *n.* amor patriae, *m.;* pietas, *f.*

patrol, *n.* vigil, *m.;* excubiae, *f. pl.;* ~, *u.i.* excubias agere, [3].

patron, *n.* patronus, *m.*

patronage, *n.* patrocinium, praesidium, *nt.*

patronize, *u.t.* faveo, studeo, [2] (*with dat.*); (be present at) adsum, (*with dat.*).

patter, *n.* crepitus, *m.*

patter, *u.i.* crepo, crepito, [1].

pattern, *n.* (sample) exemplar, exemplum; (model) specimen, *nt.*

paunch, *n.* venter, *m.*

pauper, *n.* pauper, egens, inops, *c.*

pause, *n.* pausa, mora; intermissio, *f.;* intervallum, *nt.*

pause, *u.i.* intermitto, quiesco, [3].

pave, *u.t.* (viam saxo) sterno, [3].

pavement, *n.* pavimentum, *nt.;* stratura, *f.*

pavilion, *n.* tentorium, *nt.*

paw, *n.* ungula, *f.;* pes, *m.*

paw, *u.t.* pedibus pulso (terram), [1].

pawn, *n.* pignus, *nt.*; (in chess) latrunculus, *m.*

pawn, *v.t.* pignero; oppignero, obligo, [1].

pawnbroker, *n.* pignerator, *m.*

pay, *n.* (*mil.*) stipendium, *nt.*; (wages, hire) merces, *f.*; (profit) quaestus, fructus, *m.*

pay, *v.t.* (pecuniam debitam) solvo, [3]; (stipendium) numero, [1]; *fig.* persolvo, [3]; ~, *v.i.* pendo, [3]; (be profitable) prosum, proficio, [3]; ~ **for** (hire) conduco, [3]; (buy) emo, [3]; *fig.* (suffer) poenas do, [1]; ~ **off**, dissolvo, [3].

payable, *a.* solvendus.

pay-day, *n.* dies stipendii solvendi, *m.*

payment, *n.* (act) solutio, *f.*; (sum of money) pensio, *f.*

pea, *n.* pisum, cicer, *nt.*

peace, *n.* pax; quies, *f.*; otium, *nt.*; (of mind) tranquillitas animi, *f.*

peaceable, **peaceful**, *a.* pacis amans; placabilis; (of things) pacatus; placidus, quietus.

peaceably, **peacefully**, *ad.* pacate; cum (bona) pace.

peacefulness, *n.* tranquillitas, *f.*

peacemaker, *n.* pacificator, *m.*

peach, *n.* malum Persicum, *nt.*

peacock, *n.* pavo, *m.*

peak, *n.* (of a mountain) cacumen, culmen, *nt.*; apex, vertex, *m.*

peal, *n.* (of thunder) fragor, *m.*; (of bells) concentus, *m.*

peal, *v.i.* sono, resono, [1].

pear, *n.* pirum, *nt.*; ~**-tree**, *n.* pirus, *f.*

pearl, *n.* margarita, baca, gemma, *f.*

pearly, *a.* gemmeus, gemmans.

peasant, *n.* rusticus, agrestis, agricola, *m.*

pebble, *n.* lapillus, calculus, *m.*

peck, *v.t.* rostro impeto, [3]; mordeo, [2].

peculiar, *a.* (one's own) proprius; peculiaris; (unusual) praecipuus, singularis; ~**ly**, *ad.* praesertim, imprimis; praecipue.

pedantic, *a.* litterarum ostentator, putidus; professorius; ~**ally**, *ad.* putide.

pedantry, *n.* scholasticorum ineptiae, *f. pl.*; eruditio insulsa, *f.*

pedestal, *n.* stylobates, *m.*; spira, *f.*

pedestrian, *a.* pedester; pedibus (*abl.*); ~, *n.* pedes, *m.*

pedigree, *n.* stemma, *nt.*

pedlar, *n.* institor, *m.*

peel, *n.* cutis, tunica, *f.*; cortex, *m.*

peel, *v.t.* decortico, desquamo, [1].

peep, *n.* (look) contuitus, *m.*

peep, *v.i.* per rimam speculor, [1].

peer, *n.* (equal) par.

peer at, *v.t.* (scrutinize) rimor, [1].

peevish, *a.* stomachosus, morosus, difficilis; ~**ly**, *ad.* stomachose, morose.

peg, n. paxillus, m.

pelican, n. pelicanus, onocrotalus, m.

pellet, n. globulus, m.; pilula, f.

pell-mell, ad. effuse, sine ordine, promiscue.

pelt, n. pellis, f.

pelt, v.t. peto, [3]; lapido; (beat) verbero, [1].

pen, n. (to write with) calamus, stylus, m.; (for sheep) ovile, nt.

pen, v.t. scribo, compono, [3]; (shut in) includo, [3].

penal, a. poenalis.

penalty, n. poena; mul(c)ta, f.; supplicium, n.

penance, n. satisfactio, f.; (atonement) piaculum, nt.; (punishment) poena, f.

pencil, n. graphis, f.; peniculus, penicillus, m.

pending, a. instans; (law) sub iudice.

pendulum, n. libramentum, nt.

penetrate, v.t. penetro, [1].

penetration, n. acies mentis; sagacitas, f.

peninsula, n. paeninsula, f.

penitence, n. paenitentia, f.

penitent, a. paenitens.

penknife, n. scalprum, nt.

pennant, pennon, n. vexillum, nt.

penniless, a. omnium rerum egens, inops.

penny, n. as, nummus, denarius, m.

pension, n. merces annua, f.; annuum beneficium, nt.

pensive, a. cogitabundus.

penultimate, a. paenultimus.

people, n. populus, m.; homines, m. pl.; (nation) natio, f. ~ **say,** dicunt; **common ~,** vulgus, nt.; plebs, f.

pepper, n. piper, nt.

perceive, v.t. sentio, [4]; percipio, [3]; video, [2]; intellego, [3].

percentage, n. rata portio, f.

perception, n. perceptio, animadversio, f.

perch, n. (for birds) sedile (avium), nt.; (fish) perca, f.

perch, v.i. insido, (with dat.); assido, [3] (with in with abl.).

perennial, a. perennis.

perfect, a. perfectus; absolutus; (intact) plenus, integer; **~ly,** ad. perfecte; absolute; (entirely) plane.

perfect, v.t. perficio, absolvo, [3].

perfection, n. perfectio; absolutio, summa, f.

perforate, v.t. perforo, terebro, [1].

perforation, n. (hole) foramen, nt.

perform, v.t. perficio; exsequor; fungor (with abl.); (bring to pass) efficio; (accomplish) perago, [3].

performance, *n.* exsecutio; actio, *f.*; (work) opus, *nt.*

performer, *n.* effector; (player) actor, histrio, *m.*

perfume, *n.* odor, *m.*

perfume, *v.t.* suffio, [4].

perhaps, *ad.* fortasse, forte, forsitan.

peril, *n.* periculum, discrimen, *nt.*

perilous, *a.* periculosus; **~ly,** *ad.* periculose.

period, *n.* tempus, *nt.*; aetas, *f.*

periodical, *a.* periodicus; **~ally,** *ad.* temporibus certis.

perish, *v.i.* pereo, intereo, *ir.*; extinguor, cado, [3].

perishable, *a.* fragilis, caducus, infirmus.

perjure oneself, *v.i.* peiero, periuro, [1].

perjury, *n.* periurium, *nt.*; **commit ~,** peiero, periuro, [1].

permanent, *a.* diuturnus, mansurus, perpetuus; **~ly,** *ad.* perpetuo.

permeate, *v.t.* penetro, pervagor, pererro, [1].

permission, *n.* permissio, venia, *f.*; **with your ~,** pace tua, tua bona venia.

permit, *v.t.* sino, permitto, concedo, [3]; **it is ~ted,** licet, [2].

pernicious, *a.* perniciosus; noxius; **~ly,** *ad.* perniciose.

perpendicular, *a.* directus.

perpetrate, *v.t.* perficio; facio, committo, admitto, [3]; perpetro, [1].

perpetual, *a.* sempiternus; perpetuus; perennis; continuus; **~ly,** *ad.* perpetuo, semper, usque, continenter.

perplex, *v.t.* (confound) turbo, [1]; confundo, [3].

perplexity, *n.* perturbatio; anxietas, *f.*

persecute, *v.t.* insector; vexo, [1].

persecution, *n.* insectatio; vexatio, *f.*

perseverance, *n.* perseverantia, constantia, assiduitas, *f.*

persevere, *v.i.* persevero, persto, [1].

persevering, *a.* constans; tenax (propositi); assiduus.

persist, *v.i.* persto, persevero, [1].

persistence, *n.* permansio (in aliqua re), *f.*

persistent, *a.* pertinax.

person, *n.* homo, *c.*; **any ~,** quilibet, quivis; **in ~,** ipse (ego, ille, *etc.*).

personage, *n.* homo notus, *m.*

personal, *a.* privatus; **~ly,** *ad.* per se; ipse.

perspiration, *n.* sudor, *m.*

perspire, *v.i.* sudo, [1]; sudorem emitto, [3].

persuade, *v.t.* suadeo, persuadeo, [2] (*with dat.*).

persuasion, *n.* persuasio; fides; opinio, *f.*

persuasive, *a.* suasorius; ~**ly**, *ad.* apte ad persuadendum.

pert, *a.* procax.

pertinent, *a.* appositus (ad rem), aptus, idoneus.

perturb, *v.t.* turbo, perturbo, [1].

peruse, *v.t.* lego, perlego, [3].

pervade, *v.t.* perfundo, [3]; permano, [1]; pervagor, [1].

perverse, *a.* perversus, pravus.

perversion, *n.* depravatio, *f.*

perversity, *n.* perversitas, pravitas, *f.*

pervert, *v.t.* depravo, [1]; perverto, corrumpo, [3].

pest, *n.* pestis, pernicies, *f.*

pester, *v.t.* infesto, sollicito, vexo, [1].

pet, *n.* (little favourite) corculum, *nt.*; deliciae, *f. pl.*

pet, *a.* dilectus, carus.

pet, *v.t.*, v. **caress, fondle**.

petal, *n.* floris folium, *nt.*

petition, *n.* preces, *f. pl.*; libellus, *m.*; petitio, *f.*

petrify, *v.t.* in lapidem converto, [3]; *fig.* obstupefacio, [3].

petty, *a.* minutus, angustus; (trifling) parvus.

phantom, *n.* phantasma, *nt.*; vana species, *f.*; spectrum, *nt.*

phase, *n. fig.* vices, *f. pl.*

pheasant, *n.* phasiana; avis phasiana, *f.*

phenomenal, *a.* singularis.

phenomenon, *n.* res nova, *f.*; ostentum, *nt.*

philanthropic, *a.* benignus, humanus.

philanthropist, *n.* (homo) generi humano amicus, *m.*

philanthropy, *n.* benignitas, humanitas, *f.*

philosopher, *n.* philosophus; sapiens, *m.*

philosophic(al), *a.* philosophicus; ~**ly**, *ad.* philosophice; *fig.* aequo animo.

philosophize, *v.i.* philosophor, [1].

philosophy, *n.* philosophia; sapientia; (theory) ratio, *f.*

phoenix, *n.* phoenix, *m.*

phrase, *n.* locutio, *f.*; ~, *v.t.* loquor, [3].

physical, *a.* corporis (*gen. of* corpus); physicus; ~**ly**, *ad.* natura (*abl.*); physice.

physician, *n.* medicus, *m.*

physics, *n.* physica, *nt. pl.*

physique, *n.* corpus, *nt.*

pick, *v.t.* (pluck) carpo, decerpo, [3]; lego; (choose) eligo; ~ **off**, avello, [3]; ~ **out**, eligo, [3]; ~ **up**, tollo; colligo, [3]; ~ **holes in**, carpo, rodo, [3].

pick, *n.* (tool) dolabra, *f.*; (choicest part) flos, *m.*; robur, *nt.*

pickaxe, *n.* dolabra, *f.*

picket, *n.* (*mil.*) statio, *f.*

pickpocket, *v.t. & i.* manticulor, [1].

picture, *n.* tabula, tabella; effigies; *fig.* descriptio, *f.*

picture, *v.t.* depingo, [3]; (imagine) fingo, [3].

picture-gallery, *n.* pinacotheca, *f.*

picturesque, *a.* venustus, pulcher, amoenus.

pie, *n.* (pastry) crustum, *nt.*

piece, *n.* (part) frustum, *nt.*; pars, portio, *f.*; (fragment) fragmentum, *nt.*; (coin) nummus, *m.* **tear to ~s**, dilanio, lacero, [1].

pier, *n.* pila; (massive structure) moles, *f.*; agger, *m.*

pierce, *v.t.* perforo, terebro, [1]; (with a sword, *etc.*) transfigo, perfodio, transadigo; *fig.* (with grief) (aliquem) dolore afficio, [3].

piercing, *a.* penetrabilis; (of sounds) acutissimus; *fig.* sagax; **~ly**, *ad.* acute.

piety, *n.* pietas, *f.*

pig, *n.* porcus, sus, *m.*

pigeon, *n.* columba, *f.*; columbus, *m.*

pigeon-hole, *n.* loculamentum, *nt.*

pigheaded, *a.* *fig.* obstinatus.

pigment, *n.* pigmentum, *nt.*

pigsty, *n.* hara, *f.*

pike, *n.* (spear) hasta, lancea, *f.*; (fish) lucius, lupus, *m.*

pile, *n.* (heap) acervus, cumulus, *m.*; congeries, *f.*; (of firewood) rogus, *m.*; (nap of cloth) villus, *m.*

pile up, *v.t.* coacervo, cumulo, aggero, accumulo, [1]; exstruo, congero, [3].

pilfer, *v.t.* surripio, [3]; suffuror, [1].

pilfering, *n.* direptio, *f.*

pilgrim, *n.* peregrinator, *m.*

pilgrimage, *n.* peregrinatio, *f.*

pill, *n.* pilula, *f.*

pillage, *n.* (act) vastatio, direptio; (booty) praeda, *f.*; spolium, *nt.*

pillage, *v.t.* populor, praedor, vasto, spolio, [1]; diripio, [3].

pillar, *n.* (support, prop) columna; pila, *f.*

pillow, *n.* pulvinus, *m.*; cervical, *nt.*

pilot, *n.* gubernator, rector, *m.*; **~**, *v.t.* guberno, [1]; rego, [3].

pimp, *n.* leno, *m.*

pimple, *n.* pustula, pusula, *f.*

pin, *n.* acus; acicula, *f.*; (nail, peg) clavus, *m.*

pin, *v.t.* acu figo; affigo, [3].

pincers, *n.* forceps, *f.*

pinch, *v.t.* vellico, [1]; (as cold) (ad)uro, [3]; (hurt) laedo, [3].

pinch, *n.* vellicatio, *f.* **feel the ~**, urgeor, [2], premor, [3].

pine, *n.* pinus, *f.*

pine, *v.i.* (away) tabesco, [3]; marcesco, conficior, [3].

pink, *a.* (of colour) roseus.

pinnacle, *n.* fastigium, *nt.*

pint, *n.* (measure) sextarius, *m.*

pioneer, n. (mil.) cunicularius; explorator viae; fig. praecursor, m.

pious, a. pius; (pure) sanctus; ~ly, ad. pie, sancte.

pip, n. (of fruit) semen, nt.; nucleus, m.; (of grapes) acinus, m.

pipe, n. (tube) tubus, m.; (mus.) fistula, f.; tibia, arundo, f.; calamus, m.

piper, n. fistulator, tibicen, m.

piquant, a. fig. salsus, facetus; acutus.

pique, n. offensio, f.; offensa, f.; odium, nt.

piracy, n. piratica, f.

pirate, n. praedo maritimus, pirata, m.

pit, n. fossa, fovea, scrobis, f.; puteus, m.; (abyss, gulf) barathrum, nt.; (in theatre) cavea, f.; (quarry) fodina, f.

pitch, n. pix, f.; (highest point) summum fastigium, nt.; (mus.) sonus, m.

pitch, v.t. (a tent, the camp) pono, [3]; (fling) conicio, [3]; ~, v.i. fluctuo, [1].

pitch-black, pitch-dark, a. fuscus, niger; obscurus, caliginosus.

pitcher, n. urceus, m.

pitchfork, n. furca, f.

pith, n. medulla, f.

pithy, a. medulla abundans; nervosus; fig. sententiosus.

pitiable, a. miserabilis; flebilis; lamentabilis; afflictus.

pitiful, a. misericors; (pitiable) miserabilis; (contemptible, mean) abiectus; ~ly, ad. misericorditer; miserabiliter; abiecte.

pitiless, a. immisericors; durus, v. **cruel.**

pity, n. misericordia, miseratio, f.

pity, v.t. & i. miseret (me alicuius), misereor, [2]; miseror, [1]; miseresco, [3] (all with gen.).

pivot, n. cardo, m.

placard, n. edictum, nt.

place, n. locus, m.; (office) munus, nt.; **in the first ~,** fig. primum, primo.

place, v.t. pono, [3]; loco, colloco, [1].

placid, a. placidus, tranquillus; quietus; ~ly, ad. placide, tranquille, quiete.

plague, n. pestilentia; fig. pestis, f.

plague, v.t. vexo, crucio, [1].

plain, n. campus, m.; planities, f.; aequor, n.

plain, a. (smooth) planus; (not ornamented) inornatus; (distinct) clarus; (simple) simplex; (evident) apertus, manifestus; sincerus.

plainly, ad. distincte, clare, plane; simpliciter; (evidently) manifeste, aperte, perspicue.

plaintiff, n. petitor, m.; accusator, m.

plaintive, a. flebilis; querulus; ~ly, ad. flebiliter.

plait, v.t. implico, [1]; intexo, [3].

plan, n. (project) consilium. propositum, nt.; (of ground) forma, designatio, f

plan, v.t. (scheme) excogito, [1]; (draw) designo, [1].

plane, n. (tool) runcina, f; (level surface) superficies, f

plane, v.t. runcino, [1].

planet, n. planeta, m.; stella erratica, f

plane-tree, n. platanus, f

plank, n. axis, m.; tabula, f

plant, n. herba, planta, f

plant, v.t. planto, [1]; sero, [3].

plantation, n. plantarium, nt.

plaque, n. tabula, f

plaster, n. tectorium; gypsum; (med.) emplastrum, nt.

plaster, v.t. trullisso, gypso, [1]; induco; illino, [3].

plasterer, n. tector, m.

plate, n. (thin sheet of metal) lamina, brattea, f; (silver for table) vasa argentea, nt. pl.; (dish) patella, f

plated, a. bratteatus.

platform, n. suggestus, m.; suggestum, nt.

plaudit, n. plausus, clamor, m.

plausible, a. probabilis; speciosus.

play, n. (act of playing) ludus; lusus, m.; (movement) motus. m.; (scope) area, f; locus, m.; (at a theatre) fabula, comoedia, tragoedia, f; **fair ~,** aequitas, f

play, v.t. & i. ludo, [3]; (frolic, etc.) lascivio, [4]; luxurio, [1]; (on musical instruments) cano, [3]; (gamble) aleam exerceo, [2]; (as actor) partes ago, [3].

player, n. (on the stage) histrio, actor; (on an instrument) fidicen, tibicen, citharista, m.; (of a game) lusor, m.

playful, a. lascivus, iocosus, ludibundus; **~ly,** ad. iocose.

plaything, n. (rattle) crepundia, nt. pl.; (doll) pupa, f

plea, n. (excuse) excusatio, causa, f

plead, v.t. & i. causas ago; (for one) (aliquem) defendo; (against) contra aliquem causam dico, [3]; (in excuse) excuso, [1].

pleasant, a. amoenus, iucundus, gratus; urbanus, lepidus.

please, v.t. & i. (give pleasure) placeo, [2] (with dat.); delecto, [1]; **as you ~,** ut vobis libet.

pleased, a. laetus, felix.

pleasing, a. gratus; lepidus; iucundus.

pleasure, n. voluptas; iucunditas, f; deliciae, f pl.; (caprice) libido, f; (will) arbitrium, nt.

plebeian, a. & n. plebeius; vulgaris.

pledge, n. pignus, nt.; (surety) vas, praes, m.; (proof) testimonium, nt.

pledge, v.t. pignero, [1]; spondeo, [2]; promitto, [3].

plentiful, _a._ largus, affluens, uber, copiosus, abundans; **~ly**, _ad._ large, abunde, copiose, ubertim.

plenty, _n._ copia, abundantia, ubertas, _f._

pliable, **pliant**, _a._ flexibilis; lentus, mollis; flexilis; tractabilis; mansuetus.

plight, _n._ condicio, _f.;_ status, _m._

plot, _n._ (conspiracy) coniuratio, _f.;_ (of land) agellus, _m.;_ (surveying) designatio, _f.; fig._ (of a play, _etc._) argumentum, _nt._

plot, _v.i._ coniuro, [1]; ~, _v.t._ molior, [4]; excogito, [1].

plotter, _n._, v. **conspirator**.

plough, _n._ aratrum, _nt.;_ ~, _v.t._ aro, [1].

ploughman, _n._ arator, _m._

pluck, _n._ (courage) animus, _nt._

pluck, _v.t._ (pull) vello, [3]; vellico, [1]; (gather) carpo, decerpo; (off) avello; deripio; (out) evello; eripio; _fig._ ~ **up** (courage) colligo, [3].

plug, _n._ obturamentum, _nt.;_ ~, _v.t._ obturo, [1].

plum, _n._ prunum, _nt.;_ ~ **tree**, _n._ prunus, _f._

plumage, _n._ plumae, pennae, _f. pl._

plumber, _n._ plumbarius, _m._ (worker in lead).

plumb-line, _n._ perpendiculum, _nt.;_ linea, _f._

plume, _n._ penna, pluma; (crest) crista, _f._

plummet, _n._ perpendiculum, _nt.;_ linea, _f._

plump, _a._ nitidus, obesus; corpulentus.

plumpness, _n._ obesitas, _f.;_ nitor, _m._

plunder, _n._ (booty) praeda, _f.;_ spolium, _nt.;_ (act of plundering) rapina, direptio, _f.;_ (stolen goods) furta, _nt. pl._

plunder, _v.t._ praedor, [1]; diripio, [3]; spolio, vasto, populor, [1].

plunge, _v.t._ mergo, summergo; (a sword) condo, subdo (in _with abl._) [3]; ~, _v.i._ immergor; _fig._ se mergere in . . . , [3].

plural, _a._ pluralis.

ply, _v.t._ exerceo, [2].

pocket, _n._ (pouch) marsupium, _nt.;_ crumena, _f._

pocket-money, _n._ peculium, _nt._

pod, _n._ siliqua, _f._

poem, _n._ poema, carmen, _nt._

poet, _n._ poeta, vates, _m._

poetess, _n._ poetria, _f._

poetic(al), _a._ poeticus; **~(al)ly**, _ad._ poetice.

poetry, _n._ (art) poetice; (poems) poesis, _f.;_ carmen, _nt._

point, _n._ punctum, _nt.;_ (pointed end) acumen, _nt.;_ (of swords, _etc._) mucro, _m.;_ (of a spear) cuspis, _f.; fig._ quaestio, _f.;_ casus, _m.;_ res, _f.;_ argumentum, _nt.;_ ~ **of view**, iudicium, _nt.;_ **main** _or_ **chief ~,** caput, _nt._

point, _v.t._ (aim) intendo [3]; ~ **at**, monstro, [1]; ~ **out**, monstro, [1].

pointed, *a.* praeacutus; acutus; *fig.* salsus; (stinging) aculeatus.

pointedly, *ad.* acriter, acute; plane, aperte.

pointer, *n.* index, *c.*

pointless, *a. fig.* insulsus, frigidus.

poise, *n.* (equilibrium) aequipondium, *nt.*; *fig.* (sophistication) urbanitas, *f.*

poised, *a.* libratus.

poison, *n.* venenum, virus, *nt.*

poison, *v.t.* (a thing) veneno; (a person) veneno neco; *fig.* vitio, [1].

poisoner, *n.* veneficus, *m.*; venefica, *f.*

poisoning, *n.* veneficium, *nt.*

poisonous, *a.* venenatus; veneficus; venenifer.

poke, *v.t.* (alicui) latus fodico, [1]; (touch) tango, [3]; (move) moveo, [2].

poker, *n.* rutabulum, *nt.*

polar, *a.* arctous.

pole, *n.* (staff) asser, *m.*; pertica, *f.*; contus, *m.*; (of the earth) polus, axis, *m.*

police, *n.* securitatis urbanae cura *or* custodia, *f.*

policeman, *n.* vigil, lictor, *m.*

policy, *n.* reipublicae administratio; (craft) astutia, calliditas, *f.*; (stratagem) ars, *f.*; dolus, *m.*; (in good sense) consilium, *nt.*

polish, *v.t.* polio; expolio, [4]; limo, levo, [1].

polish, *n.* nitor, levor, *m.*; *fig.* lima, *f.*

polite, *a.* comis, urbanus; affabilis, humanus.

politely, *ad.* comiter, humane.

politeness, *n.* urbanitas, comitas, humanitas, *f.*

politic, *a.* prudens.

political, *a.* publicus, civilis; ~ly, *ad.* quod ad rempublicam attinet.

politician, *n.* vir rerum publicarum peritus, *m.*

politics, *n.* res publica, *f.*

poll, *n.* (voting) suffragium, *nt.*

pollen, *n.* pollen, *nt.*

polling-booth, *n.* saeptum, ovile, *nt.*

poll tax, *n.* exactio capitum, *f.*

pollute, *v.t.* inquino, contamino, maculo, commaculo, foedo, [1]; polluo, [3].

pollution, *n.* colluvio; impuritas, macula, labes, *f.*

polygon, *n.* polygonum, *nt.*

polygonal, *a.* polygonius, multangulus.

pomp, *n.* pompa, *f.*; splendor, apparatus, *m.*

pompous, *a.* magniloquus; *fig.* inflatus.

pond, *n.* stagnum, *nt.*; lacus, *m.*

ponder, *v.t. & i.* considero, pensito, meditor, [1]; perpendo, [3].

pony, *n.* mannulus, *m.*

pool, *n.* lacuna, *f.*; stagnum, *nt.*

poop, *n.* puppis, *f.*

poor, *a.* pauper; egenus, inops; (of soil) macer; *fig.* tenuis; mediocris; miser.

poorly, *a.* aeger.

poplar, *n.* populus, *f.*

poppy, *n.* papaver, *nt.*

populace, *n.* vulgus, *nt.*; plebs, *f.*

popular, *a.* popularis; gratiosus; (common) vulgaris; **~ly**, *ad.* populariter, vulgo.

popularity, *n.* favor populi, *m.*; studium populi, *nt.*; gratia, *f.*

population, *n.* incolae urbis, civitatis, *etc., c. pl.*

populous, *a.* populo frequens, celeber.

porcelain, *n.* murra, *f.*; murrina, *nt. pl.*

porch, *n.* vestibulum, *nt.*; porticus, *f.*

porcupine, *n.* hystrix, *f.*

pore, *v.i.* (over) incumbo, [3] (*with dat.*).

pork, *n.* porcina, suilla, *f.*

porous, *a.* rarus.

porpoise, *n.* porculus marinus, *m.*

porridge, *n.* puls, *f.*

port, *n.* portus, *m.*

portable, *a.* quod (facile) portari potest.

portcullis, *n.* cataracta, *m.*

portend, *v.t.* praesagio, [4]; auguror, [1]; portendo, [3]; praemonstro, significo, [1].

portent, *n.* ostentum, portentum, prodigium, *nt.*

porter, *n.* ianitor, ostiarius, custos; (carrier) baiulus, *m.*

portfolio, *n.* scrinium, *nt.*

portico, *n.* porticus, *f.*

portion, *n.* pars; portio, *f.*

portly, *a.* obesus.

portrait, *n.* imago, effigies, *f.*

portray, *v.t.* pingo, [3]; delineo, [1]; *fig.* depingo, describo, [3].

pose, *n.* status, *m.*; (pretence) simulatio, *f.*

position, *n.* situs, positus; *fig.* status, *m.*; condicio, *f.*

positive, *a.* certus; *fig.* confidens; pervicax; **~ly**, *ad.* praecise; confidenter; pervicaciter.

possess, *v.t.* possideo, teneo, habeo, [2]; (of feelings) occupo, [1]; invado, [3]; (induce) animum induco, [3].

possession, *n.* (occupancy) possessio, *f.*; (goods) bona, *nt. pl.*; **in the ~ of**, penes (*with acc.*).

possessor, *n.* possessor, dominus, *m.*

possibility, *n.* possibilitas, *f.*; (opportunity) facultas, copia, potestas, *f.*

possible, *a.* possibilis; **as (quickly) as ~**, quam celerrime.

possibly, *ad.* (perhaps) fortasse.

post, *n.* (stake) sudis, *f.*; stipes, palus, *m.*; (doorpost) postis, *m.*; (letter-carriers) tabellarii, *m.*

pl.; (station) statio, sedes, *f.*, locus, *m.*; (office) munus, *nt.*

post, *v.t.* (put up) colloco, [1]; pono; constituo, [3]; (a letter) tabellario litteras do, [1].

poster, *n.* tabula, *f.*

posterior, *a.* posterior.

posterity, *n.* posteri; minores, *m. pl.*

posthumous, *a.* postumus.

postman, *n.* tabellarius, *m.*

postpone, *v.t.* differo, profero, [3]; prorogo, [1].

posture, *n.* status, habitus, gestus, *m.*

posy, *n.*, *v.* bouquet.

pot, *n.* olla, *f.*; aenum, vas, *nt.*

potent, *a.* potens.

potion, *n.* potio, *f.*

potter, *n.* figulus, *m.*

pottery, *n.* (trade) figlina, *f.*; (ware) figlinum, *nt.*; fictilia, *nt. pl.*; (workshop) figlina, *f.*

pouch, *n.* pera, *f.*; sacculus, *m.*

poultice, *n.* malagma, fomentum, cataplasma, *nt.*

poultry, *n.* aves cohortales, *f. pl.*

pounce, *n.* (swoop) impetus, *m.*

pounce, *v.i.* involo, [1]; insilio, [4].

pound, *n.* (weight and money) libra, *f.*; (for cattle) saeptum, *nt.*

pound, *v.t.* (crush) contundo, contero; (cattle) includo, [3].

pour, *v.t. & i.* fundo; fundor, [3]; ~ **down,** (of rain, *v.i.*) ruo; *fig.*

ingruo, [3]; ~ **out,** effundo, profundo, [3]; *v.i.* effundor, [3].

poverty, *n.* paupertas, pauperies, inopia, penuria, egestas, *f.*

powder, *n.* pulvis, *m.*

powder, *v.t.* pulvere conspergo, [3]; (reduce to powder) in pulverem redigo, [3].

power, *n.* vis; potestas, *f.*; (authority) ius; imperium, *nt.*; (mil.) copiae, *f. pl.*; *fig.* (of mind) dos animi, *f.*; **in (one's)** ~, penes (with acc.).

powerful, *a.* (prae)validus; potens; (effectual) efficax; ~**ly,** *ad.* potenter; efficaciter.

powerless, *a.* invalidus; infirmus, imbecillus; impotens; (vain) irritus; inefficax; **be** ~ **to,** non possum, *ir.*, nequeo, [4].

practicable, *a.* quod fieri potest.

practical, *a.* (opposite to theoretical) activus; (taught by experience) usu doctus; ~**ly,** *ad.* ex usu; (almost) paene.

practice, *n.* usus, *m.*; exercitatio; experientia; (custom) consuetudo, *f.*

practise, *v.t. & i.* exerceo, [2]; tracto, [1]; (do habitually) factito, [1].

praetor, *n.* praetor, *m.*

praetorian, *a.* praetorius.

praetorship, *n.* praetura, *f.*

praise, *n.* laus, laudatio; *f.* praeconium, *nt.*

praise, *v.t.* laudo, collaudo, praedico, [1]; effero, [3].

praiseworthy, *a.* laudabilis, laudandus.

prance, *v.i.* exsulto, [1].

prank, *n.* ludus, *m.*; fraus, *f.*

prattle, *n.* garrulitas, *f.*

prattle, *v.i.* garrio, [4]; blatero, [1].

prawn, *n.* squilla, *f.*

pray, *v.t.* precor, exoro, supplico, flagito, [1]; oro, [1]; ~ **for,** intercedo, [3] (*with* pro *with abl.*); (for a thing) peto, posco, [3]; ~ **to,** adoro; supplico, [1].

prayer, *n.* preces, *f. pl.*; precatio, *f.*

preach, *v.t. & i.* praedico, [1].

preamble, *n.* exordium, prooemium, *nt.*

precarious, *a.* incertus, precarius; ~**ly,** *ad.* precario.

precaution, *n.* cautio, provisio, *f.*

precede, *v.t.* antecedo, praegredior, praecurro, [3]; anteeo, praeeo, *ir.*

precedence, *n.* ius praecedendi, *nt.*; principatus, *m.*

precedent, *n.* exemplum, *nt.*

preceding, *a.* praecedens, antecedens.

precept, *n.* praeceptum, *nt.*

precinct, *n.* termini, limites, *m. pl.*

precious, *a.* pretiosus, carus; dilectus.

precipice, *n.* locus praeceps, *m.*; praeruptum, *n.*

precipitate, *v.t. & i.* praecipito, [1]; (hurry) accelero, festino, maturo, [1].

precipitate, *a.* praeceps; *fig.* inconsultus.

precipitous, *a.* praeceps, praeruptus, declivis.

precise, *a.* certus, definitus; (very) ipse; *fig.* (exact) accuratus, exactus; (of manner) rigidus; ~**ly,** *ad.* accurate.

precision, *n.* accuratio, *f.*

preclude, *v.t.* praecludo, [3]; arceo, prohibeo, [2].

precocious, *a.* praecox; festinus, praematurus.

preconception, *n.* praeiudicata opinio, *f.*

precursor, *n.* praenuntius, praecursor, *m.*

predatory, *a.* praedatorius; rapax.

predecessor, *n.* decessor, antecessor, *m.*

predestination, *n.* praedestinatio, *f.*

predestine, *v.t.* praedestino, [1].

predicament, *n.* praedicamentum, *nt.*; (difficulty) angustiae, *f. pl.*

predict, *v.t.* praedico, [3]; augur, vaticinor, [1].

prediction, *n.* praedictio, *f.*; praedictum; vaticinium, *nt.*; vaticinatio, *f.*

predominant, *a.* praepollens; **be ~,** praevaleo, [2].

predominate, *v.i.* praevaleo, [2].

pre-eminence, *n.* excellentia, praestantia, *f.*; (supreme rule) principatus, *m.*

pre-eminent, *a.* insignis, praestans, praecipuus; **~ly,** *ad.* praestanter, praecipue.

preface, *n.* praefatio, *f.;* exordium, prooemium, *nt.*

prefer, *v.t.* praefero, praepono, antefero, antepono, [3]; (like better) malo, *ir.*

preferable, *a.* potior, praestantior; **it is ~,** praestat.

preferably, *ad.* potius.

preference, *n.* **give ~** (to), antepono, [3].

pregnancy, *n.* graviditas; praegnatio, *f.*

pregnant, *a.* gravida, praegnans, gravis.

prejudge, *v.t.* praeiudico, [1].

prejudice, *n.* opinio praeiudicata, *f.;* detrimentum, *nt.*

prejudice, *v.t.* in suspicionem adduco, [3]; (injure) laedo, [3]; **be ~d against,** suspicor, [1].

prejudicial, *a.* noxius.

preliminary, *n.* prooemium, *nt.;* prolusio, *f.;* **~,** *a.* primus.

prelude, *n.* prooemium, *nt.; fig.* prolusio, *f.*

premature, *a.* praematurus; *fig.* praeproperus.

premeditation, *n.* praemeditatio, *f.*

premises, *n.* (house) domus, *f.;* (estate) fundus, *m.;* villa, *f.;* praedium, *nt.*

premiss, *n.* praemissa, *f.;* praemissa, *nt. pl.*

premium, *n.* praemium, *nt.*

premonition, *n.* praesagium, *nt.*

preoccupation, *n.* praeoccupatio, *f.*

preoccupy, *v.t.* praeoccupo, [1]; (also *fig.*).

preparation, *n.* praeparatio, *f.;* paratus, apparatus, *m.*

prepare, *v.t.* paro, comparo, praeparo, [1]; (furnish) orno, adorno; (study) meditor, [1]; **~,** *vi.* comparo, [1]; se accingere, [3].

prepared, *a.* paratus.

preposterous, *a.* praeposterus; perversus; absurdus; **~ly,** *ad.* perverse, absurde.

prerogative, *n.* praerogativa, *f.;* privilegium, *nt.*

presage, *n.* praesagium; augurium, omen, portentum, *nt.*

presage, *v.t. & i.* portendo, [3]; significo, [1]; praesagio, [4]; praedico, [3]; vaticinor, [1].

prescribe, *v.t.* praecipio; praescribo; propono, [3].

prescription, *n.* praescriptum, *nt.;* (custom) usus, *m.*

presence, *n.* praesentia, *f.;* **in my ~,** me praesente; **in the ~ of,** coram (*with abl.*).

present, *a.* praesens; hic, haec, hoc; **for the ~,** in praesens; **be ~,** adesse.

present, *n.* donum, munus, *nt.*

present, *v.t.* offero, [3]; dono, do, [1]; largior, [4]; introduco; (law) sisto, [3]; *fig.* (~ itself) obvenio, [4].

presentation, *n.* donatio, *f.*

presentiment, *n.* praesagium, *nt.*; **have a ~ of,** praesentio, [4].

presently, *ad.* (soon) mox; (immediately) illico, statim.

preservation, *n.* conservatio, *f.*

preserve, *v.t.* servo, conservo, [1]; tueor, [2]; (fruits) condio, [4].

preside over, *v.i.* praesideo, [2]; praesum (*both with dat.*).

presidency, *n.* praefectura, *f.*

president, *n.* praeses, praefectus, *m.*

press, *n.* (for wine, oil, clothes, *etc.*) prelum, *nt.*; (of people) turba, *f.*

press, *v.t.* premo; comprimo, [3]; *fig.* urgeo, [2]; insto, flagito, [1]; (force to serve) vi comparo, [1]; **~ on** *or* **upon,** insto, [1], insisto, [3] (*both with dat.*).

pressing, *a.* instans.

pressure, *n.* pressura, *f.*; *fig.* angor, *m.*; aerumna, *f.*

prestige, *n.* gloria, *f.*

presume, *v.t. & i.* (be conceited) arrogo, (hope) spero, [1]; (suppose) conicio, [3]; (dare) audeo, [2].

presumption, *n.* arrogantia; (conjecture) suspicio, *f.*; (opinion) sententia, *f.*

presumptuous, *a.* arrogans; audax, temerarius; **~ly,** *ad.* arroganter, audacter.

pretence, *n.* simulatio, *f.*; v. **pretext.**

pretend, *v.t. & i.* simulo, dissimulo, [1].

pretension, *n.* (claim) postulatio; (display) ostentatio, *f.*

pretext, *n.* species, *f.*; praetextum, *nt.*; (cause) **under the ~ of,** specie (*with gen.*).

prettiness, *n.* elegantia, venustas, *f.*

pretty, *a.* bellus; lepidus; venustus; **~ well,** mediocriter.

prevail, *v.i.* praevaleo, polleo; persuadeo, [2]; (become current) increbresco, [3]; **~ upon,** impetro, [1] (*with* ab *with* abl.).

prevalent, prevailing, *a.* vulgatus; **be ~,** increbresco, [3].

prevaricate, *v.i.* tergiversor, praevaricor, [1].

prevarication, *n.* praevaricatio, tergiversatio, *f.*

prevent, *v.t.* praevenio, [4]; praeverto, [3]; (stop) impedio, [4]; prohibeo, [2].

prevention, *n.* prohibitio, *f.*

previous, *a.* antecedens, prior; **~ly,** *ad.* antea, antehac, prius.

prey, *n.* praeda, *f.*; **beast of ~,** animal rapax, *nt.*, fera, *f.*

prey, *v.i.* (on, upon) praedor, [1]; rapio, [3]; *fig.* vexo, [1].

price, *n.* pretium, *nt.*; **at what ~?** quanti?

priceless, *a.* inaestimabilis.

prick, *n.* punctus, *m.*; (god) stimulus, *m.*

prick, *v.t.* pungo, [3]; *fig.* stimulo, [1]; **~ up,** (aures) arrigo, [3].

prickle, *n.* aculeus, *m.*; spina, *f.*

prickly, *a.* spinosus.

pride, *n.* superbia, *f.*; fastidium, *nt.*; fastus, *m.*

pride, *v.t.* (oneself on) iacto, [1]; superbio, [4] (*with abl.*).

priest, *n.* sacerdos, antistes, vates, *m.*

priestess, *n.* sacerdos, antistita, vates, *f.*

priesthood, *n.* (office) sacerdotium, *nt.*; (collectively) sacerdotes, *m. pl.*

prim, *a.* rigidus.

primarily, *ad.* praecipue.

primary, *a.* principalis; praecipuus.

prime, *n.* (of life) florens aetas, *f.*; *fig.* flos, *m.*; robur, *nt.*

prime, *a.* egregius, optimus.

primeval, *a.* primigenius, primaevus; priscus.

primitive, *a.* principalis, primitivus; (simple) simplex.

prince, *n.* rex, princeps, regulus; (king's son) regis filius, *m.*

princess, *n.* regina; regia puella; regis filia, *f.*

principal, *a.* principalis, praecipuus; maximus, potissimus; ~ly, *ad.* maxime, praecipue; potissimum, praesertim.

principal, *n.* caput, *nt.*; praeses, praefectus, *m.*

principle, *n.* principium, *nt.*; origo, *f.*; (in philosophy) ratio, *f.*;

(precept) praeceptum, *nt.*; (maxim) institutum, *nt.*

print, *v.t.* imprimo, [3].

print, *n.* (mark) nota, *f.*; vestigium, *nt.*

prior, *a.* prior.

prise, *v.t.* ~ open, vecti refringo, [3].

prison, *n.* carcer, *m.*; custodia, *f.*

prisoner, *n.* (of war) captivus; (law) reus, *m.*; rea, *f.*

privacy, *n.* solitudo, *f.*; secretum, *nt.*

private, *a.* privatus; (domestic) domesticus; ~ly, *ad.* privatim, secreto; clam.

privation, *n.* privatio; (need) inopia, *f.*

privilege, *n.* privilegium, beneficium, *nt.*; immunitas, *f.*

prize, *n.* (reward) praemium, *nt.*; (victory) palma, *f.*

prize, *v.t.* (value) aestimo, [1]; (highly) magni facio, [3].

probability, *n.* similitudo veri, probabilitas, *f.*

probable, *a.* verisimilis, probabilis.

probably, *ad.* probabiliter.

probation, *n.* probatio, *f.*

probe, *n.* specillum, *nt.*; ~, *v.t.* specillo tento, [1].

problem, *n.* (problems) problemata, *nt. pl.*; quaestio, *f.*

problematical, *a.* incertus, dubius.

procedure, *n.* ratio agendi, *f.*; ordo, *m.*; forma, *f.*; (proceedings) acta, facta, *nt. pl.*

proceed, *v.i.* progredior; procedo, incedo; (continue) pergo, [3]; (advance) proficio, [3]; (arise, spring from) orior, [4]; proficiscor, [3].

proceeding, *n.* facinus, factum, *nt.*; ~s, acta, facta, *nt. pl.*; **legal** ~s, actio, *f.*; controversia iudiciaria, *f.*

proceeds, *n.* reditus, proventus, *m.*

process, *n.* processus, *m.*; (method) ratio, *f.*; (law) lis, actio, *f.*

procession, *n.* pompa, *f.*

proclaim, *v.t.* promulgo, pronuntio, [1]; edico, propono, [3].

proclamation, *n.* pronuntiatio, promulgatio, *f.*; edictum, *nt.*

proconsul, *n.* proconsul, *m.*; pro consule.

proconsular, *a.* proconsularis.

proconsulship, *n.* proconsulatus, *m.*

procrastinate, *v.t.* differo, [3]; ~, *v.i.* cunctor, [1].

procrastination, *n.* tarditas, procrastinatio, cunctatio, *f.*

procure, *v.t.* (get) acquiro, adipiscor, consequor, [3]; comparo, [1].

prod, *v.t.* pungo, [3].

prodigal, *a.* prodigus; profusus, effusus.

prodigious, *a.* (monstrous) prodigiosus; (great) immanis; ingens; ~**ly,** *ad.* prodigiose; valde.

prodigy, *n.* prodigium, monstrum; portentum; *fig.* miraculum, *nt.*

produce, *v.i.* (bring forward) produco, profero, [3]; (bring forth) pario; (yield) fero, effero, profero; (cause) facio, [3]; creo, [1]; cieo, moveo, [2].

produce, *n.* fructus, *m.*

product, *n.* (of earth) fructus, *m.*; fruges, *f. pl.*; (of work) opus, *nt.*

production, *n.* prolatio; (manufacture) fabricatio, *f.*

productive, *a.* ferax, fertilis, fecundus; *fig.* efficiens.

profane, *a.* profanus; *fig.* impius.

profane, *v.t.* violo, profano, [1].

profanity, *n.* impietas, *f.*; nefas, *nt.*

profess, *v.t.* profiteor, [2].

profession, *n.* (avowal; calling, trade) professio, *f.*; (business, trade) ars, *f.*

professional, *a.* ad professionem pertinens.

professor, *n.* (literary) professor, *m.*

proffer, *v.t.* offero, propono, [3].

proficiency, *n.* ars, peritia, *f.*

proficient, *a.* peritus.

profile, *n.* facies obliqua, *f.*; (as portrait) catagrapha, *nt. pl.*

profit, *n.* emolumentum; lucrum, *nt.*; reditus, fructus, quaestus, *m.*

profit, *v.t.* prosum (*with dat.*); ~, *v.i.* proficio, [3]; (get advantage) lucror, [1]; fructum percipio, [3].

profitable, *a.* fructuosus, quaestuosus; lucrosus; utilis; **be ~,** prodesse.

profligate, *a.* perditus, flagitiosus, nequam, *indecl.*

profound, *a.* (deep) altus; *fig.* subtilis; abstrusus; ~ly, *ad.* penitus; subtiliter, abscondite.

profundity, *n.* altitudo, subtilitas, *f.*

profuse, *a.* effusus, profusus; ~ly, *ad.* effuse, profuse.

profusion, *n.* effusio, profusio, ubertas; abundantia, *f.*

programme, *n.* libellus, *m.*

progress, *n.* iter, *nt.*; progressus, processus, *m.*

progress, *v.i.* progredior, *fig.* proficio, [3].

progression, *n.* progressus, *m.*

progressively, *ad.* (gradually) paulatim, sensim, gradatim.

prohibit, *v.t.* veto, [1]; interdico, [3]; prohibeo, [2].

prohibition, *n.* interdictum, *nt.*

project, *n.* propositum, consilium, *nt.*

project, *v.t.* molior, [4]; ~, *v.i.* consilium capio, [3]; (jut out) promineo, emineo, [2].

projectile, *n.* missile, *nt.*

projecting, *a.* prominens; proiectus.

projection, *n.* proiectum, *nt.*; proiectura, *f.*

proletariat, *n.* plebs, *f.*; vulgus, *nt.*

prolific, *a.* fecundus, ferax, fertilis.

prologue, *n.* prologus, *m.*

prolong, *v.t.* produco, [3]; prorogo, [1]; extendo, traho, [3].

prominence, *n.* eminentia, *f.*

prominent, *a.* eminens; conspicuus.

promiscuous, *a.* promiscuus; mixtus; ~ly, *ad.* promiscue, sine ullo discrimine.

promise, *n.* promissum, *nt.*; (act) promissio, fides, *f.*

promise, *v.t. & i.* promitto, [3]; polliceor, spondeo, [2].

promising, *a.* bona *or* summa spe.

promote, *v.t.* augeo, [2]; tollo, effero, proveho, [3]; (serve) consulo (*with dat.*), [3].

promotion, *n.* amplior gradus, *m.*; dignitas, *f.*

prompt, *a.* promptus, paratus; (speedy) maturus; ~ly, *ad.* prompte; (speedily) mature.

prompt, *v.t.* subicio, [3]; (incite, *etc.*) impello, [3].

prone, *a.* pronus; propensus; proclivis.

prong, *n.* dens, *m.*

pronounce, *v.t.* pronuntio; (articulate syllables) enuntio, [1]; loquor, [3].

pronouncement, *n.* iudicium, *nt.*; sententia, *f.*

pronunciation, *n.* pronuntiatio, *f.*

proof, *n.* documentum, argumentum; indicium; signum; specimen, *nt.*; ratio demonstrandi *or* probandi, *f.*; (trial) experimentum, *nt.*

prop, *n.* fulcrum; *fig.* columen, *nt.*

prop up, *v.t.* fulcio, [4]; adminiculor, [1].

propagate, *v.t.* propago; (spread) dissemino, [1].

propagation, *n.* propagatio, *f.*

propel, *v.t.* impello; propello, [3].

propensity, *n.* proclivitas, *f.*

proper, *a.* proprius; (suitable) aptus; (becoming) decorus; ~**ly**, *ad.* proprie; apte; decore.

property, *n.* fortuna, *f.*; bona, *nt. pl.*; (characteristic) proprium, *nt.*

prophecy, *n.* praedictum, *nt.*; vaticinatio; (power) praedictio, divinatio, *f.*

prophesy, *v.t. & i.* vaticinor, divino, auguror, [1]; praedico, [3].

prophet, *n.* vates, *c.*; fatidicus, propheta, *m.*

prophetess, *n.* vates, *f.*

prophetic, *a.* fatidicus; (of inward feeling) praesagus.

propitious, *a.* propitius; faustus, felix, secundus; ~**ly**, *ad.* fauste, feliciter.

proportion, *n.* ratio, proportio; symmetria, *f.*; **in** ~, pro portione.

proposal, *n.* condicio, *f.*; (plan) consilium, *nt.*

propose, *v.t.* condicionem offero, [3]; (intend) cogito, [1]; (marriage) condicionem quaero, [3]; (a toast) propino, [1]; (a law) fero, [3]; promulgo, [1].

proposition, *n.* condicio; (bill) rogatio, *f.*; (advice) consilium, *nt.*; (logic) propositio, *f.*

propound, *v.t.* propono, profero, [3].

proprietor, *n.* dominus, erus, *m.*

propriety, *n.* decorum, *nt.*; convenientia, *f.*

propulsion, *n.* impulsus, *m.*

prosaic, *a.* pedester, solutae orationi proprior; *fig.* aridus, ieiunus.

proscribe, *v.t.* proscribo, [3].

proscription, *n.* proscriptio, *f.*

prose, *n.* oratio soluta, prosa, *f.*; pedester sermo, *m.*

prosecute, *v.t.* exsequor, persequor, [3]; insto (alicui), [1]; persevero in, [1] (*with abl.*); (accuse) reum facio, [3].

prosecution, *n.* executio; (law) accusatio, *f.*

prospect, *n.* prospectus, despictus, *m.*; (hope, expectation) spes, exspectatio, *f.*

prospective, *a.* futurus.

prospectus, *n.* titulus, *m.*, index, *c.*

prosper, *v.i.* prospera fortuna utor, [3]; successus prosperos habeo, [2]; bene cedo, cedo, [3].

prosperity, n. res secundae, f. pl.; prospera fortuna, prosperitas, f.

prosperous, a. secundus, prosperus; florens; ~ly, ad. prospere; bene.

prostitute, n. scortum, nt.; meretrix, f.

prostitution, n. meretricium, nt.

prostrate, a. prostratus, proiectus; fig. afflictus, fractus; fall ~, me (ad pedes alicuius) proicio; procumbo, [3].

prostration, n. fig. animus fractus, m.

protect, v.t. tueor, [2]; protego; defendo, [3]; servo, [1]; custodio, [4].

protection, n. tutela, custodia, f.; praesidium, tutamen, nt.

protector, n. patronus, defensor, propugnator, m.

protest, n. acclamatio; intercessio; interpellatio, f.

protest, v.i. & t. obtestor, acclamo, interpello, [1]; (against) aegre fero, intercedo (v.i.); (profess) profiteor, [3].

prototype, n. exemplar, nt.

protract, v.t. traho, protraho, differo, produco, [3].

protrude, v.i. promineo, emineo, [2].

protuberance, n. tuber, nt.; tumor, gibbus, m.

proud, a. superbus, arrogans; magnificus; **be ~,** superbio, fastidio, [4]; ~ly, ad. superbe; arroganter; (of things) magnifice.

prove, v.t. probo, [1]; evinco, arguo, [3]; (try) experior, [4]; (as false) refello, [3]; (show) monstro, demonstro; (make good) praesto, [1]; ~, v.i. (become) fio, ir.; (turn out to be) evado, [3].

proverb, n. proverbium, nt.

proverbial, a. proverbialis.

provide, v.t. paro, comparo, [1]; (supply) praebeo, [2]; suppedito, [1]; ~, v.i. (against) provideo (ne with subj.), praecaveo, [2]; (for) provideo (alicui), [2]; (with) instruo, [3] (with acc. and dat.).

provided, c., ~ that, dummodo, dum, modo.

providence, n. providentia, diligentia, cura; (divine) providentia, f.

provident, a. providus; cautus.

province, n. provincia; regio, f.; fig. provincia, f.; munus, nt.

provincial, a. provincialis; fig. rusticus.

provision, n. praeparatio, f.; apparatus, m.; copia, f.; ~s, (food) alimentum, nt.; victus, m.; penus, c.; (for an army) commeatus, m.; cibaria, nt. pl.; (for a journey) viaticum, nt.

provisional, a. temporarius; ~ly, ad. ad tempus.

proviso, n. exceptio, cautio, condicio, f.

provocation, n. provocatio, f.; (wrong) iniuria, f.

provoke, v.t. lacesso, [3], provoco, irrito, stimulo, [1].

prow, *n.* prora, *f.*

prowess, *n.* virtus, *f.*

prowl, *v.i.* praedor; (roam about) vagor, [1]; ~ **round,** obambulo, oberro, [1]

prowler, *n.* praedator, *m.*

proximity, *n.* propinquitas, proximitas, *f.*

proxy, *n.* vicarius, *m.*; **by** ~, vice, vicem (*both with gen.*).

prudence, *n.* prudentia; circumspectio, *f.*

prudent, *a.* cautus, prudens, consideratus; ~**ly,** *ad.* caute; considerate.

prune, *n.* prunum, *nt.*

prune, *v.t.* (trees) decacumino, amputo, puto, [1]; *fig.* reseco, [1]; recido, [3].

pruning-knife, *n.* falx, *f.*

pry, *v.i.* scrutor, perscrutor, exploro, [1].

prying, *a.* curiosus.

pseudo, *a.* fictus, simulatus.

puberty, *n.* pubertas, pubes, *f.*

public, *a.* publicus; communis; (known) pervulgatus; ~**ly,** *ad.* in publico; palam, aperte.

public, *n.* homines, *m. pl.*; *fig.* vulgus, *nt.*; multitudo, *f.*

publican, *n.* (farmer of taxes) publicanus; (innkeeper) caupo, *m.*

publication, *n.* promulgatio; (of a book) editio, *f.*; (published book) liber, *m.*

publicity, *n.* celebritas, *f.*; *fig.* lux, *f.*

publish, *v.t.* (make known) vulgo, divulgo, [1]; patefacio, [3]; (a book) edo, [3].

publisher, *n.* bibliopola, librarius, *m.*

publishing, *n.* (of a work) editio, *f.*

puddle, *n.* lacuna, *f.*

puerile, *a.* puerilis.

puff, *n.* (of wind) flatus, *m.*

puff, *v.t.* inflo, sufflo; ~, *v.i.* (pant) anhelo, [1]; ~ **up,** inflo, [1]; **be** ~**d up,** intumesco, [3].

puffy, *a.* sufflatus; tumens; turgidus; inflatus.

pugnacious, *a.* pugnax.

pull, *v.t.* vello, [3]; vellico, [1]; (drag) traho, [3]; ~, *v.i.* vires adhibeo, [2]; annitor, [3]; ~ **away,** avello, [3]; ~ **apart,** diripio; ~ **back,** revello, retraho, [3]; ~ **down,** (houses, *etc.*) demolior, [4]; destruo; (violently) everto, [3]; ~ **off,** avello; detraho, [3]; ~ **out,** extraho, evello, eximo, [3]; ~ **up,** extraho; eripio, eruo, [3].

pull, *n.* (act) tractus; (effort) nisus, *m.*

pulley, *n.* trochlea, *f.*

pulp, *n.* (flesh) caro, pulpa, *f.*

pulpit, *n.* rostra, *nt. pl.*; suggestus, *m.*; tribunal, *nt.*

pulsate, *v.i.* vibro, [1].

pulsation, *n.* pulsus, *m.*

pulse, *n.* (venarum) pulsus, *m.*

pulverize, v.t. pulvero, [1].

pumice(-stone), n. pumex, m.

pump, n. antlia, f.

pump, v.t. haurio, [4]; fig. (question) exploro, [1].

pumpkin, n. pepo, melopepo, m.; cucurbita, f.

pun, n. lusus verborum, iocus, m.

punch, n. (blow) pugnus, ictus, m.; (tool) terebra, f.

punch, v.t. (perforate) terebro, [1]; (strike) pugno percutio, [3].

punctilious, a. scrupulosus, religiosus.

punctual, a. promptus, accuratus, ad tempus veniens or rediens; **~ly,** ad. ad tempus, accurate.

punctuate, v.t. interpungo, [3].

punctuation, n. (act) interpunctio, f.; (break between sentences) interpunctum, nt.

puncture, n. (act) punctio, f.; (hole) punctum, nt.

pungent, a. (to the senses) acutus; fig. mordax; aculeatus.

Punic, a. Punicus.

punish, v.t. punio, [4]; castigo, [1]; animadverto, [3]; vindico, [1]; **be ~ed,** poenas do, [1].

punishment, n. (act) castigatio; poena, f.; supplicium, nt.

punt, n. ratis, f.

puny, a. pusillus, exiguus.

pup, n. catulus, m.

pupil, n. discipulus, m.; discipula, f.; (of the eye) pupilla, pupula, f.

puppet, n. pupa, f.

puppy, n. catulus, m.

purchase, n. (act) emptio; (merchandise) merx, f.

purchase, v.t. emo, [3]; (procure) comparo, [1].

purchaser, n. emptor; mercator, m.

pure, a. mundus; purus; (unmixed) merus; fig. purus; (chaste) castus; (of character) integer.

purge, v.t. purgo, mundo, [1].

purge, n. purgatio, f.

purification, n. purgatio; purificatio; expiatio; lustratio, f.; lustrum, nt.

purify, v.t. purifico, purgo; lustro, expio, [1].

purity, n. munditia; fig. castitas; integritas, f.

purple, n. purpura, f.; ostrum, conchylium, nt.; mureux, m.; **dressed in ~,** purpuratus.

purple, a. purpureus.

purpose, n. propositum, consilium, nt.; animus, m.; (end, aim) finis, c.; (wish) mens, voluntas, f.; **on ~,** de industria; consulto; **to the ~,** ad rem . . . ; **to no ~,** frustra.

purpose, v.t. propono, statuo, constituo, decerno, [3].

purposely, ad. consulto, consilio, de industria.

purr, v.i. murmuro, susurro, [1].

purr, n. murmur, nt.; susurrus, m.

purse, *n.* crumena; (money-belt) zona, *f.*

purse, *v.t.* (up) corrugo, [1]; contraho, [3].

pursue, *v.t.* sequor, persequor, insequor; *fig.* insisto (*with dat.*); utor, [3] (*with abl.*).

pursuit, *n.* insectatio, *f.*; (occupation) studium, *nt.*

pus, *n.* pus, *nt.*; sanies, *f.*

push, *v.t.* trudo, pello, [3]; urgeo, [2]; ~ **forward,** protrudo, propello, [3]; ~ **in,** *v.t.* intrudo, [3]; ~ **on,** impello, [3]; urgeo, [2]; (*v.i.*) contendo, [3]; (hasten) festino, [1].

push, *n.* pulsus, impetus, impulsus, *fig.* conatus, *m.*; (energy) strenuitas, *f.*

put, *v.t.* pono, [3]; loco, colloco, [1]; (a question) quaero; (again) repono; (aside) sepono; [3]; ~ **away,** sepono, [3]; amoveo, [2]; (in safety) recondo; (send away) dimitto, [3]; ~ **back,** repono; ~ **by,** (place in safety) condo; ~ **down,** depono; (lower, let down) demitto; (suppress, abolish) supprimo; tollo; (in writing) scribo; (in an account) fero, [3]; ~ **forward,** (promote) promoveo, [2]; (excuses, *etc.*) profero, [3]; (as a candidate) produco, [3]; ~ **in,** impono; (forcibly) immitto; interpono, [3]; ~ **off,** (deter) repello, [3]; (disconcert) perturbo, [1]; (distract) distraho, [3]; (postpone) differo; fero; ~ **on,** impono; (dress, clothes) induo; (add) addo, [3]; ~ **out,** expello, eicio; (fire, light)

exstinguo; (stretch out) extendo; *fig.* (disconcert, *etc.*) confundo, [3]; perturbo, [1]; (dislocate) extorqueo, [2]; ~ **together,** compono, confero; ~ **up,** erigo; arrigo, [3]; (for sale) propono; (as a candidate) peto; (at auctions) auctionor, [1]; (with) fero, [3]; ~ **upon,** super(im)pono; addo, [3] (*both with acc. and dat.*); (impose upon) verba do (alicui), [1].

putrefy, *v.i.* putresco, [3], putrefio, *ir.*

putrid, *a.* puter, putridus.

puzzle, *n.* quaestio abstrusa *or* obscura; *fig.* difficultas, *f.* nodus, *m.*

puzzle, *v.t.* confundo, [3]; perturbo, [1]; ~, *v.i.* haereo, [2].

puzzling, *a.* perplexus, obscurus.

pygmy, *n.* nanus, pumilio, *m.*

pyramid, *n.* pyramis, *f.*

pyre, *n.* rogus, *m.*; bustum, *nt.* pyra, *f.*

······································

······································

quadrangular, *a.* quadriangulus.

quadruped, *n.* quadrupes, *c.*

quadruple, *a.* quadruplex; quadruplus; ~, *n.* quadruplum, *nt.*

quadruple, *v.t.* quadruplico, [1].

quaestor, *n.* quaestor, *m.*

quaestorship, *n.* quaestura, *f.*

quagmire, *n.* palus, lacuna, *f.*

quail, *n.* coturnix, *f.*

quail, *v.i.* despondeo, [2]; paveo, [2].

quaint, *a.* mirus, insolitus; (strange, odd) rarus; ~**ly**, *ad.* mire.

quake, *v.i.* tremo, [3].

qualification, *n.* (endowment) indoles; (condition) condicio, *f.*; status, *m.*

qualified, *a.* aptus, idoneus; capax, dignus; (moderate) mediocris.

qualify, *v.t.* aptum reddo; instruo, [3]; (limit, restrict, *etc.*) tempero; extenuo, [1].

quality, *n.* qualitas; natura, *f.*; *fig.* dos, (degree) ordo, gradus, *m.*

qualm, *n.* (of conscience) religio, *f.*

quandary, *n.* angustiae, *f.*

quantity, *n.* quantitas; magnitudo, *f.*; numerus, *m.*; copia, *f.*

quarrel, *n.* iurgium, *nt.*; altercatio; rixa, simultas, *f.*

quarrel, *v.i.* iurgo; altercor; rixor, [1].

quarrelsome, *a.* iurgiosus, rixosus, pugnax.

quarry, *n.* (stone-quarry) lapicidinae, lautumiae, *f. pl.*; (prey) praeda, *f.*

quarter, *n.* quarta pars, *f.*; quadrans, *m.*; (side, direction, district) regio, *f.*; ~**s**, *pl.* (dwelling) tectum, *nt.*; habitatio, *f.*; (temporary abode) hospitium, deverticulum, *nt.*; (*mil.*) castra; **winter** ~**s**, hiberna, *nt. pl.*; **at close** ~**s**, comminus.

quarter, *v.t.* in quattor partes divido, [3]; (soldiers, *etc.*) colloco, [1]; dispono, [3]; (receive in one's house) hospitium praebeo, [2].

quarterly, *a.* (for three months) trimestris; (by the quarter) tertio quoque mense; ~, *ad.* tertio quoque mense.

quash, *v.t.* (law) rescindo, [3]; aboleo, [2]; abrogo, [1].

queen, *n.* regina, *f.*

queer, *a.* (strange) ineptus, insulsus, ridiculus.

quell, *v.t.* opprimo, restinguo, [3]; sedo, domo, [1].

quench, *v.t.* exstinguo, restinguo, [3]; (thirst) (sitim) sedo, [1], restinguo, [3].

querulous, *a.* querulus; queribundus.

query, *n.* quaestio; interrogatio; dubitatio, *f.*

quest, *n.* investigatio, *f.*

question, *n.* interrogatio; dubitatio, *f.*; (doubt) dubitatio, *f.*; (disputed point) quaestio, *f.*; controversia; *fig.* (matter) res, causa, *f.*; **call in** ~, dubito, [1]; **without** ~, non dubium est, haud dubie.

question, *v.t. & i.* interrogo; dubito; (examine) in ius voco; (investigate) scrutor, [1].

questionable, *a.* dubius, incertus.

quibble, *n.* captio; cavillatio, *f.*

quibble, *v.i.* captiose dico, [3]; cavillor, [1].

quick, *a.* (nimble, swift) agilis, celer; pernix; (keen, sharp) acer, acutus; *fig.* (of mind; clever) sollers; **be ~,** (go fast) propero; maturo, [1].

quick, quickly, *ad.* cito; velociter; propere; (hastily) festinanter.

quicken, *v.t.* (enliven) animo; (hasten) celero, propero; maturo; (rouse) excito, instigo, [1].

quickness, *n.* (nimbleness) agilitas; (liveliness) vivacitas; *fig.* sagacitas, *f.*; acumen (ingenii), *nt.*

quicksand, *n.* syrtis, *f.*

quick-witted, *a.* sollers.

quiet, *a.* quietus, tranquillus; placidus; (silent) tacitus; silens, mutus; **be** *or* **keep ~,** quiesco, [3]; (be silent) sileo; taceo, [2]; conticesco, [3].

quiet, *n.* quies, tranquillitas, *f.*; (silence) silentium, *nt.*; (peace) pax, *f.*

quiet, quieten, *v.t.* tranquillo; paco, sedo, [1].

quietly, *ad.* quiete, tranquille; sedate; tacite.

quietness, *n.* quies, requies, *f.*; pax, *f.*; silentium, *nt.*

quill, *n.* penna, *f.*; calamus, *m.*; (of porcupines) spina, *f.*

quilt, *n.* stragulum, *nt.*

quit, *v.t.* (leave) relinquo, desero, [3]; **~,** *v.i.* discedo, [3]; migro, [1].

quite, *ad.* (completely) omnino, penitus, prorsus; valde; (fairly) satis; **~ so,** ita est.

quiver, *v.i.* tremo, contremisco, [3]; trepido, [1].

quiver, *n.* pharetra, *f.*; corytus, *m.*

quota, *n.* rata pars, portio, *f.*

quotation, *n.* (passage quoted) locus allatus, *m.*

quote, *v.t.* affero, profero, [3]; cito, [1].

·····················

R

·····················

rabbit, *n.* cuniculus, *m.*

rabble, *n.* plebecula, faex populi, *f.*; vulgus, *nt.*; (crowd) turba, *f.*; grex, *m.*

rabid, *a.* rabidus, rabiosus.

rabies, *n.* rabies, *f.*

race, *n.* genus, *nt.*; stirps; prosapia; proles; (nation) gens, *f.*; (running) cursus, *m.*; (contest) certamen, *nt.*

race, *v.i.* cursu contendo, [3].

racecourse, *n.* stadium, spatium, *nt.*; hippodromus, *m.*

racehorse, *n.* celes, *m.*

racing, *n.* cursus, *m.*; certamen, *nt.*

rack, *n.* (for punishment) eculeus, *m.*; tormentum, *nt.*; (for holding fodder) falisca, *f.*

rack, *v.t.* (torture) torqueo, [2]; (one's brain) cum animo reputo, [1].

racket, *n.* (noise, stir) strepitus, *m.*; tumultus, *m.*

racy, *a.* salsus.

radiance, *n.* fulgor, splendor, *m.*

radiant, *a.* radians, nitidus, clarus, fulgidus, splendidus.

radiate, *v.i.* radio, [1]; fulgeo, niteo, [2]; ~, *v.t.* spargo, [3].

radiation, *n.* radiatio, *f.*

radically, *ad.* radicitus; penitus.

radish, *n.* raphanus, *f.*

radius, *n.* radius, *m.*

raft, *n.* ratis, *f.*

rafter, *n.* canterius, *m.*; trabs, *f.*; tignum, *nt.*

rag, *n.* pannus; *m.*; (ragged clothes) pannuli, *m. pl.*; dilabidae vestes, *f. pl.*

rage, *n.* furor, *m.*; rabies, *f.*; ira, *f.*

rage, *v.i.* furo, [3]; saevio, [4]; (as the sea) aestuo, [1].

ragged, *a.* (in tatters) lacer; (wearing such clothes) pannosus.

raging, *a.* furens, furiosus; furibundus, rabidus.

raid, *n.* incursio, irruptio, *f.*

raid, *v.t.* invado, [3].

rail, *n.* (fence) saepimentum, *nt.*; (baluster) cancelli, *m. pl.*

railing, *n.* (fence) saepimentum, *nt.*

rain, *n.* pluvia, *f.*; imber, *m.*

rain, *v.i.*; **it is ~ing.** pluit.

rainbow, *n.* arcus pluvius, arcus, *m.*

rainwater, *n.* aqua caelestis, *f.*; aquae pluviae, *f. pl.*

rainy, *a.* pluvius, pluvialis; pluviosus.

raise, *v.t.* attollo, [3]; elevo, [1]; (erect) erigo, [3]; (build) ex(s)truo, [3]; (money) cogo, [3]; (an army) exercitum contraho, [3]; (a siege) solvo, [3]; (increase) augeo, [2]; (up) sublevo, [1].

raisins, *n.* uva passa, *f.*

rake, *n.* rastrum, *nt.*, irpex, *m.*

rake, *v.t.* rado; (together) corrado [3]: *fig.* ~ **up,** colligo, [3].

rally, *v.t.* (troops) reduco; (recover) recolligo, [3]; ~, *v.i.* ex fuga convenio, [4].

ram, *n.* aries, *m.*; (also a battering ram).

ram, *v.i.* (ram down) festuco, [1]; pavio, [4]; (stuff) infercio, [4].

ramble, *n.* vagatio, ambulatio, *f.*

ramble, *v.i.* vagor, erro, ambulo, [1].

rambler, *n.* ambulator, *m.*

rambling, *a.* vagus.

rampage, *v.i.* saevio, [4].

rampart, *n.* vallum, propugnaculum, *nt.*; agger, *m.*

rancid, *a.* rancidus.

rancorous, *a.* infensus, infestus; invidus; malignus.

rancour, *n.* simultas, *f.*; odium, *nt.*

random, *a.* fortuitus; **at ~,** temere.

range, *n.* series, *f.*; ordo, *m.*; (class) genus, *nt.*; (of mountains) iugum, *nt.*; (tract) tractus, *m.*; (reach) teli iactus, *m.*; (great size) magnitudo, *f.*

range, *v.t.* (wander through) pervagor, lustro, [1].

rank, *n.* series, *f.*; ordo; gradus, *m.*; dignitas, *f.*

rank, *v.t.* colloco; ordino, [1]; **~,** *v.i.* collocor, numeror, [1].

rank, *a.* luxurians; immodicus; (of smell) fetidus; rancidus.

ransack, *v.t.* diripio, [3]; (search) exquiro, [3].

ransom, *n.* redemptio, *f.*; pretium, *nt.*

rant, *v.i.* superbe loquor, [3]; bacchor, [1].

rap, *n.* (slap) alapa, *f.*; (blow) ictus, *m.*; (with the knuckles) talitrum, *nt.*; (at the door) pulsatio, *f.*

rap, *v.t. & i.* pulso, [1]; ferio, [4].

rapacious, *a.* rapax; avidus.

rapacity, *n.* rapacitas; aviditas, *f.*

rape, *n.* raptus, *m.*; vitium virginis, stuprum, *nt.*

rape, *v.t.* constupro, violo, [1].

rapid, *a.* rapidus, celer; velox, citus; **~ly,** *ad.* rapide; cito; velociter, celeriter.

rapidity, *n.* rapiditas; velocitas, *f.*

rapist, *n.* stuprator, violator, *m.*

rapture, *n.* animus exsultans (laetitia); furor, *m.*

rapturous, *a.* (of things) mirificus; iucundus; (of persons) laetitia elatus.

rare, *a.* rarus; inusitatus; (infrequent) infrequens; mirus; *fig.* eximius, singularis.

rarely, *ad.* raro.

rarity, *n.* raritas; paucitas; (thing) res rara *or* singularis, *f.*

rascal, *n.* homo nequam, scelestus, *m.*

rash, *a.* praeceps, temerarius; inconsultus; **~ly,** *ad.* temere; inconsulte.

rash, *n.* formicatio, *f.*

rashness, *n.* temeritas, imprudentia, *f.*

rat, *n.* mus, *m.*

rate, *n.* (price) pretium; (of interest) faenus, *nt.*; (speed) celeritas, *f.* (tax) census, *m.*; (manner) modus, *m.*

rate, *v.t.* aestimo, [1]; (tax) censeo, [2].

rather, *ad.* potius; libentius; (slightly, somewhat) aliquantum, paulo, sub . . . ; expressed also by the comparative of adjectives; **I had ~,** malo, *ir.*

ratification, *n.* confirmatio, *f.*

ratify, *v.t.* ratum facio, [3]; confirmo, [1]; sancio, [4].

ratio, *n.* proportio, *f.*

ration, *n.* (portion) demensum, *nt.*; (*mil.*) cibaria, *nt. pl.*

rational, *a.* rationis particeps; intellegens; sapiens; **~ly,** *ad.* sapienter.

rattle, *n.* crepitus, strepitus; fragor, *m.*; (children's ~) crepitaculum *nt.*; crepundia, *nt. pl.*

rattle, *v.t. & i.* crepito; crepo, [1].

ravage, *v.t.* vasto, spolio, populor, [1]; diripio, [3].

rave, *v.i.* furo, [3]; saevio, [4]; *fig.* (be in a frenzy) bacchor, [1].

raven, *n.* corvus, *m.*

ravenous, *a.* rapax, vorax; edax.

ravine, *n.* angustiae, fauces, *f. pl.*; saltus, *m.*

raving, *a.* furiosus, furens, insanus, rabiosus, rabidus.

ravish, *v.t.* rapio, [3]; (a woman) constupro, [1]; (delight) delecto, [1].

ravisher, *n.* raptor; stuprator, *m.*

ravishing, *a.* iucundus, suavis, mirificus.

raw, *a.* crudus, incoctus; (of wounds) crudus; (unripe) immaturus; (unwrought) rudis; (of weather) frigidus; *fig.* rudis; imperitus.

ray, *n.* (of the sun) radius, *m.*

raze, *v.t.* (a town, *etc.*) solo aequo, [1]; everto, [3].

razor, *n.* novacula, *f.*

reach, *v.t. & i.* attingo, [3]; (come up to) assequor, [3]; (approach) appropinquo, [1]; (hand) trado, [3]; (arrive at) pervenio ad (*with acc.*), [4]; consequor; (stretch) extendor, [3].

reach, *n.* tractus, *m.*; spatium, *nt.*; (of a missile) iactus; (capacity) captus, *m.*

read, *v.t. & i.* lego, [3]; verso; (aloud) recito, [1].

readable, *a.* legibilis, lectu facilis.

reader, *n.* lector; recitator, *m.*

readily, *ad.* (willingly) libenter; (easily) facile.

readiness, *n.* facultas, facilitas, *f.*; **in ~,** in promptu.

reading, *n.* lectio; recitatio; (interpretation) lectio, *f.*

ready, *a.* paratus; promptus; expeditus; (willing) libens; (easy) facilis; **~ money,** *n.* praesens pecunia, *f.*; **be ~,** praesto sum.

real, *a.* verus; certus; germanus; **~ly,** *ad.* re vera; (surely) sane, certe.

reality, *n.* res; veritas, *f.*; verum, *nt.*

realization, *n.* effectio, *f.*; effectus, *m.*; (of ideas) cognitio rerum, *f.*

realize, *v.t.* (fulfil) efficio, ad exitum perduco; (convert into money) redigo; (understand) comprehendo, [3].

realm, *n.* regnum, *nt.*

reap, *v.t.* meto, [3]; deseco, [1]; *fig.* capio, percipio, [3].

reaper, *n.* messor, *m.*

reaping-hook, *n.* falx, *f.*

reappear, *v.i.* rursus appareo, [2]; redeo, [4]; resurgo, [3].

rear, *v.t.* educo, [1]; alo, [3]; ~, *v.i.* (of horses) arrectum se tollere, [3].

rear, *n.* tergum, *nt.*; (*mil.*) novissimum agmen; extremum agmen, *nt.*

reason, *n.* mens, intelligentia; (faculty) ratio; (motive) causa, *f.*; (understanding) consilium, *nt.*; (right) ius, aequum, *nt.*

reason, *v.i.* ratiocinor, disputo, [1].

reasonable, *a.* (rational) rationalis, rationis particeps; (sane) sanus; (judicious) prudens; (just) iustus, aequus; (moderate) mediocris, modicus.

reasonably, *ad.* merito; iure; iuste.

reasoning, *n.* ratio; ratiocinatio; disceptatio, *f.*

reassemble, *v.t.* recolligo, [3].

reassure, *v.t.* confirmo, [1].

rebel, *a. & n.* rebellis, seditiosus, *m.*

rebel, *v.i.* deficio, descisco, [3]; rebello, [1]; rebellionem facio, [3].

rebellion, *n.* rebellio, seditio, defectio, *f.*

rebellious, *a.* rebellis, seditiosus; (disobedient) contumax.

rebound, *v.i.* resilio, [4]; resulto, [1].

rebuff, *n.* repulsa, *f.*

rebuff, *v.t.* repello, reicio; sperno, [3].

rebuild, *v.t.* reficio, restituo, [3].

rebuke, *v.t.* vitupero, [1]; reprehendo, [3].

rebuke, *n.* vituperatio, reprehensio, *f.*

recall, *v.t.* revoco, [1]; (to the mind) in memoriam redigo, [3].

recapitulate, *v.t.* breviter repeto, summatim colligo, [3].

recapture, *v.t.* recipio, [3]; recupero, [1].

recede, *v.i.* recedo; refugio, discedo, [3].

receipt, *n.* (act) acceptio; (verbal release from an obligation) acceptilatio, *f.*; (money received) acceptum, *nt.*

receive, *v.t.* accipio, recipio, excipio; (get) percipio, [3].

recent, *a.* recens; ~**ly**, *ad.* nuper, modo.

receptacle, *n.* receptaculum, *nt.*; cisterna, *f.*

reception, *n.* aditus, *m.*; admissio, *f.*; (of a guest) hospitium, *nt.*

recess, *n.* (place) recessus, secessus, *m.*; latebra, *f.*; (vacation) feriae, *f. pl.*; iustitium, *nt.*

recipe, *n.* praescriptum, *nt.*; compositio, *f.*

recipient, *n.* acceptor, *m.*

reciprocal, *a.* mutuus; ~**ly**, *ad.* mutuo; vicissim.

reciprocate, *v.t.* alterno, [1].

recital, *n.* narratio; enumeratio; recitatio, *f.*

recitation, *n.* recitatio; lectio, *f.*

recite, *v.t.* narro; recito, [1].

reciter, *n.* recitator, *m.*

reckless, *a.* neglegens; (rash) temerarius; imprudens; ~**ly**, *ad.* temere.

recklessness, *n.* neglegentia, incuria; temeritas, *f.*

reckon, *v.t.* numero; computo, aestimo, [1]; (consider, estimate) duco, pendo, [3]; (on) confido (alicui aliqua re); ~ **up**, enumero, [1].

reckoning, *n.* numeratio; (account) ratio, *f.*

reclaim, *v.t.* reposco; repeto, [3].

recline, *v.i.* recubo, [1]; recumbo, [3]; iaceo, [2]; (at table) accubo, [1]; accumbo, [3].

recognition, *n.* recognitio, *f.*; **in** ~ **of**, pro (*with abl.*).

recognize, *v.t.* agnosco; recognosco, cognosco, [3].

recoil, *v.i.* resilio, [4], recido, [3]; (from) recedo, refugio, discedo, [3].

recollect, *v.t.* (remember) recordor, [1]; reminiscor, [3]; memini (perfect in form).

recollection, *n.* memoria; recordatio, *f.*

recommence, *v.t.* itero, renovo, [1]; repeto, [3].

recommend, *v.t.* commendo, [1].

recommendation, *n.* commendatio, *f.*

recompense, *n.* praemium, *nt.*; merces, remuneratio, *f.*

recompense, *v.t.* remuneror; (indemnify) compenso, [1].

reconcile, *v.t.* reconcilio, [1]; in gratiam restituo, [3]; **be** ~**d to**, aequo animo fero, [3]; **be** ~**d** (in harmony) convenio, [4].

reconciliation, *n.* reconciliatio, *f.*; reditus in gratiam, *m.*

reconnoitre, *v.t.* exploro, speculor, [1].

reconsider, *v.t.* recognosco, [3]; retracto, [1].

record, *v.t.* memoro, commemoro, narro, [1].

record, *n.* mentio, narratio, *f.*; monumentum, *nt.*; historia, *f.*; ~**s**, *pl.* annales, *m. pl.*

recount, *v.t.* refero, [3]; memoro, narro, enarro, [1].

recoup, *v.t.* (regain) recipero, [1].

recourse, *n.* have ~ to, confugio, perfugio, [3], adeo, [4] (*all with* ad *with* acc.).

recover, *v.t.* (get back) recipero, [1]; recipio, [3]; ~, *v.i.* convalesco, [3].

recovery, *n.* reciperatio; (from illness) recreatio, refectio, *f.*

recreation, *n.* animi remissio, oblectatio, *f.*; (for children) lusus, *m.*

recrimination, *n.* mutua accusatio, *f.*

recruit, *v.t.* (troops) suppleo, [2].

recruit, *n.* tiro, *m.*

recruitment, *n.* delectus, *m.*; supplementum, *nt.*

rectangular, *a.* orthogonius.

rectify, *v.t.* corrigo, [3]; emendo, [1].

recur, *v.i.* recurro, [3].

recurrence, *n.* reditus, *m.*

recurrent, *a.* recurrens.

red, *a.* ruber; (ruddy) rubicundus; (of hair) rufus; be ~, rubeo, [2]; grow ~, rubesco, erubesco, [3].

redden, *v.t.* rubefacio, [3]; ~, *v.i.* rubesco; erubesco, [3].

reddish, *a.* surrufus, surrubicundus, rubicundulus.

redeem, *v.t.* redimo, [3]; libero; (a pledge) repignero, [1].

red-hot, *a.* candens.

redness, *n.* rubor, *m.*

redouble, *v.t.* gemino, ingemino, [1].

redress, *v.t.* emendo, [1]; corrigo, [3]; medeor, [2].

redress, *n.* (remedy) remedium, *nt.*

reduce, *v.t.* reduco; redigo (*both* ad *or* in *with* acc.); (lessen) minuo, [3].

reduction, *n.* deminutio, *f.*

redundancy, *n.* redundantia, *f.*

redundant, *a.* redundans, supervacaneus, superfluus.

reed, *n.* arundo, *f.*; calamus, *m.*; canna, *f.*

reef, *n.* scopulus, *m.*; dorsum, *nt.*; cautes, *f.*

reel, *v.i.* (stagger) vacillo, titubo, [1].

re-enter, *v.t.* iterum intro, [1].

re-establish, *v.t.* restituo, reficio, [3].

refectory, *n.* cenatio, *f.*

refer, *v.t.* refero; remitto (*both with* ad *with* acc.), [3]; ~, *v.i.* (allude to) perstringo, attingo, [3]; (regard) specto, [1].

referee, *n.* arbiter, disceptator, *m.*

reference, *n.* (respect) ratio, *f.*

refill, *v.t.* repleo, [2].

refine, *v.t.* purgo, [1]; excolo, [3]; expolio, [4]; (metals) excoquo, [3].

refined, *a. fig.* cultus, politus; elegans; urbanus; humanus.

refinement, *n. fig.* urbanitas, humanitas; elegantia, *f.*

reflect, *v.t.* repercutio, [3]; ~, *v.i.* considero, meditor, reputo, [1]; revolvo, [3].

reflection, *n.* repercussus, *m.*; (thing reflected) imago; *fig.* consideratio, *f.*

reform, *v.t.* reficio; (amend) corrigo, [3]; emendo, [1]; ~, *v.i.* se corrigere, [3].

reform, *n.* correctio, *f.*

reformer, *n.* corrector, emendator, *m.*

refrain, *n.* versus intercalaris, *m.*

refrain, *v.i.* abstineo, [2] (*with* ab *with abl.*); parco, [3] (*with dat.*).

refresh, *v.t.* (restore) recreo, [1]; reficio, [3]; (the memory) redintegro, [1]; (cool) refrigero, [1].

refreshing, *a.* (cool) frigidus; (pleasant) iucundus.

refreshment, *n.* refectio, *f.*; (food) cibus, *m.*

refuge, *n.* refugium, perfugium, asylum, *nt.*; **take** ~, (in), confugio (in *with acc.*), [3].

refugee, *n.* profugus, *m.*; ex(s)ul, *c.*

refund, *v.t.* reddo, [3].

refusal, *n.* recusatio; repudiatio; detrectatio; repulsa, *f.*

refuse, *v.t.* recuso, nego; repudio, [1]; renuo, [3]; denego, detrecto, [1].

refuse, *n.* recrementum, purgamentum, *nt.*; faex, *f.*; quisquiliae, *f. pl.*

refute, *v.t.* refuto, confuto, [1]; refello, redarguo, [3].

regain, *v.t.* recipio, [3]; recupero, [1].

regal, *a.* regalis, regius, regificus; **~ly,** *ad.* regie, regaliter, regifice.

regard, *n.* respectus, *m.*; ratio; (care, *etc.*) cura, *f.*

regard, *v.t.* respicio, [3]; intueor, [2]; (observe) observo; (concern) specto; (mind, care) curo; (esteem) aestimo, [1]; pendo, [3]; (respect) rationem habeo, [2].

regarding, *pr.,* v. **concerning**.

regardless, *a.* neglegens, incuriosus; v. heedless; ~, *ad.* nihilominus.

regenerate, *v.t.* regenero; *fig.* redintegro, renovo, restauro, [1].

regime, *n.* (government) rerum administratio, *f.*

regiment, *n.* legio, caterva, *f.*

regimental, *a.* legionarius.

region, *n.* regio, plaga, *f.*; tractus, *m.*; (neighbourhood) vicinitas, *f.*

register, *n.* tabulae, *f. pl.*; index, *c.*

register, *v.t.* in tabulas refero, [3].

registrar, *n.* tabularius; ab actis; actuarius, *m.*

registration, *n.* perscriptio, *f.*

registry, *n.* tabularia, *f.*; tabularium, *nt.*

regret, *v.t.* (be sorry for) aegre fero, [3]; (bemoan) doleo; piget, [2]; (repent) paenitet, [2]; (miss) desidero, [1].

regret, *n.* paenitentia, *f.*; dolor, *m.*; (feeling of loss) desiderium, *nt.*

regular, *a.* (fixed) certus; (according to law) legitimus, iustus; (usual) usitatus; **~ly,** *ad.* ordine; iuste, legitime; (at fixed times) certis temporibus.

regularity, *n.* symmetria; constantia; (uniformity) aequabilitas, *f.*

regulate, *v.t.* ordino, [1]; dispono; praescribo, [3]; administro, [1].

regulation, *n.* ordinatio; moderatio, temperatio, *f.*; (law) lex, *f.*; (rule) praescriptum, *nt.*

rehabilitate, *v.t.* restituo, [3].

rehearsal, *n.* (recital) narratio, recitatio; (of a play, *etc.*) prolusio, exercitatio, meditatio, *f.*

rehearse, *v.t.* recito, [1]; repeto, [3]; (practise) meditor, [1]; praeludo, [3].

reign, *n.* regnum, *nt.*; **~,** *v.i.* regno; dominor, [1].

reimburse, *v.t.* rependo, [3].

rein, *n.* habena, *f.*; frenum, lorum, *nt.*; **~,** *v.t.* freno, [1]; *fig.* cohibeo, [2].

reindeer, *n.* tarandrus, *m.*

reinforce, *v.t.* suppleo, [2]; auxiliis confirmo, [1].

reinforcement, *n.* (*mil.*) novae copiae, *f. pl.*; subsidium, *nt.*

reinstate, *v.t.* restituo, [3].

reiterate, *v.t.* itero, [1].

reject, *v.t.* reicio, [3]; repudio, [1]; repello; (scorn) sperno, [3].

rejection, *n.* reiectio, repudiatio, repulsa, *f.*

rejoice, *v.i.* gaudeo, [2]; exsulto, laetor, [1].

rejoin, *v.t.* (meet) convenio, [4] (with cum *with abl.*); **~,** *v.i.* (answer) respondeo, [2]; resequor, [3].

rejoinder, *n.* responsum, *nt.*

rekindle, *v.i.* refoveo, [2]; excito, [1].

relapse, *v.i.* recido, relabor, [3].

relapse, *n.* morbus recidivus, *m.*

relate, *v.t.* refero, [3]; memoro; narro, [1].

related, *a.* (by blood) consanguineus; (by marriage) affinis; *fig.* propinquus, cognatus; coniunctus.

relation, *n.* narratio; (reference) ratio; (relationship) cognatio, *f.*; (person) cognatus, *m.*; cognata, *f.*

relationship, *n.* propinquitas; necessitudo; cognatio; (by blood) consanguinitas; (by marriage) affinitas; *fig.* coniunctio, *f.*

relative, *a.* cognatus; **~ly,** *ad.* pro ratione.

relative, n. cognatus, m.; cognata, f.; v. **related.**

relax, u.t. remitto, [3]; laxo, relaxo, [1]; resolvo, [3]; ~, u.i. relanguesco; (abate) remittor, [3].

relaxation, n. remissio; relaxatio, f.

relay, n. cursus publici, m. pl.

release, u.t. libero, [1]; resolvo, [3]; laxo, [1]; (relieve) exonero, levo, relevo, [1].

release, n. liberatio; absolutio; (discharge) missio, f.

relegate, u.t. relego, [1].

relent, u.i. mitesco, [3]; mitigor, [1]; lenior, [4].

relentless, a. immisericors, inexorabilis, atrox, durus.

relevant, a. aptus, appositus.

reliable, a. fidus, certus.

reliance, n. fiducia, f.; fides, f.

relic, n. reliquiae, f. pl.; monumentum, nt.

relief, n. (comfort) solacium; (alleviation) levamentum; (help) auxilium, nt.; (remedy) medicina, f.; remedium, nt.; (in sculpture) caelatura, f.

relieve, u.t. levo, allevo; mitigo, [1]; (aid) succurro, [3]; (succeed) subeo, [4] (both with dat.); (take over a duty) excipio, [3].

religion, n. religio, pietas, f.

religious, a. religiosus; pius.

relinquish, u.t. relinquo, [3]; derelinquo, demitto, omitto, depono, [3].

relish, n. (flavour) sapor, m.; (seasoning) condimentum; (fondness) studium, nt.

relish, u.t. (like) gusto, [1]; (enjoy) fruor, [3] (with abl.).

reluctance, n. aversatio, f.

reluctant, a. invitus; ~ly, ad. invitus (adj.); aegre.

rely, u.i. (trust) confido (alicui or aliqua re), [3].

remain, u.i. (stay) maneo, permaneo, [2]; resto, [1]; (last) sto, duro, [1], (be left over) supersum, ir.

remainder, n. reliquum, nt.

remaining, a. reliquus.

remains, n. pl. reliquiae, f. pl.

remark, u.t. observo, [1]; animadverto, [3].

remark, n. observatio, animadversio, f.; (something said) dictum, nt.

remarkable, a. insignis, memorabilis, notabilis; mirus; egregius.

remarkably, ad. insigniter; mire; egregie.

remedial, a. medicus, medicabilis.

remedy, n. remedium, nt.; medicina, f.

remedy, u.t. sano, [1]; medeor, [2]; corrigo, [3].

remember, u.t. memini (perfect in form); recordor, [1]; reminiscor, [3].

remind, *v.t.* commoneo, [2]; commonefacio, [3].

reminiscence, *n.* recordatio, *f.*

remiss, *a.* neglegens; incuriosus.

remission, *n.* remissio; venia, *f.*

remit, *v.t.* (abate) remitto, [3]; (forgive) condono, [1]; (money) transmitto, [3]; ∼, *v.i.* relaxor, [1].

remittance, *n.* remissio, *f.*

remnant, *n.* reliquum, *nt.*; reliquiae, *f pl.*

remonstrate, *v.t.* obtestor, acclamo, interpello, [1]; aegre fero, [3].

remorse, *n.* angor conscientiae, *m.*; stimuli, *m. pl.*

remorseless, *a.* immisericors; durus; crudelis.

remote, *a.* remotus; amotus, ultimus; longinquus; disiunctus.

removal, *n.* remotio; exportatio; (banishment) amandatio; relegatio; (changing one's dwelling) migratio, *f.*

remove, *v.t.* amoveo, [2]; depello, tollo, detraho, [3]; amando, [1].

remunerate, *v.t.* remuneror, [1].

remuneration, *n.* remuneratio, *f.*

render, *v.t.* reddo; facio; (hand over) trado; (a town, *etc.*) dedo; (translate) verto, [3].

rendezvous, *n.* locus praescriptus (ad conveniendum); (meeting itself) conventus, *m.*

renegade, *n.* transfuga, *m.*

renew, *v.t.* renovo; novo; redintegro, [1].

renewal, *n.* renovatio; integratio, *f.*

renounce, *v.t.* missum facio; pono, depono, [3]; (deny) nego, [1].

renovate, *v.t.* renovo, redintegro, [1]; (repair) reparo, instauro, [1].

renovation, *n.* renovatio, *f.*

renown, *n.* fama, gloria, *f.*; nomen, *nt.*

renowned, *a.* insignis, celeber, clarus; praeclarus.

rent, *n.* reditus, *m.*; vectigal, *nt.*; merces, pensio, *f.*; (fissure) scissura, rima, *f.*

rent, *v.t.* (let out) loco, [1]; (hire) conduco, [3].

renunciation, *n.* abdicatio, repudiatio, *f.*

reopen, *v.t.* iterum aperio, [4]; *fig.* (a case) retrecto, [1].

reorganize, *v.t.* restituo, [3].

repair, *v.t.* (buildings) reparo, instauro, [1]; (make good) reficio; restituo, [3]; (clothes) resarcio, [4]; (cure) sano, [1]; (make amends for) sarcio, [4].

repair, *n.* refectio, *f.*

repairer, *n.* refector, *m.*

reparation, *n.* restitutio, *f.*; (amends) satisfactio, *f.*

repartee, *n.* salsum dictum, *nt.*

repay, *v.t.* repono, retribuo, [3]; remuneror, [1]; (compensate) penso, compenso, repenso, [1].

repayment, *n.* solutio; remuneratio, *f.*

repeal, *v.t.* abrogo, [1]; rescindo, tollo, [3].

repeal, *n.* abrogatio, *f.*

repeat, *v.t.* itero, [1]; repeto, [3].

repeatedly, *ad.* iterum atque iterum, saepius.

repel, *v.t.* repello, [3]; *fig.* aspernor, [1].

repent, *v.i.* paenitet (me), [2].

repentance, *n.* paenitentia, *f.*

repentant, *a.* paenitens.

repercussion, *n.* repercussio, *f.*

repetition, *n.* iteratio; repetitio, *f.*

replace, *v.t.* repono; (restore) restituo; (substitute) substituo, suppono, [3].

replenish, *v.t.* repleo, suppleo, [2].

reply, *n.* responsum, *nt.*; responsio, *f.*; ~, *v.t. & i.* respondeo, [2]; refero, [3].

report, *v.t.* fero, [3]; narro, nuntio, [1]; (state) propono, [3].

report, *n.* (rumour) fama, *f.*; rumor, *m.*; (hearsay) auditio, *f.*; (noise) fragor, crepitus, *m.*; relatio; narratio, *f.*

repose, *v.i.* (rest) quiesco, requiesco, [3].

repose, *n.* quies, requies, *f.*

represent, *v.t.* repraesento, [1]; exprimo; propono, [3]; (act on behalf of) vicem impleo (*with gen.*), [2]; loco sum (*with gen.*).

representation, *n.* (act) repraesentatio; (statement) editio; (likeness) imago, *f.*;

representative, *n.* vicarius; procurator, *m.*

repress, *v.t.* reprimo, comprimo, [3]; coerceo, [2]; (tame) domo, [1].

repression, *n.* refrenatio, coercitio, *f.*

reprieve, *n.* dilatio (supplicii), *f.*; ~, *v.t.* diem prorogare damnato.

reprimand, *v.t.* reprehendo, [3]; ~, *n.* reprehensio, *f.*

reprisal, *n.* talio; vindicta, *f.*

reproach, *v.t.* obicio, [3]; exprobro; vitupero; accuso, [1].

reproachful, *a.* obiurgatorius.

reproduce, *v.t.* refero, [3].

reproof, *n.* reprehensio, vituperatio, obiurgatio, *f.*

reprove, *v.t.* obiurgo, vitupero, [1]; reprehendo, [3].

reptile, *n.* repens animal, *nt.*

republic, *n.* respublica, civitas popularis, libera civitas, *f.*

republican, *a.* popularis.

repudiate, *v.t.* repudio, [1]; respuo, renuo, abnuo, sperno, [3].

repugnance, *n.* aversatio, *f.*; fastidium, *n.*; fuga, *f.*

repugnant, *a.* odiosus; alienus.

repulse, *v.t.* repello, [3]; propulso, fugo, [1].

repulsion, *n.* repulsus, *m.*; (dislike) odium, *nt.*

repulsive, *a.* odiosus; foedus.

reputable, *a.* honestus, bonae famae.

reputation, **repute**, *n.* fama, existimatio, *f.*; nomen, *nt.*

request, *n.* preces, *f. pl.*; **at the ~ of**, rogatu (*with gen.*).

request, *v.t.* rogo, [1]; peto, [3]; supplico, precor, [1].

require, *v.t.* (demand) postulo, [1], posco, [3]; (need) egeo, [2] (*with abl.*); desidero, [1].

requirements, *n.* necessaria, *nt. pl.*

requisite, *a.* necessarius.

rescue, *v.t.* libero, recupero; (save) servo, [1].

rescue, *n.* liberatio, recuperatio, *f.*

research, *n.* investigatio, *f.*

resemblance, *n.* similitudo, *f.*; in-star, *nt.* (*indecl.*).

resemble, *v.i.* similis sum.

resent, *v.t.* aegre *or* graviter fero, [3]; indignor, [1].

resentful, *a.* iracundus; indig-nans.

resentment, *n.* indignatio, *f.*

reservation, *n.* retentio, *f.*

reserve, *v.t.* reservo, [1]; repono, condo, recondo, [3]; retineo, [2].

reserve, *n.* (silence) taciturnitas, *f.*; (*mil.*) subsidium, *nt.*

reserved, *a.* (silent) taciturnus, tectus.

reservoir, *n.* cisterna, *f.*; recepta-culum, *nt.*; lacus, *m.*

reside, *v.i.* habito, commoror, [1].

residence, *n.* habitatio; sedes, *f.*; domicilium, *nt.*; (sojourn) com-moratio, *f.*

resident, *n.* habitator, *m.*

residue, *n.* residuum, reliquum, *nt.*

resign, *v.t.* cedo, depono, [3]; abdi-co, [1]; **~ oneself to**, aequo animo fero, [3].

resignation, *n.* (act) abdicatio; (surrendering (in law)) cessio, *f.*; *fig.* aequus animus, *m.*

resin, *n.* resina, *f.*

resist, *v.i.* resisto, [3]; obsto, ad-versor, [1] (*with dat.*).

resistance, *n.* repugnantia; (*mil.*) defensio, *f.*

resolute, *a.* audax; constans; for-tis; firmus; **~ly**, *ad.* constanter; fortiter; audacter; firme.

resolution, *n.* (plan) consilium, *nt.*; (of mind) constantia, *f.*; (courage) animus, *m.*; (of an as-sembly) decretum, *nt.*

resoluteness, **resolve**, *n.* con-stantia, *f.*; consilium, *nt.*

resolve, *v.t.* decerno, statuo, con-stituo, [3]; (solve) solvo, [3]; re-solvo, reduco, redigo, [3].

resonant, *a.* resonus.

resort, *v.i.* (have recourse to) con-fugio, [3]; convenio, [4] *both with* ad *with acc.*

resort, *n.* (refuge) refugium, per-fugium, *nt.*

resound, *v.i.* resono, persono, [1].

resource, *n.* refugium, auxilium, *nt.*; ~s, opes, *f. pl.*

resourceful, *a.* callidus.

respect, *v.t.* revereor, [2]; veneror; observo, [1].

respect, *n.* (regard) respectus, *m.*; (reverence) reverentia, observantia, *f.*; (relation, reference) ratio, *f.*; **with ~ to**, ad (*with acc.*), de (*with abl.*); (as regards) quod attinet ad (*with acc.*).

respectability, *n.* honestas, *f.*

respectable, *a.* honestus; (fairly good) tolerabilis.

respectful, *a.* observans; reverens; ~**ly**, *ad.* cum summa observantia; reverenter.

respecting, *pr.* ad (*with acc.*), de (*with abl.*), quod attinet ad (*with acc.*).

respiration, *n.* respiratio, *f.*

respite, *n.* (delay) mora; cessatio; intermissio, *f.*

resplendent, *a.* resplendens, clarus, nitidus; ~**ly**, *ad.* clare, nitide.

respond, *v.i.* respondeo, [2].

response, *n.* responsum, *nt.*

responsible, *a.* obnoxius; (trustworthy) fidus; (able to pay) locuples; **be ~ for**, praesto, [1] (*with dat.*).

rest, *n.* quies; requies; pax, *f.*; (prop) fulcrum, *nt.*, statumen, *nt.*; (remainder) residuum, reliquum, *nt.*; (of people) reliqui, ceteri, *m. pl.*

rest, *v.i.* (re)quiesco, [3]; (pause) cesso, [1]; (lean) nitor; (on) innitor, [3] (*with dat.*); ~, *v.t.* (lean) reclino, [1].

restaurant, *n.* caupona, *f.*

restive, *a.* sternax, petulans.

restless, *a.* inquietus; turbidus, tumultuosus; (agitated) sollicitus; ~**ly**, *ad.* turbulente.

restoration, *n.* refectio; (recall) reductio, *f.*

restore, *v.t.* restituo, reddo, [3]; restauro, reparo, [1]; (health, *etc.*) sano, [1]; (recall) reduco, [3].

restrain, *v.t.* refreno, [1]; coerceo, [2]; (limit) circumscribo, [3]; contineo, [2]; (prevent) impedio, [4]; prohibeo, [2].

restraint, *n.* coercitio; moderatio, *f.*

restrict, *v.t.* cohibeo, [2]; restringo, circumscribo, [3].

restriction, *n.* restrictio, limitatio, *f.*

result, *v.i.* (ex)orior, [4]; proficiscor, [3]; fio, *ir.*; (follow) consequor, [3].

result, *n.* (effect) exitus, eventus, *m.*; (conclusion) summa, *f.*

resume, *v.t.* resumo; repeto, [3]; redintegro, [1].

resuscitate, *v.t.* resuscito, revoco, [1].

retain, *v.t.* retineo, [2]; servo, [1].

retaliate, *v.i.* ulciscor, [3]; par pro pari refero, [3].

retaliation, *n.* lex talionis; ultio, *f.*

retch, *v.i.* nauseo, [1].

reticent, *a.* taciturnus.

retinue, *n.* comitatus, *m.*; pompa; turba clientium, *f.*

retire, *v.i.* recedo, regredior, decedo, [3]; abeo, [4].

retirement, *n.* solitudo, *f.*; recessus, *m.*; (from office) abdicatio, *f.*

retort, *v.t.* regero, refero, [3]; ~, *v.i.* respondeo, [2].

retort, *n.* responsum, *nt.*

retrace, *v.t.* repeto, [3]; ~ one's steps, revertor, [3].

retract, *v.t.* retracto, recanto, [1].

retreat, *v.i.* recedo, refugio, [3]; pedem refero, *ir.*

retreat, *n.* recessus, *m.*; refugium, *nt.*; latebrae, *f. pl.*; lustrum, *nt.*; (*mil.*) receptus, *m.*

retribution, *n.* poena, vindicta, *f.*; supplicium, *nt.*

retrieve, *v.t.* (recover) recupero, [1]; (make good) sarcio, [4]; sano, [1].

return, *v.t.* (give back) restituo, reddo, [3]; (send back) remitto, [3]; ~, *v.i.* (go back) redeo, [4]; revertor, [3]; (come back) revenio, [4].

return, *n.* (coming back) reditus; regressus, *m.*; (giving back) restitutio; (repayment) remuneratio, *f.*; (income, profit, *etc.*) fructus, quaestus; reditus, *m.*

reunion, *n.* reconciliatio, *f.*

reunite, *v.t. & i.* reconcilio, [1].

reveal, *v.t.* retego; recludo, patefacio, prodo, [3]; nudo; (unveil) revelo, [1]; (make known) evulgo, divulgo, [1].

revel, *v.i.* debacchor, comissor, [1].

revelation, *n.* patefactio, *f.*

revelry, *n.* comissatio, *f.*; orgia, *nt. pl.*

revenge, *v.t.* ulciscor (ultus sum), [3].

revenge, *n.* ultio, vindicta, *f.*; take ~ (on), vindico (in aliquem), [1]; poenas repeto ab (aliquo), [3].

revenger, *n.* ultor, *m.*; ultrix, *f.*; vindex, *c.*

revenue, *n.* reditus, fructus, *m.*; vectigal, *nt.*

reverberate, *v.t.* repercutio, [3]; *v.i.* resono, persono, [1].

reverberation, *n.* repercussus, *m.*

revere, *v.t.* revereor, [2]; veneror, observo, [1]; colo, [3].

reverence, *n.* reverentia, veneratio, observantia, *f.*

reverent, *a.* reverens; pius; ~ly, *ad.* venerabiliter, reverenter.

reversal, *n.* rescissio, infirmatio, *f.*

reverse, *n.* (change) conversio, commutatio (fortunae); (defeat) clades, *f.*; (contrary) contrarium, *nt.*; (of a medal) aversa pars, *f.*

reverse, *v.t.* inverto; (alter) converto; (annul) rescindo, [3].

revert, *v.i.* revertor, recurro, [3]; redeo, [4].

review, *n.* recensio, *f.*; recensus, *m.*; (critique) censura, *f.*

review, *v.t.* recenseo, [2]; lustro, [1].

reviewer, *n.* censor, *m.*

revise, *v.t.* recenseo, [2]; retracto, [1]; relego, corrigo, [3]; *fig.* limo, [1].

revision, *n.* correctio; (of a literary work), *fig.* lima, *f.*

revisit, *v.t.* reviso, [3].

revival, *n.* renovatio, *f.*

revive, *v.t.* resuscito, [1]; (renew) renovo; (encourage) animo; (refresh) recreo; (recall) revoco, [1]; ~, *v.i.* revivisco, [3].

revoke, *v.t.* revoco, [1]; (a law) rescindo, tollo, [3].

revolt, *v.t.* offendo, [3]; ~, *v.i.* rebello, [1]; descisco, secedo, deficio, [3].

revolt, *n.* rebellio; defectio, *f.*

revolution, *n.* circuitus, *m.*; circumversio, *f.*; circumactus, *m.*; (change) commutatio, *f.*; (of planets) cursus, meatus, *m.*; (political) res novae, *f. pl.*

revolutionary, *a.* seditiosus, novarum rerum cupidus; ~, *n.* rerum novarum molitor, *m.*

revolve, *v.t.* volvo, [3]; voluto, [1]; ~, *v.i.* circumvolvor, circumvertor, circumagor, [3].

revolving, *a.* versatilis, versabundus.

revulsion, *n.* taedium, *nt.*

reward, *v.t.* remuneror, [1].

reward, *n.* praemium, *nt.*; merces, *f.*; fructus, *m.*

rewrite, *v.t.* rescribo, [3].

rhetoric, *n.* rhetorice, oratoria, *f.*; rhetorica, *nt. pl.*

rhetorical, *a.* rhetoricus; oratorius.

rheumatism, *n.* dolor artuum, *m.*

Rhine, *n.* Rhenus, *m.*

rhinoceros, *n.* rhinoceros, *m.*

rhododendron, *n.* rhododendron, *nt.*

Rhone, *n.* Rhodanus, *m.*

rhyme, *n.* versus, *m.*

rhythm, *n.* numerus, rhythmus, *m.*

rhythmic(al), *a.* numerosus, rhythmicus.

rib, *n.* costa, *f.*

ribald, *a.* obscenus, spurcus, turpis.

ribbon, *n.* taenia, vitta, fascia, *f.*; lemniscus, *m.*

rice, *n.* oryza, *f.*

rich, *a.* dives, locuples, pecuniosus, opimus; abundans, copiosus; (of the soil, *etc.*) fertilis, uber (of things).

riches, *n.* divitiae, opes, *f. pl.*

richness, *n.* opulentia, abundantia, copia; ubertas, fertilitas, *f.*

rickety, *a.* instabilis.

rid, *v.t.* libero, [1]; **get ~ of,** amolior, [4]; amoveo, removeo, [2]; dimitto, depono, [3]; (also *fig.*).

riddle, *n.* aenigma, *nt.*; ambages, *f. pl.*

riddle, *v.t.* (with wounds, *etc.*) confodio, [3].

ride, *v.t.* (a horse) equo vehor, [3]; ~, *v.i.* equito, [1]; ~ **away or off,** avehor, [3]; ~ **past,** praetervehor, [3].

ride, *n.* equitatio; vectatio, vectio, *f.*

rider, *n.* eques; vector, *m.*; (addition) adiectio, *f.*

ridge, *n.* iugum, dorsum; culmen, *nt.*

ridicule, *n.* ludibrium, *nt.*; risus, *m.*; ~, *v.t.* rideo, irrideo, [2].

ridiculous, *a.* ridiculus; ~**ly,** *ad.* ridicule.

riding, *n.* equitatio, *f.*

riding-school, *n.* hippodromos, *m.*

rife, *a.* frequens, vulgatus; **become** ~, increbresco, [3].

riffraff, *n.* plebecula, *f.*; vulgus, *nt.*; faex populi, *f.*

rig, *v.t.* adorno, armo, [1]; instruo, [3].

rigging, *n.* armamenta, *nt. pl.*

right, *a.* rectus; (hand, side) dexter; *fig.* verus; iustus; aequus; idoneus, aptus; ~**ly,** *ad.* recte; iuste; iure; vere; rite; **you are** ~, vera dicis.

right, *n.* (hand) dextra, *f.*; (law) ius, aequum, fas, *nt.*; (permission, licence) licentia, venia, *f.*; **on the** ~, dextrorsus; **I have a** ~ **to,** mihi licet (*with inf.*).

righteous, *a.* aequus, iustus; pius, sanctus.

rightful, *a.* legitimus, iustus; ~**ly,** *ad.* legitime, iure, iuste.

rigid, *a.* rigidus.

rigidity, *n.* rigor, *m.*

rigorous, *a.* asper, severus, rigidus.

rigour, *n.* asperitas, severitas, *f.*

rim, *n.* labrum, *nt.*; ora, *f.*; margo, *c.*

rind, *n.* crusta, cutis, *f.*; cortex, liber, *m.*

ring, *n.* anulus; (hoop) circulus, orbis, *m.*; (of people) corona, *f.*; (ground for fighting) arena, *f.*; (sound) sonitus, *m.*; (of bells) tinnitus, *m.*

ring, *v.i.* tinnio, [4]; resono, [1].

ringleader, *n.* caput, *nt.*; dux, auctor, *c.*

ringlet, *n.* (of hair) cincinnus, cirrus, *m.*

rinse, *v.t.* alluo, eluo, [3].

riot, *n.* tumultus, *m.*

riot, *v.i.* tumultuor, [1].

rioter, *n.* seditiosus, turbulentus, *m.*

riotous, *a.* seditiosus, tumultuosus, turbulentus.

rip, *v.t.* (unsew) dissuo; (tear) diffindo, divello, [3].

ripe, *a.* maturus; tempestivus.

ripen, *v.t.* maturo, [1]; ~, *v.i.* maturesco, [3].

ripeness, *n.* maturitas, *f.*

ripple, *n.* fluctus, *m.*; unda, *f.*; ~, *v.i.* murmuro, lene sono, [1].

rise, *v.i.* orior, coorior, [4]; surgo, consurgo, [3]; (out of, from) exorior, [4]; (mount) ascendo, [3]; (as a bird) evolo, [1]; (up) assurgo, [3]; (increase) cresco, [3]; (of rebels) consurgo, [3]; rebello, [1]; ~ **again**, resurgo; revivisco, [3].

rise, *n.* (ascent) ascensus; (increase) augmentum, *nt.*; (of the sun) ortus, *m.*; (rising ground) tumulus, *m.*; (origin) origo, *f.*; fons, *m.*; **give ~ to**, pario, [3].

rising, *a.* (sloping) acclivis; (about to be) futurus.

rising, *n.* (of the sun, *etc.*) ortus, *m.*; (insurrection) tumultus, *m.*; seditio, *f.*

risk, *v.t.* periclitor, [1].

risk, *n.* periculum, discrimen, *nt.*

risky, *a.* periculosus.

rite, *n.* ritus, *m.*; solemne, *nt.*

ritual, *a.* sollemnis; ~, *n.* sollemne, *nt.*

rival, *n.* rivalis, aemulus, competitor, *m.*

rival, *v.t.* aemulor, [1].

rivalry, *n.* aemulatio, *f.*; certamen, *nt.*; (in love) rivalitas, *f.*

river, *n.* flumen, *nt.*; amnis, rivus, *m.*; ~**-bed**, *n.* alveus, *m.*

rivet, *n.* clavus, *m.*

rivet, *v.t. fig.* clavo figo, [3]; *fig.* teneo, [2].

road, *n.* via, *f.*; iter, *nt.*; **on the ~**, in itinere.

roam, *etc.*, v. **ramble**, *etc.*

roar, *v.i.* fremo, rudo, [3] mugio, [4]; (of voices) vociferor, [1].

roar, *n.* fremitus, *m.*; strepitus, mugitus, clamor, *m.*

roast, *v.t. & i.* torreo, [2]; (in a pan) frigo, [3]; asso, [1]; coquo, [3].

rob, *v.t.* latrocinor; furor; praedor; spolio, despolio, [1]; diriplo, [3]; (deprive) privo, orbo, [1].

robber, *n.* latro, praedo, raptor, fur, *m.*

robbery, *n.* latrocinium, *nt.*; spoliatio, direptio, rapina, *f.*

robe, *n.* vestis, palla, *f.*

robust, *a.* robustus, validus, lacertosus, firmus.

rock, *n.* rupes, cautes, *f.*; saxum, *nt.*; scopulus, *m.*

rock, *v.t.* moveo, [2]; agito, [1]; ~, *v.i.* vibro, [1]; moveor, [2]; agitor, fluctuo, [1].

rocky, *a.* saxosus, saxeus, scopulosus.

rod, *n.* virga; ferula, *f.*

roe, *n.* (of fishes) ova, *nt. pl.*

rogue, *n.* nequam (homo), furcifer, mastigia, *m.*

role, *n.* persona, *f.*; partes, *f. pl.*

roll, *v.t.* volvo, [3]; verso, [1]; ~, *v.i.* volvor, [3].

roll, *n.* volumen, *nt.*; (coil) spira, *f.*; orbis, *m.*; (of names) index, *c.*; album, *nt.*

roller, *n.* (tool) cylindrus, *m.*

Roman, *a. & n.* Romanus; Quiris, *m.*

romance, *n.* (story) fabula, narratio ficta, *f.*; (love) amor, *m.*

romantic, *a.* fabulosus, commenticius; (chivalrous) sublimis; (pleasing) gratus;

romp, *n.* lusus, *m.*

romp, *v.i.* exsulto, [1]; ludo, [3]; lascivio, [4].

roof, *n.* tectum; fastigium; (of the mouth) palatum, *nt.*

roof, *v.t.* contego, intego, [3].

roofing, *n.* tegulae, *f. pl.*

rook, *n.* corvus, *m.*

room, *n.* (space) spatium, *nt.*; locus, *m.*; (apartment) conclave, cubiculum, cenaculum, *nt.*

roomy, *a.* laxus; spatiosus; amplus.

roost, *v.i.* insisto, [3]; insideo, [2].

root, *n.* radix, stirps, *f.*; *fig.* fons, *m.*; origo, *f.*; **by the ~s,** radicitus; **take ~,** coalesco, [3]. *fig.* inveterasco, [3].

root, *v.i.* radices ago, [3]; **~ out** *or* **up,** exstirpo, eradico, [1].

rope, *n.* funis, *m.*; rudens, *m.*

rose, *n.* rosa, *f.*

rosebud, *n.* calyx rosae, *m.*

rose-bush, *n.* rosa, *m.*

rostrum, *n.* rostra, *nt. pl.*

rosy, *a.* roseus.

rot, *v.i.* putresco, putesco, [3]; **~,** *v.t.* corrumpo, putrefacio, [3].

rot, *n.* putor, *m.*; caries, *f.*

rotate, *v.i.* volvor, [3].

rotation, *n.* ordo, *m.*

rote, *n.* **by ~,** memoriter; **learn by ~,** edisco, perdisco, [3].

rotten, *a.* puter, putidus, putridus; cariosus.

rough, *a.* asper; (with hair, thorns) hirsutus; horridus; scabrous; scaber; (of weather) procellosus; *fig.* agrestis, durus, incultus.

roughen, *v.t.* aspero, [1].

roughly, *ad.* aspere; duriter; horride; inculte; (approximately) fere, ferme.

roughness, *n.* asperitas, *f.*; (of surface) scabies; *fig.* (coarseness) rusticitas; (brutality) feritas, *f.*

roughshod, *a.* ride **~ over,** calco, proculco, [1]; obtero, [3].

round, *a.* rotundus; globosus; (as a circle) circularis; (rounded) teres.

round, *n.* orbis, circulus, *m.*; **go the ~s,** circumeo, *ir.*

round, *v.t.* (make round) rotundo; torno, [1]; (go round) circumeo, *ir.*; **~ off,** (end) concludo, [3].

round, *ad.* & *pr.* circum, circa (*with acc.*); **~ about,** undique.

roundabout, *a.* devius.

rouse, *v.t.* excito; stimulo; animo, [1]; cieo, moveo, [2]; (awaken) expergefacio, [3].

rout, *n.* tumultus, *m.*; turba; (defeat) clades, *f.*; (flight) fuga, *f.*

rout, *v.t.* fugo, profligo, [1]; fundo, [3].

route, *n.* via, *f.*; iter, *nt.*

routine, *n.* mos, usus, *m.*; consuetudo, *f.*

row, *n.* series, *f.*; ordo, *m.*; (quarrel) rixa, *f.*; (riot) turba, *f.*; **in a ~**, deinceps.

row, *v.t. & i.* remigo, [1]; remis propello, [3]; (quarrel) rixor, [1].

rower, *n.* remex, *m.*

rowing, *n.* remigatio, *f.*; remigium, *nt.*

royal, *a.* regalis, regius, regificus.

royalty, *n.* maiestas regia; dignitas regia; regia potestas, *f.*

rub, *v.t. & i.* frico, [1]; tero, [3]; **~ against**, attero, [3]; **~ off**, detergeo, [2]; **~ out**, deleo, [2].

rubbish, *n.* rudus, *nt.*; *fig.* quisquiliae, *f. pl.*; (nonsense) fabulae, gerrae, *f. pl.*

ruby, *n.* carbunculus, *m.*

rudder, *n.* gubernaculum, *nt.*; clavus, *m.*

rude, *a.* rudis, incultus; rusticus, inurbanus; (artless) incomptus, incompositus; inconditus; (insolent) insolens; (rude) asper; (unskilful) inexpertus, imperitus.

rudeness, *n.* rusticitas; inhumanitas; insolentia, *f.*

rudiment, *n.* elementum, initium, rudimentum, principium, *nt.*

rudimentary, *a.* rudis.

rueful, *a.* maestus, tristis.

ruffian, *n.* homo perditus, sicarius, latro, *m.*

ruffle, *v.t.* agito, turbo, [1].

rug, *n.* stragulum, *nt.*

rugged, *a.* asper, inaequalis, confragosus; (precipitous) praeruptus.

ruin, *n.* pernicies, *f.*; exitium, excidium, *nt.*; ruina, *f.*; **~s**, *pl.* ruinae, *f. pl.*; **in ~**, ruinosus.

ruin, *v.t.* perdo; corrumpo, [3]; depravo, vitio, [1].

ruinous, *a.* damnosus; exitiosus; exitialis, perniciosus, funestus.

rule, *n.* (for measuring) regula, *f.*; *fig.* praeceptum, *nt.*; lex, norma, regula, formula, *f.*; (government) regimen, *nt.*

rule, *v.t.* (a line) duco, [3]; (govern) rego, [3]; praesum (*with dat.*); **~**, *v.i.* dominor; impero, [1] (*with dat.*); (of a custom) obtineo, [2].

ruler, *n.* rector; regnator, gubernator, dominus, moderator, *m.*; (for drawing lines) regula, *f.*

ruling, *a.* potens; regius; (chief, most powerful) potentissimus.

rumble, *v.i.* murmuro; crepo, [1].

rumble, *n.* murmur, *nt.*; crepitus, sonitus, *m.*

ruminate, *v.i.* ruminor, [1]; *fig.* meditor, [1].

rummage, *v.t.* rimor, perscrutor, [1].

rumour, *n.* rumor, *m.*; fama, *f.*

rumple, *v.t.* corrugo, [1].

run, *v.i.* curro; (flow) fluo; (of rivers) labor, [3]; **~ about**, curso, [1]; **~ after**, sequor, [3]; sector,

[1]; ~ **away**, fugio, aufugio, [3]; ~ **down**, decurro; (as water) defluo, [3]; *fig.* vitupero, [1]; ~ **off**, aufugio; (as water) defluo, [3]; ~ **out**, excurro, [3]; (of time) exeo, *ir.*; ~ **over**, (a person) obtero; *fig.* percurro; (touch lightly) perstringo; (of fluids) (*v.i.*) superfluo, [3]; ~ **through**, percurro; (also *fig.*); (with a sword) transfigo, traicio, transigo, [3]; (squander) dissipo, [1]; ~ **together**, concurro, [3]; ~ **up**, (*v.t.*) erigo, exstruo; (*v.i.*) accurro, [3].

run, *n.* cursus, *m.*

runaway, *n.* fugitivus, *m.*; transfuga, *m.*

rung, *n.* gradus, *f.*

runner, *n.* cursor, *m.*

running, *a.* (of water) perennis, iugis; (consecutive) continuus.

rupture, *n.* violatio, seditio; dissensio; (*med.*) hernia, *f.*

rupture, *v.t.* violo, [1]; rumpo, abrumpo, [3].

rural, *a.* rusticus; agrestis.

rush, *n.* iuncus, scirpus, *m.*; (hurry) festinatio, *f.*

rush, *v.i.* ruo, feror, [3]; praecipito, [1]; (on, forward) irruo, irrumpo, prorumpo, (out) erumpo, [3]; evolo, [1].

rust, *n.* robigo; (of copper) aerugo; (of iron) ferrugo, *f.*

rust, *v.i.* robiginem contraho, [3]; *fig.* torpeo, [2].

rustic, *a.* rusticus; agrestis.

rustle, *v.i.* crepito; murmuro; susurro, [1].

rustle, *n.* stridor; susurrus, *m.*; murmur, *nt.*; crepitus, *m.*

rusty, *a.* robiginosus, aeruginosus; (rust-coloured) ferrugineus.

rut, *n.* (made by a wheel) orbita, *f.*

ruthless, *a.* immisericors; immitis; immansuetus, crudelis, ferus, saevus.

rye, *n.* secale, *nt.*

....

S

....

sack, *n.* saccus, *m.*

sack, *v.t.* (pillage) vasto, [1]; diripio, [3].

sacking, *n.* spoliatio, vastatio, *f.*; (coarse cloth) cilicium, *nt.*

sacred, *a.* sacer; sanctus; sacrosanctus; religiosus.

sacrifice, *n.* (act) sacrificium, *nt.*; (victim) victima, *f.*; *fig.* detrimentum, damnum, *nt.*

sacrifice, *v.t.* immolo, sacrifico, macto, [1]; *fig.* posthabeo, [2]; (give up) devoveo, [2]; profundo, [3].

sacrilege, *n.* sacrilegium, *nt.*; impietas, *f.*

sacrilegious, *a.* sacrilegus; impius.

sad, *a.* tristis, maestus, miser, miserabilis.

sadden, *v.t.* contristo, [1].

saddle, *n.* ephippium, stratum, *nt.*

saddle, *v.t.* (equum) sterno; *fig.* impono, [3]; onero, [1].

sadness, *n.* tristitia, maestitia, miseria, *f.*

safe, *a.* tutus; (without hurt) incolumis; (sure) certus; ~ **and sound,** salvus.

safeguard, *n.* praesidium, *nt.*; tutela, *f.*

safety, *n.* salus, incolumitas, *f.*

saffron, *n.* crocus, *m.*; ~, *a.* croceus.

sail, *n.* velum, *nt.*; carbasa, lintea, *nt. pl.*; (excursion) navigatio, *f.*

sail, *v.i.* vela facio, [3]; navigo, [1]; (set out to sea) vela do, [1]; solvo, [3]; ~, *v.t.* navigo, [1].

sailing, *n.* navigatio, *f.*; (of a ship) cursus, *m.*

sailor, *n.* nauta, *m.*

saint, *n.* vir sanctus, *m.*; femina sancta, *f.*

saintly, *ad.* sanctus, pius.

sake, *n.* for the ~ of, gratia, causa (*with gen.*); pro (*with abl.*); (on account of) propter, ob (*with acc.*).

salad, *n.* acetaria, *nt. pl.*

salary, *n.* merces, *f.*; stipendium, salarium, *nt.*

sale, *n.* venditio, *f.*; (auction) auctio, *f.*; for ~, venalis; **be on ~,** veneo, *ir.*; **put up for ~,** venalem propono, [3].

salesman, *n.* venditor, *m.*

salient, *a.* prominens; (chief) praecipuus.

saliva, *n.* saliva, *f.*; sputum, *nt.*

sallow, *a.* pallidus, luridus.

sally, *n.* eruptio, *f.*; ~, *v.i.* (*mil.*) erumpo, excurro, [3].

salmon, *n.* salmo, *m.*

salt, *n.* sal, *m.*

salt, *a.* salsus.

salt, *v.t.* salio, sale condio, [4].

salty, *a.* salsus.

salt-cellar, *n.* salinum, *m.*

salubrious, *a.* salubris (saluber), salutaris.

salutary, *a.* salutaris, salubris; utilis.

salute, *n.* salus, salutatio, *f.*; ~, *v.t.* saluto, [1].

salvation, *n.* salus, salvatio, *f.*

same, *a.* idem; **it is all the ~ thing,** nihil interest; **at the ~ time,** eodem tempore; **in the ~ place,** ibidem.

sample, *n.* exemplum; exemplar; specimen, *nt.*

sanctify, *v.t.* sanctifico; (consecrate) consecro, [1].

sanctimonious, *a.* sanctitatem affectans.

sanction, *n.* auctoritas, confirmatio, *f.*

sanction, *v.t.* ratum facio, [3]; sancio, [4]; confirmo, firmo, [1].

sanctity, *n.* sanctitas; sanctimonia, religio, *f.*

sanctuary, *n.* asylum, adytum, sacrarium, *nt.*

sand, *n.* sabulo, *m.*; arena, *f.*

sandal, *n.* solea, crepida, *f.*

sandstone, *n.* tofus, tophus, *m.*

sandy, *a.* (full of sand) arenosus, sabulosus; arenaceus; (of colour) rufus.

sane, *a.* sanus, mentis compos.

sanity, *n.* sanitas, mens sana, *f.*

sap, *n.* sucus, *m.*; lac, *nt.*

sapling, *n.* surculus, *m.*

sapphire, *n.* sapphirus, *f.*

sarcasm, *n.* dictum acerbum, *nt.*

sarcastic, *a.* acerbus, mordax.

sarcophagus, *n.* sarcophagus, *m.*

sardine, *n.* sarda, *f.*

sardonic, *a.* acerbus.

sash, *n.* cingulum, *nt.*

satchel, *n.* saccus, sacculus, *m.*; pera, *f.*; loculi, *m. pl.*

sate, *v.t.* satio, saturo, [1].

satellite, *n.* satelles, *c.*; (planet) stella minor *or* obnoxia, *f.*

satiate, *v.t.* satio, saturo, [1].

satiety, *n.* satietas, *f.*; fastidium, *nt.*

satire, *n.* satura, *f.*

satirical, *a.* satyricus, acerbus.

satirist, *n.* scriptor (*or* poeta) satyricus.

satirize, *v.t.* derideo, [2]; perstringo, [3].

satisfaction, *n.* satisfactio, *f.*; *fig.* oblectatio animi; voluptas, *f.*

satisfactory, *a.* (suitable) commodus; (pleasant) gratus, iucundus.

satisfy, *v.t.* (please) satisfacio, [3] (*with dat.*); (fill) satio, saturo, [1]; *fig.* persuadeo; (one's expectations) respondeo, [2] (*both with dat.*); (be satisfied) contentus esse.

saturate, *v.t.* saturo, [1]; imbuo, madefacio, [3].

satyr, *n.* satyrus, *m.*

sauce, *n.* condimentum; ius, *nt.*

saucepan, *n.* cacabus, *m.*

saucer, *n.* patella, *f.*

saucy, *a.* petulans, procax, protervus.

saunter, *v.i.* ambulo, [1]; incedo, [3].

sausage, *n.* farcimen, tomaculum, *nt.*

savage, *a.* ferus; ferox, immansuetus; immanis; saevus; atrox; (furious) efferus; (uncivilized) ferus, incultus; **~ly,** *ad.* crudeliter; immaniter; atrociter; saeve.

savagery, *n.* feritas; immanitas; saevitia, *f.*

save, *v.t.* servo, conservo; (from danger) libero, [1]; eripio (periculo aliquem); (spare) parco, [3] (*with dat.*); (gain) lucror, [1].

savings, *n.* peculium, *nt.*

saviour. *n.* servator, *m.*

savour, *n.* sapor, odor, nidor, *m.*

savour, *v.i.* sapio, [3]; ~, *v.t.* fruor, [3] (*with abl.*)

savoury, *a.* sapidus.

saw, *n.* (tool) serra, *f.;* ~, *ut. & i.* serra seco, [1]; serram duco, [3].

sawdust, *n.* scobis, *f.*

say, *v.t. & i.* dico, loquor, aio, [3]; fari (infin.), [1]; **he ~s,** inquit; **they ~,** dicunt, ferunt; **that is to ~,** scilicet.

saying, *n.* dictum, *nt.*

scab, *n.* (of a wound) crusta, *f.*

scabbard, *n.* vagina, *f.*

scaffold, *n.* tabulatum, *nt.;* catasta, *f.*

scaffolding, *n.* tabulatum, *nt.*

scald, *v.t.* fervente aqua macero, [1].

scale, *n.* (of a fish) squama; (of a balance) lanx, *f.;* ~s, *pl.* libra; trutina, *f.;* (degree) gradus, *m.*

scale, *v.t.* (walls) ascendo, [3]; scalas admoveo, [2] (*with ad with acc.*).

scaling-ladder, *n.* scalae, *f. pl.*

scallop, *n.* (shell-fish) pecten, *m.*

scalp, *n.* calva, *f.*

scalpel, *n.* scalpellum, scalprum, *nt.*

scaly, *a.* squamosus; squameus.

scamper, *v.i.* ruo, [3]; provolo, [1]; ~ **away,** aufugio, effugio, [3].

scan, *v.t.* examino, exploro, lustro, [1].

scandal, *n.* ignominia, turpitudo, *f.;* opprobrium, *nt.*

scandalize, *v.t.* offendo, [3].

scandalous, *a.* ignominiosus, probrosus, turpis.

scant, scanty, *a.* angustus, exiguus, tenuis.

scapegoat, *n.* caper emissarius, *m.*

scar, *n.* cicatrix, *f.;* ~, *v.t.* noto, [1].

scarce, *a.* rarus; ~**ly,** *ad.* vix, aegre.

scarcity, *n.* paucitas; penuria, inopia, *f.*

scare, *v.t.* terreo, [2]; territo, formido, [1].

scarecrow, *n.* terricula, *nt. pl.*

scared, *a.* territus.

scarf, *n.* fascia, *f.*

scarlet, *n.* (colour) color coccineus, *m.;* ~, *a.* coccineus.

scatter, *v.t.* spargo, dispergo, [3]; dissipo, [1]; (put to flight) fundo, [3]; fugo, [1]; ~, *v.i.* dilabor, [3].

scene, *n.* scaena, *f.;* (spectacle) spectaculum, *nt.;* (place) locus; (landscape) prospectus, *m.*

scenery, *n.* (of nature) species regionis, *f.;* **beautiful ~,** amoena loca, *nt. pl.;* (of a theatre) scaena, *f.*

scenic, *a.* scaenicus.

scent, *n.* (sense) odoratus; (fragrance) odor, *m.;* (of dogs) sagacitas, *f.*

scent, *v.t.* (perfume) odoro; (get wind of, scent out) odoror, [1];

scent-bottle, *n.* olfactorium, *nt.*

scented, *a.* odoratus, odorifer, odorus, fragrans.

sceptical, *a.* (suspicious) suspicax.

sceptre, *n.* sceptrum, *nt.*

schedule, *n.* libellus, *m.*

scheme, *n.* consilium, *nt.*; ~, *v.t. & i.* molior, [4].

scholar, *n.* discipulus, *m.*; discipula, *f.*; (learned man) homo doctus, *m.*

scholarship, *n.* litterae, *f. pl.*; eruditio, humanitas, *f.*

school, *n.* schola (also *fig.*); secta, *f.*; ludus, *m.*

schoolboy, *n.* discipulus, *m.*

school-fellow, *n.* condiscipulus, *m.*; condiscipula, *f.*

schoolmaster, *n.* ludi magister, magister, praeceptor, *m.*

schoolmistress, *n.* magistra, praeceptrix, *f.*

sciatica, *n.* ischias, *f.*

science, *n.* scientia; doctrina; disciplina, ars; (theory) ratio, *f.*

scientific, *a.* ad scientiam conformatus; ~ly, *ad.* ex disciplinae praeceptis.

scissors, *n.* forfices, *f. pl.*

scoff, *v.i.* irrideo, derideo, [2]; cavillor, [1].

scold, *v.t. & i.* obiurgo, increpo, increpito, [1].

scolding, *n.* obiurgatio, *f.*; iurgium, *nt.*

scoop, *n.* trulla, *f.*; ~, *v.t.* cavo, excavo, [1].

scope, *n.* finis, *m.*; propositum, *nt.*; *fig.* campus, *m.*; area, *f.*; spatium, *nt.*

scorch, *v.t.* uro, aduro, [3]; torreo, [2].

score, *n.* nota; (bill) ratio, *f.*; (twenty) viginti.

score, *v.t.* (mark) noto, [1]; *fig.* ~ **a point**, superior sum.

scorn, *v.t.* temno, contemno, sperno, [3]; aspernor, [1]; fastidio, [4].

scorn, *n.* contemptio, *f.*; contemptus, *m.*; supercilium, fastidium, *nt.*

scornful, *a.* fastidiosus; ~ly, *ad.* contemptim; fastidiose.

scorpion, *n.* scorpio, scorpius, *m.*

scotch, *v.t.* incido, [3]; vulnero, [1].

scot-free, *a.* impunitus; ~, *ad.* impune.

scoundrel, *n.* nebulo, furcifer, *m.*

scour, *v.t.* (de)tergeo, [2]; *fig.* pervagor, [1]; percurro, [3].

scourge, *n.* flagellum, *nt.*; *fig.* pestis, *f.*; ~, *v.t.* caedo, [3]; verbero, [1].

scout, *n.* explorator, speculator, emissarius, *m.*; ~, *v.t.* speculor, exploro, [1].

scowl, *v.i.* frontem contraho, [3]; ~, *n.* frontis contractio, *f.*

scramble, *u.i.* nitor, enitor, [3].

scrap, *n.* fragmentum, fragmen, frustum, *nt.*

scrape, *u.t. & i.* rado; (together) corrado, [3].

scraper, *n.* (tool) radula, *f.;* rallum, *nt.*

scratch, *u.t.* rado; scalpo; [3]; scabo, [1]; (inscribe) inscribo, [3]; ~ **out,** erado, [3].

scratch, *n.* vulnus, *nt.*

scream, screech, *u.i.* strideo, [2]; vociferor, [1]; (of a child) vagio, [4].

scream, screech, *n.* stridor, *m.;* vociferatio, *f.;* (of an infant) vagitus, *m.*

screen, *n.* umbraculum, *nt.;* (protection) praesidium, *nt.;* defensio, *f.;* ~, *u.t.* occulo, protego, defendo, [3].

scribe, *n.* scriba, amanuensis, librarius, *m.*

scroll, *n.* volumen, *nt.*

scrub, *u.t.* frico, [1]; tergeo, [3].

scrub, *n.* (brushwood) virgulta, *nt. pl.*

scruple, *n.* scrupulus, *m.;* religio, dubitatio, *f.;* ~, *u.i.* dubito, [1].

scrupulous, *a.* religiosus, scrupulosus; ~**ly,** *ad.* religiose; scrupulose.

scrutinize, *u.t.* scrutor, perscrutor, [1].

scrutiny, *n.* scrutatio, perscrutatio, *f.*

scuffle, *n.* rixa; turba, *f.;* ~, *u.i.* rixor, [1].

sculptor, *n.* sculptor, scalptor, *m.;* artifex, *m.;* caelator, *m.*

sculpture, *n.* (art) sculptura; scalptura, *f.;* (work) opus (marmoreum, *etc.*), *nt.;* ~, *u.t.* sculpo, scalpo, [3]; caelo, [1].

scum, *n.* spuma; (of metals) scoria; *fig.* sentina, *f.*

scurrilous, *a.* scurrilis, probrosus.

scurvy, *n.* scrofula, *f.*

scuttle, *u.t.* navis fundum perforo, [1].

scythe, *n.* falx, *f.*

sea, *n.* mare, aequor, marmor, *nt.;* pontus, *m.*

seacoast, *n.* ora, *f.;* litus, *nt.*

seafaring, *a.* maritimus.

seagull, *n.* larus, *m.;* gavia, *f.*

seahorse, *n.* hippocampus, *m.*

sea-urchin, *n.* echinus, *m.*

seal, *n.* signum, *nt.;* (animal) phoca, *f.*

seal, *u.t.* signo, consigno, obsigno, [1]; *fig.* sancio, [4].

sealing-wax, *n.* cera, *f.*

seam, *n.* sutura; commissura, *f.*

seaman, *n.* nauta, *m.*

seamanship, *n.* navigandi peritia, *f.*

search, *u.t. & i.* (per)scrutor, [1]; (into) inquiro, [3]; investigo, [1].

search, *n.* scrutatio; investigatio; inquisitio, *f.*

seasick, *a.* nauseabundus; **be ~,** nauseo, [1].

seasickness, *n.* nausea, *f.*

seaside, *n.* ora, *f.*

season, *n.* tempus (anni), *nt.*; (right moment) opportunitas, *f.*

season, *v.t.* condio, [4]; *fig.* assuefacio, [3]; duro, exercito, [1].

seasonable, *a.* tempestivus, opportunus.

seasoned, *a.* exercitatus.

seasoning, *n.* (act) conditio, *f.*; (the seasoning itself) condimentum, *nt.*

seat, *n.* sedes, sella, *f.*; sedile, subsellium, *nt.*; (dwelling-place) domicilium, *nt.*; (place) locus, *m.*; (dwelling) sedes, *f.*

seat, *v.t.* sede loco, [1]; (oneself) consideo, [2].

seaweed, *n.* alga, *f.*; fucus, *m.*

seaworthy, *a.* navigandi capax.

secluded, *a.* solitarius; remotus.

seclusion, *n.* solitudo, *f.*; secessus, *m.*; locus remotus, *m.*

second, *a.* secundus; alter; **for the ~ time,** iterum.

second, *n.* (person) adiutor, *m.*; (of time) punctum temporis, *nt.*

secondary, *a.* secundarius; inferior.

secondly, *ad.* deinde, tum.

secrecy, *n.* secretum, *nt.*; taciturnitas, *f.*; (keeping secret) silentium, *nt.*

secret, *a.* arcanus; secretus; occultus; furtivus; clandestinus; **in ~,** clam; **keep ~,** celo, [1]; **~ly,** *ad.* clam; occulte, furtim.

secret, *n.* secretum, arcanum, *nt.*; res arcana, *f.*

secretary, *n.* scriba; amanuensis, *m.*

secrete, *v.t.* celo, occulto, [1]; abdo, [3]; **~ oneself,** lateo, [2]; delitesco, [3].

sect, *n.* secta, schola, *f.*

section, *n.* pars; (geometry) sectio, *f.*

sector, *n.* sector, *m.*

secular, *a.* saecularis; (worldly) profanus.

secure, *a.* securus; tutus; **~ly,** *ad.* tuto, secure.

secure, *v.t.* confirmo, [1]; munio, [4]; a periculo defendo, [3]; in custodiam trado, [3]; (bring about, get) pario, [3]; paro, [1].

security, *n.* salus; incolumitas; (pledge) satisdatio, *f.*; pignus, *nt.*; (person) vas, sponsor, praes, *m.*

sedan (-chair), *n.* lectica, *f.*

sedate, *a.* gravis, sedatus.

sedentary, *a.* sedentarius, sellularius.

sediment, *n.* faex, *f.*

sedition, *n.* seditio, rebellio, *f.*; tumultus, *m.*

seditious, *a.* seditiosus, turbulentus.

seduce, *v.t.* corrumpo, [3]; depravo, [1]; decipio, [3].

seducer, *n.* corruptor, *m.*

seduction, *n.* illecebra; corruptela, *f.*

seductive, *a.* blandus.

see, *v.t.* & *i.* video, [2]; specto, [1]; cerno, conspicio, aspicio, [3]; (take precautions) caveo, video, [2]; (understand) intellego, [3]; go to ~, viso, [3]; ~ to, curo, [1].

seed, *n.* semen, *nt.*

seedling, *n.* planta, *f.*

seeing, *c.* ~ that, quandoquidem, quoniam.

seek, *v.t.* & *i.* quaero, peto, expeto, sequor, [3]; (endeavour) conor; (strive to attain) affecto, consector, [1].

seem, *v.i.* videor, [2].

seeming, *a.* speciosus.

seemingly, *ad.* in speciem, ut videtur.

seemly, *a.* decorus, decens.

seer, *n.* vates, fatidicus, augur, propheta, *m.*

seethe, *v.i.* ferveo, [2]; aestuo, [1].; (with rage) furo, [3].

segment, *n.* segmentum, *nt.*

segregate, *v.t.* segrego, [1]

seize, *v.t.* prehendo, comprehendo; arripio, [3]; (take possession) occupo, [1]; (attack) invado; incesso; *fig.* afficio, [3].

seizure, *n.* comprehensio; occupatio, *f.*

seldom, *ad.* raro.

select, *v.t.* seligo, eligo, deligo, [3].

select, *a.* exquisitus.

selection, *n.* selectio, electio, *f.*; delectus, *m.*

self, *pn.* ipse, se(se); by one's ~, solus.

self-confidence, *n.* sui fiducia, *f.*

self-conscious, *a.* verecundus.

self-control, *n.* temperantia, *f.*

selfish, *a.* nimis se amans.

selfishness, *n.* amor sui, *m.*

self-possessed, *a.* placidus, tranquillus, imperturbatus.

self-willed, *a.* obstinatus, contumax.

sell, *v.t.* vendo, [3]; ~, *v.i.* veneo, [4].

seller, *n.* venditor, *m.*

semblance, *n.* similitudo, species, *f.*

semicircle, *n.* semicirculus, *m.*

semicircular, *a.* semicirculus, semicirculatus.

senate, *n.* senatus, *m.*; curia, *f.*

senate-house, *n.* curia, *f.*

senator, *n.* senator, *m.*

senatorial, *a.* senatorius.

send, *v.t.* mitto, [3]; (on public business) lego, [1]; (away) dimitto, [3]; ~ for, arcesso, [3].

senile, *a.* senilis.

senior, *a.* natu maior.

seniority, *n.* aetatis privilegium, *nt.*

sensation, *n.* sensus, *m.*; (astonishment) stupor, *m.*; (subject of talk) fabula, *f.*

sense, *n.* (faculty) sensus, *m.*; (intellect) mens; (opinion) opinio,

sententia, *f.;* (meaning) signifi-catio, *f.*

senseless, *a.* nihil sentiens; (life-less) exanimis; *fig.* mentis ex-pers; absurdus.

sensible, *a.* sensilis; sensu praedi-tus, sensibilis; *fig.* sapiens.

sensitive, *a.* mollis; ~ **to,** impa-tiens (*with gen.*).

sensual, *a.* voluptarius; libidino-sus.

sentence, *n.* iudicium, *nt.;* (set of words) sententia, *f.;* ~, *ut.* damno, condemno, [1].

sentiment, *n.* sententia, opinio, *f.;* sensus, *m.*

sentimental, *a.* animi mollioris (*gen.*); (in contempt) flebilis.

sentinel, sentry, *n.* excubitor, vigil, *m.;* excubiae, *f. pl.;* ~**-box,** *n.* specula, *f.*

separate, *ut.* separo, [1]; disiun-go, seiungo, secerno, [3]; ~, *ui.* separor, [1]; disiungor, [3]; (go different ways) digredior, [3].

separate, *a.* separatus; disiunc-tus.

separation, *n.* separatio; disiunc-tio, *f.;* (going different ways) di-gressus, *m.*

September, *n.* September, *m.*

sequel, *n.* exitus, eventus, *m.*

sequence, *n.* ordo, *m.;* series, *f.*

serene, *a.* serenus; tranquillus.

serenity, *n.* serenitas; tranquilli-tas, *f.*

series, *n.* series, *f.*

serious, *a.* gravis, serius, seve-rus; ~**ly,** *ad.* graviter; serio; severe.

seriousness, *n.* gravitas, *f.;* se-rium, *nt.;* severitas, *f.*

sermon, *n.* oratio, contio, *f.*

serpent, *n.* serpens, anguis, *c.;* coluber, draco, *m.*

servant, *n.* minister; famulus, *m.;* ministra, ancilla, *f.;* famula, *f.*

serve, *ut. & i.* servio (alicui), [4]; (for wages) stipendia mereo *or* mereor, [2]; (be useful) prosum; (be sufficient) sufficio, [3] (*both with dat.*); ~ **up,** offero, [3].

service, *n.* servitium; (kindness) officium, *nt.;* (advantage) utili-tas, *f.;* (mil.) militia, *f.*

serviceable, *a.* utilis; commodus; **be** ~, prosum (*with dat.*)

servile, *a.* servilis, humilis.

servility, *n.* humilitas, *f.;* animus abiectus, *m.*

session, *n.* sessio, *f.;* consessus, conventus, *m.*

set, *v.t.* pono, sisto, [3]; loco, collo-co, [1]; (prescribe) praescribo, [3]; (an example) do, [1]; (en-close) includo, [3]; (on fire) ac-cendo, [3]; ~, *ui.* (of sun) occido, [3]; ~ **about,** incipio, [3]; ~ **apart** *or* **aside,** sepono; *fig.* res-cindo, [3]; ~ **down,** (in writing) noto, [1]; perscribo, [3]; ~ **forth,** expono; propono, profero, [3]; *ui.* proficiscor, [3]; ~ **in,** insero, [3]; ~ **off,** (adorn) adorno; illustro, [1]; (praise) extollo, [3]; (*u.i.*) abeo, [4]; proficiscor, [3]; ~ **on,**

(incite) instigo, [1]; (attack) invado; ~ **out**, (u.i.) discedo, proficiscor, [3]; ~ **up**, erigo; exstruo; (institute) instituo, constituo, [3].

set, a. (well-ordered) compositus.

settee, n. lectulus, m.

setting, n. collocatio, f.; (of the sun) occasus, m.

settle, u.t. statuo, constituo; (a quarrel) dirimo, [3]; (adjust) compono; (an account) solvo, [3]; ~, u.i. (reside) consido; (sink) subsido, [3].

settlement, n. constitutio; (dowry) dos, f.; (agreement) pactum, nt.; (colony) colonia, f.

settler, n. colonus, m.

seven, a. septem; ~ **times,** septies.

seven hundred, a. septingenti.

seventeen, a. septendecim, decem et septem.

seventeenth, a. septimus decimus.

seventh, a. septimus.

seventieth, a. septuagesimus.

seventy, a. septuaginta.

sever, u.t. separo, [1]; dissolvo, [3]; dissocio, [1]; disiungo, [3]; ~, u.i. disiungor, [3], etc.

several, a. plures, complures; diversus, varius.

severe, a. severus; gravis; durus; ~**ly,** ad. severe, graviter.

severity, n. severitas; gravitas; inclementia, f.

sew, u.t. & i. suo, consuo, [3].

sewer, n. cloaca, f.

sewing, n. sutura, f.

sex, n. sexus, m.

sexual, a. sexualis; naturalis.

shabby, a. pannosus; sordidus.

shackles, n. vincula, nt. pl.; pedica, compes, f.

shade, n. umbra, f.; fig. (difference) discrimen, nt.; (parasol) umbraculum, nt.

shade, u.t. opaco; obscuro; obumbro; adumbro, [1].

shadow, n. umbra, f.

shadowy, a. umbrosus, opacus; fig. tenuis, inanis, vanus.

shady, a. opacus, umbrosus.

shaft, n. sagitta, f.; (of a spear) hastile, nt.; (in a mine) puteus, m.; (of a column) scapus, m.

shaggy, a. hirsutus, hirtus, villosus.

shake, u.t. quatio, concutio, [3]; quasso, [1]; (the head) nuto, [1]; (undermine) labefacio, [3]; labefacto, [1]; ~, u.i. concutior; (with fear) tremo, [3]; (totter) vacillo, nuto, [1].

shallow, a. vadosus; fig. levis.

shallows, n. vada, nt. pl.

sham, a. fictus, simulatus; fallax; ~, n. fallacia, f.; dolus, m.; simulatio, species, f.

sham, u.t. simulo, [1]; fingo, [3].

shame, n. pudor, m.; (disgrace) dedecus; opprobrium, nt.; ignominia, f.

shame, v.t. ruborem incutio, [3] (with dat.).

shamefaced, a. pudens, pudibundus, verecundus.

shameful, a. turpis, probrosus; ~ly, ad. turpiter; probrose.

shameless, a. impudens; ~ly, ad. impudenter.

shape, n. forma, figura; species, facies, f.

shape, v.t. formo, figuro, [1]; fingo, [3].

shapeless, a. informis; deformis, indigestus, rudis.

share, n. pars, portio, f.

share, v.t. partior, [4]; (with another) communico, [1] (with cum with abl.); ~, v.i. particeps sum; in partem venio, [4].

sharer, n. particeps, c.; socius, m.; socia, f.; consors, c.

shark, n. (fish) pristis, f.; (person) fraudator, m.

sharp, a. acutus; acer; (bitter) acerbus; (tart) acidus; fig. mordax; argutus; subtilis; ~ly, ad. acute; (keenly) acriter; (bitterly) acerbe; (cleverly) subtiliter.

sharpen, v.t. acuo, exacuo, [3].

sharpness, n. (of edge) acies; (sourness) acerbitas; fig. subtilitas, perspicacitas, f.; acumen, nt.

sharp-sighted, a. perspicax.

shatter, v.t. quasso, [1]; frango, confringo; elido, [3].

shave, v.t. rado, [3]; tondeo, [2]; ~ off, abrado, [3].

shaving, n. ramentum, nt.; scobis, f.

shawl, n. amiculum, nt.

she, pn. haec, illa, ea.

sheaf, n. manipulus, fascis, m.; merges, f.

shear, v.t. tondeo, [2]; fig. spolio, nudo, [1].

shears, n. forfex, f.

sheath, n. vagina, f.; (wrapper) involucrum, nt.

sheathe, v.t. (in vaginam) recondo, [3].

shed, v.t. fundo, effundo, profundo, spargo, [3]; (blood) (one's own) do, [1]; (another's) haurio, [4]; (tears) effundo, profundo, [3].

shed, n. tugurium, nt.

sheep, n. ovis, pecus, bidens, f.

sheepish, a. timidus, modestus.

sheepskin, n. pellis ovilla, mastruca, f.

sheer, a. merus; purus; (precipitous) praeceps.

sheet, n. linteum, nt.; (of metal) lamina, f.

shelf, n. pluteus, m.; tabula, f.

shell, n. concha; crusta, testa, f.; (husk) folliculus, m.; (of nuts, etc.) putamen, nt.

shellfish, n. concha, f.

shelter, n. tegmen, fig. refugium, perfugium; (asylum) receptaculum, nt.

shelter, v.t. tego; protego; defendo, [3].

shepherd, *n.* pastor, upilio, pecorum custos, *m.*

shield, *n.* scutum, *nt.*; clipeus, *m.*; ~, *v.t.* tego, protego, defendo, [3].

shift, *v.t.* muto, [1]; amoveo, [2]; ~, *v.i.* (as the wind) verto, [3]; (shuffle) tergiversor, [1].

shift, *n.* (expedient) ratio, *f.*; modus, *m.*; (remedy) remedium, *nt.*; (trick) dolus, *m.*; ars, *f.*

shin(-bone), *n.* tibia, *f.*

shine, *v.i.* luceo, fulgeo, niteo, splendeo, [2]; corusco, mico, [1]; ~ **forth,** eluceo; eniteo, [2]; exsplendesco, [3]; ~ **on,** affulgeo, [2] (*with dat.*).

shingle, *n.* glarea, *f.*; scandula, *f.*

shining, *a.* lucidus, fulgidus, nitidus.

shiny, *a.* nitidus.

ship, *n.* navis, *f.*; navigium, *nt.*

ship, *v.t.* in navem (*or* naves) impono; accipio, [3].

shipbuilder, *n.* naupegus, *m.*

ship owner, *n.* navicularius, *m.*

shipping, *n.* navigia, *nt. pl.*

shipwreck, *n.* naufragium, *nt.*; *fig.* ruina, *f.*; interitus, *m.*

shipwrecked, *a.* naufragus; be ~, naufragium facio, [3].

shipyard, *n.* navale, *nt.*, navalia, *nt. pl.*

shirk, *v.t.* detrecto, [1].

shirt, *n.* indusium, *nt.*; tunica, *f.*

shiver, *v.i.* contremisco, horresco, [3]; horreo, [2].

shiver, *n.* (shudder) horror, *m.*; cold ~, frigus, *nt.*

shoal, *n.* (of fishes, *etc.*) caterva, *f.*; grex, *m.*; (shallow) brevia, vada, *nt. pl.*

shock, *n.* concussio, *f.*; impetus, concursus, *m.*; *fig.* (of feeling) offensio; (blow) plaga, *f.*

shock, *v.t.* percutio, percello; *fig.* offendo, [3].

shocking, *a.* foedus; atrox.

shoe, *n.* calceus, *m.*; caliga; (slipper) solea, *f.*; soccus, *m.*; (for horses) solea, *f.*

shoe, *v.t.* calceos induo, [3]; (a horse) soleas apto, [1] (*with dat.*).

shoemaker, *n.* sutor, *m.*

shoot, *v.t.* (telum) mitto; conicio, [3]; iaculor, [1]; (a person) figo, transfigo, [3]; ~, *v.i.* (of plants) germino, [1]; (of pains) vermino, [1].

shoot, *n.* (of plants) surculus, *m.*; propago, [2]; germen, *nt.*

shooting star, *n.* fax (caelestis) stella, *f.*

shop, *n.* taberna, officina, *f.*

shopkeeper, *n.* tabernarius, *m.*

shore, *n.* litus, *nt.*; ora, *f.*

short, *a.* brevis; (little) exiguus; in ~, breviter, denique; be ~ of, egeo (*with abl.*).

shortcoming, *n.* defectus, *m.*; (fault) delictum, vitium, *nt.*; (failure) inopia, *f.*

shorten, v.t. coarto, [1]; contraho, [3]; ~, v.i. contrahor; minuor, [3].

shorthand, n. notae breviores, f. pl.

short-lived, a. brevis.

shortly, ad. (of time) brevi; mox; ~ **after,** haud multum post.

shortness, n. brevitas; exiguitas, f.; (of breath) anhelitus, m.

short-sighted, a. myops; fig. improvidus.

short-sightedness, n. myopia; fig. minima imprudentia, f.

shot, n. ictus, m.; (reach, range) iactus; (marksman) iaculator, m.; (bullet) glans, f.; tormentum, nt.

shoulder, n. umerus, m.

shoulder-blade, n. scapulae, f. pl.

shout, n. clamor, m.; acclamatio, vox, f.

shout, n. clamo; acclamo; vociferor, [1].

shove, v.t. trudo, [3]; pulso, [1].

shovel, n. pala, f.; batillum; (for the fire) rutabulum, nt.

show, v.t. monstro, declaro; indico, [1]; ostendo, [3]; (display) exhibeo; (teach) doceo, [2]; (prove) confirmo, [1]; (qualities) praebeo, [2]; ~ **off,** ostento, vendito, [1].

show, n. (appearance) species; (display) ostentatio; (pretence) simulatio; (parade) pompa, f.; (spectacle) spectaculum, nt.

shower, n. imber, nimbus, m.; fig. vis, multitudo, f.

shower, v.t. superfundo, effundo; fig. ingero, [3].

showery, a. pluviosus, nimbosus, pluvius, pluvialis.

showy, a. speciosus.

shred, n. segmentum, nt.

shrewd, a. acutus, astutus, callidus; sagax; prudens; ~**ly,** ad. acute, callide; sagaciter; astute, prudenter.

shrewdness, n. calliditas; astutia; sagacitas, f.; acumen, nt.; prudentia, f.

shriek, v.i. ululo, eiulo, [1]; ~, n. eiulatio, f.; ululatus, m.

shrill, a. (per)acutus; stridulus.

shrimp, n. squilla, f.

shrine, n. (for holy things) sacrarium, sacellum, adytum, nt.; cella, f.

shrink, v.t. contraho, [3]; ~, v.i. contrahor; (withdraw) refugio, [3]; (from) abhorreo, [2]; detrecto, [1].

shrivel, v.t. corrugo, [1]; torreo, [2]; ~, v.i. corrugor, [1]; torreor, [2].

shroud, n. (of ships) rudentes, m. pl.; (of corpse) linteum (mortuorum), nt.

shroud, v.t. involvo; obduco, [3].

shrub, n. frutex, m.; arbuscula, f.

shrubbery, n. fruticetum, nt.

shrug, n. umerorum allevatio, f.; ~, v.i. umeros allevo, [1].

shudder, n. horror, tremor, m.; ~, v.i. horreo, [2]; horresco, [3].

shuffle, *v.t.* misceo, [2]; ~, *v.i.* tergiversor, [1].

shun, *v.t.* vito, devito, evito, declino, detrecto, [1]; fugio, [3].

shut, *v.t.* claudo, occludo, [3]; (out) excludo, [3]; (up) concludo, [3].

shutter, *n.* claustrum, *nt.*

shuttle, *n.* radius, *m.*

shy, *a.* timidus; pudibundus; verecundus.

shyness, *n.* timiditas; verecundia, *f.*

Sibyl, *n.* Sibylla, *f.*

sick, *a.* aeger, aegrotus; **be** ~, aegroto, [1]; (of, with) taedet (me rei), [2], fastidio, [4].

sicken, *v.t.* fastidium moveo, [2] (*with gen.*); satio, [1]; ~, *v.i.* in morbum incido, [3].

sickle, *n.* falx, *f.*; ~-shaped, *a.* falcatus.

sickly, *a.* infirmus; (pale) pallidus.

sickness, *n.* aegrotatio, aegritudo, *f.*; morbus, *m.*

side, *n.* latus, *nt.*; (part, quarter) pars; regio; (edge) ora, *f.*; (of a hill) clivus, *m.*; (party in a contest) partes, *f. pl.*

side, *a.* lateralis.

side, *v.i.* (with) partes sequor, [3] (*with gen.*); ab aliquo sto, [1].

sideboard, *n.* abacus, *m.*

sideways, *ad.* in obliquum, oblique.

sidle, *v.i.* obliquo incessu progredior, [3].

siege, *n.* oppugnatio, obsessio, obsidio, *f.*

siesta, *n.* meridiatio, *f.*; **take a** ~, meridior, [1].

sieve, *n.* cribrum, *nt.*

sift, *v.t.* cribro, [1]; cerno, [3]; *fig.* exploro, scrutor, [1].

sigh, *n.* suspirium, *nt.*; ~, *v.i.* suspiro, [1]; (for) desidero, suspiro, [1].

sight, *n.* (sense) visus; (act of seeing) aspectus, conspectus, *m.*; (of the eye) acies (oculi *or* oculorum), *f.*; (show) spectaculum, *nt.*; (appearance) species, *f.*; visum, *nt.*; **in** ~, in conspectu, **out of** ~, e conspectu.

sign, *n.* signum, indicium, *nt.*; (mark) nota, *f.*; (of a shop, etc.) insigne; *fig.* portentum, omen; augurium, *nt.*

sign, *v.t. & i.* subscribo; annuo, [3]; signum do, [1].

signal, *n.* signum; (*mil.*) classicum, *nt.*; ~, *v.t.* signum do, [1].

signature, *n.* nomen, *nt.*; subscriptio, *f.*

signet-ring, *n.* anulus, *m.*; signum, *nt.*

significance, *n.* (meaning) significatio, *f.*; sensus, *m.*; *fig.* vis, *f.*; momentum, *nt.*

significant, *a.* significans; *fig.* magni momenti.

signify, *v.t. & i.* significo, [1]; valeo, [2]; portendo, [3].

silence, *n.* silentium, *nt.*; taciturnitas, *f.*; ~! *i.* tace! tacete! ~, *v.t.*

silentium facio, [3]; (confute) refuto, [1]; (allay) sedo, [1]; compesco, [3].

silent, *a.* tacitus, silens; **~ly**, *ad.* (cum) silentio, tacite.

silk, *n.* sericum, *nt.*; bombyx, *c.*

silk, silken, *a.* sericus, bombycinus.

sill, *n.* limen inferum, *nt.*

silliness, *n.* stultitia, fatuitas, insulsitas, insipientia, *f.*

silly, *a.* stultus, fatuus, ineptus, insipiens, insulsus.

silver, *n.* argentum, *nt.*

silver, silvery, *a.* argenteus; (of hair) canus.

silversmith, *n.* faber argentarius, *m.*

similar, *a.* similis; **~ly**, *ad.* similiter.

similarity, *n.* similitudo; vicinitas, proximitas, *f.*

simile, *n.* similitudo, *f.*

simmer, *v.t.* fervefacio, [3]; ~, *v.i.* aestuo, [1]; ferveo, [2].

simple, *a.* simplex; rudis; *fig.* (silly) ineptus; ingenuus.

simpleton, *n.* stultus, fatuus, ineptus, *m.*

simplicity, *n.* simplicitas, *f.*

simplify, *v.t.* simpliciorem reddo, [3].

simply, *ad.* simpliciter; (merely) solum, modo, tantummodo.

simulate, *v.t.* simulo, [1].

simulation, *n.* simulatio, *f.*

simultaneous, *a.* eodem tempore; **~ly**, *ad.* simul, una.

sin, *n.* peccatum; delictum, flagitium, nefas, vitium, *nt.*

sin, *v.t.* pecco, [1]; delinquo, [3].

since, *pr.* post (*with acc.*); ~, *c.* cum, ex quo; (seeing that) cum; quando; quoniam; ~, *ad.* abhinc; **long ~**, iamdudum

sincere, *a.* sincerus, candidus; simplex, verus; **~ly**, *ad.* sincere, vere.

sincerity, *n.* sinceritas, simplicitas, *f.*; candor, *m.*

sinew, *n.* nervus; lacertus, *m.*

sinful, *a.* impius, pravus; flagitiosus, sceleratus.

sing, *v.t. & i.* cano, [3]; canto, [1].

singe, *v.t.* aduro, amburo, [3].

singer, *n.* cantor, *m.*

singing, *n.* cantus, *m.*; carmen, *nt.*

single, *a.* solus, unicus, unus.

single, *v.t.* (out) eligo, [3].

singly, *ad.* singillatim.

singular, *a.* unicus, singularis; (exceptional) peculiaris; egregius, eximius.

sinister, *a.* mali ominis; malevolus, iniquus.

sink, *v.i.* (fall to the ground) consido, subsido; (into ruins) collabor; (of a ship) deprimor, summergor, [3]; ~, *v.t.* deprimo; demergo, summergo; (a well) demitto, [3].

sinner, *n.* peccans, *c.*

sinuous, *a.* sinuosus.

sip, *v.t.* sorbillo, degusto, libo, delibo, [1]; ~, *n.* sorbitio, *f.*

siphon, *n.* sipho, *m.*

sir, *n.* (knight) eques, *m.*; ~! *i.* (title of respect in address) bone vir! vir clarissime!

Siren, *n.* Siren, *f.*

sister, *n.* soror, *f.*

sisterhood, *n.* societas, *f.*; collegium, *nt.*

sister-in-law, *n.* glos, *f.*

sisterly, *a.* sororius.

sit, *v.i.* sedeo; (at) assideo, [2]; (down) consido, [3]; (on) insideo, [2] (*with dat.*).

site, *n.* situs; positus, *m.*; (space) area, *f.*

sitting, *n.* (act *and* session) sessio, *f.*

situated, *a.* situs, positus.

situation, *n.* situs, positus, *m.*; *fig.* condicio, *f.*; status, *m.*

six, *a.* sex; ~ times, sexies.

six hundred, *a.* sescenti.

sixteen, *a.* sedecim.

sixteenth, *a.* sextus decimus.

sixth, *a.* sextus.

sixtieth, *a.* sexagesimus.

sixty, *a.* sexaginta.

size, *n.* magnitudo; moles; mensura; forma, *f.*

skeleton, *n.* sceletus, *m.*; (bones) ossa, *nt. pl.*; ~ key, clavis adulterina, *f.*

sketch, *n.* adumbratio, *f.*; ~, *v.t.* adumbro; delineo, [1]; *fig.* describo, [3].

skewer, *n.* veru, *nt.*

skilful, skilled, *a.* dexter, expertus, peritus; sollers, ingeniosus; ~ly, *ad.* perite, sollerter, ingeniose.

skilfulness, skill, *n.* ars, sollertia, calliditas, peritia, *f.*

skim, *v.t.* despumo, [1]; *fig.* percurro, stringo; perstringo, attingo, [3]; (fly over) volo per (*with acc.*), [1]; perlabor, verro, [3].

skin, *n.* (of people) cutis; (of animals) pellis, *f.*; (prepared) corium, *nt.*; (membrane) membrana; (of vegetables) cutis, membrana, tunica, *f.*

skin, *v.t.* pellem detraho, [3] (*with gen.*).

skinny, *a.* rugosus; macilentus; macer.

skip, *v.i.* salio, exsilio, [4]; exsulto, [1]; lascivio; ~ over, transilio, [4]; (leave out) omitto, [3]; ~, *n.* saltus, *m.*

skirmish, *n.* leve proelium, *nt.*; ~, *v.i.* velitor, [1].

skirt, *n.* (dress) vestis, *f.*; ~, *v.t.* lego, [3].

skull, *n.* calvaria, calva, *f.*

sky, *n.* caelum, *nt.*; aether, *m.*

skylark, *n.* alauda, *f.*

slab, *n.* quadra, *f.*

slack, *a.* remissus, laxus; *fig.* piger, neglegens.

slack, slacken, *v.t.* remitto, [3]; laxo, relaxo, [1]; minuo, [3]; ~, *v.i.* minuor, remittor, [3]; laxor, relaxor, [1].

slag, *n.* scoria, *f.*

slake, *v.t.* exstinguo, [3]; sedo, [1]; depello, [3].

slander, *v.t.* calumnior, detrecto, [1]; ~, *n.* calumnia; obtrectatio, *f.*

slanderous, *a.* maledicus.

slant, slanting, *a.* obliquus.

slap, *n.* alapa, *f.*; ~, *v.t.* alapam do, [1].

slash, *n.* (cut) incisura, *f.*; (blow) ictus, *m.*; (wound) vulnus, *nt.*; ~, *v.t.* concido, incido, [3].

slaughter, *n.* caedes, trucidatio, *f.*; ~, *v.t.* macto, trucido, neco, iugulo, [1].

slaughterhouse, *n.* macellum, *nt.*

slave, *n.* servus, *m.*; serva, *f.*; verna, *c.*; mancipium, *nt.*; famulus, *m.*; famula, *f.* ~, *v.i.* *fig.* sudo, [1].

slavery, *n.* servitus, *f.*; servitium, *nt.*

slave-trade, *n.* venalicium, *nt.*

slave-trader, *n.* venalicius, *m.*

slavish, *a.* servilis; humilis.

slay, *v.t.* interficio, caedo, perimo, interimo, occido, [3]; trucido, obtrunco, [1].

sledge, *n.* traha, trahea, *f.*

sleek, *a.* levis, politus; nitidus.

sleep, *n.* somnus; sopor, *m.*; quies, *f.*; ~, *v.i.* dormio, [4]; quiesco, [3]; ~ **off,** edormio, [4].

sleepiness, *n.* somnolentia, *f.*; sopor, *m.*

sleepless, *a.* insomnis; exsomnis, vigil, vigilax; pervigil.

sleeplessness, *n.* insomnia; vigilantia, *f.*

sleepy, *a.* somniculosus; *fig.* iners.

sleet, *n.* nivosa grando, *f.*

sleeve, *n.* manica, *f.*; **laugh up one's ~,** furtim rideo, [2].

sleight, *n.* (of hand) praestigiae, *f.* pl.

slender, *a.* gracilis; tenuis; (sparing) parcus.

slenderness, *n.* gracilitas; tenuitas, *f.*

slice, *n.* segmentum, frustum, *nt.*; offula; (tool) spatha, *f.*; ~, *v.t.* seco, [1].

slide, *v.i.* labor, [3].

slide, *n.* lapsus, *m.*

slight, *a.* levis; exiguus, tenuis, parvus; ~**ly,** *ad.* leviter; paulum, paulo.

slight, *n.* neglegentia; repulsa, iniuria, *f.*; contemptus, *m.*

slight, *v.t.* neglego; contemno, despicio, [3].

slim, *a.* gracilis; *v.* **slender**.

slime, *n.* pituita, *f.*; (mud) limus, *m.*

slimy, *a.* limosus, mucosus.

sling, n. funda; (for the arm) fascia, mitella, f.; ~, v.t. e funda iaculor, [1]; (hang) suspendo, [3].

slink, v.i. (away) furtim me subduco, [3]; (in) irrepo, [3].

slip, v.i. labor, [3]; ~ away, elabor, clanculum me subtraho; ~ out, excido, [3].

slip, n. lapsus, m.; fig. peccatum, nt.; culpa, f.; error, m.

slipper, n. solea, crepida, f.

slippery, a. lubricus; fig. (deceitful) subdolus; (dangerous) periculosus.

slipshod, a. neglegens.

slit, n. incisura, rima, f.; ~, v.t. incido, [3].

slope, n. acclivitas, declivitas, f.; clivus, m.

slope, v.i. proclinor, [1]; demittor, [3]; ~, v.t. demitto, [3].

sloping, a. acclivis; declivis; pronus.

sloppy, a. lutulentus, sordidus.

sloth, n. ignavia, pigritia, inertia; socordia, f.

slothful, a. iners, piger, segnis; ignavus, socors; ~ly, ad. pigre, ignave, segniter.

slough, n. (marsh) palus, f.

slow, a. tardus, lentus; piger; (gentle) lenis; ~ly, ad. tarde, lente; pigre; sensim.

slug, n. limax, c.

sluggish, a. piger, ignavus.

sluice, n. obiectaculum, nt.; catarracta, f.

slumber, n. somnus, sopor, m.; ~, v.i. obdormisco, [3]; dormito, [1]; dormio, [4].

slur, v.t. (smear) inquino, [1]; ~, n. macula, labes, f.

slut, n. mulier neglegens, f.

sly, a. astutus, vafer, callidus; on the ~, clam, clanculum; ~ly, ad., callide, vafre.

smack, n. (relish) sapor, m.; (slap) alapa, f.; (ship) lenunculus, m.

smack, v.t. (taste) gusto, [1]; (strike) ferio, [4]; ~ of, v.i. sapio, [3] (with acc.).

small, a. parvus, exiguus, tenuis; brevis; pusillus; (insignificant) levis.

smallness, n. exiguitas, tenuitas, parvitas; gracilitas; brevitas, f.

smart, a. (clever) acutus, sollers, callidus; (energetic) alacer; (elegant) lautus, nitidus; (elegantly) nitide, laute.

smartness, n. sollertia, f.; acumen, nt.; alacritas; (elegance) lautitia, f., nitor, m.

smash, n. ruina, f.; ~, v.t. confringo, [3].

smattering, n. (a small quantity) aliquantum, nt.

smear, v.t. lino, illino, oblino, ungo, [3].

smell, v.t. olfacio, [3]; odoror, [1]; ~, v.i. oleo; redoleo, [2]; fragro, [1].

smell, n. (sense) odoratus, m.; (odour) odor, m.

smelly, *a.* olidus, graveolens.

smile, *v.i.* subrideo, renideo, [2]; (at) arrideo, [2]; ~, *n.* risus, *m.*

smiling, *a.* renidens, subridens.

smith, *n.* faber, *m.*

smithy, *n.* fabrica; officina, *f.*

smoke, *v.t.* (suf)fumigo; (dry by smoke) infumo, [1]; ~, *v.i.* fumo, vaporo, [1].

smoke, *n.* fumus, vapor, *m.*

smoky, *a.* fumeus, fumidus, fumosus; fumificus; (blackened by smoke) decolor fuligine.

smooth, *a.* levis; glaber; (slippery) lubricus; (polished) teres; (calm) placidus; lenis; *fig.* blandus; ~ly, *ad.* leniter, placide; *fig.* blande.

smooth, *v.t.* levigo, [1]; polio, [4]; (with the plane) runcino; *fig.* complano, [1].

smother, *v.t.* suffoco, [1]; opprimo, [3]; (conceal) celo, [1].

smoulder, *v.i.* fumo, [1].

smudge, *n.* sordes, *f.*; ~, *v.t.* inquino, [1].

smug, *a.* sibi placens.

smuggle, *v.t.* furtim importo, sine portorio importo, [1].

smut, *n.* (soot) fuligo, *f.*

snack, *n.* pars, portio; gustatio, *f.*

snail, *n.* coclea, *f.*; limax, *c.*

snake, *n.* anguis, *c.*; serpens, *f.*; vipera, *f.*; v. **serpent.**

snap, *v.t. & i.* (one's fingers *or* a whip) concrepo, [1]; (break) frango, [3]; ~, *v.i.* dissilio, [4]; ~

at, mordicus arripio, [3]; *fig.* hianti ore capto, [1].

snap, *n.* crepitus, *m.*

snare, *n.* laqueus, *m.*; pedica, *f.*; *fig.* insidiae, *f. pl.*

snare, *v.t.* illaqueo, implico, [1]; irretio, [4].

snarl, *v.i.* (as a dog) ringor, [3]; hirrio, [4].

snarl, *n.* hirritus, *m.*

snatch, *v.t.* rapio, corripio, [3]; (away) eripio; surripio, avello, [3].

sneak, *v.i.* repo, serpo, [3]; latito, [1]; ~ **off,** me subtraho, [3].

sneer, *v.i.* irrideo, derideo, [2]; ~, *n.* irrisio, *f.*; irrisus, *m.*

sneeze, *v.i.* sternuo, [3]; ~, *n.* sternumentum, sternutamentum, *nt.*

sniff, *v.i.* naribus capto, [1]; haurio, [4].

snip, *v.t.* amputo, [1]; (off) decerpo, praecido, [3].

snob, *n.* homo novus et arrogans, divitum cultor, *m.*

snobbish, *a.* fastidiosus.

snore, *v.i.* sterto, [3]; ~, *n.* rhonchus, *m.*

snort, *v.i.* fremo, [3]; ~, *n.* fremitus (equorum), *m.*

snout, *n.* rostrum, *nt.*

snow, *n.* nix, *f.*; ~, *v.i. impers.* it is ~**ing,** ningit, [3].

snowy, *a.* niveus, nivalis; (full of snow) nivosus.

snub, *v.t.* repello, [3].

snub, *n.* repulsa, *f.*

snub-nosed, *a.* simus, resimus.

so, *ad.* sic, ita; tam; adeo; ~ **far,** eatenus; ~ **much,** tantum; tam; ~ **so,** mediocriter; ~ **that,** ita ut.

soak, *v.t.* macero, [1]; madefacio, imbuo, tingo, [3]; ~, *v.i.* (be soaked) madeo, [2]; madesco, madefio, [3]; ~ **through,** percolor, [1].

soap, *n.* sapo, *m.*

soar, *v.i.* in sublime feror, [3]; (of birds) subvolo, [1].

sob, *n.* singultus *m.*; ~, *v.i.* singulto, [1].

sober, *a.* sobrius; *fig.* moderatus.

sobriety, *n.* sobrietas, *f.*

sociable, *a.* sociabilis, socialis; facilis, affabilis, comis.

social, *a.* socialis; communis; civilis.

society, *n.* societas, *f.*; (fraternity) sodalicium, collegium, *nt.*

sock, *n.* pedale, *nt.*; udo, *m.*

socket, *n.* cavum, *nt.*

sod, *n.* (clod) caespes, *m.*

sofa, *n.* lectulus, grabatus, *m.*

soft, *a.* mollis, tener; (gentle) lenis; clemens; mitis; (not loud) mollis; *fig.* delicatus; effeminatus; ~**ly,** *ad.* molliter; leniter; clementer.

soften, *v.t.* mollio, [4]; mitigo, [1]; *fig.* lenio, [4]; placo, levo, [1]; ~, *v.i.* mollesco, (fruits) mitesco; *fig.* mansuesco, mitesco, [3].

softness, *n.* mollitia; teneritas; lenitas; (effeminacy) mollitia, *f.*

soil, *n.* solum, *nt.*; terra, *f.*

soil, *v.t.* inquino, contamino, maculo, [1].

solace, *n.* solacium, lenimen, levamen, levamentum, *nt.*

solar, *a.* solaris; solis (genitive).

solder, *v.t.* ferrumino, [1]; ~, *n.* ferrumen, *nt.*

soldier, *n.* miles, *m.*

sole, *a.* solitarius, unus, unicus, solus; ~**ly,** *ad.* solum, modo, tantum.

sole, *n.* (of the foot) planta; (of a shoe) solea, *f.*

solecism, *n.* soloecismus, *m.*

solemn, *a.* sollemnis; severus; gravis; serius; ~**ly,** *ad.* sollemniter, graviter, severe, serio.

solemnity, *n.* sollemne, festum, *nt.*; sollemnitas, *f.*

solicit, *v.t.* rogo; flagito; (tempt) sollicito, [1].

solicitor, *n.* iuris consultus, causidicus; advocatus, *m.*

solid, *a.* solidus; densus; *fig.* verus; firmus.

solid, *n.* corpus solidum, *nt.*

solitary, *a.* solitarius; (of places) desertus, solus.

solitude, *n.* solitudo, *f.*; locus solus, *m.*

soluble, *a.* solubilis.

solution, *n.* dilutum, *nt.*; *fig.* solutio, explicatio, *f.*

solve, *v.t.* solvo, [3]; explico, [1].

sombre, *a.* (severe) tristis.

some, *a.* aliqui, nescio qui; nonnullus; quidam; ~ . . . other, alius . . . alius.

somebody, *n.* nescio quis, aliquis.

somehow, *ad.* nescio quo modo.

something, *n.* aliquid, *nt.*

sometime, *ad.* aliquando; quandoque; ~ or other, aliquo tempore.

sometimes, *ad.* quandoque, interdum; nonnunquam; (when repeated) modo . . . modo.

somewhat, *ad.* paullulum.

somewhere, *ad.* alicubi.

son, *n.* filius, natus, *m.*; ~-in-law, *n.* gener, *m.*

song, *n.* cantus, *m.*; carmen, *nt.*; (tune) melos, *nt.*

soon, *ad.* brevi, postmodo, mox; ~ after, paulo post; as ~ as, simulatque, simulac; as ~ as possible, quam primum.

sooner, *ad.* (earlier) citius, temperius, prius . . . quam; (rather) libentius; potius; no ~ said than done, dicto citius.

soot, *n.* fuligo, *f.*

soothe, *v.t.* mulceo, permulceo, [2]; mitigo, levo, [1]; delenio, [4].

soothsayer, *n.* hariolus, sortilegus, *m.*; fatidicus, haruspex, *m.*; augur, vates, *c.*

sooty, *a.* fuliginosus.

sop, *n.* offa, offula, *f.*

sophisticated, *a.* lepidus.

soporific, *a.* soporus, soporifer, somnifer.

sorcerer, *n.* magus, veneficus, *m.*

sorceress, *n.* maga, saga, venefica, *f.*

sorcery, *n.* fascinatio, *f.*; veneficium, *nt.*; magice, *f.*

sordid, *a.* sordidus, turpis, foedus.

sore, *a.* tener; ~ly, *ad.* graviter, vehementer.

sore, *n.* ulcus, *nt.*

sorrow, *n.* dolor, maeror, luctus, angor, *m.*; anxietas, *f.*

sorrowful, *a.* luctuosus, tristis, miser, maestus.

sorry, I am ~, aegre fero, [3]; paenitet me (alicuius rei); **feel** ~ for, misereor, [2] (*with gen.*).

sort, *n.* (kind) genus, *nt.*; species, *f.*; (manner) modus, mos, *m.*; (quality, of things) nota, *f.*

sort, *v.t.* ordino, [1]; dispono, digero, [3].

sortie, *n.* eruptio, excursio, *f.*; excursus, *m.*

soul, *n.* anima, *f.*; (person) homo, *c.*

sound, *a.* (healthy) validus, sanus; (strong) robustus; (entire) integer; (in mind) mentis compos; (true, genuine) verus; (valid) ratus, *f.*; (of sleep) profundus; altus.

sound, *n.* sonus, sonitus, *m.*; vox, *f.*; (of a trumpet) clangor, *m.*; (noise) strepitus, *m.*

sound, *v.t.* (a trumpet) cano, [3]; (try) tento, sollicito, [1]; ~, *v.i.* sono, persono, [1]; strepo, [3].

soup, *n.* ius, *nt.*

sour, *a.* acidus, acerbus; amarus; *fig.* morosus.

source, *n.* fons, *m.*; *fig.* origo, *f.*; principium, *nt.*

sourness, *n.* acor, *m.*; acerbitas; *fig.* morositas, *f.*

south, *n.* meridies, auster, *m.*

southern, *a.* australis, meridianus.

southwards, *ad.* in meridiem, meridiem versus.

south wind, *n.* Auster, Notus, *m.*

sovereign, *n.* princeps, *c.*, rex, regnator, *m.*; ~, *a.* supremus.

sovereignty, *n.* imperium, *nt.*; dominatio, *f.*; principatus, *m.*

sow, *n.* sus; porca, *f.*

sow, *v.t.* sero, [3]; semino, [1].

space, *n.* spatium, *nt.*; area, *f.*; (of time) intervallum, *nt.*

spacious, *a.* spatiosus, amplus.

spade, *n.* (implement) ligo, *m.*; pala, *f.*

Spain, *n.* Hispania, *f.*

span, *n.* (width of the palm) palmus, *m.*

Spanish, *a.* Hispanicus, Hispaniensis.

spar, *n.* (beam) trabs, *f.*

spar, *v.i.* dimico; *fig.* digladior, [1].

spare, *v.t.* & *i.* parco, [3] (*with dat.*); parce utor, [3] (*with abl.*).

spare, *a.* parcus; exilis.

sparing, *a.* parcus.

spark, *n.* scintilla, *f.*; igniculus, *m.*

sparkle, *v.i.* scintillo, corusco, radio, mico, [1].

sparkling, *a.* nitidus, coruscus.

sparrow, *n.* passer, *m.*

Sparta, *n.* Sparta, Lacedaemon, *f.*

Spartan, *a.* Laconicus, Spartanus, Lacedaemonius.

spasm, *n.* spasmos, *m.*

spasmodic, *a.* spasticus; *fig.* rarus.

spasmodically, *ad.*, *fig.* raro.

spatter, *v.t.* inquino, [1]; aspergo, [3]; *fig.* calumnior, [1].

spatula, *n.* spatha, *f.*

spawn, *n.* ova (piscium) *nt. pl.*; ~, *v.i.* ova gignere, [3].

speak, *v.i.* & *t.* loquor, [3]; for, [1]; dico, [3]; ~ **of,** dico (de *with abl.*); (mention) memoro, [1]; ~ **out,** eloquor, proloquor, [3]; ~ **to,** alloquor, [3].

speaker, *n.* orator, *m.*

spear, *n.* hasta, lancea, *f.*; telum, pilum, iaculum, *nt.*; ~, *v.t.* transfigo, [3].

special, *a.* peculiaris, specialis; praecipuus; ~**ly,** *ad.* specialiter, praecipue, peculiariter, praesertim.

speciality, *n.* proprietas, *f.*; quod peculiare est.

species, *n.* species, *f.*; genus, *nt.*

specific, *a.* specialis; (definite) certus; ~**ally,** *ad.* specialiter.

specify, *v.t.* enumero, [1]; describo, [3].

specimen, *n.* exemplum, documentum, specimen, *nt.*

speck, *n.* macula, *f.*

speckled, *a.* maculosus.

spectacle, *n.* spectaculum, *nt.*; species, *f.*; aspectus, *m.*

spectator, *n.* spectator, *m.*; spectatrix, *f.*

spectre, *n.* simulacrum, umbra, visum, *nt.*

speculate, *v.t. & i.* meditor, [1]; coniecturam facio, [3].

speculation, *n.* contemplatio, *f.*

speech, *n.* lingua, loquela, *f.*; sermo, *m.*; contio, oratio, *f.*

speechless, *a.* mutus, elinguis; *fig.* obstupefactus.

speed, *n.* celeritas; festinatio, *f.*; impetus, *m.*; ~, *v.t.* propero, festino, adiuvo, prospero, [1]; ~, *v.i.* (hasten) propero, festino, [1].

speedy, *a.* citus, properus.

spell, *n.* (charm) incantamentum, cantamen, carmen, *nt.*; cantus, *m.*

spell, *v.t. & i.* ordino [1] syllabas litterarum.

spelling, *n.* orthographia, *f.*

spend, *v.t.* impendo; consumo; (time) ago, dego, consumo, contero; (exhaust) effundo, [3]; (squander) dissipo, [1].

spendthrift, *n.* nepos, prodigus, *m.*

spew, *v.t. & i.* vomo, [3].

sphere, *n.* sphaera, *f.*; globus, *m.*; *fig.* provincia, area, *f.*

spherical, *a.* sphaericus, sphaeralis, globosus.

sphinx, *n.* sphinx, *f.*

spice, *n.* aroma, *nt.*; odores, *m. pl.*; ~, *v.t.* condio, [4].

spicy, *a.* aromaticus, conditus, fragrans, odorus, odorifer.

spider, *n.* aranea, *f.*; ~'**s web,** araneum, *nt.*; casses, *f. pl.*

spike, *n.* clavus, *m.*; (point) cuspis; (of corn) spica, *f.*

spiky, *a.* acutus, spinosus.

spill, *v.t.* effundo, [3].

spin, *v.t.* neo, [2]; (draw out) duco, protraho, [3]; (as a top) verso, [1]; ~, *v.i.* (be turned round) versor, [1]; circumferor, [3].

spinal, *a.* dorsualis.

spindle, *n.* fusus; (of a wheel) axis, *m.*

spine, *n.* (vertebrae & thorn) spina, *f.*

spinster, *n.* innupta, *f.*

spiral, *a.* spirae formam habens; ~, *n.* spira, *f.*

spire, *n.* spira; (tower) turris, *f.*

spirit, *n.* spiritus, *m.*; anima, *f.*; *fig.* ingenium, *nt.*; vigor, *m.*; (ghost) simulacrum, *nt.*; umbra, imago, *f.*; (god) deus, *m.*

spirited, *a.* animosus; alacer.

spiritual, *a.* animi, mentis (genitives); incorporalis; ecclesiasticus.

spit, *n.* veru, *nt.*; (of land) lingua, *f.*; *v.* **spittle**; ~, *v.t. & i.* (from the mouth) spuo, [3]; excreo, [1].

spite, *n.* livor, *m.*; invidia, malevolentia, *f.*; odium, *nt.*; **in ~ of,** ablative absolute with perfect participle passive of *contemno*.

spite, *v.t.* vexo, [1].

spiteful, *a.* lividus, malevolus, invidus.

spittle, *n.* sputum, *nt.*; saliva, *f.*

splash, *v.t.* aspergo, respergo, [3].

splendid, *a.* splendidus; nitidus; lautus, sumptuosus; magnificus; **~ly,** *ad.* splendide; magnifice; laute, nitide, sumptuose.

splendour, *n.* splendor, nitor, *m.*; *fig.* magnificentia, lautitia, *f.*

splint, *n.* (in medicine) ferula, *f.*

splinter, *n.* assula, *f.*; ~, *v.t.* confringo, [3]; ~, *v.i.* dissilio, [4].

split, *v.t. & i.* findo; findor, [3]; ~, *n.* fissura, rima, *f.*

split, *a.* fissilis.

spoil, *n.* spolium, *nt.*; praeda, *f.*; exuviae, *f. pl.*; ~, *v.t.* spolio, [3]; praedor; vasto, [1]; diripio, [3]; (mar, *etc.*) corrumpo; (ruin) perdo, [3]; depravo, vitio, [1].

spoke, *n.* radius, *m.*

spokesman, *n.* orator, *m.*

sponge, *n.* spongia, *f.*; ~, *v.t.* spongia detergeo, [2].

spongy, *a.* spongiosus.

sponsor, *n.* sponsor, vas, praes, *m.*

spontaneously, *ad.* sua sponte, ultro.

spool, *n.* fusus, *m.*

spoon, *n.* coclear, *nt.*

spoonful, *n.* coclear, *nt.*

sport, *n.* ludus, lusus, *m.*; (hunting) venatio; (mockery) irrisio, *f.*; **in ~,** per iocum; ~, *v.i.* ludo, [3]; lascivio, [4].

sportive, *a.* iocosus, ludicer.

sportsman, *n.* athleta, *m.*

spot, *n.* macula; (mark) nota; (stain) labes, *f.*; (place) locus, *m.*; ~, *v.t.* (stain) inquino, maculo, commaculo; (speckle) maculis noto, [1].

spotless, *a.* expers maculis; *fig.* purus; integer; **~ly,** *ad.* sine labe.

spotted, *a.* maculosus, maculis distinctus.

spouse, *n.* coniunx, *c.*; maritus, *m.*; uxor, *f.*

spout, *n.* canalis; (of water) torrens, *m.*; ~, *v.t.* eiaculor (in altum); (speeches) declamo, [1]; ~, *v.i.* prosilio, [4]; emico, [1].

sprain, *v.t.* intorqueo, [2]; convello, [3]; luxo, [1]; ~, *n.* luxatura, *f.*

sprawl, *v.i.* humi prostratus iaceo, [2].

spray, *n.* aspergo, spuma, *f.*; (branch) ramus, *m.*; virga, *f.*

spray, *v.t.* spargo, [3].

spread, *v.t.* pando, tendo, expando, distendo, extendo; diffundo,

[3]; (make known) divulgo, [1]; ~, *v.i.* pandor, tendor, distendor, extendor, expandor, diffundor, [3]; (become known) divulgor; (of a disease, *etc.*) evagor, [1]; glisco, [3].

sprig, *n.* ramulus, *m.*; virga, *f.*

sprightly, *a.* alacer; hilaris.

spring, *n.* (season) ver, *nt.*; (leap) saltus, *m.*; (of water) fons, *m.*

spring, *a.* vernus.

spring, *v.i.* (grow from) orior, [4]; enascor, [3]; (as rivers, *etc.*) scateo, [2]; effluo, [3]; (leap) salio, exsilio, [4]; ~ **a leak,** rimas ago, [3].

springtime, *n.* vernum tempus, *nt.*

sprinkle, *v.t.* spargo, aspergo, respergo, [3]; roro, irroro, [1].

sprout, *n.* surculus, *m.*; germen, *nt.*; ~**s,** *pl.* cauliculi, *m. pl.*; ~, *v.i.* pullulo, germino, [1].

spruce, *a.* lautus, nitidus, comptus.

spur, *n.* calcar; *fig.* incitamentum, irritamen, irritamentum, *nt.*; ~, *v.t.* equum calcaribus concito, [1]; equo calcaria subdo, [3]; *fig.* incito, excito, [1].

spurious, *a.* subditus, suppositus, falsus.

spurn, *v.t.* aspernor, repudio, [1]; sperno, [3]; proculco, [1].

spurt, *v.i.* (as liquids) exsilio, [4].

spy, *n.* explorator; speculator; emissarius, *m.*

spy, *v.t. & i.* exploro; speculor, [1].

squabble, *v.i.* rixor, [1]; ~, *n.* iurgium, *nt.*; rixa, *f.*

squad, *n.* manipulus, *m.*

squadron, *n.* (of cavalry) turma, ala; (of ships) classis, *f.*

squalid, *a.* squalidus, spurcus, sordidus, turpis.

squall, *n.* vociferatio, *f.*; (sudden storm) procella, *f.*

squalor, *n.* squalor, situs, *m.*; sordes, *f. pl.*; illuvies, *f.*

squander, *v.t.* dissipo, [1]; profundo, [3].

square, *a.* quadratus; *fig.* honestus, probus; ~, *n.* quadratum, *nt.*; quadra; (tool) norma, *f.*; (*mil.*) agmen quadratum, *nt.*

squash, *v.t.* contero, confringo, [3].

squat, *v.i.* succumbo, recumbo, subsido, [3].

squeak, *v.i.* strideo, [2].

squeamish, *a.* fastidiosus.

squeeze, *v.t.* comprimo, premo, [3]; (out) exprimo, [3].

squint, *v.i.* limis oculis intueor, [2].

squint, squinting, *a.* strabus, limis oculis.

squirrel, *n.* sciurus, *m.*

squirt, *v.t.* proicio, [3]; ~, *v.i.* emico, [1]; exsilio, [4].

stab, *n.* vulnus, *nt.*; ictus, *m.*; plaga, *f.*; ~, *v.t.* fodio, [3]; perforo, [1]; perfodio, transfigo, [3].

stability, *n.* stabilitas, *f.*

stable, *a.* stabilis, solidus.

stable, *n.* stabulum, *nt.*; ~-**boy**, *n.* stabularius, *m.*

stack, *n.* acervus, *m.*; strues, *f.*; ~, *v.t.* coacervo, [1].

stadium, *n.* (running-track) stadium, *nt.*

staff, *n.* baculum, *nt.*; fustis; (baton) scipio, *m.*; (officers) legati, *m. pl.*; *fig.* (support) subsidium, fulcimentum, *nt.*

stag, *n.* cervus, *m.*

stage, *n.* proscaenium; pulpitum; suggestum; theatrum, *nt.*; *fig.* (field of action) campus, *m.*; area, *f.*; (on a journey) iter, *nt.*

stagger, *v.i.* vacillo, titubo, [1]; ~, *v.t.* obstupefacio, [3].

stagnant, *a.* stagnans; torpens; piger; iners.

stagnate, *v.i.* stagno, [1]; *fig.* refrigesco, [3].

stagnation, *n.* torpor, *m.*

staid, *a.* gravis, severus.

stain, *n.* macula, labes; *fig.* infamia, nota, *f.*

stain, *v.t.* maculo, commaculo, contamino, [1]; (dye) tingo, inficio, imbuo, [3].

stainless, *a.* immaculatus, purus; *fig.* integer.

stair, *n.* gradus, *m.*; scala, *f.*

staircase, *n.* scalae, *f. pl.*

stake, *n.* palus, stipes, vallus, *m.*; sudis, *f.*; (wager) depositum, *nt.*; ~, *v.t.* depono, [3]; pignero, oppignero, [1]; **be at** ~, in discrimine esse.

stale, *a.* vetus; obsoletus; tritus.

stalk, *n.* caulis; (of corn) culmus, *m.*

stalk, *v.i.* incedo, ingredior, [3]; spatior, [1]; (in hunting) venor, [1].

stall, *n.* stabulum; (seat) subsellium, *nt.*

stallion, *n.* (equus) admissarius, *m.*

stammer, *n.* haesitatio linguae, *f.*

stammer, *v.t. & i.* balbutio, [4]; lingua haesito, [1].

stamp, *n.* (mark) nota, *f.*; signum, *nt.*; (with the foot) vestigium, *nt.*; (kind) genus, *nt.*

stamp, *v.t.* imprimo, [3]; noto, [1]; (money) cudo, [3]; (with the feet) supplodo, [3]; pulso, [1]; ~ **out**, deleo, [2].

stand, *n.* locus, *m.*; statio; mora, *f.*; (platform) suggestus, *m.*; (counter) mensa, *f.*; **make a** ~, subsisto, [3].

stand, *v.i.* sto, [1]; consisto, [3]; (remain) maneo, [2]; (endure) tolero, [1]; sustineo, [2]; (against) resisto, [3] (*with dat.*); (aloof) absto, [1]; (by) asto, [1]; assisto, [3] (*both with dat.*); *fig.* persto, [1]; (out) exsto, [1]; promineo, [2]; (still) consisto, subsisto, [3].

standard, *n.* signum, vexillum, *nt.*; (pattern of practice or behaviour) norma, (yardstick) mensura, *f.*; ~-**bearer**, *n.* vexillarius, signifer, *m.*

standing, *n.* status, ordo, *m.*; condicio, *f.*

standstill, be at a ~, *v.i.* consisto, [3]; haereo, [2].

star, *n.* stella, *f.*; sidus, astrum; *fig.* lumen, *nt.*

stare, *n.* obtutus, *m.*; ~, *v.t. & i.* inhio, [1]; stupeo, [2]; ~ (at) intueor, [2]; haereo [2] defixus in aliquo.

stark, *a.* rigidus; ~, *ad.* omnino, penitus.

starling, *n.* sturnus, *m.*

starry, *a.* sidereus, stellans, stellatus, stellifer.

start, *v.i.* (in agitation) trepido, [1]; subsilio, [4]; contremisco, [3]; (begin) ordior, [4]; incipio, [3]; (set out) proficiscor, [3]; ~, *v.t.* (game) excito, [1]; (set on foot) instituo, [3]; (put in motion) commoveo, [2]; (begin) incipio, [3].

start, *n.* subita trepidatio, *f.*; tremor, *m.*; (departing) profectio, *f.*; (leap) saltus, *m.*; (beginning) initium, principium, *nt.*

starting-place, *n.* (at the races) carceres, *m. pl.*; claustra, *nt. pl.*

startle, *v.t.* territo, [1]; terreo, [2].

starvation, *n.* fames, inedia, *f.*

starve, *v.t.* fame interficio, [3]; ~, *v.i.* fame enecor, [1].

state, *n.* status; locus, *m.*; (political) civitas, respublica, *f.*; (pomp) magnificentia, *f.*; *fig.* condicio, *f.*

state, *v.t.* narro; declaro, indico, [1]; perscribo, [3].

stately, *a.* superbus; splendidus, lautus, augustus.

statement, *n.* affirmatio, *f.*; testimonium, indicium, *nt.*

statesman, *n.* peritus qui in republica versatur, *m.*

station, *n.* statio, *f.*; locus, *m.*; *v.t.* loco, [1]; dispono, [3].

stationary, *a.* stabilis, loco fixus, immotus.

stationer, *n.* chartarius, *m.*; ~'s **shop**, taberna chartaria, *f.*

stationery, *n.* charta, *f.*; res chartariae, *f. pl.*

statue, *n.* statua, imago, effigies, *f.*; signum, simulacrum, *nt.*

stature, *n.* statura, *f.*; habitus, *m.*

status, *n.* status, *m.*

statute, *n.* statutum; decretum, *nt.*; lex, *f.*

staunch, *a.* firmus, fidus, constans.

staunch, *v.t.* sisto, [3]; cohibeo, [2].

stay, *v.i.* maneo, [2]; commoror, (loiter) cunctor, [1]; ~, *v.t.* detineo, [2]; sisto, [3]; (curb) coerceo, [2].

stay, *n.* (sojourn) commoratio, mansio; (delay) mora, *f.*; (prop) fulcrum, *nt.*; *fig.* subsidium, columen, *nt.*

steadfast, *a.* stabilis, firmus, constans; ~ly, *ad.* constanter, firmiter.

steadiness, *n.* firmitas, stabilitas, constantia, *f.*

steady, *a.* firmus, stabilis; constans; *fig.* (serious) gravis.

steal, *v.t.* furor, [1]; (away) surripio, [3]; ~, *v.i.* repo, serpo, [3]; insinuo, [1].

stealth, *n.* (act) furtum, *nt.*; by ~, furtim, clam.

stealthy, *a.* furtivus.

steam, *n.* (aquae) vapor, *m.*; ~, *v.t. & i.* vaporo; fumo, [1].

steel, *n.* chalybs, *m.*; *fig.* ferrum, *nt.*

steep, *a.* praeceps, arduus, praeruptus.

steep, *v.t.* madefacio, [3]; macero, [1]; imbuo, tingo, [3].

steeple, *n.* turris, *f.*

steeply, *ad.* in praeceps.

steepness, *n.* acclivitas, declivitas, *f.*

steer, *v.t. & i.* guberno, moderor, [1]; dirigo, rego, [3].

stem, *n.* (of a plant) stirps, *f.*

stem, *v.t.* obsisto, obnitor (*both with dat.*); reprimo, [3].

stench, *n.* fetor, odor, *m.*

step, *n.* passus, gradus, gressus, *m.*; by ~, *ad.* gradatim, sensim, pedetentim.

step, *v.i.* gradior, [3].

stepbrother, *n.* (of father's side) vitrici filius; (of mother's side) novercae filius, *m.*

stepdaughter, *n.* privigna, *f.*

stepfather, *n.* vitricus, *m.*

stepmother, *n.* noverca, *f.*

stepson, *n.* privignus, *m.*

sterile, *a.* sterilis, infecundus.

sterility, *n.* sterilitas, *f.*

stern, *a.* durus, severus; torvus.

stern, *n.* puppis (navis), *f.*

stethoscope, *n.* stethoscopium, *nt.*

steward, *n.* administrator, procurator; vilicus, *m.*

stick, *n.* baculus, scipio, fustis, *m.*; baculum, *nt.*

stick, *v.t.* affigo, [3]; ~, *v.i.* haereo; adhaereo, [2]; ~, promineo, [2].

sticky, *a.* lentus, tenax.

stiff, *a.* rigidus; *fig.* severus; frigidus.

stiffen, *v.t.* rigidum facio, [3]; ~, *v.i.* rigesco, derigesco, [3].

stiffness, *n.* rigor, *m.*; *fig.* pertinacia, *f.*; rigor, *m.*

stifle, *v.t.* suffoco; strangulo, [1]; *fig.* opprimo, [3].

stigma, *n.* nota, ignominia, *f.*

still, *a.* quietus, immotus, tacitus.

still, *ad.* nihilominus; (yet) adhuc; (however) tamen, attamen; (even now) etiam nunc; (always) semper.

stillness, *n.* silentium, *nt.*; quies, *f.*

stilts, *n. pl.* grallae, *f. pl.*

stimulant, *n.* irritamentum, irritamen, *nt.*; stimulus, *m.*

stimulate, *v.t.* stimulo, exstimulo, excito, [1].

stimulus, *n.* v. **stimulant**.

sting, *n.* (of insects and plants) aculeus, *m.*; spiculum, *nt.*;

(wound) ictus, morsus, *m.*; *fig.* (of conscience) angor conscientiae, *m.*; ~, *u.t.* pungo, [3]; mordeo, [2]; (as nettles) uro, [3]; *fig.* excrucio, [1].

stingy, *a.* sordidus, parcus.

stink, *v.i.* feteo, male oleo [2]; ~, *n.* fetor, *m.*

stint, *v.t.* moderor, [1]; coerceo, [2]; circumscribo, parco, [3] (*with dat.*).

stipulate, *v.t.* paciscor, [3]; stipulor, [1].

stipulation, *n.* stipulatio; condicio, *f.*; pactum, *nt.*

stir, *n.* tumultus, motus, *m.*; turba, *f.*; ~, *v.t.* (arouse) excito, [1]; (move) moveo, [2]; ~, *v.i.* se movere, [2].

stitch, *v.t.* suo, [3].

stoat, *n.* mustela, *f.*

stock, *n.* (of a tree) caudex, truncus, stipes, *m.*; (handle) lignum, *nt.*; (race) genus, *nt.*; (of goods) copia, vis, *f.*; (cattle) pecus, *nt.*; stirps, *f.*; (of cattle) res pecuaria, *f.*

stock, *v.t.* instruo, [3]; orno, suppedito, [1].

stockade, *n.* vallum, *nt.*

stock-still, *a.* immotus, immobilis.

stoic(al), *a.* stoicus; *fig.* patiens.

stoicism, *n.* Stoica disciplina, *f.*; *fig.* patientia.

stolen, *a.* furtivus; clandestinus; ~ **goods,** furta, *nt. pl.*

stomach, *n.* stomachus, venter, ventriculus; (appetite) appetitus, *m.*; ~, *v.t.* (put up with) fero, [3]; tolero, [1].

stone, *n.* lapis, *m.*; saxum, *nt.*; (*med.*) calculus; (gem) gemma, *f.*; **leave no ~ unturned,** nihil reliqui facio, [3]; (of fruit) nucleus, *m.*; ~, *u.t.* lapido, [1].

stone, *a.* lapideus, saxeus.

stony, *a.* (full of stones) lapidosus; saxeus, saxosus.

stool, *n.* scabellum, scamnum, *nt.*; sella, *f.*

stoop, *v.i.* proclino, [1]; *fig.* se summittere, [3].

stop, *v.t.* prohibeo, [2]; sisto, [3]; moror, tardo, retardo, [1]; ~, *v.i.* subsisto; (cease) desisto; desino, omitto, [3]; (remain) maneo, [2]; (sojourn) commoror, [1]; ~ **up,** obturo, [1]; intercludo, [3].

stop, *n.* (delay) mora, *f.*; impedimentum, *nt.*; pausa, *f.*; (end) finis, *c.*

stoppage, *n.* obstructio, *f.*

stopper, *n.* obturamentum, *nt.*

store, *n.* copia, *f.*; apparatus; (provisions) commeatus, *m.*; ~, *u.t.* coacervo, [1]; condo; (with) instruo, [3].

storehouse, *n.* cella, *f.*; promptuarium; (granary) horreum, *nt.*

storey, *n.* (of a house) tabulatum, *nt.*

stork, *n.* ciconia, *f.*

storm, *n.* procella, tempestas; (*mil.*) expugnatio, *f.*; ~, *v.t.* expugno, [1]; ~, *v.i.* saevio, desaevio, [4].

stormy, *a.* turbidus; procellosus; *fig.* tumultuosus.

story, *n.* (tale) narratio; fabula; (history) historia, *f*; (lie) mendacium, *nt.*

storyteller, *n.* narrator; (liar) mendax, *m.*

stout, *a.* robustus; firmus; validus; (fat) pinguis; (brave) fortis.

stove, *n.* fornax, *f*; caminus, *m.*

stow, *v.t.* condo, recondo, repono, [3].

straddle, *v.i.* varico, [1].

straggle, *v.i.* palor, vagor, [1].

straggler, *n.* vagus; erro, *m.*

straight, *a.* rectus, directus; ~, *ad.* (directly) recte, recta; ~ **away,** statim, confestim, protinus.

straighten, *v.t.* rectum facio, [3]; corrigo, [3].

straightforward, *a.* simplex, apertus, directus, sincerus.

strain, *v.t.* (stretch) contendo, [3]; (a joint) luxo, [1]; (filter) percolo, [1]; (press out) exprimo, [3]; ~, *v.i.* percolor, [1]; enitor, [3].

strain, *n.* contentio; vis; (nervorum) intentio *f*; (effort) conamen, *nt.*; nisus, *m.*

strainer, *n.* colum, *nt.*

strait, *n.* fretum, *nt.*; *fig.* difficultas, *f*; angustiae, *f. pl.*

strand, *n.* (shore) litus, *nt.*; (thread) filum, *nt.*; ~, *v.i.* (of ships)

strange, *a.* peregrinus; *fig.* inusitatus; rarus; novus; mirus; mirificus.

stranger, *n.* advena, *c.*; hospes; peregrinus, *m.*

strangle, *v.t.* strangulo, suffoco, [1].

strangulation, *n.* strangulatio, suffocatio, *f*; strangulatus, *m.*

strap, *n.* lorum, *nt.*; struppus, *m.*; amentum, *nt.*

strapping, *a.* robustus.

stratagem, *n.* insidiae, *f. pl.*; *fig.* dolus, *m.*

strategy, *n.* ars imperatoria, *f.*

straw, *n.* stramentum, stramen, *nt.*; stipula, *f*; ~, *a.* stramineus.

strawberry, *n.* fragum, *nt.*

stray, *v.i.* erro, aberro, palor, vagor, [1].

stray, *a.* vagus; (sporadic) rarus.

streak, *n.* linea, virga, *f*; ~, *v.t.* distinguo, [3].

streaky, *a.* virgatus.

stream, *n.* flumen, *nt.*; amnis, *m.*; ~, *v.i.* fluo, curro, effundor, [3]; mano, [1].

street, *n.* via; (with houses) platea, *f*; vicus, *m.*

strength, *n.* robur, *nt.*; firmitas; (power) potentia, potestas, *f*; vires, *f. pl.*

strengthen, *v.t.* roboro, confirmo, [1]; munio, [4].

strenuous, *a.* strenuus; fortis; acer; ~**ly,** *ad.* strenue, fortiter, acriter.

stress, n. (anxiety) angor, m.; (chief point) summa, f.; caput, nt.; (emphasis) vis, f.; pondus, nt.

stretch, v.t. tendo; produco, extendo; distendo, [3]; ~, v.i extendo; producor; distendor; (of country) patesco, [3]; ~ out, porrigo, [3]; (oneself) pandiculor, [1].

stretch, n. (effort) intentio, contentio, f.; (expanse) spatium, nt.; tractus, m.

stretcher, n. lecticula, f.

strew, v.t. spargo, conspergo, (in)sterno, [3].

stricken, a. vulneratus, afflictus.

strict, a. (precise) accuratus, exactus; (severe) rigidus, severus; ~ly, ad. accurate; rigide; severe.

strictness, n. severitas, f.; rigor, m.

stride, v.i. varico, [1]; ~, n. gradus, m.; **make ~s,** fig. proficio, [3].

strife, n. iurgium, nt.; lis; pugna; discordia, rixa, f.

strike, v.t. ferio, [4]; pulso, [1]; percutio, [3]; (cudgel) verbero, [1]; (stamp) cudo, [3]; (the mind) subeo, [4]; succurro, [3] (with dat.); **be struck,** fig. commoveor, [2].

string, n. linea, f.; filum, nt.; (for a bow; sinew) nervus, m.; (for musical instruments) chorda; fig. series, f.; ~, v.t. persero, [3].

stringent, a. severus.

strip, v.t. (off) spolio; nudo; denudo, [1]; (clothes) exuo, [3]; (the rind, etc.) decortico, [1].

strip, n. particula, lacinia, f.; (of paper) schida, f.

stripe, n. (mark of a blow) vibex, f.; (blow) ictus, m.; verbera, nt. pl.; (for garments) virga, f.; **purple ~,** n. clavus, m.

striped, a. virgatus.

strive, v.i. (e)nitor, [3]; molior, [4]; conor, [1]; contendo, [3]; (after, for) annitor, [3]; sector, [1]; (against) obnitor, [3] (with dat.).

stroke, n. ictus, m.; plaga, f.; (of an oar) pulsus, m.; ~, v.t. (per)mulceo, [2].

stroll, v.i. (about) perambulo, obambulo, spatior, [1]; ~, n. ambulatio, f.

strong, a. robustus; fortis; firmus, valens; (powerful) potens, validus; fig. vehemens; gravis; ~ly, ad. robuste; valide; firme; fortiter; vehementer; graviter.

stronghold, n. arx, f.; castellum, nt.

structure, n. (construction) structura, f.; (building) aedificium, nt.

struggle, v.i. contendo, [3]; certo, luctor, [1]; (ob)nitor, [3]; (fight) pugno, [1]; ~, n. certamen, nt.; pugna; luctatio, f.; luctamen, nt.

strut, v.i. spatior, [1].

stubble, n. stipula, f.; culmus, m.

stubborn, a. obstinatus, pervicax, contumax; ~ly, ad. pervicaciter, obstinate, contumaciter.

stubbornness, *n.* pervicacia, contumacia, *f.*

stud, *n.* bulla, *f.*; clavus, *m.*

student, *n.* litterarum studiosus, *m.*

studious, *a.* diligens, industrius, navus.

study, *n.* studium; (room) umbraculum, *nt.*; bibliotheca, *f.*; ~, *v.t. & i.* studeo, [2] (*with dat.*), exploro; meditor, [1].

stuff, *n.* (material) materia, *f.*; (furniture, *etc.*) supellex, *f.*; (cloth) pannus, *m.*; (things) res, *f. pl.*; (woven ~) textile, *nt.*

stuff, *v.t.* farcio, [4]; sagino, [1]; (fill) expleo, repleo, [2].

stuffing, *n.* (in cookery) fartum; (for chairs, *etc.*) tomentum, *nt.*

stumble, *v.i.* offendo, [3]; (falter) haesito, [1]; (upon) incido, [3] (*with* in *with acc.*); ~, *n.* offensio, *f.*

stumbling-block, *n.* offensio, *f.*

stump, *n.* truncus, caudex, stipes, *m.*

stun, *v.t.* obstupefacio, obtundo, stupefacio, [3]; perturbo, [1]; sopio, [4].

stunt, *v.t.* incrementum (alicuius, *etc.*) impedio, [4].

stupefy, *v.t.* obstupefacio, [3]; terreo, [2]; perturbo; hebeto, [1]; sopio, [4].

stupid, *a.* stupidus, fatuus, stultus; ~**ly,** *ad.* stulte.

stupidity, *n.* stupiditas, fatuitas, stultitia, *f.*

stupor, *n.* stupor; torpor, *m.*

sturdiness, *n.* firmitas, *f.*; robur, *nt.*

sturdy, *a.* robustus, validus, firmus.

stutter, *v.i.* balbutio, [4].

sty, *n.* hara, *f.*

style, *n. fig.* sermo; modus, *m.*; genus, *nt.*

stylish, *a.* nitidus, lautus.

suave, *a.* blandus.

suavity, *n.* suavitas, dulcedo, *f.*; blanditia, *f.*

subdue, *v.t.* subicio, subigo, vinco, [3]; domo, [1].

subject, *a.* subiectus; (liable to) obnoxius (*with dat.*).

subject, *n.* (homo) subditus; civis, *m.*; (theme) materia, *f.*; argumentum, *nt.*

subject, *v.t.* subicio, subigo, [3].

subjection, *n.* servitus; patientia, *f.*

subjugate, *v.t.* subigo, [3]; domo, [1].

sublime, *a.* altus, celsus; *fig.* excelsus, sublimis.

submerge, *v.t. & i.* summergo, [3]; inundo, [1].

submersion, *n.* summersio, *f.*

submission, *n.* obsequium, *nt.*

submissive, *a.* submissus; supplex; ~**ly,** *ad.* summisse, suppliciter.

submit, *v.t.* summitto, subicio; ~, *v.i.* (condescend) descendo, [3]; (endure) subeo, [4]; (yield) cedo, [3].

subordinate, *v.t.* posthabeo, [2].

subordinate, *a.* & *n.* inferior, *m.*

subscribe, *v.t.* subscribo, [3]; subsigno, [1]; assentior, [4]; (give money) pecuniam do, [1].

subscriber, *n.* subscriptor, *m.*

subscription, *n.* (act) subscriptio, collecta, *f.*

subsequent, *a.* sequens, posterior; ~ly, *ad.* deinde, postea.

subservient, *a.* summissus.

subside, *v.i.* sido, consido, resido, subsido, [3].

subsidiary, *a.* subsidiarius.

subsidize, *v.t.* pecunias suppedito, [1].

subsidy, *n.* collatio, *f.*; subsidium, *nt.*

subsistence, *n.* victus, *m.*; vita, *f.*

substance, *n.* substantia; materia, res, *f.*; (wealth) opes, *f. pl.*

substantial, *a.* solidus, firmus; (real) verus; (chief) praecipuus; (rich) opulentus; ~ly, *ad.* solide; (truly) vere; (by nature) natura.

substantiate, *v.t.* confirmo, [1]; ratum facio, [3].

substitute, *n.* vicarius, *m.*

substitute, *v.t.* substituo, suppono, [3].

substitution, *n.* substitutio, *f.*

subterfuge, *n.* tergiversatio, *f.*; effugium, *nt.*; praetextus, *m.*

subtle, *a.* subtilis; acutus, vafer.

subtlety, *n.* subtilitas; tenuitas, astutia, *f.*; acumen, *nt.*

subtract, *v.t.* subtraho, adimo, aufero, [3].

suburb, *n.* suburbium, *nt.*

suburban, *a.* suburbanus.

subversion, *n.* excidium, *nt.*

subvert, *v.t.* everto, subverto, [3].

succeed, *v.i.* succedo, sequor, [3]; *fig.* succedo, [3]; prospere evenio, [4]; ~ to, (take over) excipio, [3].

success, *n.* bonus *or* felix exitus, successus, *m.*

successful, *a.* fortunatus, prosperus, faustus, felix; ~ly, *ad.* fortunate, prospere, fauste, feliciter.

succession, *n.* series, successio, *f.*

successive, *a.* continuus; ~ly, *ad.* in ordine; continenter; deinceps.

successor, *n.* successor, *m.*

succinct, *a.* succinctus; brevis, concisus; ~ly, *ad.* succincte, brevi.

succulent, *a.* sucosus, suculentus.

succumb, *v.i.* succumbo, cado, [3].

such, *a.* talis; eius modi; ~, *ad.* sic, adeo, tam; ~ as, qualis.

suck, *v.t.* sugo, [3]; (in, up) sorbeo, [2]; exsugo, [3]; ~, *v.i.* ubera duco, [3].

suckle, *v.t.* ubera do (alicui), do mammam, [1].

suction, *n.* suctus, *m.*

sudden, *a.* subitus, repentinus, inexpectatus; inopinatus, inopinus, necopinus; ~**ly**, *ad.* subito, repente.

sue, *v.t.* in ius voco, [1]; ~, *v.i.* oro, precor, flagito, [1]; posco, peto, [3].

suet, *n.* sebum, *nt.*; adeps, *c.*

suffer, *v.t.* patior, fero, [3]; tolero, [1]; sustineo, [2]; ~, *v.i.* laboro, [1].

suffering, *n.* perpessio, toleratio, *f.*; (labours) labores, *m. pl.*

suffice, *v.i.* sufficio, [3]; satis esse.

sufficiency, *n.* satias, *f.*

sufficient, *a.* sufficiens; ~**ly**, *ad.* satis, affatim.

suffocate, *v.t.* suffoco, [1].

suffocation, *n.* suffocatio, *f.*

suffrage, *n.* suffragium, *nt.*

sugar, *n.* saccharon, *nt.*

suggest, *v.t.* subicio, suggero, [3]; moneo, [2].

suggestion, *n.* admonitio, *f.*

suicide, *n.* mors voluntaria, *f.*; **commit** ~, mihi mortem conscisco, [3].

suit, *n.* (lawsuit) lis, causa, *f.*; (of clothes) vestimenta, *nt. pl.*, synthesis, *f.*

suit, *v.t.* accommodo, apto, [1]; ~, *v.i.* convenio, [4]; congruo, [3] (*both with dat.*).

suitable, *a.* aptus, idoneus, opportunus, congruus.

suite, *n.* (of rooms) series, *f.*

suitor, *n.* (suppliant) supplex, *c.*; (wooer) procus, *m.*

sulky, *ad.* morosus.

sullen, *a.* taetricus; morosus.

sullenness, *n.* morositas, *f.*

sulphur, *n.* sulpur, *nt.*

sultry, *a.* aestuosus, torridus, fervidus.

sum, *n.* (total) summa; (money) pecunia, *f.*; *fig.* caput, *nt.*

sum, *v.t.* (up) consummo, [1]; *fig.* breviter repeto, [3].

summary, *n.* epitome, *f.*; summarium, *nt.*; ~, *a.* brevis.

summer, *n.* aestas, *f.*; ~**-house**, *n.* umbraculum, *nt.*; ~, *a.* aestivus.

summit, *n.* culmen, cacumen, *nt.*; apex, vertex, *m.*; fastigium, *nt.*

summon, *v.t.* cito; (challenge) provoco, [1]; (send for) accio, [4]; accesso, [3]; (up) excito, [1]; (animum) erigo, [3].

summons, *n.* accitus, *m.*; evocatio, *f.*

sumptuous, *a.* sumptuosus; magnificus, lautus.

sun, *n.* sol, *m.*; ~, *v.t.* insolo, [1].

sunburnt, *a.* adustus.

sundial, *n.* solarium, *nt.*

sundry, *a.* diversus, varius.

sunny, *a.* apricus.

sunrise, *n.* solis ortus, *m.*

sunset, n. solis occasus, m.

sunshine, n. sol, m.; apricitas, f.

superb, a. magnificus, speciosus, splendidus.

supercilious, a. arrogans, superbus, fastidiosus; ~**ly,** ad. superbe, arroganter, fastidiose.

superficial, a. levis, indoctus; ~**ly,** ad. leviter.

superfluous, a. supervacaneus; superfluus; supervacuus.

superintend, v.t. praesum (alicui rei), ir.; administro, [1].

superintendent, n. praefectus; curator, m.

superior, a. superior, melior; ~ n. praepositus, m.

superiority, n. praestantia, f.

superlative, a. eximius.

supersede, v.t. aboleo, [2]; in locum (alicuius) succedo, [3].

superstition, n. superstitio, f.

superstitious, a. superstitiosus; ~**ly,** ad. superstitiose.

supervise, v.t. curo, procuro, [1].

supervision, n. cura, curatio, f.

supervisor, n. curator, m.

supper, n. cena, f.

supplant, v.t. supplanto, [1]; per dolum deicio, praeverto, [3].

supple, a. flexibilis, flexilis; mollis.

supplement, n. supplementum, nt.; appendix, f.

suppleness, n. mollitia, f.

suppliant, n. supplex, c.

supplicate, v.t. supplico, obsecro, [1].

supplication, n. obsecratio, f.; preces, f. pl.

supply, n. supplementum, nt.; copia, vis, f.; (supplies) commeatus, m.; ~, v.t. suppleo; praebeo, [2]; suppedito, [1].

support, n. (prop) fulcrum, nt.; fig. subsidium, nt.; (favour) gratia, f.; favor, m.; ~, v.t. sustineo, [2]; (prop) fulcio, [4]; (maintain) alo, [3]; (aid) adiuvo, [1]; (favour) faveo, [2] (with dat.).

supporter, n. adiutor; fautor, m.

suppose, v.t. (imagine) opinor, puto, [1]; credo, [3]; reor, [2]; arbitror, [1].

supposition, n. opinio, coniectura, f.

suppress, v.t. supprimo, comprimo, [3]; aboleo, coerceo, [2].

suppurate, v.i. suppuro, [1].

supremacy, n. principatus, m.; imperium, nt.

supreme, a. supremus, summus; ~**ly,** ad. prae omnibus aliis, summe.

sure, a. certus; (reliable) fidus; (safe) tutus; ~**ly,** ad. certe; tuto; firme; ne, profecto.

surf, n. fluctus, m.; unda, f.

surface, n. superficies, f.; aequor, nt.

surfeit, n. satietas, f.; taedium, fastidium, nt.

surge, n. fluctus, aestus, m.; ~, v.i. tumesco, [3]; aestuo, [1].

surgeon, *n.* chirurgus, *m.*

surgery, *n.* chirurgia, *f.*

surgical, *a.* chirurgicus.

surly, *a.* morosus, difficilis.

surmise, *n.* coniectura, *f.*; ~, *v.t.* coniecto, [1]; conicio, [3]; suspicor, [1].

surmount, *v.t.* supero, [1]; vinco, [3].

surname, *n.* cognomen, *nt.*

surpass, *v.t.* supero, [1]; excedo, excello, [3].

surplus, *n.* reliquum, residuum, *nt.*

surprise, *n.* admiratio, *f.*; (sudden attack) repens adventus hostium, *m.*; ~, *v.t.* deprehendo, [3].

surprising, *a.* mirus, mirabilis; inexpectatus; inopinatus; ~ly, *ad.* mirandum in modum.

surrender, *n.* (*mil.*) deditio; (law) cessio, *f.*; ~, *v.t.* cedo; dedo; trado, [3] ~, *v.i.* me dedo, [3].

surreptitious, *a.* furtivus, clandestinus; ~ly, clam, furtim.

surround, *v.t.* circumdo; circumsto, [1]; cingo, [3]; circumvallo, [1].

surplus, *n.* residuum, reliquum, *nt.*

survey, *n.* (act) inspectio; contemplatio; (measuring) mensura, *f.*; ~, *v.t.* inspicio, [3]; contemplor, [1]; (measure land) permetior, [4].

surveyor, *n.* mensor, metator, decempedator, *m.*

survive, *v.i.* superstes sum, supersum, *ir.*; supero, [1].

survivor, *n.* superstes, *c.*

susceptible, *a.* mollis; (capable) capax.

suspect, *v.t.* suspicor, [1].

suspend, *v.t.* suspendo, [3]; *fig.* intermitto; differo, [3]; abrogo, [1].

suspense, *n.* dubitatio, *f.*; **in ~,** incertus, dubius.

suspicion, *n.* suspicio, *f.*

suspicious, *a.* suspicax; suspiciosus; (suspected) suspectus; suspiciosus.

sustain, *v.t.* (prop) sustineo, [2]; sustento, [1]; fulcio, [4]; (bear, *etc.*) tolero, [1]; fero, [3]; (defend) defendo, [3]; (strengthen) corroboro, [1].

sustenance, *n.* victus, *m.*

swallow, *n.* hirundo, *f.*

swallow, *v.t.* glutio, [4]; voro; devoro, [1]; haurio, [4].

swamp, *n.* palus, *f.*; ~, *v.t.* demergo, [3]; inundo, [1].

swampy, *a.* paludosus, palustris, uliginosus.

swan, *n.* cycnus, *m.*; olor, *m.*

swarm, *n.* (of bees) examen, *nt.*; *fig.* turba, *f.*; ~, *v.i.* examino, [1]; confluo, [3].

swarthy, *a.* fuscus, subniger.

sway, *n.* dicio, *f.*; imperium, *nt.*; (motion) aestus, *m.*; ~, *v.t.* rego, [3]; ~, *v.i.* aestuo, titubo, [1].

swear, *v.i.* iuro; (curse) exsecror, [1].

sweat, *n.* sudor, *m.*; ~, *v.i.* sudo, [1].

sweep, *n.* ambitus; iactus, *m.*

sweep, *v.t.* (brush, *etc.*) verro, [3]; purgo, [1]; (pass quickly over) percurro; verro, [3].

sweet, *a.* dulcis, suavis; blandus; iucundus.

sweeten, *v.t.* dulcem facio *or* reddo, [3]; *fig.* lenio, [4]; mulceo, [2].

sweetheart, *n.* deliciae, *f. pl.*; amica, *f.*

sweetness, *n.* dulcedo; suavitas, *f.*

swell, *v.t.* inflo, [1]; tumefacio, [3]; ~, *v.i.* tumeo, turgeo, [2]; intumesco, [3]; ~, *n.* aestus, *m.*

swelling, *n.* tumor, *m.*

swerve, *v.i.* aberro, vagor; declino, [1].

swift, *a.* celer, velox, rapidus, citus; ~**ly**, *ad.* celeriter, velociter, cito.

swiftness, *n.* celeritas, velocitas, *f.*

swill, *v.t.* haurio, [4]; ingurgito, [1].

swim, *v.i.* nato, no; fluito, [1]; madeo, [2].

swimmer, *n.* natator, *m.*

swimming, *n.* natatio, *f.*

swindle, *v.t.* fraudo, [1]; circumvenio, [4].

swindler, *n.* fraudator, *m.*

swing, *n.* oscillatio, *f.*; impetus, *m.*; ~, *v.t.* huc illuc iacto, vibro,

[1]; ~, *v.i.* fluito, [1]; pendeo, [2]; huc illuc iactor, [1].

swivel, *n.* verticula, *f.*

swoop, *n.* impulsus, impetus, *m.*

sword, *n.* ensis, gladius, *m.*; ferrum, *nt.*

sycamore, *n.* sycamorus, *f.*

sycophant, *n.* sycophanta, adulator, *m.*

syllable, *n.* syllaba, *f.*

symbol, *n.* signum, symbolum, *nt.*

symmetrical, *a.* symmetrus, concinnus.

symmetry, *n.* symmetria, concinnitas, *f.*

sympathetic, *a.* (gentle) lenis, mitis, humanus; ~**ally**, *ad.* humane.

sympathize, *v.i.* (pity) misereor, [2] (*with gen.*).

sympathy, *n.* (agreement) consensus, *m.*; (fellow-feeling) sympathia, *f.*

symphony, *n.* symphonia, *f.*; concentus, *m.*

symptom, *n.* signum, indicium, *nt.*

synagogue, *n.* synagoga, *f.*

synonym, *n.* vocabulum idem declarans, synonymum, *nt.*

synonymous, *a.* idem declarans.

syntax, *n.* syntaxis, *f.*; constructio verborum, *f.*

synthesis, *n.* synthesis, *f.*

syringe, *n.* sipho, *m.*

system, *n.* systema, *nt.*; ratio, disciplina, *f.*

systematic, *a.* ad certam disciplinam redactus, ordinatus.

systematically, *ad.* ordinate.

....

T

....

table, *n.* mensa, *f.*; (register) index, *m.*

tablecloth, *n.* mantele, *nt.*

tablet, *n.* tabula, tabella, tessera, *f.*

tacit, *a.* tacitus; ~**ly,** *ad.* tacite.

taciturn, *a.* taciturnus.

taciturnity, *n.* taciturnitas, *f.*

tactful, *a.* dexter.

tack, *n.* clavulus, *m.*; ~, *v.t.* assuo; affigo, [3].

tackle, *v.t.* tracto, [1].

tackle, *n.* armamenta, arma, *nt. pl.*

tact, *n.* dexteritas; prudentia, *f.*

tactless, *a.* ineptus, insulsus, molestus.

tactics, *n.* ars militaris, ratio, *f.*

tadpole, *n.* ranunculus, *m.*; ranula, *f.*

tag, *n.* ligula, *f.*

tail, *n.* cauda, *f.*; (of a comet) crinis, *m.*

tailor, *n.* vestitor, *m.*

taint, *v.t.* inficio, [3]; contamino, [1]; polluo; *fig.* corrumpo, [3]; ~, *n.* contagio, *f.*; vitium, *nt.*; contactus, *m.*

take, *v.t.* capio; sumo; accipio, recipio; rapio, [3]; (consider, *etc.*) interpretor, [1]; accipio, [3]; ~, *v.i.* (be successful) efficax esse, *ir.*; bene succedere; (fire) accendor, [3]; ~ **after,** similem esse (*with dat.*); ~ **away,** adimo, aufero, [3]; ~ **back,** recipio, [3]; ~ **down,** demo, [3]; ~ **for,** habeo, [2]; puto, [1]; ~ **in,** percipio, intellego, [3]; *fig.* decipio, [3]; ~ **off,** exuo, demo, [3]; *fig.* imitor, [1]; ~ **up,** sumo, [3].

tale, *n.* narratio; fabula, *f.*; ~-**bearer,** famigerator, *m.*; delator, *m.*

talent, *n. fig.* ingenium, *nt.*; facultas, *f.*

talented, *a.* ingeniosus.

talk, *n.* sermo, *m.*; colloquium, *nt.*; (idle ~) fabulae, *f. pl.*; (rumour) rumor, *m.*; fama, *f.*

talk, *v.i.* loquor, colloquor, [3]; confabulor, [1].

talkative, *a.* loquax, garrulus.

tall, *a.* altus, celsus, procerus.

tallness, *n.* proceritas; altitudo, *f.*

tally, *n.* tessera, *f.*; ~, *v.i.* convenio, [4].

talon, *n.* unguis, *m.*; ungula, *f.*

tambourine, *n.* tympanum, *nt.*

tame, *a.* cicur; mansuefactus, mansuetus; *fig.* frigidus, insulsus.

tame, *v.t.* perdomo, domo, [1]; mansuefacio, subigo, [3].

tangible, *a.* tractilis.

tangle, v. **entangle**; ~**d**, *a.* irreligatus, incomptus.

tank, *n.* cisterna; piscina, *f.*; lacus, *m.*

tankard, *n.* cantharus, *m.*

tantalize, *v.t.* crucio, [1].

tantamount, *a.* tantusdem, par.

tap, *n.* (blow) ictus, *m.*; (pipe) fistula, *f.*; ~, *v.t.* leviter pulso, [1]; (wine, *etc.*) relino, [3].

tape, *n.* taenia, *f.*

taper, *n.* cereus, *m.*; funale, *nt.*

taper, *v.t. & i.* fastigo; fastigor, [1].

tapestry, *n.* aulaeum, tapete, *nt.*

tapeworm, *n.* taenia, *f.*

tar, *n.* pix, *f.*; ~, *v.t.* pice oblino, [3].

tardy, *a.* tardus, lentus.

target, *n.* parma, *f.*; (mark to aim at) scopus, *m.*

tarnish, *v.t.* infusco; hebeto; *fig.* obscuro, [1]; ~, *v.i.* hebesco, [3].

tart, *n.* scriblita, *f.*; crustulum, *nt.*; (girl) scortillum, *nt.*

tart, *a.* acidus; acerbus; *fig.* mordax; ~**ly**, *ad.* acerbe; mordaciter.

task, *n.* pensum, opus, *nt.*; labor, *m.*

tassel, *n.* cirrus, *m.*

taste, *n.* (sense) gustátus; (flavour) gustus, sapor, *m.*; *fig.* iudicium; palatum, *nt.*; ~, *v.t.* (de)gusto, [1]; ~, *v.i.* sapio, [3].

tasteful, *a.* elegans; ~**ly**, *ad.* fig. eleganter.

tasteless, *a.* insulsus; inelegans; ~**ly**, *ad.* ineleganter, insulse.

tasty, *a.* sapidus, conditus.

tatters, *n.* panni, *m. pl.*

taunt, *n.* convicium, *nt.*; convitumelia, *f.*; ~, *v.t.* exprobro, [1].

tavern, *n.* taberna, caupona, *f.*

tawdry, *a.* speciosus.

tawny, *a.* fuscus, fulvus, ravus, flavus.

tax, *n.* vectigal; tributum, stipendium, *nt.*; ~, *v.t.* vectigal impono, [3].

taxable, *a.* vectigali solvendo obnoxius.

tax-collector, *n.* exactor, *m.*

teach, *v.t.* doceo, perdoceo, [2]; instruo, [3]; erudio, [4].

teacher, *n.* magister, praeceptor, *m.*

teaching, *n.* doctrina, eruditio, *f.*

team, *n.* protelum, *nt.*; iugales, *m. pl.*

tear, *n.* lacrima; *fig.* gutta, *f.*; (rent) scissura, *f.*

tear, *v.t.* scindo, [3]; (in pieces) (di)lacero, (di)lanio, [1]; *v.i.*, ~ **rush**.

tear, *n.* scissura, *f.*

tease, *v.t.* vexo, crucio, [1].

echnical, *a.* artificialis; (word) arti proprium (verbum).

edious, *a.* tardus, lentus; longus; diuturnus, molestus; ~**ly,** *ad.* tarde; moleste.

edium, *n.* taedium, *nt.*; molestia, *f.*

eem, *v.i.* scateo, [2]; redundo, [1]; abundo.

eeming, *a.* gravidus; *fig.* frequens.

ell, *v.t.* (say) dico, [3]; (relate) narro, [1]; (inform) aliquem certiorem facio, [3].

emper, *v.t.* tempero, [1]; diluo, [3]; commiseo, [2]; (mitigate) mitigo, [1]; remitto, [3]; ~, *n.* temperatio, *f.*; animus, *m.*; ingenium, *nt.*; (anger) iracundia, *f.*

emperament, *n.* temperamentum, *nt.*

emperate, *a.* temperatus; sobrius; abstinens; ~**ly,** *ad.* temperanter, sobrie.

emperature, *n.* temperatura, temperies, *f.*

emple, *n.* templum, fanum, *nt.*; aedes, *f.*; (of the head) tempora, *nt. pl.*

emporary, *a.* temporarius, ad tempus.

empt, *v.t.* tento, sollicito, [1]; allicio, [3].

emptation, *n.* sollicitatio; illecebra, *f.*

empter, *n.* tentator, *m.*

empting, *a.* illecebrosus.

en, *a.* decem; ~ **times,** decies.

tenacious, *a.* tenax; ~**ly,** *ad.* tenaciter.

tenacity, *n.* tenacitas, *f.*

tenant, *n.* conductor; inquilinus, *m.*

tend, *v.t.* curo, [1]; ~, *v.i.* tendo, [3]; specto, [1].

tendency, *n.* inclinatio, *f.*; **having a ~ to,** proclivis ad (*with acc.*).

tender, *a.* tener, mollis; *fig.* misericors; ~**ly,** *ad.* tenere; molliter; misericorditer.

tender, *v.t.* offero, [3].

tenderness, *n.* teneritas, mollitia; misericordia, bonitas, *f.*

tendon, *n.* nervus, *m.*

tendril, *n.* (of a vine) pampinus, *c.*; (of climbing plants) clavicula, *f.*

tenement, *n.* insula, *f.*

tenet, *n.* dogma, institutum, *nt.*; doctrina, *f.*

tense, *a.* tensus, rigidus.

tension, *n.* intentio, *f.*

tent, *n.* tentorium, tabernaculum, *nt.*; **general's ~,** praetorium, *nt.*

tenterhook, *n.* **on ~s,** *a.* suspensus.

tenth, *a.* decimus; ~, *n.* decima pars, *f.*

tenure, *n.* possessio, *f.*

tepid, *a.* tepidus.

term, *n.* (word) verbum, *nt.*; (limit) terminus, *m.*; (period) spatium, *nt.*; (condition) condicio, lex, *f.*

term, *v.t.* dico, [3]; appello, voco, [1].

terminate, *v.t.* termino, [1]; finio, [4]; concludo, [3]; ~, *v.i.* terminor, [1]; finem habeo, [2].

termination, *n.* terminatio, *f.*; finis, *c.*; exitus, *m.*

terrace, *n.* solarium, *nt.*

terrible, *a.* terribilis, horribilis, dirus; **terribly,** *ad.* horrendum in modum.

terrific, *a.* terrificus, terribilis, formidabilis.

terrify, *v.t.* terreo, perterreo, [2]; territo, [1].

territory, *n.* regio; terra, *f.*; fines, *m. pl.*; (around a town) territorium, *nt.*

terror, *n.* terror, metus, pavor, *m.*; formido, *f.*

terse, *a.* (neat, polished) tersus; brevis; pressus.

test, *n.* (trial) tentamentum, tentamen, periculum, *nt.*; ~, *v.t.* tento, exploro, [1]; experior, [4]; periclitor, [1].

testify, *v.t.* testificor, testor, [1].

testimonial, *n.* litterae testimoniales, *f. pl.*

testimony, *n.* testimonium, indicium, *nt.*

testy, *a.* stomachosus, morosus.

tetanus, *n.* tetanus, *m.*

tether, *n.* retinaculum, *nt.*; ~, *v.t.* religo, [1].

text, *n.* verba scriptoris, *nt. pl.*; contextus, *m.*

textile, *a.* textilis.

texture, *n.* textum, *nt.*; textura, *f.*

than, *c.* quam.

thank, *v.t.* gratias ago, [3] (*with dat.*); ~ **you,** tibi gratias ago.

thankful, *a.* gratus.

thankless, *a.* ingratus.

thanks, *n.* gratia, *f.*; grates, *f. pl.*

that, *a. & pn.* ille, is, iste; (who, which) qui; ~, *c.* ut.

thatch, *n.* stramentum, *nt.*; ~, *v.t.* stramento tego, [3].

thaw, *v.t.* (dis)solvo, liquefacio, [3]; ~, *v.i.* regelo, [1]; solvor, liquesco, [3].

theatre, *n.* theatrum, *nt.*; scaena, cavea, *f.*

theatrical, *a.* theatralis; scaenicus.

theft, *n.* furtum, *nt.*

their, theirs, *a.* suus, eorum, illorum, earum, illarum.

theme, *n.* argumentum, *nt.*; materies, *f.*

themselves, *pn. pl.* se, sese; they ~, illi ipsi, illae ipsae; **of** ~, sui.

then, *ad.* (at that time) tum, tunc (after that) deinde, inde; (therefore) igitur; **now and** ~, non nunquam, interdum, aliquando.

theologian, *n.* theologus, *m.*

theology, *n.* theologia, *f.*

theorem, *n.* theorema, *nt.*

theoretic(al), *a.* theoreticus.

theory, *n.* theoria, ratio, ars, *f.*

here, *ad.* ibi, illic; (thither) illo, illac, illuc; ~**abouts**, circiter; ~**after**, exinde; ~**by**, inde; ~**fore**, igitur, idcirco; propterea; ~**upon**, exinde; deinde; tum.

thesis, *n.* thesis, *f.*; propositum, *nt.*

they, *pn. pl.* ii, eae, illi, illae.

thick, *a.* densus, spissus; (gross) crassus; (fat) pinguis; (muddy) turbidus, lutosus; (crowded) frequens; creber.

thicken, *v.t.* denso; condenso; spisso, [1]; ~, *v.i.* densor, [1]; spissor, [3].

thicket, *n.* dumetum, *nt.*; virgulta, *nt. pl.*

thickness, *n.* densitas; crassitudo, *f.*

thief, *n.* fur, *m.*

thieve, *v.t.* furor, [1].

thigh, *n.* femur, *nt.*

thin, *a.* tenuis; angustus; rarus; (lean) macer.

thin, *v.t.* (at)tenuo, extenuo, [1].

thing, *n.* res, *f.*; (affair) negotium, *nt.*; ~**s**, *pl.* bona, *nt. pl.*

think, *v.t. & i.* cogito, [1]; (imagine, believe, *etc.*) puto, [1]; credo, [3]; opinor, [1]; reor, [2]; arbitror, [1].

thinker, *n.* philosophus, *m.*

thinness, *n.* tenuitas; raritas, *f.*

third, *a.* tertius; ~**ly**, *ad.* tertio; ~, *n.* tertia pars, *f.*

thirst, *n.* sitis, *f.* (also *fig.*).

thirsty, *a.* sitiens; aridus, siccus; bibulus; **be** ~, sitio, [4].

thirteen, *a.* tredecim.

thirteenth, *a.* tertius decimus.

thirtieth, *a.* tricesimus.

thirty, *a.* triginta.

this, *a. & pn.* hic, haec, hoc.

thistle, *n.* carduus, *m.*

thong, *n.* lorum, amentum, *nt.*

thorn, *n.* spina, *f.*; aculeus, *m.*

thorny, *a.* spinosus; spineus; *fig.* difficilis.

thorough, *a.* germanus, perfectus; accuratus; ~**ly**, *ad.* penitus, plane, prorsus, funditus.

thoroughfare, *n.* pervium, *nt.*; via pervia, *f.*

though, *c.* etsi, etiamsi, quamvis, quamquam, licet.

thought, *n.* (thinking, idea & opinion) cogitatio, sententia, mens, *f.*

thoughtful, *a.* cogitabundus; providus; humanus.

thoughtless, *a.* incuriosus, neglegens, inconsultus; ~**ly**, *ad.* temere.

thousand, *a.* mille; **a** ~ **times**, millies.

thousandth, *a.* millesimus.

thrash, *v.t.* tero, tundo, [3]; *fig.* verbero, [1].

thread, *n.* filum, *nt.*; linea, *f.*; *fig.* tenor, *m.*

threadbare, *a.* tritus, detritus.

threat, *n.* minae, *f. pl.*

threaten, *v.t.* minor, [1]; ~, *v.i.* impendeo, immineo, [2] *(all with dat.).*

three, *a.* tres; ~ **times,** ter.

threefold, *a.* triplex, triplus.

thresh, *v.t.* tero, tundo, [3]; ~**ing-floor,** area, *f.*

threshold, *n.* limen, *nt.*

thrift, *n.* frugalitas, parsimonia, *f.*

thrifty, *a.* parcus, frugalior.

thrill, *v.t.* percello; ~, *v.i.* percellor, [3].

thrill, *n.* (excitement) animi concitatio, *f.*

thrilling, *a.* periculosus.

thrive, *v.i.* vireo, floreo; valeo, [2].

thriving, *a.* prosperus.

throat, *n.* iugulum, guttur, *nt.*; gula, *f.*

throb, *v.i.* palpito, [1]; ~, *nt.* palpitatio, *f.* pulsus, *m.*

throne, *n.* solium, *nt.*; *fig.* regia dignitas, *f.*; (kingdom) regnum, *nt.*

throng, *n.* multitudo, turba, frequentia, *f.*; ~, *v.t. & i.* premo; circumfundor; confluo, [3].

throttle, *v.t.* strangulo, [1].

through, *pr.* per, propter, ob *(all with acc.)*

throughout, *ad.* penitus, prorsus.

throw, *v.t.* iacio, conicio; mitto, [3]; iaculor, iacto, [1]; (away) abicio; (down) deicio, sterno, everto, [3]; (oneself) me prae-

cipito, [1]; (open) patefacio; (off) excutio; deicio; (clothes) exuo (out) eicio; (together) conicio (up) egero, [3].

throw, *n.* iactus, *m.*; iaculatio, *f.*

thrush, *n.* turdus, *m.*

thrust, *v.t.* trudo, impello; (with sword) perfodio, [3]; ~ **out,** ex trudo, [3]; ~, *n.* ictus; impetus *m.*; petitio, *f.*

thumb, *n.* pollex, *m.*; ~, *v.t.* (book) pollice verso, [1].

thump, *v.t.* contundo, [3]; ~, *n* ictus, *m.* percussio, *f.*

thunder, *n.* tonitrus; fragor, *m* ~, *v.t. & i.* tono, intono, [1].

thunderbolt, *n.* fulmen, *nt.*

thunderstruck, *a.* attonitus; ob stupefactus.

thus, *ad.* ita, sic; **and** ~, itaque.

thwart, *v.t.* obsto *(with dat.)*; fru stror, [1].

thyme, *n.* thymum, *nt.*

tiara, *n.* tiara, *f.*; tiaras, *m.*

ticket, *n.* tessera, *f.*; titulus, *m.*

tickle, *v.t. & i.* titillo, [1].

ticklish, *a. fig.* difficilis, periculo sus, lubricus.

tide, *n.* aestus, *fig.* cursus, *m.*

tidings, *n.* rumor, *m.*; (message nuntius, *m.*; (news) novum, *nt*

tidy, *a.* mundus.

tie, *v.t.* (al)ligo; nodo, [1]; vinci [4]; ~, *n.* vinculum, *nt.*; nodu *m.*; coniunctio, necessitas, *f.*

tier, *n.* ordo, gradus, *m.*

tiger, *n.* tigris, *c.*

tight, *a.* artus, astrictus; **~ly,** *ad.* arte, stricte.

tighten, *v.t.* stringo, astringo, [3].

tightness, *n.* soliditas, firmitas, *f.*

tile, *n.* tegula, imbrex, *f.*; **~,** *v.t.* tegulis tego, [3].

till, *ad.* (*pr.*) usque ad (*with acc.*); **~,** *c.* dum, donec.

tiller, *n.* (helm) gubernaculum, *nt.*; clavus, *m.*

tilt, *n.* (inclination) inclinatio, *f.*; (rush) impetus, *m.*; **~,** *v.t.* proclino, [1].

timber, *n.* materia, *f.*; lignum, *nt.*; tignum, *nt.*; trabs, *f.*

time, *n.* tempus, *nt.*; dies, *m.*; (age, *etc.*) aetas, *f.*; aevum, *nt.*; (century) saeculum, *nt.*; (leisure) otium, *nt.*; (opportunity) occasio, *f.*; (hour) hora, *f.*; **at this ~,** in praesenti; **at any ~,** unquam; **if at any ~,** siquando; **at a ~,** una; **all the ~,** continuo.

timely, *a.* tempestivus, opportunus.

timid, *a.* timidus, anxius.

timidity, *n.* timiditas, *f.*

tin, *n.* stannum, plumbum album, *nt.*

tinge, *v.t.* tingo, imbuo, inficio, [3].

tinkle, *n.* tinnitus, *m.*

tinkle, *v.i.* tinnio, [4]; crepito, [1].

tint, *v.t.* tingo, [3]; **~,** *n.* color, *m.*

tiny, *a.* parvulus, exiguus.

tip, *n.* (top) cacumen; acumen, *nt.*; apex, *m.*; **~,** *v.t.* (attach to end of) praefigo; (incline) inverto, [3].

tipsy, *a.* ebrius, temulentus, vinosus.

tiptoe, on ~, in digitos erectus.

tire, *v.t.* fatigo, lasso; **~,** *v.i.* defatigor, [1].

tired, *a.* fessus, defessus, lassus.

tiresome, *a.* laboriosus; molestus; operosus.

tissue, *n.* textum, *nt.*

titbit, *n.* cuppedia, *nt. pl.*

title, *n.* titulus, *m.*; inscriptio, *f.*; (label) index, *c.*; (name, *etc.*) appellatio, dignitas, *f.*

titter, *v.i.* subrideo, [2].

to, *pr.* ad (*with acc.*); (in comparison with) prae (*with abl.*); **~ and fro,** huc illuc; (until) usque ad (*with acc.*); (in order to) ut.

toad, *n.* bufo, *m.*

toadstool, *n.* fungus, *m.*

toast, *n.* (health drunk) propinatio, *f.*

toast, *v.t.* torreo, [2]; (in drinking) propino, [1].

today, *ad.* hodie.

toe, *n.* digitus, *m.*

together, *ad.* simul, una; coniunctim.

toil, *n.* labor, *m.*; opera, *f.*; sudor, *m.*; **~,** *v.i.* laboro, [1].

toilet, *n.* cultus, ornatus, *m.*; (lavatory) latrina, *f.*

token, *n*. signum, pignus, *nt*.

tolerable, *a*. tolerabilis; mediocris.

tolerance, *n*. tolerantia, toleratio, indulgentia, *f*.

tolerant, *a*. tolerans, patiens, indulgens.

tolerate, *v.t*. tolero, [1]; patior, fero, [3].

toleration, *n*. toleratio; indulgentia, *f*.

toll, *n*. vectigal, tributum, *nt*.

tomb, *n*. sepulcrum, bustum, *nt*.; tumulus, *m*.

tomorrow, *n*. crastinus dies, *m*.; ~, *ad*. cras; **the day after** ~, perendie.

tone, *n*. sonus, *m*.; *fig*. color, *m*.; vox, *f*.

tongs, *n*. forceps, *f*.

tongue, *n*. lingua, *f*.

tonight, hac nocte.

too, *ad*. nimis, nimium; (also) etiam, insuper.

tool, *n*. instrumentum; (of iron) ferramentum, *nt*.; *fig*. minister, *m*.

tooth, *n*. dens, *m*. (also *fig*.).

toothache, *n*. dolor dentium, *m*.

toothless, *a*. edentulus.

top, *n*. cacumen, culmen, *nt*.; apex, *m*.; (of a house) fastigium, *nt*.; (toy) trochus, turbo, *m*.; ~, *a*. summus (summus mons = the top of the mountain).

topic, *n*. res, *f*.; argumentum, *nt*.; quaestio, *f*.

topical, *a*. hodiernus.

topmost, *a*. summus.

topsy-turvy, *ad*. sursum deorsum.

torch, *n*. fax, taeda, *f*.; funale, *nt*.

torment, *v.t*. (ex)crucio, [1]; torqueo, [2]; ~, *n*. cruciatus, *m*.; tormentum, *nt*.

torrent, *n*. torrens, *m*. (also *fig*.).

tortoise, *n*. testudo, *f*.; ~-**shell**, *n*. testudo, *f*.

torture, *n*. tormentum, *nt*.; cruciatus, *m*.; ~, *v.t*. torqueo, [2]; (also *fig*.).

torturer, *n*. tortor, *m*.

toss, *v.t*. iacto; agito, verso, [1]; ~, *v.i*. iactor, [1]; aestuo, [1]; ~, *n*. iactus, *m*.; iactatio, *f*.

total, *a*. totus, universus; ~**ly**, *ad*. omnino, prorsus.

total, *n*. summa, *f*.

totter, *v.i*. vacillo, titubo, labo, [1].

touch, *v.t*. tango, attingo, [3]; moveo, [2]; afficio, [3]; ~, *n*. tactus, contactus, *m*.; *fig*. commotio, *f*.; **finishing** ~, *fig*. manus extrema, *f*.

touchy, *a*. offensioni pronior, stomachosus.

tough, *a*. tenax, lentus; durus; *fig*. difficilis; (stout) strenuus.

toughness, *n*. tenacitas, *f*.; lentor, *m*.; duritia; *fig*. difficultas; (courage) fortitudo, *f*.

tour, *n*. circuitus, *m*.; peregrinatio, *f*.; iter, *nt*.

tourist, *n.* viator, peregrinator, *m.*

tournament, *n.* decursio equestris, *f.*; ludus equester, *m.*

tow, *v.t.* (a ship) navem remulco trahere, [3]; **~-rope,** *n.* remulcum, *nt.*

toward(s), *pr.* adversus, ad, (of people) erga; contra, in; (of time) sub. (*all with acc.*).

towel, *n.* mantele, sudarium, *nt.*

tower, *n.* turris, arx, *f.*; castellum, *nt.*; ~, *v.i.* emineo, superemineo, [2].

town, *n.* urbs, *f.*; oppidum, municipium, *nt.* ~ **hall,** curia, *f.*

toy, *n.* crepundia, *nt. pl.*

trace, *n.* vestigium; indicium; signum; *nt.*; (for horse) helcium, *nt.*; ~, *v.t.* delineo; (down) indago, [1].

track, *n.* vestigium, *nt.*; (path) semita, *f.*; ~, *v.t.* vestigo, investigo, [1].

tract, *n.* tractus, *m.*; regio, *f.*; (small treatise) tractatus, *m.*

trade, *n.* mercatura, *f.*; commercium, negotium, *nt.*; (calling) ars, *f.*; quaestus, *m.*; ~, *v.i.* mercaturas facio, [3]; negotior, [1].

trader, *n.* mercator, *m.*

tradesman, *n.* negotiator; caupo, *m.*

tradition, *n.* fama, *f.*

traditional, *a.* ab maioribus traditus; translaticius.

traffic, *n.* (trade) commercium, *nt.*; mercatura, *f.*; ~, *v.i.* negotior, mercor, [1].

tragedy, *n.* tragoedia, *f.*; cothurnus, *m.*

tragic, *a.* tragicus; **~ally,** *ad.* tragice.

trail, *v.i.* traho, verro, [3]; ~, *n.* vestigium, *nt.*; ductus, *m.*

train, *n.* series, *f.*; ordo, *m.*; (of a robe) peniculamentum, *nt.*; (retinue) comitatus, *m.*

train, *v.t.* educo, [1]; instruo; *fig.* assuefacio, [3].

trainer, *n.* exercitor, *m.*

training, *n.* disciplina; exercitatio, *f.*

traitor, *n.* proditor, *m.*

traitorous, *a.* perfidus; perfidiosus; **~ly,** *ad.* perfide, perfidiose.

tramp, *n.* homo vagus, *m.*

trample, *v.i.* (on, upon) conculco, [1]; opprimo, obtero, [3].

trance, *n.* animus a corpore abstractus, *m.*

tranquil, *a.* tranquillus, placidus, aequus.

tranquillity, *n.* tranquillitas, quies, *f.*; tranquillus animus, *m.*

transact, *v.t.* transigo, gero, ago, perficio, fungor, [3].

transaction, *n.* negotium, *nt.*; res, *f.*

transcribe, *v.t.* transcribo, exscribo, [3].

transcription, *n.* transcriptio, *f.*

transfer, *v.t.* transfero; transmitto, [3]; ~, *n.* translatio, *f.*

transform, *v.t.* transformo, transfiguro, [1]; verto, [3].

transformation, *n.* mutatio, *f.*

transgress, *v.t.* violo, [1]; contra leges facio, [3].

transient, *a.* (fleeting) fragilis, fluxus, caducus.

transition, *n.* transitus, *m.*

transitory, *a.*, v. **transient.**

translate, *v.t.* verto, transfero, [3].

translation, *n.* translatio, *f.*; liber translatus, *m.*

translator, *n.* interpres, *c.*

transmission, *n.* transmissio, *f.*

transmit, *v.t.* transmitto, [3].

transparency, *n.* perspicuitas, *f.*

transparent, *a.* pellucidus, perspicuus, translucidus; **be ~,** pelluceo, transluceo, [2].

transpire, *v.i.* evenio, [4]; fio, *ir.*

transplant, *v.t.* transfero, [3].

transport, *v.t.* transporto, [1]; transveho, transmitto, [3]; *fig.* delecto, [1].

transport, *n.* transvectio, *f.*; (ship) navigium vectorium, *nt.*; *fig.* elatio, *f.*

transpose, *v.t.* transpono, [3].

transposition, *n.* traiectio, *f.*

transverse, *a.* transversus.

trap, *n.* laqueus, *m.*; tendicula, pedica, *f.*; *fig.* insidiae, *f. pl.*

trap, *v.t.* irretio, [4].

trash, *n.* scruta, *nt. pl.*; nugae, res vilissimae, *f. pl.*

travel, *v.i.* iter facio, [3]; peregrinor, [1].

travel, *n.* iter, *nt.*; (abroad) peregrinatio, *f.*

traveller, *n.* viator, peregrinator, *m.*

tray, *n.* repositorium, *nt.*

treacherous, *a.* perfidus; perfidiosus; dolosus; **~ly,** *ad.* perfide, perfidiose.

treachery, *n.* perfidia, *f.*

tread, *v.t.* calco, conculco, [1]; **~,** *v.i.* incedo, [3]; **~,** *n.* gradus, incessus, *m.*

treason, *n.* perduellio, proditio, *f.*

treasure, *n.* thesaurus, *m.*; gaza, *f.*; opes, *f. pl.*; **~,** *v.t.* (value) magni aestimo, [1].

treasurer, *n.* aerarii praefectus, *m.*

treasury, *n.* fiscus, *m.*; aerarium; (building) thesaurus, *m.*

treat, *v.t.* (handle) tracto, [1]; (use) utor, [3] (*with abl.*); (entertain) convivio (aliquem) accipio, [3].

treatise, *n.* libellus, *m.*

treatment, *n.* tractatio; cura, curatio, *f.*

treaty, *n.* foedus; pactum, *nt.*

treble, *a.* triplex, triplus; **~,** *v.t.* triplico, [1].

tree, *n.* arbor, *f.*

tremble, *v.i.* tremo, contremisco, [3]; trepido, [1].

trembling, *n.* trepidatio, *f.*; tremor, *m.*

tremendous, *a.* formidolosus, ingens, immanis.

trench, n. fossa, f.; vallum, nt.; agger, m.

trespass, v.i. ~ **on,** ingredior, [3].

trial, n. tentatio, f.; (law) iudicium, nt.; (attempt) conatus, m.; periculum, nt.

triangle, n. triangulum, nt.

triangular, a. triangulus, triquetrus.

tribe, n. tribus, natio, f.

tribunal, n. tribunal; (court) iudicium, nt.

tribune, n. tribunus, m.

tributary, n. amnis in alium influens, m.

tribute, n. tributum; vectigal, nt.; fig. **pay ~ to,** laudo, [1].

trice, n. **in a ~,** momento temporis, f.

trick, n. dolus, m.; artificium, nt.; fraus, f.; ~, v.t. dolis illudo, [3]; circumvenio, [4].

trickery, n. fraus, f.; dolus, m.; ars, f.

trickle, v.i. stillo, mano, [1].

trident, n. tridens, m.

trifle, n. res parvi momenti, f.; nugae, f. pl.

trifling, a. levis, exiguus, parvi momenti, frivolus.

trim, a. nitidus, comptus, bellus; ~, v.t. (prune) puto, [1]; tondeo, [2].

trinket, n. gemma, f.

trip, n. (stumble) pedis offensio, f.; (journey) iter, nt.; ~, v.t. sup-planto, [1]; ~, v.i. pedem offendo, [3]; fig. erro, [1].

triple, a. triplex, triplus; ~, v.t. triplico, [1].

tripod, n. tripus, m.; cortina, f.

trireme, n. (navis) triremis, f.

trite, a. tritus; pervulgatus.

triumph, n. triumphus, m.; ovatio; fig. victoria; exsultatio, f.; ~, v.i. triumpho, ovo, [1].

triumphant, a. triumphans, victor.

triumvirate, n. triumviratus, m.

trivial, a. levis.

triviality, n. levitas, f.; nugae, ineptiae, f. pl.

troop, n. turma, caterva, f.; grex; globus, m.; manus, f.; ~s, pl. copiae, f. pl.

trophy, n. tropaeum, nt.

tropical, a. tropicus.

trot, n. gradus, m.; ~, v.i. tolutim eo, [4].

trouble, n. (nuisance) molestia, f.; incommodum; (business) negotium, nt.; labor; (grief) dolor, m.; aerumna, f.; ~, v.t. turbo; vexo, [1]; ango, [3].

troublesome, a. molestus; operosus; difficilis.

trough, n. alveus, m.

trousers, n. feminalia, nt. pl.; bracae, f. pl.

trowel, n. trulla, f.

truant, a. otiosus; vagus.

truce, n. induciae, f. pl.

truck, *n.* carrus, *m.*

true, *a.* verus; sincerus; germanus; rectus.

truly, *ad.* vere; sincere; profecto.

trump, *v.i.* (up) conflo, [1]; confingo, [3]; machinor, [1].

trumpet, *n.* tuba, bucina, *f.;* lituus, *m.;* cornu, *nt.;* ~, *v.t. fig.* praedico, vendito, celebro, [1].

trumpeter, *n.* tubicen, *m.*

trundle, *v.t.* volvo; ~, *v.i.* volvor, [3].

trunk, *n.* truncus, *m.;* (of an elephant) proboscis; (chest) cista, *f.*

trust, *n.* fiducia, *f.;* fides, *f.;* ~, *v.t.* fido; confido; credo, [3] (*all with dat. of person*); (entrust) commendo, [1]; permitto, [3].

trustworthy, *v.* trusty.

trusty, *a.* fidus, fidelis; constans.

truth, *n.* veritas; fides, *f.;* verum, *nt.*

truthful, *a.* verax; ~ly, *ad.* veraciter.

try, *n.* conatus, *m.*

try, *v.t.* tento, probo, periclitor, [1]; experior, [4]; (law) cognosco, [3]; in ius voco, [1]; ~, *v.i.* conor, [1]; nitor, [3]; tento, [1]; molior, [4].

tub, *n.* labrum, *nt.;* lacus, *m.*

tube, *n.* tubulus, tubus, *m.*

tubular, *a.* tubulatus.

tuck, *v.t.* succingo, [3].

tuft, *n.* (of hair) cirrus, *m.*

tug, *v.t. & i.* traho; nitor, [3].

tuition, *n.* disciplina, *f.*

tumble, *v.i.* corruo, labor, collabor, cado; volvor, [3].

tumour, *n.* tumor, tuber, *m.*

tumult, *n.* tumultus, *m.;* turba, *f.*

tumultuous, *a.* tumultuosus, turbulentus.

tune, *n.* numeri, moduli, *m. pl.;* **in ~,** *a.* consonus; **out of ~,** *a.* dissonus.

tuneful, *a.* canorus.

tunic, *n.* tunica, *f.*

tunnel, *n.* canalis, *m.;* cuniculum, *nt.*

turbid, *a.* turbidus; (muddy) caenosus.

turbulence, *n.* tumultus, *m.;* seditio, *f.;* animus turbulentus, *m.*

turbulent, *a.* turbulentus.

turf, *n.* caespes, *m.;* herba, *f.*

turgid, *a.* turgidus, tumidus; inflatus.

turmoil, *n.* turba, perturbatio, *f.;* tumultus, *m.*

turn, *n.* (circuit) circuitus, *m.;* (bend) flexus, *m.;* (turning round) conversio, *f.;* circumactus, *m.;* (change, course) vicissitudo; (inclination) inclinatio, *f.;* **good ~,** officium, beneficium, *nt.;* **by ~s,** alternis, in vicem; vicissim.

turn, *v.t.* (bend) flecto, verto; (round) volvo, circumago, [1]; (change) muto, [1]; converto, [3]; (on the lathe) torno, [1]; ~, *v.i.*

convertor; flector; volvor, [3]; torqueor, [2]; mutor, [1]; (become) fio, *ir.* evado, [3]; ~ **aside**, deflecto, [3]; detorqueo, [2]; ~ **away**, (*v.t. & i.*) averto, [3]; ~ **back**, reflecto, [3]; recurvo, [1]; (*v.i.*) reverto, [3]; redeo, [4]; ~ **down**, inverto, [3] (reject) reicio, [3]; ~ **off**, averto, [3]; derivo, [1]; (*v.i.*) deflecto, [3]; ~ **out**, eicio, [3]; (*v.i.*) evenio, [4]; evado; contingo, [3]; ~ **over**, everto, [3]; (a page) verso, [1]; (cede) transfero, [3]; ~ **round**, (*v.t.*) circumago, [3]; contorqueo, [2]; (*v.i.*) versor, [1]; circumagor, [3]; ~ **up**, recurvo, [1]; (come into view) appareo, [2].

urning-point, *n.* cardo, *m.*; momentum, discrimen, *nt.*

urnip, *n.* rapum, *nt.*

urret, *n.* turricula, *f.*

urtle, *n.* testudo, *f.*

urtle-dove, *n.* turtur, *m.*

usk, *n.* dens, *m.*

utor, *n.* educator; praeceptor, paedagogus, *m.*; ~, *v.t.* doceo, [2].

weezers, *n.* volsella, *f.*

welfth, *a.* duodecimus; **for the** ~ **time,** duodecimo.

welve, *a.* duodecim; ~ **times,** duodecies.

wentieth, *a.* vicesimus.

wenty, *a.* viginti.

wice, *ad.* bis.

wig, *n.* surculus, *m.*; virga, *f.*

wilight, *n.* (evening) crepusculum; (dawn) diluculum, *nt.*

twin, *n. & a.* geminus, gemellus.

twine, *v.t.* circumvolvo, [3]; circumplico, [1]; contorqueo, [2]; ~, *v.i.* circumvolvor, circumplector, [3].

twinge, *n.* dolor, *m.*

twinkle, *v.i.* mico, corusco, [1].

twirl, *v.t.* verso, [1]; circumago, [3]; ~, *v.i.* versor, [1].

twist, *v.t.* torqueo, [2]; flecto, [3]; ~, *v.i.* torqueor, [2]; flector, [3].

two, *a.* duo.

twofold, *a.* duplex, duplus.

type, *n.* exemplar, exemplum, *nt.*; forma, *f.*

typical, *a.* typicus.

tyrannical, *a.* tyrannicus.

tyranny, *n.* tyrannis, dominatio, *f.*

tyrant, *n.* tyrannus, *m.*

U

udder, *n.* uber, *nt.*; mamma, *f.*

ugliness, *n.* deformitas, foeditas, *f.*

ugly, *a.* deformis, foedus, turpis.

ulcer, *n.* ulcus, *nt.*

ulterior, *a.* ulterior.

ultimate, *a.* ultimus; **~ly,** *ad.* denique, tandem.

umpire, *n.* arbiter, disceptator, *m.*

unable, *a.* invalidus; **be ~,** *v.i.* non possum, nequeo, [4].

unacceptable, *a.* ingratus, odiosus.

unaccompanied, *a.* incomitatus, solus.

unaccountable, *a.* inexplicabilis, inenodabilis.

unaccountably, *ad.* praeter opinionem; sine causa.

unaccustomed, *a.* insolitus, insuetus, inexpertus.

unadorned, *a.* inornatus; incomptus; simplex.

unadulterated, *a.* merus, sincerus.

unaided, *a.* non adiutus, solus.

unanimity, *n.* unanimitas, consensio, *f.*; consensus, *m.*

unanimous, *a.* unanimus, concors; **~ly,** *ad.* consensu omnium, omnium sententiis.

unapproachable, *a.* inaccessus.

unarmed, *a.* inermis, inermus.

unassailable, *a.* inexpugnabilis.

unassuming, *a.* modestus, moderatus; demissus.

unattainable, *a.* arduus, quod consequi non potest.

unattempted, *a.* intentatus, inexpertus; inausus.

unattended, *a.* incomitatus.

unauthorized, *a.* inconcessus.

unavailing, *a.* inutilis, inanis.

unavoidable, *a.* inevitabilis.

unaware, *a.* inscius, nescius, ignarus.

unawares, *ad.* (de) improviso, inopinato.

unbearable, *a.* intolerabilis.

unbecoming, *a.* indecorus, indecens, indignus, inhonestus.

unbelievable, *a.* incredibilis.

unbending, *a.* inflexibilis, rigidus.

unbiased, *a.* incorruptus; integer; sine ira et studio.

unblemished, *a.* purus, integer, intactus.

unborn, *a.* nondum natus.

unbreakable, *a.* infragilis.

unbroken, *a.* irruptus; integer.

unburden, *v.t.* exonero, [1].

unburied, *a.* inhumatus, insepultus.

uncanny, *a.* inscitus.

uncared, *a.* (~ for) neglectus.

unceasing, *a.* perpetuus, assiduus; **~ly,** *ad.* perpetuo, continenter.

uncertain, *a.* incertus, dubius ambiguus, anceps.

uncertainty, *n.* quod incertum est; dubitatio, *f.*

unchangeable, *a.* immutabilis constans.

unchanged, unchanging, *a.* immutatus, perpetuus.

uncharitable, *a.* immisericors, iniquus, inhumanus.

uncivilized, *a.* incultus, barbarus.

uncle, *n.* (on the father's side) patruus; (on the mother's side) avunculus, *m.*

uncombed, *a.* impexus, incomptus.

uncomfortable, *a.* incommodus, molestus, gravis, anxius.

uncommon, *a.* rarus, insolitus; enormis; insignis; singularis; ~**ly,** *ad.* raro; praeter solitum, plus solito.

unconcerned, *a.* neglegens; incuriosus; securus.

unconditional, *a.* simplex.

unconscious, *a.* (unaware) inscius; nescius; ~**ly,** *ad.* nesciens.

uncontrollable, *a.* impotens, effrenatus.

uncouth, *a.* barbarus, impolitus, rudis; vastus.

uncover, *v.t.* detego, recludo, retego, [3]; revelo, [1].

undaunted, *a.* impavidus, intrepidus.

undecided, *a.* incertus, dubius, sine exitu; par; integer.

undeniable, *a.* quod negari non potest.

under, *pr.* sub, subter; infra (*all with acc.*); (in number) minor (*with abl.*).

undercurrent, *n.* torrens subterfluens, *m.*

underdone, *a.* minus percoctus, subcrudus.

underestimate, *v.t.* minoris aestimo, [1].

undergo, *v.i. & t.* subeo, [4]; patior, [3]; tolero, [1]; fero, [3].

underground, *a.* subterraneus.

undergrowth, *n.* virgulta, *nt. pl.*

underhand, *a.* clandestinus; ~, *ad.* clam.

underline, *v.t.* subnoto, [1].

underling, *n.* administer, *m.*; assecla, satelles, *c.*

undermine, *v.t.* suffodio, [3]; *fig.* supplanto, labefacto, [1].

underneath, *ad.* subter, infra (*with acc.*).

understand, *v.t. & i.* intellego; sapio, [3]; scio; (hear) audio, [4].

understanding, *a.* peritus; sapiens, prudens; (sympathetic) humanus; ~, *n.* mens, *f.*; intellectus, *m.*; intelligentia, *f.*

undertake, *v.t. & i.* suscipio; incipio; aggredior, [3]; conor, [1].

undertaker, *n.* (of funerals) libitinarius, *m.*

undertaking, *n.* ausum, inceptum; propositum, *nt.*

undervalue, *v.t.* parvi facio, [3]; parvi aestimo, [1].

underworld, *n.* Tartarus, *m.*

undeserved, *a.* immeritus; indignus; iniustus; ~**ly,** *ad.* immerito, indigne.

undisciplined, *a.* rudis, inexercitatus.

undisputed, *a.* indubitabilis, certus.

undisturbed, *a.* imperturbatus; immotus.

undivided, *a.* indivisus.

undo, *v.t.* solvo, dissolvo; resolvo; dissuo; irritum facio; (ruin) perdo, [3].

undone, *a.* infectus; imperfectus; perditus.

undoubted, *a.* indubitatus; certus; ~ly, *ad.* haud dubie.

undress, *v.t.* vestem exuo; (another) vestem detraho (alicui), [3].

undue, *a.* indebitus; iniquus.

undulate, *v.i.* undo, fluctuo; vibro, [1].

unduly, *ad.* iniuste, plus iusto.

undying, *a.* immortalis; sempiternus.

unearth, *v.t.* recludo; detego, [3].

unearthly, *a.* humano maior; terribilis.

uneasy, *a.* anxius.

unemployed, *a.* otiosus.

unencumbered, *a.* liber, expeditus.

unenviable, *a.* haud invidiosus.

unequal, *a.* inaequalis, dispar, impar; ~ly, *ad.* inaequaliter, impariter.

unerring, *a.* certus.

uneven, *a.* inaequalis; iniquus; (of ground) asper.

unexpected, *a.* inexpectatus, insperatus, improvisus, inopinatus, inopinus; ~ly, *ad.* (ex) improviso.

unfailing, *a.* certus.

unfair, *a.* iniquus; ~ly, *ad.* inique.

unfaithful, *a.* infidus, perfidus; ~ly, *ad.* perfide.

unfamiliar, *a.* peregrinus; ignarus; ignotus.

unfasten, *v.t.* laxo, [1]; solvo, resolvo, [3].

unfathomable, *a.* profundus.

unfavourable, *a.* sinister; adversus.

unfeeling, *a.* durus, inhumanus, crudelis; ~ly, *ad.* dure, crudeliter, inhumane.

unfinished, *a.* imperfectus.

unfit, *a.* inhabilis, incommodus, inutilis; (not physically fit) impiger.

unfold, *v.t.* explico, [1]; aperio, [4]; pando, [3]; ~, *v.i.* dehisco, [3].

unforeseen, *a.* inexpectatus, insperatus.

unforgiving, *a.* inexorabilis.

unfortunate, *a.* infelix; infortunatus; ~ly, *ad.* infeliciter.

unfounded, *a.* vanus; sine causa.

unfriendly, *a.* parum amicus.

unfulfilled, *a.* infectus, imperfectus.

unfurl, *v.t.* expando, solvo, (vela) facio, [3].

ungainly, *a.* inhabilis, rusticus.

ungovernable, *a.* impotens, effrenatus.

ungrateful, *a.* ingratus.

unguarded, *a.* incustoditus; *fig.* inconsultus.

unhappiness, *n.* miseria, tristitia, *f.*

unhappy, *a.* infelix, infortunatus, miser.

unhealthiness, *n.* infirmitas; pestilentia, gravitas, *f.*

unhealthy, *a.* ad aegrotandum proclivis; morbosus; (things) insalubris.

unharmed, *a.* incolumis, integer.

unholy, *a.* impius; profanus.

unhoped, *a.* (~ for) insperatus.

unhurt, *a.* inviolatus, illaesus.

unicorn, *n.* monoceros, *m.*

uniform, *a.* uniformis, sibi constans.

uniform, *n.* ornatus, habitus, *m.*

uniformity, *n.* uniformitas, *f.*

unimaginable, *a.* quod animo fingi non potest.

unimportant, *a.* levis, parvus.

uninhabitable, *a.* inhabitabilis, non habitabilis.

uninhabited, *a.* cultoribus inanis; desertus.

uninjured, *a.* incolumis, illaesus.

unintelligent, *a.* crassus.

unintelligible, *a.* obscurus.

unintentional, *a.* haud meditatus.

uninterrupted, *a.* continuus, perpetuus, inoffensus.

uninvited, *a.* invocatus.

union, *n.* (act) coniunctio; (alliance) consociatio; consensio; societas, *f.*; (marriage) matrimonium, *nt.*

unique, *a.* unicus, singularis.

unison, *n.* concentus, *m.*

unite, *v.t.* consocio, [1]; coniungo; ~, *v.i.* coalesco, [3]; coniuro, [1].

unity, *n.* (oneness) unitas; *fig.* concordia, *f.*

universal, *a.* universus; ~ly, *ad.* universe; (everywhere) undique, ubique.

universe, *n.* mundus, *m.*

university, *n.* academia, *f.*

unjust, *a.* iniustus, iniquus; ~ly, *ad.* iniuste, inique.

unkempt, *a.* incomptus.

unkind, *a.* inhumanus, parum officiosus; ~ly, *ad.* inhumane.

unkindness, *n.* inhumanitas, *f.*

unknown, *a.* ignotus, incognitus.

unlawful, *a.* illicitus; inconcessus; ~ly, *ad.* contra leges.

unless, *c.* nisi, ni, nisi si.

unlike, *a.* dissimilis, dispar, diversus.

unlikely, *a.* non verisimilis.

unlimited, *a.* infinitus, immensus.

unload, *v.t.* exonero, [1].

unlock, *v.t.* recludo, [3]; resero, [1].

unluckily, *ad.* infeliciter.

unlucky, *a.* infelix, infaustus.

unman, *v.t.* (castrate) castro; *fig.*
enervo, [1].

unmanageable, *ad.* intract-
abilis; contumax.

unmarried, *a.* caelebs, innuptus,
innubus.

unmask, *v.t.* detego, [3]; nudo, [1].

unmerciful, *a.* immisericors.

unmindful, *a.* immemor; incuriosus; securus.

unmistakable, *a.* certus.

unmixed, *a.* merus, sincerus.

unmoved, *a.* immotus (also *fig.*).

unnatural, *a.* crudelis, monstruosus, immanis; (preter-
natural) praeter naturam.

unnecessary, *a.* haud necessarius.

unnerve, *v.t.* debilito, infirmo,
enervo, [1].

unnoticed, *a.* praetermissus.

unobserved, *a.* inobservatus.

unoccupied, *a.* otiosus, vacuus;
(of land) apertus.

unpack, *v.t.* expedio, [4]; eximo,
[3].

unpaid, *a.* quod adhuc debetur;
gratuitus.

unpalatable, *a.* molestus.

unparalleled, *a.* unicus; eximius.

unpardonable, *a.* non ignoscen-
dus.

unpatriotic, *a.* patriae non
amans.

unpleasant, *a.* iniucundus; incommodus; molestus; ~ly, *ad.*
iniucunde; incommode.

unpleasing, *a.* ingratus.

unpopular, *a.* populo ingratus,
invidiosus.

unpopularity, *n.* invidia, *f.*;
odium, *nt.*

unprecedented, *a.* novus, in-
auditus, unicus.

unpremeditated, *a.* subitus, non
elaboratus.

unprepared, *a.* imparatus.

unprincipled, *a.* corruptis mori-
bus, improbus.

unproductive, *a.* infecundus, in-
fructuosus.

unprofitable, *a.* inutilis, vanus.

unprotected, *a.* indefensus.

unpunished, *a.* impunitus.

unqualified, *a.* haud idoneus, inhabilis; merus.

unquestionable, *a.* certus.

unravel, *v.t.* extrico, enodo, [1];
expedio, [4].

unreasonable, *a.* contra rationem, rationis expers, absurdus;
iniquus.

unrelenting, *a.* implacabilis, inexorabilis.

unreliable, *a.* infidus.

unremitting, *a.* continuus, perpetuus, assiduus.

unrepentant, *a.* impaenitens.

unrequited, *a.* non mutuus, sine
mercede.

unreserved, *a.* apertus, candidus; ~**ly,** *ad.* aperte, libere, candide.

unrest, *n.* tumultus, *m.*

unripe, *a.* immaturus, crudus.

unrivalled, *a.* singularis.

unroll, *u.t.* evolvo, [3]; explico; [1]; pando, [3]; expedio, [4].

unruffled, *a.* tranquillus, immotus.

unruly, *a.* effrenatus; turbulentus; petulans.

unsafe, *a.* intutus; periculosus.

unsatisfactory, *a.* non idoneus; improbabilis.

unsavoury, *a. fig.* insulsus, foedus.

unscathed, *a.* salvus.

unseal, *u.t.* resigno, [1]; aperio, [4].

unseemly, *a.* indecorus, indecens.

unseen, *a.* invisus; invisitatus; inobservatus.

unselfish, *a.* suae utilitatis immemor.

unselfishness, *n.* suarum utilitatum neglegentia, *f.*

unsettled, *a.* dubius, instabilis, inconstans, inquietus.

unshaven, *a.* intonsus.

unsheath, *u.t.* e vagina educo; (gladium) destringo, [3].

unsightly, *a.* deformis; turpis, foedus.

unsociable, unsocial, *a.* insociabilis.

unsolicited, *a.* ultro oblatus.

unsophisticated, *a.* simplex, sincerus, incorruptus.

unsought, *a.* non quaesitus.

unspeakable, *a.* ineffabilis, infandus, inenarrabilis.

unstable, *a.* instabilis; fluxus; incertus.

unsteadily, *a.* infirme, instabiliter.

unsteadiness, *n.* instabilitas; infirmitas; levitas, inconstantia, *f.*

unsteady, *a.* instabilis; infirmus; tremulus; vagus, levis.

unsuccessful, *a.* improsper; infaustus; infelix; (vain) irritus, vanus; ~**ly,** *ad.* infeliciter, improspere; (in vain) frustra, re infecta.

unsuitable, *a.* incongruens, inhabilis, incommodus.

unsuspecting, *a.* minime suspicax.

untamed, *a.* indomitus, ferus.

untidy, *a.* immundus.

untie, *u.t.* solvo, resolvo, [3]; laxo, [1].

until, *c.* dum; quoad; donec; ~, *pr.* ad, in; usque ad (*all with acc.*).

untimely, *a.* immaturus; importunus; intempestivus.

untold, *a.* indictus; immemoratus; (vast) vastus.

untouched, *a.* intactus; integer; immotus.

untoward, *a.* adversus, contumax.

untrained, *a.* inexercitatus.

untrodden, *a.* non tritus; avius.

untroubled, *a.* placidus; aequus; securus, imperturbatus.

untrue, *a.* falsus, mendax.

untruth, *n.* mendacium, *nt.*

unused, *a.* inusitatus; novus, non tritus.

unusual, *a.* inusitatus, insuetus; insolitus, novus, rarus; ~**ly**, *ad.* praeter solitum, raro.

unvarnished, *a.* non fucatus; *fig.* sincerus, nudus.

unveil, *v.t.* velamen detraho; *fig.* patefacio, [3].

unwarlike, *a.* imbellis.

unwary, *a.* imprudens, incautus, inconsultus, temerarius.

unwelcome, *a.* non acceptus, ingratus, iniucundus.

unwell, *a.* aeger, invalidus, infirmus.

unwieldy, *a.* inhabilis, pinguis.

unwilling, *a.* invitus; coactus; ~**ly**, *ad.* invite, non libenter.

unwind, *v.t.* revolvo, retexo, [3].

unwise, *a.* imprudens; inconsultus; stultus; ~**ly**, *ad.* stulte; imprudenter, inconsulte.

unwitting, *a.* inscius.

unwonted, *a.* insolitus, insuetus, inusitatus.

unworthy, *a.* indignus; immeritus.

unwrap, *v.i.* explico, [1]; evolvo, [3].

unwritten, *a.* non scriptus, inscriptus.

unyielding, *a.* obstinatus.

unyoke, *v.t.* abiungo, disiungo, [3].

up, *ad. & pr.* sursum; ~ **to**, tenus; (of time) usque ad (*both with acc.*) ~**stream**, in adversum flumen; ~ **and down**, sursum deorsum; huc illuc.

uphill, *a.* adverso colle.

uphold, *v.t.* sustineo, [2]; sustento [1]; tueor, [2].

upland, *a.* editus, montanus.

upon, *pr.* super, supra; (of time) e, ex; (on) in (*all with abl.*).

upper, *a.* superus; superior; ~**most**, summus.

upright, *a.* erectus; rectus; *fig.* honestus; integer.

uproar, *n.* tumultus, *m.*; turba, *f.*

uproot, *v.t.* radicitus tollo, eruo, [3].

upset, *a.* sollicitatus, perculsus.

upset, *v.t.* everto, subverto; sterno, [3].

uprising, *n.* tumultus, *m.*

upshot, *n.* exitus, eventus, *m.*

upside, *n.* ~ **down**, sursum deorsum; **turn** ~ **down**, *v.t.* misceo, [2]; confundo, [3].

upstart, *n.* homo novus, terrae filius, *m.*

upwards, *ad.* sursum; sublime; superne; (of number) plus.

urban, *a.* urbanus.

urge, *n.* incitamentum, *nt.*

urge, *v.t.* urgeo, [2]; impello, [3]; insto, [1]; suadeo, [2] (*both with dat.*); (on) stimulo, [1].

urgent, *a.* instans; vehemens; gravis; **~ly**, *ad.* vehementer.

urine, *n.* urina, *f.*

urn, *n.* urna; (water-pot) hydria, *f.*

usage, *n.* mos, *m.*; consuetudo, *f.*; usus, *m.*

use, *n.* usus, *m.*; utilitas, *f.*; commodum, *nt.*; consuetudo, *f.*; (interest) faenus, *nt.*; **be of ~**, valeo, [2]; prosum, *ir.* (*with dat.*).

use, *v.t.* utor, [3] (*with abl.*); adhibeo, [2]; in usum verto, [3]; (treat) tracto, [1]; **~ up**, consumo, [3].

used, be ~ to, *v.i.* soleo, [2]; consuesco, [3].

useful, *a.* utilis; aptus, commodus; salutaris; **~ly**, *ad.* utiliter; apte, commode.

usefulness, *n.* utilitas; commoditas, *f.*

useless, *a.* inutilis; inhabilis; irritus, vanus; **~ly**, *ad.* inutiliter; nequicquam, frustra.

uselessness, *n.* inutilitas, *f.*

usher, *v.i.* praeeo, [4]; introduco, [3].

usher, *n.* apparitor, *m.*

usual, *a.* usitatus, solitus, consuetus; cottidianus; **~ly**, usitate; vulgo; plerumque, fere.

usurp, *v.t.* usurpo; vindico (mihi), [1]; assumo, [3].

usurper, *n.* usurpator, *m.*

utensils, *n. pl.* utensilia; vasa, *nt. pl.*; supellex, *f.*

utility, *n.* utilitas, commoditas, *f.*

utmost, *a.* extremus; ultimus; summus; **do one's ~**, summis viribus contendo, [3].

utter, *a.* (total) totus; **~ly**, *ad.* omnino, penitus; funditus.

utter, *v.t.* eloquor, dico, mitto, fundo, profero, [3]; pronuntio, [1].

utterance, *n.* elocutio; pronuntiatio, *f.*; dictum, *nt.*; vox, *f.*

....

V

....

vacancy, *n.* (emptiness) inanitas, *f.*; inane, *nt.*; (place) locus, *m.*

vacant, *a.* vacuus, inanis; *fig.* mentis vacuus.

vacate, *v.t.* vacuefacio; (leave) relinquo, [3].

vacation, *n.* (law) iustitium, *nt.*; (holidays) feriae, *f. pl.*

vacillate, *v.i.* vacillo, fluctuo, [1].

vacuum, *n.* inane, vacuum, *nt.*

vagabond, **vagrant**, *n.* homo vagus, erro, *m.*

vague, *a.* dubius; ambiguus; incertus.

vain, *a.* (pointless) vanus; futtilis; inanis, irritus; (proud) superbus, arrogans; (boastful) gloriosus; **in ~, ~ly,** *ad.* frustra; nequicquam, incassum.

valet, *n.* cubicularius, famulus, *m.*

valiant, *a.* fortis; audax, animosus; **~ly,** *ad.* fortiter; audacter, animose.

valid, *a.* validus; legitimus, ratus.

validity, *n.* firmitas; auctoritas, *f.*

valley, *n.* vallis, convallis, *f.*

valour, *n.* fortitudo, virtus, *f.*; animus, *m.*

valuable, *a.* pretiosus; carus.

valuation, *n.* aestimatio, *f.*

value, *n.* pretium, *nt.*; aestimatio, *f.*; ~, *v.t.* aestimo, [1]; pendo, [3]; **~ highly,** magni aestimo, [1].

valueless, *a.* vilis, parvi pretii.

valve, *n.* valvae, *f. pl.*

vanguard, *n.* primum agmen, *nt.*

vanish, *v.i.* vanesco, diffugio, evanesco, [3]; abeo, pereo, [4].

vanity, *n.* (pointlessness) vanitas; levitas, *f.*; nugae, *f. pl.*; (boastfulness) iactatio, ostentatio, *f.*

vapour, *n.* vapor, *m.*; exhalatio, *f.*; halitus, *m.*

variable, *a.* mutabilis; varius; levis, inconstans.

variance, *n.* discordia; discrepantia, dissensio, simultas, *f.*;

be at **~,** *v.i.* discrepo, [1]; dissideo, [2].

variation, *n.* varietas; variatio; vicissitudo, *f.*

varied, *a.* varius, diversus.

variety, *n.* varietas; diversitas; multitudo, *f.*

various, *a.* varius, diversus; **~ly,** *ad.* varie, diverse.

varnish, *n.* atramentum, *nt.*; *fig.* fucus, *m.*; ~, *v.t.* coloro, [1].

vary, *v.t.* vario, [1]; distinguo, [3]; ~, *v.i.* vario, [1].

vase, *n.* amphora, *f.*; urceus, *m.*; vas, *nt.*

vast, *a.* vastus; ingens, immensus; **~ly,** *ad.* vaste; valde; multum.

vastness, *n.* immensitas, *f.*

vat, *n.* cupa, *f.*; dolium, *nt.*

vault, *n.* fornix, *m.*; camera, *f.*; (underground) hypogeum, *nt.*; (leap) saltus, *m.*; ~, *v.t.* (cover with a vault) concamero, [1]; ~, *v.t.* (leap over) transilio, [4].

vaunt, *v.t.* iacto, [1]; glorior, [1], vendo, [3]; ostento, [1].

veal, *n.* vitulina, *f.*

veer, *v.i.* vertor, vergo, [3].

vegetable, *n.* holus, *nt.*

vegetation, *n.* herba, *f.*

vehemence, *n.* vehementia, vis, *f.*; fervor, impetus, *m.*

vehement, *a.* vehemens, violentus; fervidus; acer; **~ly,** *ad.* vehementer; acriter.

vehicle, *n.* vehiculum, *nt.*

veil, *n.* velamen; flammeolum, *nt.*; amictus; *fig.* praetextus, *m.*; simulacrum, *nt.* species, *f.*; ~, *v.t.* velo, [1]; tego, [3].

vein, *n.* vena, *f.* (also *fig.*).

velocity, *n.* velocitas, celeritas, *f.*

veneer, *n.* ligni brattea, *f.*; *fig.* species, *f.*

venerable, *a.* venerabilis, reverendus.

venerate, *v.t.* veneror, adoro, [1]; colo, [3].

veneration, *n.* veneratio, adoratio, *f.*; cultus, *m.*

venereal, *a.* venereus.

vengeance, *n.* ultio; vindicta, poena, *f.*; **take** ~, ulciscor, [3]; **with a** ~, valde.

venison, *n.* caro ferina, *f.*

venom, *n.* venenum, virus, *nt.*

venomous, *a.* venenosus, virulentus.

vent, *n.* spiramentum, *nt.*; exitus, *m.*; foramen, *nt.*; **give** ~ **to** (utter), fundo, promo, [3]; (exercise) exerceo, [2]; ~, *v.t.* aperio, [4]; per foramen emitto, [3].; ~ **one's anger on**, stomachum in aliquem effundo, [3].

ventilate, *v.t.* ventilo, [1]; *fig.* in medium profero, [3].

ventilation, *n.* ventilatio; *fig.* prolatio, *f.*

venture, *n.* discrimen, periculum, *nt.*; (hazard) alea, *f.*; (deed of daring) ausum, *nt.*; **at a** ~, temere.

venture, *v.t.* periclitor, [1]; ~, *v.i.* (dare) audeo, [2].

verandah, *n.* subdiale, *nt.*

verb, *n.* verbum, *nt.*

verbatim, *ad.* ad verbum.

verbose, *a.* verbosus; ~**ly**, *ad.* verbose.

verbosity, *n.* loquacitas, *f.*

verdant, *a.* viridis, virens; florens.

verdict, *n.* (of a jury) iudicium, *nt.*; sententia, *f.*

verge, *n.* (border) confinium, *nt.*; margo, *c.*; ora, *f.*; (limit) limes, *m.*; ~, *v.i.* vergo, [3]; **on the** ~ **of**, use future participle.

verification, *n.* affirmatio, *f.*

verify, *v.t.* ratum facio, [3]; confirmo, [1].

vermin, *n.* bestiolae molestae, *f. pl.*

vernacular, *a.* vernaculus.

vernal, *a.* vernus.

versatile, *a.* versatilis; versabilis, agilis; varius.

versatility, *n.* agilitas, *f.*

verse, *n.* versus, *m.*; carmen, *nt.*

versed, *a.* peritus, exercitatus.

version, *n.* translatio, *f.*

vertebra, *n.* vertebra, *f.*

vertex, *n.* vertex, *m.*

vertical, *a.* rectus, directus; ~**ly**, *ad.* ad lineam; recta linea.

vertigo, *n.* vertigo, *f.*

very, *a.* verus; ~, *ad.* valde, admodum; multum.

vessel, *n.* vas; (ship) navigium, *nt.*

vest, *n.* vestimentum, *nt.*; tunica, *f.*; (of a charioteer) pannus, *m.*

vestal, *n.* (virgo) vestalis, *f.*

vestige, *n.* vestigium; indicium, *nt.*

veteran, *a.* veteranus; ~, *n.* veteranus miles, *m.*

veterinary, *a.* veterinarius.

veto, *n.* intercessio, *f.*

veto, *v.t.* veto, [1].

vex, *v.t.* vexo, inquieto, [1].

vexation, *n.* vexatio; offensio, *f.*; stomachus, dolor, *m.*

vibrate, *v.i.* vibro, [1]; tremo, [3].

vibration, *n.* vibratus, motus, tremor, *m.*

vicarious, *a.* vicarius.

vice, *n.* vitium, *nt.*; turpitudo, *f.*; (instrument) forceps, *m.*

vicinity, *n.* vicinitas, vicinia, *f.*

vicious, *a.* vitiosus; perditus; turpis.

victim, *n.* victima, hostia, *f.*

victimize, *v.t.* (*fig.*) noceo, [2] (*with dat.*); laedo, [1].

victor, *n.* victor, *m.*; victrix, *f.*

victorious, *a.* superior; victor (*m.*), victrix (*f.*); ~ly, *ad.* victoris instar.

victory, *n.* victoria, *f.*; triumphus, *m.*; palma, *f.*

victuals, *n. pl.* cibaria, *nt. pl.*; victus; (*mil.*) commeatus, *m.*

vie, *v.i.* (with) aemulor, [1]; contendo, [3]; certo, [1] (*both with cum with dat.*).

view, *n.* (act) aspectus, conspectus, *m.*; oculi, *m. pl.*; species, *f.*; spectaculum, *nt.*; (prospect) prospectus, *m.*; *fig.* (opinion) sententia; opinio, *f.*; **have in ~,** cogito, [1].

view, *v.t.* viso, inviso, conspicio; inspicio, [3]; contemplor; investigo; lustro, [1]; (regard, feel) sentio, [4].

vigil, *n.* vigilia, pervigilatio, *f.*; pervigilium, *nt.*

vigilance, *n.* vigilantia, cura, *f.*

vigilant, *a.* vigil, vigilans; ~ly, *ad.* vigilanter.

vigorous, *a.* vigens, validus, acer, fortis, strenuus; ~ly, *ad.* strenue; acriter; fortiter.

vigour, *n.* vigor, *m.*; robur, *nt.*; impetus, *m.*

vile, *a.* vilis, abiectus; (wicked) perditus, flagitiosus; foedus.

villa, *n.* villa, *f.*

village, *n.* vicus, pagus, *m.*

villager, *n.* vicanus, paganus, rusticus, *m.*

villain, *n.* scelus, *nt.*; scelestus; nequam, *m.* (*indecl.*).

villainous, *a.* sceleratus, scelestus, nefarius.

villainy, *n.* improbitas, nequitia, *f.*; scelus, *nt.*

vindicate, *v.t.* vindico, [1]; assero, [3]; (justify) purgo, [1]; (defend) defendo, [3].

vindication, *n.* defensio, *f.*

vindictive, *a.* ultionis cupidus, acerbus.

vine, *n.* vitis, *f.*

vinegar, *n.* acetum, *nt.*

vineyard, *n.* vinea, *f.*; vinetum, *nt.*

vintage, *n.* vindemia, *f.*

violate, *v.t.* violo, [1]; rumpo, frango, [3].

violation, *n.* violatio, *f.*

violence, *n.* violentia; vis, *f.*; (energy) impetus, *m.*; (cruelty) saevitia, *f.*

violent, *a.* violentus; furiosus; vehemens; ~**ly**, *ad.* violenter, vehementer.

violet, *n.* (flower) viola; (colour) viola, *f.*

viper, *n.* vipera, *f.*

virgin, *n.* virgo, *f.*; puella, *f.*; ~, *a.* virginalis, virgineus.

virginity, *n.* virginitas, *f.*

virile, *a.* virilis, masculus.

virility, *n.* virilitas, *f.*

virtual, *a.* insitus, innatus.

virtue, *n.* virtus; probitas; fortitudo; (efficacy) vis, virtus, *f.*

virtuous, *a.* virtute praeditus, probus; integer; ~**ly**, *ad.* cum virtute; integre.

virulence, *n.* acerbitas, gravitas, *f.*

virulent, *a.* virulentus; acerbus, gravis.

virus, *n.* virus, *nt.*

viscous, *a.* viscosus, lentus.

visibility, *n.* visibilitas, *f.*

visible, *a.* aspectabilis, conspicuus; manifestus; **visibly**, *ad. fig.* aperte, manifesto.

vision, *n.* (faculty of sight) visus, *m.*; *fig.* visio, *f.*; visum; somnium, *nt.*

visit, *n.* aditus, *m.*; salutatio, *f.*; ~, *v.t.* viso, [3]; visito, [1]; adeo, [4].

visitor, *m.* salutator, *m.*; salutatrix, *f.*

visor, *n.* (cheek-piece of helmet) buccula, *f.*

vital, *a.* vitalis; *fig.* necessarius.

vitality, *n.* vitalitas, *f.*; vigor, *m.*

vivacious, *a.* vivax; vividus, alacer.

vivacity, *n.* vivacitas; alacritas, *f.*

vivid, *a.* vividus; (plain) manifestus; ~**ly**, *ad.* vivide; (plainly) manifesto.

vocabulary, *n.* vocabulorum index, *m.*

vocal, *a.* vocalis; canorus; ~**ly**, *ad.* voce, ore.

vocation, *n.* officium, munus, *nt.*

vociferous, *a.* clamosus.

vogue, *n.* mos, *m.*; fama, aestimatio, *f.*; **be in ~**, invalesco, [3].

voice, *n.* vox, *f.*; sonus, *m.*; (vote) suffragium, *nt.*

void, *a.* vacuus, inanis; *fig.* sterilis; invalidus, irritus, cassus; **be ~**, vaco, [1].

void, n. vacuum, inane, nt.; ~, v.t. vacuefacio, [3]; vacuo, [1]; *fig.* irritum facio, rescindo, [3].

volatile, a. volatilis; *fig.* levis, volaticus, inconstans.

volcano, n. mons igneus, m.

volley, n. nubes, f.

voluble, a. volubilis, loquax, garrulus.

volume, n. volumen, nt.; tomus, m.; (size) magnitudo, f.

voluntarily, ad. sponte, libenter.

voluntary, a. voluntarius.

volunteer, n. (miles) voluntarius, m.; ~, v.i. me offero, [3]; audeo, [2].

voluptuous, a. voluptarius, voluptuosus.

vomit, v.t. & i. vomo, evomo, [3]; eructo, [1].

vomit, n. vomitus, m.

voracious, a. vorax, edax; ~**ly,** ad. voraciter.

voracity, n. voracitas, edacitas, gula, f.

vortex, n. vertex, turbo, gurges, m.

vote, n. suffragium, nt.; *fig.* (judgment) sententia, f.; ~, v.t. censeo, [2]; ~, v.i. suffragium fero, [3].

voter, n. suffragator, m.

voting-tablet, n. tabella, f.

votive, a. votivus; ~ **tablet,** tabella, f.

vouch, v.t. & i. testificor, testor, affirmo, [1].

voucher, n. (ticket) tessera, f.

vow, n. votum, nt.; ~, v.t. (de)voveo, [2]; spondeo, [2]; (promise) promitto, [3].

vowel, n. vocalis, f.

voyage, n. navigatio, f.; ~, v.i. navigo, [1].

voyager, n. navigator, m.

vulgar, a. vulgaris, plebeius; inurbanus; rusticus; ~**ly,** ad. vulgo; rustice.

vulgarity, n. mores vulgi, m. pl.; rusticitas, f.

vulnerable, a. quod vulnerari potest.

vulture, n. vultur, vulturius, m.

W

wad, n. fasciculus, m.

waddle, v.i. anatis in modum incedo, [3].

wade, v.i. per vada eo, [4].

waft, v.t. deduco, defero, fero; traicio, [3].

wag, v.t. agito, vibro, [1]; (the tail) moveo, [2].

wager, n. sponsio, f.; pignus, nt.; ~, v.t. & i. spondeo, [2]; sponsione provoco, [1]; pignore contendo, [3].

wages, n. merces, f; stipendium, nt.

wagon, n. carrus, m.; plaustrum, nt.

waif, n. erro, m.

wail, v.t. & i. ploro, [1]; plango, [3]; fleo, [2].

wailing, n. ploratus, planctus, m.

waist, n. medium corpus, nt.

waistcoat, n. subucula, f.

wait, v.i. (stay) maneo, [2]; (for) exspecto, [1]; (on) inservio, [4] (with dat.).

wait, n. (delay) mora, f; lie in ~, insidior, [1].

waiter, n. minister, pedisequus, m.

waive, v.t. decedo (de with abl.), remitto, [3].

wake, v.t. exsuscito, excito, [1]; expergefacio, [3]; ~, v.i. expergiscor, [3].

wakeful, a. exsomnis, insomnis, vigil, vigilans.

waken, v.t.i. v. wake.

walk, n. (act) ambulatio, f; (place) ambulacrum, nt.; ambulatio, f; (manner of walking) incessus, m.; ~, v.i. incedo, [3]; ambulo, [1]; gradior, [3].

walker, n. ambulans; pedes, m.

walking, n. ambulatio, f; ~ stick, baculum, n.

wall, n. paries; (of a town, etc.) murus, m.; (mil.) moenia, nt. pl.

wallet, n. pera; mantica, f; saccus, m.

wallow, v.i. volutor, [1].

walnut, n. iuglans, nux iuglans, f.

wan, a. pallidus, exsanguis.

wand, n. virga, f; caduceus, m.

wander, v.i. vagor, erro, palor; (about) pervagor; (over) pererro, [1].

wandering, a. errabundus; vagus; erraticus; ~, n. erratio, f; error, m.

wane, v.i. decresco; minuor; tabesco, [3].

want, n. egestas, inopia, penuria, defectio, f; ~, v.t. (lack) egeo, indigeo, [2] (both with abl.); desidero, [1]; (wish) volo, [3]; opto, [1]; cupio, [3]; ~, v.i. deficio, [3]; desum, absum.

wanting, a. be ~, deficio, [3], desum, ir.

wanton, a. petulans, procax; libidinosus; lascivus; protervus.

war, n. bellum, nt.; Mars, m.; arma, nt. pl.

warble, v.i. cano, [3]; fritinnio, [4].

ward, n. (minor) pupillus, m.; pupilla, f; ~, v.t. (off) arceo, [2]; averto, [3]; prohibeo, [2].

warden, n. custos, c.

warder, n. excubitor, m.; vigil; custos, c.

wardrobe, n. arca vestiaria, f; vestiarium, nt.; (clothes) vestimenta, nt. pl.

wares, n. merces, f. pl.

warehouse, n. mercium receptaculum, nt.; cella, f.

warfare, *n.* bellum, *nt.*; res militaris, *f.*

warily, *ad.* caute, circumspecte.

wariness, *n.* cautio, circumspectio, *f.*

warlike, *a.* militaris, bellicosus, bellicus, pugnax.

warm, *a.* calidus; tepidus; *fig.* acer; iracundus.

warm, *v.t.* tepefacio, calefacio, [3]; foveo, [2].

warmth, *n.* calor, tepor, *m.*

warn, *v.t.* moneo; praemoneo, [2].

warning, *n.* monitio, *f.*; monitum, *nt.*; monitus, *m.*; *fig.* exemplum, *nt.*

warp, *v.t.* perverto, [3]; ~, *v.i.* (as wood) curvor, [1]; *fig.* pervertor, [3].

warrant, *n.* cautio; auctoritas, fides; licentia, facultas, *f.*; mandatum, *nt.*; ~, *v.t.* (securum) praesto, [1]; promitto, [3]; sancio, [4]; copiam do, [1] (*with dat.*); (excuse) excuso, [1].

warranty, *n.* satisdatio, *f.*

warrior, *n.* miles, *m.*; homo militaris, bellator, *m.*

wart, *n.* verruca, *f.*

wary, *a.* cautus, providus; prudens, circumspectus.

wash, *v.t.* lavo, [1]; abluo, [3]; ~, *v.i.* lavor, [1]; perluor, [3].

wash, *n.* lavatio, *f.*; (colour) fucus, *m.*

washtub, *n.* alveus, *m.*; labrum, *nt.*

washing, *n.* lavatio; lotura, *f.*

wasp, *n.* vespa, *f.*

waste, *n.* (laying waste) vastatio, *f.*; (loss) detrimentum; (financial) dispendium, *nt.*; (refuse) ramenta, *nt. pl.*

waste, *v.t.* (lay waste) vasto, [1]; (spend) prodigo, profundo, consumo, absumo, [3]; ~ away, *v.i.* tabesco, [3].

wasteful, *a.* profusus, prodigus.

wasteland, *n.* solitudo, *f.*; deserta, *nt. pl.* (desert)

watch, *n.* (guard) vigilia, *f.*; excubiae, *f. pl.*; (clock) horologium, *nt.*; ~, *v.t.* custodio, [4]; observo, [1]; ~, *v.i.* vigilo, [1].

watchful, *a.* vigilans; vigil, vigilax.

watchman, *n.* vigil, excubitor, custos, *m.*

watch-tower, *n.* specula, *f.*

watchword, *n.* tessera, *f.*; signum, *nt.*

water, *n.* aqua, *f.*; latex, *m.*; lympha, *f.*; (urine) urina, *f.*

water, *v.t.* rigo, irrigo, [1]; aqua misceo, [2].

watercress, *n.* nasturcium, *nt.*

waterfall, *n.* aqua desiliens, *f.*; cataracta, *f.*

water-mill, *n.* mola aquaria, *f.*

waterproof, *a.* impervius.

waterworks, *n.* aquarum ductus, aquaeductus, *m.*

watery, *a.* aquaticus; aquosus; (in appearance) aquatilis.

wave, *n.* unda, *f.*; fluctus, *m.*; ~, *v.i.* fluctuo, undo, fluito, [1]; ~, *v.t.* moveo, [2], agito, [1].

waver, *v.i.* fluctuo; (vacillate) labo; *fig.* dubito, [1].

wavering, *a.* dubius, incertus.

wavy, *a.* undans; undosus; (curling) crispus.

wax, *n.* cera, *f.*; ~, *v.t.* cero, incero, [1].

wax, *v.i.* cresco, [3]; augeor, [2].

waxy, *a.* cerosus.

way, *n.* via, *f.*; iter, *nt.*; *fig.* (manner, *etc.*) ratio, *f.*; modus; (custom) mos; (course) cursus, *m.*

wayfarer, *n.* viator, *m.*

waylay, *v.t.* insidior, [1] (*with dat.*).

wayward, *a.* libidinosus; inconstans; levis; mutabilis.

we, *pn.* nos; ~ **ourselves,** nosmet ipsi.

weak, *a.* infirmus, debilis, enervatus, imbecillus, invalidus.

weaken, *v.t.* infirmo, debilito, enervo; (things) extenuo, [1].

weakness, *n.* infirmitas, debilitas; imbecillitas, *f.*; (failing) vitium, *nt.*

wealth, *n.* divitiae, opes, *f. pl.*; opulentia; abundantia, *f.*

wealthy, *a.* opulentus, dives; locuples; abundans.

wean, *v.t.* infantem ab ubere depello, [3]; *fig.* dedoceo, [2].

weapon, *n.* telum, *nt.*; arma, *nt. pl.*

wear, *v.t.* (on the body) gero, [3]; gesto, [1]; ~, *v.i.* duro, [1]; (be worn out) atteror, [3]; ~ **out,** tero, exedo, consumo, [3].

weariness, *n.* lassitudo, fatigatio, *f.*; languor, *m.*

weary, *a.* lassus, fessus, defessus, fatigatus; languidus; operosus.

weary, *v.t.* lasso, fatigo, defatigo, [1]; conficio, [3]; ~, *v.i.* defatigor, [1].

weasel, *n.* mustela, *f.*

weather, *n.* caelum, *nt.*; tempestas, *f.*

weather-beaten, *a.* adustus, tempestate iactatus.

weave, *v.t.* texo; necto, [3].

weaver, *n.* textor, *m.*

web, *n.* textura, *f.*; textum, *nt.*; **spider's** ~, aranea, *f.*

web-footed, *a.* palmipes.

wedding, *n.* nuptiae, *f. pl.*

wedding-day, *n.* dies nuptiarum, *m.*

wedge, *n.* cuneus, *m.*; ~ **in,** *v.t.* cuneo, [1].

wedge-shaped, *a.* cuneatus.

wedlock, *n.* matrimonium, *nt.*

weed, *n.* herba inutilis *or* noxia, *f.*

weed, *v.t.* (e)runco, [1]; sarrio, [4].

week, *n.* hebdomas, septimana, *f.*

weekly, *a.* hebdomadalis.

weep, *v.i.* fleo, [2]; lacrimo, [1]; (for) deploro, [1].

weeping, *n.* ploratus, fletus, *m.*; lacrimae, *f. pl.*

weigh, *v.t.* pendo, [3]; pondero; penso; *fig.* meditor, [1]; (down) gravo, degravo, [1]; opprimo, [3].

weight, *n.* pondus, *nt.*; (heaviness) gravitas, *f.*; (burden) onus, *nt.*; *fig.* momentum, pondus, *nt.*

weighty, *a.* ponderosus, onerosus, (heavy, important) gravis.

welcome, *a.* gratus, acceptus; ~, *n.* gratulatio, salutatio, *f.*; ~! salve!

welcome, *v.t.* salvere iubeo, [2]; excipio, [3].

weld, *v.t.* (con)ferrumino, [1].

welfare, *n.* salus; utilitas, prosperitas, *f.*; bonum, *nt.*

well, *n.* puteus, fons, *m.*

well, *a.* sanus, validus; integer; be ~, valeo, [2]; ~, *ad.* bene; recte; scite, scienter; praeclare; **very ~,** optime.

well-being, *n.* salus, *f.*

well-born, *a.* nobilis, nobili genere ortus.

well-bred, *a.* liberaliter educatus; comis.

well-known, *a.* pervulgatus; notus; celeber, nobilis.

well-wisher, *n.* benevolus, amicus, *m.*

west, *n.* occidens, occasus; ~ **wind,** *n.* Favonius, Zephyrus, *m.*

westerly, western, *a.* occidentalis, occiduus.

westward(s), *ad.* in occasum, occasum versus.

wet, *a.* umidus, uvidus, madidus, udus; ~, *v.t.* madefacio, [3]; rigo, umecto, [1].

wetness, *n.* umor, *m.*

whale, *n.* balaena, *f.*; cetus, *m.*

what, *pn.* quid, quidnam, ecquid; ~, *a.* qualis, quantus; qui.

what(so)ever, *a. & pn.* quodcumque, quicquid.

wheat, *n.* triticum, *nt.*

wheedle, *v.t.* blandior, delenio, [4]; adulor, [1].

wheel, *n.* rota, *f.*; (lathe) tornus, *m.*; ~, *v.t.* (& *i.*) circumago(r), [3], roto(r), [1]; converto(r), [3].

wheelbarrow, *n.* pabo, *m.*

wheeze, *v.i.* anhelo, [1].

when, *ad. & c.* cum, ubi; ut, postquam; (interrog.) quando?

whence, *ad.* unde.

whenever, *rel. ad.* quandocunque, quoties, quotiescunque.

where, *ad.* ubi? qua? (*rel.*) qua, ubi; ~**as,** quoniam, quandoquidem, cum; quo; ~**upon,** quo facto.

wherever, *rel. ad.* quacunque, ubicumque.

whet, *v.t.* acuo; exacuo, [3].

whether, *c.* ~ . . . **or,** seu, sive; utrum . . . an, -ne . . . an, anne.

whey, *n.* serum, *nt.*

which, *a.* quis, qui? *m.*; uter? (*rel.*) qui, quae, quod; ~**ever,** quicunque, quisquis.

whiff, *n.* halitus, *m.*

while, *n.* tempus, spatium, *nt.*; mora, *f.*; **in a little ~,** brevi, postmodo; **for a ~,** paullulum.

while, whilst, *c.* dum, quoad; donec.

whim, *n.* libido, *f.*

whimper, *v.i.* vagio, [4].

whimsical, *a.* ridiculus, absurdus.

whine, *v.i.* vagio, [4]; queror, [3]; **~,** *n.* vagitus, *m.*; querela, *f.*

whip, *n.* flagellum, *nt.*; scutica, *f.*; **~,** *v.t.* flagello, verbero, [1].

whipping, *n.* verberatio, *f.*

whirl, *n.* vertex, turbo, *m.*; (of a spindle) verticillus, *m.*; vertigo, *f.*; **~,** *v.t.* torqueo, intorqueo, [2]; roto, [1]; **~,** *v.i.* rotor, [1]; torqueor, [2].

whirlpool, *n.* vertex, gurges, *m.*

whirlwind, *n.* turbo, typhon, *m.*

whisk, *n.* scopula, *f.*; **~,** *v.t.* verro, [3]; **~,** *v.i.* circumagor, [3].

whisper, *n.* susurrus, *m.*; murmur, *nt.*; **~,** *v.t. & i.* insusurro; susurro, murmuro, [1].

whistle, *v.i.* sibilo, [1]; **~,** *n.* (pipe) fistula, *f.*; (sound) sibilus, *m.*; sibila, *nt. pl.*; stridor, *m.*

white, *a.* albus, candidus; (of hair) canus; **~,** *n.* album, *nt.*; candor, *m.*

whiten, *v.t.* dealbo, [1]; candefacio, [3]; **~,** *v.i.* albesco; candesco; canesco, [3].

whiteness, *n.* albitudo, *f.*; candor, *m.*; (of hair) canities, *f.*

whitewash, *v.t.* dealbo, [1].

whither, *ad. & rel.* quo; quorsum; **~soever,** quocunque.

whitish, *a.* albidus, subalbus.

who, *pn.* quis? quae? quid? (*rel.*) qui; **~ever,** quicumque; quisquis.

whole, *a.* totus, omnis, cunctus; integer; plenus, solidus; (safe) salvus; **~,** *n.* summa, *f.*; omnia, *nt. pl.*; **on the ~,** plerumque.

wholesome, *n.* salubris, salutaris.

wholly, *ad.* omnino, prorsus.

whoop, *n.* ululatus, clamor, *m.*; **~,** *v.i.* clamo, vociferor, [1].

whore, *n.* meretrix, *f.*; scortum, *nt.*

whose, *rel. pn.* cuius.

why, *ad.* cur; quare? quamobrem?

wick, *n.* ellychnium, *nt.*

wicked, *a.* impius, nefarius, flagitiosus; malus, scelestus, sceleratus.

wickedness, *n.* nequitia, impietas, *f.*; scelus, flagitium, *nt.*

wicker, *n.* vimen, *nt.*; **~,** *a.* vimineus.

wide, *a.* latus, amplus; spatiosus; **far and ~,** late, passim, undique; **~ly,** *ad.* late, spatiose.

widen, *v.t.* (& *i.*) dilato(r); laxo(r), [1]; extendor, [3]; promoveor, [2].

widespread, *a.* longe lateque diffusus, pervulgatus.

widow, *n.* vidua, *f.*

widowed, *a.* viduatus, viduus.

widower, *n.* viduus vir, *m.*

width, *n.* latitudo; amplitudo; laxitas, *f.*

wield, *v.t.* tracto; guberno, [1]; gero, [3]; exerceo, [2].

wife, *n.* coniunx; uxor, marita, *f.*

wig, *n.* capillamentum, caliendrum, *nt.*

wild, *a.* ferus, silvestris; (of places) vastus; immanis; *fig.* incultus; saevus; insanus.

wilderness, *n.* locus desertus, *m.*; vastitas, solitudo, *f.*

wile, *n.* fraus, *f.*; dolus, *m.*; ars, *f.*

wilful, *a.* pervicax, obstinatus; ~ly, *ad.* pervicaciter; (deliberately) de industria.

will, *n.* voluntas; libido; auctoritas, *f.*; arbitrium, *nt.*; (purpose) propositum; (last ~) testamentum, *nt.*; ~, *v.t.* volo, *ir.*; iubeo, [2]; **leave by** ~, lego, [1]; relinquo, [3].

willing, *a.* libens, facilis, promptus; ~ly, *ad.* libenter; prompte.

willow, *n.* salix, *f.*

wily, *a.* vafer, astutus, callidus, dolosus, subdolus.

win, *v.t. & i.* lucror, [1]; lucrificio, [3]; (obtain) potior, [4] (*with abl.*); consequor, adipiscor, [3]; *fig.* expugno, [1]; (the battle, *etc.*) victoriam adipiscor, [3]; supero, [1]; vinco, [3].

wince, *v.i.* abhorreo, [2].

winch, *n.* sucula, *f.*

wind, *n.* ventus, *m.*; aura, *f.*; flatus, *m.*; flabra, *nt. pl.*

wind, *v.t.* circumvolvo; circumverto, [3]; glomero, [1]; torqueo, [2]; ~, *v.i.* sinuor, glomero, [1]; circumvolvor, [3]; ~ **up,** *fig.* concludo, [3].

windfall, *n. fig.* lucrum insperatum, *nt.*

winding, *a.* flexuosus, sinuosus.

windmill, *n.* mola, *f.*

window, *n.* fenestra, *f.*; specularia, *nt. pl.*

windpipe, *n.* arteria, *f.*

windy, *a.* ventosus.

wine, *n.* vinum, merum, *nt.*; ~ **cellar,** apotheca, *f.*

wing, *n.* ala, *f.*; pennae, *f. pl.*; *fig.* cornu; latus, *nt.*

winged, *a.* alatus, aliger, penniger, pennatus.

wink, *n.* nictus, *m.*; ~, *v.i.* nicto, [1]; coniveo, [2]; *fig.* ~ **at,** ignosco, praetermitto, [3].

winner, *n.* victor; superior, *m.*

winter, *n.* hiems, bruma, *f.*; ~, *v.t. & i.* hiemo, hiberno, [1].

winter, wintry, *a.* hiemalis, hibernus.

wipe, *v.t.* (de)tergeo, [2]; (the nose) emungo, [3]; (dry) sicco, [1]; (out) deleo, [2].

wire, *n.* filum metallicum, *nt.*

wisdom, *n.* sapientia, prudentia, *f.*

wise, *a.* sapiens, prudens; **~ly**, *ad.* sapienter; prudenter.

wish, *n.* optatio, *f.*; optatum; desiderium, *nt.*; voluntas, *f.*; **~**, *vt. & i.* opto, [1]; cupio, [3] volo, *ir.*; (long for) desidero, [1].

wisp, *n.* fasciculus, manipulus, *m.*

wistful, *a.* desiderii plenus.

wit, *n.* (intelligence) ingenium, *nt.*; (humour) facetiae, *f. pl.*; sal, lepos, *m.*; (person) vir acerrimo ingenio, *m.*

witch, *n.* saga, venefica, maga, *f.*

witchcraft, *n.* ars magica, *f.*; veneficium, *nt.*

with, *pr.* cum (*with abl.*); apud, penes (*both with acc.*); in (*with abl.*).

withdraw, *vt.* seduco, [3]; avoco, [1]; **~**, *vi.* recedo, [3].

wither, *vt.* torreo, [2]; sicco, [1]; uro, aduro, [3]; **~**, *vi.* marceo, [2]; aresco, languesco, [3].

withhold, *vt.* detineo, retineo; cohibeo, [2].

within, *ad.* intus, intro; **~**, *pr.* in (*with abl.*), intra (*with acc.*); **~ a few days**, paucis diebus.

without, *pr.* sine, absque (*with abl.*).

withstand, *vt.* obsisto, resisto, [3] (*with dat.*).

witness, *n.* testis, *c.*; arbiter, *m.*; testimonium, *nt.*; **call to ~**, *vt.* testor, obtestor; **~**, *vt. & i.* testificor, testor, [1].

witticism, *n.* dictum, *nt.*; sales, *m. pl.*

wittingly, *ad.* scienter; cogitate.

witty, *a.* argutus, lepidus; salsus; facetus; dicax.

wizard, *n.* magus, veneficus, *m.*

wizened, *a.* retorridus.

woad, *n.* vitrum, *nt.*

wobble, *v.i.* titubo, [1].

woe, *n.* dolor, luctus, *m.*; calamitas, *f.*

woeful, *a.* tristis, luctuosus, miser; maestus.

wolf, *n.* lupus, *m.*; (she **~**) lupa, *f.*

woman, *n.* femina, mulier, *f.*

womanly, *a.* muliebris.

womb, *n.* uterus, venter, *m.*; alvus, *f.*

wonder, *n.* miraculum; (astonishment) miratio, *f.*; stupor, *m.*; **~**, *vi.* admiror; miror, [1]; stupeo, [2]; (would like to know) scire velim, *ir.*

wonderful, *a.* mirabilis, mirus, mirificus, admirandus.

wood, *n.* lignum, *nt.*; (timber) materies, *f.*; (forest) silva, *f.*

wooded, *a.* silvosus; saltuosus.

wooden, *a.* ligneus.

woodland, *n.* silvae, *f. pl.*; nemora, *nt. pl.*

wood-nymph, *n.* Dryas, Hamadryas, *f.*

wood-pecker, *n.* picus, *m.*

woody, *a.* silvosus; silvestris; saltuosus.

woodworm, *n.* teredo, tinea, *f.*

wool, *n.* lana, *f.*

woollen, *a.* laneus.

woolly, *a.* (of wool) laneus; (as sheep, *etc.*) lanatus, laniger.

word, *n.* verbum; vocabulum; nomen; dictum, *nt.*; ~, *v.t.* verbis exprimo, describo, [3].

wordy, *a.* verbosus.

work, *n.* opera, *f.*; opus; (task) pensum, *nt.*; (trouble) labor, *m.*; ~, *v.i.* laboro, operor, [1]; ~, *v.t.* (handle) tracto, [1]; (ply) exerceo, [2]; (fashion) fabrico, [1]; (on) persuadeo, [2] (*with dat.*).

work-basket, *n.* calathus, *m.*

worker, *n.* operarius, *m.*; opifex, *c.*

working, *a.* operans; ~ **day,** negotiosus dies, *m.*

workman, *n.* opifex, artifex, faber, operarius, *m.*

workmanship, *n.* opus, *nt.*; ars, *f.*

workshop, *n.* officina, fabrica, *f.*

world, *n.* mundus, orbis, orbis terrarum, *m.*; **the next** ~, vita futura, *f.*; **where in the** ~, ubi gentium.

worldly, *a.* terrenus, humanus; saecularis, profanus.

worm, *n.* vermis, vermiculus, *m.* ~, *v.t.* (out) *fig.* extorqueo, [2]; expiscor, [1].

worried, *a.* anxius.

worry, *n.* anxietas, sollicitudo, vexatio, *f.*

worry, *v.t.* dilacero; *fig.* vexo, excrucio, [1].

worse, *a.* peior, deterior; ~, *ad.* peius; **make** ~, corrumpo, [3];

depravo, [1]; exaspero, [1]; **get** ~, ingravesco, [3].

worsen, *v.i.* ingravesco, [3].

worship, *n.* reverentia; adoratio, *f.*; cultus, *m.*; ~, *v.t.* veneror, adoro, [1]; colo, [3].

worst, *a.* pessimus; extremus, ultimus; ~, *ad.* pessime.

worth, *n.* pretium, *nt.*; dignitas, *f.*; (excellence) virtus, *f.*; ~, *a.* dignus; **be** ~, valeo, [2]; **it is** ~**while,** operae pretium est.

worthiness, *n.* meritum, *nt.*; dignitas, *f.*

worthless, *a.* vilis, levis; inutilis; nequam, (*indecl.*).

worthlessness, *n.* levitas, *f.*; inane, *nt.*

worthy, *a.* dignus, condignus.

wound, *n.* vulnus, *nt.*; plaga, *f.*; ~, *v.t.* vulnero, saucio, [1]; *fig.* offendo, laedo, [3].

wounded, *a.* saucius.

wrangle, *n.* rixa, altercatio, *f.*; iurgium, *nt.*; ~, *v.i.* rixor, altercor, [1].

wrap, *v.t.* involvo, obvolvo, [3]; velo, [1].

wrapper, *n.* involucrum; tegmen, *nt.*

wrath, *n.* ira; iracundia, *f.*; furor, *m.*

wreath, *n.* (of flowers) sertum, *nt.*; corona, *f.*

wreathe, *v.t.* torqueo, [2]; convolvo; necto, [3].

wreck, *n.* (shipwreck) naufragium; *fig.* damnum, *nt.*; ruina, *f.*; ~, *v.t.* frango, [3].

wrecked, *a.* (shipwrecked) naufragus; *fig.* fractus.

wrench, *v.t.* detorqueo, contorqueo, [2]; luxo, [1].

wrestle, *v.i.* luctor, [1].

wrestler, *n.* luctator, *m.*

wrestling, *n.* luctamen, *nt.*; luctatio, *f.*

wrestling-school, *n.* palaestra, *f.*

wretch, *n.* miser, perditus, nequam (*indecl.*), *m.*

wretched, *a.* miser, miserabilis, infelix, malus, vilis.

wriggle, *v.i.* torqueor, [2].

wring, *v.t.* torqueo, [2].

wrinkle, *n.* ruga *f.*; ~, *v.t.* rugo, corrugo, [1]; (the brow) (frontem) contraho, [3].

wrinkled, *a.* rugosus.

wrist, *n.* carpus, *m.*

write, *v.t.* & *i.* scribo; perscribo; (a literary work) compono, [3].

writer, *n.* (author) auctor, *m.*

writhe, *v.i.* torqueor, [2].

writing, *n.* (act) scriptio, *f.*; scriptum, *nt.*; scriptura; (hand) manus, *f.*; chirographum, *nt.*; (document) tabulae, *f. pl.*

writing-desk, *n.* scrinium, *nt.*

wrong, *a.* pravus, perversus; vitiosus; *fig.* falsus; iniustus, iniquus; ~ly, *ad.* falso; male, prave, perperam; **be** ~, erro, [1]; fallor, [3].

wrong, *n.* nefas, *nt. indecl.*; iniuria, *f.*; ~, *v.t.* laedo, [3]; violo, [1]; iniuriam infero, [3].

wrongful, *a.* iniustus, iniuriosus.

wry, *a.* distortus, obliquus; curvus.

Y

yacht, *n.* celox, *f.*

yard, *n.* (court) area; (for poultry) cohors; (measure) ulna, *f.*

yarn, *n.* filum, *nt.*; lana, *f.*; linum, *nt.*; *fig.* fabula, narratio, *f.*

yawn, *v.i.* oscito; *fig.* hio, [1]; (gape open) hisco, dehisco, [3]; ~, *n.* oscitatio, *f.*

year, *n.* annus, *m.*

yearly, *a.* annuus, anniversarius.

yearn, *v.i.* desidero, [1]; requiro; cupio, [3].

yearning, *n.* desiderium, *nt.*

yeast, *n.* fermentum, *nt.*

yell, *v.i.* ululo, clamo, [1]; ~, *n.* ululatus, clamor, *m.*

yellow, *a.* flavus, luteus, croceus.

yellowish, *a.* sufflavus, fulvus, gilvus.

yelp, *v.i.* gannio, [4].

yes, *ad.* ita, ita est; recte; immo; sane, certe.

yesterday, *ad.* heri; **of** ~, a hesternus, *m.*

yet, *c.* nihilominus, quamquam; tamen; (of time) adhuc; **even ~**, etiam nunc; **not ~**, nondum.

yew, *n.* taxus, *f.*

yield, *n.* fructus, *m.*

yield, *v.t.* (bring forth) fero, pario, [3]; praebeo, [2]; (give up) (con)cedo, [3]; **~**, *v.i.* cedo, [3]; manus do, [1].

yielding, *a.* obsequiosus; *fig.* mollis; lucrum afferens.

yoke, *n.* iugum, *nt.*; *fig.* servitus, *f.*; **~**, *v.t.* iugum impono, iungo, coniungo, [3].

yolk, *n.* luteum, *nt.*; vitellus, *m.*

you, *pn.* (singular) tu; (plural) vos; **~ yourselves**, tu ipse.

young, *a.* parvus, infans; *fig.* novus; **~**, *n.* adulescens, puer, *m.*; (offspring) progenies, *f.*; genus, *nt.*; fetus, *m.*; proles, *f.*

younger, *a.* iunior, minor.

youngster, *n.* adulescentulus, *m.*

your, *pr.* tuus; vester.

yourself, *pn.* tu ipse, tute; **yourselves**, vos ipsi.

youth, *n.* (age) adulescentia; iuventus, iuventa, iuventas;

(collectively) iuventus, *f.*; (young man) adulescens, iuvenis, *m.*

youthful, *a.* iuvenilis; puerilis.

Z

zeal, *n.* studium, *nt.*; fervor, *m.*; alacritas, *f.*

zealous, *a.* studiosus, alacer, acer, ardens.

zero, *n.* nihil, *nt.*

zest, *n.* sapor, gustus; *fig.* gustus; impetus, *m.*; studium, *nt.*

zigzag, *n.* anfractus, *m.*; **~**, *a.* obliquus.

zodiac, *n.* zodiacus, signifer orbis, *m.*

zone, *n.* (region of the earth) zona, *f.*

zoology, *n.* descriptio animantium, *f.*

List of Historical and Mythological Proper Names

Achaeī, ōrum, the ruling nation among the Greeks in Homeric times.

Achillēs, is, son of Peleus and of Thetis.

Actaeōn, onis, a huntsman torn to pieces by his own dogs for having seen Diana bathing.

Adōnis, is & idis, son of Cinyras, king of Cyprus, beloved by Venus; beautiful young man.

Aegēus, ēī, father of Theseus.

Aenēās, ae, son of Anchises and Venus.

Agamemnōn, onis, king of Mycenae, commander-in-chief of the Greek forces at Troy.

Aiāx, ācis, ~ Telamōnius & ~, son of Oïleus, two Greek heroes in the Trojan war.

Alcīdēs, ae, Hercules (descendant of Alceus).

Alcyonē, ēs, wife of Ceyx; she was changed into a kingfisher.

Amphitrītē, ēs, wife of Neptune, goddess of the sea.

Anchīsēs, ae, father of Aeneas.

Andromacha, ae, Andromachē, ēs, wife of Hector.

Andromeda, ae, daughter of Cepheus and Cassiope; rescued by Perseus from a sea-monster.

Anūbis, is & idis, Egyptian dog-headed god.

Apellēs, is, renowned Greek painter.

Apollō, inis, god of the sun, prophecy, music and poetry, archery and medicine, son of Jupiter and Leto.

Archimēdēs, is, mathematician and mechanical inventor at Syracuse of the 3rd century B.C.

Argō, f. ship in which the Greek heroes under Jason sailed to Colchis to obtain the golden fleece.

Argonautae, ārum, m. pl. the heroes who sailed in the *Argo*.

Argus, ī, the hundred-eyed keeper of Io.

Ariadnē, ēs, daughter of Minos, king of Crete.

Ascanius, iī, son of Aeneas; founder of Alba Longa.

Atalanta, ae, (1) daughter of Iasius; took part in the hunt of the Calydonian boar; (2) daughter of Schoeneus; very swift of foot; engaged in a race with Hippomenes and was defeated by a ruse.

Atlās, antis, a giant who supported the heavens on his shoulders.

Atreus, ei, king of Mycenae, father of Agamemnon and Menelaus.

Bacchus, ī, god of wine, son of Jupiter and Semele.

Bellerophōn, ontis, slayer of the Chimaera; rode the winged horse Pegasus.

Bellōna, ae, goddess of war.

Bona Dea, a goddess, worshipped by Roman women as goddess of Fertility and Chastity on the 1st of May.

Boreās, ae, the north wind.

C. = Cāius.

Cācus, ī, a giant, son of Vulcan, slain by Hercules.

Calypsō, *f.* a nymph, daughter of Oceanus, ruling over the island Ogygia.

Camēnae, ārum, Roman goddesses identified with the Muses.

Cassandra, ae, prophetess, daughter of Priam and Hecuba.

Castor, oris, twin-brother of Pollux, son of Tyndareus.

Catō, ōnis, (1) the censor, author of the phrase, **dēlenda est Carthāgō** (Carthage must be destroyed); born 234 B.C.; (2) an opponent of Caesar; committed suicide at Utica when his cause was defeated, 49 B.C.

Centaurī, ōrum, *m. pl.* a wild race of Thessaly, half-man, half-horse.

Cerberus, ī, three-headed dog, guarding the entrance to Hell.

Charōn, ōnis, ferryman of the Lower World.

Chīrō(n), ōnis, a Centaur who tutored Aesculapius, Hercules and Achilles.

Cincinnātus, ī, Roman dictator (485 B.C.).

Circē, ēs & ae, a famous sorceress.

Cleopātra, ae, queen of Egypt, daughter of Ptolemy Auletes; loved by Antony.

Clīō, ūs, *f.* Muse of History.

Clōthō, ō (*acc.*), *f.* one of the Fates (who span the thread of Fate).

Clytaemnēstra, ae, wife of Agamemnon.

Coriolānus, surname of C. Marcius, who took Corioli; became an enemy of his countrymen, the Romans.

Croesus, ī, king of Lydia; a rich man.

Cyclōps, ōpos, Cyclops; ~**Cyclōpes, um,** *m. pl.* one-eyed giants, workmen in Vulcan's smithy.

Cytherēa, ae, f. Venus.

Danaē, ēs, mother of Perseus.

Daphnē, ēs, daughter of the river-god Peneus, loved by Apollo.

Dardanus, ī, ancestor of the Trojan dynasty.

Decius Mūs, consul 340 B.C.; devoted himself to death to save his country.

Deucaliōn, ōnis, king of Phthia in Thessaly, son of Prometheus; with his wife Pyrrha was the only mortal saved from the flood.

Diāna, ae, goddess of hunting, sister of Apollo.

Dīdō, ōnis, foundress of Carthage.

Dīs, Dītis =Pluto.

Dryades, um, f. pl. woodnymphs.

Echidna, ae, f. Lernaean hydra, killed by Hercules.

Ēlectra, ae, daughter of Agamemnon and Clytemnestra.

Endymiōn, ōnis, a beautiful youth, beloved by Diana.

Epēus, ī, constructor of the Wooden Horse at Troy.

Epicūrus, ī, Greek philosopher, originator of the Epicurean philosophy.

Eratō, f. one of the Muses, associated by Ovid with love poetry.

Erebus, ī, god of darkness; the Lower World.

Eurōpa, ae, Eurōpē, ēs, daughter of Agenor, king of Phoenicia; carried off by Jupiter in the form of a bull.

Eurydicē, ēs, wife of Orpheus.

Euterpē, ēs, f. a Muse, later associated with the reed-pipe.

Evander, drī, emigrated from Arcadia to Italy 60 years before the Trojan War.

Faunī, ōrum, nt. pl. Fauns.

Feretrius, iī, an epithet of Jupiter as worshipped on the Capitol at Rome.

Flōra, ae, goddess of the flowers and spring.

Fortūna, ae, the Goddess Fortune.

Galatēa, ae, a sea-nymph, beloved by Acis.

Ganymēdēs, is, Jupiter's cupbearer.

Gēryōn, onis, m. a mythical three-bodied monster who lived in Erythea, an island in the far west; his oxen were carried off by Hercules.

Gigantes, um, the Giants.

Gorgō(n), onis, Medusa, daughter of Phorcus, and her

two sisters were called the Gorgons.

Grādīvus, ī, a title of Mars.

Hamilcar, aris, father of Hannibal.

Hannibal, alis, Punic surname; great Carthaginian general during the Second Punic War, son of Hamilcar.

Hannō, ōnis, Punic surname; opponent of Hannibal.

Harpȳiae, ārum, *f. pl.* mythical rapacious monsters, half-bird, half-woman.

Hasdrubal, alis, (1) brother of Hannibal; (2) son-in-law of Hamilcar.

Hēbē, ēs, goddess of youth, cupbearer to the gods.

Hecatē, ēs, a goddess of the Lower World, worshipped as goddess of spells and enchantments.

Hector, oris, son of Priam and Hecuba.

Hecuba, ae, wife of Priam.

Helena, ae, Helenē, ēs, (1) daughter of Jupiter and Leda, wife of Menelaus; (2) mother of Constantine the Great.

Hellē, ēs, *f.* daughter of Athamas, king of Boeotia, was drowned in the narrow sea (Hellespont) called after her.

Herculēs, is & (e)ī, son of Jupiter and Alcmene, a demigod and divine hero.

Hesperidēs, um, *f. pl.* daughters of Erebus and the Night; they lived in an island garden beyond Mt Atlas and guarded the golden apples which Juno received on her wedding.

Hesperus, ī, son of Atlas, or of Cephalus, and Aurora; planet Venus as evening-star.

Hōrae, ārum, *f. pl.* the Hours, goddesses of the seasons.

Hyacinthus, ī, beautiful youth beloved by Apollo, and accidentally killed by him.

Hȳdra, ae, *f.* seven-headed serpent, killed by Hercules.

Hylās, ae, beautiful youth who accompanied Hercules on the Argonautic expedition.

Hyperīōn, ōnis, son of a Titan and the Earth; the Sun.

Iacchus, ī, Bacchus.

Iāsōn, onis, son of Aeson, king of Thessaly, Grecian hero.

Īcarus, ī, son of Daedalus; tried to fly from Crete and fell into the sea.

Īlia, ae, Rhea Silvia, mother of Romulus and Remus.

Īlium, iī, *nt.* Troy.

Īō, daughter of Inachus; beloved of Zeus, turned into a cow and pursued by Argus.

Īphigenīa, ae, daughter of Agamemnon and Clytemnestra.

Īris, idis, daughter of Thaumas and Electra, messenger of the gods and goddess of the rainbow.

Īsis, idis & is, Egyptian goddess, wife of Osiris.

Itys, yos, son of Tereus and Procne; made into pie and served up to father.

Iūlus, ī, son of Aeneas, called also Ascanius.

Iūnō, ōnis, goddess and wife of Jupiter.

Iuppiter, Iovis, Jupiter, the chief Roman god.

L. = Lūcius.

Lāocoōn, ontis, a Trojan priest of Apollo.

Lāodamīa, wife of Protesilaus.

Lāomedōn, ontis, father of Priam, king of Troy, killed by Hercules.

Latīnus, ī, king of the Laurentians.

Lātōna, ae, mother of Apollo and Diana, **Lāvīnia, ae,** daughter of Latinus, wife of Aeneas.

Lēander, drī, the lover of Hero.

Lēda, ae, Lēdē, ēs, wife of Tyndareus, mother of Clytemnestra, Helen, Castor and Pollux.

Līber, erī, Bacchus.

Lībera, ae, Proserpine.

Libitīna, ae, goddess of funerals.

Lūcifer, ī, *m.* planet Venus as morning-star.

Lūcīna, ae, goddess of childbirth.

Lūna, ae, the goddess of the Moon.

Lupercālia, ium, *nt. pl.* festival of the god Lupercus on the 15th of February.

M. = Mārcus; M'. = Mānius.

Maeonidēs, ae, Homer.

Māia, ae, mother of Mercury by Jupiter.

Marius, a, um, Roman gentile name; **C. ~,** conquered Jugurtha; crushed the Cimbri and Teutons; consul in 107 B.C. and six times subsequently.

Mars, tis, the god of war.

Mausōlus, ī, king of Caria, died 353 B.C.; his tomb was a costly monument called the Mausōlēum.

Māvors, ortis, v. **Mars.**

Maximus, Q. Fabius, surnamed **Cūnctātor;** commanded against Hannibal, 217–214 B.C.

Mēdēa, ae, daughter of Aeetes, king of Colchis; deserted by Jason, killed her own children.

Melpomenē, ēs, *f.* one of the Muses, later associated with tragedy.

Memnōn, onis, son of Tithonus and Aurora, king of the Ethiopians.

Menelāus, ī, brother of Agamemnon.

Mentor, ōris, faithful friend of Ulysses.

Mercurius, iī, son of Jupiter and Maia, the messenger of the gods; the god of eloquence and of merchants and thieves.

Midās, ae, king of Phrygia; all he touched was turned into gold.

Minerva, ae, daughter of Zeus, goddess of wisdom, of the arts, of handicraft and women's works.

Mīnōs, ōis, son of Zeus and Europa, king of Crete.

Mīnōtaurus, ī, *m.* monster with the head of a bull in the Labyrinth of Crete.

Mnēmosynē, ēs, *f.* Memory, the mother of the Muses.

Morpheus, ea (*acc.*), god of dreams.

Mūsa, ae, *f.* Muse.

Narcissus, ī, son of Cephissus, enamoured of his own beauty and turned into a flower named after him.

Nemesis, eōs, goddess of retribution.

Neptūnus, ī, the god of the sea.

Nēreus, ei & eos, a sea-god, son of Oceanus and Thetys.

Nessus, ī, *m.* a Centaur, killed by Hercules.

Nestor, oris, king of Pylos, one of the oldest of the Greek heroes at Troy.

Numitor, ōris, king of Alba, father of Ilia, grandfather of Romulus and Remus.

Olympia, ōrum, *nt. pl.* the Olympic games at Olympia.

Ops, Opis, goddess of plenty, wife of Saturn.

Orestēs, is, son of Agamemnon; killed his mother Clytemnestra.

Ōrīōn, ōnis, son of Hyrieus, a hunter; the constellation Orion.

Orpheus, eī, son of Oeagrus and Calliope, husband of Eurydice.

Osīris, is, Egyptian god, husband of Isis.

P. = Pūblius.

Palēs, is, *f.* or *m.* tutelar goddess of flocks and herds.

Palinūrus, ī, the pilot of Aeneas.

Palladium, ī, *n.* statue of Pallas in the citadel of Troy; captured by Ulysses and Diomedes.

Pallas, adis & ados, Minerva, Athena.

Pān, Pānos, son of Mercury, the god of woods and shepherds, half-man, half-goat.

Parca, ae, *f.* one of the Fates; ~Parcae, *pl.* the Fates, three sisters.

Paris, idis, a son of Priam and Hecuba; carried off Helen, wife of Menelaus.

Pāsiphaē, ēs, daughter of Helios, wife of Minos, and sister of Circe.

Patroclus, ī, friend of Achilles, slain by Hector.

Pēgasus, ī, *m.* a winged horse, sprung from the blood of the slain Medusa; with the aid of Pegasus Bellerophon slew the Chimaera.

Pēleus, eī & eos, king of a part of Thessaly, husband of Thetis, father of Achilles.

Pēnēus, ī, *m.* god of a river flowing through the vale of Tempe in Thessaly.

Pentheus, eī & eos, king of Thebes, grandson of Cadmus; opposed the worship of Bacchus and was torn in pieces by his mother.

Perseus, eī & eos, son of Jupiter and Danae, killer of the Medusa, husband of Andromeda.

Phaedra, ae, daughter of Minos, and second wife of Theseus; fell in love with Hippolytus.

Phaëthōn, ontis, son of Helios and Clymene; tried to drive the chariot of the sun.

Philomēla, ae, daughter of Pandion, sister of Procne; turned into a nightingale.

Phoebus, ī, Apollo.

Plēïades, um, the seven daughters of Atlas and Pleione.

Plūtō, Plūtōn, ōnis, the god of the Underworld.

Pollūx, ūcis, son of Tyndareus and Leda, brother of Castor.

Polyphēmus, ī, a Cyclops; son of Neptune.

Polyxena, ae, daughter of Priam; sacrificed to Achilles after the Trojan War.

Pōmōna, ae, the goddess of fruits.

Portūnus, ī, tutelar god of harbours.

Priamus, ī, king of Troy, son of Laomedon.

Priāpus, ī, *m.* a god of procreation.

Procnē, ēs, daughter of Pandion, wife of Tereus; she was turned into a swallow.

Procrustēs, ae, highwayman in Attica, slain by Theseus; had a bed which all his victims were made to fit.

Promētheus, eī & eos, son of Iapetus and Clymene; stole fire from heaven and gave it to mortals.

Proserpina, ae, daughter of Ceres, wife of Pluto.

Prōtesilāus, ī, husband of Laodamia; the first of the Greek expedition to land at Troy and the first killed.

Pygmalīōn, ōnis, king of Cyprus; fell in love with a statue he had made himself; Venus then brought it to life.

Pyladēs, is, son of king Strophius, bosom-friend of Orestes.

Pȳramus, ī, the lover of Thisbe.

Pȳthōn, ōnis, *m.* a serpent slain by Apollo near Delphi.

Q.=Quīntus.

Remus, ī, brother of Romulus.

Rhadamanthus, ī, son of Jupiter, brother of Minos, judge in the Lower World.

Rhēa Silvia, daughter of Numitor, mother of Romulus and Remus.

Rōmulus, ī, founder and first king of Rome.

S. *or* Sex. = Sextus.

Sāturnia, ae, Juno.

Sāturnus, ī, father of Jupiter, originally a mythical king of Latium.

Satyrī, ōrum, Satyrs; companions of Bacchus.

Scylla, ae, *f.* a sea-monster; lived on the Italian side of the Straits of Messina, opposite Charybdis.

Semelē, ēs, daughter of Cadmus, mother of Bacchus, by Jupiter.

Serāpis, is & idis, *m.* an Egyptian god.

Sibylla, ae, a one of a class of prophetic females variously located.

Sīlēnus, ī, tutor of Bacchus, elderly, drunken, and bestial in character.

Silvānus, ī, *m.* god of the woods.

Spartacus, ī, a Thracian gladiator, leader of the gladiators in their war against Rome; killed 71 B.C.

Sȳrīnx, ingis, *f.* a nymph changed into the reed from which Pan made his pipes.

T. = Titus.

Tantalus, ī, son of Jupiter, father of Pelops and Niobe; divulged the secrets of the gods; was punished in the Underworld by a raging thirst which he could not quench.

Tarpēia, ae, Roman maiden, who treacherously opened the citadel to the Sabines.

Tarquinius Superbus, the last king of Rome.

Tēreus, eī & eos, king of Thrace, husband of Procne, and father of Itys; cut out the tongue of his wife's sister Philomela; Procne, in revenge, killed Itys and served him up to her husband in a dish.

Terpsichorē, ēs, *f.* a Muse, in later times associated with lyric poetry (dance).

Tēthys, yos, a sea-goddess, wife of Oceanus.

Thalīa, ae, *f.* the Muse of comedy or light verse.

Themis, is, goddess of justice and order.

Thēseus, eī & eos, king of Athens, son of Aegis.

Thespis, is, a pioneer of Greek tragedy.

Thetis, idis & idos, a sea-nymph, daughter of Nereus, wife of Peleus, and mother of Achilles.

Thisbē, ēs, maiden of Babylon, beloved by Pyramus.

Ti. = Tiberius, Roman first name.

Tīresiās, ae, a blind prophet of Thebes.

Tīsiphonē, ēs, *f.* a Fury.

Tītān, ānos, one of the Titans, a race of gods descended from Heaven and Earth, who preceded the Olympians; the sun-god.

Tīthōnus, ī, son of Laomedon, husband of Aurora.

Tityos, i, a giant punished in the underworld for attempting, on Juno's orders, to rape Latona.

Trītōn, ōnis, *m.* one of a kind of supernatural marine beings, represented as blowing conches and attending on Neptune.

Trītōnis, idis & idos, Minerva, Athena.

Turnus, ī, king of the Rutuli; killed by Aeneas.

Tyndaris, idis, Helen, daughter of Tyndareus.

Typhōeus, eos, a giant, struck with lightning by Jupiter, and buried under Aetna.

Ulixēs, is & eī, Ulysses, king of Ithaca, one of the Grecian heroes at Troy.

Ūrania, ae, *f.* the Muse of Astronomy.

Venus, eris, goddess of Love.

Verrēs, is, governor of Sicily, 73-71 B.C.; denounced by Cicero for his rapacity.

Vertumnus, ī, *m.* god of the seasons.

Vesta, ae, daughter of Saturn and Rhea, goddess of the hearth-fire and of domestic life.

Volcānus, v. **Vulcānus.**

Vulcānus, ī, lame son of Juno, god of fire.

Zephyrus, ī, the west wind.

List of Geographical Names

Acadēmīa, ae, a gymnasium near Athens in which Plato taught.

Achelōus, ī, *m.* the largest river in Greece, rises in Mt Pindus and flows into the Ionian Sea.

Acherōn, ontis, *m.* river in the Underworld.

Achīvus, a, um, *a.* Achaean, Grecian.

Actium, ī, *nt.* promontory and town in Epirus; celebrated for the victory of Augustus over Antony, 31 B.C.

Aegyptius, a, um, *a.* Egyptian.

Aegyptus, ī, *f.* Egypt.

Aetna, ae, Aetnē, ēs, *f.* Mt Etna, a volcano in Sicily.

Āfrī, ōrum, *m. pl.* Africans.

Āfrica, ae, *f.* Africa; Libya.

Alba, Alba Longa, ae, *f.* mother city of Rome (between the Alban Lake and Mons Albanus).

Albānī, ōrum, *m. pl.* inhabitants of Alba Longa.

Alexandrīa, ae, *f.* town on the north coast of Egypt, founded by Alexander the Great.

Alpēs, ium, *f. pl.* the Alps.

Alpīnus, a, um, *a.* of the Alps.

Āpennīnus, ī, *m.* the Apennine mountains.

Āpūlia, ae, *f.* province of south-east Italy.

Arabia, ae, *f.* Arabia.

Arabicus, Arabus, a, um, *a.* Arabian.

Argīlētum, ī, *nt.* quarter of the city of Rome which contained many booksellers' and cobblers' shops.

Argīvus, a, um, *a.* of Argos; Greek.

Asia, ae, *f.* (1) Asia; (2) the Roman province of Asia Minor.

Ātella, ae, *f.* an Oscan town of Campania, the home of a particular kind of farce.

Athēnae, ārum, *f. pl.* Athens.

Athēniēnsis, e, *a.* Athenian.

Atlās, antis, *m.* mountain-range in the north-west of Africa.

Attica, ae, *f.* city state of Greece, the capital of which was Athens.

Atticus, a, um, *a.* Attic, Athenian.

Aulis, idis, *f.* seaport town in Boeotia from which the Greek fleet sailed for Troy.

Ausonia, ae, *f.* Italy.

Aventīnus, ī, *m.* Aventine (one of the seven hills of Rome); ~, **a, um,** *a.* relating to the Aventine.

Avernus (lacus), ī, *m.* Lago d'Averno, a lake near Naples that gave off mephitic vapours, considered to be the entrance to the Underworld.

Belgae, ārum, *m. pl.* the Belgians.

Belgicus, a, um, *a.* Belgian, Belgic.

Bēnācus, ī, *m.* Lago di Garda, a lake of North Italy.

Bīthȳnia, ae, *f.* district of Asia Minor between the Propontis and the Black Sea.

Bīthȳnicus, a, um, Bīthȳnus, a, um, *a.* Bithynian.

Boeōtia, ae, *f.* district of Greece, the capital of which was Thebes.

Bosporus, ī, or **Bosphorus, m.** ~ **Thrācius,** the strait between the sea of Marmora and the Black Sea; ~ **Cimmerius,** strait between the sea of Azof and the Black Sea.

Britannia, ae, *f.* Britain.

Britannus, a, um, Britannicus, a, um, *a.* British.

Brundisium, iī, *nt.* Brindisi, a seaport of Calabria.

Byzantium, iī, *nt.* Istanbul.

Caecubum, ī, *nt.* marshy district in southern Latium (producing the most excellent kind of Roman wine).

Calabria, ae, *f.* a district of south-east Italy.

Calēdonia, ae, *f.* northern part of Britain.

Campānia, ae, *f.* a district of Italy south of Latium.

Cannae, ārum, *f. pl.* village in Apulia; the scene of the defeat of the Romans by Hannibal in 216 B.C.

Cantium, iī, *nt.* Kent.

Cappadocia, ae, *f.* province of Asia Minor, between Cilicia and Pontus.

Cāria, ae, *f.* country in the south-west of Asia Minor.

Carthāgō, inis, *f.* Carthage; ~ **Nova,** the modern Cartagena on the south-east coast of Spain.

Castalia, ae, *f.* fountain on Mt Parnassus at Delphi sacred to Apollo and the Muses.

Castalius, a, um, *a.* Castalian.

Caucasus, ī, *m.* chain of mountains between the Black and Caspian Seas.

Caystros, ī, *m.* river in Lydia noted for its swans.

Celtae, ārum, *m. pl.* the Celts.

Celticus, a, um, *a.* Celtic.

Charybdis, is, *f.* dangerous whirlpool between Italy and Sicily opposite to Scylla.

Cherronēsus, Chersonēsus, ī, *f.* Chersonese; (1) Thracian; Gallipoli peninsula; (2) Tauric, between the Black Sea and the Sea of Azof.

Cilices, um, *m. pl.* Cilicians.

Cilicia, ae, *f.* province in the south-east of Asia Minor.

Cōcȳtus, ī, *m.* river in the Underworld.

Colchis, idis, *f.* country in Asia, east of the Black Sea; ~, Colchian woman.

Colchus, a, um, Colchicus, a, um, *a.* of Colchis.

Corinthiacus, a, um, Corinthius, a, um, *a.* Corinthian.

Corinthus, ī, *f.* a city of Greece, on the Corinthian isthmus.

Crēs, ētis, *m.*, Cretan.

Crēta, ae, *f.* Crete.

Cūmae, ārum, *f. pl.* city on the coast of Campania.

Cynthius, a, um, *a.* relating to Cynthus.

Cynthus, ī, *m.* mountain of Delos.

Cyprius, a, um, *a.* of Cyprus.

Cyprus, ī, *f.* island in the Mediterranean Sea south of Cilicia.

Dācī, ōrum, *m. pl.* the Dacians.

Dācia, ae, *f.* country of the Dacians on the north of the Danube.

Danaī, ōrum, *m. pl.* the Greeks.

Dānuvius, iī, *m.* Danube.

Dēlius, a, um, *a.* of Delos.

Dēlos, ī, *f.* the smallest of the Cyclades, famous for the worship of Apollo.

Delphī, ōrum, *m. pl.* Delphi (in Phocis), containing a famous oracle of Apollo; ~, inhabitants of Delphi.

Delphicus, a, um, *a.* of Delphi.

Dēva, ae, *f.* Chester.

Dīa, ae, *f.* Naxos.

Dictaeus, a, um, *a.* of Dicte.

Dictē, ēs, *f.* mountain in Crete.

Dōdōna, ae, *f.* town in Epirus with a famed oracle of Jupiter.

Eborācum, ī, *nt.* town in Britain, the modern York.

Elȳsium, iī, *nt.* the abode of the blessed in the Underworld.

Elȳsius, a, um, *a.* Elysian.

Ēmathia, ae, *f.* district of Macedonia.

Ēpīrōticus, a, um, *a.* of Epirus.

Ēpīrus, Ēpiros, ī, *f.* country in the north-west of Greece.

Erebus, ī, *m.* the Underworld; the god of darkness.

Eryx, ycis, *m.* mountain in Sicily, on which stood a temple of Venus.

Esquiliae, ārum, *f. pl.* one of the seven hills of Rome.

Esquilīnus, a, um, *a.* of the Esquiline hill.

Etrūria, ae, *f.* country on the west coast of central Italy.

Etruscus, a, um, *a.* Etrurian.

Eurōpa, ae, *f.* (the continent of) Europe.

Euxīnus Pontus, *m.* Black Sea.

Gādēs, ium, *f. pl.* Cadiz.

Galatia, ae, *f.* country of the Galatians; a district of Asia Minor.

Gallī, ōrum, *m. pl.* the Gauls.

Gallia, ae, *f.* Gaul.

Gallicus, a, um, Gallicānus, a, um, *a.* Gallic.

Germānī, ōrum, *m. pl.* the Germans.

Germānia, ae, *f.* Germany.

Germānicus, a, um, Germānus, a, um, *a.* German.

Glēvum, ī, *n.* Gloucester.

Graecī, ōrum, *m. pl.* Greeks.

Graecia, ae, *f.* Greece.

Graecus, a, um, *a.* Greek.

Grāiī, ōrum, *m. pl.* Greeks.

Hadria, ae, *m.* Adriatic Sea.

Helicōn, ōnis, *m.* mountain in Boeotia (sacred to Apollo and the Muses).

Hellēspontus, ī, *m.* the Dardanelles.

Helvētiī, ōrum, *m. pl.* a Gallic people, in modern Switzerland.

Helvētius, a, um, Helvēticus, a, *a.* Swiss.

Hibēria, ae, *f.* Spain.

Hibēricus, a, um, *a.* Spanish.

Hibērnia, ae, *f.* Ireland.

Hierosolyma, ōrum, *nt. pl.* Jerusalem.

Hippocrēnē, ēs, *f.* a spring on Mt Helicon, made by Pegasus with a blow of his hoof.

Hispānī, ōrum, *m. pl.* the Spaniards.

Hispānia, ae, *f.* Spain.

Hispāniēnsis, e, Hispānicus, a, um, Hispānus, a, um, *a.* Spanish.

Hymettus, Hymettos, ī, *m.* mountain near Athens, famous for its honey and marble.

Īda, ae, Īdē, ēs, *f.* (1) mountain in Crete; (2) mountain-range near Troy.

Īlium, Īlion, iī, *nt.,* **Īlios, ī,** *f.* Troy.

Īlius, a, um, *a.* of Troy, Trojan.

Indicus, a, um, Indus, a, um, *a.* Indian.

Iōnium mare, part of the Mediterranean between Italy and Greece.

Ister, trī, *m.* (lower part of the) Danube.

Italia, ae, *f.* Italy.

Italicus, a, um, Ītalus, a, um, *a.* Italian.

Ithaca, ae, *f.* island in the Ionian Sea, the kingdom of Ulysses.

Iūdaea, ae, f. Judaea, the country of the Jews.

Iūdaeus, a, um, Iūdaicus, a, um, a. Jewish.

Lacedaemonius, a, um, a. Spartan.

Latium, iī, n. a district of Italy in which Rome was situated.

Latius, a, um, Latīnus, a, um, a. Latin.

Lāvīnium, iī, n. a city of Latium.

Lerna, ae, Lernē, ēs, f. a forest and marsh near Argos, the haunt of the hydra.

Lēthē, ēs, f. river of the Underworld which conferred oblivion on those who drank of it.

Libya, ae, Libyē, ēs, f. Libya; North Africa.

Libycus, a, um, a. Libyan.

Londinium, iī, nt. London.

Lupercal, ālis, nt. grotto on the Palatine Hill, sacred to god Lupercus.

Lutētia, ae, f. the modern Paris.

Lycēum, ī, nt. a gymnasium near Athens where Aristotle taught.

Lycia, ae, f. a country in the south of Asia Minor.

Lycius, a, um, a. Lycian.

Lȳdia, ae, f. a country in western Asia Minor, the capital of which was Sardes.

Macedones, um, m. pl. the Macedonians.

Macedonia, ae, f. country of the Macedonians, a large district in the north of Greece.

Macedonicus, a, um, Macedonius, a, um, a. Macedonian.

Massicus, ī, m. Monte Massico, a mountain of Campania celebrated for its wine.

Massilia, ae, f. Marseilles.

Maurī, ōrum, m. pl. the Moors.

Maurītānia, ae, f. country of the Moors, Morocco.

Mēdī, ōrum, m. pl. the Medes.

Mēdia, ae, f. country of the Medes, situated between Armenia, Parthia, Hyrcania, and Assyria.

Mēdicus, a, um, Mēdus, a, um, a. of the Medes.

Mediolānum, ī, nt. Milan, a town of North Italy.

Melita, ae, Melitē, ēs, f. Malta, island in the Mediterranean.

Mesopotamia, ae, f. a country of Asia, between the Euphrates and Tigris.

Mīlēsius, a, um, a. of Miletus.

Mīlētus, ī, m. city of Asia Minor.

Mona, ae, f. (1) Isle of Man; (2) Isle of Anglesey.

Mycēnae, ārum, Mycēnē, ēs, f. a city in Argolis, the city of Agamemnon.

Myrmidones, um, m. pl. a people of Thessaly, ruled by Achilles.

Neāpolis, is, *f.* Naples, a city of Campania.

Neāpolītānus, a, um, *a.* Neapolitan.

Nīlus, ī, *m.* the Nile.

Nōricum, ī, *nt.* a country between the Danube and the Alps, west of Pannonia.

Nōricus, a, um, *a.* of Noricum.

Numidae, ārum, *m. pl.* a people of northern Africa.

Numidia, ae, *f.* country of the Numidians.

Numidicus, a, um, *a.* Numidian.

Olympia, ae, *f.* the grove and shrine of Olympian Zeus in Elis where the Olympian games were held.

Olympiacus, a, um, Olympicus, a, um, Olympius, a, um, *a.* Olympian, Olympic.

Olympus, ī, *m.* (1) a mountain on the boundary of Macedonia and Thessaly, seat of the gods; (2) a mountain in Mysia.

Ōstia, ae, *f.*, **Ōstia, ōrum,** *nt. pl.* a seaport town in Latium, at the mouth of the Tiber.

Padus, ī, *m.* the Po.

Palātium, iī, *nt.* the Palatine, one of the seven hills of Rome.

Pannonia, ae, *f.* a country between the Danube and the Alps, east of Noricum.

Paphlagonia, ae, *f.* a province of Asia Minor on the Black Sea.

Parnas(s)os, Parnas(s)us, ī, *m.* a mountain in Phocis sacred to Apollo and to the Muses.

Paros, ī, *f.* one of the Cyclades, noted for its marble.

Parthī, ōrum, *m. pl.* a Scythian people, the Parthians.

Parthia, ae, *f.* country of the Parthians.

Parthicus, a, um, Parthus, a, um, *a.* Parthian.

Patavium, iī, *nt.* Padua.

Patavīnus, a, um, *a.* of Padua.

Pelasgī, ōrum, *m. pl.* the oldest inhabitants of Greece; the Greeks.

Pelion, iī, *nt.* a mountain in eastern Thessaly.

Pēnēus, ī, *m.* river of Thessaly, flowing through the Valley of Tempe.

Pergamum, ī, *nt.* **Pergamos, ī,** *f.*, **Pergama, ōrum,** *nt. pl.* the citadel of Troy; Troy.

Persae, ārum, *m. pl.* the Persians.

Persis, idis, *f.* Persia.

Persicus, a, um, *a.* Persian.

Pharsālos, Pharsālus, ī, *f.* a town in Thessaly, noted for the defeat of Pompey by Caesar, 48 B.C.

Pharus, Pharos, ī, *f.* an island near Alexandria, famous for its lighthouse.

Philippī, ōrum, *m. pl.* a city in Macedonia.

Phlegethōn, ontis, *m.* a river in the Underworld.

Phoenissa, ae, *f.* a Phoenician woman.

Phrygēs, um, *m. pl.* Phrygians; Trojans.

Phrygia, ae, *f.* Phrygia; Troy.

Phrygius, a, um, Phryx, ygis, *a.* Phrygian; Trojan.

Pīeria, ae, *f.* (1) a district of Macedonia, famous for the worship of the Muses; (2) a district of Syria.

Pīrēnē, ēs, *f.* a fountain in the citadel of Corinth.

Pīsa, ae, Pīsae, ārum, *f.* a city of Elis, near which the Olympic games were held.

Poenī, ōrum, *m. pl.* the Carthaginians.

Pompēiī, ōrum, *m. pl.* a maritime city in the south of Campania, near Vesuvius.

Ponticus, a, um, *a.* of the Pontus.

Pontus, ī, *m.* (1) the Black Sea; (2) north-eastern province of Asia Minor.

Propontis, idos & idis, *f.* the Sea of Marmora.

Pūnicus, a, um, *a.* Punic, Carthaginian.

Pȳrēnaeus, a, um, *a.* of the Pyrenees.

Pȳthō(n), ōnis, *f.* old name of Delphi.

Rhēnus, ī, *m.* the Rhine.

Rhodanus, ī, *m.* the Rhone.

Rhodos, ī, Rhodus, ī, *f.* Rhodes; town of the same name in the island of Rhodes.

Rōma, ae, *f.* Rome.

Rōmānus, a, um, *a.* Roman.

Rubicō(n), ōnis, *m.* a small boundary-stream between Italy and Cisalpine Gaul; the crossing of the Rubicon by Caesar, 49 B.C., was the prelude to the civil war.

Rutulī, ōrum, *m. pl.* a people of Latium, whose capital was Ardea.

Sabellus, a, um, Sabellicus, a, um, *a.* Sabine.

Sabīnī, ōrum, *m. pl.* the Sabines, an ancient Italian people.

Samnium, iī, *nt.* a country of central Italy, inhabited by the Samnites.

Samnīs, ītis, *a.* Samnite.

Samnīticus, a, um, *a.* of the Samnites.

Scamander, drī, *m.* a river near Troy.

Scylla, ae, *f.* a rock between Italy and Sicily, opposite Charybdis.

Scythae, ārum, *m. pl.* the Scythians, people dwelling north and east of the Black Sea.

Scythia, ae, *f.* country inhabited by the Scythians.

Scythicus, a, um, *a.* Scythian.

Sēricus, a, um, *a.* Chinese; made of silk.

Siculī, ōrum, *m. pl.* Sicilians.

Siculus, a, um, *a.* Sicilian.

Sīdōn, ōnis & ōnos, *f.* a Phoenician city, the mother-city of Tyre.

Sīdonius, a, um, Sīdōnicus, a, um, *a.* of or relating to Sidon.

Simoīs, entis, *m.* a river in Troas, which runs into the Scamander.

Sirmiō, ōnis, *m.* peninsula of Lake Garda.

Sparta, ae, *f.* the capital of Laconia, in the Peloponnese.

Spartānus, a, um, Sparticus, a, um, *a.* Spartan.

Stygius, a, um, *a.* of or belonging to the Styx.

Stymphālus, ī, m., Stymphālum, ī, nt. a district in Arcadia, with a town and lake of the same name; here lived the man-eating birds killed by Hercules.

Sybaris, is, *f.* a town of Lucania on the Gulf of Tarentum, proverbial for its luxury.

Symplēgades, um, *f. pl.* two floating islands at the entrance of the Euxine.

Syrācūsae, ārum, *f. pl.* Syracuse, ancient capital of Sicily.

Syrācūsānus, a, um, Syrācūsius, a, um, *a.* Syracusan.

Syria, ae, *f.* Syria.

Syrius, a, um, Syrus, a, um, Syriacus, a, um, Syriscus, a, um, *a.* Syrian.

Syrtēs, ium, *f. pl.* two great very dangerous gulfs on the north coast of Africa.

Tamesis, is, *m.* the Thames.

Tempē, nt. indecl. a valley in Thessaly, through which ran the River Peneus.

Thēbae, ārum, *f. pl.* (1) a city in Upper Egypt; (2) the capital of Boeotia.

Thēbānus, a, um, *a.* Theban.

Thessalia, ae, *f.* Thessaly, a district in the north of Greece.

Thessalicus, a, um, Thessalus, a, um, *a.* Thessalian, Thessalic.

Thrāca, ae, Thrācē, ēs, Thrācia, ae, *f.* Thrace, a district of North Greece.

Thrācius, a, um, *a.* Thracian.

Thrāx, ācis, *m.* a Thracian.

Thūlē, ēs, *f.* an island in the far north, usually in references to Iceland or Scandinavia.

Tiberis, is, *m.* a river of Latium, on which Rome stood, the Tiber.

Tomis, is, f., Tomi, ōrum, m. pl. a town of Moesiā, on the Black Sea, to which Ovid was banished; modern Costanta.

Trīnacria, ae, *f.* Sicily.

Trīnacrius, a, um, *a.* Sicilian.

Trōas, adis & ados, *f.* a Trojan woman; the region about Troy, the Troad.

Trōicus, a, um, Trōius, a, um, Trōiānus, a, um, *a.* Trojan.

Trōia, ae, *f.* Troy, a city of Asia Minor.

Trōiugena, ae, *a.* Trojan.

Trōs, ōis, *m.* a Trojan.

Tyrr(h)ēnia, ae, *f.* Etruria.

Tyrr(h)ēnus, a, um, *a.* Etrurian, Tuscan.

Umber, bra, brum, *a.* Umbrian.

Umbrī, ōrum, *m. pl.* the people of Umbria.

Umbria, ae, *f.* country of the Umbri, a district of Italy on the Adriatic, north of Picenum.

Vāticānus (mōns, collis), ī, *m.* one of the seven hills of Rome.

Venetī, ōrum, *m. pl.* a people in the north-east of Italy; a people of the north-west of Gaul.

Vesuvius, iī, *m.* a volcano in Campania.

Vīminālis collis, *m.* one of the seven hills of Rome.

Volscī, ōrum, *m. pl.* a people in the south of Latium.

Volscus, a, um, *a.* of the Volsci.

Summary of Grammar

Nouns

| | 1st declension | 2nd declension | | 3rd declension | |
| | stems in -a | stems in -o | | stems in consonants | |
	feminine	masculine	neuter	masc. & fem.	neuter
singular					
nom.	domin-a	domin-us	bell-um	dux	caput
acc.	domin-am	domin-um	bell-um	duc-em	caput
gen.	domin-ae	domin-ī	bell-ī	duc-is	capit-is
dat.	domin-ae	domin-ō	bell-ō	duc-ī	capit-ī
abl.	domin-ā	domin-ō	bell-ō	duc-e	capit-e
plural					
nom.	domin-ae	domin-ī	bell-a	duc-ēs	capit-a
acc.	domin-ās	domin-ōs	bell-a	duc-ēs	capit-a
gen.	domin-ārum	domin-ōrum	bell-ōrum	duc-um	capit-um
dat.	domin-īs	domin-īs	bell-īs	duc-ibus	capit-ibus
abl.	domin-īs	domin-īs	bell-īs	duc-ibus	capit-ibus

3rd declension			4th declension	5th declension
stems in -i			stems in -u	stems in -e
masc. & fem.	neuter		masculine	feminine

singular				
nom.	cīvis	mare	grad-us	rēs
acc.	cīv-em	mare	grad-um	rēm
gen.	cīv-is	mar-is	grad-ūs	reī
dat.	cīv-ī	mar-ī	grad-uī	reī
abl.	cīv-e	mar-ī	grad-ū	rē

plural				
nom.	cīv-ēs	mar-ia	grad-ūs	rēs
acc.	cīv-ēs	mar-ia	grad-ūs	rēs
gen.	cīv-ium	mar-ium	grad-uum	rērum
dat.	cīv-ibus	mar-ibus	grad-ibus	rēbus
abl.	cīv-ibus	mar-ibus	grad-ibus	rēbus

Notes

1 The vocative case, used in addressing or calling someone, is the same as the nominative, except in the second declension, where nouns ending **-us** form vocative singular **-e**, e.g. **Quīnte**, and nouns ending **-ius** form vocative singular **-ī**, e.g. **fīlī**.

2 All words of the first declension are feminine except for those which are masculine by meaning, e.g. **agricola** farmer, **nauta** sailor, **poēta** poet.

3 Some second declension masculine nouns have nominative **-er**, e.g. **puer**, **ager**; of these, some keep the **-e** in their stem, e.g. **puerī**, others drop it, e.g. **agrī**.

4 Third declension. The gender of all third declension nouns has to be learnt. Genitive plural is **-um**, except for (a) nouns which have the same number of syllables in nominative and genitive, e.g. **cīvis**, **cīvis** (b) nouns whose stem ends in two or more consonants, e.g. **urbs**, **mōns**; these two classes have genitive plural **-ium**, e.g. **cīvium**, **urbium**, **montium** (see also Note 8).

5 All fourth declension nouns are masculine except for **manus** (and two or three other rare words).

6 All fifth declension nouns are feminine, except for **diēs**, which is usually masculine.

7 Locative case, expressing place where:
1st declension singular: **-ae**; **(Rōma) Rōmae**   plural: **-īs**; **(Athēnae) Athēnīs**

2nd declension singular: **-ī;** (Corinthus) Corinthī plural: **-is;** (Philippī) Philippīs
3rd declension singular: **-ī/e;** (rūs) rūrī/rure plural: **-ibus;** (Gādēs) Gādibus

8 Irregular declension

1st declension: **dea** and **fīlia** have dative and ablative plural: **deābus, fīliābus.**

2nd declension: **deus** in plural declines: **dī, deōs, deōrum/deum, dīs, dīs. vir** has genitive plural: **virōrum/virum.**

3rd declension: the following nouns have genitive plural **-um,** (not **-ium**), contrary to Note 4:

pater, māter, frāter, senex, iuvenis, canis, sēdēs.
Iuppiter declines: **Iuppiter, Iovem, Iovis, Iovī, Iove.**
vīs (force) in singular has only accusative: **vim,** and ablative: **vī.**
The plural **vīrēs** (strength) is regular, with genitive **vīrium.**

4th declension: **domus** in singular declines; **domus, domum, domūs, domuī/domō, domō, domō;** locative **domī.**

Adjectives

masculine & neuter 2nd declension: feminine 1st declension

singular	m.	f.	n.
nom.	bon-us	bon-a	bon-um
acc.	bon-um	bon-am	bon-um
gen.	bon-ī	bon-ae	bon-ī
dat.	bon-ō	bon-ae	bon-ō
abl.	bon-ō	bon-ā	bon-ō

plural			
nom.	bon-ī	bon-ae	bon-a
acc.	bon-ōs	bon-ās	bon-a
gen.	bon-ōrum	bon-ārum	bon-ōrum
dat.	bon-īs	bon-īs	bon-īs
abl.	bon-īs	bon-īs	bon-īs

Like **bonus, bona, bonum** go: **miser, misera, miserum; liber, libera, liberum; niger, nigra, nigrum; pulcher, pulchra, pulchrum; sacer, sacra, sacrum**

Third declension

consonant stems

singular	m. & f.	n.
nom.	vetus	vetus
acc.	veter-em	vetus
gen.	veter-is	veter-is
dat.	veter-ī	veter-ī
abl.	veter-e	veter-e

plural	m. & f.	n.
nom.	veter-ēs	veter-a
acc.	veter-ēs	veter-a
gen.	veter-um	veter-um
dat.	veter-ibus	veter-ibus
abl.	veter-ibus	veter-ibus

stems in -i

singular	m. & f.	n.
nom.	tristis	trīst-e
acc.	trīst-em	trīst-e
gen.	trīst-is	trīst-is
dat.	trīst-ī	trīst-ī
abl.	trīst-ī	trīst-ī

plural	m. & f.	n.
nom.	trīst-ēs	trīst-ia
acc.	trīst-ēs	trīst-ia
gen.	trīst-ium	trīst-ium
dat.	trīst-ibus	trīst-ibus
abl.	trīst-ibus	trīst-ibus

Other 3rd declension adjectives in a consonant stem are: **pauper**, genitive: **pauperis; dives**, genitive **divitis**. Other types of -i stems are: **audāx** (neuter **audāx**), genitive **audācis; ingēns** (neuter **ingēns**), genitive **ingentis**.

Adverbs

1 From **bonus** type adjectives, adverbs are normally formed by adding **-e** to the stem, e.g. **laetus** happy, **laet-ē** happily; **miser** miserable, **miserē** miserably. A few add **-ō** instead of **-ē**, e.g. **tūt-us** safe, **tūt-ō** safely.

2 From third declension adjectives, adverbs are normally formed by adding **-ter** to the stem, e.g. **fortis** brave, **forti-ter** bravely; **audāx** bold, **audāc-ter** boldly; **celer** quick, **celeri-ter** quickly.

Comparison of Adjectives and Adverbs

Adjectives

positive	laetus	miser	niger	fortis	facilis
comparative	laetior	miserior	nigrior	fortior	facilior
superlative	laetissimus	miserrimus	nigerrimus	fortissimus	facillimus*

* Adjectives which double the l in superlative are: **facilis, difficilis, similis, dissimilis, gracilis** graceful, **humilis** lowly.

Adverbs

	positive	comparative	superlative
	laetē	laetius	laetissimē
	miserē	miserius	miserrimē
	fortiter	fortius	fortissimē
	facile	facilius	facillimē

Declension of comparative

singular

	m.f.	n.
nom.	laetior	laetius
acc.	laetiōrem	laetius
gen.	laetiōris	laetiōris
dat.	laetiōrī	laetiōrī
abl.	laetiōre	laetiōre

plural

	m.f.	n.
nom.	laetiōrēs	laetiōra
acc.	laetiōrēs	laetiōra
gen.	laetiōrum	laetiōrum
dat.	laetiōribus	laetiōribus
abl.	laetiōribus	laetiōribus

Irregular comparison

Adjectives

positive	bonus	malus	parvus	multus
comparative	melior	peior	minor	plūs
superlative	optimus	pessimus	minimus	plūrimus

positive	magnus	senex	iuvenis	dīves
comparative	maior	senior/nātū maior	iūnior	dī(vi)tior
superlative	maximus	nātū maximus	nātū minimus	dī(vi)tissimus

plūs in the singular is a neuter noun, with genitive **plūris** and ablative **plūre**. The plural **plūrēs** is an adjective, declining regularly, genitive **plūrium**.

Adverbs

positive	bene	male	paul(l)um	magnopere
comparative	melius	peius	minus	magis
superlative	optimē	pessimē	minimē	maximē

positive	diū	post	prope
comparative	diūtius	posterius	propius

(Adverbs continued:)

positive	saepe
comparative	saepius

Pronouns

Personal pronouns

singular

nom.	ego (I)	tū (you)	
acc.	mē	tē	sē (himself, herself)
gen.	meī	tuī	suī
dat.	mihi	tibi	sibi
abl.	mē	tē	sē

plural

nom.	nōs (we)	vōs (you)	
acc.	nōs	vōs	sē (themselves)
gen.	nostrum	vestrum	suī
dat.	nōbīs	vōbīs	sibi
abl.	nōbīs	vōbīs	sē

Possessive adjectives

meus-a-um my
tuus-a-um your
suus-a-um his own, her own

noster, nostra, nostrum our
vester, vestra, vestrum your
suus-a-um their own
All go like **bonus-a-um**, but
meus has vocative **mī**.

Demonstrative pronouns

singular

	m.	f.	n.	m.	f.	n.	m.	f.	n.
nom.	hic	haec	hoc (this)	ille	illa	illud (that)	is	ea	id (he, she, it)
acc.	hunc	hanc	hoc	illum	illam	illud	eum	?am	id
gen.	huius	huius	huius	illīus	illīus	illīus	eius	eius	eius
dat.	huic	huic	huic	illī	illī	illī	eī	eī	eī
abl.	hōc	hāc	hōc	illō	illā	illō	eō	eā	eō

plural

	m.	f.	n.	m.	f.	n.	m.	f.	n.
nom.	hī	hae	haec	illī	illae	illa	eī/iī	eae	ea
acc.	hōs	hās	haec	illōs	illās	illa	eōs	eās	ea
gen.	hōrum	hārum	hōrum	illōrum	illārum	illōrum	eōrum	eārum	eōrum
dat.	hīs	hīs	hīs	illīs	illīs	illīs	eīs/iīs	eīs/iīs	eīs/iīs
abl.	hīs	hīs	hīs	illīs	illīs	illīs	eīs/iīs	eīs/iīs	eīs/iīs

singular

	m.	f.	n.
nom.	īdem	eadem	idem (same)
acc.	eundem	eandem	idem
gen.	eiusdem	eiusdem	eiusdem
dat.	eīdem	eīdem	eīdem
abl.	eōdem	eādem	eōdem

	m.	f.	n.
nom.	quī	quae	quod (who, which)
acc.	quem	quam	quod
gen.	cuius	cuius	cuius
dat.	cui	cui	cui
abl.	quō	quā	quō

plural

	m.	f.	n.
nom.	eīdem/īdem	eaedem	eadem
acc.	eōsdem	eāsdem	eadem
gen.	eōrundem	eārundem	eōrundem
dat.	eīsdem/īsdem } all genders		
abl.	eīsdem/īsdem } all genders		

	m.	f.	n.
nom.	quī	quae	quae
acc.	quōs	quās	quae
gen.	quōrum	quārum	quōrum
dat.	quibus/quīs } all genders		
abl.	quibus/quīs } all genders		

ipse, ipsa, ipsum (self) declines like ille (except for neuter nominative and accusative singular, ipsum, ipsum)

quis? quid? (who? what?) declines like quī, quae, quod, except in feminine nominative and neuter nominative and accusative singular.

The following have genitive singular -ius and dative singular -ī; apart from this they decline like bonus.

alius, alia, aliud other
ūllus, ūlla, ūllum any
nūllus, nūlla, nūllum no
sōlus, sōla, sōlum sole, only
tōtus, tōta, tōtum whole

alter, altera, alterum one or the other of two

uter? utra? utrum? which of two?

uterque, utraque, utrumque each of two

neuter, neutra, neutrum neither of two

The following decline like quī, quae, quod: quicumque, quaecumque, quodcumque whoever, whatever

quidam, quaedam, quoddam a certain

aliquis, aliqua, aliquid someone, something

quisquam, quidquam/quicquam anyone (after a negative)

Cardinals

1	I	ūnus	22	XXII	duo et vīgintī
2	II	duo	30	XXX	trigintā
3	III	trēs	40	XL	quadrāgintā
4	IV	quattuor	50	L	quīnquāgintā
5	V	quīnque	60	LX	sexāgintā
6	VI	sex	70	LXX	septuāgintā
7	VII	septem	80	LXXX	octōgintā
8	VIII	octō	90	XC	nōnāgintā
9	IX	novem	100	C	centum
10	X	decem	101	CI	centum et ūnus
11	XI	ūndecim	200	CC	ducenti-ae-a
12	XII	duodecim	300	CCC	trecentī
13	XIII	tredecim	400	CCCC	quadringentī
14	XIV	quattuordecim	500	D	quīngentī
15	XV	quīndecim	600	DC	sescentī
16	XVI	sēdecim	700	DCC	septingentī
17	XVII	septendecim	800	DCCC	octingentī
18	XVIII	duodēvīgintī	900	DCCCC	nōngentī
19	XIX	ūndēvīgintī	1,000	M	mīlle
20	XX	vīgintī	2,000	MM	duo mīlia
21	XXI	ūnus et vīgintī			

Ordinals

prīmus-a-um	first
secundus-a-um	second
tertius-a-um	third
quārtus-a-um	fourth
quīntus-a-um	fifth
sextus-a-um	sixth
septimus-a-um	seventh
octāvus-a-um	eighth
nōnus-a-um	ninth
decimus-a-um	tenth

4 to 100 do not decline; ducenti to nōngenti decline like the plural of **bonus**; **mīlia** declines as a third declension noun.

Declension of **unus, duo, trēs**

	m.	f.	n.
nom.	ūnus	ūna	ūnum
acc.	ūnum	ūnam	ūnum
gen.	ūnīus	ūnīus	ūnīus
dat.	ūnī	ūnī	ūnī
abl.	ūnō	ūnā	ūnō
nom.	duo	duae	duo
acc.	duōs	duās	duo
gen.	duōrum	duārum	duōrum
dat.	duōbus	duābus	duōbus
abl.	duōbus	duābus	duōbus
nom.	trēs	trēs	tria
acc.	trēs	trēs	tria
gen.	trium	trium	trium
dat.	tribus	tribus	tribus
abl.	tribus	tribus	tribus

Verbs

Active

	1st conjugation	2nd conjugation	3rd conjugation		4th conjugation	mixed conjugation
	stems in -a	stems in -e	stems in -e	stems in consonants	stems in -i	(stems in -i)

Indicative

present

		1st conj.	2nd conj.	3rd conj. (stems in cons.)	4th conj.	mixed conj.
singular	1	am-ō	mone-ō	reg-ō	audi-ō	capi-ō
	2	amā-s	monē-s	reg-is	audī-s	capi-s
	3	ama-t	mone-t	reg-it	audi-t	capi-t
plural	1	amā-mus	monē-mus	reg-imus	audī-mus	capi-mus
	2	amā-tis	monē-tis	reg-itis	audī-tis	capi-tis
	3	ama-nt	mone-nt	reg-unt	audi-unt	capi-unt

future

		amā-bō	monē-bō	reg-am	audi-am	capi-am
singular	1	amā-bō	monē-bō	reg-am	audi-am	capi-am
	2	amā-bis	monē-bis	reg-ēs	audi-ēs	capi-ēs
	3	amā-bit	monē-bit	reg-et	audi-et	capi-et
plural	1	amā-bimus	monē-bimus	reg-ēmus	audi-ēmus	capi-ēmus
	2	amā-bitis	monē-bitis	reg-ētis	audi-ētis	capi-ētis
	3	amā-bunt	monē-bunt	reg-ent	audi-ent	capi-ent

imperfect

singular	1	amā-bam	monē-bam	regē-bam	audiē-bam	capiē-bam
	2	amā-bās	monē-bās	regē-bās	audiē-bās	capiē-bās
	3	amā-bat	monē-bat	regē-bat	audiē-bat	capiē-bat
plural	1	amā-bāmus	monē-bāmus	regē-bāmus	audiē-bāmus	capiē-bāmus
	2	amā-bātis	monē-bātis	regē-bātis	audiē-bātis	capiē-bātis
	3	amā-bant	monē-bant	regē-bant	audiē-bant	capiē-bant

perfect

singular 1	amāv-ī	monu-ī	rēx-ī	audīv-ī	cēp-ī
2	amāv-istī	monu-istī	rēx-istī	audīv-istī	cēp-istī
3	amāv-it	monu-it	rēx-it	audīv-it	cēp-it
plural 1	amāv-imus	monu-imus	rēx-imus	audīv-imus	cēp-imus
2	amāv-istis	monu-istis	rēx-istis	audīv-istis	cēp-istis
3	amāv-ērunt	monu-ērunt	rēx-ērunt	audīv-ērunt	cēp-ērunt

future perfect

singular 1	amāv-erō	monu-erō	rēx-erō	audīv-erō	cēp-erō
2	amāv-eris	monu-eris	rēx-eris	audīv-eris	cēp-eris
3	amāv-erit	monu-erit	rēx-erit	audīv-erit	cēp-erit
plural 1	amāv-erimus	monu-erimus	rēx-erimus	audīv-erimus	cēp-erimus
2	amāv-eritis	monu-eritis	rēx-eritis	audīv-eritis	cēp-eritis
3	amāv-erint	monu-erint	rēx-erint	audīv-erint	cēp-erint

pluperfect

singular 1	amāv-eram	monu-eram	rēx-eram	audīv-eram	cēp-eram
2	amāv-erās	monu-erās	rēx-erās	audīv-erās	cēp-erās
3	amāv-erat	monu-erat	rēx-erat	audīv-erat	cēp-erat
plural 1	amāv-erāmus	monu-erāmus	rēx-erāmus	audīv-erāmus	cēp-erāmus
2	amāv-erātis	monu-erātis	rēx-erātis	audīv-erātis	cēp-erātis
3	amāv-erant	monu-erant	rēx-erant	audīv-erant	cēp-erant

Subjunctive (Active)

present

singular 1	am-em	mone-am	reg-am	audi-am	capi-am
2	am-ēs	mone-ās	reg-ās	audi-ās	capi-ās
3	am-et	mone-at	reg-at	audi-at	capi-at
plural 1	am-ēmus	mone-āmus	reg-āmus	audi-āmus	capi-āmus
2	am-ētis	mone-ātis	reg-ātis	audi-ātis	capi-ātis
3	am-ent	mone-ant	reg-ant	audi-ant	capi-ant

imperfect

singular	1	amār-em	monēr-em	reger-em	audīr-em	caper-em
	2	amār-ēs	monēr-ēs	reger-ēs	audīr-ēs	caper-ēs
	3	amār-et	monēr-et	reger-et	audīr-et	caper-et
plural	1	amār-ēmus	monēr-ēmus	reger-ēmus	audīr-ēmus	caper-ēmus
	2	amār-ētis	monēr-ētis	reger-ētis	audīr-ētis	caper-ētis
	3	amār-ent	monēr-ent	reger-ent	audīr-ent	caper-ent

perfect

singular	1	amāv-erim	monu-erim	rēx-erim	audīv-erim	cēp-erim
	2	amāv-eris	monu-eris	rēx-eris	audīv-eris	cēp-eris
	3	amāv-erit	monu-erit	rēx-erit	audīv-erit	cēp-erit
plural	1	amāv-erimus	monu-erimus	rēx-erimus	audīv-erimus	cēp-erimus
	2	amāv-eritis	monu-eritis	rēx-eritis	audīv-eritis	cēp-eritis
	3	amāv-erint	monu-erint	rēx-erint	audīv-erint	cēp-erint

pluperfect

singular 1	amāv·issem	monu·issem	rēx·issem	audīv·issem
2	amāv·issēs	monu·issēs	rēx·issēs	audīv·issēs
3	amāv·isset	monu·isset	rēx·isset	audīv·isset
plural 1	amāv·issēmus	monu·issēmus	rēx·issēmus	audīv·issēmus
2	amāv·issētis	monu·issētis	rēx·issētis	audīv·issētis
3	amāv·issent	monu·issent	rēx·issent	audīv·issent

Imperative

singular	amā	monē	rege	audī
plural	amāte	monēte	regite	audīte

cēp·issem
cēp·issēs
cēp·isset
cēp·issēmus
cēp·issētis
cēp·issent

cape
capite

Infinitives

present	amāre	monēre	regere	audīre
perfect	amāvisse	monuisse	rēxisse	audīvisse
future	amātūrus esse	monitūrus esse	rēctūrus esse	audītūrus esse

capere
cēpisse
captūrus esse

Participles

present	amāns	monēns	regēns	audiēns	capiēns
future	amātūrus	monitūrus	rēctūrus	audītūrus	captūrus

Passive

Indicative

	1st conjugation	2nd conjugation	3rd conjugation	4th conjugation	mixed conjugation
present					
singular 1	amor	mone-or	reg-or	audi-or	capi-or
2	amā-ris	monē-ris	reg-eris	audī-ris	cape-ris
3	amā-tur	monē-tur	reg-itur	audī-tur	capi-tur
plural 1	amā-mur	monē-mur	reg-imur	audī-mur	capi-mur
2	amā-minī	monē-minī	reg-iminī	audī-minī	capi-minī
3	ama-ntur	mone-ntur	reg-untur	audi-untur	capi-untur

future

singular	1	amā-bor	monē-bor	reg-ar	audi-ar	capi-ar
	2	amā-beris	monē-beris	reg-ēris	audi-ēris	capi-ēris
	3	amā-bitur	monē-bitur	reg-ētur	audi-ētur	capi-ētur
plural	1	amā-bimur	monē-bimur	reg-ēmur	audi-ēmur	capi-ēmur
	2	amā-bimini	monē-bimini	reg-ēmini	audi-ēmini	capi-ēmini
	3	amā-buntur	monē-buntur	reg-entur	audi-entur	capi-entur

imperfect

singular	1	amā-bar	monē-bar	regē-bar	audiē-bar	capiē-bar
	2	amā-bāris	monē-bāris	etc.	etc.	etc.
	3	amā-bātur	monē-bātur			
plural	1	amā-bāmur	monē-bāmur			
	2	amā-bāmini	monē-bāmini			
	3	amā-bantur	monē-bantur			

perfect

singular 1	amātus sum	monitus sum	rēctus sum	audītus sum	captus sum
2	amātus es	monitus es	rēctus es	audītus es	captus es
3	amātus est	monitus est	rēctus est	audītus est	captus est
plural 1	amātī sumus	monitī sumus	rēctī sumus	audītī sumus	captī sumus
2	amātī estis	monitī estis	rēctī estis	audītī estis	captī estis
3	amātī sunt	monitī sunt	rēctī sunt	audītī sunt	captī sunt

future perfect

	amātus erō	monitus erō	rēctus erō	audītus erō	captus erō
	etc.	etc.	etc.	etc.	etc.

pluperfect

	amātus eram	monitus eram	rēctus eram	audītus eram	captus eram
	etc.	etc.	etc.	etc.	etc.

Subjunctive (Passive)

present

singular 1	am-er	mone-ar	reg-ar	audi-ar	capi-ar
2	am-ēris	mone-āris	reg-āris	audi-āris	capi-āris
3	am-ētur	mone-ātur	reg-ātur	audi-ātur	capi-ātur
plural 1	am-ēmur	mone-āmur	reg-āmur	audi-āmur	capi-āmur
2	am-ēmini	mone-āmini	reg-āmini	audi-āmini	capi-āmini
3	am-entur	mone-antur	reg-antur	audi-antur	capi-antur

imperfect

singular 1	amār-er	monēr-er	reger-er	audīr-er	caper-er
2	amār-ēris	monēr-ēris	reger-ēris	audīr-ēris	caper-ēris
3	amār-ētur	monēr-ētur	reger-ētur	audīr-ētur	caper-ētur
plural 1	amār-ēmur	monēr-ēmur	reger-ēmur	audīr-ēmur	caper-ēmur
2	amār-ēmini	monēr-ēmini	reger-ēmini	audīr-ēmini	caper-ēmini
3	amār-entur	monēr-entur	reger-entur	audīr-entur	caper-entur

perfect

singular	1	amātus sim	monitus sim	rēctus sim	audītus sim	captus sim
	2	amātus sīs	etc.	etc.	etc.	etc.
	3	amātus sit				
plural	1	amātī sīmus				
	2	amātī sītis				
	3	amātī sint				

pluperfect

singular	1	amātus essem	monitus essem	rēctus essem	audītus essem	captus essem
	2	amātus essēs	etc.	etc.	etc.	etc.
	3	amātus esset				
plural	1	amātī essēmus				
	2	amātī essētis				
	3	amātī essent				

Imperative

singular	amāre	monēre	regere	audīre	capere
plural	amāminī	monēminī	regiminī	audīminī	capiminī

Infinitives

present	amārī	monērī	regī	audīrī	capī
perfect	amātus esse	monitus esse	rēctus esse	audītus esse	captus esse
future	amātum īrī	monitum īrī	rēctum īrī	audītum īrī	captum īrī

Participles

perfect	amātus	monitus	rēctus	audītus	captus

Deponent verbs

Indicative

present	cōnor cōnā-ris etc.	vere-or verē-ris etc.	sequor sequ-eris etc.	ori-or orī-ris etc.	ingred-ior ingred-eris etc.
future	cōnā-bor etc.	verē-bor etc.	sequ-ar etc.	ori-ar etc.	ingredi-ar etc.
imperfect	cōnā-bar etc.	verē-bar etc.	sequ-ēbar etc.	ori-ēbar etc.	ingredi-ēbar etc.
perfect	cōnātus sum	veritus sum	secūtus sum	ortus sum	ingressus sum
future perfect	cōnātus erō	veritus erō	secūtus erō	ortus erō	ingressus erō
pluperfect	cōnātus eram	veritus eram	secūtus eram	ortus eram	ingressus eram

Subjunctives

present	cōner	verear	sequar	oriar	ingrediar
imperfect	cōnārer	verērer	sequerer	orīrer	ingrederer
perfect	cōnātus sim	veritus sim	secūtus sim	ortus sim	ingressus sim
pluperfect	cōnātus essem	veritus essem	secūtus essem	ortus essem	ingressus essem

Imperatives

singular	cōnāre	verēre	sequere	orīre	ingredere
plural	cōnāminī	verēminī	sequiminī	orīminī	ingrediminī

Infinitives

present	cōnārī	verērī	sequī	orīrī	ingredī
perfect	cōnātus esse	veritus esse	secūtus esse	ortus esse	ingressus esse
future	cōnātūrus esse	veritūrus esse	secūtūrus esse	oritūrus esse	ingressūrus esse

Participles

present	cōnāns	verēns	sequēns	oriēns	ingrediēns
perfect	cōnātus	veritus	secūtus	ortus	ingressus
future	cōnātūrus	veritūrus	secūtūrus	oritūrus	ingressūrus

Irregular verbs

	sum, esse, fui		possum, posse, potui		eo, ire, ii	
present	*indicative*	*subjunctive*	*indicative*	*subjunctive*	*indicative*	*subjunctive*
singular 1	sum	sim	possum	possim	eō	eam
2	es	sīs	potes	possīs	īs	eās
3	est	sit	potest	possit	it	eat
plural 1	sumus	sīmus	possumus	possīmus	īmus	eāmus
2	estis	sītis	potestis	possītis	ītis	eātis
3	sunt	sint	possunt	possint	eunt	eant
future						
singular 1	erō		poterō		ībō	
2	eris		poteris		ībis	
3	erit		poterit		ībit	
plural 1	erimus		poterimus		ībimus	
2	eritis		poteritis		ībitis	
3	erunt		poterunt		ībunt	

imperfect

singular	1	eram	essem	poteram	possem	ibam	irem
	2	erās	etc.	etc.	etc.	ibās	etc.
	3	erat				ibat	
plural	1	erāmus				ibāmus	
	2	erātis				ibātis	
	3	erant				ibant	

perfect

singular	1	fuī	fuerim	potuī	potuerim	iī	ierim
	2	fuistī	fueris	etc.	etc.	istī	etc.
	3	fuit	fuerit			iit	
plural	1	fuimus	fuerīmus			iimus	
	2	fuistis	fuerītis			istis	
	3	fuērunt	fuerint			iērunt	

future perfect

	esse		posse		ire	
	fuerō etc.		potuerō etc.		ierō etc.	

pluperfect

	fueram etc.	fuissem etc.	potueram etc.	potuissem etc.	ieram etc.	iissem etc.

imperatives

singular	es/estō		—		ī	
plural	este		—		īte	

infinitives

present	esse	posse	ire
perfect	fuisse	potuisse	isse
future	futūrus esse/fore	—	itūrus esse

participles

present	—	—	iēns, euntis
perfect	—	—	
future	futūrus	—	itūrus

	volō, velle, voluī		nōlō, nōlle, nōluī		mālō, mālle, māluī	
	indicative	*subjunctive*	*indicative*	*subjunctive*	*indicative*	*subjunctive*
present						
singular 1	volō	velim	nōlō	nōlim	mālō	mālim
2	vīs	velīs	nōn vīs	nōlīs	māvīs	etc.
3	vult	velit	nōn vult	nōlit	māvult	
plural 1	volumus	velīmus	nōlumus	nōlīmus	mālumus	
2	vultis	velītis	nōn vultis	nōlītis	māvultis	
3	volunt	velint	nōlunt	nōlint	mālunt	
future						
	volam		nōlam		mālam	
	volēs		nōlēs		mālēs	
	volet		etc.		etc.	
	volēmus					
	volētis					
	volent					
imperfect						
	volēbam	vellem	nōlēbam	nōllem	mālēbam	mallem
	etc.	etc.	etc.	etc.	etc.	etc.

	volō		nōlō		mālō	
perfect	voluī etc.	voluerim etc.	nōluī etc.	nōluerim etc.	māluī etc.	māluerim etc.
future perfect	voluerō etc.		nōluerō etc.		māluerō etc.	
pluperfect	volueram etc.	voluissem etc.	nōlueram etc.	nōluissem etc.	mālueram etc.	māluissem etc.
imperatives						
singular	—		nōlī		—	
plural	—		nōlīte		—	
infinitives						
present	velle		nōlle		mālle	
perfect	voluisse		nōluisse		māluisse	
future	—		—		—	

participles

present	volēns	nōlēns
perfect	—	—
future	—	—

	ferō, ferre, tulī *active*		**feror, ferrī, lātus** *passive*	
present	*indicative*	*subjunctive*	*indicative*	*subjunctive*
singular 1	ferō	feram	feror	ferar
2	fers	ferās	ferris	ferāris
3	fert	ferat	fertur	ferātur
plural 1	ferimus	ferāmus	ferimur	ferāmur
2	fertis	ferātis	feriminī	ferāminī
3	ferunt	ferant	feruntur	ferantur
future	feram		ferar	
	ferēs		ferēris	
	etc.		etc.	

imperfect	ferēbam etc.	ferrem etc.	ferēbar etc.	ferrer etc.
perfect	tulī etc.	tulerim etc.	lātus sum etc.	lātus sim etc.
future perfect	tulerō etc.		lātus erō etc.	
pluperfect	tuleram etc.	tulissem etc.	lātus eram etc.	lātus essem etc.
imperatives				
singular	fer		ferre	
plural	ferte		feriminī	

infinitives

present	ferre	ferrī
perfect	tulisse	lātus esse
future	lātūrus esse	lātum īrī

participles

present	ferēns	
perfect		lātus
future	lātūrus	